Visual Overview Transduction from Physical Energy to Neural Signals

Each of the sensory organs—eye, ear, nose, mouth, and skin—has a unique receptor for transforming a form of physical energy (e.g., light and sound waves, chemical molecules, pressure and temperature) into a neural code that is interpreted in specific areas within the cortex.

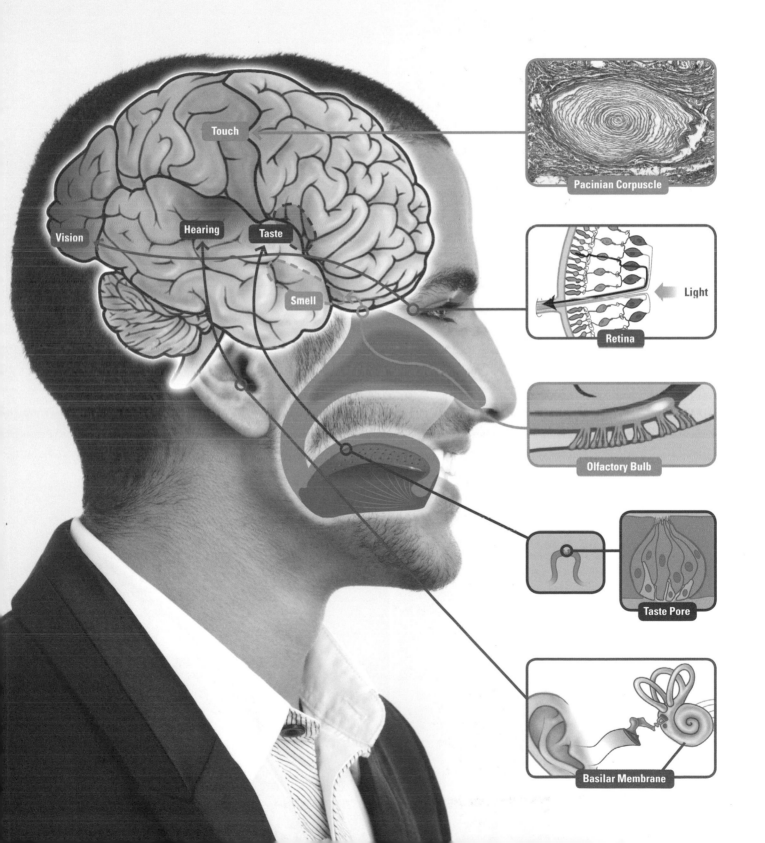

learn

Psychology

Psychology

Kenneth Carter, PhD, ABPP
Professor of Psychology
Oxford College, Emory University
Oxford, Georgia

Colleen M. Seifert, PhD
Arthur F. Thurnau Professor of Psychology
University of Michigan
Ann Arbor, Michigan

Contributions by:
Jonna Kwiatkowski, PhD
Assistant Professor of Psychology
Mars Hill College
Mars Hill, North Carolina

JONES & BARTLETT
LEARNING

World Headquarters
Jones & Bartlett Learning
5 Wall Street
Burlington, MA 01803
978-443-5000
info@jblearning.com
www.jblearning.com

Jones & Bartlett Learning books and products are available through most bookstores and online booksellers. To contact Jones & Bartlett Learning directly, call 800-832-0034, fax 978-443-8000, or visit our website, www.jblearning.com.

Substantial discounts on bulk quantities of Jones & Bartlett Learning publications are available to corporations, professional associations, and other qualified organizations. For details and specific discount information, contact the special sales department at Jones & Bartlett Learning via the above contact information or send an email to specialsales@jblearning.com.

Production Credits
Chief Executive Officer: Ty Field
President: James Homer
Senior Vice President: Eve Howard
SVP, Chief Marketing Officer: Alison M. Pendergast
VP, Production and Design: Anne Spencer
Senior Developmental Editor: William Wahlgren
Senior Editorial Assistant: Rainna Erikson
Reprints and Special Projects Manager: Susan Schultz
Associate Production Editor: Tina Chen
Production Assistant: Kristen Rogers
V.P., Manufacturing and Inventory Control: Therese Connell
Manufacturing and Inventory Control Supervisor: Amy Bacus
Rights and Photo Research Supervisor: Anna Genoese
Composition: diacriTech, Inc.
Text Design: Anne Spencer
Cover Design: Timothy Dziewit
Cover Image: © Sofia/ShutterStock, Inc.
Printing and Binding: Courier Companies
Cover Printing: Courier Companies

Library of Congress Cataloging-in-Publication Data
Carter, Kenneth, 1967-
  Learn psychology / Kenneth Carter, Colleen M. Seifert.
      p. cm.
  Includes index.
  ISBN 978-0-7637-9898-7
1. Psychology. I. Seifert, Colleen M. II. Title.
  BF81.C33 2013
  150--dc23
                              2012005228
6048

Printed in the United States of America
16 15 14 13 12   10 9 8 7 6 5 4 3 2

Brief Contents

CHAPTER 1 Psychology: An Overview 2

CHAPTER 2 A Scientific Approach to Psychology 30

CHAPTER 3 Neuroscience: The Biology of Behavior 74

CHAPTER 4 Sensation and Perception 110

CHAPTER 5 States of Consciousness 152

CHAPTER 6 Learning 184

CHAPTER 7 Memory 224

CHAPTER 8 Thinking and Language 276

CHAPTER 9 Intelligence 316

CHAPTER 10 Motivation 360

CHAPTER 11 Emotion, Stress, and Health 416

CHAPTER 12 Development Throughout the Life Span 450

CHAPTER 13 Personality 504

CHAPTER 14 Psychological Disorders 536

CHAPTER 15 Therapies for Psychological Disorders 578

CHAPTER 16 Social Psychology 614

Contents

Preface xviii
Acknowledgments xxv
About the Authors xxvii

CHAPTER 1   Psychology: An Overview 2

1.1 The Science of Psychology 5
CONCEPT LEARNING CHECK **1.1** *The Scope and Limits of the Science of Psychology 7*

1.2 The Origins and History of Psychology 8
Philosophical Roots 9
Biological Roots 9
Schools of Thought: Structuralism vs. Functionalism 10
CONCEPT LEARNING CHECK **1.2** *Comparing and Contrasting Structuralism and Functionalism 12*

1.3 Contemporary Psychology 13
The Biological Perspective 14
The Evolutionary Perspective 14
The Psychodynamic Perspective 15
The Behavioral Perspective 16
The Humanistic Perspective 16
The Cognitive Perspective 16
The Sociocultural Perspective 16
Professional Specialization and Research Areas in Psychology 17
CONCEPT LEARNING CHECK **1.3** *Contemporary Perspectives and Settings in Psychology 19*

1.4 Critical Thinking and Multiple Influences 19
Critical Thinking 19
The Importance of Multiple Influences 20
CRITICAL THINKING APPLICATION 21
Summary of Multiple Influences on Psychology 21
CONCEPT LEARNING CHECK **1.4** *Applying the Criteria of Critical Thinking 23*
VISUAL OVERVIEW: MULTIPLE PERSPECTIVES 24
Visual Summary of Psychology: An Overview 25
Chapter Review Test • Chapter Discussion Questions • Chapter Projects • Chapter Key Terms • Answers to Concept Learning Checks • Answers to Chapter Review Test • References 26

CHAPTER 2   A Scientific Approach to Psychology 30

2.1 Psychological Investigation 32
The Scientific Method in Psychology 33
Why Is the Scientific Method Important? 35
CONCEPT LEARNING CHECK **2.1** *Within or Between? 36*

2.2 Descriptive Research 37
Naturalistic Observation 37
Case Studies 38
Surveys 39
Correlational Studies 41
CONCEPT LEARNING CHECK **2.2** *What Do Correlations Mean? 46*

2.3 Experimental Research 46
CONCEPT LEARNING CHECK **2.3** *Designing an Experiment 51*

2.4 Statistical Analysis 51
Measures of Central Tendency and Variance 52
Making Inferences with Statistics 55
CONCEPT LEARNING CHECK **2.4** *Summarizing with Statistics 56*

2.5 Ethics in Psychological Research 56
Human Participants 57
Animal Studies 59
Summary of Multiple Influences on a Scientific Approach to Psychology 61
CONCEPT LEARNING CHECK **2.5** *Ethics in Psychological Studies 61*
CRITICAL THINKING APPLICATION 62
VISUAL OVERVIEW: SAMPLING FROM A POPULATION FOR SCIENTIFIC STUDY 64

Visual Summary of A Scientific Approach to Psychology 65
Chapter Review Test • Chapter Discussion Questions • Chapter Projects • Chapter Key
Terms • Answers to Concept Learning Checks • Answers to Chapter Review Test •
References 67

CHAPTER 3 **Neuroscience: The Biology of Behavior** 74

  3.1 **Overview: The Components of Biological Bases of Behavior** 76
    CONCEPT LEARNING CHECK **3.1** *Reviewing the Terminology of Neuroscience* 77

  3.2 **Neural Communication** 77
    Glia 78
    Neurons 78
    Neural Networks 82
    Multitasking Neurotransmitters 83
    CONCEPT LEARNING CHECK **3.2** *Recognizing the Parts of the Neuron* 84

  3.3 **Nervous System Organization** 84
    Peripheral Nervous System 84
    Central Nervous System 85
    CONCEPT LEARNING CHECK **3.3** *The Organization of the Nervous
    System* 86

  3.4 **The Brain** 86
    Organization 86
    Research on the Brain 86
    The Brainstem 87
    Midbrain 89
    Forebrain 89
    Plasticity 93
    CONCEPT LEARNING CHECK **3.4** *Identifying the Structures and
    Functions in the Brain* 94

  3.5 **The Endocrine System** 94
    Endorphins 95
    Adrenal Glands 95
    Gonads 95
    CONCEPT LEARNING CHECK **3.5** *Identifying the Role of Endorphins and the Endocrine
    System Functions* 96

  3.6 **Genetics** 96
    The Basic Concepts of Genetics 96
    The Research Methods of Genetics 98
    Summary of Multiple Influences on the Biology of Behavior 100
    CONCEPT LEARNING CHECK **3.6** *Reviewing the Role of Genetics in Psychology* 100
    CRITICAL THINKING APPLICATION 101
    VISUAL OVERVIEW: NERVOUS SYSTEM 102
    Visual Summary of Neuroscience: The Biology of Behavior 103
    Chapter Review Test • Chapter Discussion Questions • Chapter Projects • Chapter Key
    Terms • Answers to Concept Learning Checks • Answers to Chapter Review Test •
    References 105

CHAPTER 4 **Sensation and Perception** 110

  4.1 **The Interaction of Sensation and Perception** 112
    CONCEPT LEARNING CHECK **4.1** *Comparing Top-Down and Bottom-Up Processing* 114

  4.2 **Sensory Principles** 114
    Transduction of Physical Energy into Neural Stimulation 115
    Detection Thresholds Reflect Sensitivity 115
    Sensory Adaptation 117
    CONCEPT LEARNING CHECK **4.2** *Testing Sensory Thresholds* 118

  4.3 **The Five Major Senses** 118
    The Sense of Vision 119
    The Sense of Hearing 123
    The Sense of Smell 124
    The Sense of Taste 125
    The Sense of Touch 127
    CONCEPT LEARNING CHECK **4.3** *Methods of Sensory Transduction* 129
    CRITICAL THINKING APPLICATION 129

4.4 Perception Organizes Sensations 130
Form and Pattern Perception 130
Gestalt Organizing Principles 131
Depth Perception 133
Perception of Motion 134
Perceptual Constancy 135

CONCEPT LEARNING CHECK **4.4** *Perceptual Organization Principles* 136

4.5 Experience and Perception 137
Development 137
Learning 137
Culture 138

CONCEPT LEARNING CHECK **4.5** *The Role of Experience in Perception* 140

4.6 The Role of Attention 140
Selective Attention 140
Divided Attention 141
Summary of Multiple Influences on Sensation and Perception 142

CONCEPT LEARNING CHECK **4.6** *The Role of Attention in Perception* 142

VISUAL OVERVIEW: TRANSDUCTION FROM PHYSICAL ENERGY TO NEURAL SIGNALS 143

Visual Summary of Sensation and Perception 144
Chapter Review Test • Chapter Discussion Questions • Chapter Projects • Chapter Key
  Terms • Answers to Concept Learning Checks • Answers to Chapter Review Test •
  References 146

CHAPTER 5 **States of Consciousness**. 152

5.1 Overview: Consciousness, Brain Activity, Levels of Awareness . . . 154
CONCEPT LEARNING CHECK **5.1** *Consciousness and Psychology* 155

5.2 Sleep 155
Biological Rhythms and Stages of Sleep 156
Sleep Theories 157
Effects of Sleep Deprivation 158
Sleep Disorders 158

CONCEPT LEARNING CHECK **5.2** *Stages of Sleep* 162

5.3 Dreams. 162
Theories of Dreams 162

CRITICAL THINKING APPLICATION 163
Dream Contents 164

CONCEPT LEARNING CHECK **5.3** *Theories of Dreams* 165

5.4 Hypnosis 165
Critical Thinking About Hypnosis 165
Theories of Hypnosis 166

CONCEPT LEARNING CHECK **5.4** *Theories of Hypnosis* 167

5.5 Meditation 167
Meditation Defined 167
Effects and Benefits of Meditation 167

CONCEPT LEARNING CHECK **5.5** *The Effects and Benefits of Meditation* 168

5.6 Drug Use 168
Mechanism of Action of Psychoactive Drugs 171
Depressants 171
Stimulants 172
Hallucinogens 173
Summary of Multiple Influences on Consciousness 174

CONCEPT LEARNING CHECK **5.6** *The Effects of Psychoactive Drugs* 175

VISUAL OVERVIEW: SLEEP CYCLES 176

Visual Summary of States of Consciousness 177
Chapter Review Test • Chapter Discussion Questions • Chapter Projects • Chapter Key
  Terms • Answers to Concept Learning Checks • Answers to Chapter Review Test •
  References 179

CHAPTER 6 **Learning** 184

6.1 How We Learn. 186
CONCEPT LEARNING CHECK **6.1** *Comparing Types of Learning* 188

6.2 Classical Conditioning 188

Pavlov's Experiments 189
Review of Terminology, Processes, and Factors That Affect Classical Conditioning 192
Conditioning and Emotional Responses 192
Contemporary Views of Classical Conditioning 194
Applying Principles of Classical Conditioning 196
CONCEPT LEARNING CHECK **6.2** *Applying Principles of Classical Conditioning* 197

6.3 **Operant Conditioning** **198**
Thorndike's Law of Effect 198
Skinner's Experiments 198
Punishment 203
Review of Terminology, Processes, and Factors That Affect Operant Conditioning 204
Contemporary Views of Operant Conditioning 205
Applying Principles of Operant Conditioning 207
CONCEPT LEARNING CHECK **6.3** *Comparing Consequences of Behavior* 208

6.4 **A Cognitive Approach: Observational Learning** **208**
CRITICAL THINKING APPLICATION 209
Tolman's Latent Learning 209
Bandura's Social-Cognitive Learning Theory 210
Summary of Multiple Influences on Learning 213
CONCEPT LEARNING CHECK **6.4** *Learning by Observing* 214
VISUAL OVERVIEW: THREE TYPES OF LEARNING 215
Visual Summary of Learning 216
Chapter Review Test • Chapter Discussion Questions • Chapter Projects • Chapter Key
Terms • Answers to Concept Learning Checks • Answers to Chapter Review Test •
References 218

CHAPTER 7 **Memory** **224**
7.1 **Overview: What is Memory?** **226**
CONCEPT LEARNING CHECK **7.1** *Defining Memory* 227
7.2 **Constructing Memory** **227**
Automatic Processing 227
Effortful Processing 229
Mnemonics 232
CONCEPT LEARNING CHECK **7.2** *Applying Methods of Encoding* 233
7.3 **The Three Stages of Memory** **233**
Sensory Memory 234
Short-Term Memory or Working Memory 234
Long-Term Memory 238
Storing Memories in the Brain 239
CONCEPT LEARNING CHECK **7.3** *Movement of Information Through the Stages of
Memory* 240

7.4 Organizing Information in Memory 240
Declarative Memory 242
Procedural Memory 247

CONCEPT LEARNING CHECK **7.4** *Organizing Information in Memory* 248

7.5 Retrieval from Memory 248
Retrieval Cues 248
Adding Context 250
Retrieval Practice 251

CONCEPT LEARNING CHECK **7.5** *Practicing Retrieval* 251

7.6 Reconstructing Memories 252
Source Monitoring 252
The Misinformation Effect 252
False Memories 254

CONCEPT LEARNING CHECK **7.6** *Introducing Error in Memory* 256

CRITICAL THINKING APPLICATION 256

7.7 Forgetting 257
Measures of Forgetting 257
Theories of Forgetting 259
Motivated Forgetting 260
Amnesia 261

CONCEPT LEARNING CHECK **7.7** *Learning from Case Studies of Amnesia* 262

7.8 How to Improve Your Memory 263
Memory Principles Applied to Studying 263
Summary of Multiple Influences on Memory 264

CONCEPT LEARNING CHECK **7.8** *Developing Helpful Study Habits* 265

VISUAL OVERVIEW: TYPES OF KNOWLEDGE IN MEMORY 266

Visual Summary of Memory 267
Chapter Review Test • Chapter Discussion Questions • Chapter Projects • Chapter Key
Terms • Answers to Concept Learning Checks • Answers to Chapter Review Test •
References 269

CHAPTER 8 Thinking and Language.......................276

8.1 Overview: What Is Thinking?...............................278
CONCEPT LEARNING CHECK **8.1** *Defining Thinking* 281

8.2 Problem Solving 281
Problem-Solving Methods 281
Biases in Problem Solving 284
Expertise 286

CONCEPT LEARNING CHECK **8.2** *Applying*
Methods of Problem Solving 286

8.3 Decision Making 286
Algorithms in Decision Making 287
Heuristics in Decision Making 287

CRITICAL THINKING APPLICATION 289

CONCEPT LEARNING CHECK **8.3** *Recognizing*
Heuristics in Decision Making 290

8.4 Reasoning 290
Algorithms in Reasoning 290
Biases in Reasoning 292

CONCEPT LEARNING CHECK **8.4**
Practicing Reasoning 294

8.5 Language ....
294
What Is a "Language"? 294
Language Structure 294
Language Development 296
Theories of Language
 Acquisition 297
Language in Animals 298

CONCEPT LEARNING CHECK **8.5**
Features of Language 299

8.6 Brain, Language, and
Culture 300

Summary of Multiple Influences on Thinking and Language 302

CONCEPT LEARNING CHECK **8.6** *Multiple Influences on Language Use* 304

VISUAL OVERVIEW: TYPES OF THINKING PROCESSES 305

Visual Summary of Thinking and Language 306

Chapter Review Test • Chapter Discussion Questions • Chapter Projects • Chapter Key Terms • Answers to Concept Learning Checks • Answers to Chapter Review Test • References 309

CHAPTER 9 Intelligence 316

9.1 The Nature of Intelligence .318
Defining Intelligence 318
Theories of Intelligence 319

CRITICAL THINKING APPLICATION 323
The Brain and Intelligence 324

CONCEPT LEARNING CHECK **9.1** *Comparing Theories of Intelligence* 326

9.2 Measuring Intelligence 327
The Development of Intelligence Testing 327
Principles of Test Construction 330

CONCEPT LEARNING CHECK **9.2** *Understanding What Scores Mean* 336

9.3 Individual Differences in Intelligence 336
Intellectual Disability 336
High Intellectual Ability 338

CONCEPT LEARNING CHECK **9.3** *Varieties of Intelligence* 340

9.4 Group Differences in Intelligence 340
Differences Within Groups and Differences Between Groups 340
Bias in Intelligence Testing 343

CONCEPT LEARNING CHECK **9.4** *Expecting to Be Smarter* 346

9.5 Multiple Influences: The Roles of Genetics and Environment in Determining Intelligence 346
Evidence for Heredity 347
Evidence for Environmental Influence 347
Summary of Multiple Influences on Intelligence 350

CONCEPT LEARNING CHECK **9.5** *Understanding the Evidence on the Heredity-Environment Question* 350

VISUAL OVERVIEW: STEPS IN CREATING AN INTELLIGENCE TEST 351

Visual Summary of Intelligence 352

Chapter Review Test • Chapter Discussion Questions • Chapter Projects • Chapter Key Terms • Answers to Concept Learning Checks • Answers to Chapter Review Test • References 354

CHAPTER 10 Motivation 360

10.1 Motivational Theories 362
Instinct Theories 362
Evolutionary Theories 363
Drive Theories 363
Arousal Theories 364
Incentive Theories 365
Hierarchical Theories 366

CONCEPT LEARNING CHECK **10.1** *Theories of Motivation* 367

10.2 **Motivation of Hunger** **368**
The Physiology and Regulation of Hunger 368
Environmental Influences 373
Hunger, Eating, and Weight 374
A Comparison: Motivation of Thirst 378

CONCEPT LEARNING CHECK **10.2** *Eating Disorder or Disordered Eating?* 378

CRITICAL THINKING APPLICATION   379

10.3 **Sexual Motivation** **380**
Physiology of Sexual Response 381
Gender Norms in Sexual Motivation 382
Evolutionary Theories of Mating 384
Sexual Orientation 387

CONCEPT LEARNING CHECK **10.3** *Evolution and Gender Differences* 390

10.4 **Social Motivations** **390**
Motivation to Belong 390
Motivation to Achieve 392
Motivation for Self-actualization 393

CONCEPT LEARNING CHECK **10.4** *Fostering Achievement* 394

10.5 **Motivation and Work** **394**
Personnel Psychology 395
Organizational Psychology 397
Career Directions 400
Summary of Multiple Influences on Motivation 403

CONCEPT LEARNING CHECK **10.5** *What "Works" at Work?* 404

VISUAL OVERVIEW: MOTIVATION: SOURCES OF HUNGER 405

Visual Summary of Motivation 406
Chapter Review Test • Chapter Discussion Questions • Chapter Projects • Chapter Key
Terms • Answers to Concept Learning Checks • Answers to Chapter Review Test •
References 408

CHAPTER 11 Emotion, Stress, and Health 416

11.1 **The Role of Physiology and Evolution in Emotion** **418**
The Role of Physiology in Emotion 418
The Role of Evolution in Emotion 421

CONCEPT LEARNING CHECK **11.1** *Bodily Processes and Emotion* 421

11.2 **The Role of Behavior and Cognition in Emotion** **422**
The Role of Behavior in Emotion 422

CONCEPT LEARNING CHECK **11.2** *Behavior and Cognition and Emotion* 425

11.3 **Theories of Emotion** **425**
Common-Sense Theory 425
James-Lange Peripheral Feedback Theory 425
Cannon-Bard Simultaneous Trigger Theory 426
Schacter-Singer Two-Factor Theory of Emotion 426
Cognitive-Mediational Theory of Emotion 428

CONCEPT LEARNING CHECK **11.3** *Theories of Emotion* 428

11.4 **Expressing Emotion** **428**
Culture and Emotion 428

Gender and Emotion 429
Fear 429
Anger and Aggression 429
Love 430

CONCEPT LEARNING CHECK **11.4** *Expressing Emotion* 431

11.5 **Stress** **432**
What Is Stress? 432
Sources of Stress 432
Cognition and Stress 434
Choice as a Stress 435
Culture and Stress 435
Effects of Stress 436
Stress and Health 436
Coping with and Managing Stress 437
Interventions 437

CONCEPT LEARNING CHECK **11.5** *Sources and Effects of Stress* 438

11.6 **Positive Psychology** **438**
Happiness 438
Hardiness 439
Optimism 440
Summary of Multiple Influences on Emotion, Stress, and Health 441

CONCEPT LEARNING CHECK **11.6** *Positive Psychology* 441

CRITICAL THINKING APPLICATION 441

VISUAL OVERVIEW: THEORIES OF EMOTION 442

Visual Summary of Emotion, Stress, and Health 443
Chapter Review Test • Chapter Discussion Questions • Chapter Projects • Chapter Key
Terms • Answers to Concept Learning Checks • Answers to Chapter Review Test •
References 445

CHAPTER 12 **Development Throughout the Life Span** **450**
12.1 **The Beginnings of Development** **452**
What Is Development? 452
Prenatal Development 453
The Newborn 456

CONCEPT LEARNING CHECK **12.1** *Before and After Birth* 457

12.2 **Infancy and Childhood** **457**
Physical Development 458
Cognitive Development 461
Social Development 465

CONCEPT LEARNING CHECK **12.2** *Stages of Cognitive Development* 472

12.3 **Adolescence and Young Adulthood** **472**
Physical Development 473
Cognitive Development 475

Social Development 476

CONCEPT LEARNING CHECK **12.3** *Defining Adolescence* 478

Critical Thinking Application 478

12.4 **Adulthood and Aging** **479**

Physical Development 479

Cognitive Development 481

Social Development 483

CONCEPT LEARNING CHECK **12.4** *Is There a "Right Time" for Everything?* 486

12.5 **Nature and Nurture** **486**

Summary of Multiple Influences on Development 488

CONCEPT LEARNING CHECK **12.5** *Nature or Nurture?* 489

VISUAL OVERVIEW: STAGES OF DEVELOPMENT ACROSS THE LIFESPAN 490

Visual Summary of Development Throughout the Life Span 491

Chapter Review Test • Chapter Discussion Questions • Chapter Projects • Chapter Key
Terms • Answers to Concept Learning Checks • Answers to Chapter Review Test •
References 493

CHAPTER 13 **Personality** **504**

13.1 **Defining Personality** **506**

CONCEPT LEARNING CHECK **13.1** *Describing Personality Theories* 507

13.2 **The Psychoanalytic Perspective** **507**

The Nature of the Psychoanalytic Perspective 507

Freud's Psychoanalytic Theory 508

Jung's Analytical Psychology 511

Adler's Individual Psychology 513

Evaluating the Psychoanalytic Perspective—Is Freud in Error? 513

CONCEPT LEARNING CHECK **13.2** *Comparing the Psychoanalytic Perspectives* 514

13.3 **The Humanistic Perspective** **514**

Rogers's Person-Centered Perspective 514

Maslow's Theory of Self-actualization 515

Evaluating the Humanistic Perspectives 516

CONCEPT LEARNING CHECK **13.3** *Illustrating the Humanistic Perspective* 516

13.4 **Trait Perspectives** **517**

Factor Analysis 517

The Big Five Factors 517

Assessing Traits 518

Evaluating the Trait Perspective 518

CONCEPT LEARNING CHECK **13.4** *Identifying the Big Five Traits* 518

13.5 **The Social Cognitive Perspective** **519**

Bandura's Social Cognitive Theory 519

Mischel's Social Cognitive Theory 520

Evaluating the Social Cognitive Perspective 521

CONCEPT LEARNING CHECK **13.5** *Comparing Social Cognitive Perspectives* 521

13.6 **The Biological Perspective** **521**

Eysenck's Theory 522

Genetics and Personality 523

Evolutionary Theories of Personality 523

Explain 524

Evaluating the Biological Perspective 524

CONCEPT LEARNING CHECK **13.6** *Understanding the Biological Perspective* 524

13.7 **Personality Assessment** **524**

CONCEPT LEARNING CHECK **13.7** *Identifying Personality Assessments* 526

13.8 **Culture and Personality** **526**

Summary of Multiple Influences on Personality 527

CONCEPT LEARNING CHECK **13.8** *Examining Culture and Personality* 527

CRITICAL THINKING APPLICATION 527

VISUAL OVERVIEW: THE MAJOR THEORIES OF PERSONALITY, THEORISTS, AND CONCEPTS 528

Visual Summary of Personality 529

Chapter Review Test • Chapter Discussion Questions • Chapter Projects • Chapter Key
Terms • Answers to Concept Learning Checks • Answers to Chapter Review Test •
References 531

CHAPTER 14 Psychological Disorders 536

14.1 **Overview: Understanding Psychological Disorders** 538
Defining Psychological Disorders 538
Criteria of Abnormal Behavior 539
Classifying and Labeling Psychological Disorders 540
Etiology of Psychological Disorders 542
CONCEPT LEARNING CHECK **14.1** *Identifying Psychological Disorders* 544

14.2 **Anxiety Disorders** **544**
Generalized Anxiety Disorder 544
Panic Disorder 545
Phobic Disorders 546
Obsessive-Compulsive Disorder 547
Posttraumatic Stress Disorder 549
Etiology of Anxiety Disorders 549
CONCEPT LEARNING CHECK **14.2** *Identifying Anxiety Disorders* 551

14.3 **Somatoform Disorders** **552**
Somatization Disorder 552
Conversion Disorder 553
Hypochondriasis 553
Etiology of Somatoform Disorders 553
CONCEPT LEARNING CHECK **14.3** *Identifying Somatoform Disorders* 554

14.4 **Dissociative Disorders** **554**
Dissociative Amnesia and Fugue 554
Dissociative Identity Disorder 555
Etiology of Dissociative Disorders 556
CONCEPT LEARNING CHECK **14.4** *Identifying Dissociative Disorders* 556

14.5 **Mood Disorders** **556**
Major Depressive Disorder 556
Depression and Bipolar Disorder 557
Etiology of Mood Disorders 558
CONCEPT LEARNING CHECK **14.5** *Identifying Mood Disorders* 559

14.6 **Psychotic Disorders** **560**
Symptoms of All Schizophrenic Disorders 560
CRITICAL THINKING APPLICATION 561
Schizophrenic Subtypes 561
Etiology of Psychotic Disorders 562
CONCEPT LEARNING CHECK **14.6** *Classifying Signs and Symptoms of Schizophrenia* 563

14.7 **Personality Disorders** **564**
Antisocial Personality Disorder 565
Paranoid Personality Disorder 565
Borderline Personality Disorder 566
Summary of Multiple Influences on Psychological Disorders 567
CONCEPT LEARNING CHECK **14.7** *Categorizing Personality Disorders* 567
VISUAL OVERVIEW: DISTINGUISHING PSYCHOLOGICAL DISORDERS 568
Visual Summary of Psychological Disorders 569
Chapter Review Test • Chapter Discussion Questions • Chapter Projects • Chapter Key
Terms • Answers to Concept Learning Checks • Answers to Chapter Review Test •
References 571

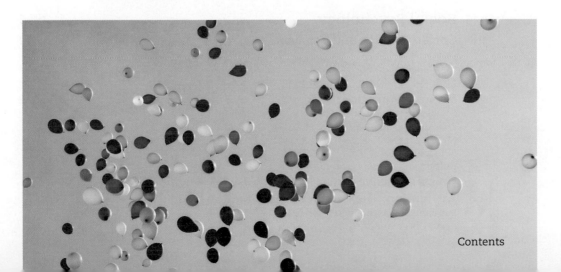

CHAPTER 15 Therapies for Psychological Disorders 578

   15.1 **Mental Health Practitioners and Settings 580**
Psychiatrists 581
Counseling and Clinical Psychologists 581
Master's-Level Therapists 582
Settings for Mental Health Practitioners 582
The Role of Psychotherapy 583
CONCEPT LEARNING CHECK **15.1** *Comparing the Roles and Settings of Mental Health Practitioners 584*

   15.2 **Psychodynamic Therapy** **584**
Techniques of Psychodynamic Therapy 584
Types of Psychodynamic Therapy 586
Short-Term Psychodynamic Therapy 586
CONCEPT LEARNING CHECK **15.2** *Understanding Psychodynamic Therapies 586*

   15.3 **Humanistic Therapy** **587**
Carl Rogers and Client-Centered Therapy 587
CONCEPT LEARNING CHECK **15.3** *Describing the Elements of Humanistic Therapy 588*

   15.4 **Behavior Therapy** **588**
Classical Conditioning Techniques 588
Operant Conditioning Techniques 590
CONCEPT LEARNING CHECK **15.4** *Designing a Behavioral Treatment Plan 590*

   15.5 **Cognitive Therapies** **590**
Aaron Beck and Cognitive Therapy 591
Albert Ellis and Rational Emotive Therapy 591
CONCEPT LEARNING CHECK **15.5** *Comparing Cognitive Therapies 591*

   15.6 **Family Systems and Group Therapy** **592**
Systems Approaches 592
Group Therapy 592
CONCEPT LEARNING CHECK **15.6** *Describing an Eclectic Systems Approach 593*

   15.7 **Biomedical Therapies** **593**
Drug Treatments 593
Medical Procedures 599
CONCEPT LEARNING CHECK **15.7** *Explaining the Use of Medicines for Psychological Conditions 600*

   15.8 **Evaluating Therapies for Psychological Disorders** **601**
Effectiveness of Therapies for Psychological Disorders 601
Effectiveness of Different Therapies 602
Common Factors That Increase Effectiveness 602
Culture, Cultural Values, and Psychotherapy 603
CRITICAL THINKING APPLICATION 603
Summary of Multiple Influences on Therapies for Psychological Disorders 603
CONCEPT LEARNING CHECK **15.8** *Summarizing the Factors of Effective Psychotherapy 604*
VISUAL OVERVIEW: COMMON MEDICATIONS USED TO TREAT PSYCHOLOGICAL DISORDERS 605
Visual Summary of Therapies for Psychological Disorders 606
Chapter Review Test • Chapter Discussion Questions • Chapter Projects • Chapter Key Terms • Answers to Concept Learning Checks • Answers to Chapter Review Test • References 608

CHAPTER 16 Social Psychology 614

   16.1 **Social Thought and Behavior** **617**
Groups 617
Core Social Motives 618
CONCEPT LEARNING CHECK **16.1** *Describing Social Roles 618*

   16.2 **Person Perception** **619**
Social Categorization 619
Physical Appearance 619
Stereotypes 620
Subjectivity 620
Culture and Person Perception 620
CONCEPT LEARNING CHECK **16.2** *Person Perception and Musical Tastes 621*

   16.3 **Attribution: The Person or the Situation? 621**
Fundamental Attribution Error 621
Actor-Observer Bias 621

Defensive Attribution 622
Self-Serving Bias 622

CONCEPT LEARNING CHECK **16.3** *Explaining Attributional Biases* 622

16.4 **Attitudes and Social Judgments**............................**623**
Components of Attitudes 623
Relieving Cognitive Dissonance 624
Influencing Attitudes: Persuasion 624
Culture and Attitudes 625

CONCEPT LEARNING CHECK **16.4** *Explaining Persuasion* 625

16.5 **Conformity and Obedience** **626**
Conformity 626
The Power of the Situation: The Stanford Prison Experiment 627
Obedience 627

CRITICAL THINKING APPLICATION 629

CONCEPT LEARNING CHECK **16.5** *Distinguishing Conformity, Obedience,*
and Compliance 630

16.6 **Social Interactions** **630**
Prejudice 630
Aggression 630
Factors in Attraction 632

CONCEPT LEARNING CHECK **16.6** *Designing for Friendships* 633

16.7 **Group Influence on the Individual**..........................**633**
Altruism 634
Effects of Group Interaction 635
Decision Making 636
Groupthink 636
Social Loafing 637
Social Facilitation 637
Deindividuation 637
Summary of Multiple Influences on Social Psychology 638

CONCEPT LEARNING CHECK **16.7** *Preventing Groupthink* 638

VISUAL OVERVIEW: THE CORE SOCIAL MOTIVES 639

Visual Summary of Social Psychology 640

Chapter Review Test • Chapter Discussion Questions • Chapter Projects • Chapter Key
Terms • Answers to Concept Learning Checks • Answers to Chapter Review Test •
References 641

Glossary 648
Index 663
Credits 675

Welcome

Welcome to *Learn Psychology*! Our goal with *Learn Psychology* is to create content for introductory psychology that establishes a new paradigm for student-centered learning.

Learn Psychology is written with the 21st-century student in mind. We have developed a fresh presentation for introductory psychology that is highly interactive, compatible with digital applications, and cognizant of the challenges of an ever-evolving economic landscape. To us, the perfect textbook makes learners want to read it and presents everything they need to know in an easy-to-use format. That's what we've done with *Learn Psychology*. We have drawn on the best practices of educational pedagogy with a "learning by doing" approach that pairs critical analysis of psychological concepts with examples from everyday life and allows readers to actively engage with the curriculum.

About The Learn Series

Learn Psychology is the flagship publication of **The Learn Series**, a completely new course curriculum solution from Jones & Bartlett Learning that aims to provide a fresh, integrated print and digital program solution for general education survey courses. **The Learn Series** is produced with today's "digitally native" students in mind by re-envisioning the learning experience and focusing not just on *what* students learn but also *how* students learn. **The Learn Series** is characterized by authoritative and notable authors; visual, modular design; student-centered pedagogy; and integrated formative and summative assessments that improve learning outcomes—features that allow instructors to easily customize and personalize course curriculum. **The Learn Series** provides the most interactive and advanced curriculum solution for today's student-centered learning environments by emphasizing the skills students need to thrive in the 21st-century knowledge-based economy.

For more information on additional titles in the series, please visit www.TheLearnSeries. com.

Skills for the 21st-Century Workforce

	Sample 21st-Century Addressable Workforce Skills			Supporting Pedagogy in The *Learn Series*
RESEARCH LITERACY	Able to determine the extent of information needed	Able to evaluate information and its sources critically	Can apply evidence to new problem solutions	Group and individual projects Online writing tutorial included in Navigate
INTERPERSONAL COMMUNICATION & PUBLIC SPEAKING	Can convey ideas and meaning through oral communication	Able to speak persuasively in a group	Can effectively work in a team structure to solve problems	Group and individual projects Discussion questions Instructor's Resource Curriculum Guide with additional group projects and activities
PROBLEM SOLVING & CRITICAL ANALYSIS	Able to analyze data Able to synthesize different types of information	Able to evaluate source material for validity, etc.	Able to make decisions based on data	Critical Thinking Applications Short essay questions in Test Bank Interactive exercises in Navigate PAL Psychology
TECHNOLOGY LITERACY	Able to use the Internet critically	Able to retrieve and manage information via technology	Able to use basic word processing and spreadsheet software/tools	Navigate Learn Psychology Chapter Projects Online activities and assignments
WRITTEN COMMUNICATION	Able to organize and outline the main topics or thesis	Uses a variety of simple and complex sentences to create a fluid writing style	Able to write complete, grammatically correct sentences	Online Writing Tutorial included in Navigate Short Essay Questions in Assessment Banks

The Themes and Approach of *Learn Psychology*

The overarching definition of psychology is the science of behavior and mental processes, and the biological, experiential, and sociocultural factors that influence behavior. In *Learn Psychology*, we highlight the multiple influences that affect psychological phenomena. Within each chapter, we explain how biological factors (including genetics, neural processing, hormones, and evolution) combine with environmental factors (such as culture, social context, and experience) to influence psychology. We offer multiple levels of explanation to aid in understanding the "why" of psychology; that is, why do people behave they way they do? In order to understand psychological questions, we must explain the interplay of biological and environmental influences jointly at work in all human behavior.

Each chapter topic is explained in terms of the multiple influences on psychology and concludes with a thought-provoking summary that emphasizes these multiple influences. Learners will see this theme of "multiple influences on psychology" repeated throughout the text, continually underscoring the fact that human psychology has roots in biology, yet is driven by social and cultural context, and that these factors work in concert to explain psychological concepts and questions. Though the field is just beginning to explore how genes and environment interact in development, for example, *Learn Psychology* encourages students to consider multiple influences as explanations for any topic within psychology.

Throughout the book we also emphasize psychological science and explain the methods involved in research. We present state-of-the-art information on psychological topics and the supporting scientific evidence. What we know about psychological phenomena comes from these studies, so it is critical that students learn about the science and the methods. These research discussions require the learner to think critically about conclusions from empirical studies and how results can be applied to behavior in the real world. The scientific foundation includes both classic and recent studies to provide the most accurate, current, and comprehensive coverage possible.

The Structure of *Learn Psychology*

Learn Psychology helps optimize learning through enhanced coverage, study, testing, and review while emphasizing the "doing" that reinforces comprehension. Pedagogical features are designed to provide a preview of the material and ensure key concepts are well understood. Each chapter contains numbered sections, or modules, that address a major concept in the introductory psychology curriculum. These modules are self-contained key content units. Each module has associated learning objectives, preview statement, illustrations, concept learning check, and finally, a summary and test. This modular content unit structure informs the entire *Learn Psychology* program.

All of the content in *Learn Psychology* is highly visual, current, and easy to understand. Visual overviews play to dynamic learning and underscore important points. Our goal with *Learn Psychology* is to present accurate core content rooted in best-in-class pedagogy while avoiding distracting off-topic add-ons. The result is an introductory psychology curriculum that is engaging, consistent, and complete—and which helps students measure their progress at every step.

Learn Psychology is fully comprehensive and designed for cutting-edge coursework. By incorporating opportunities for active learning, Learn Psychology maximizes teaching productivity, enhances student learning, and addresses the challenges of teaching and learning introductory psychology in fresh, new ways.

Pedagogical Aids and Features

Learn Psychology is based on a modular concept format that provides a clear organization of the key topics pertaining to introductory psychology. With this modular format, digital versions of *Learn Psychology* are also fully customizable, allowing faculty full control over the desired curriculum. For more information on customization options, please visit the publisher website at www.jblearning.com.

This essential textbook covers more than 100 introductory psychology topics and divides them into modules linked with learning objectives, providing students with a structured road map for learning, reviewing, and self-assessment.

Every chapter in *Learn Psychology* is organized with the following structure to help learners engage with the concepts in the textbook as they read:

Chapter Sections

The modular format dictates that each chapter opens with a series of learning objectives, which reappear whenever a topic is repeated to help guide students' learning. Each chapter contains several numbered sections that address a major topic or concept; sections are largely self-contained units of content instruction. Any element or feature labeled with a section number reflects and is relevant to that section.

Chapter Overview

Content-specific chapter overviews provide a summary of key chapter concepts and serve as a "master plan" to visually show the scope and sequence of content covered. Students use the Chapter Overviews as a map, to guide them through critical concepts and keep them connected to learning objectives.

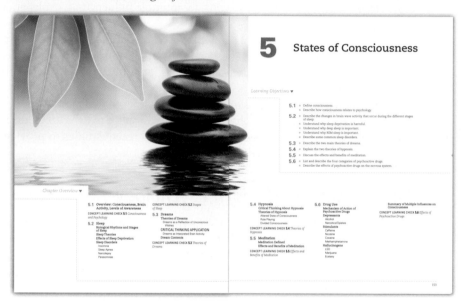

Section Preview Statement

Within each section, a preview statement summarizes the content of the section that follows. These preview statements prepare students for the content ahead, providing advance organization during reading.

14.1 Overview: Understanding Psychological Disorders

Psychologists use a number of different tools to diagnose and understand psychological disorders.

- Define psychological disorders as determined by the American Psychiatric Association (APA) and explain the criteria for abnormal behavior using the *Diagnostic and Statistical Manual of Mental Disorders*.

Figures and Tables

Figures and tables underscore key points or present complex information. They provide an effective alternative mode of instruction, presented schematically to aid the reader visually and reinforce the text. References to figures are in color to make it easier to locate the figure and pop right back into the reading.

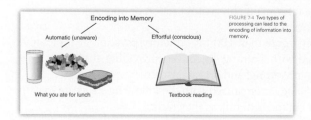

FIGURE 7-4 Two types of processing can lead to the encoding of information into memory.

Concept Learning Check

At the end of every section, a Concept Learning Check is presented to test mastery of the material in that section. These checks focus on "pain points" for students and provide extra coaching on the key concepts in the chapter. This gives learners a chance to apply what they have studied in fresh examples, or to see the material applied from a different perspective.

Critical Thinking Application

The Critical Thinking Applications within each chapter highlight a challenging or topical concept that asks learners to participate and demonstrate their understanding of the concepts.

Summary of Multiple Influences in the Chapter

The final section of each chapter ties together the discussion of biological and environmental factors affecting our psychology and highlights the multiple influences on the topic presented.

Chapter Key Terms

Key Terms appear in blue in the text at point of use and are defined in a way that doesn't interrupt the main idea of the sentence. Key terms are also provided in the margin with sharp definitions that can be used as flashcards. Key terms are also found as an alphabetical list at the very end of the chapter and in the final glossary.

Visual Overview

The Visual Overview provides a dynamic visual diagram of one or more key concepts and helps to tie chapter themes and segments into a cohesive whole.

Visual Summary

The Visual Summary is located at the end of the chapter and recaps the main ideas in each section using brief, bulleted sentences that are highlighted with an image that refers back to the section content.

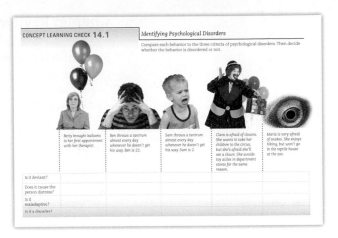

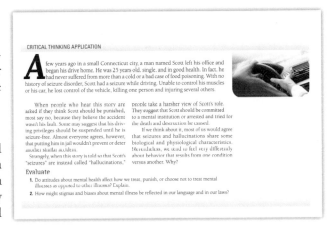

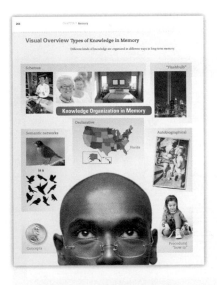

Chapter Review Test

The Chapter Review Test is a multiple-choice self-quiz covering the entire chapter. Headings correlate to chapter sections as well as objective statements. Answers that provide complete rationales are also included.

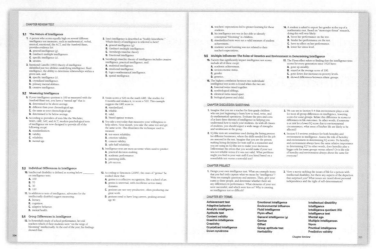

Chapter Discussion Questions

Open-ended questions provoke thoughtful discussions in the classroom or in online discussion boards. These questions are carefully chosen to illuminate key concepts of the chapter and to create a constructive experience of discussion, evaluation, and comparison in order to solidify comprehension.

Chapter Projects

Potential projects for individuals, pairs, or small groups are suggested. These can be done either in class or outside of class. They focus on an issue related to students' lives and experience, real-world applications, or media depictions of psychological concepts.

Learn Psychology Digital Curriculum

Learn Psychology is a comprehensive and integrated print and digital solution for courses in introductory psychology. Instructors and students can use the following digital resources in part, or in whole:

Navigate Learn Psychology is a simple-to-use and fully customizable online learning platform combining authoritative content written by the authors of the main text with interactive tools, assessments, and robust reporting and grading functionality. Using content that extends the core text, including objectives organized by lesson, instructors can use Navigate Learn Psychology as part of an on-ground, online, or hybrid course offering requiring little to no start-up time.

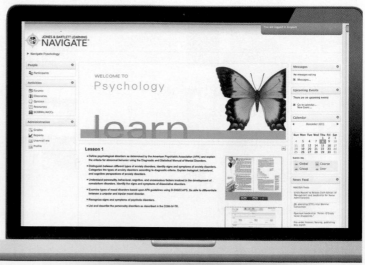

PAL Psychology is a powerful new personalized adaptive learning (PAL) program that uniquely combines study planning, homework assignments, and assessment tools all in one easy-to-use application. PAL Psychology helps students study more efficiently so they can make the most of their study time.

For students who prefer electronic textbooks, *Learn Psychology* is also available in digital formats from leading ebook retailers such as Coursesmart, Amazon, and Google.

Learn Psychology Instructor Resource Program

Every element in the Instructor Resource Program maps to chapter and section-level learning objectives. Student learning outcomes are developed by the main authors of the core text ensuring quality and consistency throughout.

The Comprehensive Instructor Resource Program includes:

- **Instructor Resource Curriculum Guide** featuring chapter overviews, chapter outlines, suggested lectures, discussion questions, projects, handouts and media resources—all keyed to chapter section and learning objectives, when and where possible. Additionally, we also include a correlation grid connecting learning objectives to APA outcomes and selected 21st-century workforce skills.
- **Brownstone's *Diploma* Testing Software** with a comprehensive bank of test questions written by the main text authors. The complete bank includes over 160 Critical Thinking, Applied, and Factual questions per chapter, each tagged to chapter learning objectives and Bloom's Taxonomy. Questions can be sorted, selected, and edited based on level of difficulty or question type.
- **PowerPoint™ Presentation Slides** in multiple formats including PowerPoint with chapter images only; PowerPoint with chapter outlines and key narrative; and PowerPoint with outlines, key narrative, and images. All of the PowerPoint slide presentations are written by the main text authors and include references to supported chapter learning objectives.
- **Psychology Instructor Place** for online access to PowerPoints, Instructor Resource Curriculum Guide, APA correlation grid, 21st-century workforce correlation grid, discussion questions file, suggested student projects, video resources links, chapter-by-chapter media bibliography, and sample syllabi.

Contact your Jones & Bartlett Learning Account Representative for more details.

More Free Resources for Students To Support Basic Writing Skills:

A Writing Tutorial for College Students

The ability to organize and outline main topics and write complete, grammatically correct sentences is a critical skill for today's freshman-level student. Combining the best of English composition manuals and various open resources available online, *Learn Psychology* includes a specially developed free resource designed to help students improve basic writing skills, analyze resources on the web, and perform critical analysis of a topic.

The website, www.AWritingTutorialforCollegeStudents.com, distills the essential skills of writing into eight succinct modules:

1. Introduction to College Writing
2. Structure and Thesis Statements
3. Mechanics and Grammar
4. Research, Citation, and Avoiding Plagiarism
5. Making an Argument
6. The Research Paper
7. The Writing Process
8. Elegance and Style

About the Authors

Dr. Antone Minard, PhD

Dr. Minard earned his PhD from the University of California, Los Angeles. He currently resides in Vancouver, British Columbia, where he teaches in the Humanities Department at Simon Fraser University and in the Department of Classical, Near Eastern, and Religious Studies at the University of British Columbia.

Dr. Amy Hale, PhD

Dr. Hale earned her PhD from the University of California, Los Angeles, and teaches introductory students in a variety of courses, disciplines, and delivery systems emphasizing writing projects and assignments.

Acknowledgments

There is an art to aiding in the creation of a textbook like this one. It's an effort that involves encouragement, opportunity, support, and constructive criticism. There are dozens of people who have mastered this art and who made the completion of this project possible. We want to start by thanking Eve Howard, Senior Vice President at Jones & Bartlett Learning. Eve's vision has been the essence of this project, and she provided wonderful motivational speeches, mentorship, understanding, and advice. We would also like to thank our editor, Bill Wahlgren, for his tireless guidance with the manuscript and for his patience and gentility. Without the help extended by each of them, we would not have developed the skills necessary to carry out this project, nor would we have as deep an appreciation of the meaning of collaboration. A special thank-you to the friendly production experts at Jones & Bartlett Learning, including Susan Schultz, Anne Spencer, and Anna Genoese. We would like to especially thank our chief marketing strategist, Alison Pendergast.

Jonna Kwiatkowski of Mars Hill College expertly jumped in and assisted us with the discussion questions and projects at the end of the chapters, taking advantage of her experience with successful online class delivery, and with several of the ancillary elements of the *Learn Psychology* resources. Wendy Ludgewait also contributed to the development of the learning objectives and assessments and the lecture materials.

We also want to thank the reviewers of *Learn Psychology*, who took time out of their hectic schedules to pore over the drafts of the chapters. Your dedication, attention to detail, and expertise helped shape this text. We learned so much from each of you. Thank you!

In-Depth Psychology Faculty Reviewers

Laura Bailey, San Joaquin Valley College
Art Beaman, University of Kentucky
Janice Hartgrove-Freile, Lonestar Community College
John Haworth, Chattanooga State Community College
Linda Jackson, Michigan State University
Jim Johnson, Central New Mexico Community College
Kevin O'Neil, Florida Gulf Coast University
Catherine Snyder, Paradise Valley Community College
John Updegraff, Kent State University

In addition to the reviewers, special thanks to the many instructors who participated in our expanded review and market research, which aided us in rounding out the strategy for **The Learn Series**, as well as refining the pedagogy and chapters of *Learn Psychology*.

Psychology Faculty Analysts

Eric D. Miller, Kent State University
Javier Alonso, Oakton Community College
Jill Norvilitis, Buffalo State College
Richard Shadick, Pace University
Timothy Hartshorne, Central Michigan University
Michelle Russell, University of Tennessee-Knoxville
Jamie Tanner, Valdosta State University
Christine Harrington, Middlesex County College
Dennis A. Gentry, University of Cincinnati Clermont
Cecile Marczinski, Northern Kentucky University
Kim Morris, Athens Technical College
Michael Davis, West Virginia Northern Community College
Steve Ellyson, Youngstown State University
Linda Bajdo, Macomb Community College
Peter Vernig, Suffolk University
Caroline Kozojed, Bismarck State College
Christopher J. Mruk, Bowling Green State University
Bob Reese, Jefferson College of Health Sciences
Amber Amspoker, University of Houston
Teri Fournier, Diablo Valley College

Sean Taylor, Des Moines Area Community College

Scot Hamilton, University of West Georgia

Kevin Kean, Central Connecticut State University

Michael Rader, Northern Arizona University

Jeffrey Green, Virginia Commonwealth University

Diane Reddy, University of Wisconsin-Milwaukee

Jeffrey Baker, Monroe Community College

Karla Lassonde, Minnesota State University, Mankato

Diane Pisacreta, Saint Louis Community College

David Gersh, Houston Community College—Central

Kelie Jones, Odessa College

Cari Cannon, Santiago Canyon College

Andrea Molarius, Shasta College

Ari Grayson, Scottsdale College

Robert Zettle, Wichita State University

Dr. Rebecca Fahrlander, University of Nebraska at Omaha

David Biek, Macon State College

Bonnie Gray, Scottsdale College

Brian Howland, University of Florida

Emily Stark, Minnesota State University, Mankato

Ryan Tapscott, Iowa State University

Mary Fraser, DeAnza College

Susie Sympson, Johnson County Community College

Mary-Ellen O'Sullivan, Housatonic Community College

Dr. Eva Szeli, Arizona State University

Michael Knepp, Mount Union

Karl L. Wuensch, East Carolina University

Barb Corbisier, Blinn College

Autumn Willard, St. Clair County Community College

Sarah Novak, Hofstra University

Lorry Cology, Owens Community College

Laura Jackman, Joliet Junior College

Melissa McCeney, Montgomery College

Jill Berger, Nova Southeastern University

Tamara Hodges, Baylor University

Amy Masnick, Hofstra University

Christine Lofgren, University of California Irvine

William Rick Fry, Youngstown State University

Michael Rader, Northern Arizona University

Aimee Callender, Auburn University

Chris Ruggiero, Tacoma Community College

Rick Howe, College of the Canyons

Finally, a very special thanks to my entire family and many friends, including Jennifer Thompson, Jack Hardy, Teddy Ottaviano, Sharon Lewis, and Susan Ashmore, for providing infinite patience, kindness, and food during adversity.
—Kenneth Carter

To my girls, Lynn Hillger, Julie Boland, and Kim Wheeler, for getting me through it; and my boys, Zeke and Victor Montalvo, for making me do it. I owe you.
—Colleen Seifert

About the Authors

Dr. Kenneth Carter received his PhD in Clinical Psychology from the University of Michigan, Ann Arbor, in 1993 and completed a postdoctoral Masters in clinical psychopharmacology at Fairleigh Dickinson University in 2007. Before joining the faculty at Emory University, Dr. Carter served as a Senior Assistant Research Scientist in the Epidemic Intelligence Service of the Centers for Disease Control and Prevention where he researched smoking as a risk marker for suicidal behaviors in adolescents. Currently he is a Professor of Psychology at Oxford College, Emory University, where he is actively involved in research and teaching. Dr. Carter has been a psychotherapist and researcher for more than 17 years. His work has garnered awards from the National Institutes of Health, the National Heart, Lung, and Blood Institute, and the University of Michigan. Dr. Carter is a past editor of *JCAL: The Journal of Cognitive-Affective Learning*. In addition to his own research, Dr. Carter authors articles in plain language on the latest research in psychology for magazines such as *mental_floss* and *Reader's Digest*, and for news programs such as *Connect With Kids* and NBC's *Today*.

Dr. Colleen Seifert received her BA in Psychology from Gustavus Adolphus College in St. Peter, Minnesota, in 1980, and her PhD in Psychology from Yale University in 1987. After a postdoctoral fellowship at the University of California at San Diego, Dr. Seifert moved to the University of Michigan, Ann Arbor, and was promoted to full Professor of Psychology in 2001. She was named Arthur F. Thurnau Professor of Psychology in 2011. Her research publications address thinking and memory, specifically, how the status and types of past experiences in memory affect current reasoning. Dr. Seifert's investigations are rooted in her interest in how people navigate through complex, real-world tasks, and her research examines planning and problem solving in the domains of legal reasoning, medicine, and creative design. She is a past President and Executive Officer of the Cognitive Science Society, past co-chair of the Institutional Review Board for the Behavioral Sciences at Michigan, and a member of several journal editorial boards.

Chapter Overview ▼

1.1 The Science of Psychology

CONCEPT LEARNING CHECK 1.1 *The Scope and Limits of the Science of Psychology*

1.2 The Origins and History of Psychology
Philosophical Roots
Biological Roots
Schools of Thought: Structuralism vs. Functionalism
  Structuralism
  Functionalism

CONCEPT LEARNING CHECK 1.2 *Comparing and Contrasting Structuralism and Functionalism*

1.3 Contemporary Psychology
The Biological Perspective
The Evolutionary Perspective
The Psychodynamic Perspective
The Behavioral Perspective
The Humanistic Perspective
The Cognitive Perspective
The Sociocultural Perspective
Professional Specialization and Research Areas in Psychology

CONCEPT LEARNING CHECK 1.3 *Contemporary Perspectives and Settings in Psychology*

1 Psychology: An Overview

Learning Objectives ▼

1.1 ▪ Define the science of psychology.
▪ Distinguish between psychological science and popular misconceptions about psychology.

1.2 ▪ Discuss the origins and history of psychology.
▪ Examine the role of philosophy and physiology in the development of psychology.
▪ Contrast structuralism and functionalism.

1.3 ▪ Compare and contrast contemporary perspectives in psychology.
▪ Describe focused specializations of research and practice.

1.4 ▪ Examine the role of critical thinking in the field of psychology.
▪ Illustrate the five criteria for critical thinking.

1.4 Critical Thinking and Multiple Influences
Critical Thinking
The Importance of Multiple Influences
CRITICAL THINKING APPLICATION
Summary of Multiple Influences on Psychology

CONCEPT LEARNING CHECK **1.4** *Applying the Criteria of Critical Thinking*

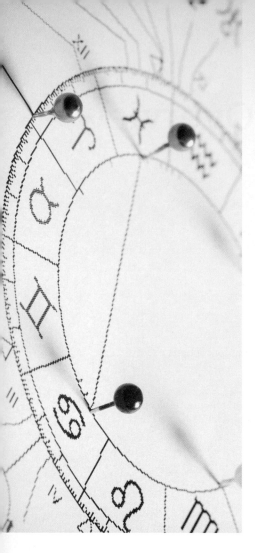

I am one of those people who always knew what I wanted to be when I grew up. Well, not always. It was around fifth grade that I stumbled upon psychology, and I knew that it was the career for me. Little did I know that I would spend the rest of my life as a psychologist and much of my social life preparing myself for a surprise each time someone discovered what I did for a living.

You see, when you are a psychologist, friends, family, and even strangers will bombard you with tons of questions about what kind of people are most compatible in a relationship and which antidepressants are best for poodles and what kind of person would keep a pet monkey and what it means when you dream about the ocean and . . . well, you get the point. Not just questions—theories, too: strange theories about behavior based on the tiniest sliver of psychology, theories based on flawed evidence, and, all too often, theories based on no evidence at all.

Psychology is a field that is vast, but not always in the ways that people think. Why are there so many questions and why so many theories? People have a natural curiosity about behavior and mental processes—a natural curiosity about psychology. But people do not always understand the difference between psychology and other ways to explain behavior. Such was the case back in graduate school one day as I was heading to campus on the shuttle. A fellow passenger noticed I was reading a book on relationships.

"Oh, you are a *psychologist*," she said, with the same kind of lilt in her voice as if I had told her I was going to school to be a pirate.

"Yes, I am just reading about a theory of relationships."

"Is it about Libras? What sign are you?"

"Oh . . . um . . . Well, you know that is astrolo—"

"I bet you are a Capricorn."

"Well, no . . . I am a Taurus."

"That is just what I thought. You are just like a Taurus. They taught you about that in grad school, right?"

"Well, no . . . nothing about Taurus. You see, that's astrolog—"

"They *didn't* teach you about personality? That's stupid. Every psychologist should know about personality."

"Oh . . . no, they did teach me about personality. I had several courses on personality theory, but horoscopes are not really psychology, that's really astrolo—"

"You do not know about personality? I cannot believe you do not know the personality of a Taurus. Exactly what do they teach you about psychology in grad school?"

"Well . . . they teach you science."

1.1 The Science of Psychology

Psychology is the scientific study of behavior and mental processes.

- Define the science of psychology.
- Distinguish between psychological science and popular misconceptions about psychology.

Tell someone you are studying psychology (go ahead—try it) and you are likely to hear some common reactions. Some people suppose you are interested in psychological disorders and may launch into a story about an uncle who collected lost keys or a friend who nibbles her food in careful counter-clockwise bites. Still others may abruptly silence themselves, admitting nervously that they fear that you are going to analyze them. Some might even huff and say that psychology is the science of the obvious. You see, misunderstandings about the field of psychology are deep and wide ranging. Often they are based on popular belief, media portrayals, or assumptions that have little or nothing to do with the science of psychology. **Psychology**, the scientific study of mental processes and behavior, is a fascinating science, and you have come to study it at a very good time. While people have pondered behavior and mental processes for ages, it is only fairly recently that we have examined them scientifically.

The word *psychology* comes from two Greek words: *psych* (meaning *mind*) and *logo* (*study*). The word *psychology* translates to *study of the mind*. Today, psychology has broadened its scope beyond the study of subjective experiences of the **mind** to answer a vast number of questions about mental processes and behavior. To name just a few: What is the best way to treat psychological conditions such as depression? How do children learn to speak? What causes us to fear or to love or to laugh? What motivates people to work hard in school and in their careers? How do we make meaning out of the sounds we hear and the things we see? How do we go about making sense of the world around us? The study of the mind is one of the most important sciences because it addresses something of natural interest to everyone who has a mind. It also offers essential insights into and understanding of what it means to be human.

If you think about it, we are all in the business of examining behavior and mental processes. After all, since we all have minds, we all know something about how they work. It is common to wonder about the attitudes and behavior of those around us, as well as our own. We try to behave appropriately (for the most part) in various situations, and often we try to influence the behavior of others. Some of us are known for understanding, and at times anticipating, the attitudes and behaviors of others. So how are psychologists any different?

Psychologists are different because they are scientists, and their work is based on scientific principles. **Science** is the operation of general laws, especially as obtained and tested through the scientific method. Wilson (1999) says that science "is the organized, systematic enterprise that gathers knowledge about the world and condenses this knowledge into testable laws and principles" (p. 58). Science emphasizes **empiricism**, or knowledge based on observation. We will discuss the principles of scientific study and the scientific method. We have a tremendous arsenal of methods that allow us to systematically

Psychology The scientific study of behavior and mental processes.

Mind Mental processes and our subjective experiences.

Science The operation of general laws, especially as obtained and tested through the scientific method.

Empiricism The theory of knowledge that assumes that knowledge should be based on observation.

THE FIRST CENTURY

of Psychological Science and Practice in America

Dr. Ludy T. Benjamin, Jr.

M	Movement or shift in field
F	Fields
E	Event/major meeting/ milestone
L	Legal or accreditation
P	Publication or new journal
S	Major study

1880s

M	Child Study Movement began
M	Psychology taught within traditional philosophy departments
E	First American psychology laboratories: Johns Hopkins, Pennsylvania, Indiana, Wisconsin, Clark, Nebraska, Kansas
P	Publication of George Trumbull Ladd's *Elements of Physiological Psychology* (1887)
P	Founding of *American Journal of Psychology* (1887) by G. Stanley Hall

1890s

M	Structuralism flourished under Titchener at Cornell University
M	Beginnings of American functionalism and its conflict with structuralism
E	Psychology laboratories founded at many universities including Columbia, Iowa, Michigan, Wellesley, Harvard, and Texas
E	American Psychological Association formed in 1892 by G. Stanley Hall and others
P	Coining of the term "mental test" in 1890 by James McKeen Cattell and development of anthropometric mental testing
P	Publication of William James's *Principles of Psychology* (1890)

Empirical evidence A type of information that is capable of being confirmed or invalidated by systematic observation.

examine behavior and the psychological factors that drive it. Today's psychology is called psychological science at some universities in recognition of the rigor of its study. The science you will read about in *Learn Psychology* is based on solid, **empirical** observations that are repeatable.

A field of study that uses the scientific method to increase knowledge is a science. Legions of scientists, from astronomers to zoologists, use scientific methodology to investigate and improve our knowledge of the world around us and beyond. For example, physicists, geologists, and astronomers improve our understanding of the universe. Biologists and chemists study the origins of life, its endless variations, and, in medical science, the preservation of life and health in humans. The study of mental processes and human behavior is reserved for psychologists, using scientific methodology to improve our knowledge about *us*, making it one of the most vital, influential, and important sciences. In addition, psychologists are the only scientists who use the *subject* of their investigations—the mind—to *perform* their investigations. It is a unique challenge. As you will learn, designing and conducting experiments that reveal important insights about our mental processes and behavior is a demanding task. For some, it is a life's work. Clearly, this approach to understanding and at times anticipating the attitudes and behaviors of others is far removed from the intuitive "horse sense" that some people seem to have about others. Further, intuition resists explanation and cannot be taught. Often it is just plain wrong. Psychology, being based on scientific principles, welcomes analysis and criticism. Some of the experimental studies you will read about have been performed dozens of times over the years with dozens of different populations. Some of the general laws of psychology you will study may indeed be predictable, but many others are guaranteed to surprise you! We hope that this text engages you in learning about the many ways the science of psychology has advanced far beyond what we as individual "users" know about the mind.

Sometimes, however, the results of scientific inquiry are unsatisfactory. This may be due to our expectations: They may be unrealistic. For example, if you asked a biologist to tell you what a goby fish eats, I am certain that any ichthyologist, a biologist who studies fish, could spout off the favorite meals of the goby quite easily. If, however, I produced a goby from a bowl and asked an ichthyologist to tell you what this specific fish ate yesterday, you would have a different story. The sentences would be full of "probably" and "likely" meals for the fish. Science is pretty good at describing and predicting trends for larger groups, but the more specific you get, the more problems there are. Things get fuzzier the more specific your demands. It is the same for planets, plants, and people. Astronomy, too, is much better at explaining the general than the specific. We can say more confidently, for example, how planets come to be than how our planet, the Earth, came to be. And with psychology, we can say why some people may be shy, but not necessarily why any particular person is or may be shy. We can predict how aggressive people are based on the area of the country they live in (Cohen, Nisbett, Bowdle, & Schwarz, 1996), the temperature on a given day (Anderson & Anderson, 1984), the levels of the hormone testosterone in their saliva (Yu & Shi, 2009), and whether they have just won or lost a soccer game (Rascle et al., 2010). But we cannot predict whether a specific individual

Figuring out what a species of fish eats is much easier than determining what a particular fish had to eat that day.

1890s *(Continued)*

M Edward Thorndike's pioneering work in animal learning

M Dominance of studies of sensation and perception in the study of human consciousness

E Joseph Jastrow organized psychology exhibition at the Chicago World's Fair (1893)

E Founding of the first psychological clinic at the University of Pennsylvania by Lightner Witmer (1896)

P Cattell bought *Science* magazine (1894)

S First study on the psychology of advertising by Harlow Gale (1895)

1900s

M Studies of learning became more prominent, especially animal learning

F Applied areas of study included: child development, educational psychology, abnormal psychology, mental testing

E First psychology laboratory in a mental hospital—McLean Hospital in Belmont, Massachusetts (1904)

P Publication of the four volumes of Titchener's *Experimental Psychology* ("The manuals") (1901–1905)

P First books on social psychology (1909)

M Founding of Titchener's Experimentalists (1904)

M Mental hygiene movement began (1908)

M Formalization of American functional psychology (functionalism) at the University of Chicago and Columbia University

E Sigmund Freud visited America for the Clark University 20th anniversary (1909)

L First eugenic sterilization law in Indiana (1907)

P New journals: *Journal of Philosophy, Psychology, and Scientific Method* (1903), *Psychological Bulletin* (1904), *Journal of Abnormal Psychology* (1906), *The Psychological Clinic* (1907)

will become a domestic abuser, even knowing his or her personal circumstances. It is understandable that this may be disappointing. After all, we are not interested in predictions of behaviors in general as much as we are interested in why people we know do—or do not do—certain things. The limits of prediction are a problem shared by all sciences.

Finally, it is important to recognize that not everything that sounds like science is science. Sometimes we come to believe things because they are dressed up as science. Information that appears scientific but is based on unsound scientific principles is **pseudoscience**. Pseudoscience that can seem somewhat scientific is often appealing. There are some famous examples of pseudoscience. Maybe you have a roommate who listens to classical music when he or she studies. Maybe you listen to it yourself. Take a moment to listen to some classical music. Do you feel yourself getting smarter? Does listening to classical music improve intelligence? Some people in Georgia thought so. They enlisted corporations to donate classical music recordings to expectant mothers. Do a quick search of the Internet for "Mozart effect" and I am sure you will locate dozens and dozens (and dozens) of websites that describe the connection between intelligence and classical music.

A peek into the original study reveals some surprising findings (Rauscher, Shaw, & Ky, 1993). The researchers examined the effect of listening to classical music—namely the first few minutes of "Mozart Sonata for 2 Pianos in D Major"—on a few dozen college students. The researchers found a temporary increase in spatial–temporal reasoning on an IQ test. Since that time, many people have tried, but no one has ever been successful at duplicating the results of the study (Pietschnig, Voracek, & Formann, 2010).

The greatest difficulty in the study of psychology is the vast number of topics that fall under its purview. Everything we do involves our mental processes in some way, so the behaviors of interest include a wide range of topics, from marriage proposals to Google circles. The only limitation to the study of human behavior is figuring out a method for observing it. In this text, we will examine some of the important topics in psychology and introduce you to them. It is a daunting task, nearly like showing a friend your favorite sites on the Internet in only a few moments. We have tried to highlight the most important research findings, the "greatest hits," and the hottest new science, all of which reveal important principles and insights about mental processes and human behavior.

Does listening to Mozart make you smarter? Some researchers thought so. Then their results sparked a pseudoscience theory called the Mozart effect.

Pseudoscience Information that appears scientific but is based on unsound scientific principles

---

CONCEPT LEARNING CHECK 1.1 | *The Scope and Limits of the Science of Psychology*

1. Wilson just read in his psychology text that most people require 8 hours of sleep to be rested, but he feels rested after only sleeping 5. Wilson now believes that the sleep researcher must be wrong. How would you respond to Wilson's claim?

2. Make a list of some topics you are excited to learn about in psychology. Use the table of contents and the index to map out where the topics might appear. Do not be surprised if you find topics in many locations.

1910s

M Rapid growth of industrial psychology

E World War I provided a significant impetus to applied psychology, particularly mental testing and abnormal psychology

E Psychologists were stationed at 40 Army hospitals during the war

E New York Psychoanalytic Society (1911), American Psychoanalytic Association (1911)

P Watson published his behaviorist manifesto (1913)

P New journals: *Journal of Educational Psychology* (1910), *Psychoanalytic Review* (1913), *Journal of Experimental Psychology* (1916), *Journal of Applied Psychology* (1917)

E First internships in psychology were begun at the Boston Psychopathic Hospital under Robert Yerkes (1912)

E Founding of American Association of Clinical Psychologists (1917)

S Research on the nature and origin of sex differences; early work on the psychology of women

P Lewis Terman's version of Binet scale, the Stanford-Binet (1917)

1920s

M Decade of greatest popularity of psychology with the public

M Gestalt psychology ideas crossed the Atlantic

M Structuralism disappeared after the death of Titchener in 1927

L APA established a certification program for consulting psychologists

E Francis Cecil Sumner is first African-American PhD in psychology (1920)

E American Vocational Guidance Association (1921)

P Appearance of several American popular psychology magazines

1.2 The Origins and History of Psychology

Psychology has roots in other disciplines such as philosophy and biology that have influenced both early and contemporary perspectives in psychology.

- Discuss the origins and history of psychology.
- Examine the role of philosophy and physiology in the development of psychology.
- Contrast structuralism and functionalism.

If you wanted to study psychology in, say, the late 1700s, you were pretty much out of luck. Psychology had not grown into its own discipline yet. It was the realm of thinkers in philosophy and biology. Philosophers were interested in what it means to be human, so they began studying the mind, or our subjective experience. Biologists, on the other hand, were busy studying our organs, including the brain. It would not be until much later that *psychological scientists* would emerge to construct a scientific approach to behavior and mental processes.

How did psychology emerge from the fringes of philosophy and biology to become one of the most popular sciences of the 21st century FIGURE 1-1? Changes in psychology were, in part, the result of debates among the early schools of psychology that turned the young discipline to science in order to answer questions about the structure and function of behavior and mental processes. Psychology as an independent discipline did not emerge until the late 19th century (around the time of the invention of the first cash register, blue jeans, and the electric light bulb).

FIGURE 1-1 Psychology has become one of the most popular undergraduate degrees.
Source: Data from Monitor on Psychology, *June 2008, Vol. 39, No. 6.*

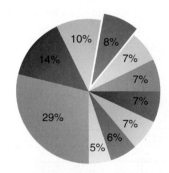

- ■ Business 311,600
- ■ Social sciences and history 156,900
- ■ Education 105,500
- ■ Psychology 85,600
- ■ Visual and performing arts 81,000
- ■ Health professions and related clinical sciences 80,700
- ■ Engineering and engineering technologies 78,600
- ■ Communications, journalism, and related programs 72,700
- ■ Biological and biomedical sciences 64,600
- ■ Computer and information sciences 54,100

1920s *(Continued)*

M Debates over nature-nurture

M Child Guidance Movement began

M Behaviorism became dominant system of psychology

E The Psychological Corporation (1921)

E Ninth International Congress of Psychology—Yale University (1929),

E Psi Chi (1929)

P Rorschach Test (1921), teaching machine (1924), Draw-a-Man Test (1926)

P First textbooks published on the history of psychology (1929)

1930s

M Emphasis on operationism and operational definitions

M Growth of projective testing

M Decade for grand theories of personality (Allport, Murray)

E Association for Consulting Psychologists (1930); Society for Research in Child Development (1933); Society for the Psychological Study of Social Issues (1936); American Association for Applied Psychology (1937)

S Kelloggs' ape and child study (1931; Psychometric Society (1935)

P Thematic Apperception Test (1935)

M Beginning of neobehaviorism (Tolman, Hull, Guthrie, Skinner)

M Beginnings of differential academic training for experimental and clinical psychologists

M Large influx of emigre psychologists from Europe, especially Germany and Austria

E Inez Beverly Prosser—first African-American woman PhD in psychology (1933)

E Boder's Psychological Museum in Chicago (1937)

P Psychological Round Table (1936)

P *Journal of Consulting Psychology* (1937); *Journal of Parapsychology* (1938)

Philosophical Roots

What motivates human behavior? What determines our personality? Psychologists certainly were not the first people to consider questions such as these: Psychology has deep roots in **philosophy**, the study of knowledge and existence, which has long considered what motivates behavior. For example, Aristotle (BCE 384–322) FIGURE 1-2 contemplated the connection of the body and soul (Benjamin, 2008). Ancient philosophers like Plato and Aristotle and even William Shakespeare and Descartes considered many of the same things that psychologists are working on today.

Biological Roots

Psychology also has roots in other sciences. **Physiology**, a branch of biology that studies internal biological processes, has focused attention on the link between the brain and human behavior. In fact, it has only been recently that the biologists and other scientists linked the brain with behavior and personality. Even today, many people point to their chest or heart when they refer to themselves rather to their head or brain. In many cultures, the "me spot" is the heart rather than the head. Ancient Greek physiologists discovered, for example, that damage to one area of the brain created problems in certain parts of the body. The ancient Greek physician Hippocrates (BCE 460–370) FIGURE 1-3 noticed that when people suffered head injuries, their behavior changed, and he surmised that the brain was linked to behavior. Seventeenth-century philosopher and physician John Locke (1632–1704)

Although we currently see the source of our consciousness as the brain. We still point to our heart when talking about ourselves.

Philosophy The study of knowledge and existence.

Physiology A branch of biology that studies internal biological processes.

FIGURE 1-2 Philosophers such as Aristotle pondered many of the same questions that psychologists do today.

FIGURE 1-3 Considered the founder of medicine, Hippocrates considered many questions about behavior and mental processes.

1940s

M Boulder Conference established scientist/practitioner model of training for clinical psychologists (1949)

E Psychologists contributions to World War II: selection of personnel, training, design of equipment, psychological warfare, therapy for victims, etc.

E National Council of Women Psychologists (1941)

L First state psychology licensure law, Connecticut (1945)

P MMPI (1942)

P Strong Vocational Interest Blank (1943)

M Joint APA/VA program to establish accreditation of clinical psychology programs developed (1946)

E New APA formed by merger of several groups (particularly AAAP). Central Office established in Washington, DC (1945)

L National Mental Health Act (1946)

E Educational Testing Service (1947)

E National Institute of Mental Health (1949)

P *American Psychologist* (1946)

S Egas Moniz won the Nobel Prize for work that led to prefrontal lobotomies (1949)

1950s

M Emphases on human factors, physiological psychology, development across the lifespan, scientific method, statistics

M Modern cognitive psychology began

F New fields: space psychology, psychopharmacology, use of computers

L APA began accreditation of counseling psychology doctoral programs (1951)

P First DSM (1952)

P Publication of first APA code of ethics (1953)

S Evelyn Hooker published research that de-pathologized homosexuality (1957)

FIGURE 1-4 suggested that our minds link together ideas that come from the things we see, feel, and experience. Biologists interested in behavior brought with them a set of tools to study biology and behavior: scientific thinking and the scientific method.

Schools of Thought: Structuralism vs. Functionalism

Psychology did not emerge from philosophy and physiology whole and exactly as it is today. Like all sciences, psychology has been shaped by events, reactions, and trends. These influences, including important early thinkers in the field, not only shaped early psychology but also continue to affect contemporary approaches to psychology.

Structuralism

Structuralism The school of psychology that studies human experience by breaking it down into smaller pieces.

The school of **structuralism** studies human experience by breaking it down into smaller pieces. Just as our physical world is made of elements such as iron, copper, and zinc, our mental world, structuralists assumed, was also made of mental elements or structures. The school of structuralism focused on determining just what these mental structures are. Structuralists like Edward B. Titchener and Wilhelm Wundt FIGURE 1-5 suggested that the key to determining mental structures would be to deconstruct human experience by recording the components of an experience, sort of like how you can describe a yummy meal by describing the flavor profiles in a new dish.

FIGURE 1-4 John Locke was an English philosopher who suggested that the mind was a blank slate at birth and knowledge was written on it by our experiences.

FIGURE 1-5 Wilhelm Wundt is often called the founder of modern psychology.

1950s *(Continued)*

M First professional school of psychology: Adelphi University

M Social psychology gained in prominence, perhaps because of psychology's role in 1954 Supreme Court Decision on desegregation, Brown vs. Board of Education

E National Science Foundation (1950), Human Resources Research Organization (1951), Nebraska Symposium on Motivation (1953)

L APA Approved Internships (1956)

L National Defense Education Act (1958)

P *Journal of Counseling Psychology* (1954)

P Wechsler Adult Intelligence Scale (1955)

1960s

M American discovery of Piagetian ideas, especially in education

M Major growth of cognitive psychology (Neisser, Bruner, Simon)

M Humanistic psychology began

E Rogers-Skinner Debate (1962)

L President Kennedy signed the Community Mental Health Centers Act (1963) that called for prevention, community based treatment, and deinstitutionalization

P History of psychology became a specialty field: Archives of the History of American Psychology founded at University of Akron (1965)

M Academic psychology flourished with excellent financial support from business and government

M B. F. Skinner's ideas achieved prominence via applications in education and clinical psychology

L Majority of states passed laws for licensure of psychologists, a process completed in the 1970s

L Texas licensure law (1969)

P *Journal of Humanistic Psychology* (1961)

P DSM-II (1968)

The first laboratory to focus on such studies was founded in 1879 at the University of Leipzig in Germany. The creation of this laboratory by Wilhelm Wundt is sometimes considered the founding of psychology (Benjamin, 2008). Wundt and his colleagues used a technique called introspection to examine the internal components of experience. **Introspection** means "looking inward," and it is a technique used to study subjective experiences such as one's own mental and emotional processes. For example, when you eat a strawberry, what is your experience? A participant would be given a strawberry and asked to speak aloud while eating it: "I am experiencing a feeling of coolness, now tartness . . . Not very sweet . . ." Introspection focuses on what people can report from their experiences. Wundt and his colleagues would, for example, play a trumpet sound and ask the participants to explain their reactions: What did it sound like, how did you feel when you heard it?

The problem—and strength—of introspection is its reliance on subjective experience. Introspection is highly individualized, and the same stimulus can result in varied reactions from different people. If 100 people eat mangoes, each may focus on different components of the experience. What is more, there was no way for the structuralists to sort out how many of these differences are important. No two people would reach the same result following this introspective method. As a result, structuralism proved too messy, and over time, new ways to examine experience were developed.

Today, some researchers use introspective activities such as a "think aloud" protocol in order to peer into the subjective aspects of conscious activities (e.g., Fonteyn, Kuipers, & Grobe, 1993). Introspective activities are useful when researchers want to explore the process of what a person is doing as he or she is doing it. People often report things differently in retrospect because they may not realize what they did. Asking them to report what they do as they are doing it provides a better look at the experience. Critics of introspection say that the technique is unscientific and relies too much on **anecdotal evidence**, or unscientific observation.

Functionalism

The school of structuralism defined early psychology but gave way in the early 1900s to a new school called functionalism. While structuralism attempted to break down the elements of experience, **functionalism** was concerned with the purposes of behavior and mental processes. William James (1842–1910) FIGURE 1-6, an early functionalist, was inspired by Charles Darwin's (1809–1882) FIGURE 1-7 work on finding meaning behind the behaviors and physical structures of animals. Darwin inspired biologists not only to describe but also to explain why animals have certain biological structures. The goal of structuralism was not simply to identify a structure but also to describe how aspects of the structure increased the likelihood of survival. Functionalists were interested in how behavior functions to adapt to the environment.

Introspection Examination of one's own mental and emotional processes.

Anecdotal evidence A type of information that relies on unscientific observation.

Functionalism A school of psychology concerned with the purposes of behavior and mental processes.

FIGURE 1-6 William James.

1970s

M Behavior modification movement

F Formation of first free-standing schools of professional psychology: California School of Professional Psychology

E National Institute of Child Health and Human Development (1963); North American Society for the Psychology of Sport and Physical Activity (1967); Association of Black Psychologists (1968)

S Roger Sperry did initial psychological research on split-brain patients and hemispheric specialization (Nobel Prize 1981)

M Debate over professional training models led to Vail Conference (1974) and development of the Doctorate of Psychology (PsyD); subsequent growth of professional schools

M Heavy government funding of research on alcoholism and drug abuse

L APA began accreditation of school psychology doctoral programs (1970)

P *Cognitive Psychology* (1970)

P *APA Monitor* (1971)

M Government interest in rural mental health care, geropsychology, substance abuse

M Organizational issues achieved prominence in forming industrial/organizational psychology

E Association of Psychologists Por La Raza (1970), became National Hispanic Psychological Association in 1979

P Skinner published *Beyond Freedom and Dignity* (1971)

FIGURE 1-7 Charles Darwin.

William James wanted the field of psychology to examine how people change as a result of their environment. He thought that consciousness, for example, must benefit survival, or it would not exist. To him, that meant that a way to study how consciousness helps us in the world was needed. James believed that consciousness shifts too continually to be studied in the way that the structuralists suggested. Instead, James was inspired to study the "stream of consciousness," because he thought that a constantly shifting consciousness could not be reduced to elements. Because structure and function always go together, James believed that it did not make sense to separate the two. Functionalism brought psychology out of the laboratory and into the real world, attempting to explain how organisms adapt within their environments.

Functionalism was important because it marked the evolution from a focus on subjectivity to an objective study of behavior and mental processes. It led the way for psychologists who later emphasized the importance of empiricism, the theory of knowledge based on observation.

Although structuralism and functionalism are no longer active schools of contemporary psychology, elements of both structuralism and functionalism can be seen in contemporary schools of psychology.

CONCEPT LEARNING CHECK 1.2　　　*Comparing and Contrasting Structuralism and Functionalism*

Compare and contrast the ways that a structuralist and a functionalist might study the taste of spoiled milk.

1. Structuralist:

2. Functionalist:

1970s *(Continued)*

M Increased Federal Government funding of programs to recruit and train ethnic minorities as psychologists

M Reduction of Federal Government role in training of psychologists, first by the VA, then by NIMH

E Asian American Psychology Association (1972); Society of Indian Psychologists (1973); DSM-III (1973); National Institute on Drug Abuse (1974); National Institute on Alcohol Abuse and Alcoholism (1974); Minority Fellowship Program (1974); Hispanic Journal of Behavioral Sciences (1979)

1980s

F The term psychology dropped from some field names to reflect their interdisciplinary nature, e.g., behavioral neuroscience, cognitive science

E Scientists left APA to form American Psychological Society (1988)

E National conference on psychology and aging held in Boulder, Colorado (1981)

E American Psychological Association of Graduate Students (1988)

E Roger Sperry, David Hubel, and Torsten Wiesel, Nobel Prize 1981

P *Psychology and Aging* (1986); *Journal of Family Psychology* (1987)

1990s

M Managed care altered nature of psychotherapy, significantly reduced insurance coverage of mental health

M Psychologists lobby for prescription privileges

F Executive coaching

E Psychology Exhibition at the Ontario Science Center (1991)

E Teachers of Psychology in the Secondary Schools (1992)

P Advanced Placement Psychology Exam (1992)

1.3 Contemporary Psychology

Contemporary perspectives in psychology offer specialized ways to study behavior and mental processes.

- Compare and contrast contemporary perspectives in psychology.
- Describe focused specializations of research and practice.

People are complex—so complex that there is no single perspective that all psychologists use to describe, examine, explain, and predict behavior and mental processes. Those looking for one simple solution will be disappointed because there is no one correct perspective. Instead, interactions of multiple perspectives are required in order to capture the richness of the influences on human behavior. Each perspective will focus on different questions and offer different ways to examine human behavior and mental processes. Perspectives in psychology continue to evolve, and you may even notice overlap in the perspectives.

Each school of psychology focuses on a single approach for behavior and mental processes, which may exclude others that are equally valid. The **eclectic model**, however, pulls together multiple ways of examining a particular problem or question. For example, the **biopsychosocial approach** recognizes three equally important aspects of human mental processes and behavior: biological, psychological, and social. We can use different **levels of analysis** to focus our attention on a part of the story and then step back and appreciate the multiple influences. Let us consider aggression. A biological approach might suggest that aggression is related to the amount of testosterone in the system (Yu & Shi, 2009). However, we also know that culture can influence violence as well (Cohen et al., 1996). What is more, there are studies that suggest that experiential factors such as learning can increase or decrease aggression, too (Rascle et al., 2010). The complex layers of influence are best appreciated when combined to examine how they interact. No one perspective provides the one and only answer, however. Each one focuses on different aspects of behavior and mental processes. A single perspective is very likely incomplete; it may take several overlapping perspectives to get a three-dimensional picture of mental and behavioral processes. **TABLE 1-1** summarizes some of the main research specialties in psychology and the proportion of psychological research that takes place in that area.

Eclectic model An approach that pulls together multiple ways of examining a particular problem or question

Biopsychosocial approach A theory that recognizes three equally important aspects of human mental processes and behavior: biological, psychological, and social.

Levels of analysis Various ways of examining the same psychological phenomenon.

TABLE 1-1 Some of the Research Subfields in Psychology

Percentage	Area	What They Do	Chapter References
36	Clinical	Researches, evaluates, and treats psychological conditions.	14 15
11	Counseling	Helps people achieve greater well-being when they are experiencing difficulty adjusting to life stressors.	14 15
3	Industrial/Organizational	Researches, evaluates, and helps to shape business, employees, and their products.	10
8	Education/School	Researches and evaluates teaching and learning practices and techniques	7
16	Generalist	Crosses the boundaries of many subfields of psychology and integrates research in several areas.	All
3	Psychobiology and comparative	Investigates the physiological processes of behavior and mental processes of humans and other animals	3, 4, 10
6	Developmental	Studies the cognitive, social, and biological changes that emerge with growth over time.	10
3	Cognitive	Examines thinking processes, including knowing, remembering, reasoning, deciding, and communicating.	4

(continues)

Neuroscience The study of the brain and nervous system; also called biological psychology.

Positron emission tomography (PET) A neuroscience imaging technique that uses radioactive glucose to indicate areas of activity.

Functional magnetic resonance imaging (fMRI) Neuroscience imaging technique used to measure changes in blood flow.

Evolutionary psychology A branch of psychology that examines the impact of natural selection on behavioral and mental processes.

Natural selection Varying success in reproduction resulting from the interaction of an organism with the environment.

TABLE 1-1 Some of the Research Subfields in Psychology *(continued)*

Percentage	Area	What They Do	Chapter References
8	Social/Personality	Social psychologist: Studies how the way people think, feel, and behave influences and is influenced by others Personality psychologist: Studies the patterns in the way people think, feel, and behave.	13, 16
2	Experimental	Conducts methods to investigate behavior and mental processes; works closely with professionals in other subfields.	2, 4
1	Health	Researches how psychological factors impact wellness, illness, and medical treatments.	11
1	Forensic	Applies psychological research to the criminal justice system.	16

Source: Data from 2009 Doctorate Employment Survey, APA Center for Workforce Studies. March 2011.

The Biological Perspective

The biological perspective examines how physiology connects with the environment to create behavior and mental processes. **Neuroscience**, also called biological psychology, is the branch of psychology that studies the connection between behavior and the body, brain, and nervous system. Neuroscientists help us understand how the brain processes thoughts and emotions, helping to link the physical body with explanations for behavior on many different levels. How are emotions linked to the physical sensations in your body? Neuroscience examines questions like these at the molecular, cellular, organ, and system levels.

While the structuralists had only the tool of introspection, the biological perspective uses a variety of research approaches, including the study of genetics, activity of individual brain cells, and patterns of activation across the brain over time. This is made possible through new tools such as complex imaging techniques, including positron emission tomography and functional magnetic resonance imaging. **Positron emission tomography (PET)** is a neuroscience imaging technique that uses radioactive glucose to indicate areas of activity in the brain, and **functional magnetic resonance imaging (fMRI)** is a noninvasive brain imaging technique that uses powerful magnets and radio equipment to produce detailed images of the soft tissue in your brain. It is particularly useful because it can be used to examine brain activity over time FIGURE 1-8. Along with older techniques such as EEG (electroencephalography) FIGURE 1-9 and FIGURE 1-10, new techniques include MEG (magnetoencephalography), a technique for recording electrical signals from the brain based on changes in magnetic fields.

The Evolutionary Perspective

Evolutionary psychology is a branch of psychology that examines the impact of natural selection on behavioral and mental processes. According to the evolutionary perspective, our behaviors and mental processes are influenced, in part, by information inherited biologically. Influenced by Charles Darwin and the functionalists, evolutionary psychologists assume that behaviors and mental processes must benefit survival. According to **natural selection**, success in reproduction varies depending on the interaction of an organism with the environment. Those with certain behaviors live longer and pass those genes to future generations.

Evolutionary psychologists study **heritability**, or how much of a characteristic can be linked to genetics as opposed to the environment.

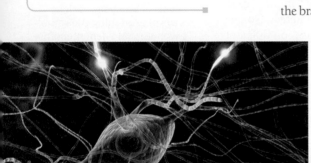

Neurons are the basic building block of the human nervous system.

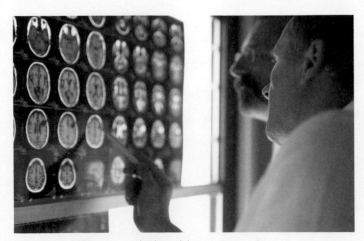

FIGURE 1-8 MRIs map out brain activity.

How much is intelligence, depression, or personality influenced by your genes as opposed to the environment? The perspective of evolutionary psychology is important because everything in the body—brain structures, hormones, fingers, and toes—are all mapped out by DNA FIGURE 1-11. In addition, comparative psychology studies behavior in other animals as models for our own evolutionary selection. Hoarding behavior in field mice may help us to understand people who save old newspapers, and topics like monogamy and tool use have been studied in animal groups in the wild.

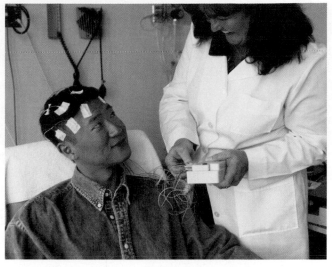

FIGURE 1-9 The EEG is a noninvasive way to measure electrical activity in the brain.

The Psychodynamic Perspective

According to the psychoanalytic perspective, unconscious processes determine your behavior. **Psychoanalytic theory** is a family of theories originated by Sigmund Freud that focus on unconscious motivation and the expression of personality. According to the psychoanalytic perspective, **unconscious** processes outside of your awareness determine your personality. Before Freud, no one considered that the reasons for one's behavior might not be obvious. But now, this idea is pervasive in everyday thought. You may have heard someone say, "He is in *denial*!" Or, "She is a little *anal* about keeping her room clean." How about, "He tried to hide it, but it *slipped* out." All of these expressions come from Freud's theories. His psychoanalytic approach emphasizes the study of unconscious conflicts that shape behavior. In psychoanalysis, our dreams' hidden meanings and our contradictory actions are studied to reveal our hidden motives.

Heritability How much of a characteristic can be linked to genetics as opposed to the environment.

Psychoanalytic theory A family of theories originated by Freud that focuses on unconscious motivation.

Unconscious According to Freud, thoughts, memories, feelings, and wishes that reside outside of awareness.

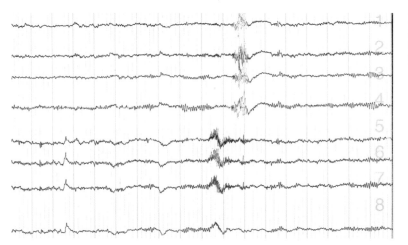

FIGURE 1-10 EEG patterns map out electrical activity in the brain.

Imagine someone named Zeke on the day that he opens his new comic book shop to the public. After weeks of stocking his store and months of planning, the big day arrived, and Zeke talked about how excited he was to finally open its door. That morning, he loaded up his car in the driveway and ran back into his house to pick up one more thing. When he came out, he discovered his car running, with all of the doors locked and windows up. He had no spare key, and his roommate was 2 hours away at school; by the time he arrived, Zeke's car had run out of gas. How did Zeke end up 4 hours late for the biggest day of his career? Freud would say Zeke had conflicting feelings that morning. Of course, he was genuinely excited to open his store but perhaps also terrified of failing. While Zeke was not aware of any conflict, his actions gave him away: After all, he had never before or since locked his keys in his running car.

The psychoanalytic school studies topics such as the meaning behind our dreams and the nature of personality. It also posits that the way to change people's behavior is to

FIGURE 1-11 The biological perspective suggests that physiology and our DNA can influence behavior and mental processes.

Sigmund Freud (1856–1939) is the founder of the psychodynamic perspective in psychology and is often considered the founder of the first well-organized theory of personality.

B. F. Skinner (1904–1990), a major figure in the behavioral perspective, examined learning in several species of animals.

Humanists such as Abraham Maslow suggested that we are motivated to become good people. Maslow suggested these motivations are in a hierarchy, from basic physiological needs to self-fulfillment needs.

understand the conflicting emotions that underlie it. Psychoanalysis relies on the "talking cure," in which a client sees a therapist regularly to talk about his or her concerns and to attempt to understand his or her inner conflicts. Though there are many criticisms of the psychoanalytic perspective, it remains a major force in psychology.

The Behavioral Perspective

Behaviorism, the study of learning based on directly observable actions, was founded by John Watson in 1913. The behavioral perspective suggests that instead of focusing on subjective experiences such as introspection, psychology should emphasize the study of objective behaviors. Behaviorism sought to predict and control behavior and to find a few simple rules for understanding behavior. The behavioral perspective explores the relationship between biological and environmental influences that allow us to learn or change through our experiences. Radical behaviorists were galled at the introspective techniques of the early structuralists and argued that we cannot know what is inside the mind. They proposed that psychologists should study only what is directly observable by others: behaviors in the world. This was, they argued, the best way to make psychology more scientific—by focusing on objective evidence.

The behavioral perspective examines such things as how we learn from the world around us and how we change what we do in response to expected outcomes.

The Humanistic Perspective

According to the **humanistic perspective**, personality, behavior, and mental processes are influenced by an innate capacity for personal growth. The humanists believed that the psychoanalytic and behavioral approaches were too deterministic. The psychoanalytic approach focused on internal, unconscious forces while the behavioral approaches emphasized the external environment. The psychoanalytic and behavioral approaches suggested that humans were at the will of something often too powerful for them to control—either internal drives or external circumstances. The humanistic approach emphasized free will and the pursuit of the best version of ourselves that we can be. Humanists such as Carl Rogers and Abraham Maslow value subjective reality and the importance of human potential.

Humanism's focus can be seen in **positive psychology**, a branch of psychology that emphasizes the constructive features of human strength and healthy living rather than sickness and pathology. Researchers in positive psychology examine human hardiness, optimism, and resilience.

The Cognitive Perspective

The cognitive perspective in psychology emphasizes the internal processes of thought that help us make sense of the world. **Cognition** encompasses all aspects of thinking, including knowing, remembering, reasoning, deciding, and communicating. In addition, the cognitive perspective studies our shortcuts in thinking and the biases and errors that can come from them. Cognitive psychologists study decision-making processes of both slow, deliberative decisions (like choosing the best car you can afford) as well as quick, intuitive choices when we make a snap judgment using our "gut."

Cognitive psychology really took off back in World War II. Knowing how people process and interpret information made psychologists a valuable resource as they helped to design cockpit displays that allowed pilots to recognize and use information from their displays efficiently. Today, cognitive psychologists continue to be interested in questions of internal thought and **cognitive neuroscientists** study brain action linked to thought, perception, and language.

The Sociocultural Perspective

The **sociocultural perspective** (featured throughout *Learn Psychology*) emphasizes the way that social and cultural elements in the world (or environment) influence behavior and mental processes. **Social psychology** is the branch of psychology that focuses on how our thoughts, feelings, and behaviors influence and are influenced by others. The sociocultural perspective helps to make psychology more representative of various cultures and to disrupt the belief that one group is superior to others and the standard by which others are judged, a reflection of **ethnocentrism**.

The sociocultural perspective includes social psychology and cultural psychology, which emphasizes the examination of differences in cultural values and norms. Social and cultural psychology examine the ways that people affect each other (Peplau & Taylor, 1997). **Cross-cultural psychology** examines and compares behaviors and mental processes between different cultures, which helps highlight the various influences of culture. The sociocultural perspective suggests that you cannot really understand behavior in the absence of a person's cultural and social context.

The sociocultural perspective has grown in the United States as the country and psychology have become more diverse. By 2050, ethnic minorities will represent nearly half of the U.S. population (U.S. Census Bureau, 2011). Women now earn three out of four doctorate and undergraduate degrees in psychology (Willard, 2011). It was not always this way. Back in 1895, Mary Calkins (1863–1930) completed all the requirements for a PhD in psychology from Harvard University and had the full support of her committee to earn the degree. But Harvard refused to grant her the degree because, at the time, women were not allowed to earn degrees from Harvard. Calkins was offered a degree from Harvard's sister school, Radcliffe, but she refused it. That did not hold her back. She later became the president of the American Psychological Association. Pioneers like Francis Cecil Sumner (1914–2005), who was the first African American granted a PhD in psychology at Clark University, and contemporary psychological scientists such as Claude Steele have broadened psychology to examine the impact of ethnicity on the individual. The sociocultural perspective is useful because it helps to describe the range of similarities and differences we see in people across the globe.

Professional Specialization and Research Areas in Psychology

The field of psychology is massive. No psychologist can study everything; therefore, many specialize in a particular subfield of psychology. You can take courses that will broaden and deepen your understanding of these topics, and in fact, universities offer doctoral degrees in the subjects of many of the chapters and topics in this book. Some psychological subfields do **basic research**, meaning that the research is driven by the quest for fundamental understanding of the concepts and the theories behind them. Basic research is concerned with expanding knowledge, even if the knowledge has no practical application. Other psychological research is **applied research**, or driven by a need to solve a specific problem. Basic and applied research interact with each other. Often, a psychologist may pursue a research topic in order to get to the bottom of a certain theory (how the eyes adjust to darkness), only to discover a practical application for the research (applications to treat night blindness).

Just knowing that someone is a psychologist might not tell you much. In fact, if someone says that she is a psychologist, the most you can figure is that she may know something about behavior and/or mental processes. Psychologists study people, animals, and even organizations. Psychologists work in clinics, private practices, hospitals, schools, prisons and other government agencies, and large Internet companies. The field of psychology includes several subfields, which are research specialties and work settings for people who research and apply their work. Psychologists in these settings apply their specific research interests to understanding populations and finding solutions to problems.

Psychologists may use data from their research areas to solve or address particular issues and research questions. For example, social psychologists, who focus on how your thoughts, feelings, and behaviors influence and are influenced by others, may apply the results of their research to explain the culture and behavior of juries.

Culture and social settings can impact our behaviors and mental processes.

Behaviorism The study of learning based on directly observable actions.

Humanistic perspective A branch of psychology that emphasizes growth, potential, and self-actualization.

Positive psychology A branch of psychology that emphasizes the constructive features of human strength and healthy living rather than pathology.

Cognition All types of thinking, including knowing, remembering, reasoning, deciding, and communicating.

Cognitive neuroscientist A scientist who studies brain action as it is linked to thought, perception, and language.

Sociocultural perspective A school of psychology that emphasizes the way that social and cultural elements in the world (or environment) influence behavior and mental processes.

Social psychology A branch of psychology that focuses on how our thoughts, feelings, and behaviors influence and are influenced by others.

Ethnocentrism Believing that your own group is superior to others and should be the standard by which other cultures are judged.

Cross-cultural psychology A branch of psychology concerned with the impact that shared attitudes, customs, and behaviors have on individual behavior and mental processes.

Basic research A type of research concerned with expanding knowledge, even if the knowledge has no practical application.

Applied research A type of research concerned with solving everyday problems.

The American Psychological Association (APA) and the Association for Psychological Science (APS) are the field's main professional organizations. The American Psychological Association has 54 divisions or specialized groups. Some of these divisions represent research fields like the ones described above, and others reflect topical interests such as APA Division 18: Psychologists for Public Service. These divisions help members to share research, stay current, and contribute to leading psychological publications. In fact, many divisions publish research journals that highlight the research agendas of the division. **TABLE 1-2** shows the diversity of the divisions of the APA.

TABLE 1-2 List of Divisions of the American Psychological Association

1. Society for General Psychology
2. Society for the Teaching of Psychology
3. Experimental Psychology
5. Evaluation, Measurement, and Statistics
6. Behavioral Neuroscience and Comparative Psychology
7. Developmental Psychology
8. Society for Personality and Social Psychology
9. Society for the Psychological Study of Social Issues (SPSSI)
10. Society for the Psychology of Aesthetics, Creativity and the Arts
12. Society of Clinical Psychology
13. Society of Consulting Psychology
14. Society for Industrial and Organizational Psychology
15. Educational Psychology
16. School Psychology
17. Society of Counseling Psychology
18. Psychologists in Public Service
19. Society for Military Psychology
20. Adult Development and Aging
21. Applied Experimental and Engineering Psychology
22. Rehabilitation Psychology
23. Society for Consumer Psychology
24. Society for Theoretical and Philosophical Psychology
25. Behavior Analysis
26. Society for the History of Psychology
27. Society for Community Research and Action: Division of Community Psychology
28. Psychopharmacology and Substance Abuse
29. Psychotherapy
30. Society of Psychological Hypnosis
31. State, Provincial and Territorial Psychological Association Affairs
32. Society for Humanistic Psychology
33. Intellectual and Developmental Disabilities
34. Society for Environmental, Population and Conservation Psychology
35. Society for the Psychology of Women
36. Society for the Psychology of Religion and Spirituality
37. Society for Child and Family Policy and Practice
38. Health Psychology
39. Psychoanalysis
40. Clinical Neuropsychology
41. American Psychology-Law Society
42. Psychologists in Independent Practice
43. Society for Family Psychology
44. Society for the Psychological Study of Lesbian, Gay, Bisexual and Transgender Issues
45. Society for the Psychological Study of Ethnic Minority Issues
46. Media Psychology
47. Exercise and Sport Psychology
48. Society for the Study of Peace, Conflict, and Violence: Peace Psychology Division
49. Society of Group Psychology and Group Psychotherapy
50. Society of Addiction Psychology
51. Society for the Psychological Study of Men and Masculinity
52. International Psychology
53. Society of Clinical Child and Adolescent Psychology
54. Society of Pediatric Psychology
55. American Society for the Advancement of Pharmacotherapy
56. Trauma Psychology

Source: Data from the American Psychological Association, http://www.apa.org

When many people think of psychologists, they imagine a therapist who listens to a person who sits on a sofa or who works in a private practice or maybe in a hospital. Psychologists, however, work in various settings, as you can see in FIGURE 1-12.

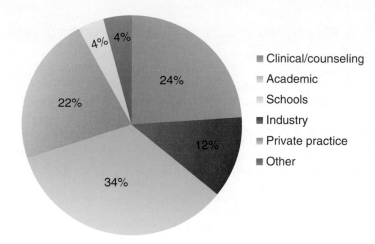

FIGURE 1-12 Settings in which psychologists work. *Source: Data from 2009 Doctorate Employment Survey, APA Center for Workforce Studies, March 2011.*

- Clinical/counseling
- Academic
- Schools
- Industry
- Private practice
- Other

CONCEPT LEARNING CHECK 1.3   *Contemporary Perspectives and Settings in Psychology.*

1. Choose a psychological topic that interests you. Then briefly describe how each of four contemporary perspectives in psychology suggests that one might investigate and analyze the topic.

2. Zoe tells her friend she wants to go to school to become a psychologist. Her friend quips, "You want to be a therapist in a private practice?" Outline a response summarizing at least four areas and three settings in which you are likely to find a psychologist but that do not involve therapy or private practice.

1.4 Critical Thinking and Multiple Influences

An understanding of the science of psychology requires critical thinking.

- Examine the role of critical thinking in the field of psychology.
- Illustrate the five criteria for critical thinking.

Good psychology, like all science, demands a certain way of thinking. This way of thinking includes an ability to take in information and decide how credible it is. Not all evidence is equal, and sometimes things can sound convincing or scientific even when they are not.

Critical Thinking

How do you determine what evidence to believe? Critical thinking is important in this process. **Critical thinking** involves identifying and evaluating evidence to guide thoughts and decision making. Critical thinking also helps you to analyze what you have learned and apply this information to unfamiliar situations. Rather than just believing what seems right, critical thinking encourages you to look for problems, assumptions, and biases in the evidence and to make the most reasoned judgments from the evidence. There are many guidelines and tips for critical thinking such as the ones offered by the American Psychological Association in **TABLE 1-3**. Although critical thinking is an important life skill, it is not always easy to apply. As you encounter information, keep the following five criteria (LEARN) of critical thinking in mind.

Critical thinking
Identification and evaluation of evidence to guide thoughts and decision making.

Five Criteria for Critical Thinking in Psychology (LEARN)

1. **L**ook for multiple influences. Often there are many causes for behavior and mental processes. Indeed, there are many levels of analysis, or various ways of examining the same psychological phenomenon.

2. **E**xamine alternatives. It may be possible that other explanations exist. Do not just accept the one that is given or adopt the first one that comes to mind. Keep in mind that many conclusions can be drawn from the same set of circumstances.

TABLE 1-3 Critical Thinking Skills in Psychology from the *APA Guidelines for the Undergraduate Psychology Major*

Respect and use critical and creative thinking, skeptical inquiry, and, when possible, the scientific approach to solve problems related to behavior and mental processes.

Evaluate the quality of information, including differentiating empirical evidence from speculation and the probable from the improbable.

- Identify and evaluate the source, context, and credibility of behavioral claims
- Challenge claims that arise from myth, stereotype, or untested assumptions
- Use scientific principles and evidence to resolve conflicting claims
- Recognize and defend against common fallacies in thinking
- Avoid being swayed by appeals to emotion or authority
- Evaluate popular media reports of psychological research
- Demonstrate an attitude of critical thinking that includes persistence, open-mindedness, tolerance for ambiguity, and intellectual engagement
- Make linkages or connections between diverse facts, theories, and observations

Engage in creative thinking.

- Intentionally pursue unusual approaches to problems
- Recognize and encourage creative thinking and behaviors in others
- Evaluate new ideas with an open but critical mind

Use reasoning to recognize, develop, defend, and criticize arguments and other persuasive appeals.

- Identify components of arguments (e.g., conclusions, premises/assumptions, gaps, counterarguments)
- Distinguish among assumptions, emotional appeals, speculations, and defensible evidence
- Weigh support for conclusions to determine how well reasons support conclusions
- Identify weak, contradictory, and inappropriate assertions
- Develop sound arguments based on reasoning and evidence

Approach problems effectively.

- Recognize ill-defined and well-defined problems
- Articulate problems clearly
- Generate multiple possible goals and solutions
- Evaluate the quality of solutions and revise as needed
- Select and carry out the best solution

Source: From APA Guidelines for the Undergraduate Psychology Major http://www.apa.org/ed/precollege/about/psymajor-guidelines.pdf

3. **A**nalyze the evidence. All evidence should be looked at carefully. Rather than accepting it at face value, inspect evidence for weaknesses, flaws, and shortcomings.

4. **R**easoned skepticism. This is a tough one. As Carl Sagan said, "Keep an open mind, but not so open that your brains fall out" (Sagan, 1986). It is important to be open minded, but if something seems incredible, it might not be credible.

5. **N**otice assumptions. Sometimes we accept evidence because it supports what we already believe. Notice your own assumptions about the supporting evidence as well as the assumptions of the person providing the evidence.

Critical thinking will help you reduce the effects of personal bias when examining evidence. The Critical Thinking Applications in each chapter will ask you to analyze a new question, problem, or situation and use critical thinking techniques to explore and better understand concepts you have studied in the chapter.

The Importance of Multiple Influences

Critical thinking suggests that in psychology it is important to consider multiple influences. Why? Often, a singular perspective is not enough to get the full picture of what is going on. For example, how much of a person's behavior and mental processes are inherited and how much is learned? The relative contributions of nature vs. nurture is a long debate and is older than psychology as an independent discipline. Are people born the way they are, or does what happens to them influence who they are? Those who believe that it is nature, or biology, genes, and evolution, would suggest that those aspects determine behavior and mental processes. On the other hand, those who suggest that nurture is responsible, would explain our behavior and mental processes as being determined by nurture, meaning our environment, learning, and culture.

CRITICAL THINKING APPLICATION

Complete the following quiz on psychological facts and myths, then compute your score by giving yourself one point for each item answered correctly.

Test your Psychology IQ

1. Jet lag is worse going from Hawaii to New York than from New York to Hawaii.

2. Hypnosis is valuable in helping witnesses recall details of a crime.

3. The world's most popular drug is alcohol.

4. People use only about 10% of their brain's capacity.

5. It is not possible to make a gay person heterosexual through psychotherapy.

6. During a full moon, people commit more crimes and behave more abnormally.

7. A few people can use their minds to influence, for example, the way that dice will fall.

8. If two things correlate highly, this does not prove that one causes the other.

9. Hypnosis can reduce the pain of surgery or childbirth.

10. Inside our brains are memories for everything we have experienced.

11. The average IQ in the USA is only about 100.

12. The moon looks much bigger on the horizon than overhead because the atmosphere acts like a magnifying glass.

13. Schizophrenia means split personality.

14. Mentally ill or retarded persons are no more likely to be violent than normal people.

15. Research shows that no significant learning occurs when information is given repeatedly during sleep.

16. As people age, they sleep less.

17. Through hypnosis, some people can remember things from the first 6 months of life.

18. Most German Nazis showed no evidence of serious psychiatric disorders.

19. Among the range of animals, the larger the brain, generally the greater the intelligence.

20. Clear evidence exists to show that a very small percentage of people can receive thoughts of others and predict the future.

Answers: 1. T, 2. F, 3. F, 4. F, 5. T, 6. F, 7. F, 8. T, 9. T, 10. F, 11. T, 12. F, 13. F, 14. T, 15. T, 16. T, 17. F, 18. T, 19. T, 20. F

Source: Standing, L. G. & Huber, H. (2003). Do Psychology Courses Reduce Belief in Psychological Myths? *Social Behavior and Personality*, 31(6), 585–592. © Society for Personality Research (Inc.)

How did you do? The maximum score is 20, which indicates you do not believe any of the myths. Do not worry if you did not answer all the questions correctly. The score of the average person who has not taken a psychology course is about 13.

Evaluate

1. What was your reaction to some of the answers? Were your answers based on your own experience, scientific research, or a personal theory?

2. Research a few of the topics in several ways. Try an Internet search as well as using scientific journals and psychology books to find the answers. Do you find differences in the evidence presented? Use critical thinking techniques, such as those mentioned above, to reexamine the questions and evaluate the evidence that supports the answers. What conclusions can you draw about your own answers to the quiz? What questions, if any, do you have about your research into some of the topics?

Summary of Multiple Influences on Psychology

Sometimes single perspectives offer flat explanations. More depth occurs when you combine the approaches, as demonstrated by two fluffy cats that share something special with each other. Take a look at the adult cat, Rainbow, and 7-week-old CC in FIGURE 1-13. Cute, are they not? Besides being fluffy, Rainbow and CC have something very special in common: CC (short for copy cat) is a clone of Rainbow. In other words, despite looking very different, Rainbow and CC are genetically identical. If you are wondering how two

FIGURE 1-13 Rainbow (left) is an adult calico cat, CC (right) is genetically identical to Rainbow although she looks different. CC has a spot above her left paw, for example, while Rainbow does not.

genetically identical cats can look so different, the answer lies in the multiple influences between nature and nurture. While genetics or nature influences the fact that CC is a calico, biology only tells part of the story FIGURE 1-14. The influence of CC's growth also influences her calico pattern, but environmental influence cannot explain the pattern either FIGURE 1-15. The exact pattern of her calico is influenced by an analysis of both genetic and environmental factors (Shin et al., 2002) FIGURE 1-16.

FIGURE 1-14 Biology alone can not explain why Rainbow and CC's calico patterns are different.

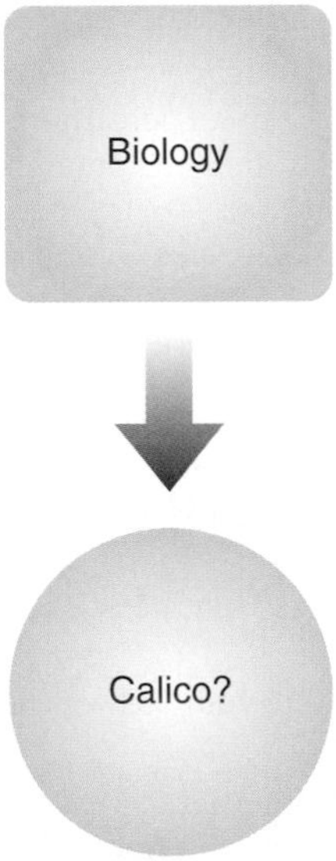

FIGURE 1-15 Environmental forces alone can not explain why Rainbow and CC's calico patterns are different.

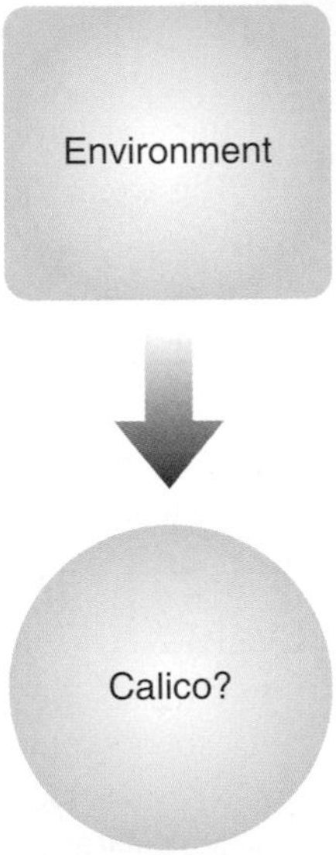

FIGURE 1-16 The multiple influences of biology and environment can provide a more complete explanation than one factor alone.

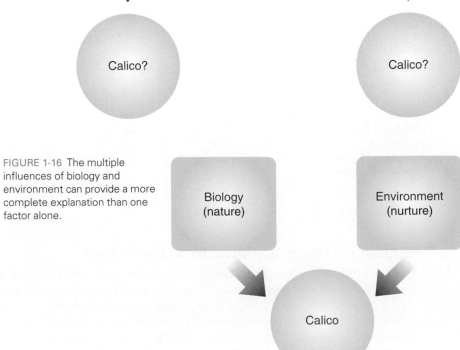

We wrote this book to include information from various sources, including biological, experiential, and cultural. We consider evidence from several types of research, looking at genetics, evolution, biology, environment, social interaction, and culture—integrated throughout the book within each topic. The end of each chapter summarizes this content. You will see a section called "Summary of the Multiple Influences" that highlights a few of the influences on the chapter's topics.

CONCEPT LEARNING CHECK 1.4 | *Applying the Criteria of Critical Thinking*

Harvey has just read an article on the Internet about the influence of the zodiac on personality that suggests that all Tauruses are stubborn and that all Capricorns are hard workers. Use the LEARN approach to critical thinking to analyze and evaluate Harvey's statement.

1. Look for multiple influences:

2. Examine alternatives:

3. Analyze the evidence:

4. Reasoned skepticism:

5. Notice assumptions:

Visual Overview Multiple Perspectives

Multiple perspectives reveal the multiple underlying causes of a psychological function. Each of these perspectives contributes understanding of a vital component of depression, yet none tells a complete story.

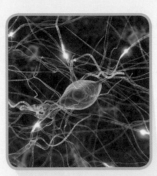

Biological
lower amounts of neurotransmitters; genetics

Evolutionary
Depression might be reaction to chronic stress, becoming depressed rather than aggressive might be a better strategy over time.

Positive psychology
Lack of connectedness

Psychoanalytic
Unresolved conflicts from early life

Depression

Behavioral
Learned helplessness

Sociocultural
Environmental conditions

Cognitive
"Self-talk" and rumination

Humanistic
Lack of unconditional positive regard

1.1 The Science of Psychology

- Psychology is the scientific study of behavior and mental processes.
- The scientific nature of psychology separates it from everyday predictions about behavior and mental processes.
- Pseudoscience is information that seems scientific but is based on unsound scientific principles.

1.2 The Origins and History of Psychology

- Psychology as an independent discipline did not emerge until the late 19th century but has roots in other fields such as philosophy and physiology.
- Structuralism was an early school of thought in psychology that studied human experience by breaking it down into smaller elements.
- Functionalism was an early school of thought in psychology that was concerned with the purposes of behavior and mental processes.

1.3 Contemporary Psychology

- Psychology's multiple contemporary perspectives are used to capture the richness of the influences of human behavior.
- The biological perspective examines how physiology connects with the environment to create behavior and mental processes.
- The evolutionary perspective examines the impact of natural selection on behavior and mental processes.
- The psychodynamic perspective examines how unconscious processes determine your behavior.
- The behavioral perspective explores the relationship between biological and environmental influences that allow us to learn or change through our experiences.
- The humanistic perspective emphasizes the innate capacity for mental growth.
- The positive psychology perspective emphasizes the constructive feature of human strength and healthy living.
- The sociocultural perspective emphasizes the way that social and cultural elements in the world influence behavior and mental processes.
- Psychologists have developed focused specializations of research and practice.
- Psychologists work in several settings, including clinical, industry, academic, private practice, and schools.
- Psychologists have specialty subfields, including clinical, counseling, industrial/organizational, education, developmental cognitive, social, and personality.

1.4 Critical Thinking and Multiple Influences

- Critical thinking involves identifying and evaluating evidence to guide your decision making.
- Principles of critical thinking include looking for multiple influences, examining alternatives, analyzing evidence, reasoned skepticism, and noticing assumptions (LEARN).
- The eclectic model suggests that no single explanation is adequate and it is important to consider multiple levels.

25

1.1 The Science of Psychology

1. Psychology is the science of:
A. personality.
B. humans.
C. diagnosis and treatment of mental disorders.
D. behavior and mental processes.

2. Television and radio personalities often give information that sounds as if it is based on psychological science, but it is not. In many cases, this is an example of:
A. pseudoscience.
B. introspection.
C. focusing on the mind rather than the brain.
D. eclecticism.

1.2 The Origins and History of Psychology

3. Early influences on understanding behavior and mental processes include the fields of philosophy and:
A. sociology.
B. anthropology.
C. physiology.
D. chemistry.

4. Charles Darwin's theory of evolution influenced the early school of psychology known as:
A. functionalism.
B. structuralism.
C. behaviorism.
D. psychoanalysis.

5. Contemporary psychological perspectives differ from the classic "armchair" schools because contemporary schools rely heavily on:
A. modern computers.
B. the scientific method.
C. introspection.
D. determining the cause of a psychological condition.

6. The founding of psychology as an independent discipline is linked to which person?
A. Aristotle
B. John Locke
C. Wilhelm Wundt
D. Sigmund Freud

7. To test a new website's ease of use, Sam watches as users interact and records the users' spoken reactions to the experience. This technique, called a "think aloud," is rooted in which structuralist technique?
A. Introspection
B. Empiricism
C. Objectivism
D. Functionalism

8. William James would have believed which of the following statements?
A. Psychology should study the structures of human experience only.
B. Structure and function cannot be separated.
C. Anecdotal evidence should be emphasized over empirical evidence.
D. Consciousness is an ongoing, rational state for most humans.

1.3 Contemporary Psychology

9. Which contemporary perspective's primary aim is to explain the impact of natural selection on behavior and mental processes?
A. The biological perspective
B. The behavioral perspective
C. The evolutionary perspective
D. The humanistic perspective

10. Didier's therapist says that Didier is anxious because of unconscious conflicts. His therapist is using the _____ perspective to explain his anxiety.
A. biological
B. psychodynamic
C. evolutionary
D. humanistic

11. Roberta's therapist says she is anxious because of underactive neurotransmitters in her nervous system. Roberta's therapist is using the _____ perspective to explain her anxiety.
A. humanistic
B. behavioral
C. biological
D. cognitive

12. Ian is studying the levels of testosterone in the body as they rise and fall during the year. He is investigating this in order to expand knowledge. This research is known as _____ research.
A. applied
B. basic
C. anecdotal
D. eclectic

13. Which of the following are settings in which you are likely to find a psychologist?
A. Private practice
B. Hospitals
C. Industry
D. Schools
E. All of the above

1.4 Critical Thinking and Multiple Influences

14. Katy believes that her brother is stressed because "stress runs in her family." However, her brother points out additional factors that are leading to his stress, such as the extra responsibility she has been given at her job and adjusting to a new neighborhood. Katy refuses to listen. Which principle of critical thinking is Katy ignoring?
  A. Reasoned skepticism
  B. Looking for multiple influences
  C. Noticing assumptions
  D. Analyzing the evidence

15. A psychologist who uses an eclectic model emphasizes:
  A. biological approaches.
  B. environmental approaches.
  C. psychodynamic approaches.
  D. multiple influences.

CHAPTER DISCUSSION QUESTIONS

1. Notice in Section 1.1 the examples of the types of questions science is better and worse at answering. In general, science is good at predicting trends but gets fuzzier with more specifics. Using this idea of trends versus specifics, examine the questions that will be answered in the chapters of this text (beginning with this section) and identify a trend that a psychologist might answer and a more specific question that would be more difficult to answer.

2. Psychology has strong roots in both philosophy and physiology, as discussed in Section 1.2. After reviewing the main contemporary approaches to psychology in Section 1.3 (biological, evolutionary, psychodynamic, behavioral, humanistic, cognitive, and sociocultural), distinguish a possible philosophical and physiological question that might influence each approach.

3. The LEARN approach is explained in Section 1.4 as a way to think critically, which may lead you to think about it as an approach to science, studying, or other academic endeavors. However, critical thinking can be useful in many realms, including understanding social situations. Assess the value of the LEARN approach in your own social life. Think of a situation in which your social interaction with a person or group was confusing or unclear. Use the LEARN approach to reevaluate the situation. Does this approach bring a new understanding to this situation? Why or why not?

CHAPTER PROJECTS

1. Section 1.3 explains seven of the main approaches to psychology today (biological, evolutionary, psychodynamic, behavioral, humanistic, cognitive, and sociocultural). Review these approaches and then find an example in the news or on the Internet that demonstrates each approach. Your examples should use a technique or make a conclusion that is specific to each approach.

2. Section 1.4 explains the LEARN approach to critical thinking. Dramatize this approach by creating two dialogs: one using the LEARN approach, and one not using the LEARN approach. First, identify a problem that a character would need to think through. Then, explain how s/he might work through the problem without the LEARN approach. Then, write a second dialog in which the character works through the problem using the LEARN approach. For each dialog, include the reflective thoughts of the character at the end of the situation.

CHAPTER KEY TERMS

Anecdotal evidence
Applied research
Basic research
Behaviorism
Biopsychosocial approach
Cognition
Cognitive neuroscientist
Critical thinking
Cross-cultural psychology
Eclectic model
Empirical evidence
Empiricism
Ethnocentrism

Evolutionary psychology
Functionalism
Functional magnetic resonance imaging (fMRI)
Heritability
Humanistic perspective
Introspection
Levels of analysis
Mind
Natural selection
Neuroscience
Philosophy
Physiology

Positive psychology
Positron emission tomography (PET)
Pseudoscience
Psychoanalytic theory
Psychology
Science
Social psychology
Sociocultural perspective
Structuralism
Unconscious

1.1 The Scope and Limits of the Science of Psychology

1. The researcher has gathered data and made a general claim based upon the nature of sleep. Science is much better at describing general trends than the needs of an individual person.

1.2 Comparing and Contrasting Structuralism and Functionalism

1. Structuralists might break down the components of the taste of spoiled milk.
2. Functionalists would examine why we dislike the taste of spoiled milk. A functionalist might also suggest the disgusting taste might make us not want to drink something that could harm us.

1.3 Contemporary Perspectives and Settings in Psychology

1. Sample answer: Psychologists from different perspectives might investigate humor and laughter in different ways. The biological perspective: What parts of the brain are involved in laughter? How does our brain react when we notice something funny?
   The evolutionary perspective: How does humor offer a reproductive advantage?
   The psychodynamic perspective: Do the things we find funny say something about our unconscious mind?
   The behavioral perspective: In what ways is humor learned? Why is it rewarding when someone laughs at a joke you tell but not when they laugh at a mistake you make?
   The humanistic and positive psychology perspective: Is laughter really the best medicine? Are there benefits to laughing?

The cognitive perspective: What makes something funny? Are there certain thinking processes at play in a joke? The sociocultural perspective: Are there cultural variations in what people find funny?

2. Use the tables in this section to guide your answers. Psychologists research and practice in several areas, including clinical, counseling, industrial/organizational, education, social, and personality. In addition to private practice, psychologists work in clinics, industry, academic settings, and schools.

1.4 Applying the Criteria of Critical Thinking

1. Look for multiple influences. [Many things influence personality, including biological, psychological, cultural, and social characteristics. Personality might be more complex than the explanation suggests.]
2. Examine alternatives. [Maybe people emphasize the kinds of personality characteristics they are hoping to see.]
3. Analyze the evidence. [Do all your friends born in May have the same personality? It might be good to cross-check by examining the "evidence" presented in Harvey's Internet article.]
4. Reasoned skepticism. [This is such a simple theory of personality, it is important to be skeptical about it.]
5. Notice assumptions. [The assumption behind this explanation is that there is something about the personality that is influenced by your birthday.]

1.1 The Science of Psychology

1. D. Rationale: Psychology is the scientific study of behavior and mental processes. Although psychology studies humans, it studies nonhumans as well. Psychology does not focus only on psychological conditions like depression.
2. A. Rationale: Pseudoscience is information that appears scientific but is not based on scientific principles.

1.2 The Origins and History of Psychology

3. C. Rationale: Physiology influenced psychology because it acknowledged the role that the health and biology of the brain had on mental processes and behavior.
4. A. Rationale: Functionalism was an early school of psychology that focused on the purpose, or function, of a behavior.
5. B. Rationale: Contemporary perspectives of psychology utilize the scientific method as a way of gathering evidence.
6. C. Rationale: While John Locke and Aristotle discussed topics that might be included in psychology, the founding of psychology is linked to Wilhelm Wundt.
7. A. Rationale: Introspection is a technique used to study subjective experiences such as one's own mental and emotional processes.
8. B. Rationale: James argued against the structuralists, suggesting that structures are there because of the function they serve.

1.3 Contemporary Psychology

9. C. Rationale: The biological perspective's primary aim is to study the body, brain, and nervous system, while the evolutionary perspective seeks to explain the impact of natural selection on behavior and mental processes.
10. B. Rationale: The psychodynamic perspective focuses on unconscious processes.
11. C. Rationale: The biological perspective studies the connection of behavior to the body, brain, and nervous system.
12. B. Rationale: The goal of basic research is to test a theory. The goal of applied research is to find a practical application.
13. E. Rationale: According to the table in Section 1.4, you can find psychologists in all of these settings.

1.4 Critical Thinking and Multiple Influences

14. B. Rationale: Looking for multiple influences is an important factor in critical thinking.
15. D. Rationale: The eclectic model pulls together multiple ways of examining a particular phenomona.

REFERENCES

Anderson, C. A., & Anderson, D. C. (1984). Ambient temperature and violent crime: Tests of the linear and curvilinear hypotheses. *Journal of Personality and Social Psychology, 46,* 91–97. doi:10.1037/0022-3514.46.1.91

Benjamin, L. T. (2008). *A history of psychology: Original sources and contemporary research.* New York: Blackwell.

Cohen, D., Nisbett, R. E., Bowdle, B. F., & Schwarz, N. (1996). Insult, aggression, and the Southern culture of honor: An "experimental ethnography." *Journal of Personality and Social Psychology, 70*(5), 945–960. doi:10.1037/0022-3514.70.5.945

Fonteyn, M. E., Kuipers, B., & Grobe, S. J. (1993). A description of think aloud method and protocol analysis. *Qualitative Health Research, 3*(4), 430–441. doi:10.1177/104973239300300403

Hughes, W., Lavery, J., & Doran, K. (2009). *Critical thinking: An introduction to the basic skills.* Toronto: Broadview Press.

Peplau, L. A. & Taylor, S. E. (1997). Sociocultural perspectives in social psychology. Englewood Cliffs, NJ: Prentice Hall.

Pietschnig, J., Voracek, M., & Formann, A. K. (2010). Mozart effect Shmozart effect: A meta-analysis. *Intelligence, 38*(3), 314–323. doi:10.1016/j.intell.2010.03.001

Rascle, O., Traclet, A., Souchon, N., Coulomb-Cabagno, G., & Petrucci, C. (2010). Aggressor-victim dissent in perceived legitimacy of aggression in soccer: The moderating role of situational background. *Research Quarterly for Exercise and Sport, 81*(3), 340–348.

Rauscher, F. H., Shaw, G. L., & Ky, C. N. (1993). Music and spatial task performance. *Nature, 365*(6447), 611. doi:10.1038/365611a0

Sagan, C. (1986). *Broca's Brain: Reflections on the Romance of Science* (1st ed.). New York: Ballantine Books.

Shin, T., Kraemer, D., Pryor, J., Liu, L., Rugila, J., Howe, L., Buck, S., et al. (2002). Cell biology: A cat cloned by nuclear transplantation. *Nature, 415*(6874), 859. doi:10.1038/nature723

U.S. Census Bureau. (2008). *United States population projections by race and Hispanic origin: 2000–2050.* Retreived from http://www.census.gov/population/www/projections/methodstatement.html

Willard, C. (2011, January). Men: A growing minority? *gradPSYCH, 9*(1), 40.

Wilson, E. (1999). *Consilience: The unity of knowledge.* New York: Vintage.

Yu, Y. Z., & Shi, J. X. (2009). Relationship between levels of testosterone and cortisol in saliva and aggressive behaviors of adolescents. *Biomedical and Environmental Sciences, 22*(1), 44–49.

Chapter Overview ▼

2.1 **Psychological Investigation**
The Scientific Method in Psychology
Why Is the Scientific Method
Important?

CONCEPT LEARNING CHECK **2.1** *Within or Between?*

2.2 **Descriptive Research**
Naturalistic Observation
Case Studies
Surveys
Correlational Studies

CONCEPT LEARNING CHECK **2.2** *What Do Correlations Mean?*

2.3 **Experimental Research**

CONCEPT LEARNING CHECK **2.3** *Designing an Experiment*

2.4 **Statistical Analysis**
Measures of Central Tendency and
Variance
Making Inferences with Statistics

CONCEPT LEARNING CHECK **2.4** *Summarizing with Statistics*

2

A Scientific Approach to Psychology

Learning Objectives ▼

2.1 ■ Define psychological science.
■ Describe the steps in the scientific method in psychology.
■ Discuss the importance of the scientific method.
■ Identify design choices in research.

2.2 ■ Explain the goals of descriptive research.
■ Discuss the components of a naturalistic observation study.
■ Compare and contrast case studies, surveys, and correlational studies in terms of descriptive research.

2.3 ■ Describe the components of a psychological experiment.

2.4 ■ Illustrate the central tendency of, and the variation among, a set of scores in describing data.
■ Describe what it means when a study shows an effect that is statistically significant.

2.5 ■ Examine the rights of participants in research identified in the Belmont Report.
■ Contrast the ethical guidelines for human research studies and animal research studies.

2.5 Ethics in Psychological Research
Human Participants
Animal Studies
Summary of Multiple Influences on a Scientific Approach to Psychology

CONCEPT LEARNING CHECK **2.5** *Ethics in Psychological Studies*
CRITICAL THINKING APPLICATION

My first month of graduate school, I was ready to run my very first experiment. The students in an introduction to psychology course at the school had begun signing up for the open slots I had posted, and I was ready for the first student who agreed to come, a man I will call Jason Porter. When I opened the door to the lab, I saw standing in front of me the most famous person I had ever seen face to face, an Oscar-winning Hollywood star with many important films to his credit. I recalled that he had taken a break from filming to get a degree at this school, and here he was, signed up for *my* experiment! I ushered him in to the observation room and gave him a consent form to sign and a written task to begin the study. Then I left the room, and ran down the hall to tell my fellow graduate students that Jason Porter was in the lab! Several of them followed me back and looked through the one-way mirror at him as he worked on the experimental task. Thinking back to that day, I confess that I am not proud of my star-struck behavior.

What protects people who volunteer for research studies? Do they have the right to confidentiality, so that others will not know what they said or did during the study or even that they participated? How are ethical guidelines enforced in practice? And are there consequences when ethical principles are violated in research? The American Psychological Association provides ethical guidelines, and federal law clarifies the rights of research participants and the responsibilities of researchers. As you will see, scientific research that involves human or animal subjects engaged in tasks that one hopes will offer insights into the mind is among the most demanding types of research in science.

2.1 Psychological Investigation

Psychology uses the scientific method to examine the mind by studying people's behaviors.

- Define psychological science.
- Describe the steps in the scientific method in psychology.
- Discuss the importance of the scientific method.
- Identify design choices in research.

What separates the science of psychology from intuition, opinion, and common sense? Like most of us, you likely have your own ideas about why people behave the way they do, and many are likely correct. For example, women cry more often than men, children are influenced by their parents, and people often want what they cannot have. These observations are of little value precisely because they are so common or obvious. There are many more observations about people's behavior that require more information, or evidence, to confirm. Do people marry others like themselves, or do "opposites attract?" Are we more motivated by money or by meaning in our lives? What is the best way to make a desired change in our behavior?

To answer these questions, psychologists use the **scientific method**. This method tests hypotheses by gathering measurable evidence to determine whether they are true. This often requires designing experiments that capture the behavior of interest and then systematically observing the resulting data. For example, one study had college-age male skateboarders attempt a series of tricks. Half of them did so while an attractive young female experimenter looked on. The skateboarders who saw the woman watching them took more risks with their tricks and had a higher level of testosterone in their saliva

Scientific method A systematic approach to organizing the collection of data and drawing conclusions from a research study.

(Ronay & von Hippel, 2010). Because the experiment kept the situation the same except for the presence of the woman, we can conclude that it was her presence alone that aroused the men and led them to take more risks. **Empirical** studies gain information by carefully collecting observations, or data. Data can include quantitative observations, such as the number of minutes a task takes or a rating on a scale for a survey question. Data can also be qualitative when the "qualities" of data are systematically described rather than counted. For example, interviews collect people's own expressions of their experiences as a source of data. Empirical studies lie at the heart of psychology because they allow us to draw conclusions about human behavior and thinking.

Psychologists want to uncover the "what" of a given phenomenon, such as "intelligence": what is the nature of intelligence? What are its features? What consequences does it have for a person? The research design, or overall structure of a study, depends on the specific questions of interest. And, because the field of psychology is so diverse in its questions, its methods are also highly varied. Psychologists seek universal truths about all people, as well as an understanding of the important differences among them, such as gender, culture, ethnicity, and personality, that result in differing experiences in life. In addition, we want to know the "why" of a phenomenon; that is, an explanation of its causes and the multiple factors that influence it. What does it mean to say that someone is "intelligent," and what causes some people to be judged as more intelligent than others? Using the scientific method, psychologists can add new knowledge about psychology.

Psychological science studies human behavior in order to learn what "makes people tick." Research on psychological topics collects data about human behavior using the same scientific method found in other sciences. This can involve creating a **theory**, with an overarching conceptualization or model about how various factors may influence behavior. Research can also begin with a testable hypothesis, from an observation about human behavior, or with the goal of looking for relationships among possible influences. Then, the scientific method involves relying on empirical evidence provided by impartial procedures and careful measurements of the results. In fact, throughout this book, you will see reference citations—names and dates within parentheses. These are references to studies that support a finding, conclusion, or fact presented in the text. To learn more about the evidence presented, you can look up the reference in the list at the end of the chapter and find a copy to read for yourself. In this chapter, we will cover the major concepts involved in psychological research. The goal is to understand research design well so that you can be an informed, critical reader when considering scientific evidence in this book and wherever it may arise.

The Scientific Method in Psychology

Perhaps you have seen it happen: People gather in a local bar and enjoy an evening of talking, drinking, and meeting new friends. Sometimes, these gatherings result in "hookups," or romantic pairings for the evening or longer. A country singer, Mickey Gilley, once observed, "Don't the Girls Get Prettier at Closing Time?" Presumably, the singer meant that a given girl might be viewed as even prettier when the bar is closing and your chance to talk with her tonight is ending. What type of psychological study could test this question? Of course, it is not enough to ask a few people, or make our own guesses; instead, we want to design a research study using scientific principles that allows us to draw a solid conclusion. And we would also want to consider whether "the boys" get more handsome. In fact, such a study was conducted, and we can consider its design and findings in light of the scientific method (Pennebaker et al., 1979).

- Step 1: Formulate a testable hypothesis. First, the question has to be turned into a clear statement that can be shown to be true or false, called a **hypothesis**. For this study, the researchers defined the hypothesis as, "Individuals are seen as more attractive as the time to decide whether to interact with them decreases." Hypotheses are statements about what will happen in a given situation; if the observations do not match the prediction, then the hypothesis is rejected.

- Step 2: Select the research method and design the study. Next, the researchers had to consider how to best test this question. There is no "best" research strategy; rather, each design has its advantages and disadvantages. What people are available to participate in the study? Where should the study take place? How should the behaviors

Empirical Research studies that gain information by carefully collecting observations, or data.

Psychological science Research conducted on topics in the field of psychology.

Theory An overarching conceptualization about how variables may cause behavior.

Hypothesis A clear statement or prediction that can be shown to be true or false in an experiment.

When college students socialize at a bar, what influences attraction?

be measured? Psychological researchers do their best to test their hypotheses in ways that represent the real-world environment in which their question, or hypothesis, has meaning. In this case, the researchers decided to use three bars near a university rather than testing the hypothesis within a laboratory. In the report of the methods used in a study, specific information is given so that someone else can reproduce the same circumstances. For this reason, we know that the researchers were careful in conducting their study.

- Step 3: Collect the data. The researchers approached more than 100 people (half male, half female) of college age in the bars, waiting until they were not engaged in conversation with anyone. They also chose **participants** (people who take part in a research study, also called *subjects*) who were not "intoxicated" or "incapacitated." An experimenter of the same gender approached the potential participant and asked if he or she would mind answering a few questions for a psychology study. Everyone approached agreed to participate. The experimenters asked, "On a scale from 1 to 10, where 1 indicates 'not attractive,' 5 indicates 'average,' and 10 indicates 'extremely attractive,' how would you rate the opposite-sex individuals here tonight?" They then asked, "If you were a member of the opposite sex, how would you rate the other (men or women) here tonight?" The experimenter thanked them and departed. The experimenters looked at the amount of time remaining before "closing time" and collected the data at 9 p.m., 10:30 p.m., and 12 midnight at bars closing at 12:30 a.m. What do you think they found?

- Step 4: Analyze the data and draw conclusions. The ratings provided by the participants were grouped by gender and by the time of the observation. The ratings were analyzed using statistics to compare the ratings based on time of evening. People rated members of the opposite sex as increasingly attractive as closing time approached FIGURE 2-1. While the ratings of their own gender changed a bit from time to time, these differences were not reliable; instead, only the ratings for the opposite gender at 12:00 increased above all of the other ratings. What conclusion is appropriate from this study? The time of night made a difference: The later time produced higher ratings of the opposite sex. So this experiment provides evidence that Mickey Gilley's common-sense observation was right!

Participant A volunteer who agrees to take part in research studies, also called a subject.

Journal A publication containing articles written by scientists that are reviewed before publication by a group of peers.

FIGURE 2-1 Bar patrons' ratings of opposite-sex based on time before closing.
Source: Data from Pennebaker, J. W., Dyer, M. A., Caulkins, R. S., Litowitz, D. L., Ackerman, P. L., Anderson, D. B., & McGraw, K. M. (1979). Don't the Girls Get Prettier at Closing Time: A country and western application to psychology. Personality and Social Psychological Bulletin, 5, *122–125.*

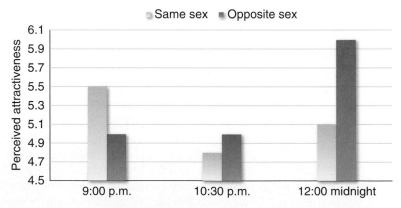

- Step 5: Report the findings. When studies are complete, researchers write a full report and submit it to a **journal**, or scientific publication. Peer reviewers—other researchers who had no part in the study—read the report and point out problems with its design or conclusions and with the way they are reported (Wilkinson, 1999). What would you say about this study? Do you think it is good evidence that the hypothesis is true? Can you think of any alternative explanations for why the observations came out this way? For example, as the evening went on, people in the bar likely had more to drink, and were perhaps more tired or more energetic? There was also no attempt to account for the fact that some in the bar may have preferred their own gender rather than the opposite sex. In addition, the study's method had the participants rate the entire group as a whole rather than individuals. As in most studies, questions about the findings remain. For example, would perceiving "the girls get prettier" make any difference in people's actual behavior toward each other? The study cannot answer this question. However, it was reviewed by experts and selected for publication and has been cited by more than 50 other studies published since it appeared.

For any study of human behavior, design choices must be made. These choices often lead to limitations in the conclusions from the study. For example, if they had conducted the study in a laboratory, they would have had more control over the participants but would the subjects have acted as naturally? There are also *confounds* in the design, or factors that may affect the results that are not intended as a part of the study. In this case, the 12 midnight measurement always happens after the participants have spent more time in the bar setting. So the length of time subjects spent in the bar before participating in the study is a confound—that is, a systematic difference between the groups that is not the one the experimenter is measuring (they measured time before closing). So are the girls prettier because the bar is about to close and opportunities to meet someone are vanishing or because you have now drunk a lot more beer?

An important choice in study design is whether to have different people in the comparison groups or whether to have the same people do the experiment more than once. These researchers chose a **between-subjects design**, in which there are different individuals in each of the groups (9 p.m., 10:30 p.m., and 12 midnight) of the study. The people who were in the bar at 9 p.m. may have been a different group than those who stayed on through the closing hour; as a result, their opinions may differ because different types of people make up the three groups. The researchers might have asked the same people to stay at the bar all night and give ratings at each time point, called a **within-subjects design**. If the same person gives a rating at each time, you may have more confidence that the difference you saw is due to the time. In fact, another group of researchers conducted this study again (Johnco et al., 2010), this time asking the same individuals to perform ratings at each time point. They found the same effect—the "girls" still do get prettier—even when blood alcohol levels are taken into account. This shows how studies may suggest further research to refine our understanding of the results and may raise new questions. We can conclude that this closing time effect does occur; however, do we really know *why* it occurs based on these studies?

The results of one study never provide all the information you may need to answer all of the questions you may have. With the scientific method, studies build upon the foundation of other studies to help us reach conclusions. And every research study has limitations in its design. Consider this when you read about studies in this book. Did the researchers make good design choices? Do their conclusions follow from the study? Are there limitations that lead you to question whether it is true in general? While research studies are always fully reported in journals, the results of every study are still open to interpretation. This requires that we be critical thinkers when considering empirical reports.

Why Is the Scientific Method Important?

Researchers in psychology follow the scientific method to perform studies that help explain and may predict human behavior. This is a much more challenging task than studying snails or sound waves. It often requires compromises, such as testing behavior within laboratories rather than natural settings, and asking those readily available (such as introduction to psychology students) to participate rather than collecting data from a true cross-section of the population. It often requires great cleverness to conceive of measures that tap into what people are thinking without altering their thinking, called **reactivity**. Simply knowing they are being observed may cause people to behave differently (such as more politely!). People may give answers they feel are more socially desirable than their true feelings. But for all of these difficulties for psychology, the payoff of the scientific method is that the findings are **replicable**; that is, if you run the same study again following the same procedures, you will be very likely to get the same results. In that sense, the scientific method provides **reliability** for the observations made about human behavior.

However, studies must always be questioned as to their **validity**: Do the research findings offer insight into the psychological question they set out to answer? The scientific

Between-subjects design A research plan in which different individuals take part in differing aspects of the study and the different groups are compared.

Within-subjects design A research plan in which each subject takes part in every aspect of the study.

Reactivity Unintentionally altering people's natural behavior by attempting to measure it.

Replicable Results from a research study that appear the same when the study is repeated.

Reliability The consistency of the results when similar studies are performed.

Validity The degree to which a research experiment captures what it claims to study.

Psychological science follows the same principles of the scientific method found in other fields of science.

Generalizability How well a study's findings can be applied to other people and circumstances.

Meta-analysis A study that examines the results of many earlier studies on a topic and compares their findings to draw conclusions.

method allows other researchers to form their own judgments about a study, and to follow it with their own study if necessary to better identify the underlying causes of behaviors. Incrementally, piece by piece, systematic observations are made and published, and the next research study builds upon them. This provides a solid basis for accumulating evidence across studies, finding consistencies and errors, and coming to a lasting conclusion that is built on fact rather than intuition, personal opinion, or guesswork. The **generalizability** of the results, or how well the findings can be applied to other people and circumstances, is supported by similar findings from other studies. One way to test whether results can be generalized to other situations is to repeat studies while changing the "who," "how," and "where" of the study. Do you think the closing time study would have the same outcome if conducted in a campus coffee shop rather than a bar? Do you think you would find the same results on Sundays, when bars close earlier? The more studies conducted that test the conclusions in new contexts, the more confidence we have that the findings apply to people's behavior in general.

An important contribution to this process is a **meta-analysis** study, in which tens or even hundreds of studies on a single topic are considered together and conclusions drawn about our current knowledge. For example, Petersen and Hyde (2010) conducted a meta-analysis of 834 studies from 87 countries (occurring between 1993 and 2007) to determine gender differences in sexuality. They concluded that men report more permissive attitudes toward casual sex and slightly more sexual experience than did women; however, the difference is disappearing, especially in cultures with greater gender equality. The variety of people participating and the great number of different studies included provide very solid evidence for this meta-analysis conclusion.

CONCEPT LEARNING CHECK 2.1   *Within or Between?*

Consider the following descriptions of research designs. For each, identify whether the research design was within-subject, in which each individual participated in every part of the study, or between-subject, in which different people took part in different tasks during the study.

1. A researcher is interested in determining whether using a highlighter helps students during reading. He has his class read a chapter from the textbook using a highlighter while reading and then take a quiz. The next week, he tells them to refrain from using any highlighter or underlining while they read the chapter, and again they take a quiz. The results show highlighters actually produce worse performance on the quizzes.

2. Dr. Brady has a theory that members of all-female groups work more cooperatively together than members of all-male groups. To test this, she assigns participants at random to same-sex groups of five. She asks them to work on a series of tasks. She then has the participants rate their own group members' performances. The results show females are rated as more cooperative, while males are rated as more competitive.

3. Dr. Mertz tries out a new presentation software package on one of his sections of psychology. He gives his traditional blackboard lecture in his morning class and a computerized slide presentation with the same lecture in his afternoon class. He gives the same test to both sections and finds that 15% of the students in the 8 a.m. section fail the test versus 30% in the 2 p.m. section. He concludes that the new presentation method does not improve learning.

4. Dr. Ricardo wants to determine the effects of hunger on aggression in a cat colony. He takes 10 cats from the colony, keeps them in individual cages, and gives them a feeding schedule that results in their losing 20% of their normal weight over a 2-week period. He also isolates 10 other cats in cages but keeps them on a normal feeding schedule. He then tests each hungry cat by putting it back in the colony. The hungry cats show the threat posture that precedes fighting much more frequently than the nonhungry cats. He concludes that hunger increases aggression in cats.

5. Dr. Cleaver believes that children do not show strong preferences for "gender-appropriate" toys. In a testing room, she finds that children often choose gender-appropriate toys, but in interviews, they tell her they like both kinds of toys. She concludes that society pressures children to limit their toy choices.

6. A national study examines factors that determine whether exercise aids weight loss. Subjects are told to begin a rigorous exercise program, and at the end of 3 months, follow-up results are examined. The study finds that people in the study lost an average of 5 pounds.

2.2 Descriptive Research

Descriptive research is intended to accurately observe and systematically define behavior.

- Explain the goals of descriptive research.
- Discuss the components of a naturalistic observation study.
- Compare and contrast case studies, surveys, and correlational studies in terms of descriptive research.

The goal of descriptive research in psychology is to make systematic observations about the "what" of our behavior. As a first step, or for some types of questions, simply observing what happens can be very informative. These studies may take the form of observing behavior as it occurs in the field, or the real world, analyzing a single example case, asking people questions about their behavior, or observing across groups of people or over time. One type of study, called a **comparative study**, looks at behaviors across species. For example, pet dogs were discovered to respond to humans pointing to food locations as a referential gesture (Soproni et al., 2002), even though other primates do not appear to use pointing as a signal. Descriptive studies are concerned with the relationships between and among behaviors, experiences, and individual attributes, also called **variables**.

Naturalistic Observation

When the behavior of interest is complex or has practical importance, it is often first observed as it occurs in "the wild" without any intervention by the researchers, called **naturalistic observation**. Have you ever noticed that the person pulling out from the parking space you are waiting for takes an especially long time once they see you waiting? This is an annoying perception, but is it true?

A naturalistic observational study (Ruback & Juieng, 1997) examined whether the amount of time drivers took to leave a parking space was related to whether another driver was waiting for the space. Two hundred drivers were observed leaving their parking spaces in front of a mall. Two researchers observed the drivers from the time they opened the driver's side door to the time when the car had completely exited the space. Thirty-eight percent of the drivers were scored as "intruded upon" when they turned their head toward an approaching car before they opened their car door. Drivers departed more quickly (averaging 32 seconds) when *not* intruded upon than when they saw a car waiting (39 seconds on average). So it is true, they are staying longer because you are waiting. However, from a descriptive study, we cannot say *why* this occurs. The authors discuss the territoriality of humans and the need to "mark" or defend their use of the location, but the study does not address these potential explanations.

In fact, observational studies are often employed to discover the behavior of other animals in comparative studies. Naturalist Jane Goodall (1934–) accomplished observations of groups of chimpanzees by spending much of her life following these primates as they moved throughout their natural environment. She noted evidence of territoriality among chimpanzees in which individuals would protect areas and objects they claimed through aggression, postures, gestures, and calls (Goodall, 1982). The "owner" must be prepared at all times to defend his or her claim from others in the group. Somehow, it seems easier to attribute the squabbling of chimpanzees to a display of territoriality, while it is harder to imagine that we ourselves are engaging in the same behavior. Comparative studies of other animals help to identify behaviors in the natural environment that may be removed from our modern awareness.

Naturalistic observation is a method by which the researcher makes no attempt to interact with or change the behavior of those observed. Instead, the research is from the standpoint of a "fly on the wall," making as little impact as possible while noting the behavior of those around them. For example, most people think of themselves as "moral," but do they behave that way? A team of researchers sat outside a university copy room and recorded the number of copies made based on the sound of the copier. Students, faculty, and staff used the copier and self-reported the number of copies they made for

Comparative study A research project that compares similarities and differences between human and animal behavior.

Variable A factor that is manipulated, measured, or controlled during an experiment.

Naturalistic observation Observing human behavior as it occurs in a real-world setting.

Jane Goodall, the world's foremost authority on chimpanzee behavior.

later billing on an honor system. How "honorable" were they? The observers found that people routinely underestimated the number of copies they actually made, with a constant percentage of unreported copies over different copy job sizes. However, when they made a lot of copies, they were more likely to be dishonest. So people seemed to feel competing motivations to maximize financial profits and to behave honestly (Goldstone & Chin, 1993). Observational studies can take place in any public forum, and people can be observed without giving their permission for the study.

Naturalistic studies are important within psychology because many studies are conducted under the controlled conditions of a laboratory or through asking people about their behavior. Then, when a study takes place "in the wild," psychologists sometimes observe that people's behavior in real settings differs. For example, more than 97% of people in Michigan reported that they wear seat belts (National Highway Traffic and Safety Administration, 2008). However, a naturalistic study in which observers watched drivers, found seat belt use ranged from 52 to 90% (Gonzalez et al., 2011). So naturalistic studies provide an important check on the generalizability and validity of research findings. On the other hand, it can be difficult to avoid bias when conducting naturalistic studies. For example, in the study of parking space territory (Ruback & Juieng, 1997), the observers always knew whether a car was waiting or not. They may have been subtly biased by that knowledge when recording the time it took for cars to exit. Objectivity is sometimes difficult to achieve in naturalistic settings.

Case Studies

Case study The extensive examination of the experience of a single individual or group.

Another important type of descriptive study is the extensive examination of the experience of a single individual or group, called a **case study**. These studies are often conducted because the individual's experience is highly unusual, and their behavior allows us to reflect on what must be happening for all individuals. For example, cognitive neuroscientists and clinical neuropsychologists study individuals who have brain injuries that produce specific, characteristic behavior. This allows scientists to infer how the injured areas function within an intact brain. One such case involved a 16-year-old boy called "Adam" (Farah et al., 2000). At 1 day old, Adam contracted meningitis and suffered brain damage to areas of his brain that process visual images FIGURE 2-2. Surprisingly, Adam was able to do well with most visual tasks at age 14, such as recognizing objects; however, he showed extreme difficulty with facial recognition. His favorite television show was *Baywatch*, and he viewed it for an hour daily. In the study, he was given 10 photos of the cast and asked to identify them. He was unable to identify a single face and refused to even guess. This case provides important evidence in support of two separate visual recognition systems in the brain, one for objects (which worked well for Adam) and one for faces (which did not). The case

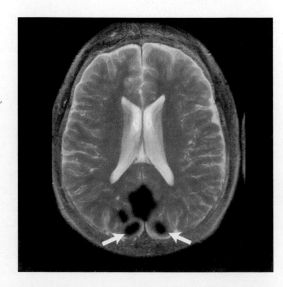

FIGURE 2-2 Arrows indicate areas of damage (represented by shading) in the occipital lobes.
Source: Adapted from Farah, M. J., Rabinowitz, C., Quinn, G. E., & Liu, G. T. (2000). Early commitment of neural substrates for face recognition. Cognitive Neuropsychology, 17*(1–3), 117–123.*

also suggests that the brain cannot recover this face recognition function after damage even in a very young infant.

With case studies, there is always a concern that something about the individual other than the brain damage identified may be taking place. Other cases can be compared, but the exact damage is not likely to be the same in other individuals. However, from case studies of adults, damage to this part of the brain is now known to cause prosopagnosia, or the inability to recognize faces (Farah et al., 1995). Damage to other areas of this visual processing region can cause object agnosia, in which individuals are unable to recognize common objects (like hats and toasters) but can recognize faces (Moscovitch et al., 1997). Together, the cases allow us to conclude that the two types of images—faces and objects—rely on separate biological networks of neurons to achieve recognition from memory. Case studies are also undertaken when an individual's life experience is unique, such as individuals who were severely abused as children, who demonstrate exceptional talent, or who display criminal behavior. Case studies address questions about human behavior that cannot be designed as a research study due to the rare qualities of the individuals; however, we can learn much from such studies on a case-by-case basis.

Surveys

We are inundated with surveys, from the "Tell us about your experience" questions when making purchases, to online pop-up surveys, to telephone and e-mailed questionnaires on politics, medical care, and community issues. Within psychology, surveys are a big business, reaching out to sample people across communities in order to register the opinions of a variety of people. **Internet-mediated research**, such as surveys posted online for volunteer respondents, allows researchers to question participants across the world. Why are surveys so popular? A major reason is that a **survey** involves the self-report of behavior, and is much easier to collect than other data. By simply asking people what they do and care about, you can gain interesting information about their psychological lives. Consider a simple survey conducted with 100 students at a mid-size Midwestern university (Ross et al., 1999). In the spring term, they asked 100 students to check items on a list of 40 sources of stress in their lives at college **TABLE 2-1**. The results can be presented in the form of a bar graph to show the differences among the categories **FIGURE 2-3**. Simply asking people important questions about their experiences can reveal interesting information for

Internet-mediated research Using the World Wide Web to collect data from remote participants.

Survey A study method in which individuals are asked to respond to a set of questions designed by an experimenter.

TABLE 2-1 Number of College Students Reporting Stress ($n = 100$)

Change in sleeping habits	89
Change in eating habits	74
Financial difficulties	71
Computer problems	69
Lower grade than expected	68
Roommate conflict	61
Public speaking	60
Fighting with boy/girlfriend	41
Personal health problem	26
Change of major	24
Trouble with parents	21
Missing too many classes	21
Death of friend or family	18
Minor law violation	14
Parental divorce	1

Source: Adapted from Ross, S. E., Niebling, B. C., & Heckert, T. M. (1999). Sources of stress among college students. College Student Journal, 33*(2). 312–318.*

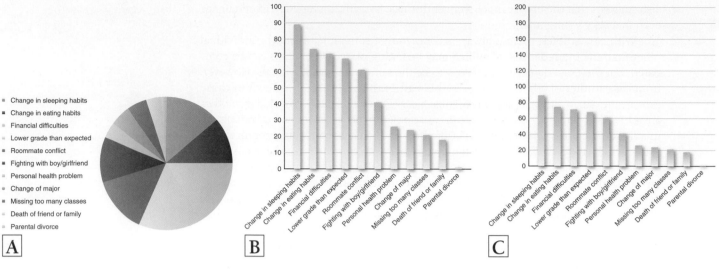

FIGURE 2-3 Results from studies can be displayed in a variety of forms. A. Pie chart showing the frequency of reported stressors. B. Bar graph of the same data. The horizontal axis (x-axis) shows the categories of stressors, and the vertical axis (y-axis) shows the frequency of reports. C. This graph shows the same data again; however this time, the scale has changed to show scores up to 200. As a result, the bars are smaller, so the impact of the stressors may *seem* smaller. Be sure to check scales to interpret carefully the picture you see.
Source: Data from Ross et al., 1999.

Population The larger group about whom a study would like to draw conclusions.

Sample The subgroup of individuals included in a study to represent a larger population.

Sampling bias The selection of a sample of individuals from within a population that fails to capture an accurate representation of the larger group.

others about what to expect in their own lives. Surveys are used across areas in psychology to assess what concerns people, what inspires them, and what drives their behavior.

However, doing so using well-conceived research designs requires several steps. First, we can ask who we want to draw conclusions about, called the **population** of the study. For example, the survey above addresses college students, while other studies may target the elderly, people in the United States, or people in general. Defining this group is important in selecting a **sample**, or the subgroup of respondents who will take part in the study FIGURE 2-4. In the survey above, one group of 100 students at one university was selected at random for the sample, and the researchers want to conclude that their findings are valid for the population of all college students. How might they improve on the validity of their design? One solution is to increase the number of participants (called *n*) in the study. If many people contribute responses, we can feel more confident we are capturing what most of this population thinks. A second solution is to collect the sample in ways that better represent the population; so they might collect data from campuses at small colleges, big research universities, and community colleges so that all types of college students are included in the sample. Some studies may show a **sampling bias**, or a limitation in the sample selected; for example, studies recruiting participants by calling through the telephone book listings will omit people who do not have listed numbers or home phones.

FIGURE 2-4 A sample, or subset, of individuals are selected from a larger population.

Most commonly, researchers choose a **convenience sample**, or participants who are readily available for the study. Since most researchers are located on college campuses, this means the vast majority of studies conducted use samples composed of undergraduates, often those studying in psychology. They are often selected through their participation in a course or presence in a particular building in which recruiting signs are posted (Schultz, 1969). Are they (and you) "typical" people who are like most other people in the world? Far from it: Study participants are smarter, more involved in volunteer activities, and more financially well off than the rest of the population, even in just the United States (Rosenthal & Rosnow, 1975). Nevertheless, findings from a college student sample are often generalized to all people, assuming a universal truth to the results. Sampling done well represents important factors about the population, including gender, age, ethnicity, and socioeconomic status. In major studies, methods of **random sampling** are used to ensure that every member of the population of interest has an equal chance of selection through the use of randomization. For example, using addresses, one could survey every 10th house listed within a community; however, you would still miss participants who do not live in homes. The cost of good sampling methods often leads to compromises on the selection of the study sample.

Survey data are very easy to collect, and tremendous numbers of psychological studies rely on the self-reports of individuals. However, surveys can have important drawbacks. For example, people can say whatever they want on a survey, so you may not capture their true thoughts or behavior. Sometimes researchers ask the same questions in different forms in order to detect when people might not be giving truthful answers or may be answering without reading the questions carefully. In addition, surveys often depend on our ability to accurately remember our past or recent experiences, and studies have shown that people are not very accurate in recalling when events occurred (Tourangeau et al., 2000). People's answers are also influenced by how the questions are stated and the order of question presentation (Schwarz & Hippler, 1995). Survey methodology is a large specialty area within psychology and provides important descriptive information about people's behavior.

Convenience sample A group of participants who are readily available for a study.

Random sampling Selecting which members of a population will participate in a study through a systematic method that gives every person an equal chance of selection.

Correlational Studies

Some descriptive studies attempt to determine the relationship between two types of observations. For example, many studies measure "satisfaction with life" (Diener et al., 1985), or your subjective "report card" on how your life is going right now TABLE 2-2. After answering the five test items, you will have a score ranging from 5 to 35. This score is a measure of your subjective well-being (SWB), or your self-perception of how satisfying your life is through evaluating life events (e.g., Diener, 2006). Now we can ask, what variables are related to high SWB? For example, is it true that money brings happiness?

TABLE 2-2 Satisfaction with Life Scale

Below are five statements that you may agree or disagree with. Using the 1 to 7 scale below, indicate your agreement with each item by placing the appropriate number on the line preceding that item. Please be open and honest in your response.

7	6	5	4	3	2	1
Strongly agree	Agree	Slightly agree	Neither	Slightly disagree	Disagree	Strongly disagree

1. _____ In most ways my life is close to my ideal.

2. _____ The conditions of my life are excellent.

3. _____ I am satisfied with my life.

4. _____ So far I have gotten the important things I want in life.

5. _____ If I could live my life over, I would change almost nothing.

Scale: Add your scores for the five items.

30–35 Very high score; highly satisfied: Respondents who score in this range love their lives and feel that things are going very well. Their lives are not perfect, but they feel that things are about as good as lives get.

(continues)

TABLE 2-2 Satisfaction with Life Scale *(continued)*

25–29 High score: Individuals who score in this range like their lives and feel that things are going well. Of course their lives are not perfect, but they feel that things are mostly good.

20–24 Average score: The average of life satisfaction in economically developed nations is in this range—the majority of people are generally satisfied, but have some areas where they very much would like some improvement.

15–19 Slightly below average in life satisfaction: People who score in this range usually have small but significant problems in several areas of their lives, or have many areas that are doing fine but one area that represents a substantial problem for them.

10–14 Dissatisfied: People who score in this range are substantially dissatisfied with their lives. People in this range may have a number of domains that are not going well, or one or two domains that are going very badly.

5–9 Extremely dissatisfied: Individuals who score in this range are usually extremely unhappy with their current life. In some cases this is in reaction to some recent bad event such as widowhood or unemployment.

Source: Data from Diener, E., & Biswas-Diener, R. (2008). The science of optimal happiness. Boston: Blackwell Publishing.

Scatterplot Graph showing the points observed from scores on two variables.

Correlation coefficient An index, called *r*, of the degree of relationship between two variables, ranging from −1.00 to +1.00.

Correlation A measure of the degree to which different factors are associated with one another.

Positive correlation An association between two variables where higher scores on one go with higher scores on the other.

We can compare people's annual incomes in relation to their SWB scores by graphing them in a **scatterplot**, in which each point represents one person's income and SWB score FIGURE 2-5. To view the pattern of relationship between the variables, the scatterplot includes a line showing the average across the points. Do the points fall close to the average along the line, together, or are they scattered in a very diffuse pattern? This degree of association—how closely the points fall to one another—is measured by the product-moment **correlation coefficient**, invented by Karl Pearson. He named the coefficient *r* to reflect the idea of "reversion," or returning to the average. If the points are clustered along the line, the value of *r* will be high, and if the points are scattered in a more diffuse pattern, the *r*-value will be very low.

In addition, the *r*-value, also called a **correlation**, provides an indicator of the *direction* of relationship between two variables. FIGURE 2-6 shows three possible patterns of scatterplots. How might income relate to SWB scores? One possible pattern reflects a **positive correlation** between the two variables, in which higher scores on one "go with" higher scores on the other, and the value of *r* is between 0.0 and +1.00. It is also possible

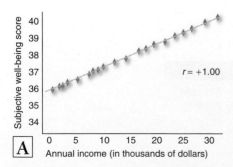
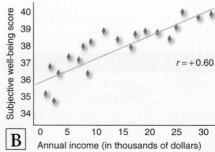
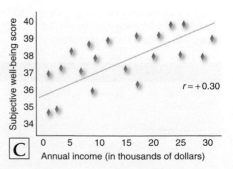

FIGURE 2-5 Three example scatterplots show possible associations between income and SWB, with one point for each observation of a person's income and their SWB score. In A, the correlation (*r* value) is close to + 1.00, so each person that is higher in income is also higher on SWB score. B shows a correlation of + 0.60, where the points are more scattered. C shows more scatter in the pattern and thus, results with a lower correlation (*r* value of + 0.30).

that we may find a **negative correlation** (between 0.0 and –1.00), between income and SWB. What if more money brings *less* happiness; for example, working at better-paying jobs brings more stress? Then *higher* income would be associated with *lower* SWB scores. A final possibility is that there is *no* systematic relationship between income and SWB. If so, then all levels of income would have some people with both high and low SWB scores.

> **Negative correlation** An association between two variables where higher scores on one go with lower scores on the other.

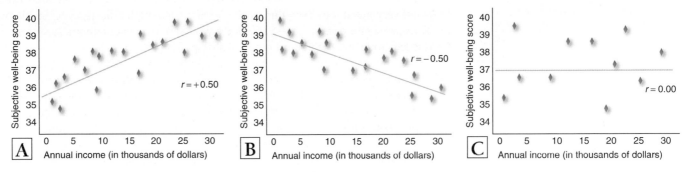

FIGURE 2-6 Correlations can be positive and negative. In A, a positive correlation is found when scores on one variable increase with scores on another. B. A negative correlation is shown, where increasing scores on one variable are matched with decreasing scores on the other. C. When two variables are unrelated, their correlation is close to zero, and there is no pattern to the spread of points in the distribution.

What is your prediction? Over several studies, the average correlation between income and life satisfaction is about +0.20 (Diener & Biswas-Diener, 2002; Lucas & Dyrenforth, 2006; Lucas et al., 2008) FIGURE 2-7. What does this mean? Because it is positive, it means *higher* incomes tend to correlate with *higher* life satisfaction scores. But the numerical size of the correlation also reveals the *strength* of the association. The strength of a correlation is measured by its distance from 0.0 on a scale of 0.0 to +1.0 or –1.0. The further the number is from 0.0, the stronger the correlation. Note that an *r*-value of –0.30 is as strong as one of +0.30; they differ in the *direction* of the correlation. So if you tell me what your income is, I can estimate your life satisfaction score to some degree. But if the *r*-value was higher (say, +0.50), there would be a stronger association between income and SWB scores, giving me a better chance of estimating your life satisfaction more accurately.

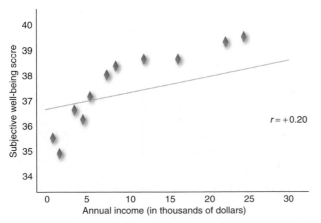

FIGURE 2-7 The actual findings showing the degree of association between income and SWB scores, *r* = 0.20.
Source: Data from Diener, E., & Biswas-Diener, R. (2008). The science of optimal happiness. Boston: Blackwell Publishing.

But knowing the relative strength of a correlation raises other questions we might want to answer. For example, can we interpret the strength of the correlation in terms of how much one variable is tied to the other? To do so, we use the concept of variance, which is an index of the amount of variation among scores. So there is an average SWB score in the United States, and there is a tremendous amount of variance around that average. Each person differs from the average by some large or small amount. What if I knew people's income: Would that help me explain why some of them have high SWB scores and some have low SWB scores? If so, income would provide a good account of the variance in subjective well-being. To determine the amount of the variance in one variable that can be attributed to the other, you can calculate "$r \times r$," or R^2; so the variance in individuals' SWB scores that is due to income is equal to 0.20^2, or 0.04. That means only 4% of the differences in SWB scores are accounted for by income level. That is not very much; however, this small correlation strength reflects a very stable pattern. The richest group (more than $200,000 a year) reports higher happiness scores than the middle group and the poorest group (less than $10,000 a year).

Is this a meaningful finding? Income explains only 4% of the variance in SWB scores. However, when you consider how many other things may also contribute to life satisfaction (e.g., relationships, religion, family, friends, ice cream), the correlation of +0.20 is indeed a helpful finding. It allows us to conclude that money can buy happiness, at least to some small degree. However, the correlation alone does not tell us about the specific patterns within the relationship between two variables. When we examine the subsets of the data, some meaningful patterns emerge. For example, it appears that money *does* make a difference to SWB when income is very low; but, once over $10,000 in annual income, there is less of a difference in SWB attributable to income level. So we might conclude that the relationship between income and SWB depends on the category (very low vs. livable incomes). However, the correlation cannot tell us this: instead, it reveals the association between all levels of both variables at the same time.

Correlations can tell us whether an association exists between two variables, its direction (positive or negative), and its strength, which tells us how well one variable accounts for the variance in the other. But you cannot stop there: You have to look at the scatterplots and examine the *patterns* of association. Consider the scatterplots in FIGURE 2-8. Distributions can have the same correlation value, but the pattern of scores can be very different. For example, age is not correlated with SWB, with no detectable pattern, so that all ages include some people with high and low SWB scores. But the same correlation may be found when there is an underlying pattern; for example, high SWB scores in childhood, young adults, and the elderly, and low scores in teenagers and older adults. The same correlation of 0 could also be found when younger and older people have high SWB and adults have lower scores. So when you see a correlation, think, "These two variables are related;" however, it cannot tell you exactly *how* they are related.

Another question is whether a correlation reveals *why* the two associated variables interact. Does greater subjective well-being cause one to be wealthier, or does greater wealth cause SWB to be higher? One might seem more logical, but a descriptive study with a correlation cannot tell us about the *causality* between the variables. Correlation is not causation; instead,

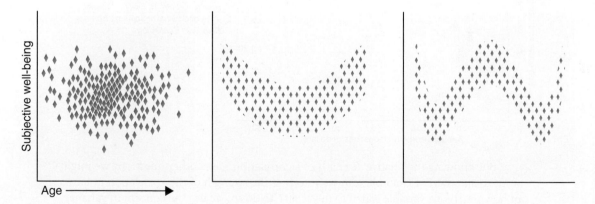

FIGURE 2-8 Three scatterplots of SWB and age with correlations of 0. From the images, it is clear that the correlation does not reveal any information about the shape or pattern of a distribution of scores.

it indicates only that the two variables are associated, or "go together." It may be that a third variable, one we are not measuring, is actually the cause of both observed variables. For example, what if getting married causes both an increase in income (for the family now) and an increase in SWB? We cannot rule out the presence of other, unmeasured factors that may be the cause behind the observed association. So, when you see a correlation, think about what other factors may be causing the relationship between the two correlated variables.

How do we decide whether the correlation strength is large enough to be meaningful to our decisions about behavior? For subjective well-being, the highest correlation found was with self-esteem ($r = +0.55$), along with satisfaction with work ($r = +0.37$) and satisfaction with health ($r = +0.29$; Campbell, 1981). The size of your social network correlates at +0.16 with life satisfaction. A meta-analysis of studies found the correlation between age and SWB to be near zero (Stock, Okun, Haring, & Witter, 1983). How can we interpret the value of these correlations? They may seem small; on the other hand, correlations, even when small, reflect real relationships between variables. For example, the ability of employment interviews to predict job success is just +0.20 (McDaniel, Whetzel, Schmidt, & Maurer, 1994); however, the small size of the correlation does not convince people that they should skip interviews when hiring! Similarly, sugar consumption was reported to be correlated at +0.01 with the behavior and cognitive processes of children (Wolraich, Wilson, & White, 1995). But parents still believe sugar makes their children act more "wired." In large enough samples, even small correlations stand up across studies.

What should our standard be in interpreting the significance of correlation strength? In psychological research, the standard for a correlation is +0.30, meaning one variable accounts for 9% of the variance in the other. As a rule of thumb, this is considered an important finding with implications about and for our behavior (Mischel, 1968). In medical studies, much smaller correlations are considered important (Meyer et al., 2001). For example, women's calcium intake and bone mass are correlated at +0.08, yet it is still recommended that women take calcium supplements to improve bone health (Welten et al., 1995). The correlation of low-level lead exposure and reduced childhood intelligence test scores is +0.11; however, laws are in place to require notification of lead paint use when a home is sold. Even small correlations that predict a small amount of the variance in a variable are important findings if they provide knowledge that is helpful to health and well-being.

A final question to consider about correlation is whether all important variables are included within a study. For example, does subjective well-being differ based on culture, or what part of the world you are living in? Researchers have found very large international differences in life satisfaction, and they appear to be much more related to differences in life circumstances than differences in psychology, or the way these circumstances are evaluated by individuals (Diener et al., 2010). FIGURE 2-9 shows that when the scope of the study is extended across cultures and nations, it is apparent that poverty has an

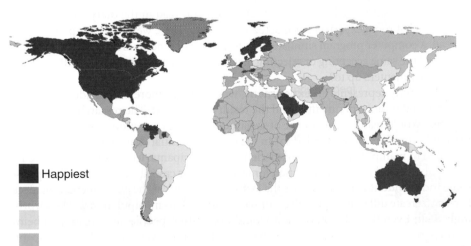

FIGURE 2-9 A depiction of countries around the world with the average subjective well-being score coded by color, with red as the happiest.
Source: White, A. (2007). A global projection of subjective well-being: A challenge to positive psychology? Psychtalk, *56, 17–20.*

Happiest

Least happy

Experimental group In an experiment, the group that receives some treatment or experience.

Control group In an experiment, the group that receives no extra treatment or experience.

Interaction between variables When the effect of one independent variable on the dependent variable depends upon the level of another independent variable.

Does walking through an underground tunnel lower your mood?

Walking in the outdoors is hypothesized to improve your mood.

random assignment cannot be done, the question becomes, "To what degree is the variable (e.g., gender) associated with the dependent measure?" For example, a meta-analysis found that girls outperformed boys on math in elementary school and middle school, but large differences with boys outperforming girls show up in high school and college (Hyde et al., 1990). However, because these studies are not true experiments, with the individuals assigned to gender randomly, we cannot conclude that gender per se causes differences in math performance. Many other things (teacher expectations, activities encouraged as interests, societal views of appropriate careers) may be affecting math scores (Eccles & Jacobs, 1986) rather than gender itself. For many important topics in psychology, we have to settle for these indications of relatedness but still think carefully about underlying causes, just as with correlational studies.

In the simplest studies, the independent variable includes an **experimental group** (that receives some treatment or experience) and a **control group** (that receives *no extra* treatment or experience). Control groups are important because of the need to compare those who receive the treatment to those who do not, allowing you to conclude the treatment has an effect. For example, one study compared people who took a campus walk using underground tunnels (the control group walked the normal paths in the cold Canadian setting) to those asked to walk for the same 15-minute period along a canal in a natural setting (the experimental group). After walking, tests showed those who walked along the greenway reported feeling more positive, more relaxed, and more fascinated with life, and reported fewer negative emotions than the tunnel walkers (Nisbett & Zelenski, 2011). The result provides a causal explanation: The level of positive mood *depends upon* the path taken; that is, the score on the dependent variable depends upon the condition of the independent variable.

The experimenters could have chosen to compare a control group of people who did not walk at all. Or perhaps walking through nature would be better compared to walking through an urban environment. Many studies include more than one comparison condition to identify the cause of any observed differences in the dependent variable. But no one study can include enough conditions to answer any question definitively; instead, it takes a series of experiments to arrive at a conclusion. More typically, experiments include more than one independent variable, allowing the exploration of the **interaction between variables**. For example, suppose we repeated the study above but added another independent variable: time stress. Now we can determine whether the positive impact of natural settings on mood is affected by whether you are under time pressure to complete the walk vs. no time pressure FIGURE 2-12. We expect to see the same pattern occur in the control group: With no time restriction, people would rate their mood higher if they walked the natural path than when they walked the

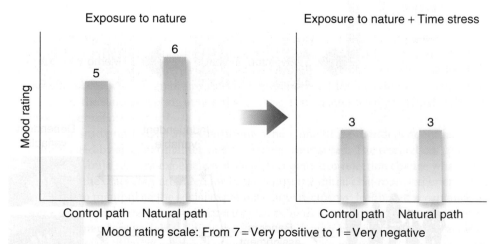

FIGURE 2-12 One study found that walking through natural areas improved people's ratings of their mood. But if we add another independent variable to the study—asking people to walk "as fast as they can"—the pattern of results may change. The control group (without time pressure) may show the same benefit of natural path on mood, but when under time pressure, both path groups may result in negative mood ratings.
Source: Data from Nisbet, E. K., & Zelenski, J. M. (2011). Underestimating nearby nature: Affective forecasting errors obscure the happy path to sustainability. Psychological Science, 22(9), 1101–1106.

control path through the tunnel. However, the time variable makes a difference in the observed pattern: When under time pressure to complete the walk "as fast as they can," *both* groups now rate their moods similarly negative after the walk. Including more variables allows researchers to determine how the impact of one variable might be affected by another.

Confounding variables, or alternative factors that might account for differences in the dependent measure, must be ruled out in order to draw solid conclusions. For example, perhaps the weather on the day of the walk affected the results. Experimenters can try to hold those factors constant in the study or conduct further studies to rule out other potential causes. The use of careful controls within studies is also needed to avoid inaccuracy of measurements due to the researcher's expectations, called **experimenter bias**, or from the participants' expectations. For example, experimenter bias might arise if judgments are made about subjects' performances and the experimenter knows whether they have received the treatment. Participants may alter their behavior in a study to be more **socially desirable** and fail to answer honestly. For example, knowing they received a medication during the study, they may believe the medication has an effect and change their behavior as a result. For this reason, researchers sometimes include placebos, or medications without active ingredients, for one group of subjects so that any **placebo effect** can be separated from the effect of the medication. When subject or experimenter bias is expected to be a problem, a **double-blind procedure** is followed in which neither the subject nor the experimenter knows which condition is assigned for that subject.

The key to a good experiment lies in how the researchers define their independent and dependent variables. In their **operational definitions**, studies attempt to describe and capture the key elements of the variables of interest while still providing a reliable measure of performance. For many areas of psychology, research has broken out in new directions as soon as someone was able to identify new ways of measuring psychological behavior. One example is the use of gaze as a dependent measure. Technology was adapted to allow researchers to pinpoint what someone was looking at and, consequently, to infer what aspect of a situation they were thinking about (called the eye-mind hypothesis; Just & Carpenter, 1980). For example, eye movements have been used to analyze how we interpret information in visual scenes (Henderson, 2003) FIGURE 2-13. This dependent measure has now been employed with infants, web page design, and classroom studies of student–teacher interaction. Examples of the wide variety of behaviors measured by psychologists are shown in TABLE 2-3.

Sometimes, it is not possible to do a true experiment given the topic of interest. For example, developmental studies are particularly challenging. Researchers may follow an individual from first grade through high school, measuring the same person each year, and compare behavior over time in a **longitudinal study**. But these studies take a long time to complete (because we have to wait until participants age), and they require staying in contact with people throughout the length of the study. Then, when it's time to compare your performance at age 6 and age 18, many things have changed in addition to their age (the independent variable of interest): The world has changed, too! Alternatively, we can try to understand development by comparing a current group of 6 year olds to others who are now 18, called a **cross-sectional study**. Because we are selecting people for the study based on their age, there is no random assignment to condition. Importantly, there may be **cohort effects**; that is, the life of a 6 year old may be different now than it was for those who are now 18 when they were 6. So the question remains, are differences observed due to age alone, or are they due to differences related to the time period in which people were raised? On questions where the participant comes into the study with their independent variable already determined (by their age,

Confounding variable An alternative factor that might account for observed differences in the dependent measure.

Experimenter bias The introduction of inaccuracy of measurements due to the researcher's expectations.

Social desirability bias Participants may alter their responses if they perceive them as depicting them negatively.

Placebo effect A participant's belief that he or she is receiving a treatment can produce changes in behavior.

Double-blind procedure A method in which both the experimenter and participant are not informed about the subject's assignment to a treatment within a study.

Operational definition The concrete implementation of a psychological concept within a study.

Longitudinal study Following a person through development by studying him or her at different points in time.

Cross-sectional study Comparing people at different ages with different people in the age groups.

FIGURE 2-13 Eye movement durations of one viewer looking at the scene. The circles represent fixations and the lines represent saccades. *Source: Data from Henderson, J. M. (2003). Human gaze control during real-world scene perception.* Trends in Cognitive Sciences, 7(11), 498–505.

Cohort effect A difference observed between age groups that may be due to differences in their experiences in addition to age.

TABLE 2-3 Examples of Behavioral Measures in Psychology Studies

Eye movements	Amount of drug self-administered
Galvanic skin reponse	Time spent working
Event-related potentials (electrical activity in the brain)	Hoarding
PET scans (images of oxygen uptake showing high-activity areas in the brain)	Amount of money donated
fMRI scans (images of high neural activity in brain areas)	Number of cookies eaten
EEG (heart rates)	Seat belt use
Cortisol hormone levels in saliva	Time survey was returned
Odor deposited on pads worn under arms	Mailing of postcards
Time to tap a response key	Detection of a stimulus
Recognition of a familiar face	Avoiding shocks
Word identification	Time of awakening
Recall from memory	School grades
Time hand is held in bucket of ice water	Attachment to parents
Decisions to purchase products	Speed of learning
Self-reports of activities, attitudes, thoughts, and feelings	Language use
Ratings of personality	Number of bar presses
Breathing rate	Political themes
Factual quizzes	Perceptions of culture
Driving	Jury decisions
Telephone answers	Hand washing
Facial expressions	Aesthetic judgments
Looking time	Intelligence test scores
Imitation of body movements	Interest in math
Survey questions	Amount of hot sauce added for another
Judgments of liking	Stories told
Distance from another	Mate choices
Group consensus	Photographs of dorm rooms
Number of ideas generated	Picking up another's dropped wallet

gender, personality, experience, etc.), random assignment cannot be accomplished, so the study does not involve a true experiment.

The reason why true experiments with random assignment are so important is that they prove the independent variable alone is the *cause* of observed differences in the dependent variable. This is the most powerful and informative conclusion you can draw from studies of behavior. A true experiment allows conclusive evidence that the independent variable causes differences in the dependent variable.

Another problem with true experiments is that achieving control of the independent variable often involves making compromises about the generalizability of a study. In order to keep elements of the experimental and control conditions constant, you may have to test the participants within a laboratory setting. For example, a study on gender differences in cocaine addiction might employ an animal model, such as a rat, and carefully measure the consequences of the rat's self-administered dosing (Hu et al., 2004). However, will the findings tell us about the differences in men's and women's real life experiences, and how their everyday lives might impact decisions to use cocaine? The ability to conduct controlled studies often requires isolating the target behavior in laboratories in order to ensure proper controls; but, this means some of the important features of real behavior are missing from the simplified (but better controlled) conditions in a study. As shown in TABLE 2-4, there are advantages and drawbacks to conducting research using each of these methods.

TABLE 2-4 Comparison of Research Methods

Type of Study	Descriptive	Correlational	Experimental
Goal	Capture existing behaviors	Detect associations between variables	To determine causes
Examples	Case studies Naturalistic observation Surveys	Surveys Group comparisons	Field Laboratory
Key feature	Watch or ask people	Compute correlation of variables	Random assignment
Strengths	Describes in natural setting	Captures existing differences	Determines causality
Weaknesses	Difficult to be objective Hard to compare studies	Can't determine causation, only association	Generalize to behavior in the world

CONCEPT LEARNING CHECK 2.3   *Designing an Experiment*

Design a study to test the hypothesis that men earn higher salaries than women. Fill in the specifics of your study for each of the study elements below.

1. Independent variable

2. Dependent variable

3. Operational definition (of dependent variable)

4. Randomization

5. Sampling

6. Population

7. True Experiment

2.4 Statistical Analysis

The data collected about behavior are summarized by standard numerical measures that describe differences.

- Illustrate the central tendency of, and the variation among, a set of scores in describing data.
- Describe what it means when a study shows an effect that is statistically significant.

To psychologists, the proof is in the data: What do the measurements show about people's actual behavior? My friend Sheri, now a clinical psychologist, demonstrated this approach when she was just a preschooler. The babysitter who cared for Sheri and her little brother sometimes hit him, but when Sheri told her parents, they interpreted this to mean it happened only rarely. So one day, Sheri took the cardboard backing from one of her father's new shirts and made a mark on it with a crayon every time the babysitter struck her brother. That night, confronted with the many markings on the cardboard, her parents quickly grasped the seriousness of the situation. In many important decisions about policies, education, and life improvement, the most convincing evidence is a conclusion drawn from data.

Measures of Central Tendency and Variance

Statistics provide a numerical representation of data, summarizing the nature of all of the observations collected into a shorthand "picture." Rather than describe each data "point" or observation, it is helpful to summarize them into a depiction that describes the most important findings. There are two important ways to describe data: the **central tendency** of, and the variation among a set of scores.

Measures of central tendency describe the "typical" value of a given variable. For example, how many dogs live in the typical American family? The number of dogs in a sample of 45 homes is shown in FIGURE 2-14. How can we summarize the results of the data collected? One measure, called the **mode**, is the most frequently observed score, or one dog per home. A second measure is the **median**, or the middle score of the distribution that divides the sample in two. If we line up the homes from the fewest to the most dogs and take the middle home in this list, the score is 2 dogs. Finally, the most common way to describe the central tendency of a set of scores is the arithmetic average of all the scores (adding up the number of dogs in all, divided by the number of homes), called the **mean**—in this case, 2.8 dogs. Which of these gives the best picture of how many dogs

Statistic A numerical summary of the results of data collection.

Central tendency The "typical value" of a group of scores, described by the mean, mode, or median.

Mode The most frequently observed score in a data sample.

Median The score at the middle of a distribution of scores from a sample.

Mean The arithmetic average, or the sum of all scores in a sample divided by the number of scores.

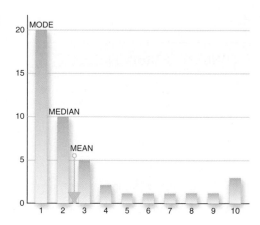

FIGURE 2-14 Measures of central tendency shown on a frequency distribution.

people own? You might say that most families with dogs own just one (the mode), while half own one or two (the median), while the average number is close to three. The best measure of central tendency to report is the one that gives the most useful summary for your purpose. For example, if you are interested in discussing the close bonds formed by people with their dogs, pointing out that most homes have just one (the mode) provides some relevant information.

In addition, we need a way to describe how the scores are distributed around the typical score: Are they spread very far apart, or are they clustered closely together? A bar graph showing the total number of observations in each category is often "smoothed" into a line drawing to show the shape of a distribution of scores. For example, suppose students' scores from a quiz are compiled, and the distribution of their scores shows that most people score close to the average score FIGURE 2-15. We might conclude that most of the students are learning the material well. On the other hand, the same average score might occur with a distribution of scores that is much more "spread out": While the central tendency is the same, there may be many more higher and many more lower scores. This suggests that the group shows more differences between scores, called **variance**. So in addition to the central tendency, it is important to give a summary of the variance observed in the data sample. A simple measure of variance is the **range**, or the

Variance The variability between scores observed on a given dependent variable.

Range A measure of variation in a data sample determined by subtracting the lowest score from the highest score.

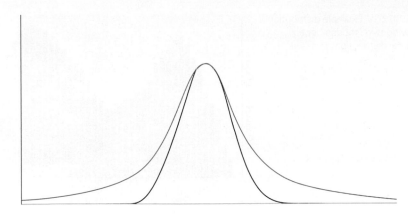

FIGURE 2-15 Scores from two quizzes demonstrate that data with the same mean can have a different variation within the group—the red group's data is much more spread out.

highest score minus the lowest score. The most frequently used measure of variation is the **standard deviation**, a measure tracking how each score in a sample differs from the mean **TABLE 2-5**. This calculation reveals in a single number whether the distribution of scores is close together or more spread out.

The pattern of scores can take on many shapes, such as a **bimodal distribution**, in which there are two clusters of frequently occurring scores FIGURE 2-16. Often, the distribution of scores in a large sample takes the shape of an upside-down bell, called the **normal distribution**. It takes this name because many common measurements fall into this distribution shape, such as people's heights FIGURE 2-17. For this special pattern of

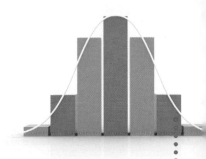

The frequency of each category observed is shown as a bar; then, the shape of the tops of the bars is smoothed into a line drawing.

TABLE 2-5 Example of Standard Deviation in Two Samples

	BOYS			GIRLS		
	Test Score	Difference from Mean	Squared Difference	Test Score	Difference from Mean	Squared Difference
	110	10	100	110	10	100
	109	9	81	110	10	100
	108	8	64	110	10	100
	107	7	49	110	10	100
	106	6	36	110	10	100
	94	−6	36	90	−10	100
	93	−7	49	90	−10	100
	92	−8	64	90	−10	100
	91	−9	81	90	−10	100
	90	−10	100	90	−10	100
Mean =	100			100		
Range =	90–100			90–110		
Sum of Deviations^2 =		660			1,000	
Sum of Deviations^2/ (n−1)		73.33			111.11	
Standard Deviation =		8.56			10.54	

Standard Deviation = $\sqrt{(Sum\ of\ Deviations^2/n-1)}$.

Standard deviation A statistical measure tracking how each score in a sample differs from the mean.

Bimodal distribution A pattern of scores with two distinct clusters with different modes (frequently occurring scores).

Normal distribution The inverted bell-shaped frequency distribution that often occurs for psychological tests and variables such as height.

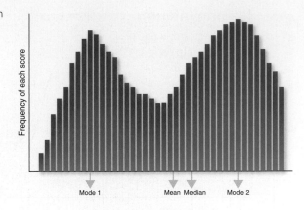

FIGURE 2-16 Example distribution showing two "modes," or a bimodal distribution.

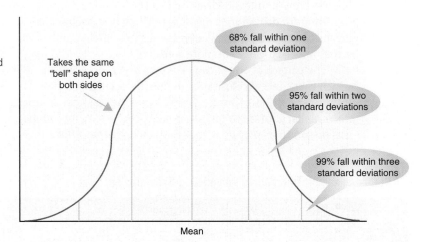

FIGURE 2-17 The normal curve has a specific distribution where certain percentages of scores fall within one, two, or three standard deviations.

distribution, the mean and the median are the same; that is, half of the scores fall lower than the mean and half higher. The "spread" of the normal distribution is related to the standard deviation. Approximately 68% of the scores lie within one standard deviation of the mean, 95% within two, and 99% within three standard deviations of the mean. Research reports often include the means and standard deviations in order to provide a complete picture of the data observed. For example, the study on nature walks found that an indoor walk produced an average positive mood rating of 2.01, with a standard deviation of 0.82, while an outdoor walk produced an average mood rating of 3.21, with a standard deviation of 0.84 (Nisbett & Zelenski, 2011). From this, we can depict the distributions of the two sets of data for indoor and outdoor walkers and about how much the two overlap FIGURE 2-18.

FIGURE 2-18 Walkers who were mostly indoors had a lower mean mood rating (in blue) than walkers out in nature (shown in red), though the variance in the two groups (shown by the spread of the frequency distributions) was very similar.
Source: Data from Nisbett, E. K., & Zelenski, J. M. (2011). Underestimating nearby nature: Affective forecasting errors obscure the happy path to sustainability. Psychological Science, 22(9), 1101–1106.

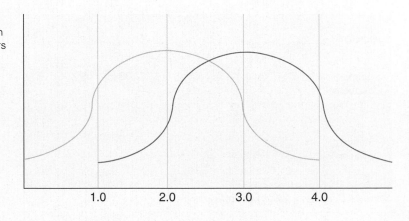

Making Inferences with Statistics

The point of using **inferential statistics** is to guide us in making conclusions from data, and to help us decide whether any differences observed are meaningful or due to random variation. In other words, can we believe the differences in the groups within an experiment, or could we be mistaken? When drawing conclusions, we want to ensure that the differences we observe are reliable and not simply a result of chance. Suppose you wanted to test whether college athletes have lower grade point averages than nonathletes. You could stop by the gym, ask five athletes and five nonathletes their GPAs, and see if the averages differ. Suppose you found that the GPAs of the five athletes were actually higher. Would you believe the result? What would it take to convince you that an observed difference between the two groups is "real" and not a result of chance?

What leads us to believe that the difference between two groups is real? One factor is the size of the difference between the two groups. A recent study found the average GPA of male recruited athletes was 2.84, while nonathletes averaged 3.04 (College Sports Project, 2010). This is a fairly small difference on a small (4.0) scale. If the averages of the two groups are even close together ("walk-on" male athletes averaged 2.97), we might be less inclined to believe there is a real difference between the groups. A second factor is the variability within each of the groups. The standard deviation for nonathletes was very small, while the GPAs among athletes had more spread from high to low. That means the nonathletes are more similar in their GPAs as a group, while the athletes show a lot more variation among them. But the variance in both groups was small in comparison to the size of the averages. That suggests reliable measurement. A third factor to consider is how many observations were collected. In the study, there were 8,951 recruited athletes and 22,734 nonathletes. With so many observations, you might feel much more confident that the differences observed are reliable differences compared to the locker room study.

These factors are combined in statistical formulas that capture the size of the difference between groups, the amount of variation observed within each, and the number of observations collected, all at the same time. From the resulting statistical value, we can determine the probability that the finding may have occurred just by chance or whether occurring by chance alone is unlikely. There may be a 1 in 10 chance of observing this data pattern or a 1 in 100 chance, so we need to set a criterion or standard to use as a cutoff for accepting that an outcome is "unlikely." For example, say you have a bag with 100 marbles inside, with 99 blue and 1 red marble. You pull 1 marble out, and it is the red one. We might agree that is highly unlikely to happen! What if there were 10 marbles that were red and 90 blue, and you pull out one that is red? Still surprised? The standard used by psychologists—purely an arbitrary convention—is a probability of less than 5%. When an observed difference occurs and the probability of its occurrence is determined to be less than 5%, psychologists call it **statistically significant**, noted as the "alpha level," or p-value. Psychologists agree that when the likelihood of finding the observed difference is less than 5%, they will consider the differences as "real" and not a fluke occurrence. So the study on GPA found a statistically significant difference (a p-value less than 0.05) and was judged not likely to be caused by chance. Though recruited male athletes do have lower GPAs than male nonathletes, the size of the difference is fairly small; in fact, the study authors concluded athletes had ". . . GPAs only slightly below those of nonathletes."

Statistics are tools used to describe the results of research and to make inferences about how likely the observations are to reflect real differences (or the result of chance alone). For each study, researchers ask whether the results could be due to chance alone, whether the findings are robust (of a large size), and whether the study was sensitive enough to detect a real difference if it was there. Statistical significance is a standard the field accepts to say that the findings are likely to be real; however, errors do occur. A replication is the running of a study again under similar circumstances to see whether the same results are found. Sometimes, results cannot be replicated, pointing out errors or important features in studies. One study found a "Mozart effect," in which 10 minutes of listening to classical music by Mozart led to a three-point improvement on a spatial reasoning test FIGURE 2-19 (Rauscher et al., 1993). Many researchers attempted

---

Inferential statistic
A numerical test to determine what conclusions can be drawn from observed data.

Statistically significant
When the probability (p) of an observed difference occurring is determined to be less than 5% (p <0.05).

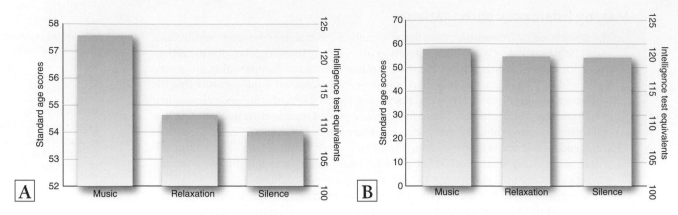

FIGURE 2-19 A. Performance on a spatial reasoning task improved more after listening to Mozart's music for a brief period. Note that the scale begins at "5;" if the scale began at "0," as in B, the small size of the "Mozart effect" is more apparent.
Source: Data from Rauscher, F., Shaw, G., & Ky, K. (1993). Music and spatial task performance. Nature, 365, 611.

to benefit from this finding by playing classical music for babies to boost their reasoning abilities. However, further studies showed the effect was difficult to replicate and did not generalize to other reasoning tasks (Steele et al., 1999). Other times, studies may show a statistically reliable result that has little importance in the world. For example, a study of swimming showed people move as quickly through syrup as they do through water (Gettelfinger & Cussler, 2004). Though statistically significant, the question of the study's significance to our understanding of psychology is an entirely separate question. This demonstrates that even statistically significant findings have to be considered for their real-world validity.

CONCEPT LEARNING CHECK 2.4 | *Summarizing with Statistics*

1. For the set of data below, compute the mean, median, mode, and range.

1, 1, 1, 1, 2, 2, 2, 3, 3, 5

A. Mean

B. Median

C. Mode

D. Range

Explain

2. In your own words, describe what it means when a study shows an effect that is "statistically significant."

2.5 Ethics in Psychological Research

Psychological research requires careful judgments and regulation regarding appropriate participation by humans and animals in studies.

- Examine the rights of participants in research identified in the Belmont Report.
- Contrast the ethical guidelines for human research studies and animal research studies.

Psychologists are interested in studying all kinds of human behavior, from our finest to our worst moments. Is it ethical to experiment on people? In order to study behavior using the scientific method, researchers sometimes create conditions in their studies that may be uncomfortable for participants. At the same time, the benefits of the research may be new psychological knowledge that not only increases our understanding but has the potential to help solve problems in the world. Do these positive ends justify the means? How do researchers protect their research participants and, at the same time, conduct studies that probe difficult issues in human behavior?

Human Participants

Historically, scientists had no guidance or regulation regarding how to treat human participants. For example, in the 1920s and 1930s, when laboratory studies were beginning in the United States, studies were conducted by well-meaning psychologists that would never be allowed now. In one, studying the experience and expression of emotion, participants were subjected to a variety of treatments designed to elicit strong emotion: plunging their hand into a pail of shallow water that, unbeknownst to them, contained three live frogs; viewing a pornographic picture; dropping a lit firecracker underneath an unsuspecting subject's chair; and a request to cut off a live rat's head with a butcher knife (Landis & Hunt, 1939). Other famous studies raised concerns about how participants were treated in research studies and motivated a national movement to regulate behavioral research.

In 1974, the National Research Act was signed into law, creating the National Commission for the Protection of Human Subjects of Biomedical and Behavioral Research. This *Common Rule* requires federally funded investigators to obtain and document the informed consent of research subjects, and describes requirements for institutional review boards at universities and hospitals to review research before it is conducted. Other subparts address additional requirements when conducting research with vulnerable populations such as pregnant women, children, and prisoners. In 1979, the National Commission published the Belmont Report (Department of Health and Human Services, 1979), identifying the rights of participants in research, including:

1. Respect for persons. Treat individuals as autonomous agents, and protect those who may not be able to make independent decisions. Respect means that subjects enter into the research voluntarily and are given adequate information. If someone has a diminished ability to give consent (children, prisoners, mentally ill), take extra steps to protect that individual's rights.

2. Beneficence. Treat people ethically by not only respecting their decisions and protecting them from harm but also making efforts to secure their well-being. First, do no harm, and second, maximize possible benefits and minimize possible harms.

3. Justice. Out of a sense of fairness, it is important to distribute both the burdens and the benefits of research. Since all of society benefits from research, all should be asked to bear the costs of participating in research.

From the principles of the Belmont Report, procedures to guide researchers in conducting their studies were created. Institutional review boards (IRBs) were created to examine planned experiments to ensure the rights of the participant are preserved. For behavioral studies, each researcher must provide information to the IRB for review, and the board determines the risk–benefit analysis for the research. In addition, each researcher commits to offering every participant privacy and confidentiality so that their participation and the data they contribute to the research are not revealed to others outside of the research team. This was the rule I breached when I revealed to other graduate students that a Hollywood star was participating in my research study. Along with the nature of participation and the contributions made, the fact that someone participated at all is also treated confidentially.

Research studies now begin with a key step called the **informed consent** process. In this process, the participants are given information about the nature of the tasks they will be asked to complete, disclosure of any risks and benefits to them, their rights to privacy and confidentiality, the length of participation requested, and any compensation provided for their participation. They are also told they have the right to withdraw from participating at any time. The participants can ask questions of the researcher, and the process concludes with signatures from the participants who decide to volunteer for that study. These consent forms document that the subjects indicated they understand their rights; however, even after signing, they may choose to end their participation at any time without consequences.

These steps help to ensure that there are no surprises in research studies; rather, the participants know what they are getting into when they decide to join a study, and they know they can choose to stop. Of course, for most studies, the participants cannot be informed about the hypothesis beforehand; otherwise, they may behave differently based on their knowledge of the study. But they can know what they will be asked to do (answer questions about their personality, solve math puzzles, talk in a chat room).

Informed consent The process through which an experimenter describes the nature of study participation to the potential volunteer, including his or her right to stop at any time.

Deception To actively provide information to the participant that is untrue.

Debriefing The process by which any deception used by researchers is fully disclosed to participants at the end of a study.

For most behavioral research in psychology, these tasks are uncontroversial. In fact, for studies involving surveys alone, informed consent is not always needed; instead, your willingness to answer a question indicates your consent to participate. But the researcher is obligated to remind you that you may choose not to answer any question at any time. Other studies fall into the realm of "public behavior": When you are in a public place, you do not have a right to privacy! Your behavior can be observed by anyone and used (anonymously) in a study report.

A more difficult situation arises when the researcher plans to use **deception** in the experiment; that is, to actively provide information to the participants that is untrue. You have already read about such an experiment in this chapter. Can you identify which study it was? The "online chat room" study used active deception because the researchers told the participants they were having a conversation with others online, while it was actually a computer program that was generating the conversation. This deception seems innocuous; that is, no one is likely to be upset when they learn the truth. However, other studies may use deception that is troubling to participants. In one study, subjects were told, "You are the type who will end up alone later in life. You may have friends and relationships now, but by your mid-20s, most of these will have drifted away. You may even marry or have several marriages, but these are likely to be short-lived and not continue into your 30s" (Baumeister et al., 2002). The experimenters argue these manipulations are necessary to create emotional responses within laboratory studies.

To deal with this problem, a standard has emerged: Is the experience one you may encounter within everyday life? It is possible you may hear swear words directed at you or have a palm reader tell you negative things about your future in the course of day-to-day living. These types of events may occur, and most people are able to withstand the short-term stress caused by such studies. In addition, the Belmont regulations require that studies using deception provide a full **debriefing** following the study, through which the untrue information is revealed and the participants can ask any questions. So, in the chat room study, researchers fully informed the participants that the conversation was a computer program and explained why it was necessary to keep that information from them (because it was intended to make them feel socially excluded). A process debriefing is used to walk the participants through the study, ensuring they understand that they were assigned to the treatment they received at random, that they know the manipulation (such as the false test results) had nothing to do with them personally, and they can have any questions answered before they leave the study.

It has been more than 30 years since the Common Rule was established, and the safety and well-being of human and animal participants has been greatly improved. However, to some, this increased regulation of behavioral research may have gone too far. Most universities review all research under the same guidelines, and the process is costly and time consuming. In most psychology studies, little or no risk is involved, so perhaps less regulation is needed. In addition, the regulations may mean that some studies of great benefit to society may never be conducted because they invoke ethically questionable procedures. For example, teenage pregnancy interventions could be tested to determine which are most successful. However, because they are under the age of consent (18), studies of teenagers require parental consent for their participation. And, for example, if parents will not approve a study plan that makes condoms accessible to their children, the possible benefits to the children cannot be determined. In some situations of urgent need, such as behaviors related to HIV transmission, lack of scientific knowledge may result in more human suffering, while studies may be conducted in areas of the world with fewer ethical protections for participants (Angell, 2000; Lurie & Wolfe, 1997).

The ethical conduct of psychological studies has come a long way since the 1920s; however, it is important to recognize that dilemmas still exist. For example, the principle of justice says that everyone in a society should bear the burden of contributing to research. In practice, however, individuals who are willing to participate for small financial payments or for credit in college courses are the ones most often recruited. In addition, studies of special populations may approach some individuals multiple times in order to recruit participants. Further, there is a difficulty in recruiting those with psychological disorders (such as bipolar disorder or schizophrenia) to participate in a study when, by definition, their thinking may be disordered. Finally, other ethical dilemmas in psychology include the fact that many potential questions are not asked, and many important members of society are not included in studies. Across all fields, university professors at doctoral institutions are still predominantly male (68%) and White (78%) (Forrest Cataldi et al., 2005). Since the lived experiences of researchers contribute to their research questions, it is important to broaden the diversity of those engaged in psychological research.

Animal Studies

Animal subjects (mostly laboratory-bred rats and mice, but also cats, dogs, and monkeys) are employed in a wide array of psychological studies. Research topics include exposure to addictive drugs, sleep, diet, stress, hormones, and disease. Increasingly, the link between behavior and genetics is examined, and animal models are much more practical for these studies due to their shorter natural lifespan. The interest in measures of neural function often involves invasive procedures such as surgery to determine how behavior relates to physiological function and performing brain anatomy studies after death. The use of animal models allows us to gain knowledge that would not be possible with human subjects based on ethical or practical concerns. The results from animal studies have been shown to greatly benefit human health and medical treatments (Miller, 1985).

The white lab rat shown here in containers, is a staple of many psychology studies.

However, animals are not given the same rights that human participants enjoy: They cannot consent to participation. Efforts are made to ensure humane treatment of research animals, and safeguards are put in place to make certain they receive adequate care. Ethical boards review all animal research treatments, and federal laws specify how animals are housed and fed in protected facilities. Animal testing is much more prevalent in consumer product testing, through which substances are proven safe for human consumption or use. However, the practice of testing animals for purely research purposes is controversial, and some argue that it is not appropriate, even if human lives are saved by the outcome of research (Shapiro, 1990). Even within the field, people differ in their opinions: A survey of researchers in the field of psychology found that a majority support animal studies involving observation but disapprove of studies involving pain or death (Plous, 1996).

In behavioral research, laboratory animals have played critical roles in developing new theories that are now improving research into human behavioral disorders. One example is research on brain activity in monkeys. In the studies, monkeys undergo testing with wires implanted in specific brain areas that record neural activity. One researcher noted that a monkey's brain responded as if it had eaten a peanut even though it was only *watching* someone else eat one (Rizzolatti, Fogassi, & Gallese, 2006). This uncovered a network in the brain that reflects others' behavior and may be responsible for creating empathy with others. Researchers are now exploring how disruptions of this "mirror neuron" system may be related to the development of autism in humans, a growing health concern (Iacoboni, 2008).

Another example comes from a study of dogs that first underwent training in which escaping from shock was impossible (Seligman & Maier, 1967). After this training, the dogs were placed in an escape learning setting where they could easily escape the coming shock by jumping over a low barrier. But the dogs had given up, a phenomenon that is termed *learned helplessness*. This behavior was tied to theories of human behavior in depression, in which people lose the sense that they can have a positive impact on their own success or environment. Many years later, Seligman is now leading a research-based movement, called positive psychology, that is using some of these insights to help change lives for the better around the world (Peterson, 2006; Seligman, 2006).

Dogs unable to escape from shocks appeared to "give up," and did not attempt to escape when tested in a new situation.

Increasingly, scientists are looking for alternatives to animal studies in psychology (Gallup & Suarez, 1985). For example, experimental methods are being devised that can tie behavior to human brain function through neuroimaging. While studies of human behavior have produced many important findings about mental processes, the ability to tie those processes to specific structures and systems within the brain has been limited. However, brain imaging devices from medicine have now been used in behavioral research to measure thinking through correlates in the brain's activity. These include measuring the uptake of oxygen (positron emission technology, or PET scans), changes in blood flow (functional magnetic resonance imagery, or fMRI scans), and electrical patterns of activity across the scalp (event-related potentials, or ERPs) that are produced by neural activity. These new methods have allowed psychologists to ask questions with human subjects that were not possible in the past.

For example, when people diagnosed with schizophrenia hear voices in hallucinations, are they actually "hearing" them? A study had volunteers lie in MRI machines and depress a button for the duration of time they were hearing voices. The results showed that the brain activity taking place during hallucinations is in the same areas that are active when we actually hear voices (Kircher et al., 2005) FIGURE 2-20. The development of new technologies for measuring human brain function may reduce the need for the use of animal models in psychology.

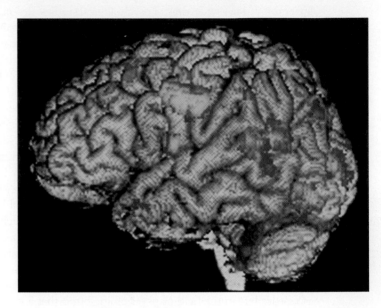

FIGURE 2-20 Positron emission tomography (PET) brain scan of a schizophrenic male patient aged 23 during an active hallucination. Highlighted in orange are areas of brain activity in the visual (right) and auditory processing (upper central) areas of brain, showing the patient has "seen" and "heard" during an hallucination.

Research in psychology strives to identify the factors that influence human behavior. The underlying model is that all humans are alike and that there are *universal* truths about psychology that apply to all humans. Clearly, this is true for many research conclusions. For example, psychologists have concluded that

- There is a special area of the human brain devoted to learning and recognizing human faces (Farah, 1996).
- People have a deep need to belong to a social group or relationship (Baumeister, 1991).
- The basic human emotions are displayed in characteristic facial expressions (Ekman et al., 1987).

At the same time, many conclusions about behavior depend upon the ways individuals *differ* from one another, including by gender, age, ethnicity, nationality, education, socioeconomic status, environment, personality, and culture. Many findings must be qualified by noting that the research studies included only Americans or college students, meaning that the validity for other groups has not yet been verified. In fact, the attempts to verify "universal" findings across cultures have quickly uncovered major differences in how individuals respond based on the culture surrounding them.

For example, social psychologists identified a reasoning pattern so pervasive it was named the "fundamental attribution error" (Nisbett & Borgida, 1975; Ross, 1977). This error is to assume that people act the way they do because the behavior is an inherent part of their nature and not because of the particular situation in which they find themselves. For example, you observe your professor lecturing in class and infer that he or she is very comfortable giving public speeches. You see the behavior and attribute it to who she or he is as a person. Then you attend a friend's wedding and see the same professor nervously reciting poetry as part of the ceremony. This tells you that the situation also plays a role: Though your professor is comfortable in the lecture hall, he or she is not likely to win a poetry slam. The "fundamental attribution error" we all make is to assume that what we see is a reflection of the person's qualities and not the situation he or she is in.

Or do we? In a study comparing American and Chinese students, a video of an individual fish swimming in front of a group of fish was shown. More American than Chinese participants described the activity of the fish as internal to the fish ("the fish is leading the group") rather than externally caused ("the school of fish is avoiding a predator;" Morris & Peng, 1994). Cultural values like individualism (in Western cultures) and collectivism (in Eastern cultures) appear to alter the inferences people draw to explain the behavior of others (Miller, 1984). In several studies, East Asians tended to attribute behavior to the situation, while Westerners attributed the same behavior to the person (Masuda & Nisbett, 2001). One explanation for this difference in attribution is that people in different cultures are more or less oriented toward perceiving themselves within a holistic environment. The fundamental attribution error was not so fundamental after all!

Summary of Multiple Influences on a Scientific Approach to Psychology

Currently, explorations of culture and psychology are burgeoning as researchers seek to compare how individuals are affected by the social environment around them. Throughout this book, we will bring to bear evidence of multiple influences on human behavior. Many influences from biology, such as genetics, heredity, hormones, and brain structure and function, unite our behavior under explanations that apply to all humans. These same biological influences may account for many differences across individuals, such as gender, age, and personality differences. Other influences from our lived experiences may similarly evoke universal behavior across individuals, such as learning to speak and forming bonds with others. At the same time, psychologists are uncovering many more ways that our lived experiences, including our culture, education, and socioeconomic environment, may give rise to differences in our behavior.

The methods available to psychologists for exploring the causes of human behavior are varied, each with strengths and limitations. Consequently, it is critical to examine evidence about multiple influences on behavior through as many different methods as possible. Throughout this book, we will bring to bear evidence from biological, environmental, cultural, and experiential influences to provide a more complete picture of psychology.

CONCEPT LEARNING CHECK 2.5 | *Ethics in Psychological Studies*

Define and describe these concepts of ethical conduct in research studies.

1. Respect for persons

2. Beneficence

3. Justice

4. Informed consent

5. Deception

6. Debriefing

CRITICAL THINKING APPLICATION

Students sometimes serve on the IRB committees that review research. Their job is to consider the risks and the potential benefits of studies, along with ensuring the researchers follow the informed consent guidelines. For each of the studies, consider whether you would approve it or whether you would stop an ongoing study. What issues might raise questions in your mind? Finally, guess whether the description came from an actual study or is an example created for illustration.

1. A subject comes to an approved experiment on hypothesis testing. The experimenter has a hidden rule that produces a number sequence, and the subject must try to figure out the rule by generating examples and asking if they fit the experimenter's rule. One subject starts using the same examples over and over again and gets very agitated when he cannot guess the experimenter's rule. He becomes unresponsive and has to be taken to the ER. Should the study be stopped?

This event happened in a famous study taking place around 1960. The pressure of the very difficult task was too much for one participant. However, it was reasonable to expect that people would be able to respond without such a reaction, and this was the only participant to have difficulty. Therefore, the study was continued (Wason & Johnson-Laird, 1968).

2. Some psychologists are interested in the effect of frustration on preschool children. They propose a study in which a 3-year-old child is able to see a desired toy through a transparent plastic box and is left alone to work on opening the box with a ring of wrong keys. After 3 minutes, the experimenter returns with the correct key and explains, "I guess I gave you the wrong keys. Let's try this one." The box is then opened; the child is encouraged to play for 1 minute with the toy. Do you think this causes harm to the child subjects?

The frustration tolerance required by this task has been used as a dependent measure in many studies (Dennis, 2006). Parents must always give permission for minors to participate in studies; however, very young children are not able to give their own assent to participate.

3. A researcher is interested in examining gender differences in attitudes toward sex. An attractive research assistant approaches students (of the opposite sex) on campus. She or he strikes up a conversation and then asks one of the following three questions: "Will you go on a date with me tonight?" "Will you come to my apartment tonight?" Or "Will you have sex with me tonight?" After the subject's response is noted, the research assistant debriefs the subject. Is it fair to ask such a question on a street corner?

This study was conducted at a major Midwestern university. Because the participants were approached in a public place and the content of the discussion was not outside of everyday experience, no consent was required for the study. The study found that almost all of the male participants said, "Yes!" (Clark & Hatfield, 1989).

4. Observations will be collected of public behavior in restrooms—specifically, of males standing at urinals. A confederate will be in the restroom and will approach the subject by standing at either a nearby urinal or two urinals away. A nearby experimenter will record latency and duration of urination by the subject. Do the investigators need consent from the participants?

This study was conducted using public restrooms, so no consent was needed from participants. The results showed the effects of social stress from violating "personal space" (Middlemist et al., 1976).

5. A researcher interested in what provokes violence invited students into the lab. Once there, they were "accidentally" bumped into by a confederate, who muttered a curse word at the student. The subjects' response to the incident ranged from ignoring it completely to chasing the confederate down the hall and pounding on the door. Is this experience along the lines of what you encounter in daily life?

This study was conducted at a major university and approved by the IRB after some consideration of what words were appropriate to use as the insult in the study. The results showed subjects from northern U.S. states were less reactive to the insult than were subjects from southern U.S. states (Cohen et al., 1996).

6. Participants in a study were asked to try on "clothing samples" in a locked laboratory room, where they were alone. They were given either a basket of sweaters or a basket of revealing swimsuits and told to put one on. Then they completed some surveys and a math test.

Because subjects were alone in the lab room, this was considered an acceptable request of participants. This study was approved by the IRB, and its findings were that women did more poorly on the math test when wearing swimsuits rather than sweaters, but for men, there was no difference (Fredrickson et al., 1998).

From the variety of studies you have seen here, it is clear that people differ in their judgments of what they consider appropriate for psychological experiments. While the guidelines help to ensure that subjects are informed about the study and that they may not be told everything until the study ends, the many studies being conducted will mean that some people become offended by the procedures. As a last resort, there is comfort in knowing that participants may always stop their participation at any time or may decide not to answer any given question. But, just like everyday experiences in the world, experiments may evoke unexpected emotions. Concerns about studies can be reported directly to the experimenter and to the IRB at any institution.

Visual Overview Sampling from a Population for a Scientific Study

The population includes all individuals for whom you would like to draw conclusions from the study. In a sample, you select a smaller group from the population for the purpose of the research study. Random sampling ensures that all members have a equal chance of being chosen for the study, so that no subgroups within the population are left out. Convenience samples (e.g., volunteers on college campuses) are often used as a shortcut due to the cost of true random sampling.

Convenience Sample

Small subset that is easy to access (e.g., college students)

Random Sample

Every person has an equal chance of being selected

Nonrandom Sample

A small subgroup that may not represent all in the population; may be biased in selection.

2.1 Psychological Investigation

- Psychological science is the study of human behavior and its underlying causes.
- The scientific approach to investigation consists of five steps.

  Step 1: Formulate a testable hypothesis.

  Step 2: Select the research method and design the study.

  Step 3: Collect the data.

  Step 4: Analyze the data and draw conclusions.

  Step 5: Report the findings.

- Every research study has limitations in its design.
- *Reliability* is the degree to which an experiment can be repeated under similar circumstances and produce the same results.
- *Validity* refers to how well the research reflects and captures what it set out to measure.
- *Generalizability* tells how well research findings can be applied to other people and circumstances.

2.2 Descriptive Research

- Descriptive studies are concerned with the qualities of human behaviors, experiences, and individuals, called variables.
- Naturalistic observation studies behavior as it occurs in "the wild", without any intervention by the researchers.
- The extensive examination of the experience of a single individual or group is called a case study.
- A well-conceived survey draws conclusions about the population from a selected sample.
- Methods of random sampling are used to ensure that every member of the population of interest has an equal chance of selection through the use of randomization
- A scatterplot provides a graph showing each person's score on two variables.
- The correlation coefficient *r* provides an indicator of the type of relationship between two variables.

- A positive correlation between two variables means that the scores of both variables rise together, and the value of *r* is between 0.0 and +1.00.
- A negative correlation means that as the score of one variable rises, the score of the other drops, and the value of *r* is between 0.0 and −1.00.
- When there is *no* systematic relationship between the two variables, *r* is close to 0.
- A correlation can tell us whether an association exists between two variables, the direction (positive or negative), the strength of the association, and even how well one variable accounts for variance in the other.
- A correlation cannot tell us about *causality* between the variables.

2.3 Experimental Research

- In experiments, the researcher intentionally manipulates variables and measures their impact on other variables.
- The independent variable is a factor that the experimenter manipulates to create different experiences for participants.
- The dependent variable measures any effect of the independent variable. Change in the dependent variable *depends* on the independent variable.
- The key feature that allows the conclusion of causality is that every participant in the study has an equal chance of being

assigned to the groups of the independent variable, called random assignment.
- In the simplest studies, the independent variable includes an experimental group (that receives some treatment or experience) and a control group (that receives no extra treatment or experience).
- The advantage of a true experiment is that the scientific method proves that the independent variable alone is the cause of observed differences in the dependent variable.

2.4 Statistical Analysis

- The data collected about behavior are summarized by standard statistics that describe differences in measurements.
- Measures of central tendency describe the "typical" value of a given variable. These include the mode, the median, and the mean.
- The variance describes how the scores are distributed around the typical score, including statistics called the range and standard deviation.

- The point of using statistics is to guide us in making generalizations from samples, and to help us decide whether any differences observed are significant.
- When the probability of a finding is determined to be less than 5%, psychologists say it reaches statistical significance, noted as the "alpha level" or $p < 0.05$.

2.5 Ethics in Psychological Research

- The Belmont Report (Department of Health and Human Services, 1979) identified the rights of participants in research, including *Respect for persons, Beneficence,* and *Justice.*
- Institutional review boards (IRBs) were created to examine planned experiments to ensure the rights of the participants are preserved.
- Research studies now begin with a key step called the informed consent process.
- In deception experiments, the researcher actively provides information to the participant that is untrue, and provides a full debriefing following the study.
- Animal subjects (mostly laboratory-bred rats and mice, but also cats,

dogs, and monkeys) are employed in a wide array of psychological studies.
- Ethical boards review all animal research treatments, and federal laws specify how animals are housed and fed in protected facilities.
- The underlying model is that there are *universal* truths about psychology that apply to all humans. At the same time, many conclusions about behavior depend upon the ways individuals *differ* from one another.
- Many influences from biology, such as genetics, heredity, hormones, brain structure and function, underly our behavior.

2.1 Psychological Investigation

1. The ability to draw a conclusion from a study that will also be true in other settings is called:
   A. reliability.
   B. validity.
   C. generalizability.
   D. probability.

2. The first step in designing a research study is to:
   A. formulate a hypothesis.
   B. collect data.
   C. report findings.
   D. select a research method.

2.2 Descriptive Research

3. A descriptive study that includes only a single subject is called:
   A. a case study.
   B. a survey.
   C. naturalistic observation.
   D. an experiment.

4. Which of the following is an example of a negative correlation?
   A. People who exercise regularly live longer than those who do not.
   B. There is no relationship between violent crime and whether a state has a death penalty.
   C. The more children watch television, the less they read.
   D. Men with high testosterone levels are more prone to violence.

5. Which of the following is an example of a positive correlation?
   A. If you take vitamin C, you are less likely to catch a cold.
   B. The more classes you attend, the higher your grades will be.
   C. People who smoke have poorer health.
   D. The more you exercise, the less you eat.

6. Sample is to population as:
   A. large is to small.
   B. not representative is to representative.
   C. valid is to invalid.
   D. part is to whole.

2.3 Experimental Research

7. The variable that an experimenter manipulates in order to measure its effects is called the _____ variable.
   A. independent
   B. controlled
   C. random
   D. dependent

8. A group of researchers wanted to determine if people tend to eat more food when they are with others, so half the participants ate in a room together and half ate in a room alone. They then measured how much food was consumed. In this study, the independent variable was:
   A. the amount of food that was consumed.
   B. how hungry the participants felt at the end.
   C. whether they ate with others or alone.
   D. the type of room that they ate in.

9. A group of researchers tested whether children's performance is affected by the presence of the experimenter. Half of the children were tested in a room alone and timed while they completed a puzzle. In this study, the length of time it takes to complete the puzzle would be:
   A. the independent variable.
   B. a confounding variable.
   C. a control variable.
   D. the dependent variable.

10. A true experiment requires:
   A. the use of humans.
   B. the research participants to manipulate the independent variable.
   C. at least three comparison groups.
   D. random assignment of research participants to conditions.

11. A researcher is carrying out a study on procrastination. In the research process, she must specify, in concrete "how-to" terms, how the dependent variable will be measured. In other words, she must provide:
   A. hypotheses.
   B. theories.
   C. operational definitions.
   D. archival records.

2.4 Statistical Analysis

12. The measure of central tendency that indicates which response occurred most frequently is the:

A. mean.

B. median.

C. mode.

D. average.

13. The measures of variation within a group of scores include the:

A. range.

B. significance.

C. *r*-value.

D. average.

14. The level of statistical significance used as a standard in psychological research is:

A. 0.05.

B. 0.50.

C. 1.00.

D. 100.

2.5 Ethics in Psychological Research

15. Stan is in a study in the subject pool in which the experimenter seems to rush him through the tasks. As a result, Stan started feeling uncomfortable. Stan should know he has a right to:

A. demand more time.

B. stop the experiment.

C. take a break for as long as he needs.

D. complain to the experimenter.

16. Mackenzie agreed to take part in an experiment in which she was asked to drink two glasses of beer over 30 minutes, was given a blood test, and then was given a questionnaire. When finished, she was not told the purpose of the study, nor that the drinks had no alcohol. In this case, the researchers:

A. failed to obtain informed consent.

B. violated Mackenzie's right to privacy.

C. did not use an adequate debriefing procedure.

D. did not provide adequate protection from harm.

17. The process at the start of a study in which the experimenter and participant discuss what will occur in the session is called the:

A. introduction to the study.

B. formulation of hypothesis.

C. informed consent process.

D. warm-up session.

CHAPTER DISCUSSION QUESTIONS

1. The scientific method is a formal approach to designing a research study with the goal of better understanding a topic, question, or problem. You may find that when you work on problems in your everyday life, you use some of the same steps. Think of a problem that you solved and compare the steps of the scientific method to the steps that you used. Are the steps the same? Did you follow the same order as the scientific method? What was different about your problem-solving approach?

2. Think of a career or job that you might like and then consider the various descriptive research techniques covered in Section 2.2 (naturalistic observations, case studies, surveys, and correlational studies). For the career you have picked, identify how someone might use each of the descriptive research techniques. In other words, for this career, describe some topics, questions, or problems for which you could investigate solutions using these descriptive research techniques.

3. One of the most interesting challenges for psychological research is figuring out how to create operational definitions for the topics we want to study. An operational definition explains how a researcher intends to measure the independent or dependent variable, an important step in developing an experiment. Identify a possible way to measure, or operationally define, each of the following topics of interest to psychology: memory, happiness, learning, depression, and motivation.

4. *Statistical significance* is used to describe research results that exceed the probability of chance. When researchers claim to have statistically significant results, it means they believe their results would happen again if they did their experiment again. In comparison, the term significant is used often in situations that have nothing to do with research (e.g., "she thought that was a significant change in his attitude"). Describe at least three situations in which it would be appropriate to call something statistically significant versus significant.

5. Review the informed consent process discussed in Section 2.5 and consider how the same type of process might be useful in nonresearch situations. Think of a situation in which you would have liked to have informed consent before participating. Relate the parts of informed consent to your own situation and describe what the informed consent process would have discussed.

CHAPTER PROJECTS

1. Think about something in psychology that you would be interested in studying. Then, starting with the steps of the scientific method discussed in Section 2.1, plan a research project. In your response, fill in details for each step of the scientific method, making sure to include information from the other sections of this chapter. For example, in step 2 of the scientific method, make sure to add information about which type of research method you would use.

2. Popular media sources often report on research results, but they try to present the results in very general terms so that many people can understand. Sometimes, these popular media sources end up misrepresenting research results through their simplification or because they want to create a more sensational story. Think about the long-term problems of popular media sources misrepresenting research results. Demonstrate how sensationalizing research results could be harmful. Imagine and describe a scenario in which a false representation of a research result could be damaging to a person or a community.

Between-subjects design
Bimodal distribution
Case study
Central tendency
Cohort effect
Comparative study
Confounding variable
Control group
Convenience sample
Correlation
Correlation coefficient
Cross-sectional study
Debriefing
Deception
Dependent variable
Double-blind procedure
Empirical
Experiment
Experimental group
Experimenter bias
Generalizability

Hypothesis
Independent variable
Inferential statistic
Informed consent
Interaction between variables
Internet-mediated research
Journal
Longitudinal study
Mean
Median
Meta-analysis
Mode
Naturalistic observation
Negative correlation
Normal distribution
Operational definition
Participant
Placebo effect
Population
Positive correlation
Psychological science

Random assignment
Random sampling
Range
Reactivity
Reliability
Replicable
Sample
Sampling bias
Scatterplot
Scientific method
Social desirability bias
Standard deviation
Statistically significant
Statistic
Survey
Theory
Validity
Variable
Variance
Within-subjects design

2.1 Within or Between?

1. Within
2. Between (males and females were compared)
3. Between
4. Within
5. Within (boys and girls did the same activities and were not compared)
6. Within (all exercised)

2.2 What Do Correlations Mean?

1. Studying with others may be an effective way to improve grades.
2. More conservative people are somewhat more likely to have a daily breakfast.
3. There is no relationship between viewing movies and reading.
4. More video game playing is related to lower likelihood of graduation.
5. Daily aerobic exercise may effectively improve mood.

2.3 Designing an Experiment

1. Independent variable. [Gender]
2. Dependent variable. [Salary]
3. Operational definition (of dependent variable). [Hourly wage paid over past 3 months]
4. Randomization. [None]
5. Sampling. [Select 100 males and 100 females from an executive education conference]
6. Population. [Employed adults]
7. True experiment. [No, because we cannot assign people at random to the independent variable groups]

2.4 Summarizing with Statistics

1. **A.** Mean. 21/10, or 2.1
   B. Median. Middle score, or 2
   C. Mode. Most frequent score, or 1
   D. Range. 1 to 5
2. The findings from the study are unlikely to occur by chance.

2.5 Ethics in Psychological Studies

1. Respect for persons. [Make sure everyone has a free, independent choice about participating.]
2. Beneficence. [Make sure you minimize any harm, and try to treat participants well.]
3. Justice. [Provide the opportunity to participate as fairly as possible.]
4. Informed consent. [Tell the participants what they will be asked to do and what the risks are. Give them a chance to ask questions, and remind them they can stop at any time.]
5. Deception. [If you give false information to participants, you must fully inform them about it after the study in the debriefing.]
6. Debriefing. [Informing the participant about the study's purpose and procedures at the conclusion of their session.]

ANSWERS TO CHAPTER REVIEW TEST

2.1 Psychological Investigation

1. C. Rationale: Generalizability; though validity is a closely related concept, it refers to the meaning of the finding.
2. A. Rationale: Formulate a hypothesis; before a study method can be selected, the hypothesis must be known.

2.2 Descriptive Research

3. A. Rationale: A case study.
4. C. Rationale: The more children watch television, the less they read; a high score on one variable goes with a low score on the other.
5. B. Rationale: The more classes you attend, the higher your grades will be; a high score goes with a high score.
6. D. Rationale: Part is to whole; a sample is a subset of the population.

2.3 Experimental Research

7. A. Rationale: Independent; it is assigned to participants and acts independently.
8. C. Rationale: Whether they ate with others or alone; it was assigned to subjects.
9. D. Rationale: The dependent variable; it is measured to determine if there were any effects.

10. D. Rationale: Random assignment of research participants to conditions; a key to true experiments.
11. C. Rationale: Operational definitions; exactly how to measure the effects.

2.4 Statistical Analysis

12. C. Rationale: Mode; it comes from the French word for "fashion" and is related to the idea of "most popular."
13. A. Rationale: Range; another is the standard deviation.
14. A. Rationale: 0.05, meaning that 5 times out of 100 studies, this finding might occur by chance.

2.5 Ethics in Psychological Research

15. B. Rationale: Stop the experiment; the participant can decide to stop at any time.
16. C. Rationale: Did not use an adequate debriefing procedure; because deception was used, debriefing is required.
17. C. Rationale: Informed consent process; this initial information is required for many studies.

REFERENCES

Angell, M. (2000). Investigators' responsibilities for human subjects in developing countries. *New England Journal of Medicine, 342,* 967–969.

Baumeister, R. F. (1991). The need to belong: Desire for interpersonal attachments as a fundamental human motivation. *Psychological Bulletin, 117*(3), 497–529.

Baumeister, R. F., Twenge, J. M., & Nuss, C. K. (2002). Effects of social exclusion on cognitive processes: Anticipated aloneness reduces intelligent thought. *Journal of Personality and Social Psychology, 83,* 817–827.

Campbell, A. (1981). *The sense of well-being in America: Recent patterns and trends.* New York: McGraw-Hill.

Clark, R. D., III, & Hatfield, E. (1989). Gender differences in receptivity to sexual offers. *Journal of Psychology and Human Sexuality, 2,* 39–55.

Cohen, D., Nisbett, R. E., Bowdle, B., & Schwarz, N. (1996). Insult, aggression, and the Southern culture of honor: An "experimental ethnography." *Journal of Personality and Social Psychology, 70,* 945–960.

College Sports Project. (2010). College Sports Project updates findings about athletics and academics in NCAA Division III. Retrieved from http://www.collegesportsproject.org/

Dennis, T. (2006). Emotional self-regulation in preschoolers: The interplay of child approach reactivity, parenting, and control capacities. *Developmental Psychology, 42*(1), 84–97.

Department of Health and Human Services. (1979). *Belmont report: Ethical principles and guidelines for the protection of human subjects of research, report of the National Commission for the Protection of Human Subjects of Biomedical and Behavioral Research.* http://www.hhs.gov/ohrp/archive/documents/19790418.pdf

Diener, E. (2006). Guidelines for national indicators of subjective well-being and ill-being. *Applied Research in Quality of Life, 1,* 151–157.

Diener, E., & Biswas-Diener, R. (2002). Will money increase subjective well-being?: A literature review and guide to needed research. *Social Indicators Research, 57,* 119–169.

Diener, E., & Biswas-Diener, R. (2008). *The science of optimal happiness.* Boston: Blackwell.

Diener, E., Emmons, R. A., Larsen, R. J., & Griffin, S. (1985). The Satisfaction With Life scale. *Journal of Personality Assessment, 49*(1), 71–75.

Diener, E., Kahneman, D., & Helliwell, J. (2010). *International differences in well-being.* New York: Oxford University Press.

Eccles, J. S., & Jacobs, J. E. (1986). Social forces shape math attitudes and performance. *Signs, 11*(2), 367–380.

Ekman, P., Friesen, W. V., O'Sullivan, M., Chan, A., Diacoyanni-Tarlatzis, I., Heider, K., Krause, R., LeCompte, W. A., Pitcairn, T., Ricci-Bitti, P. E., Scherer, K. R., Tomita, M., & Tzavaras, A. (1987). Universals and cultural differences in the judgments of facial expressions of emotion. *Journal of Personality and Social Psychology, 53*(4), 712–717.

Farah, M. J. (1996). Is face recognition special? Evidence from neuropsychology. *Behavioral Brain Research, 76*(1–2), 181–189.

Farah, M. J., Levinson, K. L., & Klein, K. L. (1995). Face perception and within-category discrimination in prosopagnosia. *Neuropsychologia, 33,* 661–674.

Farah, M. J., Rabinowitz, C., Quinn, G. E., & Liu, G. T. (2000). Early commitment of neural substrates for face recognition. *Cognitive Neuropsychology, 17*(1–3), 117–123.

Forrest Cataldi, E., Fahimi, M., & Bradburn, E. M. (2005). *2004 National Study of Postsecondary Faculty (NSOPF:04) Report on Faculty and Instructional Staff in Fall 2003* (NCES 2005–172). U.S. Department of Education. Washington, DC: National Center for Education Statistics. Retrieved from http://nces.ed.gov/pubsearch

Fredrickson, B. L., Roberts, T. A., Noll, S. M., Quinn, D. M., & Twenge, J. M. (1998). That swimsuit becomes you: Sex differences in self-objectification, restrained eating, and math performance. *Journal of Personality and Social Psychology, 75*(1), 269–284.

Gallup, G. G., & Suarez, S. D. (1985). Alternatives to the use of animals in psychological research. *American Psychologist, 40*(10), 1104–1111.

Gardner, W. L., Pickett, C. L., & Brewer, M. B. (2000). Social exclusion and selective memory: How the need to belong influences memory for social events. *Personality and Social Psychology Bulletin, 26*(4), 486–496.

Gettelfinger, B., & Cussler, E. L. (2004). Will humans swim faster or slower in syrup? *American Institute of Chemical Engineering Journal, 50,* 2646–2647.

Goldstone, R. L., & Chin, C. (1993). Dishonesty in self-report of copies made: Moral relativity and the copy machine. *Basic and Applied Social Psychology, 14*(1), 19–32.

Gonzalez, R., Seifert, C. M., Manzon, E., Yoon, C., & Cho, S. (2011). *From "part-time" to "rolling" belters: Social promotions of seat belt use.* Unpublished manuscript.

Goodall, J. (1982). Order without law. *Journal of Social and Biological Structures, 5*(4), 353–360.

Henderson, J. M. (2003). Human gaze control during real-world scene perception. *Trends in Cognitive Sciences, 7*(11), 498–505.

Hu, M., Crombag, H. S., Robinson, T. E., & Becker, J. B. (2004). Biological basis of sex differences in the propensity to self-administer cocaine. *Neuropsychopharmacology, 29,* 81–85.

Hyde, J. S., Fennema, E., & Lamon, S. J. (1990). Gender differences in mathematics performance: A meta-analysis. *Psychological Bulletin, 107*(2), 139–155.

Iacoboni, M. (2008). *Mirroring people: The new science of how we connect to others.* New York: Farrar, Straus, & Giroux.

Johnco, C., Wheeler, L., & Taylor, A. (2010). They do get prettier at closing time: A repeated measures study of the closing-time effect and alcohol. *Social Influence, 5*(4), 261–271.

Just, M., & Carpenter, P. (1980). A theory of reading: From eye fixations to comprehension. *Psychological Review, 87,* 329–354.

Kircher, T. T. J., & Thienel, R. (2005). Functional brain imaging of symptoms and cognition in schizophrenia. *Progress in Brain Research, 150,* 299–308, 604.

Landis, C., & Hunt, W. (1939). *The startle pattern.* Oxford, UK: Farrar & Rinehart.

Lucas, R. E., & Dyrenforth, P. S. (2006). Does the existence of social relationships matter for subjective well-being? In K. D. Vohs & E. J. Finkel (Eds.), *Self and relationships: Connecting intrapersonal and interpersonal processes* (pp. 254–273). New York: Guilford Press.

Lucas, R. E., Dyrenforth, P. S., & Diener, E. (2008). Four myths about subjective well-being. *Social and Personality Psychology Compass, 2*(5), 2001–2015.

Lurie, P., & Wolfe, S. M. (1997). Unethical trials of interventions to reduce perinatal transmission of the human immunodeficiency virus in developing countries. *New England Journal of Medicine, 337*(12), 853–856.

Masuda, T., & Nisbett, R. E. (2001). Attending holistically vs. analytically: Comparing the context sensitivity of Japanese and Americans. *Journal of Personality and Social Psychology, 81,* 922–934.

McDaniel, M. A., Whetzel, D. L., Schmidt, F. L., & Maurer, S. D. (1994). The validity of employment interviews: A comprehensive review and meta-analysis. *Journal of Applied Psychology, 79,* 599–616.

Meyer, G. J., Finn, S. E., Eyde, L. D., Kay, G. G., Moreland, K. L., Dies, R. R., Eisman, E. J., Kubiszyn, T. W., & Reed, G. M. (2001). Psychological testing and psychological assessment: A review of evidence and issues. *American Psychologist, 56,* 128–165.

Middlemist, R. D., Knowles, E. S., & Matter, C. F. (1976). Personal space invasions in the lavatory: Suggestive evidence for arousal. *Journal of Personality and Social Psychology, 33*(5), 541–546.

Miller, J. G. (1984). Culture and the development of everyday social explanation. *Journal of Personality and Social Psychology, 46,* 961–978.

Miller, N. E (1985). The value of behavioral research on animals. *American Psychologist, 40,* 423–440.

Mischel, W. (1968). *Personality and assessment.* New York: Wiley.

Morris, M. W., & Peng, K. (1994). Culture and cause: American and Chinese attributions for social and physical events. *Journal of Personality and Social Psychology, 67,* 949–971.

Moscovitch, M., Winocur, G., & Behrmann, M. (1997). What is special about face recognition? Nineteen experiments on a person with visual object agnosia and dyslexia but normal face recognition. *Journal of Cognitive Neuroscience, 9,* 555–604.

National Highway Traffic Safety Administration (2008). *Seat belt use in 2008: Use rates in the states and territories.* (DOT-HS-811-106). Washington, DC: U.S. Department of Transportation.

Nisbett, E. K., & Zelenski, J. M. (2011). Underestimating nearby nature: Affective forecasting errors obscure the happy path to sustainability. *Psychological Science, 22*(9), 1101–1106.

Nisbett, R. E., & Borgida, E. (1975). Attribution and the psychology of prediction. *Journal of Personality and Social Psychology, 32,* 932–943.

Pennebaker, J. W., Dyer, M. A., Caulkins, R. S., Litowitz, D. L., Ackerman, P. L., Anderson, D. B., & McGraw, K. M. (1979). "Don't the girls get prettier at closing time": A country and western application to psychology. *Personality and Social Psychological Bulletin, 5,* 122–125.

Petersen, J. L., & Hyde, J. S. (2010). A meta-analytic review of research on gender differences in sexuality, 1993–2007. *Psychological Bulletin, 136,* 21–38.

Peterson, C. (2006). *A primer in positive psychology.* New York: Oxford University Press.

Plous, S., (1996). Attitudes toward the use of animals in psychological research and education: Results from a national survey of psychologists. *American Psychologist, 51*(11), 1167–1180

Rauscher, F., Shaw, G., & Ky, K. (1993). Music and spatial task performance. *Nature, 365,* 611.

Rizzolatti, G., Fogassi, L., & Gallese, V. (2006, November). Mirrors in the mind. *Scientific American, 54* 61.

Ronay, R., & van Hippel, W. (2010). The presence of an attractive woman elevates testosterone and physical risk-taking in young men. *Social Psychological and Personality Science, 1,* 57–64.

Rosenthal, R., & Rosnow, R. L. (1975). *The volunteer subject.* Oxford, UK: John Wiley & Sons

Ross, L. (1977). The intuitive psychologist and his shortcomings: Distortions in the attribution process. In L. Berkowitz (Ed.), *Advances in experimental social psychology* (vol. 10, pp. 173–220). New York: Academic Press.

Ross, S. E., Niebling, B. C., & Heckert, T. M. (1999). Sources of stress among college students. *College Student Journal, 33*(2), 312–318.

Ruback, R. B., & Juieng, D. J. (1997). Territorial defense in parking lots: Retaliation against waiting drivers. *Journal of Applied Social Psychology, 27*(9), 821–834.

Schultz, D. P. (1969). The human subject in psychological research. *Psychological Bulletin, 72*(3), 214–228.

Schwarz, N., & Hippler, H.-J. (1995). Subsequent questions may influence answers to preceding questions in mail surveys. *The Public Opinion Quarterly, 59*(1), 93–97.

Seligman, M. E. P. (2006). *Learned optimism: How to change your mind and your life.* New York: Vintage.

Seligman, M. E. P., & Maier, S. F. (1967). Failure to escape traumatic shock. *Journal of Experimental Psychology, 74,* 1–9.

Shapiro, K. J. (1990). Animal rights vs. humanism: The charge of speciesism. *Journal of Humanistic Psychology, 30,* 9–37.

Soproni, K., Miklósi, Á., Topál, J., & Csányi, V. (2002). Dogs' (*Canis familaris*) responsiveness to human pointing gestures. *Journal of Comparative Psychology, 116*(1), 7035–7036.

Steele, K. M., Bella, S. D., Peretz, I., Dunlop, T., Dawe, L. A., Humphrey, G. K., Shannon, R. A., Kirby, J. A. Jr., & Olmstead, C. G. (1999). Prelude or requiem for the 'Mozart effect'? *Nature, 400,* 827.

Stock, W. A., Okun, M. A., Haring, M. J., & Witter, R. A. (1983). Age and subjective well-being: A meta analysis. In R. J. Light (Ed.), *Evaluation studies: Review annual* (vol. 8, pp. 279–302). Beverly Hills, CA: Sage.

Schwarz, N., & Hippler, H. -J. (1995). Subsequent questions may influence answers to preceding questions in mail surveys. *The Public Opinion Quarterly, 59*(1), 93–97.

Tourangeau, R., Rips, L. J., & Rasinski, K. (2000). *The psychology of survey response.* Cambridge, UK: Cambridge University Press.

Wason, P. C., & Johnson-Laird, P. N. (1968). *Thinking and reasoning.* Harmondsworth, UK: Penguin.

Welten, D. C., Kemper, H. C. G., Post, G. B., & Van Staveren, W. A. (1995). A meta-analysis of the effect of calcium intake on bone mass in young and middle-aged females and males. *Journal of Nutrition, 125,* 2802–2813.

White, A. (2007). A global projection of subjective well-being: A challenge to positive psychology? *Psychtalk, 56,* 17–20.

Wilkinson, L., & Task Force on Statistical Inference. (1999). Statistical methods in psychology journals: Guidelines and explanations. *American Psychologist, 54*(8), 594–604.

Wolraich, M. L., Wilson, D. B., & White, J. W. (1995). The effect of sugar on behavior or cognition in children. *Journal of the American Medical Association, 274,* 1617–1621.

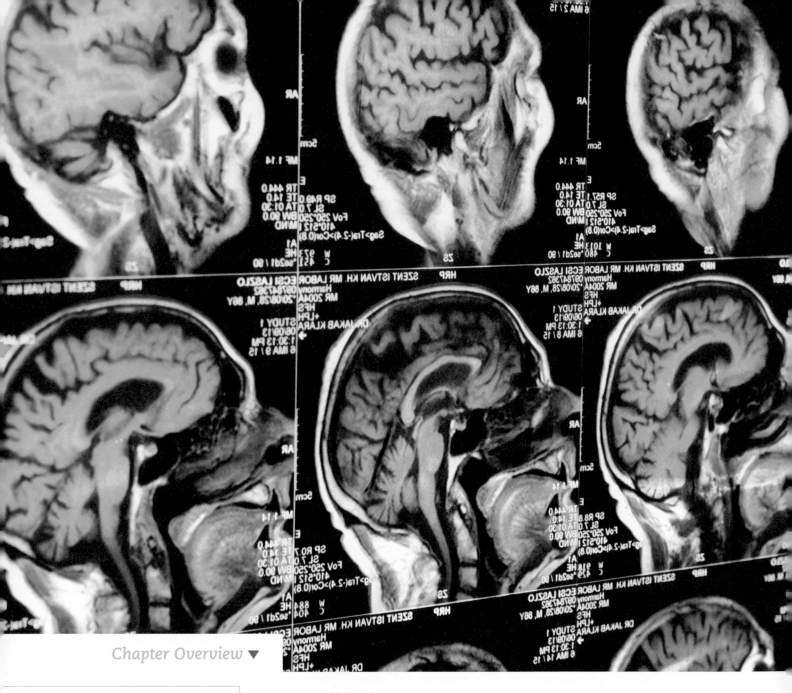

Chapter Overview ▼

3.1 **Overview: The Components of Biological Bases of Behavior**

CONCEPT LEARNING CHECK **3.1** *Reviewing the Terminology of Neuroscience*

3.2 **Neural Communication**
Glia
Neurons
  The Structure of a Neuron
  Neurotransmitters
  Synapses
  How Neurons Communicate
  Action Potentials

Neural Networks
  Pruning of Networks
Multitasking Neurotransmitters

CONCEPT LEARNING CHECK **3.2** *Recognizing the Parts of the Neuron*

3.3 **Nervous System Organization**
Peripheral Nervous System
Central Nervous System
  Spinal Cord

CONCEPT LEARNING CHECK **3.3** *The Organization of the Nervous System*

3 Neuroscience: The Biology of Behavior

Learning Objectives ▼

3.1 ■ Describe how neuropsychology and neuroscience relate to the study of psychology.
■ Explain how the nervous system conducts signals to and from various parts of the body and brain.

3.2 ■ Identify the structural elements of the nervous system.
■ Recognize the types and structure of neurons.

3.3 ■ Compare and contrast the peripheral nervous system and the central nervous system.

3.4 ■ Identify the different areas of the brain and the functions they control.

3.5 ■ Discuss the role of endorphins and the endocrine system as communication mechanisms in the nervous system.

3.6 ■ Discuss the role of genetics in psychology.

3.4 The Brain
Organization
Research on the Brain
The Brainstem
Midbrain
Forebrain
  Thalamus
  Hypothalamus
  Limbic System
  Cerebrum and Cerebral Cortex
Plasticity

CONCEPT LEARNING CHECK **3.4** *Identifying the Structures and Functions in the Brain*

3.5 The Endocrine System
Endorphins
Adrenal Glands
Gonads

CONCEPT LEARNING CHECK **3.5** *Identifying the Role of Endorphins and the Endocrine System Functions*

3.6 Genetics
The Basic Concepts of Genetics
The Research Methods of Genetics
Summary of Multiple Influences on the Biology of Behavior

CONCEPT LEARNING CHECK **3.6** *Reviewing the Role of Genetics in Psychology*

CRITICAL THINKING APPLICATION

*I*t was history-making surgery—the surgery that would restore his sight. Forty-six-year-old Mike May had been blind since he was 3, when a freak chemical explosion had damaged both of his eyes. This surgery would correct that. Stem cells, multiple operations, and even a transplanted cornea would be used—the stuff of science fiction. All of these technologies would come together for this miracle operation. News magazine shows were on hand as the doctors removed the bandages from Mike's eyes. You could hear the rapid-fire clicks of a crush of cameras. He had functioning eyes and would see his wife's face for the very first time.

Faces, Mike would later realize, would be a problem for him. A few weeks after his operation, he noticed that he had trouble distinguishing one person from another—he could not really tell his two children apart. Two months after the operation, although his eyesight was good enough for driving, he still could not tell men's faces from women's faces or that his sister was wearing Groucho glasses. Faces were enigmas. Something was wrong. His eyes were fine, but his brain had trouble interpreting what he was seeing.

We see with more than just our eyes. We see with our brains, too. Our brains have to process the information that comes in through not only our eyes but our other senses as well. Mike's brain had adapted to help him get along quite well without being able to see. After all, he set a world's record for downhill skiing by a totally blind person and received numerous medals in the Paralympic Games. It is as if the parts of his brain that might have processed sight had been reassigned new duties. We'll hear more about Mike May's story later and how the tools of neuroscience help to explain his perceptions.

3.1 Overview: The Components of Biological Bases of Behavior

The nervous system conducts signals to and from various parts of your body.

- Describe how neuropsychology and neuroscience relate to the study of psychology.
- Explain how the nervous system conducts signals to and from various parts of the body and brain.

You cannot study much psychology without some understanding of biology. It is like trying to explain the plot of a favorite book or movie without being able to name any of the characters. Know just a little about the biology of psychology, and you've added critical depth and dimension to your understanding of psychology.

Biological psychology, also called neuropsychology, is the branch of psychology that studies the connection of bodily systems and behavior with **neuroscience**, the study of the brain and the nervous system. Neuropsychology helps to link your physical body with explanations for behavior on many different levels. Neuropsychologists help us understand how the brain processes our thoughts and emotions. It also can aid in explaining how our emotions are linked to the physical sensations in our body. Why does your stomach hurt when you are nervous? Neuropsychology examines questions like these at the molecular, cellular, organ, and system levels.

Biological psychology The branch of psychology that studies the connection of bodily systems and behavior.

Neuroscience The study of the brain and nervous system.

Biologists organize the human body into different organ systems. As you know, you have a digestive system that breaks down and processes foods, a circulatory system that distributes blood to and from the various organs in your body, and a respiratory system that brings oxygen in and carbon dioxide out of your body. Neuroscientists are most interested in the **nervous system**, which is a network of organs, nerves, and supportive systems that send and receive neural signals to and from various parts of the body.

The nervous system links our experience of a changing world with our actions and attitudes. Its main job is communication. The several million signals, or messages, that the nervous system sends and receives every minute are really just electrochemical activity. The nervous system's power and complexity lie in the many ways these signals, or messages, are processed.

Communication within the nervous system generally occurs through messages between **neurons**, or nerve cells, which act like instant messengers, delivering messages that activate or deactivate parts of your nervous system. Communication also occurs through long-distance messengers, such as **hormones**, that communicate with areas of the body that lie beyond the nervous system. The central hub of activity, however, is in your brain. We'll discuss each of these aspects of the nervous system in detail and end with a discussion of genetics that highlights the interconnection of biological and environmental influences.

This chapter has a lot of terms, many of which may be unfamiliar. But like the characters in a book or a movie, once you know how they're related, they'll be less intimidating. We'll start with the basics and work our way to larger, more complex systems. By the end of this chapter, you will understand the molecules, cells, organs, and systems that underlie the biology of behavior.

Nervous system
A collection of organs including neurons and supportive systems.

Neuron A nerve cell.

Hormone A chemical messenger that is produced by endocrine glands.

CONCEPT LEARNING CHECK 3.1   *Reviewing the Terminology of Neuroscience*

Match the term with the correct definition.

A. Nervous system

B. Neuroscience

C. Neurons

D. Hormones

E. Biological psychology

1. _____ The collection of organs including neurons and supportive systems that creates and conducts signals to various parts of our body

2. _____ The long-distance messengers of our nervous system

3. _____ The branch of psychology that studies the connection of bodily systems and behavior

4. _____ The study of the brain and the nervous system

5. _____ Nerve cells that provide fast communication

3.2 Neural Communication

The nervous system is composed of glia and neurons. Glia support and protect neurons. Neurons communicate messages throughout the nervous system and the rest of the body.

- Identify the structural elements of the nervous system.
- Recognize the types and structure of neurons.

Like the rest of your body, your nervous system is composed of millions upon millions of highly specialized cells. In general, nervous system cells fall into two major categories: glia and neurons.

Glia

Glia cells Cells in the nervous system that provide support and protection for neurons.

Neural pruning The destruction of certain neurons to increase the processing speed of the nervous system.

Interneuron A neuron that communicates only with other neurons.

Afferent nerve fibers Neurons that move information toward the brain and spinal cord.

Efferent nerve fiber A type of neuron that carries impulses away from the central nervous system.

Sensory neuron A neuron that is responsible for carrying external stimuli to the central nervous system for processing.

Motor neuron A type of neuron that interfaces with muscles and glands.

Glia cells are cells of the nervous system that support and protect our neurons. *Glia*, from the Greek word for *glue*, were once thought to be the paste that held neurons together. New research has expanded our understanding of glia (sometimes referred to as glial cells). Although smaller than neurons, glial cells are more numerous. Estimates suggest that glial cells make up about 50% of the total volume of the brain (Jessen, 2004). Glial cells provide nutrients, insulation, and protection to neurons. They do not stop there—glial cells also manage and organize your nervous system by directing where neurons grow. They send survival signals to some neurons and perish signals to others to direct **neural pruning**, or the destruction of certain neurons to increase the processing speed of the nervous system. Glial cells also play a strong role in controlling how neurons communicate and in the formation of connections between neurons. In addition to this supportive role, some recent research suggests that glial cells might send communication signals of their own. Damage to glial cells can leave neurons exposed to destruction, inflammation, or slowed processing. Glial malfunction may be partially responsible for such diseases as multiple sclerosis, brain tumors, and Alzheimer's disease (Jessen, 2004).

Although we are beginning to appreciate the complex role that glial cells play, the neuron is the star of the nervous system.

Neurons

Your brain consists of tens of billions (by some estimates, up to 100 billion) of neurons, each with thousands of connections, as can be seen in FIGURE 3-1. Neurons, or nerve cells, are the basic cells of the nervous system. Groups of neurons form nerve fibers that communicate information, or special messages, throughout the nervous system. Many of these neurons communicate with other types of cells throughout the body, such as muscle cells or gland cells. Most neurons in your body, however, are **interneurons**, which are neurons that communicate only with other neurons to help you do all that you do each moment of the day.

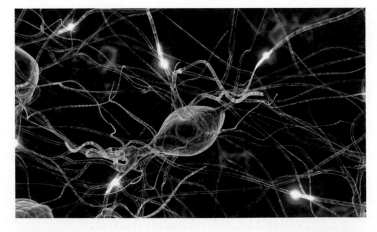

FIGURE 3-1 Neurons are the basic cell of the nervous system.

Your nervous system also requires that certain neurons be specialized in order to get the job done. In the same way you have veins that move blood away from the heart and arteries that move it back, you have **afferent nerve fibers** that move information toward the brain and spinal cord as well as **efferent nerve fibers** that carry impulses away from the brain and spinal cord.

To perform a simple physical task, such as turning a page in a book, you use different kinds of neurons. First, you use **sensory neurons**, one type of *afferent* nerve fiber. These are neurons that translate external stimuli into messages to be sent to the central nervous system for processing. When you touch the page of a book, sensory neurons send messages to your brain, allowing it to recognize the single page you intend to turn. Then you employ **motor neurons**, an example of *efferent* nerve fibers. These are the neurons that send messages to muscles and glands to activate the muscles in your hand as you pull the page toward you.

You even have specialized neurons that are activated when you watch another person perform a task. Called **mirror neurons**, they are active both when you perform a task yourself and also when you watch another person perform an action. Mirror neurons make it easier for you to perform an action while watching another person do the same action, which is very handy when in a group exercise class. In fact, new research on mirror neurons suggests that their role may include monitoring our own movements so that we are aware of the movements we make (Bonaiuto & Arbib, 2010).

The Structure of a Neuron

With more than 10,000 specialized types of neurons come various neuron structures as well. Most neurons, however, have a few things in common: dendrites, a soma, and an axon.

Dendrites are the nerve cell structures that receive messages from other neurons. They look a little like tree roots and funnel messages from other neurons to the **soma**, or **cell body**. The soma is the central part of the neuron. It keeps the cell alive and contains the genetic material for the cell. The **axon** is a long tubelike structure that carries the message away from the soma on its way to another neuron. Although axons are infinitesimally narrow, some are also infinitesimally short, while others, such as those between your spine and your toes, extend several feet. As a collection, the axons of neurons form cablelike bunches in the peripheral nervous system called **nerves**. To keep the message moving smoothly, glial cells envelop a neuron's axon in a white fatty substance called myelin. This **myelin sheath** insulates the axon and enables efficient communication along the axon. The myelin sheath also divides axons into little capsulelike sections, like sausages on a string. At the very end of the axon is the **axon terminal**, sometimes called the terminal button or terminal end bulb.

This is just a basic blueprint. As you can see in FIGURE 3-2, some neurons do not have axons and some have two, but in general, most neurons follow the same basic structure.

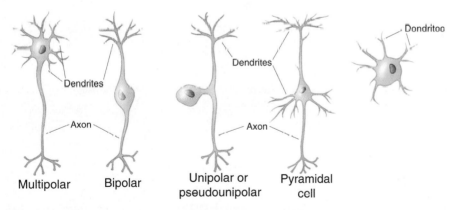

Dendrites

Dendrites

Dendrites

Axon

Axon

Multipolar   Bipolar   Unipolar or pseudounipolar   Pyramidal cell

FIGURE 3-2 Neurons come in many shapes, sizes, and configurations.

Neurotransmitters

Although the billions of neurons in your body are in constant communication with each other, they do not touch to communicate; they use (and recycle) chemicals to bridge the incredibly tiny space between one neuron and the next. Neurons communicate messages by discharging neurotransmitters. **Neurotransmitters** are molecules and act as chemical messengers that communicate, or transmit, messages from one neuron to the next. Neurotransmitters can directly or indirectly influence neurons in particular areas of the brain and therefore affect behavior.

Synapses

The space between neurons is part of an area called the **synapse** FIGURE 3-3. The synapse consists of three parts: the terminal button of the sending or **presynaptic neuron**; the space between one neuron and the next (called the synaptic gap or **synaptic cleft**); and the receptor sites on the dendrites of the receiving or **postsynaptic neuron**.

Mirror neuron A type of neuron that fires when an individual watches an action and when performing the action.

Dendrite Nerve cell structure that receives information from other cells.

Soma The part of the neuron that keeps the cell alive and contains the genetic material for the cell.

Cell body The part of a nerve cell that keeps the entire cell alive; also called the soma.

Axon The part of the neuron that carries the nerve impulse away from the soma.

Nerves Bundles of neurons.

Myelin sheath A fatty substance that insulates the axon and enables efficient transmission.

Axon terminal The part of the neuron that discharges and recycles neurotransmitters; also called the terminal button.

Neurotransmitter Chemical messenger that transmits information from one neuron to another.

Synapse An area that includes three structures; the terminal button of the sending neuron, the synaptic gap, and the dendrite of the receiving neuron.

Presynaptic neuron A neuron that sends a signal to another neuron.

Synaptic cleft The small space between the axon terminal of a sending neuron and the dendrite of the receiving neuron.

Postsynaptic neuron A neuron that receives a signal from another neuron.

Synaptic transmission
The process by which one neuron communicates with another by using neurotransmitters.

Action potential The electrical message or neural impulse that flows along a neuron's axon.

Threshold The point at which a neuron will respond to an action potential.

How Neurons Communicate

Neural communication is fast—really fast. Our fastest neurons communicate across incredibly tiny spaces, transmitting messages at rates of up to 268 miles an hour—the top speed of the world's fastest trains. Let us take a close look at how this communication works. Neurons communicate by way of **synaptic transmission** FIGURE 3-4, meaning they use neurotransmitters to send messages across the synapse to the next neuron. The message the neuron sends can generate or prevent an **action potential**. Neurons send just two types of messages: The message is either *excitatory*, which tells the next neuron, "Fire!" or *inhibitory*, which tells the next neuron, "Don't fire!" If the sum of excitation from excitatory neurons minus the sum of inhibition from inhibitory neurons is greater than the next neuron's **threshold**, then the postsynaptic neuron fires (creates an action potential). If a neuron is communicating with, say, a muscle cell, an excitatory message might cause the muscle cell to contract so you can flex your biceps in the mirror. An inhibitory message might cause a muscle to release so you can place your grocery bags on the kitchen table.

Action Potentials

So neurons send excitatory or inhibitory messages—called action potentials—that say to the next neuron, "Fire!" or "Don't fire!" But what sets these messages in motion? It is both an electrical and chemical reaction. All around the neuron, both inside and outside of a neuron's axon, are fluids that contain electrically charged atoms (or ions) of sodium and potassium. The movement of these ions determines whether a neuron generates an action potential FIGURE 3-5. When a neuron is not firing or is at rest, sodium and potassium ions flow back and forth through tiny holes in the axon's wall, or membrane.

FIGURE 3-3 The synapse is the junction between two neurons.

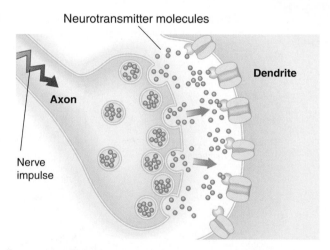

Action Potentials

Neurotransmitter molecules

Dendrite

Axon

Nerve impulse

FIGURE 3-4 Neurons don't touch, instead they communicate through synaptic transmission.

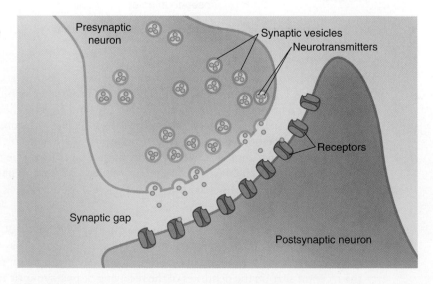

Presynaptic neuron

Synaptic vesicles

Neurotransmitters

Receptors

Synaptic gap

Postsynaptic neuron

These holes are called channels. They allow sodium and potassium to move from areas of higher concentration to areas of lower concentration on their own. Think of a drop of red dye in a glass of water. The dye will disperse through the water, moving from an area of higher concentration (where there is a lot of dye) to areas of lower concentration (where there is little or no dye). The ions of our neurons move around in the same way. The axon's membrane also contains a channel that acts like a pump, sending some of the potassium and sodium ions against the flow, back to their respective sides of the axon. This pump ensures that the inside of an axon is more negatively charged than the outside of the axon. In a resting neuron, this charge is about −70 millivolts (by contrast, a small watch battery is more than 10 times stronger at about 880 millivolts). Maintaining the negative charge, by the way, takes a huge amount of energy. It is estimated that up to one-third of our energy, even when we are sedentary, is used to power this sodium/potassium pump (Laughlin, van Steveninck, & Anderson, 1998). The inactive neuron's negative charge is called the **resting potential** FIGURE 3-6.

When a neuron is stimulated to fire, potassium channels in the first section of the axon close. Then sodium rushes into the axon and causes this section of the axon to **depolarize**, or become more positive. This generates an action potential. Once the action potential is generated and starts hurtling down the axon, it does not grow stronger or weaker, and it cannot be stopped. This is called the **all-or-nothing law**, because an action potential either happens or it does not.

The action potential continues hurtling down the axon, changing the polarity of each axon section as it passes through. Once the action potential has passed, the opened channels in the axon's membrane now close, and that section of the axon resets or **repolarizes**

Resting potential An inactive neuron's negative charge.

Depolarizes The process by which an axon becomes more positive.

All-or-nothing law The concept that either a neuron fires or it doesn't. There is no partial firing.

Repolarizes The process by which a neuron's axon will return to the resting potential.

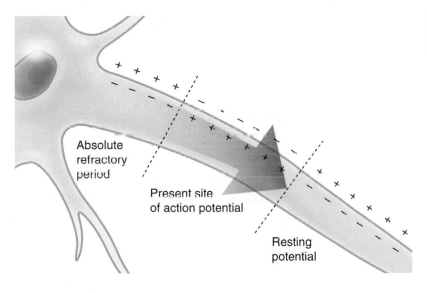

FIGURE 3-5 The action potential will determine if a neuron will fire.

FIGURE 3-6 Resting potential.

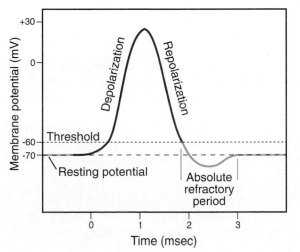

Absolute refractory period The point after an action potential when the neuron cannot produce another action potential no matter the intensity of the stimulation.

Synaptic vesicle A sac that contains neurotransmitters in the axon terminal.

Receptor site An area on the dendrite that receives neurotransmitters.

Stimulus threshold The point at which the neuron responds by changing its voltage.

Postsynaptic potential (PSP) Changes in the dendrite of the receiving neuron as the result of its binding with neurotransmitters.

Excitatory postsynaptic potential (EPSP) A voltage change caused by the binding of neurotransmitters that causes a positive voltage shift in the resting potential of the postsynaptic neuron triggering the neuron to fire.

Inhibitory postsynaptic potential (IPSP) A voltage change caused by the binding of neurotransmitters that causes a negative voltage shift in the resting potential of the postsynaptic neuron preventing the neuron from firing.

Reuptake The reabsorption of neurotransmitters back into a presynaptic neuron.

Synaptic pruning The destruction of less active synapses to organize and improve efficiency of the neural connections.

and returns to the resting potential. This reset period is called the **absolute refractory period**. It is the point after an action potential when the neuron cannot produce another action potential, regardless of the intensity of the stimulation. During this time, the action potential cannot regenerate. It is really a short time, maybe 1 to 2 milliseconds. The absolute refractory period prevents the action potential from moving backward and ensures that the action potential flows only in one direction.

This change in polarity is constantly regenerated as the action potential travels from section to section along the axon. It is somewhat like a kid careening down a water slide: The polarity of the axon returns to its resting potential after the action potential has passed—just as the water flow in a section of the slide returns to normal after the kid passes by. The action potential continues in this way until it reaches the axon terminal, where it performs a final trick.

When the action potential reaches the axon terminal, it ends at **synaptic vesicles**, which are small sacs that contain the neurotransmitters, floating down to the very end of the axon terminal or the terminal end bulb. There, the synaptic vesicles fuse with the terminal button. At this point, the neurotransmitters spill out into the synaptic gap, where they float and bounce around like Ping-Pong balls. Some will find their way to another neuron's receptor sites. **Receptor sites**, located on the neuron's dendrites, are areas that receive neurotransmitters. There, the neurotransmitters from the sending neuron bind with the receiving neuron's receptor site and deliver the message to fire or not to fire.

Once the neurotransmitter binds to the receiving, or postsynaptic, neuron's receptor site, it can help change the voltage of the postsynaptic neuron. If enough bind, the postsynaptic neuron will reach its **stimulus threshold**, the point at which it responds by changing its voltage. This change in voltage is called a **postsynaptic potential (PSP)**. A PSP is a change in the postsynaptic neuron that was the result of neurotransmitters from another neuron binding with it. The postsynaptic neuron may generate an action potential of its own, in which case the entire process repeats itself, and the postsynaptic neuron becomes a presynaptic neuron, and so on and so on.

There are two kinds of postsynaptic potentials, or PSPs: excitatory and inhibitory. **Excitatory postsynaptic potentials (EPSPs)**, cause a positive voltage shift in the resting potential of the next (postsynaptic) neuron. This triggers the channels in the axons to open and depolarize them, causing the neuron to fire. **Inhibitory PSPs (IPSPs)**, cause a negative voltage change and make the resting potential even more negative. In this case, the neuron does not fire. In fact, it may take even more stimulation for the neuron to fire because the current resting potential may be below its usual –70 millivolts.

Postsynaptic neurons do not absorb or pass on the neurotransmitters that they receive and that bind with them. Therefore, they need to be discarded or put to good use. There are two primary cleanup mechanisms in the synapse. Some neurotransmitters get gobbled up (metabolized) by an enzyme called monoamine oxidase (MAO), while some others get recycled and repackaged into new synaptic vesicles by transport proteins located on the presynaptic terminal buttons. This process of reabsorbing the neurotransmitters into a presynaptic neuron is called **reuptake**.

Neural Networks

You'll recall that neurons receive signals from a lot of other neurons all at the same time. Rather than simply passing along the signal, neurons integrate signals. An IPSP, under the right circumstances, could cancel out an EPSP. In this way, neurons incorporate information from many sources.

In addition, there are specific neurotransmitter pathways that connect various areas of the brain. These pathways are sort of like highways that connect certain brain areas and allow neurotransmitters to influence behavior in many parts of the brain.

Pruning of Networks

You might think that the more synaptic connections we have, the better. However, the nervous system forms more synapses than it needs, so, over time, it gradually gets rid of the less active synapses. This is referred to as **synaptic pruning**. Newborns, for example, have about 11 million neurons in their thalamus, a part of the brain that acts as a relay station. By adulthood, they have lost about 41% of those neurons (Abitz et al., 2007) FIGURE 3-7. Getting rid of less active connections helps to organize and improve the efficiency of the whole system. In fact, neural networks peak when a person is 1 year old and then begin their decline.

Multitasking Neurotransmitters

Neurotransmitters act like keys to the locks of receptor sites, with only certain neurotransmitters activating certain receptor sites to create inhibitory or excitatory PSPs.

Since neurotransmitters can only create either an excitatory postsynaptic potential or an inhibitory postsynaptic potential, it would seem logical that you would only need two types of neurotransmitters—one for the gas and one for the brakes. In actuality, more than 100 different types of substances play the role of neurotransmitters at least some of the time (Greengard, 2001). There are a few "classic" neurotransmitters whose functions can be found in TABLE 3-1. A single neurotransmitter can be involved in many functions and thus may have overlapping responsibilities in the nervous system. **Acetylcholine** and **norepinephrine**, for example, are both involved in memory.

In addition to influencing postsynaptic neurons, some drugs can influence the effect of neurotransmitters. An **agonist**, for example, is a substance that mimics or increases the effect of a neurotransmitter. **Gamma-aminobutric acid (GABA)** is the nervous system's primary inhibitory neurotransmitter. GABA agonists like Valium can slow down the nervous system and relax us. **Antagonists**, on the other hand, are substances that block the action of a neurotransmitter. Botulinum toxin, for instance, acts as an antagonist and blocks the release of acetylcholine. This interference with acetylcholine can cause paralysis of muscles and result in the illness known as botulism. Agonists and antagonists each can act directly (by binding or blocking) at receptor sites or indirectly (by increasing or decreasing the release of the neurotransmitter, blocking reuptake, or destroying transmitters in the synapse).

Acetylcholine Neurotransmitter that is involved in memory and muscle functions.

Norepinephrine A neurotransmitter responsible for learning and memory.

Agonist A substance that mimics or increases the effect of a neurotransmitter.

Gamma-aminobutric acid (GABA) The nervous system's primary inhibitory neurotransmitter.

Antagonist A substance that blocks the action of a neurotransmitter.

Dopamine Neurotransmitter that is involved in movement and reward systems.

Serotonin A neurotransmitter involved in sleep, mood, and appetite.

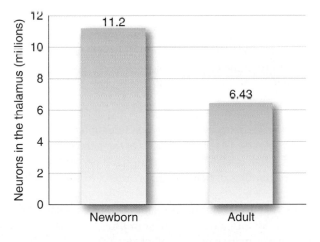

FIGURE 3-7 The number of synaptic connections declines significantly over time, but this synaptic pruning leads to more efficient processing.
Source: Data from Abitz, M., Nielsen, R. D., Jones, E. G., Laursen, H., Graem, N., & Pakkenberg, B. (2007). Excess of neurons in the human newborn mediodorsal thalamus compared with that of the adult. Cerebral Cortex, 17(11), 2573–2578. doi:10.1093/cercor/bhl163

TABLE 3-1 Neurotransmitters and Their Functions

Neurotransmitter	Function
Acetylcholine	Involved in memory and muscle functions.
Dopamine	Involved in movement and reward systems.
GABA	The nervous system's primary inhibitory neurotransmitter.
Norepinephrine	Responsible for learning and memory.
Serotonin	Involved in sleep, mood, and appetite.

CONCEPT LEARNING CHECK 3.2   *Recognizing the Parts of the Neuron*

Match the parts of the neuron and synapse with the correct area.

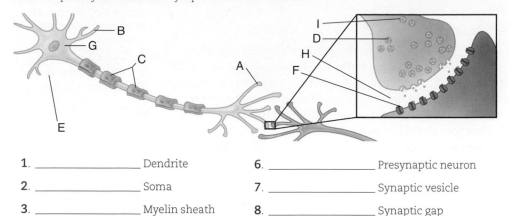

1. _____ Dendrite

2. _____ Soma

3. _____ Myelin sheath

4. _____ Axon terminal

5. _____ Neurotransmitters

6. _____ Presynaptic neuron

7. _____ Synaptic vesicle

8. _____ Synaptic gap

9. _____ Receptor site

3.3 Nervous System Organization

Our nervous system is composed of two main branches: The central nervous system integrates and controls the body and the peripheral nervous system links the rest of your body to the central nervous system.

▪ Compare and contrast the peripheral nervous system and the central nervous system.

Your nervous system is composed of two main branches: the central nervous system FIGURE 3-8, which integrates and controls the body, and the peripheral nervous system, which links the rest of the body to the central nervous system. The two parts of your nervous system work together to connect and operate the body.

Peripheral Nervous System

It might be easier to think about the peripheral nervous system in terms of what it is not. The **peripheral nervous system** consists of all the parts of the nervous system *excluding* the brain and the spinal cord. What is left? A lot. The peripheral nervous system includes miles and miles of nerves, or bundles of neurons that connect to the muscles, glands, and organs of your body.

The peripheral nervous system itself is organized into two parts: a **somatic nervous system**, which controls the voluntary movement of your muscles, and the **autonomic nervous system**, which controls internal organs and glands.

The autonomic nervous system, in turn, has two components: The **sympathetic nervous system** speeds you up to fight, freeze, or flee; the **parasympathetic nervous system** calms you down and conserves your bodily functions.

Imagine that you are in class and suddenly your professor says the words that all students fear: "Pop quiz!" All of a sudden, your sympathetic nervous system fires up. Your hands become cold and clammy; your heart rate and blood pressure shoot up. Your sympathetic nervous system is getting you ready to rumble. The problem is, there is no one to fight and nowhere to flee. In these situations, some people do freeze with test anxiety. There is some evidence that this is the kind of stress that might be linked to cardiovascular disease (Macleod et al., 2002).

Peripheral nervous system A division of the nervous system excluding the brain and spinal cord.

Somatic nervous system The division of the peripheral nervous system that connects to voluntary muscle movement and communicates sensory information.

Autonomic nervous system Part of the peripheral nervous system that interfaces with the heart, intestines, and other organs.

Sympathetic nervous system A branch of the autonomic nervous system that prepares the organs for vigorous activity.

Parasympathetic nervous system A component of the autonomic nervous system that conserves bodily functions and energy.

Events like a pop quiz, a fender bender, or even a day of riding roller coasters may lead to exhaustion. Some people attribute this tiredness to all the work their body did. However, some of your exhaustion may be due to the effects of your parasympathetic nervous system calming you down. FIGURE 3-9 highlights the features and organs that are affected by the sympathetic and parasympathetic nervous systems.

Central Nervous System

The **central nervous system** consists of your brain and your spinal cord, and it has a support system of its own. In addition to the bony skull and spinal column, the central nervous system is protected by **cerebrospinal fluid (CSF)**, a clear liquid created in the brain's ventricular system that supports and protects the central nervous system. Cradling the brain in cerebrospinal fluid creates buoyancy and reduces the net weight of the brain from around 3 pounds (about the weight of a large pineapple) to less than 2-tenths of a pound (about the weight of one medium-sized banana) because of buoyancy. CSF also acts as a transportation medium to carry hormones in and out of the brain and wash away toxins. We will explore the brain in more detail later on.

Spinal Cord

Although our brain often gets top billing, the spinal cord is no bit player. The **spinal cord** is a collection of neurons that run from the base of the brain and down your back and is protected by a spinal column. Your spinal cord can initiate actions all by itself. These **reflexes**, or involuntary motor responses, coordinated by the spinal cord are known as **spinal reflexes**. When you touch a hot stove, for example, it is easy to think that your brain coordinates your response—jerking your arm back—but it does not. The information goes directly to the spinal cord, and your spinal cord sends the signal to pull your hand back before you do any more damage to your poor finger. In the next section, we'll examine how the spinal cord does what it does.

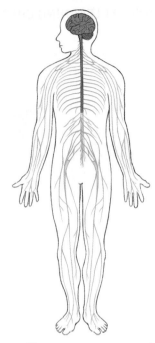

FIGURE 3-8 The nervous system consists of a central (red) and peripheral (blue) nervous system

Central nervous system
A division of the nervous system that is comprised of the brain and spinal cord.

Cerebrospinal fluid (CSF)
Clear liquid created in the ventricular system that supports and protects the central nervous system.

Spinal cord A collection of neurons that run from the base of the brain down the back.

Reflex An involuntary motor response.

Spinal reflex An involuntary motor response coordinated by the spinal cord.

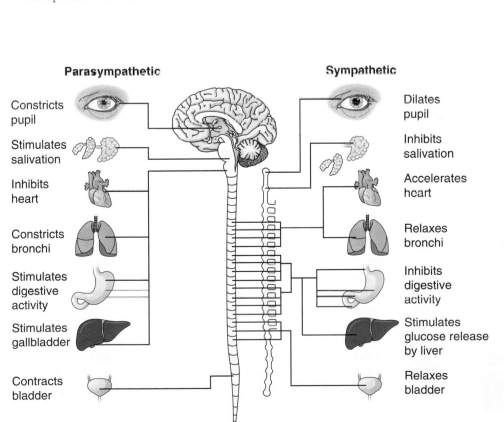

FIGURE 3-9 The sympathetic nervous system gets us ready to fight, freeze, or flee, while the parasympathetic nervous system calms us down.

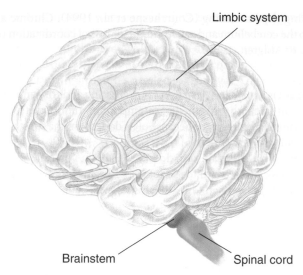

FIGURE 3-16 The limbic system is a group of structures that surround the brainstem.

Hippocampus Part of the limbic system that is involved in processing new memories.

Cerebrum The cerebrum is the largest part of the forebrain and consists of left and right hemispheres, each made up of four lobes.

Corpus callosum A dense network of fibers that connects the left and right cerebral hemispheres.

Cerebral cortex The part of the brain involved in complex cognitive functioning.

Occipital lobe An area in the back of the cerebral cortex. Its visual cortex processes image information.

Temporal lobe An area of the cerebral cortex near the temples. Includes primary auditory cortex, and language centers.

Frontal lobe The front part of the cerebral cortex involved in planning, organization, and personality.

Motor cortex A region of the cerebral cortex involved in planning, controlling, and executing motor functions.

Parietal lobe An area of the cerebral cortex located behind the frontal lobe. Its somatosensory cortex processes body sensation information.

Somatosensory cortex An area of the parietal lobe that processes body sensation information.

Association areas Areas of the cerebral cortex involved in integration of information.

Hippocampus

Being on a national news television program would be an exciting day for anyone, but Michelle would not remember it. A car crash left her hippocampus damaged. The **hippocampus** is part of the limbic system that is involved in processing new memories. Because of this damage, she cannot record any new memories. She remembers everything up until the time of the car accident that damaged her hippocampus—everything until 1994. After that, things get fuzzy—even her wedding to her husband in 1997. In fact, her memory seems to reset every day. She uses sticky notes, her cell phone, and a GPS system to get around most days. It is incredibly frustrating for her. When reading a book, by the time she gets to the middle, she may have totally forgotten how the story started. When shopping, by the time she gets to the store, she may have forgotten why she went there in the first place. Michelle's story demonstrates how important the hippocampus is to each of us in our everyday life.

Cerebrum and Cerebral Cortex

The **cerebrum** is the area most responsible for thinking and language. It is the largest part of the forebrain and is involved in complex cognitive functioning. Containing about 90% of the brain's volume, the cerebrum is only about a fourth of an inch thick (about the thickness of a cushy yoga mat). Its hills (gyri) and valleys (sulci) make it more compact and easier to carry around with you. Without this folding, the cerebrum would be about 3 feet wide by 3 feet long. The cerebrum consists of two hemispheres (left and right), each of which contains four lobes. The two hemispheres are connected by a dense network of nerve fibers called the **corpus callosum**.

Lobes of the Cerebrum

When we picture a brain, the image most of us have is of the **cerebral cortex**, the outside layer of the cerebrum. The cerebral cortex, or cortex, is the rounded mass of "gray matter" just beneath the skull. There are four lobes, or regions, in each hemisphere of the cerebral cortex FIGURE 3-17. Each lobe has been linked to different tasks. The **occipital lobes** are an area in the rear of the cerebral cortex. At the very back of the occipital lobes is the visual cortex, which processes image information. The **temporal lobes** are an area near the temples. The temporal lobes contain the primary auditory cortex, which processes sounds. The **frontal lobes** are at the front of the cerebral cortex and play a role in personality, organization, and planning. The frontal lobes also contain the **motor cortex**, which is an area that has a role in planning, controlling, and executing movements. The **parietal lobe** is located behind the frontal lobe, at the top of your head. The parietal lobes contain the **somatosensory cortex**, which processes body sensation information such as texture, warmth, weight, and how things feel. The parietal lobes also contain **association areas** that are critical in the integration of information.

Hemispheres

The cerebrum's two hemispheres, left and right, are sometimes referred to as the left brain and right brain. Each hemisphere is divided into the four lobes. These **cerebral hemispheres** operate relatively independently even though they are connected by the corpus callosum FIGURE 3-18. This highway of nerve fibers allows the hemispheres to be in constant contact with each other. The discovery of **lateralization of function**, the idea that there are hemispheric specialties, was made quite by mistake. Severing the corpus callosum, also called a callostomy, is an operation that is sometimes performed to control epileptic seizures. Seizures in epilepsy can sometimes be like electrical storms that spread across the brain. Cutting the corpus callosum, it was believed, could contain the seizure on one side of the brain. The first surgeries were done in the 1940s but did not really help those with epilepsy. Because of this, the idea was abandoned and the resulting hypothesis was that it caused no perceptible difference in thoughts or actions of the patients. It was not until 30 years later that other physicians realized that in the previous operations, the corpus callosum was not completely severed. Once that new operation was done, the seizures were controlled and researchers started noticing some differences between these new "**split-brained**" patients and those who had not had this operation.

Cerebral hemisphere One of the two regions of the cerebral cortex.

Lateralization of function The concept that each hemisphere of the cerebral cortex is primarily responsible for certain activities.

Split brain The result of severing the corpus callosum, so that the hemispheres of the cerebral cortex cannot communicate through the nerves that would usually connect them.

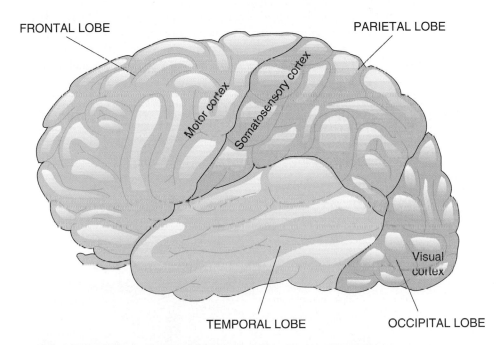

FRONTAL LOBE   PARIETAL LOBE

TEMPORAL LOBE   OCCIPITAL LOBE

Motor cortex   Somatosensory cortex

Visual cortex

FIGURE 3-17 Lobes of the cerebral cortex.

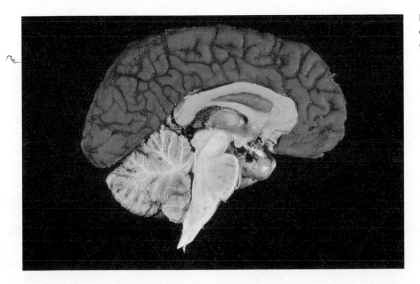

FIGURE 3-18 A photograph of the brain showing the cerebral hemisphere (purple) and the corpus callosum (green).

Severing the connection between the left and right hemispheres gave researchers a peek at how each hemisphere operates because information could no longer flow between the two hemispheres. As a result of this operation, the left hemisphere could not communicate with the right hemisphere. Lateralization of function is the concept that each hemisphere is primarily responsible for a certain function FIGURE 3-19. For example, scientists discovered a left-hemispheric dominance for language, both written and verbal. While the right hemisphere can understand some written words, it has a much harder time changing words into spoken language, something that is no problem for the language-loving left hemisphere. Despite that, the right hemisphere has some of its own strengths, including visual and spatial tasks.

Destruction of parts of the corpus callosum can stop the transfer of certain signals from the left hemisphere to the right. The back part of the corpus callosum, for example, relates to the transfer of sight, hearing, and body sensation. The frontmost part of the corpus callosum is responsible for things like attention.

Once the **split-brain surgery** is completed, the hemispheres operate independently FIGURE 3-20. Since the left hemisphere is in control of the right side of the body, and the right hemisphere is in charge of the left, combined with lateralization of function, researchers came up with some interesting findings. If researchers showed an image, let us say of a key, to only the right visual field of the patient, the patient could easily describe what he saw. The reason was that the image would go into the right visual field, get processed by the brain's left hemisphere, and the left hemisphere's strength in language could easily describe the key. However, when shown an image to the left visual field, the patient

Split-brain surgery An operation that involves severing the corpus callosum. Also called a corpus callostomy.

FIGURE 3-19 Lateralization of function suggests hemispheric specialties.

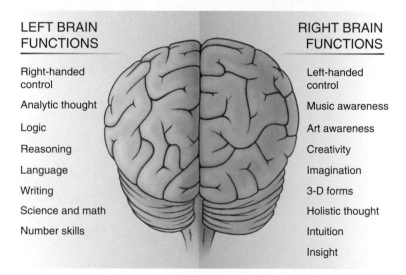

FIGURE 3-20 An example of a split-brain experiment.

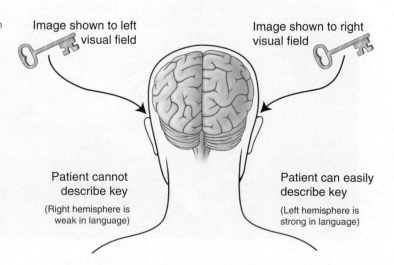

did not recognize the image because the right hemisphere is not too great at producing language. However, if given a list of images to point to, he could find the image easily.

Even though most of us have an intact corpus callosum, there are some artifacts of the left and right hemispheric dominance for certain tasks. This means that the left and right brains' particular talents can show up in everyday tasks. Since our right hemisphere is better at visual spatial tasks, for example, we tend to pay more attention to the facial information processed in our left visual field. These artifacts lead to **perceptual asymmetries** or differences in the speed of processing depending on the laterality of function. (For example, we tend to pay more attention to the left side of the face when we recognize people we know).

Plasticity

Our nervous system has an astounding ability to grow and adjust. **Plasticity** refers to the ability of the nervous system to adapt by creating new neural pathways. I'm sure you've noticed from our discussion of the biology of the brain that the structure and functions of brain areas are linked. The idea that certain areas of the brain are responsible for specific processes is known as **cortical localization**. Because of this, scientists can predict what kind of problems a person might have due to damage to certain brain areas. For example, damage to an area of the brain that processes language can lead to **aphasia**, which is an inability to understand or produce language.

But the nervous system can also change and grow. Reading this textbook can cause changes to your brain. As you learn new ideas, new synaptic connections are made. Learning a second language, for example, can create denser areas of brain matter in your left parietal lobe (Mechelli et al., 2004). In fact, the earlier you learn a second language, the denser this area becomes from that experience.

Your life experiences can alter the actual structure as well as the tasks that these structures can accomplish. **Structural plasticity** is the brain's ability to change in response to the environment. fMRIs indicate, for example, that learning to play a musical instrument can make areas in your hippocampus more dense. The environment can change the function of certain areas of the brain, too. **Functional plasticity** is the capacity to change areas of the brain that are responsible for activities. When you learn how to read, for example, there are changes to the way your brain processes information that may improve brain functioning.

It used to be thought that we were born with all of the neurons we'll ever have. More recent research, however, has suggested that **neurogenesis**, the process of the development of new neurons, is not only possible but also can be influenced by our environment. Exercise, for example, can create new neurons in the hippocampus of mice (van Praag, Shubert, Zhao, & Gage, 2005).

But what about Mike May at the beginning of this chapter? Why did Mike have so much difficulty in recognizing faces? Unfortunately, when certain experiences do not occur, this could result in some areas of the brain not developing fully. For many structures and functions, there may be a **critical period** or a window of opportunity in which certain experiences will result in the development of functions and structures in our brain. Mike May could have missed the many early experiences that would have allowed his developing brain to interpret and distinguish faces (Fine et al., 2003).

Perceptual asymmetry Because of imbalances between the left and right cerebral hemispheres, visual or auditory processing happens at different speeds depending on whether sensory input is coming from the left or right side of the body.

Plasticity The ability of the nervous system to adapt by creating new neural pathways.

Cortical localization The observation that certain areas of the brain are responsible for specific processes.

Aphasia An inability to understand or produce language based on damage to the language areas of the brain.

Structural plasticity The brain's ability to change in response to the environment.

Functional plasticity The capacity to change areas of the brain that are responsible for activities.

Neurogenesis The process of the development of new neurons.

Critical period A time when a property is most vulnerable to being established or altered.

CONCEPT LEARNING CHECK **3.4**   *Identifying the Structures and Functions in the Brain*

Match the area of the brain with the function.

A. Medulla
B. Pons
C. Reticular activating system
D. Cerebellum
E. Substantia nigra
F. Thalamus
G. Hypothalamus
H. Hippocampus

1. _____ Involved in the creation of new memories
2. _____ *B* _____ Relays information from the cortex and is involved in sleep and arousal
3. _____ Detects need states
4. _____ Sleep and wakefulness
5. _____ Relay station for sensory information
6. _____ Breathing, heartbeat, and other essential functions
7. _____ Initiation of movement
8. _____ Coordination of movement

Endocrine system A collection of glands involved in releasing hormones into the bloodstream.

3.5 The Endocrine System

The endocrine system uses endorphins and hormones to communicate over long distances and time.

- Discuss the role of endorphins and the endocrine system as communication mechanisms in the nervous system.

While neurotransmitters work their magic at the synapse level, other communication mechanisms transfer messages over much greater distances and over longer periods of time. The **endocrine system** FIGURE 3-21 is a separate and slower communication sys-

FIGURE 3-21 Structures of the endocrine system.

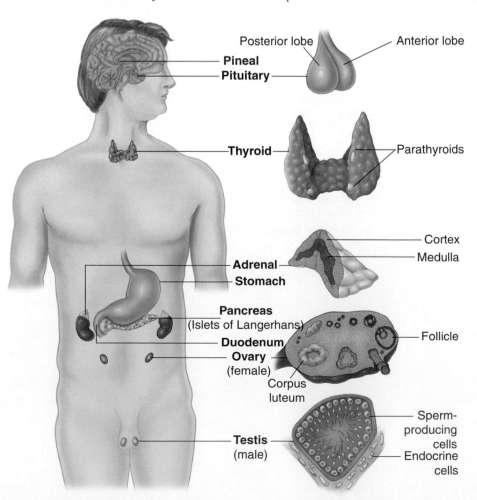

tem that uses hormones, which are chemical messengers released into the bloodstream. By releasing hormones into the bloodstream, the endocrine system can exert influence not only from long distances but for a long period of time as well. Once the body begins to produce **testosterone**, for example, there are changes in the male that last for years (such as the growth of facial hair). These chemicals can also function as or influence neurotransmitters. For example, norepinephrine, secreted by the adrenal gland, can be a neurotransmitter or a hormone depending on what function it is performing. When you are getting ready to fight, freeze, or flee because of a stressor, many parts of your body need to react. Your heart beats faster, you breathe more heavily, and your pupils dilate. Many of these changes are controlled by hormones rather than by neurotransmitters.

The endocrine system and nervous system are linked via the hypothalamus and pituitary gland for communication. The endocrine system relies on the brain's hypothalamus to regulate the production and release of hormones. It is the hormone control center for the rest of the body. The hypothalamus, in turn, relies on the pituitary gland to activate the other endocrine glands. The pituitary gland is often called the "master gland" since it influences so many other glands.

Endorphins

Endogenous opioid peptides, or **endorphins**, can reduce pain and promote pleasure. During extreme exercise, pain, or even excitement, the **pituitary gland** and hypothalamus both pour endorphins into the blood stream. Endorphins are naturally produced painkillers and get their name because they mimic the action of synthetic painkillers. The word *endorphin* is a cross between *endogenous*, meaning coming from within the body, and *morphine*, a medicine used to decrease pain. Endorphins are neither neurotransmitters nor hormones. Rather, they are neuromodulators that influence the effects of neurotransmitters. Some endorphins function like neurotransmitters when they operate in the synapse, and most will alter the effects of neurotransmitters. At other times, endorphins will be released directly into the bloodstream.

Perhaps the most common notion of endorphins comes from the idea of the "runner's high," a feeling of pleasure some report from extensive exercise. Recently, some researchers have questioned whether endorphins are linked to a runner's high at all. The discovery of endorphins in the early 1970s coincided with the start of a running and jogging craze in the United States. Some researchers believed that this may have been the origin of the idea of the runner's high. Researchers do admit that exercise can be addicting. Rats, for example, in the proper context will run themselves to death (up to 12 miles a day) if allowed to do so.

Other research (Sparling, Giuffrida, Piomelli, Rosskopf, & Dietrich, 2003) indicates that the pain-killing and out-of-body sensations experienced by some runners may be linked to another part of the brain, and the runner's high might be linked to tetrahydrocannabinol, or THC, the psychoactive substance in marijuana. THC does have mild pain-reducing effects, but it is not morphine.

Adrenal Glands

The **adrenal glands** are important glands of the endocrine system. The two adrenal glands are at the top of the kidneys (*ad* meaning adjacent and *renal* referring to the kidneys). There are two parts to the adrenal glands: an outer **adrenal cortex** (*cortex* means the outside like bark) and an inner **adrenal medulla** (*medulla* referring to the middle of the structure like marrow, the inside of a bone). The sympathetic nervous system stimulates the adrenal medulla, and it releases epinephrine and norepinephrine (more commonly known as adrenaline). Hormones secreted by the adrenal glands have a broad influence over many organs in the body. For example, the adrenal glands, in times of stress, will secrete stress hormones like epinephrine that increase blood pressure, heart rate, and the other parts of the fight, freeze, or flee response of the sympathetic nervous system.

Gonads

Gonads are organs that release male and female sex hormones. In women, the ovaries secrete **estrogen**, progesterone, and a small amount of testosterone. In men, the testes secrete testosterone. Testosterone is also produced in the adrenal glands of men and women.

Testosterone A sex hormone produced by the testes, adrenal cortex, and ovaries that is important in the male sex characteristics of the male body.

Endorphins Chemicals linked to pain perception and reward.

Pituitary gland The endocrine system's master gland.

Adrenal glands Important glands of the endocrine system consisting of the adrenal cortex and the adrenal medulla.

Adrenal cortex The outer layer of the adrenal gland that secretes hormones during stress.

Adrenal medulla The interior layer of the adrenal gland that secretes epinephrine and norepinephrine.

Gonads An organ that secretes sex hormones.

Estrogen A sex hormone produced primarily by the ovaries that is an important female sex hormone.

CONCEPT LEARNING CHECK 3.5 | *Identifying the Role of Endorphins and the Endocrine System Functions*

Match the chemical or structure with the correct function.

A. Hypothalamus

B. Pituitary gland

C. Epinephrine

D. Testosterone

E. Estrogen

1. _____ Associated with stimulation of the sympathetic nervous system

2. _____ A structure that detects need states

3. _____ Sometimes called the "master gland" because it influences hormone production in other parts of the body

4. _____ A sex hormone produced primarily by the ovaries that is an important female sex hormone

5. _____ A sex hormone produced by the testes, adrenal cortex, and ovaries that is important in the male sex characteristics in the male body

---

3.6 Genetics

Our DNA, in combination with the environment, allows us to pass along traits from parents to offspring.

- Discuss the role of genetics in psychology.

The Basic Concepts of Genetics

Packed inside nearly all of your cells is a special message—in code. This message is locked away in deoxyribonucleic acid or DNA and contains the directions to make every substance and structure in your body. There are nearly 6.5 feet of tightly bundled DNA in each cell of the body. In essence, your DNA contains the unique list of ingredients and the specific recipe to make you *you*. Anyone who has watched a crime drama lately knows that DNA is unique to each person in the world who has ever lived.

All parts of your body are produced from this instruction manual—from your earwax to the endoplasmic reticulum and from your toes to your tears. A **genome** is the sum of an organism's hereditary information, like an instruction manual for assembling the body. Our genes are the letters, each offering up a part of the story of you. Put the letters together in a genome and you have the story—provided you've put the letters together in the right order. In this section, we'll look at genetics and behavioral genetics and examine the ways in which the biology of behavior is influenced by both genetic and environmental factors.

Chromosomes are the parts of the cell that contain segments of DNA called **genes** FIGURE 3-22. You got half of your chromosomes from your mom and the other half from your dad back when you were a **zygote**, or a fertilized egg. This means, of course, that half your genes came from each of your biological parents. Our genes' ability to make copies of themselves lets our parents give us certain characteristics like freckles or big feet. But with half from mom and half from dad, what decides what gets expressed? This answer depends on many factors.

First, it is important to know that most traits are **polygenic**, meaning that multiple genes influence their expression. It is unlikely that there is only one gene for shyness, for example.

Genome The sum of an organism's hereditary information.

Chromosome Cellular organelle that contains genes.

Gene A segment of DNA.

Zygote A fertilized egg.

Polygenic Characteristics that multiple genes shape.

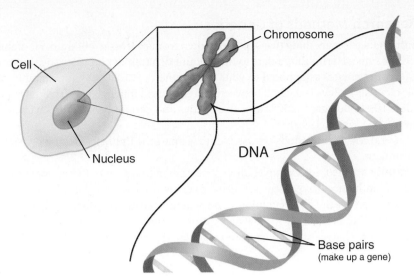

How traits are expressed also depends on the characteristics of the genes that are linked to the traits. Certain genes are more assertive than others. A **dominant gene** exercises its influence over other genes and overpowers recessive genes. This is called a **heterozygous condition**. A **recessive gene's** influence will only be seen when it teams up with an identical recessive gene. When two recessive genes pair up, the trait is likely to be expressed. When genes are alike, it is called a **homozygous condition**. Sometimes when a trait is heterozygous, the recessive trait lurks in the background. It is genetically present but not expressed. You'd never know you had it. Your **phenotype**, the expression of genetic influence, may not match your **genotype** or your personal genetic makeup. Then, if you pass on your genes to your kids by mating with someone who also has a recessive gene for the same trait, the trait may pop up. That explains how two people with straight, dark brown hair can have a child with curly red hair.

But after that, what determines which traits are expressed? According to scientists since Darwin, it is the environment. Each time an organism produces an offspring, a unique combination of DNA from the male and female parent is passed down. Some combinations of DNA can lead to infertility, diseases, or a shorter life. But, by chance, some combinations of DNA cause the offspring to remain healthier in a particular environment. Therefore, they live longer and are more likely to appear in future generations. In such cases, the combined DNA is an **adaptation**, a characteristic that increases in a population because it makes reproduction or survival more likely. These adaptations can accumulate over generations in both individuals and populations of individuals, giving them a distinct advantage.

For example, combinations of DNA caused some people in certain parts of Africa to have genes that protected them from malaria. This gene was more likely to appear in some of their children. Children who received the malarial protection gene survived and were able to pass it along to their children. The kids who did not get the trait may have died sooner and therefore were less likely to have kids of their own. Those who passed along the adaptive, malaria-resistant genes increased their family's **fitness**, or their contribution to the genetic pool of the next generation. As a group, this is called **inclusive fitness**, or kin selection, which is your family's contribution to the entire gene pool of the population.

So what do these notions of heredity and **natural selection** have to do with psychology? Everything. Earlier in this chapter, we discussed the importance of neurotransmitters, neurons, neural pathways, brain structures, other chemicals, and their links to behaviors and actions. All of these structures and molecules are mapped out by DNA. How it all comes together is influenced by the interplay of biology and the environment.

Dominant gene A unit of heredity whose influence is exerted over other genes.

Heterozygous condition A circumstance where genes are different for a given trait.

Recessive gene A unit of heredity whose influence is exerted only when paired with an identical gene.

Homozygous condition A circumstance where both genes are the same for a given trait.

Phenotype Expression of genetic influences.

Genotype An individual's genetic makeup.

Adaptation A process by which a characteristic increases in a population because it makes reproduction or survival more likely.

Fitness The contribution an individual makes to the gene pool of the next generation.

Inclusive fitness Also known as kin selection, the contributions to the next generation's gene pool of both an individual and his or her relatives.

Natural selection Varying success in reproduction resulting from the interaction of an organism with the environment.

The Research Methods of Genetics

Heritability The amount of a trait or characteristic that you can link to genetics as opposed to the environment.

Family study A method that allows researchers to test hypotheses concerning the contribution of genetic and environmental factors by examining biological relatives.

An inheritance is something that is passed down from parents to children. Heritability is much the same. **Heritability** refers to the amount of a trait or characteristic that you can link to your genetics as opposed to your environment. FIGURE 3-23, for example, shows what scientists believe is the link between our genes and intelligence (Devlin, Daniels, & Roeder, 1994; Norrgard, 2008) as well as genes and certain personality characteristics FIGURE 3-24 (Plomin, 1999).

Several research methods are used to tease apart the influence of biology versus the environment.

Family studies, for example, allow researchers to test hypotheses concerning the amount of influence that genetic factors have versus environmental factors by examining biological relatives. But just examining families cannot tell us everything. Perhaps members of one family are more likely to have depression, for example, because the family lives in an atmosphere charged with unexpressed rage. This is an environmental factor that makes

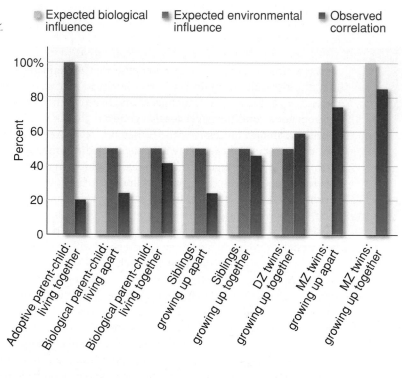

FIGURE 3-23 Heritability of human intelligence.
Source: Data from Devlin, B., Daniels, M., & Roeder, K. (1994). The heritability of IQ. Genetics, 137, 597–606.

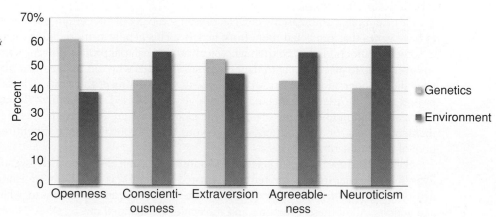

FIGURE 3-24 Heritability estimates for personality traits.
Source: Data from Jang, K.L., Lively, W.J., & Vernon, P.A. (1996). Heritability of the big five personality dimensions and their facets: a twin study. Journal of Personality, 64(3), 577–591.

it more likely that the family's members will be depressed. Here is where **adoption studies** come in. In an adoption study, researchers examine characteristics between children and their biological and adopted parents. These studies compare characteristics of parents to the characteristics of their biological or adopted kids.

Family and adoption studies are often compelling; however, they still only reveal part of the story. While family members do share genetic makeup, they are not identical. Each child has a unique combination of genes from mom and dad. To reveal the various contribution factors of the environment and biology, it would help if all mom and dad's children were exactly the same. This is the case in **twin studies**. There are two kinds of twins. One kind is **monozygotic (MZ)** (from one-egg, or identical twins). Identical twins come from a single fertilized egg that splits apart. MZ twins share 100% of their genetic material. Only 1 in 250 births are identical twins (Segal, 2010). The other types of twins are **dizygotic (DZ)** (from two-egg, or fraternal twins; FIGURE 3-25). DZ twins come from two eggs and two sperm and really are not any more genetically similar than two nontwin siblings from the same parents. Fraternal twins do have the research advantage of having the same prenatal environment. Twin studies are the gold standard, used to tease apart environmental and biological influences. Since identical twins share 100% of their genes, and twins raised together share 100% of their environment, examining twins in different families might be the ideal way to tease out the relative strength of genes versus environmental contribution. The idea of using twins to examine the relative strength of environmental and genetic influences has been around for a long time. Some classic adoption studies looked at identical twins whose natural parents had schizophrenia. Although the twins were adopted by different families with no history of schizophrenia, the studies revealed the presence of heritable genes for schizophrenia. These studies demonstrated that children whose parents had schizophrenia were still at risk for having the disorder (Heston, 1966).

As impressive as these estimates of heritability are, there may be problems with assumptions behind the twin study model. Although identical twins may share a family environment, should we assume that each twin's experience of this environment is the same? Some critics of the family study method suggest we should not (Hoffman, 1991). Birth order, gender differences, and varied experiences with teachers, friends, sports, interests, and siblings

Adoption study A method that allows researchers to test hypotheses concerning the contributions of genetic and environmental factors by examining characteristics between children and their biological and non-biological parents.

Twin study A research design in which the influences of heredity and environment are examined by comparing monozygotic or dizygotic twins.

Monozygotic (MZ) twins Twins from a single fertilized egg; also known as identical twins.

Dizygotic (DZ) twins Twins who are formed from two fertilized eggs; also known as fraternal twins.

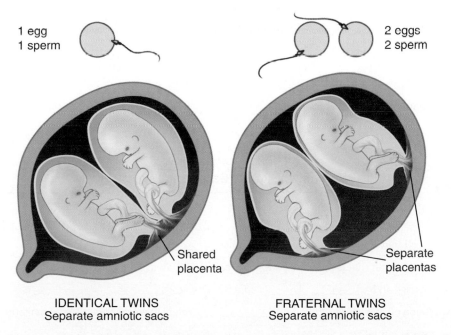

IDENTICAL TWINS
Separate amniotic sacs

FRATERNAL TWINS
Separate amniotic sacs

FIGURE 3-25 Monozygotic (identical) twins come from one egg, while dizygotic (fraternal) twins come from two.

all conspire to make your family environmental experience unique to you—maybe as unique as your mix of genes. Siblings' individual experiences within the same family can be as different as if they came from totally different families. On the other hand, some researchers have suggested that there is a "twin effect." The idea here is that twins, *because* they are twins, are raised a little differently than nontwin children. This, researchers note, makes it difficult to compare twins to nontwins (Plomin, Asbury, & Dunn, 2001). After all, how many people in the same family are routinely mistaken for one another or dress in identical clothes?

Summary of Multiple Influences on the Biology of Behavior

As this chapter has shown, neuroscientists and behavioral biologists examine behavior at many levels, as summarized in **TABLE 3-2**.

It has been a few years since Mike May's operation. The critical period has passed for his occipital lobe to be able use vision in the same way he would have before the accident. Even a year after the operation, he can correctly identify only about 25% of common objects. He has trouble discerning facial expressions most of the time, and he still has difficulty telling men's faces from women's faces. People, however, are amazingly flexible. Mike relies on secondary features such as the length of a person's hair or the shapes of eyebrows to make these judgments.

Psychology cuts across several fields. In this chapter, we have touched on many of the disciplines that help us to understand human behavior—chemistry, biology, and genetics, to name just a few. People are complex as well. You cannot separate a person from his or her body any more than you can separate psychology from neuroscience.

TABLE 3-2 What Neuroscientists Study

Level	What Does It Examine?
Behavioral	What people do
System	Systems such as the sympathetic or sympathetic nervous system reactions
Local circuit	Groups of neurons
Single neuron	An individual neurons reaction to an event such as exposure to a medicine or a neurotransmitter
Synapse	What occurs at the synapse
Membrane	Ion channels on neurons
Genetic	How genes influence the how neurons work

Source: Adapted from E. H. Chudler. Neuroscience for Kids. http://faculty.washington.edu/chudler/what.html

CONCEPT LEARNING CHECK 3.6 | *Reviewing the Role of Genetics in Psychology*

Fill in the blank with the key term that fits the statement best.

1. _____ are the parts of the cell that contain segments of DNA called _____.

2. _____ refers to the amount of a trait that is linked to your genetics rather than to your environment.

3. _____ twins come from one egg and _____ come from two eggs.

4. _____ refers to the expression of your genes while _____ refers to your actual genetic makeup.

5. Most traits come from multiple genes, meaning they have a _____ influence.

CRITICAL THINKING APPLICATION

A quick review of news magazine articles about genetics yields some interesting claims—there seems to be a gene for everything from laziness to racism to liberalism. These stories do their best to extrapolate from recent findings in neuroscience and genetics, with a hope of linking biology with our behaviors in a clean, unmuddled, precise way. But is it really that simple?

A 1980 *Science* magazine article, for example, related superior mathematical performance in men to biological factors, suggesting the male brain was better for math (Benbow & Stanley, 1980).

Biodeterminism is the belief that only your biology influences your future. It is the notion that some things are purely biologically derived and that other things come only from environmental factors. As you have learned in this chapter, there's no single part of the brain that is associated with math. There is also no single gene associated with math ability. In fact, a recent study examined nearly 500,000 individuals and found no link between math ability and gender (Else-Quest, Hyde, & Linn, 2010). There were some countries in which women were better in math and some countries in which men were better.

Evaluate

1. What examples of biodeterminism do you see stated in the nightly news about new studies?
2. What other explanations can you think of for laziness, racism, and liberalism? Are genetics the most compelling explanation?

Visual Overview Nervous System

Our nervous system is composed of two main branches: the **central nervous system** integrates and controls the body, and the **peripheral nervous system** links the rest of the body to the central nervous system.

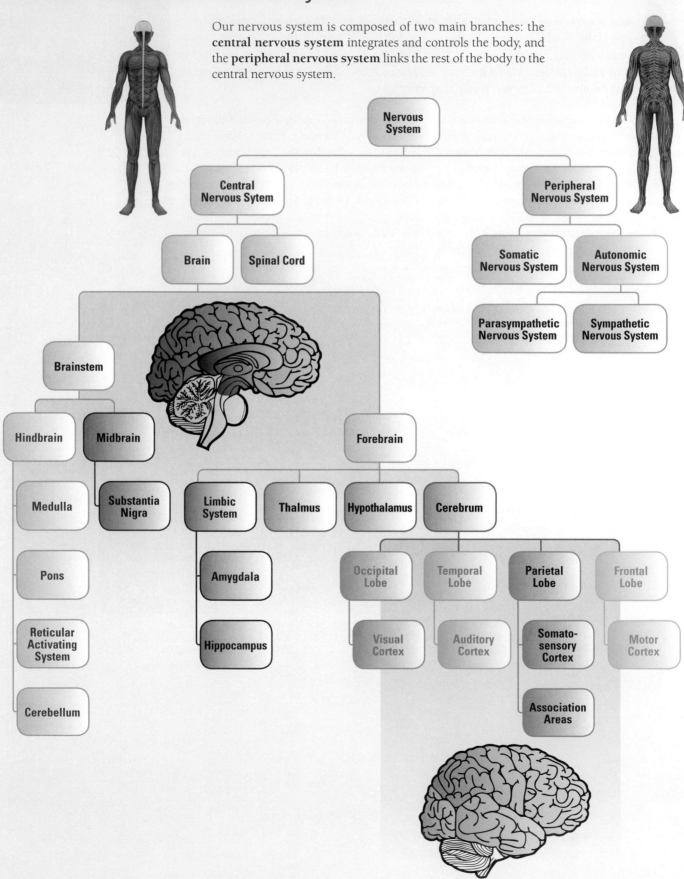

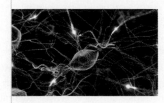

3.1 Overview: The Components of Biological Bases of Behavior

- The nervous system conducts signals to and from various parts of your body.
- Neuropsychology and neuroscience add depth and dimension to the science of psychology.
- Neuropsychology helps us to link our physical body with explanations for behavior on many different levels.

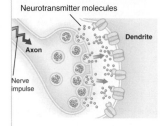

Neurotransmitter molecules
Dendrite
Axon
Nerve impulse

3.2 Neural Communication

- The nervous system is composed of glia and neurons.
- Glial cells are the cells of the nervous system that support and protect our neurons.
- Neurons are the basic cells of the nervous system.
- The basic structure of neurons includes the soma, dendrites, and axons.
- Neurons communicate via synaptic transmission.
- The action potential determines the message a neuron will send.
- Neurons integrate the messages they receive.
- Synaptic pruning results in more efficient neural networks.
- Neurotransmitters are involved in synaptic transmission.

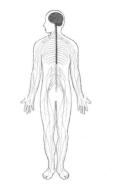

3.3 Nervous System Organization

- Our nervous system is composed of a peripheral nervous system and a central nervous system.
- The peripheral nervous system includes nerves that connect to all the glands and organs of our body.
- The peripheral nervous system is divided into the somatic and the autonomic nervous systems.
- The autonomic nervous system is divided into the sympathetic and parasympathetic nervous systems.
- The central nervous system consists of the brain and the spinal cord.

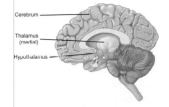

Cerebrum
Thalamus (medial)
Hypothalamus

3.4 The Brain

- Researchers use many tools to examine the inner workings of the brain, including examining lesions and the effect of electrical and magnetic stimulation, EEGs, CTs, PET scans, and MRIs.
- The brainstem consists of the hindbrain and midbrain and is involved with structures that support vital body processes.
- The midbrain is a major relay station for processing auditory and visual information and includes the substantia nigra, which is responsible for the initiation of movement.
- The forebrain is the largest part of the brain and includes the thalamus, the hypothalamus, the limbic system, and the cerebrum.
- The limbic system is a group of structures that surround the brainstem and governs emotions such as anger, happiness, and fear and stores and retrieves new memories.
- The cerebrum contains about 90% of the brain's volume. It consists of four lobes and two hemispheres that are connected by a dense network of nerve fibers called the corpus callosum.
- The occipital lobes of the cerebrum contain the visual cortex, which processes visual images.
- The temporal lobes of the cerebrum house the primary auditory cortex, which processes sound.
- The frontal lobes of the cerebrum contain the primary motor cortex, which

is an area that has a role in planning, controlling, and executing movements.

- The frontal lobes of the cerebrum play a role in personality, organization, and planning.
- The parietal lobes of the cerebrum contain the somatosensory cortex, which processes body sensation information.
- The cerebrum has a left and right hemisphere that are expert at certain tasks; this is known as lateralization of function.

- Lateralization of function was discovered by research into split-brained patients whose corpus callosum was severed. The result was that the left and right hemispheres operated without communicating to the other hemisphere.
- The brain has an amazing ability to grow and adjust. This results in both structures and functions adapting to environmental influences.

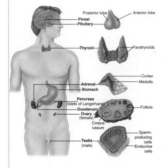

3.5 The Endocrine System

- The nervous system uses endorphins and hormones to communicate over longer distances and time.
- Endorphins can reduce pain and promote pleasure.

- The endocrine system consists of glands that create hormones.
- Hormones are chemical messengers that have a broad influence over many organs in the body.

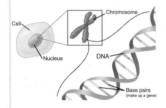

3.6 Genetics

- Chromosomes are parts of the cell that contain segments of DNA called genes.
- Most traits are polygenic, meaning they arise from multiple genes.
- Dominant genes will exercise their influence over other genes and overpower recessive genes, whose influence will only be seen when teamed up with an identical gene.
- The environment has an influence on which genes are expressed.
- A gene is considered adaptive because it leads to a characteristic that makes reproduction or survival more likely.

- Heritability refers to the amount of a trait that you can link to your genes as opposed to your environment.
- Research methods for examining heritability include family studies, adoption studies, and twin studies.
- The human brain is amazingly complex and flexible.
- Psychology draws from several fields, such as chemistry, biology, and genetics.
- A person's psychological makeup cannot be understood separately from his or her physiological makeup.

3.1 Overview: The Components of Biological Bases of Behavior

1. The branch of science that studies the connections between the brain and behavior is called:
   A. biological psychology.
   B. neuroscience.
   C. biopsychology.
   D. All of the above.

3.2 Neural Communication

2. Which of the following structures is involved in providing nutrients, insulation, and protection to neurons?
   A. Axon terminal
   B. Neurotransmitters
   C. Dendrites
   D. Glia

3. The sodium-potassium pump moves sodium ions _____ and potassium ions _____.
   A. out of the cell; out of the cell
   B. out of the cell; into the cell
   C. into the cell; into the cell
   D. into the cell; out of the cell

4. What is the approximate resting potential of the inside of a neuron?
   A. –70 millivolts
   B. +70 millivolts
   C. –10 millivolts
   D. +10 millivolts

5. What determines if a neuron has an action potential?
   A. Glial cells
   B. Both EPSPs and IPSP
   C. Only EPSPs
   D. Only IPSPs

3.3 Nervous System Organization

6. After her students surprised her, Dr. Morgan's blood pressure increased and her heart rate sped up. These physical reactions were most likely regulated by her:
   A. hippocampus.
   B. parasympathetic nervous system.
   C. sympathetic nervous system.
   D. spinal cord.

3.4 The Brain

7. The limbic system is important for:
   A. motor coordination.
   B. creating cerebrospinal fluid.
   C. connecting the cerebral hemispheres.
   D. emotional behaviors.

8. One function of the thalamus is to:
   A. regulate sleep.
   B. relay sensory information.
   C. encode new memories.
   D. motor coordination.

9. Dr. Anton is experimenting on brain function by injecting subjects with a radioactive glucose substance and then asking them to listen to recordings of sounds. The subject's heads are then scanned to determine the areas of the most radiation. What is the method being used by Dr. Anton?
   A. Electroencephalogram
   B. Computed axial tomography
   C. Positron emission tomography
   D. Magnetic resonance imaging

10. After a car accident, Roman had damage to his cerebellum. Roman is likely to have difficulty with which of the following activities?
    A. Yoga
    B. Reading
    C. Following conversations
    D. Understanding emotions

11. Memories of emotional events are especially likely to be facilitated by activation of the:
    A. amygdala.
    B. hypothalamus.
    C. sensory cortex.
    D. motor cortex.

3.5 The Endocrine System

12. People who feel a runner's high after participating in long, strenuous exercise sessions can thank which of the following chemicals?
    A. Estrogen
    B. Endorphins
    C. Pons
    D. Reticular activating system (RAS)

13. The endocrine system consists of glands that create _____.
    A. hormones
    B. neurotransmitters
    C. endorphins
    D. myelin

3.6 Genetics

14. When a trait is _____, it may increase in the population because it makes reproduction or survival more likely.
  - **A.** heritable
  - **B.** homozygous
  - **C.** recessive
  - **D.** adaptive

15. In order to determine how much the environment, as opposed to genes, influences behavior, the best type of study would compare which types of children?
  - **A.** MZ twins growing up together
  - **B.** DZ twins growing up apart
  - **C.** DZ twins growing up together
  - **D.** MZ twins growing up apart

CHAPTER DISCUSSION QUESTIONS

1. What examples from your own family suggest recessive and dominant gene expression?

2. In what ways does integrating neuroscience with psychology help psychology as a science?

3. In what ways does psychology influence the study of biology?

4. Structure and function are major themes in neuroscience. Discuss some examples.

CHAPTER PROJECTS

1. Design and construct an experiment to examine the link between psychological states and physiological response when viewing natural versus constructed environments. Collect pictures from online sources of natural environments like woods and animals versus constructed environments like cities. Consider measuring heart rate and blood pressure. Be sure in your report to indicate any confounds that may have influenced your results.

Adapted from Rowland, D. L., Kaariainen, A., & Houtsmuller, E. J., 2000. Interactions between physiological and affective arousal: A laboratory exercise for psychology. Teaching of Psychology, 27, 34–37.

2. Make a model of the brain or a neuron out of common everyday objects. See if you can link the function to the structure of what you have created.

3. Research the history of certain discoveries or technologies in neuroscience. What led to the discovery of the electroencephalogram, for example?

CHAPTER KEY TERMS

Absolute refractory period	**Cerebral hemispheres**	**Frontal lobe**
Acetylcholine	**Cerebrospinal fluid (CSF)**	**Functional magnetic resonance imagining (fMRI)**
Action potential	**Cerebrum**	**Functional plasticity**
Adaptation	**Chromosome**	**Gamma-aminobutric acid (GABA)**
Adoption study	**Computed tomography scans (CT scans)**	**Gene**
Adrenal cortex	**Corpus callosum**	**Genome**
Adrenal glands	**Cortical localization**	**Genotype**
Adrenal medulla	**Critical period**	**Glia cells**
Afferent nerve fibers	**Dendrite**	**Gonads**
Agonist	**Depolarizes**	**Heterozygous condition**
All-or-nothing law	**Dizygotic (DZ) twins**	**Heritability**
Amygdala	**Dominant gene**	**Hindbrain**
Antagonist	**Dopamine**	**Hippocampus**
Aphasia	**Efferent nerve fibers**	**Homozygous condition**
Association areas	**Electrical stimulation of the brain**	**Hormone**
Ataxia	**Electroencephalogram (EEG)**	**Hypothalamus**
Autonomic nervous system	**Endocrine system**	**Inclusive fitness (kin selection)**
Axon	**Estrogen**	**Inhibitory postsynaptic potential (IPSP)**
Axon terminal	**Endorphins**	**Interneuron**
Biological psychology	**Excitatory postsynaptic potential (EPSP)**	**Lateralization of function**
Brainstem	**Family study**	**Lesion**
Cell body	**Fitness**	
Central nervous system	**Forebrain**	
Cerebellum		
Cerebral cortex		

Limbic system
Magnetic resonance
  imaging (MRI)
Medulla
Midbrain
Mirror neuron
Monozygotic (MZ) twins
Motor cortex
Motor neuron
Myelin sheath
Natural selection
Nerves
Nervous system
Neural pruning
Neurogenesis
Neuron
Neuroscience
Neurotransmitter
Norepinephrine
Occipital lobe
Parasympathetic nervous
  system
Parietal lobe

Perceptual asymmetry
Peripheral nervous system
Phenotype
Phrenology
Pituitary gland
Plasticity
Polygenic
Pons
Positron emission tomography
  (PET scan)
Postsynaptic neuron
Postsynaptic potential (PSP)
Presynaptic neuron
Receptor site
Recessive gene
Reflex
Repolarize
Resting potential
Reticular formation
Reuptake
Sensory neuron
Serotonin
Soma

Somatic nervous system
Somatosensory cortex
Spinal cord
Spinal reflex
Split brain
Split-brain surgery
Stimulus threshold
Structural plasticity
Substantia nigra
Sympathetic nervous system
Synapse
Synaptic cleft
Synaptic pruning
Synaptic transmission
Synaptic vesicle
Temporal lobe
Testosterone
Thalamus
Threshold
Transcranial magnetic
  stimulation (TMS)
Twin study
Zygote

ANSWERS TO CONCEPT LEARNING CHECKS

3.1 Reviewing the Terminology of Neuroscience
1. A. Nervous system
2. D. Hormones
3. E. Biological psychology
4. B. Neuroscience
5. C. Neurons

3.2 Recognizing the Parts of the Neuron
1. B. Dendrite
2. G. Soma
3. C. Myelin sheath
4. A. Axon terminal
5. D. Neurotransmitters
6. E. Presynaptic neuron
7. F. Receptor site
8. I. Synaptic vesicle
9. H. Synaptic gap

3.3 The Organization of the Nervous System
1. Central nervous system
2. Spinal cord
3. Somatic nervous system
4. Sympathetic nervous system
5. Parasympathetic nervous system

**3.4 Identifying the Structures and Functions
in the Brain**
1. Hippocampus
2. Reticular activating system

3. Hypothalamus
4. Pons
5. Thalamus
6. Medulla
7. Substantia nigra
8. Cerebellum

**3.5 Identifying the Role of Endorphins and the
Endocrine System Functions**
1. Epinephrine
2. Hypothalamus
3. Pituitary gland
4. Estrogen
5. Testosterone

3.6 Reviewing the Role of Genetics in Psychology
1. **Chromosomes** are the parts of the cell that contain
   segments of DNA called **genes**.
2. **Heritability** refers to the amount of a trait that is linked to
   your genetics rather than to your environment.
3. **Monozygotic** twins come from one egg and **dizygotic**
   come from two eggs.
4. **Phenotype** refers to the expression of your genes while
   genotype refers to your actual genetic makeup.
5. Most traits come from multiple genes, meaning they have a
   polygenic influence.

3.1 Overview: The Components of Biological Bases of Behavior

1. D. Rationale: Biological psychology, biopsychology, and neuroscience are all areas that study the connections of the brain and behavior.

3.2 Neural Communication

2. D. Rationale: Glial cells are the cells in the nervous system that provide support and protection for neurons.

3. B. Rationale: The sodium-potassium pump moves sodium ions out of the cell and potassium ions into the cell.

4. A. Rationale: The resting potential inside of the neuron is −70 millivolts

5. B. Rationale: Since neurons receive and integrate signals from many different other neurons, both excitatory post-synaptic potentials and inhibitory postsynaptic potentials will determine if a neuron has an action potential.

3.3 Nervous System Organization

6. C. Rationale: The sympathetic nervous system is a branch of the autonomic nervous system that prepares the organs for vigorous activity.

3.4 Brain

7. D. Rationale: The limbic system is a group of structures that surround the brainstem and governs emotions.

8. B. Rationale: The thalamus is a forebrain structure that is a major relation station for sensory information.

9. C. Rationale: Dr. Anton is using positron emission tomography or a PET scan. A PET scan is a neuroscience imaging technique that uses radioactive glucose to indicate areas of activity.

10. A. Rationale: The cerebellum is part of the hindbrain involved in the development and coordination of movement.

11. A. Rationale: The amygdala is linked to emotions like anger and fear.

3.5 Endocrine System

12. B. Rationale: Endorphins are chemicals linked to pain perception and reward.

13. A. Rationale: The endocrine system is a collection of glands involved in releasing hormones into the bloodstream.

3.6 Genetics

14. D. Rationale: Adaptation is the process by which a characteristic increases in a population because it makes reproduction or survival more likely.

15. D. Rationale: Looking at monozygotic twins growing up apart would be the best way to examine heritability.

REFERENCES

Abitz, M., Nielsen, R. D., Jones, E. G., Laursen, H., Graem, N., & Pakkenberg, B. (2007). Excess of neurons in the human newborn mediodorsal thalamus compared with that of the adult. *Cerebral Cortex, 17*(11), 2573–2578. doi:10.1093/cercor/bhl163

Benbow, C., & Stanley, J. (1980). Sex differences in mathematical ability: Fact or artifact? *Science, 210*(4475), 1262–1264. doi:10.1126/science.7434028

Bonaiuto, J., & Arbib, M. A. (2010). Extending the mirror neuron system model, II: What did I just do? A new role for mirror neurons. *Biological Cybernetics, 102*(4), 341–359. doi:10.1007/s00422-010-0371-0

Courchesne, E., Townsend, J., Akshoomoff, N. A., Saitoh, O., Yeung-Courchesne, R., Lincoln, A. J., James, H. E., et al. (1994). Impairment in shifting attention in autistic and cerebellar patients. *Behavioral Neuroscience, 108*(5), 848–865.

Devlin, B., Daniels, M., & Roeder, K. (1994). The heritability of IQ. *Genetics, 137,* 597–606.

Else-Quest, N. M., Hyde, J. S., & Linn, M. C. (2010). Cross-national patterns of gender differences in mathematics: A meta-analysis. *Psychological Bulletin, 136*(1), 103–127. doi:10.1037/a0018053

Fine, I., Wade, A. R., Brewer, A. A., May, M. G., Goodman, D. F., Boynton, G. M., Wandell, B. A., et al. (2003). Long-term deprivation affects visual perception and cortex. *Nature Neuroscience, 6*(9), 915–916. doi:10.1038/nn1102

Greengard, P. (2001). The neurobiology of slow synaptic transmission. *Science, 294*(5544), 1024–1030. doi:10.1126/science.294.5544.1024

Herdener, M., Esposito, F., di Salle, F., Boller, C., Hilti, C. C., Habermeyer, B., Scheffler, K., et al. (2010). Musical training induces functional plasticity in human hippocampus. *Journal of Neuroscience, 30*(4), 1377–1384. doi:10.1523/JNEUROSCI.1513-09.2010

Heston, L. L. (1966). Psychiatric disorders in foster home reared children of schizophrenic mothers. *British Journal of Psychiatry, 112*(489), 819–825. doi:10.1192/bjp.112.489.819

Hoffman, L. (1991). The influence of the family environment on personality: Accounting for sibling differences. *Psychological Bulletin, 110*(2), 187–203.

Jessen, K. R. (2004). Glial cells. *The International Journal of Biochemistry & Cell Biology, 36*(10), 1861–1867.

Laughlin, S. B., van Steveninck, R. R., & Anderson, J. C. (1998). The metabolic cost of neural information. *Nature Neuroscience, 1*(1), 36–41.

Macleod, J., Davey Smith, G., Heslop, P., Metcalfe, C., Carroll, D., & Hart, C. (2002). Psychological stress and cardiovascular disease: Empirical demonstration of bias in a prospective observational study of Scottish men. *BMJ (Clinical Research Ed.), 324*(7348), 1247–1251. Retrieved from http://www.ncbi.nlm.nih.gov/pubmed/12028978.

Mechelli, A., Crinion, J. T., Noppeney, U., O'Doherty, J., Ashburner, J., Frackowiak, R. S., & Price, C. J. (2004). Neurolinguistics: Structural plasticity in the bilingual brain. *Nature, 431*(7010), 757. doi:10.1038/431757a

Melgaard, B., & Ahlgren, P. (1986). Ataxia and cerebellar atrophy in chronic alcoholics. *Journal of Neurology, 233*(1), 13–15.

Norrgard, K. (2008). Heritability of human intelligence: IQ and eugenics. *Nature Education, 1*(1). Retrieved from http://www.nature.com/scitable/topicpage /heritability-of-human-intelligence-iq-and-eugenics-796

Plomin, R. (1999). IQ and human intelligence. *American Journal of Human Genetics, 65*(5), 1476–1477.

Plomin, R., Asbury, K., & Dunn, J. (2001). Why are children in the same family so different? Nonshared environment a decade later. *Canadian Journal of Psychiatry, 46*(3), 225–233. Retrieved from http://www.ncbi.nlm.nih.gov .proxy.library.emory.edu/pubmed/11320676

Rowland, D. L., Kaariainen, A., & Houtsmuller, E. J. (2000). Interactions between physiological and affective arousal: A laboratory exercise for psychology. *Teaching of Psychology, 27,* 34–37.

Segal, N. L. (2010). Twins: The finest natural experiment. *Personality and Individual Differences, 49*(4), 317–323. doi:10.1016/j.paid.2009.11.014

Sparling, P. B., Giuffrida, A., Piomelli, D., Rosskopf, L., & Dietrich, A. (2003). Exercise activates the endocannabinoid system. *Neuroreport, 14*(17), 2209.

van Praag, H., Shubert, T., Zhao, C., & Gage, F. H. (2005). Exercise enhances learning and hippocampal neurogenesis in aged mice. *Journal of Neuroscience, 25*(38), 8680.

pieces—a pear, a cabbage leaf, and is that a gourd? You finally decide you're looking at a pile of fruits and vegetables. Examine the same image now that it has been inverted (right): This time, look for a face in the image! Do you see its eyes, nose, and hair? This time, your expectation provided a "face" organization to help you process the image. This example illustrates that what we see is not *solely* determined by what is "out there" on the page; instead, we *create* an interpretation through the interaction of top-down perceptions and bottom-up sensations.

A learned skill such as reading demonstrates how top-down perceptual processes actively guide understanding, overriding the actual information provided by sensation. For example, you can still read this sentence even though the letters are scrambled as long as the first and last letter appear in the right place: "Tihs is bcuseae the huamn mnid deos not raed ervey lteter by istlef, but the wrod as a wlohe" (Rawlinson, 1976). Another source of expectations arises from our most recent processing, called **perceptual set**. This refers to a "mindset" of top-down expectations based on your experience. For example, while reading handwriting, we interpret small black marks on the page as forming letters. The influence of perceptual set is so strong that even ambiguous figures can still be interpreted. For example, in one experiment, people viewed ambiguous figures as a different image depending upon the image they started with FIGURE 4-4 (Fisher, 1968). This suggests our recent perceptions provide top-down expectations about what is about to occur.

> **Perceptual set** The influence of recent processing as a framework for continuing perception.

FIGURE 4-4 The phenomenon of perceptual set is demonstrated by viewing these images from left to right. Processing from the left to right allows us to continue to recognize the bird in the more ambiguous middle drawings. However, processing from the right generates a different form (a cat), and that form is maintained as you continue to look leftward at the more ambiguous images in the middle.

CONCEPT LEARNING CHECK 4.1 | *Comparing Top-Down and Bottom-Up Processing*

Identify aspects of these experiences that correspond to top-down and bottom-up processing:

A. Reading a book

B. Walking down the street and recognizing a friend

C. Listening to a new song

D. Being tapped on the shoulder when you didn't notice anyone behind you

E. Taking the first spoonful of your favorite food into your mouth

4.2 Sensory Principles

Sensory organs register physical energy using very different mechanisms that share common principles of operation.

■ Apply the principles of transduction, sensitivity, and adaptation across the senses.

Though very different in physical structure, our senses share some key defining features in their task of relating our psychological experience to the reality of the external world.

Transduction of Physical Energy into Neural Stimulation

Each of our sensory organs—eyes, ears, nose, mouth, and skin—has its own method for translating external physical stimulation into neural stimulation. **Transduction** is the process in which physical energy in the world is translated into an electrochemical signal—neurons firing—that represents the incoming sensation in the brain. For example, a touch on your fingertip causes receptors within the skin to register "pressure," which in turn causes neurons located there to begin firing. These neural signals are passed through the body to the brain, where the construction of meaning takes place.

Each sense organ responds to a different type of physical energy in the world, such as sound waves, chemical molecules in the air, or light waves. So the sense organs have specialized **sensory receptor** cells that react only to particular kinds of physical stimulation. For example, in the ear, tiny hair cells move, registering a pattern of sound waves and converting this to neural firing. All five of these major sense organs register two specific features of the incoming sensation: Sensations are coded for their *intensity* (strong versus weak) and *quality* (e.g., a foul versus a pleasant smell). Typically, much of this coding about the nature of the sensation happens *after* transduction. Once in neural form, sensations follow neural pathways from the receptors to specific areas in the brain, particularly in the outer cortex. So the experience of sensation begins with the sensory receptors in the sense organs and continues in the brain.

Detection Thresholds Reflect Sensitivity

How good are our sensory systems? Humans compare unfavorably to the impressive sense of smell in dogs or the superior distance vision in birds of prey. The field of research called psychophysics examines the properties of our external sensory systems. What is the smallest sensation we can detect? **Absolute thresholds** are the lowest amount of physical energy we can detect reliably (50 percent of the time) using a given sense organ. For example, standing on the top of a building on a clear, dark night, a person can detect a lighted candle 30 miles away (Galanter, 1962). We can taste a teaspoon of sugar in 2 gallons of water, and smell a drop of perfume inside a three-room apartment. We can hear a ticking watch 20 feet away, and feel a bee's wing fall onto a cheek from a centimeter away. However, there are some problems with measuring absolute thresholds.

For example, you may recall taking a hearing test, during which you wear headphones and raise your hand whenever you hear a tone. Suppose that some time passes and you don't hear any tones. Now you may be expecting that a tone must be coming soon and be straining to hear it. This may make you *too* ready to respond and say, "Yes, I heard something." So your criterion for deciding that you did hear a very faint tone changes based on your top-down expectations. Your sensitivity—how many tones you miss and how many tones you incorrectly say you heard—will vary. **Signal detection theory** (Green & Swets, 1966) is a testing method that takes your readiness to respond into account. On some trials, a tone is played and you say, "Yes, I heard it," called a "hit." Other times, no tone is played, but you think you did hear one, called a "false alarm" **TABLE 4-1**. By comparing these trials, your ability to detect a tone can be measured along with your tendency to be more or less conservative. By correcting for changes in your top-down expectations and criteria for responding, signal detection theory can provide a more accurate measure of thresholds.

We can also define the sensitivity of our senses by examining how accurately we can detect *changes* in stimulation. If you turn up the volume on your iPod, how much louder

Transduction The process in which physical energy in the world is translated into an electrochemical signal—neurons firing—that represents sensation in the brain.

Sensory receptor Specialized cells in each sense organ that react to only particular kinds of external physical stimulation.

Absolute threshold The lowest amount of physical energy that can be detected reliably 50 percent of the time using a given sense organ.

Signal detection theory A sensory testing method that takes into account both the actual stimulus intensity and your readiness to respond.

TABLE 4-1 Signal Detection Theory

Signal Is Played		
You say:	"Yes"	"No"
	Hit	Miss
Signal Is Not Played		
You say:	"Yes"	"No"
	False alarm	Correct rejection

Source: Adapted from Green, D. M., & Swets, J. A. (1966). Signal detection theory and psychophysics. New York: Wiley.

is perceived as "louder?" If you have ever been fitted for eyeglasses or contact lenses, you have experienced a test of your ability to detect subtle differences in sensation. As you sat in a chair, you looked through a lens to find the best correction for your vision. You were asked repeatedly, "Which is better, the first lens or the second?" The doctor was, in effect, checking whether adding more correction to your lenses results in any noticeable improvement in your vision. When you can no longer detect a difference with additional lenses, the best correction to your vision has been found. A **difference threshold** is defined as the difference in stimulus strengths that you can correctly identify at least 50 percent of the time. The smallest amount of change between two stimuli that a person can detect at least half of the time is defined as the **just noticeable difference (jnd)**.

Your ability to notice a difference between sensations depends directly upon the *strength* of the stimulus. For example, turning your headphones down may be quite noticeable when the sound is already low, whereas turning it down by the same amount when it's blasting loudly might not be noticeable. As the stimulus becomes stronger or larger, so, too, does the *jnd*, and vice versa, a relationship known as **Weber's Law** (Hess & Hayes, 1993). Imagine carrying a heavy (20-pound) bag of groceries and adding a 1-pound bag of coffee to it. The difference in the weight of the bag is not as noticeable compared to adding the same coffee bag to a very light (2-pound) grocery bag. It is the *proportion* of the difference between the two stimuli (20 vs. 21 pounds or 2 vs. 3 pounds) that matters in detecting differences, not the *size* of the difference (adding 1 pound to both bags). Weber's Law says that the size of the *just noticeable difference* (i.e., the change in stimulus intensity) is a constant proportion of the original stimulus value. And this proportion is different for each sense modality (e.g., hearing, seeing, touch). For example, a 10-decibel difference in volume is easy to notice at low volumes, so you may hear a mosquito buzzing in a quiet room. But at high volumes, the 10-decibel difference between a jet engine and a machine gun may be harder to detect **TABLE 4-2**.

If sensation falls "below threshold," we may be unaware that it occurred, called **subliminal perception** (without conscious awareness). We may be unsure that we even *saw* a particular stimulus; however, its effect can be measured. In one study, pairs of kaleidoscope images were flashed on a screen for 2 seconds. Later, the volunteers couldn't say which of the pair they had seen, but when told to "just guess," they were up to 80 percent accurate (Voss & Paller, 2009). Advertisers sometimes use subliminal perception to attempt to influence consumers **FIGURE 4-5**. Does it work?

In 1957, an advertising expert named James Vicary reported he had secretly flashed, at a third of a millisecond, the words "Eat Popcorn" and "Drink Coke" onto the screen during a movie at a public theater (Pratkanis, 1992). His studies involved thousands of moviegoers who received a subliminal message every 5 seconds during the film. Vicary claimed an increase in Coke sales of 18 percent and a rise in popcorn sales of almost 58 percent. However, this was too good to be true for advertisers: 5 years later, after investigation by the Federal Communications Commission, Vicary admitted his studies were a "gimmick" intended to save his failing business and that they had no scientific or practical validity.

Difference threshold The smallest difference in sensation that is reliably detectable.

Just noticeable difference (jnd) The smallest amount of change between two stimuli that a person can detect at least half of the time.

Weber's Law As the stimulus becomes stronger or larger, so does the just noticeable difference between it and other similar stimuli.

Subliminal perception Sensation registered "below threshold," without conscious awareness of its occurrence.

FIGURE 4-5 In the 2000 presidential campaign, a 30-second televised advertisement discussed a prescription drug plan for the elderly. Alongside images of Vice-President Al Gore, the ad shows fragments of the slogan, "Bureau**rats** decide." The letter string "RATS" was flashed for a split second. The advertisement was withdrawn after complaints.

TABLE 4-2 Weber's Law

Sound	Decibel Level	Times Louder than Threshold
Jet engine	140	100,000,000,000,000
Threshold of pain	120	1,000,000,000,000
Rock band	110	100,000,000,000
Vacuum cleaner	80	100,000,000
Traffic	70	10,000,000
Conversation	60	1,000,000
Mosquito	40	10,000
Breathing	10	10
Threshold of hearing	0	1

Source: Data from Center for Hearing and Communication, 2012, http://www.chchearing.org/noise-center, Retrieved 2/22/12.

There is little evidence that subliminal perception leads to actual changes in behavior (Vokey & Read, 1985). For example, one claim for subliminal perception is that you can learn while you sleep! Commercials for self-help and language recordings claim you can play them while you sleep, and your subliminal perception will take in the information. In double-blind procedures (in which both subject and tester don't know what was on the recordings), no benefit from listening while sleeping has been found (Greenwald et al., 1991). So save your money!

Sensory Adaptation

Another important principle is that our sense organs *adapt* to the stimulation they receive over time. For all senses, repeated exposure to a stimulus will lead, over time, to reduced responding. For example, if you are exposed to the smell of a skunk, you will initially find it noxious; but, over time, your sense of smell will adapt so that the odor is much less noticeable. **Sensory adaptation** is change in responsiveness to the same sensation over time. For example, are you wearing a watch right now? If so, you were likely unaware of the sensation of the pressure it causes on your skin because your sense of touch adapted to its presence over time. Adaptation allows you to ignore the ever-present watch and to notice immediately when your watch falls off. Sensory adaptation results in sense organs that are great at detecting *changes* in sensation rather than at maintaining the same sensation over time.

For example, if you could stabilize your eye so that it remained completely still while you stared at this page, you would only be able to see it for about 10 seconds; then everything would go dark. Sensory receptors that are repeatedly stimulated in exactly the same way will begin to adapt and will stop passing forward the neural message to the brain (Martinez-Conde et al., 2004). We don't experience this because our eyes make automatic movements called *saccades*, creating a fresh sensation to process FIGURE 4-6.

> **Sensory adaptation** A change in responsiveness to the same stimulation in a sensory organ over time.

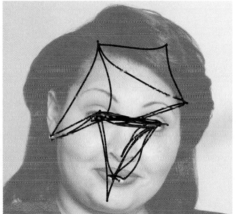

FIGURE 4-6 When viewing a still image, our eyes move across it quickly, stopping briefly at points, and then moving on to refresh the sensations. The movement of the eye fixations is depicted by the dots and lines shown in the figure on the right.

Our perceptual processes experience fatigue when a sensation remains the same and excite when sensation changes. Consider the image in FIGURE 4-7. Once information is perceived, we don't need to attend closely to it. However, if some portion of the image moves, this may provide vital information about a threat (or food source) that requires immediate attention. Our sensory processes are adapted through evolution to process changes in sensation, increasing our chances of survival.

In summary, our experience of the external world is created by the transduction of physical energy into neural stimulation, by the sensitivities of our sense organs, and by our adaptation to stimulation over time. These principles are consistent across each of our sensory systems; however, each sense has its own "hardware" for implementing these principles. Said another way, the transduction of physical to neural energy is accomplished in different ways within each sensory organ.

FIGURE 4-7 In a visual scene, movement may be the only visual cue that reveals the presense of danger; in this case, an alligator in a plant-covered swamp.

Answer the following question.

1. How would you determine the absolute and difference thresholds for the sense of taste? Describe the testing method you would use to measure the sensitivity of your sense of taste.

4.3 The Five Major Senses

Five major sources of external information provide sensory data.

- Identify the five main external senses.
- Describe how each sensory organ achieves transduction.
- Follow the path of signals within the brain.

How many senses are there, and what defines a "sense?" By convention, we often describe "the five senses"—seeing, hearing, smelling, tasting, and touching—as the main sources of sensations from the world. These relate to five external sense organs on the body, namely, the eyes, ears, nose, mouth, and skin (see **TABLE 4-3**). However, there are additional sources of information about the world that are internal to the body.

For example, the vestibular sense (based on movement of fluid within the ear canals) provides sensations of balance and indicates the position of your body relative to the ground. Imagine a gymnast tumbling through the air; with eyes closed, the vestibular sense provides information about where the body is in space. Another internal body sense, kinesthetic sense, provides you with information about the movement and position of your muscles and joints. Motion simulators used in entertainment rides make use of these bodily senses to give you the impression of driving fast around a curve; the seat tilt provides the same internal sensations you would have in a real car. We also have internal detectors of muscle stretch. So our bodies provide some internal senses to help us relate to the external world.

In this chapter, we will focus on our five main external senses to illustrate the most relevant principles of sensation for psychology. Keep in mind, however, that we rarely function in the world using only one sense. Texting on your cell phone combines sight and touch; eating combines smell and taste. And understanding speech involves both visual and auditory cues, which explains why it's easier to understand each other when talking face to face (McGurk & MacDonald, 1976). And for a small number of people, perceptions can appear to blend across modes, such as smelling a color or hearing a visual movement (Simner et al., 2006). Synesthesia refers to a rare, genetic neurological condition in which stimulation of one sensory or cognitive pathway leads to automatic experiences in a second (Sagiv & Robertson, 2005). Often, this involves combining types of stimuli, like seeing colors around days of the week or saying words that evoke tastes

Virtual reality devices present visual images adjusted to show what you would see if you moved your head and body within a simulated world.

TABLE 4-3 Overview of the Five Major Senses

Sense	Stimulus	Receptors	Location	Psychological Phenomenon
Seeing	Visible light waves	Rod and cone cell	Retina	Color vision
Hearing	Sounds waves	Hair cells	Cochlea	Locating sound sources
Smelling	Chemicals floating in air	Receptor cells	Olfactory bulb	Pheromones
Tasting	Chemicals dissolved in water	Taste buds	Papillae	Supertasters
Touching	Pressure	Pacinian corpuscles	Skin	Differing sensitivity of body surfaces

in the mouth (Ward & Simner, 2003). But only 1 percent of us have such experiences, so we will focus on five major senses separately in this chapter.

The Sense of Vision

Humans are visual creatures; for us, "seeing is believing." In the span of evolutionary time, vision went from a primitive recognition of light versus dark to the detection of features like shape, texture, motion, and color in higher-order animals (Land & Fernald, 1992). What makes the sense of vision in humans possible? Light waves have three physical properties that create sensations: The **wavelength** of light—the horizontal distance between wave peaks—determines its color or hue. The amplitude—how high the peaks are—determines its brightness. And the number of different wavelengths present determines its saturation, or the purity and richness of color. For example, red, green, and blue light each have a characteristic wavelength, and white light combines all three. The physical properties of the external stimulus—the light—result in our internal sensation of color, brightness, and richness. But how does light in the external world form our psychological experience?

We commonly describe vision as taking place in the eye, but it only begins there. Light from an object comes in through the eye's pupil and passes through the lens (a transparent organ that helps to focus light). It is then flipped upside down and falls onto the back wall of the eyeball, a layer of nerve cells called the **retina** FIGURE 4-8.

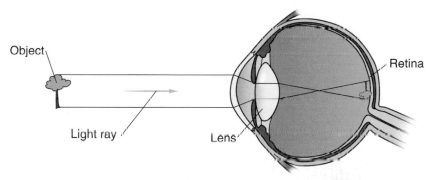

FIGURE 4-8 Rays of light entering the eye pass through the lens to fall on the back wall of the eyeball, called the retina.

Wavelength The distance between peaks of incoming light waves that determines their color.

Retina The layer of sensory receptor cells lining the back wall of the eye.

Rod cells Rod-shaped cells in the retina that register degrees of lightness and darkness.

Cone cells Cone-shaped cells on the retina that recognize colors.

Dark adaptation The increased sensitivity experienced when your eyes adjust to lower levels of available light.

Fovea The focal point of the retina where image processing is sharpest due to more cone cells.

Photoreceptors The rod and cone cells in the retina that register the presence of light waves.

Bipolar cells Cells that process incoming information from the rods and cones in the retina.

Ganglion cells More complex cells that process patterns of receptor activation within the retina.

So an image of a person actually falls on the retina with the feet at the top of the retina and the head at the bottom. Two types of cells line the interior wall of the retina: **rod cells**, which recognize degrees of darkness and light, and **cone cells** that recognize colors (see FIGURE 4-9). The rod cells operate under low illumination, and night vision occurs using this type of receptor. Located around the periphery of the eye, the rod cells detect light but are not good at sharp images. As you enter a dark room, your rod cells become more than 10,000 times more sensitive to light after time passes, and you experience **dark adaptation**. Similarly, when you go from a dark to light room, you experience light adaptation, in which your eyes adjust to the higher illumination of a room.

The cone cells operate under high illumination. These cells are packed around the **fovea**, or focal point of the eye. This means the perception of sharp images is best in the area at the center of our gaze. Rod and cone cells are known as **photoreceptors**: cells that respond to the electromagnetic energy of light. Photoreceptor cells *transduce*, or translate, the light's energy into neural signals. These neural signals pass to another layer of cells, called **bipolar cells**, which process and pass them to another layer called **ganglion cells**. More than 130 million photoreceptor cells feed neural signals into about one million ganglion cells. So within the retina itself, layers of connected cells begin to process sensory information first absorbed by the photoreceptors (Palmer, 1999).

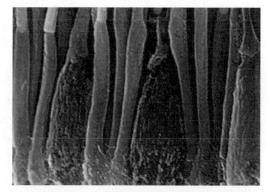

FIGURE 4-9 This image shows the distinctive shapes of rod and cone cells. There are 20 rod cells for every one cone cell, and the cones are clustered in the center of the retina. Rods respond to dim light, and cones detect color and detail.

Because the photoreceptor cells lie at the back, or interior wall, of the retina FIGURE 4-10, incoming light must pass through the ganglion and bipolar cell layers to reach the photoreceptor cells. It's as if the wiring of a car headlight was placed in front of rather than behind the light. Ganglion cells' axons then carry neural signals within a complex strand of neural pathways, called the **optic nerve**, that leaves the back of the eye and extends into the brain. The point at which the optic nerve leaves the back of the eye causes a **blind spot**, where light falling on that part of the retina cannot be processed (see FIGURE 4-11). As neural activity exits the eyes through the optic nerves, the signals travel to visual centers in the brain FIGURE 4-12.

Close one eye and imagine a vertical line in the middle of what you can see. Everything to the left of that line is in your left visual field and on the right, your right visual field. Each eye has its own left and right visual fields. So the neural pathway from each eye crosses

Optic nerve The bundle of neural fibers collecting sensation in the retina that passes out of the eyeball in a pathway to the brain.

Blind spot The small area of the retina where the optic nerve leaves the eyeball.

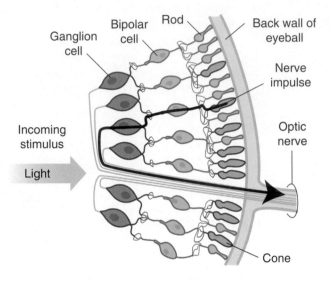

FIGURE 4-10 A depiction of the eye, where the layers of cells in the retina are enlarged.

FIGURE 4-11 To experience your blind spot, close your right eye and look at the red dot on the right with your left eye. From about 18 inches away, move your face slowly towards the page. At a critical distance, the circle on the left will fall entirely on your blind spot, the area of the retina where there are no receptor cells (where the optic nerve leaves the eye). When the circle disappears it is seen as the same as the background because that area is "filled in" by nearby receptors.

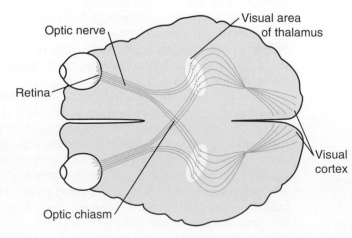

FIGURE 4-12 Neural stimulation takes place in the retina, where the processing of signals begins. From there, signals travel to a cross-over point called the optic chiasm, the thalamus "relay center," and finally to the occipital lobes of the cortex.

over at a point called the **optic chiasm**. Here, all the neural signals from the left visual fields of both eyes are gathered and sent to the right hemisphere of the brain. Similarly, all the neural signals from the right visual fields of both eyes are gathered and sent to the brain's left hemisphere. Then neural pathways within each hemisphere send the neural signals to the thalamus, the "sensory relay center" of the brain. The thalamus reroutes incoming neural messages to processing areas in the visual cortex and then to more than 30 different areas of the occipital cortex.

Within the occipital cortex, groups or "columns" of cells further analyze the neural signals to make sense of the incoming information. These cells are called **feature detectors**. Each feature detector cell responds to a unique, specific aspect, or feature, of the visual stimulus (e.g., a horizontal line, a vertical line, or line at a specific angle). Each feature detector cell performs its task independently from all other feature detector cells, known as **parallel processing**. However, a feature detector also sends messages to nearby cells, acting to amplify and inhibit the action of its neighbors.

Nobel Prize–winning research (Hubel & Weisel, 1962) studied the function of these feature detector cells in the visual cortex. The experiment involved tapping into individual cells with microelectrodes. Anesthetized (unconscious) cats (with their eyes open) saw a stimulus projected on a screen in front of them. The microelectrode captured the activity of an individual feature detector cell while a stimulus was displayed in different places on the screen. By carefully testing which stimuli activated each cell, the experimenters determined that individual cells in the visual cortex responded only to certain types of visual information. For example, a cell may respond only to a line moving up and down at a 45-degree angle. This particular cell's receptive field is limited only to a small area that, when stimulated in a specific way by specific visual information, causes a change in its firing rate.

Each feature detector cell looks for a specific pattern, such as color, form, movement, and depth (Hubel, 1996). The visual cortex is made up of millions of these cells, each tuned to recognize simple or complex features. Other cells look at the results of this process and attempt to recognize patterns formed by overlapping fields of feature detectors (Tanaka, 1996). It's a bit like putting together the pieces of a jigsaw puzzle: By detecting the edges of forms—abrupt transitions between light and dark—the visual system begins to put together the outlines of an image, and the stimulus takes on a recognizable form.

For example, a simple stimulus like the letter "A" consists of three separate lines. Using bottom-up processing, feature analysis by the differing types of detector cells identifies each separate line (/ - \), and the pattern they form is pieced together by further processing in the visual cortex (A). At the end of this (split-second) journey from retina to cortex, the pattern, spread across columns of cells, is recognized as the letter "A." Now, imagine how much easier this process would be had you just read the letters "B – A – N – A – N –"! Your top-down expectations for the letter to come would help you tie the pieces into a pattern much more quickly!

To perceive color, our eyes use the same method as television and computer screens. In order to produce the entire spectrum of colors, only three primary colors of light are needed: red, blue, and green. This **trichromatic theory** of color vision—that the eye contains only red, blue, and green color detectors—was advanced by Thomas Young (1773–1826) and Hermann von Helmholtz (1821–1894). In fact, evidence shows that each cone in the retina is tuned to detect only red, or blue, or green light (Bowmaker & Dartnall, 1980). The patterns of light detected by cones are then analyzed to capture individual hues made up of varying combinations of these three colors. Color mixing with light is *additive*, in that two colors with different wavelengths combine to produce a new color; so, red and blue light together make pink light

However, there is more to color vision than cones. For example, consider the images comprised of dots in FIGURE 4-13. Some individuals (about 8 percent of men and 0.5 percent of women, with men more at risk because of mutations linked to X chromosomes) cannot see numbers formed by certain colors of dots. This indicates a form of **colorblindness**, a condition marked by difficulty in distinguishing one color, such as red, from others, such as green. If trichromatic theory were the correct account of color vision, these patterns should not be problematic.

Optic chiasm The place in the front of the brain where the neural tracts following from the optic nerve of each eye cross over so that some tracts lead to both the right and left hemispheres.

Feature detectors Individual cells in the visual cortex that respond only to certain types of visual patterns, such as lines, circles, or angles.

Parallel processing Analyzing information in groups or "columns" of cells in the cortex at the same time in order to understand an overall pattern.

Trichromatic theory The notion that color vision relies on sensory receptors in the retina that process only red, blue, and green.

Colorblindness A condition marked by difficulty in distinguishing among some shades of red, green, or, more rarely, blue.

Opponent process theory The theory that opposing, or complementary, colors (yellow/blue, white/black, and red/green) are produced by differences in firing rates by complex cells within the retina.

Afterimage The appearance of an illusion of color (e.g., red) on a white surface after viewing its complementary color (e.g., green) for a prolonged period.

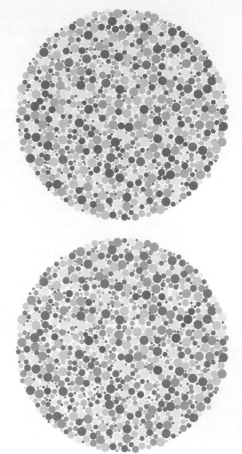

FIGURE 4-13 Some individuals have trouble picking out the numbers "23" in the image (top) and the number "57" (bottom) among the dot patterns, indicating an impairment of color processing that can't be explained by trichromatic theory.

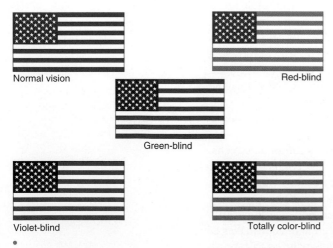

Most people see the American flag in the colors shown on the flag labeled "normal vision". With variants of color blindness, people have difficulty in distinguishing among colors due to a problem in one type of receptor, causing the flag to appear in different colorations.

A different theory of color vision was proposed by Ewald Hering (1834–1918), called **opponent process theory**. This arose from observation of phenomena called negative **afterimages**. In some conditions, viewing red for a time leads to seeing its complementary color, green, on a white background. Similarly, viewing blue can lead to an afterimage of its complementary color, yellow, and black to white. When processing the same stimulus over a period of time fatigues the receptor cells on the retina, they respond by presenting the *opposing* color to what was processed. This "opponent process" suggests that yellow and blue are linked, as are red and green, and black and white. The occurrence of afterimages demonstrates a link in our sensation of color that cannot be explained by trichromatic theory FIGURE 4-14.

What accounts for afterimages? The answer lies in the characteristics of the ganglion cells that process information coming from the cone cells. There are three types of ganglion cells: red/green cells, blue/yellow cells, and black/white cells. When cones sensitive to one color fire, the ganglion cell inhibits the processing of the opposing color. So a single ganglion cell that fires faster when a red cone is active may fire slowly when the complementary green cones become active FIGURE 4-15. As a result, the color we see as an afterimage is a reflection of the processing in ganglion cells adapting to the repeated neural messages from the cones. For example, a ganglion cell firing rapidly to signal "red" will eventually fatigue and slow down, resulting in the passing on of a signal from that cell as "green" (Vimal et al., 1987).

The occurrence of afterimages shows that as soon as cones register information, the next layer of cells has already begun to piece together information and transmit an interpretation of the stimulus. So both the trichromatic theory and the opponent process

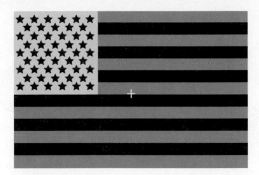

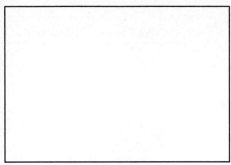

FIGURE 4-14 To see an afterimage, focus on the cross in the middle of the left figure. Be sure to keep your eyes as still as possible. Stare at the cross for at least 30 seconds. Then, switch your eyes quickly to the white box on its right. You should see an afterimage of the American flag!

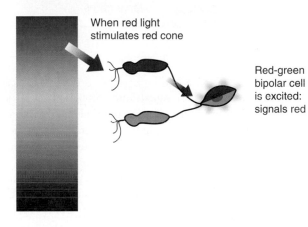

When red light stimulates red cone

Red-green bipolar cell is excited: signals red

FIGURE 4-15 Opponent process theory posits the presence of processing cells that respond to pairs of complementary colors: red or green, blue or yellow, or black or white. These cells help to refine the color detected in the red, blue, and green cone cells.

theory together help to explain color vision (Abramov & Gordon, 1994). Perceptual **illusions** like afterimages remind us that our sensory systems can go astray. By examining some of these exceptions, we can glimpse how our sensory and perceptual systems build our internal sense of the external world.

The Sense of Hearing

Audition, or the sense of hearing, depends on the movement of air in the external world. As the proverbial question goes, "If a tree falls in the forest and no one is around to hear it, does it make a sound?" The falling tree does make sound waves, but audition occurs when someone hears it.

Our sense of hearing registers a sound when an object in the world vibrates, setting air molecules into motion against the ear. Imagine striking a metal bar; as it vibrates, it creates small pressure waves of air that travel out in all directions. These are called *sound waves* and are invisible to the eye. These waves have amplitude or height, which creates the experience of loudness (Knight, 1960). The number of sound waves arriving within a given time period reflects their **frequency**, which we experience as pitch (whether a sound is high or low). Combinations of sound waves contribute to our psychological sense of the complexity or purity of sound, called *timbre* (pronounced "TAM-ber"). To accomplish this, our ears rely on a lot of "hardware" to amplify the incoming sound waves and detect the three major properties of sound.

FIGURE 4-16 shows the ear, its internal canal, and a delicate translation system that captures the sound waves on the eardrum in the outer ear and replicates them in the middle ear through a mechanism involving the hammer, anvil, and stirrup bones to produce pressure on a membrane called the **oval window**. The **cochlea** is a semicircular canal formed by three spiral-shaped fluid-filled tubes. Movement of the oval window causes the fluid in the cochlea to move, reproducing the sound wave that struck the eardrum. The cochlea is lined with the **basilar membrane**, which includes tiny hair cells on its surface. Each of these **hair cell receptors** is connected to the auditory nerve. When sound waves

Illusion A visual image that creates a misperception of the world.

Frequency The wavelength of sound or light waves (the time distance between peaks).

Oval window Membrane in the ear that collects sound waves and translates them into fluid movement in the cochlea.

Cochlea The semicircular canal of fluid-filled tubes that captures movements of the oval window to transduce vibrations into neural firing.

Basilar membrane A neural pathway within the cochlea that registers the movement of fluid through tiny hair cells on its surface.

Hair cell receptors Sound receptors in the cochlea that transduce fluid movement into neural impulses.

FIGURE 4-16 The external portion of the ear acts to collect sound waves, while the middle ear replicates them on an internal mechanism called the basilar membrane. The movement of this membrane stimulates receptor cells that create neural impulses.

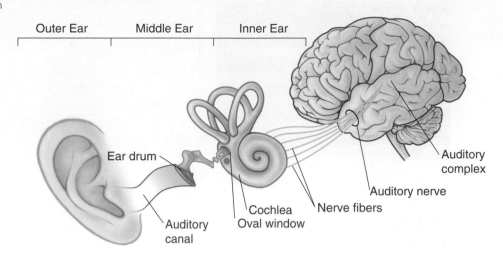

Place theory The notion that the pitch of a sound is determined by the location of the stimulation on the basilar membrane inside the ear.

Frequency theory The notion that the firing rate of neurons is determined directly by the frequency (length of time between sound waves) of the sound.

Chemical senses The two external senses that involve the detection of chemical molecules either dissolved in water (taste) or floating in the air (smell).

cause them to move, the hair cells transduce these signals into patterns of neural activity. This activity then follows a pathway from the inner ear to the thalamus. From there it travels on to either the left or the right *auditory cortex* in the temporal lobes of the brain. All of the neural connections from the right ear go to the left auditory cortex, and all of the connections from the left ear go to the right auditory cortex.

How does the stimulation of hair cell receptors create the experience of hearing? Loudness is recorded by the firing rate of the individual nerve cells and in the total amount of neural activity occurring. However, two theories attempt to explain how we hear pitch. **Place theory** proposes that sound waves of differing frequencies affect different locations along the basilar membrane (Bekesy, 1947). High-frequency sounds move the part of the membrane nearest the oval window, while low-frequency sounds move the entire membrane. **Frequency theory** (Wever, 1949) suggests the firing rate of neurons is determined directly by the frequency (length of time between sound waves) of the sound. In fact, both factors are at work, depending on the particular pitch of the incoming sound: Lower-pitched sounds are detected through increased firing rates, and higher-pitched sounds are detected according to where the neurons are located. Intermediate pitches use both methods. Unlike light, sound is not additive; instead, we hear each low and high pitch in sound separately rather than mixed into a single pitch.

Given this delicate system, our sense of hearing can be very vulnerable to overstimulation. How loud is "too loud"? The measurement unit of sound is the decibel (dB). Daily exposure to sounds over 85 decibels (vacuum cleaners, subways, and lawnmowers) can flatten hair cells over time and cause a gradual hearing loss. Even brief exposure to stimuli over 140 dB (gunshots, amplified rock band, rocket launch) can cause permanent hearing loss (Kryter, 1994). Listening to music at high volumes through the earphones of MP3 players and similar devices can also cause hearing loss (Vogel et al., 2009), and this loss is permanent.

Why are our ears on the sides of our heads? Imagine walking through the woods and hearing a sound nearby. Immediately, you swing your head in the direction of the sound. How does our sense of hearing tell us which way to look? The positions of the ears on opposite sides of the head results in differences in the timing of the sensations they register. The brain calculates a sound's location—below or above; right or left; near or far—by using these differences in the volume and timing of the arrival of sound waves at each ear (Phillips & Brugge, 1985). In trying to find sound sources, we often tilt our heads one way or another, providing further cues about where sounds are occurring in the world around us.

The Sense of Smell

Taste and smell are **chemical senses** because they involve the detection of chemical molecules either dissolved in water (taste) or floating in the air (smell). The proximity of the mouth and nose also means that the two senses work together to produce the sensations we experience in a process called **sensory interaction**. If you can recall eating a meal when you have a cold, the food may have seemed less tasty. These two senses provide important clues about the foods we eat, such as whether they are potentially nutritious or poisonous. These sensory systems also help motivate us to eat.

Olfaction is far less important to us than to other mammals; for example, dogs have about 100 million smell receptors, compared to just 10 million in people. We take in odors through olfactory receptors located at the top of our nasal cavity (and some in the throat). The neurons leading from these receptors are bundled together in the olfactory nerve, which travels to the **olfactory bulb** located at the base of the brain FIGURE 4-17. The receptors for odors appear to be highly specialized, with thousands of different types, each responding to a different odor molecule in the air (Buck & Axel, 1991). The *lock-and-key theory* (Amoore et al., 1964) suggests that odor molecules may fit into differently shaped sites on the receptors, triggering the transduction to neural stimulation. Unlike the visual and auditory senses, much of the processing of the neural activity from odor receptors occurs in the sensory organ rather than the brain. Olfaction is the only sense that does not pass through the thalamus for further processing in the cortex but is sent directly to the amygdala within the limbic system, which processes emotion and memory. As a result, smell is a link to memories and feelings, even after many years (Chu & Downes, 2000).

Olfaction The sense of smell.

Olfactory bulb The processing center for smell located at the base of the brain.

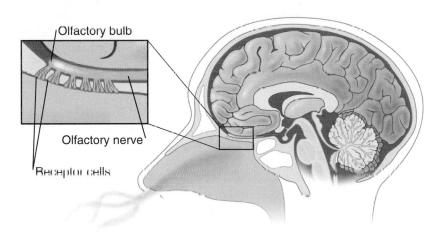

FIGURE 4-17 Unlike other senses, much of the neural processing of smell takes place in the sense organ itself, rather than the cortex.

You may find there are some smells you react to strongly and others you can't detect. Studies have found that individuals can't be characterized as more or less sensitive to odors than others (Koelega, 1994); instead, you may be more sensitive than someone else to some specific odor. **Pheromones** are biochemical odors emitted by people that others can recognize. Parents can recognize their children by smell, and infants respond to the smell of their mother's breast (Russell, 1976). Women are sensitive to the pheromones produced during the menstrual cycle. In one study, women were exposed to armpit sweat (applied to their upper lips) from other women, and they developed coordinated menstrual cycles even though they had no other contact (Stern & McClintock, 1998). Pheromones may also play important roles in sexual attraction, so our sense of smell may affect our social relationships.

The Sense of Taste

Clearly, our sense of taste, or **gustatory** sense, greatly affects our behavior, motivating us to eat when we're not hungry, to choose some foods over others, and to avoid some foods completely. Taste buds are neural receptors located mostly on the tongue FIGURE 4-18, and they are shaped like the segments of an orange. The buds have tiny hair-like projections through a central pore. Water-soluble chemicals in food stimulate the taste buds to transduce this chemical energy into neural signals. There can be several hundred buds located in and around each **papillae** (the visible bumps we see on the tongue). If you've ever burned your tongue on hot food or liquids, you've experienced the death of some of your taste buds! Fortunately, our bodies regenerate taste buds constantly in order to repair the damage.

Pheromone A characteristic biochemical odor emitted by an individual.

Gustatory The sense of taste.

Papillae Visible bumps on the tongue.

FIGURE 4-18 Taste buds are the chemical receptors located in and around papillae in the tongue and mouth. The taste buds are embedded within the papillae, and are made up of taste receptor cells.

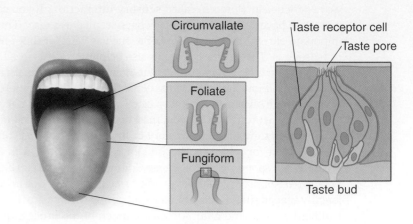

Our sense of taste registers at least five primary qualities: sweet, salty, sour, bitter, and "umami," thought to relate to tastes with high concentrations of proteins (Yamaguchi & Ninomiya, 2000). These tastes may help us to select food, because sweet-tasting foods like fruit are generally safe to eat, while the "salty" detectors help us maintain levels of sodium needed in the blood. "Sour" detectors may aid in avoiding spoiled foods, and "bitter" usually signals something poisonous, or at least something to be avoided. However, a wide range of chemical stimuli can activate each type of receptor. For example, more than 50 different binding sites are activated by an equal number of different bitter-tasting chemicals. Our experience of different tastes arises from the combinations of stimulated receptors.

While people don't differ in the qualities of receptors, they do show a large variation in the number of taste buds present. Some individuals have as few as 500 taste buds, while others have as many as 10,000 (Bartoshuk, 1993). No other sense involves such large differences in numbers of receptors among individuals. Researchers have found that 25 percent of us are "supertasters" and have a greater number of structures that house taste buds FIGURE 4-19. If you're a supertaster, you may experience an overall higher level of tasting ability than others (Bartoshuk, 2000). And the burning heat set off by the chili pepper ingredient, capsaicin, is more intense in supertasters than in others. But be careful how you test yourself: An aspiring chef challenged his friend to a chili-eating contest and ate a plateful of his hottest sauce to his friend's spoonful. Later that night, the chef was found unconscious and died just hours later (Sims, 2008). Mild adverse reactions to chili peppers can include burning eyes, a streaming nose, and uncontrollable hiccups.

FIGURE 4-19 Some people, called supertasters, are born with many more taste buds. This figure shows two tongues stained with blue food coloring. The top image shows a supertaster, with about 60 fungiform papillae within a 6 mm circle (shown in red). The bottom image shows a tongue with just 16 in the same size area.

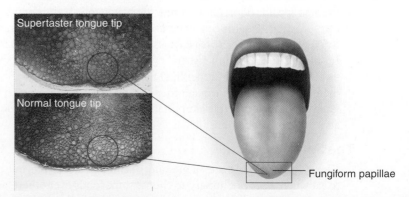

Is it good to be a supertaster? It may not help you, but to a social group, having some individuals who can detect poisonous food would be an advantage. Supertasters appear to be more responsive to many bitter compounds, including those in coffee, grapefruit juice, and green tea. So supertasters may have an advantage in detecting the poisonous compounds in plants, which often taste bitter. They also perceive saccharin and sucrose as sweeter than other people do and are more sensitive to oral pain. It is possible to self-diagnose supertasters at home by careful examination of the tongue. Use blue food dye and look for the number of papillae. Being a supertaster or nontaster represents normal variation in the human population, just like eye or hair color.

The Sense of Touch

Touch is a very important sense for psychology because it connects us to other people. Consider this example: Can you tickle yourself? Tickling is defined as the act of touching a part of the body so as to cause involuntary twitching movements or laughter. Harris and Christenfeld (1999) presented subjects with a "mechanical tickle machine," and found that people laughed just as much when they believed a machine was tickling them. But the tickle response is something you can't do for yourself: It may be a reflex, similar to the startle reflex, that is contingent upon the element of surprise. You can't tickle yourself because you can't surprise yourself in this way. This shows that the physical stimulus—the touch—is interpreted differently based on your knowledge of its source. Clearly, top-down expectations play a role in determining how incoming sensations are perceived and whether sensation is pleasurable.

Our perception of touch relies on separate sensory systems for pressure, temperature, and pain. The entire surface of our bodies responds to pressure against it. Tiny receptors, called **Pacinian corpuscles**, are located in the fatty layer beneath the surface of the skin FIGURE 4-20. These receptors transduce changes in pressure on the skin into neural signals that travel to the brain and "tell" it how much force has been applied and where it is located. Pacinian corpuscles send the brain a pattern that looks exactly like the object itself. So pressing a coin onto the skin registers in the brain as the shape of a circle, called **isomorphic** perception (Burton & Sinclair, 1996).

Pacinian corpuscles are not evenly distributed across the skin; instead, they are gathered more densely in some areas where more sensitivity to touch is required. Think for a minute about what parts of your skin are most sensitive. Your fingers and face are more sensitive than the calf, trunk, and arm, so less pressure is required to register sensation. It makes sense that the face and hands are most sensitive when you consider how important they are for eating, social behavior, and fine movements. FIGURE 4-21 shows how pressure sensation differs across the body, where the lips, hands, feet, and sex organs have more sensory neurons than other parts of the body. To demonstrate this difference in sensitivity, try this experiment: Hold two toothpicks together and press them gently onto your skin, beginning at your shoulder. Reposition the toothpicks, advancing a little farther down your arm and toward your hand and fingers. At your shoulder, the two toothpick points should feel like one. By the time you reach your hand and fingers, you should clearly feel two separate points of pressure.

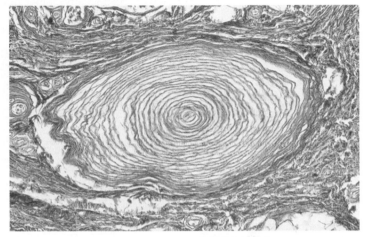

FIGURE 4-20 A sensory receptor called the Pacinian corpuscle is located within the skin.

Pacinian corpuscles Tiny pressure receptors located in the fatty layer beneath the skin.

Isomorphic A representation taking on the same shape or form as the object itself.

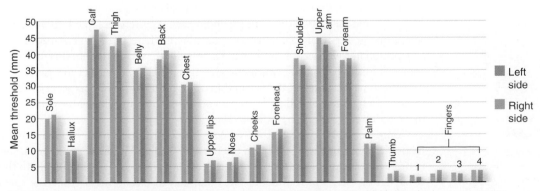

FIGURE 4-21 This map of the body shows that some areas have greater sensitivity (require less pressure to recognize touch, shown by shorter bars) than others. For example, touch on the face is easier to detect than on the trunk of the body.
Source: Data from Weber, E. H. (1978.) E. H. Weber: The sense of touch. [translated from De pulsu, resorptione, auditu et tactu: Anatationes anatomicae et physiologicae by E. H. Weber, 1834]. New York: Academic Press.

Imagine grasping a toasted marshmallow and an ice cube in your hand at the same time. What sensation would you expect to feel? When a person grasps two braided water pipes—one with cold water running through it and one with warm water—the sensation they experience is, "very hot!" This surprising result is based on how the sensory receptors recognize temperature (Casey et al., 1993). Parts of the skin have receptors responding to cold, while nearby areas have receptors responding to warmth. When both types of responses occur at the same time, the brain interprets simultaneous firing as "burning hot." Neuroimaging studies show that gripping warm and cold bars at the same time activates brain regions responsive to pain (Craig et al., 1996). While you may think of pain as occurring on the skin, pain can and does register through any sensory receptor. Deafening sounds, blinding lights, and spicy-hot foods produce pain as readily as sunburn. But most importantly, pain goes beyond sensation in that many psychological factors affect our perception of pain. When asked by his dentist "Where does it hurt?" the philosopher Bertrand Russell replied, "In my mind, of course." Our top-down expectations about pain can greatly change our experience of it.

How does sensation translate to the perception of pain in the mind? Pain is critically important for survival, as it indicates damage to the body. Unlike other senses, there are multiple sensory receptors that detect pain and multiple routes for the processing of pain sensations. First, there is a simple reflex in the interneurons located in the spine that connect incoming sensory fibers and outgoing movement fibers. This circuit allows us to rapidly respond to a painful stimulus even before the perception of pain occurs in the brain FIGURE 4-22. Second, there are pain receptors of two types: fast-acting ones

Gate-control theory The notion that interneurons in the spinal cord act as a gate to block some sensory signals from going to the brain.

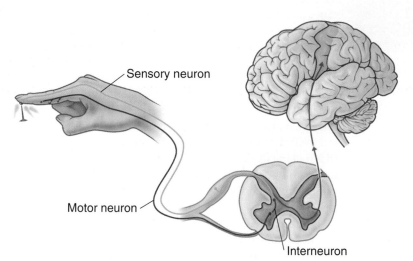

FIGURE 4-22 Pain messages can be quickly responded to based on "interneurons" in the spinal cord that link incoming sensory and motor neurons. As a result, the movement away from the painful stimulus happens well before the pain message reaches the brain.

Sensory neuron

Motor neuron

Interneuron

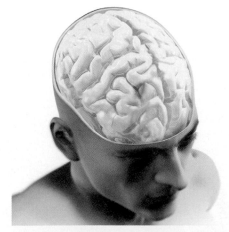

FIGURE 4-23 This drawing shows an area of the cortex called the anterior cingulate cortex. In a study where people played a virtual ball-tossing game, social exclusion showed activation in this area, just as when experiencing physical pain.

that transmit sharp initial pains and slower-acting receptors that provide the sensation of longer-lasting, duller pain. These neural signals for pain travel through two separate pathways and cause two different psychological experiences (Treede et al., 1999). The sensation of pain involves not just a registration of where and what is happening but also an emotionally aversive response that motivates us to avoid the stimulus. In fact, there is some evidence that social pain, such as being rejected by a partner in a game, can cause the same brain response as the perception of physical pain (Eisenberger et al., 2003). The reaction to both social and physical pain activates the same area of the cortex, known as the anterior cingulate (see FIGURE 4-23).

Gate-control theory (Melzack & Wall, 1965) proposes that too much sensory information coming in can overwhelm the nervous system. When that happens, the interneurons in the spinal cord act as a gate, blocking some signals from going to the brain while letting others pass through. The brain may also send messages to the spinal cord to open or close these gates, controlling the amount of sensation transmitted. Pain can be also be "gated" by skin receptors, so that massaging your bumped elbow acts to "close the gate" and prevent pain signals from reaching the brain. Top-down processing can be very influential in the processing of pain signals. For example, while playing a sport, you may not feel a cut until after you stop playing. Pain can be controlled by changing the context, such as the generation of endorphins, drugs, massage, acupuncture, and competing stimulation. One particularly helpful method is distraction. In studies of pain tolerance, managing intense discomfort is aided by focusing attention on a pleasant picture, music, film, or even just a familiar mental image (Villemure & Bushnell, 2002). Expectant mothers are taught this "focal point" technique, along with breathing exercises, to help cope with labor pain.

The mind exerts plenty of control over what we experience as pain. In the **placebo effect**, people are given a treatment that is known to have no effect on pain, such as a sugar pill; nonetheless, some report their experience of pain is reduced significantly. This is a great example of how top-down processing provides expectations for our experience. In the placebo effect, expectations are so strong that we actually experience what we believe we should! One study of postoperative pain following the extraction of a molar tooth found that a saline injection was as potent as a 6- to 8-mg dose of morphine (Levine et al., 1981). In addition, our memory for pain may be quite inaccurate, focusing on the peak amount of pain and the amount of pain perceived at the end of an experience, called the "peak-end rule" (Kahneman et al., 1993). What if you had to choose whether to have your colonoscopy extended for a short interval? It would seem obvious that a shorter duration would be less painful; however, people with the added time reported less pain because the extra period involved less pain at the end of the experience. Tapering the experience so that the end period was less painful actually changed people's perception of the total pain they endured (Redelmeier et al., 2003). Pain perception clearly demonstrates the interaction of bottom-up sensory processes and top-down perceptual processes. It is to these perceptual processes that we now turn.

Placebo effect Feeling benefit or improvement from a treatment known to have no effect.

Extrasensory perception (ESP or psi) Detecting information without knowing its sensory source.

CONCEPT LEARNING CHECK 4.3 | *Methods of Sensory Transduction*

Each of the five sensory organs has a different means of transducing physical energy to neural stimulation. Identify which sense fits with each description of neural stimulation:

1. _____ Movement of a tiny hair cell on a membrane

2. _____ Fitting of a chemical molecule into a specific site

3. _____ Breakdown of pigment after exposure to light

4. _____ Compression of a receptor's shape

5. _____ Dissolved chemicals matching one of five qualities

CRITICAL THINKING APPLICATION

As we've seen, sensation and perception involve the interaction of the external stimulus with internal expectations. If we don't know or recognize the sensory source of our perception, it is termed **extrasensory perception (ESP or psi)**. People have reported having the experience of clairvoyance (knowing something beyond the usual senses), telepathy (transferring information between people), psychokinesis (influence of thought on physical events), and premonition (awareness of a future event; Bem, 2011).

For example, one student reported having a premonition: "A week before my grandma died I was on my way to school and for some reason felt compelled to think about her. And then, a week later, she died. I always knew she had health problems, but for some reason, I knew her time was up."

It's tempting to apply a mystical interpretation to these experiences and decide that ESP must be involved. About 57 percent of U.S. adults believe in some form of ESP (CBS News, 2002). Moreover, over one-quarter of Americans say they believe in psychic phenomena, such as communicating with someone who has died,

(Continues)

FIGURE 4-24 The set of five distinct "Zener" cards created by Rhine and Zener to test for extrasensory perception in laboratory studies.

that extraterrestrials have visited earth, or that houses can be haunted (Lyons, 2005). Others enjoy psychics, astrology, and palm-reading sessions. What is the basis for these beliefs?

Parapsychology, the study of extrasensory phenomena, has produced hundreds of controlled studies attempting to document extrasensory perception. In the 1930s, J. B. Rhine and K. Zener created a set of cards with symbols on one side FIGURE 4-24. One procedure tested for *telepathy*, where a "sender" would look at each card in sequence and the "receiver" would try to read the sender's mind. In another procedure, the subject would try to read the card face down (*clairvoyance*, detecting something hidden from view) or try to predict the sequence of cards before they were shuffled (*precognition*). Rhine accumulated more than 100,000 responses from a variety of subjects. In 1934, he reported the results: Using a 25-card deck, his subjects averaged 7.1 correct card identifications, a better-than-chance performance. Another procedure had a sender concentrate on a single visual stimulus, and the receiver chose the stimulus that "matches their thoughts the best" from among four stimuli. Receivers were found to be 32 percent correct, higher than the 25 percent expected by chance (Bem & Honorton, 1994).

Most recently, Bem (2011) presented a set of studies in which people guessed which of two positions on the screen would show a stimulus; after their guess, the position was determined at random by a computer program. Some of the pictures were erotic and others nonerotic. The results were that for erotic pictures only, a very small (53 percent vs. 50 percent expected by chance) but reliable effect occurred in which subjects guessed better than chance. Despite these findings, the vast majority of existing documented studies fail to find evidence of ESP.

It is difficult to conduct rigorous research on ESP and avoid alternative interpretations. Great care must be taken to ensure that no other sensory information is reaching the recipient and that no other non–ESP information will allow them to select their responses (Swets & Bjork, 1990).

Evaluate

1. How would you account for experiences such as those cited previously without appealing to ESP?
2. What type of study would provide convincing evidence about extrasensory perception? Think through the details of your study and how you would rule out any alternative explanations.
3. What type of study would convince you that ESP does not exist?

4.4 Perception Organizes Sensations

Perceptual processes organize incoming sensations by providing patterns and organizing principles to help us navigate and understand the outside world.

- Describe the principles that organize perception of images.

In order to make sense of the incoming flow of sensations, we need the help of top-down perceptual processes. Sensation and perception processes work together to interpret information using bottom-up sensory stimulation and top-down expectations about what we are going to see or experience. Much of the research on perception has examined the visual system and the cues we use to make sense of incoming images, and we will focus on examples of visual perception.

Form and Pattern Perception

As we saw, the visual system picks out specific features from the stimulus for further processing; then, these features have to be reassembled to recognize objects. To do this, our perception relies on organizational principles—that is, ways of putting together information. As we've seen, visual sensations begin at the retina and are pieced together by feature detectors to create a neural pattern. But how do we then recognize the neural pattern as a familiar form or object, such as an apple? Our perceptual processes have to give meaning to the pattern.

One theory argues that objects are represented in memory by **distinctive features**—that is, those essential physical features that uniquely specify an object (Treisman, 1999). For example, there is a distinctive set of features that allows you to identify a letter even

Parapsychology The study of paranormal or extrasensory phenomena.

Distinctive features The essential physical properties that uniquely identify an object.

MNMMNNMNMMN

FIGURE 4-25 Feature analysis tolerates variation in specific features, while detecting the distinctive features that distinguish among similar objects like letters.

though many specific aspects of the image may vary FIGURE 4-25. The more distinctive the differences from objects around it, the easier it is to pick out a given object. On the other hand, the presence of more perceptual cues may make some features "pop out" during a visual search, indicating that some features are just easier to detect than others FIGURE 4-26. The feature detection cells in the occipital lobe detect more complex patterns of features, and may look for complex forms called **geons** that capture geometrical shapes like cylinders and pyramids (Biederman, 1987; see FIGURE 4-27). Organizing principles help by providing top-down expectations for the objects we're looking for within the incoming stimulus information.

Gestalt Organizing Principles

Gestalt psychologists (Wertheimer, 1912) identified organizing principles we use to identify objects. **Gestalt** means "whole," reflecting the belief that the whole emerges in perception and is more than simply "the sum of its parts." In other words, perception involves both what is "out there" and what comes from "inside the mind." Both bottom-up information from a sensory system and top-down perceptual processes are needed to create understanding.

Figure and Ground

A major problem that must be solved by our visual system is figure and ground—that is, determining what aspects in a scene are the figure (the object of interest) and what parts comprise the background. Sometimes the difference between a target figure and its surrounding ground is unclear. To the retina, the patterns of brown and white in this illustration have no meaning. The retina can only faithfully reproduce where the shapes occur on the image. To perceive the figure, our sense of sight draws on organizational principles.

> **Geon** A simple three-dimensional form that, in combination, can create any shape.
>
> **Gestalt** The "whole," reflecting the belief that the whole emerges in perception and is more than simply "the sum of its parts."

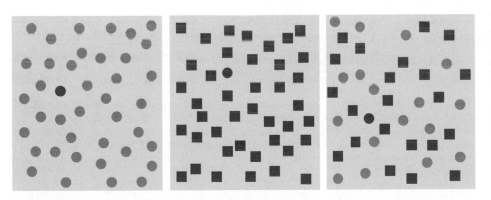

FIGURE 4-26 Scan through the figures looking for a red circle. Is it equally easy to find in all three panels? Chances are good you found the red circle easiest to find in the first panel, where it "pops out," and hardest in the last where it blends in with other red objects.

Geons   Objects

FIGURE 4-27 Recognition of the form of an object like a cup may require piecing together constituent parts, represented as "geons."

Our top-down expectations lead us to "fill in" missing edges of shapes, and finally to pick out the figure of interest from the background.

Perceptual Grouping

Our perception of visual images depends on organizing principles called the **laws of perceptual grouping**. One principle is *similarity*, in which pieces of images that appear similar in some way (in color, size, or orientation) are assumed to part of the same object. A second principle is *proximity*: If images are close together, they are likely to be part of the same object. The principle of *continuity* tells us that objects that touch each other are also likely to be parts of the same object. Finally, closure helps us fill in missing parts of images in order to perceive a whole object. These perceptual organization principles, summarized in FIGURE 4-28, help us to group related information within an image and figure out what parts belong to which objects.

These laws of perceptual grouping take us beyond what we physically see in the world to a pattern of perception based on expectations about visual objects. When patterns are incomplete, we tend to fill in the missing information in order to perceive the whole we expect to see (Rumelhart et al., 1986; FIGURE 4-29). The laws of perceptual grouping allow us to perceive a whole based on fragments and create an image where nothing is actually visible. The importance of organizational principles is illustrated by **reversible figures** in which two separate interpretations are suggested by the same image FIGURE 4-30. Another example of how organizational principles operate comes from **impossible figures**, which employ cues suggesting multiple, conflicting organizing principles FIGURE 4-31.

Visual **illusions** are images that create a misperception of the world. They make the point that what is "out there" in the stimulus goes through a great deal of perceptual processing to arrive at a meaningful interpretation of an image. By examining how illusions mislead our perceptions, we gain insight into how perceptual processing works. For the

Laws of perceptual grouping Simple organizational principles that help to interpret image elements, including similarity, proximity, continuity, and closure.

Reversible figure An image that can be understood with two different interpretations.

Impossible figure An image that can't be resolved into a single consistent interpretation.

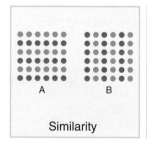
Similarity

Proximity

Continuity

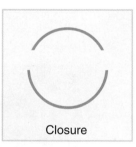
Closure

FIGURE 4-28 Organizing principles help us create a coherent image. **A** is seen as rows of dots, while **B** is seen as columns of dots. The *similarity* of their color helps to organize the image. The second image shows "four sets of double lines" rather than "eight lines" because *proximity* organizes the information. The *continuity* of line segments helps us see two lines overlapping in the top image; however, the two images below it suggest they could be two non-overlapping lines. Finally, the principle of *closure* fills in missing parts to help us perceive a whole object.

FIGURE 4-29 Missing information is readily filled in by our perceptual processes based on what we expect to see.
Source: Adapted from Kanizsa, G, (1955). Margini quasi-percettivi in campi con stimolazione omogenea. Rivista di Psicologia 49*(1): 7–30.*

FIGURE 4-30 Two opposing images. One shows a series of white urns, while the other shows two figures facing one another in silhouette.

Depth perception The detection of the distance of a stimulus from the body.

Binocular cues Ways to determine depth of field that require having two eyes.

Retinal disparity Two slightly different images falling on each retina because of their distance from one another on the face.

most part, the laws of perceptual grouping work so well at processing outside stimuli that we don't even notice occasional inconsistencies in our perception.

Depth Perception

Accurately estimating how far away an object is may be useful and sometimes essential. **Depth perception** tells us how far to reach for an object, how to navigate through space, or whether to duck when a ball is flying at us (Gibson, 1988). We perceive depth through principles that make the best use of the limited information that reaches our sensory organs. Remember that the retina provides only two dimensions (height and width in a two-dimensional plane), while the world has three! The missing dimension, depth, is the distance to a given object. We need ways to translate a proximal (nearby) stimulus (the sensations registering on our receptors) into a perceived distal (distant) stimulus—the actual object out there in the world. Our visual system uses two sources of information for depth: binocular cues and monocular cues.

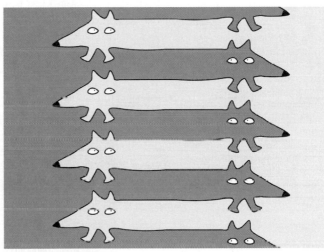

FIGURE 4-31 In some visual illusions, the laws of perceptual organization help to construct an image that is impossible in the physical world. In this image space between a series of orange foxes becomes a series of white foxes.

You might expect that having two eyes is a big advantage in perceiving depth, but **binocular cues** are of limited use. One such cue, **retinal disparity**, arises from our eyes being a couple of inches apart. Close both of your eyes, then open one at a time. You can see that each eye has a slightly different image. Your brain merges the images, and as it does so, it uses their differences to create an effect of depth. You can prove this to yourself by rapidly blinking first one eye, then the other. This provides some information about how far away the object is because the closer the object is, the more the locations of the images on the two retinas will differ. However, very distant objects will produce very similar images on the two retinas. Special neurons located in the visual cortex use this retinal information to determine depth (Cumming & DeAngelis, 2001). Technology for three-dimensional viewing of movies makes use of retinal disparity cues by projecting a slightly different image to each eye using special viewing glasses.

The second binocular cue is literally right in front of your face: **convergence**. Your eyes provide muscle movement cues as they work to coordinate focus on objects just in front of you. If you hold your arm out to focus on your finger and then draw your finger close to your nose, you reach a point where your eyes appear to "cross" the images. This muscular cue tells you when an object is very close to you.

Most commonly, we judge distance from cues that are available to a single eye, called **monocular cues**. If you close one eye, you can still use all of these cues to detect the distance of an object on the single retinal image you see. These cues have long been used in art to portray three dimensions on the two-dimensional surface of a canvas FIGURE 4-32. Our visual system uses these same cues to give us the impression of depth in the physical world FIGURE 4-33. By exaggerating these same cues, artists can create two-dimensional

Convergence A cue to depth based on the muscle movement of your eyes as they work to coordinate focus on objects in front of you.

Monocular cues Ways of determining the distance of an object that require a single eye.

FIGURE 4-32 Pictorial cues are used to suggest the depth of field in artistic images. Spot the depth cues in this image. We automatically perceive the foreground as closer to us because of its coarser texture, its greater detail, the relative size of the posts, relative heights of objects in the image, the interposition of objects, and the linear perspective of walls appearing to converge in the distance.

images that convey the illusion of three-dimensionality in an extremely realistic way FIGURE 4-34. In addition to pictoral cues, **accommodation** of the eye muscles as we focus our vision on near or far objects also provides a monocular cue about depth of field. These binocular and monocular cues to depth, and those for detection of motion, are shown in TABLE 4-4.

Perception of Motion

Motion perception involves only monocular cues, even though the objects are moving in three-dimensional space. In perceiving real movement, we rely on two types of cues to tell us how far away objects are. **Motion parallax** involves noting that objects close to you are moving past you faster than objects farther away. This effect is seen along the road where the edges of the roadway move past you faster than faraway objects on the horizon FIGURE 4-35. The second movement cue to depth is called **kinetic depth effect**. Imagine watching the shadow from an object (like a cat) lit by a car headlight. If the object rotates, a viewer can readily perceive the shape of the object just from seeing the changing shadow pattern (Wallach & O'Connell, 1953). We also readily extract structure from motion of points of light we see in a moving image, even with little information available. When viewed as a video, people can readily see a dozen moving light points, attached to the joints of the body, as a moving human figure (Johansson, 1973). Biological motion is a highly complex motion pattern and demonstrates the sophistication of pattern analysis in the brain.

FIGURE 4-33 We use a variety of cues to interpret visual depth in the physical world. A. Relative height: Objects higher in the image are more distant. B. Texture gradient: Closer images have more coarse texture. C. Linear perspective: Parallel lines appear to converge in the distance. D. Shading: Patterns of light and shadow suggest angles and shapes.

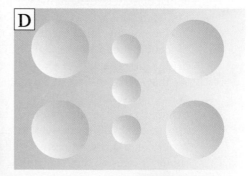

FIGURE 4-34 Artist Julian Beever demonstrates how three-dimensional perception can be created from two-dimensional cues in his art using chalk drawings on pavement. From the perspective shown, the image appears to be three dimensional; however, the actual drawing exaggerates the swimmer's extended leg disproportionately in order to create the impression of depth.

TABLE 4-4 Summary of Distance Cues

	Cues
Binocular (requires both eyes)	Convergence
	Retinal disparity
Monocular (requires one eye)	
Eye muscle	Accommodation
Movement	Motion parallax
	Kinetic depth effect
Pictorial	Size of object
	Height in plane
	Linear perspective
	Interposition
	Texture gradient
	Shading
	Atmospheric perspective

Accommodation Movement in an eye's muscles as we focus our vision on near or far objects provides a monocular depth cue.

Motion parallax The interpretation that objects close to you are moving past you faster than objects farther away.

Kinetic depth effect The movement of a three-dimensional object reveals its shape.

Phi phenomenon A series of static images viewed in sequence are interpreted as a moving image.

Constancy The assumption that objects in the physical world do not change spontaneously, but maintain their size, shape, color, and brightness over time.

Interestingly, our perception of motion is independent of retinal motion. An early demonstration of this was the **Phi phenomenon**, in which light bulbs turned on and off in a series appear to us as a moving light. For example, a lighted sign with bulbs flashed on and off in sequence appears as a moving light to the viewer. Following the Gestalt principle of continuity, we "see" a moving light rather than the actual independent sources in sequence. Film presents a series of still images to the eye, and the mind connects them to give the perception of continuous movement. Another type of motion illusion arises when a static image appears to be moving due to the effects of interacting color contrasts. If you look at the image in FIGURE 4-36, it appears that the forms are moving; however, if you keep your eyes still on a corner of the image, you will see that it is not. The illusion of motion results primarily from differences in the speed of processing the contrast in colors where the neurons respond faster to the higher-contrast white and black elements than to the lower-contrast light gray and dark gray elements (Backus & Oruc, 2005). But even these movement illusions depend only on monocular cues. We rely on organization provided by the laws of perceptual grouping to perceive three-dimensional objects from two-dimensional retinal images.

Perceptual Constancy

We assume that objects in the physical world don't change spontaneously. Instead, real objects maintain **constancy** in their size, shape, color, and brightness over time. Our perceptual system uses this knowledge to account for the many changes in form or shape that appear on the retina, and we automatically link them together to produce a mental image in which the object remains constant. For example, if you hold a coin in your fingers, you can turn it from a front view, where you see a circle shape, to a side view, where you see only the thin edge. That means the shape of the coin on the retina has drastically changed, but it still looks like the same quarter to you. Shape constancy allows us to recognize an object even though its shape might appear quite different. The sensations registered on the retina are overridden by the higher-order, top-down processing in the brain, which is saying, "Yes, this looks a little different now than before, but it's really the same object. It must have spun in the air." Constancy is important because it allows us to see very different sensory input as part of the same external object.

FIGURE 4-35 The faster moving objects near to you, such as the car, are compared to objects in the distance (such as the trees behind) in the depth cue of motion parallax.

We perceive an object as having a set size even though its size on the retina changes with its distance, a principle known as size constancy. As a person walks towards you,

FIGURE 4-36 This image uses color contrast to give the impression of concentric movement. As your eyes naturally move while examining the image, the change in color contrast falling on receptors gives you the illusion that the circles are moving.

their image on the retina gets larger; however, we know people don't grow or shrink instantly in the world. We rely on this knowledge to conclude that a person that appears larger on the retina must be closer to us. The relative size of each person in the figure provides a cue about how far away each person is from the viewer. Since physical size stays constant, the perceived size on the retina as we move closer or farther away from an object tells us how far away it is. However, we have no problem recognizing that it's the same object even though its shape on the retina is quite different. These constancies in shape and size are important because, as observers, we move around in the world and our sensory information changes however, we don't perceive the objects themselves as changing.

Light and shadow also produce different patterns on the retina, where the brightness of parts of an object may make it appear dramatically different in the image formed on the retina. However, we have no trouble recognizing the whole object based on our assumption of brightness constancy. We are adept at "filling in" our perception so that the object appears as a whole even if we actually see only its parts. Similarly, inconsistencies in color are "filled in" by the perceptual processes so that missing spots of color are not detected, called color constancy. For example, a shadow falling across the hood of a car doesn't change your perception of the car as a single solid color.

The **Ames room** illusion (named after American ophthalmologist Adelbert Ames, Jr., in 1934) plays with our sense of size constancy by making two people look very different in size FIGURE 4-37. The room's normal cues about depth (the straight line of the floor and window sills) are hidden by distortions. This illusion shows that our usual perceptual processes can be fooled. Most of the time, however, our perceptual system effectively provides us with the information we need to recognize objects, to determine where they are in space, and to coordinate our actions in relation to them. The key to its success is our ability to provide top-down perceptual processing of incoming, bottom-up information to make sense of the world around us.

CONCEPT LEARNING CHECK 4.4   *Perceptual Organization Principles*

Match the example to the perceptual organization principle.

A. Laws of perceptual grouping: similarity, proximity, continuity, and closure

B. Binocular depth cue: retinal disparity and convergence

C. Monocular depth cue: linear perspective, relative height, interposition, texture gradient, shading, atmospheric perspective, and relative size

D. Motion cues: kinetic depth and motion parallax

E. Constancy: size, shape, brightness, and color

1. _____ Noticing the faces of the first few rows of people sitting in a stadium

2. _____ Seeing a "double" image of a pencil held close to your face

3. _____ Recognizing a globe from the half of a sphere lit by a flashlight

4. _____ Finding two groups of three people sitting near each other in a waiting room

5. _____ Stopping to pick up a quarter stuck on its edge in a sidewalk grate

6. _____ Noticing which wolf standing in a pack is the closest to you

7. _____ Detecting the shape of a tumbling box by watching its shadow

8. _____ Seeing a large train approaching at a distance

9. _____ Recognizing a black snake as it moves through the shadows of a bush

10. _____ Following a straight line when two paths in the wood intersect

4.5 Experience and Perception

Perception can be influenced by biological and experiential factors.

■ Give examples of how perception may be altered by experience.

We've seen that perceptual processes rely on experience. Researchers have confirmed that perception is also determined by the habits, tendencies, and styles we bring to bear on our sensations (Wehner & Stadler, 1994).

Development

Are we born with the ability to construct perceptions, or do they depend on experience with the world? In other words, is perception based on "nature," our built-in biology, or on "nurture," the experiences we have? An early experiment tested the relative contributions of nature and nurture in the perceptual ability of babies who can crawl (Gibson & Walk, 1960). A "visual cliff" was designed on a tabletop with a patterned surface on one half and a glass surface on the other half, with the patterned area on the floor below. Would a 6- to 14-month-old baby placed on the table perceive the apparent dropoff and refuse to crawl across it? (See FIGURE 4-38.) Even with their mothers calling them from the "cliff" side, most babies refused to crawl onto the glass surface. This suggests that the ability to perceive depth—so important to survival—may be inborn and not require any experience with the world.

However, 6-month-old babies do have some experience with perception, which may amplify an innate fear of heights. What about younger babies? The difficulty is determining how to ask an infant what she perceives when she is as yet unable to perform many actions upon the world. In a follow-up study with the visual cliff, 2-month-olds showed changes in heart rate when placed over the glass top but not over the patterned top (Campos et al., 1970). These infants showed signs of noticing the difference in depth. So some perceptual abilities are built in to our perceptual system.

Learning

A key aspect of perception that demonstrates the importance of experience is identifying faces (LeGrand et al., 2010). Based on our experience, we "fill in" the expected details of the face and may miss details that differ from our expectations. In FIGURE 4-39, the top two images of an upside-down face may look the same; however, when viewed right side up, as we normally see them, we readily detect the differences in the two images. Unlike most objects, faces are processed holistically rather than as a collection of independent features. Our tendency to see patterns of features as faces, even when occurring in objects like rocks and trees, is illustrated by FIGURE 4-40. This suggests

Ames room An illusion created by adding physical distortions to make a room appear to have a normal rectangular shape so that its contents appear to violate size constancy.

FIGURE 4-37 This room is designed to give the appearance of a level floor, with parallel lines formed by the juncture of the wall and ceiling. The person on the left is thus perceived as bigger because the distance cues are hidden from us. The left corner is actually closer and has a lower ceiling than the right.

FIGURE 4-38 The "visual cliff" apparatus is a table with one half covered by a patterned surface. The other half is made of glass, and the patterned surface is dropped down to the floor. A baby is placed on the patterned side, and its mother attempts to coax the baby to crawl over the glass top to reach her.

FIGURE 4-39 When faces are viewed in an unusual orientation (two top images), they look similar. When viewed right side up, our experience allows us to readily detect the alterations in the left hand image.

Müller-Lyer illusion Two lines of the same length appear to be different if one has inward "arrowhead" extensions compared to outward extensions.

face recognition may be built into the development of perception. In addition, our experience seeing specific faces and similarities among those faces can lead to difficulties in detecting specific kinds of differences among faces. Many studies have shown an "own race" bias in which people are much more accurate in remembering faces of individuals from their own racial group (Meissner & Brigham, 2001). Presumably, greater familiarity with individual faces within your family and ethnic group (called kinship) makes it easier to recognize the subtle variations in new faces.

Culture

Because perception is informed by our experience, culture also plays a role in altering our perception. One example from anthropologist Colin Turnbull (1961) describes a man from the BaMbuti pygmy people, Kenge, whose life experience was limited to densely forested settings. For someone growing up in a rainforest, a view with a very distant horizon perspective would be rare. Turnbull describes taking Kenge from the rainforest to a savanna, where for the first time he viewed a wide plain with very distant objects, such as trees FIGURE 4-41. One of the objects was a large buffalo that was completely unfamiliar to him. Kenge referred to the buffaloes as "insects." To him, their small size on the retina was a cue about their physical size. Because he had no experience with the animal or this depth of perspective, he was unable to interpret the large animal in the distance as different from closer, small insects. This example suggests that the way we interpret objects and scenes depends heavily on our experience within those environments.

Research in anthropology suggests that some perceptual illusions may arise from our experiences with the world and are therefore potentially different among different cultures. The **Müller-Lyer illusion** is experienced by people in Western cultures as the appearance of the "arrowhead" line as shorter than the same line with outward ends FIGURE 4-42. But where does this illusion come from? One theory is

FIGURE 4-40 We readily notice facial images even where unexpected.

FIGURE 4-41 The long distance perspective of a savanna (left) provides many different depth cues than the shorter views in the rain forest (right).

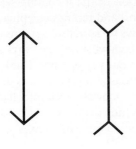

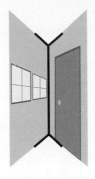

FIGURE 4-42 The Müeller-Lyer figure embedded in the "carpentered world," where the angles adjacent to the vertical line provide information about its distance from the viewer. In contrast, experience with alternative architecture, such as this Zulu kraal, would not provide the same visual experiences.

that these figures suggest depth by perspective, representing familiar lines seen in the world that correspond to depth (Nijhawan, 1991). So the "arrowhead" lines suggest the vertical line is nearer to the viewer, while the open-ended line suggests the vertical line is at a greater distance. Early research suggested that those in environments without these "carpentered world" characteristics would not necessarily see the same meaning in the lines. People from non-Western cultures were found to be less susceptible to the Müller-Lyer illusion (Segall et al., 1966). Perhaps experience with straight lines, rectangular rooms, and right angles is required to develop this organizing principle in perception. The **Ponzo illusion** also relies on the linear perspective cue to judge the distance of objects FIGURE 4-43. Even though all three figures are the same size, the one furthest to the right appears larger because the linear perspective cue makes it appear farther away. Because it relies on constructed lines in the world, this illusion is strongest in Western cultures (Leibowitz et al., 1969).

Comparing people with East Asian and Western cultural backgrounds has revealed other differences in interpretations of images. When asked to describe a simple scene of fish swimming in a tank, Japanese students were much more likely to include descriptions of the context information, while American students described the more salient, focal objects first FIGURE 4-44. Overall, Japanese made 65 percent more observations about the background than did Americans (Masuda & Nisbett, 2001). Cultural experiences may include how information is attended to and processed, resulting in differences in how we see the world based on the social and physical world in which we live.

> **Ponzo illusion** The misjudgment based on linear perspective that identical objects placed within converging lines appears to be of different sizes.

FIGURE 4-43 How do the three men compare? If you perceive the top as bigger than the bottom, you are subject to the Ponzo Illusion, because all three cast the same size image on the retina. The linear perspective cue makes it seem as though the top figure is farther away, and thus it is perceived as larger.

FIGURE 4-44 After viewing a short video of fish moving in a tank, people were asked to describe what they saw. American and Japanese participants differed in what they emphasized in their reports, and how much attention they paid to the background context.

All instances of perception involve the interpretation of the incoming sensory information based on our experiences, cultural definitions, and recent perceptual processing. Perceptual habits develop over time so that the ways we structure our sensations reflect our life history (Gibson, 1992). Further, our beliefs about what we *expect* to perceive play a critical role in matching the incoming sensations to our perceptions. Think back to the story at the beginning of the chapter: My expectations about professors did not yet include an individual like the one I encountered on the sidewalk. Examples like this illustrate that our perception depends heavily on the interaction of the external sensation and the top-down perceptual expectations we bring to bear on our experiences.

CONCEPT LEARNING CHECK 4.5   *The Role of Experience in Perception*

1. Imagine that you were raised in a rainforest environment. The vegetation is very dense, little light reaches the ground, and the coloration of plants and animals is vivid. Now, imagine you are transplanted at your current age to Greenland, an open plain with little vegetation ringed with jagged cliffs. Based on your experience, what specific perceptual cues would be more difficult to make use of in your new home?

4.6 The Role of Attention

Sensation and perception depend on our choices about what available information to attend to given the limits of our capacity for attention.

■ Describe how attention enhances and limits perception.

To further understand our perceptions, we return to the idea that all of the information available in the physical world—what's "out there"—is not necessarily included in the internal representation created in the mind—what's "in here." **Attention** involves awareness of the sensations and perceptions that are a focus of thinking at any given time. When we miss information in the world that could be detected, it reveals more about how normal perceptual processing takes place.

Selective Attention

A compelling demonstration of this phenomenon is provided by research on **inattentional blindness**. Imagine watching a video in which six people throw two basketballs to each other. Your job is to pay attention to the team of three people wearing black t-shirts and to count the number of passes that take place among them throughout the video. Most people focus on the team they are assigned to, and they closely monitor the number of passes that take place within the two-minute video. Now suppose that, midway through the video, someone in a gorilla suit enters the scene, stands in the middle of the picture, and pounds his chest. Surely anyone would notice something so unusual! However, most of the subjects in the study did not notice the gorilla shown in FIGURE 4-45. For those counting the passes, more than 70 percent completely missed the presence of the gorilla in the midst of this

Attention Awareness of the sensations and perceptions that are a focus of thinking at any given time.

Inattentional blindness Failing to process an object clearly present in a scene.

FIGURE 4-45 Three frames from the opaque "gorilla" event in the selective-looking paradigm. The unexpected object (a person in a gorilla suit) was visible for 5 seconds as it traversed the visual scene.

scene (Simons & Chabris, 1999). When not told to count passes, everyone watching the video readily detects the presence of the gorilla. This study demonstrates that what appears in front of us is not necessarily what appears in our perception of the world. Rather, our impressions of the world around us are caused by our attention to sensory information as well as the perceptual principles we use to process sensations in the physical world.

We have the ability to focus on some information while ignoring other stimuli. Our attention to external stimulation is selective, meaning we do not simultaneously attend to all of the stimuli occurring around us (Lavie & Tsal, 1994). In **selective attention**, you choose to perceive only what's currently relevant to you (Johnston & Dark, 1986). For example, you listen to your friend's voice in a crowded restaurant, ignoring the many other sounds present. Selective attention narrows your awareness to particular sensations, at the same time leaving you unaware of others. Your perception depends both on what sensory information is present around you and which stimuli you decide to attend to and which you decide to ignore (Simons & Levin, 1998).

The fact that we often miss very obvious external stimuli may lead to some concerns about our abilities to process needed information. Why don't we simply process all of the information our sensory receptors capture? The reason is that our capacity for processing sensory information is limited. Only so much information can be processed at one time. It is as if we have a "gatekeeper" to control the flow of information over time (Broadbent, 1958). Therefore, we sometimes experience **change blindness**, in which some features of a scene change (such as a car pulling in front of you), but you fail to notice because you are not attending to that information. Even though real objects are there in the environment, we may sometimes completely miss them because we choose not to pay attention (Galpin, Underwood, & Chapman, 2008).

At the same time, we may be unable to resist processing some information despite our intention to ignore it. When experienced readers look at a familiar word, they process its name and meaning automatically. It is very difficult to look at a word and not think about its name, even when doing so interferes with a task. In a classic study, Stroop (1935) demonstrated this by asking people to look at a series of words and report only the color of the ink for each FIGURE 4-46. Most people cannot completely ignore the words and simply name the colors, even when we try to suppress this well-practiced skill of reading. Somtimes, automatic processes break through our attempts to control attention.

However, most often, we can decide to select and focus our attention on specific aspects of the world around us. Doing so allows us to process some information deeply and to use our cognitive resources to our best advantage. It also means that we may miss important information even when it's right in front of us. As we've seen, some aspects of our environment seem to demand our attention, especially when their use is well practiced. The result is that we are not always in control of whether important information in our environment becomes part of our perception of the world.

Selective attention Intentionally attending to one specific task.

Change blindness A change occurs between two viewings of a scene, but it is not noticed.

Divided Attention

What happens to those sensations that are not given attention? It appears they are not "turned off" but continue to receive some level of processing. For example, if you are

Blue **Red** Yellow **Green Orange** Purple

Yellow Blue Orange **Blue Purple** Red

Red Green **Purple** Yellow Blue **Orange**

Purple Red **Green Blue** Yellow **Purple**

FIGURE 4-46 Try to say the name of the color of ink only, as quickly as you can, for each of the words in the figure. You will find it difficult to ignore what the words say.

Cocktail party phenomenon
Hearing your name mentioned despite not attending to its source.

Divided attention The process of attending to two or more tasks to perform them at the same time.

listening to a conversation at a party, you may be aware of a nearby conversation but not of its content. Then, when someone in the other group mentions your name, your attention is immediately and automatically drawn to that conversation, referred to as the **cocktail party phenomenon** (Cherry, 1953; Moray, 1970). So if the unattended information is being filtered out at some level, it must occur after the sounds have been identified as words.

But how do we sort out one message from several others? And when do we become overloaded by incoming information? People often report that they are quite good at doing two things at once, such as listening to music while studying or having a conversation while watching a movie. When you try to do two things at once—say, driving while talking on a cell phone—you are juggling two different sources of sensory input at the same time. **Divided attention** is the process of attending to two or more tasks to perform them at the same time (Pashler, 1998). Coordinating senses often works well; however, when you must react suddenly to changes in sensation, your response time is slowed if you are trying to follow two sources of sensory input. For example, people in driving simulators showed slower reactions to brake lights and stop signs when talking on cell phones (Strayer et al., 2003).

An active task like a cell phone conversation detracted from driving performance, while a passive task like listening to the radio did not. Using a phone—hands free or not—resulted in dangerous delays in driving responses. One study estimated that using a cell phone while driving makes an accident four times more likely (McEvoy et al., 2005). A University of Utah study found motorists who talk on cell phones while driving are as impaired as drunken drivers with blood-alcohol levels at the legal limit of 0.08 percent (Strayer et al., 2006). Dividing attention between tasks is sometimes possible, but not when one of the tasks requires full attention in order to respond to important changes (Levy & Pashler, 2008). Studies show that, while practice improves performance, it is simply not as good as undivided attention (Wickens et al., 1983).

Summary of Multiple Influences on Sensation and Perception

Our minds direct our perception, piecing together information, filling in missing pieces, and looking for confirming evidence that gives us our psychological sense of constancy in the world. These top-down processes work to provide organization for the incoming bottom-up information arriving from the sensory organs.

Multiple influences contribute to our sensations and perceptual processes. We share many biological features of our sensory organs with other animals. However, we differ from them, and even from other mammals, in our use of these organs; for example, we are much less likely to use our sense of smell to recognize others. Human evolution presumably led to our greater emphasis on visual and auditory processing. Biological influences have created specific sensory receptors capable of transducing different forms of physical energy (e.g., light waves, odor molecules) into neural impulses. Similarly, areas of the brain in the cortex have specialized to process sensory information, such as visual information in the occipital lobe and auditory information in the temporal lobe. However, the environment we experience also plays an important role in sensation and perception. We recognize objects and sensations through our familiarity with them, and choose to attend to them or ignore them. Our experiences provide key principles to help us organize the chaotic information coming from our senses into patterns we recognize. And interpreting these patterns often depends on the special, formative social and cultural experiences that shape our understanding of the external world.

Our minds make sense of what is "out there" in the world to produce our internal psychological experience. Said another way, we tend to "see what we believe" rather than "believe what we see." As Albert Einstein said, "Reality is merely an illusion, albeit a very persistent one."

CONCEPT LEARNING CHECK **4.6**   *The Role of Attention in Perception*

---

1. Design a cell phone system that would be safe to use while driving. How would you use the principles of attention to help organize the incoming and outgoing information?

Visual Overview Transduction from Physical Energy to Neural Signals

Each of the sensory organs—eye, ear, nose, mouth, and skin—has a unique receptor for transforming a form of physical energy (e.g., light and sound waves, chemical molecules, pressure and temperature) into a neural code that is interpreted in specific areas within the cortex.

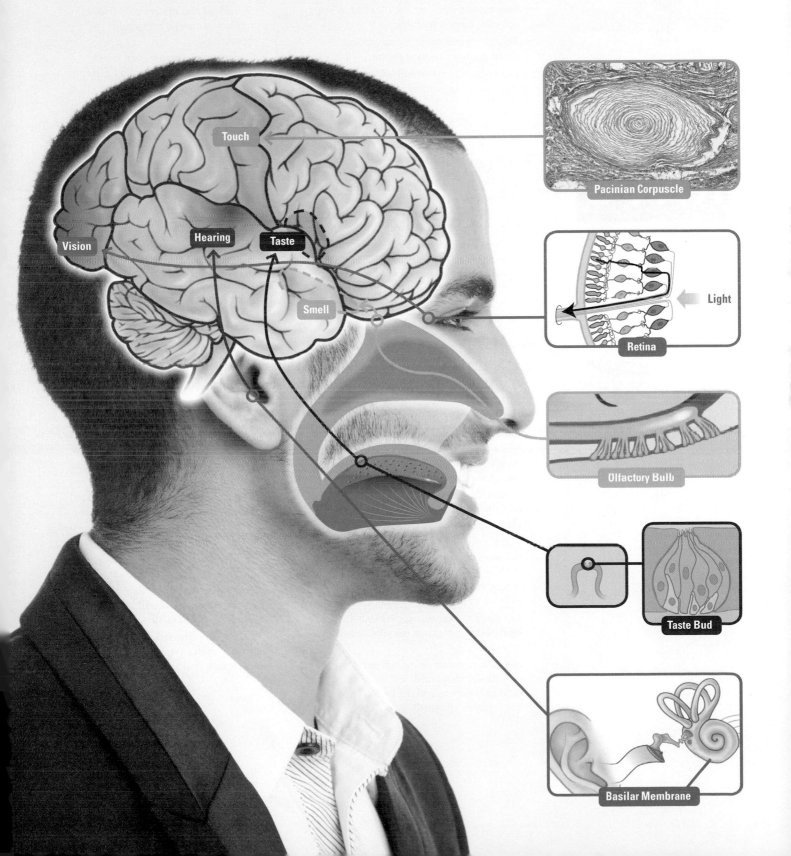

Touch

Vision

Hearing

Taste

Smell

Pacinian Corpuscle

Light

Retina

Olfactory Bulb

Taste Bud

Basilar Membrane

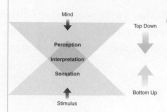

4.1 The Interaction of Sensation and Perception

- We actively create our understanding of the external world around us.
- Sensations result from the stimulation of a sense organ by a stimulus.
- Perception makes use of expectations based on experiences in memory.
- Sensation occurs through bottom-up processing of incoming information, while perception organizes sensations into patterns through top-down processing.
- Sensations and perceptual processes interact to create a meaningful interpretation.
- Perceptual set occurs when recent processing guides continuing perception.

4.2 Sensory Principles

- Our sensory organs share common principles of operation, but each has its own specialized receptor cells to encode stimulus intensity and quality.
- Transduction is the process through which physical energy in the world is translated into neural firing.
- Signal detection theory helps to measure the sensitivity of the senses, called absolute and difference thresholds.
- Some sensation is registered subliminally, without conscious awareness.
- Sensory adaptation occurs quickly when the same stimulation is present over time.

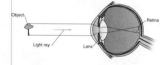

4.3 The Five Major Senses

- The five major sources of external sensations are the eye, ear, nose, mouth, and skin; internal sources include vestibular and kinesthetic senses.
- The sense of vision occurs through the retina, a layer of rod and cone nerve cells lining the back wall of the eye that registers the wavelengths of light.
- Feature detector cells in the visual cortex of the brain pick out patterns and piece them together to recognize objects.
- Color vision is based on a trichromatic theory of red, blue, and green color detectors, and on opponent process theory in which opposing colors are tied together in processing by complex cells.
- The sense of hearing registers sound waves originating from the vibrations of an object.
- Hair cell receptors detect vibrations in the ear's basilar membrane, and recognition of sounds depends on the location and frequency of vibrations.
- Taste and smell involve the detection of chemical molecules in water or air, and they work together in a process called sensory interaction.
- Smell receptors located at the top of the nasal cavity lead into the olfactory bulb and are adept at recognizing individual biochemical odors called pheromones.
- Taste buds are neural receptors located mostly on the tongue's visible bumps called papillae.
- The sense of touch occurs through Pacinian corpuscle receptors located in the fatty layer beneath the skin surface.
- The perception of pain depends on sensory receptors as well as on other psychological influences.
- Information detected without a known sensory source is called extrasensory perception (ESP).

4.4 Perception Organizes Sensations

- Perceptual processes organize incoming sensations into recognizable patterns through a variety of principles.
- We recognize objects by piecing together forms and patterns of distinctive features.
- The whole ("Gestalt") that emerges is more than simply "the sum of its parts."
- In every image, we determine what aspects represent the figure of interest vs. the background.
- Organizing pieces into images is aided by the laws of perceptual grouping, including similarity, proximity, continuity, and closure.
- Depth perception is important to perception because it helps us decide how far away objects are in the world.

- Binocular cues depend on two eyes and include retinal disparity and convergence.
- Most often, we judge distance from monocular cues that are available to a single eye, including linear perspective, relative height, interposition, texture gradient, shading, atmospheric perspective, relative size, and accommodation.
- Perception of motion involves cues including motion parallax and the kinetic depth effect.
- Perceptual constancy is the assumption that real objects don't change their shape, size, brightness, or color despite changes in how they appear to our senses.

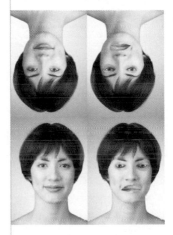

4.5 Experience and Perception

- Biology determines the sensations we can detect, and inborn tendencies to detect depth and faces may exist.
- Perception can be altered by culture, context of processing, and experience.

- Cultural differences in perceptions have been demonstrated with illusions related to a "constructed world."

4.6 The Role of Attention

- Our perception is affected by what we choose to attend to and the limits to our attentional capacity.
- Inattentional blindness results from ignoring stimuli, and change blindness occurs when we fail to notice changing features in a scene.
- Selective attention allows us to choose to perceive only what's currently relevant.

- The cocktail party phenomenon shows some sensations may be processed even without attention.
- We are limited in our ability to divide attention across different sources of sensory input or tasks at the same time.

4.1 The Interaction of Sensation and Perception

1. Your ability to sing along in time with your favorite song on the radio relies on:
   A. perceptual constancy.
   B. top-down processing.
   C. auditory pitch.
   D. absolute thresholds.

2. When getting up at night to use the bathroom, you can navigate in the dark hallway and return without running into any obstacles by using your memory of the rooms. This is an example of:
   A. top-down processing.
   B. bottom-up processing.
   C. perceptual constancy.
   D. absolute threshold.

3. When perceiving our surroundings, we use both top-down and bottom-up processes to make sense of the stimuli. But we rely even more on top-down processing when we find ourselves in _____ contexts.
   A. familiar
   B. unfamiliar
   C. perceptual
   D. artistic

4.2 Sensory Principles

4. Sonja put on a new watch this morning and found it uncomfortable because it was so heavy. However, later, when a friend asked her what time it was, she forgot she was even wearing a watch. This change in sensitivity is known as:
   A. perceptual constancy.
   B. sensory adaptation.
   C. absolute threshold.
   D. just noticeable difference.

5. The smallest difference between two sounds that you can reliably detect (at least half the time) is called the:
   A. absolute threshold.
   B. just noticeable difference.
   C. signal detection.
   D. transduction.

4.3 The Five Major Senses

6. The retina can detect color images with red, blue, and green detector cells called:
   A. cones.
   B. rods.
   C. feature detectors.
   D. ganglions.

7. Each of the five main external senses travels from the sensory organ through the sensory relay station in the brain, the thalamus, and then on to cortical areas, except for:
   A. vision.
   B. hearing.
   C. smell.
   D. touch.

8. Eric has been wearing yellow welding goggles for the past 30 minutes. Based on the opponent-process theory of color vision, when Eric takes off the goggles, he should expect that white objects may temporarily appear to be:
   A. more distant.
   B. less distant.
   C. blue.
   D. green.

4.4 Perception Organizes Sensations

9. The sand at Jason's feet appeared coarse, and he could see the individual grains of sand. However, the sand farther down the beach appeared to be a smooth, tan surface. This apparent difference provides the depth cue of:
   A. light and shadow.
   B. interposition.
   C. texture gradient.
   D. relative size.

10. One binocular visual cue that provides information about how far away something is called:
    A. linear perspective.
    B. interposition.
    C. convergence.
    D. relative size.

11. An oil painting itself can include all of the following cues to depth perception except:
    A. linear perspective.
    B. retinal disparity.
    C. texture gradient.
    D. relative image size.

4.5 Experience and Perception

12. When viewing a complex scene, students from East Asian cultures tended to describe _____ more than those from Western cultures.
   A. the focal figure
   B. carpentered figures
   C. binocular cues
   D. the background context

13. The Müller-Lyer illusion may be interpreted differently by some people based on their:
   A. experience with constructed corners.
   B. artwork.
   C. reading.
   D. perceptual set.

4.6 The Role of Attention

14. People feel able to divide attention between highly practiced, automatic tasks, like reading or driving, and more demanding tasks, like conversation. A recent study of motorists in accidents found:
   A. the accident rate was higher when on the phone.
   B. the accident rate was the same for callers and noncallers.
   C. the accident rate was higher for callers but not those with speakerphones.
   D. the accident rate was lower for those on the phone.

15. Failing to notice the sudden disappearance of an object within a scene is a phenomenon known as:
   A. change blindness.
   B. perceptual set.
   C. selective attention.
   D. divided attention.

CHAPTER DISCUSSION QUESTIONS

1. A surprising fact about human perception is that top-down processes can change how we understand external sources of sensation. Why do you think top-down processes are so important? What advantages and disadvantages does it provide?

2. If you had to live without one of your senses, which one might you choose, and why? How would the lack of that sense affect your everyday life? How might your other senses begin to compensate for the loss?

3. Think of a perceptual illusion you have experienced. What caused the illusion? What does it suggest about how our perceptual processes normally operate?

4. What differences in perception may arise from differences in cultural perspectives? How do culture and experience play roles in sensation and perception? Think of specific examples of how top-down processing may result in two people having different perceptions.

5. Eyewitnesses are often called upon to testify about specific elements of their experiences, such as whether a door was open when they arrived at home or what color shirt a person was wearing. Based on what you read about attention, what kinds of information do you think eyewitnesses will be inaccurate about?

CHAPTER PROJECTS

1. Try to experience limited or altered sensation in one of your sensory organs. For example, wear a thick pair of work gloves, smear Vaseline on a pair of sunglasses, or wear earplugs. See if you can describe the specific problems that arise from your changed sensory processes. What evidence do you find about how other senses make up for the lost sensation?

2. Watch the movie *Rashomon* (1950) by Akira Kurosawa. The film depicts the assault of a woman and her samurai husband through the mutually contradictory accounts of four people. It was remade as a Western, *The Outrage* (1964), and has influenced a variety of subsequent films, such as *Hero*, *Vantage Point*, *Courage Under Fire*, *Basic Instinct*, and *One Night at McCool's*. How is the difference between sensation and perception illustrated by differences in how people perceive the same external event?

CHAPTER KEY TERMS

Absolute threshold	**Bipolar cells**	**Colorblindness**
Accommodation	**Blind spot**	**Cone cells**
Afterimage	**Bottom-up processing**	**Constancy**
Ames room	**Change blindness**	**Convergence**
Attention	**Chemical senses**	**Dark adaptation**
Basilar membrane	**Cochlea**	**Depth perception**
Binocular cues	**Cocktail party phenomenon**	**Difference threshold**

Distinctive features
Divided attention
Extrasensory perception
 (ESP or psi)
Feature detectors
Fovea
Frequency
Frequency theory
Ganglion cells
Gate-control theory
Geon
Gestalt
Gustatory
Hair cell receptors
Illusion
Impossible figure
Inattentional blindness
Isomorphic
Just noticeable difference (jnd)
Kinetic depth effect

Laws of perceptual grouping
Monocular cues
Motion parallax
Müller-Lyer illusion
Olfaction
Olfactory bulb
Opponent process theory
Optic chiasm
Optic nerve
Oval window
Pacinian corpuscles
Papillae
Parallel processing
Parapsychology
Perception
Perceptual set
Pheromone
Phi phenomenon
Photoreceptors
Placebo effect

Place theory
Ponzo illusion
Retina
Retinal disparity
Reversible figure
Rod cells
Selective attention
Sensation
Sensory adaptation
Sensory receptor
Signal detection theory
Stimulus
Subliminal perception
Top-down processing
Transduction
Trichromatic theory
Wavelength
Weber's Law

ANSWERS TO CONCEPT LEARNING CHECKS

4.1 Comparing Top-Down and Bottom-Up Processing

A. Reading a book. [Bottom-up: Piecing together lines to recognize letters; top-down: Anticipating the next word.]

B. Walking down the street and recognizing a friend. [Bottom-up: Identifying the features of a face; top-down: Looking for that friend in the crowd.]

C. Listening to a new song. [Bottom-up: Piecing together tones to recognize melody; top-down: Anticipating the next lyric.]

D. Being tapped on the shoulder when you didn't notice anyone behind you. [Bottom-up: Feeling pressure on your skin at the shoulder; top-down: Recognizing someone wants your attention.]

E. Taking the first spoonful of your favorite food into your mouth. [Bottom-up: Processing the taste spreading on your tongue; top-down: Anticipating what the taste will be.]

4.2 Testing Sensory Thresholds

1. For absolute threshold, you might begin by tasting a sample of 1 ounce of water with no sugar added; then, a sample with one grain of sugar added, then two, and so on until you notice a sweet taste in the water. For difference thresholds, compare the difference between two samples in the series. Does a sample with one more grain taste sweeter to you? Once the water solution is already sweet (contains many grains), adding one more grain to the sample might not make it noticeably sweeter.

4.3 Methods of Sensory Transduction

1. Movement of a tiny hair cell on a membrane. [Hearing]

2. Fitting of a chemical molecule into a specific site. [Smell]

3. Breakdown of pigment after exposure to light. [Vision]

4. Compression of a receptor's shape. [Touch]

5. Dissolved chemicals matching one of five qualities. [Taste]

4.4 Perceptual Organization Principles

1. C [texture gradient]

2. B [retinal disparity]

3. D [kinetic depth]

4. A [proximity]

5. E [shape constancy]

6. C [interposition]

7. D [kinetic depth]

8. E [size constancy]

9. E [brightness constancy]

10. A [continuity]

4.5 The Role of Experience in Perception

1. Living in a dense rainforest would provide little experience with some visual depth cues due to the limited distance you can view. These cues include atmospheric perspective, linear perspective, relative height, relative size, and texture gradient. Once in Greenland, the newness of the open sky perspective would make it harder to make use of the available distance cues.

4.6 The Role of Attention in Perception

1. From studies, we know that talking on a cell phone can compete with responding to visual cues while driving. One solution might be to add tactile or touch alarms to grab attention from drivers when needed. The rumble strips on highways before tollbooths act as an attentional cue using a different physical modality (the sensations of movement produced when the car tires roll over studded cement strips).

4.1 The Interaction of Sensation and Perception

1. B. Rationale: Singing along requires anticipating what stimulus is going to occur next. This requires top-down processing using expectations about what you will perceive.

2. A. Rationale: Navigating from memory involves using your expectations about where objects are, a top-down process, rather than your sensations arising from the actual objects.

3. A. Rationale: Because top-down processing involves expectations from memory, they are made possible by what we already know: the familiar.

4.2 Sensory Principles

4. B. Rationale: The sensations arising from the pressure of the watch on the skin are quickly adapted to by our sensory processing so that the same stimulus over time stops receiving attention, known as sensory adaptation.

5. B. Rationale: The just noticeable difference is defined as the ability to notice a difference between two similar stimuli at least half of the time.

4.3 The Five Major Senses

6. A. Rationale: The cones are the receptor cells in the retina that respond to these three color wavelengths.

7. C. Rationale: Smell is a unique sense in that more of its perceptual processing takes place in the sense organ and in the limbic system rather than in the cortex.

8. C. Rationale: The opponent process theory states that some cells process the presence of opposing colors, blue or yellow and red or green, resulting in afterimages of the opposing color.

4.4 Perception Organizes Sensations

9. C. Rationale: The fine detail of texture that can be detected nearby fades to a more smooth appearance on surfaces farther away.

10. C. Rationale: The only binocular cue (requiring two eyes) is convergence, the muscle movements that coordinate focus on nearby objects.

11. B. Rationale: Retinal disparity is a binocular cue in which the images on the two retinas are slightly different, and unlike the other cues, this cannot be depicted in a two-dimensional image like a painting.

4.5 Experience and Perception

12. D. Rationale: Cultural experiences may include how information is attended to and processed, resulting in differences in how we see the world based on the social and physical world in which we live.

13. A. Rationale: Studies show people are more likely to experience this illusion if they have experience viewing the right angles of constructed rooms.

4.6 The Role of Attention

14. A. Rationale: Dividing attention by talking on the phone while driving showed problems regardless of whether the mode was hands free.

15. A. Rationale: The study involved showing two scenes that were identical except for a missing object. This type of change blindness may be caused by divided or selective attention.

REFERENCES

Abramov, I., & Gordon, J. (1994). Color appearance: On seeing red, or yellow, or green, or blue. *Annual Review of Psychology, 45,* 451–485.

Amoore, J. E., Johnston, J. W., & Rubin, M. (1964). The stereochemical theory of odor. *Scientific American, 210,* 42–49.

Backus, B. T., & Oruc, I. (2005). Illusory motion from change over time in the response to contrast and luminance. *Journal of Vision, 5*(11), 1055–1069.

Bartoshuk, L. M. (1993). The biological basis of food perception and acceptance. *Food Quality and Preference, 4,* 21–32.

Bartoshuk, L. M. (2000). Comparing sensory experiences across individuals: Recent psychophysical advances illuminate genetic variation in taste perception. *Chemical Senses, 25,* 447–460.

Bekesy, G. V. (1947). The variation of phase along the basilar membrane with sinusoidal vibration. *Journal of the Acoustical Society of America, 19,* 452–460.

Bem, D. J. (2011). Feeling the future: Experimental evidence for anomalous retroactive influences on cognition and affect. *Journal of Personality and Social Psychology, 100,* 407–425.

Bem, D. J., & Honorton, C. (1994). Does psi exist? Replicable evidence for an anomalous process of information transfer. *Psychological Bulletin, 115,* 4–18.

Biederman, I. (1987). Recognition-by-components: A theory of human image understanding. *Psychological Review, 94,* 115–147.

Bowmaker, J. K., & Dartnall, H. J. (1980). Visual pigments of rods and cones in a human retina. *Journal of Physiology, 298,* 501–511.

Broadbent, D. E. (1958). *Perception and communication.* London: Pergamon Press.

Buck, L., & Axel, R. (1991). A novel multigene family may encode odorant receptors: A molecular basis for odor recognition. *Cell, 65,* 175–181.

Burton, H., & Sinclair, R. (1996). Somatosensory cortex and tactile perceptions. In L. Kruger (Ed.), *Pain and touch* (pp. 105–177). San Diego: Academic Press.

Campos, J. J., Langer, A., & Krowitz, A. (1970). Cardiac responses on the visual cliff in prelocomotor infants. *Science, 170,* 196–197.

Casey, K. L., Zumberg, M., Heslep, H., & Morrow, T. J. (1993). Afferent modulation of warmth sensation and heat pain in the human hand. *Somatosensory and Motor Research, 10,* 327–337.

CBS News. (2002, April 28). Poll: Most believe in psychic phenomena. CBSNEWS.com.

Cherry, E. C. (1953). Some experiments on the recognition of speech, with one and two ears. *Journal of the Acoustical Association, 25,* 975–979.

Chu, S., & Downes, J. J. (2000). Odour-evoked autobiographical memories: Psychological investigations of Proustian phenomena. *Chemical Senses, 25,* 111–116.

Craig, J. C., Reiman, E. M., Evans, A., & Bushnell, M. C. (1996). Functional imaging of an illusion of pain. *Nature, 384,* 258–260.

Cumming, B. G., & DeAngelis, G. C. (2001). The physiology of stereopsis. *Annual Review of Neuroscience, 24,* 203–238.

Eisenberger, N. I., Lieberman, M. D., & Williams, K. D. (2003). Does rejection hurt? An fMRI study of social exclusion. *Science, 302*(5643), 290–292.

Fisher, G. H. (1968). Ambiguity of form: Old and new. *Perception and Psychophysics, 4,* 189–192.

Galanter, E. (1962). Contemporary psychophysics. In R. Brown, E. Galanter, H. Hess, & G. Mandler (Eds.), *New directions in psychology.* New York: Holt, Rinehart, & Winston.

Galpin, A., Underwood, G., & Chapman, P. (2008). Sensing without seeing in comparative visual search. *Consciousness and Cognition, 17,* 672–687,

Gibson, E. J. (1988). Exploratory behavior in the development of perceiving, acting and the acquiring of knowledge. *Annual Review of Psychology, 39,* 1–41.

Gibson, E. J. (1992). How to think about perceptual learning: Twenty-five years later. In H. L. Pick, P. van den Broek, & D. C. Knill (Eds.), *Cognition: Conceptual and methodological issues* (pp. 215-237). Washington, DC: American Psychological Association.

Gibson, E. J., & Walk, R. D. (1960, April). The "visual cliff." *Scientific American,* 153–154.

Green, D. M., & Swets, J. A. (1966). *Signal detection theory and psychophysics.* New York: Wiley.

Greenwald, A. G., Spangenberg, E. R., Pratkanis, A. R., & Eskenaz, J. (1991). Double-blind tests of subliminal self-help audiotapes. *Psychological Science, 2*(2), 119–122.

Harris, C. R., & Christenfeld, N. (1999). Can a machine tickle? *Psychonomic Bulletin & Review, 6,* 504–510.

Hess, R. F., & Hayes, A. (1993). Neural recruitment explains "Weber's law" of spatial position. *Vision Research, 33,* 1673–1684.

Hubel, D. H. (1996). A big step along the visual pathway. *Nature, 380,* 197–198.

Hubel, D. H., & Weisel, T. (1962). Receptive fields, binocular interaction and functional architecture in the cat's visual cortex. *Journal of Physiology, 160,* 106–154.

Johansson, G. (1973). Visual perception of biological motion and a model of its analysis. *Perception and Psychophysics, 14,* 201–211.

Johnston, W. A., & Dark, V. J. (1986). Selective attention. *Annual Review of Psychology, 37,* 43–75.

Kahneman, D., Fredrickson, B. L., Schreiber, C. A., & Redelmeier, D. A. (1993). When more pain is preferred to less: Adding a better end. *Psychological Science, 4,* 401–405.

Knight, D. C. (1960). *The first book of sound: A basic guide to the science of acoustics.* New York: Franklin Watts.

Koelega, H. S. (1994). Sex differences in olfactory sensitivity and the problem of the generality of smell acuity. *Perceptual and Motor Skills, 78,* 203–213.

Kryter, K. D. (1994). *The handbook of hearing and the effects of noise.* San Diego: Academic Press.

Land, M. F., & Fernald, R. D. (1992). The evolution of eyes. *Annual Review of Neuroscience, 15,* 1–29.

Lavie, N., & Tsal, Y. (1994). Perceptual load as a major determinant of the locus of selection in visual attention. *Perception and Psychophysics, 56,* 183–197.

Le Grand, R., Mondloch, C. J., Maurer, D., & Brent, H. P. (2010). Impairment in holistic face processing following early visual deprivation. *Psychological Science, 15*(11), 762–768.

Leibowitz, H. W., Birslin, R., Perlmutter, L., & Hennessy, R. (1969). Ponzo perspective illusion as a manifestation of space perception. *Science, 166,* 1174–1176.

Levine, J. D., Gordon, N. C., Smith, R., & Fields, H. L. (1981). Analgesic responses to morphine and placebo in individuals with postoperative pain. *Pain, 10*(3), 379–389.

Levy, J., & Pashler, H. (2008). Task prioritization in multitasking during driving: Opportunity to abort a concurrent task does not insulate braking responses from dual-task slowing. *Applied Cognitive Psychology, 22,* 507–525.

Lyons, L. (2005). Paranormal beliefs come (super) naturally to some. *Gallup News,* November 1.

Martinez-Conde, S., Macknik, S. L., & Hubel, D. H. (2004). The role of fixational eye movements in visual perception. *Nature Reviews Neuroscience, 5*(3), 229–240.

McGurk, H., & MacDonald, J. (1976). Hearing lips and seeing voices. *Nature, 264*(5588), 746–748.

McEvoy, S. P., Stevenson, M. R., McCartt, A. T., Woodward, M., Haworth, C., Palamara, P., & Cercarelli, R. (2005). Role of mobile phones in motor vehicle crashes resulting in hospital attendance: A case-crossover study. *British Medical Journal, 331,* 428–433.

Masuda, T., & Nisbett, R. E. (2001). Attending holistically vs. analytically: Comparing the context sensitivity of Japanese and Americans. *Journal of Personality and Social Psychology, 81,* 922–934.

Meissner, C. A., Brigham J. C. (2001). Thirty years of investigating the own-race bias in memory for faces: A meta-analytic review. *Psychology, Public Policy, and Law, 7*(1), 3–35.

Melzack, R., & Wall, P. (1965). Pain mechanisms: A new theory. *Science, 150,* 971–979.

Moray, N. (1970). *Attention: Selective processes in vision and hearing.* New York: Academic Press.

Nijhawan, R. (1991). Three-dimensional Müeller-Lyer illusion. *Perception and Psychophysics, 49,* 333–341.

Palmer, S. E. (1999). *Vision science: Photons to phenomenology.* Cambridge, MA: MIT Press.

Pashler, H. (1998). The psychology of attention. Cambridge, MA: MIT Press.

Phillips, D. P., & Brugge, J. F. (1985). Progress in neurophysiology of sound localization. *Annual Review of Psychology, 36,* 245–274.

Pratkanis, A. R. (Spring 1992). The cargo-cult science of subliminal persuasion. *Skeptical Inquirer* (Committee for the Scientific Investigation of Claims of the Paranormal), 260–272.

Rawlinson, G. E. (1976). The significance of letter position in word recognition. Unpublished PhD Thesis, Psychology Department, University of Nottingham, Nottingham UK.

Redelmeier D. A., Katz, J., & Kahneman, D. (2003). Memories of colonoscopy: A randomized trial. *Pain, 104*(1–2), 187–194.

Rumelhart, D. E., McClelland, J. L., Hinton, G., & the PDP Research Group. (1986). *Parallel distributed processing: Vol. 1. Foundations.* Cambridge, MA: MIT Press.

Russell, M. J. (1976). Human olfactory communication. *Nature (London), 260,* 520–522.

Sagiv, N., & Robertson, L. C. (2005). *Synesthesia: Perspectives from cognitive neuroscience.* Oxford: Oxford University Press.

Segall, M. H., Campbell, D. T., & Herskovits, M. J. (1966). *The influence of culture on visual perception.* Indianapolis, IN: Bobbs-Merrill.

Simner, J., Mulvenna, C., Sagiv, N., Tsakanikos, E., Witherby, S. A., Fraser, C., Scott, K., & Ward, J. (2006). Synaesthesia: The prevalence of atypical cross-modal experiences. *Perception, 35*(8), 1024–1033.

Simons, D. J., & Chabris, C. E. (1999). Gorillas in our midst: Sustained inattentional blindness for dynamic events. *Perception, 28,* 1059–1074.

Simons, D. L., & Levin, D. T. (1998). Failure to detect changes to people in real world interaction. *Psychonomic Bulletin and Review, 5,* 644–649.

Sims, P. (2008). Aspiring chef dies hours after making ultra-hot sauce for chili-eating contest. Daily Mail Online, 29th September 2008. http://www.dailymail.co.uk/news/article-1063598/Aspiring-chef-dies-hours-making-ultra-hot-sauce-chilli-eating-contest.html.

Stern, K., & McClintock, M. K. (1998). Regulation of ovulation by human pheromones. *Nature, 392,* 177–179.

Strayer, D. L., Drews, F. A., & Crouch, D. J. (2006). Comparing the cell-phone driver and the drunk driver. *Human Factors, 48,* 381–391.

Strayer, D. L., Drews, F. A., & Johnston, W. A. (2003). Cell phone induced failures of visual attention during simulated driving. *Journal of Experimental Psychology: Applied, 9,* 23–52.

Stroop, J. R. (1935). Studies of interference in serial verbal reactions. *Journal of Experimental Psychology, 18,* 643–662.

Swets, J. A., & Bjork, R. A. (1990). Enhancing human performance: An evaluation of "new age" techniques considered by the U.S. Army. *Psychological Science, 1,* 85–96.

Tanaka, K. (1996). Inferotemporal cortex and object vision. *Annual Review of Neuroscience, 19,* 109–139.

Treede, R. D., Kenshalo, D. R., Gracely, R. H., & Jones, A. K. (1999). The cortical representation of pain. *Pain, 79*(2–3), 105–111.

Treisman, A. (1999). Feature binding, attention, and object perception. In G. W. Humphrys, J. Duncan, & A. Triesman (Eds.), *Attention, space, and action* (pp. 91–111). New York: Oxford University Press.

Turnbull, C. M. (1961). *The forest people: A study of the Pygmies of the Congo.* New York: Clarion.

Villemure, C., & Bushnell, M. C. (2002). Cognitive modulators of pain: How do attention and emotion influence pain processing? *Pain, 95,* 195–199.

Vimal, R. L. P., Pokorny, J., & Smith, V. C. (1987). Appearance of steadily viewed lights. *Vision Research, 27,* 1309–1318.

Vogel, I., Verschuure, H., van der Ploeg, C. P. B., Brug, J., & Raat, H. (2009). Adolescents and MP3 players: Too many risks, too few precautions. *Pediatrics, 123,* e953–e958.

Vokey, J. R., & Read, J. D. (1985). Subliminal messages: Between the devil and the media. *American Psychologist, 40*(11), 1231–1239.

Voss, J. L., & Paller, K. A. (2009). An electrophysiological signature of unconscious recognition memory. *Nature Neuroscience, 12,* 349–355.

Wallach, H., & O'Connell, D. N. (1953). The kinetic depth effect. *Journal of Experimental Psychology, 45*(4), 205–217.

Ward, J., & Simner, J. (2003). Lexical-gustatory synaesthesia: Linguistic and conceptual factors. *Cognition, 89*(3), 237–261.

Wehner, T., & Stadler, M. (1994). The cognitive organization of human errors: A Gestalt theory perspective. *Applied Psychology: An International Review, 43,* 565–584.

Wertheimer, M. (1912). Experimentelle Studien über das Sehen van Bewegung. *Zeitschrift für Psychologie, 60,* 321–378.

Wever, E. G. (1949). *Theory of hearing.* New York: Wiley.

Wickens, C. D., Kramer, A. F., Vanasse, L., & Donchin, E. (1983). Performance of concurrent tasks: A psycho-physiological assessment of the reciprocity of information-processing resources. *Science, 221,* 1080–1082.

Yamaguchi, S., & Ninomiya, K. (2000). Umami and food palatability. *Journal of Nutrition, 130*(4S Suppl.), 912S–962S.

Larger doses of marijuana are associated with hallucinations and dissociative experiences. While some research suggests that marijuana can cause problems with long-term memory and motor coordination, others find only minor impairment in memory and learning in a group of long-term users versus nonusers (Grant, Gonzalez, Carey, Natarajan, & Wolfson, 2003).

The medicinal benefits of marijuana have led to its use in some medical areas. Medicinal benefits include increased appetite and reduction of nausea and vomiting, tremors, and the number and severity of seizures (Voth & Schwartz, 1997).

Ecstasy

Ecstasy (MDMA) A stimulant-hallucinogenic drug that can induce euphoria and diminish anxiety.

Methylenedioxymethamphetamine **(MDMA)** or **ecstasy** is a stimulant-hallucinogenic drug that can induce euphoria and diminish anxiety. Under the influence of ecstasy, users report feelings of enhanced intimacy, increased sensitivity to sensory stimuli, and more emotional openness. Ecstasy produces its full effect about an hour after it is ingested and lasts about 4 to 6 hours. Long-term use of MDMA is associated with dehydration, depression, and insomnia and can create long-term damage to serotonin neurons. Some people experience heart, liver, or kidney failure from taking large doses.

Transport proteins are one of the cleanup mechanisms in the synapses. Molecules of ecstasy are attracted to these sites and are taken into the axon terminal. This can cause changes in the reuptake site, causing the transport proteins to work backward. Instead of recycling serotonin, the axon terminal pumps it out of the cell. With fewer ways to clean up the synaptic gap, serotonin floods the synapse, overstimulating the receptor sites. This overstimulation can produce permanent damage and reduce the amount of healthy serotonin in the brain.

Serotonin pathways in the cerebral cortex influence multiple areas. Because there's so much serotonin in the synapse, ecstasy affects the user's emotions, appetite, sleep, wakefulness, and consciousness. In addition to serotonin, ecstasy can also impact dopamine, which is involved in our nervous system's reward system.

Summary of Multiple Influences on Consciousness

Eventually I did get to sleep. Turns out I was worried about a television interview that I was scheduled for later on that week. It's probably not a big surprise that something as simple as that, even though I wasn't thinking about it, could have such an impact on my ability to get to sleep. In this chapter, we have seen how our awareness of our internal and external environments is influenced by biological factors like the effects of psychoactive substances and natural sleep cycles but also by environmental factors like meditation and hypnosis. Social and cultural influences have an impact not only on your wanting to alter your consciousness through psychoactive drugs, but as in the case of LSD, your actual experience of the drug. Our awareness and experiences of our internal and external worlds depend on how we interact with these experiences. There are multiple influences on our awareness of both.

CONCEPT LEARNING CHECK **5.6** | *The Effects of Psychoactive Drugs*

Match the class of psychoactive drug to the specific substance.

A. Depressant   **1**. _____ Alcohol

B. Stimulant   **2**. _____ Amphetamines

C. Hallucinogen   **3**. _____ Caffeine

                              4. _____ Cocaine

                              5. _____ Ecstasy

                              6. _____ LSD

                              7. _____ Marijuana

                              8. _____ Methamphetamines

                              9. _____ Narcotics

                              10. _____ Nicotine

                              11. _____ Opiates

Visual Overview Sleep Cycles

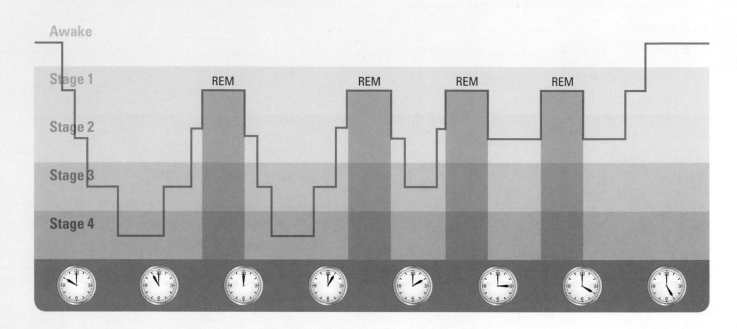

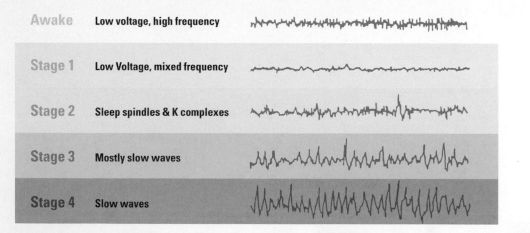

Awake	Low voltage, high frequency		
Stage 1	Low Voltage, mixed frequency		
Stage 2	Sleep spindles & K complexes		
Stage 3	Mostly slow waves		
Stage 4	Slow waves		

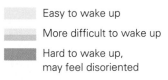

Easy to wake up

More difficult to wake up

Hard to wake up, may feel disoriented

REM   Low voltage, mixed frequency + rapid eye movement and muscle atonia

5.1 Overview: Consciousness, Brain Activity, Levels of Awareness

- Neuroscience imaging gives us a peek into what occurs in consciousness.
- Consciousness is dynamic and fluid.
- Our ability to selectively attend helps us to focus and attend.

- Dual processing ability of your nervous system helps you to attend to and manage stimuli from a variety of sources.
- Cognitive neuroscience is the science that studies thought, perception, and language from a biological perspective.

5.2 Sleep

- Your brain is active during sleep.
- You progress through four distinct phases during sleep.
- Stage 1 is the phase between relaxed wakefulness and sleep.
- Stage 2 is distinguished by sleep spindles and K-complexes on the EEG.
- In Stage 3, delta waves emerge on the EEG.
- In Stage 4, delta waves are more prominent on the EEG.
- REM sleep emerges the second time you enter Stage 1 sleep and is associated with memory sorting and dreams.
- The restorative theory of sleep suggests that sleep regenerates the body.

- The adaptive theory of sleep maintains that sleep is an evolved biological process.
- Sleep deprivation can cause many psychological and physical problems.
- Chronic sleep deprivation and sleep debt can also cause problems in daily functioning.
- Sleep disorders are conditions in which the quality or quantity of sleep is disturbed.
- Parasomnias are abnormal behaviors associated with sleep.
- Dyssomnias are conditions that affect the quantity or timing of sleep.
- Insomnia is characterized by difficulty falling or staying asleep.

5.3 Dreams

- Dreams are an array of sensory events experienced during sleep.
- The Freudian theory of dreams suggests that dreams are a reflection of unconscious id wishes.

- The activation-synthesis theory of dreams maintains that dreams are the result of interpreted brain activity during the consolidation of our memories.

5.4 Hypnosis

- Hypnosis is a trancelike state induced by a person whose suggestions of changes in consciousness or sensations are readily accepted by the subject.
- Not everyone is hypnotizable; about 20% of people can't be hypnotized, even by highly skilled practitioners.
- Hypnosis can help many medical conditions like pain.
- Researchers can't consistently find changes in the brain that would indicate

that hypnosis is a special state of consciousness.
- The sociocognitive theory of hypnosis suggests that you respond to the suggestions of the hypnotist because you are expected to do so.
- Dissociation theories of hypnosis suggest that the hypnotic state produces a split in consciousness and separates the executive control system from the rest of the brain.

5.5 Meditation

- Meditation refers to any mental practice that focuses on regulating attention and awareness.

- The techniques of meditation hold promise for the treatment of several conditions.

5.6 Drug Use

- A psychoactive drug is a chemical used to alter consciousness.

- The abuse of psychoactive substances can lead to addiction, tolerance, and symptoms of withdrawal.

- A mechanism of action refers to the way a drug functions, and psychoactive drugs influence the functioning of the nervous system through their influence on neurotransmitter functioning.

- Depressants are drugs that reduce the level of activity in the nervous system and include tranquilizers, alcohol, narcotics, barbiturates, and opiates.

- Stimulants are drugs that increase activity in the nervous system and include caffeine, nicotine, amphetamines, methamphetamine, cocaine, and ecstasy.

- Hallucinogens are a class of drugs that distort conscious experience and include LSD, mescaline, and marijuana.

5.1 Overview: Consciousness, Brain Activity, Levels of Awareness

1. The interdisciplinary study of how brain action is linked to thoughts, perception, and language is called
   A. change blindness.
   B. cognitive neuroscience.
   C. dual processing.
   D. selective attention.

2. Your ability to pay attention to only one voice among many is called
   A. change blindness.
   B. dual processing.
   C. selective attention.
   D. consciousness.

3. Consciousness includes which of the following?
   A. Awareness of your internal sensations
   B. Awareness of your own thoughts
   C. Your awareness of yourself as a person separate from others
   D. All of the above

5.2 Sleep

4. As the night goes on:
   A. it becomes increasingly difficult to wake up.
   B. REM periods get longer.
   C. Stage 4 periods get longer.
   D. Stage 3 periods get longer.

5. About an hour after falling asleep, Dane sits up in bed screaming. After his roommate wakes him, he doesn't remember anything. It seems that Dane is suffering from
   A. narcolepsy.
   B. nightmares.
   C. night terrors.
   D. sleep apnea.

6. The bursts of EEG activity that occur during Stage 2 sleep are called
   A. night terrors.
   B. REM sleep.
   C. sleep spindles.
   D. sleep apnea.

7. The part of your hypothalamus that is involved in sleep and wakefulness is called
   A. suprachiasmatic nucleus.
   B. circadian.
   C. melatonin.
   D. CPAP.

8. A person who experiences sleep attacks where he or she suddenly lapses into sleep during the day is likely suffering from which sleep disorder?
   A. Sleep apnea
   B. Narcolepsy
   C. Primary insomnia
   D. Night terrors

9. Sarah snores a lot when she sleeps. In addition, she has periods during which her breathing will stop. It's likely that Sarah suffers from which sleep disorder?
   A. CPAP
   B. Cataplexy
   C. Obstructive sleep apnea
   D. Hypocretin

10. Stopping someone from getting REM sleep would result in what changes in sleep when the person is then allowed to sleep normally?
    A. More restful sleep
    B. No change in REM when allowed to sleep normally
    C. Increased REM in Stage 4 sleep when allowed to sleep normally
    D. Increased REM in Stage 1 sleep when allowed to sleep normally

5.3 Dreams

11. As Anton remembered his dream, he was running a race. A person utilizing the psychoanalytic or Freudian theory of dream would say that Anton's account of the dream represents the _____ content of the dream.
    A. manifest
    B. latent
    C. activated
    D. synthesis

12. Roberta had a dream in which she was ice skating while reading a psychology book. Earlier that day, she was watching ice skating on TV while reading her book. Which model or theory of dreams would suggest that this dream is just a way to combine the memories she had that day?
    A. Manifest content
    B. Latent content
    C. Psychoanalytic
    D. Activation-synthesis

5.4 Hypnosis

13. The theory of hypnosis that suggests that the hypnotic state that separates the executive control system from the rest of the mind is called
    A. the dissociative theory of hypnosis.
    B. the role-playing theory of hypnosis.
    C. hypermnesia.
    D. the sociocognitive theory of hypnosis.

Chapter Overview ▼

6.1 How We Learn

CONCEPT LEARNING CHECK **6.1** *Comparing Types of Learning*

6.2 Classical Conditioning
  Pavlov's Experiments
    Acquisition
    Extinction and Spontaneous
      Recovery
    Generalization
    Discrimination
  Review of Terminology, Processes,
  and Factors That Affect Classical
  Conditioning

Conditioning and Emotional
Responses
Contemporary Views of Classical
Conditioning
  Learning to Predict
  Biological and Evolutionary
    Predispositions
Applying Principles of Classical
Conditioning
  Watson and Behaviorism
  Little Albert Experiment

CONCEPT LEARNING CHECK **6.2** *Applying Principles of Classical Conditioning*

6 Learning

Learning Objectives ▼

6.1 ▪ Distinguish among three major types of learning theories focusing on behavior.

6.2 ▪ Identify the principles of classical conditioning involving reflexive behaviors.

6.3 ▪ Apply the principles of operant conditioning based on the consequences of behavior.

6.4 ▪ Explain the evidence that learning can occur without acting out behavior.

6.3 Operant Conditioning
Thorndike's Law of Effect
Skinner's Experiments
  Reinforcement
  Acquisition and Shaping
  Generalization and Discrimination
  Extinction
  Schedules of Reinforcement
Punishment
Review of Terminology, Processes, and Factors That Affect Operant Conditioning
Contemporary Views of Operant Conditioning
  Learned Helplessness
  Intrinsic Motivation
  Biological Influences on Operant Conditioning

Applying Principles of Operant Conditioning
CONCEPT LEARNING CHECK **6.3** *Comparing Consequences of Behavior*

6.4 A Cognitive Approach: Observational Learning
CRITICAL THINKING APPLICATION
Tolman's Latent Learning
Bandura's Social-Cognitive Learning Theory
  Acquisition vs. Performance
  Basic Processes
  Biological Basis: Mirrors in the Brain
  Applying Principles of Observational Learning

Summary of Multiple Influences on Learning
CONCEPT LEARNING CHECK **6.4** *Learning by Observing*

At 6, my son Victor just barely reached the "You must be this tall to ride!" sign at the community pool. He eagerly climbed the stairs after his older cousins, excited for his first trip on a waterslide. He jumped on at the top, rode the waterslide down twisting turns, and landed on his back in the foot-deep pool of water at the bottom. Completely, and unexpectedly, submerged, Victor coughed and cried from the rush of water into his nose. He was done riding the slide, but not just for the day: Two years later, Victor doesn't recall that August day, but he still avoids waterslides, saying, "I just don't like them."

Something happened during Victor's first waterslide experience: He learned an enduring connection between waterslides and feelings of discomfort. In what ways does our biological heritage explain how we learn basic responses like "fear?" And how does our experience in the world shape what we learn about it? As we'll see in this chapter, our biological tendencies interact with environmental factors to produce learning like Victor's. Psychologists investigate events like these to understand the processes underlying learning. Their research explores topics such as:

- how emotional experiences affect our actions and attitudes
- how we learn to change our behavior in response to expected outcomes
- how we learn from the behavior of others around us.

In this chapter, we'll explore the relationships between the biological and environmental influences that allow us to change through our experiences; that is, to learn from them.

6.1 How We Learn

Learning can occur through associating events that occur together, responding to the consequences of our behavior, and observing the behavior of others.

■ Distinguish among three major types of learning theories focusing on behavior.

Learning A lasting change in knowledge or behavior based on experience.

Acquisition Gaining new knowledge or behavior to use in the future.

Psychologists think about **learning** as a lasting change in knowledge and/or behavior as a consequence of experience. It is a central problem for psychology because people, and in fact all living things, must learn in order to survive. The world is constantly changing, and our capacity to learn means we can adjust to a changing world by changing our behaviors accordingly. The field of psychology has devoted an immense amount of research to the ways in which we learn from experience. Learning is certainly a central, defining topic within psychological science.

At the heart is a basic question: How can I, as a scientist, determine that you, as a research subject, have learned? Right now, as you're reading this text, you are learning (I sincerely hope!), forming connections to what you already know, and creating new memories containing this new information, called **acquisition** of information or behaviors. But to an outside observer, how can your change in knowledge be verified? Typically, we use language to demonstrate whether we have learned something. But people are often unable to report how or why they know something; for example, Victor can't say how he learned to avoid waterslides. So historically, psychologists focused on defining learning in a way that does not depend on language. If you meet someone who doesn't speak your language, how could you determine what he or she can learn? You would have to depend on the person's behaviors, or actions that can be directly observed in the world.

For this reason, a well-established psychological theory, called **behaviorism**, argues that we can't know what is inside the mind, but we can know what actions are observable in the world (Watson, 1913).

"Radical behaviorists" thought we should investigate the basic processes of learning by completely ignoring what people are thinking and study only their discrete, observable behaviors. They chose to refer to learning as **conditioning**, emphasizing the role of training to produce changes in behavior. In addition, behaviorists study the properties of human learning by testing animal behaviors, arguing that the important processes of learning are just as evident in animals as they are in humans. To understand why people do what they do, behaviorists argue, we don't need language; instead, we need only observe behavior as it changes with experience.

From this behaviorist perspective, there are two types of learning exhibited by humans and other animals: classical conditioning and operant conditioning FIGURE 6-1. In **classical conditioning**, we learn through our experience with the world that two things are associated with one another, just as a flash of lightning goes with the roar of thunder. By watching for signs that predict what will happen next, we can learn to seek out or avoid situations that may benefit or harm us. This type of learning is basic to survival, helping us seek out the good and avoid the bad. For example, if you eat a new food and then become sick, you will quickly associate sickness with that food and avoid it in the future. Classical conditioning involves *instinctive and reflexive* behaviors that are elicited (or brought out) by specific events. The key to classical conditioning is to remember that it involves only reflexive behaviors: specifically, our basic physiological responses, such as feeling sexually aroused, nauseated, anxious, or startled.

The second type of learning from the behaviorist perspective ties a behavior to its consequence in the world. In **operant conditioning**, we "operate" on our environment, and our behavior is rewarded with consequences; if we are positively rewarded, we will perform this behavior again, and more often. Operant conditioning involves behaviors that we emit (*freely choose*) to perform. Why do you put change in the soda machine or talk to that cute student or read this assignment? Because these behaviors have been rewarded, or **reinforced**, in the past. For example, drinking a soda tastes good, so that behavior is likely to be repeated. The key to operant conditioning is to remember that it predicts how we will behave based on how we've been rewarded for these behaviors in the past.

Following the behaviorist approach, a second approach to learning, the **cognitive** approach, focused on learning as changes in knowledge within the mind. Cognitive theories of learning address mental processes that cannot be accounted for in strictly behavioral terms. Even in rats, learning can occur without behavior, so we need explanations for how

Behaviorism The study of learning based on directly observable actions.

Conditioning Training, or learning as displayed by an animal's or human's behavior.

Classical conditioning A neutral stimulus is associated with an unlearned stimulus and its automatic response.

Operant conditioning Training emitted behaviors to make them more likely to occur again.

Reinforce To strengthen behavior, making it more likely to occur again.

Cognitive The explanations of behavior based on changes in knowledge within the mind.

Classical Conditioning

The monkey avoids snakes after being bitten by one.

Operant Conditioning

The monkey works to peel the banana, and is rewarded with food.

Observational Learning

The monkey copies a new method for cracking open coconuts

FIGURE 6-1 Learning theories in psychology address only observable behaviors and apply to all types of organisms.

Observational learning Acquiring new behaviors from watching a model.

changes occur in knowledge within the mind. For example, **observational learning** allows us to watch and learn from the behaviors of others without moving a muscle. In fact, it appears that our brains are wired with special neural systems that "mirror" the experiences of others within our own minds. By observing others, we can quickly gain knowledge about which behaviors are likely to lead to good outcomes. For example, wild monkeys have been shown to rapidly learn to fear snakes from watching other monkeys (Mineka, Keir, & Price, 1980). In fact, studies of animal groups show the benefits of "culture" similar to ours, in which a chimp that learns to swim leads to a whole pack of swimming chimps, while other groups never venture into the water. The phrase "Monkey see, monkey do" is not about humans, but it aptly describes how readily we learn from others around us.

Behavioral theories of learning describe how behavior changes with experience (see **TABLE 6-1**). Because they focus on our external, observable actions in the world, they do not take into account the thinking we do or the language we use. In later chapters, we will more fully explore cognitive theories of learning in terms of memory processes and language. In this chapter, we will see how far theories of learning can go in accounting for our behavior without appealing to the special cognitive abilities of the human animal.

TABLE 6-1 Summary of Behavioral Learning Theories

Type of Learning	Training Method	After Training	Example
Classical conditioning	A neutral stimulus is paired with an unconditioned stimulus that elicits an unconditioned response.	The neutral stimulus becomes the conditioned stimulus and elicits the conditioned response.	A bell now elicits salivation just like meat does.
Operant conditioning	A behavior is followed by reinforcement.	The behavior is now more likely to occur.	A rat presses a bar for food.
Observational learning	A behavior is modeled for the learner.	The observer performs the same behavior at will.	A child hits a doll just like what was seen on a video.

CONCEPT LEARNING CHECK 6.1   *Comparing Types of Learning*

For each example, determine whether it best fits classical conditioning, operant conditioning, or observational learning theory.

1. Sydney liked the comments and attention she received when she wore provocative clothing, so she started wearing even shorter skirts to school.

2. Raoul was home alone when a bad storm brought down the power lines, leaving him in the dark for several hours. Now, he insists that his roommate stay in whenever it's raining.

3. Mandy was very disappointed when her daughter was caught playing hooky from middle school. The school had to send a letter to their home because Mandy herself was not at work on the days that the school attempted to call her.

4. Dedre had several humiliating moments when her history teacher called on her to explain concepts in class. Now, whenever he calls on her during class, she starts trembling uncontrollably.

5. When Pete went to his girlfriend's home for dinner, he watched to see which fork she used for the salad.

6. Malay was trying to study, but every time she answered one of her sister's comments, her sister talked even more.

6.2 Classical Conditioning

We learn to connect events that predict our important physiological responses, including reflexes and fear.

■ Identify the principles of classical conditioning involving reflexive behaviors.

In associative learning, we learn that when Event A happens, Event B is likely to follow soon after. For example, you may learn to stay out of dusty attics after finding a spider lurking in one. How we learn these sorts of associations between events is called classical conditioning, because it was the first modern learning theory developed. It was originally discovered—by accident—by a Russian physiologist, Ivan Pavlov. You may have heard of the famous "Pavlov's dogs," as they provided the insight behind this learning theory (Pavlov, 1927).

Pavlov's Experiments

Pavlov was interested in digestion in dogs, not in psychology. In fact, he later won a Nobel Prize for his studies of the reflexes involved in digestive functioning. Part of his scientific procedure involved putting food (in this case, meat powder) on dogs' tongues and measuring their salivary secretions in long tubes hanging from the corners of their mouths. Dogs naturally produce saliva, or drool, whenever they are exposed to food. But Pavlov soon noticed a surprising thing: The dogs salivated as soon as they saw the assistant entering the lab! The dogs learned to associate the sight of the attendant with food because the two occurred together in time. This phenomenon, called psychic secretions by Pavlov and Pavlovian conditioning by others, came to be called classical conditioning.

Acquisition

Let's walk through the steps involved in the process of classical conditioning for Pavlov's dogs. Before any learning takes place, there is an existing link between the food, called the **unconditioned stimulus** (the event that elicits a response) and the resulting salivating, called the **unconditioned response** (the reflexive behavior elicited by the stimulus). When dogs are exposed to food, they automatically begin to salivate as a basic physiological reflex. Conditioning refers to the learning and training that results in this response. Whenever you see the term *conditioned*, think *learned*, and for *unconditioned*, think *unlearned* (occurring without learning).

The first step in conditioning involves a new stimulus, called the **neutral stimulus** because it does not yet cause any response. For example, Pavlov rang a bell, which at first caused no salivary reaction in the dogs at all. During the conditioning trials, the neutral stimulus (the bell) was presented with the unconditioned stimulus (the food). So on each trial, a bell was rung just before food was given to the dogs, which produced the unconditioned response (salivating). By repeatedly pairing the neutral stimulus with the unconditioned stimulus, the dogs learned that the bell reliably predicts the arrival of food. Soon, the dogs didn't wait for the food but began salivating as soon as they heard the bell. After conditioning, the bell is called a **conditioned stimulus**. That is, the bell changes from a neutral or meaningless stimulus into a stimulus that, on its own, now leads to a **conditioned response** (salivation). In addition, salivation changes from a reflexive, unconditioned response into a trained or "conditioned" response. This sequence of learning trials in classical conditioning is shown in FIGURE 6-2. The key is to remember that *unconditioned* refers to the *unlearned*, already-present connection between a stimulus and a reflexive response. *Conditioned*, then, refers to the *learned* association acquired between a new stimulus and the reflexive response.

Unconditioned stimulus An unlearned signal that leads to an automatic, reflexive response.

Unconditioned response A physiological behavior that is involuntarily elicited by a stimulus.

Neutral stimulus An event or signal that causes no reflexive, automatic response.

Conditioned stimulus A learned signal that predicts another stimulus is about to occur.

Conditioned response A physiological behavior that is associated with a learned stimulus.

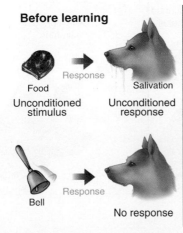

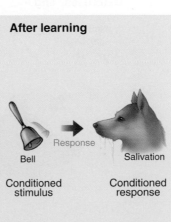

FIGURE 6-2 The sequence of events in Pavlov's classical conditioning experiment.

The positive emotions from cooking with family may become associated with specific foods, which later give rise to the same feelings on their own.

Higher-order conditioning Learning to associate a neutral stimulus with an already-learned conditioned stimulus and conditioned response.

Extinction The tendency to stop responding to the conditioned stimulus when repeatedly presented without the unconditioned stimulus.

The famous example of Pavlov's dogs is all well and good, but what does it tell us about learning by people? Classical conditioning is very specific in terms of what you can learn with it: It refers *only* to learning that involves an existing reflex, instinct, or automatic response. An example of a reflex that can be classically conditioned is the "startle" response, induced by any loud, sudden noise. Imagine you're driving along in your car, and you suddenly hear a police siren behind you: You will feel an unsettling startle reflex in response. The loud sound (the unconditioned stimulus) will cause your body to become active, alert, alarmed, and likely upset (the unconditioned response). Now imagine you drive past a police car sitting on the side of the road (a previously neutral stimulus). You may cringe and feel the same unpleasant startle reaction. Through classical conditioning, you have learned that police cars (now the conditioned stimulus) signal the unconditioned stimulus (the siren), which evokes your startle response. Now, just seeing a police car is enough to cause the (conditioned) startle response, even without hearing the siren.

Through **higher-order conditioning**, a neutral stimulus can become a new conditioned stimulus just by being paired with an existing conditioned stimulus FIGURE 6-3. In Pavlov's study, after the connection between the bell and salivation is well established, he added a new neutral signal, a flashing light, *before* the bell rang. Any signal that predicts the conditioned stimulus (the bell) will *itself* be learned as a conditioned stimulus. These second-order associations can have important consequences in our everyday lives. For instance, you may later feel an unpleasant startle reaction just from seeing a police officer. Anything related to the conditioned stimulus can be a signal that it may now occur.

Classical conditioning theory states that we are ready to associate *any* sign with our reflexive, unconditioned responses. And we may learn the association, as Victor did with the waterslide, through a single trial. Victor's unpleasant experience of being unexpectedly submerged at the bottom of the slide (the unconditioned stimulus) naturally resulted in fear and pain (the unconditioned response). This experience turned a previously neutral stimulus (going on the waterslide) into a conditioned stimulus that now, by itself, elicits fear (the conditioned response). He may also associate other signals with that event, such as the specific pool where it took place. We are often unaware of the higher-order associations we develop, but our physiological responses can be so pleasant or unpleasant that we quickly learn to associate new cues that predict their occurrence. A familiar signal like the smell of a favorite food can be enough to evoke our conditioned responses from past experiences.

Extinction and Spontaneous Recovery

It's important to realize that, just as we learn an association between a signal and our physiological reaction, we can *un*learn it. In the process of **extinction**, the conditioned stimulus is repeatedly presented without the unconditioned stimulus. For example, if

FIGURE 6-3 In higher-order conditioning, a new neutral stimulus (a light) is paired with an already learned conditioned stimulus (the bell) instead of with the unconditioned stimulus (the food).

Before learning

Neutral stimulus

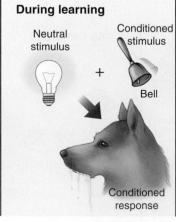

During learning

Neutral stimulus

Conditioned stimulus

+

Bell

Conditioned response

After learning

Conditioned stimulus

Conditioned response

Victor were to go down that waterslide every day and never again experience that painful submersion, he would eventually unlearn that association. However, it also appears that past associations "wait in the wings," ready to reappear if needed. New learning appears to suppress but not erase previous learning. If some time goes by without any experience of the conditioned stimulus, and then it suddenly occurs again, it may again evoke the conditioned response. This partial recovery of an association, called **spontaneous recovery**, occurs even after the conditioned stimulus has undergone extinction FIGURE 6-4. When in doubt, we fall back on the strength of prior associations. In fact, conditioned responses can show resistance to extinction, where the conditioned response is particularly difficult to unlearn.

Generalization

Classically conditioned responses may occur with a new stimulus even though it is not exactly the same as the one first learned. For example, you may have heard the whining tone of the dentist's drill as its painful work on your teeth was about to occur. After acquisition, the sound of the drilling tone has become a conditioned stimulus, eliciting a feeling of fear whenever you hear it. But what about other drilling sounds? In classical conditioning, you may **generalize** learning so that you have the same conditioned response (fear) to other, similar sounds, a process called stimulus generalization. The process of generalization in classical conditioning forms a reliable relationship, called the generalization gradient: The closer the new stimulus is to the one you learned, the more likely you are to experience the same conditioned response. FIGURE 6-5 shows this pattern, in which the strength of a conditioned response is highest when the stimulus is most similar to the conditioned stimulus. When new stimuli are less like the original, the conditioned response is weaker.

Discrimination

The opposite side of generalization is the process of **discrimination**, in which the learner comes to recognize differences among similar stimuli. Perhaps the dentist's drill has led you to fear all such sounds; but over time, you may demonstrate a reduced fear response when

Spontaneous recovery The reappearance of an extinguished conditioned response.

Generalization Learning to respond to stimuli similar to the one experienced.

Discrimination Learning to see the difference between two similar stimuli.

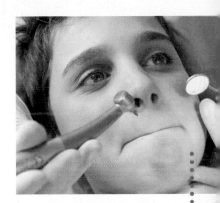

The sounds of the dentist's drill become associated with pain, so that the sound alone may give rise to fear in the future.

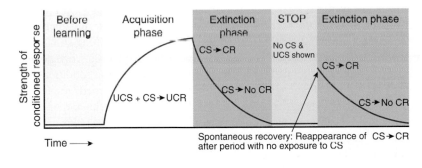

FIGURE 6-4 The rising line shows an increase in the conditioned response during acquisition, and a decrease during extinction. Then, after some time passes, the response may return, called "spontaneous recovery."

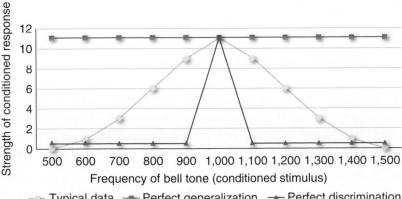

FIGURE 6-5 If Pavlov's dogs only responded to a bell tone like the one they learned, they would show a steep generalization gradient (the green line). If they generalized their learning so that similar sounding bells also produced the conditioned response, a pattern like the blue line would be observed. And, if they responded to any bell at all, they would show the complete generalization indicated by the orange line.

you hear a woodworking drill. As you learn stimulus discrimination, the generalization gradient narrows so that a smaller range of stimuli elicits the same conditioned response. This allows us to learn which aspects of the earlier experience predict real danger.

Review of Terminology, Processes, and Factors That Affect Classical Conditioning

An example will help to illustrate the terms and processes just described FIGURE 6-6. Classical conditioning is learning that two events go together; when one happens, the other happens. But most importantly, classical conditioning happens with behaviors that are elicited from the learner and are *not* voluntary. For example, if a strange dog bites you, you will have the automatic response of pain and fear, and that is not a choice or decision on your part. It occurs because an unconditioned stimulus—the dog bite—produces an unconditioned response—pain and fear. This existing link is the cornerstone of classical conditioning, and new learning builds upon this unconditioned association.

FIGURE 6-6 The three stages in classical conditioning are depicted: before, during, and after conditioning (learning).

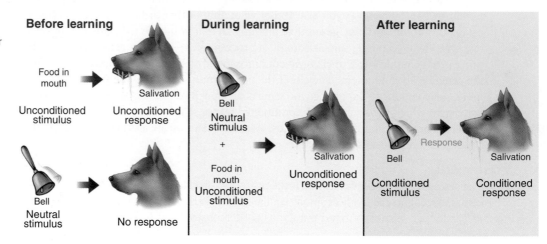

Before learning

Food in mouth → Salivation

Unconditioned stimulus → Unconditioned response

Bell → No response

Neutral stimulus

During learning

Bell
Neutral stimulus
+
Food in mouth
Unconditioned stimulus
→ Salivation
Unconditioned response

After learning

Bell → Response → Salivation

Conditioned stimulus → Conditioned response

Now, in this example, we pair the dog's bark—a neutral stimulus—with the bite. Before learning, the bark is neutral because it elicits no response from you. But after your experience of hearing barking, then of being bitten and feeling the resulting pain and fear, you have now learned that the bark is associated with the bite. Now, even when no bite occurs, a barking dog—the conditioned (or learned) stimulus—elicits the conditioned (learned) response: You feel fear! Remember that the unconditioned (unlearned) response becomes the conditioned (learned) response, so they are always the same behavior. And, in classical conditioning, this is always a basic physiological response such as a reflex or an emotion.

Once learned, these associations can undergo extinction. If a barking dog never bites, you may get used to the bark eventually. On the other hand, you may generalize your fear response to any animal that makes noise or you may learn to discriminate among noises that signal danger. What is most impressive about classical conditioning is that an experience can occur only once, but the learning from it can stay with you forever. Classical conditioning helps us readily learn the signs associated with our intense experiences of pain and pleasure.

Conditioning and Emotional Responses

In humans, events or images may elicit important reflexes or instinctive responses that involve emotions like fear, sexual arousal, joy, sadness, disgust, or anxiety. Our emotional responses are easy to train through classical conditioning, and they matter very much to our sense of safety and well-being. For example, when children have been abused, they associate angry faces with the painful violence that follows. Pollak and colleagues (1998) found that abused children's brain wave responses to angry faces were much stronger and longer lasting compared to those of nonabused children. A similar phenomenon may occur in couples experiencing marital discord. Repeated experiences of conflict and pain may lead to deep, emotional responses becoming associated with the other

Reflexive or automatic emotional arousal may occur from some events; in this case, a fly in your soup elicits the emotion of disgust.

partner (Gottman, 1998; Driver & Gottman, 2005). As a result, even when not engaged in fighting, the mere presence of the partner may evoke the emotional discomfort they have experienced so often. Through classical conditioning, we quickly learn the signs that predict upcoming emotional pain or pleasure, and we remain sensitive to those cues long after the original learning takes place.

Associations may also be positive. Using the principles of classical conditioning, it is easy to explain why specific associations occur with feelings of sexual arousal. For example, an unconditioned stimulus, such as a kiss, will lead to the unconditioned response of sexual arousal FIGURE 6-7. Through experience, however, another stimulus associated with the kiss may on its own lead to feelings of sexual arousal. For example, the smell of perfume, when paired with the kiss, can become associated with the resulting sexual arousal. Eventually the scent of the perfume alone leads to the conditioned response of sexual arousal.

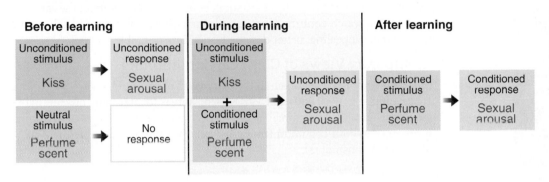

FIGURE 6-7 Through classical conditioning, a perfume scent (conditioned stimulus) can become associated with sexual arousal (conditioned response).

In addition, we may be drawn to particular people without realizing they have tapped into classically conditioned responses from our past. For example, you may really enjoy listening to a new friend's deep voice as he tells you about his life and find his manner reassuring and supportive. The similarity to your long talks with your own father may not be apparent until you see them together. Or a friend stopping by with fresh-baked chocolate chip cookies may bring out warm feelings not just for the taste but also for the feelings of comfort you experienced when your Mom baked the same cookies for you. A "lucky" sweater or beat-up old car may become tied to intense feelings from experiences in which they happened to be with you, leading to a residue of past emotions on familiar objects. It is easy to underestimate the influence of our associations to past emotional experiences. We even prefer specific numbers and letters of the alphabet; specifically, those of our own birthdates and letters from our own names (Koole et al., 2001)!

In fact, we learn so well from classical conditioning that changes may occur in our physiological responses below our conscious awareness. In particular, it may be possible to train the body's immune system, affecting our general health (Ader & Cohen, 1985). Using classical conditioning procedures, sugar water was paired with a drug that caused nausea. As expected, rats quickly developed an aversion to the taste of the sugar water. Many of these rats died because this drug weakens the immune system by destroying white blood cells. Later, surviving rats were then fed sweetened water on its own (the conditioned stimulus) without the drug (the unconditioned stimulus). Consuming the sweetened water associated with the drug was enough to suppress the immune system (the conditioned response), leading to sickness and death in these rats FIGURE 6-8. Other studies show promise in *increasing* activity levels in the immune system through classical conditioning (Miller & Cohen, 2001). **Biofeedback** methods, which provide external signals of physiological responses, have been successfully used to train people to lower their blood pressure, slow their heartbeat, relax muscle tension, and control pain (deCharms et al., 2005).

Another place where emotional conditioning takes place is in advertising. One technique is to pair images that evoke pleasant responses (such as sexual images, the unconditioned stimulus) with a neutral product image (which becomes the conditioned stimulus). By repeatedly associating the product with an image that elicits a positive unconditioned response (arousal), advertisers hope their products will also come to evoke

Biofeedback Using instruments that display physiological functions to help learn to control responses.

FIGURE 6-8 Suppression of the immune system occurred through classical conditioning when a sweet taste was paired with exposure to an immune-suppressing drug. Later, the animals experienced immune suppression from drinking the sweetened water alone. *Source: Data from Miller, G., & Cohen, N. (2001). Psychological interventions and the immune system: A meta-analytic review and critique. Health Psychology, 20, 47–63.*

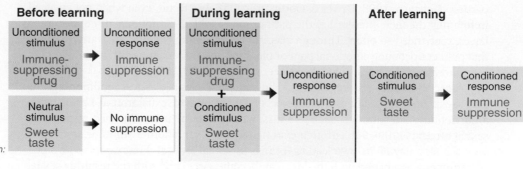

Before learning		During learning	After learning	
Unconditioned stimulus **Immune-suppressing drug** →	Unconditioned response **Immune suppression**	Unconditioned stimulus **Immune-suppressing drug** **+** Conditioned stimulus **Sweet taste** → Unconditioned response **Immune suppression**	Conditioned stimulus **Sweet taste** →	Conditioned response **Immune suppression**
Neutral stimulus **Sweet taste** →	**No immune suppression**			

Car advertisements with sexy models are intended to build your positive associations with the automobile.

Taste aversion Learning to dislike foods that were followed by nausea.

Avoidance learning Learning to stay away from stimuli that predict negative events.

the same reaction. Car ads, for example, often feature an attractive female model draped across the hood; since the model is not for sale, her purpose in the ad must be to evoke positive sexual feelings and, by association, boost your feelings about the car. Advertisers know (and research confirms) that car ads including an attractive female are rated (by men) as more appealing, better designed, and more desirable.

Contemporary Views of Classical Conditioning

The dominance of behaviorism in the early years of psychology gave way to the cognitive revolution in the 1960s and 1970s. Behaviorists focused only on external behavior and worked mainly with animal models; as a result, they sometimes underestimated the importance of both cognition (thoughts, beliefs, language) and biology (built-in and evolutionary constraints).

Learning to Predict

Pavlov's account of dogs responding to bells led to a view of learning as a mindless, mechanical process. Yet even dogs may be thinking more than Pavlov would suggest: Perhaps what the dogs learned about the bell was not a simple association but, rather, the *prediction* that food was about to arrive. Based on years of research in animal learning, Rescorla (1988) concluded that the simple pairing of events is not sufficient for conditioning to occur. Instead, classical conditioning results in *predicting* that Event A (the conditioned stimulus) will be followed by Event B (the unconditioned stimulus). A study demonstrated the difference by pairing a tone and an electrical shock. For one group of rats, the tone always perfectly predicted the shock, while for another group, the shock occasionally occurred without the tone. Only the first group learned to fear the tone; for the second group, the conditioned stimulus simply didn't reliably predict the unconditioned stimulus. Classical conditioning requires more than a simple association or pairing of stimuli; rather, it requires a *reliable, predictive* relationship.

Biological and Evolutionary Predispositions

Pavlov and other early behaviorists assumed that any organism (pigeon, rat, or human) can be conditioned with any stimulus (bell, light, or odor). But can we learn to associate any signal with any physiological response? Imagine dining out in a restaurant where you happen to try a dish with hollandaise sauce. At home later that night, you become violently ill. How do you think you will feel about eating hollandaise sauce again? Most likely, you will not be eager. However, you could have associated many other things in the situation with your illness, such as the people you dine with or the music playing in the restaurant. John Garcia proposed an explanation for this experience: People—and all animals—develop **taste aversions** that associate feelings of nausea with whatever food was last consumed, and this causes them to avoid that taste in the future. He suggested that we are biologically prepared to easily learn some signals and not others as predictors for some responses.

To test his theory, Garcia and Koelling (1966) exposed rats to an unconditioned stimulus (radiation), and they experienced an unconditioned response (illness). For different groups of rats, he provided different neutral stimuli as potential cues: clicking noises, flashing lights, and sweet-tasting water. Would the rats learn to associate these neutral stimuli with illness equally well? The measure of their associations would be their **avoidance learning**; that is, whether the animals tried to escape from these cues. As Garcia suspected, some pairings were easier to learn than others: The rats were much quicker to learn that the taste of sugar water predicts nausea compared to lights or sounds FIGURE 6-9. Garcia also performed versions of the study in which the unconditioned stimulus was electrical shock and the unconditioned response was pain and fear. For these rats, it was much easier to learn that lights predicted the shock and difficult to learn that sweetened water did. His conclusion was that not all conditioned stimuli are equal; rather, some associations between stimuli and responses are easier to learn than others.

Our readiness to learn the signals for important physiological responses can result in problems in real-world situations. One example comes from the administration of chemotherapy to patients with cancer FIGURE 6-10. When patients begin treatment, the drugs given to fight the cancer frequently cause terrible nausea as a side effect. The patient experiences this unconditioned stimulus—the drug—that produces the unconditioned response of nausea. However, this occurs repeatedly in the presence of the same neutral stimulus: a waiting room. Over time and experience, the patient begins to associate the waiting room itself with the impending nausea that will result from the drug. Eventually, even when no drug is administered, the patient will enter the waiting room (the conditioned stimulus) and begin to feel the nausea that usually results (the conditioned response). Humans are so good at pairing signals to physiological reactions that events far removed from the unconditioned stimulus, such as the freeway exit sign on the way to the treatment center, may become conditioned to begin the unpleasant response. Many cancer patients report that they continue to feel nauseous in response to any reminders of their treatment, even 20 years later (Cameron et al., 2001).

Biological preparedness describes inborn tendencies that point us toward the signals that are most likely to be related to the cause of our reactions. These tendencies vary across species and play a very valuable role in preserving us from harm. It makes sense that the scavenging rat would be quick to learn to avoid foods that make it sick, while birds, on the other hand, are more likely to learn visual cues. We humans also show preparedness to learn to fear specific dangerous objects and situations, such as spiders, thunder, snakes, darkness, and heights. Öhman and Mineka (2001) proposed that we have "fear modules" to protect us from the dangers experienced by our ancestors. As a result, we are biologically prepared to learn associations that help us adapt to our world

Biological preparedness
Built-in tendencies to learn some associations more easily.

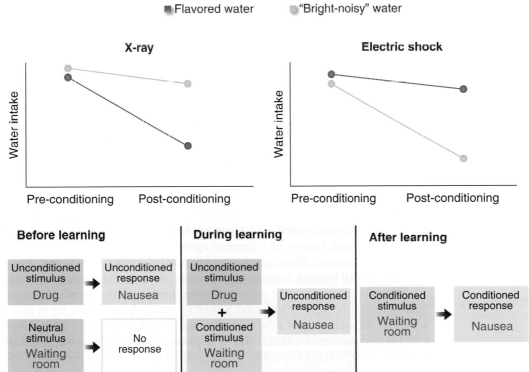

FIGURE 6-9 Water intake is shown before (pre-) and after (post-) conditioning. The left panel shows learning when X-rays were the unconditioned stimulus, and the right panel shows learning when electric shock was the unconditioned stimulus. The results show that the rats learned some pairings more readily: the taste of flavored water to nausea, and "bright lights and noise" to shock. *Source: Data from Garcia, J., & Koelling, R. A. (1966). Relation of cue to consequence in avoidance learning.* Psychonomic Science, 4, 123–124.

FIGURE 6-10 Through classical conditioning, a waiting room (conditioned stimulus) can become associated with nausea (conditioned response).

6.3 Operant Conditioning

We learn based upon the consequences that follow our behavior in the world.

■ Apply the principles of operant conditioning based on the consequences of behavior.

Operant A behavior freely initiated or displayed, which can be conditioned.

Law of Effect Behaviors that lead to positive outcomes are likely to be repeated.

Reinforcer A consequence (either positive or negative) following a behavior that makes it *more* likely to occur again.

As we know, classical conditioning always involves an unconditioned, involuntary response *elicited from* the individual whenever an unconditioned stimulus occurs. These reflexes involve important physiological reactions that greatly affect our everyday lives, particularly in our experience of emotion. However, a second theory of learning involves voluntary responses *emitted by* the subject: That is, the individual freely chooses to make a particular response at a given time. This kind of conditioning is called operant conditioning, where **operant** refers to a behavior "operating" in the world. The choice of whether and when to perform a given behavior is purely at the discretion of the individual. So what controls operant behavior, or the decision to perform a given action?

Thorndike's Law of Effect

In 1898, Edward Thorndike decided to look at this problem using cats as his subjects. Thorndike put cats into large wooden crates containing an escape lever inside. These puzzle boxes required the cat to pull on a lever to release the latch and open the door to escape. Thorndike was interested in animal intelligence and wanted to see how long it would take the cats to learn to open the box. What he found was that the behaviors followed by pleasant consequences were more likely to be repeated in that situation FIGURE 6-11. So when the cat was first trapped inside the puzzle box, it scratched at the bars, pushed at the ceiling, nosed the floor, howled, and performed many other behaviors, until finally it happened to press the lever that opened the door. After many trials, the cat learned to press the lever right away to release itself from the box. The animal had learned

FIGURE 6-11 The cat in a puzzle box would perform many different behaviors, until finally it learned to press the lever and escape.
Source: Data from Thorndike, E. L. (1898). Animal intelligence: An experimental study of the associative processes in animals. Psychological Monographs, 2 (Whole No, 8).

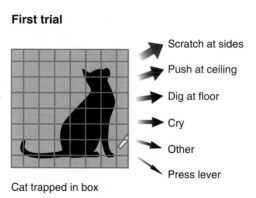

First trial

Scratch at sides
Push at ceiling
Dig at floor
Cry
Other
Press lever

Cat trapped in box

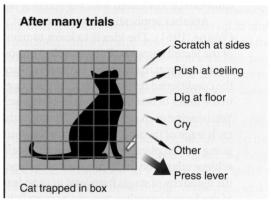

After many trials

Scratch at sides
Push at ceiling
Dig at floor
Cry
Other
Press lever

Cat trapped in box

to perform the specific actions that led to positive outcomes. Thorndike summarized his findings as the **Law of Effect**: Behaviors that lead to positive outcomes in a situation are likely to be repeated again in the future (Thorndike, 1898).

Skinner's Experiments

B. F. Skinner FIGURE 6-12, another major figure in behaviorism, pursued this finding to determine how individuals learn from the consequences of their actions. In Skinner's theory, the individual freely chooses to emit some behavior, which is followed by some kind of consequence (Skinner, 1938). When the consequences are pleasant, the individual is much more likely to do that behavior again. Skinner called this "reinforcement learning," because positive outcomes reinforce, or strengthen, the chance of performing that specific behavior again. This comes from its everyday meaning: If something is reinforced, it is made stronger. So if your dog sits and you hand him a treat, the treat is the **reinforcer**: It acts to make the behavior (sitting) more likely to occur again.

Skinner conducted the bulk of his research using laboratory rats and pigeons. The tasks they learned to perform and the reinforcers he used in the studies were very simple. However, by varying which behaviors received reinforcement and how the rewards were

FIGURE 6-12 B. F. Skinner was very influential learning theorist, and a major figure in 20th-century American culture.

provided, Skinner was able to characterize many important principles that predict the behaviors people do even in complex situations. He started with the simplest design possible, known as the **Skinner box (operant chamber)** FIGURE 6-13. The box was large enough for the animal to move about but was starkly empty except for a single response mechanism and a feeding tray. For the rat, the response bar could be pressed with its paws, and for a pigeon, a disk could be pecked to register a response. When the animal performed the desired response (pushed down the bar or pecked the disk), the box would automatically drop a pellet of food into the tray. This food served as the reinforcer: The animal learned to perform whatever action led to the appearance of the food. A recorder was connected to the box to measure the animal's responses over time. This simple setup allowed Skinner to investigate how reinforcement affected behavior.

FIGURE 6-13 The Skinner box is a controlled environment where animals could be trained while recording their responses automatically.

Reinforcement

Skinner studied how animals learned to perform specific behaviors and how their learning was affected by reinforcement FIGURE 6-14. The key idea about reinforcement is that it always brings on a more pleasant state for the learner. **Positive reinforcement** is like getting a reward, where a behavior is followed by a pleasant stimulus (for example, a food pellet). Behavior can also be reinforced—made stronger—by a "negative reinforcer." **Negative reinforcement** occurs when a behavior is followed by the termination of a negative stimulus. For example, a loud noise may be sounding in the box, and when the rat pushes down the lever, the noise stops. This is "negative" because it means taking something away from the learner, but it results in a more pleasant outcome (no loud noise). It is important to remember that reinforcement always makes the behavior stronger and more likely to happen again because it produces a desirable outcome for the learner. *Positive* refers to applying a reinforcer (like giving a medal), and *negative* refers to taking away something as a reinforcer (like a loud noise). But both always lead to increases in the target behavior.

Skinner box (operant chamber) A testing apparatus with a response mechanism that also delivers reinforcement.

Positive reinforcement A consequence that creates a pleasant state, making behavior more likely to occur.

Negative reinforcement A consequence that takes away an unpleasant state, making behavior more likely to occur.

Primary reinforcer A reward that provides basic needs.

FIGURE 6-14 Skinner's view was that "reinforcement" always makes the behavior grow stronger.

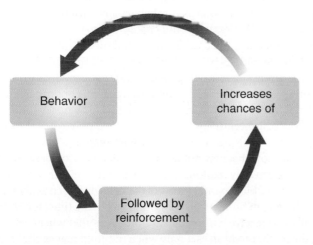

These examples work well within the Skinner box, but do human behaviors also receive positive and negative reinforcers? Yes! An example of a positive reinforcer is a smile; when you receive one, you are more likely to keep doing whatever behavior you are doing. An example of a negative reinforcer is the mechanism in your car that encourages you to put on your seatbelt. If you sit in the car without your belt, a pinging sound will occur that is unpleasant, and it will continue until you click on your seatbelt. Immediately, the obnoxious pinging noise is terminated. Therefore, your behavior of buckling up is negatively reinforced; that is, the annoying noise ends once you perform the desired behavior. In both cases, the reinforcement strengthens the behavior (makes it more likely to occur again); however, reinforcement occurs both by applying a positive reward and by removing a negative stimulus (see **TABLE 6-2**).

Skinner defined two types of reinforcers. **Primary reinforcers** bring about a pleasant state by fulfilling some biological need. These reinforcers are the basics—food, water,

TABLE 6-2 Reinforcement Learning

	Positive	Negative
Pleasant outcome increases behavior	Add something "Give a medal"	Take something away "Turn off alarm"

FIGURE 6-15 Food is a primary reinforcer because its positive value to the learner is already established.

FIGURE 6-16 A kiss is a secondary reinforcer for this dolphin because it had to learn that affection from its trainer means positive consequences for it.

Secondary reinforcer (conditioned reinforcer) A reward that can be exchanged for ones meeting basic needs.

Shaping Reinforcing an approximation of a behavior initially, and then increasing successively to reach the target behavior.

air—so any behavior that brings these primary reinforcers is quickly repeated FIGURE 6-15. **Secondary reinforcers** (also called **conditioned reinforcers**, because they are learned) are pleasing because they are associated with a primary reinforcer. They don't, in and of themselves, fulfill any biological need, but they are positively viewed because they can be turned into a primary reinforcer FIGURE 6-16. The secondary reinforcer that is very effective for people is money. Money is not a primary reinforcer because you can't eat it; however, people will work hard for it because it can buy the primary reinforcers you need. Examples of secondary reinforcers used by Skinner in his studies include tokens that are given meaning because they can be exchanged for primary reinforcers like food. So a monkey will happily work for a pile of tokens it can exchange for a banana.

Acquisition and Shaping

The acquisition of behaviors in Skinner boxes was straightforward: The researcher would wait until the animal (say, a rat) did the desired behavior (let's say, pushed down on the response bar), and then she would press a button to release the food pellet into the tray. The rat would quickly learn to perform that behavior (push the bar) in order to receive the food reinforcer. But what if the animal in training never does push the bar? How can behaviors be acquired if you have to wait until the animal does them before you can reinforce them? Skinner's answer is a procedure called **shaping**, or rewarding successive approximations of the target behavior. The trainer chooses a target behavior that is short of the eventual goal; so, rather than pushing the bar, the initial goal would be to move in the direction of the bar. As soon as this behavior occurred, the rat would be reinforced. Then the trainer would change the goal to be closer to pushing, such as touching the bar. The rat would then be reinforced only if it touched the bar with its paw. By successively meeting and then changing the goal, shaping allows a complex behavior to be gradually trained.

Using shaping, Skinner demonstrated that pigeons can learn to play Ping-Pong! Initially, the pigeons received rewards whenever their beaks touched the ball. Eventually, they received food only when they actually scored a point on the pigeon across the table. Shaping allows the development of behaviors that may not occur on their own. And because operant conditioning can only reinforce the behaviors the animal emits, it is critical to come up with a way to establish partial forms of the behavior, eventually requiring the complete behavior. Shaping in human behavior occurs all of the time; for example, a child learning to talk will often receive reinforcement from its mother whenever it makes any sound. Over time, the mother reinforces it only when the child makes a "Ma" sound. Eventually, the mother waits until a full "Mama" is heard before rewarding her with attention. Skinner believed that the principles of learning he studied in his boxes were all that were needed to explain even the most complex human behaviors.

Generalization and Discrimination

Just as with classical conditioning, operant conditioning follows the principles of generalization and discrimination. When the rat learns to press the lever for a food reward, it may press it with its left paw, then its right, and then its nose; as long as the pellets keep falling with each bar press, the actual behavior can be of a general type that works to depress the bar. Alternatively, behaviors can be discriminated so that only a particular type of press—say, using both paws—releases the food. The rats will quickly learn which aspects of their behaviors are required and which can be varied. With any learning task, the learner will adapt to perform what is necessary to achieve the reinforcer and will stop performing behaviors that don't lead to reinforcement.

But what happens when reinforcement occurs by accident? Skinner (1948) discussed the problem of superstition through reinforcement. He set up a Skinner box that dropped a food pellet at varied time intervals. The reinforcement in this case had nothing to do with the animal but simply occurred on a random, predetermined basis. Now, imagine you are the pigeon in the box. You are waiting around for food and decide to try bobbing your head. Coincidentally, the food drops, reinforcing your head bobbing. Now you think you've got it: Keep bobbing, and the reinforcer will come. It may take some repetitions, but again, food drops, and you become convinced that your bobbing is the cause. In this way, Skinner argues, learners can become convinced that certain behaviors lead to reinforcements because it has happened in the past. Baseball players, for example, are known to repeat the meals they ate and actions they performed just before hitting that home run. Then, because they believe in the connection, they perform these rituals every time, and consequently, they again occur before the reinforcement of a home run happens. Learners are on the watch for reinforcements, and consequently they may "learn" from them even when no real connection to the outcome exists!

Extinction

As in classical conditioning, operant conditioning uses the term *extinction* to refer to "unlearning" the behavior. Imagine that you've trained a rat to press a bar for food. Now you unplug the box, and no more food will fall. How long do you think the rat will continue pressing, hoping for its food reward? It may do so for quite a while, but eventually, the rat will give up and stop emitting the bar pressing behavior. When it does, we say that the behavior has been **extinguished**. Animals are fairly quick to learn that the gravy train has stopped and are efficient with their efforts. People, on the other hand, are notorious for not giving up in the face of extinction. For example, Orne (1962) did a study to determine how long people would continue working on a task with no clear reward. He sat his subjects in a room full of papers with multiplication problems on them and asked them to begin working. Then he asked them to begin tearing up each piece of paper once they had solved the problems to show them that their work had no purpose. Still, they continued working. After 3 hours, Orne called a halt to the study, failing to see the extinction point any other animal would have reached. When asked, the people in the study said they had developed their own rationales for why they were asked to do the problems, and they kept going even though no reinforcement appeared to be coming. Later in this chapter, we will return to the role that cognition plays in learning.

Schedules of Reinforcement

Ideally, you would follow every behavior with a reinforcer every time it occurs, called **continuous reinforcement**. This makes the behavior very reliable, and very rapid, in response. Immediately reinforcing the behavior is much more effective than delaying it until later. In fact, for some animals like rats, a 30-second delay in delivering the reinforcement may mean they fail to learn the behavior. People, however, are much better at working for delayed reinforcement. (For example, some students work for 4 years to receive their college degrees!)

However, it may not be practical to provide reinforcement with every behavior. Instead, an **intermittent reinforcement** may be used, in which the reinforcer is delivered after only some of the responses. The benefit of using intermittent reinforcement, also called partial reinforcement, is that you don't have to supply the reinforcer each time the desired behavior occurs. For example, if a rat is working for food pellets, it may eventually become full and stop the behavior. However, if it must perform the behavior multiple times in order to receive the reward once, it will be able to work longer. Another benefit is that intermittent reinforcement is more resistant to extinction. If you are paid $10 every time you mow the lawn, it only takes one time of not getting paid for you to notice. But if you are paid only every 10th time, it may be a while before you notice that the reinforcement has stopped.

A **schedule of reinforcement** refers to planning the timing of the application of reinforcers **TABLE 6-3**. If the reinforcement occurs, for example, after every other response, or every fifth response, the schedule is called a **fixed-ratio schedule** FIGURE 6-17. If you frequent a particular coffee shop, you may be given a card with which, after 10 purchases, you

Extinguish To stop the display of a given behavior.

Continuous reinforcement Following every behavior with a consequence.

Intermittent reinforcement Following behavior with a consequence sometimes, but not every time.

Schedule of reinforcement A plan for applying consequences following a behavior.

Fixed-ratio schedule Providing reinforcement after a set number of repeated behaviors.

TABLE 6-3 Schedules of Reinforcement

Name	Time of Reinforcement
Continuous	After each behavior occurs
Intermittent (partial)	Only after some repetitions of the behavior
Fixed ratio	Only after a set number of repeated behaviors
Variable ratio	After an average (with some variation) number of repetitions
Fixed interval	Only after a set time has passed and the behavior occurs
Variable interval	Only after an average (with some variation) amount of time has passed and the behavior occurs

FIGURE 6-17 A fixed-ratio schedule of reinforcement.

receive a free coffee. This fixed-ratio schedule provides a reward—the free coffee—only after you perform the behavior 10 times. Another type of reinforcement schedule is the **variable-ratio schedule** FIGURE 6-18. This involves setting an average number of times the behavior must occur before the reward is given, but the actual number varies around that average. An effective example of a variable-ratio schedule is a slot machine found in casinos. The machines are set to pay off on a variable ratio: For example, after an average of 10,000 quarters are played, a payout of winnings will occur. But it is not predictable exactly when that will occur, because the payoff may occur much earlier or much later than that average. This variable-ratio schedule works well to keep the response coming because of the uncertainty about exactly when the reward will occur.

Both of these **ratio schedules** are based on the number of times the behavior occurs. As a result, the learner tends to perform frequent, rapid responses because the reward is contingent—depends upon—the number of responses made. The ratio schedules are very effective in motivating fast responses, with the fixed-ratio schedule producing the most responses over the shortest amount of time FIGURE 6-19. For example, with your coffee card, you know exactly how many more coffees you have to buy before you will get your free one! But with the variable-ratio schedule, you are never certain about how many times you'll have to repeat the behavior before the reinforcement will come your way. As a result, variable-ratio schedules show greater resistance to extinction. It's harder to know when reinforcements have actually ended!

Two other reinforcement schedules are based on the amount of time that elapses between rewards. On time **interval schedules**, no amount of responding is going to hurry the reward; instead, some time must pass before the reinforcer is given. Most of

FIGURE 6-18 A variable-ratio schedule of reinforcement.

Variable-ratio schedule Providing reinforcement after an average number of repeated behaviors.

Ratio schedules Reinforcement is provided after behaviors are repeated a number of times.

Interval schedule Reinforcement is provided after time passes, and then a behavior is repeated.

FIGURE 6-19 The delivery schedule for reinforcement makes a difference in how quickly the learner will perform the behavior.

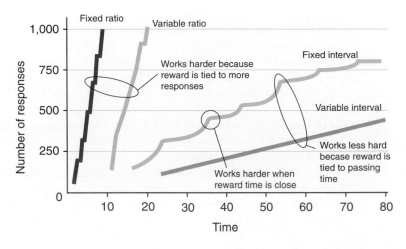

us are employed on a **fixed-interval schedule**—that is, we receive a paycheck after some period of work FIGURE 6-20. So, for example, our reward—the check—comes every 2 weeks, even though our behavior of working is spread over that 2-week interval. This type of schedule is more convenient for administering the reinforcement. But it is not as effective in getting frequent, fast behavior to occur because the learner knows he or she has to wait, and that the speed or frequency of responding does not determine when the reinforcement will occur. The slowest responding is seen in the **variable-interval schedule**, in which a reward will occur after a variable period of time FIGURE 6-21. An example is checking your mailbox for new mail: After time passes, you will likely receive more mail, but you can't predict when, and the number of times you check for the mail does not affect whether you will receive it. What is the best schedule of reinforcement for motivating fast, frequent responding? Continuous reinforcement! That way, you know you will be reinforced as soon as you perform the response.

FIGURE 6-20 A fixed-interval schedule of reinforcement.

Punishment

In reinforcement learning, you are attempting to strengthen or increase the likelihood of the behavior occurring again. Unlike the reinforcement learning we've been discussing, the goal of punishment is to *extinguish* a behavior rather than reinforce it. That is, you want the behavior that is punished to stop and never occur again. This key difference separates reinforcement learning from punishment FIGURE 6-22. Punishment places the learner in a more negative situation by either applying a bad consequence or removing a positive state. In contrast, the outcome for learners is always more *positive* following reinforcement. That is, they are enjoying their reinforcer (such as food), or they are enjoying the removal of a negative reinforcer (the absence of the pinging noise now that their seatbelts are latched). Punishment creates a negative state in the learner through **punishment by application** of a negative event, such as a spanking, or **punishment by removal** of a positive event or state, such as being grounded (not allowed to leave the house).

Studies of learning show that punishment is not an effective tactic for learning. One reason is that punishment informs the learner about what *not* to do, but it does not inform him or her about what to do instead. So if someone steals food for her family and is then arrested, the punishment may stop the behavior of stealing, but it does not solve the problem of needing food. Another problem with punishment is that it may lead to imitation of the

FIGURE 6-21 A variable-interval schedule of reinforcement.

	Add to situation	**Remove from situation**
Reinforcement (always increases behavior)	Positive reinforcement	Negative reinforcement
Punishment (may decrease behavior)	Punishment by application	Punishment by removal

FIGURE 6-22 The key difference is that reinforcement always strengthens behavior, while punishment is intended to decrease it.

Fixed-interval schedule Providing reinforcement for the first behavior after a set amount of time passes.

Variable-interval schedule Providing reinforcement for the first behavior after a set average amount of time has passed.

Punishment by application Attempting to extinguish a behavior by applying a negative consequence.

Punishment by removal Attempting to extinguish a behavior by removing a positive state.

Yelling at children may teach them to act similarly toward others.

punisher rather than stopping the targeted behavior. For example, if a child hits another child and then receives a spanking, the child may have difficulty learning to stop hitting others due to modeling (discussed in the next section).

A review of studies on physical punishment concluded that children subjected to physical punishment tend to become more aggressive themselves (Gershoff, 2002). Many countries have made physical punishment illegal (such as Germany, Norway, Finland, and Israel), while others employ physical punishment for mild transgressions such as vandalism. In the United States, a parent can be prosecuted for injuring a child through physical punishment. According to Alan Kazdin (2008), "More than one-third of all parents who start out with relatively mild punishments end up crossing the line drawn by the state to define child abuse, such as hitting with an object, harsh and cruel hitting, and so on."

Finally, punishment may also lead to negative emotional consequences through classical conditioning. The application of punishment, such as a spanking by a parent, may lead to emotional responses and fear in the child. These feelings then become associated with the parent who performs the punishment. So, through punishment, the child may feel fearful in the presence of the parent as a classically conditioned response to the experience of being punished. However, there are some situations in which some form of punishment may be necessary. If so, punishment that removes the learner from a desirable situation, such as having to sit on a "time out" chair rather than play, are much less problematic than physical punishment. In addition, some behaviors may post a danger to the learner. For example, some disturbed clinical patients may pull their own hair or hit themselves repeatedly; in these situations, punishments such as a short burst of sprayed water or even a mild electrical shock have been employed (Lovaas, 1987).

If punishing undesirable behavior is not effective, then what does work? It is much more effective to stop "attending to" undesirable behaviors and start rewarding desired ones. This can be tricky, because to the learner, punishment may be interpreted as a positive reinforcer. A classic example is a child having a tantrum in the grocery store aisle. This is undesirable behavior, and the parent wants it to stop. However, the actual response may be to stop shopping, pay attention to the child, soothe him, and perhaps bargain with him to gain his cooperation. The parent may feel she is obviously displeased by the behavior, but to the child, the response is reinforcing the tantrum: The child received attention, appeasement, and an early exit from shopping following the tantrum. In any learning situation, it is important to look at what outcome follows the behavior: If the behavior increases in frequency, it is likely that something about the situation is providing reinforcement to the learner. Solving behavior problems often requires careful attention to what response is occurring after a behavior. From years of study of reinforcement learning, we know that behaviors that are reinforced—in any way—are more likely to happen again. Consequently, the advice from learning theorists is that undesired behaviors should be absolutely ignored. Then quickly jump in to reinforce any positive behaviors once they occur.

Review of Terminology, Processes, and Factors That Affect Operant Conditioning

Operant conditioning refers to the ways we "operate" on our environment: We do behaviors and then experience their reinforcement or lack thereof. Here's an example of reinforcement in its purest form: karaoke. You stand in front of a room full of friends and strangers and belt out "I Wanna Know What Love Is" by Foreigner. How do you know whether to do that ever again? By the tremendous applause that follows your performance! Your behavior is reinforced by the clapping, and you're much more likely to sing again. If, instead, your performance is followed by painful silence, you may be less likely to volunteer again. Our behavior in the world is constantly shaped by the reinforcement we receive: Do something, see what the result is, and act based on that feedback. Reinforcement can be positive, where a good thing is given, or negative, where a bad thing is taken away. The key is that reinforcement always makes the behavior more likely to happen again.

Shaping is important in operant conditioning because you have to wait until the learner emits the desired behavior—voluntarily—before you can reinforce it. So you might start by rewarding her for doing part of the behavior at first, then hold off until she does more of it, and so on, shaping the behavior into what you want to see. Just as with classical conditioning, you may see generalization (now you are happy to dance as well as sing) or discrimination (you learn to sing only when your mom is in the crowd to start the applause). But if the applause stops, you will also eventually stop singing. Operant conditioning depends on the reinforcement to maintain the behavior, and a variety of schedules for reinforcement have been identified. Reinforcing behaviors you want to see again works much better for learning than punishing behaviors you want to extinguish.

Contemporary Views of Operant Conditioning

B. F. Skinner was one of the most important intellectual figures in psychology, but his theory was quite controversial. He raised the question of whether we ever truly act without expectations of consequences or whether "free will" is limited by the realities of reinforcement:

> "In the traditional view, a person is free. He is autonomous in the sense that his behavior is uncaused. He can therefore be held responsible for what he does and justly punished if he offends. That view, together with its associated practices, must be re-examined when a scientific analysis reveals unsuspected controlling relations between behavior and environment" (Skinner, 1972, p. 17).

If our behavior is determined by the reinforcements it will receive, then are we really free to do as we choose?

Skinner's strong beliefs in the power of the environment in controlling behavior led him to minimize any contributions of internal, cognitive processes. At one point, he claimed that the mental thoughts we experience are also behaviors, in the form of "subvocal" speech (Skinner, 1957; 1990). He remained unwilling to consider any role for cognition in determining behavior or that the principles of operant conditioning might be altered by biological influences. However, other researchers quickly found evidence that operant conditioning is not the only influence on our behavior.

Learned Helplessness

Some studies of operant conditioning use an **escape learning** procedure (Durgam, 2001). Animals are placed in a shuttle box with two compartments. An electrical current, mildly painful but not harmful, is passed through the floor on one side of the box, and the animal quickly learns to jump over a partition or through an opening to the other side to escape the shock. Rats quickly learn signals, such as flashing lights or buzzers, that predict when the shocks will occur and jump into the safe area in advance ("avoidance learning"). However, Seligman and Maier (1967) altered this procedure by giving dogs advance training. First, they were exposed to electrical shocks that they could neither control nor escape from. After this initial training, they were placed in the shuttle box for the escape learning procedure. However, these dogs acted in a way that no previous animal had: They simply failed to learn to escape from the shocks, even when escape was easy and readily learned by dogs without the initial training.

Seligman called this phenomenon "**learned helplessness**." The dogs initially unable to escape the shock seemed unable to learn that they were *now* able to escape. They seemed to have generalized their learning to feel they no longer had any control of consequences. As a result, they were unable to learn to respond when the consequences changed. Seligman extended this concept to human behavior in people suffering from depression. When you feel your efforts at controlling events in your life repeatedly fail, you may become depressed and give up at even trying to succeed. Later, you may be in situations in which you can control the consequences, but you may still fail to act, believing you are not able to control the outcome. For example, if you were to enroll in an advanced language course without any background and receive failing grades on every assignment, you may quickly give up on your efforts. Later, even if the instructor makes the assignments much easier, you may still put out little effort, believing you have no control over whether you will do well in the course.

The feeling of personal control over outcomes—that your behaviors will lead to appropriate reinforcements—is key to feeling effective and in control in life. When people feel their setbacks are temporary and are limited to a specific area, they are more motivated to keep working and may then end up successful. People are more likely to become depressed if they believe that their lack of control over outcomes is permanent or a part

Escape learning An acquired behavior performed to avoid a noxious stimulus.

Learned helplessness When an animal fails to take action to escape a noxious stimulus.

of their own basic personality rather than based in the situation (Abramson, Seligman, & Teasdale, 1978). These findings were important because operant conditioning theory would never have predicted them. In reinforcement learning, no animal would stop trying to repeat behaviors that lead to good outcomes. The results showing that dogs—and people—can give up trying to learn posed a problem for operant conditioning theory. It also led Seligman to develop the field of positive psychology to counteract these effects.

Intrinsic Motivation

It would seem that rewards are always good, leading to more of the desired behavior. But rewards can also result in discouraging rather than reinforcing behavior. A classic study (Lepper, Greene, & Nisbett, 1973) gave preschool children felt markers to play with, and most children enjoyed this new toy. One week later, the children were divided into three groups. Children in the first group were told they would receive a reward (a gold star and a ribbon) for playing with the markers. Children in the second group were not told about the reward but received one when they finished playing, just like the first group. Children in the third group were not told about the reward, nor did they receive one when they finished playing. After a week, their teachers put out the markers in the classroom with no instructions. How much time would the children spend playing with the markers? The children who had played with them for the reward—Group 1—now played with them less! Those who had no reward or had the surprise reward (so they didn't feel they had participated just for the reward) chose to play more. What explains why reinforcing the first group backfired?

One possible explanation is that pleasurable activity (like playing with the markers) feels less so when it is rewarded. Lepper and colleagues argued that "playing" follows from **intrinsic motivation**, in which an internal drive or interest gives rise to the behavior. By providing **extrinsic motivation**—giving the reward—for this behavior, the reinforcement had provided an external source to account for their behavior. This explanation is quite cognitive: When considering whether to play with the markers again, the children who received rewards could justify their earlier playing as driven by the reward, not by their own interest. As a result, they may conclude they don't really have an inherent, or intrinsic, interest in playing with them. Providing reinforcements for behaviors that people would choose to do anyway may backfire, convincing them that the only reason to behave in this way is to receive the reward. Then, when the reward is withdrawn, the behavior stops. When people are intrinsically motivated to read, to create, and to learn, adding artificial reinforcements may take away the joy that arises from the behavior itself. Consequently, adding external rewards can decrease the performance of some behaviors.

These studies raise issues about the role of cognition in learning, and their results are clear: People do not simply and mindlessly repeat behaviors that are followed by reinforcements. Accounting for learning will require that we include more cognitive variables in the mix.

Biological Influences on Operant Conditioning

Biological influences are also apparent in the use of operant principles for training animals. In movies and television, live animal shows at outdoor aquariums, theme parks, and zoos, and in our homes, the principles of operant conditioning have been successfully applied to train animals to do very unusual things. Two of Skinner's students, Keller and Marian Breland (1961), successfully trained a wide variety of animals, including dogs, cats, chickens, parakeets, turkeys, pigs, ducks, hamsters, porpoises, and killer whales—eventually training more than 10,000 animals from more than 100 different species. However, in their work, the Brelands noticed that not all behaviors were readily learned by all species. For example, it was quite simple to train a dog or cat to jump, since that is a behavior it naturally performs. However, teaching them to crawl on their bellies proved much more difficult.

The reason is that animals are biologically predisposed to perform certain actions related to their survival, and those behaviors are specific to the ways each animal hunts for food and defends itself. In addition, the animals showed a tendency to revert to their typical behaviors, called **instinctual drift** (see FIGURE 6-23). For a bank commercial, trainers attempted to teach a raccoon to pick up coins and deposit them in a piggy bank. However,

Intrinsic motivation Behavior is repeated without any external reinforcement.

Extrinsic motivation Behavior is repeated only when external reinforcement is provided.

Instinctual drift The tendency for new behaviors to revert to ones familiar to that species.

FIGURE 6-23 It is easier to train a pig to play soccer than other sports because they naturally "root" into the ground, behavior that helps them learn to move the ball.

while readily able to manipulate the coins, the raccoon proved reluctant to release the shiny objects into the bank, pulling them back out again and again. Contrary to operant principles, you can't train every response in every animal equally easily. As with classical conditioning, biological constraints intervene to guide learning.

Applying Principles of Operant Conditioning

Because reinforcement learning is so effective, it has been applied in many circumstances in which other types of learning are not possible. For example, in training animals, the principles of operant conditioning work well to produce the desired behavior. The same principles are applied to humans in a therapy called behavior analysis, or **behavior modification**. In this therapy, concrete rewards are offered for specific, easy-to-perform behaviors, allowing the establishment of successful change. For example, Ivar Lovaas (1987) worked with children with severe forms of autism. He was able to use immediate rewards, such as food, drink, and hugs, to reinforce simple requests such as sitting in a chair. By working on these simple, successful behaviors, other types of learning experiences were then possible. Behavior modification is especially effective for individuals for whom language-based instruction is not possible. Because all organisms can understand positive outcomes, reinforcement learning can train all types of learners. Behavior modification is in widespread use in clinical therapy and now has gained favor for encouraging socially beneficial activities. In Ann Arbor, Michigan, recycling behaviors are tracked by weighing containers from each household, and points are awarded that can be used to purchase prizes. In schools, sports, and clinics, operant conditioning is working to help people learn to perform beneficial behaviors.

One prominent example of operant conditioning occurs in the workplace. You may have noticed that salespeople are sometimes paid on commission rather than by the hour; that is, their pay is based on the number of sales they make while on the job. Realtors, too, earn money only once they successfully sell a house. Does making your paycheck contingent upon making a sale motivate people to sell more? A study in a major department store set out to test this idea (Luthans, Paul, & Baker, 1981). More than 80 retail clerks were observed on the job over a period of 60 days, and their performance was scored for sales, stock work, idle periods, and absence from their stations. After 20 days, half of the staff were told about a new incentive program that would take place for the next 20 days: Those with the best performance would earn paid time off, equivalent cash, and a chance for a paid vacation. After the incentive period ended, both groups were still monitored for another 20 days. FIGURE 6-24 shows the results of the study. In the "baseline" period, before the incentives were introduced, performance measures in the control and experimental groups looked very similar. But beginning on day 20, and for the next 20 days while the incentives were given, the experimental group outperformed the control group by a large margin. Reinforcements worked to motivate better performance in the salespeople. Interestingly, this improved performance continued in the final phase even

Positive reinforcement has been shown to be effective in changing behaviors of children with severe autism.

Behavior modification An operant conditioning program designed to achieve a goal.

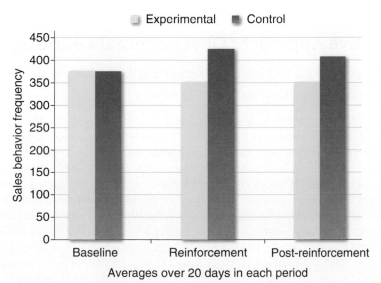

FIGURE 6-24 In the baseline period, both groups performed the same. However, once the experimental group began receiving reinforcements, their performance was much better than that of the control group, even when the reinforcement period ended.
Source: Data from Luthans, F., Paul, R., & Baker, D. (1981). An experimental analysis of the impact of contingent reinforcement on salesperson's performance behavior. Journal of Applied Psychology, 66 (3). 314–323.

when no incentives were offered. The experimental group maintained better performance even when the reinforcement ended.

Token economies Situations in which easy-to-use secondary reinforcers are traded in for a meaningful reward.

Behavioral contract The learner signs a written specification of an operant conditioning program.

Token economies are another method for developing long-term behavior changes. Tokens redeemable for privileges or rewards can be given out to reinforce behaviors on the spot. One example of a token economy occurs at a language-learning camp in Minnesota, where teachers reward campers when they attempt to speak in the new language. Then, when camp ends, tokens are traded in for large prizes. Token economies help by reinforcing the behavior whenever it occurs with an immediate symbol of reward, even though the reward itself is not given until later. For children, tokens such a ribbons, trophies, and gold stars are used to reinforce new behaviors, such as completing assignments, competing in sport, or participating in science fairs. Even for adults, the use of token economies can help people to reinforce new behaviors immediately and learn to maintain them over time. For individuals who have difficulty understanding the consequences of their behavior, a **behavioral contract** may be created to make an explicit link from behavior to reward. For example, a homeless shelter may require specific behaviors every day in order to stay overnight, such as making beds or returning by a certain time. Contracts may be especially helpful for adolescents or individuals with communicative or emotional disorders. Clear expectations that can be successfully met can help individuals establish desired behaviors.

CONCEPT LEARNING CHECK 6.3 | *Comparing Consequences of Behavior*

For each example below, determine what type of operant conditioning has occurred. First, identify the subject and his or her behavioral response. Decide whether the response was (a) strengthened through reinforcement or stopped through punishment. If the response was strengthened through reinforcement, decide whether it was (b) the result of positive (something added) or negative (something taken away) reinforcement.

1. Every time Billy says "please" when he makes a request, his parents do as he asks. After 1 week, Billy almost always remembers to say "please."

2. When Sarah interrupts her mom when she's talking on the phone, her mom stops the conversation to tell Sarah not to do that, and asks, "What is so important it can't wait?" After a month, Sarah interrupts her mom every time she makes a call.

3. Whenever Pete brings home a paper with an "A," he is excused from doing his usual household chores for the rest of the week. He begins to get more "A" grades.

4. Maxell did a terrific job on a sales report in just 1 day, so her boss asked her to do all of the reports for the office. A week later, Maxell had not yet finished any more reports.

6.4 A Cognitive Approach: Observational Learning

We readily benefit in our own learning by observing the behavior of others.

- Explain the evidence that learning can occur without acting out behavior.

A third type of learning involves no response and no reinforcement: In observational learning, knowledge or behavior changes simply from watching others. Without ever experiencing a situation yourself, you can watch what unfolds when others take action around you. This is also called **modeling**, because we imitate the behavior of a model provided by another person. As social animals, we are constantly in a position to observe and learn from the behavior of others. Where does the line form in this coffee shop? Should you take your shoes off when entering this home? What's the speed limit on this road? We constantly gain needed information simply by matching the behavior of others around us.

Modeling Performing specific behaviors that others observe.

Behavioral theorists would never agree to such a cognitive description of learning. But a great deal of evidence has accumulated to suggest that what the animal—or human—*knows* about events matters. Modern behaviorists see that it is necessary to make inferences about what is occurring in the mind, or cognition, even to explain learning in rats. As Rescorla (1988) stated, "Conditioning is not a stupid process by which an organism willy-nilly forms associations between any two stimuli that happen to co-occur. Rather the organism is better seen as an information seeker using logical and perceptual relations among events and its own preconceptions to form a sophisticated representation of its world" (p. 154).

How did learning theories change from the radical view that only external behavior matters?

CRITICAL THINKING APPLICATION

Can the principles of operant conditioning be used to change your own behavior? Here's an experiment on behavior modification you can attempt. First, review the major terms from our discussion of operant conditioning. Can you design a behavior modification program to help you achieve a goal?

Step 1: Goal. First, think about your goal. Select a behavior that you want to perform more often (e.g., floss your teeth), not one that you want to stop (e.g., smoking). Ideally, the behavior would be something you do at least several times a day; for example, "Increase the amount of time I study every day." Then, propose an operational definition (quantitative rather than qualitative) of your target behavior so you can measure the change. For example, if your target behavior is to study more, how many hours each day would constitute studying "more"?

Step 2: Baseline. Next, keep a written record of your behavior for 3 days without beginning any conditioning. Just note whenever you do the behavior (e.g., study, and for how long), for several days.

Step 3: Conditioning. Now you are ready to begin the conditioning. But first, you have to identify a reinforcer that works for you. It must be something that you can control, that you will make use of only when you do the target behavior, and that you find pleasurable. Some examples might be watching a video, calling a friend to talk, or eating a cookie. Decide on the contingencies, or how you will administer the reinforcer; for example, "For every hour I study, I can eat one cookie." Or, "For every day I study for 4 hours, I can watch 1 hour of television." Try to think of a variety of possible reinforcers, and choose one that will motivate you but will not be too expensive or have harmful, unpleasant, or unintended consequences. Be very specific about what you must do to receive the reinforcement. If you can't trust yourself as your own trainer,

ask a roommate or friend to apply the reinforcer for you. Next, think about the schedule of reinforcement: Will it be continuous, such as eating a cookie after every assignment you complete? Or will it be a partial reinforcement schedule in which you receive the reinforcement only after some responses? Will it be a ratio (depending on the number of responses that occur) or interval (depending on how much time has passed) schedule? Then, for at least 5 days, follow the reinforcement plan you designed.

Step 4: Extinction. During this period, no reinforcement is given. Continue writing down the number (or length) of times your behavior occurs. Keep a record for at least 3 days.

Step 5: Principles of operant conditioning. Now examine your records. How much did you do your target behavior before conditioning started? How many times did you receive reinforcement during the training period? And how often did you perform the behavior when it was no longer being reinforced? What do you conclude about your behavior modification program? Did your desired behavior decrease during extinction, when the reinforcement period stopped? If so, perhaps reinforcement will be required to maintain your new behavior. If your desired behavior continued even though it was no longer being reinforced, what do you conclude about operant conditioning? Are there other aspects of the situation that may be providing rewards for your new behavior? For example, perhaps you are enjoying your studying more, and that is causing you to continue studying more even without the cookies!

Tolman's Latent Learning

One learning theorist who raised issues with behaviorist theories was Edward C. Tolman (1886–1959). He identified **latent learning**, in which learning takes place without any

Latent learning
Knowledge that is not displayed in behavior until reinforcement is provided.

change in displayed behavior (Tolman, 1948). One study (Tolman & Honzik, 1930) had rats learn to run through mazes for a food reward at the goal box. With the reward, this group showed steady improvement by making fewer errors over the 17 days in the study FIGURE 6-25. Another group was allowed to run the maze each day, but there was no food in the goal box. This group showed continued wrong turns and errors, and just a small improvement in their performance over the days. This result appears to support operant conditioning theory because they didn't improve without reinforcement. But a third group started out with no reinforcement for their first 10 days in the maze. On the 11th day, and every day after that, a food reward awaited them in the goal box. If these rats had learned nothing in the first 10 days without reward, as predicted by operant theory, they should now begin to learn just like the first group of rats did on Day 1 and show the same steady improvement over days.

FIGURE 6-25 Tolman and Honzik's results showed that rats that were reinforced only after 11 days of wandering the maze (the no reinforcement then reinforcement group) quickly responded to reinforcement, performing better than rats always reinforced (the always reinforced group). The never reinforced group never received any reinforcement. *Source: Data from Tolman, E. C. (1948). Cognitive maps in rats and men. Psychological Review, 55, 189–208; Tolman, E. C., & Honzik, C. H. (1930). Introduction and removal of reward and maze performance in rats.* University of California Publications in Psychology, 4, 257–275.

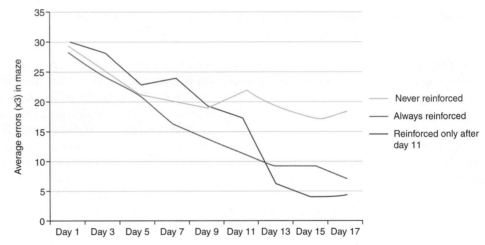

But they didn't! On the remaining days of the study, these rats showed an immediate reduction in errors and even performed better than the rats that had received reinforcement all along. Clearly, this third group had learned from its "purposeless" wanderings in the maze, because as soon as there was a reward, the rats quickly found it. The evidence Tolman collected showed that learning does take place without reinforcement. In addition, the studies showed that learning can occur in the absence of any displayed behavior. Tolman suggested the rats had developed **cognitive maps** of the maze, so that when they wanted to reach the goal quickly for the reward, they had an internal representation leading them there. As evidence from these and other studies accumulated, learning psychologists were forced to begin incorporating cognitive processes into their theories.

Cognitive map A mental representation of a physical path to a goal location.

Tolman demonstrated that cognition must be incorporated into learning theories. His rats learned about the maze without any reinforcement taking place and were ready to use their knowledge when needed. This opened the door for theories that explicitly discussed the cognitive changes taking place during learning.

Bandura's Social-Cognitive Learning Theory

In an experiment to demonstrate this point, a researcher named Albert Bandura set out to test observational learning in a study with 5- and 6-year-old children (Bandura, Ross, & Ross, 1961). In this study, children watched a videotape in which an adult model played with a large inflatable doll called a Bobo doll. In the video, the adult model performed violent actions upon the doll: kicking it, punching it, lifting it up and throwing it, and so forth. Next, the child was brought into a second room full of toys, and to introduce a feeling of frustration, they were told the toys in that room were for "the other children." Left alone in a third playroom, they soon found one of the toys there was the same Bobo doll shown in the video. Would there be any effects of seeing the violence in the video when the children were allowed to play on their own?

Bandura found plenty of evidence that the children were affected by the modeling they saw in the video. Not only were the children more violent with the Bobo doll, but they

Mice who wander in a maze without any reward will then run through it quickly once cheese is added to the goal box as a reward.

also performed actions very similar to the model's actions FIGURE 6-26. For example, they also lifted the large doll up and threw it and repeated phrases the model used ("Sock him in the nose!"). The children appeared to learn how to behave with this novel toy by copying the actions they had seen in the video. Learning, in the form of acquiring specific behaviors, had taken place simply through observing the model's behavior.

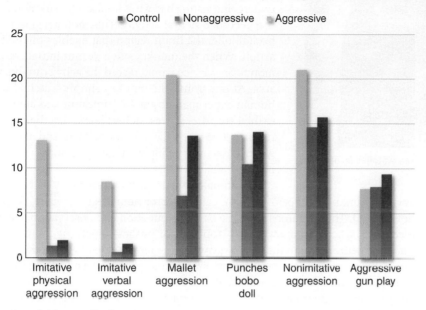

FIGURE 6-26 The results of Bandura's study of modeling aggression. Control (green) and nonaggressive model subjects (orange) showed less aggressive behaviors than the aggressive model subjects (blue).
Source: Data from Bandura, A., Ross, D., & Ross, S. A. (1961). Transmission of aggression through imitation of aggressive models. Journal of Abnormal and Social Psychology, 63, *575–582.*

Acquisition vs. Performance

Bandura proposed that two stages are required in observational learning: an acquisition stage and a performance stage. Recall the rats in Tolman's demonstration of latent learning: First, they wandered through the maze without any rewards. However, when the reward trials began, the rats were quick to find them, showing they had learned (during an acquisition stage) but had not demonstrated their knowledge until the rewards appeared (in the performance stage). Similarly, Bandura noted that observational learning can take place in an acquisition phase without any display of behavior from the learner. Then, in a performance stage, their behavior reveals the change they gained from having observed the model. Any parent can verify that children readily learn from observation but can show no sign until they perform the behavior—usually at a most embarrassing time!

Basic Processes

In later work, Bandura proposed four processes required for successful learning by observation (Bandura, 1977).

1. Attention. To learn by observation, you have to pay attention to the behavior being modeled and to the consequences of the behavior. While you may have witnessed someone preparing a meal many times, you may not have attended closely enough to perform the actions on your own. We also choose our models; so peers, movies, and celebrities may become effective models because they capture our attention.

2. Retention. Once observed, time may pass before you have the opportunity to take action. Will you recall the behavior you observed and remember its specific nature? Taking steps to mentally rehearse or think about the observations will aid in recall.

3. Reproduction. Even though you saw the necessary behaviors, you must be able to perform them yourself. You may have watched a chef throw pizza dough into the air, but you may not be able to reproduce that behavior and execute it correctly.

4. Motivation. Whether an observer ever takes action will be determined by whether he or she feels the behavior will be reinforced, or lead to a desirable consequence. People are more likely to imitate when models are rewarded for their behavior and observers see the behavior as accomplishing something they desire.

Observational learning proves that learning can occur without firsthand experience. The real question is what behaviors people will choose to imitate and where those behaviors will lead.

FIGURE 6-27 Some of the same neurons fire when a monkey watches an action as when it performs the same action.

Mirror neurons Neurons in the frontal lobe that respond to motor behavior in oneself and in others.

Biological Basis: Mirrors in the Brain

Recent evidence suggests that not only are we prepared to imitate others, but we also may have a built-in biological advantage in doing so. Researchers in Parma, Italy, were studying motor behavior in monkeys. A laboratory monkey undergoing testing had wires implanted in its motor cortex that recorded neural activity. This motor region is in the frontal lobe, the brain region that enables planning and action. When the monkey put a peanut into its mouth, a monitoring device would record the activity in this motor area. At one point, the monkey simply watched while a human experimenter grabbed a peanut and ate it. Much to their surprise, the researchers found that the same brain region active when the monkey grabbed and ate a peanut was made active by simply watching the human (or another monkey) do it FIGURE 6-27.

Eventually, the scientists realized they had discovered a previously unknown type of neuron, called **mirror neurons** (Rizzolatti, Fogassi, & Gallese, 2006). These neurons form the basis for imitation and observational learning. For example, when a monkey grasps, touches, or pushes something, neural activity occurs. The neurons fire in the same way when the monkey observes another monkey (or a person) performing the same behaviors. Brain scans reveal that humans, like monkeys, have a mirror neuron system (Iacoboni, 2008). As we observe others' actions, our brains generate an internal simulation of their activity. For example, watching a child eat an ice cream cone, we can imagine the sense of pleasure it generates, along with the sense of loss when she drops it to the ground. We may learn to understand another person's feelings by imitating them within our own neural system and playing out their consequences. Our mirror neurons may help us understand how others are feeling when we see a smile, a passionate kiss, or a painful blow. Some scientists speculate this system may be involved in our ability to develop empathy for others. In fact, the lack of connection to others displayed by individuals with autism may be linked to "broken mirrors" in this system (Iacoboni & Dapretto, 2006; Oberman & Ramachandran, 2007).

Certainly, the discovery of mirror neurons identified a potential biological mechanism to support our ability to learn by observing others.

Applying Principles of Observational Learning

By the time most children in this country reach adolescence, they have seen countless acts or portrayals of violence in the media. Think about your own exposure to violence. How many fights, gunshots, and killings have you seen depicted? Do you think this exposure has ever led to violence on your part? In the 1970s, it was believed that watching violence might lead to less aggression. The idea was that seeing violence was cathartic: It released your aggressive feelings to see aggression by others. However, experiments like Bandura's suggest that simply observing violence may make violence less offensive. Are we perhaps more accepting of violent behavior and therefore more likely to respond aggressively in some situations? Recent studies using video have shown that people do act more aggressively following viewing of aggression (Bushman & Huesmann, 2001). For example, in one study, college students' aggressive cognitions increased with the level of violence in a video, and their measured hostility and systolic blood pressure were higher in response to the most violent video (Bushman & Geen, 1990).

What about the effects of exposure to violent models on your sensitivity toward violence? One study (Carnagey, Anderson, & Bushman, 2007) tested college students who played 20 minutes of either violent (*Duke Nukem*, *Mortal Kombat*, and *Future Cop*) or nonviolent (*3D Pinball*, *3D Munch Man*, and *Tetra Madness*) games FIGURE 6-28. The researchers found that both groups showed similar results when having their heart rate and galvanic skin response tested. Next, they watched a 10-minute videotape of real-life violence, including police confrontations, fights among prisoners, people shooting at each other, and the like. Results showed that those who had played violent video games had weaker physiological responses to images of violent, real-life events than those who

FIGURE 6-28 Frequent exposure to violent images results in lowered physiological, and therefore psychological, responses.

played nonviolent games. Their findings suggest that violent video game exposure can cause a psychological desensitization to violence. The researchers warn: "It appears that individuals who play violent video games habituate, or 'get used to,' all the violence and eventually become physiologically numb to it. The modern entertainment media landscape could accurately be described as an effective systematic violence-desensitization tool." After repeated exposure in video games, violent images may no longer evoke the same psychological response (Carnagey et al., 2007).

A meta-analysis of studies of video game play across cultures found that exposure to violent video games is a causal risk factor for increased aggressive behavior and decreased empathy (Anderson et al., 2010). These studies show a direct relationship between violent media and feelings of aggression. Considering how much exposure to violence occurs in our everyday lives, these studies pose real concern. Based on a review of more than 50 years of research, violence depicted on television, in films, and in video games raises the risk of aggressive behavior in adults and young viewers (Huesmann, 2007). It also poses a public health risk second only to smoking as a risk factor. The health of young people is placed at greater risk by media violence than by unprotected sex among populations at risk of contracting AIDS, or by passive smoking. However, in 2011, the U.S. Supreme Court struck down a California law that banned the sale of violent video games to children on the grounds that it violated the right to free speech (Liptak, 2001).

Observational learning can also be used to motivate positive social encounters, called **prosocial behavior** (Rosenhan, 1972). Seeing others donate to charity, volunteer in the community, or help others can motivate the imitation of that behavior. Unfortunately, there has been relatively little research on purely prosocial video game effects, largely because there are few games that have the main characters modeling helpful behavior. However, one recent study found that playing a prosocial (relative to a neutral) video game reduced hostile expectations and decreased the accessibility of antisocial thoughts (Greitemeyer & Osswald, 2009). Prosocial behavior is another instance in which the main tenants of operant conditioning may not appear to hold. In charitable giving, for example, you are performing an action that is not rewarded by an external reinforcer but actually results in a financial loss. However, giving can be its own reward, pointing out how any account of learning must also provide for internal motivations, cognition, and emotions as influences on our behavior.

Observational learning greatly speeds the amount of information and behavior we can acquire by benefitting from the behavior of others. In some social animals, a "culture" develops in which new behaviors are shared among the group but may never be picked up by other groups. For example, chimpanzees were thought to be unable to swim; however, one individual tried it and liked the water play. Soon, the entire group was in the water, and this behavior was maintained over time. However, no other chimpanzee group has been observed playing in water. A recent study introduced new foraging techniques to individual chimps in different groups (Whiten et al., 2007). They found that foraging behaviors carried across two separate groups of chimpanzees, and within a group, most of the troop were observed using the special techniques. This suggests other social animals can gain the advantage of cultural learning, which provides faster adaptation than genetic changes through generations.

Summary of Multiple Influences on Learning

Like the other forms of learning, observational learning again demonstrates how biological (in the form of mirror neurons) and environmental factors (in the form of other people whose behavior we model) work together to produce learning. Throughout this chapter, both in the behavioral theories of classical and operant conditioning and in the cognitive theory of observational learning, we've seen the multiple causal influences determining whether learning occurs. We have seen how learning depends on biological factors (e.g., physiological reflexes, biological preparedness, mirror neurons) and environmental factors (e.g., associations, experiences, reinforcements) including social factors (observation of others). What and how we learn depends on our biological and evolutionary heritage, and to a very large extent, on the experiences we have in the world. The theories of learning in this chapter point out the complex interweaving of biological and environmental influences in psychology.

Violent images in emotionally arousing video games may lead to desensitization toward aggression.

Prosocial behavior Actions that help others at a cost to oneself.

Chimpanzees have been found to develop novel methods of foraging for foods that are shared within social groups.

CONCEPT LEARNING CHECK 6.4 | *Learning by Observing*

Consider the principles of observational learning. Which of these outcomes may follow from observation? Explain how each of these relates to the principles of observational learning.

1. New behaviors

2. Stopping of previously learned behaviors

3. Start of previously forbidden behaviors

4. Similar behaviors

Visual Overview Three Types of Learning

There are three basic types of learning exhibited by humans and other animals: classical conditioning ("learning"), operant conditioning, and observational learning. In classical conditioning, we learn to anticipate events that cause basic physiological responses (UCS: Unconditioned Stimulus, UCR: Unconditioned Response, CS: Conditioned Stimulus, CR: Conditioned Response). In operant conditioning, whether we perform a given behavior again depends on its "reinforcement," or reward. Finally, observational learning occurs by "mirroring" the experiences of others within our own minds. These three methods of learning explain how our behavior changes with experience.

Classical Conditioning

BEFORE   AFTER

Operant Conditioning

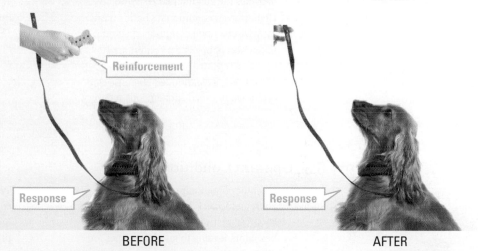

BEFORE   AFTER

Observational Learning

BEFORE   AFTER

6.1 How We Learn

- Learning describes a lasting change in knowledge or behavior based on experience.
- Behaviorism defines learning based on changes in observable behaviors.
- Classical conditioning describes linking events that occur together.

- Operant conditioning describes responding to the consequences of our behavior.
- In observational learning, a cognitive theory, new behaviors are modeled by others.

6.2 Classical Conditioning

- We learn to connect events that signal important physiological responses.
- Pavlov's dogs learned to associate a bell with receiving meat and began salivating.
- Acquisition takes place by pairing a neutral stimulus with the unconditioned stimulus.
- After learning, the neutral stimulus becomes the conditioned stimulus.
- After learning, the unconditioned response becomes the conditioned response.
- Higher-order conditioning builds more associations upon conditioned stimuli.
- Extinction happens if a conditioned stimulus repeatedly appears alone.
- After a rest, a conditioned response can occur again, called spontaneous recovery.

- In generalization, similar stimuli evoke the same conditioned response.
- In discrimination, distinctions between meaningful stimuli (signs) are made.
- Emotional responses like fear, arousal, and anxiety can be classically conditioned.
- More recent work suggests classical conditioning is more like learning a prediction.
- Taste aversion shows we are biologically prepared to more easily learn some associations.
- Phobias can be classically conditioned and treated using these techniques.

6.3 Operant Conditioning

- Operant conditioning is learning from consequences.
- Thorndike's Law of Effect predicts behaviors leading to good outcomes are repeated.
- B. F. Skinner's experiments show the principles of operant conditioning.
- Reinforcement (or reward) of behavior leads to learning.
- Shaping involves rewarding partial behavior in successive approximations.
- Operant or voluntary behaviors also show generalization and discrimination.

- When behaviors no longer occur, they enter extinction.
- Schedules of reinforcement are training programs for delivering rewards.
- Punishment is not an effective method of operant learning.
- Intrinsic motivation can make external reinforcers more complicated to apply.
- Not all behaviors are equally easy to learn for every species of animal.
- Behavior modification programs can change problematic behaviors.

6.4 A Cognitive Approach: Observational Learning

- We readily learn by observing the behavior of others.
- Cognition is evident in even animal learning as shown in latent learning.
- Both negative and prosocial behavior can be acquired from models.
- Bandura's experiments showed children learn aggressive behavior from models.
- Learning can take place well before performance shows it has occurred.

- Basic processes include attention, retention, reproduction, and motivation.
- Mirror neurons in the brain respond the same whether you are performing or observing.
- Observational learning provides the benefit of others' experiences.

6.1 How We Learn

1. When 2-year-old Clarice was playing in the basement, a large burst of thunder scared her at the same time she saw a cat. Now Clarice has a cat phobia. Clarice's experience is an example of which type of learning?
- **A.** operant conditioning
- **B.** observational learning
- **C.** superstition
- **D.** classical conditioning

2. When Harold watched the cheerleaders at the first Michigan football game he attended, he learned to do their new cheer flawlessly. This type of learning is most likely due to:
- **A.** operant conditioning.
- **B.** mirror neurons.
- **C.** classical conditioning.
- **D.** observational learning.

3. Your coworker gives you a compliment, and you smile back. The probability that she will give you another compliment now increases. This is an example of the type of learning called:
- **A.** mirror neurons.
- **B.** operant conditioning.
- **C.** observational learning.
- **D.** classical conditioning.

6.2 Classical Conditioning

4. After several visits to the doctor for chemotherapy treatments, Courtney finds she begins to feel nauseous just sitting in the waiting room before her appointment begins. According to the principles of classical conditioning, Courtney's feeling of nausea in the absence of any chemotherapy drugs is:
- **A.** an unconditioned stimulus.
- **B.** an unconditioned response.
- **C.** a conditioned stimulus.
- **D.** a conditioned response.

5. In Little Albert's experience with classical conditioning, a neutral stimulus (the white rat) was paired with a very loud crash of metal, which startled him and made him cry. After Little Albert learns this, the rat will become a(n):
- **A.** unconditioned stimulus.
- **B.** conditioned stimulus.
- **C.** controlled stimulus.
- **D.** generalized stimulus.

6. In a classic study on taste aversion, rats tasted sweetened water, saw a flash of light, and heard a loud clicking noise simultaneously. When they were then exposed to X-rays, which caused nausea, the rats learned to avoid the:
- **A.** loud clicking noise.
- **B.** sweetened water, light flashes, and clicks.
- **C.** sweetened water.
- **D.** flashes of light.

7. Wolpe's research on treating phobias with systematic desensitization showed that the best way to "unlearn" an association developed through classical conditioning is to:
- **A.** focus on consistent training.
- **B.** add learning by rewards.
- **C.** retrain with relaxation training.
- **D.** understand the basis for irrational fears.

6.3 Operant Conditioning

8. Denisa works hard on studying for her psychology exam. As a result, she gets an "A" on the first exam. Now, she is much more likely to study hard for the second exam. In this example, the grade is:
- **A.** positive punishment.
- **B.** positive reinforcement.
- **C.** negative reinforcement.
- **D.** superstitious behavior.

9. Stanley gets annoyed when his mom nags him to do his homework. When he finally does it, his mom stops nagging. Now he does his homework without any nagging. "Nagging" has served as a:
- **A.** punishment by application.
- **B.** positive reinforcement.
- **C.** negative reinforcement.
- **D.** punishment by removal.

10. You are a manager at a telemarketing firm and want to get your employees to make the most calls possible while at work. To do so, you should provide bonus money after they make calls using a schedule of reinforcement called:
- **A.** variable ratio.
- **B.** fixed ratio.
- **C.** fixed interval.
- **D.** variable interval.

11. Oskar listens regularly to a radio station that gives prizes to listeners who are asked to call in once every few hours, after either 1, 2, or 3 hours have gone by. This is an example of a schedule of reinforcement called:
- **A.** fixed interval.
- **B.** variable interval.
- **C.** variable ratio.
- **D.** fixed ratio.

6.4 A Cognitive Approach: Observational Learning

12. In a classic experiment by Bandura, nursery-school children observed an adult model interact with a Bobo doll, an inflatable clown-like toy, and then were given a chance to play with Bobo. The results of this research showed that:
A. classical conditioning explains kids' behavior.
B. rewards can provide reinforcements for learning.
C. antisocial actions are instinctual action patterns.
D. exposure to aggression leads to aggression.

13. Scientists were surprised to find activation in prefrontal cortex neurons involved in planning motor actions whenever a monkey in their experiment:
A. saw a picture of a peanut.
B. saw a peanut.
C. saw a man reach for and eat a peanut.
D. went for a swim in a pond.

14. Observational learning is distinguished from both classical conditioning and operant conditioning by the fact that:
A. no behavior occurs during learning.
B. another person is usually present.
C. no "conditioning" (training or learning) takes place.
D. more repetitions or trials are needed to learn.

CHAPTER DISCUSSION QUESTIONS

1. A surprising fact about theories of human learning in this chapter is that they focus on behavior rather than on knowledge. How far can a behavioral theory go in explaining learning? What aspects of learning are not well addressed by the theories here, and what must knowledge-based theories account for?

2. Think of an example of your own emotional experience. Were any associations made to the experience? Do any of those associations elicit an emotional reaction now? How can you "unlearn" undesirable associations?

3. Is punishment ever a useful training technique? What are the arguments against using punishment? Do you feel physical punishment should be illegal in your country?

4. What differences in cultural perspectives may arise from experience? How do culture and experience play roles in how people learn in a given situation? Think of specific examples of how two people may learn differently in the same situation based on cultural experiences.

5. Based on what you read about aggression arising from violence in videos, do you think some behaviors should be banned from entertainment media for children?

CHAPTER PROJECTS

1. Read an article or book about the experiences of people who have social phobia. How would a treatment technique like systematic desensitization work for social phobia? Would a behavior modification program also address issues with social interaction? What would a behavioral contract to increase social behaviors look like?

2. Read the short story "Flowers for Algernon" (1959) by Daniel Keyes or see the Hollywood film called *Charley* (1968) directed by Ralph Nelson. The story captures issues of animal ethics, cognitive maps and operant training, and the treatment of the disabled. How is the intelligence of people perceived as different from that of animals, and what does that imply about people who are less able to learn?

Acquisition
Avoidance learning
Behavior modification
Behavioral contract
Behaviorism
Biofeedback
Biological preparedness
Classical conditioning
Cognitive
Cognitive map
Conditioned response
Conditioned stimulus
Conditioning
Continuous reinforcement
Discrimination
Escape learning
Extinction
Extinguish
Extrinsic motivation
Fixed-interval schedule
Fixed-ratio schedule

Flooding
Generalization
Higher-order conditioning
Instinctual drift
Intermittent reinforcement
Interval schedule
Intrinsic motivation
Latent learning
Law of Effect
Learned helplessness
Learning
Mirror neurons
Modeling
Negative reinforcement
Neutral stimulus
Observational learning
Operant
Operant conditioning
Phobia
Positive reinforcement
Primary reinforcer

Prosocial behavior
Punishment by application
Punishment by removal
Ratio schedules
Reinforce
Reinforcer
Schedule of reinforcement
Secondary reinforcer (conditioned reinforcer)
Shaping
Skinner box (operant chamber)
Spontaneous recovery
Systematic desensitization
Taste aversion
Token economies
Unconditioned response
Unconditioned stimulus
Variable-interval schedule
Variable-ratio schedule

6.1 Comparing Types of Learning

1. This fits operant conditioning because the behavior is followed by consequences that make performing the behavior again more likely.

2. This fits classical conditioning because the storm has become associated with the fear from the electrical outage.

3. This fits observational learning because the mother's behavior is the model for the daughter's (not going to work or school).

4. This fits classical conditioning because an emotional response is elicited by a conditioned stimulus (the teacher calling her name).

5. This fits observational learning because he learns what to do by watching his girlfriend.

6. This is operant conditioning because Malay's responses reinforce her sister's talking.

6.2 Applying Principles of Classical Conditioning

1. Unconditioned stimulus: shock

   Unconditioned response: fear

   Conditioned stimulus: flash of light

   Conditioned response: fear

2. Unconditioned stimulus: poison

   Unconditioned response: nausea

   Conditioned stimulus: smell of sheep

   Conditioned response: nausea

6.3 Comparing Consequences of Behavior

1. **a.** Reinforcement: It led to more of the behavior.

   b. Positive reinforcement: His requests with "please" always led to a pleasant outcome by his parents doing what he wanted.

2. **a.** Reinforcement: It led to more of the behavior.

   b. Positive reinforcement: Her mother's attention when interrupted was positive for Sarah.

3. **a.** Reinforcement: It led to more of the behavior.

   b. Negative reinforcement: A negative (chores) is removed after the behavior, leading to a positive outcome for the learner.

4. **a.** Punishment: The behavior decreased or stopped.

   b. Not applicable

6.4 Concept Learning Check 6.4 Learning by Observing

1. Observation is good at helping learners gain new behaviors they see modeled by others.

2. Observation does not involve any behavior during learning, so it is difficult to observe that a behavior is not happening.

3. Studies on aggression show that people can learn negative behaviors they see modeled.

4. Observing behaviors may result in the learner acquiring similar behaviors to what is modeled; for example, they may try their own aggressive actions on the Bobo doll in Bandura's study.

ANSWERS TO CHAPTER REVIEW TEST

6.1 How We Learn

1. D. Rationale: The thunder elicited fear and now the cat is associated with fear. The automatic response signals that this is classical conditioning.

2. D. Rationale: The learner didn't perform any actions but watched another perform the behavior. So this is an example of observational learning.

3. B. Rationale: The smile worked to reinforce the behavior of smiling in the learner, making her more likely to smile again. So this is reinforcement learning, also called operant conditioning.

6.2 Classical Conditioning

4. D. Rationale: The drugs (unconditioned stimulus) elicited nausea (unconditioned response). After learning, the waiting room (conditioned stimulus) elicits the same nausea, now a conditioned (learned) response.

5. B. Rationale: The loud crash (unconditioned stimulus) elicited fear (unconditioned response), and now, after learning, the rat (conditioned stimulus) is associated with fear (conditioned response).

6. C. Rationale: Not all associations are equally easy to learn. For taste aversion, animals are biologically prepared to associate taste with nausea and have a harder time learning to associate other neutral stimuli (like light or sound) with nausea.

7. C. Rationale: The presence of the conditioned stimulus now elicits a conditioned response. Systematic desensitization provides gradual practice being in the presence of the conditioned stimulus while learning to relax.

6.3 Operant Conditioning

8. B. Rationale: The grade is a reinforcement because it makes the behavior more likely to occur again. It is a positive reinforcement because it is the introduction of a positive reward for the learner.

9. C. Rationale: The nagging makes the behavior (doing homework) more likely to happen again, so it is a reinforcement. When the nagging stops, it is the removal of a negative feature, so it is negative reinforcement.

10. B. Rationale: The schedules of reinforcement vary in how quickly the learner responds and works for further reinforcement. The schedule that motivates the fastest responses is a fixed-ratio schedule.

11. B. Rationale: The reinforcement occurs to a behavior that happens after a given time interval, which varies (1, 2, or 3 hours), so it is a variable-interval schedule.

6.4 A Cognitive Approach: Observational Learning

12. D. Rationale: The children in the study showed the same aggressive play behaviors they had observed in the models, so that watching aggressive behavior led to more aggressive actions by the children.

13. C. Rationale: The mirror neurons respond to actions that the animal plans and performs itself and to the same actions when performed by another. They likely play a role in learning by observation.

14. A. Rationale: Unlike the two other types of learning, observational learning occurs without the learner performing any behaviors, but simply by watching a model. Other people can be involved in all three types of learning, and all three types may produce learning within a single trial.

REFERENCES

Abramson, L., Seligman, M., & Teasdale, J. (1978). Learned helplessness in humans: Critique and reformulation. *Journal of Abnormal Psychology, 87,* 49–74.

Ader, R., & Cohen, N. (1985). CNS-immune system interactions: Conditioning phenomena. *Behavioral and Brain Sciences, 8,* 379–426.

Anderson, C. A., Ihori, N., Bushman, B. J., Rothstein, H. R., Shibuya, A., Swing, E. L., Sakamoto, A., & Saleem, M. (2010). Violent video game effects on aggression, empathy, and prosocial behavior in eastern and western countries: A meta-analytic review. *Psychological Bulletin, 136*(2), 151–173.

Bandura, A. (1977). *Social learning theory.* Englewood Cliffs, NJ: Prentice-Hall.

Bandura, A., Ross, D., & Ross, S. A. (1961). Transmission of aggression through imitation of aggressive models. *Journal of Abnormal and Social Psychology, 63,* 575–582.

Breland, K., & Breland, M. (1961). The misbehavior of organisms. *American Psychologist, 16,* 661–664.

Bushman, B. J., & Geen, R. G. (1990). Role of cognitive-emotional mediators and individual differences in the effects of media violence on aggression. *Journal of Personality and Social Psychology, 58*(1), 156–163.

Bushman, B. J., & Huesmann, L. R. (2001). Effects of televised violence on aggression. In D. G. Singer and J. Singer (eds.), *Handbook of children and the media* (pp. 223–254). Thousand Oaks, California: Sage.

Cameron, C. L., Cella, D., Herndon, J. E. II, Kornblith, A. B., Zuckerman, E., Henderson, E., Weiss, R. B., Cooper, M. R., Silver, R. T., Leone, L., Canellos, G. P., Peterson, B. A., Holland, J. C. (2001). Persistent symptoms among survivors of Hodgkin's disease: An explanatory model based on classical conditioning. *Health Psychology, 20,* 71–75.

Carnagey, N. L., Anderson, C. A., & Bushman, B. J. (2007). The effect of video game violence on physiological desensitization to real-life violence. *Journal of Experimental Social Psychology, 43,* 489–496.

deCharms, R. C., Maeda, F., Glover, G. H., Ludlow, D., Pauly, J. M., Soneji, D., Gabrieli, J. D. E., Mackey, S. C., & Raichle, M. E. (2005). Control over brain activation and pain learned by using real time functional MRI. *Proceedings of the National Academy of Sciences of the United States of America, 102*(51), 18626–18631.

Driver, J. L., & Gottman, J. M. (2005). Dysfunctional marital conflict and everyday marital interaction. *Journal of Divorce & Remarriage, 43*(3–4), 63–77.

Durgam, R. C. (2001). Rodent models of depression: Learned helplessness using a triadic design in rats. *Current Protocols in Neuroscience,* 8.10B.1–8.10B.12.

Garcia, J., & Koelling, R. A. (1966). Relation of cue to consequence in avoidance learning. *Psychonomic Science, 4,* 123–124.

Gershoff, E. T. (2002). Corporal punishment by parents and associated child behaviors and experiences: A meta-analytic and theoretical review. *Psychological Bulletin, 128*(4), 539–579.

Gottman, J. M. (1998). Psychology and the study of marital processes. *Annual Review of Psychology, 49,* 169–197.

Greitemeyer, T., & Osswald, S. (2009). Prosocial video games reduce aggressive cognitions. *Journal of Experimental Social Psychology, 45,* 896–900.

Huesmann, L. R. (2007). The impact of electronic media violence: Scientific theory and research. *Journal of Adolescent Health, 41*(6), S6–S13.

Iacoboni, M. (2008). *Mirroring people: The new science of how we connect to others.* New York: Farrar, Straus, & Giroux.

Iacoboni, M., & Dapretto, M. (2006). The mirror neuron system and the consequences of its dysfunction. *Nature Review Neuroscience, 7,* 942–951.

Kazdin, A. E. (2008). *The Kazdin method for parenting the defiant child: With no pills, no therapy, no contest of wills.* Boston: Houghton Mifflin Harcourt.

Koole, S. L., Dijksterhuis, A., & van Knippenberg, A. (2001). What's in a name: Implicit self-esteem and the automatic self. *Journal of Personality and Social Psychology, 80*(4), 669–685.

Lepper, M. R., Greene, D., & Nisbett, R. E. (1973). Undermining children's intrinsic interest with extrinsic reward: A test of the "overjustification" hypothesis. *Journal of Personality and Social Psychology, 28,* 129–137.

Liptak, A. (2011). Minors can buy violent games, justices decide. *New York Times,* June 27, p. A1.

Lovaas, O. I. (1987). Behavioral treatment and normal educational and intellectual functioning in young autistic children. *Journal of Consulting and Clinical Psychology, 55*(1), 3–9.

Luthans, F., Paul, R., & Baker, D. (1981). An experimental analysis of the impact of contingent reinforcement on salesperson performance behavior. *Journal of Applied Psychology, 66*(3), 314–323.

Miller, G., & Cohen, N. (2001). Psychological interventions and the immune system: A meta-analytic review and critique. *Health Psychology, 20,* 47–63.

Mineka, S., Keir, R., & Price, V. (1980). Fear of snakes in wild- and laboratory-reared rhesus monkeys (*Macaca mulatta*). *Animal Learning and Behavior, 8,* 653–663.

Öhman, A., & Mineka, S. (2001). Fears, phobias, and preparedness: Toward an evolved module of fear and fear learning. *Psychological Review, 108,* 483–522.

Orne, M. T. (1962). On the social psychology of the psychological experiment: With particular reference to demand characteristics and their implications. *American Psychologist, 17,* 776–783.

Pavlov, I. P. (1927). *Conditioned reflexes.* London: Oxford University Press.

Pollak, S., Cicchetti, D., & Klorman, R. (1998). Stress, memory, and emotion: Developmental considerations from the study of child maltreatment. *Developmental Psychopathology 10,* 811–828.

Oberman, L. M., & Ramachandran, V. S. (2007) The simulating social mind: The role of the mirror neuron system and simulation in the social and communicative deficits of autism spectrum disorders. *Psychological Bulletin, 133,* 310–327.

Rescorla, R. A. (1988). Pavlovian conditioning: It's not what you think it is. *American Psychologist, 43,* 151–160.

Rizzolatti, G., Fogassi, L., & Gallese, V. (2006). Mirrors in the mind, *Scientific American, 54* 61.

Rosenhan, D. L. (1972). Learning theory and prosocial behavior. *Journal of Social Issues, 28*(3), 151–163.

Seligman, M. E. P., & Maier, S. F. (1967). Failure to escape from traumatic shock. *Journal of Experimental Psychology, 74,* 1–9.

Skinner, B. F. (1938). *The behavior of organisms.* New York: Appleton-Century-Crofts.

Skinner, B. F. (1948). "Superstition" in the pigeon. *Journal of Experimental Psychology, 38,* 168–172.

Skinner, B. F. (1957). *Verbal behavior.* New York: Appleton-Century-Crofts.

Skinner, B. F. (1972). *Beyond freedom and dignity.* New York: Bantam Vintage.

Skinner, B. F. (1990). Can psychology be a science of mind? *American Psychologist, 45,* 1206–1210.

Thorndike, E. L. (1898). Animal intelligence: An experimental study of the associative processes in animals. *Psychological Monographs, 2*(Whole No, 8).

Tolman, E. C. (1948). Cognitive maps in rats and men. *Psychological Review, 55,* 189–208.

Tolman, E. C., & Honzik, C. H. (1930). Introduction and removal of reward and maze performance in rats. *University of California Publications in Psychology, 4,* 257–275.

Watson, J. B. (1913). Psychology as the behaviorist views it. *Psychological Review, 20,* 158–177.

Watson, J. B. (1924). The unverbalized in human behavior. *Psychological Review, 31,* 339–347.

Watson, J. B. (1925). *Behaviorism.* New York: W. W. Norton.

Watson, J. B., & Rayner, R. (1920). Conditioned emotional responses. *Journal of Experimental Psychology, 3,* 1–14.

Whiten, A., Spiteri, A., Horner, V., Bonnie, K. E., Lambeth, S. P., Schapiro, S. J., & de Waal, F. B. (2007). Transmission of multiple traditions within and between chimpanzee groups. *Current Biology, 17*(12), 1038–1043.

Wolpe, J. (1961). The systematic desensitization treatment of neuroses. *Journal of Nervous and Mental Diseases, 132,* 180–203.

Chapter Overview ▼

7.1 Overview: What Is Memory?

CONCEPT LEARNING CHECK **7.1** *Defining Memory*

7.2 Constructing Memory
Automatic Processing
Effortful Processing
Mnemonics

CONCEPT LEARNING CHECK **7.2** *Applying Methods of Encoding*

7.3 The Three Stages of Memory
Sensory Memory
Short-Term Memory or Working Memory
Long-Term Memory
Storing Memories in the Brain
Synaptic Changes
The Anatomy of Memory

CONCEPT LEARNING CHECK **7.3** *Movement of Information Through the Stages of Memory*

7.4 Organizing Information in Memory
Declarative Memory
Semantic Memory
Episodic Memory
"Flashbulb" Memories
Procedural Memory

CONCEPT LEARNING CHECK **7.4** *Organizing Information in Memory*

7.5 Retrieval from Memory
Retrieval Cues
Adding Context
Retrieval Practice

CONCEPT LEARNING CHECK **7.5** *Practicing Retrieval*

7 Memory

Learning Objectives ▼

7.1 ■ Explain how human memory differs from an objective video recording of events.

7.2 ■ Identify the ways that effortful processing can help to encode information into memory.

7.3 ■ Discuss how the three memory stages are involved in encoding new information into memory.

7.4 ■ Describe the main ways that information is organized in long-term memory.

7.5 ■ Examine the successful retrieval of information from long-term memory.

7.6 ■ Explain how information from long-term memory may include misinformation.

7.7 ■ Analyze how forgetting improves memory.

7.8 ■ Identify principles that can improve memory.

7.6 Reconstructing Memories
Source Monitoring
The Misinformation Effect
False Memories

CONCEPT LEARNING CHECK 7.6 *Introducing Error in Memory*
CRITICAL THINKING APPLICATION

7.7 Forgetting
Measures of Forgetting
Theories of Forgetting

Motivated Forgetting
Amnesia

CONCEPT LEARNING CHECK 7.7 *Learning from Case Studies of Amnesia*

7.8 How to Improve Your Memory
Memory Principles Applied to Studying
    Actively Construct Memory
    Schedule Study Sessions
    Test to Learn
    Cue Retrieval

Summary of Multiple Influences on Memory

CONCEPT LEARNING CHECK 7.8 *Developing Helpful Study Habits*

One December day, I spent a lunch hour buying Michigan sweatshirts as holiday gifts for my nephews. At the end of the workday, I returned to my car and was startled to find the bag of gifts missing. Living in a small college town, security was not on my mind, and I had left my car unlocked. I filed a police report by phone, and sent an e-mail to the entire department: "The Grinch Has Stolen Christmas," I warned, cautioning them not to leave their vehicles open.

The next day at lunch, I returned to the local college sportswear store, and approached the counter to tell them what had happened. "There you are!" the clerk immediately said, handing over a large package, "You forgot your purchase yesterday!"

I returned to the office and e-mailed the police and department, revealing that the missing bag had been my error alone. But that night, after I got out of my car, I locked the door behind me—for the first time ever.

7.1 Overview: What Is Memory?

Memory is an active process that constructs, encodes, stores, alters, and retrieves information.

- Explain how human memory differs from an objective video recording of events.

Memory The enduring consequence in the mind of our experiences with the world.

Is memory accurate? I know perfectly well that there was no theft from my car, and yet my sense of possible danger was inflated by an event I know never actually occurred. We may want to believe our memory is like a videotape of the past that we can call to mind at will. However, as we will see in this chapter, memory is not at all a static "picture;" instead, **memory** is an active, constructive, and dynamic process. When we examine the psychology of memory, we discover that vivid memories can be true and untrue, accurate and distorted, all at the same time. How can an experience become a life-long memory when it never really happened? In this chapter, we'll discover how memory processes shape what we know and remember about the world.

As a student, you already know a lot about memory; in fact, you are an expert at getting information into memory and ways of testing whether it is there. But in psychology, memory refers to the much broader topic—the enduring consequences in the mind of our experiences with the world. Every event you witnessed, fact you read, view you have seen, voice and song you have heard, and step you've taken has passed through your memory system, even if only for an instant. What is left behind in memory for you to now recall? The processing of our experiences can lead to little effect on memory; for example, what did you eat for lunch last Wednesday? Alternatively, it can lead to memories that last a lifetime, such as the day you met your boy or girlfriend for the first time. Memories are created through actions we take in the world, such as how to execute your improved tennis stroke. And memories are formed from wholly internalized processes, such as thinking about what has happened in the past and what you would like to have happen in the future.

With every new experience, memory effortlessly brings our past to mind. In many ways, the person you are is entirely determined by what you remember about your past. Do you like lemonade? Have you ever been to Ohio? Do you speak Spanish? Our memories define us as individuals and give us our sense of belonging in our relationships to others, and in our own personal histories. Should you become completely unrecognizable through physical characteristics, your memory identifies you as the unique person you are.

Memory plays a role in every other psychological function. Consciousness involves thinking about experiences in memory, and perception requires recognizing when an object is familiar. Learning requires remembering that a behavior was previously rewarded. It is difficult to imagine how thinking occurs without relying on memory, even if just in the language we might use to express a current thought. Later, we'll address how cognitive processes such as thinking and deciding go hand in hand with memory processes. In this chapter, we will focus specifically on how memory internalizes the world within the mind.

CONCEPT LEARNING CHECK 7.1 | *Defining Memory*

As an experienced student, you've likely taken many tests designed to capture your memory for knowledge. The formats of some test items commonly used include:

A. Essay

B. Multiple choice

C. Fill in the blank

1. _____ Which of these is the most difficult type of question to answer, and why?

2. _____ Which is the easiest type of question to answer, and why?

3. _____ Which question type aids memory retrieval by providing cues?

7.2 Constructing Memory

Adding information into memory can be automatic, but constructing new memories requires effortful processing.

- Identify the ways that effortful processing can help to encode information into memory.

Learning brings new knowledge into memory. A first question to consider is how information enters memory, a process called **encoding**. Many things seem to enter memory with no effort on our part; for example, you can probably draw a floor plan of your current bathroom even though you've not likely thought about it before now. However, other things seem to require a great deal of effort to encode into memory. For example, what is the name of the person you last met? While it seems like memory should be a record of whatever occurs around us, memories are not passive observances. Instead, we actively construct our memories based on information around us. Encoding information into memory often requires much more effort in its construction.

Automatic Processing

We can encode large amounts of information without conscious effort, called **automatic processing**. Many things are encoded into memory even though little interest is paid to them. **Incidental memory** includes information you process and remember without any specific effort to do so. For example, advertisements are designed to be memorable even though you are explicitly not trying to remember them FIGURE 7-1. They are frequently repeated, designed to be "catchy," and sometimes add music or emotional cues to aid recall. Given examples like these, it's easy to think information lands in memory with little effort on our part. But you know, for example, from attempting to learn the names for

Encoding The process of taking new information and storing it in short- and long-term memory.

Automatic processing Information made available without conscious effort.

Incidental memory Explicit knowledge you did not intentionally encode.

1. Reach out and touch someone.	**A.** AT&T®
2. The real thing	**B.** Coca-Cola®
3. Finger lickin' good	**C.** KFC®
4. He keeps going and going and going . . .	**D.** Energizer® batteries
5. It's everywhere you want to be.	**E.** VISA®
6. Live in your world, play in ours.	**F.** Sony PlayStation®
7. When it absolutely, positively has to be there overnight	**G.** FedEx®
8. Snap, Crackle, Pop!	**H.** Kellogg's® Rice Krispies®
9. Just do it.	**I.** NIKE

FIGURE 7-1 Identify the brand name associated with each of these advertising slogans. What factors help you recall them even though you are not trying to remember them?

all of the parts of the brain, that even repetition is not enough to ensure that information will "stick" in memory.

Often, information is encoded automatically, without your conscious attempt to attend to it. You may find yourself humming the song you keep hearing on the radio. Or you may think about fortune cookies when you pass the pungent smells of a Chinese restaurant. **Priming** refers to the activation of information in memory from a related cue (Meyer & Schvaneveldt, 1971). We are often unaware of these memory associations acquired from our environment, but they constantly bring past memories to mind. Automatic associations predict what will happen next, and that can influence our behavior. In one study (Bargh et al., 1996), students performed a laboratory task, and for some, it included the words, "worried, Florida, old, lonely, grey, sentimental, wise, bingo, retired, wrinkle." After the study, the time it took the students to walk down the hallway to the exit was measured (see FIGURE 7-2). Those who had read the elderly-related words took longer to exit, even though they were unaware of the stereotype contained in the task. We constantly encode and recall associations from information in the world without our conscious awareness.

> **Priming** The activation of information in memory from a related cue.

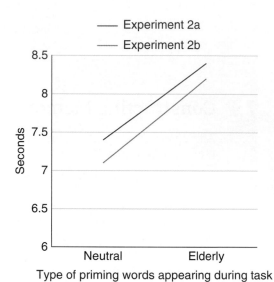

FIGURE 7-2 Mean time (in seconds) to walk down the hallway after the conclusion of the experiment for subjects primed by "elderly" stereotyped words compared to neutral words. The graph shows a replication in experiment 2a and 2b.
Source: Data from Bargh, J. A., Chen, M., & Burrows, L. (1996). Automaticity of social behavior: Direct effects of trait construct and stereo-type activation on action. Journal of Personality and Social Psychology, *71(2), 230–244.*

However, most often, we must put effort into constructing a memory for an event. This is not a videotape of our experience that we can replay later. Instead, constructing memories requires paying attention, or focusing our mental "spotlight" on specific information. In fact, the fundamental requirement for encoding information into memory is paying attention to it. This fact is illustrated by information we believe to be in memory but that may not be there. What does a penny look like? You have handled them countless times, but can you recall the correct face of a penny? (See FIGURE 7-3.) Why is this information hard to recall? Most likely, it was never encoded into your memory in the first place. After all, to use a penny, all you need to know is its color and size to distinguish it from other coins. So your memory for a penny is constructed from the available information but does not include everything that could have been encoded. Constructing memories involves attending to, selecting from, and encoding specific information

FIGURE 7-3 What does a penny look like? You have used it many times, and can surely recognize one when it is shown to you. But can you identify which of the drawings accurately depicts the face of the coin?
Source: Reproduced from Nickerson, R. S., & Adams, M. J. (1979). Long term memory for a common object. Cognitive Psychology, 11, *287–307.*

about your experiences. In this sense, memory is highly selective: It depends on you to construct the information, and it requires your effort.

Effortful Processing

In contrast to automatic processing, memory construction requires a great deal of effortful processing in order to ensure that information is encoded into memory. As experienced learners, you know this very well: Simple repetition, or experience with information, is not sufficient to guarantee that the target information will be encoded (see FIGURE 7-4). One fundamental finding is that we tend to remember the *meaning* of an experience rather than the incidental details surrounding its encoding. In other words, people perform effort after meaning, attempting to understand the point of a communication or experience, and we tend to encode the meaning that we assign to it.

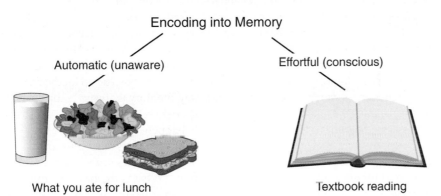

Encoding into Memory

Automatic (unaware)   Effortful (conscious)

What you ate for lunch   Textbook reading

FIGURE 7-4 Two types of processing can lead to the encoding of information into memory.

This is illustrated by an early study of reading (Sachs, 1967), where this story was presented: "There is an interesting story about the telescope. In Holland, a man named Lippershey was an eyeglass maker. One day his children were playing with some lenses. They discovered that things seemed very close if two lenses were held about a foot apart. Lippershey began experimenting and his "spyglass" attracted much attention. He sent a letter to Galileo, the great Italian scientist. Galileo at once realized the importance of the discovery and set about to build an instrument of his own. He used an old organ pipe with one lens curved out and the other in. On the first clear night he pointed the glass toward the sky. He was amazed to find the empty dark spaces filled with gleaming stars! Night after night Galileo climbed to a high tower, sweeping the sky with his telescope. One night he saw Jupiter, and to his great surprise discovered near it three bright stars" (Sachs, 1967).

What will you remember about this story in a few minutes? In the study, students read the passage sentence by sentence and were interrupted for a test at various points. The results (see FIGURE 7-5) show that, after some further sentences were read, memory for the words, ordering, and syntax of the sentences was poor: Only the meaning of the

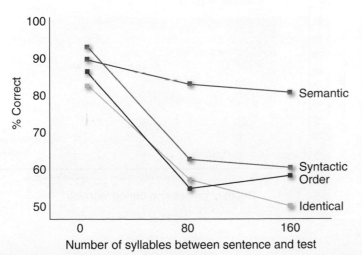

FIGURE 7-5 The results show that as more syllables were presented, memory for the literal words seen, word order, and syntax of the sentences grew worse. Only the meaning remained in memory after reading further sentences.
Source: Data from Sachs, J. (1967). Recognition memory for syntactic and semantic aspects of connected discourse. Perception and Psychophysics, 2, *437–442.*

sentences was remembered after further reading. This shows that, though we process many types of information, we are most likely to recall the gist, or meaning, of the information we comprehend. In many other studies, information presented in a variety of formats such as visual, auditory, text, or multimedia tends to be "boiled down" to its gist when encoded into memory. So you may not remember much of what was actually said during an important conversation, but you will encode the main "point" of the experience into memory.

In this sense, a memory is a construction of available information. Two people watch the same YouTube clip, but what they recall about the video may differ. Each will construct his or her own "take" on the information, organize the pieces in a way that make sense to him or her, and then encode his or her own version into memory. In a sense, a memory is a "story" that we tell ourselves about what we experienced (Schank & Abelson, 1995). As an example, consider the congressional testimony of Supreme Court Justice Clarence Thomas and Anita Hill, a lawyer who had worked for years with Thomas. Hill testified that Thomas had subjected her to sexually explicit comments that she felt constituted harassment. Thomas denied making each of the specific comments Hill attributed to him and blamed politicians for trying to derail his nomination to the court. Though these two people have many shared memories, the memories they constructed for themselves about their experiences were very different. In this way, memory is always "subjective," relying on the meaning we take from the events we experience. The memory we construct is not necessarily the same as the events that actually happened (Bartlett, 1932).

Suppose your goal is to construct a memory that will be available to you in the future. How can you best construct and encode information? Let's say you want to use a new password for your online bank account, "bandit." What is the best way to encode this new password into memory so you will remember it next time you try to log in? Most people will say that repeating it over and over is the best way to "burn" something into memory. But repetition is a fairly "shallow" way to process the information. A "deeper" level of processing would be to think about the *meaning* of the new password: A "bandit" steals money, and money is what you're storing in the online bank account you are setting up; so, you hope the password will keep out any "bandit" that tries to steal your money. Now, which of these encoding methods will be better for helping you remember your new password? A study of **levels of processing** demonstrated that the deepest, most mean-ingful level for encoding information results in the best recall (Craik & Tulving, 1975). One group read words and thought about whether they were shown in all capital letters versus all lowercase letters. This visual encoding task is a "shallow" process, since they didn't even need to read the words to perform this task. A second group made up rhymes for each word, focusing on the acoustic sounds. The final group was told to think about the semantics, or meaning, of each word they read. The results (see FIGURE 7-6) show the deepest level of encoding, thinking about meaning, produced the best recall. Thinking about deep, meaningful associations with information is the best way to fully process it, and deeper thinking results in better memory.

Levels of processing The depth of thinking with new information affects the likeli-hood of remembering it.

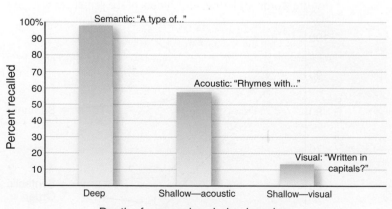

FIGURE 7-6 Processing a word by encoding its meaning (semantic encoding) results in better recognition at test time than more shallow processing of its visual appearance or sound. *Source: Data from Craik, F. I. M, & Tulving, E. (1975). Depth of processing and the retention of words in episodic memory.* Journal of Experimental Psychology: General, 104, *268–294.*

Suppose you want to remember the date of the first moonwalk. Another principle of memory, called **elaboration**, involves drawing connections to information already in memory. This helps encoding because establishing multiple, meaningful links to information provides more ways to access it again in the future. For example, you might think about the circumstances of the first moonwalk—that it was televised at 8:17 p.m., so many people were able to watch it as it happened in real time. That same year, Richard Nixon became U.S. president, and the Beatles gave their last live performance on the rooftop of Apple Records. Adding connections to "play out" the meaning of the timing of the first moonwalk elaborates its connections to other information in memory, and so makes it more memorable.

There are many ways to elaborate on meaning, such as thinking of examples ("An example of an *aphorism* is, 'No good deed goes unpunished'"), implications ("What happened after the Civil War ended in 1863?"), or comparisons ("Prime numbers have only two divisors, while even numbers always have 2 as a divisor"). Focusing on meaning helps encode information by tying it to information that is already present in memory, providing multiple ways to link the new information into memory. More links means it's well encoded, and more ways to access it are available. Surprisingly, you can spend *less* time studying if you are careful to elaborate on new information rather than attempting to memorize it in isolation.

What is the easiest way to elaborate on new information? To think about how it relates to you! Like all humans, we are attuned to information that reflects upon us personally. So a very helpful method of encoding is to tie new information to personally relevant information, called the **self-reference effect**. You will likely remember who the candidates were in a presidential election if you were able to place your first vote that year. If you are female, you may be more likely to recall that one vice-presidential nominee was also a woman. And you'll be more likely to remember your college football team's season if you attended games. Since we are (necessarily) thinking a lot about ourselves, tying information into our personal memories really helps in constructing memories. In one study, the self-reference effect was examined by having subjects rate 40 personality traits (for example, "friendly, hostile, ambitious"). Some subjects judged whether the words were self-descriptive. Others judged the same words' length, sound, or meaning. Later, subjects remembered more of the words if they were asked to think about them with regard to themselves (Rogers, Kuiper, & Kirker, 1977). This is not surprising when you consider we are most interested in information about ourselves.

In fact, our memory is better for information that we have to *construct* ourselves instead of having it simply given to us. This is called the **generation effect**. For example, imagine being introduced to someone new and having a conversation with him or her. If you say his or her name yourself during the conversation, you'll be more likely to recall it later than if you hear someone else say it. The reason is that the act of generating the name is more cognitively active than simply passively hearing it. A study by Slamecka and Graf (1978) demonstrated this effect by asking some subjects to generate rhymes, such as, "nose - r ___." Other subjects had the same word pairs read aloud to them. Who showed better memory? Even though the generation of rhymes required little effort, the simple act of generating the associated word improved memory by 28%. This suggests that testing your memory by simply reading over the material is not as effective as trying to generate the answers for yourself.

Active construction works to get information encoded into memory. "Watching" the information pass by is ineffective at making an impression on your memory. College texts are often resold covered in highlighter markings; however, while highlighting key information is better than just reading (Fowler & Barker, 1974), effective studying involves far more than simply underlining (Wade & Trathen, 1989). The reason is that the amount of cognitive processing you do with new information and how you construct the information for yourself makes a huge difference in your memory for the material. In fact, research on college learning in physics has shown the value of memory construction in the form of self-explanation. In one study, college students read physics texts including worked-out examples (Chiet et al., 1989; 1994). Some students were asked to explain, or talk through, the worked-out problem to themselves rather than simply reading through it. These students learned new problem-solving skills and showed superior performance on

Elaboration Tying new information to that already stored in memory.

Self-reference effect Associating information with oneself to aid in retrieval.

Generation effect Memory is better for information that we create ourselves.

posttests compared to students who simply studied the material for the same amount of time. By talking through the example in their own words, the self-explanation students were able to tie the new problem skills to their previous knowledge in memory.

Mnemonics

Sometimes, the information we would like to encode is difficult to tie to our past knowledge. Constructing memories sometimes calls for the use of strategies to make information more memorable, called **mnemonics** (nih-MON-iks). These "tricks" make use of our ability to construct and organize information to help us encode it into memory. One mnemonic, called the **method of loci**, uses imagery to construct a memory including specific items. The trick is to think of a very familiar path, such as the route you take often between your home and your classroom. Picture the route, the turns you take, the street names and buildings. Then you can add in visual images of the set of items you want to remember (such as a grocery list). So you imagine leaving your home and picture a newspaper propped across the doorframe. Next, you turn at the sidewalk and have to step over a giant loaf of bread. On the corner where you turn left, you imagine a tall salami serving as the light pole. After encoding all of the items, you needn't think about the list again. Later, at the store, you simply "walk" the imagined path again in your mind and notice the objects you have placed in your path. Newspaper, bread, salami—your constructed list is easy to recall.

Mnemonics are a great method for constructing memories that include pieces that are difficult to connect together. Another mnemonic, called the "first letter" mnemonic, associates a set of things together with an acronym created by the first letter of each item. For example, the order of colors in the visual spectrum (red, orange, yellow, green, blue, indigo, and violet) may be hard to recall. So the phrase "ROY G BIV" can be constructed, and that serves as a cue to help you remember all of the colors in order. Or, if you need to recall all of the Great Lakes, you can construct the acronym "HOMES" to help recall lakes Huron, Ontario, Michigan, Erie, and Superior. One reason mnemonics work is that you can create associations between items in a way that is unusual and therefore memorable. For example, the whimsical phrase, "Never Eat Soggy Waffles," helps to recall the directions on the compass starting at the top and going clockwise. We tend to have better memory for items that "stick out" as different or unusual compared to other items in memory (von Restorf, 1933).

Another mnemonic, called the **link method**, can help you construct organization in memory, such as, "Hippos are like elephants, which never forget; and, the "hippocampus" is the brain area where memories are formed." Constructions of memory are often culturally based, where tricks for creating memories are passed on to other people. Remembering the spelling trick, "I before E, except after C"? Or the tip for recalling how to change the clocks for Daylight Savings Time ("spring forward, fall back")? Mnemonic tricks are very helpful in constructing memories of information you need in courses, such as the bones of the hand or the orders of the animal kingdom.

A mnemonist is an expert at using these methods to learn new information. One college student practiced for more than 200 hours over several months and then was tested. He was able to correctly repeat a string of 80 individual digits in order (Ericsson & Chase, 1982). His mnemonic trick was based on his extensive knowledge of long-distance running. He encoded the digits in clumps that matched times he recognized; for example, "3492" was recalled as "3 minutes and 49.2 seconds, a near world-record time for the mile." With practice, he established an elaborate set of mnemonic associations he could use to recall groups of digits. With practice and the right mnemonics, anyone can become an exceptional mnemonist.

Any mnemonic that adds meaning to the material can be helpful; for example, you might make up a story of "The Three Little Memory Stages" along the lines of "The Three Little Pigs." Special tricks include using vivid visual imagery (your mom jumping out of a giant cake with 16 candles on it to remember her birthdate) and exaggerated, even silly associations ("Obama rhymes with llama") as ways of making memories stand out.

Memories are not like videos; instead, they are "stories" we create for ourselves to tie information together for later recall. This requires not only attention but also active, effortful processing.

Mnemonic Encoding "trick" that ties to-be-remembered information to something familiar.

Method of loci Mnemonic for remembering items by placing them on a familiar path.

Link method Forming links between concepts to make them more memorable.

CONCEPT LEARNING CHECK 7.2   *Applying Methods of Encoding*

For each example, determine which type of effortful encoding strategy is illustrated.

Strategies

A. Elaboration

B. Generation

C. Depth of processing

D. Self-reference effect

E. Self-explanation

F. Mnemonic devices

1. _____ "Let me try to think of an example of when classical conditioning happens in my everyday life."

2. _____ "Observational learning reminds me of when I learned how to make pancakes, and I watched my Dad cook them for me until I remembered all of the steps."

3. _____ "I remember it's called 'operant conditioning' because the learner 'operates' in the environment and gets reinforced for it."

4. _____ "Once I read a book section, I draw my own visual outline to understand the meaning of the material."

5. _____ "The answer is classical conditioning. Let me trace through the problem so I can see for myself which stimulus is the UCS, and which is the CS."

7.3 The Three Stages of Memory

There are three different memory stages for the conscious processing of memories.

■ Discuss how the three memory stages are involved in encoding new information into memory.

How is new information processed and stored in memory? One proposed model is the **stage model of memory** (Atkinson & Shiffrin, 1968), in which three separate stages are involved in consciously forming a lasting memory (see FIGURE 7-7). The three stages include:

1. We experience a flash of input information through our senses, called **sensory memory**.
2. Some information from this stage is encoded into a short-term memory buffer, where we hold it in our current thoughts.
3. Some information from this stage is encoded into a long-term memory store, where it remains indefinitely for future access.

Stage model of memory
Atkinson and Shiffrins's three stages of memory—sensory, short-term, and long-term memory.

Sensory memory The brief flash of input information through the senses.

Working memory
Synonym for short-term memory that reflects its role in thinking.

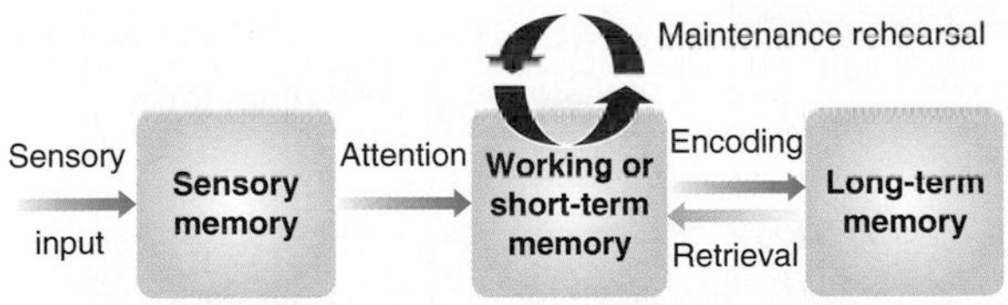

FIGURE 7-7 The Atkinson-Shiffrin (1968) stage model proposes three separate memory storage areas. Information moves between them as shown by the green arrows, within short-term memory as shown by the red arrows, and out of long-term memory as shown by the blue arrow. *Source: Data from Atkinson, R. C., & Shiffrin, R. M. (1968). Human memory: A proposed system and its control processes. In K. W. Spence & J. T. Spence (Eds.), The psychology of learning and motivation, 2, 89–195. New York, NY: Academic Press.*

A wealth of research has taken place since the model was proposed, and many aspects have been updated. For example, short-term memory is now called **working memory** to reflect the "work" it performs in our thinking processes (Baddeley, 2001). This middle stage is the "hot seat" of action, where new information is constantly flowing in through sensory memory, and past information is also constantly brought in from long-term memory.

For example, imagine you are searching online for a present for your young niece or nephew. You come across a picture of a book, *Green Eggs and Ham*. The entire image of the book enters into your sensory memory as you view the page. However, most of this information falls away while you pay attention to just the author's name, Dr. Seuss. Only that information enters into short-term memory, where you retain the name while thinking about it. That leads to retrieval from long-term memory—specifically, the memory that you once read and liked the book as a child. You stop thinking about the author as a writer, so that information falls out of short-term memory; but meanwhile, you decide you want the book for your relative. In the end, you encode your intention to buy the book, and that is stored in your long-term memory. This example shows how selective the memory processes can be: A great deal of information is presented in sensory memory, but a limited piece is attended to in short-term memory, and then finally, a different piece stored in long-term memory. In the next sections, we will further discuss each of these three stages and their operations.

Sensory Memory

The first stage of memory is essentially a sensory register. The sensory memory stage is capable of taking in a large amount of information, but it retains it only very briefly. For example, lift your eyes from the page to take in the scene in front of you right now, and then shut your eyes. Your memory for the visual scene rapidly fades from sensory memory in less than a second. However, there can be quite a bit of information contained in that visual scene, including all of the objects in a room, the lights, furniture patterns, people, and many other details. If it fades so fast, how do we make use of the impressions provided by our senses?

Consider the display in FIGURE 7-8. At a glance, then looking away, can you report all 12 letters correctly? Most can't because even though complete, the sensory image fades quickly, before you can report all of the letters. However, Sperling (1960) devised a way to show that we can selectively access parts of the complex stimulus and read some informa-tion from it in time. Just *after* the stimulus in the figure was flashed on a screen, subjects were signaled with a high tone to report the top row, a medium to report the middle row, or a low tone to report the bottom row. With the tone signal, subjects were able to report all four digits on the specified line before the image faded. This study demonstrates that our sensory store has a very large capacity for holding information; but it decays, or fades from memory, very quickly (in a fraction of a second). In order to "read" in any informa-tion from it (or, in other words, to perceive it), we have to *select* which information we want by attending to it.

FIGURE 7-8 When an image of letters is flashed for just 1/20th of a second, subjects remember less than half of the letters. But, when a tone follows the flash to signal which row to report, their performance is nearly perfect. *Source: Adapted from Sperling, G. A. (1960). The information available in brief visual presentation.* Psychological Monographs: General and Applied, *74(11), 1–29.*

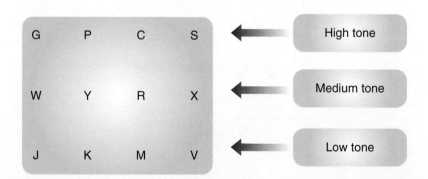

So we can select out a small amount of information from the sensory register before the information disappears. This **iconic memory** registers what the eye sees in vivid detail, but very briefly. These properties hold true for other senses like audition. **Echoic memory** holds the last few sounds that arrived at your ears for a fleeting moment before it, too, is wiped clean. While sensory memory is quite short, it allows us to select out the information we want—to perceive its meaning—if we attend to it while it is there. Thus, attention is the key to what gets encoded from sensory memory into short-term memory. Unfortunately, though many have claimed it, no one has been shown to have a long-lasting "photographic memory" (FIGURE 7-9).

Short-Term Memory or Working Memory

The second stage of memory is called short-term memory, more recently also referred to as "working memory." **Short-term memory (STM)** consists of the conscious thoughts

Iconic memory Sensory memory for visual information taken in.

Echoic memory Sensory memory for the sound reaching your ears.

Short-term memory (STM) The memory stage consisting of whatever infor-mation is in consciousness.

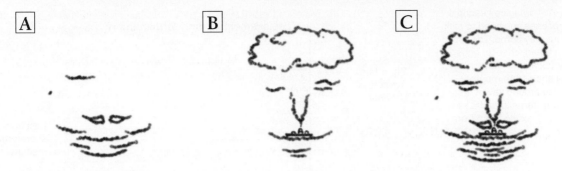

FIGURE 7-9 A true photographic memory would not fade, but would persist in the "mind's eye" so that you could pass this test: View the image in A, then look at the image in B. With a photographic memory, you could combine the features and produce the image in C.
Source: Adapted from Miller, S., & Peacock, R. (1982). Evidence for the uniqueness of eidetic imagery. Perceptual and Motor Skills, 55, *1219–1233.*

you can keep in mind at any given moment. STM has multiple components, including a phonological buffer that holds the sounds of speech and a visuo-spatial sketch pad that stores information like a mental map of a route (Baddeley & Hitch, 1974). How much information can be held in short-term memory at one time? Let's "seed" your short-term memory with a series of numbers. Look at the numbers presented in FIGURE 7-10. First, read only the row labeled "A." Read the set of numbers aloud, one at a time, slowly, until

FIGURE 7-10 Read the line of numbers next to the letter, and then look away, trying to keep the numbers you read in mind.

A:	7	3	5	6	2	1	8	4	9
B:	9	5	6	2	7	4	1	8	3
C:	1	8	3	2	9	5	4	6	7

you reach the end of the series. Then, look away from the book, and try to keep the numbers in mind for 30 seconds. Then, try to say all of the numbers out loud, in order. Most people find they can't keep all nine digits in memory, and they work hard to maintain them in their conscious mind. **Maintenance rehearsal** is the practice of saying the numbers over and over to yourself to refresh their activation and keep them available to your conscious mind. You can keep them in mind as long as you keep rehearsing them. If you stop and wait about a minute, you will find you now have little memory for the series. Short-term memory decays within 15 to 30 seconds unless you actively rehearse the information.

Now, look back at Row B, read through it completely, and then go on to Row C. Certainly, there are too many numbers now to keep them all in mind in the correct sequence. This demonstrates that short-term memory has a limited capacity. As new numbers in the sequence come in, they displace the earlier items from memory and are now remembered while the old information is lost. FIGURE 7-11 illustrates displacement with a grocery list. As new items fill up the list, the earlier items are bumped off. Our short-term

Maintenance rehearsal
Reactivating information in short-term memory to keep it in mind.

FIGURE 7-11 Imagine hearing a list of groceries you need to pick up on your way home. The list includes: bread, cheese, eggs, peas, syrup, apples, flour, milk. Because short-term memory is limited to around seven items, early items (bread) can be displaced, losing them from memory.

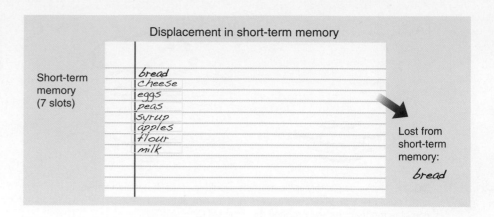

Displacement in short-term memory

Short-term memory (7 slots)

bread
cheese
eggs
peas
syrup
apples
flour
milk

Lost from short-term memory:

bread

memory appears to be limited to approximately seven items at any one time, with a range from five to nine. This very limited capacity was called "The Magical Number Seven, plus or minus two" by George Miller (1956). To illustrate, listen to someone speaking. How many of their actual words can you recall at the end of a sentence? Usually, the later words can be retrieved, but the earlier items are quickly lost from your short-term memory. In fact, the original telephone numbers created by Bell Telephone used this limited-capacity principle to design seven-number sequences for local phone numbers. These seven digit strings were short enough to look up in a phone book and keep in mind while people dialed the number.

But you may be wondering, "7 ± 2 *what*?" We can remember seven digits, or letters, or even seven grocery items: What matters is the number of items. However, the same information can be presented as a list of seven separate items ("R – E – C – E – I – V – E") or as a single item ("receive"). By grouping items into larger sets of information, through a process known as "**chunking**," more information can be maintained in short-term memory. A chunk is a meaningful memory unit consisting of related elements (Cowan, 2001). By changing digit strings into meaningful units (like the "Zip code plus 4"), you can keep more items in short-term memory (see FIGURE 7-12).

The synonymous concept of "working memory" emphasizes that this second memory stage is where the real "work" of thinking takes place. Imagine trying to perform mental arithmetic by adding a series of numbers in your head: 897 + 364 = ? To accomplish this, you must recall the operations you need (7 + 4 = 11) and then maintain memory of this result while you move to the tens column, and so on. If you are unable to keep results in mind while recalling and applying operations, you will be unable to complete the task. So your **working memory span**, or the number of items you can keep in mind at once, will have a direct impact on the thinking you can do. FIGURE 7-13 provides an example of an intelligence test item that depends on short-term memory span for success (Raven, 1936).

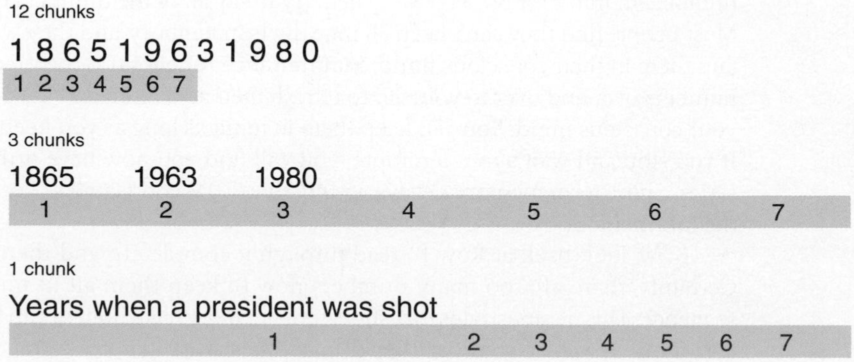

Chunking Grouping separate elements into a related unit in memory.

Working memory span The amount of different pieces of information (such as digits) that can be held in conscious memory for a short time and reported back correctly.

FIGURE 7-12 While each digit can be considered as one item to remember, four together as a year can be recalled as a single "chunk" in memory.
Source: Data from Miller, G. A. (1956). The magical number seven, plus or minus two: some limits on our capacity for processing information. Psychological Review, 63(2), 81–97.

12 chunks

1 8 6 5 1 9 6 3 1 9 8 0
1 2 3 4 5 6 7

3 chunks

1865   1963   1980
1   2   3   4   5   6   7

1 chunk

Years when a president was shot
1   2   3   4   5   6   7

Raven's Matrices

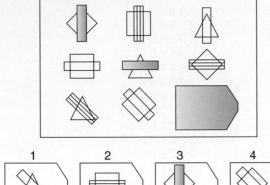

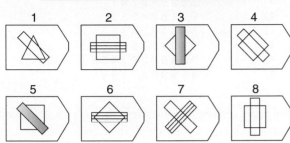

FIGURE 7-13 Raven's matrices. *Source: Adapted from Raven, J. C. (1936). Mental tests used in genetic studies: The performance of related individuals on tests mainly educative and mainly reproductive. MSc Thesis, University of London.*

Raven's matrices show a set of figures that are related, with the final figure missing. Select the final shape that completes the set from the group shown above. Look across rows and then look down the columns to determine the rules. Then, use the rules to determine the missing figure.

1. The background figures in each row are a rectangle, a triangle, and a diamond. So the third row needs a square.
2. The bar has three possible orientations. The third figure in the third row needs a bar oriented obliquely.
3. The bar has three possible patterns: clear, striped, and solid. The bar in the third figure in the third row must be solid.
4. So, the answer is alternative 5.

Working memory allows you to store partial information, information you have to keep in mind as you are analyzing each row.

You also need to process the information, and "work" on it (hence "working" memory). For example, you not only need to hold the geometric figures in mind, but you also need to compare them.

Holding all of this information in mind to successfully complete the task is the function of working memory. Much of the variation in problem difficulty and in differences among people in problem solving ability is due to working memory, according to this model.

People differ on the size of their memory span when tested. The memory span test FIGURE 7-14 was created to test individuals on their ability to remember sequences. For most of us, on richer tasks, four is a more likely span than the seven that Miller claimed (Cowan, 2001). But interestingly, individual differences in the size of memory span have been shown to relate to measures of thinking ability. Reading is correlated with memory span because it's easier to process complex sentences when you can keep more information in mind. For example, reading the sentence "There is a sewer near our house who makes terrific suits" requires the reader to back up and find an alternate meaning for *sewer*. Having a larger short-term memory span makes initially ambiguous sentences easier to process. One longitudinal study found that a child's working memory span at age 5 is a better predictor of later academic success than her or his IQ score (Alloway & Alloway, 2010).

Sequence Test

FIGURE 7-14 Memory span test.

1	9 2 4 1
2	6 3 8 5
3	2 7 9 4 1
4	5 3 2 6 9
5	4 9 5 2 8 3
6	1 8 4 6 3 5
7	7 4 2 9 6 8 1
8	3 5 8 4 6 9 2
9	2 6 9 7 4 1 3 5
10	5 8 3 7 6 9 2 4
11	3 8 2 5 4 6 7 9 1
12	9 7 1 6 2 4 8 5 3
13	3 4 9 1 6 2 8 7 5 3
14	9 4 3 4 5 2 8 1 7 6
15	7 3 4 6 9 2 7 1 4 5 8
16	4 1 9 3 8 2 7 1 9 6 5

For this test, take a blank piece of paper and number the lines 1 through 16. To begin the test, read the top row of digits, at a pace of one per second; then, look away, and write them down in order on the paper. Next, try the second row, and the third, until you have tested yourself on all of the lines. Compare your paper to the figure: the highest number of digits where you got both lines correct is your short-term memory span.

Long-Term Memory

Most importantly, the processing that takes place in short-term memory also determines whether the information gets encoded into the next stage, called long-term memory. As long as you keep rehearsing information in short-term memory, it will stay there. However, eventually, you will want to encode the information into long-term memory, where it can remain available for an unlimited amount of time. **Long-term memory (LTM)** refers to what most people mean when they talk about "memory": an essentially limitless store of information that appears to persist indefinitely. In this way, long-term memory appears to be like the hard drive of a computer: Once information is written on a computer disk, it stays forever. However, while short-term memory feeds information into long-term memory, encoding it into long-term memory takes effort. As a student, you are well aware of this! A summary of each of the three memory stages and their characteristic features is shown in TABLE 7-1.

Long-term memory (LTM) The enduring stage of memory that is unlimited in capacity and duration.

TABLE 7-1 The Atkinson-Shiffrin Stage Model of Memory

	Sensory Information Storage	Short-Term Memory	Long-Term Memory
Nickname	Register	"Working memory" buffer	Storehouse
Function	Get information in	Hold in current thought	Hold for later use
Format	Literal image	Labels	Semantic meaning
Capacity	Unlimited	7 ± 2 items	Unlimited
Duration	Less than a second	15–30 seconds	Unlimited
Retains	Attention selects information	Attention maintains information	Attention required to encode
Input source	External senses	Sensory and long-term memory	Short-term memory
Forgetting	Decay	Displace	Interference

Source: Atkinson, R.C., & Shiffrin, R.M. (1968). Human memory: A proposed system and its control processes. In K.W. Spence (Eds.), The psychology of learning and motivation, 2, 89–195. New York, NY: Academic Press.

Storing Memories in the Brain

To understand how information is written into your long-term memory, we will have to investigate the biology of human memory. You may think of the information in the brain as a library full of books, each in its own place. However, from the earliest days of brain research, it seemed that memory for information is not organized into specific places. In a series of experiments, rats were trained to find their way out of mazes, and then a portion of the cortex was removed. No matter which area was taken out, the rats were still able to solve the mazes (Lashley, 1950). The *amount* of cortical tissue removed affected their performance, but the *location* of the removed cortex had no effect on later performance in the maze. This led Lashley to conclude that memories are not localized but widely distributed across the cortex.

Synaptic Changes

Neuroscientists searched for the "engram," the neuronal processes that form and store new memories. We know from studies of other species that synapses between neurons show changes as a result of experience. Working with sea slugs, which have only 20,000 nerve cells, or neurons, Kandel and Schwartz (1982) trained the animals through classical conditioning. They then observed changes in the amount of the neurotransmitter serotonin at certain synapses. These synapses then became more efficient at passing signals to the dendrites of other neurons. Specifically, the sending neurons became more sensitive, so it took less stimulation to cause them to fire; at the same time, the receiving neurons developed more receptor sites. As a consequence, the neural circuit is more sensitive and more responsive to the specific patterns of neural activities that have been experienced.

This change in neurons is called **long-term potentiation**, reflecting greater potential for transmitting neural signals in the future (Lynch & Stabli, 1991). So synapses are responsible for **consolidation**, the process that converts information into structural changes in the brain to form long-term memories (Dudai, 2004).

The Anatomy of Memory

While synapses change all over the cortex to reflect the specifics of learning, there is an anatomical structure that is critical in the formation of all new memories: the **hippocampus** (see FIGURE 7-15). This structure, part of the limbic system deep in the brain, is highly interconnected with every area of the cortex (Gluck & Myers, 1997). Through these connections, the hippocampus plays an essential role in consolidating or forming long-term memories. This consolidation process takes more time, but once it is accomplished, the hippocampus is no longer needed to access the learned information. So the hippocampus appears to play its role in developing the long-term structural changes in the cortex that maintain information over time.

How do we know that the hippocampus plays this unique role in memory consolidation? The main evidence comes from an inadvertent experiment with a human subject known as "H.M." Treated surgically for extreme epileptic seizures in 1953 when he was 27, H.M. awoke to life with his hippocampus removed from both hemispheres. The surgery was successful in its primary goal of controlling his epilepsy. However, its side effects were catastrophic: Since the operation, H.M. was unable to learn anything new. He could not

Long-term potentiation The process of changes in neuronal receptivity that encodes information into memory.

Consolidation The stabilization of information in long-term memory through structural changes in the brain.

Hippocampus Limbic system structure that acts to consolidate information into long term memory.

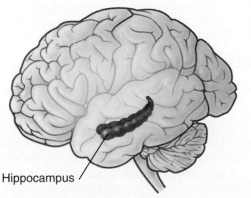

FIGURE 7-15 The hippocampus, part of the limbic system, plays a vital role in the formation of new memories.

Hippocampus

identify by name the researchers he worked with daily until his death in 2008. His family moved to a new home, but he was unable to learn his way around the new neighborhood. He read the same newspaper over and over again and always found it of interest. He remained quite amiable and was able to hear the same joke repeatedly, laughing every time.

H.M.'s short-term memory appeared to be intact, so that he could remember a small amount of verbal information as long as he was not distracted. So he could carry on a conversation as long as the content remained in his short-term memory. However, a few minutes later, he had no memory for the conversation he just had.

Researcher: Do you know what you did yesterday?

H.M.: No, I don't.

R: How about this morning?

H.M.: I don't even remember that.

R: Could you tell me what you had for lunch today?

H.M.: I don't know, to tell you the truth.

Interestingly, all of his memories for events before the surgery were intact, and he remembered earlier life experiences, such as schoolyard events, quite easily. However, he remained completely unable to form any new memories following his surgery.

In his own words, H.M. described his conscious experience:

"Every day is alone in itself, whatever enjoyment I've had, and whatever sorrow I've had . . . Right now, I'm wondering. Have I done or said anything amiss? You see, at this moment everything looks clear to me, but what happened just before? That's what worries me. It's like waking up from a dream; I just don't remember." (Milner, 1970, p. 37)

For H.M., his conscious experience was limited to what he could keep in short-term memory or recall from long-term memory prior to the surgery. Each moment was sensible, but he had no memory at all for what happened a few minutes, hours, days, or years ago. The loss of memory in clinical patients is called **amnesia**. H.M.'s complete inability to form new memories proved conclusively that the hippocampus is the seat of new memory formation. Many other clinical cases since have replicated this finding, and we'll return to this topic in the section on forgetting.

Amnesia The loss of memory in clinical patients.

CONCEPT LEARNING CHECK 7.3   *Movement of Information Through the Stages of Memory*

For each scenario presented below, identify how information flows through the three memory stages by indicating which stage the information resides in during the example.

| Sensory Memory | | Short-Term or Working Memory | | Long-Term Memory |

A. Sensory memory

B. Long-term memory

C. Non-working memory

D. Short-term or working memory

1. You see a flash of lightning out of the corner of your eye and go back to your conversation. The flash likely made it into your memory system only to _____.

2. You are introduced to Peter and talk to him for a while, but you forget his name after a minute. Peter's name likely made it as far as _____.

3. You study neurotransmitter properties and tie them in with their functions within psychology, along with thinking of examples. You score an "A" on the quiz the next day. The neurotransmitter information likely made it into _____.

7.4 Organizing Information in Memory

Different kinds of knowledge are organized in different ways in long-term memory.

■ Describe the main ways that information is organized in long-term memory.

This stage model of memory provides a good account of how sensory information is taken into conscious short-term memory and eventually encoded into long-term memory. However, studies on human memory quickly uncovered the fact that the content of memory, that is, the type of information our memory contains, resulted in differences in how that information was organized and stored in long-term memory. Remembering how to ride a bike involves qualitatively different knowledge than remembering that a fox has pointed ears or that waiters will come to take your order in a restaurant. In this section, we discuss different ways of organizing information in long-term memory.

Within long-term memory, are there different kinds of memories? Yes, there are different kinds of information stores, and their organization is accomplished in different ways. This has consequences for how the information is encoded and recalled. The organizational structure that is imposed on information influences what is "remembered." Organization seems to be the key to finding things in memory again. For finding your favorite pair of socks, or information about your bank PIN in long-term memory, organizing the information makes it much easier to locate than having it thrown together in a heap. And a lot of evidence suggests that information in long-term memory is not stored in a haphazard fashion, but is instead highly organized.

Different types of memory organizations hold different forms of memory. The major divisions in long-term memory are shown in FIGURE 7-16. The major division in long-term memory is between memories that are declarative and those that are procedural. **Declarative memory** is information that can be explicitly stated; for example, your name, the date for Halloween each year, and a recipe for carrot cake. This is also called explicit memory in that you can identify clearly exactly what information is contained in each idea (see FIGURE 7-17). Nondeclarative memory includes information that can't be stated. This includes **procedural memory**, which contains information about how to do specific tasks, such as riding a bike, styling your hair, or flipping pizza dough. You can describe what the task is, but you can't describe the specific muscle movements that produce the activity. In this sense, procedural knowledge is implicit memory; you can ride a bike or tie a bow in your shoelace, but you can't just tell someone how to do it. Procedural memories arise from repeated practice with actions.

Declarative memory Memory for knowledge of which we are consciously aware; also called explicit memory.

Procedural memory Implicit, nonstated memory for how to do things; also called implicit memory.

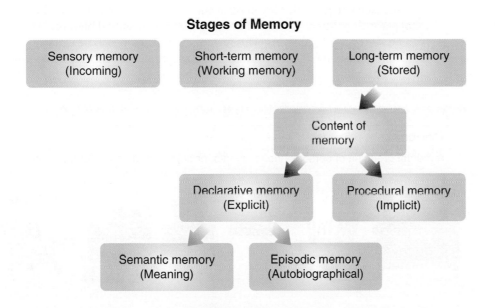

Stages of Memory

FIGURE 7-16 A taxonomy of types of knowledge in long-term memory.

Procedural Memory

Knowledge of "how to do"

Skills, implicit, hard to verbalize

Declarative Memory

Knowledge "that . . ."
Factual, explicit, accessible

Republic of Chile

FIGURE 7-17 An important distinction between types of knowledge in long-term memory is that of declarative vs. procedural memories.

Declarative Memory

Several different types of knowledge are encoded in the declarative memory system, which captures explicit knowledge of which we are consciously aware. One is called **semantic memory** because it refers to the meaning, or semantics, we associate with concepts. Semantic memory is also broken down into distinct types.

Semantic Memory

One of the basic "building blocks" of declarative memory is the **concept**, or a grouping of similar objects and events. Consider the idea of the "chair": What does this concept involve? You can describe the act of sitting and conclude that chairs must have a flat area. But must they have seat backs, legs, or arms? When you see an object, even if it is entirely new to you, you have no difficulty recognizing that it can be used as a chair (see FIGURE 7-18). So, for example, even though each of these instances looks different, we recognize them all as chairs. One of the most powerful aspects of concepts is that they allow us to know things about new instances. And therefore we can make inferences about them. For example, we know about how big each one is in life, that it is for sitting on, that it is likely to be movable, and that it is a designed piece of furniture. Concepts are central to how we understand the world. So it's natural and effective for us to divide the world into concepts.

Concepts can also be organized into categories based on their common properties. A **category** is a hierarchical cluster of similar concepts; for example, the category "birds" includes its members, (e.g., robins, sparrows, and cardinals). Knowing from memory that a concept fits into a category can provide useful knowledge (see FIGURE 7-19). For example, if I am told that an object is a pomegranate, a type of fruit, I know I can eat it. Categories provide information at a general level for the entire group of concepts within them and efficiently store information at the group level. So I know my new pomegranate can be made into juice, that it will ripen and then decay, and that it should be stored in a cool place. By grouping concepts into categories or **conceptual hierarchies**, information can be shared across concepts. This memory organization is more efficient, because the shared information (e.g., that fruit can be made into juice) only has to be stored in one place (e.g., with "fruit") rather than with each concept.

Semantic memory
Memory for the meaning of material.

Concept A "building block" or basic unit of knowledge.

Category A cluster of similar concepts.

Conceptual hierarchy Organization of related concepts into levels of categories.

FIGURE 7-18 The concept of "chair" includes a diverse set of objects that may appear hard to define; but, we recognize a chair instantly.

Concept
A mental grouping of persons, ideas, events, or objects that share common properties.

FIGURE 7-19 This concept hierarchy shows the sets of concepts grouped under "foods," and the set of concepts grouped under "fruits." The importance of this memory organization is that shared information has to be stored in only one place—with the higher level concept.

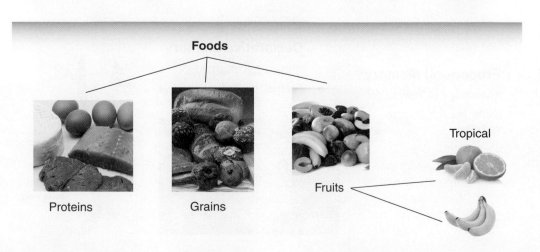

Foods

Proteins   Grains

Fruits

Tropical

How do we know that long-term memory makes use of these efficient concept hierarchies? A series of studies used the speed of finding needed information to uncover its organization (Collins & Loftus, 1975). For example, which would you answer faster: (a) Does a chicken have wings? or (b) Does a bird have wings? The results show that knowledge about the properties of birds (flies, have wings) is stored in memory with "bird," and the concept of "chicken" is stored as an associated concept. So to answer the question about chickens having wings, this link between the concepts has to be searched, taking more time. (This is true even though "chickens" and "wings" are associated through experiences with eating them!) In FIGURE 7-20, we see what a small part of a concept hierarchy, also called a **semantic network**, of related ideas might look like. As you can see, the concept "bird" is closely associated with "flies, wings, and feathers." It is more distantly connected to "blood" (stored with "animals") or "farm" (stored with "chicken"). The result is that related concepts are clustered together in ways that reflect their meaningful associations.

Semantic network model Organization of information that captures meaningful relationships between concepts.

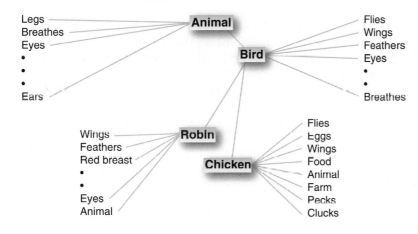

FIGURE 7-20 A semantic network showing the organization of the concept hierarchy for "birds." *Source: Reproduced from Collins, A. M., & Loftus, E. F. (1975). A spreading activation theory of semantic processing. Psychological Review, 82, 407–428.*

Another consequence of organization in long-term memory is that concepts that are frequently accessed together are more tightly linked, so that accessing one makes it easier to access the other. For example, think of a "bird". You are much more likely to answer "robin" than "ostrich," because the first is much more frequently accessed. Try again: Think of a fruit. Did "apple" come to mind, or the more unusual "kiwi"? Our long-term memory keeps track of the associations between concepts simply by tracking the frequency of their occurrence together. Then, the strength of the links between concepts aids in accessing one given the other, in the form of priming (Meyer & Schvaneveldt, 1971). This process, also called **spreading activation**, is very important in bringing the right concepts to mind to help us process what is happening in the world around us. For example, when you are seeing a zebra, you are much more likely to access a related concept like "tiger" than "dentist" (Bousfield, 1953). Theories of memory that embody these interconnections are called **connectionist models**, or parallel distributed processing (PDP) models. These approaches focus on representing every level of information in memory as interconnected elements, so that the activation of a concept creates an active network of smaller pieces of knowledge.

Another idea about how we store information in memory is the **schema** (Bartlett, 1932), a pattern of knowledge that occurs across experiences. Consider an example story using a schema called the "restaurant script" (Schank & Abelson, 1977): "John went into a restaurant and sat down. He ate spaghetti. He left." Not exactly a scintillating story, but if I ask you about it later, you are likely to add lots of substance to its bare bones. Did he order from a waitress? Did he leave a tip? Was he satisfied with his meal? Schemas provide a scaffold for events so that you can track the action as it occurs and make assumptions to fill in any gaps. And it helps to organize our behavior by shaping perceptions and encoding our experiences (e.g., "Why is this waiter giving me a list of sushi?").

So, if you have a schema, you have a basic framework to fit new experiences into as they occur. We have thousands of schemas in memory, organizing our memories for

Spreading activation The links between concepts in memory help to access one given another.

Connectionist models Memory theories that capture the distributed interconnections between concepts.

Schema Organizer for information about events, people, and groups.

Think of a . . .

bird?   fruit?

Concepts that are frequently accessed together are more tightly linked, thus, when you think of "bird" you are much more likely to think of the common robin, rather than the more unusual ostrich. What if you were asked to think of a fruit?

experiences with individuals (Michael Jackson), groups (college football fans), and events (weddings, baseball games, bat mitzvahs; see FIGURE 7-21). Rather than remembering every experience separately, schemas group them together in memory and so provide a general description of what usually happens. Studies show that people agree on the knowledge included in schemas, such as the ordering of steps (e.g., you eat before you pay in a restaurant; Bower et al., 1979).

Schemas play an important role in reconstructing memories, filling in the usual events when we can't recall the specifics (e.g., did you wait in the waiting room at the dentist's office on your last visit?). Studies show people report parts of schemas even when not actually mentioned in a story (Bower et al., 1979). Imagine you are brought into a graduate student's office shown in FIGURE 7-22. You are left there for 10 minutes and then brought into

FIGURE 7-21 Schemas in memory organize information and guide our behavior.

Person Schema
About particular people

Group Schema
About groups of people

Event Schema
About particular events

FIGURE 7-22 Look around in this office, then look away. Write down everything you can remember in the office.

another room and asked to now write down everything you can remember in the office. What will you recall? People tend to remember items consistent with their schema for an office, like the desk and chair, but not the basket (Brewer & Treyens, 1981). More interestingly, people often report items not in the actual office, but typically found there (for example, books!). So, while schemas aid memory by facilitating the recall of related items, they can also result in the intrusion of items that were not present in the scene.

In this way, schemas introduce distortions or inaccuracies in memory. Many times, we may "remember" something because it is consistent with a schema, not because it really happened. For example, you may recall that you have eaten at a particular restaurant and so must have ordered there. Or you may remember that you once didn't have enough money to leave a tip but not recall which restaurant you were in. The power of the schema is that it organizes information very efficiently. Rather than storing a complete record of each restaurant visit, your schema for restaurants preserves the common elements (e.g., ordering, eating, paying) while leaving out details that appear unimportant.

Episodic Memory

So far, we have been discussing types of semantic memory, such as concepts, categories, semantic networks, and schemas. All of these memory structures work to organize information and bring it to mind just when it is needed. A second type of declarative memory is episodic memory (see FIGURE 7-23). **Episodic memory** refers to the recall of

Episodic memory Recall of your own personal, autobiographical experiences.

Semantic Memory

Definitions, knowledge, and facts

A 15-year-old invented ear muffs because his ears were cold

= Dog

Episodic Memory

Personal experiences

FIGURE 7-23 Declarative memory includes both semantic (meaning-based) and episodic (autobiographical) memories.

your own personal experiences, also called autobiographical memory. The events from your last birthday, your walk home last night, and your earliest childhood memories are all examples of this special type of memory. We saw that declarative memory structures were focused on grouping similar information together for greater efficiency. In episodic memory, the focus is on the distinctive differences between experiences. The more your experience is novel, unusual, and unlike any other, the more likely you will recall it well. For example, can you recall what you ate for lunch last Thursday? How about what you ate for lunch last Thanksgiving? Or the first time you ate octopus, or a special meal someone made for you? We're more likely to remember the personal experiences that mean the most to us and so stand out from the everyday experiences we enjoy.

"Flashbulb" Memories

One type of episodic memory stands out from all others due to its vividness. Consider for a moment where you were when you first heard the news about 9/11, when two airliners crashed into the Twin Towers in New York City in 2001 FIGURE 7-24. I can still clearly recall my spouse coming into the room and asking me to turn on the television because a plane had crashed into the towers. I was very skeptical, and we watched together as the second plane later crashed into the buildings. This is called a **flashbulb memory** because the notion is that this moment is indelibly recorded in your memory, just like a flashbulb went off to capture a photograph of that specific moment. You likely had the feeling that you will never forget where you were when you heard about the events of 9/11. The heightened emotion we feel during some episodes in life signals to us that the

Flashbulb memory An emotional or vivid event that appears to be well remembered.

FIGURE 7-24 The attack on the World Trade Center on 9/11 was a surprising event that many people experienced as a "flashbulb memory" that they will never forget.

event is salient and should be paid attention to and remembered. In fact, the place where memory consolidation takes place, the hippocampus, is adjacent to the amygdala, the area of the brain that processes primitive emotions like fear. Our emotions appear to highlight special memories.

You likely also believe that your memory for that episode is highly accurate. One research group set out to examine this assumption through a controlled study. In 1986, millions watched the launch of the space shuttle *Challenger*. One crew member aboard was a schoolteacher, Christa McAuliffe, who was chosen as the first member of the Teacher in Space Project. Disaster occurred when the spacecraft broke apart 73 seconds into its flight, leading to the deaths of its seven crew members. Media coverage of the accident was extensive, and 85% of Americans heard the news within an hour of the accident. Researchers at Emory University then surveyed students in psychology the next day, and again several years after that day (Neisser & Harsch, 1992). Here are two examples of reports from students who were asked, "Where were you when you heard the news about the *Challenger* disaster?"

A: "I was in my religion class and some people walked in and started talking about [it]. I didn't know any details except that it had exploded and the schoolteacher's students had all been watching which I thought was so sad."

B: "When I first heard about the explosion I was sitting in my freshman dorm room with my roommate and we were watching TV. It came on a news flash and we were both totally shocked."

Which report do you think is the most accurate? In fact, both reports are from the same student! She wrote the first report a day after the explosion, and the second two and a half years later. She was so confident in her later report that she asked to see her earlier one from the day after the disaster. Even seeing her own handwriting, she could not explain why she had such a different flashbulb memory after time had passed. Memories, especially emotional ones, may seem quite salient, and we may indeed never forget. But studies like this one show that people do forget even very vivid memories and can be very mistaken about what they believe to have experienced at the time.

Procedural Memory

Episodic and semantic memories involve explicit knowledge. We can state the content of the memories and describe exactly what they involve. Another type of memory, procedural memory, captures actions: how we move, perform, and manipulate objects. For procedural knowledge, we learn through practicing sequences of actions over time. As a result, we are left unable to describe the content of procedural memories even though we can demonstrate the knowledge. For this reason, it is called implicit memory, evident in our actions even if we can't describe its content.

Procedural memory is the type of memory that allows you to remember how to tie your shoelaces or play a guitar without consciously thinking about these activities. After many sessions of practice, your fingers fly through the procedures on autopilot, expertly performing well-tuned actions in a very specific manner. Becoming truly expert at an activity such as playing the piano appears to take on the order of 10,000 hours of practice (Ericsson, Krampe, & Tesch-Romer, 1993). That would mean 10 years of practicing more than 2 hours a day! After all of that practice, your fingers move automatically as you think, just as when you're typing or texting on a cell phone. Procedural memories are also very durable, so that skills you learned as a child are still "in there" waiting to be used again. As they say, "Once learned, you never forget how to ride a bicycle." In a sense, it's "muscle memory," stored in the cerebellar area at the base of the brain.

The strongest evidence that suggests a separation of implicit and explicit memory focuses on studies of amnesic patients. Amnesia, as illustrated by the case of H.M., demonstrated the critical role of the hippocampus in forming new memories. Yet H.M. would provide another startling finding about memory. Psychologist Brenda Milner tested H.M. on a task called "mirror tracing." A device holds an image of a large star, but you can only see its reflection through a mirror while you trace it on a blank page. It's a hard task for anyone, but with practice, people learn to do it. The first time H.M. tried it, he performed poorly. But the next time he tried, he did it a little better. Soon, after practicing the task over a 3-day period, he completed the task as well as anyone (see FIGURE 7-25).

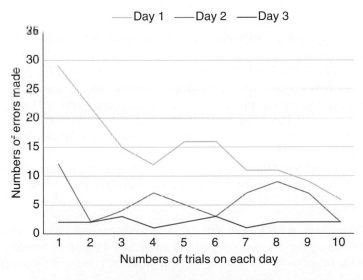

FIGURE 7-25 H.M. showed improvement in learning skilled movements in this mirror-tracing task. He was taught to trace a line between the two outlines of a star while viewing his hand and the star in a mirror. He showed steady improvement over the 3 days of testing, though he continued to have no memory of having attempted the task before. *Source: Data from Milner, B., Squire, L. R., & Kandel, E. R. (1998). Cognitive neuroscience and the study of memory. Neuron, 20, 445–468.*

However, H.M. showed no memory for his experiences tracing the star. He was asked to do so again, and after tracing it almost perfectly, said, "I thought this would be difficult, but I seem to have done this well" (Milner, Squire, & Kandel, 1998). Because H.M. was incapable of consciously remembering the task but seemed to be able to unconsciously remember how to perform it, the human mind must contain at least two separate and independent memory systems. One system, explicit memory, appears to be processed through the hippocampus. In H.M.'s case, the surgery removing his hippocampus in both hemispheres completely obliterated his ability to form new memories. However, another memory path exists in the brain, involving the cerebellum (the area at the base of the brain controlling complex, voluntary movements) and the nearby basal ganglia. Studies on other amnesic patients also support the possibility of an intact implicit memory despite a severely impaired explicit memory (Cohen et al., 1985).

CONCEPT LEARNING CHECK 7.4   *Organizing Information in Memory*

Determine what type of memory organization is illustrated in each example and match it to this list:

A. Concepts   **1.** _____ A pig has a curly tail.

B. Concept hierarchies   **2.** _____ The moment you found out you got into college.

C. Semantic networks   **3.** _____ Taking a seat in the waiting room at the dentist.

D. The schema   **4.** _____ A whale is a mammal, not a fish.

E. Episodic memory   **5.** _____ Name a vehicle that is red and has a siren: a fire truck.

7.5 Retrieval from Memory

The key to retrieving information from memory is to think about the context surrounding learning.

■ Examine the successful retrieval of information from long-term memory.

In the last sections, we saw the many ways information is organized in long-term memory and the processes involved in adding information to this enduring store. So why can't we remember everything that was once placed in long-term memory? Think back on courses you have completed in the past. Even though you may have correctly recalled the information on the final exam, can you recall it now? Your high school French may be "in there," but what does it take to successfully gain access to it again? *Retrieval* refers to the process of bringing information from long-term memory back into consciousness in short-term or working memory (see FIGURE 7-26). Sometimes, retrieval of memories occurs spontaneously and without effort. When your favorite song is playing, you can sing along without having to concentrate on the lyrics. Many other times, retrieving information from long-term memory, just like encoding into it, requires a lot of work!

> **Tip-of-the-tongue phenomenon** The feeling of knowing a word but being unable to recall it from long-term memory.

The **tip-of-the-tongue phenomenon** (James, 1890) illustrates this difficulty. James described it as "a gap that is intensely active," where a word appears to be known but cannot be recalled from memory. You would be able to recognize the right answer, but you couldn't retrieve it from memory on your own. The examples listed in FIGURE 7-27 are selected based on the difficulty of retrieving the appropriate word from memory (Yaniv & Meyer, 1987). When you have entered a state in which you feel you know an answer but cannot recall it from long-term memory, you are having a tip-of-the-tongue experience. Studies suggest these (1) are a nearly universal experience, across languages, (2) happen to most people about once a week, (3) increase with age, (4) frequently occur when one is trying to think of a person's name, and (5) are resolved during the experience about half of the time (Brown, 1991).

Retrieval Cues

What "work" can you do at the time of retrieval to help bring information to mind? You need a way to "prime" the information, just like you prime a pump by pouring water into it, so that the target word will become active in memory. This can be accomplished

FIGURE 7-26 Retrieval involves reactivating information in long-term memory and placing it within conscious access in short-term or working memory. *Source: Data from Atkinson, R. C., & Shiffrin, R. M. (1968). Human memory: A proposed system and its control processes. In K. W. Spence & J. T. Spence (Eds.), The psychology of learning and motivation, 2, 89–195. New York: Academic Press.*

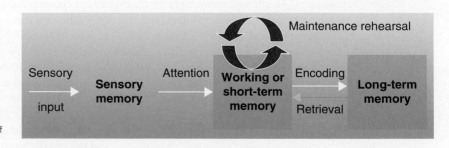

Recall the word.

1. A navigational instrument used in measuring angular distances, especially the altitude of the sun, moon, and stars at sea.

2. A small boat used in the river and harbor traffic of China and Japan, propelled with an oar.

3. An infectious and usually fatal bacterial disease of animals, especially cattle and sheep.

4. A person who believes that nothing can be known about God; expressing ignorance of God; not an atheist.

5. In old Greek stories, the food of the Gods; supposed to give immortality to any human who eats it; anything that has a delightful taste.

Answers: 1. Sextant, 2. Sampan, 3. Anthrax, 4. Agnostic, 5. Ambrosia.

FIGURE 7-27 Read these definitions one at a time and try to think of the word. When you can't, but feel you do know the answer, you will have reached a "tip-of-the-tongue" phenomenon, where you can recognize the answer but can't retrieve it from long-term memory.
Source: Adapted from Yaniv, I., & Meyer, D. E. (1987). Activation and metacognition of inaccessible stored information: Potential bases for incubation effects in problem solving. Journal of Experimental Psychology: Learning, Memory, and Cognition, 13(2), 187–205.

by trying to access information related to the word you are trying to recall. Suppose you are stuck while trying to retrieve author Mark Twain's real name. You might think about other facts you know about him, such as the names of his books, famous quotes, the time in history when he lived, and so forth. Each of these facts can serve as a retrieval cue or an aid in recall. One cue would be his first name, "Samuel." Does this cue help you retrieve the name? By continuing to add as many related cues as possible, you may use **cued recall** to finally retrieve his name.

Retrieval cues can help in recall by providing activation of related concepts, boosting the activation of the target concept through spreading activation (see FIGURE 7-28) (Collins & Loftus, 1975). These principles work the same no matter how complex the target information in memory. If you need to recall the name of the brain structure responsible for encoding new long-term memories, you can aid its retrieval by thinking about related concepts, which then serve as retrieval cues. Remember H.M. and his tragic amnesia, living each day without remembering what occurred. Did you recall "hippocampus?" Retrieval cues work by filling out the network of concepts related to the target you are trying to recall. Imagine playing a heated game of charades with your friends. A wide variety of unusual cues can work to help you access a particular piece of knowledge in memory.

These memory principles also explain why encoding strategies work the way they do. Elaboration, for example, is tying a new concept to other concepts already in memory. So, rather than learn about canaries in isolation, comparing them to other types of birds and thinking about how they differ in size, eating behavior, and singing helps to tie the new concept into the network of past concepts. Then, the ties from encoding can serve as cues at the time of retrieval, "retracing" your steps during encoding to bring the target concept to mind. In fact, the more you can tie the cues at retrieval to the ones you used during encoding, the more likely you are to retrieve the information. This principle, called **encoding specificity**, says that the cues present at encoding will be the best cues at retrieval (Thompson & Tulving, 1973). In that experiment, people learned two separate lists of words, one while sitting on the side of a pool and one while underwater, in scuba gear! Next, they were tested for both lists, either in the water or on the deck. The results showed

Cued recall Retrieving information from related pieces of information.

Encoding specificity The principle that cues present at encoding will be the best cues for retrieval.

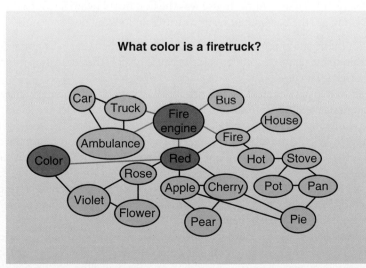

What color is a firetruck?

FIGURE 7-28 In a semantic network, accessing concepts tied to your target concept in memory spreads activation to it, making successful retrieval more likely. To remember "fire engine," for instance, you can add retrieval cues like "color" and "red" to make the concept more active.
Source: Adapted from Collins, A. M., & Loftus, E. F. (1975). A spreading activation theory of semantic processing. Psychological Review, 82, 407–428.

that more words were retrieved when the encoding conditions (e.g., being underwater) *matched* the retrieval conditions (e.g., being in the water).

Physiological states, such as being under the influence of alcohol, can similarly serve as a cue in memory (Goodwin et al., 1969). Finally, there is a role for mood in memory. Perhaps you had an unpleasant experience during which you felt very afraid; luckily, this experience may not come to mind very often. However, at future times when you experience that emotion again, the unpleasant memories may come quickly to mind. Bower (1981) documented this effect by inducing pleasant or depressed states in subjects and found that the emotional state during learning could aid in the retrieval of word lists. Depending on their mood, their free associations, imaginative fantasies, social perceptions, and snap judgments about others' personalities changed. And, when the feeling-tone of a narrative agreed with the reader's emotion, the salience and memorability of events in that narrative were increased. So the **mood congruence** of information at encoding and retrieval can serve as a memory cue.

Mood congruence
Matching emotional mood as a cue at encoding and retrieval to improve memory.

Adding Context

Just like specific cues, encoding specificity suggests the *context* of an event, or the circumstances surrounding it, is very important for retrieval. For example, returning to your childhood home may lead to the retrieval of memories you may not have thought about in a long time. The specific place cues help to retrieve memories that took place in that location. Reinstating the context of an event, even if only in your mind, can help with retrieval. For example, if you try to recall events from the year you were 5, you may have a difficult time recalling many. But if I help you to reinstate the context by talking about kindergarten, your first teacher, how you got to school every day, whether you went on any field trips, and so on, memories may start to come back to you. The idea is that long-term memories are still "in there," but they may require cues from their original encoding to bring them to mind again.

In everyday life, this suggests you're likely to remember more of that high school algebra if you return to the classroom where you learned it! In fact, some studies have shown a (very) small benefit to studying in the same classroom in which the test takes place. However, the power of encoding specificity lies more in the specific set of features related to a specific memory than in a general cue like where you learned it. The key to retrieval is to have ways to label memories so that you can bring them back up again by thinking about those labels. For example, one study asked people to recall other students from their yearbooks between 5 and 20 years after graduating from high school (Williams & Hollan, 1981). People recalled some names immediately, and then used contextual cues to help recall other names; for example:

> "trying . . . I'm—Okay I was imagining the whole room and we were imagining the instruments set up and I'm trying to remember the name of this guy—who used to . . . Art! And he was also in our 10th-grade art class . . . he would also bring a whole lot of people to—first on that—what's his name now? Let's see—[whistle] I'm trying to—remember his name. At his house was the first time I heard a Jefferson Airplane album. Umm . . . the bass guitar, really a strungout looking dude . . . uhh . . . wow."

Clearly, lots of information remained in memory, though the name was not accessible; however, recalling the name was still possible because of all of the contextual information that served as retrieval cues.

The need to reinstate context in order to recall experiences in memory may be the cause of an amnesia we all suffer from: childhood amnesia (Usher & Neisser, 1993). Think back now to your earliest memory in life. For most people, this dates between ages 2 and 5 (Barrett, 1980). Why? A possible cause may be the difficulty in reinstating the context of early memories to help to retrieve them. What else was on your mind when you were 4? What were the salient moods, places, and thoughts at that time? What labels, if any, were you likely to have created for your memories? If we were able to reinstate the context for those memories, we may find they are indeed still there in our long-term memories, awaiting the right cues to unlock them.

Another explanation is that memory may improve as we develop our sense of "self" (around age 2), since we organize memories autobiographically (Howe & Courage, 1997). Similarly, language learning at about the same age may allow children to describe experiences in ways that add to memorability (Hayne & Simcock, 2002). A final possibility is biological: Perhaps the networks of neurons that encode memories may require some time to fully mature (Bachevalier & Vargha-Khadem, 2005).

Very often, we have the sense of knowing information is in memory but being unable to explicitly state it. An example is the "50 states problem": You are likely able to recognize that Alabama and Arkansas are states in the United States, but can you name the other 48? What can we do when "it's in there," but we can't quite recall it from memory? As noted about retrieval, putting in effort to try to retrieve the information can lead to success. Accessing related information in memory (thinking about road trips you've made), invoking the context in which the information was originally encoded (remembering your fifth grade classroom), and generating retrieval cues (there must be other states that start with "A") are all ways to work at retrieval. When you are being tested and experience a retrieval cue failure, try to keep this playful perspective in mind and vary the cues you use to help with retrieval.

Retrieval Practice

Recent studies have shown that testing can be a means of improving learning, not just of assessing its results. Suppose you are given the task of learning 40 new words in a new language, say, Swahili. Most people would spend the entire time allotted to studying the words and their meanings. However, if you spent the same amount of time but used it to repeatedly test your recall of the words, you would actually learn more (Karpicke & Roediger, 2008). Taking a memory test enhances later retention, a phenomenon known as the *testing effect*. The simple act of practicing recall can boost your ability to retrieve the information later (Carrier & Pashler, 1992). The steps involved in retrieval benefit from practice.

But testing facilitates learning beyond offering an opportunity to restudy the material. In one experiment, students studied prose passages and took either one or three immediate free-recall tests, without any feedback, or restudied the material the same number of times. Students then took a final retention test 5 minutes, 2 days, or 1 week later. When the final test was given after only 5 minutes, repeated studying produced the best performance. However, on the delayed tests, repeated testing produced substantially greater retention than studying, even though repeated studying increased students' confidence in their ability to remember the material. Testing is a powerful means of improving learning (Roediger & Karpicke, 2006).

In fact, testing helps even if you don't know the answers! Studies of pretesting, where you attempt to answer questions about material you haven't read yet, find substantial benefits simply from considering the questions. Unsuccessfully attempting to answer questions about new topics proved more beneficial than having extended time to study the text (Richland et al., 2009). For example, a question such as, "What is total color blindness caused by brain damage called?" was posed before reading. The subjects who saw the question were more likely to learn the answer (cerebral achromatopsia) from the text than those who simply studied it on their own. The pretest questions served to prepare learners to look for important information in the text.

Once information appears to be solidly in memory, it is tempting to stop studying. However, the **overlearning** principle shows that performance can still be improved even when accuracy is at 100%. When you keep practicing retrieval past the point of perfect recall, you are still strengthening connections between concepts. So we can continue to learn even after we think we know the information perfectly.

Overlearning Continuing learning even when recall appears successful.

CONCEPT LEARNING CHECK 7.5 | *Practicing Retrieval*

Consider the principles of memory retrieval. Explain how these strategies would help you recall a word on the tip of your tongue.

1. Generating retrieval cues

2. Adding context

3. Retrieval practice

7.6 Reconstructing Memories

Memory is a dynamic process that constructs both old and new information.

■ Explain how information from long-term memory may include misinformation.

As we learned about perception, what is "out there" is not necessarily what makes it into the mind, and so with memory. Our experience of an event is not wholly encoded into memory, but may be "filled in" using our schemas. So when you attempt to recall a particular time you were in a restaurant, you may recall elements of the event, but you may also reconstruct, or regenerate, memories of the event using your knowledge of what usually happens. This process of "filling in" the details of a memory is called **reconstruction**.

For example, think of a family holiday that took place several years ago. Can you actually recall the details of the event, such as who was there, what time you gathered, what food was served and what you ate and drank, and what was discussed? While some notable details may be recalled ("the ham Mom cooked all day that turned out looking like a football"), most of our "memory" for the event is constructed by what we know must have occurred: "Surely Uncle Bob was there because he always comes, and we always have turkey, and we gather at noon. . . ." We can construct, or reconstruct, a memory for that holiday, and bits of actual memories may be included; however, a large part of our memory for that day is filled in by knowledge rather than specific recollection. In a study of college students, Brewer (1988) had students and their roommates keep detailed diaries of their daily lives. While they could recall specific memories that same day, the common events were likely to be reconstructed memories. We seem to keep vivid memories of unusual, surprising, and important events (such as flashbulb memories), while our everyday experiences are grouped together under schemas, recording only minimal information from each event. Reconstruction is a guess at what happened based on the frequency of occurrence; as a result, it can be incorrect. We lose many details of our experiences and combine reconstruction with recall when remembering, potentially introducing inaccuracies in memory.

Source Monitoring

When we reconstruct memories, we may get some of the specifics wrong. A common error is remembering some information but being unable to recall its source. **Source monitoring** errors refers to recalling information without identifying its original source (Lindsay & Johnson, 1991). If I ask you to do a series of mundane tasks, such as lick an envelope and staple some papers, or ask you to watch while someone else does those actions, will you remember which you did? Laboratory studies show that it's easy to forget such inconsequential actions and to recall that you did them when you actually watched (Johnson, Hashtroudi, & Lindsay, 1993). Source-monitoring error is observed for important events as well, such as when people incorrectly recalled how they heard about the *Challenger* disaster.

An example of a source monitoring error with important consequences occurred when psychologist Donald Thompson was identified by a rape victim as a physical match for the face of her attacker. Just before the attack, Thompson had appeared on a live television show to discuss his work (ironically) on face recognition. The police determined that the victim must have accurately remembered his face but mistaken the source as the attacker rather than the show (Powell & Freckelton, 2008). Other studies suggest simply imagining possible events make you more likely to misremember them as occurring. For example, after the crash of an El Al Boeing 747 into an apartment building in the Netherlands, 60% of study participants reported seeing video of the crash on television (Crombag et al., 1996). However, no such video exists! This suggests we should be suspicious of our memories and seek to validate them externally rather than believing whatever we recall. Though it goes against our belief that our memories are the truth, we have seen that memory is far from a videotape of our experiences.

The Misinformation Effect

Can memory for a specific episode be altered by new information? In one study (Loftus, Miller, & Burns, 1978), subjects were shown a series of color slides depicting an accident

Reconstruction Creating a memory of what likely occurred based on information you can recall.

Source monitoring Memory for the circumstances of acquiring information.

in which an automobile hit a pedestrian. At the beginning, a sports car is seen passing a yield sign, then moving on to where the accident occurred. FIGURE 7-29 Later, the subjects were asked questions about what they remembered. One of the questions included a "presupposition," or a phrase that is assumed to be true when it was not: "Did another car pass the red car while it was stopped at the stop sign?" This information was misleading because it was actually a yield sign, but most people don't notice the contradiction. For other subjects, consistent information was presented ("the yield sign") or no sign was mentioned. Then, after a delay, subjects were tested again about their memory for the accident. The partcipants had to say whether they had seen the image with a stop sign or the yield sign before. If the subjects never saw the misinformation, they said the correct sign 75% of the time; however, if they saw the question asking about the stop sign, fewer people (41%) correctly reported the yield sign. FIGURE 7-30 shows that misinformation led to even poorer performance on giving correct answers if introduced after a delay rather than right after seeing the slides. Overall, the results suggest that information seen after an event, whether consistent or misleading, is integrated into the witness's memory of the event.

FIGURE 7-29 People saw an image of a car stopped at a yield sign, and were later asked if anyone passed the car when it was at the stop sign.

FIGURE 7-31 shows what may be happening in memory when new information is added after an event. If a contradiction is not detected, the misinformation may remain in memory and may change later descriptions of the event. This **misinformation effect** (Loftus, 1979) leads to the inclusion of incorrect information along with the original memory in a way that the person can't distinguish. Then, when they reconstruct the original event, they may include other information that came later within their own account. This means that memories can include information encoded at the original time of the event and information that is added to that memory when it is discussed or thought about at a later time. This is strong evidence that memory is dynamic (Schank, 1982); that is, it is changeable based on reaccessing it and adding to it at later times. Studies show that questions about events, even if they occur long after the events took place, can influence memory by adding misinformation (Loftus, 1975; 1979; 1980).

Misinformation effect
Adding new, incorrect information to a memory after the event.

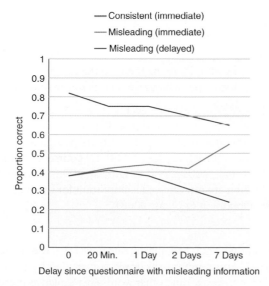

— Consistent (immediate)
— Misleading (immediate)
— Misleading (delayed)

Proportion correct

Delay since questionnaire with misleading information

FIGURE 7-30 Introducing misleading information during later questions impacts the accuracy of memory for the original event. In a control group, no misinformation was introduced. In another group of participants, misleading information was given immediately following viewing the slides of an accident. In a third group, the misleading information came after a 20-minute filler test. Some participants in all three groups were tested for their memory of the original slides either immediately, after 20 minutes, 1 day, 2 days, or 1 week later. The results show the misled groups were significantly less accurate than the control groups.
Source: Data from Loftus, E. F., Miller, D. G., & Burns, H. J. (1978). Semantic integration of verbal information into a visual memory. Journal of Experimental Psychology: Human Learning and Memory, 4(1), 19–31.

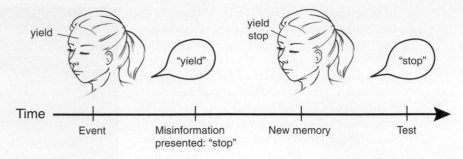

FIGURE 7-31 When new information is added about a past episode, it may become incorporated into memory without noting an inconsistency.

Loftus (1996) points out that questions asked of eyewitnesses may commonly introduce error by including information that the witness unwittingly incorporates into his or her memories of events. In a typical investigation, witnesses may be questioned multiple times, and hypotheses about what occurred are often expressed. Even when trying to accurately report what you witness, you may be influenced by the questions posed by the police, lawyers, and other authorities. In a dramatic 1984 case in Scott County, Minnesota, prosecutors investigated a child-abuse ring (Press et al., 1985). It started when two mothers accused a local trash collector of sexually abusing their girls; he, in turn, confessed and accused 15 others (he later recanted). As the investigation continued, 45 adults were targets, and 24 were eventually charged. Many of the children involved were taken from their parents and placed in foster homes. There, they were repeatedly interviewed by prosecutors or social workers, who encouraged them to recall detailed stories. For children, and even for adults, the questions asked by authorities, even when well intentioned, can lead to answers that the questioner seeks.

In the end, only one trial of two adults was held in Scott County, and they were acquitted; all remaining charges were dropped. Cases like this raise the question of whether a child's testimony about events can be trusted. To investigate, Loftus and others conducted a study in which preschoolers were asked repeatedly (7–10 times over a 10 week period) about a fictitious event (Ceci et al., 1994). They were told, "I'm going to read some things that may have happened to you, and I want you to think real hard about each one of them that I am going to read. Try to remember if it really happened. Think real hard, and tell me if this ever happened to you." Then, they were asked about several events, some provided by parents such as a sibling's birth or vacation, and some fictitious. In particular, one event was getting their hand caught in a mousetrap and going to the hospital to have it removed.

The results showed the children's memory for true events was very nearly always accurate. But, by the seventh questioning, around one-third of the children reported recalling the fictitious event actually happening to them. One 4-year-old's statement describes his report (Ceci et al., 1994, p. 399):

> "My brother Colin was trying to get Blowtorch (an action figure) from me, and I wouldn't let him take it from me, so he pushed me into the wood pile where the mousetrap was. And then my finger got caught in it. And then we went to the hospital, and my mommy, daddy, and Colin drove me there, to the hospital in our van, because it was far away. And the doctor put a bandage on this finger [indicating]."

Perhaps because they trusted the source, and other events were true, some preschool children incorporated the story into their memories and added details to establish its reality. Later studies support the finding that preschool children are particularly vulnerable to a variety of suggestive influences (Bruck & Ceci, 1999). Of course, children can be accurate witnesses to events (Ceci et al., 2002; Poole & Lindsay, 1998). Studies show that when, how, and how often children are interviewed is important for the accuracy of their reports. (Garven et al., 1998; Goodman & Quas, 2008).

False Memories

False memory Inaccurate information incorporated into memory.

What about memory accuracy in adults? They, too, may create new, **false memories** for events that never actually occurred. An innocuous example is provided by studies in which words are presented (e.g., *bed, rest, awake*) and other words are recalled as presented (e.g., *sleep*; Deese, 1959; Roediger & McDermott, 1995), a phenomenon called *implicit memory*. However, adults are also capable of generating false memories for episodic events (Loftus, 1997). Suppose you are told, "I talked to your parents, who shared a story about how you had been lost in the mall when you were about 5 years old. You may not feel like you remember this event. But you were lost for an extended period, were crying, and found aid and comfort in an elderly woman who finally reunited you with your family. Now, try to recall as much detail as possible about that event. Are you starting to remember now?" Twenty-nine percent of college students stated they remembered, either partially or fully, the false event constructed for them. Another study provided false photographs of subjects on a hot air balloon ride as a child, and more than 50% recalled specifics of the event (Wade et al., 2002).

Suggesting memories that never happened and coming to feel you can recall them is a very rare experience. But you may have experienced something like this; for example, perhaps you have heard a family story about your childhood so often you become convinced you remember the scene. Or, while you remember an event, discussing it with others adds information to that memory so that it contains new elements not there when you initially experienced it. It is even possible to imagine events so vividly that you may misremember them as something that happened, called *imagination inflation* (Loftus & Davis, 2006). This points out a danger in our memory system: We may have vivid memories of events that never actually occurred. For example, spurious memories of unidentified flying object (UFO) abductions are created and maintained, and in these cases, there is at least some reason to doubt their literal accuracy (Newman & Baumeister, 1996).

In fact, even when we know information in memory is incorrect, it can still affect our thinking. In the *continued influence effect*, people rely on information they *know* is not true when making later decisions (Johnson & Seifert, 1994). For example, imagine you heard about a family of four found dead in their home, having dined the night before at a local Chinese restaurant. The police report that food poisoning was not the cause of their deaths, and you believe that. But do you want to go eat at that restaurant? No! The best way to counteract misinformation is to provide an alternative account for the cause; in this case, it was carbon monoxide poisoning. Even information known to be incorrect stays in memory, and we may fall back on it. Think about the example of the "stolen" Christmas gifts at the beginning of the chapter; even though I knew perfectly well there was no theft, I still believed the parking lot was more dangerous after this event! This use of asserted information, even when corrected, can have serious consequences for our reasoning about events in the world (Lewandowsky et al., 2005).

After learning about the processes involved in memory, it may be surprising that memory is ever really accurate; rather, we each carry in our minds a changing version of the reality we experienced. But memory is most often surprisingly accurate. In one study, people saw a series of travel scenes for just a second or two but were very accurate in identifying whether they had seen them before—more than 90% correct—even when thousands of pictures were shown (Shepard, 1967; Standing, 1973). Memory for familiar faces surpasses 95% accuracy (Bruce & Le Voi, 1983). Procedural memory is maintained for very long periods of time; in fact, it is often said that you never forget how to ride a bicycle once you have learned. And your own test scores should convince you that, if you put in effort, it is possible to encode and maintain any information in memory. In this section, we have focused on the question of how distortions enter into memory because they have important consequences. But even so, your memory most often serves as an accurate record of your experiences, preferences, and emotions over time.

CONCEPT LEARNING CHECK 7.6 | *Introducing Error in Memory*

For each example, identify the principle involved in introducing error into memory.

A. Reconstruction

B. Source-monitoring error

C. Misinformation effect

D. False memory

1. _____ Carrie mistakenly thinks her roommate was along when she saw Third Eye Blind perform because she does everything with her roommate.

2. _____ The professor told the class when the quiz would take place but gave a different date on the syllabus.

Peter recalls the syllabus date and is upset that the quiz is a surprise.

3. _____ Raoul sees a woman who looks very familiar but can't think of how he knows her. Later, he sees her picture on a poster for school election candidates.

4. _____ Little Colleen always shudders when her family drives by the municipal trash facility. She recalls the smell inside the trucks because her brothers always tell her that when she was born, they picked her up at the garbage dump.

CRITICAL THINKING APPLICATION

A witness to a crime says, "I'll never forget that face!" As jurors, we believe them. Eyewitness testimony is the gold standard in the courtroom and the most convincing short of DNA evidence (Loftus, 1996). But after what you have learned about memory in this chapter, what do you predict about the veracity of eyewitness memory?

Very influential in trials, juries find eyewitnesses quite convincing (Kassin et al., 1989). How could someone be wrong about identifying an attacker at the center of an extremely traumatic event? One case involved a woman (see FIGURE 7-32) who identified her male attacker in court. Based largely on her testimony, he served more than 10 years in jail for the crime; however, he was then freed based on DNA evidence. FIGURE 7-33 shows the actual assailant and the man she mistakenly identified. Remarkably, the accused man and the victim have written a book together describing their painful journey through this case (Thompson-Cannino & Cotton, 2009). In recent years, hundreds of cases have been overturned based on DNA testing, and more than 80% of these contained mistaken identifications (http://www.innocenceproject.org/).

A great deal of psychological research has identified factors that influence the accuracy of eyewitnesses (see **TABLE 7-2**), and there is a strong consensus among legal professionals that these principles are sufficiently reliable to present in court. However, jurors are still most influenced by the apparent confidence of the eyewitness in their identification (Penrod & Cutler, 1995). Unfortunately, an eyewitness's confidence is not a good predictor of accuracy; in studies of actual crime witnesses, very confident identifications occurred even when the witness was wrong. This suggests our judgments about eyewitness memory may not be very different from other types of memory. If it feels real, we believe it must be, despite plenty of psychological evidence to the contrary.

FIGURE 7-32 Jennifer Thompson identified the man she believed attacked and raped her during an assault in 1984.

FIGURE 7-33 Ronald Cotton (right), is shown in this 1984 police photo. Cotton was convicted of the rape of Jennifer Thompson, but DNA testing eventually showed the real rapist was Bobby Poole (left).

TABLE 7-2 Factors that Impair the Accuracy of Eyewitness Testimony

- Very high levels of stress during the event
- The occurrence of violence during the event
- The presence of a weapon that captures attention
- The duration of the event
- Longer amount of time since the event until questioning occurs
- Identification of a person from a race other than your own
- Information about the event is provided by others after it occurred
- Exposure to a person is experienced in other settings
- The witness's own attitudes and beliefs about the event

Source: Kassin, S. M., Ellsworth, P. C., & Smith, V. L. (1989). The "general acceptance" of psychological research on eyewitness testimony: A survey of the experts. American Psychologist, 44(8), 1089–1098.

7.7 Forgetting

The ability to forget informs us about the processes of remembering.

■ Analyze how forgetting improves memory.

We often think of "forgetting" as a mistake, as in forgetting our keys or a phone number. But the ability to forget may be a key feature of human memory that aids, rather than inhibits, our intelligence (Schank & Abelson, 1977). A case study illustrates how important it is to select out information for later recall versus recalling everything that occurs. A woman was identified who spends an excessive amount of time recalling autobiographical memories. If given a date, she can tell you what she was doing and what day of the week it fell on. Based on hers and other cases, a syndrome called **hyperthymesia** was identified (Parker et al., 2006). However, this special memory ability is not very helpful; indeed, it gets in the way of thinking about life. While it can take work to encode information into memory, the fact that we can also forget a great deal of information may be the feature of human memory that makes us "smart."

Hyperthymesia Recalling past autobiographical events to an excessive degree and accuracy.

Forgetting curve Graph showing that much information is immediately lost from memory after study.

Measures of Forgetting

As students, you are experts in memory tests: Free recall of information is tested by writing essays, recognition by a multiple-choice test, and cued recall by fill-in-the-blank and matching questions. All of these methods are used in education to see how much a student remembers from information in lessons. But what if you wanted to study how much information students *forget*?

In the early days of psychology, Herman Ebbinghaus (1885) attempted to look at memory performance using novel stimuli, ones that he had never been exposed to before. So he created the nonsense syllable, three-letter strings that did not form recognizable words (e.g., *puh*, *ret*, and *miw*). He then tested his own memory for them after varied amounts of time and measured what information was lost or forgotten. The result was a **forgetting curve** (see FIGURE 7-34), the shape of which holds true for just about any learned material. Initially, there is a steep loss in the amount of information retained, and then this levels out to a baseline maintained over time. Other, more meaningful material shows the same type of forgetting curve. For example, Bahrick's (1984) study of high school Spanish students showed that they forgot a lot in the initial years after studying (see FIGURE 7-35), but surprisingly still retained around 40% of the material up to 50 years later! Most relevant for you, a similar pattern was found for material from an introduction to psychology class up to 12 years later (Conway, Cohen, & Stanhope, 1991).

The speed of forgetting depends on the difficulty of the learned material (e.g., how easy it is to encode deeply), its organization, and physiological factors such as stress and sleep. This basal forgetting rate differs little between individuals. However, improvement in forgetting rates occurs through the repetition of learning (see FIGURE 7-36). With each study session, the starting point of full recall (at the end of the study session) falls off, but not as far with the second repetition and even less with the third. The notion is that each session is raising the "floor" of the forgetting function, even though each session shows a

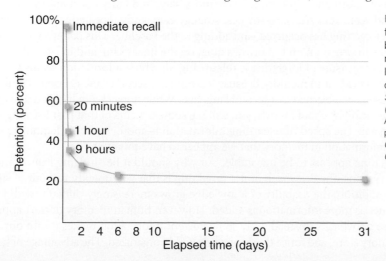

FIGURE 7-34 Ebbinghaus's forgetting curve is characterized by an initial sharp dropoff in remembered material, which then levels off to a baseline maintained over time.
Source: Data from Ebbinghaus, H. (1885; reprinted in 1913). Memory: A contribution to experimental psychology. (Translation by H. Roger & C. Bussenius). New York: Teacher's College Press.

FIGURE 7-35 Bahrick's (1984) study of high school Spanish students showed that they forgot a lot in the initial years, but still retained around 40% of the material 50 years later.
Source: Data from Bahrick, H. P. (1984). Semantic memory content in permastore: Fifty years of memory for Spanish learned in school. Journal of Experimental Psychology: General, 113, *1–35.*

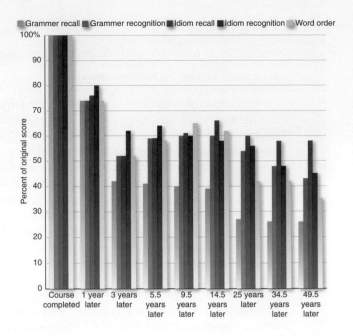

FIGURE 7-36 Forgetting curves showing repeated study sessions, where each acquires the maximum, and then the fall off to the base rate is less with each session.

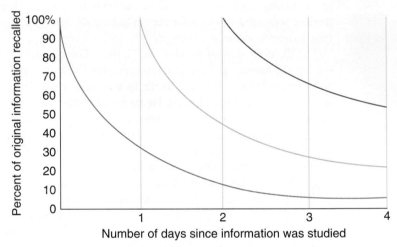

marked dropoff immediately following learning. Each repetition in studying increases the optimum interval before the next repetition is needed (for near-perfect retention, initially repetitions may need to be made within days, but later they can be made after years).

Since a great deal of forgetting happens right away, this may suggest a strategy of studying just before exams, before the dropoff happens. However, that would result in a very big dropoff! With each repetition of study, the recall floor is boosted so that the retention of information in long-term memory stays at a fairly constant level for days, weeks, and years after study. So the best strategy is to study repeatedly, picking up after the initial forgetting has occurred, and adding to the baseline. This pattern will help you to recall the information on tomorrow's quiz, on the final exam, and in later life!

Another measure of forgetting is **relearning**, in which information seems to be forgotten but is evident in memory because learning it a second time is faster. Think back on any lessons you learned in a second language. While it may seem like you don't recall much of your high school French, you will see some benefits of that past learning if you study it again. The speed of relearning information is another way to demonstrate that we have information in memory that we appear to have forgotten.

Forgetting appears to be inevitable, but why should it be? Judging from computer memory systems, the drawback of not forgetting is that you quickly run out of storage space. In addition, the usability of knowledge grows increasingly difficult, with longer access times as more information is added. However, human memory doesn't appear to have these drawbacks. Instead, only some current information makes it into our long-term memory store, and, once there, remains highly organized. The advantage of human

Relearning A measure of forgetting and learning that is based on how easy it is to learn information again at a later time.

memory is that the material we think about the most is the most likely to be encoded into long-term memory and is therefore less likely to be forgotten.

Theories of Forgetting

There are many reasons we remember some information, such as its personal importance, its emotional tone, and the frequency of thinking about it. Similarly, there are many reasons we may forget. The endless details we experience, such as where the ketchup is found in the cafeteria, are arguably not needed. Indeed, retaining that information in memory would work against our ability to focus on meaningful information we may need again. Through the efficient organization of information in memory, we don't need to remember all the times we've seen a robin or every trip to the dry cleaner's; instead, we remember only general information about some episodes in life. A memory without the ability to forget would face an overwhelming problem of organization (a glance at your computer storage drive should convince you that keeping everything quickly becomes a problem for retrieval)! But if information is desirable, why is it sometimes forgotten?

The primary reason we can't recall information we want—the formula for the circumference of a circle, the name of your new neighbor, or where you left your car keys—is that the information was never encoded into long-term memory in the first place. Think about meeting someone new: Are you attending to his or her name and attempting to tie it into your existing knowledge? Most often, we're too busy shaking hands and preparing what we'll say to fully encode their name. We have identified a number of ways you can increase the odds of getting information into long-term memory, and the key factor is effort. Some things go right without any help, and some things stay in memory that we wish we could forget. But for the most part, forgetting happens because the current contents of short-term memory never make it any further into long-term memory, causing encoding failure.

If information is encoded into long-term memory, it appears to endure there. There is no evidence that memories decay, or fade in their strength over time. Based on **decay theory**, we would expect all memories to fade over time; however, there are some old memories that you still vividly recall. No physiological evidence has been discovered that suggests well-encoded memories fade over time. Instead, memories appear to be retained: The problem with forgetting seems to involve getting information encoded in the first place or regaining access to it.

Another important factor in forgetting is **interference** from other information. Neuropsychological evidence suggests that sleep is necessary in order to allow the consolidation process in the hippocampus to occur (Stickgold, Hobson, Fosse, & Fosse, 2001). In a very early study of learning, Jenkins and Dallenbach (1924) compared learning a set of new concepts (A) to learning those concepts followed by a new set (B). They found subjects remembered more information from set A if they went to sleep rather than learning another set. They concluded that "forgetting is not so much a matter of the decay of old impressions and associations as it is a matter of interference, inhibition, or obliteration of the old by the new." If the two sets of information are very similar, such as sets of nonsense words as in Ebbinghaus's study, learning one may cause interference with memory for the other. As long as the materials are distinctive, interference between study sessions is not a major problem.

This raises the question of how to schedule study sessions so as to maximize what is recalled. A great wealth of evidence indicates that spacing out your study sessions produces much better performance than studying once for the same amount of time (Cepada et al., 2006). This **spacing effect** is that we retain information better if the learning effort is distributed over time (see FIGURE 7-37). Many students plan to cram their learning into a long session just before a test, called "massed practice." This can feel like it's leading to a lot of progress, but it is actually an inefficient process. In general, shorter practice sessions spaced widely apart produce the best memory. There are few findings in psychology as robust as the spacing effect; even so, many modern educational systems fail to build in repeated practice sessions as part of learning (Dempster, 1988). In many cases, two spaced presentations are about *twice* as effective as one massed session (Hintzman, 1974). Now that you know how important it is to space out your learning sessions, you can build this principle into your study habits.

Decay theory The notion that information fades from memory on its own.

Interference theory New knowledge can disrupt recently learned memories.

Spacing effect Learning is improved if study effort is distributed over time.

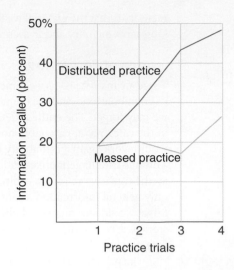

FIGURE 7-37 Graph showing the advantage of spaced vs. massed practice for long-term memory retention.
Source: Data from Cepada, N. J., Pashler, H., Vul, E., Wixted, J. T., & Rohrer, D. (2006). Distributed practice in verbal recall tasks: A review and quantitative synthesis. Psychological Bulletin, 132*(3), 354–380.*

Repression Mentally pushing away explicit recall of unpleasant memories.

Motivated Forgetting

Can our conscious intention to forget an event be helpful in making it disappear from memory? *Motivated forgetting* is a concept introduced by Freud (1957) as a defense mechanism against unpleasant memories. Through **repression**, or submerging painful memories away from consciousness, we may choose to avoid traumatic memories. Recent evidence suggests it is possible to prevent unwanted declarative memories from entering consciousness (Anderson & Green, 2001). So do people sometimes intentionally forget the past? Williams (1994) interviewed women who had documented histories of sexual victimization in childhood. A large proportion of the women (38%) did not recall the abuse that had been reported 17 years earlier. Women who were younger at the time of the abuse or molested by someone they knew were more likely to have no recall of the abuse. Of the more than 60% of victims who recalled the events, 10% reported they had, at some time in the past, forgotten about the abuse. Those with "recovered memories" tended to be younger at the time of the event and had received less support from their mothers (Williams, 1995). There were no differences in the accuracy of those with recovered memories from those who reporting always remembering.

Another study surveyed professional psychologists and found approximately 25% who reported childhood abuse. Of these, 40% reported a period of forgetting some or all of the abuse (Feldman-Summers & Pope, 1994). Both sexual and nonsexual abuse were subject to periods of forgetting, and the most frequently reported factor related to recall was being in therapy. This suggests that traumatic events can be "missing" from memory for some period of time and later accessed as a result of available cues or therapeutic intervention (Palm & Gibson, 1998). Some psychologists argued that recovered memories are more likely in some types of trauma, such as the betrayal of trust (Freyd, 1995). In the practice of therapy, clinicians became interested in pursuing repressed memories as explanations for their clients' difficulties as adults (Frederickson, 1992). Perhaps as a result, the 1990s brought an increasing number of reports of the recovery of previously repressed memories of childhood abuse.

However, Loftus and Ketchum (1994) argued that many ways of attempting to retrieve memories can cause them to be unwittingly created. As we saw with false memories from repeated suggestive questions, it may be possible to induce false memories of abuse (Loftus, 1993). By asking clients to imagine that abuse had occurred, repeatedly raising questions, and use of hypnosis, therapists may have unintentionally encouraged the creation of false memories of traumatic events (Loftus & Davis, 2006). The result can be unintended yet have tragic consequences. An example from a 1989 criminal case involved an adult woman coming forward with a 20-year-old "recovered memory" of her 8-year-old friend's rape and murder: She now recalled that the perpetrator was her own father (Morain, 1995). The father spent more than 6 years in jail before his conviction was overturned.

While some cases of recovered memories have been documented (Schooler, 2001; Schooler et al., 1997), they are extremely rare. One explanation for them is that how the person thinks about events at the time may be different from his or her views of events later in life (Geraerts et al., 2007). In addition, people who recovered their memories of abuse through suggestive therapy also exhibit a heightened susceptibility to the construction of false memories (Geraerts et al., 2009). While some memories may indeed come to mind unexpectedly, more often, the key problem with traumatic memories is learning to live with them. Cases of posttraumatic stress disorder and the trauma of war experiences (Sargant & Slater, 1941) suggest memories we would like to forget more often haunt us (Rubin, Berntsen, & Bohni, 2008).

Amnesia

Perhaps the most eloquent descriptions of forgetting come from those who suffer from a neurological impairment, demonstrating both the loss of memory and its importance in defining us as individuals. Cases like that of H.M. show the consequences of the loss of hippocampal function, resulting in an inability to create new memories. While H.M.'s case was unique in terms of the destruction of the hippocampus in both hemispheres, a similar case of amnesia resulted from a stab wound. When a fencing foil entered his brain through the right nostril, taking a slightly oblique course to the left, patient N.A. also suffered a loss of the ability to encode new verbal information (Teuber et al., 1968). Other patients have been found to have explicit memory for events lasting no more than 1 minute. In one study, two patients (on three occasions each) readily consumed a second lunch when it was offered 10 to 30 minutes later, and usually began to consume a third meal 10 to 30 minutes after that. These findings suggest that memory for the recent past is important even for simple behaviors like eating (Rozin, Dow, Moscovitch, & Rajaram, 1998).

Amnesia also occurs after damage to the medial temporal lobe, often caused by encephalitis. However, one recent, very rare case resulted from trauma, which restricted blood flow (and so cut off oxygen) to the right temporal lobe. Scott Bolzan, a former NFL player, slipped in the bathroom and landed on the back of his head (Bolzan et al., 2011). He lost his memories of the 46 years of his life, including his teenage sons, his wife, and even his own parents. Bolzan can add new memories of life since the accident, but lost all memory for his life prior to the injury. However, he continues to have intelligence and reasoning, as well as language function. He retained some skills like bike riding, which are part of procedural memory. However, he could not remember how to start the car the first time he drove months later, though knew the meaning of road signs and lights. Simply telling him about the events of his life did not lead to recovery of his experiences from his own memory. Balzan also understands that he has a memory disorder, and retains the fact.

With Bolzan, as well as H.M., explicit memory was impaired, but implicit memory still functioned. One historical case of implicit learning involved a woman with Korsakoff's syndrome (see FIGURE 7-38). Korsakoff's syndrome is marked by the loss of explicit memory, usually as a result of chronic alcoholism. In 1911, physician Edouard Claparède hid a pin in his right hand before meeting her, which pricked her painfully when they shook hands. When he returned the next day, the patient did not recall having met him previously, but

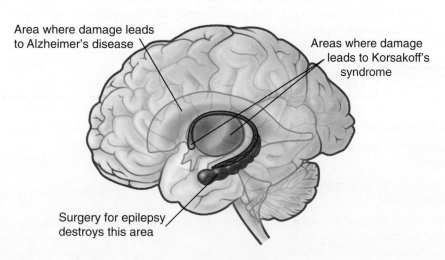

Area where damage leads to Alzheimer's disease

Areas where damage leads to Korsakoff's syndrome

Surgery for epilepsy destroys this area

FIGURE 7-38 Brain areas involved in damage to memory based on clinical cases.

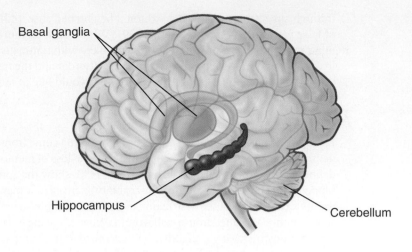

FIGURE 7-39 Brain areas involved in processing explicit (hippocampus) and implicit (cerebellum and basal ganglia) memories.

Basal ganglia

Hippocampus

Cerebellum

Alzheimer's disease A progressive memory disorder in which people lose access to explicit memory.

Dementia Clinical diagnosis of major memory loss with age or disease.

she refused to shake his hand, saying, "Sometimes pins are hidden in people's hands" (Schwartz & Resiberg, 1991). Patients with **Alzheimer's disease**, a progressive memory disorder, also show an ability to perform visual tasks in the occipital cortex involving implicit knowledge while showing no signs of explicit recall in the tasks (Golby et al., 2005). As a result, patients can continue to perform a routine task like bathing by following implicit cues while forgetting many of their explicit memories (such as recognizing family members).

Studies of malfunctions of memory, in particular forms of **dementia** or memory loss, have helped researchers understand how we encode, store, and retrieve memories. Cases like H.M.'s support the stage model of memory, in which explicit memories are recorded as sensory memory (the immediate initial stage), then short-term memory (or working memory), and only then into long-term memory. However, studies of patients with memory loss also show that an important type of memory—implicit memory—does not appear to rely on the same brain areas thought to support the stage model of memory.

The evidence from studies of patients who experience loss of explicit memory but retain intact implicit memory (including patient H.M.) suggest an alternate route for storing memories in the brain that bypasses the hippocampus. Procedural knowledge in memory, such as riding a bike or learning to type, can remain intact in these patients (Schacter, 1992). The reason is that motor movements involved in performing procedures are processed through the cerebellum and basal ganglia areas of the brain (see FIGURE 7-39). As a result, damage to the hippocampal area shows no impact on implicit memory for procedural knowledge. In some studies, patients were taught a new motor task successfully even though they always reported that they had never performed the task before (Schacter, 1992). This alternate route explains why memory appears to be divided between explicit and implicit knowledge.

CONCEPT LEARNING CHECK 7.7   *Learning from Case Studies of Amnesia*

Identify which type of forgetting is illustrated in these case examples.

A. Implicit memory

B. Amnesia

C. Dementia

1. _____ Mary suffers from Korsakoff's syndrome and can't encode any new experiences.

2. _____ Despite suffering from amnesia, Bill has learned how to type, even though he doesn't remember learning.

3. _____ Helen is able to function well at home, but she can no longer hold conversations on the phone about the past.

7.8 How to Improve Your Memory

The principles of memory reveal helpful strategies for improving retention.

■ Identify principles that can improve memory.

Memory Principles Applied to Studying

From evidence about the encoding process, it is clear that active effort by the learner is required. The following guidelines group the principles of memory into active steps you can take to improve your recall.

Actively Construct Memory

Learning is not the same as reading; instead, you need to actively construct your memory for the material. Several principles help with constructing memory, including elaboration, generation, depth of processing, self-reference, self-explanation, and mnemonic devices. For all of these principles, you will want to ensure that you are *actively* processing the information you want to remember. Simply rereading, highlighting, and repeating it (such as replaying a lecture podcast) are *not* effective ways to help encode new material. *You* must be thinking about it in as many different ways as possible to construct your own view of the material. If you can rephrase the information in your own words, in ways that are relevant to you and tie in to what you already know, you will have prepared an excellent account to encode into long-term memory.

Our knowledge of the many types of memory organizations points out how critical it is to encoding and retrieval. Unlike computer disks, we can't afford endless searches through random lists of information. Human memory is built around organizing related information together, grouping meaningful units for easier retrieval. Judging from its importance in memory research, taking the time to organize the information you are attempting to learn is key to accomplishing this goal. One trick is to spend time after each class rewriting your notes, organizing clusters of information in hierarchies and related lists. This also helps to point out any missing connections between concepts and prepares you to ask questions at the next class session. You can't rely on your processing during the frantic note taking in lectures to lead to a thoughtful organization that suits your learning.

Schedule Study Sessions

A second set of related principles addresses how you should schedule study sessions. The spacing effect says that studying two different times for an hour each time is twice as effective as studying once for 2 hours. This explains why cramming your studying into one massive session before an exam is less effective than studying for shorter periods over the term. Rehearsing material a day later greatly promotes memory for the material when tested at a later time. You will save time and have better learning if you study regularly rather than all at once. In general, shorter practice sessions spaced widely apart produce the best effects for long-term memory. Now that you know how important it is to space out your learning sessions, you can build this principle into your study habits. In addition, try to avoid studying similar material back to back to avoid interference effects. Instead, switch to a less-related course after you finish one session. Finally, don't forget the lessons from forgetting: Sleep is critically important in forming new memories, and failing to sleep enough will limit how much of your new knowledge can be encoded into long-term memory. It's a hard lesson for busy college students, but sleep is your best friend when it comes to learning.

Test to Learn

Testing is also a critical part of learning. Asking questions, even ones you can't answer correctly, works to draw associations to the material you're learning. Repeated attempts to retrieve the information help you build up intermediate cues that aid recall. This even works for simple tasks like remembering where you parked your car today. When you are first out of sight of the car, ask yourself to remember where it is. This simple act of practicing recall can boost your ability to repeat this feat later. Surprisingly, testing even without feedback promotes the mindset and connections among ideas you will need for mastery of the material. We learn from testing as well as studying, so include self-testing in your study plans. And keep studying even when you know the answers. Overlearning works to practice the associations you've learned and strengthen them for later access.

Cue Retrieval

Retrieval problems can lead to frustration because you feel the knowledge is "in there," but you can't access it. The principles of retrieval cuing can help when you're drawing a blank. In the moment, think about related information and any mnemonic cues you used during studying to help you come across the information through an alternate route. Try reinstating the context of the time of initial learning. This includes your state of mind, mood, the physical setting, and related concepts in mind at the time of learning. Context is very important in guiding you towards the knowledge in memory. In addition, state-dependent and mood-dependent memory effects suggest you should also maintain a rested, calm mind while studying and testing.

Summary of Multiple Influences on Memory

Multiple influences color our psychological experience of memory. Biology plays a significant role, as demonstrated by the importance of sleep in forming new memories. Failing to sleep enough will limit how much new knowledge can be encoded into long-term memory. The consolidation of information into long-term memory takes some time for neuronal processes to work. Another source of biological evidence is the devastating impact of brain injury and disease on memory functions. Damage to some areas, such as the hippocampus, can destroy the possibility of encoding new memories.

Another source of influence on memory is our past experiences. When we experience similar things, we automatically group them together in memory: faces of family members or celebrities, words or pictures, are all associated together in memory based on how we experienced them. Our networks of memories provide access to information based on how things belong together. "Bread and butter" or "tofu and edamame" are connections formed in our memories as patterns of associations. Human memory is built around organizing related information together, grouping meaningful units as we experience them for easier retrieval.

Finally, the environment around us plays an important role in memory. It's easier to recall information in the same context, so you recognize schoolmates on campus that you may pass by at the mall. Retrieval is aided by reinstating the context at the time of initial learning. This assists in accessing information by invoking the same state of mind, a similar mood, the physical setting, or concepts in mind at the time of learning. Context is very important in guiding access to knowledge in memory. In addition, state-dependent and mood-dependent memory effects suggest your state of mind is part of this environment.

Knowing the multiple influences affecting memory, we can identify ways to take advantage of this knowledge and improve our memory for new information. Suggestions for how to improve your memory are summarized in **TABLE 7-3**.

TABLE 7-3 Techniques for Improving Memory

Technique	Description	Guideline	Example
Context effects	Cues from the learning context help to retrieve information	Reestablish the context to aid in recall.	"Let's see, the other types of memory were declarative and procedural, so implicit must be paired with . . ."
Depth of processing	The more deeply you think about the meaning, the better you will learn	Rephrase the point in your own words: How can you best describe the meaning?	"So to me, "procedural learning" is something you can't forget as long as you can do it."
Elaboration	Link the material to information you already have in your memory	Think of how the new information relates to concepts you know.	"So semantic nets organize a bunch of concepts."

(continues)

TABLE 7-3 Techniques for Improving Memory *(continued)*

Technique	Description	Guideline	Example
Forgetting curve	Learned information drops off quickly over time	Review the material again before a quiz to keep it accessible in memory.	"Since the quiz is tomorrow, I'll make time to go back over Chapter 8 tonight."
Generation	Make up a new idea or example on your own.	Tie the new information to clear examples	"Procedural knowledge is like riding a bike."
Mnemonic devices	Create memorable links between new concepts	Try to break down new terms into easy-to-remember pieces.	"Declarative knowledge is the kind you can 'declare' out loud."
Organization	Organize new information into related units to learn together	Outline new information to understand which parts fit together.	"Here are all the ways I can improve my studying."
Overlearning	Learning continues even after we think we know the information well	Continue to study the information even if you get it right on quizzes.	"I got them all right, but I'm going to go over them and explain why they're right."
Self-explanation	Create an explanation of why specific concepts work the way they do.	Talk your way through the material in your own words.	"So, the amygdala is close to the hippocampus, and emotion plays a role in memory!"
Self-reference effect	Link the material to thoughts about yourself	Remember a time that this concept happened to you.	"One of my 'flashbulb' memories is the inauguration of President Obama."
Spacing effect	Study periods spaced out over time results in the best learning	Study the material every day throughout the term.	"I'm going to study one topic in Chapter 7 every day this week."
Testing effects	Help your learning by giving yourself frequent practice recall tests.	After learning, practice recalling what you just learned.	"Let me try to recall the three stages of memory."
Visual imagery	Changing formats from verbal to visual can help to create complementary memories.	Think of a visual representation of the information.	"The sensory store trickles some information into short-term memory which trickles some information into long-term memory.

CONCEPT LEARNING CHECK 7.8 | *Developing Helpful Study Habits*

Select three principles from Table 7-3 that have been shown to improve memory.

Describe how you could incorporate each principle into your study routine. Example: Organization. I can reorganize the material to group related concepts together and create an overall outline that captures the relationships among them.

Visual Overview Types of Knowledge in Memory

Different kinds of knowledge are organized in different ways in long-term memory.

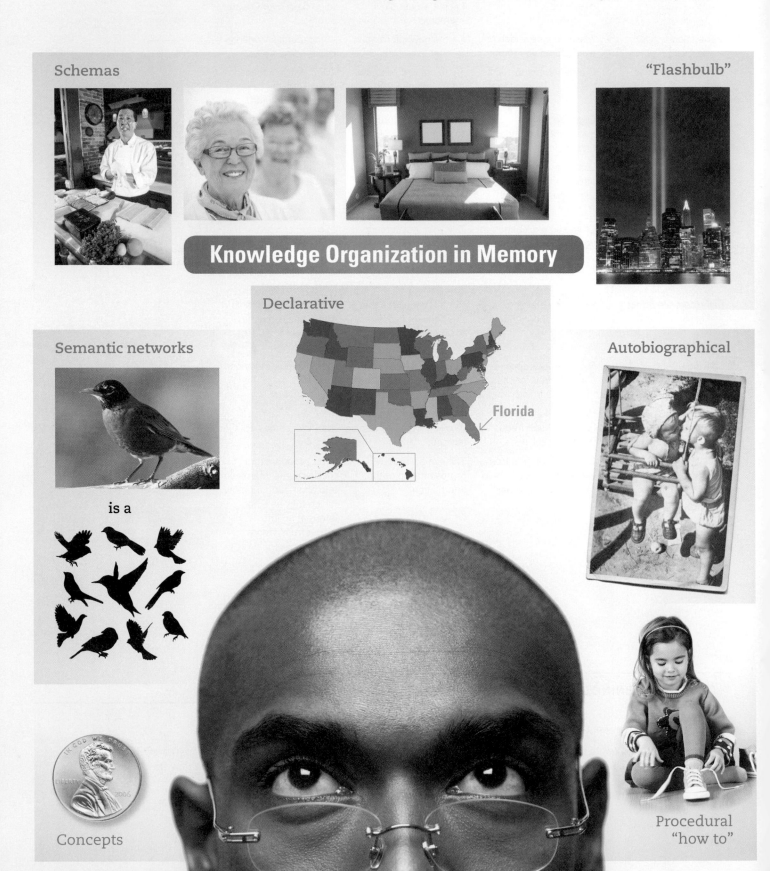

Schemas

"Flashbulb"

Knowledge Organization in Memory

Declarative

Semantic networks

Florida

Autobiographical

is a

Concepts

Procedural
"how to"

7.1 Overview: What Is Memory?

- Memory is the enduring consequence in the mind of our experiences with the world.
- It is an active process that interprets our experiences, not simply recording them.

- Memory is central to every other psychological process.

7.2 Constructing Memory

- Automatic processing occurs when information is encoded into memory without conscious awareness.
- Attention is needed to select from the information currently available and encode it into memory.
- Effortful processing is needed to ensure that information is successfully transferred into memory.
- *Levels of processing* refers to the notion that the more "deeply" the meaning is understood, the more likely it will be stored in memory.
- Elaboration is the process of drawing out the meaning of information and connecting it to related information already in memory.
- Self-reference effects show that we are

most likely to remember things that are tied to ourselves in some way.
- Generation effects show that actively processing by "going beyond the information given," such as coming up with examples, enhances memory.
- Self-explanation facilitates memory through a deeper processing of why concepts work the way they do.
- Visual encoding makes use of our rich visual sense to make information more memorable.
- Mnemonics are tricks for making information more memorable through rhymes, acronyms, and other memory aids.

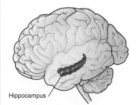

Hippocampus

7.3 The Three Stages of Memory

- There are three different memory stages for the conscious processing of memories.
- Sensory memory takes in sensory input in a rich display, but it fades in a fraction of a second.
- Short-term memory is information you are currently conscious of, and it fades in less than a minute or is displaced by new thoughts.
- Short-term memory is limited to around seven items at any one time, but "chunking" information can make this more efficient.
- Working memory refers to the same stage as short-term memory but highlights that

work is needed to keep information in mind and that it supports cognitive tasks.
- Long-term memory is the permanent stage of memory that can hold an unlimited amount of information indefinitely.
- Memories are stored in the brain by long-term potentiation, which changes the interaction of neurons at the receptor sites to preserve information.
- Memories are stored in a distributed fashion all over the cortical areas of the brain and in the cerebellum.
- The hippocampus is the memory structure that helps to consolidate new information into long-term memory.

7.4 Organizing Information in Memory

- Knowledge in memory is organized into groupings based on content.
- Declarative memory is memory for information you can state explicitly.
- Semantic memory is a type of declarative memory that includes factual information.
- Concepts, concept hierarchies, and semantic networks capture the building blocks of information and their rich interconnections in memory.

- The schema organizes memory for events and captures the repetition of experiences like a "script."
- Episodic memory includes autobiographical experiences along with "flashbulb" memory events.
- Procedural memory includes information that is known implicitly and is "performed" through action.

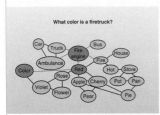

7.5 Retrieval from Memory

- Context provides the key to retrieving information from memory.
- Retrieval cues work by spreading activation from related concepts in memory.
- Adding context promotes retrieval by providing cues like the ones at encoding.

- Encoding specificity is the principle that matching context at encoding and retrieval maximizes recall.
- The act of practicing retrieval makes future retrievals more likely to be successful. So test often!

7.6 Reconstructing Memories

- Memory is a dynamic process that constructs both old and new information.
- Reconstruction involves creating a memory by filling in information from memory.
- Source monitoring involves knowledge about when, where, and how information was acquired.

- False memories include information encoded into memory that is inaccurate.
- The misinformation effect shows that incorrect information can be added to a memory at a later time.

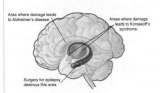

7.7 Forgetting

- The forgetting curve shows that we lose a lot of knowledge immediately after learning.
- Repeated study sessions boost the baseline of long-term knowledge.

- Forgetting is useful because it limits our memory to information we expect to be useful later.
- Cases of memory loss inform us about the principles of successful memory.

7.8 How to Improve Your Memory

- The principles of memory reveal many helpful strategies for improving retention.

- Study habits can improve the likelihood of encoding and retrieving information when you need it.

7.1 Overview: What Is Memory?

1. Memory is:
   A. an accurate record of what we experience.
   B. the enduring consequences of our experiences.
   C. our ability to recall facts.
   D. the outcome of trying to learn.

7.2 Constructing Memory

2. The process by which we transform what we perceive, think, or feel into an enduring memory is called:
   A. encoding.
   B. remembering.
   C. reconstructing.
   D. storing.

3. Long-term retention of information is greatly enhanced by:
   A. repetitive processing.
   B. visual assessment.
   C. elaborative encoding.
   D. rhyme judgment.

4. When learning a new word, like *hippocampus*, you will remember it best if you:
   A. think about what the word means.
   B. think of another word that rhymes with it.
   C. picture how the word looks.
   D. write the word in large block letters.

7.3 The Three Stages of Memory

5. Memory storage is composed of sensory memory, short-term memory, and:
   A. working memory.
   B. long-term memory.
   C. potentiated memory.
   D. retrieval.

6. The process of keeping information in short-term memory by mentally repeating it is called:
   A. maintenance rehearsal.
   B. chunking.
   C. memorizing.
   D. mnemonic storage.

7. Short-term memory can hold:
   A. a seven-digit telephone number but not a list of seven words.
   B. approximately seven meaningful items.
   C. information for no more than 3 minutes.
   D. an unlimited amount of information.

8. When rats are given drugs that block long-term potentiation:
   A. they develop stronger synaptic connections.
   B. they lose their ability to encode information.
   C. they get easily lost in familiar mazes.
   D. neurotransmitter release is enhanced.

7.4 Organizing Information in Memory

9. Emile said that he vividly remembers the day he turned 21. This is an example of a(n):
   A. explicit memory.
   B. procedural memory.
   C. implicit memory.
   D. iconic memory.

10. Every year around the anniversary of her father's death, without realizing why, Judy experiences a feeling of sadness. This reaction is an example of a(n):
    A. explicit memory.
    B. implicit memory.
    C. state-dependent retrieval cue.
    D. emotional retrieval cue.

11. A network of associated facts and concepts that make up our general knowledge of the world is called:
    A. semantic memory.
    B. episodic memory.
    C. explicit memory.
    D. implicit memory.

7.5 Retrieval from Memory

12. Of the following, the best example of using retrieval context is:
    A. learning the material so thoroughly that it comes right to mind.
    B. sitting in your usual desk in your usual classroom when taking an exam.
    C. using memory drugs to enhance neural processing.
    D. drinking coffee while studying.

13. When Jorge studies for a test in his noisy dorm, he always has his favorite energy drink at hand. The encoding specificity principle would suggest that he should:
    A. have some of the energy drink a few hours before the test.
    B. have a sip of the energy drink right before going to sleep to enhance memory.
    C. take a can of the energy drink with him to the test.
    D. ask the instructor if he can use an iPod to listen to soothing music during the test.

7.5 Retrieval from Memory

14. A world-famous musician left his multimillion-dollar instrument in the trunk of a taxi. What might have caused him to forget something so important to him?
  A. The lack of retrieval cues
  B. Source memory
  C. The novel context
  D. Mood-dependent memory

7.6 Reconstructing Memories

15. Recall of when, where, and how information was acquired is called:
  A. constructive memory.
  B. retrospective memory.
  C. source memory.
  D. misinformation in memory.

16. When subjects in Loftus's experiment on misinformation saw a picture of a yield sign and then read a question about a stop sign, they were more likely than control subjects to report having seen:
  A. a yield sign.
  B. a stop sign.
  C. both signs.
  D. neither sign.

17. Defense attorneys often protest prosecutors' use of eyewitness testimony because:
  A. source errors may cause an eyewitness to make a false identification.
  B. eyewitnesses are more prone to forgetting.
  C. poor eyesight in eyewitnesses tends to invalidate their testimony.
  D. a confident eyewitness is usually right.

7.7 Forgetting

18. Research by Hermann Ebbinghaus using nonsense syllables demonstrated that:
  A. memories of new information fade at a constant rate over time.
  B. new memories remain strong for up to 4 weeks before they begin to fade.
  C. most forgetting of new information happens soon after learning.
  D. individuals remember much more than they think they do.

19. Information can be kept for hours, days, weeks, or years in the:
  A. retrieval terminal.
  B. hippocampus.
  C. remembrance database.
  D. long-term memory store.

20. Johan has difficulty remembering events in his life that occurred after his recent surgery; his neurosurgeon has diagnosed him as suffering from:
  A. dementia.
  B. long-term potentiation.
  C. synaptic enhancement.
  D. amnesia.

7.8 How to Improve Your Memory

21. Studies show that, following a heavy session of studying, you should:
  A. exercise.
  B. sleep.
  C. switch to a different course topic to study.
  D. avoid thinking about the material.

22. The following are all methods of elaborative encoding except for:
  A. generation.
  B. self-reference.
  C. self-explanation.
  D. highlighting.

23. For optimal results in terms of longest-term memory for the material, is it best to plan your study sessions so that they:
  A. switch back and forth between class topics.
  B. occur in one marathon session for each course.
  C. occur in widely spaced out shorter sessions.
  D. repeat the material over and over.

CHAPTER DISCUSSION QUESTIONS

1. You have an exam coming up. Remind yourself of helpful ways to prepare for it. What are the terms for these techniques?

2. Describe one of your flashbulb memories and explain why that memory is so firmly imprinted in your mind.

3. You are a juror in a case involving the robbery of a convenience store. An eyewitness identifies the accused. In considering this evidence, what should you bear in mind?

4. The head of your study group has asked you to obtain 10 items for tomorrow's meeting; unfortunately, you're not in a position to make a written list. The items are pens, a ruler, 3 × 5 cards, ice, sodas, a master key, a list of members, cookies, cups, and a carton to use as a waste basket. Discuss two methods you might use to remember the 10 items.

5. Imagine that a reliable, effective memory-enhancing drug were available for purchase. Describe some of the pros and cons of this drug.

CHAPTER PROJECTS

1. Read an article or book about the experiences of people who have memory disorders. Oliver Sacks has written several, including *The Man Who Mistook His Wife for a Hat*. What does the experience of the patients described tell you about normal memory functions? Are there any limits to the use of this type of data in learning about memory?

2. Several popular films have investigated short-term memory loss:

Memento (2003)
50 First Dates (2004)
Finding Nemo (2003)

Watch one of these commercial movies. Is the movie accurate in its depiction of how memory works?

CHAPTER KEY TERMS

Alzheimer's disease
Amnesia
Automatic processing
Category
Chunking
Concept
Conceptual hierarchy
Connectionist models
Consolidation
Cued recall
Decay theory
Declarative memory (explicit memory)
Dementia
Echoic memory
Elaboration
Encoding
Encoding specificity
Episodic memory
False memory

Flashbulb memory
Forgetting curve
Generation effect
Hippocampus
Hyperthymesia
Iconic memory
Incidental memory
Interference theory
Levels of processing
Link method
Long-term memory (LTM)
Long-term potentiation
Maintenance rehearsal
Memory
Method of loci
Misinformation effect
Mnemonic
Mood congruence
Overlearning
Priming

Procedural memory (implicit memory)
Reconstruction
Relearning
Repression
Schema
Self-reference effect
Semantic memory
Semantic network model
Sensory memory
Short-term memory (STM)
Source monitoring
Spacing effect
Spreading activation
Stage model of memory
Tip-of-the-tongue phenomenon
Working memory
Working memory span

ANSWERS TO CONCEPT LEARNING CHECKS

7.1 Defining Memory

1. A. Essay. Essays are the most difficult because you have to retrieve all of the information from memory, and there are very few cues offered to help.

2. B. Multiple-choice. These questions are easier because the information is presented to you, and you can match it to what you have in memory. All you need to do is recognize the right answer. Fill-in-the-blank questions also require recalling information, but having the surrounding information helps you retrieve the needed term.

3. C. Fill-in-the-blank. Memory retrieval can be difficult, but having some cues to help you find the information in memory is very helpful.

4. Recognizing information in memory is easier when you don't have to do the step of retrieval. You might conclude that retrieval is the hard part, and cues from the surrounding context or choices help a lot.

7.2 Applying Methods of Encoding

1. D. This fits the self-reference effect because effort is made to turn the concept into a personal example.

2. D. This fits self-reference encoding because the concept is being tied to specific events in the learner's own life.

3. F. This fits mnemonics because the learner is using the words' relationship to remember the concepts.

4. C. This fits depth of processing because they are capturing the deeper meaning of the material.

5. E. Self-explanation is the method that tries walking through examples to make sure you understand why every step occurs.

7.3 Movement of Information Through the Stages of Memory

Information flows from sensory memory to short-term memory to long-term memory. Sensory and short-term memory can drop information, but long-term memory does not.

A. Sensory memory.
B. Short-term memory.
C. Long-term memory.

7.4 Organizing Information in Memory

1. A pig has a curly tail. [A. Concepts]

2. The moment you found out you got into college. [E. Episodic memory]

3. Taking a seat in the waiting room at the dentist. [D. The schema]

4. A whale is a mammal, not a fish. [B. Concept hierarchies]

5. Name a vehicle that is red and has a siren: a fire truck. [C. Semantic networks]

7.5 Practicing Retrieval

1. Generating retrieval cues. [Thinking of related words will help by spreading activation to the word you're trying to recall.]

2. Adding context. [Matching the context of retrieval to the context of learning helps in accessing the word in memory.]

3. Retrieval practice. [Studies show practice with retrieval, even without feedback, helps with later retrieval; so practicing trying to retrieve the word will help when you try to access it again later.]

7.6 Introducing Error in Memory

1. A. [Reconstruction, because she is filling in the participants based on what usually happens.]

2. C. [Misinformation effect, because two dates were given in two separate communications, and the contradiction was not noted.]

3. B. [Source monitoring error, because the face was familiar from the poster, not from knowing the woman.]

4. D. [False memory, because the story is not true, but Colleen has invented some details to support it.]

7.7 Learning from Case Studies of Amnesia

1. B. [Amnesia refers to the inability to form new memories since an event.]

2. A. [Implicit memory can provide the ability to perform functions without explicit knowledge.]

3. C. [Dementia refers to the loss of explicit memories of the past.]

7.8 Developing Helpful Study Habits

Self-reference effect. I can think about an example of when a topic happened in my own life and work through it to illustrate the important properties of the concept.

Spacing effect. I can plan to study my calculus material every day the class meets, so I'll stretch the study sessions out over the week.

Testing effects. At the end of each study session, I can test myself on the key terms.

More examples are in Table 7-3.

ANSWERS TO CHAPTER REVIEW TEST

7.1 Overview: What Is Memory?

1. B. Rationale: Memory involves more than facts or what we try to learn, and it can be a distorted picture of our experiences; however, it captures what remains from our experiences.

7.2 Constructing Memory

2. A. Rationale: Unlike the two other stages of memory, *encoding* refers to taking information into memory.

3. C. Rationale: *Elaboration* refers to enhancing memory through meaning, unlike the other options listed.

4. A. Rationale: Unlike the other strategies listed, encoding based on meaning works best.

7.3 The Three Stages of Memory

5. B. Rationale: The two other stages of memory lead to the encoding of information into long-term memory.

6. A. Rationale: The only means of maintaining information in short-term memory that involves repetition is maintenance rehearsal.

7. B. Rationale: The capacity of short-term memory is reflected in the "magic 7 ± 2."

8. B. Rationale: The function of long-term potentiation is to make changes in the receptivity of neuronal connections, making it possible to store new knowledge in long-term memory.

7.4 Organizing Information in Memory

9. A. Rationale: The only option reflecting conscious awareness of the information is explicit memory.

10. B. Rationale: This option reflects the lack of conscious awareness of the information, and D is not a term covered in the chapter.

11. A. Rationale: This option reflects stated knowledge and is more specific than option C (explicit memory).

7.5 Retrieval from Memory

12. B. Rationale: This option reflects matching the context of learning to the context at testing.

13. C. Rationale: This option reflects matching the context of learning to the context at testing, the principle of encoding specificity.

14. A. Rationale: This option reflects the lack of potential cues to remind him of the instrument in the trunk, while there is no information to suggest C or D are relevant.

7.6 Reconstructing Memories

15. C. Rationale: This option reflects the definition of source memory.

16. A. Rationale: This option reflects the results of the study in which subjects were misled by information included in a follow-up question but didn't notice any contradiction.

17. A. Rationale: This option reflects the example of eyewitness error discussed in the text, and the other options are incorrect statements.

7.7 Forgetting

18. C. Rationale: This option reflects the major point about the forgetting curve.

19. D. Rationale: This option reflects the fact that only the long-term memory store holds information without decay.

20. D. Rationale: This option reflects the fact that only memories since the event are not recalled.

7.8 How to Improve Your Memory

21. B. Rationale: This option reflects the fact that sleep is needed to encode information into long-term memory. The alternatives are either not mentioned (A and D) or explicitly incorrect based on the text.

22. D. Rationale: This option reflects the fact that highlighting simply repeats rather than elaborates on the information, while the other alternatives add meaning to the information.

23. C. Rationale: This option reflects the spacing effect, while the other alternatives are explicitly incorrect based on the text.

REFERENCES

Alloway, T. P., & Alloway, R. G. (2010). Investigating the predictive roles of working memory and IQ in academic attainment. *Journal of Experimental Child Psychology, 80*(2), 606–621.

Anderson, M. C., & Green, C. (2001). Suppressing unwanted thoughts by executive control. *Nature, 410,* 366–369.

Atkinson, R. C., & Shiffrin, R. M. (1968). Human memory: A proposed system and its control processes. In K. W. Spence & J. T. Spence (Eds.), *The psychology of learning and motivation* (Vol. 2, pp. 89–195). New York: Academic Press.

Bachevalier, C., & Vargha-Khadem, F. (2005). The primate hippocampus: Ontogeny, early insult and memory. *Current Opinion in Neurobiology, 15*(2), 168–174.

Baddely, A. D. (2001). Is working memory still working? *American Psychologist, 56,* 849–864.

Baddeley, A. D., & Hitch, G. J. L. (1974). Working memory. In G. A. Bower (Ed.), *The psychology of learning and motivation: Advances in research and theory* (Vol. 8, pp. 47–89). New York: Academic Press.

Bahrick, H. P. (1984). Semantic memory content in permastore: Fifty years of memory for Spanish learned in school. *Journal of Experimental Psychology: General, 113,* 1–35.

Bargh, J. A., Chen, M., & Burrows, L. (1996). Automaticity of social behavior: Direct effects of trait construct and stereotype activation on action. *Journal of Personality and Social Psychology, 71*(2), 230–244.

Barrett, D. (1980). The first memory as a predictor of personality traits. *Journal of Individual Psychology, 36*(2), 136–149.

Bartlett, F. C. (1932). *Remembering: A study in experimental and social psychology.* Cambridge, UK: Cambridge University Press.

Bolzan, S., Bolzan, J., & Rother, C. (2011). *My life, deleted: A memoir.* New York: HarperOne.

Bousfeld, W. A. (1953). The occurrence of clustering in the recall of randomly arranged associates. *Journal of General Psychology, 49,* 229–240.

Bower, G. H. (1981). Mood and memory. *American Psychologist, 36*(2), 129–148.

Bower, G. H., Black, J. B., & Turner, T. J. (1979). Scripts in memory for texts. *Cognitive Psychology, 11*(2), 177–220.

Brewer, W. F. (1988). Memory for randomly sampled autobiographical events. In U. Neisser & E. Winograd (Ed.), *Remembering reconsidered: Ecological and traditional approaches to the study of memory* (pp. 21–90). Cambridge, MA: Cambridge University Press.

Brewer, W. F., & Treyens, J. C. (1981). Role of schemata in memory for places. *Cognitive Psychology, 13,* 207–230.

Brown, A. S. (1991). A review of the tip-of-the-tongue experience. *Psychological Bulletin, 109*(2), 204–223.

Bruce, V., & Le Voi, M. E. (1983). Recognizing faces [and discussion]. *Philosophical Transactions of the Royal Society of London. Series B, Biological Sciences, 302*(1110), 423–436.

Bruck, M., & Ceci, S. J. (1999). The suggestibility of children's memory. *Annual Review of Psychology, 50,* 419–439.

Carrier, M., & Pashler, H. (1992). The influence of retrieval on retention. *Memory & Cognition, 20*(6), 633–642.

Ceci, S. J., Crossman, A. M., Scullin, M. H., Gilstrap, L., & Huffman, M. L. (2002). Children's suggestibility research: Implications for the courtroom and the forensic interview. In H. L. Westcott, G. M. Davies, & R. H. C. Bull (Eds.), *Children's testimony: A handbook of psychological research and forensic practice* (pp. 117–130). West Sussex, England: John Wiley & Sons Ltd.

Ceci, S. J., Huffman, M. L. C., Smith, E., & Loftus, E. F. (1994). Repeatedly thinking about a non-event: Source misattribution among preschoolers. *Consciousness & Cognition, 3,* 388–407.

Cepada, N. J., Pashler, H., Vul, E., Wixted, J. T., & Rohrer, D. (2006). Distributed practice in verbal recall tasks: A review and quantitative synthesis. *Psychological Bulletin, 132*(3), 354–380.

Chi, M. T. H., Bassok, M., Lewis, M. W., Reimann, P., & Glaser, R. (1989). Self-explanations: How students study and use examples in learning to solve problems. *Cognitive Science, 13*(2), 145–182.

Chi, M. T. H., De Leeuw, N., M-H., & Lavancher, C. (1994). Eliciting self-explanations improves understanding. *Cognitive Science, 18*(3), 439–477.

Cohen, N. J., Eichenbaum, H., Deacedo, B. S., & Corkin, S. (1985). Different memory systems underlying acquisition of procedural and declarative knowledge. *Annals of the New York Academy of Sciences, 444,* 54–71.

Collins, A. M., & Loftus, E. F. (1975). A spreading activation theory of semantic processing. *Psychological Review, 82,* 407–428.

Conway, M., Cohen, G., & Stanhope, N. (1991). On the very long-term retention of knowledge acquired through formal education. *Journal of Experimental Psychology: General, 120,* 395–409.

Cowan, N. (2001). The magical number four in short-term memory: A reconsideration of mental storage capacity. *Behavioral and Brain Sciences, 24,* 87–185.

Craik, F. I. M., & Tulving, E. (1975). Depth of processing and the retention of words in episodic memory. *Journal of Experimental Psychology: General, 104,* 268–294.

Crombag, H. F. M., Wagenaar, W. A., & Van Koppen, P. J. (1996). Crashing memories and the problem of "source monitoring." *Applied Cognitive Psychology, 10,* 95–104.

Deese, J. (1959). On the prediction of occurrence of particular verbal intrusions in immediate recall. *Journal of Experimental Psychology, 58,* 17–22.

Dempster, F. N. (1988). The Spacing Effect: A case study in the failure to apply the results of psychological research. *American Psychologist, 43*(8), 627–634.

Dudai, Y. (2004). The neurobiology of consolidations, or, how stable is the engram? *Annual Review of Psychology, 55,* 51–86.

Ebbinghaus, H. (1885; reprinted in 1913). Memory: A contribution to experimental psychology. (Translation by H. Roger & C. Bussenius). New York: Teacher's College Press.

Ericsson, K. A., & Chase, W. G. (1982). Exceptional memory. *American Scientist, 70*(6), 607–615.

Ericsson, K. A., Krampe, R. T., & Tesch-Romer, C. (1993). The role of deliberate practice in the acquisition of expert performance. *Psychological Review, 100*(3), 363–406.

Feldman-Summers, S., & Pope, K. S. (1994). The experience of forgetting childhood abuse: A national survey of psychologists. *Journal of Consulting and Clinical Psychology, 62,* 636–639.

Fowler, R. L., & Barker, A. S. (1974). Effectiveness of highlighting for retention of text material. *Journal of Applied Psychology, 59*(3), 358–364.

Frederickson, R. (1992). *Repressed memory: A journey to recovery from sexual abuse.* New York: Fireside (Simon & Schuster).

Freud, S. (1957). Repression. In J. Strachey (Ed. & Trans.), *The standard edition of the complete psychological works of Sigmund Freud* (Vol. 14, pp. 146–158). London: Hogarth.

Freyd, J. J. (1995). *Betrayal trauma: The logic of forgetting childhood abuse.* Cambridge, MA: Harvard University Press.

Garven, S., Wood, J. M., Malpass, R. S., & Shaw, J. S., III. (1998). More than suggestion: The effect of interviewing techniques from the McMartin preschool case. *Journal of Applied Psychology, 83*(3), 347–359.

Geraerts, E., Schooler, J. W., Merckelbach, H., Jelicic, M., Hauer, B. J. A., & Ambadar, Z. (2007). The reality of recovered memories: Corroborating continuous and discontinuous memories of childhood sexual abuse. *Psychological Science, 18,* 564–567.

Gerarts, E., Lindsay, D. S., Merckelbach, H., Jelicic, M., Raymaekers, L., Arnold, M. M., & Schooler, J. W. (2009). Cognitive mechanisms underlying recovered-memory experiences of childhood sexual abuse. *Psychological Science, 20*(1), 92–98.

Gluck, M. A., & Myers, C. E. (1997). Psychobiological models of hippocampal function in learning and memory. *Annual Review of Psychology, 48,* 481–514.

Golby, A., Silverberg, G., Race, E., Gabrieli, S., O'Shea, J., Knierim, K., Stebbins, G., & Gabrieli, J. (2005). Memory encoding in Alzheimer's disease: An fMRI study of explicit and implicit memory. *Brain, 128*(4), 773–787.

Goodman, G. S., & Quas, J. A. (2008). Repeated interviews and children's memory: It's more than just how many. *Current Directions in Psychological Science, 17*(6), 386–390.

Goodwin, D., Powell, B., Bremer, D., Hoine, H., & Stern, J. (1969). Alcohol and recall: State-dependent effects in man. *Sciences, 163*(3873), 1358–1360.

Hayne, H., & Simcock, G. (2002). Breaking the barrier? Children fail to translate their preverbal memories into language. *Psychological Science, 13*(3), 225–231.

Hintzman, D. L. (1974). Theoretical implications of the spacing effect. In R. L. Solso (Ed.), *Theories in cognitive psychology: The Loyola Symposium* (pp. 77–99). Potomac, MD: Erlbaum.

Howe, M. L., & Courage, M. L. (1997). The emergence and early development of autobiographical memory. *Psychological Review, 104*(3), 499–523.

James, W. (1890). *The principles of psychology, Vol. 1 and 2.* New York: Dover Publications, 1950.

Jenkins, J. G., & Dallenbach, K. M. (1924). Oblivescence during sleep and waking. *American Journal of Psychology, 35,* 605–612.

Johnson, H. M., & Seifert, C. M. (1994). Sources of the continued influence effect: When misinformation in memory affects later inferences. *Journal of Experimental Psychology: Learning, Memory, and Cognition, 20*(6), 1420–1436.

Johnson, M. K., Hashtroudi, S., & Lindsay, D. S. (1993). Source monitoring. *Psychological Bulletin, 114*(1), 3–28.

Kandel, E. R., & Schwartz, J. H. (1982). Molecular biology of learning: Modulation of transmitter release. *Science, 218,* 433–443.

Lashley, K. S. (1950). In search of the engram. In the *Symposium of the Society for Experimental Biology* (Vol. 4). New York: Cambridge University Press.

Lewandowsky, S., Stritzke, W. G. K., Oberauer, K., & Morales, M. (2005). Memory for fact, fiction, and misinformation: The Iraq War 2003. *Psychological Science, 16,* 190–195.

Lindsay, D. S., & Johnson, M. K. (1991). Recognition memory and source monitoring. *Psychological Bulletin, 29*(3), 203–205.

Loftus, E. F. (1975). Leading questions and the eyewitness report. *Cognitive Psychology, 7,* 560–572.

Loftus, E. F. (1979). The malleability of human memory. *American Scientist, 67*(3), 312–320.

Loftus, E. F. (1980). *Memory: Surprising new insights into how we remember and why we forget.* Reading, MA: Addison-Wesley.

Loftus, E. F. (1993). The reality of repressed memories. *American Psychologist, 48,* 518–537.

Loftus, E. F. (1996). *Eyewitness testimony.* Cambridge, MA: Harvard University Press.

Loftus, E. F. (1997). Creating false memories. *Scientific American, 277,* 70–75.

Loftus, E. F., & Davis, D. (2006). Recovered memories. *Annual Review of Clinical Psychology, 2,* 469–498.

Loftus, E. F., & Ketchum, K. (1994). *The myth of repressed memory: False memories and the allegations of sexual abuse.* New York: St. Martin's Press.

Loftus, E. F., Miller, D. G., & Burns, H. J. (1978). Semantic integration of verbal information into a visual memory. *Journal of Experimental Psychology: Human Learning and Memory, 4*(1), 19–31.

Lynch, G., & Stabli, U. (1991). Possible contributions of long-term potentiation to the encoding and organization of memory. *Brain Research Reviews, 16,* 204–206.

Meyer, D. E., & Schvaneveldt, R. W. (1971). Facilitation in recognizing pairs of words: Evidence of a dependence between retrieval operations. *Journal of Experimental Psychology, 90,* 227–234.

Miller, G. A. (1956). The magical number seven, plus or minus two: some limits on our capacity for processing information. *Psychological Review, 63*(2), 81–97.

Milner, B. (1970). Memory and the temporal regions of the brain. In K. H. Pribram & D. E. Broadbent (Eds.), *Biology of memory.* New York: Academic Press.

Milner, B., Squire, L. R., & Kandel, E. R. (1998). Cognitive neuroscience and the study of memory. *Neuron, 20,* 445–468.

Morain, D. (1995). Recovered memory murder case unravels. *Los Angeles Times,* December 25, Ret. 11/11/2011, http://articles.latimes.com/1995-12-25/news/mn-17740_1_memories-cases-recovered.

Neisser, U., & Harsch, N. (1992). Phantom flashbulbs: False recollections of hearing the news about *Challenger.* In E. Winograd and U. Neisser (Eds.), *Affect and accuracy in recall: Studies of "flashbulb" memories* (pp. 9–31). New York: Cambridge University Press.

Newman, L. S., & Baumeister, R. F. (1996). Toward an explanation of the UFO abduction phenomenon: Hypnotic elaboration, extraterrestrial sadomasochism, and spurious memories. *Psychological Inquiry, 7*(2), 99–126.

Nickerson, R. S., & Adams, M. J. (1979). Long term memory for a common object. *Cognitive Psychology, 11,* 287–307.

Palm, K. M., & Gibson, P. (1998). Recovered memories of childhood sexual abuse: Clinicians' practices and beliefs. *Professional Psychology: Research and Practice, 29*(3), 257–261.

Parker, E. S., Cahill, L., & McGaugh, J. L. (2006). A case of unusual autobiographical remembering. *Neurocase, 12,* 35–49.

Penrod, S., & Cutler, B. (1995). Witness confidence and witness accuracy: Assessing their forensic relation. *Psychology, Public Policy, and Law, 1*(4), 817–845.

Poole, D. A., & Lindsay, D. S. (1998). Assessing the accuracy of young children's reports: Lessons from investigations of child sexual abuse. *Applied and Preventive Psychology, 7*(1), 1–26.

Powell, M. B., & Freckelton, I. (2008). The contribution to forensic psychology by professor Donald Thomson. *Psychiatry, Psychology and Law, 15*(3), 361–361.

Press, A., Hager, M., King, P., Namuth, T., Sherman, D., & Walters, S. (1985). The youngest witnesses. *Newsweek,* February 19, 72–74.

Raven, J. C. (1936). *Mental tests used in genetic studies: The performance of related individuals on tests mainly educative and mainly reproductive.* MSc Thesis, University of London.

Richland, L. E., Kornell, N., & Kao, L. S. (2009). The pretesting effect: Do unsuccessful retrieval attempts enhance learning? *Journal of Experimental Psychology: Applied, 15*(3), 243–257.

Roediger, H. L. III, & Karpicke, J. D. (2006). Test-enhanced learning: Taking memory tests improves long-term retention. *Psychological Science, 17*(3), 249–255.

Roediger, H. L., & McDermott, K. B. (1995). Creating false memories: Remembering words not presented in lists. *Journal of Experimental Psychology: Learning, Memory, and Cognition, 21*(4), 803–814.

Rogers, T. B., Kuiper, N. A., & Kirker, W. S. (1977). Self-reference and the encoding of personal information. *Journal of Personality and Social Psychology, 35,* 677–688.

Rozin, P., Dow, S., Moscovitch, M., & Rajaram, S. (1998). What causes humans to begin and end a meal? A role for memory for what has been eaten, as evidenced by a study of multiple meal eating in amnesic patients. *Psychological Science, 9*(5), 392–396.

Rubin, D. C., Berntsen, D., & Bohni, M. K. (2008). A memory-based model of posttraumatic stress disorder: Evaluating basic assumptions underlying the PTSD diagnosis. *Psychological Review, 115*(4), 985–1011.

Sachs, J. (1967). Recognition memory for syntactic and semantic aspects of connected discourse. *Perception and Psychophysics, 2,* 437–442.

Sargant, W., & Slater, E. (1941). Amnesic syndromes in war. *Proceedings of the Royal Society of Medicine, 34*(12), 757–764.

Schacter, D. L. (1992). Understanding implicit memory: A neuroscience approach. *American Psychologist, 47,* 559–569.

Schank, R. C. (1982). *Dynamic memory.* Cambridge: Cambridge University Press.

Schank, R. C., & Abelson, R. P. (1977). *Scripts, plans, goals, and understanding: An inquiry into human knowledge structures.* Hillsdale, NJ: Lawrence Erlbaum Assoc.

Schank, R. C., & Abelson,. P. (1995). Knowledge and memory: The real story. In R. S. Wyer, Jr. (Ed.), *Advances in knowledge and memory:* The real story (pp. 1–85). Hillsdale, NJ: Lawrence Erlbaum Associates.

Schooler, J. W. (2001). Discovering memories in the light of metaawareness. *Journal of Aggression, Maltreatment and Trauma, 4,* 105–136.

Schooler, J. W., Ambadar, Z., & Bendiksen, M. A. (1997). A cognitive corroborative case study approach for investigating discovered memories of sexual abuse. In J. D. Read & D. S. Lindsay (Eds.), *Recollections of trauma: Scientific research and clinical practices* (pp. 379–388). New York: Plenum.

Schwartz, B., & Reisberg, D. (1991). *Learning and memory.* New York: Norton.

Shepard, R. N. (1967). Recognition memory for words, sentences, and pictures. *Journal of Verbal Learning and Verbal Behavior, 6,* 156–163.

Slamecka, N. J., & Graf, P. (1978). The generation effect: Delineation of a phenomenon. *Journal of Experimental Psychology: Human Learning and Memory, 1*(6), 592–604.

Sperling, G. A. (1960). The information available in brief visual presentation. *Psychological Monographs: General and Applied, 74*(11), 1–29.

Standing, L. (1973). Learning 10,000 pictures. *Quarterly Journal of Experimental Psychology, 25,* 207–222.

Stickgold, R., Hobson, J. A., Fosse, R., & Fosse, M. (2001). Sleep, learning, and dreams: Off-line memory reprocessing. *Science, 294*(5544), 1052–1057.

Teuber, H. L., Milner, B., & Vaughan, H. G., Jr. (1968). Persistent anterograde amnesia after stab wound of the basal brain. *Neuropsychologia, 6*(3), 267–282.

Thompson-Cannino, J., & Cotton, R. (2009). *Picking Cotton: Our memoir of injustice and redemption.* New York: St. Martin's Griffin.

Tulving, E., & Thompson, D. M. (1973). Encoding specificity and retrieval processes in episodic memory. *Psychological Review, 80,* 352–373.

Usher, J., & Neisser, U. (1993). Childhood amnesia and the beginnings of memory for four early life events. *Journal of Experimental Psychology, 122*(2), 155–165.

von Restorff, H. (1933). Über die Wirkung von Bereichsbildungen im Spurenfeld. *Psychologische Forschung, 18,* 299–342.

Wade, K. A., Garry, M., Read, J. D., & Lindsay, D. S. (2002). A picture is worth a thousand lies: Using false photographs to create false childhood memories. *Psychonomic Bulletin & Review, 9,* 597–603.

Wade, S. E., & Trathen, W. (1989). Effect of self-selected study methods on learning. *Journal of Educational Psychology, 81*(1), 40–47.

Williams, L. M. (1994). Recall of childhood trauma: A prospective study of women's memories of child sexual abuse. *Journal of Consulting and Clinical Psychology, 62*(6), 1167–1176.

Williams, L. M. (1995). Recovered memories of abuse in women with documented child sexual victimization histories. *Journal of Traumatic Stress, 8*(4), 649–673.

Williams, M. D., & Hollan, J. (1981). The process of retrieval from very long-term memory. *Cognitive Science, 5,* 87–119.

Yaniv, I., & Meyer, D. E. (1987). Activation and metacognition of inaccessible stored information: Potential bases for incubation effects in problem solving. *Journal of Experimental Psychology: Learning, Memory, and Cognition, 13*(2), 187–205.

Chapter Overview ▼

8.1 **Overview: What Is Thinking?**

CONCEPT LEARNING CHECK 8.1 *Defining Thinking*

8.2 **Problem Solving**
Problem-Solving Methods
Biases in Problem Solving
Expertise

CONCEPT LEARNING CHECK 8.2 *Applying Methods of Problem Solving*

8.3 **Decision Making**
Algorithms in Decision Making
Heuristics in Decision Making

CRITICAL THINKING APPLICATION

CONCEPT LEARNING CHECK 8.3 *Recognizing Heuristics in Decision Making*

8 Thinking and Language

Learning Objectives ▼

8.1 ▪ Explain the dual processes of thinking.

8.2 ▪ Compare and contrast the processes for problem solving.
　　 ▪ Discuss how bias impacts problem solving.
　　 ▪ Explain problem representation.

8.3 ▪ Examine the pros and cons of heuristic use in decision making.

8.4 ▪ Explain how presented knowledge may bias reasoning.
　　 ▪ Demonstrate how beliefs impact reasoning.

8.5 ▪ Define language and describe the unique characteristics of human language.
　　 ▪ Describe the theories of language acquisition.

8.6 ▪ Explain how language use reveals its impact on our thinking.
　　 ▪ Describe the influence of biology and culture on how we think.

8.4 Reasoning
Algorithms in Reasoning
Biases in Reasoning

CONCEPT LEARNING CHECK **8.4** *Practicing Reasoning*

8.5 Language
What Is a "Language"?
Language Structure

Language Development
Theories of Language Acquisition
Language in Animals

CONCEPT LEARNING CHECK **8.5** *Features of Language*

8.6 Brain, Language, and Culture
Summary of Multiple Influences on Thinking and Language

CONCEPT LEARNING CHECK **8.6** *Multiple Influences on Language Use*

A friend mentioned he was visiting his cousin in California, Uma Thurman. Later, I told my colleague, Sam, who is a big fan. "Wow," said Sam, "Do you think you can get your friend to introduce me to her?" I looked over at Sam, a nice looking 30-year-old cognitive psychologist, and thought of Uma, a famous actor in films like the *Kill Bill* series, and the classic *Pulp Fiction*. With the skepticism apparent on my face, I promised to ask. The next day was April 1st, and I could not resist. I phoned Sam and left a message saying I had talked to my friend, and it was a go: "Uma is dying to meet you!" After a couple of hours, I called back to say, "April Fool's!" But Sam was already planning his big date, and called a few friends to share the good news. He has never really forgiven me for that April Fool's joke. Was it rational thinking for professor Sam to think a Hollywood star would be "dying to meet him"?

8.1 Overview: What Is Thinking?

Thinking involves dual processes that help us make sense of our experiences in the world.

- Explain the dual processes of thinking.

Thinking The internal mental processes that make sense of our experiences.

Cognition All types of thinking, including knowing, remembering, reasoning, deciding, and communicating.

Rational thinking Thinking marked by the use of deliberate reasoning.

Deliberation Slow, careful thinking aimed at considering all alternatives.

Is thinking "rational?" In psychology, **thinking** is defined by the many kinds of mental processes we perform as we experience the world. Within psychology, we use the term **cognition** to refer to thinking processes, including knowing, remembering, reasoning, deciding, and communicating. In Chapter 7, we discussed the variety of concepts in memory and the different ways concepts can be represented in memory. These concepts obviously form the core content of thinking, and their nature influences how we are able to refine, combine, and create new concepts through thinking. We are all very familiar with our internal thoughts, yet our awareness of the influences on our thinking may be somewhat limited. Our emotions, associations in memory, biological functions in the brain, and cultural experiences may affect our thinking but are not considered to be thinking processes. With so much on our minds, cognitive researchers have developed a rich set of theories to describe how thinking is accomplished. A central point is that our thinking is often far from a rational process.

People often believe that thinking should be logical, follow rules, and arrive at a "correct" answer or conclusion. **Rational thinking** is marked by the use of reason, or coming to conclusions when considering facts fully and carefully. This form of thinking is slow and deliberate, with the goal of avoiding errors and arriving at the best conclusion (Kuo et al., 2009). It takes a great deal of effort to consider all of the relevant information. For example, when you chose a college to attend, you may have felt the need to figure out all of the relevant factors, including the programs available at each college, the cost, the location, and so forth. In this type of slow **deliberation**, writing down all of the pros and cons of the options can be helpful, along with searching for information to help identify the best choices. This rational approach may seem like the "right" way to approach thinking; after all, one of the worst things someone can say is that we are being illogical. But consider how often you perform this type of careful thinking: Did you do it today or yesterday? We think constantly, yet we choose to do this deliberative thinking only sometimes.

Most of us believe that our thinking is of this deliberative style. However, more often, our thinking can be described as intuitive, quick, and easy. We try to make fast, efficient judgments because we need to make so many of them. When to cross the street at the intersection, what drink to order with a meal, and who to call next? We are constantly making decisions, and life is too short to always perform careful deliberation. Instead, we may rely on first impressions, instincts, or emotions to drive our choices without given them much thought. Sometimes, even though all of the evidence points toward a choice, we may have a "gut feeling" about what to do. This fast **intuition** (Kahneman et al., 1982) seems to describe a lot of our day-to-day thinking, from which route to take to which jam to buy. This type of thinking has been called "fast and frugal," because it helps us to arrive at a decision quickly while minimizing the effort we have to expend (Gigerenzer, 2007). We resort to "quick and dirty" thinking, or use our intuition, so we can move on to more important matters. However, this does leave us open to making errors in our thinking.

When you have a "gut instinct" but cannot consciously explain it, what does it reveal about your thinking? A study in cognitive neuroscience demonstrated the power of gut instincts (Bechara, Damasio, Tranel, & Damasio, 1997). In the study, people played the Iowa Gambling Task FIGURE 8-1. Four decks of virtual cards are presented on a screen in front of you, and you can select which deck to draw from. The decks pay off differently; some provide a small gain and others a steep loss. To win, you have to figure out the incentive value of the deck choices available to you. As you play, you gradually figure out which are the "good" decks, leading to wins, and which deck to avoid drawing from. After about 40 or 50 selections, people are fairly good at picking from only the good decks. But much sooner, after only 10 tries, people show a "stress" reaction (sweaty palms) as they reach for a bad deck, as measured by galvanic skin response FIGURE 8-2. This "gut-level" recognition that a deck is bad happened well before people fully understood or could explain why it was bad. Only after playing much longer did they get to the point where they could explain what was happening with the differing deck payoffs.

Interestingly, a part of the brain that processes emotion may play a big role in our ability to choose well. When clinical patients with orbitofrontal cortex (OFC) dysfunction play the card game, they continue to choose from the bad decks, sometimes even though they know consciously that they are losing money overall. It is as if they do not experience the same emotional reaction to bad events that other players do. These patients point out that our gut reactions to choices are important indicators of what is important to us in the world. Damasio called this a **somatic marker** through which the body reveals a response about an outcome. This physical response may then influence our decision-making processes, both unconsciously and consciously. As a result, our gut reactions may provide a better measure of how we should choose next.

These "**dual processes**" in thinking—slow, deliberative, conscious reasoning versus fast, automatic, and emotional reactions—describe the major ways we think across many tasks (Stanovich & West, 1998). What determines whether we will do one of these two types of thinking? First, people are more likely to rely on the fast and easy strategies if they are tired or pressed for time. When you are feeling stressed, you are much more likely to grab an easy answer (like a cheeseburger). Second, we are much more likely to use deliberative thought if the stakes are high (as in making a decision about a medical procedure) and the decision is infrequent, compared to decisions (like what to have for lunch) that we make over and over again. One mode of thinking is not "better" than the other; rather, giving each decision the appropriate type of effort is the key. Later in this chapter, we will illustrate this difference of slow and careful versus fast and easy, the dual modes of thought.

Intuition The "gut feeling" that leads to a fast and easy conclusion.

Somatic marker A visceral, physiological response that reveals underlying emotion about an event or decision.

Dual processes The two modes of thinking, one fast and easy, one slow and careful.

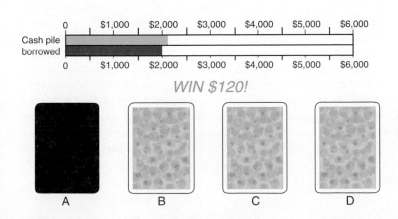

FIGURE 8-1 Four decks of cards are presented to participants, and they choose which deck to play next. The decks have differing payoffs, so participants learn over time which decks tend to provide better payoffs.
Source: Reproduced from Bechara, A., Damasio, H., Tranel, D., Damasio, A. R. (1997). Deciding advantageously before knowing the advantageous strategy. Science, *275(5304), 1293–1295.*

FIGURE 8-2 Average numbers of cards selected from the bad decks versus the good decks, and the mean magnitudes of anticipatory skin conductance responses (SCRs) associated with the same cards.
Source: Reproduced from Bechara, A., Damasio, H., Tranel, D., Damasio, A. R. (1997). Deciding advantageously before knowing the advantageous strategy. Science, 275(5304), 1293–1295.

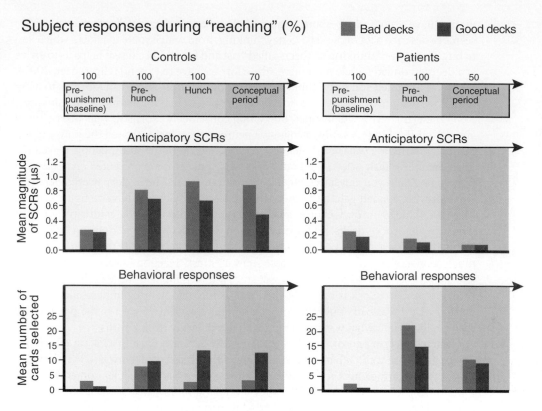

Metacognition Reflective thoughts about your own thinking processes.

When given a choice between two identical nylon stockings, people still managed to select one over the other and generate an explanation for their choice.

A final question in defining thinking is our awareness of our own thinking processes, also called **metacognition**. You might expect we would be experts on cognition, since we observe our own internal thoughts constantly. However, we are often unaware of the internal mental activities that give rise to our conscious experience of thinking. A physician once asked me, "Isn't thinking really just *random*?" Hopefully, it does not seem too random to him as he performs surgery, but more likely as he drives home and lets his thoughts flow freely. As we observe our own internal thoughts, we find that ideas come to mind spontaneously, new ideas interrupt others, and staying on track to arrive at conclusions can sometimes be very difficult. It is a problem for us to consider what processes are driving our thoughts, what is influencing our decisions, and why we want ice cream. Let us practice "thinking about your thinking": Now, for one minute, stop reading and reflect about your thinking.

What did you notice? You may have found that you had *some* awareness of what you were thinking, what brought ideas to mind, or what caused you to become distracted. However, your own thinking may take place outside of your conscious awareness. A clever example comes from research in which people are asked to say what they think about a decision even when, objectively, there is no real reason for the decision. In one study, people were asked to choose one of two identical nylon stockings and then explain their choice (Nisbett & Wilson, 1977). Logically, there is no reason to prefer one, and people tended to choose the one on the right (as most were right handed). However, people did choose one and then came up with a plausible reason for preferring it, such as, "It is more sheer." We are constantly influenced during thinking in ways we are not consciously aware of, and so we are often left to explain our thinking without key information. In fact, some studies show that trying to think about our own thinking processes can lead to decisions we are *less* happy with (Wilson & Schooler, 1991). So making good decisions may not depend on being aware of our thinking process but, rather, on choosing the right thinking process for a certain situation.

CONCEPT LEARNING CHECK **8.1** | *Defining Thinking*

Consider the dual processes of thinking discussed in this section.

1. Which process would you choose to use when deciding what college to attend? Why?

2. What process would you follow when deciding what to order for lunch today? Why?

8.2 Problem Solving

We solve problems through trial and error, deterministic algorithms, heuristic "guesses," and insight.

- Compare and contrast the processes for problem solving.
- Discuss how bias impacts problem solving.
- Explain problem representation.

Much of our thinking is focused on solving a specific problem; for example, how can I get this paper done before the deadline, or how can I find a ride to the airport? A **problem** is any given situation that differs from a desired goal state, and there is a *nonobvious* way to get from one to the other. Turning on the TV is not a problem when the remote control is in your hand; however, it is a problem when you cannot find the remote! To solve problems, you have to think about how to get from the current state to the **goal** (the situation you want to achieve), and getting there involves some novel thinking. For example, if your goal were to become president of your college student body, how would you go about doing so? Some goals have clear, practiced paths, and some require creative new plans. By studying problem solving, cognitive psychologists have identified key features of successful solutions.

> **Problem** A situation with a starting point, a goal state, and a nonobvious way to get to it.
>
> **Goal** A situation you would like to achieve.

Problem-Solving Methods

The experimental study of problem solving began with some classic demonstrations of thinking (Köhler, 1929). Consider a famous problem called the two string problem (Maier, 1931). The experiment was carried on in a large room in which two cords hung from the ceiling. As a participant, you soon learn that if you hold either cord in one hand, you cannot reach the other cord FIGURE 8-3. The goal is to tie the two cord ends together, and you can use anything in the room: poles, ring stands, clamps, pliers, extension cords, tables, and chairs. People think of solutions such as using the extension cord to lengthen one of the cords, using a pole as an arm extension to pull one string over, and anchoring one string in place with a chair while the other is brought over to it. A third of

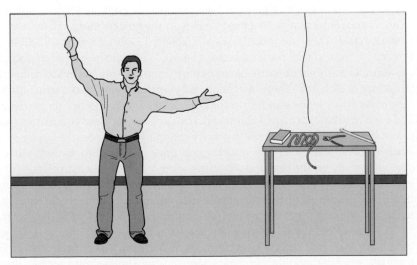

FIGURE 8-3 In the two string problem, the participant is asked to tie the ends of two cords together; however, the cords are spaced far enough apart that you can't reach them using just your hands. What solutions can you think of?
Source. Data from Maier, N. R. F. (1931). Reasoning in humans: II. The solution and its appearance in consciousness. Journal of Comparative Psychology, *12, 181–194.*

Trial and error Creating a solution, testing to see if it works, and then starting over if unsuccessful.

Generate and test Guess at the answer and see if it works on a trial-and-error basis.

Algorithm A well-defined process that is guaranteed to produce a solution.

Means-end analysis A problem-solving strategy that reduces differences between the current and the goal states.

Heuristic A mental shortcut, or rule of thumb, that may or may not lead to a correct solution.

participants implement a pendulum, using the pliers as a weight and setting the weighted cord swinging so that it can be caught in position near the other cord. How do we solve problems like the two string problem?

There are a variety of methods to follow in trying to generate solutions to problems. Typically, we use a **trial and error** process in which we create a solution, test to see whether it worked, and then start over if unsuccessful. This method is also known as **generate and test**, because you generate a solution and then test to see whether it is correct. So, in creating your course schedule for next term, you might start by choosing four courses and then find that two of them conflict. Since that solution failed, you would try again to select courses and see if that new set works. Trial and error is a slow method that is likely to lead to failures. It would be a bad choice for something like guessing a locker combination because there are so many possibilities. However, trial and error might work when you need to recover a computer logon password you cannot recall: You may try your past passwords one at a time in hopes that you might come across the solution. When there is a small set of possible solutions, trial and error can work to solve a problem. Though most people start with this approach, it is not a helpful method for a problem like the two string problem because you are not likely to generate a solution.

Sometimes, you want to choose a well-defined process that is guaranteed to produce a solution, called an **algorithm**. For example, if your goal is to find out how much money you have, you would follow an algorithm to identify each money source and its amount and each debt owed, summing them carefully and determining the final correct figure. This requires deliberative thinking (and a pencil and paper, bank statements, a calculator, or a spreadsheet). However, if you are careful in performing the algorithm, you *will* arrive at the correct solution. A useful way to determine whether a process is an algorithm is to think about whether it could be programmed into a computer. If it can, it follows sequential steps that, when done correctly, will lead to the right solution. However, for many problems and for the two string problem, there are no known algorithms (or computer programs) that can devise a solution.

Another problem-solving method is to break problems into subparts. **Means-end analysis** compares differences between where you are now and your goal state (Newell & Simon, 1972). In using this strategy, you try to reduce the differences between the current state and the goal. For example, you may decide to eat a healthier diet. By identifying key differences in how you would like to eat, you can figure out ways to reduce these differences and get you closer to your goal. For example, you might decide to substitute a multigrain bagel for a donut because the bagel has more nutritional value. The means-ends approach may help you with the two string problem: The goal involves having both strings located at the same point in space at the same time. So you can reduce the difference between your current state and the goal state by fixing one of the strings at that meeting point. Thinking this way may break the problem down into the subpart of getting each string to that location (by tying it to a chair or swinging it into place).

Often, even when an algorithm is known, people prefer to take a "mental shortcut" to a solution. For example, suppose you are in the grocery store to buy a box of Cap'n Crunch cereal. There are three boxes available: a 12-ounce box for $2.88, a 17-ounce box for $3.58, and a 27.5-ounce box for $4.50. Which is the best deal? You can use an algorithm like arithmetic to divide the cost by the number of ounces to compare the cost per ounce of each box. This is a difficult and effortful algorithm requiring time, and you may make errors while standing in the aisle. Instead, you may decide to take a shortcut and use a **heuristic**, or mental shortcut that may or may not lead to a correct solution. An example of a heuristic people use in grocery shopping is to choose the largest-size package available because it usually provides the best price (Lave, 1988). By using this heuristic, you will usually get the best deal. However, there are times when it will fail; for example, a promotion may have a smaller-size box marked down to a lower price per ounce. With heuristics, you are using a shortcut method that minimizes the time and effort required to make a selection, and you are willing to settle for the mistakes that will sometimes occur.

The "rules of thumb" provided by heuristics are useful in our day-to-day thinking because they are fast, require little effort, and usually lead to the right answer. For something like grocery shopping, estimation heuristics are a good choice because the cost of an error is not too high. However, if you are building a bridge, you want to follow algorithms

Shoppers often follow heuristic shortcuts, like "bigger boxes are better bargains," rather than computing the best value using math (an algorithm).

guaranteed to get to the correct solution! The main conclusion from psychological research is that people very often use heuristics in their thinking even when more accurate algorithms are available. The reason seems to be that heuristics often lead to good answers and require much less time and effort. For other problems, there are no known algorithms to guide your solution. For example, whom should you marry? Given the uncertainly about what will happen in your future and in the difficulty of predicting whether you will have a happy marriage, it is difficult to determine the best candidate. Your approach to a given problem may involve choosing from a variety of heuristics observed in problem solving, decision making, and reasoning (see **TABLE 8-1**).

New situations automatically bring past experiences to mind from memory. Consequently, we often rely on our past experiences to solve new problems. **Analogy** involves recalling a previous problem with a known solution to apply to a novel, or new, problem. An example is the "curved tube" problem shown in FIGURE 8-4 (Kaiser, McCloskey, & Proffitt, 1986). Once a ball travels through a curved tube, what path will it take when exiting the tube? Even children as young as 4 are able to solve this problem correctly by thinking by analogy: When you see water coming out of a garden hose, it travels in a straight line even if the hose is tangled and twisted. And, in the curved tube problem, this analogy can help you correctly choose the straight path solution. School-age students sometimes choose the curved path, perhaps confused by new knowledge about physics (such as centripetal and centrifugal forces). However, when they view a special-effects video showing a curved path, even these students recognize that it "looks funny" through analogy to their past experiences. While analogy should help to solve problems, studies show people often have difficulty recognizing when a new problem is similar to an old one (Gick & Holyoak, 1980). This is called **lack of transfer**.

Another problem-solving process is called **insight**, or the sudden appearance in consciousness of a solution. We have all experienced the flash of insight, sometimes with a feeling of "Aha!" Insight occurs when the representation of the problem is **restructured**, or changed to alter your perspective. Consider this problem (Davidson & Sternberg, 1984):

A man has black socks and blue socks in a drawer mixed in a ratio of 4 to 5. It is dark, and so the man cannot see the colors of the socks he removes from the drawer. How many socks must he take out to make sure to have a pair of the same color?

To most people, this looks like a math problem; instead, think about what you do when you put on a pair of socks in the morning. As you do, you may feel insight dawn on you: If there are two colors, you need just three socks to make a pair. In one study, people

Analogy A problem-solving process that makes use of a previous solution.

Lack of transfer The failure to use a past analogy that offers a solution.

Insight The sudden appearance in consciousness of a solution.

Restructuring Changing the representation of a problem to remove unnecessary constraints.

TABLE 8-1 The Role of Information in Cognitive Biases

Information Source	Heuristic Leading to Bias	Correction Method for Bias
Problem Solving		
Irrelevant information	Unnecessary constraints	Change your representation of the problem
Past experience	Mental set	Approach it as if it is a completely novel task
Usual uses and habits	Functional fixedness	Imagine using an object in novel ways
Decision Making		
Schemas in memory	Representativeness	Ignore "what it looks like" and focus on statistics
Recall from memory	Availability	Recall additional possibilities from memory
Description provided	Framing	Restate the problem in neutral or opposite terms
Reasoning		
Initial belief formed	Confirmation bias	Look for contradictory evidence
Existing beliefs	Belief perseverance	Consider the possibility that your belief is wrong
Self-knowledge	Overconfidence	Consider what you don't (and can't) know

Bias A preexisting perspective applied to a problem or decision.

Representation An internal, mental description of a problem or information.

Irrelevant information Knowledge referred to in a problem that is not needed in its solution.

Unnecessary constraint An apparent requirement for a solution that is not really needed.

FIGURE 8-4 The curved tube problem (A), its correct solution (B), and the most common incorrect response (C).
Source: Reproduced from Kaiser, M. K., McCloskey, M., & Proffitt, D. R. (1986). Development of intuitive theories of motion: Curvilinear motion in the absence of external forces. Developmental Psychology, 22(1), 67–71.

were asked to solve math problems or insight problems, and to give a "close to solution?" rating every 15 seconds as they worked. On math problems, more people give higher ratings as time passes. For insight problems, ratings of closeness to solution do not go up during the work period, but stay low right up to the moment when solution occurs (Metcalfe & Wiebe, 1987). Then, suddenly, the ratings rise at once as they see the insightful solution. However, the feeling of insight may not necessarily include a solution. The insight may instead indicate you have found a new way of looking at the problem. Evidence from neuroimaging and event related potential (ERP) studies have identified neurological correlates of the feeling of "Aha!" Insight solutions are associated with a burst of high-frequency neural activity starting about 300 milliseconds *before* participants signaled they had arrived at a solution by pressing a button (Jung-Beeman et al., 2004; Kounios & Beeman, 2009). The location of the activity is in the right anterior temporal lobe FIGURE 8-5.

Biases in Problem Solving

A bias refers to holding a belief that affects your ability to think objectively. In problem solving, **bias** can occur when we approach a problem with past experiences and assumptions that alter our perspective. Often, these beliefs are helpful in finding solutions; however, they can lead to the inability to find solutions because they affect your mental **representation**, or internal description, of the problem. For example, the socks problem above is difficult because it includes **irrelevant information**, or details not needed, about the ratio of socks that makes the problem appear to be a math problem. Sometimes, it is important to reduce the information you have in your representation because it is not needed, or even distracting. In the nine-dot problem FIGURE 8-6 (Burnham & Davis, 1969), we perceive requirements for a solution that are actually **unnecessary constraints**. From the appearance of the rows and columns of dots, we assume the solution must fit inside the apparent "box" of dots. Now, if I tell you that the solution involves going "outside the box" formed by the dots, you may have an idea about how to solve it

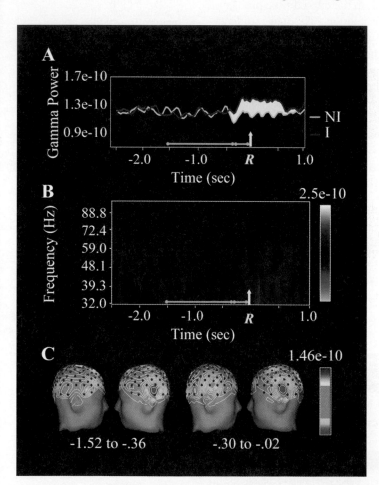

FIGURE 8-5 A high-frequency EEG shows activity associated with problem solution. Panel A shows neural activity over time. The activity for "insight" begins just before the response (yellow R). Panel B shows frequency over time, with red areas where insight EEG power is greater than noninsight, beginning 0.3 seconds before the response. Panel C shows the topographic distribution of this neural activity located in the right anterior temporal lobe.

FIGURE 8-6 The nine-dot problem (left) asks the solver to draw four straight lines that go through the middle of all of the dots without taking the pencil off the paper. The solution (right) is possible only by going outside the perceived box of dots.
Source: Data from Jung-Beeman, M. Bowden, E. M., Haberman, J., Frymiare, J. L., Arambel-Liu, S., Greenblatt, R., Reber, P. J., & Kounios, J. (2004). Neural activity when people solve verbal problems with insight. PLoS Biology, 2, 502–505.

(though you will still need to work out a specific solution). The phrase "thinking outside the box," derived from the nine-dot problem (Kihn, 2005), has become synonymous with removing constraints, leading to more creative solutions. Creating an appropriate problem representation, or description of the problem elements, is critical to solving it.

Another type of bias in problem solving is the use of habits we learn from solving past problems. For example, after seeing a series of math problems involving ratios, you will have an even harder time figuring out the answer to the socks problem above. By finding the solution to a series of problems using a specific method first, you will have a harder time switching to a new method. In other words, you have become "stuck in a rut." Your **mental set**, a preexisting state of mind, habit, or attitude, can affect and mislead your attempt to solve a new problem (Luchins, 1942). Once you have latched onto a particular approach, it can be very difficult to consider alternatives, called **fixation**. People often become stuck on a dead end in their solution path, which may block the consideration of alternatives (Kaplan & Simon, 1990). In effect, your initial ideas can limit your effectiveness in solving problems (Smith, 1995).

A related obstacle to solution arises from our previous use of objects in specific ways. In the candle problem FIGURE 8-7 (Duncker, 1945), you are asked to affix a candle to a wall using only a box of tacks, a candle, and a book of matches. There is an object available in the problem that leads to an elegant solution; however, **functional fixedness**, the tendency to see an object as having only a familiar function, prevents us from seeing it (Maier, 1937). In a different version of the study, the objects are presented with the tacks dumped out of the box; now people are much more likely to see the box as a potential holder for the candle and tack it onto the wall for the solution. In order to get around functional fixedness, you need a fresh, unbiased view of the objects and their properties. And once again, to be creative, you need to think "outside the box"; this time, outside the box of tacks!

The biases in our problem solving may be obvious, but we often fail to notice them. When faced with a difficult problem, it often helps to take a fresh perspective toward the problem. Taking a break from the problem, doing something else, and returning with a different mindset can help to break through some problem-solving obstacles. **Incubation** is defined as a period of time in which a problem is set aside prior to further attempts to solve it. An early study suggested an incubation period produced better solution rates than working straight through for the same amount of time (Silveira, 1972). A meta-analysis of incubation studies found that tasks with open-ended solutions show more benefit from incubation (Sio & Ormerod, 2009). One possible explanation is that you are able to approach the problem after a break with a new perspective. It is also possible that you will be exposed to information during the incubation interval that might help you to solve the problem (Seifert et al., 1995). When in doubt, taking a break may be helpful in jump-starting you toward a solution.

Mental set An existing state of mind, habit, or attitude that affects new problem solving.

Fixation Getting stuck on an approach to a problem and failing to see alternative approaches.

Functional fixedness Seeing objects for use only in their intended roles.

Incubation A period of time in which a problem is set aside prior to further attempts to solve it.

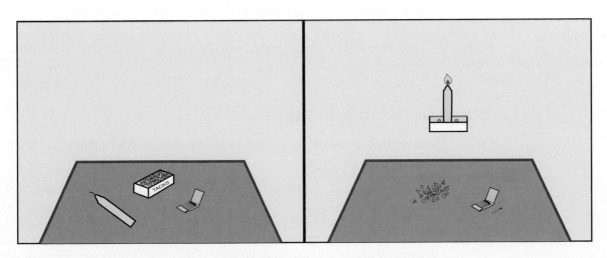

FIGURE 8-7 How can you affix the candle to the wall and light it?
Source: Data from Duncker, K. (1945). On problem solving. Psychological Monographs, 58*(270).*

Deliberative practice Working on skills just beyond your current level of comfort.

Decisions Thinking that requires a choice among alternatives.

Judgment Making an informed guess about something unknown or uncertain.

Uncertainty The state of not being determined, either because the event has not occurred or cannot be known logically.

Expertise

How much practice do you need to get better at problem solving? Studies of skill building over time, including chess experts, pianists, and athletes, found that approximately 10,000 hours of practice are needed to produce outstanding performance (Ericsson et al., 1993) FIGURE 8-8. A great deal of time and experience are needed to acquire a large enough knowledge base to excel (Chi, Glaser, & Farr, 1988). Experts have *more* knowledge, and their knowledge is *organized* around important patterns in the domain (Chase & Simon, 1973; Chi, Feltovich, & Glaser, 1981; Ericsson & Ward, 2007). For example, a chess expert can look at a board during play and see the styles of attack and the history of the game so far, while a novice may recognize only specific moves (de Groot, 1965). This knowledge enables experts to think in larger units, tackling problems in bigger steps. A most surprising conclusion from this research is that experts are made, not born. All performers, including the most naturally gifted or talented, need a minimum of approximately 10 years of intense practice before they can win at international levels in highly competitive domains. **Deliberative practice** (focusing on tasks just beyond your current level of competence and comfort) leads to success (Ericsson et. al, 1993). The good news is that *anyone* can be an expert: All it takes is 10 years!

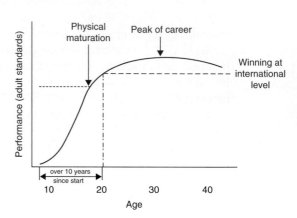

FIGURE 8-8 The development of expert performance as related to age. Elite performers typically reach their peak career performance in the middle to late 20s for vigorous sports, and two decades later for chess, billiards, arts, and sciences.
Source: Reproduced from Ericsson, K. A., & Ward, P. (2007). Capturing the naturally occurring superior performance of experts in the laboratory. Current Directions in Psychological Science, 16*(6), 346–350.*

CONCEPT LEARNING CHECK 8.2   *Applying Methods of Problem Solving*

For each example, determine which type of problem solving strategy is illustrated.

A. Generate and test

B. Algorithm

C. Means-ends analysis

D. Analogy

1. _____ Let me try to think of a good name for our team. How about Sunday Strikers?

2. _____ I will try 1-1-1, then 1-1-2, then 1-1-3, and keep going until the locker opens.

3. _____ This chemistry lab reminds me of cooking, so I had better measure each portion carefully.

4. _____ I will get to my home in LA by first flying into town, then taking a taxi to the house.

8.3   Decision Making

Rather than following algorithms, our decisions are often guided by heuristics.

- Examine the pros and cons of heuristic use in decision making.

In addition to solving problems, we are called upon to make **decisions** where we must choose among alternatives, or whether to take some action. **Judgment** refers to a type of decision making in which we project beyond what we already know and draw our "best guess" conclusion. Judgments take place under **uncertainty**: That is, we do not know definitively whether the defendant committed the crime, whether we will enjoy this first date, or whether it will rain tomorrow. However, we often must use whatever evidence we have to make our best estimate of what might be true, or most likely. In sum, the evidence suggests people often use heuristics, or shortcuts, in decision making that can lead to biases and errors. This main conclusion led to a 2002 Nobel Memorial Prize in Economics for Daniel Kahneman for his work with Amos Tversky (1937–1996).

Algorithms in Decision Making

Just as in problem solving, there are algorithms available to help you determine the best decision. For judgments, we can use **probability theory** to take into account all contingencies and their likelihoods and determine the best estimate of what will occur. For example, in judging whether to go camping on July 4, you could look up the weather on this date for the past 100 years to determine how many times it rained, providing a statistical estimate. Similarly, if you are deciding whether to drive or fly home for Thanksgiving, you can create a **decision tree** showing all of your choices (share ride, drive, bus, train, plane) and weigh each one based on its value to you (the cost, ease of scheduling, and risks; Hastie, 2001) FIGURE 8-9. Then, with all of the options given specific values, you can choose the best one. Algorithms using principles of probability and statistics provide methods for how we "should" make judgments—but do we use them?

Many people find it difficult and time consuming to use algorithms in their everyday lives (Arkes, 1991). Even when you are presented with this information, you may not

Probability theory A statistical algorithm that takes into account all contingencies and their likelihoods to determine the best estimate of an uncertain event.

Decision tree A decision-support tool that uses a tree-like graph of options, including chance event, resources, cost, and value.

Representativeness heuristic Making a guess based on how much the situation "looks like" something known.

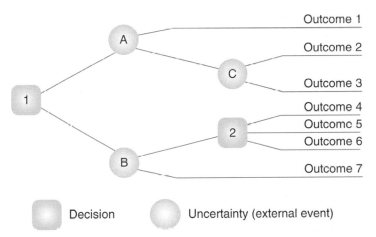

FIGURE 8-9 A decision tree is a method for analyzing the possible choices, along with uncontrollable events, to forsee potential outcomes of all possible choices.

Decision   Uncertainty (external event)

FIGURE 8-10 Would you guess these are more likely to be future environmentalists or future lawyers?

use it. For example, the National Highway Traffic Safety Administration estimates that your chance of getting in a car accident increases by 300% if you are talking on your cellular phone. Will this information stop you from talking while driving? Using the algorithm to determine the answer, it is rational to stop calling or texting while driving! Yet you may still choose to do it. We must be influenced by other factors as well when we make decisions.

Heuristics in Decision Making

Just as with problem solving, people often use heuristics, or rules of thumb, to help us make decisions (Nisbett & Ross, 1980). For example, imagine you go to a class on environmental studies, and you know that 30% of its students are prelaw and 70% are environmental studies majors. You meet Chris, who is wearing a suit and carrying a leather briefcase FIGURE 8-10. Would you guess Chris is a lawyer? Most people would; however, since there are more environmental studies students in the class, that is, statistically, a better guess. Instead, we are influenced by the **representativeness heuristic**; that is, whether things "look like" what we expect (Kahneman & Tversky, 1972). If Chris looks more like a pre-law major, we make that assumption even though, statistically, it is not as likely. Most of the time, using the representativeness heuristic leads

Availability heuristic Using the ease of memory access as a measure of the likelihood of an event.

Framing effect A bias in decisions based on the description of the problem.

Loss aversion Preferring options that will avoid losing rather than maximize gains.

Choice overload The presence of too many options, causing problems in decisions.

We tend to overestimate how often events occur if they are readily available in memory; events covered by the press seem to us to occur more often than ones not receiving coverage.

It seems decisions would improve if more options are made available. How many choices are enough, and can there be too many?

to a quick and easy decision that is often correct (Kunda & Nisbett, 1986). However, "judging a book by its cover" can lead to errors, and in important ways. Representativeness can lead to judgments based on stereotypes, in which assumptions are unfairly made based on gender, ethnicity, and socioeconomic status. First impressions and are just one small sample of someone's behavior are often inaccurate.

Another source of information used in decisions is what is already in your memory. When thinking about familiar things, this information comes readily to mind, allowing us to conclude it happens frequently. For example, you have likely heard of Michael Jackson, but perhaps not Johnny Hallyday, so you would be correct in guessing that Jackson has sold more records. The **availability heuristic** is the tendency to estimate the likelihood of an event in terms of how easily it can be recalled (Tversky & Kahneman, 1974). The effort in retrieving the information determines your judgment of how frequently it occurs. This heuristic can backfire: Has Johnny Hallyday sold more music than Jennifer Lopez? From the availability heuristic, you may incorrectly say Lopez has sold more. Another example is that people overestimate the frequency of death by car accident, tornados, and botulism while underestimating the frequency by diabetes, stroke, and asthma (Slovic et al., 1979). This may occur because media coverage more frequently reports the first set, leading to greater accessibility of examples in memory (Schwarz et al., 1991).

Decision making can also be biased by the way the choices are presented, known as the **framing effect** (Tversky & Kahneman, 1981). For example, would you prefer to purchase ground beef with a label saying "75% lean" or one saying "25% fat"? The fat content is the same, but the information "frame" led 82% of participants to choose the "75% lean" beef (Keren, 2007). A study with beachgoers during spring break showed that framing of information can have direct effects on behavior. People were approached on the beach and given a free coupon toward the purchase of condoms. One coupon boasted a "95% effectiveness" rate, while the other mentioned a "5% failure" rate. The safety information was the same, but the decision framing made a difference in how many coupons were redeemed. The "95% effective" coupons were much more likely to be used for purchases (Linville, Fischer, & Fischhoff, 1993). How we tell the story can impact people's understanding of the relevant information. In all cases, framing effects follow a simple pattern: People try to make choices that will minimize losses, called **loss aversion** (Tversky & Kahneman, 1991). People prefer to make a choice that involves the least risk and avoids any chance of loss.

How can we avoid making decision errors based on heuristics? One way to try to "debias" your thinking is to examine how any given information can help—or hurt—your decision making. We assume that information in front of us is relevant and informative about the situation. Imagine that it could be in error, or just not informative for making a good decision. One strategy is to either ignore or at least question the information you are given. Another strategy is to "change the frame" by thinking of risks or probabilities over time. For example, some drivers fail to wear seat belts every time because they know the probability of a fatal accident on any one trip is very small (1 in 3.5 million "person trips"). However, over 50 years of driving (around 40,000 trips), the probability is 0.01, and for a disabling accident, 0.33 (Slovic et al., 1978). People asked to think about this longer-term perspective were more likely to say they would buckle up every time.

In today's world, you may often face decisions in which *too much* information is available. **Choice overload** refers to having too many choices to handle in decision making. If you were buying a new jam, how many options would you like to choose from? Should the number of options matter? A field study showed that people might be happier when facing *fewer* choices! Iyengar and Lepper (2000) offered grocery shoppers the choice of either 24 new jam flavors or just 6. Shoppers stopped at a table for a taste and were given a $1 coupon. Would having more choices result in more jam purchases? The results showed people presented with more choices were *more* likely to taste jams but *less* likely to buy one! FIGURE 8-11 We may be overstating the appeal of variety when what we really prefer is the same strawberry jam every day.

In such cases, when we are faced with too many choices, we may be more likely to resort to heuristics. For example, in the supermarket, we could determine the best buy using math (Lave, 1988). But, we may instead choose the bigger "bargain" bottle

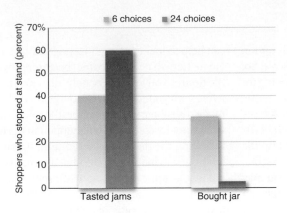

FIGURE 8-11 Percentage of customers who tasted vs. purchased jam based on number of choices presented.
Source: Data from Iyengar, S. S., & Lepper, M. R. (2000). When choice is demotivating: Can one desire too much of a good thing? Journal of Personality and Social Psychology, 79(6), 995–1006.

or whichever is on sale this week. When we generate rules to handle frequent decisions, it saves us the time and effort of deciding. For example, you may have a rule about what you order to drink when in a restaurant. While we may believe "variety is the spice of life," we tend to choose our favorites when the time comes (Schwartz et al., 2002). And, we are influenced by factors such as what *other* people are ordering. One study found that groups of people ordering beer privately tended to all choose the same kind FIGURE 8-12; however, when they took turns ordering aloud (as in the usual restaurant situation), people chose different types of beer, apparently to avoid making the same choice as others (Ariely & Levav, 2000). This suggests we have a social expectation that variety in choice is good, and we feel compelled to follow it despite our personal preferences for our old favorite. It may be important to consider your gut reaction when making choices, and let emotion be your guide when the decision is one of personal preference.

FIGURE 8-12 When you order your drink privately, you may order differently than when you hear others' orders.

CRITICAL THINKING APPLICATION

What do experts recommend as strategies for making good decisions? When the decision is important, it is worthwhile to take extra care to consider all possible consequences, along with ways to increase your alternative choices. For example, imagine that you have several options for the upcoming summer break, including an internship in marketing in New York City, a summer job in a social service agency in your college town, or the job you had in your hometown last year, now accompanied by a substantial raise. Each alternative has many advantages and disadvantages, so which one is the best option for you?

Researchers have identified a variety of methods to help you weigh your options (Yates, 1990). One approach keeps things simple by selecting just one most important aspect to focus on within the decision, called the Single-Feature Model. For example, you may decide that your financial needs must take precedence, so no matter how tempting the other offers, living at home

and getting more pay takes priority. A second approach, called Elimination by Aspects (Tversky, 1972), involves looking at each alternative and ruling out ones that do not meet your minimum requirements. For example, you may decide you need to earn at least $250 each week and then rule out the social service alternative because it cannot provide that salary. Finally, you may, with the

(Continues)

CRITICAL THINKING APPLICATION *(Continued)*

help of a pencil and paper, consider each option on each of its features, rating them on a scale. So, the marketing job is in New York (+10 rating for location) and provides a good salary (+5 rating for salary) but will have expensive living costs (–10 on costs). Once you have rated each of the features for each of the options, you add up the ratings to see which alternative has a better score.

When you do a decision analysis, you may be surprised by the results: Even though, on paper, working at home is the "best" option, your emotions may make it difficult to give up the opportunity to be in New York or the rewards of helping others in the social service job. The exercise of writing down the pros and cons and considering what is most important to you

can help to make your gut feelings more evident. No matter what the outcome, becoming aware of the desires you feel is very helpful in making and living with your decision (Naqvi et al., 2006). For many decisions, there is no "best" choice because we cannot foresee what will happen in the future following the decision. In addition, if you keep looking, you may discover other alternatives that are just as appealing (say, a summer course on film making in San Francisco). At some point, people choose to **satisfice** (Simon, 1955), or find a choice that is satisfactory given what is known. With the large number of decisions we face daily and the uncertainty about the future, we often have to decide when we have arrived at a "good enough" decision.

CONCEPT LEARNING CHECK 8.3   *Recognizing Heuristics in Decision Making*

For each heuristic below, give an example and identify how it makes difficult or time-consuming decisions easier.

1. Representativeness

2. Availability

3. Framing

4. Satisficing

8.4 Reasoning

Rather than always rational, our reasoning may be biased by what we think we know.

- Explain how presented knowledge may bias reasoning.
- Demonstrate how beliefs impact reasoning.

Satisfice Finding a satisfactory choice rather than the best one.

Reasoning Thinking through our knowledge and beliefs to reach a conclusion.

Inductive reasoning Generalizing from specific information to form a rule.

Deductive reasoning A logical task in which new assertions are derived from what is known.

Syllogism A simple deduction task with three statements or premises.

A third type of thinking is called **reasoning**, or evaluating information (including facts, assumptions, and beliefs) to draw a conclusion. In **inductive reasoning**, we move from some specific information to a more general conclusion. For example, you might see several stories about a pit bull attack and conclude that this type of dog is more aggressive than others. In inductive reasoning, you draw from specific instances to conclude in general terms, even though it may not always be correct. The use of stereotypes and schemas illustrate that people readily draw conclusions from a small amount of specific information. Alternatively, in **deductive reasoning**, you start with a general rule and apply it to a specific instance. If I know that "All state residents are charged in-state tuition" and you mention you are a state resident, I can conclude you are charged in-state tuition. Deductive reasoning involves drawing valid, new assertions from what is already known.

Algorithms in Reasoning

The rules of logic provide algorithms for drawing conclusions; unfortunately, studies in psychology show that people do not use the rules of logic very often (Wilkins, 1928). You may recognize logic problems called **syllogisms**; for example, "All As are Bs.

EXAMPLE 1

A. Some As are Bs;
All Bs are Cs:

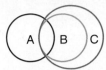

Therefore, all As are Cs:

Invalid

B. Some pets are dogs;
All dogs are mammals:

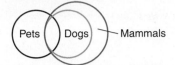

Therefore, all pets are mammals:

Invalid

EXAMPLE 2

A. All As are Bs;
Some Bs are Cs:

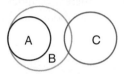

Therefore, some As are Cs:

Invalid

B. All dogs are mammals;
Some mammals are pets:

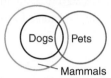

Therefore, some dogs are pets:

Valid?

FIGURE 8-13 Mental models for examples one and two show there are two different ways to interpret the given statements. For example 1, "some" can mean some or all; and in problem 2, not enough information is given to say whether A and C overlap. So, you have to keep both possibilities in mind to answer the question. In addition, in example 1, the content in 1B helps you see the right answer (what about geckos?), while in 2, the content in B (we know dogs are pets!) can mislead you.

All Bs are Cs. Does it follow that all As are Cs?" People are able to solve simple logic problems, but they make errors on the majority of problems (Revlis, 1975). Instead, people try to reason logically by creating a **mental model** (a spatial representation of the possibilities; Johnson-Laird, 2001). People construct models, like the ones shown in FIGURE 8-13, to help them think about the problem. These models help us to consider possibilities that may not be obvious without the diagram. For example, "some As are Bs" can means that some As are not Bs, or that *all* As are Bs, leading to a common logical error. Another factor in solving logic problems is that people are influenced by the **content**, or meaning, of the words used in the problem, even though they do not matter in logic. Consider the same problem in a concrete context: "All boys are children. All children are humans. Does it follow that all boys are humans?" People are more likely to get this version right because the content of the question—boys, children, and humans—is familiar, and they can judge its truth without using logic. Studies of deduction have demonstrated that people are very prone to judge statements on their content rather than on their logic (Johnson-Laird & Byrne, 2002).

To illustrate, a problem called the **Wason selection task** (Wason and Johnson-Laird, 1972) asked people to determine which of four cards have to be turned over to test a rule FIGURE 8-14. The rule is, "If a vowel is on one side, an even number is on the other side." This task is notoriously difficult; most people check the card that shows the rule is followed (card a), but they fail to check the card that would show if the rule was *not* followed (card d). However, a new version of the problem was created that showed much better success (Griggs & Cox, 1982). This time, FIGURE 8-15 the rule was, "If they are drinking beer, they must be over 21." Now, people recognize that they have to check the "underage card" (card d) to make sure no one is breaking the rule. When the problem is framed as "checking for cheaters," people were much more likely to check for cases that

Mental model A visual, spatial, or content-based representation of a problem or situation.

Content The surface meaning of the words in a problem.

Wason selection task A card game that requires checking for rule violations.

 E   K   4   7

FIGURE 8-14 Which card or cards must you turn over to determine whether this rule is correct: "If a vowel is on one side, an even number is on the other side."
Source: Data from Wason, P. C., & Johnson-Laird, P. N. (1972). Psychology of reasoning: Structure and content. Cambridge, MA: Harvard University Press.

FIGURE 8-15 Which card or cards must you turn over to determine whether this rule is correct: "If they are drinking beer, they must be over 21."
Source: Data from Cheng, P. N., & Holyoak, K. J. (1985). Pragmatic reasoning schemas. Cognitive Psychology, 17, 391–416.

disconfirm the rule (Cheng & Holyoak, 1985). Content is highly influential in reasoning, so that there are some topics that people find very challenging to reason about and others about which they are able to be much more logical. Evolutionary theorists have argued that our ability to reason may have been affected by our long history of living in social groups and the resulting need to reason about interactions with others (Cosmides, 1989). This may have led to a survival advantage for those able to reason about social matters like catching cheaters.

Biases in Reasoning

Confirmation bias
Seeking out information consistent with what is believed to be true.

The information that we have in memory is used to process new information. As a result, our thinking processes are also affected by the **confirmation bias**, in which it is easier to process and incorporate new information that is consistent with what we already know (Klayman, 1985). As a result, we tend to seek out information that confirms what we know rather than looking for new evidence that might prove us wrong. Consider a detective working on a crime case: She will look for witnesses to verify that the suspect was in the crime location, but may not look for witnesses to identify the suspect in other places at that time. We follow through on our beliefs by "piling on" new evidence consistent with them. In its extreme form, this can cause us to discount or ignore conflicting information when it is available. In a study with law students, their initial assessment of guilt following reading about a case also determined how likely they were to pursue further investigation of it (Rassin et al., 2010). The schemas that organize information in memory, lead us to predict and expect information in the world to match.

Cultural styles of reasoning may produce some variation in how people handle discrepant information. Consider whether you agree with these statements:

A. Nothing is identical to itself because everything is dynamic and changeable over time.

B. Contradictions like "good and bad" and "old and new" exist in the same object or event.

C. Nothing is ever isolated or independent, but instead, everything is related.

These principles capture aspects of dialectical thinking, which involves accepting contradiction among ideas FIGURE 8-16. Peng and Nisbett (1999) found differences in how people think about contradictory or dialectical ideas based on their cultural background. Specifically, they found evidence that when Chinese and American students were presented

FIGURE 8-16 In dialectical thinking, opposing ideas are considered valid at the same time, and a synthesis is created.

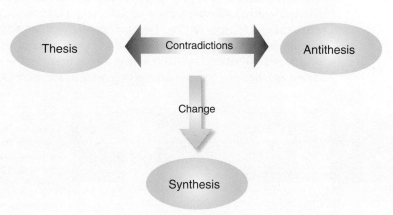

with contradictions from everyday social life, they differed in their responses. When given scenarios about conflicts between mothers and daughters, Americans tended to give responses that were one-sided (e.g., "Mothers should respect their daughters' independence"). Chinese students, in contrast, found merit and fault on both sides (e.g., "The mothers and daughters have failed to understand each other"). Of course, while both groups are capable of thinking dialectically and logically ("No statement can be both true or false"), they differed in how often they used specific styles of thinking. The style of thinking was more likely to be dialectical in nature, reflecting both "black and white," when from Chinese students. So cultural influences can alter our characteristic ways of reasoning.

Across cultures, when we hold beliefs, we try very hard to maintain them, even in the face of conflicting evidence. Once established, we have a tendency to reject evidence against our beliefs and favor evidence that supports them, called **belief perseverance**. In one study, students both for and against the death penalty were given "information from research studies" (Lord, Ross, & Lepper, 1979). Some of the reports provided evidence that the death penalty is an effective crime deterrent, and others offered evidence that it has no effect on crime rates. For example, one study reported was: "Palmer & Crandall (1977) compared murder rates in 10 pairs of neighboring states with different capital punishment laws. In 8 of the 10 pairs, murder rates were *higher* in the state *with* capital punishment. The research opposes the deterrent effect of the death penalty." The students interpreted this study differently based on their existing beliefs. A proponent of the death penalty concluded, "It seems that the researchers studied a carefully selected group of states and that they were careful in interpreting the results." An opponent of the death penalty viewed the same report and said, "There might be very different circumstances between the two sets of states, even though they were sharing a border." No matter what their opinion was, the students raised more doubts and criticism about the evidence that was *against* their existing belief and claimed the evidence in favor of their belief was stronger. If we only accept evidence that supports our beliefs and reject other information, our beliefs become impervious to evidence. We stop looking to see *whether* our beliefs are right and look for evidence *that* they are right. These reasoning errors can make it quite difficult to change our beliefs even when overwhelming evidence is presented.

Perhaps as a result of these processes, we are also very prone to show **overconfidence** about our beliefs, in which we overestimate how likely we are to be correct. In these studies, people are asked about facts and then asked to estimate how likely they are to be correct in their answers (e.g., "What is the capital of Bolivia? How sure are you of your answer?"). People consistently overestimate the odds of their being correct by about 15% (Koriat et al., 1980). People are also overconfident about how well they drive, how quickly they can get tasks done, and whether they are doing well on a test (Dunning et al., 2004). The problem may be that you know a lot about what you know; but, by definition, you *do not* know what you do not know. In fact, studies have shown that the *less* knowledge you have in a domain, the *more* likely you are to overestimate your success in it (Kruger & Dunning, 1999). These factors may at last explain why Sam was so ready to fall for my April Fool's joke about Uma Thurman. Sam has a healthy self-image, so why would Uma Thurman not want to date him? Sam was perhaps overconfident about his own ability to interest possible dates and failed to consider what other options Uma Thurman may have. Of course, perhaps Sam was right; so, I would like to apologize here to Sam, and to Uma!

In problem solving, decision making, and reasoning, we have seen repeated examples of how heuristic use may be fast and easy, often leading to good outcomes. However, heuristics can also be viewed as biases that lead you astray in your thinking. The heuristics and biases in this chapter are shown in Table 8-1, along with suggestions of ways to correct your thinking. Of course, noticing your own biases is not trivial; in fact, studies have shown that people can be unaware of their own cognitive biases. When judging your own possible bias, you tend to rely on introspection; however, for other people, you may think of other ways to assess their bias (Pronin, Lin, & Ross, 2002). Just as in overconfidence, you have more information about your internal thinking, and that may mislead you rather than help you recognize your limitations in thinking. Metacognition, or the ability to reflect on your own thinking, may be limited in recognizing the use of

Belief perseverance Holding onto a belief in the face of evidence against it.

Overconfidence Being more certain about your beliefs than you should be.

heuristics and resulting biases. As an alternative, ask someone else what they think about your reasoning: Our peers may be able to provide more accurate assessments of how we are doing in our thinking processes.

CONCEPT LEARNING CHECK 8.4 | *Practicing Reasoning*

Consider the need to reason about whether you are prepared for your upcoming test on this material. Suppose that, after studying, you decide you are ready for the exam. How might each of these factors influence the validity of your conclusion? And how might you correct for these influences?

1. Content effects

2. Confirmation bias

3. Belief perseverance

4. Overconfidence

8.5   Language

Learning a language provides evidence of special thinking skills.

- Define language and describe the unique characteristics of human language.
- Describe the theories of language acquisition.

Learning theorist B. F. Skinner famously referred to thinking as "sub-vocal speech" (McGuigan, 1970). He meant that we cannot know what is occurring inside the mind, but we can observe the communications it produces. **Language**, one form of communication, is a core and defining process of human thinking and it identifies the human species as different from all others. While many animals have elaborate and sophisticated communication systems ("It's me!" "Where are you guys?" "Look out for that owl!"), only human communication meets some definitions of a "language."

What Is a "Language"?

Why is this? A few key properties separate human language use from communications in other species. First, our language has **semanticity**, or meaning. While animals likely express a great variety of experiences and emotions through squeaks and growls, human language offers meaningful units that, in combination, convey meaning quite unlike their sounds. A high school graduate knows about 45,000 different words, and a college graduate at least twice that amount (Miller, 1991). Our language has a code for meaning that is extensive beyond the one hundred basic sounds we are capable of making. Another property is **generativity**, the capacity to use a finite set of words and rules for combining them to generate an endless variety of unique things to say. In fact, whenever you begin to suspect that every possible combination of words has already been expressed, someone invents something like "twittering." Finally, our language includes **displacement**, the ability to communicate about things that are not in our immediate surroundings. Imagine what a limitation it would be if we were unable to refer to objects, locations, and people not present, or to express abstract or imaginary ideas. Our language provides a new method of thinking that takes us far beyond the world in front of us.

Language Structure

There are at least seven thousand distinct languages worldwide, and tens of thousands of differing dialects. Each is based on the same structures, though they differ in which specific elements are included. The smallest units of speech are **phonemes**, the basic sounds of all languages. English has up to 45 distinct phonemes, such as *t*, *sh*, and *ch*. The smallest unit that carries meaning is called a **morpheme**. For example, *dog* is a morpheme, but *dof* is not, even though each contains three phonemes. Every **word** has one or more morphemes, including prefixes like *anti-* and suffixes like *-able*. Combining groups of words leads to

---

Language A form of thinking used to communicate with others and ourselves.

Semanticity Containing meaning or reference to things in the world.

Generativity The capacity to use a finite set to create endless variety of unique combinations.

Displacement The ability to refer to things not visible in our immediate surroundings.

Phonemes The basic sounds of human languages.

Morpheme The smallest unit of sounds that carries meaning.

Word A meaningful pattern of sound defined within a language.

phrases, and phrases are then combined into **sentences**. An organized sequence of words can convey facts, hypotheses, questions, requests, intentions, and thoughts.

The organization of words within a language, or **grammar**, involves two levels: the **surface structure**, or the ordering of a sequence of words in time, and the **deep structure**, or the composition of meaning within a phrase FIGURE 8-17. You may recall drawing sentence trees to learn proper grammar in school. These trees capture the difference between the surface structure, such as "The horse that raced past the barn fell," and the underlying deep structure meaning, "The horse (that raced past the barn) fell" (Frazier & Rayner, 1982). Linguists study how languages create meaning through the words and rules of combination they allow. Psycholinguists show how the language is used, how it impacts comprehension, and what is later recalled from memory. For example, consider this story:

> There is an interesting story about the telescope. In Holland, a man named Lippershey was an eye-glass maker. One day his children were playing with some lenses. They discovered that things seemed very close if two lenses were held about a foot apart. Lippershey began experimenting, and his "spyglass" attracted much attention. He sent a letter to Galileo, the great Italian scientist. Galileo at once realized the importance of the discovery and set about to build an instrument of his own. He used an old organ pipe with one lens curved out and the other in. On the first clear night he pointed the glass toward the sky. He was amazed to find the empty dark spaces filled with gleaming stars! Night after night Galileo climbed to a high tower, sweeping the sky with his telescope. One night he saw Jupiter, and to his great surprise discovered near it three bright stars.

Now, write down the story without looking back at the text. What do you recall? Sachs (1967) measured people's memory for specific sentences either right away, after they had read another 80 syllables of story, or after they had read another 160 syllables. The results are shown in FIGURE 8-18. He found that people could correctly identify the

Phrase Two or more words combined to convey meaning.

Sentence Organized sequence of words that conveys facts, hypotheses, questions, requests, intentions, and thoughts.

Grammar Rules within a language that determine whether a sentence is properly formed and complete.

Surface structure The ordering of a sequence of words in time.

Deep structure The meaning composed by a phrase or sentence.

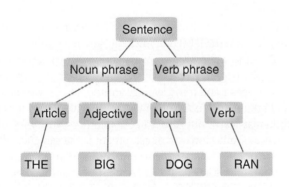

FIGURE 8-17 A tree diagram maps out the words in a sentence, organizing them into the parts of language that reveal their "deep structure" or underlying meaning.

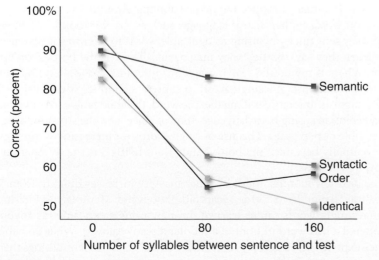

FIGURE 8-18 After reading a story, only semantics, or the meaning of the text (green), stays available in memory.
Source: Adapted from Sachs, J. (1967). Recognition memory for syntactic and semantic aspects of connected discourse. Perception and Psychophysics, 2, 437–442.

Gist The semantic meaning of a sentence.

Paraphrase A description of the same meaning using different elements.

Pragmatics The social context of language that adds to its meaning.

Extralinguistic factors Information outside of language that aids in comprehension.

Babbling The initial vocalizing performed by babies learning to speak.

Holophrastic The use of a single word to represent more complex ideas in early language learning.

semantic structure, order, syntactic structure, and the identical sentence if tested right away. However, after reading further, the only format recalled was the semantic structure. People preserve the semantics, or **gist**, of the information, but they "forget" other aspects of the language expression. After reading, you can recall a **paraphrase** or description of the meaning it contained, but you do not preserve other linguistic elements.

Of course, language is a social vehicle, and the **pragmatics**, or social context, of language is also critical to comprehension. Consider the question, "Can you pass the salt?" If you answer, "yes," you are answering the literal meaning of the question, but not the pragmatic meaning, which is, "Give me the salt!" Studies by Gibbs (1986) showed that you are actually faster to process the intended meaning ("Pass the salt!") than the literal meaning ("Are you able to pass the salt?") for these types of indirect requests. If you listen carefully to speech, you will see that we often use the pragmatics of the situation around us to guide our understanding. For example, when someone says, "Good job!" to you, they may be sincerely complimenting you, or insulting you by being sarcastic. Determining which meaning the speaker intends is part of communication, but it depends on **extralinguistic factors**—that is, information outside of the literal content of language that aids in comprehension.

Many extralinguistic factors play into our comprehension of meaning in communication. For example, the speaker's intonation ("Good job?") can suggest a question. Facial expressions also provide cues, where falling down laughing might suggest they were being sarcastic. Gestures such as shaking the head, pointing, or giving a "thumbs up" also play a critical role in deriving meaning from communication. For all of these reasons, the medium of communication makes an important difference in how easily we understand each other. Over a phone, by text or e-mail, or even video link, important cues about the other person can be degraded. Studies have found that, despite advances in technology, no medium produces better communication between people than face-to-face interaction (Baltes et al., 2002). Given the long history of human evolution, it makes sense that we came to rely on many cues from the speaker in interpreting the meaning behind communications.

Language Development

Stop to think for a moment about how long you have been in school and how many years of instruction have gone into the level of knowledge you have attained. Now think about this: Children of all cultures absorb the words and grammar of language without any instruction at all! Just by being exposed to language, children learn an average of nine words per day between ages 1 and 6 and average around 14,000 words by then. They also learn to use rules of grammar that are often too complicated even for adults to explain. While some children may learn to speak earlier than others, and some may struggle with language, the sequence of milestones in development is the same for all (Brown, 1973).

Newborns cry to communicate. In the second month of life, infants begin using their tongues to coo, making sounds like *oh* and *ah*. At about 4 months, babies begin **babbling**, vocalizing in ways that sound like human speech. These three stages are consistent regardless of the language heard (and occur even in babies that cannot hear). However, sounds not used in your own language (e.g., for Japanese speakers, the phenome "r" is not present) are eventually dropped out of the babbling. Around 1 year, babies produce their first, short words in their native language, such as "ba" for "bottle." Even year-old toddlers display semanticity by using recognizable words to refer to specific meanings. However, when they say, "Bottle," they may mean, "There is the bottle," or "I want a bottle," or "Where is my bottle?" Such one-word utterances are called **holophrastic**, referring to this early use of a single word to express a complex idea (Braine, 1971). Though the linguistic utterance is limited to the word, the child is able to convey actions, desires, and emotions using body language, tone of voice, and the surrounding context (the dinner table or nap time). This use of single words for increasingly complex ideas ("bottle" eventually becomes "my bottle" and "want bottle") is the foundation of the child's growing vocabulary.

For the next few months, toddlers' word mastery increases quickly, from 5 at 12 months to 30 at 18 months to 250 at 2 years old (Woodward, Markman, & Fitzsimmons, 1994). Interestingly, words can be learned through a single exposure (as anyone who has ever uttered a bad word in front of a toddler already knows). What do babies talk about? They express their desires (people, toys, "more") and point out things that move (dogs, cars, birds). Around 2 years of age, their vocabulary explodes to hundreds of new words each year. Toddlers also begin **telegraphic speech**, in which they combine two- and three-word phrases ("More milk" for "I want more milk"). Exposure to enriched environments, including *Sesame Street* on TV, can increase vocabularies more rapidly (Rice et al., 1990). As they enter grade school, children's vocabulary continues to expand, and they construct longer and more complex sentences. They display generativity, constructing phrases of their own they have never heard said by others. They learn to correctly apply rules of grammar, such as using the past tense, plurals, and pronouns. For example, initially, children learn that you can add "-ed" to the end of a word to say it happened already, such as "added," "played," and "barked." They may **overregularize** the rule, adding "-ed" to words where the past tense does not require it, such as "runned," "drinked," and "falled" (Marcus, 1995). Eventually, the unusual past tenses ("ran," "drank," fell") are learned as well. The unique, rule-breaking variations are the most difficult to acquire, as any English as a Second Language learner will tell you. By speaking in the past tense, children display the property of displacement, or referring to events no longer in the immediate environment.

Later in grade school, children begin to understand that words can have double meanings. After visiting the petting zoo, 6-year-old Stephanie held up her chicken nugget at dinner and said, "Isn't it funny that 'chicken' sounds just like 'chicken'?" Young children find knock-knock jokes so funny because they are beginning to realize that one word can have two very different meanings ("Knock knock." "Who's there?" "Dewey." "Dewey who?" "Do we have to go to school today?") Later in grade school, children begin to understand abstract concepts, like "mammals," "freedom," and "abstract." Metaphors, analogies, and adages become more interpretable, such as, "The grass is always greener on the other side of the fence" (Vosniadou, 1987). These developmental milestones are quite consistent across gender, language, and cultures. What would happen if children were not exposed to a rich language environment as they learn? Would language develop if the child was not surrounded by other speakers? Of course, no one would attempt an experiment that would intentionally isolate a child from others' language.

But for some individuals, language isolation has occurred. A 13-year-old victim of lifelong child abuse, Genie was discovered in her home in November of 1970, strapped to a potty chair (Rymer, 1994). Her father and mother had isolated her in the basement, and she was rarely exposed to speech. After her rescue, she appeared unable to acquire language as completely as other children (Fromkin et al., 1974). Through cases where normal development did not occur, we have learned that early childhood is a **critical period** for learning language (Lennenberg, 1967). This critical period is a window of time required for successful language development to take place. Children not exposed to language by around age 7 gradually lose their potential for learning the complexities of language. Other evidence comes from studies of American Sign Language (ASL), a complete language using hand gestures to represent morphemes and letters. A study by Newport (1990) compared deaf children who learned American Sign Language from infancy (native speakers), *early* learners (first exposed to ASL at age 4 to 6), and *late* learners (first exposed after age 12). Late learners can still master words and order but never become as fluent in signing as native signers and have less crisp and more grammatically inconsistent forms FIGURE 8-19. Deaf children can sometimes be given cochlear implants that allow them to hear sounds, and their language learning then appears the same as in hearing children (Svirsky, 2000). The critical period for language learning also appears in second-language learning. If you learn another language before puberty, you will likely be able to speak it without an accent. As an adult, the initial language leaves its trace in new language learning (Oyama, 1976). Hakuta and colleagues (2003) have shown that later age at emigration predicts more difficulty in learning a second language.

Theories of Language Acquisition

How language acquisition takes place is a question hotly debated within psychology. **Behaviorist theories**, such as that of B. F. Skinner, argue there is nothing special about language learning; instead, it follows the same principles identified in general learning theories. In this view, the principles of association, imitation, and reinforcement are adequate to explain

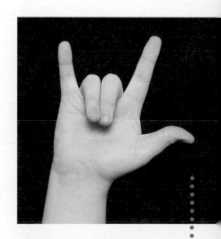

The American Sign Language sign for, "I love you."

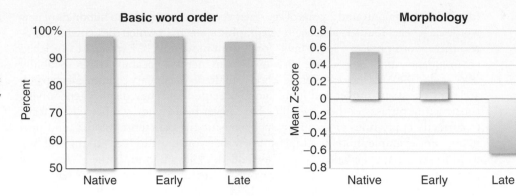

FIGURE 8-19 This graph shows control over basic word order in ASL. There are effects of age of acquisition, but the scores on seven tests of ASL morphology (form) show consistent effects of age, with natives outscoring early learners, who in turn outscore late learners.
Source: Adapted from Newport, E. L. (1990). Maturational constraints on language learning. Cognitive Science, *14, 11–28.*

Nativist theory The view that language is a special skill we are born with.

Interactionist theory The view that language combines inborn abilities with special environmental triggers.

how language acquisition occurs. **Nativist theories**, such as that of Noam Chomsky, argue that language learning is too remarkable to be explained by experience alone; instead, some built-in capacity must account for our language capacity. Chomsky (1972) argued that the human brain is biologically hardwired as a "language acquisition device" or "LAD." In other words, we are born with "programs" to help infants readily acquire language. As evidence, Chomsky argued that all people have language, and all languages have particular properties (like nouns and verbs) in common. Children all over the world learn to fluently speak the language they hear, at about the same age, and without much effort or instruction. Pinker (1995) argues that humans are genetically prepared for language, and evidence shows that humans are born with unique sensitivities to the sounds and structures of speech (Mac-Whinney, 1998).

Language is another example of multiple influences in thinking. Nature may prepare us to learn language remarkably quickly; however, without the external situation around us—hearing and interacting with others—language skills do not develop normally. **Interactionist theories** attempt to combine explanations of inborn tendencies with the special environmental triggers that enhance the development of language. Other aspects of social interaction, such as gestures, also assist in language learning (Goldin-Meadow, 2003). Social interaction is, after all, the purpose of learning language, and aspects of the social environment greatly impact it. In particular, being spoken to frequently by caregivers speeds the development of language (Richards, 1994). Even the dreaded "baby talk" that parents lapse into serves a purpose: Its high pitch and exaggerated intonation are preferred to normal speech by 4 month olds (Fernald, 1985). While we have developed ways of using language that are far removed from any specific recipient, such as writing textbooks and messages in bottles, at heart, language is social thought.

Language in Animals

Many animals are also social. So why is their communication, however rich and complex, not considered the equivalent of human language? What language capacities exist in animals? Researchers have studied communication in apes, dolphins, and even parrots to uncover what makes human language so special. However, the question has not been, "What are they saying to each other?" The question for psychologists has been, "Are any of them able to talk to *us*?"

Irene Pepperberg (2002) and colleagues spent more than 20 years teaching English to an African gray parrot named Alex. Because parrots can mimic sounds, they have the potential to produce spoken language sounding like human speech, unlike any other species. Alex knows more than 70 words, can count objects up to six, and can compare two objects ("smaller," "bigger") and choose objects based on multiple features ("What is blue and triangular?"). Alex can name an object placed in front of him ("block") and respond to questions about it ("red," "wood," and "square") with 80% accuracy. This is quite impressive, but imagine how annoying this performance would be in a friend. Alex learned from watching a human model be scolded or rewarded for his or her answers, and eye contact along with pointing were important parts of learning. While Alex was a well-trained bird (he died in 2007), his mastery of language left something to be desired.

Psychologist Irene Pepperberg and her research team worked with an African gray parrot named Alex on his speech sounds for over 20 years.

On the other hand, studies of communication among dolphins have demonstrated rudimentary semantics and syntax use (Hillix & Rumbaugh, 2004; Linden, 1993). Two bottlenose dolphins, Phoenix and Akeakamai, were trained to communicate with trainers through hand gestures and electronic whistles. When given commands of two to five words, such as "Right water left Frisbee fetch," the dolphins correctly took the Frisbee to the water on the right. Dolphins are good candidates for language capacity, as their brains are very large, and they normally live in a highly complex and very social environment. However, like Alex, their ability to learn human language seems more like behavior captured by learning theories rather than the spontaneous burst of untrained language learning in human toddlers. To answer whether any animal could learn human language, researchers turned to our nearest evolutionary relatives: The great apes.

As social animals, dolphins have sophisticated communication skills and have learned to respond to complex signals from humans.

Early researchers working with chimpanzees quickly realized they lacked the anatomy to produce speech sounds like ours. Premack (1971) was able to teach a chimp named Sarah to communicate by placing colored chips onto a magnetic board (though Sarah later bit off Premack's fingers, in another form of communication). American Sign Language use proved more successful, when Allen and Beatrice Gardner (1989) successfully taught four chimpanzees, including their star pupil, Washoe. She learned more than 132 signs and was able to combine signs into simple sentences. She also showed innovation in sign use, combining them in ways she had not seen expressed by others, such as calling a swan a "water bird" and describing a toy doll in a teacup as "Baby in my cup." Washoe also communicated with other chimps in sign language and taught her son 68 different signs. A gorilla named Koko, trained by Patterson and Linden (1981), holds the record with a 600-word vocabulary.

These smart animals clearly learned a lot, but how was their learning like human language learning? Sue Savage-Rumbaugh and colleagues (1998) set out to see if chimps could learn like humans do—through exposure to language in context rather than through instruction. Kanzi, a pygmy chimp, learned to talk by making hand signals, pointing to symbols on a board, and pressing symbols on a keyboard, and he can understand spoken English. Kanzi reacted appropriately to requests that varied, such as, "Turn on the light," "Show me the light," and "Bring me the light." Without seeing the speaker, Kanzi once heard, "Jeanie hid the pine needles in her shirt"; immediately, he walked up to Jeanie and searched her shirt. Clearly, apes are able to understand and produce communications at a level showing language properties like semanticity and generativity.

Koko, a gorilla, learned to communicate with trainers through American Sign Language.

But how does this compare to human language learning? Savage-Rumbaugh performed a head-to-head test of Kanzi and a 2-year-old human named Alia. In tests over a 9-month period, the two were tested on more than 650 commands in spoken English. The sentences were designed to be new (not previously heard) and to combine objects in unusual ways (e.g., "Can you pour the ice water in the potty," and "Make the doggie bite the snake"). Both Kanzi (with 74% correct) and Alia (with 65% correct) showed they understood spoken language, semantics, and syntax, even though they were unable to produce it. Clearly, Kanzi mastered more language comprehension than most people ever thought possible for a chimp. However, his learning peaked there, while Alia, at 2, was just beginning her language "burst." While it is clear that animals may understand much more than they can say, it is also unlikely they are able to give speeches, write poetry, or think about particle physics. Language, and the deep thoughts it captures, appear to be a uniquely human capacity.

CONCEPT LEARNING CHECK **8.5**   *Features of Language*

Consider the principles of semanticity, generativity, and displacement.

1. Identify examples of these three language capacities in other animal species.

2. Which of these principles is missing from animal language use?

8.6   Brain, Language, and Culture

Our language use reveals its impact on our thinking and the influence of biology and culture.

- Explain how language use reveals its impact on our thinking.
- Describe the influence of biology and culture on how we think.

Broca's area Part of the left frontal lobe that produces speech sounds.

Wernicke's area Part of the left temporal lobe that comprehends spoken words.

Linguistic relativity The notion that language shapes our ideas and not the other way around.

What is special about humans that allowed us to develop language and to think abstract thoughts? One answer can be determined from our "hardware," the specific functions supported in the brain that allow us to comprehend and produce spoken language. Early clues about brain function arose from clinical cases of brain injury. In 1865, Paul Broca noticed his medical patients sometimes suffered from an inability to speak. One man was called the Tan Man because he was only able to produce the word *tan*. He was able to comprehend what was spoken to him and even to sing familiar songs, but his production of spoken language was limited to that single word. The damaged area of the brain was in the left frontal lobe, called **Broca's area**. Another area located in the left temporal lobe, called **Wernicke's area**, produced different behavior when damaged by strokes. In these cases identified by Carl Wernicke in patients in 1874, words still flowed freely but made little sense, described as "word salad." The right ingredients—the individual words—were produced correctly, but the meaning in word combinations was lacking. These patients also had trouble comprehending speech.

As brain injury cases suggested, language processing in the brain has been found to occur mainly in the left hemisphere. In all right-handed people and even most left-handed people, these language-processing centers are located only in the left hemisphere FIGURE 8-20. Wernicke's area is active when hearing words, and Broca's area is active when speaking words. In addition to brain anatomy, the mouth, throat, and larynx allow us to systematically vary the sounds we create, and our faces express meaning, along with our gestures. Humans are gifted with the hardware that allows language to take place with minimal effort. In fact, the close ties between our use of language and the development of thinking raises the question of which came first, the thought or its description?

Linguistic relativity is the idea that language shapes our ideas and not the other way around. The language we speak may determine the ways we conceptualize the world

FIGURE 8-20 In this image, Broca's area for speech generation (in the left frontal lobe) is shown in blue, and Wernicke's area for speech comprehension (in the left temporal lobe) is shown in green.

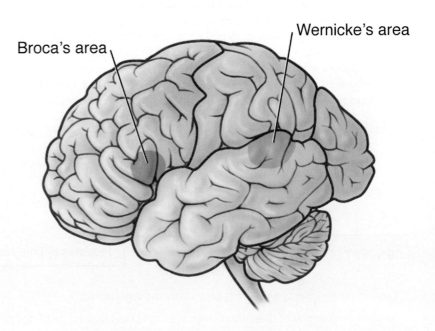

Broca's area

Wernicke's area

(Whorf, 1956). For example, German contains a word, *Schadenfreude*, which is translated as "delighting in others' misfortune." Is this a concept you knew before you heard this word? If not, your thinking about this concept is relative, or dependent on, the language you speak. This notion, that language creates thought, is called the Sapir-Whorf hypothesis (Kay & Kempton, 2009). Of course, anyone who speaks more than one language knows it is possible to express the same idea in different languages. The idea here is that the *ways* of expression created by language may in turn influence how we think. Whorf's study of the Hopi led him to conclude that their language contained no words or grammatical forms that refer directly to past, present, or future. This suggested that people living in different cultures and speaking different languages may be thinking about time in different ways.

Imagine you had four pictures of a person at various ages. As an English speaker, you would almost certainly order the pictures chronologically left to right, with the oldest pictures to the right. Or you could arrange them "east to west," as do the Pompuraawan, a remote tribe in Australia. Their language does not have words such as *left* or *in front of*; instead, they use the cardinal directions, such as "my south arm." How a culture thinks spatially influences how they think about time (Boroditsky & Gaby, 2010). In one study, Mandarin Chinese and English speakers were examined because they differ in the spatial metaphors used to describe time (Boroditsky, 2001). In English, we think of a line extending horizontally to describe time, looking "forward" to events and putting past events "behind" us. In Mandarin, people speak about time on a vertical axis, with the past as *shang*, or up, and later events as *xia*, or down. In a laboratory study, native speakers were reminded of either horizontal or vertical space and then had to quickly answer temporal questions, such as, "May comes earlier than April, true or false?" English speakers answered more quickly with reminders of horizontal space, while Mandarin speakers were quicker with reminders of vertical space FIGURE 8-21. How we think also influences what we understand in language comprehension. If I tell you, "Next Wednesday's meeting has been advanced by two days," which day is the new meeting day? If you say "Friday,"

Image of Hopi woman from Whorf's study of language and culture.

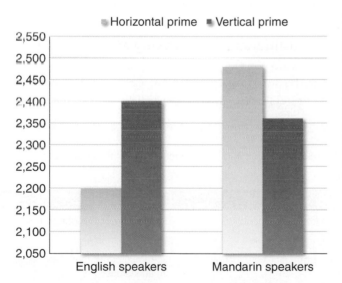

FIGURE 8-21 English speakers think of time horizontally, so they performed better with a horizontal prime when making a time judgment. Mandarin speakers think of time vertically, so they performed worse with the horizontal prime on the same task. *Source: Data from Boroditsky, L. (2001). Does language shape thought? English and Mandarin speakers' conceptions of time.* Cognitive Psychology, *43(1), 1–22.*

you are thinking of time as a horizontal line stretching ahead of you, and advancing the meeting means moving it further into the future. However, if you thought "Monday," your thinking may use a metaphor of time as a horizontal river flowing past you. So, if something is "advanced" in time, it is moved closer toward you (McGlone & Harding, 1998).

Another place where language may drive the concepts we use is the topic of gender. Many languages, such as French, have gender marked in reference to objects; for example, *window* is preceded by the feminine *la* rather than the masculine *le*. German has three genders for things: masculine, feminine, and neutral, while English has one: neutral. Does "gendered" language affect the way we think, or is it a harmless practice to talk about "fresh*man*," "chair*man* of the board," and the "evolution of *man*"? Studies show that the use of masculine pronouns such as *he*, even when intended to be inclusive, lead people to think of males. For example, students were asked to write short stories starting with, "In a large co-ed institution, the average student will feel isolated in his courses." Sixty-five percent of the resulting stories focused on a male student (Moulton et al., 1978). The fact that gender is built into references in languages—some more than others—suggests that linguistic relativity is readily evident in our language use and thinking.

The complexity of the interactions between thought and language makes it a wonder that we ever understand each other at all. It suggests the study of second languages may be an important way to increase understanding across cultures. When we examine language and thinking in different cultures, we find evidence that they reflect the lived experiences that greatly vary across cultures. Given that the culture surrounding us influences our modes of thinking, thought may be subject to "cultural relativity." Individualism-collectivism describes the degree to which a culture relies on and has allegiance to the self (independence) or the group (interdependence; see **TABLE 8-2**). Those in Western cultures like Americans tend to focus on independence in their self-descriptions, while those in East Asian cultures identify interdependence as a value (Markus & Kitayama, 1991; Triandis et al., 1988). A worldwide study of 116,000 employees of IBM found the most independent people were from the United States, Australia, Great Britain, Canada, and the Netherlands, while the most interdependent people were from Venezuela, Colombia, Pakistan, Peru, and Taiwan (Hofstede, 1980). FIGURE 8-22 illustrates the difference between an individual view versus a collectivist view of the self. Which description fits how you think about yourself? When asked to complete the fragment, "I am . . .," will your responses be characteristics of yourself ("an athlete," "a risk taker"), or of your relationship to others ("a sister," "a son")? This difference between an individualist versus a collectivist view of oneself varies across the two types of cultures (Markus & Kitayama, 1991) FIGURE 8-23. And it varies even within people who happen to be bicultural. When Chinese Americans were "primed" by answering in Chinese, they focused on duties to others, fitting in, and harmonious interdependence FIGURE 8-24. When primed by writing in English, Chinese Americans focused on individual descriptors (Hong et al., 2001). The language we speak influences our thinking about ourselves—a core aspect of cognition—and the cultural values we hold.

Summary of Multiple Influences on Thinking and Language

The ways we think and how we use language are clearly subject to multiple influences from biology and culture. The functional specialization of brain areas plays an important role in the comprehension and production of language. It also reveals that our decisions

TABLE 8-2 Summary of Key Differences Between an Independent and an Interdependent Construal of Self

Feature Compared	Independent	Interdependent
Definition	Separate from social context	Connected with social context
Structure	Bounded, unitary, stable	Flexible, variable
Important features	Internal, private (abilities, thoughts, feelings)	External, public (statuses, roles, relationships)
Tasks	Be unique	Belong, fit-in
	Express self	Occupy one's proper place
	Realize internal attributes	Engage in appropriate action
	Promote own goals	Promote others' goals
	Be direct; "say what's on your mind"	Be indirect; "read other's mind"
Role of others	*Self-evaluation:* others important for social comparison, reflected appraisal	*Self-definition:* relationships with others in specific contexts define the self
Basis of self-esteem	Ability to express self, validate internal attributes	Ability to adjust, restrain self, maintain harmony with social context

Source: Data from Markus, H. R., & Kitayama, S. (1991). Culture and the self: Implications for cognition, emotion, and motivation. Psychological Review, 98*(2), 224–253.*

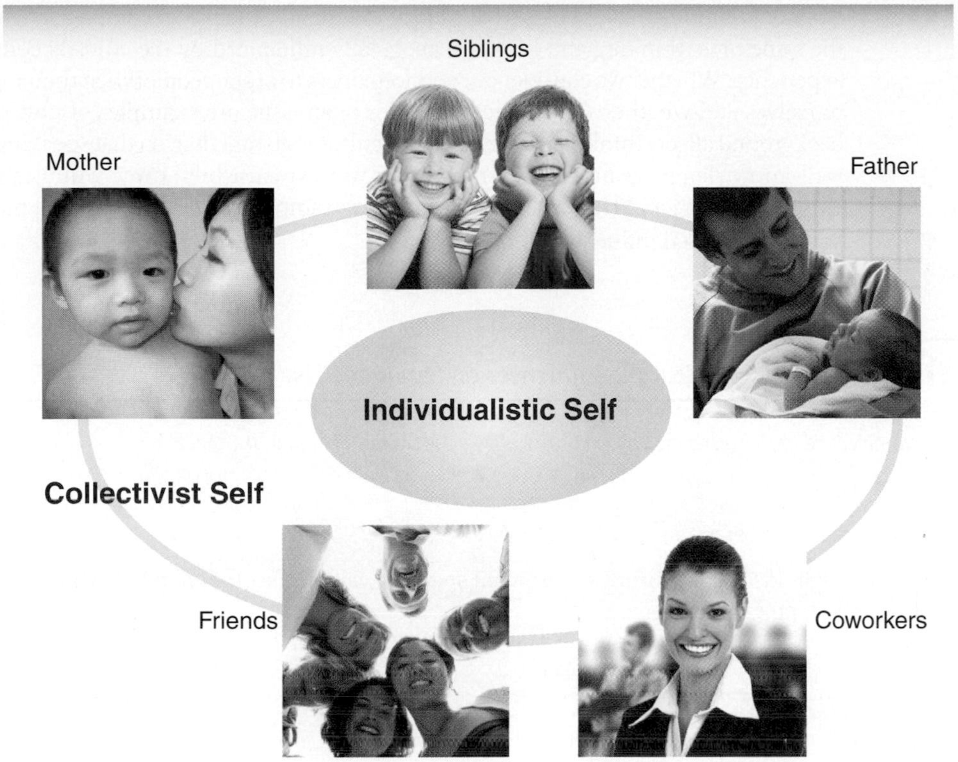

Siblings

Mother

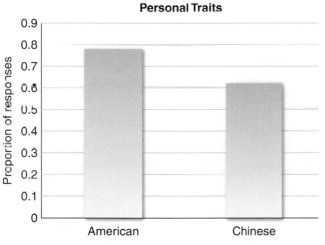

Father

Individualistic Self

Collectivist Self

Friends

Coworkers

FIGURE 8-22 An identity focused on individualism defines the self independently from other people.

Personal Traits

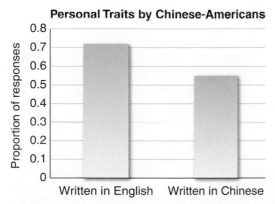

FIGURE 8-23 American students were more likely to report personal traits in their self descriptions, while Chinese students reported more interdependent relationships to define themselves.
Source: Data from Markus, H. R., & Kitayama, S. (1991). Culture and the self: Implications for cognition, emotion, and motivation. Psychological Review, 98(2), 224–253.

Personal Traits by Chinese-Americans

FIGURE 8-24 People who held both Chinese and American identities (biculturals) were asked to complete the self-identity task writing in English or in Chinese. When primed by the language, they altered their descriptions to fit the cultural identity of the language in which they were writing.
Source: Data from Hong, Y., Ip, G., Chiu, C., Morris, M. W., & Menon, T. (2001). Cultural identity and dynamic construction of the self: Collective duties and individual rights in Chinese and American cultures. Social Cognition, 19(3), 251–268.

are influenced not just by the content stored in the cerebral cortex but also by the flow of emotion in the orbital-frontal cortex and limbic system. Biology plays a role in determining which of the dual thinking processes—the slow, deliberate reasoning or the fast, associative instinct—drives our decisions. The biology of our brains certainly produces a kind of thinking that appears to be unique to humans: the use of complex language. At the same time, thinking and language are greatly influenced by the cultural context we experience. Whether we consider our connectedness to other people when thinking about ourselves and whether we can see both sides of an issue are examples of how cultural background affects thinking. Languages and cultures go together, so that speaking in one well-known language may change not just the word you use but how you think about the world. Thinking and language provide another example of the importance of biological and sociocultural influences in psychology.

CONCEPT LEARNING CHECK 8.6 | *Multiple Influences on Language Use*

Identify the concept illustrated in each example, and explain how biology or culture affects the sample of language provided.

1. (Holding teacup) "Could dogs nurse the television?"

2. "To describe myself: I am a biker, I love cats, and I enjoy sudoku."

3. "On the one hand, Republicans have the right idea about cutting government spending, but on the other hand, they are wrong about the high costs of social welfare programs."

4. "G-g-go . . . go . . . go . . . h-h-home."

5. "That was a long time ago, I cannot go back there."

Visual Overview Types of Thinking Processes

Three main types of thinking—problem solving, decision making, and reasoning—are identified in the chapter. Each has a distinct set of methods and algorithms that can be used to think through the question, and each has specific heuristics (or short cuts in thinking) and biases (or errors) to watch out for.

How can we increase sales?

What makes you a good candidate?

Do you want the job?

Cognitive Processes		
Types of thinking	Methods and algorithms (Systematic approaches to try)	Heuristics and biases (Shortcuts and errors to avoid)
Solving a problem	• Trial and error • Means-ends analysis • Analogy • Insight	• Mental set • Fixation • Functional fixedness
Making a decision	• Probability theory • Decision tree	• Representativeness • Availability • Framing
Reasoning to a conclusion	• Inductive reasoning • Deduction and logic • Mental models	• Confirmation bias • Belief perseverance • Overconfidence

8.1 Overview: What Is Thinking?

- Thinking includes the internal processes of the mind that help us make sense of the world.
- Rational thinking is marked by the use of reason, or coming to conclusions when considering facts fully and carefully. This form of thinking has the goal of avoiding errors and arriving at the best conclusion.

- Intuition is using first impressions, instincts, or emotions to drive our choices without given them much thought.
- These dual processes in thinking—slow, deliberative, conscious reasoning versus fast, automatic, and efficient reactions—describe the major ways we think across many tasks.

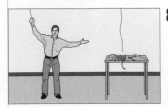

8.2 Problem Solving

- We solve problems through both deterministic algorithms and heuristic guesses.
- A problem is any given situation that differs from a desired goal state, and there is a *nonobvious* way to get from one to the other.
- An algorithm is a well-defined process that is guaranteed, eventually, to produce a solution. When one is available, and when the problem is important, this is a good choice for finding a solution.
- A heuristic is a mental shortcut in thinking that may or may not lead to a correct solution. The rules of thumb provided by heuristics are fast, require little effort, and usually lead to the right answer.
- Trial and error, means-ends analysis, analogy, and insight identify different approaches to solution.

- A bias is a tendency to hold on to one familiar perspective at the expense of (possibly equally valid) alternatives.
- Irrelevant information and unnecessary constraints can be distracting in a representation.
- Mental set is a preexisting state of mind, habit, or attitude, that can affect and mislead thinking.
- Fixation is when the solver sticks to an initial approach and cannot consider alternatives.
- Incubation helps by setting aside a problem for a break before further attempts to solve it.
- Ten thousand hours of practice are needed to produce expertise.
- Deliberative practice involves working on skills just beyond your current level.

8.3 Decision Making

- Rather than following algorithms, our decisions are often guided by heuristics.
- Making decisions involves choosing among alternatives or whether to take some action.
- Judgment is when we reach beyond what we already know and draw a conclusion.
- Probability theory is an algorithm that takes into account all contingencies and their likelihoods.
- A decision tree shows all choices and weighs each one based on its value.
- Heuristics are easy shortcuts that usually work but sometimes cause errors.

- The representativeness heuristic guides judgments based on what things "look like."
- The availability heuristic uses the ease of recall from memory to estimate the likelihood of an event.
- Decision making can also be biased by the way the choices are presented, known as the framing effect.
- People try to make choices that will minimize or avoid losses, called loss aversion.
- Choice overload refers to having too many choices to handle in decision making.

8.4 Reasoning

- Rather than always being rational, our reasoning may be biased by what we think we know.
- Reasoning is attempting to go beyond what we now know to draw a conclusion.
- Algorithms for reasoning are based on deduction and logic.
- Inductive reasoning draws more general conclusions from specific information.
- People are influenced by the content or meaning of the words used in a problem.

- Mental models are visual or graphical representations of the problem.
- In confirmation bias, we seek information that matches what we already know.
- Belief perseverance maintains beliefs even in the face of contradictory evidence.
- People show overconfidence by overestimating how likely we are to be correct.

8.5 Language

- Learning a language provides evidence of special thinking skills unique to humans.
- Language is a core and defining process of human thinking.
- A few key properties of human language are: semanticity, or meaning; generativity, the capacity to use a finite set of words to generate an endless variety of statements; and displacement, the ability to communicate about things that are not in the immediate surroundings.
- The structure of language includes phonemes, morphemes, words, phrases, and sentences.
- The organization of words within a language, or grammar, involves two levels:
  - the surface structure, or the ordering of a sequence of words in time.
  - the deep structure, or the composition of meaning within a phrase.
- People preserve the semantics, or gist, of the information, but they "forget" other aspects of the language expression.
- Pragmatics, or the social context, of language is also critical to comprehension.
- Extralinguistic factors outside of the literal content of language aid in comprehension, such as facial expressions and gestures.
- Children of all cultures absorb the words and grammar of language without any instruction.

- The sequence of milestones in language development is the same for all children.
- There is a critical period for learning language at around age 7, when we gradually lose the potential for learning language.
- Behaviorist theories argue there is nothing special about language and that it follows general learning theories.
- Nativist theories argue that language learning is built in or hardwired in the brain.
- Interactionist theories attempt to combine explanations of inborn tendencies with the special environmental triggers that enhance language learning.
- Studies of communication among dolphins and apes have demonstrated use of semantics and grammar.
- Chimpanzees have shown innovation in sign language use and can learn like humans do through exposure to language in context.
- However, animal learning of human languages peaks at the level attained by humans at age 2 or 3.
- Language and the complex thought it captures appear to be uniquely human capacities.

8.6 Brain, Language, and Culture

- The brain comprehends and produces language in two areas of left hemisphere: Broca's area for producing words and Wernicke's area in comprehension.

- Linguistic relativity is the idea that language shapes our ideas and not the other way around.

- Language reveals a culture's way of thinking, such as conceptions about time.

- People think similarly within cultures and differently from those in other cultures on topics like dialectical ideas and relationships to others.

- The ways we think and how we use language are clearly subject to multiple influences from biology and culture.

8.1 Overview: What Is Thinking?

1. Thinking marked by the use of reason, or coming to conclusions when considering facts fully and carefully, is called:
   A. rational.
   B. instinct.
   C. intuitive.
   D. metacognition.

8.2 Problem Solving

2. A step-by-step sequence of rules that always leads to the correct solution for a problem is called:
   A. an algorithm.
   B. a heuristic.
   C. representation.
   D. an analogy.

3. A mental shortcut in thinking that may or may not lead to a correct solution is called:
   A. an algorithm.
   B. a heuristic.
   C. representation.
   D. an analogy.

4. Jarrod approaches his problem by identifying the differences between the current state and the goal state he desires. He is likely to use using the problem-solving approach called:
   A. trial and error.
   B. means-ends analysis.
   C. analogy.
   D. insight.

5. Approaching a problem using the same strategies you always use reflect a bias called:
   A. mental set.
   B. mental models.
   C. analogy.
   D. insight.

6. You need to tighten a screw but have no screwdriver, so you pull a penny out of your pocket and use it to fix the faucet. What problem-solving bias have you just overcome?
   A. Means-end analysis
   B. Anchoring
   C. Brainstorming
   D. Functional fixedness

7. The process that helps by setting aside a problem for a break before further attempts to solve it is called:
   A. incubation.
   B. insight.
   C. intuition.
   D. means-ends analysis.

8. Studies found that expert performance at the highest levels requires:
   A. 1,000 hours of practice.
   B. 10,000 hours of practice.
   C. 100,000 hours of practice.
   D. true talent.

8.3 Decision Making

9. Simon is meek, tidy, quiet, and overly concerned with order and detail. People who meet him and guess that he is probably a bookkeeper are relying on:
   A. the confirmation bias.
   B. the representativeness heuristic.
   C. the availability heuristic.
   D. the framing effect.

10. People will accept a bet when they have a 10% chance of winning but are less likely to accept a bet in which they are told they have a 90% chance of losing. This is an example of which cognitive bias?
    A. The availability heuristic
    B. The representativeness heuristic
    C. The confirmation bias
    D. The framing effect

11. Selma estimates that breast cancer is the leading cause of death for women because it readily comes to mind. This example illustrates using:
    A. the framing heuristic.
    B. the availability heuristic.
    C. the representativeness heuristic.
    D. the confirmation bias.

12. Laying out all of the possible alternatives and their possible outcomes is a method for decision making called:
    A. logic.
    B. heuristics.
    C. trial and error.
    D. decision tree.

8.4 Reasoning

13. We often seek information that matches what we already know, called the:

   A. confirmation bias.

   B. belief perseverance.

   C. overconfidence.

   D. availability heuristic.

8.5 Language

14. The language property that separates human language use from other species is called:

   A. semanticity.

   B. generativity.

   C. displacement.

   D. grammar.

8.6 Brain, Language, and Culture

15. The area of the brain found to be involved in difficulties in producing spoken language, as in patients like the Tan Man, who could only say *tan*, is called:

   A. Broca's area.

   B. Wernicke's area.

   C. Chomsky's area.

   D. cerebellum.

CHAPTER DISCUSSION QUESTIONS

1. Identify one situation in which you think you would use rational thinking and one situation where you think you would use intuitive thinking. For each situation, evaluate the pros and cons of using the opposite style of thinking. For example, for your rational situation, what would happen if you used intuitive thinking instead?

2. Problem solving involves identifying a strategy to go from where you are to your goal. Think of a problem you have in your life and then examine how you would use the following problem-solving strategies to work toward your goal. Strategies: generate and test, algorithm, means-ends analysis, analogy.

3. Advertisers and marketing executives are very aware of the heuristics that we use in decision making. In fact, they often capitalize on our natural tendencies in the hope that we will decide to use their products. Find an example of a heuristic that is being used to sell a product in an advertising campaign. Identify the heuristic and then explain how it is being used in the advertising campaign.

4. Sections 8.5 and 8.6 review many of the factors that influence our ability to use language, including development, biology, and culture. Assess the role of each factor—development (8.5), biology (8.6), and culture (8.6)—in your own language skills. Would each factor have the same importance if you were to learn a new language now as it did when you learned your first language?

CHAPTER PROJECTS

1. Problem solving, decision making, and reasoning are three important aspects of thinking that are separate but related. Write a story in which the main character is confronted with at least three different situations, so one is best solved with problem solving, one with decision making, and one with reasoning. Highlight and number the beginning of each situation. Then, in a separate paragraph, identify whether the situation requires problem solving, decision making, or reasoning and how the character used a strategy from the book to continue toward the story's conclusion.

2. Imagine that you are the country's top language expert, and as such, the president has asked you to come and work on a very special project. Your job is to develop a plan to help infants learn to speak. As this language expert, develop a plan for the President, explaining how your strategy fits with our current understanding of how humans learn and develop language skills.

CHAPTER KEY TERMS

Algorithm	Generate and test	Paraphrase
Analogy	Generativity	Phonemes
Availability heuristic	Gist	Phrase
Babbling	Goal	Pragmatics
Behaviorist theory	Grammar	Probability theory
Belief perseverance	Heuristic	Problem
Bias	Holophrastic	Rational thinking
Broca's area	Incubation	Reasoning
Choice overload	Inductive reasoning	Representation
Cognition	Insight	Representativeness heuristic
Confirmation bias	Interactionist theory	Restructuring
Constraints	Intuition	Satisfice
Content	Irrelevant information	Semanticity
Critical period	Judgment	Sentence
Decisions	Lack of transfer	Somatic marker
Decision tree	Language	Surface structure
Deductive reasoning	Linguistic relativity	Syllogism
Deep structure	Loss aversion	Telegraphic speech
Deliberation	Means-end analysis	Thinking
Deliberative practice	Mental model	Trial and error
Displacement	Mental set	Uncertainty
Dual processes	Metacognition	Unnecessary constraint
Extralinguistic factors	Morpheme	Wason selection task
Fixation	Nativist theory	Wernicke's area
Functional fixedness	Overconfidence	Word
Framing effect	Overregularize	

ANSWERS TO CONCEPT LEARNING CHECKS

8.1 Defining Thinking

1. Because the stakes are high (you only go to college once in your life), this calls for the slow, deliberation mode of thinking.

2. Lunch is something you decide daily, so using a quick, intuitive decision mode will not have serious consequences.

8.2 Applying Methods of Problem Solving

1. Let me try to think of a good name for our team. How about Sunday Strikers? [A. Generate and test]

2. I will try 1-1-1, then 1-1-2, then 1-1-3, and keep going until the locker opens. [B. Algorithm]

3. This chemistry lab reminds me of cooking, so I had better measure each portion carefully. [D. Analogy]

4. I will get to my home in LA by first flying into town, then taking a taxi to the house. [C. Means-ends analysis]

8.3 Recognizing Heuristics in Decision Making

1. You might use representativeness to decide that someone in a coffee shop near campus looks like another student. This provides stereotypical guesses that are often correct.

2. Which have you done more often, brushed your teeth or brushed your shoes? Ease of access in memory works most times to tell us what has happened more often.

3. How you "frame" a decision ("You don't want to go to the party, do you?" vs. "Let's go to the party!") can lead to the answer you want to hear.

4. Choosing shoes that fit and look okay may be a good decision compared to continuing to hunt for the perfect shoe. (Fashionistas may disagree!) Satisficing helps by letting you settle for a "good enough" answer to meet your needs.

8.4 Practicing Reasoning

1. Content effects may make the concepts easy to understand but unclear in another setting. So make sure you can generate your own example of each concept.

2. Confirmation bias may lead you to look for examples showing you do understand the materials but not to test yourself in ways that show you do not. So be sure to really test yourself and not just read over the information and affirm that you know it.

3. Belief perseverance may make it hard to see the evidence that you are not performing well. So use some objective measures of whether you have mastered the material, such as asking someone to verify your definitions of key terms.

4. Overconfidence may lead you to estimate a higher level of mastery than you have achieved. So continue studying even after you feel confident you know it.

8.5 Features of Language

1. Dolphins showed semanticity by demonstrating use of semantics and syntax; Washoe the chimpanzee showed generativity in that she created novel sentences.

2. No evidence is provided that the animals described referred to things outside their current view, which shows a lack of displacement.

8.6 Multiple Influences on Language Use

1. This "word salad" statement shows a lack of meaning, associated with damage to Wernicke's area.

2. This self-description is typical of an individualist view of oneself, often found in Western cultures.

3. This statement reflects dialectical thinking, in which opposing views are held at the same time, more common in Eastern cultures.

4. This speech difficulty is associated with damage to Broca's area.

5. This view of time as "behind us" reflects an English cultural model with time as horizontal.

ANSWERS TO CHAPTER REVIEW TEST

8.1 Overview: What Is Thinking?

1. A. Rational thinking requires slow, deliberative thought in contrast to quick intuitive judgments.

8.2 Problem Solving

2. A. The definition of an algorithm is that it always leads to a correct solution when executed properly.

3. B. A heuristic is a "rule of thumb" that leads to a fast answer, but is not always correct.

4. B. Means-ends analysis attempts to "reduce the differences" between your current situation and your goal.

5. A. Mental set is a specific way of approaching problems based on your past experience, potentially causing you to miss new ways.

6. D. You don't normally use a penny as a screwdriver, so you are considering a new function rather than the "fixed" function it usually serves.

7. A. Incubation involves taking a break in your solution attempts so you can take a fresh approach.

8. B. Experts practice for 10,000 hours before reaching elite levels of performance in many fields.

8.3 Decision Making

9. B. Representativeness involves making judgments based on what things look like.

10. D. Framing is the story told about the information that can bias you towards a given focus.

11. B. Availability involves judging how likely something is based on how easily it comes to mind.

12. D. The decision tree method for making decisions involves identifying all of the options and what they might lead to in the future.

8.4 Reasoning

13. A. Looking for what we expect to see is a bias that confirms what we know rather than challenges it.

8.5 Language

14. C. Animals communicate, but there is limited evidence that they refer to things not present in the current environment.

8.6 Brain, Language, and Culture

15. A. Broca's area is involved in producing speech, and the Tan Man could only repeat that word.

REFERENCES

Ariely, D., & Levav, J. (2000). Sequential choice in group settings: Taking the road less traveled and less enjoyed. *Journal of Consumer Research, 27*(3), 279–290.

Arkes, H. (1991). Costs and benefits of judgment errors: Implications for debiasing. *Psychological Bulletin, 110*(3), 486–498.

Baltes, B. B., Dickson, M. W., Sherman, M. P., Bauer, C. C., & LaGanke, J. S. (2002). Computer-mediated communication and group decision making: A meta-analysis. *Organizational Behavior and Human Decision Processes, 87*(1), 156–179.

Bechara, A., Damasio, H., Tranel, D., Damasio, A. R. (1997). Deciding advantageously before knowing the advantageous strategy. *Science, 275*(5304), 1293–1295.

Boroditsky, L. (2001). Does language shape thought? English and Mandarin speakers' conceptions of time. *Cognitive Psychology, 43*(1), 1–22.

Boroditsky, L., & Gaby, A. (2010). Remembrances of times east: Absolute spatial representations of time in an Australian Aboriginal community. *Psychological Science, 21*(11), 1635–1639.

Braine, M. D. S. (1971). On two types of models of the internalization of grammars. In D. I. Slobin (Ed.), *The ontogenesis of grammar: A theoretical symposium.* New York: Academic Press.

Brown, R. (1973). *A first language: The early stages.* Cambridge, MA: Cambridge University Press.

Burnham, C. A., & Davis, K. G. (1969). The nine-dot problem: Beyond perceptual organization. *Psychonomic Science, 17*(6), 321–323.

Chase, W. G., & Simon, H. A. (1973). Perception in chess. *Cognitive Psychology, 4*, 55–81.

Cheng, P. N., & Holyoak, K. J. (1985). Pragmatic reasoning schemas. *Cognitive Psychology, 17*, 391–416.

Chi, M. T. H., Feltovich, P., & Glaser, R. (1981). Categorization and representation of physics problems by experts and novices. *Cognitive Science, 5*(2), 121–152.

Chi, M. T. H., Glaser, R., & Farr, M. J. (1988). *The nature of expertise.* Englewood Cliffs, NJ: Lawrence Erlbaum Associates.

Chomsky, N. (1972). *Language and mind.* New York: Harcourt, Brace, Jovanovich.

Cosmides, L. (1989). The logic of social exchange: Has natural selection shaped how humans reason? *Cognition, 31*, 187–276.

Davidson, J. E., & Sternberg, R. J. (1984). The role of insight in intellectual giftedness. *Gifted Child Quarterly, 28*(2), 58–64.

de Groot, A. D. (1965). *Thought and choice in chess.* The Hague: Moulton

Duncker, K. (1945). On problem solving. *Psychological Monographs, No. 58* (270).

Dunning, D., Heath, C., & Suls, J. M. (2004). Flawed self-assessment: Implications for health, education, and the workplace. *Psychological Science in the Public Interest, 5*(3), 69–106.

Ericsson, K. A., Krampe, R. T., & Tesch-Römer, C. (1993). The role of deliberate practice in the acquisition of expert performance. *Psychological Review, 100*(3), 363–406.

Ericsson, K. A., & Ward, P. (2007). Capturing the naturally occurring superior performance of experts in the laboratory. *Current Directions in Psychological Science, 16*(6), 346–350.

Fernald, A. (1985). Four-month-old infants prefer to listen to motherese. *Infant Behavior and Development, 8*(2), 181–195.

Frazier, L., & Rayner, K. (1982). Making and correcting errors during sentence comprehension: Eye movements in the analysis of structurally ambiguous sentences. *Cognitive Psychology, 14*(2), 178–210.

Fromkin, V., Krashen, S., Curtiss, S., Rigler, D., & Rigler, M. (1974). The development of language in Genie: A case of language acquisition beyond the critical period. *Brain and Language, 1*, 81–107.

Gardner, R. A., Gardner, B. I., & Van Cantfort, T. E. (Eds.). (1989). *Teaching sign language to chimpanzees.* Albany: State University of New York Press.

Gibbs, Jr., R. W. (1986). What makes some indirect speech acts conventional? *Journal of Memory and Language, 25*(2), 181–196.

Gick, M. L., & Holyoak, K. J. (1980). Analogical problems solving. *Cognitive Psychology, 12*, 306–355.

Gigerenzer, G. (2007). *Gut feelings: The intelligence of the unconscious.* New York: Viking.

Goldin-Meadow, S. (2003). *Hearing gesture: How our hands help us think.* Cambridge, MA: Harvard University Press.

Griggs, R. A., & Cox, J. R. (1982). The elusive thematic-materials effect in Wason's selection task. *British Journal of Psychology, 73*, 407–420.

Hakuta, K., Bialystok, E., & Wiley, E. (2003). Critical evidence: A test of the Critical-Period Hypothesis for second-language acquisition. *Psychological Science 14*(1), 31–38.

Hastie, R. (2001). Problems for judgment and decision making. *Annual Review of Psychology, 52*, 653–683.

Hillix, W. A., & Rumbaugh, D. M. (2004). *Animal bodies, human minds: Ape, dolphin, and parrot language skills.* New York: Kluwer.

Hofstede, G. (1980). *Culture's consequences: International differences in work-related values.* Newbury Park, CA: Sage.

Hong, Y., Ip, G., Chiu, C., Morris, M. W., & Menon, T. (2001). Cultural identity and dynamic construction of the self: Collective duties and individual rights in Chinese and American cultures. *Social Cognition, 19*(3), 251–268.

Iyengar, S. S., & Lepper, M. R. (2000). When choice is demotivating: Can one desire too much of a good thing? *Journal of Personality and Social Psychology, 79*(6), 995–1006.

Johnson-Laird, P. N. (2001). Mental models and deduction. *Trends in Cognitive Sciences, 5*(10), 434–442.

Johnson-Laird, P. N., & Byrne, R. M. J. (2002). Conditionals: A theory of meaning, pragmatics, and inference. *Psychological Review, 109*(1), 646–678.

Jung-Beeman, M. Bowden, E. M., Haberman, J., Frymiare, J. L., Arambel-Liu, S., Greenblatt, R., Reber, P. J., & Kounios, J. (2004). Neural activity when people solve verbal problems with insight. *PLoS Biology, 2*, 502–505.

Kahneman, D., Slovic, P., & Tversky, A. (Eds.) (1982). *Judgment under uncertainty: Heuristics and biases.* New York: Cambridge University Press.

Kahneman, D., & Tversky, A. (1972). Subjective probability: A judgment of representativeness. *Cognitive Psychology, 3*(3), 430–454.

Kaiser, M. K., McCloskey, M., & Proffitt, D. R. (1986). Development of intuitive theories of motion. Curvilinear motion in the absence of external forces. *Developmental Psychology, 22*(1), 67–71.

Kaplan, C. A., & Simon, H. A. (1990). In search of insight. *Cognitive Psychology, 22*(3), 374–419.

Kay, P., & Kempton, W. (2009). What is the Sapir-Whorf hypothesis? *American Anthropologist, 86*(1), 65–79.

Keren, G. (2007). Framing, intentions, and trust–choice incompatibility. *Organizational Behavior and Human Decision Processes, 103*(2), 238–255.

Kihn, M. (2005). "Outside the box": The inside story. *FastCompany, 95*, 40.

Klayman, J. (1995). Varieties of confirmation bias. *Psychology of Learning and Motivation, 32*, 385–418.

Köhler, W. (1929). *Gestalt psychology.* Oxford, England: Liveright.

Koriat, A., Lichtenstein, S., & Fischhoff, B. (1980). Reasons for confidence. *Journal of Experimental Psychology: Human Learning and Memory, 6*(2), 107–118.

Kounios, J., & Beeman, M. (2009). The aha! moment: The cognitive neuroscience of insight. *Current Directions in Psychological Science, 18*(4), 210–216.

Kruger, J., & Dunning, D. (1999). Unskilled and unaware of it: How difficulties in recognizing one's own incompetence lead to inflated self-assessments. *Journal of Personality and Social Psychology, 77*(6), 1121–1134.

Kunda, Z., & Nisbett, R. E. (1986). Prediction and the partial understanding of the law of large numbers. *Journal of Experimental Social Psychology, 22*(4), 339–354.

Kuo, W-J., Sjöström, T., Chen, Y-P., Wang, Y-H., & Huang, C-Y. (2009). Intuition and deliberation: Two systems for strategizing in the brain. *Science, 324*(5926), 519–522.

Lave, J. (1988). *Cognition in practice: Mind, mathematics, and culture in everyday life*. Cambridge: Cambridge University Press.

Lennenberg, E. H. (1967). *Biological foundations of language*. New York: Wiley.

Linden, E. (1993, March 22). Can animals think? *Time*, 52–61.

Linville, P. W., Fischer, G. W., & Fischhoff, B. (1993). AIDS risk perceptions and decision biases. The social psychology of HIV infection. In J. B. Pryor & G. D. Reeder (Eds.), *The social psychology of HIV infection* (pp. 5–38). Hillsdale, NJ, England: Lawrence Erlbaum Associates.

Lord, C. G., Ross, L., & Lepper, M. R. (1979). Biased assimilation and attitude polarization: The effects of prior theories on subsequently considered evidence. *Journal of Personality and Social Psychology, 37*, 2098-2109.

Luchins, A. S. (1942). Mechanization in problem solving—the effect of Einstellung. *Psychological Monographs*, No. 54(6). Washington, DC: American Psychological Association.

MacWhinney, B. (1998). Models of the emergence of language. *Annual Review of Psychology, 49*, 199–227.

Maier, N. R. F. (1931). Reasoning in humans: II. The solution and its appearance in consciousness. *Journal of Comparative Psychology, 12*, 181–194.

Maier, N. R. F. (1937). Reasoning in rats and human beings. *Psychological Review, 44*(5), 365–378.

Marcus, G. F. (1995). The acquisition of the English past tense in children and multilayered connectionist networks. *Cognition, 56*(3), 271–279.

Markus, H. R., & Kitayama, S. (1991). Culture and the self: Implications for cognition, emotion, and motivation. *Psychological Review, 98*(2), 224–253.

McGlone, M. S., & Harding, J. L. (1998). Back (or forward?) to the future: The role of perspective in temporal language comprehension. *Journal of Experimental Psychology: Learning, Memory, and Cognition, 24*, 1211–1223.

McGuigan, F. J. (1970). Covert oral behavior during the silent performance of language tasks. *Psychological Bulletin, 74*(5), 309–326.

Metcalfe, J., & Wiebe, D. (1987). Intuition in insight and non-insight problem solving. *Memory and Cognition, 15*, 238–246.

Miller, G. A. (1991). *The science of words*. New York: Freeman.

Moulton, J., Robinson, G. M., & Elias, C. (1978). Sex bias in language use: "Neutral" pronouns that aren't. *American Psychologist, 33*(11), 1032-1036.

Naqvi, N., Shiv, B., & Bechara, A. (2006). The role of emotion in decision making: A cognitive neuroscience perspective. *Current Directions in Psychological Science, 15*(5), 260–264.

Newell, A., & Simon, H. A. (1972). *Human problem solving*. Englewood Cliffs, NJ: Prentice-Hall.

Newport, E. L. (1990). Maturational constraints on language learning. *Cognitive Science, 14*, 11–28.

Nisbett, R. E., & Ross, L. (1980). *Human inference: Strategies and shortcomings of social judgment*. Englewood Cliffs, NJ: Prentice-Hall.

Nisbett, R. E., & Wilson, T. D. (1977). Telling more than we can know: Verbal reports on mental processes. *Psychological Review, 84*(3), 231–259.

Oyama, S. (1976). A sensitive period for the acquisition of a nonnative phonological system. *Journal of Psycholinguistic Research, 5*, 261–285.

Patterson, F. G. P., & Linden, E. (1981). *The education of Koko*. New York: Holt, Rinehart, & Winston.

Peng, K., & Nisbett, R. E. (1999). Culture, dialectives, and reasoning about contradiction. *American Psychologist, 54*, 741–754.

Pepperberg, I. M. (2002). *The Alex studies: Cognitive and communicative abilities of grey parrots*. Cambridge, MA: Harvard University Press.

Pinker, S. (1995). *The language instinct: How the mind creates language*. New York: Harper-Collins.

Premack, D. (1971). Language in the chimpanzee. *Science, 172*, 808–822.

Pronin, E., Lin, D. Y., & Ross, L. (2002). The bias blind spot: Perceptions of bias in self versus others. *Personality and Social Psychology Bulletin, 28*(3), 369–381.

Rassin, E., Eerland, A., & Kuipers, I. (2010). Let's find the evidence: An analogue study of confirmation bias in criminal investigations. *Journal of Investigative Psychology and Offender Profiling, 7*, 231–246.

Revlis, R. (1975). Two models of syllogistic reasoning. *Journal of Verbal Learning & Verbal Behavior, 14*, 180–195.

Rice, M. L., Huston, A. C., Truglio, R., & Wright, J. (1990). Words from "Sesame Street:" Learning vocabulary while viewing. *Developmental Psychology, 26*, 421–428.

Richards, B. J. (1994). Child-directed speech and influences on language acquisition: Methodology and interpretation. In C. Gallaway & B. Richards (Eds.), *Input and interaction in language acquisition* (pp. 74–106). New York: Cambridge University Press.

Rymer, R. (1994). *Genie: A scientific tragedy*. New York: Harper Perennial.

Sachs, J. (1967). Recognition memory for syntactic and semantic aspects of connected discourse. *Perception and Psychophysics, 2*, 437–442.

Savage-Rumbaugh, S., Shanker, S., & Taylor, T. J. (1998). *Apes, language, and the human mind*. New York: Oxford University Press.

Schwartz, B., Ward, A., Monterosso, J., Lyubomirsky, S., White, K., & Lehman, D. R. (2002). Maximizing versus satisficing: Happiness is a matter of choice. *Journal of Personality and Social Psychology, 83*(5), 1178–2119.

Schwarz, N., Bless, H., Strack, F., Klumpp, G., Rittenauer-Schatka, H., Simons, A. (1991). Ease of retrieval as information: Another look at the availability heuristic. *Journal of Personality and Social Psychology, 61*(2), 195–202.

Seifert, C. M., Meyer, D. E., Davidson, N., Patalano, A. L., & Yaniv, I. (1995). Demystification of cognitive insight: Opportunistic assimilation and the prepared-mind perspective. In R. J. Sternberg & J. E. Davidson (Eds.), *The nature of insight* (pp. 65–124). Cambridge, MA: MIT Press.

Silveira, J. (1972). *Incubation: The effect of interruption timing and length on problem solution and quality of problem processing*. Unpublished doctoral dissertation, University of Oregon.

Simon, H. (1955). A behavioral model of rational choice. *Quarterly Journal of Economics, 69*(1), 99–118.

Sio, U. N., & Ormerod, T. C. (2009). Does incubation enhance problem solving? A meta-analytic review. *Psychological Bulletin, 135*(1), 94–120.

Slovic, P., Fischhoff, B., & Lichtenstein, S. (1978). Accident probabilities and seat belt usage: A psychological perspective. *Accident Analysis and Prevention, 10*, 281–285.

Slovic, P., Fischhoff, B., & Lichtenstein, S. (1979). Rating the risks. *Environment, 21*(3), 14–20, 36–39.

Smith, S. M. (1995). Fixation, incubation, and insight in memory and creative thinking. In S. M. Smith, T. B. Ward, & R. A. Finke (Eds.), *The creative cognition approach* (pp. 135–155). Cambridge, MA: MIT Press.

Stanovich, K. E., & West, R. F. (1998). Individual differences in rational thought. *Journal of Experimental Psychology: General, 127*, 161–188.

Svirsky, M. A., Robbins, A. M., Kirk, K. I., Pisoni, D. B., & Miyamoto, R. T. (2000). Language development in profoundly deaf children with cochlear implants. *Psychological Science, 11*(2), 153–158.

Triandis, H., Bontempo, R., Villareal, M., Asai, M., & Lucca, N. (1988). Individualism and collectivism: Cross-cultural perspectives on self-ingroup relationships. *Journal of Personality and Social Psychology, 54*, 323–338.

Tversky, A. (1972). Elimination by aspects: A theory of choice. *Psychological Review, 79*(4), 281–299.

Tversky, A., & Kahneman, D. (1974). Judgment under uncertainty: Heuristics and biases. *Science, 185,* 1124–1131.

Tversky, A., & Kahneman, D. (1981). The framing of decisions and the psychology of choice. *Science, 211,* 453–458.

Tversky, A., & Kahneman, D. (1991). Loss aversion in riskless choice: A reference-dependent model. *Quarterly Journal of Economics, 106*(4) 1039–1061.

Vosniadou, S. (1987). Children and metaphors. *Child Development, 58*(3), 870–885.

Wason, P. C., & Johnson-Laird, P. N. (1972). *Psychology of reasoning: Structure and content.* Cambridge, MA: Harvard University Press.

Whorf, B. J. (1956). In J. B. Carroll (Ed.), *Language, thought and reality: Selected writings of Benjamin Lee Whorf.* Boston: MIT Press.

Wilkins, M. C. (1928). The effect of changed material on the ability to do formal syllogistic reasoning. *Archives of Psychology, 16,* 83.

Wilson, T. D., & Schooler, J. W. (1991). Thinking too much: Introspection can reduce the quality of preferences and decisions. *Journal of Personality and Social Psychology, 60*(2), 181–192.

Woodward, S. A., Markman, E. M., & Fitzsimmons, C. (1994). Rapid word learning in 13- to 18-month-olds. *Developmental Psychology, 30,* 538–553.

Yates, J. F. (1990). *Judgment and decision making.* Englewood Cliffs, NJ: Prentice Hall.

Chapter Overview ▼

9.1 The Nature of Intelligence
Defining Intelligence
Theories of Intelligence
Intelligence as a General Ability
Intelligence as Multiple Abilities
Expanding the Concept of Intelligence

CRITICAL THINKING APPLICATION
The Brain and Intelligence

CONCEPT LEARNING CHECK 9.1 *Comparing Theories of Intelligence*

9.2 Measuring Intelligence
The Development of Intelligence Testing
Alfred Binet: Predicting School Achievement
Lewis Terman and the Stanford-Binet Intelligence Text

The Wechsler Intelligence Scales
Group Intelligence Testing
Principles of Test Construction
Selecting Questions for Intelligence Tests
Standardization
Reliability
Validity

CONCEPT LEARNING CHECK 9.2
Understanding What Scores Mean

9.3 Individual Differences in Intelligence
Intellectual Disability
High Intellectual Ability

CONCEPT LEARNING CHECK 9.3 *Varieties of Intelligence*

9 Intelligence

Learning Objectives ▼

9.1
- Define intelligence from an adaptation perspective.
- Compare and contrast theories of intelligence.
- Explain how brain size and neural efficiency relate to intelligence.

9.2
- Examine the development of intelligence testing.
- Describe the principles of test construction.
- Discuss reliability and predictive validity of intelligence testing.

9.3
- Illustrate the varieties of intelligence including high intellectual ability and intellectual disability.

9.4
- Explain reasons for gender and ethnic gaps in standardized intelligence tests.
- Identify types of biases in intelligence testing.

9.5
- Describe the roles of genetics and environment, and their interaction, in determining intelligence.

9.4 Group Differences in Intelligence
Differences Within Groups and Differences Between Groups
Gender Group Differences
Ethnic Group Differences
Bias in Intelligence Testing
Cultural Bias in Intelligence Tests
Stereotype Threat
Expectations

CONCEPT LEARNING CHECK **9.4** *Expecting to Be Smarter*

9.5 Multiple Influences: The Roles of Genetics and Environment in Determining Intelligence
Evidence for Heredity
Evidence for Environmental Influence
Generational Changes: The Flynn effect
Environmental Differences

Summary of Multiple influences on Intelligence

CONCEPT LEARNING CHECK **9.5**
Understanding the Evidence on the Heredity-Environment Question

Mrs. Nola looked angry as she told me my intelligence test results. I had produced the highest score in my second grade class, but I had missed one question: "Can you hear cabbage boiling in a pot?" I had answered, "No." She scolded me, "Of course the answer should be, 'Yes!' Anyone knows that! You can hear the water boiling away!" A tear fell as I watched her turn and walk away. I did not dare tell her what I was thinking: "Yes, you can hear it boiling, but you *cannot* know that it is *cabbage* in the pot!" Even to my 7-year-old mind, my answer seemed more intelligent than hers. (Not that I am holding a grudge!) Ever since that day, I have been suspicious of tests that claimed to measure how smart I was, how much potential I had in school, and how likely I was to succeed in life. It seemed patently unfair to judge my intelligence based on whether I had ever cooked cabbage. Are intelligence tests capable of measuring true intellectual ability? And if so, what is "intelligence"?

9.1 The Nature of Intelligence

While we may perceive a basic intellectual ability in others, there is little agreement about what that entails.

- Define intelligence from an adaptation perspective.
- Compare and contrast theories of intelligence.
- Explain how brain size and neural efficiency relate to intelligence.

We are often struck by the intelligence of individuals around us. They may quickly figure out a math problem you are struggling with, or come up with a surprising idea you have never thought about. The variation in intelligence among people seems like a fact of life: Some are particularly "gifted," while others struggle with mental tasks you find quite easy. Are these apparent differences in intelligence real? Or is it possible that we are all operating with the same basic mental capacity, and the differences we see are due to specific knowledge, training, or experience? Often, and with little evidence, we believe that someone who excels in the classroom will also be intelligent in other areas of life. What have psychologists learned about these common assumptions?

Defining Intelligence

What do we mean when we say someone is "intelligent?" When people are asked to define it, they give answers such as, "profits from experience," "reasons logically," "knows a lot about the world," "well-read and well-spoken," and "does well in school" (Sternberg et al., 1981). The word derives from *intellect*, meaning the capacity for thinking and acquiring knowledge, especially of a high or complex order. Most commonly, we think of intelligence as a general capacity to comprehend and reason, emphasizing cognition (Spearman, 1904). Though they differ in emphasis, psychologists define **intelligence** as a very general mental capability involving the ability to reason, plan, solve problems, think abstractly, comprehend complex ideas, learn quickly, and learn from experience (Gottfredson, 1997a). This emphasizes the role of learning appropriate behaviors in intelligence. To be smart, we both avoid doing things that lead to failure and figure out which things lead to success in life.

When we say someone excels in athletics, we mean that they are good at particular sports; but we would also expect them to be better than average at any physical task. For example, an NFL football player may not be great at basketball, but he would likely be better than the average person due to his strength and conditioning. Similarly, with intelligence, we expect a highly intelligent person to do well in school, perform at the top of her or his profession, and make good choices in her or his personal life. It is

Intelligence The capacity to learn from experience, acquire knowledge, adapt to the environment, and solve problems.

surprising (and makes for big new stories) when someone accomplishes a high level of achievement, such as becoming a state governor, yet displays poor judgment in financial or personal matters. We expect an intelligent person to be well rounded in mental prowess so that he or she does well in every task.

We also think of intelligence as a capacity that stays with an individual throughout life. We think that a smarter child is also going to be a smarter adult, and a straight-A college student is more likely to become a judge. In fact, people tend to maintain the same measured level of intelligence throughout their life span, with very little measurable change even in middle childhood and early adolescence (Moffitt et al., 1993). Correcting for education, there is no drop-off in test scores on vocabulary measures, but a small decline on performance tasks in the oldest group (Kaufman et al., 1989) FIGURE 9-1. However, all of us go through changes in mental capabilities as our neural systems continue to develop in adolescence and well into our twenties.

Because we view intelligence as the capacity to adapt appropriately, we expect this ability to be beneficial in whatever domain a person enters. So we expect a future doctor to have good grades in high school, run his or her personal and financial lives successfully, and succeed if they switch to law school instead. But is there flexibility in intelligence? Are "smart" people smart all of the time and in all things? Or is there more variation, so that exceptional intelligence is shown in some areas but not in every arena?

Myron Rolle, 23, is a professional football player for the Tennessee Titans. He graduated from Florida State as a pre-med major in 2½ years with a 3.75 GPA.

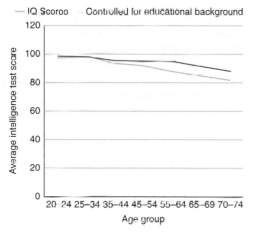

IQ Scores — Controlled for educational background

FIGURE 9-1 Scores from seven adult age groups (ranging from 20–24 to 70–74) in the WAIS-R intelligence test standardization sample, comprising a sample of 1480 men and women.
Source: Data from Kaufman, A. S., Reynolds, C. R., & McLean, J. E. (1989). Age and WAIS-R intelligence in a national sample of adults in the 20- to 74-year age range: A cross-sectional analysis with educational level controlled. Intelligence, 13(3), 235–263.

Theories of Intelligence

To answer these questions, psychologists have developed theories of intelligence. A central question is whether intelligence is best viewed as one core capacity or as a combination of different cognitive skills. For example, Albert Einstein is renowned as a physicist who invented the theory of relativity, Thurgood Marshall was a brilliant lawyer and Supreme Court justice, Marie Curie was the first person honored with two Nobel Prizes (in physics and chemistry), and Kenneth Wayne Jennings III holds the record for the longest winning streak (74 games) and highest money won (more than $3 million) on the game show *Jeopardy!*. Are these intellectual standouts demonstrating the same underlying "intelligence"? Psychologists have addressed this question by comparing how individuals perform on multiple tasks that vary in the type of cognitive skill required. Several different theories of intelligence have resulted (see **TABLE 9-1**).

Intelligence as a General Ability

Charles Spearman proposed that a **general intelligence (g)** capacity was the sole source of all mental abilities. Spearman gave individuals a variety of mental tasks to perform, including solving puzzles, running mazes, copying spatial designs, and forming verbal analogies (1904). While different people scored the highest on different tasks, Spearman noted that those who excelled at one task also tended to perform well on the others. So while some individuals may be more skilled in some tasks than in others, their performances in these tasks were moderately correlated. (Recall that a "moderate" correlation coefficient ranges from 0.3 to 0.7). This pattern of results led Spearman

General intelligence (g) Spearman's theory that all mental abilities reflect a single underlying capacity.

TABLE 9-1 Psychological Theories of Intelligence

Theorist	Major Concept	Key Points
Charles Spearman (1904)	General intelligence	A single, general intelligence capacity ("*g*") is the source of all mental abilities
Louis Thurstone (1938)	Primary mental abilities	Discovered a set of seven different factors related to varied task scores
Raymond Cattell (1963)	Fluid and crystalized	Discovered just two underlying abilities: fluid intelligence and crystallized intelligence
Robert Sternberg (1985)	Triarchic theory	Broadened Cattell's concept into three categories of intelligence: analytic, creative, and practical
Howard Gardner (1983)	Multiple intelligences	Proposed a theory of seven separate intelligence abilities operating independently
Mayer, Salovey, Caruso, & Sitarenios (2001)	Emotional intelligence	The ability to perceive, understand, integrate, and regulate emotions to promote personal growth

Ken Jennings III is the winningest game show participant in television history. In February, 2011, he played Jeopardy against an IBM computer program called "Watson" and lost.

Specific intelligences (s) Spearman's theory of performance factors only involved in each particular task.

Primary mental abilities Thurstone's theory of a set of seven different factors related to intelligence.

Fluid intelligence The ability to figure out relationships between new concepts within a given task.

Crystalized intelligence The ability to draw upon previously learned knowledge and skills.

Intelligence test A measure intended to identify the relative mental ability of individuals.

to conclude that there is a single, general intelligence underlying performance in all intellectual tasks. So a single "intelligence" score could be determined that will predict how a person will perform on any mental task.

Of course, this correlation between tasks is not perfect. Spearman also proposed **specific intelligences (s)** that accounted for skilled performance, specific to each particular task. Any cognitive task draws upon multiple abilities, some of which are unique to the specific task (such a pressing a particular key) and others that also apply to other tasks (such as detecting a stimulus). More recent work has shown that the single *g* score predicts success in many areas of life, including work, physical health, and accidents (Gottfredson, 2004). Simply by knowing someone's *g* score, you can estimate to some degree how well that person will do on a wide variety of tasks involving intellectual and personal-life outcomes.

Intelligence as Multiple Abilities

While Spearman focused on how similar people's performances were across tasks, others focused on how performances differed. Why are some people really exceptional in math and only above average on language tasks? Louis Thurstone (1938) set out to determine how many different types of mental abilities might exist. Thurstone gave college students many different tests capturing differing aspects of intelligence. He then compared their performances to see which tasks were correlated; that is, where an individual scoring high on one (say, mental arithmetic) also scored high on the other (say, geometry). Thurstone's results showed a set of seven different types of tasks, which he called **primary mental abilities**. These include perceptual speed, verbal comprehension and fluency, number, spatial visualization, memory, and reasoning. To predict how people might perform on a task, you would need to know their abilities in all seven areas.

Raymond Cattell (1963) performed further analyses and found just two underlying abilities: **fluid intelligence**, the ability to determine relationships among new concepts, and **crystalized intelligence**, the ability to draw upon previously learned knowledge and skills. The tasks used in assessing intelligence were separable into those that rely on past learning and those that require on-the-spot processing in a novel problem context (Deary et al., 2010). An example of a test of fluid intelligence is Raven's Progressive Matrices (Raven, 2000). This test is designed to require no specific prior knowledge to perform well. Crystalized intelligence captures the facts you learned over time. Cattell further proposed that crystalized intelligence would continue to grow with age, while fluid intelligence would diminish at older ages (Cattell, 1987) FIGURE 9-2.

Analytical ability is the focus of **intelligence tests**, designed to measure intellectual ability. Both Spearman and Thurstone's work involved tasks focused on cognitive components or mental steps, such as comparing two items or solving computations. For example, consider this analogy problem: "Lawyer is to client as doctor is to . . ." To solve it, you must determine the meaning of each word, compare the relationship between

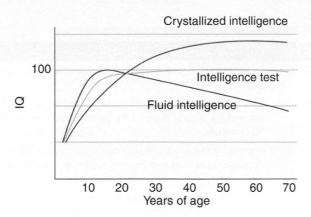

FIGURE 9-2 A theoretical depiction of intellectual abilities over the life span. *Source: Data from Intelligence: Its structure, growth and action (p. 206) by R. B. Cattell, 1987, Amsterdam: North-Holland. Copyright 1987 by Elsevier Science Publishers.*

lawyer and *client*, map that relationship onto *doctor*, and then generate the matching word. Intelligence would be revealed on this problem by how quickly you could perform these cognitive operations and select the right answer on a multiple-choice test (*patient*; Sternberg, 1985). Analytic problems come with all the information needed to solve them and have only a single right answer, which can be reached by only a single method. These theories focused on clearly "cognitive" tasks in which a stimulus is presented and the subject thinks and then produces a written or verbal response. So the intelligence displayed involves a limited range of tasks, all very similar to "schoolwork." But what if the tasks were expanded to include a wider range of problems?

Practical problems, in contrast, require work on formulating the problem, gathering information, and using your prior experience (Neisser et al., 1996). Sternberg's (1985) **triarchic** (three-part) **theory of intelligence** extends the concept of intelligence to include not just the mental operations you perform (**analytic intelligence**) but also the ability to vary your approach to problems (**creative intelligence**) and manage your cognitive resources (**practical intelligence**) to get the job done. Creative intelligence includes the ability to decide which information is relevant, how the old connects to the new, how to combine ideas in novel ways, and to see the "big picture" when faced with a problem. The third component in Sternberg's theory is practical intelligence, the ability to assess the situation and do what is necessary to be successful. Key aspects are identifying what is expected of you, knowing your strengths and weaknesses, and working effectively within the time provided. The ability to solve the problem may not be sufficient to be successful; instead, you also need to be innovative in how you approach a task and be smart about how you work on the problem.

Expanding the Concept of Intelligence

Other theorists have expanded the notion of intelligence to include movements, audition, and even "reading" other people. Seeing the genius of a speed skater or surgeon, it seems logical to extend the notion of intelligence outside of academic tasks. Most prominently, Howard Gardner (Gardner, 1983) proposed a theory of **multiple intelligences** in which separate abilities operate independently. Gardner proposed eight types of intelligence, including linguistic, logical-mathematical, musical, spatial, bodily-kinesthetic, naturalist, interpersonal, and intrapersonal (Gardner & Hatch, 1989; see **TABLE 9-2**). To Gardner,

Triarchic theory of intelligence Sternberg's theory positing three underlying aspects of cognition: analytic, creative, and practical.

Analytic intelligence Sternberg's theory posited the ability to break problems down into component parts for analysis.

Creative intelligence Sternberg's theory suggests an underlying component of applying mental abilities to your experience in novel and helpful ways.

Practical intelligence Sternberg's theory proposed the ability to assess a situation and do what is necessary to be successful.

Multiple intelligences Gardner's theory proposed seven separate types of cognitive abilities operating independently.

TABLE 9-2 Gardner's Multiple Intelligences

Type of Intelligence	Exemplar	Core Components
Linguistic	Poet, journalist	Sensitivity to the sounds, rhythms, and meanings of words; sensitivity to the different functions of language
Logical—mathematical	Scientist, mathematician	Sensitivity to and capacity to discern logical or numerical patterns; ability to handle long chains of reasoning
Musical	Composer, violinist	Ability to produce and appreciate rhythm, pitch, and timbre; appreciation of the forms of musical expressiveness
Spatial	Navigator, sculptor	Capacity to perceive the visual-spatial world accurately and to perform transformations on initial perceptions

(continues)

TABLE 9-2 Gardner's Multiple Intelligences *(continued)*

Type of Intelligence	Exemplar	Core Components
Body—kinesthetic	Dancer, athlete	Ability to control bodily movements and to handle objects skillfully
Naturalist	Botanist, chef	Ability to make fine discriminations among the flora and fauna of the natural world or the patterns and designs of human artifacts
Interpersonal	Therapist, salesperson	Capacity to discern and respond appropriately to the moods, temperaments, motivations, and desires of other people
Intrapersonal	Person with detailed, accurate self-knowledge	Access to one's own feelings and the ability to discriminate among them and draw on them to guide behavior; knowledge of one's own strengths, weaknesses, desires, and intelligence

Source: H. Gardner & T. Hatch, Multiple intelligences go to school: Educational implications of the theory of multiple intelligences, Educational Researcher, 18(8) (1989), with adaptation based on personal communication from H. Gardner (1996).

Emotional intelligence
The ability to perceive, understand, integrate, and regulate emotions to be self-motivated and socially skilled.

individuals like Einstein, Marshall, Curie, and Jennings are "geniuses" in different ways, and a single conception of "intelligence" is not adequate to account for the varieties of intelligence they display (Gardner, 1993). More recently, Gardner has expanded this list to include spiritual or existential intelligence (Gardner, 2000).

Others have expanded the notion of intelligence to include **emotional intelligence**, or the ability to perceive, understand, integrate, and regulate emotions to promote personal growth (Mayer et al., 2001). You may have the ability to notice how others are feeling or to recognize your own emotions and use that information to guide your thoughts and behaviors (see **TABLE 9-3**) (Goleman, 1998). And it is helpful to regulate your emotions by doing things that can improve your mood. Further studies have found significant correlations between tests of emotional intelligence and general intelligence (g) (Schulte et al., 2004; Schutte et al., 1998). While general intelligence is important, purely intellectual ability must be managed well in order to produce desired outcomes.

TABLE 9-3 A Test of Emotional Intelligence

Take this test to determine your emotional intelligence (Schutte et al., 1998). Rate your response to each item on a five-point scale, where "1" means, "Strongly disagree," "2" is "Disagree," "3" is "Neutral," "4" is "Agree," and "5" is "Strongly agree."

1. I know when to speak about my personal problems to others _____
2. When I am faced with obstacles, I remember times I faced similar obstacles and overcame them _____
3. I expect that I will do well on most things I try _____
4. Other people find it easy to confide in me _____
5. I find it easy to understand the non-verbal messages of other people _____
6. Some of the major events of my life have led me to re-evaluate what is important and not important _____
7. When my mood changes, I see new possibilities _____
8. Emotions are one of the things that make my life worth living _____
9. I am aware of my emotions as I experience them _____
10. I expect good things to happen _____
11. I like to share my emotions with others _____
12. When I experience a positive emotion, I know how to make it last _____
13. I arrange events others enjoy _____
14. I seek out activities that make me happy _____
15. I am aware of the non-verbal messages I send to others _____

(continues)

TABLE 9-3 A Test of Emotional Intelligence *(continued)*

16. I present myself in a way that makes a good impression on others _____
17. When I am in a positive mood, solving problems is easy for me _____
18. By looking at their facial expressions, I recognize the emotions people are experiencing _____
19. I know why my emotions change _____
20. When I am in a positive mood, I am able to come up with new ideas _____
21. I have control over my emotions _____
22. I easily recognize my emotions as I experience them _____
23. I motivate myself by imagining a good outcome to tasks I take on _____
24. I compliment others when they have done something well _____
25. I am aware of the non-verbal messages other people send _____
26. When another person tells me about an important event in his or her life, I almost feel as though I have experienced this event myself _____
27. When I feel a change in emotions, I tend to come up with new ideas _____
28. When I am faced with a challenge, I don't give up because I believe I will succeed _____
29. I know what other people are feeling just by looking at them _____
30. I help other people feel better when they are down _____
31. I use good moods to help myself keep trying in the face of obstacles _____
32. I can tell how people are feeling by listening to the tone of their voice _____
33. It is not difficult for me to understand why people feel the way they do _____

Scoring: Sum the number of your scale points for each of the 33 items. A higher score suggests better emotional intelligence, and a lower score suggests lower emotional intelligence. For comparison, some average scores for female prisoners: 120.1; men: 124.8; women: 130.9; therapists: 134.9 (Schutte et al., 1998).

Source: Schutte. N. S., Malouff, J. M., Hall, L. E., Haggerty, D. J., Cooper, J. T., Golden, C. J., & Dornheim, L. (1998). Development and validation of a measure of emotional intelligence. Personality and Individual Differences, 25, *167–177.*

Creativity Novel thinking in which we redefine problems, see gaps in knowledge, generate ideas, and take reasonable risks in implementing them.

CRITICAL THINKING APPLICATION

Creativity may be a very different cognitive ability than intelligence. **Creativity** has been described as novel thinking in which we redefine problems, see gaps in knowledge, generate ideas, and take reasonable risks in implementing them (Sternberg, 2001; Treffinger et al., 2000; Weisberg, 1986). Creativity involves combining and connecting ideas in new ways (Finke, Ward, & Smith, 1992).

Consider this problem: Design a new application (app) for a cell phone. Take a minute now to think about what problems you might be able to solve with an app, what enjoyment it might provide, and what desirable features could be added to a phone though apps. When you have generated several ideas, choose one and write it out, including a drawing of what it might look like.

Now, should you consider your proposed app "creative"? One of the most widely accepted definitions of a creative outcome is one that is both "novel" and "useful" (Amabile, 1996). Does yours meet both criteria? Usually, people feel that it is not too difficult to think of an app that would be useful. Imagine an app that would find the closest public restroom in the vicinity of the phone—very useful! But what about

novelty? Is your idea one that may already exist among the thousands of apps already available on phones? Or is it one that no one is likely to have thought of yet?

While we think of intelligence as a set capacity that does not change much over a lifetime, studies have shown that creativity can be trained in any individual (Scott et al., 2004). What can you do to improve your creative skills? Here is a set of suggestions drawn from research on creativity:

Find the problem. Studies of successful artists found that they did not just "jump" into creating; instead, they stopped, considered, and developed their ideas about what the "problem" really was (Csikszentmihalyi & Getzels, 1988). What essence or emotion did they want to capture in their art? For the app design, think

(Continues)

CRITICAL THINKING APPLICATION *(Continued)*

Many applications have been designed for cell phones. Can you create a new one, suggesting a novel and useful idea?

through how you use your phone and about the bugs or problems of everyday life with which it could potentially be helpful. Before you can create a "genius" solution, you need to deeply understand and then capture the problem.

Generate as many ideas as possible. You only need one really good idea for a successful business. But, to find one, it is best to first generate as many ideas as possible! Then, you can select among them to find the best (Smith, 1998). To do so, you want to try a wide variety of techniques and approaches. For example, you might think about ways that people used their home phones in the 1960s and then think of what people carry in their purses or wallets as ways to generate more ideas.

Break your "set." Psychological studies show that people have a hard time thinking of a *second* idea. Once the first becomes established, you tend to like it, and this becomes your "mental set" (Bilalic et al., 2010). As a result, you may get "stuck" on that solution and fail to see alternatives. So try to produce variation among your ideas by taking a set-breaking attitude. What if you *could not* use your cell phone? What apps does that suggest? Or what if you could only use it underwater? Try to switch the ways in which you think about the problem so that you can get to varied ideas.

Combine two very different things. Some studies have shown the power of analogies in creating new ideas (Dahl & Moreau, 2002). For example, think about ways animals communicate and what that may suggest for cell phones. Or use conceptual combination (Finke et al., 1992), in which you put two very different ideas together. For example, how could your cell phone serve as a kitchen? These techniques help you consider "far-out" ideas that do not come readily to mind.

Take a break and incubate. A final approach is to take a step away from the problem and come back at a later time. This period in which you are not working on the problem, called "incubation," may help by exposing you to information that may help in your task (Seifert et al., 1995). At the least, you will come back refreshed with a new approach to your problem.

Creativity is linked to intelligence because, certainly, some intelligence is required for the purposeful act of creation (Sternberg, 2001). However, the fact that creative potential changes with training, such as music lessons, cooking experience, and creativity programs, means it is not a fixed capacity. Instead, every individual can become more creative by practicing techniques like the ones listed above.

Now, about that cell phone app design . . . Try it again, with these ideas in mind!

The Brain and Intelligence

Cognitive theories have not yet explained the nature of intelligence. Can we gain any evidence about intelligence from studies of the brain? The long-standing assumption has been that "size matters": Bigger brains have long been thought to relate to better mental functioning. For example, researchers preserved Albert Einstein's brain, hoping to find that the great theoretical physicist would show different features in the anatomy of his brain. On autopsy, they discovered that Einstein's brain was actually a bit smaller than that of other men his size. However, they did find that the area of the brain devoted to mathematical thinking was 15% wider than in other comparison samples (Witelson, Kigar, & Harvey, 1999) FIGURE 9-3. This area was also unusual in that it lacked a sulcus, or cleft, seen in all control brain samples. Visuospatial cognition, mathematical thought, and imagery of movement are associated with this inferior parietal lobe area. And as it happens, Einstein said he came up with visual images and then translated them into the language of mathematics (the theory of special relativity, for example, was triggered by his musings on what it would be like to ride through space on a beam of light).

What about for the rest of us? Is brain size related to intelligence? The clearest evidence is that, in healthy people, total brain volume (measured using structural MRI) is moderately correlated ($r = 0.35$) with intelligence test scores (Deary et al., 2010). But is this true for the entire brain, or are there specific areas of brain function most related to intelligence? Based on a review of existing fMRI studies, Jung and Haier (2007) proposed that the parietal and frontal brain regions, along with the association cortex, show the

Albert Einstein, physicist and Nobel prize winner.

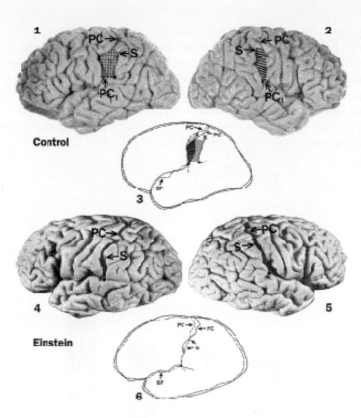

FIGURE 9-3 Comparison of a male control brain (1, 2, 3) and the brain of Einstein (4, 5, 6). Notice the relatively larger posterior parietal area.

greatest relationship to scores on tests of intelligence. These regions are thought to be connected by a special neural tract to facilitate communication between them FIGURE 9-4. Keep in mind that studies are correlational in nature, so how the quantity of brain tissue relates to the quality of cognitive functions is unknown (Deary et al., 2010).

However, when it comes to intelligence, size may be less important than efficiency in brain functioning. Neural circuits that link areas and offer fast movement of signals between areas may be important to intelligence. Deary and colleagues (2010, using functional neuroimaging findings) suggest intelligent brains process information more efficiently (that is, use fewer neural resources when performing cognitive tasks) than do less intelligent brains. So the sheer size of the brain may be less important than the development of interconnections between brain areas supporting intelligence. So brains

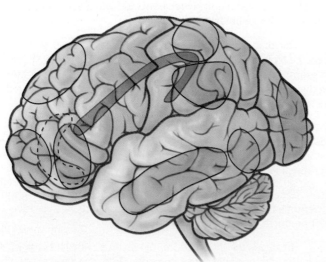

FIGURE 9-4 The brain areas correlated with intelligence (Jung and Haier, 2007). The yellow areas show left-hemispheric correlations, and in green, right-hemispheric correlations. The arcuate fasciculus (shown in pink) is a white matter tract that connects the involved brain regions.

of more intelligent people may simply work faster than the brains of others. Supporting this idea, research has found that the speed with which people can perform simple tasks is correlated with intelligence (Deary, Der, & Ford, 2001). The tasks include determining which of two lines is longer (called inspection speed; Deary & Stough, 1996) or pressing (as quickly as possible) one of eight buttons that is currently lighted. People with higher conduction speed also had higher scores on an intelligence test FIGURE 9-5. Brains that are better wired to pass along signals faster may be responsible for some of the differences observed in intelligence.

FIGURE 9-5 Performance by subjects ordered from slowest (1st) to fastest (5th)
Source: Adapted from Deary, I. J., Der, G., & Ford, G. (2001). Reaction times and intelligence differences: A population-based cohort study. Intelligence, 29(5), 389–399.

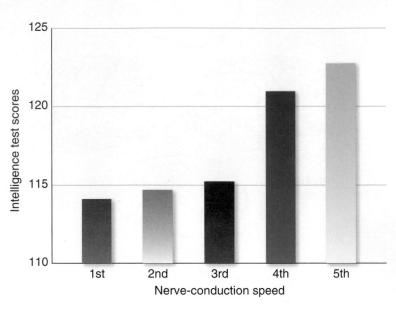

CONCEPT LEARNING CHECK 9.1   *Comparing Theories of Intelligence*

Several different theories have been proposed to account for the nature of intelligence. For each example below, identify the theory most related, and explain how it accounts for the example.

A. Spearman's *g*

B. Thurstone's primary abilities

C. Cattell's fluid and crystalized intelligence

D. Sternberg's triarchic theory of intelligence

E. Gardner's theory of multiple intelligences

F. Emotional intelligence

1. _____ Ben works part time as a bagger at the grocery store, where he excels in imagining how the individual items can be put together within the space of a paper bag to produce the best fit.

2. _____ Ellie is going on 80, and while she has slowed down some in her thinking, she can still quickly recall her knowledge of books from her years of work as a librarian.

3. _____ Thurman is undecided about his career direction, so while in college, he took the MCAT (premedical school exam), the LSAT (the prelaw exam), and the GRE (the graduate study exam). Thurman was hoping the tests would make his decision for him; however, he scored in the 95th percentile on all three exams.

4. _____ Katrina loves math and does really well in her math courses and on tests of mathematical ability. However, whenever the test involves verbal material, Katrina has difficulty reading and receives much lower scores.

5. _____ Sharan has a difficult time in her courses, but she excels in her entrepreneurship club and is able to come up with very creative ideas for products.

6. _____ Helaina is the "house mom" of her dorm: She loves meeting new people, learning about them, and connecting to them emotionally.

9.2 Measuring Intelligence

Tests are designed to measure intelligence, but what they measure is debatable.

■ Examine the development of intelligence testing.
■ Describe the principles of test construction.
■ Discuss reliability and predictive validity of intelligence testing.

Intelligence is one of the most debated topics within the field of psychology. One reason is that the stakes involved are extremely high. Many opportunities—such as attending top schools, selection for important jobs, and appointments to leadership positions—are reserved for the "most intelligent" candidates. Clearly, selecting intelligent candidates for medical school would make good use of human resources. But how do we determine who is most intelligent? Tests depend on underlying theories of the nature of intelligence, and as we have seen, there is little agreement on this question. As a result, intelligence is defined, practically speaking, as "whatever the tests test" (Boring, 1923). In this section, we will uncover the history of the intelligence test and explain the state of the art.

The Development of Intelligence Testing

Intelligence is a controversial topic because some people have tried to use intelligence tests for their own political agenda, claiming one group of people is superior to others. Sir Francis Galton (1822–1911), a cousin of naturalist Charles Darwin, noted that some families (including his own) in English society at the time seemed to have a wealth of intelligent individuals. This led him to suspect that intelligence was based on genetics. One of the problems with his reasoning is that most "intelligent" people he studied also happened to be well educated, while the less intelligent people he tested were often poor and not well educated. But which factor caused the other? Galton concluded that wealth and power were caused by intelligence, and one of his followers developed the idea of "eugenics," through which society could be improved by "weeding out" people who were not intelligent and encouraging those who were to have more children. It was suggested that some individuals of low intelligence should be sterilized, and such programs for developmentally disabled individuals ended as recently as 1981 in the United States (Sullivan, 2002).

Street scene in France, 1904, at the time of Binet's development of the first modern intelligence test.

Alfred Binet: Predicting School Achievement

The modern study of intelligence testing began with Alfred Binet (1857–1911), who was asked by the French Ministry of Education in 1904 to come up with a way to identify children who were "sub-normals." Binet and his colleague, Theodore Simon, collected a wide variety of tasks, including memory, math, vocabulary, and logical reasoning, focusing on schoolwork. He then tested many children on these tasks and found which ones predicted academic success. Binet selected 30 items of increasing difficulty for the test's final version. **TABLE 9-4** provides examples of the test items

TABLE 9-4 Items from Binet's Tests of Intelligence for Children

Year 3
1. Point to eyes, nose, and mouth
2. Repeat two digits
3. Identify objects in a picture
4. Repeat a sentence of six syllables

Year 7
1. Show right hand and left ear
2. Describe a picture
3. Carry out three commands given simultaneously
4. Count the value of six coins

Year 15
1. Repeat seven digits
2. Find three rhymes for a given word in one minute
3. Repeat a sentence of twenty-six syllables
4. Interpret a set of given facts

Source: Binet, A. & Simon T. (1916). The development of intelligence in children: The Binet-Simon Scale. E.S. Kite (Trans.), Training School at Vineland New Jersey, Department of Research No. 11. Baltimore, MD: Williams & Wilkins.

Males and females also differ in their *interests*, as measured by the field of study they choose during college: Women are more likely to choose a major in the biological or social sciences FIGURE 9-16. Lawrence Summers (2005), then president of Harvard University, suggested that the underrepresentation of women in science and engineering could be due to a "different availability of aptitude at the high end." However, psychological studies of children's school performance have documented that the observed differences in career paths may be due to social variables rather than intellectual ability. Math grades in middle school and students' plans to take more math courses are related to students' own estimates of their math abilities, their perceptions of the value of math courses, and their levels of math anxiety (Eccles & Jacobs, 1986). The students' beliefs, in turn, are related most strongly to the beliefs of their *mothers* concerning the difficulty of mathematics for their children. Stereotypes about genders play a significant role in whether students decide to pursue mathematics very early in life—as early as second grade (Cvencek, Meltzoff, & Greenwald, 2011).

FIGURE 9-16 Women tend to earn more degrees in the social sciences, whereas men earn more in the physical sciences. *Source: Data from the National Survey of Recent College Graduates, National Science Foundation, 2008.*

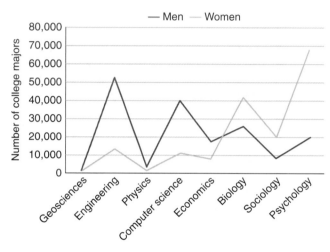

Girls tend to perform less well on math tests beginning in middle school, perhaps due to social factors.

Ethnic Group Differences

In designing intelligence tests, gender is presumed to play no role in predicting test scores, so the tests are designed to produce the same average score for males as for females. No such assumptions are made about the relationship between ethnicity or race and intelligence. Historically, the groups tested during the development of intelligence tests were located in France and in Northern California, and the ethnicity of the individuals tested was predominantly white or European. These same tests have been given to individuals all over the world, and as more data became available, people began to compare the scores of groups based on race. It is important to recognize that "race" has no biological definition based on genetics (American Anthropological Association, 1994). Instead, race is a social categorization defined—and self-defined—by social conventions based on country or ethnic origin, as well as physical characteristics such as skin color FIGURE 9-17. Any category combines some people that may not feel an affiliation, such as "Asian American" including people with diverse familial backgrounds in China, Japan, Korea, Laos, Vietnam, the Philippines, India, and Pakistan.

FIGURE 9-17 Estimated population of the United States by race and ethnicity, 2009. *Source: Data from the US Census Bureau, 2009.*

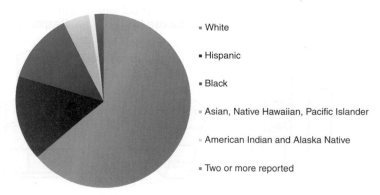

Because claims about ethnic differences have been used in racial discrimination in the past, any claims must be subject to very careful scrutiny (Neisser et al., 1996). Just as eugenicists argued that some races were superior to others, there are people today who claim that whites are "smarter" than blacks (Hermstein & Murray, 1994). To support their claim, they point out that the average intelligence test score for whites (100) is higher than the average score for blacks (85; Gottfredson, 1997a), called a **racial gap**. Rushton and Jensen (2005) recently stated that the difference in average scores remains as large today as it was 100 years ago. But on the most recent review of available data, this difference is smaller, with an estimate of 90.5 for black schoolchildren in 2002 (Dickens & Flynn, 2006). Because blacks have gained 4 to 7 IQ points on whites over the past 30 years, differences based on genetics are not likely to be responsible for the gap.

Environmental influences are social, cultural, physical, or family settings that affect an individual. Several lines of evidence support the role of environmental factors in lower scores for blacks. For example, one study followed children born to German mothers and American fathers working in the armed services in Germany after World War II (Eyferth, 1961). There was no difference between the intelligence test scores of children with white or black fathers. Other studies have attempted to compare intelligence test scores for blacks based on population genetics. African Americans average about 20 percent European genes, largely as a legacy of slavery. But the proportion of European genes ranges widely among individuals, from near zero to more than 80 percent. If the racial gap is mostly genetic, then blacks with more European genes ought to have higher scores on average. In fact, they do not: The proportion of European genes bears no relationship to measured intelligence among African-American children (Loehlin, Vandenberg, & Osborne, 1973; Loehlin, Willerman, & Horn, 1988). Finally, a study of black children adopted by white families (Scarr, Weinberg, & Waldman, 1993) found their intelligence test scores averaged 106, exceeding the national average for both blacks and whites.

Adoption studies identify another factor as significant in intelligence test scores—namely, socioeconomic status. When upper-middle-class families adopt poor children, they show a test score gain of 12 to 16 points. Because blacks are disproportionately represented in lower incomes, this factor may explain why average scores are lower. What about other groups? Hispanics' scores are typically between those of blacks and whites (Gottfredson, 1997a). Are there any groups scoring higher than whites? You might expect Asian Americans to score higher, based on their higher school grades and higher scores on achievement tests like the SAT and GRE (Neisser et al., 1996). However, in more than a dozen studies from the 1960s and 1970s, the average scores of Japanese and Chinese American children were around 97 or 98; none was over 100 (Flynn, 1991). One smaller group does have a higher average intelligence test score: Ashkenazi Jews average somewhere between 110 and 115. Across all of these groups; however, when you statistically control for factors like socioeconomic status and school quality, differences between group scores are not evident (Nisbett, 2009).

Bias in Intelligence Testing

While there are different types of intelligence tests, they all seem to measure the same underlying "intelligence," as shown by their high correlations. Some use words or numbers and require specific cultural knowledge (e.g., vocabulary), while others avoid this by using shapes or designs and simple, universal concepts (e.g., many/few, open/closed, up/down; Gottfredson, 1997a). Researchers and **psychometricians** (those who study the principles of psychological measurement) claim to produce a test that is fair and free of bias. Are they successful?

Cultural Bias in Intelligence Tests

Americans and other Westernized groups typically outperform members of traditional societies on intelligence tests, even those designed to be culture fair. But then, it is primarily Western science that has created the industry of intelligence testing, and the tests may provide an advantage to those from the same culture. For example, the 1937 Stanford-Binet test was used from 1937 to 1960 based on norms collected only with white children. How do cultural factors shape differences in intelligence test scores? Fagan and Holland (2002) tested blacks and whites on their knowledge and ability to learn and reason with words and concepts. The whites had substantially more existing knowledge of the various

Racial gap Differences on average test scores between groups associated by racial or ethnic definitions.

Environmental influence A factor in the social, cultural, physical, or family setting that may influence an individual.

Psychometrician A scientist who studies the principles of psychological measurement.

Though small differences are reported in group performance, environment is influential in the development of intelligence.

words and concepts, but when tested on their ability to learn new words, the blacks did just as well as the whites. When the tests used words and concepts known equally well to blacks and whites, on both comprehension and analogies, there were no differences. These data support the view that cultural differences in information and processes provided to children may account for group differences in intelligence scores (Fagan & Holland, 2007; Irvine & Berry, 1988).

If the children all live in the United States, where do cultural differences arise? The experience of individuals is different based on area of the country, schooling, socioeconomic status, gender, and race and ethnicity. Cultural environment includes how people live, what they value, and what they do with their time, which differs for each family. For example, in poorer black families, children are rarely asked "known-answer" questions (in which the asker already knows the right answer), such as, "What color is an elephant?" (Nisbett, 2009). These children may be confused by hearing this type of question at school (e.g., "Doesn't the teacher already know that elephants are gray?"). If the answer is obvious, then why is the question being asked? Even tests designed to avoid any cultural influences seem to be unsuccessful at doing so. For example, in one study, the Cattell Culture-Fair Intelligence Test was given to American, Nigerian, and Indian adolescents, and 59% of the items were found to be culturally biased (Nenty, 1986). Despite this fact, some researchers attempt to compare whole countries' average intelligence scores and draw conclusions about their economic prospects (Lynn & Vanhanen, 2006).

Even the ability to take intelligence tests depends on experience with formal schooling (Neisser, 1976). To college students, taking tests is second nature, and you are able to respond quickly to test items from long years of practice. If you hand your exam to a parent or grandparent, their lack of practice will make it more difficult for them to respond even if they know the answers. This is illustrated by researchers' stories of testing individuals from non-Western cultures without literacy experience. For example, Smith (1996) reported that his research team recruited native Mayans in Guatemala to participate in research on syllogism problems. The problems included fictional concepts (e.g., "sesamoid bones"), and the subjects were told to reason about categories. For example, "Fish have sesamoid bones. Birds have sesamoid bones. How likely are all animals to have sesamoid bones?" American college students answered the question easily, while one Mayan protested, "You are the one who knows about 'sesamoid bones,' so you tell *me* the answer." While the individual was capable of performing the reasoning, answering questions with made-up words was not a familiar task.

Achi Maya preserve traditional farming and building practices in rural Guatemala, but may score less well on tests involving school experience.

Stereotype Threat

Imagine that I ask you to take a math test right now. How do you feel you will do on it? Now, imagine I ask you to do so wearing either a bikini or a Speedo swim brief. Do you think you can perform at your best? In a study looking at how people feel when their body is "objectified" (they are made aware of others' perspectives on their body), students were asked to put on either a bulky sweater or a tiny swimsuit. Then, they took a math test wearing the outfit. Do you think this would make a difference in math test scores? After all, we have been discussing mathematical ability as a stable, reliable measure of intelligence. However, Fredrickson and colleagues (1998) found wearing a revealing swimsuit produced lower scores on a math test, but only for the female students FIGURE 9-18.

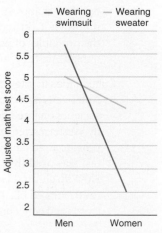

FIGURE 9-18 Math performance by experimental condition and gender. Means are corrected for guessing and past performance on standardized math tests. *Source: Reproduced from Fredrickson, B. L., Roberts, T-A., Noll, S. M., Quinn, D. M., & Twenge, J. M. (1998). That swimsuit becomes you: Sex differences in self-objectification, restrained eating, and math performance.* Journal of Personality and Social Psychology, *75(1), 269–284.*

They argued that making women more aware of others' views about their bodies (by wearing the swimsuit) drew their attention and disrupted their intellectual performance.

In the same way, our knowledge of stereotypes about ourselves (e.g., "girls are not good at math," "boys are not good at language," and "Asians are good at math") may alter how we behave when we face a test. Knowing what people expect of you may change how much attention you pay to the task, how hard you work, and how confident you are in performing at your best. Because Asian American students are aware of the stereotype, reminding them of it before they take a difficult math test can improve their performance on the test (Walton & Cohen, 2003). On the other hand, sometimes stereotypes are negative and can cause people to perform more poorly. Claude Steele and Joshua Aronson (1995) discovered that black students are affected by negative stereotypes about the racial gap in intelligence test scores. In their study, African American college students were asked to take a test containing standardized questions. Some were told the test was "an exercise in problem solving," while others were told it was a "test diagnostic of verbal ability," and thus related to intelligence. The students performed worse (in comparison to their prior test scores) on the questions when they thought the test was related to intelligence FIGURE 9-19. This phenomenon, called **stereotype threat**, was demonstrated in another study in which black students asked to indicate their race before a math test (activating the stereotype) performed more poorly than they had on prior exams. The scores of white students were not affected by being asked to indicate their race.

Steele and Aronson (1995) argued that thinking about negative stereotypes related to a task that you are performing creates stereotype threat. This is defined as decrements in performance caused by knowledge of cultural stereotypes. The negative impact of race on standardized tests may be caused, at least in part, by the knowledge that you, as a black student, are expected to perform poorly. Stereotype threat has been demonstrated in a variety of tasks and groups. For example, when a math task is described as "diagnostic of intelligence," Latinos and Latinas perform more poorly than do whites (Gonzales, Blanton, & Williams, 2002). White men perform more poorly on a math

If male, would wearing this swimsuit affect your performance on a math test?

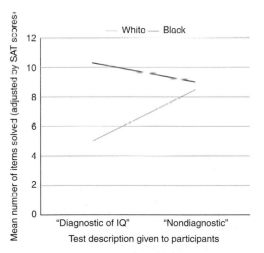

FIGURE 9-19 When African American students were told a test would be diagnostic of intelligence, they performed worse than their prior performance; however, white students showed no change. *Source: Reproduced from Steele, C. M., & Aronson, J. (1995). Stereotype threat and the intellectual test performance of African Americans.* Journal of Personality and Social Psychology, 69(5), 797–811.

test when they told that their performance will be compared to Asian American men (Aronson et al., 2005). And capturing another stereotype, whites perform more poorly than blacks on a sports task when it is described as measuring "natural athletic ability" (Stone, 2002). Stereotype threat is created by testing situations that raise concerns about your performance relative to that of others. When stereotypes lead others to believe that we are likely to perform poorly, we are more likely to do so. However, these effects can be reduced by reminding people of the positive characteristics of themselves or their group (Cohen et al., 2006).

When white students were told a test involved natural athletic ability, they performed worse.

Expectations

In addition to the test-taker's beliefs, expectancies, or expectations about performance, from other people may play a role in performance differences. In a groundbreaking study by Rosenthal and Jacobson (1968), the expectations teachers had for their students were manipulated. At the beginning of a school year, Rosenthal got permission from

Stereotype threat Performance decrements caused by knowledge of cultural stereotypes.

If female, how would you feel taking a math test in a bikini?

grade school teachers to administer a special test to their students. He told them these new tests would predict the development of intelligence in schoolchildren. Then, he instituted a specific manipulation: "Do not let this influence you," he said, "But I thought you would like to know that in your classroom, these students scored particularly high on the test. Their intellects will bloom in the coming year." In fact, there was nothing special about the selected students: Rosenthal chose them at random among the students in the class. But their teachers now expected them to show some sort of intellectual leap during the year. And they did! By the end of the year, the selected students' grades improved, and their performance on conventional intelligence tests greatly improved! How did the manipulation succeed in causing real changes in the students' test performances?

The explanation is that the teachers who heard that some of their students were about to "bloom" must have treated them differently. Maybe they spent more time with them, encouraged them, or challenged them more than the other students. So, as a result of the expectancies planted by Rosenthal, the actual academic outcomes of these students were changed. This effect is called a self-fulfilling prophecy, meaning an event that happens *because* you have predicted it. Rosenthal's finding is one of the most important in psychology, and one that should be recalled by every teacher and parent: You will get what you expect from a child! If a teacher's expectations can affect academic performance and intelligence tests for the better, they can also change them for the worse. If teachers expect that some students are not as intelligent, perhaps because of their ethnicity, social class, or cultural background, they may end up treating them in ways that lead to worse outcomes. All children are encouraged by adults expecting the best from them!

Teachers' increased expections for some individual students resulted in actual gains on intelligence tests for those students.

CONCEPT LEARNING CHECK 9.4   *Expecting to Be Smarter*

1. Based on the concept of stereotype threat, which of these situations is most relevant?

    A. A male taking a math test

    B. An Asian male taking a math test

    C. A female taking an intelligence test

    D. A Hispanic male taking an intelligence test

2. What was caused by the expectancies of the teachers in the Rosenthal study?

    A. They believed some students would "bloom" in class.

    B. Some students received higher grades.

    C. Some students improved on standardized intelligence tests.

3. Based on self-fulfilling prophecy, what should you tell yourself about your next psychology test?

9.5 Multiple Influences: The Roles of Genetics and Environment in Determining Intelligence

Both genes and environment contribute to intelligence, but the relationship is complex.

■ Describe the roles of genetics and environment, and their interaction, in determining intelligence.

We have seen that intelligence as measured by tests is a fairly stable characteristic of a person over his or her life span. But are the underlying causes of differences in intelligence a result of nature ("in the genes") or of nurture (the environment)? Let us examine the available evidence.

Evidence for Heredity

The relationship between heredity and IQ is continually debated within the field. **Heritability** is the proportion of the variance (differences between individuals) that is due to genetic factors. Note that heritability describes differences *between* people and cannot be applied to a single individual. People vary in eye color and blood type, and the variance in these traits is accounted for by genetics. But for traits like the specific religion you practice or the language you use, there is no genetic influence: These traits are not "heritable" at all. Instead, environmental factors determine how people differ. In the middle are traits for which there is a moderate genetic influence on the variation observed. Even psychological traits, such as how religious you are, how proficient you are with language, and how liberal or conservative you are, may be partially heritable (Pinker, 2004). The scale for heritability goes from 0, or not influenced at all by genetics, to 1, meaning completely determined by genetics.

How can we determine whether genetics or heritability impacts intelligence? We can look at people that are biologically related and see if their intelligence test scores are also related. Estimates of heritability come from comparing the intelligence test scores of blood relatives, such as identical twins (who share all of their genes), fraternal twins and siblings (who share half of their genes), and less-related family members. If intelligence is heritable, then the relatives of a person with a high intelligence test score should exhibit a comparably high score. Bouchard and McGue (1981), in a review of 111 studies, concluded the mean correlation of scores between identical twins was 0.86, between siblings, 0.47, between half-siblings, 0.31, and between cousins, 0.15. This pattern is what you might expect if genetics played an important role in intelligence: The greater the genetic similarity between two individuals, the more similar their intelligence scores FIGURE 9-20.

Heritability The proportion of variance (differences between individuals) in an observable trait that is due to genetic factors.

Twin study Examining the heritability of traits by comparing identical twins (who share all of their genes) to fraternal twins (who share 50% of their genes).

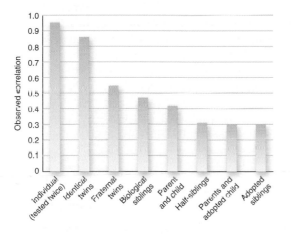

FIGURE 9-20 Correlations between individuals by family relationship.
Source: Data from Kaufman, A. S., & Lichtenberger, E. (2006). Assessing adolescent and adult intelligence (3rd ed.). Hoboken, NJ: Wiley.

Estimates of the heritability of intelligence range from 0.4 to 0.8 (Gottfredson, 1997a). This relationship is also seen in studies of brain structure in related siblings. Evidence from brain studies of twins shows a higher similarity in the patterns of cortical grey matter, made up of neuronal cell bodies. These studies suggest that genetic links in intelligence are caused by brain structure, which is determined by genetics. In FIGURE 9-21, the high heritability of grey matter is evident in identical compared to fraternal twins (Toga & Thompson, 2005). Genetic influences on brain structure may be the cause of the similarities in intelligence that arise from biological relatedness.

Evidence for Environmental Influence

If genetics alone determines intelligence, we would expect people within biologically related families to have very similar scores. But members of the same family can differ substantially in intelligence test scores (by an average of about 12 points). In fact, studies of twins and other blood relatives *also* show that environment has an effect on intelligence. These **twin studies** compare intelligence test scores for siblings that were raised together to pairs that were adopted by two different families. If two individuals are raised together, the correlation in intelligence test score is always higher than if they were raised or are living apart FIGURE 9-22. So the shared environment of being from the same family makes two people *more* similar in their intelligence test scores. And the scores of unrelated individuals living together are correlated at $r = +0.23$, while the scores of any two

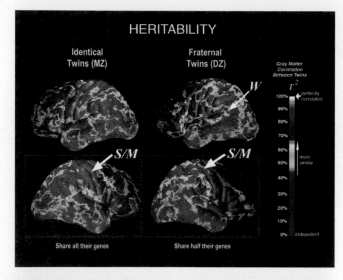

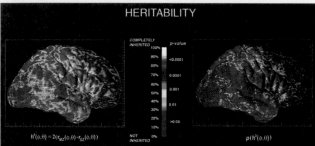

FIGURE 9-21 "Heritable" means that the correlation is greater for identical twins than for fraternal twins. Results show similarities from genetics appear in frontal and temporal lobe regions. *Source: Data from Toga, A. W., & Thompson. P. M. (2005). Genetics of brain structure and intelligence.* Annual Review of Neuroscience, *28, 1–23.*

Flynn effect The increase in intelligence test scores have (about three points per decade, across the globe) over generations taking the tests.

individuals at random are not correlated, showing a shared environment does affect intelligence scores. This data shows the importance of environment as well.

Studies of twins may overestimate heritability because we all share environment in important ways (for example, in the United States, we all attend school). That makes identical twins raised apart more similar because they share many elements of the environment *except* immediate family, but we count all similarity in twins raised apart as attributable to genes. To see this, imagine we all grew up in the same environment; then, all differences in intelligence would seem to be solely genetic. This is especially true for adoptive families, which Nisbett (2009) argues, "are all alike." Not only are they more affluent than average, they also tend to give children lots of cognitive stimulation and emphasize the importance of education. So, comparison data of those raised apart provide erroneously high estimates of heritability. Identical twins adopted into different families are raised with different parents, but in the United States, they attend the same suburban public schools, enjoy the same financial advantages, watch *Sesame Street*, and eat at McDonald's. The available evidence from intelligence test scores cannot separate out the contribution solely from genetics because some aspects of environment are always shared.

Generational Changes: The Flynn Effect

Another source of evidence that intelligence is not determined by heredity alone is that average intelligence scores appear to be changing over time. James Flynn noticed this trend, later termed the **Flynn effect**. Intelligence test scores have increased by about three points per decade, across the globe, for as long as there have been recorded tests (Flynn, 1984). Of course, the tests are repeatedly standardized over time, and this process resets the mean score to 100 again, so the increase is not apparent. But if 20 years have passed since the last time the test was standardized, people who now score 100 on the new version would probably average about 106 on the old (Neisser et al., 1996). If everyone alive today is smarter (by more than 15 points, a full standard deviation) than everyone alive in 1940, what does that tell us about the concept of intelligence, or at least its measurement?

FIGURE 9-22 Pairs of people living together are shown in blue bars, living apart in red; the difference indicates the impact of environmental factors. *Source: Data from Kaufman, A. S., & Lichtenberger, E. (2006). Assessing adolescent and adult intelligence (3rd ed.). Hoboken, NJ: Wiley.*

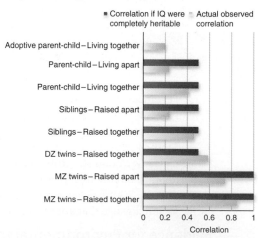

Flynn (1984) states that the fact that there are significant generational gains in intelligence means that the scores cannot be determined by genetics. The highest gains are on culturally loaded subtests with questions like, "How are dogs and rabbits similar?" Today, we are more likely to answer using abstract categories ("dogs and rabbits are mammals") than more concrete categories ("dogs and rabbits are pets"; Flynn, 2007). Our genes could not have changed enough over 60 years to create this difference in thinking; instead, it must result from environmental factors like education. As noted earlier, the difference between black and white average intelligence test scores has also changed over time, from 15 to less than 10 points. If intelligence changes within the population over a short period of time, environmental factors must be the cause.

Environmental Differences

What factors in the environment predict intelligence test scores? One clear factor is schooling: Intelligence is correlated at about $r = +0.60$ with the number of years spent in school (Neisser, 1996). In part, this may be because people with higher intelligence scores may enjoy taking classes and thus are more likely to stay in school. But education itself also has a causal effect on intelligence scores. Because of school year calendars, some children who are very close in chronological age just miss the deadline to enroll and have to wait until the next year to begin school. Children who make the deadline for entering school have higher intelligence scores than those who just missed it, even though they are nearly identical in age. So schooling, and not the extra year alone, accounts for the improvements in scores.

Another major influence from the environment is social and economic deprivation, experienced disproportionately by black and other minority families. When poor children are adopted by upper-middle-class families, they show a gain of 12 to 16 points on intelligence tests (Nisbett, 2009). Households without enough money to cover living expenses have children with lower intelligence test scores even when controlling for other factors, like education, race, and parenting (Brooks-Gunn & Duncan, 1997). Many other stressors follow with low socioeconomic status, such as poor nutrition, parental alcohol and drug use, younger age of parenting, less prenatal care, and lower birth weight. Lower-class children are also less likely to be breastfed, which offers a seven-point advantage in intelligence test scores if carried through for 8 months (Horwood et al., 2001). Moving households is also a source of instability: In inner-city schools, the turnover of children in a single classroom throughout an academic year can be as high as 100%. This means that, for the poor, improvements in childhood environment have great potential to bring about increases in intelligence. As Nisbett (2009) says, "If we want the poor to be smarter, we should just make them richer."

A. Japanese family's possessions. B. Malian family's possessions. C. Mexican family's possessions. D. South African family's possessions.

Nisbett (2009) also argues that parenting in upper-class homes is also very different: By the age of 3, children with parents employed professionally have heard 30 million words. With working-class parents, this drops to 20 million, and to as low as 10 million for black welfare mothers. Parents also speak differently to their children, with many more encouragements per reprimand (six) in professional homes, and a reversed ratio of two reprimands for each encouragement in lower-class families. When parents prepare their children to face the world they perceive around them, this may lead to very different ways of raising children, affecting their intellectual development.

Our unique, individual experiences may make the largest environmental contribution to intelligence. One of these factors may be birth order. You differ from your siblings because your family was very different before and after you joined it. For the first child, the average intelligence for the family combines two adults and one child; but, for a fourth child, the average now includes three other children. Research has shown that intelligence scores decrease as the number of children in the family increases and decrease based on order of birth (Zajonc, 1976). A recent study confirmed that this effect is likely explained through simple resource allocation: When there are more children, the resources will be more scarce for everyone compared with the firstborn (who gets all the attention with no competition); (Kristensen & Bjerkedal, 2007). Many other yet to be uncovered experiential factors may contribute to differences measured by intelligence tests.

Jenny Ferrill, of Danville, Ill.,
plays with her 2-year-old
quintuplets at their home.
The number of children in the
family may affect intelligence
by competition for adult
interaction.

Summary of Multiple Influences on Intelligence

The evidence provided from empirical studies shows that genetic contributions are one cause of individual differences in intelligence test scores. But what does it mean to say that intelligence is heritable? We think of genes as causing traits like eye color. However, genes also produce traits that require certain environments, actions, or triggers to be expressed. (Plomin, DeFries, & Loehlin, 1977). For example, a trait like shyness might be caused by genes but only observed when someone is alone with strangers. Further, even if genes are critical, we may be able to alter their impact (e.g., we wear glasses to correct vision) and prevent poor outcomes. At the same time, environmental factors also contribute substantially to the development of intelligence (Mackenzie, 1984). Just what those factors are or how they influence development is also not yet clear (Neisser et al., 1996). Attendance at school is certainly important, for example, but *which* aspects of schooling are critical? Clearly, early childhood development requires adequate nutrition and care, and exposure to learning environments seems to benefit all children. But once the basic needs of children are met, it is still difficult to predict children's intellectual potential.

Studies have attempted to compare the contributions of genetics and the influence of environment. For example, intelligence test scores are roughly five points higher if a child has highly educated parents (van der Sluis et al., 2008). But is this due to genetics or to the environment that parents provide, or are both required to produce higher intelligence? The childhood home environment can influence the extent to which genetic factors and environmental factors contribute to the differences observed in children's cognitive ability (van der Sluis et al., 2008). Findings with adults suggest that genetics plays a role across types of environment, while for children, genes and environment interact to influence intelligence (Tucker et al., 2011). In particular, the impact of genetics is more readily observed in poorer environments, while children from more affluent homes do well regardless of their genetic makeup (Turkheimer et al., 2003).

In sum, it is clear that intelligence tests measure something, and that it is related to school performance. Genetics plays a role in influencing intellectual growth, and environment plays a role in providing a supportive base for development. But do not forget the importance of expectancies, as seen in the Rosenthal study of classroom teachers. A related factor not yet discussed is self-motivation: You can control your school performance through more practice. In studies of middle school students, those who hold a "fixed" theory of intelligence are mainly concerned with how smart they are and prefer tasks they can already do well (Blackwell et al., 2007). They avoid tasks on which they may make mistakes and not look smart. In contrast, people who believe in an "expandable" or "growth" theory of intelligence want to challenge themselves to increase their abilities, even if they fail at first. One researcher, Carol Dweck, recalled a young boy who was a ringleader of the troublemakers in his class. "When we started teaching this idea about the mind being malleable, he looked up with tears in his eyes, and he said, 'You mean, I don't have to be dumb?'" she said. "A fire was lit under him" (Trei, 2007).

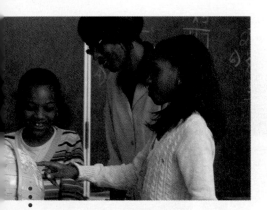

Teaching children to believe in their
own capacity to learn has benefits
for education and intelligence

CONCEPT LEARNING CHECK 9.5 | *Understanding the Evidence on the Heredity-Environment Question*

Heritability for traits in humans is estimated by comparing resemblances between twins. Fraternal (DZ) twins on average share half their genes, and so identical (MZ) twins on average are twice as similar genetically as DZ twins. A crude estimate of heritability, then, is approximately twice the difference in correlation between MZ and DZ twins. Refer to the data in Figure 9-20 to answer these questions:

1. How do identical twins differ from fraternal twins in the correlation between their intelligence test scores? Describe how the two correlations compare and what that says about heritability.

2. Environmental influence is shown by comparing twins raised together versus twins raised apart. How do identical twins' intelligence test scores differ based on whether they grow up together? Describe how the two correlations compare and what that says about heritability.

3. What do you conclude from this evidence?

Visual Overview Steps in Creating an Intelligence Test

Creating a new test of intelligence requires selecting test items, verifying them against a criterion group, establishing reliability and standardization, and determining whether the test has predictive validity.

1 Pick questions for the test

2 Test Against Criterion

Do "smart" students get it right, and "not smart" get it wrong? If so, include on test.

3 Establish Reliability

Test, retest, scores the same?

5 Validity

Does the test predict which students will succeed in life?

4 Standardization

Test with large numbers of people to refine, establish norms.

9.1 The Nature of Intelligence

- While we may perceive a basic intellectual ability in others, there is little agreement about what that entails.
- Charles Spearman (1904) proposed that a general intelligence capacity (called *g*) was the source of all mental abilities.
- Louis Thurstone's (1938) results showed a set of seven different factors related to task scores, which he called primary mental abilities.
- Raymond Cattell (1963) found just two underlying abilities: fluid intelligence, the ability to determine relationships within a given task, and crystalized intelligence, the ability to draw upon previously learned knowledge and skills.

- Sternberg's (2001) triarchic theory of intelligence placed intelligence within three categories: analytic, creative, and practical.
- Howard Gardner (1983) proposed a theory of multiple intelligences in which seven separate cognitive abilities operate independently.
- Mayer and colleagues (2001) expanded the concept further by examining emotional intelligence, or the ability to perceive, understand, integrate, and regulate emotions to promote personal growth.
- The speed with which people can perform simple tasks is predictive of intelligence.

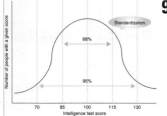

9.2 Measuring Intelligence

- Tests are designed to measure intelligence, but what they measure is debatable.
- The modern study of intelligence testing began with Alfred Binet (1857–1911), who created a way to predict school achievement in all children through testing.
- Binet defined "mental age" as the average level of intellectual development for a child of a particular age.
- The intelligence quotient, or IQ, was defined by Terman as a child's mental age divided by his or her chronological age.
- David Wechsler (1896–1981) created more efficient measures of adult intelligence called the Wechsler Adult Intelligence Scale (WAIS).
- Most tests include a wide variety of types of questions in order to tap intelligence in differing domains.
- Working memory capacity strongly predicts a person's performance on a battery of intelligence tests that measure everything from abstract problem-solving to social intelligence.

- Modern intelligence test scores, along with aptitude and achievement tests, are always converted from the number of correct answers to your relative performance compared to that of others on the same test, called standardization.
- The "normal distribution" for intelligence tests refers to the "bell curve" shape of scores falling around an average of 100.
- Reliability refers to repeating the measurement and getting the same outcome.
- Content validity (also called face validity) is how well they get at what we really mean when we say someone is "intelligent."
- Predictive validity refers to how well test scores correlate with intelligence as displayed in the world.
- Intelligence test scores predict school performance, the number of years of education you will complete, occupational status, income, and how well employees perform in their jobs.

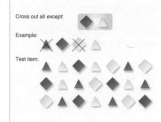

9.3 Individual Differences in Intelligence

- Intellectual disability is defined as an intelligence test score of less than 70 originating before the age of 18, and was historically classified into four levels: "mild," "moderate," "severe," with limited potential to learn to speak; and "profound," requiring complete care.

- The origins of intellectual disability include a wide range of physical causes, but about 75% of cases cannot be linked to any physical cause, and may be due to socioeconomic, cultural, or environmental factors in early childhood.

- Savants are individuals who are average (or even deficient) in most areas of cognitive functioning but display an extraordinary talent in one area.

- A prodigy is defined as a child with a special skill or talent far exceeding the norm for his or her age.

- Terman's study found that high-scoring students were also more athletic, healthy, socially well adjusted, and emotionally stable; however, they did not become famous for their career successes.

- Geniuses are defined within domains rather than universally, are very productive, work hard over a long period of time (more than 10 years), and have long careers.

9.4 Group Differences in Intelligence

- Designed to compare individuals, intelligence test scores have sometimes been used to compare groups of people.

- There is always variation (differences between individuals) within a given group, and that variation far outweighs the differences between groups.

- There is absolutely *no* difference between the mean intelligence test scores for males and females, but there are more males than females that score in the extreme ends of the intelligence score distribution (above 130 or below 70).

- Women tend to do better than men on some verbal tasks, including spelling, writing, and pronouncing words.

- Boys surpass girls (on average) in tests of math (after grade school) and on spatial tasks.

- Historically, the groups used to develop intelligence tests were predominantly white or Eastern European.

- Tests find the average IQ score for whites (100) is higher than the average score for blacks (85). However, holding economic status and school quality constant, there is little difference between group IQ scores.

- Adoption studies suggest the differences in intelligence test score averages may be based on environmental factors.

- Our knowledge of stereotypes about us ("girls are not good at math," "boys are not good at language," and "Asians are good at math") may alter how we behave when we face a test.

- The teachers who heard that some of their students were about to "bloom" intellectually expected they would do so, treated them differently, and they did.

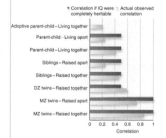

9.5 Multiple Influences: The Roles of Genetics and Environment in Determining Intelligence

- Both genes and environment contribute to intelligence, but the relationship is complex.

- If intelligence is heritable (that is, based on genetics alone), then the heritability, or the correlation of phenotype (the gene's behavioral expression) and genotype (squared), would be 1.0; but, estimates of the heritability of intelligence range from 0.4 to 0.8.

- Flynn effect: IQ scores have increased by about three points per decade, across the globe, for as long as there have been recorded tests.

- Intelligence is correlated at about $r = +0.6$ with the number of years spent in school.

- When poor children are adopted by upper-middle-class families, they show a gain of 12 to 16 points on intelligence tests.

- Genetics plays a role in influencing intellectual growth, and environment plays a role in providing a supportive base for intellectual development.

9.1 The Nature of Intelligence

1. A person who scores equally high on several different intelligence test measures, such as mathematical, verbal, musical, emotional, the ACT, and the Stanford-Binet, provides evidence for:
   A. general intelligence (*g*).
   B. Gardner's multiple intelligences.
   C. specific intelligence (*s*).
   D. savants.

2. Raymond Cattell's (1963) theory of intelligence identified just two abilities underlying intelligence: fluid intelligence, the ability to determine relationships within a given task, and:
   A. specific intelligence (*s*).
   B. crystalized intelligence.
   C. primary mental abilities.
   D. creative intelligence.

3. Sam's intelligence is described as "bodily kinesthetic." Which theory of intelligence is referred to here?
   A. general intelligence (*g*)
   B. Gardner's multiple intelligences
   C. Sternberg's triarchic theory
   D. Emotional intelligence

4. Sternberg's triarchic theory of intelligence includes creative intelligence, practical intelligence, and:
   A. analytical intelligence.
   B. emotional intelligence.
   C. logico-mathematical intelligence.
   D. spatial intelligence.

9.2 Measuring Intelligence

5. If your intelligence quotient is 100 as measured with the Stanford-Binet test, you have a "mental age" that is:
   A. determined to be above average.
   B. different than your chronological age.
   C. the same as your chronological age.
   D. determined to be below average.

6. According to providers of tests like the Wechsler, WAIS, GRE, SAT, and ACT, modern psychological tests of intelligence are now designed to provide all of the following *except*:
   A. standardization.
   B. validity.
   C. reliability.
   D. mental age.

7. Susan scores a 520 on the math GRE. She studies for 6 months and retakes it, to score a 520. This example suggests the GRE score is:
   A. standardized.
   B. reliable.
   C. valid.
   D. biased against women.

8. You take a test today that measures your willingness to help others. Next month, you take the same test and get the same score. This illustrates the technique used to measure:
   A. test-retest reliability.
   B. criterion validity.
   C. content validity.
   D. split-half reliability.

9. Intelligence tests are most accurate when used to predict:
   A. practical decision-making.
   B. academic performance.
   C. parenting skills.
   D. job success.

9.3 Individual Differences in Intelligence

10. Intellectual disability is defined as scoring below _____ on intelligence tests.
    A. 100
    B. 70
    C. 30
    D. 120

11. In addition to tests of intelligence, advocates for the intellectually disabled suggest measuring:
    A. literacy.
    B. cognition.
    C. adaptive behavior.
    D. mental health.

12. According to Simonton (2009), the cases of "genius" he studied show that:
    A. genius is a collective recognition, like a school of art.
    B. genius is universal, with excellence across many domains.
    C. geniuses are not very productive, often producing one great work.
    D. geniuses tend to have long careers, peaking around age 40.

9.4 Group Differences in Intelligence

13. In Rosenthal's study of school performance, he told teachers which of their students were "on the verge of blooming" intellectually. At the end of the year, his findings showed that:

A. teachers' expectations led to greater learning for those students.

B. his intelligence test was in fact able to identify conceptual "blooming" in children.

C. standardized tests were not a valid measure of student achievement.

D. students' actual learning was not related to their teacher's expectations.

14. A student is asked to report her gender at the top of a mathematics test. Based on "stereotype threat" research, doing this will very likely:

A. boost her performance on the test.

B. hinder her performance on the test.

C. have no effect on her performance.

D. lower her stress level.

9.5 Multiple Influences: The Roles of Genetics and Environment in Determining Intelligence

15. Factors that significantly impact intelligence test scores include all of these *except*:

A. academic achievement.

B. socioeconomic status.

C. gender.

D. genetics.

16. The highest correlation between two individuals' intelligence test scores is found when the two are:

A. fraternal twins raised together.

B. nonbiological siblings.

C. identical twins raised apart.

D. biological parent and child.

17. The Flynn effect refers to finding that the intelligence tests scores for every generation since 1920 have:

A. gone up steadily.

B. stayed at the average score of 100.

C. gone down due increases in poverty levels.

D. showed differences between ethnic groups.

CHAPTER DISCUSSION QUESTIONS

1. Imagine that you are a teacher for first-grade children who are just beginning to learn how to read, write, and do mathematical operations. Evaluate the pros and cons of at least three theories of intelligence in helping you understand how to teach your students. As with all classes of students, you should expect a wide range of strengths and weaknesses in the group.

2. IQ-like tests are sometimes used during the hiring process for different businesses, where the skills needed for the job are assessed in the test. Imagine that you are the person making hiring decisions for wait staff in a restaurant and you are using an IQ-like test to make your decisions. Differentiate the errors that you would make if your test was not reliable versus if it was not valid. What problems might you find in your wait staff if you hired based on a nonreliable test versus a nonvalid test?

3. We can see in Section 9.4 that environment plays a role for most all group differences in intelligence, lowering scores for some groups. Relate this difference in scores to differences in life outcomes. In other words, if someone is at risk for a lower IQ score due to environmental circumstances, what areas of his/her life are likely to be affected?

4. Section 9.5 reviews evidence for both heredity and environment in intelligence. Assess the role of heredity and environment in determining IQ scores. Do heredity and environment always have the same relative importance in determining IQ? In other words, does heredity play a bigger role for some groups versus others? Or is the role of heredity and environment always about the same for everyone?

CHAPTER PROJECT

1. Design your own intelligence text. What are example items that you feel truly capture what we mean by "intelligence"? Write ten example questions and answers. Then, give your exam to three people, and determine whether there are any differences in performance. What elements of your test were successful, and which were less so? Why is creating an intelligence test so difficult?

2. View a movie tackling the issues of life for a person with intellectual disability. Are there any aspects of the depiction that surprised you? What issues are raised about personal independence and the right of self-determination?

CHAPTER KEY TERMS

Achievement test	Emotional intelligence	Intellectual disability
Adaptive behavior	Environmental influence	Intelligence
Analytic intelligence	Fluid intelligence	Intelligence quotient (IQ)
Aptitude test	Flynn effect	Intelligence test
Content validity	General intelligence (*g*)	Mental age
Creative intelligence	Genius	Multiple intelligences
Creativity	Gifted	Norm
Crystalized intelligence	Group aptitude test	Practical intelligence
Down syndrome	Heritability	Predictive validity

Primary mental abilities
Prodigy
Psychometrician
Racial gap
Reliability
Savant syndrome
Scale

Specific intelligences (*s*)
Split-half reliability
Standardized procedure
Standardization
Stanford-Binet Scale
Stereotype threat
Test-retest reliability

Triarchic theory of intelligence
Twin study
Validity
Wechsler Adult Intelligence
   Scale (WAIS)
Working memory capacity

ANSWERS TO CONCEPT LEARNING CHECKS

9.1 Comparing Theories of Intelligence

1. Spatial intelligence is proposed as a separate ability in Gardner's multiple intelligences theory to account for individuals' exceptional performance on visual imagination tasks.

2. Cattell's theory distinguished fluid intelligence, or the processing of information, from crystalized intelligence, or the recall of knowledge and skills learned in the past. Ellie is able to make good use of her previous knowledge, but shows decreased functioning in fluid intelligence with age.

3. Spearman's theory of g, or general intelligence, says that there is a single underlying intellectual capacity that is reflected in all tests of cognition. His theory predicts that someone who scores high on one of these tests will likely score high on the others.

4. Thurstone's theory of primary abilities recognizes different specialized abilities that comprise intelligence. So Katrina might excel in math and do less well on tests of verbal comprehension and fluency.

5. Sharan shows great creativity. This skill is posited by Sternberg as one of the core intelligences in his triarchic theory of intelligence.

6. Helaina's ability to make interpersonal connections is an ability described in two different theories: Gardner's multiple intelligences theory includes interpersonal intelligence, and the theory of emotional intelligence describes a similar ability to "read" other people's emotions and make connections to them.

9.2 Understanding What Scores Mean

Question 1

A. A score of 100 is exactly at the average and median score of the population; 50% score higher and 50% score lower.

B. A score of 115 falls at one standard deviation above the mean; 84% of people score lower than Susan.

C. A score of 70 falls at two standard deviations below the mean; more than 97% of people score higher than Bill.

D. A score of 170 is very high, with less than 1 in 1,000 people scoring higher than Kate.

Question 2

A. Intelligence tests are much more refined in terms of reliability. The tests are very consistent across time, so

that the same person scores similarly when he or she retakes the test, and the test items are consistent across the test.

B. Validity is much more difficult to achieve with testing.

Question 3

Content validity asks whether the items appear on the surface to capture what is meant by "intelligence." Predictive validity is whether the test captures the intended outcomes the tests are designed to assess; for example, college success and career achievement.

9.3 Varieties of Intelligence

1. Mensa [C. Gifted]

2. Carl Friedrich Gauss [B. Prodigy]

3. Gottfried Mind [A. Savant]

4. Leonardo di ser Piero da Vinci [D. Genius]

9.4 Expecting to Be Smarter

1. Only item D reflects stereotype threat, because the concept only applies when the test taker expects the test to confirm a negative stereotype about him or her.

2. All three outcomes were caused by the teachers' expectancies, showing their beliefs actually created better intellectual development in the students.

3. You should expect that you will work hard and learn the concepts well and then do well on the test. Believing this will make it more likely to happen!

9.5 Understanding the Evidence on the Heredity-Environment Question

1. The correlation for identical twins (around +0.80) is larger than the correlation for fraternal twins (+.45). So the difference between these two correlations shows heritability.

2. The correlation for identical twins raised together is about +0.85, and raised apart, about +0.75. So intelligence is somewhat less correlated when raised apart. So the size of contribution from nongenetic factors is small.

3. The correlations are larger for biological relatedness, and being raised in different environments has a small effect.

ANSWERS TO CHAPTER REVIEW TEST

9.1 The Nature of Intelligence

1. A. Rationale: Spearman's theory holds that one major factor accounts for the display of intelligence across different tasks.

2. B. Rationale: Cattell posited fluid intelligence relating to processing new information, and crystalized intelligence reflected what is already stored in memory.

3. B. Rationale: Gardner's multiple intelligences theory included a variety of types of intelligence offered in no other theories.

4. A. Rationale: Sternberg's third component is the analytical ability posited in most theories.

9.2 Measuring Intelligence

5. C. Rationale: Your intelligence quotient is your mental age divided by your chronological age; for example, a 9-year-old who tests at the level of other 9-year-olds would have an IQ of 100.

6. D. Rationale: Mental age is no longer measured by modern tests.

7. B. Rationale: Reliability means scoring about the same when the same person takes the test at a different time.

8. A. Rationale: This illustrates taking the test and then retesting, so it is a measure of test-retest reliability.

9. B. Rationale: Intelligence tests are much like school tests, so it is not surprising that they predict who will do well on school tasks.

9.3 Individual Differences in Intelligence

10. B. Rationale: Individuals scoring lower than a 70 are two standard deviations below the average of 100, and so are a small proportion of the population.

11. C. Rationale: Rather than skill at tests, the ability to adapt to situations is critical for living independently.

12. D. Rationale: The body of work recognized as "genius" seems to require a long career within a field.

9.4 Group Differences in Intelligence

13. A. Rationale: The teachers were given false information about their students' test scores, but their belief in them caused the teachers to expect certain performance from those students, and they lived up to those expectations.

14. B. Rationale: A female knows that girls tend to score lower in math, so she may feel threatened by the test and perform worse than her best.

9.5 Multiple Influences: The Roles of Genetics and Environment in Determining Intelligence

15. C. Rationale: Intelligence tests are designed so that the average for both males and females is the same.

16. C. Rationale: Genetics play a large role in intelligence as measured by current tests.

17. A. Rationale: The increase in test scores every 10 years shows the population as a whole is getting "smarter" (or more educated) based on current intelligence tests.

REFERENCES

Ackerman, P. L., Beier, M. E., & Boyle, M. O. (2005). Working memory and intelligence: The same or different constructs? *Psychological Bulletin, 131*(1), 30–60.

Alon, S., & Tienda, M. (2007). Diversity, opportunity, and the shifting meritocracy in higher education. *American Sociological Review, 72,* 487–511.

Amabile, T. M. (1996). *Creativity in context: Update to the social psychology of creativity.* Boulder, CO: Westview Press.

American Anthropological Association. (1994). Statement on "race" and intelligence. http://www.aaanet.org/stmts/race.htm

Aronson, J., Fried, C. B., & Good, C. (2005). Reducing the effects of stereotype threat on African American college students by shaping theories of intelligence. *Journal of Experimental Social Psychology, 38,* 113–125.

Barnett, W. S. (1995). Long-term effects of early childhood programs on cognitive and school outcomes. *The Future of Children, 5*(3), Long-Term Outcomes of Early Childhood Programs, 25–50.

Batty, G. D., Whitley, E., Deary, I. J., Gale, C. R., Tynelius, P., & Rasmussen, F. (2011). Psychosis alters association between IQ and future risk of attempted suicide: Cohort study of 1,109,475 Swedish men. *British Medical Journal, 340,* 1348.

Bilalic, M., McLeod, P., & Gobet, F. (2010). The mechanism of the Einstellung (Set) Effect: A pervasive source of cognitive bias. *Current Directions in Psychological Science, 19,* 111–115.

Blackwell, L. S., Trzesniewski, K. H., & Dweck, C. S. (2007). Implicit theories of intelligence predict achievement across an adolescent transition: A longitudinal study and an intervention. *Child Development, 78*(1), 246–263.

Blumer, D. (2002). The illness of Vincent van Gogh. *American Journal of Psychiatry, 159,* 519–526.

Boring, E. G. (1923). Intelligence as the tests test it. *New Republic, 35,* 35–37.

Bouchard, T. J., & McGue, M. (1981). Familial studies of intelligence: A review. *Science, 212*(4498), 1055–1059.

Brooks-Gunn, J., & Duncan, G. J. (1997). The effects of poverty on children. *The Future of Children, 7*(2), 55–71.

Cattell, R. B. (1949). *The culture-free intelligence test.* Champaign, IL: Institute for Personality and Ability Testing.

Cattell, R. B. (1963). Theory of crystalized and fluid intelligence: A critical experiment. *Journal of Educational Psychology, 54,* 1–22.

Cattell, R. B. (1987). *Intelligence: Its structure, growth and action* (p. 206). Amsterdam: Elsevier Science Publishers.

Cohen G. L., Garcia, J., Apfel, N., & Master, A. (2006). Reducing the racial achievement gap: A social-psychological intervention. *Science, 313*(5791), 1307–1310.

Csikszentmihalyi, M., & Getzels, J. W. (1988). Creativity and problem finding in art. In F. Farley & R. Neperud (Eds.), *The foundations of aesthetics, art, and art education* (pp. 91–116). New York: Praeger.

Cvencek, D., Meltzoff, A. N., & Greenwald, A. G. (2011). Math–gender stereotypes in elementary school children. *Child Development,* 766–779.

Dahl, D. W., & Moreau, P. (2002). The influence and value of analogical thinking during new product ideation. *Journal of Marketing Research, 39,* 47–60.

Darlington, R. B., Royce, J. M., Snipper, A. S., Murray, H. W., & Lazar, I. (1980). Preschool programs and later school competence of children from low-income families. *Science, 208*(4440), 202–204.

Deary, I. J., Der, G., & Ford, G. (2001). Reaction times and intelligence differences: A population-based cohort study. *Intelligence, 29*(5), 389–399.

Deary, I. J., Leaper, S. A., Murray, A. D., Staff, R. T., & Whalley, L. J. (2003). Cerebral white matter abnormalities and lifetime cognitive change: A 67-year follow-up of the Scottish Mental Survey 1932. *Psychology and Aging, 18,* 140–148.

Deary, I. J., Penke, L., & Johnson, W. (2010). The neuroscience of human intelligence differences. *Nature Reviews: Neuroscience, 11,* 201–211.

Deary, I. J., & Stough, C. (1996). Intelligence and inspection time: Achievements, prospects, and problems. *American Psychologist, 51*(6), 599–608.

Deary, I. J., Thorpe, G., Wilson, V., Starr, J. M., & Whalley, L. J. (2003). Population sex differences in IQ at age 11: The Scottish mental survey 1932. *Intelligence, 31*(6), 533–542.

Del Banco, N. (2011). *Lastingness: The art of old age.* New York: Grand Central Publishing.

Deutsch Smith, D. (2005). *Introduction to special education: Teaching in an age of opportunity.* New York: Allyn & Bacon/Longman.

Dickens, W. T., & Flynn, J. R. (2006). Black Americans reduce the racial gap: Evidence from standardization samples. *Psychological Science, 17*(10), 913–920.

Eccles, J. S., & Jacobs, J. E. (1986). Social forces shape math attitudes and performance. *Signs, 11*(2), 367–380.

Einfeld, S. L., Piccinin, A. M., Mackinnon, A., Hofer, S. M., Taffe, J., Gray, K. M., Bontempo, D. E., Hoffman, L. R., Parmenter, P. T., & Tonge, B. J. (2006). Psychopathology in young people with intellectual disability. *Journal of the American Medical Association, 296,* 1981–1989.

Engle, R. W., Tuholski, S. W., Laughlin, J. E., Conway, A. R. A. (1999). Working memory, short-term memory, and general fluid intelligence: A latent-variable approach. *Journal of Experimental Psychology: General, 128,* 309–331.

Eyferth, K. (1961). Leistungen verschiedener Gruppen von Besatzungskindern in Hamburg-Wechsler Intelligenztest fur Kinder (HAWIK) [Performance of different groups of occupation children on the Hamburg-Wechsler Intelligence Test for Children]. *Archiv fur die gesamte Psychologie, 113,* 222–241.

Fagan, J. F., & Holland, C. R. (2002). Equal opportunity and racial differences in IQ. *Intelligence, 30*(4), 361–387.

Fagan, J. F., & Holland, C. (2007). Racial equality in intelligence: Predictions from a theory of intelligence as processing. *Intelligence, 35*(4), 319–334.

Feldman, D. H. (1980). *Beyond universals in cognitive development.* Norwood, NJ: Ablex.

Finke, R. A., Ward, T. B., & Smith, S. M. (1992). *Creative cognition: Theory, research, and applications.* Cambridge, MA: MIT Press.

Flynn, J. R. (1984). The mean IQ of Americans: Massive gains 1932 to 1978. *Psychological Bulletin, 95*(1), 29–51.

Flynn, J. R. (1991). *Asian Americans: Achievement beyond IQ.* Hillsdale, NJ: Lawrence Erlbaum Assoc.

Flynn, J. R. (2007). *What is intelligence?: Beyond the Flynn Effect.* Cambridge, MA: Cambridge University Press.

Fredrickson, B. L., Roberts, T-A., Noll, S. M., Quinn, D. M., & Twenge, J. M. (1998). That swimsuit becomes you: Sex differences in self-objectification, restrained eating, and math performance. *Journal of Personality and Social Psychology, 75*(1), 269–284.

Garces, E., Thomas, D., & Currie, J. (2002). Longer-term effects of Head Start, *American Economic Review, 92*(4), 999–1012.

Gardner, H. (1983). *Frames of mind: The theory of multiple intelligences.* New York: Basic Books.

Gardner, H. (1993). *Creating minds.* New York: Basic Books.

Gardner, H. (2000). A case against spiritual intelligence. *International Journal for the Psychology of Religion, 10*(1), 27–34.

Gardner, H., & Hatch, T. (1989). Multiple intelligences go to school: Educational implications of the theory of multiple intelligences. *Educational Researcher, 18*(8), 4–9.

Goleman, D. (1998). *Working with emotional intelligence.* New York: Bantam Books.

Gonzales, P. M., Blanton, H., & Williams, K. J. (2002). The effects of stereotype threat and double-minority status on the test performance of Latino women. *Personality and Social Psychology Bulletin, 28*(5), 659–670.

Gottfredson, L. S. (1997a). Mainstream science on intelligence: An editorial with 52 signatories, history, and bibliography. *Intelligence, 24,* 13–23.

Gottfredson, L. S. (1997b). Why *g* matters: The complexity of everyday life. *Intelligence, 24*(1), 79–132.

Gottfredson, L. S. (1998). The general intelligence factor. *Scientific American Presents, 9,* 24–29.

Gottfredson, L. S. (2003). The challenge and promise of cognitive career assessment. *Journal of Career Assessment, 11*(2), 115–135.

Gottfredson, L. S. (2004). Intelligence: Is it the epidemiologists' elusive "fundamental cause" of social class inequalities in health? *Journal of Personality and Social Psychology, 86*(1), 174–199.

Halpern, D. F., Benbow, C. P., Geary, D. C., Gur, R. C., Hyde, J. S., & Gernsbache, M. A. (2007). The science of sex differences in science and mathematics. *Psychological Science in the Public Interest, 8*(1), 1–51.

Hedges, L. V., & Nowell, A. (1995). Sex differences in mental test scores, variability, and numbers of high-scoring individuals. *Science, 269*(5220), 41–45.

Hermstein, R. J., & Murray, C. (1994). *The bell curve: Intelligence and class structure in American life.* New York: Free Press.

Horwood, L. J., Darlow, B. A., & Mogridge, N. (2001). Breast milk feeding and cognitive ability at 7–8 years. *Archives of Disease in Childhood: Fetal and Neonatal, 84*(1), F23–27.

Hunt, E., & Carlson, J. (2007). Considerations relating to the study of group differences in intelligence. *Perspectives on Psychological Science, 2,* 194–213.

Hunter, J. E., & Hunter, R. F. (1984). Validity and utility of alternative predictors of job performance. *Psychological Bulletin, 96*(1), 72–79.

Hyde, J. S., & Linn, M. C. (1988). Gender differences in verbal ability: A meta-analysis. *Psychological Bulletin, 104*(1), 53–69.

Irvine, S. H., & Berry, J. W. (Eds.). (1988). *Human abilities in culture.* Cambridge, MA: Cambridge University Press.

Jaeggi, S. M., Buschkuehl, M., Jonides, J., & Perrig, W. J. (2008). Improving fluid intelligence with training on working memory. *Proceedings of the National Academy of Sciences, 105*(19), 6829–6833.

Jaeggi, S. M., Buschkuehl, M., Jonides, J., & Shah, P. (2011). Short- and long-term benefits of cognitive training. *Proceedings of the National Academy of Sciences, 108*(25), 10081–10086.

Jensen, A. R. (1980). *Bias in mental testing.* New York: Free Press.

Jordan, T. J., Grallo, R., Deutsch, M., & Deutsch, C. P. (1985). Long-term effects of early enrichment: A 20-year perspective on persistence and change. *American Journal of Community Psychology, 13*(4), 393–415.

Jung, R. E., & Haier, R. J. (2007). The Parieto-Frontal Integration Theory (P-FIT) of intelligence: Converging neuroimaging evidence. *Behavioral and Brain Sciences, 30,* 135–154.

Kaufman, A. S. (2009). *IQ testing 101.* New York: Springer.

Kaufman, A. S., & Lichtenberger, E. (2006). *Assessing adolescent and adult intelligence* (3rd ed.). Hoboken, NJ: Wiley.

Kaufman, A. S., Reynolds, C. R., & McLean, J. E. (1989). Age and WAIS-R intelligence in a national sample of adults in the 20- to 74-year age range: A cross-sectional analysis with educational level controlled. *Intelligence, 13*(3), 235–253.

Kline, P. (1991). *Intelligence: The psychometric view.* New York: Rutledge, Chapman, & Hall.

Kristensen, P., & Bjerkedal, T. (2007). Explaining the relation between birth order and intelligence. *Science, 316*(5832), 1717.

Lazar, I., Darlington, R., Murray, H., Royce, J., & Snipper, A. (1982). Lasting effects of early education: A report from the Consortium for Longitudinal Studies. *Monographs of the Society for Research in Child Development* (Series No. 195), *47,* 2–3.

Lee, V. E., Brooks-Gunn, J., Schnur, E., & Liaw, F.-R. (1990). Are Head Start effects sustained? A longitudinal follow-up comparison of disadvantaged children attending Head Start, no preschool, and other preschool programs. *Child Development, 61,* 495–507.

Lemann, N. (1999). *The big test: The secret history of the American meritocracy.* New York: Farrar, Strauss, & Giroux.

Loehlin, J. C., Vandenberg, S. G., & Osborne, R. T. (1973). Blood group genes and Negro–White ability differences. *Behavior Genetics, 3,* 263–270.

Loehlin, J. C., Willerman, L., & Horn, J. M. (1988). Human behavior genetics. *Annual Review of Psychology, 39,* 101–133.

Lynn, R., & Vanhanen, T. (2006). *IQ and global inequality.* Augusta, GA: Washington Summit Publishers.

Maccoby, E. E., & Jacklin, C. N. (1974). *The psychology of sex differences.* Stanford, CA: Stanford University Press.

Mackenzie, B. (1984). Explaining Race Differences in IQ: The Logic, the Methodology, and the Evidence. *American Psychologist, 39*(2), 1214–1233.

Mayer, J. D., Salovey, P., Caruso, D. L., & Sitarenios, G. (2001). Emotional intelligence as a standard intelligence. *Emotion, 1,* 232–242.

Mercer, J. R. (1973). IQ: The lethal label. *Education Digest: Essential Readings Condensed for Quick Review, 38*(5), 17–20.

Miller, L. K. (1998). Defining the savant syndrome. *Journal of Developmental and Physical Disabilities, 10*(1), 73–83.

Moffitt, T. E., Caspi, A., Harkness, A. R., & Silva, P. A. (1993). The natural history of change in intellectual performance: Who changes? How much? Is it meaningful? *Journal of Child Psychology and Psychiatry, 3,* 455–506.

Neisser, U. (1976). General, academic, and artificial intelligence. In L. B. Resnick (Ed.), *The nature of intelligence* (pp. 135–144). Hillsdale, NJ: Erlbaum.

Neisser, U., Boodoo, G., Bouchard, T. J. Jr., Boykin, A. W., Brody, N., Ceci, S. J., Halpern, D. F., Loehlin, J. C., Perloff, R., Sternberg, R. J., & Urbina, S. (1996). Intelligence: Knowns and unknowns. *American Psychologist, 51*(2), 77–101.

Nenty, H. J. (1986). *Cross-Cultural bias analysis of Cattell Culture-Fair Intelligence Test.* 67th Annual Meeting of the American Educational Research Association, San Francisco, CA, April 16–20.

Nisbett, R. E. (2009). *Intelligence and how to get it: Why schools and cultures count.* New York: Norton.

Olszewski-Kubilius, P., & Lee, S. Y. (2004). Parent perceptions of the effects of the Saturday Enrichment Program on gifted students' talent development. *Roeper Review, 26,* 156–165.

Pinker, S. (2004). Why nature & nurture won't go away. *Dædalus, 133*(4), 5–17.

Plomin, R., DeFries, J. C., & Loehlin, J. C. (1977). Genotype–environment interaction and correlation in the analysis of human behavior. *Psychological Bulletin, 84*(2), 309–322.

Powers, D. E., & Rock, D. A. (1999). Effects of coaching on SAT I: Reasoning test scores. *Journal of Educational Measurement, 36*(2), 93–118.

Pyryt, M. C. (1993). Career development for the gifted and talented: Helping adolescents chart their futures. *Journal of Secondary Gifted Education, 5*(1), 18–21.

Raven, J. (2000). The Raven's Progressive Matrices: Change and stability over culture and time. *Cognitive Psychology, 41*, 1–48.

Reynolds, A. J., Temple, J. A., & Robertson, D. L. (2001). Long-term effects of an early childhood intervention on educational achievement and juvenile arrest: A 15-year follow-up of low-income children in public schools. *Journal of the American Medical Association, 285*(18), 2339–2346.

Robinson, A., Shore, B. M., & Enersen, D. (Eds.). (2007). *Best practices in gifted education.* Waco, TX: Prufrock Press.

Robinson, N. M., Zigler, E., & Gallagher, J. J. (2000). Two tails of the normal curve: Similarities and differences in the study of mental retardation and giftedness. *American Psychologist, 55*, 1413–1424.

Roid, G. H., & Barram, R. A. (2004). *Essentials of Stanford-Binet Intelligence Scales (SB5) assessment.* Hoboken, NJ: John Wiley & Sons.

Rosenthal, R., & Jacobson, L. (1968). *Pygmalion in the classroom: Teacher expectation and pupils' intellectual development.* New York: Holt, Rinehart, & Winston.

Rushton, J. P., & Jensen, A. R. (2005). Thirty years of research on race differences in cognitive ability. *Psychology, Public Policy, and Law, 11*, 235–294.

Schulte, M. J., Ree, M. J., & Carretta, T. R. (2004). Emotional intelligence: Not much more than g and personality. *Personality and Individual Differences, 37*, 1059–1068.

Schutte, N. S., Malouff, J. M., Hall, L. E., Haggerty, D. J., Cooper, J. T., Golden, C. J., & Dornheim, L. (1998). Development and validation of a measure of emotional intelligence. *Personality and Individual Differences, 25*, 167–177.

Scarr, S., Weinberg, R. A., & Waldman, I. D. (1993). IQ correlations in transracial adoptive families. *Intelligence, 17*, 541–555.

Scott, G., Leritz, L. E., & Mumford, M. D. (2004). The effectiveness of creativity training: A quantitative review. *Creativity Research Journal, 16*(4), 361–388.

Seifert, C. M., Meyer, D. E., Davidson, N., Patalano, A. L., & Yaniv, I. (1995). Demystification of cognitive insight: Opportunistic assimilation and the prepared-mind hypothesis. In R. J. Sternberg & J. E. Davidson (Eds.), *The nature of insight* (pp. 65–124). Cambridge, MA: MIT Press.

Shalock, R. L., Borthwick-Duffy, S. A., Bradley, V. J., Buntinx, W. H. E., Coulter, D. L., Craig, E. M., Gomez, S. C., Lachapelle, Y., Luckasson, R., Reeve, A., Shogren, K. A., Snell, M. E., Spreat, S., Tassé, M. J., Thompson, J. R., Verdugo-Alonso, M. A., Wehmeyer, M. L., & Yeager, M. H. (2010). *Intellectual disability: Definition, classification, and systems of supports* (11th Ed.). Annapolis Junction, MD: AAIDD Publications.

Shepard, R. N., & Metzler, J. (1971). Mental rotation of three-dimensional objects. *Science, 171*, 701–703.

Shurkin, J. N. (1992). *Terman's kids: The groundbreaking study of how the gifted grow up.* New York: Little, Brown and Co.

Simonton, D. K. (2009). *Genius 101.* New York: Springer.

Smith, E. E. (1996). Personal communication.

Smith, G. F. (1998). Idea-generation techniques: A formulary of active ingredients. *Journal of Creative Behavior, 32*(2), 107–133.

Spearman, C. (1904). General intelligence objectively determined and measured. *American Journal of Psychology, 15*, 201–293.

Steele, C. M., & Aronson, J. (1995). Stereotype threat and the intellectual test performance of African Americans. *Journal of Personality and Social Psychology, 69*(5), 797–811.

Sternberg, R. J. (1985). *Beyond IQ: A triarchic theory of human intelligence.* New York: Cambridge University Press.

Sternberg, R. J. (2001). What is the common thread to creativity: Its dialectical relation to intelligence and wisdom. *American Psychologist, 56*, 360–362.

Sternberg, R. J., Conway, B. E., Ketron, J. L., & Bernstein, M. (1981). People's conceptions of intelligence. *Journal of Personality and Social Psychology, 41*(1), 37–55.

Stone, J. (2002). Battling doubt by avoiding practice: The effects of stereotype threat on self-handicapping in white athletes. *Personality and Social Psychology Bulletin, 28*, 1667–1678.

Streissguth, A. P., Aase, J. M., Clarren, S. K., Randels, S. P., LaDue, R. A., & Smith, D. F. (1991). Fetal alcohol syndrome in adolescents and adults. *Journal of the American Medical Association, 265*, 1961–1967.

Subotnik, R. F., Olszewski-Kubilius, P., & Worrell, F. C. (2011). Rethinking giftedness and gifted education: A proposed direction forward based on psychological science. *Psychological Science in the Public Interest, 12*(1) 3–54.

Sullivan, J. (2002). State will admit sterilization past. *Portland Oregonian,* November 15, 2002. (Mirrored in *Eugene Register-Guard,* November 16, 2002, at Google News.)

Summers, L. H. (2005). Archive of Remarks at the National Bureau of Economic Research Conference on Diversifying the Science & Engineering Workforce. Cambridge, MA. January 14, 2005.

Taggart, L., Taylor, D., McCrum-Gardner, E. (2010). Individual, life events, family and socio-economic factors associated with young people with intellectual disability and with and without behavioural/emotional problems. *Journal of Intellectual Disability, 14*(4), 267–288.

Terman, L. M. (1925). *Genetic studies of genius. Mental and physical traits of a thousand gifted children.* Oxford, UK: Stanford University Press.

Thorndike, A. L., & Hagen, E. P. (1977). *Measurement and evaluation in psychology and education.* New York, NY: Macmillan.

Thurstone, L. L. (1938). *Primary mental abilities.* Chicago: University of Chicago Press.

Toga, A. W., & Thompson, P. M. (2005). Genetics of brain structure and intelligence. *Annual Review of Neuroscience, 28*, 1–23.

Treffert, D. (1989). *Extraordinary people.* New York: Harper and Row.

Treffinger, D., Isaksen, S., & Dorval, B. (2000). *Creative problem solving: An introduction* (3rd ed.). Waco, TX: Prufrock Press.

Trei, L. (2007). New study yields instructive results on how mindset affects learning. *Stanford Report,* February 7. http://news.stanford.edu/news/2007/february7/dweck-020707.html

Tucker-Drob, E. M., Rhemtulla, M., Harden, K. P., Turkheimer, E., & Fask, D. (2011). Emergence of a gene x socioeconomic status interaction on infant mental ability between 10 months and 2 years. *Psychological Science, 22*(1), 125–133.

Turkheimer, E., Haley, A., Waldron, M., D'Onofrio, B., & Gottesman, I. I. (2003). Socioeconomic status modifies heritability of IQ in young children. *Psychological Science, 14*(6), 623–628.

van der Sluis, S., Willemsen, G., de Geus, E. J. C., Boomsma, D. I., & Posthuma, D. (2008). Gene–environment interaction in adults' IQ scores: Measures of past and present environment. *Behavior Genetics, 38*(4), 348–360.

Vernon, P. A. (1983). Speed of information processing and general intelligence. *Intelligence, 7*(1), 53–70.

Walton, G. M., & Cohen, G. L. (2003). Stereotype lift. *Journal of Experimental Social Psychology, 39*(5), 456–467.

Weisberg, R. W. (1986). *Creativity: Genius and other myths.* New York: Freeman.

Williams, R. L. (1972). *The BITCH-100: A culture-specific test.* American Psychological Association Annual Convention, Honolulu, HI.

Witelson, S. F., Kigar, D. L., & Harvey, T. (1999). The exceptional brain of Albert Einstein. *The Lancet, 353*, 2149–2153.

Woods, E., & McDaniel, P. (1997). *Training a Tiger: Raising a winner in golf and in life.* New York: HarperCollins Publishers.

Yeargin-Allsopp, M., Murphy, C. C., Cordero, J. F., Decouflé, P., & Hollowell, J. G. (1997). Reported biomedical causes and associated medical conditions for mental retardation among 10-year-old children, metropolitan Atlanta, 1985 to 1987. *Developmental Medicine and Child Neurology, 39*(3), 142–149.

Yeargin-Allsopp, M., Murphy, C. C., Oakley, G. P., & Sikes R. K. (1992). A multiple-source method for studying the prevalence of developmental disabilities in children: The Metropolitan Atlanta Developmental Disabilities Study. *Pediatrics, 89*(4 Pt 1), 624–630.

Zajonc, R. B. (1976). Family configuration and intelligence: Variations in scholastic aptitude scores parallel trends in family size and the spacing of children. *Science, 192*, 227–229.

Zigler, E. (1984). Personal communication.

Zigler, E., & Berman, W. (1983). Discerning the future of early childhood intervention. *American Psychologist, 38*(8), 894–906.

Zigler, E., & Muenchow, S. (1992). *Head Start: The inside story of America's most successful educational experiment.* New York: Basic Books.

Chapter Overview ▼

10.1 Motivational Theories
Instinct Theories
Evolutionary Theories
Drive Theories
Arousal Theories
Incentive Theories
Hierarchical Theories

CONCEPT LEARNING CHECK **10.1** *Theories of Motivation*

10.2 Motivation of Hunger
The Physiology and Regulation of Hunger
  The Stomach
  The Brain
  Hormones
  Metabolism
  Glucose Monitoring
  Genetics

Environmental Influences
Hunger, Eating, and Weight
  Eating Disorders
  Obesity
A Comparison: Motivation of Thirst

CONCEPT LEARNING CHECK **10.2** *Eating Disorder or Disordered Eating?*

CRITICAL THINKING APPLICATION

10.3 Sexual Motivation
Physiology of Sexual Response
Gender Norms in Sexual Motivation
Evolutionary Theories of Mating
Sexual Orientation
  Biological Factors
  Environmental Factors

CONCEPT LEARNING CHECK **10.3** *Evolution and Gender Differences*

10 Motivation

Learning Objectives ▼

10.1
- Define the concept of motivation.
- Discuss the theories about what moves individuals toward the fulfillment of a goal.

10.2
- Illustrate the biology/physiology of hunger.
- Explain environmental influences on hunger.
- Describe the eating disorders and self-regulation.

10.3
- Examine the physiology of human sexual response.
- Compare and contrast gender norms in sexual motivation.
- Discuss evolutionary theories of mating.
- Describe the biological and environmental factors in sexual orientation.

10.4
- Define the social motivations and give examples of each.

10.5
- Explain the relationship between human motivation and work.

10.4 Social Motivations
Motivation to Belong
Motivation to Achieve
Motivation for Self-actualization

CONCEPT LEARNING CHECK **10.4** *Fostering Achievement*

10.5 Motivation and Work
Personnel Psychology
Organizational Psychology

Career Directions
Summary of Multiple Influences on Motivation

CONCEPT LEARNING CHECK **10.5** *What "Works" at Work?*

O n a rare visit to my hometown, I ran into a high school classmate, Terri. "What have you been doing in the last 10 years since graduation?" she asked. Terri had already filled me in on her life on a Montana ranch, working on a ski patrol in Aspen, and marriage with two children. When I answered, I surprised even myself by observing, "I have been in school since I last saw you!" Following 4 years of college, I was finishing my sixth year of a PhD program in psychology. I realized that I was 28 and had never been out of school! The end goal—becoming a professor—was not even within reach. Two years of postdoctoral study followed before I began my first full-time job at age 30. Terri's look of amazement matched my own: What motivates us to work for years toward long-term goals? It is no wonder that there are many theories developed to explain motivation. But as we shall see, no one theory has yet satisfactorily explained every aspect of motivation.

10.1 Motivational Theories

A variety of theories have been proposed to explain what moves us toward the fulfillment of a goal.

- Define the concept of motivation.
- Discuss the theories about what moves individuals toward the fulfillment of a goal.

Why did you get out of bed today? Sometimes, it is hard to see our true motivations because our daily lives are quite routine. So, for a moment, imagine your life without alarm clocks, cell phones, or schedules. If you had a day with unstructured time, what would you do first when you woke up? Biological requirements for maintaining your body would likely come first, such as thirst, urination, keeping warm or cool, and eating. The human body can live for only 3 minutes without oxygen, 3 days without water, and 3 weeks without food. But a human can live a lifetime without sex, even though it is required to propagate our species. Once beyond biological needs, you may soon want to talk to someone you care about or eventually feel the need to accomplish something during your day. How can we capture the many reasons for our decisions to act?

Motivation An inner state that energizes people toward the fulfillment of a goal.

Motive The pursuit of pleasure and the avoidance of pain or displeasure.

Instinct theories Motivation from biologically programmed behaviors occurring in response to environmental cues.

Motivation is described as an inner state that energizes people toward the fulfillment of a goal. Importantly, motivation is considered to arise internally, as an act of will, rather than an external force compelling you to take action (like pulling your hand back from a hot stove). Motivation is also related to an intention or outcome that you desire; so you are motivated to achieve some goal or state, such as being financially independent, or in a happy relationship. At the base level, a **motive** is the pursuit of pleasure in some form and the avoidance of pain or displeasure. Just about any goal can be termed a motive as long as it motivates a person to pursue it for any reason. Throughout the history of psychology, several theories of motivation have been proposed. Theories of motivation try to explain how and why we are energized to move toward specific goals.

Instinct Theories

Comparative psychology grew from the study of animal behavior. Understanding the built-in behaviors that occur in animals led to **instinct theories**, or motivation as inborn, programmed behaviors occurring in response to a cue (Weiner, 1972). An instinct can be triggered by internal cues (such as the menstrual cycle in mammals) as well as external (environmental) cues (e.g., the presence of a receptive partner for mating). Humans, too, have instincts, or behavior that arises across cultures, apparently without learning. For example, if a newborn is placed near a woman's breast, it will "root" around with its mouth, attempting to suck on the nipple. This is a basic behavior that appears to be inborn in all humans. Other instincts include smiling, fear of snakes and spiders, and protecting your children. However, most of human behavior cannot be considered instinctual because it can be overridden even in the presence of a cue. For example, a basic motivation like eating when you are hungry can occur or not occur based on a willful decision. As a result, the theory of instincts that accounts for animal behaviors cannot explain our voluntary decisions about whether to take specific actions. The theory's greatest weakness is the fact that humans are motivated to do many things, particularly at higher levels of control (like earning a college degree!), that cannot be explained as simple instincts.

Evolutionary Theories

Evolutionary psychologists apply the theory of evolution to explain the psychology behind our behaviors (Buss, 1995). They believe there exist **universals** in human behavior—that is, behaviors that people perform regardless of their cultures. Further, these universal behaviors are the product of millions of years of human history and have little to do with the modern environment surrounding us today. Instead, the behaviors of early humans that led to their survival also led to children more likely to pursue the same behaviors. As a species, their behaviors thus **evolved** or were selected over generations to leave the ones best fit for that environment. For example, throughout the history of humans, food supplies tended to wax and wane. Some groups had to live through periods of scarcity during which little food was available. Some of these humans liked to overeat when food was available, preferring fatty and sweet foods that were stored as body fat. Then, when food was not available, these individuals had the advantage of stored body fat to help them through the lean times. So the question of why we overeat may relate back to our ancestors: Those who ate more were more likely to survive and, therefore, become the ancestors of today's ice cream lovers.

Evolutionary theories of motivation focus on motives that affect the success of the population over time. While we may think of these as primarily biological, such as acquiring food, human evolution is thought to reflect the increasing importance of social motives in the survival of an individual. The individual needed the group to provide safety, a partner to provide the opportunity to mate, a larger family to assist with raising the young, and the skills to cooperate and compete for resources within the group (Bernard et al., 2005). As a result, humans were selected based on their interest, desire, and success at solving problems within the social domain. The generations of humans who survived to raise children shaped the patterns of motivations we see in people today.

Considering the theory of evolution in psychology may seem a bit odd. However, it is important to remember how many generations of humans lived before our recorded history. More than 150,000 years ago, *Homo sapiens* lived in roving groups of 50 to 80 people and, around 90,000 years ago, lived on the African Savanna. About 60,000 years ago, *Homo sapiens* moved out around the world. They lived as hunters and gatherers for the last 50,000 years. Less than 10,000 years ago, they began farming, and modern settlements became possible. Large groups of people living in close proximity are a recent development in human history. The early environments in which humans lived and survived were very different from our own. For example, modern humans in Western cultures know more individuals at age 6 than most early humans would have encountered over their lifetimes! For humans in prehistory, much of their time was devoted to finding food on a daily basis by hunting and gathering; in today's world, grocery stores make this a minor effort each day. More recent developments playing a large role in our lives, such as the Internet and cell phones, are just a blip on the time scale of evolution. That leaves plenty of room for evolutionary factors that shaped human behaviors to impact the motivations of people today.

Drive Theories

A **drive** is defined as tension arising from within our physiological systems, which in turn motivates action (Hull, 1943). For example, over time, your cells need more water, so you become motivated to drink. As more time passes, the need for water causes a tension within your system. Eventually, you are driven to take action and satisfy the drive, releasing the tension. When our bodies need something, the states of tension caused are quite unpleasant (such as the feeling of being thirsty or hungry). The body attempts to

Evolutionary psychologist A researcher who applies the theory of evolution to explain the psychology behind behaviors.

Universals Behaviors that all people perform regardless of their cultures.

Evolved behaviors Behaviors selected over generations to best fit the environment.

Drive A tension arising from within physiological systems that motivates action.

Homeostasis The process of maintaining a stable or balanced physiological state over time.

Drive theory A theory that states of tension motivate us to take action to reduce them.

Arousal theory The theory that we are motivated to seek out a particular level of arousal.

Optimal arousal A level of activation that is sufficient but not overwhelming.

Yerkes-Dodson law of arousal The theory that performance is best at medium levels of arousal.

maintain **homeostasis**, or a steady internal state. **Drive theory** says these states are what motivate us to take action to reduce those unpleasant feelings. Drives are usually thought of as biological needs, such as thirst, eating, and sex. Drive theory is helpful for explaining why we get hungry and eat, or why we scratch when we itch. For many people in the world today, satisfying the drives for food, water, and safety are daily occurrences; in the more developed world, we may devote much less effort toward the pursuit of drives.

Unconscious drives, such as the drive to stay alive and to be aggressive, self-destructive, or to die, have also been proposed by psychologists such as Sigmund Freud (1856–1939). However, drives cannot predict when specific behaviors will occur. In particular, people sometimes perform actions that *increase* feelings of tension. Skydiving, driving too fast, and watching scary movies all add to our feelings of unresolved tension, yet some people sometimes enjoy increasing the tension they feel.

Arousal Theories

If people sometimes choose to reduce tension and other times to increase it, perhaps we are attempting to manage the level of tension we experience. **Arousal theory** states that we are motivated to seek out a particular level of arousal, one that is stimulating but not overwhelming (Fiske & Maddi, 1961). If your arousal level is too low and you are bored, you may seek out environments, people, and situations that will increase your arousal. And if it is too high, you may decrease your arousal by practicing meditation, avoiding stimulation, or isolating yourself from others. Arousal theory suggests that tension is not a bad thing, but it should be regulated so that you have just the right amount, or **optimal arousal**.

The relationship between your level of arousal and your performance is described as curvilinear, according to the **Yerkes-Dodson law of arousal** FIGURE 10-1. Consider taking a standardized test before applying to college. If you considered the test to be routine, you might have had a very low level of anxiety or arousal about it and may not have performed your best (as quickly or accurately) during the hours of the exam. On the other hand, if you felt very anxious about the exam, your arousal may have been too high and interfered with your performance. This predicts that your best performance will occur when your arousal level is "optimal"—when you feel excited, but not too excited. For example, one experienced psychology instructor now runs up and down a flight of stairs just before his large lectures begin. After years of teaching, he does not feel the edge of tension about his performance, so he recreates the feeling by stimulating his level of arousal through exercise. Athletic teams do this, too, through "pumped up" pep talks just before games. Arousal theory may explain getting out of bed in the morning; as pleasant as it is to lie quietly for some time, eventually the boredom of the setting may cause you to initiate some other action. So, if your arousal is too low, you may try some more stimulating behavior to keep your arousal level within a target range. Arousal theory takes the environment around you into account in explaining why you are motivated to make changes. However, arousal theory is not very helpful in explaining long-term motivation. Why might you continue studying throughout college? It may relate to keeping your level of arousal at an

According to arousal theory, people may be motivated to increase their level of arousal through acts like skydiving.

FIGURE 10-1 At both high and low levels of arousal, performance on a task is worse.

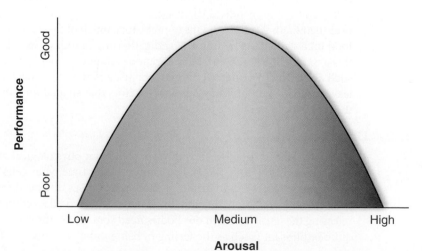

optimal level; however, it may more likely be caused by a desire to be successful, make money, gain power, or do something that you find rewarding.

Incentive Theories

Another view of motivation, known as **incentive theories**, focuses on the reward or payoff for behaviors. We quickly learn to perform behaviors that lead to desirable consequences. So perhaps the explanation for more complex behaviors involves incentives. **Incentives** are the rewards and punishments associated with different actions that lure people into taking action. This account of motivation says we can explain why you took a particular action by looking into the incentives that followed it. Incentives can have complex relationships with behaviors; for example, coming late to a party seems bad, but it may result in your skipping out on paying for the pizza. So incentives for taking action can be hidden or explicit and can work differently for different people (e.g., some people do not like ice cream; Atkinson, 1964).

Incentive theory says we are motivated to do things by two types of incentives: intrinsic and extrinsic. **Intrinsic incentives** involve internal feelings. These incentives motivate you to do things because they make you happy, make you feel good, or at least make you feel less bad. Donating change at the Salvation Army bucket leads to a warm feeling through knowing you are helping others, and holding a job that you love serves as its own reward. These behaviors reflect **intrinsic motivations**, or behaviors performed for an internal reward. **Extrinsic incentives** are external rewards or punishments that motivate you to perform a specific action. So, you may hold a job because you want the pay you receive, or you earn good grades because you want your parents' approval. **Extrinsic motivation** refers to the desire to gain external rewards for behavior. There is a reason we do not have to pay people to watch cartoons but do pay them to sell hotdogs. When we are not motivated by intrinsic motivations, external incentives are used to help motivate us. The world is organized around incentives, as are social relationships, and they often mix intrinsic and extrinsic rewards.

Are the effects of intrinsic and extrinsic incentives the same? That is, does paying people to do something (extrinsic incentive) have the same psychological effect as their doing it because they enjoy it (intrinsic incentive)? To answer this question, researchers brought college students into a lab for three test sessions (Deci, 1971). In all three sessions, the control group was given block puzzles to solve and then left alone while researchers watched to see how many more puzzles these students would solve on their own time. For the incentive group, the students were paid to complete each puzzle, but only during the second work session. During the third session, both groups were again tested without any incentives. The control group voluntarily spent time on the puzzles during the breaks between sessions, and there was no difference in how many they did across the three sessions. They appeared to do the puzzles because they enjoyed doing so. But the incentive group behaved differently: They spent a lot more time on the puzzles in the session for which they were paid, and a lot less time on them during the third session, when they were not paid FIGURE 10-2.

The results showed that paying people to do a task they already enjoyed (and did for free in the first session) made them lose interest in doing it for free. This effect is called the **overjustification effect**, in that the extrinsic reward provides a complete rationale for doing the task, so no intrinsic

Incentive theories Motivation that focuses on the reward or payoff for behaviors.

Incentive The rewards and punishments associated with different actions.

Intrinsic incentives Feelings of reward created within the individual.

Intrinsic motivation The desire to perform behaviors for an internal reward.

Extrinsic incentives Rewards (such as pay) given to motivate people to perform certain behaviors.

Extrinsic motivation The desire to gain external rewards for behavior.

Overjustification effect When a task provides an extrinsic reward, no intrinsic motive is needed.

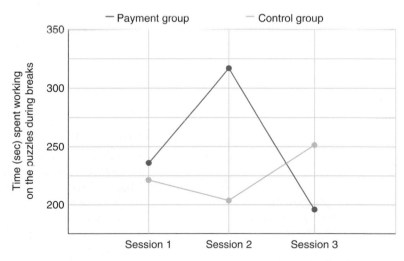

FIGURE 10-2 Students who were paid to solve puzzles during their free time (red) completed more puzzles in the second session (when paid), but fewer in the third session (when not paid), compared to the control group (blue).
Source: Data from Deci, E. L. (1971). Effects of externally mediated rewards on intrinsic motivation. Journal of Personality and Social Psychology, 18(1), 105–115.

motive is needed (Lepper et al., 1973). To say you were paid to do it *and* that you enjoyed doing it would be *over*justifying your behavior. Does being paid really undermine your intrinsic interest in a task? One study looked at the work of professional artists who completed pieces either on commission (paid for by an art patron) or for their own collection (for potential sale at a later time). Commissioned works were judged as "less creative" than noncommissioned work (Amabile, 1996).

Further, *more* external incentives do not necessarily improve performance. In a recent study, students were given a variety of tasks to complete, involving remembering strings of digits, performing motor skills, or creative games (Ariely et al., 2009). Different groups were given either small, medium, or large financial rewards based on their performance. For mechanical skills, for which no thinking was involved, higher rewards did lead to better performance. But if the task involved cognitive skill in even a rudimentary way, the larger reward led to poorer performance FIGURE 10-3. Increasing the incentives made performance *worse* on tasks that involved thinking.

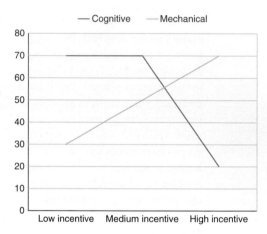

FIGURE 10-3 Results showing performance based on level of incentives for mechanical skills and cognitive skills. *Source: Data from Ariely, D., Gneezy, W., Lowenstein, G., & Mazar, N. (2009). Large stakes and big mistakes.* Review of Economic Studies, 76, *451–469.*

So extrinsic incentives have a complex relationship to our behavior. A meta-analysis of 111 randomized controlled studies concluded that "Financial incentives, if they are big enough, can influence discrete behavior at the individual level in the short run" (Kane et al., 2004). But the fundamental fact of motivation is that human beings cannot be compelled to change their behaviors, such as what and how much they eat, or whether they smoke or exercise. These behavior changes can be *initiated* by "extrinsic" motivators like rewards (Curry et al., 1991). But human nature is such that we do not necessarily internalize motivation based on rewards (Pink, 2009). The incentive approach does not work to build up the intrinsic motivation needed to sustain behavior change over time (Amabile, 1996). External incentives get people to perform a behavior but not necessarily to believe in—or understand—its value.

Hierarchical Theories

How do these differing accounts of motivation fit together? One important approach to motivation attempts to understand the needs and motivations of humans in terms of levels. That is, there are basic or primary needs, like hunger and thirst, that we fulfill before considering other types of needs. Abraham Maslow (1908–1970) identified a **hierarchy of needs** FIGURE 10-4 in which each level of need depends on satisfying the lower levels. So we focus first on physiological needs like hunger and thirst before considering the importance of safety, which is dealt with before addressing our need for love or belonging, and so on. Higher-level needs like esteem, including status, power, and respect, can only be addressed once the lower-level needs are satisfied.

At the highest level, once our biological and social needs are met, Maslow posited the idea of **self-actualization**, or the goal of fulfilling your potential, or "being all that you can be." Maslow is identified with the humanist tradition in psychology, which proposes that the greatest goal for humankind is for each individual to develop into his or her greatest potential. Maslow developed his theory by studying the lives of eminent people, who had often succeeded in reaching the pinnacle of self-actualization. While the needs Maslow proposed are intuitively appealing, there is little evidence in support of this

Hierarchy of needs
Maslow's theory that each level of need depends on satisfying lower levels.

Self-actualization
Maslow's concept that the highest need is to fulfill individual potential.

Self-actualization — — — — — — — — — — — — — — Passions, creativity, morality, problem solving

Esteem — — — — — — — — — — — — — — Self-esteem, confidence, respect of and by others

Love / belonging — — — — — — — — Friendship, family, social interaction, intimacy, affection

Safety — — — — — — — — — Security of: body, morality, family, resources, property, health

Physiological — — — — — Food, water, health, sleep, breathing

FIGURE 10-4 Maslow's hierarchy of needs shows basic needs as a foundation, with higher level needs built upon them.

model. For example, in a cross-cultural study with participants from 39 countries, the fulfillment of "esteem" needs was considered more important only in Western cultures, where independence is stressed over interdependence (Oishi et al., 1999).

For many of us, our basic needs are met each day without much effort. But what if you live in a dangerous environment in which you must be concerned about walking home at night or being safe while you sleep? These needs would prevent you from working on your goals for relationships and self-actualization. Across the world, most people expend their effort in meeting basic needs for clean water, enough food, and a safe environment. Similarly, in some contexts, social goals of building relationships with family and maintaining social status might limit your search for self-actualization, requiring your service or duty to the family or group. Finally, consider an emergency situation, such as the impact of Hurricane Katrina. After the storm and flooding subsided, would you begin thinking about your basic physiological needs? Or would contacting your family members be your priority? Clearly, many factors, from biological to social to achievement needs, play into the psychology of motivation.

Natural disasters and emergencies can reveal psychological differences in our motivation to act.

CONCEPT LEARNING CHECK 10.1 | *Theories of Motivation*

Match each example to the theory that gives the best account of the motivation described.

A. Instinct

B. Evolution

C. Drive

D. Arousal

E. Incentive

F. Hierarchy of needs

1. _____ Harry finds his mind wandering after studying for hours in a carrel in the library. He heads to the local bar to find some action.

2. _____ Jamal dislikes his job, but he sticks with it because he needs the money.

3. _____ Karen eventually stops playing and leaves the soccer game in progress to head to the sidelines for some water.

4. _____ Even though she knows it is not a healthy choice, Rebecca loves the taste of fried foods.

5. _____ Tommy saw a spider and ran from it.

6. _____ Francesca has to work to provide for her family before she can attend college.

Explain

7. For each of these theories, explain whether they can account for motivational differences observed for people living in different environments, such as a modern Japanese high-rise apartment versus a remote desert hut.

A. Instinct

B. Evolution

C. Drive

D. Arousal

E. Incentive

F. Hierarchy of needs

10.2 Motivation of Hunger

Many biological and environmental factors affect the system that regulates hunger and eating.

- Illustrate the biology/physiology of hunger.
- Explain environmental influences on hunger.
- Describe the eating disorders and self-regulation.

Hunger provides an example of how a basic motivation can require a complex system for regulation. The human body has not just one system to regulate eating behavior but many. A great deal of research has examined why we eat, what we eat, and, increasingly, what to do when we eat too much.

The Physiology and Regulation of Hunger

Many biological factors contribute to the regulation of hunger and eating. These systems are located throughout the body, including the stomach and digestive organs, the brain, the endocrine system, the blood, and our genes. The hunger motivation ensures that we maintain a nourished body using feedback from all of these biological sources.

The Stomach

The first thing to think of is the stomach: Its growls seem to signal that food is needed, and when full, its stretching signals that you have had enough. To test the idea of the stomach as the regulator of hunger, an early study involved intentionally swallowing a balloon (Cannon & Washburn, 1912). The balloon was inflated with air to fill the stomach, and a recording device registered whenever the stomach contracted. Meanwhile, the subject (A. J. Washburn) pushed a button whenever he felt hungry FIGURE 10-5. Sure enough, the reports of feelings of hunger were directly related to the contractions of the empty stomach.

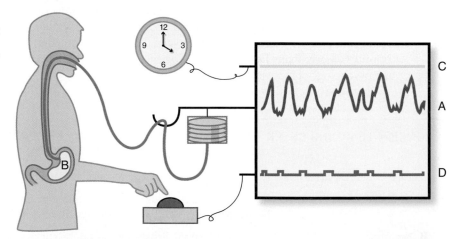

FIGURE 10-5 Cannon and Washburn's study showed that stomach contractions were the cause of feelings of hunger pangs.

It seemed the case was closed; however, patients who had their stomachs removed due to disease still reported feelings of hunger. In addition, an experiment with rats showed that they continued to eat even though their stomachs were surgically removed. So while hunger pangs in the stomach play a role in motivating you to eat, they are not the only mechanism that regulates our eating behavior.

The Brain

Early studies examined the role the brain plays in hunger and eating. The limbic system, located in the center of the brain, controls motivation, emotion, and memory FIGURE 10-6. The structure called the **hypothalamus**, located just below the thalamus, is the functional center of motivation in the brain. Studies of animals tested what happens to eating behavior when the hypothalamus was either destroyed or was stimulated by placing an electrode within it. The results showed two separate areas of the hypothalamus that activate and deactivate eating behavior.

One area of the hypothalamus, called the **lateral hypothalamus**, appears to be a "start eating" center. When it is activated, it "turns on" hunger, and the animal starts eating. When stimulated with a small amount of electricity through an electrode in this area,

Hypothalamus The functional center of motivation in the brain.

Lateral hypothalamus The "start eating" functional center in the brain.

Limbic system

FIGURE 10-6 The limbic system including the amygdala, hippocampus, and hypothalamus, is responsible for motivated behavior, memory, and emotion.

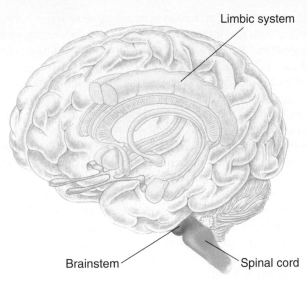

Brainstem   Spinal cord

Ventromedial hypothalamus
The functional "stop eating" center in the brain.

Endocrine system The network of glands throughout the body that manufacture and secrete hormones.

a rat will eat even after it is full (Teitelbaum & Epstein, 1962). However, if this area is destroyed by killing cells, the "start button" no longer works. Animals with lesions in this lateral (or side) area of the hypothalamus will not initiate eating on their own FIGURE 10-7.

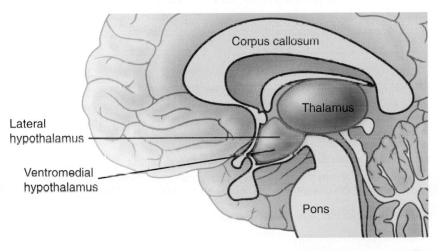

Corpus callosum

Thalamus

Lateral hypothalamus

Ventromedial hypothalamus

Pons

FIGURE 10-7 Two areas of the hypothalamus, the lateral and the ventromedial, are responsible for motivating the starting and stopping of eating.

Another area of the hypothalamus is called the **ventromedial hypothalamus**, located below and toward the center of the structure. This area appears to be a "stop eating" center, turning hunger off. When the ventromedial area of the hypothalamus is stimulated, a rat will not eat. It will act as if it is full even though it has not been fed. And, when this area is damaged, the rat appears to lose the ability to "shut off" its hunger. These rats consume endlessly, growing to more than three times their normal body weight FIGURE 10-8 (Wyrwicka & Dobrzecka, 1960). So there appear to be brain centers located in the hypothalamus that control the initiation and the cessation of eating.

FIGURE 10-8 When the ventromedial hypothalamus is destroyed, rats will continue eating to the point of tripling their body weight.

Hormones

But what signals these centers to make eating stop and start? The hypothalamus is a brain area that regulates the **endocrine system**, the network of glands throughout the body that manufacture and secrete hormones. The hypothalamus is the neural center

Hormones Chemicals that influence body growth, mood, and sexual characteristics.

Ghrelin A hormone secreted by the empty stomach to stimulate hunger.

Leptin A protein secreted by fat cells to signal adequate stores.

Metabolism The physiological processes used to convert energy from nutrients.

Basal metabolic rate The body's ability to use nutrients efficiently to maintain itself when at rest.

that communicates with the endocrine system to produce more or fewer hormones as needed. **Hormones** are chemicals that influence body growth, mood, eating, and sexual characteristics. Some hormones function as neurotransmitters, providing a connection between the brain and the endocrine system. **TABLE 10-1** shows the major endocrine glands and the effects of the hormones they produce. In particular, digestive hormones in the stomach, gut, and pancreas work to control the processing of food and signal when more food is needed. In particular, a hormone called **ghrelin** is secreted by the empty stomach to stimulate hunger. Another, called *obestatin*, sends out a "fullness" signal. Other hormones also suppress hunger, including peptide *PYY* in the digestive tract, *orexin* from the hypothalamus, and **leptin**, a protein secreted by fat cells to signal that adequate fat stores already exist.

For those who have successfully lost weight, hormones may work against maintaining the loss: After losing weight, hormonal changes occur that increase appetite. In one study, participants' hormone levels and appetites were assessed after they ate breakfast (Sumithran et al., 2011). They then spent 10 weeks on a very-low-calorie (less than 550 calories a day) diet and lost an average of 14% of their body weight. The hormone, leptin, which tells the brain how much body fat is present fell by two-thirds immediately after the weight loss. When leptin falls, appetite increases, and subjects said they were hungrier than when they started the study. A year later, the subjects were gaining the weight back despite a maintenance diet (on average, half of what they had lost). And leptin levels were still one-third lower than they were at the start of the study. Other hormones that stimulate hunger, such as ghrelin and peptide *PYY*, were also changed in a way that increased subjects' appetites. After being overweight, that weight becomes the new "normal" that your body attempts to maintain.

Metabolism

Hormones impact the body through the regulation of the **metabolism** of the body, or the physiological processes used to convert energy from nutrients. The **basal metabolic rate** is the ability to use nutrients efficiently to maintain the body when at rest for functions like breathing and digesting. The body strives for a state of homeostasis, maintaining a

TABLE 10-1 Major Endocrine Glands and the Functions of the Hormones They Produce

Gland(s)	Produce Hormones that Regulate
Adrenals	Fight-or-flight responses Metabolism Sexual desire in women
Anterior pituitary	Testes and ovaries Breast milk production Metabolism Reactions to stress
Gut	Digestion
Hypothalamus	Release of pituitary hormones
Ovaries	Development of female sexual traits Ova production
Pancreas	Glucose metabolism
Parathyroid	Calcium levels
Posterior pituitary	Water conservation Breast milk excretion Uterus contraction
Testes	Development of male sexual traits Sperm production Sexual desire in men
Thyroid	Metabolism Growth and development

stable or balanced physiological state over time. Individuals vary in how much energy their bodies expend when at rest, with some at a faster rate of calorie burn and some requiring very few calories when not in motion. Regulation of metabolism is handled through the thyroid gland. About 65 to 70% of calories burned each day are used to keep up the routine body functions—heart, kidneys, and liver. About 10 to 15% are spent eating and assimilating food. And the rest are spent by the exercising of muscles. Your metabolic rate makes a difference in how much food you need to consume to provide enough energy to keep your body functioning. Each body has a weight that it naturally gravitates to, and researchers have found that all people, fat or thin, adjust their metabolism to maintain that weight (Leibel et al., 1995). This individual **set point** seems to maintain a particular range of body weight FIGURE 10-9. So, if food intake is sharply cut back, the metabolism slows to maintain the usual weight, and if too much food is taken in, metabolism increases to burn off extra calories (Keesey & Powley, 1986). The body responds to changes in weight by attempting to maintain its present weight, though some studies have not found evidence of metabolic adaptation to weight loss (Weinsier et al., 2000).

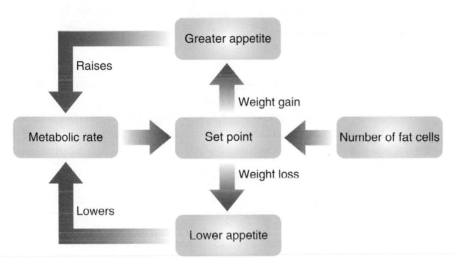

FIGURE 10-9 Set point theory suggests the body works to maintain a particular weight, so that when intake is reduced, metabolism slows to burn fewer calories.
Source: Data from Keesey, R. E., & Powley, T. L. (1986). The regulation of body weight. Annual Review of Psychology, 37, 109–133.

Many obese people eat about the same amount as those of normal weight (Spitzer & Rodin, 1981). When pairs of individuals are matched by weight, height, age, and activity level, differences in metabolic rate are apparent (Rose & Williams, 1961). So one person may eat twice as many calories in a day as another but maintain the same weight due to differences in metabolism. If your metabolism is very efficient, it stores more calories as body fat in reserve, and over time, weight gain occurs. As mentioned earlier, leptin (a protein) is secreted by fat cells and acts as a signal to make the metabolism less efficient, burning more calories. While obese individuals still produce leptin, the receptors in the brain that respond to this signal appear to be deficient (Maffei et al., 1995). As a result, it can be difficult to lose or gain weight beyond a range in which your body comfortably operates. However, because changes in weight do occur, the tendency to maintain a set weight is sometimes called a **settling point** instead. The National Weight Control Registry (Wing & Hill, 1994) tracks individuals who have successfully lost more than 100 pounds, demonstrating that it is possible to change this system over time.

Glucose Monitoring

In addition to regulating endocrine mechanisms, the brain also controls the level of **glucose** (or sugar) in the bloodstream FIGURE 10-10. The brain automatically monitors the levels of glucose in the blood and changes the level of hormones produced by the endocrine system in response. After eating, the levels of glucose in the blood rise as the food is processed. This leads the hypothalamus to stimulate the endocrine system to process the glucose using the hormone **insulin**, secreted by the pancreas and used to convert glucose

Set point The tendency to maintain a particular range of body weight.

Settling point Tendency to maintain an approximate but changeable weight range.

Glucose The form of sugar that carries nutrients in the bloodstream.

Insulin A hormone secreted by the pancreas and used to convert glucose into energy for muscle use.

FIGURE 10-10 The hypothalamus coordinates the work of the endocrine system to use and store glucose throughout the body.
Source: Data from Campfield, L. A., Smith, F. J., Rosenbaum, M., & Hirsch, J. (1996). Human eating: Evidence for a physiological basis using a modified paradigm. Neuroscience and Biobehavioral Reviews, 20(1), 133–137.

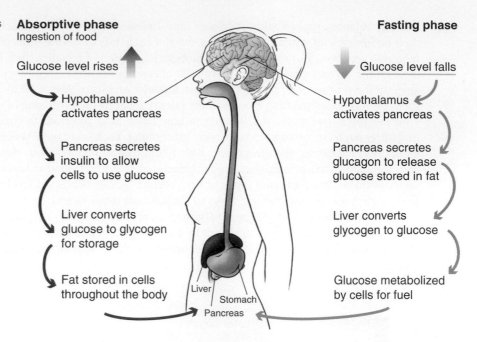

Absorptive phase
Ingestion of food

Glucose level rises

Hypothalamus activates pancreas

Pancreas secretes insulin to allow cells to use glucose

Liver converts glucose to glycogen for storage

Fat stored in cells throughout the body

Liver
Stomach
Pancreas

Fasting phase

Glucose level falls

Hypothalamus activates pancreas

Pancreas secretes glucagon to release glucose stored in fat

Liver converts glycogen to glucose

Glucose metabolized by cells for fuel

Diabetes A disease in which sugar in the blood is ineffectively used due to resistance to or an absence of insulin.

Adipose tissue Fat cells stored beneath the skin and throughout the abdomen.

into energy for muscle use. The inability to produce insulin, or resistance to it, leads to the disease called **diabetes**. Unused glucose is converted into glycogen, a form of animal starch, and stored in the liver. For longer-term storage, fat tissue (called **adipose tissue**) is stored beneath the skin and throughout the abdomen. Adipose tissue absorbs nutrients from blood and converts them to triglycerides (fats). In obese individuals, the size of the fat cells increases to hold more stored energy.

The result of these processes is that when blood sugar is low, people feel hungry and want food (Campfield et al., 1996). When food intake raises glucose levels, hunger is reduced FIGURE 10-11. However, this regulatory system takes time to operate. We can eat quickly, but it takes some time for the food in the stomach to be processed and for blood glucose to rise. As a result, it is easy to eat more than necessary to restore glucose levels or to wait too long to eat again and then feel extreme effects of deprivation. Foods also differ in how quickly they are converted into glucose. Simple sugars such as fruit juices have a high glucose index, meaning they are taken up quickly to affect sugar in the bloodstream, while complex carbohydrates take longer to process, leading to extended periods of glucose uptake. All of these biological processes work together to signal when to start or stop eating.

FIGURE 10-11 The cycle of consumption is started by detecting lowered glucose levels, and ended by raised glucose levels.

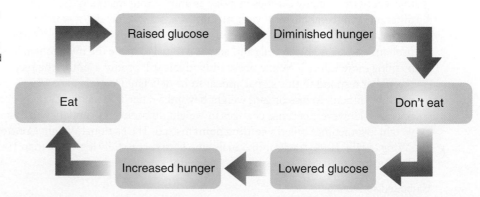

Raised glucose

Diminished hunger

Eat

Don't eat

Increased hunger

Lowered glucose

Genetics

Genetics also plays a major role in regulating hunger. Studies of twins demonstrate that adult body weight is more similar in identical twins than in fraternal twins (Stunkard et al., 1990) FIGURE 10-12. These correlations occur even when twins are raised apart and so experience different environments. Adoptive siblings do not resemble each other in weight even when they share a family environment, but they do resemble their biological

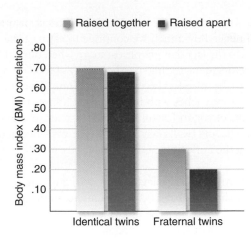

■ Raised together ■ Raised apart

FIGURE 10-12 Identical twins have a more similar body weight than fraternal twins, even if they were not raised together.
Source: Data from Bulik, C. M., Wade, T. D., Heath, A. C., Martin, N. G., Stunkard, A. J., & Eaves, L. J. (2001). Relating body mass index to figural stimuli: population-based normative data for Caucasians. International Journal of Obesity and Related Metabolic Disorders, *25(10), 1517–1524.*

parents (Grilo & Pogue-Geile, 1991). The factor that puts children at greatest risk of being overweight is having obese parents (Agras et al., 2004). This provides strong evidence that the many physiological factors regulating hunger are influenced by genetic heritage (Schwartz et al., 2000).

This brings us back to evolutionary theories of motivation. The limbic system that controls motivation evolved in mammals that lived in very different environments than we do today. Then, food was often scarce and took a great deal of energy to acquire, and little storage was possible. So each day was consumed with efforts toward securing enough food to eat. The ability to store fat was an advantage through early human history, when food sources were sometimes unavailable (Assanand et al., 1998). Today, the average American consumes 150 cups of sugar a year. Such abundance of pure calories was never possible in the environment of early humans, and our system for regulating hunger never had to cope with too much food. As a result, the delicate biological machinery regulating our food consumption is faced with environmental challenges unlike any experienced in the history of human evolution. Perhaps it is not surprising that hunger, eating, and weight have become important health concerns today.

Environmental Influences

Apart from the many biological factors involved in the motivation to eat, a wealth of environmental factors plays a role as well. Imagine standing at a buffet. Which foods will you select for your plate? People have individual taste preferences, such as a "sweet tooth" or an addiction to hot sauce. But in all people, sweetness causes neural systems to actively generate a "liking" reaction, so sweet tastes are more desirable than other tastes (Pecina et al., 2003). We have a specific hunger for sodium if our bodies lack it, leading us to seek out salty foods. More typically, we seek out foods with tastes we enjoy and prefer those foods when available (Murphy, 1947). One strategy to test whether you are truly "hungry" is to ask whether you would eat something you do not enjoy. And deprivation can make foods seem more enticing. Dieting in which specific foods are not eaten can increase your desire for (and consumption of) the forbidden foods (Stirling & Yeomans, 2004). Culture also influences what we eat, so that certain familiar foods are desired, while foods regularly eaten in some cultures may seem unpalatable in others.

We are also sensitive to food cues in the environment. You may not have thought about eating a cupcake recently, but seeing them in the store may make you decide to try one again. Exposure to food cues leads to increased consumption, which forms the basis of modern advertising. But can exposure to food cues ever help to curb your appetite? A recent study asked some people to imagine placing 30 individual pieces of candy one by one into a bowl. Another group was told to imagine eating 30 pieces, concentrating on the taste, chewing, and swallowing of each one. Then, both groups were given real candies, and the amount they chose to eat was measured. Those who had imagined simply placing the candies in a bowl ate more than the control group; but, those who had imagined *eating* the candy ate less! This finding demonstrates the principle of habituation in which the first bite is delicious and the 20th bite is not as satisfying. Specifically imagining repeatedly eating a certain food can lead to a decrease in our desire for it (Morewedge et al., 2010).

Foods eaten in some cultures, like these grasshoppers, are unacceptable in others.

Unit bias Tendency to eat the amount provided as a serving.

Anorexia nervosa An eating disorder in which an individual feels he or she is overweight despite objective evidence.

Why doesn't habituation always work to curb eating? It does in most people and situations. But other factors can influence how much we continue to eat past the point of satisfying hunger. **Unit bias** refers to the fact that people eat more when offered larger servings (Geier et al., 2006). Even factors in the setting like the variety of food on display can influence eating, while exposure to the same food every day can diminish your intake. People ate a third more when offered sandwiches with four different fillings rather than one and more when given three flavors of yogurt (distinctive in taste, texture, and color) compared to just one of their favorite flavors (Rolls et al., 1981). The presence of others also affects eating: As the group size at the buffet increases, the meal size increases as well (Herman et al., 2003).

In addition, we often eat "mindlessly," watching television or socializing without being aware of how much we consume (Wansink & Sobel, 2007). We tend to report only a fraction of the food decisions we make, and we seem to be unaware (or unwilling to admit) that our environment influences these decisions. Environmental factors like package size, plate shape, lighting, seating, and music can influence consumption far more than we realize. The environment affects how much we eat by inhibiting our self-monitoring and by suggesting alternative norms for amounts of food we "should," or wish to, consume (Wansink, 2004). We also respond to external incentives around eating, such as eating what is served to you as a guest, a situation in which refusal may be viewed as insulting. And have you ever been admonished to finish the food on your plate? Avoiding the wasting of food, eating a complete meal, or demonstrating that the chef's work was excellent can lead to consuming more than is truly desired.

In American culture, there is pervasive exposure to food that is highly caloric, heavily marketed, and readily available. This creates a "toxic environment" for eating in which nutritious food is harder to find and more expensive than less healthy choices (Horgen & Brownell, 2002). These forces include the explosion of fast food outlets, increasingly large restaurant portion sizes, "all-you-can-eat" buffets, the proliferation of mini markets that sell high-calorie snacks and drinks, widespread food advertising, and contracts between schools, snack food, and soft drink companies to sell products in school cafeterias. And the prevalence of severely overweight children, 15%, has doubled during the past 20 years.

With these environmental factors surrounding eating, it is easy to see how hunger changes from "what the body needs" to "what the person wants." The attraction to eat something pleasurable becomes even larger when you are hungry or stressed, leading you to eat more. Individuals with high responses to stress (measured by cortisol reactivity) eat more after stressful tasks and eat significantly more sweet food on both stressful and nonstressful days (Epel et al., 2001). Stressors also lead to increases in negative mood and then greater food consumption. These results suggest that psychophysiological responses to stress lead to uncontrolled eating behavior for some people. Combined with the availability of food, the college environment appears to promote an average weight gain of 2.9 pounds during the first year on campus (Hoffman et al., 2006). Over time, these environments can impact both weight and health (Epel et al., 2001).

Hunger, Eating, and Weight

When any of these biological or environmental factors goes awry, there is the potential for difficulty in maintaining a healthy weight. Most commonly, the problem is obesity: Two-thirds of American adults and one-third of school-age children are either overweight or obese. These proportions increased by 50% for adults and 300% for children in the past 50 years (Arkowitz & Lilienfeld, 2009). Obesity is considered a medical problem because it often leads to diseases like diabetes, high blood pressure, and heart disease. But, as we have seen, many factors influence whether someone is overweight; so being overweight alone is not considered to be the result of an "eating disorder." Three specific eating disorders have been identified by the American Psychiatric Association based on research in psychology and psychiatry: anorexia nervosa, bulimia, and binge eating disorder.

Eating Disorders

Anorexia nervosa is an eating disorder in which individuals continue to feel they are overweight despite objective evidence that they are actually underweight. This disorder is defined as involving weight loss of at least 25%, restriction of intake, fear of becoming obese, and problems with body image. Disturbance of body image, or **body dysmorphia**, involves an overly self-critical attitude toward your own appearance and occurs in both men and women. For example, anorexics asked to estimate the size of their body parts by drawing on paper or making a belt consistently overestimated their true size (Pierloot & Houben, 1978). They may follow extreme diets in the attempt to control their weight or overdo their exercise regimens to gain a sense of control over their weight. With too little body fat, cessation of the menstrual cycle sometimes occurs. This disorder has appeared throughout history, as this description from the 17th century shows (Silverman, 1983):

> *Mr. Duke's daughter in St. Mary Axe, in the year 1684, and the Eighteenth year of her Age*
> *... fell into a total suppression of her monthly courses from a multitude of Cares and Passions*
> *of her mind. From which time her Appetite began to abate ... She wholly neglected to care*
> *for herself for two years ... (like a skeleton only covered with skin) ...*
> —Richard Morton (1689) (cited in Bliss & Branch, 1960, pp. 9–11).

Anorexia typically develops in early adolescence, and approximately 2% of girls are affected. Boys make up only 10% of cases, though this number is growing. Anorexia is very difficult to treat, often involving longer-term in-hospital stays and relapses, with around 10% of cases resulting in death from heart problems caused by lack of proper nutrition.

A second type of eating disorder is called **bulimia nervosa** and refers to individuals that binge eat large amounts of food but maintain relatively normal weights by purging (vomiting) or using laxatives to avoid absorbing food. The diagnostic criteria for bulimia include episodes of binging followed by purging, an inability to stop voluntarily, depression with self-deprecating thoughts, and binges followed by dieting. Other health problems arise from this cycle of behavior, such as damage to the teeth or esophagus from repeated purging. It, too, can be a fatal disease. Some estimates show around 4% of college-age women show some symptoms of bulimia (Drewnowski et al., 1988).

Binge eating disorder is a pattern of frequently consuming unusually large amounts of food (Pull, 2004). Almost everyone overeats on occasion, but for some people, overeating becomes a regular occurrence. Someone with binge eating disorder often eats in secrecy and does not compensate by purging or overexercising so is often overweight.

Perceptions of body weight can play a role in these eating disorders. In anorexics, perceptual distortions (body dysmorphia) prevent them from perceiving their shrinking size. For others, trying on small swimsuits in the mirror may be anxiety provoking. A recent study suggests that culture may play a role in the perceptions of weight and body image. Think about your ideal body at age 18. Which figure FIGURE 10-13 fits your ideal best? Now, which figure fits your real body at age 18? Most people find a mismatch, suggesting the ideal body is different from their own. But where did your idea of the "ideal body" come from?

Researchers asked both African American and white teenage girls to describe their "ideal" (Parker et al., 1995). White teens suggested someone blue-eyed, 5 feet 7 inches tall, weighing between 100 and 110 pounds, a rather narrow definition of beauty. African American teens, however, described personal qualities such as a sense of style, a nice personality, or "having a good head on one's shoulders." For a physical description, most

Body dysmorphia A disturbance of body image including an overly self-critical attitude.

Bulimia nervosa A disorder involving binge eating large amounts of food but maintaining relatively normal weight by purging.

Binge eating disorder An eating disorder marked by repeated overeating without the compensatory strategies found in bulimia.

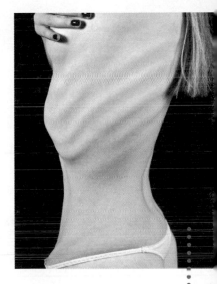

To someone with anorexia, a thin appearance may be perceived as grossly overweight.

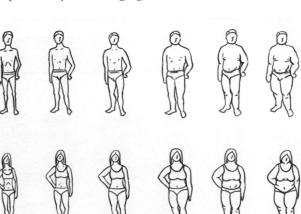

FIGURE 10-13 Which body image most resembles our culture's ideal? Which image most resembles your own body?
Source: Adapted from Bulik, C. M., Wade, T. D., Heath, A. C., Martin, N. G., Stunkard, A. J., & Eaves, L. J. (2001). Relating body mass index to figural stimuli: population-based normative data for Caucasians. International Journal of Obesity and Related Metabolic Disorders, *25(10), 1517–1524.*

Nicole Richie (May 2007) was "outed" as pregnant based on the "baby bump" in this photo.

responded that fuller hips, large thighs, and a small waist were desirable. Close to 90% of the white teens were dissatisfied with their weight, versus 30% of the black respondents. For white girls, weight seemed a central aspect of their self-image, promoting unrealistic expectations. However, other research suggests this is changing, and an increase in anorexia and bulimia is occurring among African American women of all socioeconomic levels (Crago et al., 1996). Other studies have found strong correlations between levels of eating disturbance, self-esteem, and body dissatisfaction in male homosexuals (Williamson & Hartley, 1998), suggesting this may also be a vulnerable population.

Perceptions of body image are clearly influenced by values that vary from one culture to another (Striegel-Moore & Builk, 2007). In Western cultures, unrealistic images of beauty are propagated through movies, television, and print advertisements (Bulik et al., 2001). Do these images impact our views of ourselves and others? One study demonstrated that viewing ideal images can make you more critical of the real people in your life. Men and women saw slides depicting either opposite-sex nudes or abstract art. Then they were asked how attractive they found their current romantic partner, and how "in love" they were with this partner. Women were unaffected; however, men were more dissatisfied with their current partner after looking at the nudes (Kenrick, Gutierres, & Goldberg, 1989). People tend to perform social comparison, so that considering the appearance of others around us may influence how we view ourselves (Suls et al., 2002) and our partners.

Another consequence of an overemphasis on low body fat manifests as poor reproductive health. Infertility and cessation of menses occur with lower weights, and while doctors recommend gaining 20 pounds during a pregnancy, this can be frightening to those concerned about being overweight. This also may negatively affect attitudes about breastfeeding. While we see media reports on "body after baby," showing celebrities who get back into shape quickly following birth, a slower-paced recovery to normal weight is more typical.

Obesity

The most common problem with hunger motivation is overeating, resulting in excess body weight. Obesity itself is not considered an eating disorder because excess weight can arise from multiple influences. Sometimes there is a problem with a biological mechanism, such as genetics, a too-slow metabolism, a problem in the response to sugar in the blood, or a disease of the endocrine system such as Cushing's disease, caused by high levels of cortisone in the blood. For other people, excess weight is caused by physical inactivity, overeating, or "disordered eating," in which specific foods are eaten to excess. Other times, obesity results from situational factors, such as the "freshman 15" (which turns out to be more often 5 pounds of extra weight in first-year students) resulting from the variety and availability of residence hall food combined with the stress of college study (Holm-Denoma et al., 2008). Obesity is a problem that must be considered in the context of the multiple influences of biology and environment.

Obesity is defined as an excess level of fat in the body, when someone is at least 15% above ideal weight for a given height. A ratio of weight to height called the **body mass index (BMI)** is used to classify degrees of obesity as a function of excess weight FIGURE 10-14

Obesity An excess level of fat in the body, at least 15% above ideal weight for a given height.

Body mass index (BMI) A ratio of height and weight that includes comparison to others.

FIGURE 10-14 The body mass index (BMI) shows the categories of weight based on the larger population.
Source: Data from the CDC/Division of Nutrition, Physical Activity, and Obesity, National Center for Chronic Disease Prevention and Health Promotion.

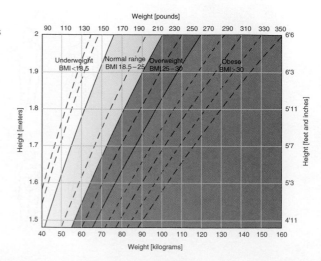

(Eknoyan, 2008; Keys et al., 1972). The index requires only height and weight and provides comparison based on the general population. Currently, Western cultures are experiencing an epidemic of obesity at rates never seen before, and weight increases are spreading across the globe. With abundantly available processed foods high in sugar and fat and a decline in physical exercise or exertion at work and school, more people than ever before in history are currently well above their ideal weight (NIH, NHLBI Obesity Education Initiative, 1998).

Why does this matter? Obesity is a leading preventable cause of disease and one of the most serious public health problems of today (Barness et al., 2007) FIGURE 10-15. For example, in women, a BMI above 32 has been associated with a doubled mortality rate

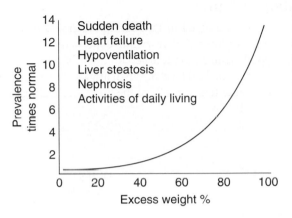

FIGURE 10-15 Prevalence increases exponentially when excess weight is 60% or more above desirable weight. *Source: Reproduced from Kral, J. G. (1985). Morbid obesity and related health risks.* Annals of Internal Medicine, 103*(6), 1043–1104.*

(Manson et al., 1995). In addition, excess weight increases the risk of heart disease, diabetes, and stroke FIGURE 10-16. Research shows that as BMI approaches the "overweight" and "obese" categories, risk of cancers (endometrial, breast, and colon), hypertension (high blood pressure), high cholesterol, liver and gallbladder diseases, sleep apnea and respiratory problems, osteoarthritis, and infertility also greatly increase (Kral, 1985). In addition, these diseases often combine to create metabolic syndrome, a combination of type 2 diabetes, high blood pressure, high blood cholesterol, and high triglyceride levels (Haslam & James, 2005).

Clearly, from the evolutionary perspective, human bodies are not suited to carrying so much extra fat. In some times and places, obesity was widely perceived as a symbol of wealth and fertility and still is in some areas (Haslam & James, 2005). When food is scarce, extra body weight is viewed as attractive; in some areas, young girls are encouraged to overeat to gain excess weight as a sign of beauty. In Mauritania, women are fighting back against force-feeding, but up to one-third of the country's women risk their health by putting on weight to conform to a cultural aesthetic standard (IRIN, 2009). But when food is plentiful, thin is "in"; in fact, social class differences are associated with weight, presumably because nutritious food is more expensive.

In addition to health risks, there are many psychological, social, and economic consequences to being overweight. Obesity is stigmatized in much of the world. Being overweight leads to negative stereotypes such as laziness, slothfulness, and lower class status. The obese are often discriminated against in employment, salary determinations, and housing. For example, one study found weight discrimination in employment is greater than bias about ethnicity and gender (Roehling et al., 2007). And the obese may have difficulty in romantic relationships and friendships and have been found to suffer bullying during grade school (Lumeng et al., 2010).

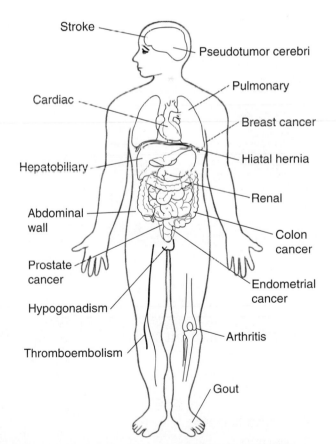

FIGURE 10-16 Organ systems with complications and conditions associated with obesity.

While there is a wealth of information available on weight loss, there is no magic solution. Studies suggest several strategies. First, decide to make permanent changes in eating habits (rather than dieting) so that weight loss is more likely to be permanent. Track your food intake to keep aware of how much you are eating (Lichtman et al., 1992). New recommendations for preventing weight gain have increased from 30 minutes of moderate-intensity activity daily to 45 to 60 minutes per day (Saris et al., 2003). Intrinsic sources of motivation (e.g., interest and enjoyment in exercise) play a more important role than extrinsic rewards in longer-term weight management (Teixeira et al., 2006). It helps to want to change for your own sake, such as to feel healthier and enjoy life, rather than simply wanting to look good in someone else's eyes.

A Comparison: Motivation of Thirst

We have just seen the many factors involved in motivating when and what we eat. In contrast, consider the motivation of "thirst." Here, a simple mechanism detects when fluid in the body is low (the hypothalamus monitors cell fluid levels, and the pituitary gland and kidneys monitor blood plasma fluid levels). When low levels are detected, we feel thirst, take in fluid, and as water enters the cells of the body, our feelings of thirst subside FIGURE 10-17 (Blass & Hall, 1976).

When you see someone drinking from a large water bottle, do you think of their behavior as driven by psychology?

FIGURE 10-17 Compared to the complex mechanisms responsible for hunger, the motivation for thirst involves a much simpler mechanism based on cell and blood plasma hydration.
Source: Data from Blass, E. M., & Hall, W. G. (1976). Drinking termination: Interactions among hydrational, orogastric, and behavioral controls in rats. Psychological Review, 83(5), 356–374.

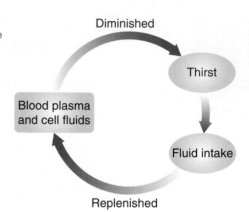

When you see someone drinking water, no one thinks, "Look at her drinking all of that water! What a hog!" No one pays you less because you drink a lot of water or sees you as a less desirable mate, nor do you hate yourself for doing it. What if our motivation to eat were more like the system that controls thirst? With the notable exception of alcohol, no one consumes too much by drinking. Imagine that as your goal for hunger: That you eat what your body needs as it needs it.

CONCEPT LEARNING CHECK 10.2 | *Eating Disorder or Disordered Eating?*

For each concept, explain the behavior and whether it is considered an eating disorder:

1. Bulimia

2. Binge eating disorder

3. Obesity

4. Anorexia

CRITICAL THINKING APPLICATION

*I*magine that I place a marshmallow in front of you (and imagine you enjoy eating them). I leave you alone with the marshmallow, and you can eat it any time you wish; however, if you wait until I return to eat it, I will give you an extra marshmallow. Left alone, how long will you resist the temptation to eat the marshmallow in front of you? In a study of 5-year-olds, this task turned out to be an excellent measure of **self-regulation**, or the ability to control behavior through intentional strategies (Mischel et al., 1972). Some of the children went ahead and ate the marshmallow right away. Some focused their attention on the marshmallow and were led to eat it a short time later. But the children who managed to distract themselves from the reward, by looking or turning away, singing, or talking to themselves about other things, lasted the longest without eating and thereby won the second reward.

This ability to postpone rewards, called the **delay of gratification**, is viewed as a sign of maturity. Can you work for a long time toward a goal without a taste of the reward? Getting a college degree, an MD, or a PhD, as in the opening story, may be one of the longest delays of gratification in life. Most often, we overemphasize the present rather than the future. It tastes good now, and that feels more important than the upcoming swimsuit season. Resisting temptation is often considered an act of willpower in which you resolve not to give in. One theory suggests that willpower requires effort, and exerting that effort requires energy (Baumeister et al., 1998). Since energy is a limited resource, you may run out of it; however, after some time, it is replenished. But if you use up your energy on other things, you will have less energy available for self-control.

The prediction from this theory is that using your willpower in one situation will reduce the probability of successfully using it again later. In one study, participants came into a lab filled with the smell of fresh-baked chocolate chip cookies (Baumeister et al., 2007). A plate containing both cookies and radishes was presented. They were assigned at random to taste only one food (either the cookies or the radishes). In a control condition, no food (and no cookie smell) was presented. They were left alone in the room to taste the food for 5 minutes. Next, the participants worked on a puzzle, and the time they spent on it was measured. In fact, the puzzle was unsolvable, and eventually, all of them gave up on it. But would their use of self-control make a difference in how long they kept trying? The cookie participants were allowed to smell and then eat then cookies. However, the radish participants had to see and smell the cookies but taste only the radishes. Did exercising their self-control by not eating the cookies affect how much willpower they applied to the puzzle?

The results in **TABLE 10-2** show that it did. The group eating the chocolate chip cookies worked about as long (on average) as the control participants. However, the group eating the radishes kept working half as long on the frustrating puzzle task. This suggests that using their willpower to avoid eating the cookies took a toll on them, making them less able to sustain their effort on the puzzle. The self-control of behavior—doing what you think is best rather than what you feel you really want—takes effort. It is also influenced by situational factors, like stress and exhaustion. You may notice that you tend to eat more junk food around exam times or miss your exercise when you are feeling tired. Just as a muscle gets tired from exertion, using your self-control can cause difficulty doing so again in the short term, even on unrelated tasks. Bouncing back depends on, of all things, your blood glucose level. Laboratory tests showed that initial acts of self-control decrease self-control on later tasks, but consuming a glucose drink restored it (Baumeister et al., 2007). So exerting

Self-regulation The ability to control behavior through intentional strategies.

Delay of gratification The ability to postpone rewards until a later time.

TABLE 10-2 Persistence on Unsolvable Puzzles (Experiment 1)

Condition	Time (min)	Attempts
Radish	8.4	19.4
Chocolate	18.9	34.3
No food control	20.9	32.8

Note: Standard deviations for Column 1, top to bottom, are 4.67, 6.86, and 7.30. For Column 2, SDs = 8.12, 20.16, and 13.38.
Source: Baumeister, R. F., Vohs, K. D., & Tice, D. M. (2007). The strength model of self-control. Current Directions in Psychological Science, 16*(6), 351–355.*

(Continues)

your self-control requires a certain amount of glucose in your system. This provides another reason to keep your blood sugar levels constant by eating healthy meals and snacks throughout the day.

How can you improve your self-regulation? Studies of dieters found that people eat more while watching television because they are distracted from monitoring their behavior. Binge eating may even be motivated by the desire to escape from self-awareness (Heatherton & Baumeister, 1991). Those with high standards for themselves and sensitivity to opinions of others feel anxious when they fall short. To escape such negative pressures and feelings, binge eaters narrow their attention to the immediate stimulus (the food) and avoid thinking more broadly about themselves. Other behaviors can also help us escape from feelings of negative self-awareness; for example, drinking alcohol provides the feeling of escape, but also makes it especially hard to regulate how much you drink. Fortunately, you can find harmless means of escape through other behaviors. In particular, exercise (even a single session!) has been shown to be an effective way to narrow focus and improve your mood while providing benefits to your health (Yeung, 1996).

Recommendations for improving your self-control include:

- Set realistic goals.
- Think in terms of "health*ier*" rather than perfection.
- Keep a record of your behavior to raise your awareness.

- Keep trying to align your behavior with your goals in "baby steps."
- Save your self-control resources by managing your exposure.

If self-control takes effort, it can help to use care in exposing yourself to situations in which you will have to exert it. For example, if you know you will be attending a party with lots of fattening food, you might consider eating a healthy meal beforehand so that you are not as tempted to eat the treats at the party. Controlling your home environment by keeping only healthy foods around will mean you will not have to exercise control to avoid eating the cookies in the kitchen. By choosing environments that support your goals, you can avoid having to exercise self-control in the moment (stay out of bakeries and donut shops!).

The good news is that what seems challenging now and requires a great deal of willpower will become easier as you successfully practice the behavior. For example, if you are currently drinking a lot of soda, choosing not to do so requires exercising your self-control. However, the more you do not drink it, the easier it will be to choose not to drink it the next time. This is another reason to keep records of your behavior: After some time passes, you can look back and see what your behavior was like and see how you were able to make changes successfully. Taking even "baby steps," like cutting back on soft drinks, makes a big difference in your health over time.

10.3 Sexual Motivation

The motivation for sex is present in all animals and is necessary to ensure their reproduction.

- Examine the physiology of human sexual response.
- Compare and contrast gender norms in sexual motivation.
- Discuss evolutionary theories of mating.
- Describe the biological and environmental factors in sexual orientation.

Mating Male-to-female intercourse for the purpose of reproduction.

While biology plays a central role in **mating** (male-to-female intercourse for the purpose of reproduction) in animals, psychological forces motivate human sexual desire and behavior. Giving and receiving pleasure and feeling and expressing love and value with another person are important motivators for human sexual behavior. But in humans, *sex* refers to many behaviors in addition to intercourse, including manual or oral sex with a partner, same-sex partners, individual masturbation, or even erotic dreams and fantasies. So it is important to understand the basic biology of human sexual response.

Physiology of Sexual Response

William H. Masters and Virginia E. Johnson initiated research on sexual response in the 1960s (Masters & Johnson, 1966). Until the publication of their work, societal attitudes about sex required secrecy. As a result, there was little scientific information available about what happens physically during sexual activities. To study sexual responses in the laboratory, Masters and Johnson came up with elaborate methods for their studies. In addition to physiological measures like respiration and heart rate, they created devices to measure erection, vaginal lubrication, and orgasmic contraction. They brought individuals into the lab and observed them as they masturbated or performed intercourse in a variety of positions. At the time, it was challenging to find volunteers for the studies; while men were willing, some women were recruited based on their experience with prostitution.

In their initial studies, the team observed more than 10,000 complete sexual responses. Masters and Johnson found certain predictable consistencies across individuals. While we may differ in what kinds of stimulation are most exciting to us, our physical responses to stimulation are very similar. Masters and Johnson described four phases of physiological responses during sex, called the **human sexual response cycle**: excitement, plateau, orgasm, and resolution TABLE 10-3. During the **excitement phase**, as arousal begins, blood circulates into all the erectile structures in the body (e.g., penis, clitoris, nipples), a process called **vasocongestion**. A sex flush, or reddening of the skin, can occur, along with an increase in heart rate and breathing. Males experience an erection, while females display vaginal lubrication and swelling of the clitoris, labia, and uterus. In both men and women, the breasts, nipples, and areola enlarge slightly with excitement.

In the **plateau phase**, there is a leveling off of excitement, as arousal remains elevated and deepens. The penis can produce a few drops of fluid at this stage. In females, the glans of the clitoris retracts under the clitoral hood, becoming less available for stimulation. As a result, most women do not receive enough stimulation from intercourse alone to result in orgasm. In the **orgasmic phase**, the climax of arousal occurs. Short in duration (around 15 seconds), the pelvic muscles contract at a rate of less than a second between 3 and 15 times, and in males, ejaculation occurs. What does an orgasm feel like? Men and women report similar experiences, including sensations throughout the genitals and pelvic area. Male and female descriptions of orgasms are very similar, including pleasure and satisfaction, emotional intimacy, ecstasy, relaxation, and sensations like flooding, flushing, and throbbing (Mah & Binik, 2005).

However, as seen in FIGURE 10-18, the response cycle does differ between genders. Most importantly, the female response cycle takes longer in the excitement and plateau stages. And they differ in the final **resolution phase**, in which excitement levels return to base rate. After orgasm, men experience a return to baseline levels of excitement and require some time before another orgasm is possible, called a **refractory period**. In women,

Masters and Johnson were married during their research studies of sexuality, but later divorced.

Human sexual response cycle Phases of excitement, plateau, orgasm, and resolution that complete a sexual act.

Excitement phase Sexual arousal begins with blood circulation into all the erectile structures in the body.

Vasocongestion Blood circulates into all the erectile structures in the body (e.g., penis, clitoris, nipples).

Plateau phase The second stage of the sexual response cycle, during which there is a leveling off of excitement.

Orgasmic phase The climax of arousal during which orgasm and ejaculation occur.

Resolution phase Final stage of the sexual response cycle, during which excitement levels return to base rate.

Refractory period Period of time following orgasm during which males cannot achieve another.

TABLE 10-3 The Human Sexual Response Cycle for Males and Females

Phase	Arousal Level	Characteristics
Excitement phase	Increasing	Vasocongestion, increased heart rate and breathing, penile erection, vaginal lubrication and swelling of the clitoris, labia, and uterus. Slight enlargement of the breasts, nipples, and areola.
Plateau phase	High	Arousal remains elevated, seminal fluid released from penis. In females, the glans of the clitoris retracts under the clitoral hood.
Orgasmic phase	Highest	Orgasm occurs (~15 seconds), pelvic muscles contract at a rate of less than a second between 3 and 15 times, and in males, ejaculation occurs.
Resolution phase	Decreasing	Arousal returns to base rate. Males require some time before another orgasm is possible, called a refractory period.

Source: Data from Masters, W. H., & Johnson, V. E. (1966). Human sexual response. Oxford, England: Little, Brown.

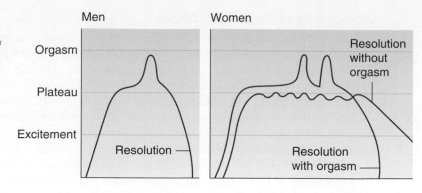

FIGURE 10-18 Differences by gender in the response cycle. *Source: Data from Masters, W. H., & Johnson, V. E. (1966). Human sexual response. Oxford, England: Little, Brown.*

Sexual disorder Problems occurring in the sexual response cycle.

Testosterone The male sex hormone that stimulates production of sperm and sex organs in males and sex drive in males and females.

Oxytocin "Feel-good" hormone released after orgasm.

Sex norms Typical behaviors observed across people.

further stimulation can cause another orgasm before excitement tapers off. Or, if orgasm is not reached (as is frequent from intercourse alone), a longer resolution phase may occur.

This research changed our basic knowledge of how the body responds during sex. The work was important in medicine and psychology because it offered identification of problems in sexual responses (**sexual disorders**) that were undiagnosable in the past. A great deal of research since that time has identified the importance of sex hormones in causing responses. **Testosterone**, the male sex hormone, stimulates production of sperm and is responsible for the development of sex organs in males, In addition, testosterone levels in the blood have been shown to correlate with sexual desire in men and must also be present in women in order for them to feel sexual interest (Meston & Frohlich, 2000). Now, treatment involving replacing hormones could help individuals with sexual disorders. Another hormone, **oxytocin**, is released during orgasm in both genders and leads to sensations of emotional well-being. And dopamine, the neurotransmitter associated with the pleasure response, increases during sex to convey qualitative or interpretive information about its rewarding value (Becker et al., 2001). This suggests the purpose of orgasm goes beyond pleasure to lead to bonding between two people experiencing sex together.

Gender Norms in Sexual Motivation

Sex norms, or typical behaviors for males and females, may arise from both evolutionary pressures and from cultural learning. For example, adults experience intercourse two to three times per week on average; of course, this includes many individuals who are not sexually active and those who experience it daily. It is very difficult to define "normal" sexual behavior because your own preferences define what is normal for you.

Nevertheless, one common observation is that men seem to desire sex more than women (Baumeister et al., 2001). Masturbation rates show that males are much more likely to experience orgasms than are females, start at an earlier age, and do so more often (Peplau, 2003). While almost all boys learn to masturbate for pleasure FIGURE 10-19, about half of girls do so as teenagers. What is happening to sexual impulses in young girls? One idea is that boys experience sexual arousal very directly through erections (Ramsey, 1943). But because sexual arousal is more diffuse in female bodies, girls learn to associate arousal with more general stimuli, developing "crushes" and placing boy band posters on their

FIGURE 10-19 Percentage of boys reporting masturbation to orgasm. *Source: Data from Ramsey, G. V. (1943). The sexual development of boys. American Journal of Psychology, 56(2), 217–233.*

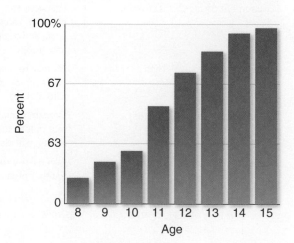

bedroom walls. Freud (1915) described this as **sublimation**, in which sexual urges are disguised by pursuing more acceptable behaviors.

Even as adults, however, the observed norm is that men think about and desire sex more often than women, rate the strength of their drive higher, initiate sex with their partners more frequently, and desire more frequent sex than women (Peplau, 2003). Considering only heterosexual intercourse, 98% of men reach orgasm, while 75% of married women and 62% of single women do so. Years ago, newspaper advice columnist Ann Landers asked her female readers, "Would you rather cuddle or have sex?" Of the 90,000 women who responded, 72% preferred cuddling to intercourse, while the vast majority of men responding far preferred sexual activity with their partners (Angier, 1985).

Men and women also appear to differ in the age of **sexual peak**, or highest point of interest and engagement in sex over the lifetime. One of the earliest studies of men's self-reported sexual behavior found that frequency of orgasm is highest in the teens and 20s, peaking at 30 and then declining. For males, sexual performance in terms of strength and number of erections decreases with age past the 20s. Women, on the other hand, report more frequent orgasms beginning at 30 and continuing into their 40s (Kinsey et al., 1953). In one study, people over 35 were asked to estimate the age of males' and females' sexual peaks, highest frequency of sexual activity, highest rate of sexual satisfaction, and highest rate of sexual desire (Barr et al., 2002). Women report greatest interest in their 30s, and men in their 20s FIGURE 10-20. Why is the sexual peak so differently timed?

Sublimation The notion that sexual urges may be disguised by pursuing more acceptable behaviors.

Sexual peak The highest point of interest and engagement in sex.

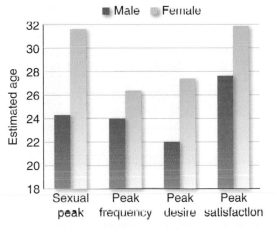

FIGURE 10-20 Reported age at sexual peak overall and for each dimension of sexuality (Barr, 2002).
Source: Data from Barr, A., Bryan, A., & Kenrick, D. T. (2002). Sexual peak: Socially shared cognitions about desire, frequency, and satisfaction in men and women. Personal Relationships, 9, 287–299.

Another difference in sex norms by gender is in the number of different sexual partners. Ideally, how many partners should a person have over his or her lifetime? Is the number different for men than for women? A study by the National Center for Health Statistics, a branch of the Centers for Disease Control and Prevention, examined this for 1999 to 2002. Twenty-five percent of women and 17% of men reported having no more than one partner of the other sex in their lifetime, while 9% of women and 29% of men reported having more than 15 partners FIGURE 10-21. (The median number of partners for women was four and for men, seven.) The survey found only about 11% of never-married adults had never experienced intercourse (Fryar et al., 2007).

NBA Hall of Famer Wilt Chamberlain said he had sex with 20,000 women. In his 1991 biography, A View from Above, Chamberlain devoted an entire chapter to sex. He wrote, "At my age, that equals out to having sex with 1.2 women a day, every day since I was 15 years old."

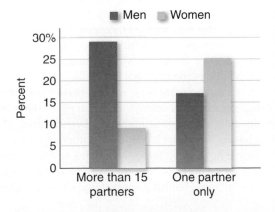

FIGURE 10-21 Average number of sexual partners reported over the lifetime by gender.
Source: Data from Fryar, C. D., Hirsch, R., Porter, K. S., Kottiri, B., Brody, D. J., & Louis, T. (2007, June 28). Drug use and sexual behaviors reported by adults: United States, 1999–2002. Advance Data from Vital and Health Statistics, No. 384, 1–16.
http://www.cdc.gov/nchs/data/ad/ad384.pdf

Another sex norm is that men are more likely to seek casual sex with an acquaintance. A classic study took place on a college campus in which researchers hired "attractive" male and female assistants (Clark & Hatfield, 1989). Individuals of the opposite sex were approached, and the assistant stopped them to say, "I've been noticing you around campus. I find you very attractive." This was followed by one of three straightforward requests: "Would you go out with me tonight?" "Would you come over to my apartment tonight?" or "Would you go to bed with me tonight?" Men and women responded to the request for a date about equally; in one study, 50% of both sexes agreed. But a noticeable difference was found for the sex request. In two experiments, around 70% of the men agreed to the request for sex, compared to not one of the women FIGURE 10-22. In fact, a common response among these men was along the lines of, "Why do we have to wait until later?" Recent research suggests many factors play into women's rejection of the offer (Conley, 2011). Women are more likely to be concerned about sexual assault. And men can almost be guaranteed a pleasurable sexual encounter with an attractive partner, while women experience orgasm only 35% as often in first-time sexual encounters. So maybe women accept fewer casual sexual relations because they are more relaxed, and thus more receptive, when they are with partners they know and trust.

Reproductive strategies The preferences males and females show in their mating behavior.

Paternal uncertainty Historically, men could not be sure whether a child was their genetic offspring.

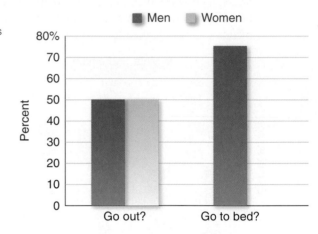

FIGURE 10-22 Results from a study inviting males and females for a date vs. sexual activity. *Source: Data from Clark, R. D., III, & Hatfield, E. (1989). Gender differences in receptivity to sexual offers.* Journal of Psychology and Human Sexuality, 2, 39–55.

These sex norms suggest men prefer having sex more strongly, earlier in life, more frequently, and with more partners than do women. Cases in which men risk their families and jobs by engaging in sex outside of marriage appear regularly in the headlines, suggesting that sex remains a powerful motive for men throughout their lives.

Evolutionary Theories of Mating

What might explain these behavioral differences between genders? Evolutionary theory suggests differences in sex norms fit well with gender differences in **reproductive strategies** (Buss, 1994, 1995). These are the preferences males and females show in their mating behavior. First, note that evolutionary theory attempts to account for sexual behavior within the species, and not differences among individuals. Its focus is on the survival of the species and what the best strategies are for procreation, considered in just the same way as for other animals. This account does not say that any behavior is "right" or appropriate; however, it does suggest that different strategies for mating lead to reproductive advantages. Individuals benefit if they successfully mate, produce children, and have those children survive to adulthood. That way, their own genetic contribution is most likely to be passed down to future generations. The "winning" strategies are "naturally selected" over time by their success and so are increasingly likely to occur.

First, consider the case of male reproductive strategy. For males, the cost of procreation is small, limited to the acts of intercourse, and there is no waiting period until they can father more children. So men would benefit from following a strategy of impregnating many different women while minimizing investment in them or their children. That is, the male strategy is "quantity." By having a number of mates, an individual male could produce more surviving children than if he devoted himself to raising children with only one mate. An additional complication is that until very recently, men had no way of knowing whether a child was their genetic offspring (called **paternal uncertainty**); so, rather

Monica Lewinsky, a White House intern, alleged nine sexual encounters occurred between her and President Clinton from 1995 to 1997 in or near the Oval Office.

than investing in each child, they are more likely to be successful by attempting to father as many children as possible.

For females, on the other hand, the costs of reproduction are much higher. First, pregnancies and giving birth are dangerous. A much greater investment of resources is needed to carry, breastfeed, and care for the limited number of offspring a woman can produce over her lifespan. As a result, women should be more selective in their reproductive choices, because each child matters much more to her success in passing on her genes. The female strategy is "quality." Choosing high-status mates could enhance a woman's reproductive potential by raising her own social status, providing material and nutritional benefits, and providing access to social and economic resources. This is especially important given that our species produces the slowest-maturing offspring among all animals—for some of us, maturation takes more than 20 years!

Because their reproductive investments differ, males and females may use different reproductive strategies, called **parental investment theory**. Evolutionary theory does not suggest that any individual person is consciously thinking about these strategies. Instead, the theory argues that some people happened to behave in these ways, and as a result, their genes were more likely to be passed on. So, over generations, these different strategies provided an advantage and were then passed on to their children FIGURE 10-23. Over many generations, these reproductive strategies would give some people and their offspring a selective advantage and so occur more often in the population as a whole. This rather cold view of reproduction ignores all of the psychological aspects of relationships between individuals and focuses on which strategies are successful in transferring genes to the next generation.

Parental investment theory The required investment in offspring differs between genders, resulting in differing strategies.

Fertile A female able to conceive and bear children.

Status High economic and social status within the group is a desirable quality in male mates.

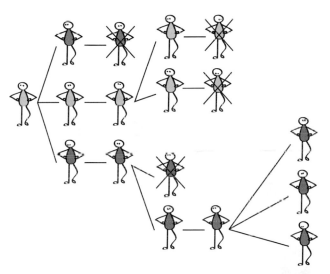

FIGURE 10-23 Variation in features of individuals, and in their preferences for mates, occur. Some of these lead to reproduction and success of offspring, and so are passed on to later generations. Some are not as successful, and are therefore not passed on to surviving generations.

Interestingly, differences in reproductive strategies by gender fit well with the sex norms observed (Buss, 1994). Based on their smaller investment in offspring, men should want to have more sex, more often, with more partners, and earlier in life. Women, on the other hand, should be more selective about their mates, waiting to find ones that can provide resources to support them and their children. Further, it would also explain why women would experience a sexual peak later in life, motivating them to continue reproducing throughout the lifespan (which was much shorter throughout human evolutionary history). So the differences in sex norms by gender fit well with this evolutionary account of differences in reproductive strategies.

In addition, strategy differences predict which types of partners should be most attractive to men and women (Buss, 1995). Men should look for mates that are **fertile**, or able to conceive and bear children. This is a problem because, in humans, it is not obvious when a woman is fertile. Women are sexually responsive throughout their menstrual cycles, while other female animals are capable of sexual responses only during periods when they are fertile. So men should look for signs related to fertility, such as youthfulness and good health. Women, on the other hand, should look for mates that can support them and their offspring by providing resources. This is referred to as **status**, since having a

Businessman Donald Trump and his third wife, Melania. "I continue to stay young, right? I produce children, I stay young," said the 59-year-old Trump. Their baby is Trump's fifth child and his wife's first.

Alfred Kinsey founded the Institute of Sex Research in 1947.

the middle zones of the continuum. They acknowledged some experiences (including fantasies, dreams, emotions, and behaviors) with both same- and opposite-sex partners. So individuals may be characterized as predominantly heterosexual or homosexual, or anywhere in between FIGURE 10-26. **Bisexual** refers to those with more than incidental involvement with both male and female partners.

While the challenges and cultural messages may be very different for homosexuals, there are far more similarities than differences between homosexual and heterosexual relationships. Most gays and lesbians form close, enduring relationships that are happy and functional and enjoy similar family and social support networks. In fact, overall satisfaction in a relationship is about the same for homosexuals as for heterosexuals (Gottman et al., 2003). Freed from the gender roles of "husband" and "wife," homosexual relationships can balance power and responsibility more flexibly. Homosexuals can legally marry in a growing number U.S. states or file legal domestic partnerships. Many gay and lesbian couples feel the same desire as other couples to have and nurture children. And studies show that the children of homosexuals are as well-adjusted as children of heterosexuals and are no more likely to be homosexual (Fitzgerald, 1999).

Bisexual A person with more than incidental involvement with both male and female partners.

Coming out Sharing one's same-sex orientation with others or the public.

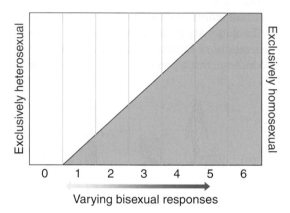

FIGURE 10-26 Kinsey characterized orientation as falling along a continuum from solely heterosexual to exclusively homosexual, with most people falling in between.

Does someone *choose* who they will be attracted to? Can you change your sexual orientation? One way to think about this question is to examine your own experience (Rochlin, 1982). When did you first decide to be heterosexual or homosexual? What do you think caused your sexual orientation? How do you know you would not enjoy sex with other types of partners? Just like most heterosexuals, most homosexuals feel they did not have to be told their orientation; rather, it became clear to them through the relationships and emotions they experienced as they matured. However, because of strong cultural biases, homosexuals are likely to experience many challenges during their development, including prejudice, the need to come to terms with their identity, and the need to share their orientation with others, called "**coming out**" (Rhoads, 1995).

However, the question of what factors may cause sexual orientation has been hotly debated, and historically, there was much interest in attempting to change sexual orientation. What evidence exists about how sexual orientation originates?

Biological Factors

Biologically speaking, male and female heterosexuals and homosexuals are highly similar. Only a few small biological differences have been identified. Three biological factors have been correlated with sexual orientation: brain structure and function, prenatal hormones, and genetic influences. One study has identified a possible relationship in an area of the brain within the hypothalamus. Called the third interstitial nucleus, this area is related to emotions and sexual urges. It is larger in men than in women; however, it was found to be larger in straight men than in gay men, and about the same size in gay men as in women (LeVay, 1991). More recent studies have found the degree of symmetry between the hemispheres and connections between them are also different in gay and heterosexual individuals (Savic & Lindstrom, 2008). These imaging results also show similar patterns in gay men and straight women and in straight men and gay women.

Mourners at a prayer vigil for murder victim Matthew Shepherd. This event prompted legislation to expand the definition of hate crime to include persecution based on sexual orientation.

Another biological factor affecting sexual development is the presence of hormones in the prenatal period. In fact, whether an individual develops male genitals depends on the presence of testosterone during the first 2 months of prenatal development (by default, all fetuses are initially female). Sexual differentiation in the brain starts in the second half of pregnancy (Garcia-Falgueras & Swaab, 2010). **Estrogen** is the hormone central to female sexual development and fertility, and overexposure to synthetic estrogen during pregnancy has been related to later bisexuality and homosexuality (Meyer-Bahlburg et al., 1995). This suggests hormonal exposure in the womb correlates with differences in orientation.

Another factor may be the number of older brothers you have! Mothers who carry male fetuses may develop antibodies to male hormones. When they are carrying later boys, these antibodies may interfere with hormonal development. In men, sexual orientation correlates with the number of older brothers, with each additional older brother increasing the odds of homosexuality by approximately 33% (Blanchard & Klassen, 1997). However, no such relationship in sibling births has been found in females (Blanchard et al., 1998).

Genetic explanations would mean sexual orientation is determined at conception. Twin studies of gays and lesbians show that the concordance rate, or likelihood of one twin having a characteristic if the other has it, is around 20 to 40% for homosexuality (Långström et al., 2008). As the genetic similarity increases, the similarity of orientation also increases, independently of environment (Pillard & Bailey, 1998) FIGURE 10-27. Sibling, twin, and adoptee concordance rates are compatible with the hypothesis that genes account for at least half of the variance in sexual orientation. The role of genes in determining orientation is now widely accepted, but specific mechanisms and how they influence orientation are not yet known.

> **Estrogen** The hormone central to female sexual development and fertility.

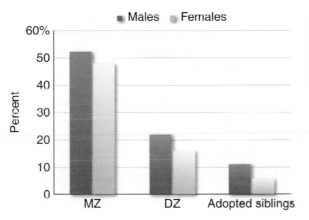

FIGURE 10-27 Concordance rates for homosexuality.
Source: Data from Pillard, R. C., & Bailey J. M. (1998). Human sexual orientation has a heritable component. Human Biology, 70(2), 347–365.

Environmental Factors

Theories of environmental causes of sexual orientation have abounded, yet *none* have received scientific support. For example, domineering mothers and absent fathers, sex play experiences or molestation during childhood, and homosexual parents have all been posited but rejected by numerous studies. In fact, no exclusively environmental factor has ever been shown to relate to differences in sexual orientation. This is a powerful statement given the many studies that have attempted to find differences in experiences that might account for orientation.

Another possibility is that an interaction of biology and environment may play a role in orientation. One such account (Bem, 2000) suggests we are born not with a specific orientation but with many personality predispositions. Our tendencies to be aggressive, shy, or agreeable seem to be built in. As a result, children are attracted to certain types of activities and playmates. For some, it is play behavior that fits within gender norms, like roughhousing in boys and dolls with girls. For most children in the grade school years, gender segregation is evident on the playground and in social groups, as well as in the activities they choose to pursue. As a result, they spend most of their time with others of the same gender (following the "cootie" theory of grade schoolers). Because they are rarely exposed to the opposite gender, they later become interested in them as "exotic," leading to sexual attraction in adolescence. Bem called this theory **"exotic becomes erotic"** (Bem, 1996).

> **"Exotic becomes erotic"** Bem's theory that typical gender preferences lead to less exposure to the opposite sex and, thus, later attraction.

Some children's personalities may lead them to choose activities and playmates of the opposite gender. Then, their early play experiences are with the opposite sex, and they may feel they are very different from others of their own gender. They may then see children of their own gender as strange and exotic, eventually leading to feelings of arousal toward their own gender. In fact, there is little evidence that differences in play preferences are involved in sexual orientation. Bem's theory suggests we find someone attractive simply because that person is so different from us; but in fact, similarity is often the basis of attraction. In summary, we know very little about what environmental factors may affect sexual orientation or about how our experiences affect our sexual preferences and activities as adults. While the motivation for sex is powerful, we have much to learn about what drives our sexual behavior.

CONCEPT LEARNING CHECK 10.3   *Evolution and Gender Differences*

Explain the evolutionary account of gender differences in sexual behavior.

1. Why do males and females differ in their reproductive strategies?

2. What do men look for in a mate?

3. What do women look for in a mate?

4. How does a preference, such as males preferring younger mates, become prevalent in the population?

10.4 Social Motivations

After our basic biological needs are satisfied, we move up the hierarchy to higher-level social and achievement needs.

- Define the social motivations and give examples of each.

Abraham Maslow (1943) suggested that, after our basic biological needs are met, we can begin to pursue the higher-level needs in the hierarchy of motivations. Safety has received little research attention outside of dangerous work settings. However, more research has addressed the need to belong and love and the need for esteem for oneself and from others. Finally, research on self-fulfillment suggests how motivation to achieve may fit into Maslow's description of self-actualization.

Need to belong Motivation to feel a part of relationships or groups of people.

Motivation to Belong

First among the social motives is the **need to belong**. We may want to feel a part of a relationship or group in the form of friendship, romantic relationship, closeness to family, religious or professional groups, shared activities, or even starting a family of our own. Humans are social animals, and the need to belong is a fundamental human motive (Baumeister & Leary, 1995). Humans have a pervasive drive to form and maintain lasting, positive, and significant interpersonal relationships. This requires frequent interactions with the same individuals over time.

Wanting to belong with others would obviously be a competitive advantage for survival in the physical world; in the social world, belonging may provide considerable assistance. Deprivation of good relationships has been linked to a variety of negative consequences. People who lack belongingness suffer higher levels of mental and physical illness and are more prone to behavioral problems ranging from traffic accidents to criminality (Baumeister & Leary, 1995). Social isolation is strongly related to unhappiness; in fact, it is about the only objective factor that shows a substantial (negative) correlation with feelings of well-being (Baumeister, 1991).

People seem widely and strongly inclined to form social relationships quite easily, even in the absence of any special set of circumstances. If you ask couples how they met, you will find many circumstances quite unremarkable, even though the outcome of their meeting was very meaningful. Friendships seem to arise spontaneously and readily, and people invest a great deal of time and effort in others. For example, first-year college

Groups often encourage feelings of belonging by sharing identifiable signs. Are you wearing anything right now that signals your belonging to a group?

students interact with whomever is in their immediate proximity and form long-term friendships with a subset of those people (Marmaros & Sacerdote, 2006). And people are just as reluctant to break social bonds as they are eager to form them. In fact, the tendency to respond with distress and protest to the end of a relationship is nearly universal across different ages and genders (Davis et al., 2003).

Clearly, we were meant to be together. Being accepted, included, or welcomed leads to a variety of positive emotions (e.g., happiness, elation, contentment, and calm), whereas being rejected, excluded, or ignored leads to strong negative feelings (e.g., anxiety, depression, grief, jealousy, and loneliness; Baumeister, 1991). The near universality of distress associated with divorce and bereavement is consistent with the belongingness hypothesis; indeed, there is little evidence that significant social bonds can ever be broken without suffering or distress. Moreover, changes in belongingness status are an important cause of emotions. In fact, one of the basic functions of emotion may be to regulate our behavior in forming and maintaining our social bonds (Baumeister & Leary, 1995).

As evidence, we are finely tuned to be highly sensitive to signs of **social rejection**, or exclusion from contact by others. Anyone who has lived through middle and high school knows well the experience of acceptance and rejection from peers and how deeply it affects us. In fact, recent studies show the pain of social rejection is quite similar to physical pain. One set of studies had people play a computer game of ball tossing, and some were systematically left out of the cooperative game (Eisenberger et al., 2003). When excluded from the game, compared to when included, participants showed increased activity in two neural regions that are frequently associated with the unpleasantness of physical pain—the dorsal anterior cingulate cortex and the anterior insula. Those who showed greater activity reported feeling more upset by the rejection episode. Thus, neural responses to social exclusion recruited some of the same neural regions that are involved in physical pain, supporting the commonsense notion that rejection really does "hurt."

Real-world experiences of social rejection have also shown activation of the same regions of the brain that are involved in the sensory experience of physical pain (Kross et al., 2010). This study recruited people who had gone through a romantic breakup during the past 6 months, leading to intense feelings of rejection and pain. Participants underwent fMRI (functional magnetic resonance imaging) scans while they looked at photos of their ex or else a friend and thought about their experiences. They were also measured while a device caused tolerable pain on their arms. These were compared to scans of other people's brain responses to physical pain and activated the same regions of the brain. We are motivated to maintain good relationships and try to repair them when problems arise because breakups and rejections really hurt. Other research shows that taking acetaminophen, a physical pain reliever, diminishes the pain of hurt feelings and social exclusion (DeWall et al., 2010) FIGURE 10-28. If the experience of not belonging feels as important as physical pain, our motivation to maintain ties with others must be very strong indeed.

Social rejection Exclusion from contact by others causes emotional pain.

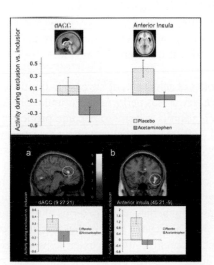

FIGURE 10-28 Changes in neural activity (during social exclusion or inclusion) were observed in two brain areas: (a) dorsal anterior cingulate cortex (dACC) and (b) right anterior insula. Participants took either acetaminophen or a placebo. The change in intensity of neural activity (shown in color bar) was greater for those who took placebo. Taking acetaminophen reduced social pain.

Motivation to Achieve

Esteem motivation Desire to feel appreciation from others.

Achievement motivation A desire to accomplish difficult jobs in an area with a standard of excellence.

Maslow (1943) suggested the next level of motivation was desire for **esteem**, or appreciation from others. What fuels the drive to succeed, excel, and advance in the world and to have others recognize our accomplishments? **Achievement motivation** is a desire to accomplish difficult tasks in an area with a standard of excellence (Murray, 1938). To determine your inner need for achievement, an indirect test called the **thematic apperception test (TAT)** measures your fantasies about the outcomes of situations (Morgan & Murray, 1935). A participant looks at a drawing and creates a story about it FIGURE 10-29. For example, what is the person thinking about in the image, what will they do next, and what will happen to them? Murray (1938) found that people projected their own desires onto characters, and the stories they created showed systematic differences that revealed their own motivations. This method worked better than asking people about their motivations because they did not worry about what the experimenter wanted to hear. Instead, they mentioned the ideas they themselves were most interested in through the content of the stories they created.

FIGURE 10-29 Thematic apperception test card showing an image. What do you think the woman in the image is thinking? This test draws out people's implicit motivations.

Thematic apperception test (TAT) An indirect test measuring your fantasies about the outcomes of situations, reflecting your motivations.

Need for achievement Desire to succeed at challenging tasks.

Achievement gap The difference in U.S. school test scores and grades for white compared to African American children.

By scoring TAT responses systematically, McClelland and colleagues (1953, 1976) identified which people were high in their **need for achievement**, or desire to succeed at challenging tasks. This measure was shown to relate to how hard people work, how persistent they are at tasks, and how innovative they are. Individuals with a high need for achievement also get better grades in school, are more successful in their careers, and are more "upwardly mobile." People who are motivated to succeed set high but realistic goals so that they are challenged yet can succeed. But what about the process of achievement? How are we affected by successes and setbacks along the way to a goal?

It is clear that cultures differ in their expectations for achievement, and family, social, and school pressures may influence your desire to accomplish goals in the world. Parental attitudes and practices provide the foundation for children's development of beliefs about school achievement and thus are critical determinants of children's school experiences (Taylor et al., 2004). For example, one stereotype in American culture is that Asian-Americans are more driven to perform well academically. Research has concluded that Asian Americans perceive and have experienced restrictions in upward mobility unrelated to education. Consequently, education has assumed greater importance within the culture as a means of escaping limited options (Sue & Okazaki, 1990). For groups defined by gender, race, ethnicity, or socioeconomic status, an **achievement gap** appears on measures such as standardized test scores, grade point averages, dropout rates, and college enrollment and completion rates (Ladson-Billings, 2006). The possible reasons for differences in achievement for whites and ethnic minorities are under debate. However, a meta-analysis showed that the most accurate predictor of student achievement is the ways in which the family is involved in a child's education (Henderson et al., 1994; Lee & Bowen, 2006).

Within educational psychology, two modes of achievement have been identified that predict different outcomes from learning: mastery versus performance orientation (Ames, 1992; Ames & Archer, 1988). Mastery orientation is a desire to become proficient in a skill to the best of your ability. With this goal, you are concerned not about external evaluation but with your own sense of your ability to perform well at the target task. Mastery orientation is associated with deeper engagement with the task and greater perseverance in the face of setbacks. Performance orientation, on the other hand, is the desire to achieve on external indicators of success, such as grades. If your sense of satisfaction is highly influenced by your grade, you may be defining your achievement in terms of this external standard for success. Performance orientation is associated with higher anxiety because you feel less control over whether you can be successful, since an external judge decides whether your achievement is adequate. In addition, performance orientation can make the actual learning seem secondary to doing well on tests, rather than focusing on the goal of learning the material well.

Another key factor in achieving your goals is your mindset (Dweck, 2006). **Mindsets** are beliefs about yourself and your abilities, such as intelligence, talents, and personality. Are these fixed traits, things you cannot change? Or are they things you can, with effort, develop and improve throughout your life? People with a **fixed mindset** believe that their traits are predetermined, and nothing can change that. People with this mindset worry about their traits and whether they are adequate. On the other hand, a **growth mindset** sees these qualities develop through dedication and effort.

Does how you think about your achievements make a difference in your success? Dweck (2006) and her research team studied the effect of praise. Fifth grade students were given a series of puzzles easy enough so they all did fairly well. Half were praised for their intelligence: "You must be smart at this." The other half were praised for their *effort*: "You must have worked really hard." Then the students were allowed to choose the next test: a more difficult one that they would learn a lot from, or another just like the first. Of those praised for their effort, 90% chose the *harder* set of puzzles. Of those praised for their intelligence, a majority chose the *easy* test. They had chosen to avoid the risk of embarrassment. Next, all of the students were given a difficult test, which all failed. A final round of tests was as easy as the first round. The results showed those who had been praised for their effort improved by about 30%. Those who had been told they were smart did worse than they had at the very beginning—by about 20%.

The ability to repeatedly respond to failure by exerting more effort (instead of giving up) is the key to achievement. People with **persistence** rebound well from failures and can sustain their motivation through long periods of delayed gratification. Specific brain circuitry has been identified in the orbital and medial prefrontal cortex (Gusnard et al., 2003). This area monitors the reward center of the brain, and like a switch, it intervenes when there is no immediate reward. When it switches on, it is telling the rest of the brain that the reward is coming later, so do not stop trying. The brain has to learn that frustrating events can be worked through without reward. As a result, a person who grows up getting rewards infrequently will have persistence, because he or she will keep going even when rewards are not yet in sight.

Motivation for Self-actualization

Maslow's hierarchy points to the self as the ultimate motivation. Self-actualization involves working toward becoming the best version of yourself you can be—specifically, "The full use and exploitation of talents, capacities, and potentialities" (Maslow, 1970, p. 50). Achieving this is the ultimate motivation, that of fulfilling your human potential. For most, life goals include spirituality, community, family, career, lifestyle, and other interests. Maslow suggests that we strive to become the best version of ourselves out of an inner motivation. So we work to achieve our full potential, increasing our complexity, independence, and social responsibility (Bozarth & Brodley, 1991). Self-actualization theory says we know what is good for us, and we are motivated to achieve it.

However, there is plenty of evidence that people pursue behaviors that are damaging to themselves, including smoking, procrastinating, and overeating. Why do we have difficulty reaching our full potential given our motivation to self-actualize? Work in **humanistic psychology** explains potential causes of problems in developing self-actualization (Rogers, 1951). Taking a motivational view, we can look at studies of health behavior that attempt to help people stop smoking, lose weight, and stop drinking. People's lack of interest in or reluctance to participate in health and wellness programs is the "No. 1 obstacle" to changing health behaviors (National Business Group on Health, 2010).

The good news is that people do not need to depend on external rewards for their behavior. Instead, we can identify internal incentives for behaviors and, as a result, be less dependent on external rewards. This process involves integrating new behaviors within your own internal values. Through integration, the regulation of behavior is taken into your core sense of self. As a result, the behavior becomes "self-determined." Decades of studies have demonstrated that self-determination is the key factor in long-term motivation. **Self-determination theory** (Deci & Ryan, 1985) points to three factors that promote internalization. First, a meaningful rationale must be provided because people want to know why the behavior change is important. Second, it is important to acknowledge people's feelings about the behavior change. Third, as much as possible, choices should be provided about the behavior.

Mindset A belief about yourself and your abilities, such as intelligence, talents, and personality.

Fixed mindset The belief that your traits are predetermined and nothing can change them.

Growth mindset Belief that your qualities and capacities develop through effort.

Persistence The ability to repeatedly respond to failure by exerting more effort.

Humanistic psychology Theories of motivation emphasizing the goal to develop to the highest potential for each individual.

Self-determination theory Motivation involves integrating new behaviors into your internal values.

Choice appears to be the key to intrinsic motivation. Imagine being assigned a movie to watch or choosing one for yourself. Even if it is the same movie, the mere act of choosing makes your experience of it much more personal. In building intrinsic motivation, the key is in the personal: It must mean something to *you* (Ryan, et al., 1983). For example, losing weight for a partner's sake is much less likely to be successful than when you decide to do so for your own health reasons (Teixeira et al., 2006). So making choices based on your own internal values will help to integrate your desired behavior with your goals. Based on these findings about motivation, some suggestions for making improvements (or self-actualizing) your behaviors include:

- Make choices in novel ways: It is easy to be "stuck in a rut" in which you do the same thing every time you are in a given situation. Try going out to eat someplace new rather than the old favorite, or switch your usual beverage to something you have never tried. If you add to your behavioral repertoire, it may be easier to make good choices and avoid problem areas.
- Link the present with long-term goals: It is important to keep the goal state in mind, knowing that you do not have to enjoy the process to relish the rewards. Walking every day may seem a small step, but after 6 months, the benefits from it will be very rewarding. So keep the long-term goal in mind to help you initiate the first steps.
- Make use of higher-level thinking processes: We are sensitive to cues in the environment that can alter our intentions, like advertisements, habits, and cultural customs. So take a moment to step back and think about why you are making a choice. Is it relevant to your long-term goals or motivated by something specific in your environment? Try to be vigilant about the factors affecting your choices, and think through which ones are positive for you.
- Practice self-regulation: We all perform self-regulation of a variety of important behaviors; otherwise, we would be unable to meet even our basic needs. But while we may feel we cannot regulate some behaviors—we fail to exercise, eat poorly, or drink too much alcohol—the truth is that we *are* regulating it already. To move it in the direction you desire, try to think in terms of baby steps: Have one less drink than you want, or eat one less treat per day. By practicing your regulation, you will get better at moving in the desired direction.

Changing your intentions is the first step in changing behavior, and it leads directly to success. A meta-analysis of 47 experiments found that changes in behavioral intentions do lead to significant behavior changes (Webb & Sheeran, 2006). By taking advantage of what you know about motivation, you can guide your own behavior toward your goals. Self-actualization is, by definition, a motivation that continues throughout life, encouraging us to strive to become better people. It represents the best of human nature through its motivation to continually improve ourselves.

CONCEPT LEARNING CHECK 10.4 | *Fostering Achievement*

Based on information you just read in this section, answer the following question.

1. What can you do to foster your own need for achievement?

10.5 Motivation and Work

For most adults, the workplace provides a setting that tests our motivation.

- Explain the relationship between human motivation and work.

Industrial and organizational psychology Field of study addressing the psychology of work.

For most people, basic motivations drive their everyday behavior. Across the world, many people travel great distances every day for clean water and spend the majority of their day earning money for food, housing, and other basic needs. Fewer people enjoy the luxury of combining their need to earn a living with their higher-level motivations to belong, achieve, and find self-fulfillment. The subfield of **industrial and organizational**

psychology addresses the psychology of "work," including motivation at work, the personality qualities and skills ideally suited to differing occupations, hiring and evaluation procedures, maximizing performance at work, and organizing workplaces to help achieve the best outcomes. These psychologists use their knowledge of psychological principles to provide consultation to employers. Hiring, salary, and promotion practices must follow legal guidelines from the Civil Rights Act, the Americans with Disabilities Act, and other legislation surrounding issues like harassment in the workplace. In addition to laboratory studies, research in this field often tests theories in actual workplaces to determine the best practices for motivating employees within work organizations.

One of the earliest studies in the field attempted to determine what factors lead to improved motivation. The study took place in the late 1920s at a large electric company in which parts were assembled. A special testing room and a control room were set up to allow the comparison of the effects of specific interventions on worker productivity. In the test room, the management tried changing to very bright lighting, changing to very dim lighting, adding rest periods, shortening the work day, shortening the work week, interviewing the employees, and adding financial incentives to see what worked best. The surprising finding was that the test room workers performed better for *every* intervention tested. Apparently, the increased interest shown toward the workers in the test room was, by itself, enough to improve their motivation. This phenomenon was called the **Hawthorne effect** after the plant in the study (Mayo, 1933). Hawthorne effects may last anywhere from a few days to years, depending on the situation (Roethlisberger & Dickson, 1939). It demonstrates that people are motivated not just by financial rewards but also by their own higher motivations and needs. Industrial and organizational psychologists have been examining workplaces ever since to identify how to make workplaces more rewarding to employees.

The Hawthorne study of plant workers found that any increase of interest toward the workers led to improved motivation.

Hawthorne effect Improvement in a test group (compared to a control group) caused by the increased interest shown toward them.

Personnel psychology Field focusing on the selection, training, and evaluation of employees.

Personnel Psychology

Personnel psychology focuses on selection, training, and evaluation of employees (Schuler, Farr, & Smith, 1993). As in personality psychology, industrial psychologists have sought to measure individuals' interests and aptitudes and identify guidelines for career selection. One such test is the Strong Interest Inventory (Donnay et al., 2011). This survey compiled responses from individuals in many varied types of occupations. Then, when a new individual takes the survey, the responses are compared to determine the best fit to workers in each career field. For example, someone who is interested in interacting with a wide variety of people, from intellectuals to the sports-minded to fun-loving friends, may find "military officers" as a match because officers regularly deal with a broad range of types. The test places you in a work category with others who report sharing the same interests and aptitudes, suggesting you may enjoy the same jobs. Studies show that people flourish when there is a good fit between their personality type and the characteristics required by the job (Holland, 1996) TABLE 10-4. Career centers and coaches offer similar tests to help determine which professions are a "best match" for an individual.

TABLE 10-4 Types of Personalities and Complementary Jobs

Personality Type	Preferences	Description	Occupation Type	Jobs
Realistic	Machines, tools, objects	Practical, frank	Concrete, mechanical	Carpenter, driver
Investigative	Gaining knowledge	Asocial, intellectual	Analytic, problem solving	Psychology, scientist
Artistic	Literature, music, art	Unconventional, creative	Innovative, imaginative	Musician, designer
Social	Interpersonal, emotional	Nurturant, agreeable	Working with others	Counselor, clergy
Enterprising	Directing or persuading	Energetic, gregarious	Selling, leading	Lawyer, manager
Conventional	Orderly routines	Careful, conforming	Meet goals and standards	Editor, accountant

Source: Reproduced from Holland, J. L. (1996). Exploring careers with a typology: What we have learned and some new directions. American Psychologist, 51(4), 397–406.

Other types of tests examine your cognitive abilities, integrity, job knowledge, physical ability, and personality, as well as your background and experiences. A meta-analysis of procedures for selecting employees analyzed later job and training performance (Schmidt & Hunter, 1998). General mental ability was an important predictor of eventual success in all types of jobs. Other selection methods also predicted success on the job. Work sample tests are hands-on simulations of the job performed by applicants, such as a welding test. Consulting and technology firms sometimes pose difficult puzzles in interviews to assess how the candidate reasons about problems (Poundstone, 2004). Integrity tests screen for behaviors like drinking or drugs, fighting, stealing, and absenteeism. And structured interviews provide a fixed procedure and ordering of questions, along with standards for scoring; as a result, they provide much better prediction than open-ended interviews. Virtually every major organization in the United States uses interviews to select personnel; however, interviews have been shown to be poor at assessing abilities (Arvey & Campion, 1982).

How do employers know what to look for in a potential employee? **Job analysis** is one of the most widely used techniques (McCormick et al., 1972). This method determines the tasks that a worker is responsible for, as well as the knowledge, skills, and abilities needed in the job. Then recruiting can take place with those qualities in mind. This approach led to the Job Diagnostic Survey, designed to determine whether (and how) jobs might be redesigned to improve employee motivation and productivity (Hackman & Oldham, 1975). However, one of the best indicators of whether a person and a job are a good match is a **realistic job preview**. This involves having the potential employee sample the work experience to determine his or her interest in the job and whether the job requirements are a good match for the candidate. Job previews tend to lower initial expectations from the potential employee and increase self-selection, organizational commitment, job satisfaction, performance, and job survival (Premack & Wanous, 1985). Internships, paid and unpaid, are one route to preview jobs and can lead to employment prospects.

And how do potential employees know what to look for in a job? This is quite challenging for those entering their first full-time jobs as professionals after graduation from college. While the liberal arts prepare students to read, write, analyze, and discuss, they provide little information about the world of work. The biggest knowledge gap for students is what kinds of jobs exist in the world outside of college and how to gain access to them. To learn more about the working world during college, visit your campus career center early and look at the opportunities it offers to explore jobs, including informational interviews and internships. And when the time comes to search for jobs, as you might expect, job-search behavior is significantly and positively related to finding employment (Kanfer et al., 2001). Effort put into the search and the intensity of your effort do pay off in the likelihood of success.

Just like many other areas of human interaction, hiring is subject to biases in perception. Interviewers tend to believe in their own intuitive abilities to find good candidates in the absence of evidence, called the **interviewer illusion** (Nisbett, 1987). As a result, they can be resistant to using testing or other decision aids to help in selecting employees (Highhouse, 2008). In a study in which managers viewed resumes and photos, both gender and attractiveness affected their ratings of candidates (Marlowe et al., 1996). The extent of the bias was generally smaller for the most experienced managers, but less-attractive female applicants were routinely at a disadvantage regardless of managerial experience. Racial bias is a key issue in hiring discrimination, while black hiring officers were found to hire a greater proportion of blacks who apply (Stoll et al., 2004). Homosexuals were also found to be discriminated against in a survey study (Crow et al., 1998), as were overweight people in a laboratory study (Pingitore et al., 1994). Those hiring, managing, and evaluating workers have an obligation to avoid bias in these processes.

Most people feel their work provides more than economic benefits. As evidence, 65 to 95% of the workforce across Western countries state they would continue to work even if they had enough money to live comfortably for the rest of their lives (Harpaz, 1988). People attach a broader social and psychological significance to their work lives; after all, we spend a third of our days in full-time employment and often socialize with coworkers outside of work. A study of the meaning of work across countries measured the centrality of work to life, economic and self-expressive goals, and the sense of social obligation (England, 1990). Patterns identified included a "balanced" worker, one for whom work

Job analysis Determination of the tasks, knowledge, skills, and abilities needed in a job.

Realistic job preview A potential employee samples the work experience to determine his or her interest in a job.

Interviewer illusion Belief in one's own intuitive abilities to find good candidates in the absence of evidence.

is central to life and includes economic and expressive goals; a duty-oriented worker who feels obligation and is very satisfied with his or her work; an economic worker who focuses on pay and security; and the "alienated" worker, who does not feel invested in any of these goals. These patterns led to differences in the effort made by workers and, thus, to outcomes on the job.

What makes people feel most engaged and interested in their work? Early research focused on **job burnout**, defined as a prolonged response to chronic emotional and interpersonal stress on the job (Maslach et al., 2001). Extensive research has established that stressful jobs lead to exhaustion, cynicism, and lack of effectiveness. More recently, research has focused on **engagement**, or feelings of involvement and interest in work. One study asked employees whether they "have the opportunity to do what they do best every day." Only one in five employees strongly agreed with this statement; but, if they did, their work units showed substantially higher performance (Harter, Schmidt, & Hayes, 2002). When employees feel engaged, businesses are more successful, employees use their talents, and there is lower turnover in the staff. So why is not every employer concerned about engagement at work? The incentive theory, with the premise that we work for the paycheck, has been pervasive in business. Increasingly, however, organizations are working to help employees structure their jobs in ways that help them feel more engaged in their work as a way of improving retention.

Balancing the characteristics of jobs can improve engagement and result in feelings of **flow** (Csikszentmihalyi, 1990). This state of mind arises during activities you greatly enjoy, when attention is focused on the task in front of you, and the challenge of the task is met by your own expertise. Work sessions feel seamless, and "time flies" when you are working in a state of flow. This requires changing the nature of a job over time in order to keep up with the changing development of the employee. This quality is hard to capture in performance evaluations for raises, promotions, and layoffs. Evaluation often focuses on what can be counted (number of sales, number of products completed) or on qualitative judgments of managers (global ratings of success in the job; Landy & Farr, 1980). With subjective judgments, there is potential for bias from a supervisor. An alternative approach, called **360-degree feedback**, solicits evaluation (sometimes anonymously) from everyone who interacts with an employee, including customers, peers, subordinates, and supervisors (Ghorpade, 2000) FIGURE 10-30. By 1996, this approach had become standard among Fortune 500 companies.

Job burnout A prolonged response to chronic emotional and interpersonal stress on the job.

Engagement Feelings of involvement and interest in work.

Flow A state of mind arising during activities when the challenge of the task is met by expertise.

360-degree feedback Evaluation method that solicits input from everyone who interacts with an employee.

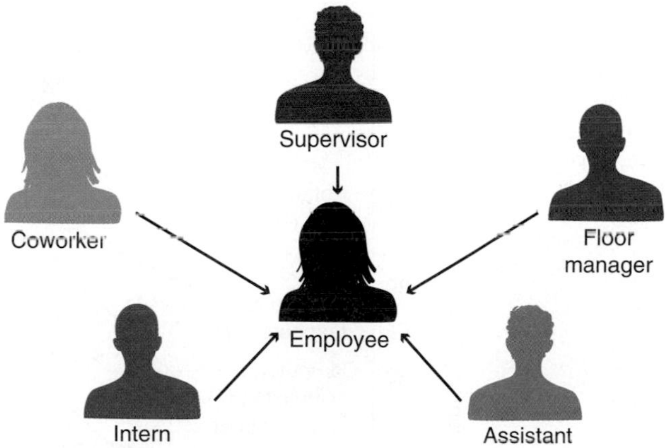

FIGURE 10-30 360-degree feedback seeks information from all of those who interact with an employee to evaluate their performance and identify goals for improvement.

Organizational Psychology

Rather than studying individuals, **organizational psychology** examines how the structure of jobs and the workplace affects the success of group efforts. Policy decisions, working teams, and management style all affect how work gets accomplished and the ultimate success of organizations.

One important factor in work organization is management. Better performance in top management teams occurs when there is more positive than negative communication among teams (Losada & Heaphy, 2004). The most profitable, productive, and

Organizational psychology Field examining how the structure of jobs and the workplace affects the success of group efforts.

effective teams had a ratio of five positive statements for each negative statement during their work interactions. The lowest-performing teams had a ratio of three negative for every positive statement. This same "five positive to one negative" ratio was discovered by Gottman (1994) in studies of successful marriages. The best predictor of whether a marriage will last was a large majority of positive communications. "Toxic" workplaces—and people—are ones whose negative communications wear down your initiative to make changes. Recent work in organizational psychology has identified the "positive organization" as a way to implement ideas from positive psychology into the workplace (Bakker & Schaufeli, 2008).

A surprising trend in the modern workplace is the increased presence of incivility in the workplace, defined as interpersonal mistreatment such as disrespect, condescension, and degradation (Andersson & Pearson, 1999). Almost 70% of workers reported some experience with workplace incivility, from as many as one-third of the most powerful individuals within organizations (Cortina et al., 2001). For example, do you think it is appropriate to use curse words during heated discussions? Can you imagine being called a "bitch" on the job? Surprisingly, this is becoming more common in less formal workplaces. While women reported more occurrences of incivility at work, it has been found to have negative impacts on job satisfaction for all (Cortina et al., 2001). Another problem is **sexual harassment** on the job, a situation in which unwelcome sexual comments or advances are imposed in the workplace. On average, 58% of women report having experienced potentially harassing behaviors, and 24% report having experienced sexual harassment at work (Ilies et al., 2003). These results suggest that sexual harassment is more prevalent in organizations with relatively large power differentials between organizational levels. Training managers to improve interactions and team-building skills can help to set standards for interactions in the workplace.

Organizational psychologists are also interested in the factors that affect workplaces on a broader scale. For example, societal factors such as gender norms may affect how an organization works. Of the 21 million professional jobs in the United States., women hold 53%. But of the 8 million better-paying jobs (averaging more than $40,000 in 1998), women hold only 28% (Doyle, 2000). These jobs include physicians, lawyers, engineers, computer and natural scientists, and college instructors FIGURE 10-31. Women in these professions also have lower compensation, on average, because they work fewer hours and are in lower-paying positions. Valian (1999) argues that cultural values and assumptions

Sexual harassment
Unwelcome sexual comments or advances imposed in the workplace.

FIGURE 10-31 The percent of women in major professions by year, with data from the 1950–1980 census and 5-year moving averages. The figures in parentheses indicate women's earnings as a percent of men's in 1998 dollars.
Source: Data from U.S. Bureau of the Census and Bureau of Labor Statistics.

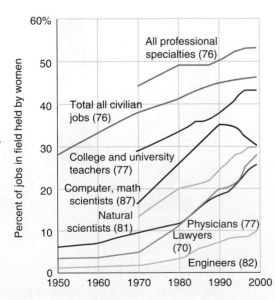

are the cause of the resulting pay differences. Women are expected to carry more of the family and homemaking responsibilities, resulting in less availability for work. And when comparing candidates for positions, gender stereotypes about success favor males. While women are catching up in higher education, in which the percentage gaining PhDs in some fields outstrips men, those in professorships are still disproportionately male. This suggests that factors beyond any individual affect the experience of work in organizations.

Gender stereotyping also results in differences in perception on the job. While many women are advancing in business, there appears to be a "glass ceiling," a situation in which women find it harder to break through to the top ranks of a field, such as chief executive officer, director, or dean (Lynness & Thompson, 1997). In this study, financial services executives in comparable jobs had less authority, received fewer stock options, and had less international mobility if they were female. Women at the highest executive levels reported more obstacles than lower-level women and had lower satisfaction with future career opportunities. In 1987, Ann B. Hopkins was the only female among 88 candidates for partnership at Price Waterhouse, Inc. Though noted as an outstanding performer, she was not accepted as a partner. A colleague explained that, in order to improve her chances, she should "walk more femininely, talk more femininely, dress more femininely, wear make-up, have her hair styled, and wear jewelry." Hopkins brought a gender discrimination lawsuit against her employer, which eventually reached the Supreme Court. The court ruled that gender-based stereotyping had influenced perceptions of her behavior, and she won the case (Fiske et al., 1991).

The problem with differences in treatment or pay is that people want to perceive their outcomes as fair. **Equity theory** posits that people want their effort and pay to be fair compared to others' (Adams, 1962). Relative to other workers, if you work harder or produce more, you expect to be paid more. Even monkeys have a sense of equity. In a study by Brosnan & Dewahl (2003), monkeys (brown capuchins) performed tasks for rewards (like grapes). If another monkey received the same reward with less or no effort, the monkeys objected vociferously. This suggests there may be an evolutionary origin for our aversion to inequity.

> **Equity theory** The notion that people want their effort and pay to be fair compared to that of others.

A field study at an insurance firm demonstrated that people adjust their work to match their perceptions of equity. In the study, more than 200 employees were temporarily relocated to other offices (Greenberg, 1988). They were assigned at random to offices that belonged to others that were higher, the same, or lower in rank at the company. The number of cases processed and decision quality were measured before, during, and after this relocation period. The results showed that those placed in better offices actually worked harder to produce better work, while those placed in lower offices felt undercompensated and lowered their performance FIGURE 10-32. Perceptions of unfair treatment can interfere with work performance.

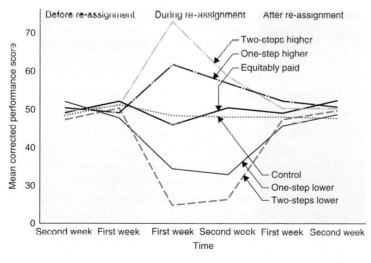

FIGURE 10-32 Insurance workers' performance over time, including a middle period during which some were assigned to better, or worse, offices than their peers. Perceptions of unfair treatment undermined work performance. *Source: Modified from Greenberg, J. (1988). Equity and workplace status: A field experiment.* Journal of Applied Psychology, 73(4), 606–613.

A great deal of research in organizational psychology has asked what causes exceptional group or team performance. Group work is central to many jobs, so understanding what leads to well-functioning groups could greatly improve productivity. The face-to-face group is preferred in most workplaces, yet studies of performance show that it can lead to group **process loss**, or time spent coordinating discussion rather than working on the task itself (Hill, 1982). As a result, for many tasks, summing the work of individuals working alone results in better performance than asking a group to work together. Interventions that structure group interactions to minimize process loss have been shown to improve effectiveness for certain kinds of groups and tasks (Hackman, 1987). There is

> **Process loss** Time a group spends coordinating discussion rather than working on the task itself.

less evidence that interventions around group composition affect the success of groups. Interventions that focus directly and primarily on the quality of relationships among members usually succeed in changing attitudes and sometimes behavior but have no consistent effects on group performance (Hackman, 1987). Nevertheless, some evidence suggests that using personality tests to set up work teams with specific characteristics can be effective (Bell, 2007). Some of the first research in the field was on group compatibility (Schutz, 1955) and suggested that groups that are happy together are more productive.

Leadership provided by managers is a key component to a well-functioning workplace. The focus of many leadership theories is on traits, such as intelligence and originality (Yukl &Van Fleet, 1992). But on the job, the main function of a leader is the development and shaping of team processes and the monitoring and management of ongoing team performance (Kozlowski & Bell, 2003). One experimenter worked with intact management teams from a Fortune 500 high-technology company (Korsgaard et al., 1995). Some team leaders showed high consideration by listening to members' input. As a result, their groups had higher perceptions of fairness and higher commitment to the recommendations that were reached, and attachment and trust in the leader increased. If team leaders showed low consideration by listening but not commenting on input from the team, member attachment and trust in the leader decreased. Even though the members of these groups had a history of working together, leaders who actively listened to team members and incorporated their ideas into a final recommendation significantly affected the quality of decisions made. This has considerable ramifications for the impact of leader behavior in an ongoing work context: Listen to employees and incorporate their input!

Career Directions

As a college student, you may soon face the problem of career and work: How can you best determine which career direction or job possibilities are your best options? The average American changes jobs 10 times between the ages of 18 and 42 (Bureau of Labor Statistics, 2006). In addition, people in a wide range of work contexts are not only looking for a job or paid employment; instead, they may also be looking for a career or a related sequence of jobs with increasing responsibilities and compensation. Finally, some people may look for a "calling." A **calling** is defined as an occupation that an individual (1) feels drawn to pursue, (2) expects to be intrinsically enjoyable and meaningful, and (3) sees as a central part of his or her identity (Berg et al., 2010). The example at the beginning of the chapter fits this description: Becoming a professor was not just a career choice but also a choice of identity. The short-term sacrifices on the path to becoming a professor are worth it for someone who would rather be in a bookstore on Friday night!

In a survey across types of workers, about a third identified their work as a "job," another third as a "career," and another third as a "calling" (Wrzesniewski et al., 1997). So there is a range of possibilities in careers, and you can choose the approach that is the best fit for you:

- If you approach work as a job, you focus primarily on the financial rewards. The nature of the work itself may hold less interest for you. What is important is the money, which is motivating for you. If a job with more pay comes your way, you will likely move on. And you find the remuneration very satisfying.
- If you approach work as a career, you are likely interested in advancement. You may want to climb the career ladder as far as possible or be among the most highly regarded professionals in your field. You are motivated by the status, prestige, and power that come with the job and by becoming one of the top performers as well as part of a group.
- If you approach your work as a calling, you focus on the work itself. You are less interested in financial gain or career advancement, preferring instead to find a sense of fulfillment from the work. You are less concerned about financial payoff and greatly desire the identity the career provides.

Experiencing work as a calling is associated with a series of psychological benefits, including increased life, health, and job satisfaction (Wrzesniewski et al., 1997). Callings inspire feelings of passion—strong emotional inclinations toward work-related

Calling Choice of occupation you feel drawn to pursue for intrinsic meaning and identity.

activities that individuals find interesting, important, and worthy of their time and energy. One of America's largest job-search companies (Monster.com) urges job seekers to "find your calling." Today, individuals are exposed to—and can consider—many more occupational choices than in the past (Twenge, 2006). A calling can be much more motivating than a job because the rewards are personal as well as financial.

However, the world of work is structured in a way that restricts your ability to pursue all of the occupations that may "call" to you. You may feel called toward different occupations or may choose less satisfying but more financially lucrative or socially desirable occupations (Iyengar et al., 2006). Or you may feel shut out of your desired options through lack of skills or opportunities to succeed (Twenge, 2006). Finally, you may discover callings in other fields after you have chosen your occupation, making it difficult or impossible to pursue these other callings. For others, a job may become a "calling" as the challenges and rewards from success lead you to invest in a career. Many people find their careers through happenstance, a connection through a relative or friend, and end up feeling very invested because they devote themselves to it.

There are steps you can take to "craft" your current job into your calling (Berg et al., 2010). In this study, some workers described taking active steps to alter their jobs and leisure activities to pursue their unanswered callings. Two core dimensions are enjoyment and meaning or a sense of purpose and personal growth. Participants reported using three techniques to create opportunities for their unanswered callings: task emphasizing, job expanding, and role reframing TABLE 10-5. In addition, they crafted their leisure pursuits to meet their achievement needs outside of work.

TABLE 10-5 Crafting Techniques

Technique	Explanation	Illustration
Job Crafting		
Task emphasizing *(highlighting assigned tasks to pursue an unanswered calling)*	Changing the nature of an assigned task to incorporate aspects of an unanswered calling	"I still get to help families in my job . . . like when I run events here in the library, I make sure to talk with students and parents not just about media stuff, which is my job, but also about them as people. . . . So I feel like there are parallels there . . . [because] I'm doing something valuable and something good." (Fannie)
	Dedicating additional time, energy, or attention to an assigned task that is related to an unanswered calling	"I try to use the technology [involved in my job] as much as possible . . . I have a Smart Board in my room. I'm on the technology district committee, and the technology committee for our school. I really like being on those committees. I'm excited that I'm going to start to be able to use more technology in the classroom." (Amy)
Job expanding *(adding tasks to pursue an unanswered calling)*	Taking on short-term or temporary tasks to incorporate aspects of an unanswered calling	"We had a request into the office for someone to speak at a university a couple months ago, and so I volunteered. . . . It gave me a chance to talk with a whole group of college students about what we do, and why, and how we're effective. I really enjoyed it and it was really exciting and fun for me." (Paula)
	Increasing the number of tasks continually expected of individual to incorporate aspects of an unanswered calling	"I think I've become kind of the go-to person on a junior level for just anything that has to do with communications or writing, someone who's not at the management level. So I work with a lot of the other Associates when they have ideas or questions about writing and things like that. . . . It makes me feel like I'm important. . . . It's not exactly the writing that I want to do in my life, but I think it's helped me understand the nuances of word choice and how to message things, and I enjoy it." (Emma)

(continues)

TABLE 10-5 Crafting Techniques *(continued)*

Technique	Explanation	Illustration
Role reframing *(altering one's perception of a role to pursue an unanswered calling)*	Establishing a cognitive connection to align the conventional social purpose of a job responsibility with an unanswered calling	"I think the question for me has always been 'How can I grow and how can I make a contribution?' . . . and therapy felt that way for me. I mean, I thought I could make a contribution in other people's lives, and I knew that in hearing their stories and being intimate, on that sort of intellectual level with them, would make a contribution to their lives. And it seems to me that teaching is really about the whole of the student and the faculty member. It's about their interaction, and about how what you're talking about in class might relate to what you are living in your life. It's not therapy in the sense that you don't intrude on the privacy of folks, but I really think if education doesn't help you live more joyfully and creatively and love better, then it's not worth much." (Craig)
	Broadening the conventional social purpose of a job responsibility to incorporate an unanswered calling	"I often liken teaching to being a musician because of when I'm in front of a classroom, I put on my performance face. I can be talking in a rather soft voice like this to you outside a classroom, and as soon as I enter that classroom, [Guitarist Gary] the performer is on. And it's the same way with music; you kind of put on your stage face. . . . It's entertaining education: edu-tainment. And I'm doing that all the time. I'm trying to make class time interesting and fun and entertaining because research on education demonstrates when people are in a good mood, they tend to learn better and learn more. . . . I remember when I was performing and I had my rock band and my other bands, the high which I got from playing in front of people was very similar to the high which I get from performing teaching in front of people." (Gary)

Leisure Crafting

Vicarious experiencing	Seeking fulfillment through others' participation in an unanswered calling	"Whenever we do go to a concert or musical theatre . . . I will fantasize a little bit and daydream about if I was the one up there singing, or I was the one up there playing the piano. . . . I really don't think I have the talent to really do anything very important from the musical end, but I'm happy that I still have it in my life for my own enjoyment." (Mary)
Hobby participating	Pursuing leisure and volunteer activities related to an unanswered calling	"I'm not going to retire from either. As long as I can hold a guitar in my hands, I'm going to be playing. And as long as I can stand in front of a class and teach, and somebody lets me, I'm going to be doing that. . . . Music more so. I can see somebody getting too old to teach. But I can't imagine somebody, or at least I can't imagine myself, ever getting too old to at least once in a while, pick up my instrument and play it. Because it's just a different world. It's a totally different world." (Abe)

Source: Reproduced from Berg, J. M., Grant, A. M., & Johnson, V. (2010). When callings are calling: Crafting work and leisure in pursuit of unanswered occupational callings. Organization Science, 21*(5), 973–994.*

Working with fewer external incentives may actually increase your sense of self-determination. Many people are choosing jobs not for the financial benefits but for the achievements they can experience through them. Programs like Teach for America and the Peace Corps work well because people join in order to enjoy the sense of contributing and "doing good" in the world and are willing to work for very low pay compared to other jobs. Field studies show that doing good on the job, when combined with intrinsic motivation, results in better performance and increased persistence (Grant, 2008).

People have different reasons for the career choices they make. None are "good" or "bad," but the key is the match to what you value. Are you willing to delay gratification through a long training period, sacrifice a normal lifestyle, and do what it takes to become a medical doctor? Or are you better suited to a career path that puts you into the action sooner and allows you to learn through the challenges along the way? Take some time to reflect about what motivates and inspires you and how you plan to approach your work. Talk to your parents and others who work to hear about their motivations and their satisfaction with their jobs.

Many resources are available to help with the important career decisions ahead. A place to start is your campus career center, which typically offers help with job searches and interview preparation. There are many online resources, books, and articles about career selection and guides to help you think about careers. You can even find counselors at your school or professional career coaches that can help you identify a path. The best advice is to start considering your options now and attempt to gain experience in a variety of workplaces to discover what best serves to motivate you.

Summary of Multiple Influences on Motivation

As we saw from the discussions of motivation based on physiological needs, humans have elaborate systems for controlling behavior. Like other animals, we have sophisticated biological systems that monitor and regulate basic behaviors like eating and sex. At the same time, these same behaviors are influenced by social factors, environmental contexts, and cultural conventions.

For example, we examined the elaborate system that regulates the motivation of hunger. From physiology, stomach receptors and hormones motivate eating when the stomach is empty and suppress it when full. "Start" and "stop" eating areas in the hypothalamus control the initiation of eating based on signals from sugar in the bloodstream. The hypothalamus also communicates with glands throughout the digestive system through hormones to coordinate eating. A longer-term monitoring system, the metabolism, affects the maintenance of weight as a set or settling point. And genetics plays a major role in the long-term outcome of these mechanisms.

To this, many additional environmental factors join in to affect whether eating takes place. Food preferences, availability, cues from the environment like advertisements, and moods affect what and how much we eat. In addition, the social setting can lead to eating more when we are joined by others. Our cultural practices also tell us which food to savor and which to avoid. Even our cultural depictions of "ideal" others can affect how we feel about our own and others' bodies and, therefore, how we choose to eat (or not to eat).

These environmental and biological factors combine to stimulate eating. As a result, there are many ways in which the hunger motivation can lead us astray. When obesity or eating disorders occur, it is tempting to think they share the same cause. However, each of the influences described can lead to changes in eating behavior, so the underlying cause(s) can be different for each person. Causes of increased weight may involve disruptions of processes in genetics, the brain, the endocrine system, the stomach, and behaviors responsive to the environment. The number of processes involved suggests there may be many different causes for the same symptom of excess weight.

The same argument holds for higher-level motivations: Why are some people driven by a need for achievement while others are content to do "well enough?" The roots of our higher-level motivation may lie in early parenting relationships, experiences in childhood, "self-talk" about what is needed to accomplish goals, environmental influences like education, competition with others, and physiological influences like arousal. These motivations present complex pictures of the influence of biological and environmental factors.

Motivation clearly illustrates how the expression of a specific behavior can be caused by biological and environmental factors, some of which are outside of our awareness. This makes understanding and changing our behavior a challenging task!

CONCEPT LEARNING CHECK **10.5** | What "Works" at Work?

Complete this true or false quiz and explain why each answer is correct.

1. Interviews provide good evidence of the best person to hire.   T   F

2. Most people say their work is their true "calling."   T   F

3. General mental ability is a good predictor of success in any job.   T   F

4. Gender makes no difference in career outcomes.   T   F

5. Productive work teams communicate more positives than negatives.   T   F

Visual Overview Motivation: Sources of Hunger

The motivation to eat has characteristic influences in our physical bodies (shown in blue) and in our environment (shown in green).

Are You Hungry?

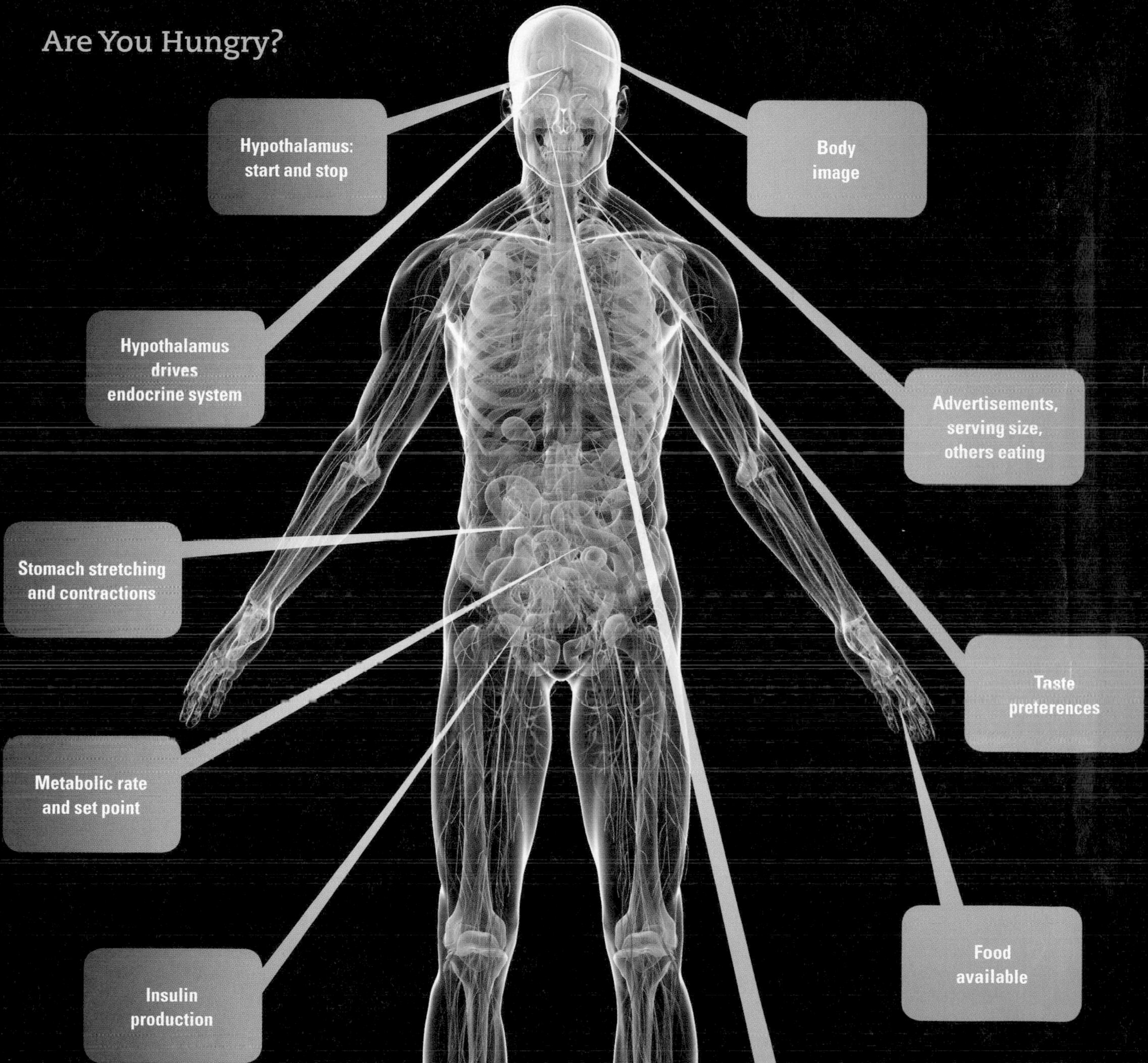

Hypothalamus: start and stop

Body image

Hypothalamus drives endocrine system

Advertisements, serving size, others eating

Stomach stretching and contractions

Metabolic rate and set point

Taste preferences

Insulin production

Food available

10.1 Motivational Theories

- Motivation is described as an inner state that energizes people toward the fulfillment of a goal.
- Understanding built-in behaviors led to instinct theories, or motivation as programmed behavior occurring in response to environmental cues.
- Evolutionary psychologists apply the theory of evolution to explain behaviors.
- A drive is defined as tension arising from within our physiological systems, which in turn motivates action.

- Arousal theory states that we are motivated to seek out an optimal level of arousal.
- Incentive theories focus on the reward or payoff for behaviors.
- Maslow posited that the needs and motivations of humans form levels, called the hierarchy of needs.

10.2 Motivation of Hunger

- Our physiological system attempts to manage our hunger and keep our energy stores in a steady state.
- Hunger pangs in the stomach play a role, but are not our only motivation for eating.
- The structure called the hypothalamus is the functional center of motivation in the brain.
- The hypothalamus also regulates the endocrine system, the network of glands throughout the body that manufacture and secrete hormones.
- Another source of regulation for hunger occurs through the metabolism of the body, or the physiological processes used to convert energy from nutrients.
- When the level of glucose (or sugar) in the bloodstream is low, people feel hungry, and when food raises the glucose levels, hunger is reduced.
- Genetics also plays a major role in metabolism, set point, and body type.

- A wealth of environmental factors play a role in motivating us to eat.
- Anorexia nervosa is an eating disorder in which someone feels he or she is overweight despite objective evidence.
- Binge eating disorder and bulimia nervosa refer to individuals who binge eat large amounts of food. In bulimia, relatively normal weight is maintained by purging.
- Perceptions of body image are influenced by personal, social, and cultural values that may vary from one culture to another.
- Obesity, defined as an excess level of fat in the body, at least 15% above ideal weight for a given height, is a leading preventable cause of disease and one of today's most serious public health problems.

Hourglass shape   Rectangle shape

10.3 Sexual Motivation

- The motivation for sex is present in all animals, necessary to ensure their reproduction.
- Masters and Johnson described four phases of physiological responses during sex called the human sexual response cycle: excitement, plateau, orgasm, and resolution.

- The male sex hormone testosterone has been shown to correlate with sexual desire, and another hormone called oxytocin is released during orgasm, leading to sensations of emotional well-being.
- Differences between genders may follow from different reproductive strategies, called parental investment theory.

- Sexual orientation refers to the gender preferred for emotional and sexual intimacy.
- Kinsey defined a continuum of sexual orientation, from exclusively heterosexual (opposite sex) to bisexual to exclusively homosexual (same sex).

- No theories of environmental causes of sexual orientation have ever received scientific support.

10.4 Social Motivations

- Maslow suggested that, after our basic biological needs are satisfied, we move up the hierarchy to social and achievement needs.
- We all want to feel a part of a relationship or group, called the need to belong.
- Motivated people set high but realistic goals so that they are challenged, yet can succeed.
- Mindsets, or beliefs about yourself and your abilities, oriented toward growth

help to develop skills through dedication and effort.
- Self-actualization involves working toward the full use and exploitation of your talents, capacities, and potentials.
- Decades of studies have demonstrated that self-determination, or choice, is the key factor in long-term motivation.

10.5 Motivation and Work

- The subfield of industrial and organizational psychology addresses the psychology of work.
- The Hawthorne effect occurs when increased interest directed toward a worker results in improved performance.
- Interviewers tend to believe in their own intuitive abilities to find good candidates in the absence of evidence, called the interviewer illusion.
- Race, gender, sexual orientation, obesity, and attractiveness have been shown to influence the selection and hiring of employees.

- There is more positive than negative communication within effective teams, in a ratio of five positive to one negative.
- Gender norms still affect career choices and compensation in the workplace.
- A calling is defined as an occupation that an individual (1) feels drawn to pursue, (2) expects to be intrinsically enjoyable and meaningful, and (3) sees as a central part of his or her identity.
- Motivation clearly illustrates how the expression of a specific behavior can be caused by biological and environmental factors, some outside of our awareness.

10.1 Motivational Theories

1. The fact that Jack enjoys racing on dirt bikes but not sky diving supports the _____ theory of motivation.
   A. instinct
   B. arousal
   C. drive
   D. incentive

2. Patrick ate a large breakfast. When he arrived for class, a friend offered him a muffin. Even though Patrick was still quite full, he wanted to make his friend happy, so he ate it anyway. Patrick's behavior can best be explained by the _____ theory of motivation.
   A. self-awareness
   B. instinct
   C. drive
   D. incentive

3. According to Maslow's hierarchy of needs, which of these is the most primary need?
   A. Safety
   B. Intimacy
   C. Self-actualization
   D. Belonging

4. Tevin's dad paid him a dollar for every "A" grade he brought home in high school. Now that Tevin is in college, his grades have started to drop. This suggests Tevin's high school study efforts were motivated:
   A. instinctually.
   B. extrinsically.
   C. as needed.
   D. intrinsically.

10.2 Motivation of Hunger

5. Because the _____ regulates the glands, it could be considered to be the connection between the brain and the endocrine (hormonal) system.
   A. hypothalamus
   B. hippocampus
   C. thalamus
   D. amygdala

6. Several motivations, such as hunger and sex, are accomplished through hormones (such as testosterone) secreted directly into the bloodstream through the _____ system.
   A. endocrine
   B. autonomic nervous
   C. limbic
   D. peripheral nervous

7. If a rat has a brain tumor that results in a disruption of "start eating" behavior, which of the following areas is the most likely location of the tumor?
   A. Hypothalamus
   B. Thalamus
   C. Cerebellum
   D. Brainstem

8. Patients diagnosed with anorexia nervosa have been shown to have:
   A. bouts with bulimia.
   B. failed at diets repeatedly.
   C. distorted body images.
   D. lived in a modern culture.

10.3 Sexual Motivation

9. Masters and Johnson studied female and male sexual responses. Which of these statements expresses their main findings about sexual response?
   A. Female sexual satisfaction depends on penis size.
   B. There is no refractory period.
   C. Men have greater orgasmic capabilities than women.
   D. The sexual response cycle is the same in men and women.

10. Evolutionary theory predicts that, due to differences in parental investment, women should seek mates who are:
    A. physically attractive.
    B. intelligent.
    C. muscular.
    D. high in status.

11. Evolutionary theory predicts that, due to differences in parental investment, men should seek mates who:
    A. are physically attractive.
    B. are of normal weight.
    C. have a low waist-to-hip ratio.
    D. are high in status.

12. The correlations in homosexual orientation between identical twins compared to fraternal twins and other siblings suggest that sexual orientation:
    A. is influenced more by environment.
    B. is influenced more by genetics.
    C. is affected equally by both.
    D. is not known to be related to either environment or genetics.

10.4 Social Motivations

13. Sarah and Alice meet at a student group meeting. They begin talking and eventually become friends. Even though Sarah is not always nice to Alice, they continue to be friends. This best demonstrates the human:
    A. need for belonging.
    B. need for self-actualization.
    C. need for achievement.
    D. need for power.

14. Patrice really enjoys solving difficult equations. Whenever she has free time, she plops down and does some calculations. She is then asked to be in a study in which she gets paid $5 for every equation she solves. According to results from Deci's puzzle experiment on intrinsic and extrinsic motivation, Patrice will now be likely to:

    A. enjoy doing calculations just as much.
    B. like doing calculations even more.
    C. get less satisfaction out of doing calculations on her own.
    D. refuse to participate in any more research studies.

15. At the top of Maslow's hierarchy of needs, he proposed that we all share the deep motivation to:
    A. make the most of our potential.
    B. form a significant relationship.
    C. provide for ourselves and loved ones.
    D. receive the respect of others around us.

10.5 Motivation and Work

16. The Hawthorne effect, first observed with workers in a special "test" room versus a control room, showed that:
    A. better pay increased production.
    B. none of the interventions applied to the test room led to increased production.
    C. all interventions applied to the test room led to increased production.
    D. improving the brightness in the room led to increased production.

17. The best predictor of later job success is:
    A. the need to belong.
    B. general mental ability.
    C. an outgoing personality.
    D. the need to achieve.

18. The study of insurance workers assigned at random to offices of others of higher, the same, and lower status on the corporate structure showed that people:
    A. benefit from changed surroundings.
    B. will work harder for more money.
    C. are sensitive to equity in compensation.
    D. dislike changes in leadership.

CHAPTER DISCUSSION QUESTIONS

1. Section 10.1 defines motivation as an inner state that energizes people toward the fulfillment of a goal. However, you will find that each theory of motivation (instinct, evolutionary, drive, arousal, incentive, and hierarchical) places a different emphasis on the role of the internal state. Evaluate each theory of motivation by how strong an influence it places on internal states in driving goal fulfillment.

2. Compare and contrast the physiological factors and environmental factors involved in feeling hungry. Are some factors more powerful than others? Should you expect individual differences in how much each factor influences a person's eating patterns?

3. Think of a common theme about sex and relationships that you have seen depicted in movies or television shows. Relate the information in this chapter about sexual motivation to the theme you have selected. Does the information in the chapter support the ideas in movies and television? Why or why not?

4. Assess the relationship between the higher motivations discussed in section 10.4 (belonging, achievement, self-actualization) and work motivation. How might your higher motivations influence your success in getting hired, maintaining a job, and getting promoted?

CHAPTER PROJECTS

1. How would your life be different without one of your motivations? Review hunger, sexual, and the higher motivations and pick one that is particularly interesting to you. Then, create a scenario that illustrates how your life would be different without that motivation. How would it change your daily life? How would it change your long-term life planning?

2. Advertisers and marketers use information about our motivations when they create advertising campaigns. Find video (e.g., YouTube) clips of commercials for a particular product and identify which motivations are being targeted in the ads. In your evaluation of the commercials, make sure that you refer to specific knowledge of motivation discussed in the chapter.

CHAPTER KEY TERMS

360-degree feedback
Achievement gap
Achievement motivation
Adipose tissue
Anorexia nervosa
Arousal theory
Basal metabolic rate
Binge eating disorder
Bisexual
Body dysmorphia
Body mass index (BMI)
Bulimia nervosa
Calling
Coming out
Continuum of sexual orientation
Delay of gratification
Diabetes
Drive
Drive theory
Endocrine system
Engagement
Equity theory
Esteem motivation
Estrogen
Evolutionary psychologist
Evolved behaviors
Excitement phase
"Exotic becomes erotic"
Extrinsic incentives
Extrinsic motivation
Fertile
Fixed mindset
Flow
Ghrelin
Glucose

Growth mindset
Hawthorne effect
Heterosexual
Hierarchy of needs
Homeostasis
Homosexual
Hormones
Humanistic psychology
Human sexual response cycle
Hypothalamus
Incentive
Incentive theories
Industrial and organizational
    psychology
Instinct theories
Insulin
Interviewer illusion
Intrinsic incentives
Intrinsic motivation
Job analysis
Job burnout
Lateral hypothalamus
Leptin
Mating
Metabolism
Mindset
Motivation
Motive
Need for achievement
Need to belong
Obesity
Optimal arousal
Organizational psychology
Orgasmic phase
Overjustification effect

Oxytocin
Parental investment theory
Paternal uncertainty
Persistence
Personnel psychology
Plateau phase
Process loss
Realistic job preview
Refractory period
Reproductive strategies
Resolution phase
Self-actualization
Self-determination theory
Self-regulation
Set point
Settling point
Sex norms
Sexual disorder
Sexual harassment
Sexual orientation
Sexual peak
Social rejection
Status
Sublimation
Testosterone
Thematic apperception
    test (TAT)
Unit bias
Universals
Vasocongestion
Ventromedial hypothalamus
Waist-to-hip ratio (WHR)
Yerkes-Dodson law of arousal

ANSWERS TO CONCEPT LEARNING CHECKS

10.1 Theories of Motivation

1. D. He is seeking increased arousal.

2. E. He is motivated by pay.

3. C. The biological drive to drink overrides the social game.

4. B. Preferred tastes for sweet and fat may have helped human ancestors survive in environments in which food was scarce.

5. A. Some inborn fears and reflexes occur when certain stimuli are presented.

6. F. Meeting physiological needs by gaining resources comes before higher-level needs in hierarchy theory.

7. Instinct, evolutionary, and drive theories posit the same motivations for everyone. However, satisfying drives may be more effortful for some people. Arousal theory takes the situation into account, so it would predict different motivations for people in different environments. Incentive theory is very sensitive to the features of the environment that reward behavior; so someone in Japan may work longer hours because there are more goods available to buy with the financial incentives they received for work.

Finally, the hierarchy of needs theory is designed to take differences in situations into account. People that have their basic needs met (such as the Japan example) are free to pursue their higher-level motivations.

10.2 Eating Disorder or Disordered Eating?

1. Bulimia. [Binging by overeating followed by purging the body through vomiting or laxatives; eating disorder.]

2. Binge eating disorder. [Binging by overeating large quantities not followed by purging but compulsively performed in secret; eating disorder.]

3. Obesity. [Gaining weight to more than 15% of the ideal body weight for your height; not an eating disorder.]

4. Anorexia. [Losing at least 25% of your weight with restriction of eating and fear of becoming obese; eating disorder.]

10.3 Evolution and Gender Differences

1. They differ in strategy because they differ in parental investment. Strictly speaking, males need only donate sperm, and they may have a large number of offspring. Females must invest in pregnancy and birth, then nursing

and raising the child and can produce fewer children over their lifetime.

2. Based on cues that predict fertility, males would be attracted based on youth, health, and low waist-to-hip ratio signals.

3. Based on cues that predict status, females would be attracted to older males, high social status, and high material wealth signals, as these help to support her.

4. First, within a population, there are some males who prefer younger mates, some who prefer older, and some the same. Over generations, the successful males are ones who chose younger mates and thus were able to reproduce and pass their genes on to the next generation. As a result, the preference for younger mates spreads so more men have that tendency in progressive generations.

10.4 Fostering Achievement

1. Following Dweck's work, you can focus on your process toward achievement rather than ability. So rewarding yourself for hours of study is more beneficial than rewarding yourself for the outcome of the grade. This reflects a growth mindset. Belief in hard work and effort to accomplish goals ("You worked really well today; You put so much effort into learning the material!") is more effective than encouragement based on ability ("You are a smart person; You always do badly at math."), which reflects an unchanging and fixed mindset.

Following self-determination theory, you can work to integrate your externally rewarded behavior into your personal values. Identify intrinsic motivations in your behavior that will sustain it when the external reward is no longer available.

10.5 What "Works" at Work?

1. F. The interviewer illusion shows people believe they can learn the most from interviews, but only structured interviews show benefits.

2. F. Only a third of those surveyed said their work was their calling.

3. T. Intelligence is the strongest factor related to job success across fields.

4. F. Women are less likely to end up in higher-paying fields and jobs.

5. T. The ratio is five positive statements for each negative.

ANSWERS TO CHAPTER REVIEW TEST

10.1 Motivational Theories

1. B. Rationale: Arousal theory says we seek the optimum level of arousal, not the highest level.

2. D. Rationale: Since he is not hungry, he is eating for an external reason, the incentive of making his friend happy.

3. A. Rationale: Safety is the most basic need listed, and Maslow proposed basic needs come first.

4. B. Rationale: The extrinsic incentive of money was motivating him, and without it, he does not continue the behavior.

10.2 Motivation of Hunger

5. A. Rationale: The hypothalamus is the brain structure involved in motivation.

6. A. Rationale: The endocrine system releases hormones.

7. A. Rationale: The hypothalamus region, specifically the lateral hypothalamus.

8. C. Rationale: They are overly self-critical about their bodies.

10.3 Sexual Motivation

9. D. Rationale: Males and females go through similar response cycles (with some differences).

10. D. Rationale: High status commands more resources and help from others, which benefits her.

11. C. Rationale: Males should be concerned with fertility, which is predicted by waist-to-hip ratio.

12. B. Rationale: The more related, the more concordance of orientation, and there is little evidence about environmental influences.

10.4 Social Motivations

13. A. Rationale: We need to belong and avoid rejection when possible.

14. C. Rationale: Once paid for an activity, people find it not as enjoyable to do for fun.

15. A. Rationale: Maximizing our potential is Maslow's self-actualization.

10.5 Motivation and Work

16. C. Rationale: All of the interventions showed improvement due to increased interest in the workers.

17. B. Rationale: General intelligence was found to be the best predictor; need to achieve may be a mismatch in some jobs.

18. C. Rationale: People worked harder in nicer offices and less in less nice offices, showing they were sensitive to the "perks" that come with jobs.

REFERENCES

Adams, J. S. (1963). Toward an understanding of inequity. *Journal of Abnormal and Social Psychology, 67,* 422–436.

Agras, W. S., Hammer, L. D., McNicholas, F., & Kraemer, H. C. (2004). Risk factors for childhood overweight: A prospective study from birth to 9.5 years. *Journal of Pediatrics, 145*(1), 20–25.

Amabile, T. M. (1996). Motivational synergy: Toward new conceptualizations of intrinsic and extrinsic motivation in the workplace. *Human Resource Management Review, 3*(30), 185–201.

Ames, C. (1992). Classrooms: Goals, structures, and student motivation. *Journal of Educational Psychology, 84*(3), 261–327.

Ames, C., & Archer, J. (1988). Goals in the classroom: Students' learning strategies and motivation processes. *Journal of Educational Psychology, 80*(3), 260–267.

Andersson, L. M., & Pearson, C. M. (1999). Tit for tat? The spiraling effect of incivility in the workplace. *Academy of Management Review, 24,* 452–471.

Angier, N. (1985, January 28). Finding trouble in paradise: Do women really prefer cuddling over "the act"? *Time, 125,* 76.

Ariely, D., Gneezy, W., Lowenstein, G., & Mazar, N. (2009). Large stakes and big mistakes. *Review of Economic Studies, 76,* 451–469.

Arkowitz, H., & Lilienfeld, S. O. (2009). Environment and weight. *Scientific American Mind, 20,* 68–69.

Arvey, R. D., & Campion, J. E. (1982). The employment interview: A summary and review of recent research. *Personnel Psychology, 35,* 281–322.

Assanand, S., Pinel, J. P. J., & Lehman, D. R. (1998). Personal theories of hunger and eating. *Journal of Applied Social Psychology, 28,* 998–1015.

Atkinson, J. W. (1964). *An introduction to motivation.* New York: Van Nostrand.

Bakker, A. B., & Schaufeli, W. B. (2008). Positive organizational behavior: Engaged employees in flourishing organizations. *Journal of Organizational Behavior, Special Issue: Contexts of Positive Organizational Behavior, 29*(2), 147–154.

Barness, L. A., Opitz, J. M., & Gilbert-Barness, E. (2007). Obesity: Genetic, molecular, and environmental aspects. *American Journal of Medical Genetics, 143A*(24), 3016–3034.

Barr, A., Bryan, A., & Kenrick, D. T. (2002). Sexual peak: Socially shared cognitions about desire, frequency, and satisfaction in men and women. *Personal Relationships, 9,* 287–299.

Baumeister, R. F. (1991). The need to belong: Desire for interpersonal attachments as a fundamental human motivation. *Psychological Bulletin, 117*(3), 497–529.

Baumeister, R. F., Bratslavsky, E., Muraven, M., & Tice, D. M. (1998). Is the active self a limited resource? *Journal of Personality and Social Psychology, 74,* 1252–1265.

Baumeister, R. F., Catanese, K. R., & Vohs, K. D. (2001). Is there a gender difference in strength of sex drive? Theoretical views, conceptual distinctions, and a review of relevant evidence. *Personality and Social Psychology Review, 5*(3), 242–273.

Baumeister, R. F., & Leary, M. R. (1995). The need to belong: Desire for interpersonal attachments as a fundamental human motivation. *Psychological Bulletin, 117,* 497–529.

Baumeister, R. F., Vohs, K. D., & Tice, D. M. (2007). The strength model of self-control. *Current Directions in Psychological Science, 16*(6), 351–355.

Becker, J. B., Rudick, C. N., & Jenkins, W. J. (2001). The role of dopamine in the nucleus accumbens and striatum during sexual behavior in the female rat. *Journal of Neuroscience, 21*(9), 3236–3241.

Bell, S. T. (2007). Deep-level composition variables as predictors of team performance: A meta-analysis. *Journal of Applied Psychology, 92*(3), 595–615.

Bem, D. J. (1996). Exotic becomes erotic: A developmental theory of sexual orientation. *Psychological Review, 103*(2), 320–335.

Bem, D. J. (2000). Exotic becomes erotic: Interpreting the biological correlates of sexual orientation. *Archives of Sexual Behavior, 29*(6), 531–548.

Berg, J. M., Grant, A. M., & Johnson, V. (2010). When callings are calling: Crafting work and leisure in pursuit of unanswered occupational callings. *Organization Science, 21*(5), 973–994.

Bernard, L. C., Mills, M., Swenson, L., & Walsh, R. P. (2005). An evolutionary theory of human motivation. *Genetic, Social, and General Psychology Monographs, 131,* 129–184.

Blanchard, R., & Klassen, P. (1997). H-Y antigen and homosexuality in men. *Journal of Theoretical Biology, 185*(3), 373–378.

Blanchard, R., Zucker, K. J., Siegelman, M., Dickey, R., & Klassen, P. (1998). The relation of birth order to sexual orientation in men and women. *Journal of Biosocial Science, 30,* 511–519.

Blass, E. M., & Hall, W. G. (1976). Drinking termination: Interactions among hydrational, orogastric, and behavioral controls in rats. *Psychological Review, 83*(5), 356–374.

Bliss, E. L., & Branch, C. H. H. (1960). *Anorexia Nervosa: Its history, psychology and biology.* New York: Paul B. Hoeber.

Bozarth, J. D., & Brodley, B. T. (1991). Actualization: A functional concept in client-centered therapy. *Journal of Social Behavior & Personality, 6*(5), 45–59.

Brosnan, S. F., & de Waal, F. B. M. (2003). Monkeys reject unequal pay. *Nature, 425*(6955), 279–299.

Bulik, C. M., Wade, T. D., Heath, A. C., Martin, N. G., Stunkard, A. J., & Eaves, L. J. (2001). Relating body mass index to figural stimuli: Population-based normative data for Caucasians. *International Journal of Obesity and Related Metabolic Disorders, 25*(10), 1517–1524.

Buss, D. M. (1989). Sex differences in human mate selection: Evolutionary hypotheses tested in 37 cultures. *Behavior and Brain Sciences, 12,* 1–49.

Buss, D. M. (1994). The strategies of human mating: People worldwide are attracted to the same qualities in the opposite sex. *American Scientist, 82,* 238–249.

Buss, D. M. (1995). Evolutionary psychology: A new paradigm for psychological science. *Psychological Inquiry, 6,* 1–30.

Buss, D. M., & Schmitt, D. P. (1993). Sexual strategies theory: An evolutionary perspective on human mating. *Psychological Review, 100*(2), 204–232.

Campfield, L. A., Smith, F. J., Rosenbaum, M., & Hirsch, J. (1996). Human eating: Evidence for a physiological basis using a modified paradigm. *Neuroscience and Biobehavioral Reviews, 20*(1), 133–137.

Cannon, W. B., & Washburn, A. L. (1912). An explanation of hunger. *American Journal of Physiology, 29,* 441–454.

Clark, R. D., III, & Hatfield, E. (1989). Gender differences in receptivity to sexual offers. *Journal of Psychology and Human Sexuality, 2,* 39–55.

Conley, T. D. (2011). Perceived proposer personality characteristics and gender differences in acceptance of casual sex offers. *Journal of Personality and Social Psychology, 100*(2), 309–329.

Cortina, L. M., Magley, V. J., Williams, J. H., & Langhout, R. D. (2001). Incivility in the workplace: Incidence and impact. *Journal of Occupational Health Psychology, 6*(1), 64–80.

Crago, M., Shisslak, C. M., & Estes, L. S. (1996). Eating disturbances among American minority groups: A review. *International Journal of Eating Disorders, 19,* 239–248.

Crow, S. M., Fok, L. Y., & Hartman, S. J. (1998). Who is at greatest risk of work-related discrimination—Women, blacks, or homosexuals? *Employee Responsibilities and Rights Journal, 11*(1), 15–26.

Csikszentmihalyi, M. (1990). *Flow: The psychology of optimal experience.* New York: Harper & Row.

Curry, S. J., Wagner, E. H., & Grothaus, L. C. (1991). Evaluation of intrinsic and extrinsic motivation interventions with a self-help smoking cessation program. *Journal of Consulting and Clinical Psychology, 59,* 318–324.

Davis, D., Shaver, P. R., & Vernon, M. L. (2003). Physical, emotional, and behavioral reactions to breaking up: The roles of gender, age, emotional involvement, and attachment style. *Personality and Social Psychology Bulletin, 29*(7), 871–884.

Deci, E. L. (1971). Effects of externally mediated rewards on intrinsic motivation. *Journal of Personality and Social Psychology, 18*(1), 105–115.

Deci, E. L., & Ryan, R. M. (1985). *Intrinsic motivation and self-determination in human behavior.* New York: Plenum Press.

DeWall, C. N., MacDonald, G., Webster, G. D., Masten, C. L., Baumeister, R. F., Powell, C., Combs, D., Schurtz, D. R., Stillman, T. F., Tice, D. M., & Eisenberger, N. J. (2010). Acetaminophen reduces social pain: Behavioral and neural evidence. *Psychological Science, 21*(7), 931–937.

Donnay, D. A. C., Morris, M. L., Schaubhut, N. A., Thompson, R. C., Grutter, J., & Hammer, A. L. (2011). *Strong Interest Inventory(r) [Newly Revised].* Mountain View, CA: CPP.

Doyle, R. (2000). Women and the professions. *Scientific American,* April, 30–31.

Drewnowski, A., Yee, D. K., & Krahn, D. D. (1988). Bulimia in college women: Incidence and recovery rates. *American Journal of Psychiatry, 145*(6), 753–755.

Dweck, C. (2006). *Mindset: The new psychology of success.* New York: Random House.

Eisenberger, N. I., Lieberman, M. D., & Williams, K. D. (2003). Does rejection hurt? An fMRI study of social exclusion. *Science, 302,* 290–292.

Eknoyan, G. (2008). Adolphe Quetelet (1796–1874)—the average man and indices of obesity. *Nephrology, Dialysis, & Transplantation, 23*(1), 47–51.

England, G. W. (1990). The patterning of work meanings which are coterminous with work outcome levels for individuals in Japan, Germany and the USA. *Applied Psychology, 39*(1), 29–45.

Epel, E., Lapidus, R., McEwen, B., & Brownell, K. (2001). Stress may add bite to appetite in women: A laboratory study of stress-induced cortisol and eating behavior. *Psychoneuroendocrinology, 26*(1), 37–49.

Fiske, D. W., & Maddi, S. R. (1961). *The function of varied experience.* Homewood, IL: Dorsey.

Fiske, S. T., Bershoff, D. N., Borgida, E., Deaux, K., & Heilman, M. E. (1991). Social science research on trial: Use of sex stereotyping research in *Price Waterhouse v. Hopkins. American Psychologist, 46*(10), 1049–1060.

Fitzgerald, B. (1999). Children of lesbian and gay parents: A review of the literature. *Marriage and Family Review, 29,* 57–75.

Freud, S. (1915). Instincts and their vicissitudes. Reprinted in J. Strachey (Ed.) (1957), The standard edition of the complete psychological works of Sigmund Freud, volume XIV (1914–1916): On the history of the Psycho-Analytic movement, papers on metapsychology and other works, pp. 109–140. London: The Hogarth Press and the Institute of Psycho-analysis.

Fryar, C. D., Hirsch, R., Porter, K. S., Kottiri, B., Brody, D. J., & Louis, T (2007, June 28). Drug use and sexual behaviors reported by adults: United States, 1999–2002. *Advance Data from Vital and Health Statistics,* No. 384, 1–16. http://www.cdc.gov/nchs/data/ad/ad384.pdf

Garcia-Falgueras, A., & Swaab, D. F. (2010). Sexual hormones and the brain: An essential alliance for sexual identity and sexual orientation. In S. Loche, M. Cappa, L. Ghizzoni, M. Maghnie, & M. O. Savage (Eds.), *Pediatric neuroendocrinology: Endocrine development, Vol. 17* (pp. 22–35). Basel: Karger.

Geier, A. B., Rozin, P., & Doros, G. (2006). Unit bias: A new heuristic that helps explain the effects of portion size on food intake. *Psychological Science, 17,* 521–525.

Ghorpade, J. (2000). Managing five paradoxes of 360-degree feedback. *Academy of Management Executive, 14*(1), 140–150.

Gottman, J. M. (1994). *Why marriages succeed or fail.* New York: Simon & Schuster.

Gottman, J. M., Levenson, R. W., Gross, J., Frederickson, B., McCoy, K., Rosenthal, L., Ruef, A., & Yoshimoto, D. (2003). Correlates of gay and lesbian couples' relationship satisfaction and relationship dissolution. *Journal of Homosexuality, 45*(1), 23–43.

Grant, A. M. (2008). Does intrinsic motivation fuel the prosocial fire? Motivational synergy in predicting persistence, performance, and productivity. *Journal of Applied Psychology, 93*(1), 48–58.

Greenberg, J. (1988). Equity and workplace status: A field experiment. *Journal of Applied Psychology, 73*(4), 606–613.

Griebel, T. (2006). Self-portrayal in a simulated life: Projecting personality and values in The Sims 2. *International Journal of Computer Game Research, 6*(1).

Grilo, C. M., & Pogue-Geile, M. F. (1991). The nature of environmental influences on weight and obesity: A behavior genetics analysis. *Psychological Bulletin, 110,* 520–537.

Gusnard, D. A., Ollinger, J. M., Sulman, G. L., Cloninger, C. R., Price, J. L., Van Essen, D. C., & Raichle, M. E. (2003). Persistence and brain circuitry. *Proceedings of the National Academy of Sciences, 100*(6), 3479–3484.

Hackman, J. R. (1987). The design of work teams. In J. W. Lorsch (Ed.), *Handbook of organizational behavior* (pp. 315–342). Englewood Cliffs, NJ: Prentice-Hall.

Hackman, J. R., & Oldham, G. R. (1975). Development of the Job Diagnostic Survey. *Journal of Applied Psychology, 60*(2), 159–170.

Harpaz, I. (1988). Variables affecting non-financial employment commitment. *Applied Psychology, 33,* 235–247.

Harter, J. K., Schmidt, F. L., & Hayes, T. L. (2002). Business-unit-level relationship between employee satisfaction, employee engagement, and business outcomes: A meta-analysis. *Journal of Applied Psychology, 87*(2), 268–279.

Haslam, D. W., & James, W. P. (2005). Obesity. *Lancet, 366*(9492), 1197–1209.

Heatherton, T. F., & Baumeister, R. F. (1991). Binge eating as escape from self-awareness. *Psychological Bulletin, 110*(1), 86–108.

Henderson, A. T., Berla, N., & The National Committee for Citizens in Education. (1994). *A new generation of evidence: The family is critical to student achievement.* Columbia, MD: National Committee for Citizens in Education.

Herman, C. P., Roth, D. A., & Polivy, J. (2003). Effects of the presence of others on food intake: A normative interpretation. *Psychological Bulletin, 129,* 873–886.

Highhouse, S. (2008). Stubborn reliance on intuition and subjectivity in employee selection. *Industrial and Organizational Psychology, 1,* 333–342.

Hill, G. W. (1982). Group versus individual performance: Are N+1 heads better than one? *Psychology Bulletin, 91,* 517–539.

Hoffman, D. J., Policastro, P., Quick, V., & Lee, S. K. (2006). Changes in body weight and fat mass of men and women in the first year of college: A study of the "freshman 15." *Journal of American College Health, 55*(1), 41–45.

Holland, J. L. (1996). Exploring careers with a typology: What we have learned and some new directions. *American Psychologist, 51*(4), 397–406.

Holm-Denoma, J., Joiner, T., Vohs, K., & Heatherton, T. (2008). The "freshman fifteen" (the freshman five actually): Predictors and possible explanations. *Health Psychology, 27,* S3–S9.

Horgen, K. B., & Brownell, K. D. (2002). Confronting the toxic environment: Environmental and public health actions in a world crisis. In T. A. Wadden & A. J. Stunkard (Eds.), *Handbook of obesity treatment* (pp. 95–106). New York: Guilford Press.

Hull, C. L. (1943). *Principles of behavior.* New York: Appleton-Century-Crofts.

Ilies, R., Hauserman, N., Schwochau, S., & Stibal, J. (2003). Reported incidence rates of work-related sexual harassment in the United States: Using meta-analysis to explain reported rate disparities. *Personnel Psychology, 56,* 607–631.

Integrated Regional Information Networks (IRIN). (2009, June 26). *Mauritania: Force-feeding on decline, but more dangerous.* http://www.unhcr.org/refworld /docid/4a4885d540.html

Iyengar, S. S., Wells, R. E., & Schwartz, B. (2006). Doing better but feeling worse: Looking for the "best" job undermines satisfaction. *Psychological Science, 17*(2), 143–150.

Kane, R. L., Johnson, P. E., Town, R. J., & Butler, M. (2004). A structured review of the effect of economic incentives on consumers' preventive behavior. *American Journal of Preventive Medicine, 27*(4), 327–352.

Kanfer, R., Wanberg, C. R., & Kantrowitz, T. M.. (2001). Job search and employment: A personality–motivational analysis and meta-analytic review. *Journal of Applied Psychology, 86*(5), 837–855.

Keesey, R. E., & Powley, T. L. (1986). The regulation of body weight. *Annual Review of Psychology, 37,* 109–133.

Kenrick, D. T., Gutierres, S. E., & Goldberg, L. L. (1989). Influence of popular erotica on judgments of strangers and mates. *Journal of Experimental and Social Psychology, 25,* 159–167.

Kenrick, D. T., & Keefe, R. C. (1992). Age preferences in mates reflect sex differences in reproductive strategies. *Behavioral and Brain Sciences, 15,* 75–133.

Keys, A., Fidanza, F., Karvonen, M. J., Kimura, N., & Taylor, H. L. (1972). Indices of relative weight and obesity. *Journal of Chronic Disease, 25*(6), 329–343.

Kinsey, A. C., Pomeroy, W. B., & Martin, C. E. (1948). *Sexual behavior in the human male.* Philadelphia: Saunders.

Kinsey, A. C., Pomeroy, W. B., Martin, C. E., & Gebhard, P. H. (1953). *Sexual behavior in the human female.* Philadelphia: Saunders.

Korsgaard, M. A., Schweiger, D. M., & Sapienza, H. J. (1995). Building commitment, attachment, and trust in strategic decision-making teams: The role of procedural justice. *Academy of Management Journal, 38*(1), 60–84.

Kozlowski, S. W. J., & Bell, B. S. (2003). Work groups and teams in organizations. In W. C. Borman, D. R. Ilgen, & R. J. Klimoski (Eds.), *Handbook of psychology (Vol. 12): Industrial and organizational psychology* (pp. 333–375). New York: Wiley.

Kral, J. G. (1985). Morbid obesity and related health risks. *Annals of Internal Medicine, 103*(6), 1043–1104.

Kross, E., Berman M. G., Mischel, W., Smith, E. E., & Wager, T. D. (2010). Social rejection shares somatosensory representations with physical pain. *Proceedings of the National Academy of Sciences, 108*(15), 6270–6275.

Ladson-Billings, G. (2006). From the achievement gap to the education debt: Understanding achievement in U.S. schools. *Educational Research, 35*(7), 3–12.

Landy, F. J., & Farr, J. L. (1980). Performance rating. *Psychological Bulletin, 87*(1), 72–107.

Långström, N., Rahman, Q., Carlström, E., & Lichtenstein, P. (2008). Genetic and environmental effects on same-sex sexual behavior: A population study of twins in Sweden. *Archives of Sexual Behavior, 39*(1), 75–80.

Lee, J.-S., & Bowen, N. K. (2006). Parental involvement, cultural capital and the achievement gap among elementary school children. *American Educational Research Journal, 43*(2), 193–218.

Leibel, R. L., Rosenbaum, M., & Hirsch, J. (1995). Changes in energy expenditure resulting from altered body weight. *New England Journal of Medicine, 332,* 621–628.

Lepper, M. R., Greene, D., & Nisbett, R. E. (1973). Undermining children's intrinsic interest with extrinsic reward: A test of the "overjustification hypothesis." *Journal of Personality and Social Psychology, 28*(1), 129–137.

LeVay, S. (1991). A difference in hypothalamic structure between heterosexual and homosexual men. *Science, 253*(5023), 1034–1037.

Lichtman, S. W., Pisarska, K., Berman, E. R., Pestone, M., Dowling, H., Offenbacher, E., Weisel, H., Heshka, S., Matthews, D. E., & Heymsfield, S. B. (1992). Discrepancy between self-reported and actual caloric intake and exercise in obese subjects. *New England Journal of Medicine, 327*(27), 1893–1898.

Losada, M., & Heaphy, E. (2004). The role of positivity and connectivity in the performance of business teams—A nonlinear dynamics model. *American Behavioral Scientist, 47,* 740–765.

Lumeng, J. C., Forrest, P., Appugliese, D. P., Kaciroti, N., Corwyn, R. F., & Bradley, R. H. (2010). Weight status as a predictor of being bullied in third through sixth grades. *Pediatrics, 125*(6), e1301–e1307.

Lynness, K. S., & Thompson, D. E. (1997). Above the glass ceiling? A comparison of matched samples of female and male executives. *Journal of Applied Psychology, 82*(3), 359–375.

Maffei, M., Halaas, J., Ravussin, E., Praley, R. E., Lee, G. H., Zhang, Y., Fei, H., Kinm, S., Lallone, R., & Ranganathan, S. (1995). Leptin levels in human and rodent: Measurement of plasma leptin and ob RNA in obese and weight-reduced subjects. *Nature Medicine, 11,* 1155–1161.

Mah, K., & Binik, Y. M. (2005). Are orgasms in the mind or the body? Psychosocial versus physiological correlates of orgasmic pleasure and satisfaction. *Journal of Sex & Marital Therapy, 31,* 187–200.

Manson, J. E., Willett, W. C., Stampfer, M. J., Colditz, G. A., Hunter, D. J., Hankinson, S. E., Hennekens, C. H., & Speizer, F. E. (1995). Body weight and mortality among women. *New England Journal of Medicine, 333*(11), 677–685.

Marlowe, C. M., Schneider, S. L., & Nelson, C. E. (1996). Gender and attractiveness biases in hiring decisions: Are more experienced managers less biased? *Journal of Applied Psychology, 81*(1), 11–21.

Marmaros, D., & Sacerdote, B. (2006). How do friendships form? *Quarterly Journal of Economics, 121*(1), 79–119.

Maslach, C., Wilmar, B., Schaufeli, W. B., & Leiter, M. P. (2001). Job burnout. *Annual Review of Psychology, 52,* 397–422.

Maslow, A. H. (1943). A theory of human motivation. *Psychological Review, 50*(4), 370–396.

Maslow, A. H. (1970). *Motivation and personality* (2nd Ed.). New York: Harper & Row.

Masters, W. H., & Johnson, V. E. (1966). *Human sexual response.* Oxford, UK: Little, Brown.

Mayo, E. (1933). *The human problems of industrial civilization.* New York: Macmillan.

McClelland, D. C., Atkinson, J. W., Clark, R. A., & Lowell, E. L. (1953). *The achievement motive.* New York: Appleton-Century.

McClelland, D. C., Atkinson, J. W., Clark, R. A., & Lowell, E. L. (1976). *The achievement motive.* Oxford, UK: Irvington.

McCormick, E. J., Jeanneret, P. R., & Mecham, R. C. (1972). A study of job characteristics and job dimensions as based on the position analysis questionnaire (PAQ) [Monograph]. *Journal of Applied Psychology, 56,* 347–368.

Meston, C. M., & Frohlich, P. F. (2000). The neurobiology of sexual function. *Archives of General Psychiatry, 57,* 1012–1030.

Meyer-Bahlburg, H. F. L., Ehrhardt, A. A., Rosen, L. R., Gruen, R. S., Veridiano, N. P., Vann, F. H., & Neuwalder, H. F. (1995). Prenatal estrogens and the development of homosexual orientation. *Developmental Psychology, Special issue: Sexual Orientation and Human Development, 31*(1), 12–21.

Mischel, W., Ebbesen, E. B., & Raskoff Zeiss, A. (1972). Cognitive and attentional mechanisms in delay of gratification. *Journal of Personality and Social Psychology, 21*(2), 204–218.

Morewedge, C. K., Huh, Y. E., & Vosgerau, J. (2010). Thought for food: Imagined consumption reduces actual consumption. *Science, 330*(6010), 1530–1533.

Morgan, C. D., & Murray, H. A. (1935). A method for investigating fantasies. *Archives of Neurology and Psychiatry, 34,* 289–306.

Murphy, G. (1947). *Personality: A biosocial approach to origins and structures.* New York: Harper.

Murray, H. A. (1938). *Explorations in personality.* New York: Oxford University Press.

National Business Group on Health (15th Annual) and the Towers Watson. (2010). *Survey on Purchasing Value in Health Care, with 507 employers of 1,000 or more employees that collectively employ 11.5 million workers.* http://www.businessgrouphealth.org/pressrelease.cfm?ID=151

NIH, NHLBI Obesity Education Initiative. (1998). *Clinical guidelines on the identification, evaluation, and treatment of overweight and obesity in adults.* http://www.nhlbi.nih.gov/guidelines/obesity/ob_gdlns.pdf

Nisbett, R. E. (1987). Lay personality theory: Its nature, origin, and utility. In N. E. Grunberg, R. E. Nisbett, J. Singer (Eds.), *A distinctive approach to psychological research: The influence of Stanley Schacter* (pp. 87–117). Hillsdale, NJ: Erlbaum.

Oishi, S., Diener, E. F., Lucas, R. E., & Suh, E. M. (1999). Cross-cultural variations in predictors of life satisfaction: Perspectives from needs and values. *Personality and Social Psychology Bulletin, 25*(8), 980–990.

Parker, S., Nichter, M., Nichte, M., Vuckovic, N., Sims, C., & Ritenbaugh, C. (1995). Body image and weight concerns among African American and White adolescent females: Differences that make a difference. *Human Organization, 54*(2), 103–114.

Pecina, S., Cagniard, B., Berridge, K. C., Aldridge, J. W., & Zhuang, X. (2003). Hyperdopaminergic mutant mice have higher "wanting" but not "liking" for sweet rewards. *Journal of Neuroscience, 23*(28), 9395–9402.

Peplau, L. A. (2003). Human sexuality: How do men and women differ? *Psychological Science, 12*(2), 37–40.

Pierloot, R. A., & Houben, M. E. (1978). Estimation of body dimensions in anorexia nervosa. *Psychological Medicine, 8,* 317–324.

Pillard, R. C., & Bailey, J. M. (1998). Human sexual orientation has a heritable component. *Human Biology, 70*(2), 347–365.

Pingitore, R., Dugoni, B. L., Tindale, R. S., & Spring, B. (1994). Bias against overweight job applicants in a simulated employment interview. *Journal of Applied Psychology, 79*(6), 909–917.

Pink, D. H. (2009). *Drive: The surprising truth about what motivates us.* New York: Riverhead Books.

Poundstone, W. (2004). *How would you move Mount Fuji?: Microsoft's cult of the puzzle—How the world's smartest companies select the most creative thinkers.* New York: Little, Brown.

Premack, S. L., & Wanous, J. P. (1985). A meta-analysis of realistic job preview experiments. *Journal of Applied Psychology, 70*(4), 706–719.

Pull, C. B. (2004). Binge eating disorder. *Current Opinion in Psychiatry, 17*(1), 43–48.

Ramsey, G. V. (1943). The sexual development of boys. *American Journal of Psychology, 56*(2), 217–233.

Rhoads, R. A. (1995). Learning from the coming-out experiences of college males. *Journal of College Student Development, 36*(1), 67–74.

Rochlin, M. (1982). *The language of sex: The heterosexual questionnaire, Changing Men.* Waterloo, ON: University of Waterloo.

Roehling, M. V., Roehling, P. V., & Pichler, S. (2007). The relationship between body weight and perceived weight-related employment discrimination: The role of sex and race. *Journal of Vocational Behavior, 71*(2), 300–318.

Roethlisberger, F. J., & Dickson, W. J. (1939). *Management and the worker: An account of a research program conducted by the Western Electric Company, Hawthorne Works, Chicago.* Cambridge, MA: Harvard University Press.

Rogers, C. R. (1951). *Client-centered therapy: Its current practice, implications, and theory.* Oxford, England: Houghton Mifflin.

Rolls, B. J., Rolls, E. T., Rowe, E. A., & Sweeney, K. (1981). Sensory specific satiety in man. *Physiology & Behavior, 27*(1), 137–142.

Rose, G. A., & Williams, R. T. (1961). Metabolic studies of large and small eaters. *British Journal of Nutrition, 15*, 1–9.

Ryan, R. M., Mims, V., & Koestner, R. (1983). Relation of reward contingency and interpersonal context to intrinsic motivation: A review and test using cognitive evaluation theory. *Journal of Personality and Social Psychology, 45*(4), 736–750.

Saris, W. H. M., Blair, S. N., Van Baak, M. A., Eaton, S. B., Davies, P. S. W., Di Pietro, L., Fogelholm, M., Rissanen, A., Schoeller, D., Swinburn, B., Tremblay, A., Westerterp, K. R., & Wyatt, H. (2003). How much physical activity is enough to prevent unhealthy weight gain? Outcome of the IASO 1st Stock Conference and consensus statement. *Obesity Reviews, 4*, S101–S114.

Savic, I., & Lindstrom, P. (2008). PET and MRI show differences in cerebral asymmetry and functional connectivity between homo- and heterosexual subjects. *Proceedings of the National Academy of Sciences of the United States of America, 105*(27), 9403–9408.

Schmidt, F. L., & Hunter, J. E. (1998). The validity and utility of selection methods in personnel psychology: Practical and theoretical implications of 85 years of research findings. *Psychological Bulletin, 124*(2), 262–274.

Schuler, H., Farr, J. L., & Smith, M. (1993). *Personnel selection and assessment. Individual and organizational perspectives.* Hillsdale, NJ: Erlbaum.

Schutz, W. C. (1955). What makes groups productive? *Human Relations, 8*, 429–465.

Schwartz, M. W., Woods, S. C., Porte, D. Jr., Seeley, R. J., & Baskin, D. G. (2000). Central nervous system control of food intake. *Nature, 404*(6778), 661–671.

Silverman, J. A. (1983). Richard Morton, 1637–1698, limner of anorexia nervosa: His life and times, a tercentenary essay. *Journal of the American Medical Association, 250*(20), 2830–2832.

Singh, D. (1993). Adaptive significance of waist-to-hip ratio and female physical attractiveness. *Journal of Personality and Social Psychology, 65*, 293–307.

Singh, D. (1994). Is thin really beautiful and good? Relationship between waist-to-hip ratio (WHR) and female attractiveness. *Personality & Individual Differences, 16*(1), 123–132.

Spitzer, L., & Rodin, J. (1981). Human eating behavior: A critical review of studies in normal and overweight individuals. *Appetite, 2*, 293–329.

Stirling, L. J., & Yeomans, M. R. (2004). Effect of exposure to a forbidden food on eating in restrained and unrestrained women. *International Journal of Eating Disorders, 35*(1), 59–68.

Stoll, M. A., Raphael, S., & Holzer, H. J. (2004). Black job applicants and the hiring officer's race. *Industrial and Labor Relations Review, 57*(2), 267–287.

Striegel-Moore, R. H., & Bulik, C. M. (2007). Risk factors for eating disorders. *American Psychologist, Special Issue: Eating Disorders, 62*(3), 181–198.

Stunkard, A. J., Harris, J. R., Pedersen, J. L., & McClearn, G. E. (1990). The body-mass index of twins who have been reared apart. *New England Journal of Medicine, 332*, 1483–1487.

Sue, S., & Okazaki, S. (1990). Asian-American educational achievements: A phenomenon in search of an explanation. *American Psychologist, 45*(8), 913–920.

Suls, J., Martin, R., & Wheeler, L. (2002). Social comparison: Why, with whom, and with what effect? *Current Directions in Psychological Science, 11*(5), 159–163.

Sumithran, P., Prendergast, L. A., Delbridge, E., Purcell, K., Shulkes, A., Kriketos, A., & Proietto, J. (2011). Long-term persistence of hormonal adaptations to weight loss. *New England Journal of Medicine, 365*, 1597–1604.

Taylor, L. C., Clayton, J. D., Rowley, S. J. (2004). Academic socialization: Understanding parental influences on children's school-related development in the early years. *Review of General Psychology, 8*(3), 163–178.

Teitelbaum, P., & Epstein, A. N. (1962). The lateral hypothalamus syndrome: Recovery of feeding and drinking after lateral hypothalamic lesions. *Psychological Review, 69*(2), 74–79.

Teixeira, P. J., Going, S. B., Houtkooper, L. B., Cussler, E. C., Metcalfe, L. L., Blew, R. M., Sardinha, L. B., & Lohman, T. G. (2006). Exercise motivation, eating, and body image variables as predictors of weight control. *Medicine & Science in Sports & Exercise: Applied Sciences: Psychobiology and Behavioral Strategies, 38*(1), 179–188.

Twenge, J. M. (2006). *Generation "Me:" Why today's young Americans are more confident, assertive, entitled—and more miserable than ever before.* New York: Free Press.

Valian, V. (1999). *Why so slow? The advancement of women.* Cambridge: MIT Press.

Wansink, B. (2004). Environmental factors that increase the food intake and consumption volume of unknowing consumers. *Annual Review of Nutrition, 24*, 455–479.

Wansink, B., & Sobel, J. (2007). Mindless eating: The 200 daily food decisions we overlook. *Environment and Behavior, 39*(1), 106–123.

Webb, T. L., & Sheeran, P. (2006). Does changing behavioral intentions engender behavior change? A meta-analysis of the experimental evidence. *Psychological Bulletin, 132*(2), 249–268.

Weiner, B. (1972). *Theories of motivation: From mechanism to cognition.* Oxford, UK: Markham.

Weinsier, R. L., Nagy, T. R., Hunter, G. R., Darnell, B. E., Hensrud, D. D., & Weiss, H. L. (2000). Do adaptive changes in metabolic rate favor weight regain in weight-reduced individuals? An examination of the set-point theory. *American Journal of Clinical Nutrition, 72*(5), 1088–1094.

Williamson, I., & Hartley, P. (1998). British research into the increased vulnerability of young gay men to eating disturbance and body dissatisfaction. *European Eating Disorders Review, 6*(3), 160–170.

Wing, R. R., & Hill, J. O. (1994). Successful weight loss maintenance. *Annual Review of Nutrition, 21*, 323–341.

Wrzesniewski, A., McCauley, C., Rozin, P., & Schwartz, B. (1997). Jobs, careers, and callings: People's relations to their work. *Journal of Research in Personality, 31*, 21–33.

Wyrwicka, W., & Dobrzecka, C. (1960). Relationship between feeding and satiation centers of the hypothalamus. *Science, 132*, 805–806.

Yeung, R. R. (1996). The acute effects of exercise on mood state. *Journal of Psychosomatic Research, 40*(2), 123–141.

Yukl, G., & Van Fleet, D. D. (1992). Theory and research on leadership in organizations. In M. Dunnette & L. Hough (Eds.), *Handbook of I/O psychology* (Vol. 3, pp. 147–198). Palo Alto, CA: Consulting Psychologists Press.

Chapter Overview ▼

11.1 The Role of Physiology and Evolution in Emotion
The Role of Physiology in Emotion
The Role of Evolution in Emotion

CONCEPT LEARNING CHECK **11.1** *Bodily Processes and Emotion*

11.2 The Role of Behavior and Cognition in Emotion
The Role of Behavior in Emotion
Facial Feedback and Emotion

CONCEPT LEARNING CHECK **11.2** *Behavior and Cognition and Emotion*

11.3 Theories of Emotion
Common-Sense Theory
James-Lange Peripheral Feedback Theory
Cannon-Bard Simultaneous Trigger Theory
Schacter-Singer Two-Factor Theory of Emotion
Cognitive-Mediational Theory of Emotion

CONCEPT LEARNING CHECK **11.3** *Theories of Emotion*

11 Emotion, Stress, and Health

Learning Objectives ▼

11.1
- Define how bodily processes are involved in emotion.
- Discuss how physiological processes are involved in emotion.
- Discuss the evolutionary basis of emotion.

11.2
- Explain the impact that thoughts and behaviors have on emotion.
- Explain the connection between behavior and emotion.

11.3
- Identify and discuss the main theories of emotion.

11.4
- Examine and explain the special factors and situations that can influence the expression of emotions.

11.5
- Examine the various factors that lead to stress.
- Discuss the physical and psychological effects of stress.

11.6
- Illustrate how positive psychology emphasizes the constructive features of human strength and healthful living rather than pathology.

11.4 Expressing Emotion
Culture and Emotion
Gender and Emotion
Fear
Anger and Aggression
Love
CONCEPT LEARNING CHECK **11.4** *Expressing Emotion*

11.5 Stress
What Is Stress?
Sources of Stress

Cognition and Stress
Choice as a Stress
Culture and Stress
Effects of Stress
Stress and Health
  Stress and the Immune System
Coping With and Managing Stress
Interventions
CONCEPT LEARNING CHECK **11.5** *Sources and Effects of Stress*

11.6 Positive Psychology
Happiness
Hardiness
Optimism
Summary of Multiple Influences on Emotion, Stress, and Health
CONCEPT LEARNING CHECK **11.6** *Positive Psychology*

CRITICAL THINKING APPLICATION

Twack! Thud! Plonk! Bam! Crash! Those were the sounds I heard at 3 a.m. My first groggy thought was a grumpy, "What's Bailey knocked over this time?!" I always thought cats were supposed to be stealthy, but mine didn't get that memo, especially Bailey, who seems to intentionally topple mugs and flick pens onto the floor in order to get my attention. But this crash was different. This crash grabbed my attention and shook most of the house. I opened my eyes and I saw both my cats, Barnum and Bailey, on the bed. I looked at them; they looked at me. Then, as we all realized at the same time that it must be something else, they darted from the bedroom as I stumbled to the front of the house.

What I saw through the window stopped me in my tracks. A man with a bat in his hand was slamming his body against the screen door to my front porch. He had already torn off the screen and moved his attention to the door. I didn't know what to do: Save the cats, scare away the intruder, call the police, cry? Then, for a brief second, I caught the invader's eye. I gave my most menacing grimace and he fled.

I was simultaneously terrified and angry as I called the police. When the police arrived about 20 minutes later, I was still shaking. Unless you count my recent ride on the Daredevil roller coaster, it was the most frightened I can remember being. I was exhausted. It was 5:30 a.m. and in an hour I needed to leave for work, but I was drained and wanted to go back to sleep. I had experienced a flood of emotions that had swept over me, leaving me exhausted.

What are emotions and where do they come from? Many emotions are linked to stress. What are the effects of stress on your body? What explains where I found the strength to try to protect my cats and house instead of cowering under the covers?

When thinking about emotions, it's important to consider the vast array of experiences that are part of emotion. We think of an emotion as a feeling, but really it's more than that. Emotion is a class of subjective reactions brought on by an event, including four types: physiological (my heart beat faster when I saw the intruder), behavioral (I ran to the door and scowled at the intruder), cognitive (I perceived the noise as harmless at first, and then dangerous), and affective (I was afraid).

Emotion A class of subjective feelings elicited by stimuli that have high significance to an individual.

Fight-or-flight response A reaction to danger in which the sympathetic nervous system prepares the organs for vigorous activity.

11.1 The Role of Physiology and Evolution in Emotion

Biological processes are involved in emotion.

- Define how bodily processes are involved in emotion.
- Define how physiological processes are involved in emotion.
- Discuss the evolutionary basis of emotion.

The Role of Physiology in Emotion

There are many physiological reactions that occur with emotions. Your sympathetic nervous system prepares you to fight, freeze, or flee. This **fight-or-flight response**

FIGURE 11-1 is a reaction to danger in which the sympathetic nervous system prepares the organs for vigorous activity. Once stimulated, your autonomic nervous system signals the adrenal glands to release stress hormones like **corticosteroids**, which are hormones produced in the adrenal cortex in reaction to stress, and **catecholamines**, which are stress hormones released by the adrenal glands FIGURE 11-2. Your muscles tense, blood pressure increases, heart rate quickens, endorphins release. In this state, your pupils dilate, your attention focuses, and your digestive functioning slows to a crawl (which explains butterflies in the stomach).

Corticosteroids
Hormones produced in the adrenal cortex in reaction to stress.

Catecholamines Stress hormones released by the adrenal glands.

Yerkes Dodson law
A theory that performance is best at medium levels of arousal.

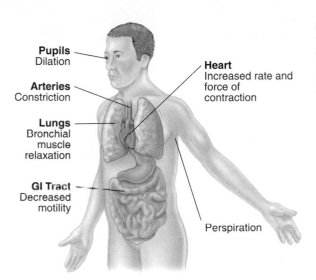

Pupils
Dilation

Arteries
Constriction

Lungs
Bronchial muscle relaxation

GI Tract
Decreased motility

Heart
Increased rate and force of contraction

Perspiration

FIGURE 11-1 Stress can activate the hypothalamus, which can cause increased heart rate, perspiration, and dilation of pupils. This is the first stage of the stress response: alarm.

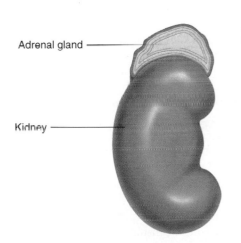

Adrenal gland

Kidney

FIGURE 11-2 The adrenal glands sit on top of the kidneys.

When the parasympathetic nervous system takes over, things slow down. You may feel sleepy or relaxed after an anxiety-producing situation. The parasympathetic nervous system helps you to recover, digest, and rest.

Is arousal always bad? Not really. A little bit of stress or arousal can be helpful. According to the **Yerkes Dodson law**, optimal levels of arousal may be helpful, while too little arousal can be problematic. For example, during an exam, being sleepy can be a problem, on the other hand, too much arousal can lead to test anxiety and cause you to freeze up. As you can see in FIGURE 11-3, the Yerkes Dodson law looks like an upside down U, with optimal outcomes occurring at moderate levels of arousal for most behaviors (Teigen, 1994). However, the more complicated a behavior, the lower the best arousal level. This is also true for new behaviors or ones that require careful judgment or creativity. If you are playing chess, you might need complete silence and zero distractions. On the other hand, simple, instinctual, and well-rehearsed tasks, like washing the dishes or folding laundry, might have higher optimal arousal levels.

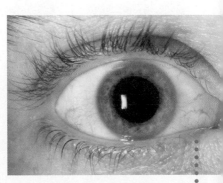

Dilated pupils are a sign of the fight-or-flight response.

FIGURE 11-3 According to the Yerkes Dodson law, optimal levels of arousal occur in the moderate range.

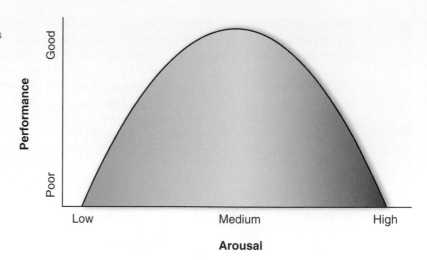

Activities such as video games may have a high level of optimal arousal.

Polygraph A machine that uses physiological measurements to detect lies.

Galvanic skin response (GSR) A measurement of the conductivity of your skin.

Anthropomorphism Assigning human emotions or behaviors to nonhumans.

The Yerkes Dodson law may explain why you can do so well playing video games with music blaring and sensory overload coming from the screen and your friends screaming "Jump! Jump!" at you. Each person has a level of arousal that works best for her or him—an optimal level of arousal. Too much arousal causes problems, and too little leaves you disengaged.

Knowing the physiological elements of emotions and the nervous system can be handy. One way that this knowledge is used is in a **polygraph**, a machine that uses biological measurement to detect lies FIGURE 11-4. From *poly*, meaning many, and *graph*, meaning write, a polygraph will test autonomic nervous system arousal in multiple ways including pulse, blood pressure, breathing, fidgeting, and **galvanic skin response (GSR)**, which is a measurement of the conductivity of your skin. Why skin conductivity? Well, when you have a sympathetic nervous system spike, the tips of your fingers begin to release tiny beads of sweat. This sweat makes your skin more conductive, and electricity can pass along the skin more quickly. These sweat glands are activated by the sympathetic nervous system and deactivated by the parasympathetic nervous system. Because of this relationship, skin conductivity is a handy measure of your stress response.

One idea behind the polygraph is that lies produce different stress patterns from nondeceptive responses. Polygraphs assume that lying leaves distinctive physiological cues. Once a baseline of arousal is established by answering a series of questions, the polygrapher will ask questions and look for spikes of sympathetic nervous system activity.

An alternative way to use a polygraph is the guilty knowledge test (GKT). A GKT is used to determine if the subject has "guilty knowledge" about a situation, such as a crime. In the guilty knowledge test, the subject is asked about key elements of a case, knowledge that only someone that knows intimate details of the case would know. People tend to respond physiologically to things that are familiar, so the autonomic nervous system will answer the questions for them. The polygrapher will ask a series of multiple-choice questions and look for sympathetic nervous system reactions to the correct answer, which indicate guilty knowledge of the situation. For example, a polygrapher might say "The gun was left on the desk. The gun was left on the floor. The gun was left in the bathroom. The gun was left under the bed." If the gun was left under the bed and the subject knows that, the polygrapher would notice a sympathetic nervous system reaction when he or she read that question.

The use of polygraphs is controversial and admissible in court in a minority of states in the United States. There are arguments about the validity of the tests in the scientific community, with some experts suggesting that the

FIGURE 11-4 A polygraph uses physiological measurement to detect lies.

tests are accurate (Grubin, 2010), while others suggest that the science behind the tests is weak (National Research Council, 2003).

The Role of Evolution in Emotion

Evolution suggests that certain traits are more likely to be passed along if they make reproduction or survival more likely. If you know about this theory, you may not be surprised to learn that Charles Darwin FIGURE 11-5 had a theory that emotions were evolved behaviors. In his classic text, *The Expression of Emotions in Man and Animals* FIGURE 11-6 (Darwin, 2009; Feinstein, Adolphs, Damasio, & Tranel, 2011), Darwin suggested that emotions were innate and evolved adaptive responses. People who had the ability to create and understand the emotions on the faces of others had a reproductive advantage because they can, for example, instill fear or anticipate aggression.

Look at the photos in FIGURE 11-7. Can you tell what emotions these animals are experiencing? Bared teeth might represent anger. Dogs growl and bare their teeth. Cats hiss and bare their teeth. You may have even bared your teeth in anger at a driver who cut you off in traffic. Showing your teeth is a way of communicating, "See these teeth? I could bite you with them!" Hopefully it won't come to biting, but animals that can communicate and understand nonverbal signals are at an advantage. However, seeing emotional expressions in the faces of nonhuman animals can easily lead to **anthropomorphism**, assigning human emotions or behaviors to nonhumans. Thinking that golden retrievers and dolphins are cheerful because their faces look like they are smiling or that King Charles spaniels have a yearning sadness because they have huge pools of eyes may say more about humans than it does about the animals. Anthropomorphism may also explain why I describe my cat Bailey as manipulative because of his pen-flicking behavior.

FIGURE 11-5 Charles Darwin had a theory that emotions were evolved behaviors.

FIGURE 11-6 "Fear" from Charles Darwin's *The Expression of Emotions in Man and Animals* (1872).

FIGURE 11-7 Can you tell what emotions these animals are experiencing?

CONCEPT LEARNING CHECK 11.1 | *Bodily Processes and Emotion*

Match the term to the situation or statement that explains it.

A. Fight-or-flight response

B. Galvanic skin response

C. Anthropomorphism

D. Yerkes Dodson law

1. _____ It is really hard to concentrate on studying neuroscience when I have had too much caffeine.

2. _____ We think that dolphins look happy because they look like they are smiling.

3. _____ After my friends yelled "SURPRISE!," I noticed my heart was racing.

4. _____ Carol attached small pads to the fingertips of the suspect in order to measure conductivity.

5. _____ A physiological process that might cause us to freeze when we are confronted with danger.

Explain

6. Explain, using the Yerkes Dodson law, why it might be easier to clean your room when it's noisy in your house than when it's quiet.

Showing your teeth is a way your face expresses anger.

Doesn't this horse look happy? Anthropomorphism refers to assigning human emotions or behaviors to nonhumans.

11.2 The Role of Behavior and Cognition in Emotion

Thoughts and behaviors can have an impact on emotion.

- Explain the impact that thoughts and behaviors have on emotion.
- Explain the connection between behavior and emotion.

Your emotional experience is made up of more than physiological reactions. How you interpret those reactions also influences how you feel. For example, people who tend toward **catastrophic thinking** will distort the scale and impact of a stressful event and may interpret an event as more threatening than others would. Indeed, our emotional experience incorporates our evaluation of an event.

But can you have an emotional response that isn't prompted by a thought? Absolutely. Robert Zajonc (pronounced ZI-yence; rhymes with science; Zajonc, 1980) suggested that thoughts and emotional responses are not always tied together. Sometimes you can have an emotional response without a thought tied to it. One morning, while at the beach, I was enjoying breakfast and reading the newspaper. In the background, I heard a song and started to feel very, very sad. I had no idea why. Later on when I was headed to the shore, it hit me: That was the song I played to soothe my dog when he was very sick. Since then, I'd never been able to hear that song without feeling very sad. In this case, the sadness was linked to the song, but there was no thought that accompanied it.

Why is this so? There are multiple influences on how emotions are processed. Some emotions are the result of a neural shortcut. Rather than being processed in the cortex, visual and auditory sensations can hop on neural pathways from your eyes and ears to the **amygdala**, a cluster of neurons in the temporal lobe linked to emotions such as anger and fear FIGURE 11-8. This means that things you see or hear can activate the amygdala. The amygdala, in turn, can influence your thoughts and feelings (LeDoux, 1998). This gives biological support to the idea that thoughts and simple feelings can sometimes be disconnected.

The Role of Behavior in Emotion

Your friend returns from class and you know instantly that she's had a bad day. How do you know? You can tell by the look on her face. Facial expressions send social signals.

People don't usually express their emotion in facial expressions unless others are around (Buck, Losow, Murphy & Costanzo, 1992). Facial expressions convey different

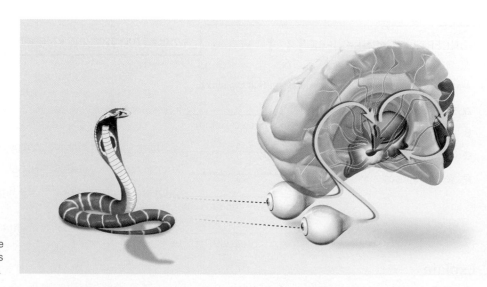

FIGURE 11-8 Some emotions take a shortcut and pass from the eyes and ears directly to the amygdala.

meanings depending on the circumstances. People often use facial expressions to lie about their feelings as well as to express them.

Darwin suggested that facial expressions were evolved behaviors to communicate information. For this to be true, other people have to be able to recognize those facial expressions. To test this theory, Paul Ekman FIGURE 11-9; (Ekman, Friesen, O'Sullivan, & Chan, et al., 1987) showed photographs of people displaying emotions. He took these photographs (like the ones in FIGURE 11-10) to several countries: Argentina, Brazil,

FIGURE 11-9 Paul Ekman researched basic emotions.

FIGURE 11-10 Ekman used photos like these in his research.

Chile, Japan, New Guinea, and the United States. He discovered that people from those countries were pretty good at recognizing the emotions of anger, fear, disgust, happiness, sadness, and surprise. Because they are thought to be universally expressed, anger, fear, disgust, happiness, sadness, and surprise are known as **basic emotions**—feeling states thought to be expressed in a common way. In fact, many of these facial expressions occur in children blind from birth (Galati, Miceli, & Sini, 2001). Since then, Ekman and others have proposed additional nominees for basic emotions, as you can see listed in TABLE 11-1 (Ekman, 1999).

Facial expressions do vary a bit from culture to culture (Mesquita & Frijda, 1992), which could explain why people are better at identifying emotional expression from faces from their own culture than those of people from other cultures FIGURE 11-11.

Facial Feedback and Emotion

While some researchers debated about which came first, the emotion or the physiological response, others debated what seemed like an obvious order—the emotion or the facial expression. After all, aren't facial expressions just a reaction to your emotions? Well, the **facial feedback hypothesis** suggests that an emotion is regulated, in part, by the feedback

Catastrophic thinking A cognitive distortion of the scale and impact of a stressful event.

Amygdala A cluster of neurons in the temporal lobe linked to emotions such as anger and fear.

Basic emotions Feeling states that are thought to be expressed in a universal way.

Facial feedback hypothesis A theory that suggests that the position of the facial muscles influences emotional expression.

Facial expressions can also send social signals.

TABLE 11-1 Additional Basic Emotions

Amusement
Contempt
Contentment
Embarrassment
Excitement
Guilt
Pride in achievement
Relief
Satisfaction
Sensory pleasure
Shame

Source: Adapted from T. Dalgleish, & M. J. Power (Eds.), Handbook of cognition and emotion *(pp. 45–60). New York: John Wiley & Sons Ltd.*

FIGURE 11-11 Percent of people from different countries who were able to correctly identify facial expressions. *Source: Adapted from Ekman, P., & Friesen, W. V. (2003). Unmasking the Face: A Guide to Recognizing Emotions From Facial Expressions. Malor Books.*

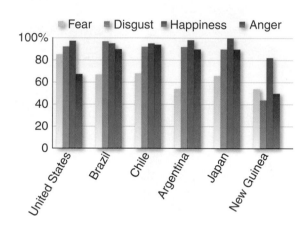

your brain gets from the way your face is arranged (Kraut, 1982). This would mean that frowning can make you sad and smiling can make you feel happy.

According to facial feedback, the way you hold your face can produce emotions. You are sad because you cry. To test this hypothesis, researchers (Strack, Martin, & Stepper, 1988) asked participants to look at cartoons while holding a pen in one of three positions: between their teeth, between their lips, or in their hand FIGURE 11-12. The idea was that holding a pen between your teeth forces you to smile and a frown results from lip holding. Those who were asked to hold the pen between their teeth rated the cartoons the funniest, and those who held the pen between their lips rated them the least funny.

Facial expressions of emotion are sometimes blunted when we are alone.

FIGURE 11-12 Holding a pencil between the teeth (A) forces a smile, while between the lips (B) produces a frown.

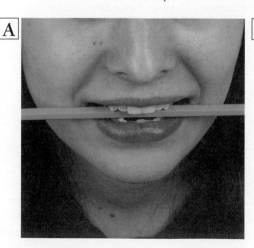

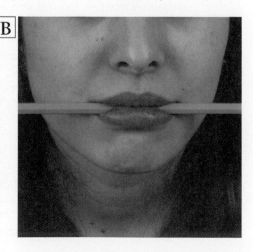

Some theorists suggest that facial feedback alone influences emotion. Other theories suggest that facial muscles act in a way to control blood flow to your brain. Smiles, the theory proposes, cool the brain, while frowns increase brain temperature (McIntosh, Peter, Stephen, & Emerick, 1997).

CONCEPT LEARNING CHECK 11.2 | *Behavior and Cognition and Emotion*

Indicate if the statement is true or false.

1. You can have an emotion without a thought.

2. The amygdala is a cluster of neurons linked to sadness.

3. Sensory signals can take a neural shortcut from the eyes to the brain in order to create emotions.

4. Thinking about things differently can impact emotions.

Fill in the blank with the correct term.

5. Children born without the ability to see will often smile when they are happy. Some researchers say that this is evidence that happiness is a _____ emotion.

6. The _____ suggests that smiling more can make you feel happier.

Explain

7. Some people use botulinum toxin to temporarily reduce the wrinkles in the face by making them unable to move some of their facial muscles. Explain the impact of this procedure on their emotional experience, according to the facial feedback hypothesis.

11.3 Theories of Emotion

Psychologists have various theories of emotion.

- Identify and discuss the main theories of emotion.

But which comes first—the thoughts, the physiological reactions, or the feelings? Or do they all flood in at the same time? Different theories of emotion offer different angles on how emotions arise. In general, theories will highlight the multiple influences of biology and sociocultural influences on emotion. The **biopsychosocial model** recognizes three equally important aspects of human mental processes and behaviors: biological (including brain chemistry), psychological (thoughts, emotions, and behaviors), and social (cultural and societal influences).

Common-Sense Theory

If you ask most people where emotions come from, you are likely to get a common description. Common sense might suggest that the perception of an event would elicit an emotion, which would then cause your body to react FIGURE 11-13. Thinking back to the story of the attempted break-in, this would mean that first I saw the intruder, then I recognized him as something dangerous, and finally I was afraid. That feeling set off the typical physiological fear response, such as a pounding heart and sweating.

James-Lange Peripheral Feedback Theory

The James-Lange theory of emotion, created by William James and Carl Lange (James, 1948), suggests exactly the opposite. According to the **James-Lange theory**, our emotional experience is really just an interpretation of the specific physiological recipe for that emotion: "We feel sad because we cry." As we experience that unique combination of biological events, we experience that emotional reaction. In other words, perception of a stimulus causes bodily arousal, which leads to an emotion FIGURE 11-14.

Biopsychosocial model
A theory that recognizes three equally important aspects of human mental processes and behaviors: biological (including brain chemistry), psychological (thoughts, emotions, and behaviors), and social (cultural and societal influences).

James-Lange theory
A concept of emotion that suggests that emotions are composed of our awareness of biological reactions to stimuli.

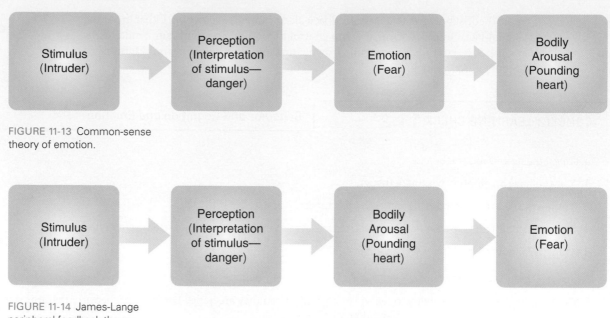

FIGURE 11-13 Common-sense theory of emotion.

FIGURE 11-14 James-Lange peripheral feedback theory.

This means that after seeing the intruder, I perceived him as something threatening. This perception generated a specific combination of body responses—an increase in blood pressure and heart rate, sweating—that was interpreted as fear. The experience of emotion is, according to this theory, an awareness of the physiological responses to emotion-arousing stimuli.

Cannon-Bard Simultaneous Trigger Theory

The James-Lange theory has one (huge) problem, according to physiologist Walter Cannon. If emotions were observations of unique bodily reactions, then that would mean you'd need a unique combination of physiological reactions for every emotion: one set of reactions for fear, one for sadness, one for love. The problem is that this doesn't seem to be the case—at least, not in any way we can measure. If you hook a person up to a machine that measures different physiological responses, like heart rate and blood pressure, it's hard to distinguish between the physiological responses that come with different emotions. Does a pounding heart mean the person is in love, or afraid, or excited, or angry? And what about emotion mash-ups, like when you are both frightened and angry at the same time? All that psychologists have been able to determine is a general level of sympathetic nervous system arousal. In fact, this general arousal was all the emotions seemed to have in common, according to some researchers (Cacioppo, Berntson, Klein, & Poehlmann, 1997). Perhaps physiological arousal and affect, or feelings, were two different components of emotions that arose simultaneously. That's the idea behind the Cannon-Bard theory of emotion.

The **Cannon-Bard theory** of emotion suggests that perception of a stimulus causes bodily arousal and emotion at the same time. Emotion-arousing stimuli simultaneously trigger physiological responses and subjective experience of emotion FIGURE 11-15. This would mean that once I saw the intruder, two things happened at the same time: My heart started to race and I felt an emotional experience of fear.

Schacter-Singer Two-Factor Theory of Emotion

Schacter and Singer (1962) proposed a cognition-plus-feedback theory of emotion. They suggested that perceiving and thinking about a stimulus influence the kind of emotion that is felt. The degree of body arousal can also influence the intensity of the emotion. Schacter and Singer (1962) suggested that our bodily reaction (physiology) as well as our thoughts, influenced by our interpretations, previous experiences, and memories, create

Cannon-Bard theory
A theory of emotion that suggests that events cause emotions by triggering biological and psychological experience of emotions at the same time.

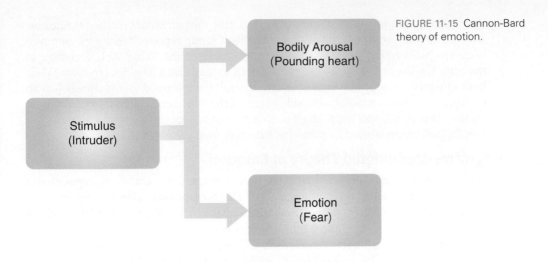

FIGURE 11-15 Cannon-Bard theory of emotion.

the emotion. Remember the story about the break-in? At first I heard the CRASH. Since my previous experience with crashes meant that my cat had knocked over something, my interpretation of that event didn't trigger the emotion of fear. In fact, my first reaction was anger since I thought the crash was Bailey's fault.

The **Schacter-Singer two-factor theory** of emotion suggests that feelings are a combination of bodily arousal and how we interpret that arousal. This theory suggests that all emotions are physiologically similar—basically just sympathetic nervous system arousal—and what distinguishes them is the label we place on that emotion. Emotion = arousal + labels FIGURE 11-16.

In 1962, Schacter and Singer attempted to test their two-factor theory of emotion. They created a fake vitamin called Suproxin that was supposed to improve vision. Suproxin was simply a shot of adrenalin that would have caused a temporary spike of blood pressure, heart rate, and breathing rate, with most of the effects subsiding in 10 to 15 minutes. Over several days, they brought nearly 200 subjects to their lab and randomly divided them into two groups. One group would be informed of the possible side effects of Suproxin. They were told that their hands might shake and their hearts might beat faster. The other group was not informed of any possible side effects; they were told only that the shot was harmless. After being informed (or not), the subjects were put in a variety of situations that might elicit emotion. For example, one group was subjected to an insulting and intrusively personal questionnaire. In that group was a member of the research team, disguised as a participant in the experiment, who was becoming increasingly agitated and vocal about how annoying the questionnaire was. The questions, too, became increasingly obnoxious, ending in, "With how many men (other than your father) has your mother had extra marital relationships? A. 4 and under; B. 5–9; C. 10 and over." You'll notice that the lowest number is "4 and under." By this time in the experiment, the disguised research team member sitting next to the study participant

Schacter-Singer two-factor theory A theory of emotion that suggests that feelings are a combination of body arousal and how we think about that arousal.

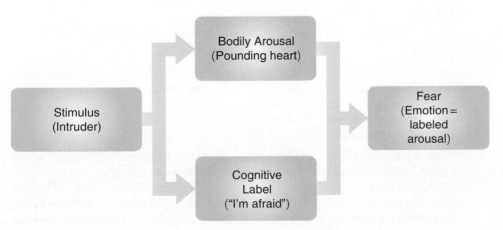

FIGURE 11-16 Schacter-Singer two-factor theory of emotion.

Disguised research team members faked anger to test the two-factor theory of emotion.

Cognitive-mediational theory of emotion
A theory that feelings are caused by what we think caused our thoughts.

rips up the questionnaire and storms out. Soon after, the participant is asked to rate how irritated or annoyed he or she felt. The "informed" group reported feeling less annoyed while the "uniformed" group reported feeling more annoyed. Why? Well, according to the Schacter-Singer two-factor theory, you need arousal and a label for emotion. While both groups were provided with adequate arousal, the informed group already had an explanation for their arousal—the side effects of the Suproxin. The uninformed group, on the other hand, was left to itself to surmise the source of their extra arousal. The uninformed group labeled its arousal as irritation from the obnoxious survey.

Cognitive-Mediational Theory of Emotion

Some emotion researchers emphasize physiological reactions, while others emphasize cognitive labels attached to emotions, and still others emphasize certain behaviors, such as facial expressions. The **cognitive-mediational theory of emotion** suggests that feelings are caused by our cognitive appraisal. Different cognitive appraisals explain why similar situations can create different emotions in different people. It may even explain why a situation may create the emotional mash-up of anger and fear that I felt during my porch invasion, since I had multiple explanations for my feelings. The cognitive-mediational theory also creates an intervention point. Changing your appraisal of the situation can change your emotion.

Lazarus (Lazarus, 1991b) suggested that cognitive appraisals could happen outside of awareness and without a thought, or a thought that occurs so quickly that you don't know you had it. Incidents can create situation–feeling pairings, so that when a situation happens again, the feeling is generated automatically. Remember the story about the song that suddenly made me sad? The music was paired to a sad situation, so now every time I hear it, I feel sad.

CONCEPT LEARNING CHECK 11.3   *Theories of Emotion*

For each theory, identify the components.

1. James-Lange: Each emotion has a _____.

2. Cannon-Bard: This theory suggests that a stimulus that leads to emotions triggers both _____ and _____ at the same time.

3. Schacter and Singer: This theory suggests that emotion is caused by _____ plus a _____.

11.4 Expressing Emotion

Special factors and situations have the potential to influence how and when emotions are expressed.

■ Examine and explain the special factors and situations that can influence the expression of emotions.

You will recall that emotions involve four components: physiological, behavioral, cognitive, and affective. However, many special factors and situations have the potential to influence how and when emotions are expressed.

Culture and Emotion

Emotion is influenced by culture. Not only does culture determine what makes people feel angry, sad, lonely, happy, ashamed, or disgusted, it can also affect the behavioral component of the emotion. **Display rules** are guidelines about how you should express emotions. In some cultures, for example, it's considered impolite not to cover your mouth while you laugh FIGURE 11-17. Also, people in cultures that favor individualistic behavior are more comfortable with public displays of negative emotions, like anger (Matsumoto,

FIGURE 11-17 In some cultures, display rules suggest that it is polite to cover your mouth when you are laughing.

Yoo, & Fontaine, 2008). Individualistic cultures, like the United States, may have more instances of couples fighting in public, for example.

While growing up, we learn an emotional script that outlines how we are expected to behave and show emotion in different situations. These norms reflect not only how people react, but when.

Gender and Emotion

Display rules also govern how men and women express their emotions. Some suggest that men tend to show their feelings less often and less intensely (Plant, Hyde, Keltner, & Devine, 2000), except for power presentations like anger (LaFrance & Banaji, 1992). This doesn't, however, mean that men feel emotions less than women do. Women may report more emotions because of social and cultural norms of display rules (Grossman & Wood, 1993). Women may be more likely to pick up on emotional cues than men (Klein et al., 2004) and may score higher on tests of **emotional intelligence**, the capacity to understand and manage feelings.

Fear

Except for the occasional horror movie or haunted house, most of us don't like to experience fear. Fear is an emotion that lets us know that something dangerous is about to happen or is happening. Sometimes, we need to tolerate fear in order to get things done. However, what if nothing scared you—if you were immune to fear? What would happen if you could remove the part of your brain that's linked to the fear response? Would your life be better if you had no reaction to fear? That's what patient SM feels (or rather doesn't feel). Lesions and scars created by lipoid protenosis, also known as Urbach-Wiethe disease, destroyed her amygdala, and as a result she experiences no fear (Feinstein et al., 2011).

What's more, SM can't recognize fear in the faces of others. The part of the brain that's most involved in fear is the amygdala. The amygdala is the brain area most involved in the processing, memory, and emotional reactions to fear. It lights up on an MRI when you see something that makes you feel fearful. In fact, even thinking about something scary can trigger the amygdala. It seems that the brain areas that are responsible for our sensation of fear are also linked to our recognition of fear responses in others.

Anger and Aggression

Early views of anger regarded this emotion as a reaction to a goal blocked or unattained. Known as the **frustration-aggression hypothesis**, this theory suggests that **frustration** occurs when a goal is blocked and leads to anger and **aggression**, which are words or physical acts a person does to cause harm. A blocked goal, however, can produce more than just aggression. Embarrassment, guilt, and nervousness can all be reactions to a thwarted goal. What makes anger different? In anger, you see someone else as responsible for blocking your goal. Anger assumes that the other person had control over his or her actions, and, for some reason, acted without considering your needs. Lazarus (Lazarus, 1991a) defined anger as an emotional reaction to a perceived "demeaning offence against me and mine."

You may remember that anger is one of the basic six emotions. But anger is also governed by display rules. People who think that venting their anger is useful because it provides **catharsis** or releases pent-up emotions and prevents the anger from exploding are more likely to express their anger. The display rules for anger in their family may even encourage them to show their anger when they are frustrated. Research, unfortunately, doesn't support the theory that venting anger is healthy or useful. Venting anger actually makes people more angry rather than less (Lohr, Olatunji, Baumeister, & Bushman, 2007). While venting may make you feel a little better at first, in the long run it may make matters worse.

If venting your anger only makes it worse, what can you do? Sometimes the best thing you can do is to wait it out. Anger often passes if you don't feed it by rehearsing

Display rules Guidelines about how one should express emotions.

Emotional intelligence The capacity to understand and manage your own feelings as well as the feelings of others.

Frustration-aggression hypothesis Early theory of anger suggesting that anger is a reaction to a goal blocked or unattained.

Frustration Anxiety felt when attempts to reach a goal are hindered.

Aggression Words or physical acts a person does in order to cause harm.

Catharsis A release of pent-up emotions.

The amygdala regulates our own fear response and also helps us to recognize fear in the faces of others.

in your head or out loud to other people what made you angry. Exercising or listening to calming (not angry) music can also help. Once the anger dissipates a bit, it might be time to discuss what angered you. Controlled displays of anger can be more beneficial than the scorched-earth approach of hostile venting and retaliation (even though that may feel good at first).

Love

Love is an emotion featured in books, music, movies, poems . . . well, nearly everywhere. Love is a complex emotion and concept. Robert Sternberg (Sternberg, 1986) proposed what he called a **triangular theory of love** FIGURE 11-18. His theory suggested that all interpersonal relationships are composed of one or more of three components:

1. Intimacy: close feelings; sharing private and personal thoughts and emotions;
2. Passion: physical attraction; and
3. Commitment: a pledge to maintain the connection into the future.

These ingredients of relationships can be combined in different amounts to create eight different kinds of love, according to Sternberg.

1. Nonlove represents an absence of all three. Nonlove may describe how you feel about people you pass on the street or have no connection with.

2. Friendship/liking involves intimacy only, no commitment or passion. You may have close feelings and share important details about your life.

3. Infatuation involves passion only but lacks any sharing or commitment. Infatuation can burn bright and hot but can easily vanish.

4. Empty love involves commitment only, no passion and no intimacy. There is commitment to maintaining the relationship. When couples "stay together for the children" or a marriage is arranged for them, it can result in empty love.

5. Romantic love consists of intimacy and passion, but no commitment. Often a couple early in a relationship experiences romantic love before they have made a long-term commitment to each other.

Triangular theory of love Sternberg's theory that relationships are composed of three components: intimacy, passion, commitment.

FIGURE 11-18 The triangular theory of love.

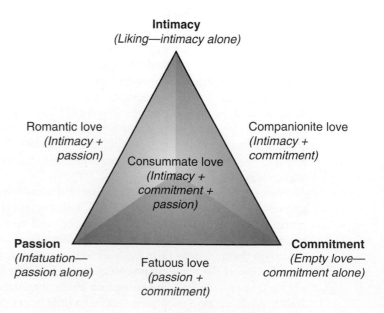

6. Companionate love consists of intimacy combined with commitment, without passion. Long-term best friends, family, and even couples for whom passion has faded are examples of companionate love.

7. Fatuous love involves passion and commitment but not intimacy. *Fatuous* (meaning foolish) suggests that the commitment without any intimacy is a problem with this kind of love. People who get married after knowing each other for only a few hours could be accused of fatuous love.

8. Consummate love is love that consists of all three forms: intimacy, passion, and commitment.

Neuropsychologists have something to say about love, too. Oxytocin, sometimes called the "cuddle chemical," is involved in attachment. Oxytocin is a pituitary hormone and is released during breastfeeding and sexual intercourse and may work as a physiological mark for empathy (Barraza & Zak, 2009). Other chemicals involved in love and passion include estrogen, testosterone, dopamine, and serotonin.

CONCEPT LEARNING CHECK 11.4 | *Expressing Emotion*

Match the components to the kind of love indicated.

A. Intimacy

B. Passion

C. Commitment

1. _____ Companionate

2. _____ Consummate

3. _____ Empty

4. _____ Fatuous

5. _____ Friendship

6. _____ Infatuation

7. _____ Nonlove

8. _____ Romantic

Explain

9. People who think that venting their anger is useful because it provides _____ or releases pent-up emotions and prevents the anger from exploding are more likely to express their anger.

10. Describe the research on venting anger and describe some alternative solutions.

11.5 Stress

Various factors lead to stress; stress has multiple effects.

- Examine the various factors that lead to stress.
- Discuss the physical and psychological effects of stress.

Stress A response that occurs from events seen as a challenge.

Stressors Anything perceived as a challenge.

Acute stressors Brief events that require a period of coping.

Chronic stressors Long-lasting events that require adaption.

Cope To reduce the impact of an event.

Stress is a response that occurs from events seen as a challenge (Lazarus & Folkman, 1984). We all have experienced stress when late for an appointment, during relationship problems, in quarreling with a roommate, or from lack of money. When studying stress, some psychologists emphasize exposure to events that are linked to the stress reaction, or **stressors**. Anything perceived as a challenge can be a stressor. Some stressors can be acute. **Acute stressors** are brief events that require a period of coping, like figuring out a new way to get to the airport because of road construction. **Chronic stressors** are long-lasting events that require you to adapt, such as starting college or adjusting to life in a new city.

What Is Stress?

"Stressed out," "freaking out"—these are some terms people use to describe how they feel when they question whether they can **cope**, meaning to reduce the impact of an event or handle what's in front of them. If you are stressed out over midterms, then you wonder if you can do all the things you need to do in order to be successful—read, organize your notes, and prepare for the exam. Psychologists have examined the components and implications of stress in our lives.

Sources of Stress

Researchers Holmes and Rahe realized that different stressors require different amounts of life change and coping (Holmes & Rahe, 1967). To measure the impact of life change, they created the Social Readjustment Rating Scale. The Holmes and Rahe Social Readjustment Rating Scale is a scale of stressful events. Different events such as the ones in TABLE 11-2

TABLE 11-2 Items from the Social Readjustment Rating Scale

Shown below are sample items from the Social Readjustment Rating Scale. Users of the complete scale simply add up the values for the listed life events that have occurred within the past year. Totals are categorized using specific ranges for: no significant problems, mild, moderate, or major life crisis.

Item	Life Event Value
Death of Spouse	100
Divorce	73
Death of close family member	63
Personal injury or illness	53
Marriage	50
Marital reconciliation	45
Pregnancy	40
Sex difficulties	39
Death of close friend	37
Begin or end school	26
Trouble with boss	23
Change in work hours or conditions	20
Change in schools	20
Change in recreation	19
Change in social activities	18
Change in sleeping habits	15
Total: _____	

For those using the complete scale, the 37% who had scores in the mild range suffered from illness, compared with 61% of those in the moderate range and 79% of those in the major range.

Source: Reproduced from Holmes, T. H., & Rahe, R. H. (1967). The social readjustment rating scale, Journal of Psychosomatic Research, 11(2), 213–218. doi:10.1016/0022-3999(67)90010-4

were assigned different numbers of life change units, with higher numbers indicating more adjustment needed and therefore more stress. After adding up all the numbers, the Social Readjustment Scale indicates how likely it is that the stressors will lead to health difficulties.

Students often have different stressors than the ones listed in the original scale. Inspired by Holmes and Rahe, other researchers (Mullen, 1981) have created a scale for young college students that reflect the kinds of stressors most common for them (see **TABLE 11-3** for some examples).

TABLE 11-3 Items from the Student Stress Scale

Item	Stress Rating
Divorce between parents	65 points
Failed important course	47
Serious argument with close friend	40
Change of major	39
Trouble with parents	39
New girl or boyfriend	38
Increased workload at school	37
First quarter/semester in college	36
Serious argument with instructor	30
Lower grades than expected	29
Too many missed classes	25
Change of college	24
Dropped more than one class	23

Source: Adapted from Mullen, K. D. & Costello, G. (1981). Health awareness through self-discovery: A workbook. Minneapolis: Burgess Publishing.

Rude people, traffic jams, and lost keys can be a hassle. Daily hassles can build up over time to be as much of a stressor as a major life event.

Daily hassles (microstressors) Minor irritations that produce stress.

While Holmes and Rahe focused on major life events as bringing about stress, other researchers (DeLongis, Coyne, Dakof, Folkman, & Lazarus, 1982) focused on small events that can build up over time. Called **daily hassles** or **microstressors**, these small events can affect you even more than a rare major life event. Researchers suggested that things like rude people and traffic jams affect us more due to the seemingly unending aggravation and annoyance triggered by these hassles **TABLE 11-4**.

Cognition and Stress

But stress isn't just an event. Something can be stressful to one person but not to someone else. Whether something creates a stress reaction also depends on how it is perceived. The ways in which we see, or appraise, a situation can help to determine if it is stressful for us. We appraise not only the threat but also our ability to handle such a threat. These appraisals are subjective in nature. A move to a new city can be a negative stress for one person, while another might experience it as a positive event and not at all stressful.

TABLE 11-4 Examples of Daily Hassles

- Misplacing keys
- Arguments
- Traffic jams
- Time pressures
- Lack of sleep
- Fear of crime
- Shopping
- Bureaucracy
- Waiting
- Loneliness
- Waiting in line
- Pollution
- Gossip
- Relatives
- Excess noise
- Inconsiderate people
- Difficult neighbors
- Car breakdown
- Meal preparation
- Job dissatisfaction
- Office politics

The stress reaction depends, in part, on how you experience and appraise an event and how you think you can and will handle the event. If you think you have all of the resources you need to overcome the event, then you may not see it as stressful. If you have only some of the resources, you may perceive the event as a challenge and feel moderate stress if you can overcome the event with some effort. You feel lots of stress if you think you don't have the resources to overcome the event. This means that you assess not only the event, but also your potential ways of dealing with the event.

Choice as a Stress

Choice also causes stress. You might think that having choices in your life makes things great. Variety is the spice of life, isn't it? If you've ordered an expensive coffee from a specialty coffee shop lately, you've likely been flooded by beverage possibilities (up to 87,000 combinations of syrups and toppings). Even if you like all your options, choosing (approaching) something means not choosing (avoiding) something else. Making a choice can cause a situation involving incompatible goals or a **conflict**. With choices come four kinds of conflict, each with the potential to cause stress (Lewin, 1935).

An **approach-approach conflict** is a situation in which a decision must be made between two incompatible choices that both have positive features. An approach-approach conflict carries the smallest amount of stress since you like both options. However, you may have some regret since you can't choose both.

The flipside occurs in an avoidance-avoidance conflict. An **avoidance-avoidance conflict** is a situation in which a decision must be made between two undesirable choices. Since you have to choose between two things that are unlikable, you might have a problem deciding and experience more stress than you'd expect with an approach-approach conflict.

In an **approach-avoidance conflict**, a decision must be made about a goal that has both positive and negative features. Sometimes people get stuck in the decision-making process and can't stop thinking about what to do (Emmons & King, 1988). Working through approach-avoidance conflicts requires that you calm down, understand the relative benefits of each choice, gather information, and maybe even outsource the decision to someone you trust. Sometimes the decision process feels bigger than the actual decision itself.

Most of the time, we are confronted with many choices, each with positive and negative consequences, as in the **multiple-approach-avoidance conflict**. If you have ever gotten choice paralysis over deciding what to do over a vacation or spring break, you've experienced the multiple-approach-avoidance conflict. Should you go to the beach, a theme park, the mountains? Welcome to the multiple-approach-avoidance conflict. The conflict, unfortunately, doesn't always dissolve once your choice has been made. This can sometimes result in a postdecision remorse, like buyers' remorse, if your final choice doesn't end up being as rosy as you imagined.

Conflict A situation that involves incompatible objectives.

Approach-approach conflict A situation in which a decision must be made between two incompatible choices that both have positive features.

Avoidance-avoidance conflict A situation in which a decision must be made between two undesirable choices.

Approach-avoidance conflict A situation in which a decision must be made about a goal that has both positive and negative features.

Multiple-approach-avoidance conflict A situation in which a decision must be made between many choices, each with positive and negative consequences.

Acculturative stress The anxiety felt in response to challenges from new cultural expectations.

Culture and Stress

Adjusting to anything new can cause stress, including being part of a new culture. **Acculturative stress** is the anxiety felt in response to challenges from new cultural

Aerobic activity has been shown to reduce the negative impact of stress.

General adaptation syndrome (GAS) Selye's term for the body's stress response that occurs in three stages: alarm, resistance, and exhaustion.

Psychosomatic diseases Disorders in which a real medical syndrome is exacerbated by psychological factors. Also known as psychophysiological illness.

Type A personality A style characterized by difficulty relaxing, impatience, and anger when delayed.

Type B personality A style characterized by being relaxed about time, slow to anger, and relative ease at relaxing.

Coronary heart disease A medical condition that results in narrowing of the vessels that supply blood to the heart.

Immune system Processes the body uses to protect against disease.

Lymphocytes A type of cell involved in the immune system that works to attack foreign substances.

expectations. Knowing and understanding the nuances of display rules, a new language, and unfamiliar customs can be exhausting.

There is also stress associated with not being a member of a dominant group. In a study of around 500 African-Americans in California, 95% of them reported racial discrimination in the previous 12 months (Klonoff, Landrine, & Ullman, 1999). Similar outcomes have been uncovered for other minority groups, including Hispanics, Asian-Americans (Jackson, Williams, & Torres, 1997), bisexuals, and homosexuals (Stotzer, 2010). In fact, even expecting to be discriminated against can be stressful (Flores et al., 2008).

Effects of Stress

Stress has two main fronts: physical and psychological. Stress is a biological and psychological reaction to a provocative event. An early theory of how humans react to stress was created by Walter Cannon. Cannon (1939) suggested that when your body identifies a danger it prepares to fight, freeze, or flee. More commonly known as the fight-or-flight response, your sympathetic nervous system is activated. Over time, chronic activation of your sympathetic nervous system can cause wear and tear on your body.

Stress is also a process. Stressors, according to Hans Selye (Selye, 1936) produce a predictable pattern of reactions. After studying people who experienced stress, Selye described the **general adaptation syndrome (GAS)**, a process by which any organism organizes itself against stress. The GAS begins with resistance as the organism gathers the resources needed to confront the event. If the event is defeated—great. If not, the organism moves on to the next phase, alarm, in which more resources are gathered. The last phase is exhaustion, when the resources are depleted, and illness may occur. An example of exhaustion from an unresolved stressor can be seen in burnout.

Stress and Health

"You'll worry yourself sick" is something my mom used to say to me as a kid. The connection between stress and illness is well established. Links between stress and ulcers (Sharma, Ghosh, & Sharma, 2004) as well as headaches (Martin, Lae, & Reece, 2007) have been made in the literature. When there is a link between an illness and stress, it's thought of as a psychosomatic illness. A **psychosomatic disease** is a disorder in which a real medical syndrome is exacerbated by psychological factors. While it is common to think that a psychosomatic illness is all in your head, stressors can create or worsen real illness. Headaches, for example can be made worse when under stress.

Personality, stress, and illness interact. Back in the 1960s, cardiologists uncovered a link between reactions to stress and cardiac disease (Friedman & Rosenman, 1974). This led to the discovery of two personality types.

Type A personalities tend to be competitive, hostile, and impatient. They are the type of people who not only will walk up an escalator but be gruff when they are passing you. The type A personality is so aware of time that even the slightest delays in a schedule will cause them a lot of anxiety. They also escalate to anger pretty quickly.

On the other hand, **Type B personalities** are relaxed and patient. Seemingly unflappable, the Type B personalities are more resistant to time pressure, more cooperative, easy going, and patient. Researchers discovered that Type A personalities have a greater likelihood for **coronary heart disease**, a medical condition that results in narrowing of the vessels that supply blood to the heart.

If you are watching the clock as you read this chapter, it's not time to worry—it seems that the dangerous mix of ingredients in the Type A personality is anger and hostility (Smith & Ruiz, 2002).

Stress and the Immune System

Stress can impact the body and the immune system. The **immune system** consists of processes the body uses to protect against disease. Your immune system defends against external invasions such as bacteria and viruses, in part by employing **lymphocytes**, cells that attack foreign substances FIGURE 11-19. Without the immune system, you would be vulnerable to illness and disease.

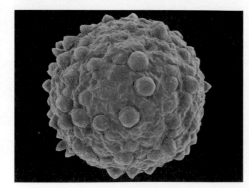

FIGURE 11-19 Lymphocytes are cells involved in immune functioning.

Hormones such as endorphins and corticosteroids flow into your body during stress and can weaken the immune response. Called **immunosuppression**, stress makes the immune system work less efficiently—in essence, stressing your immune system. Constantly alerting your immune system can, over time, reduce your ability to react and defend against the foreign substances, which invade your body and can lead to more increased illness (Glaser, Rice, Sheridan, & Fertel, 1987).

Coping with and Managing Stress

While stress causes discomfort and even leads to illness, stress also leads to motivation to reduce the stress. The things that you do to get rid of the stress are called coping. While stress is the response to the event you see as a challenge, **coping** is the way that you manage the stress.

Coping with the stress doesn't always lead to resolving the cause of the stress. Some forms of coping might involve escaping or avoiding the stressful situation altogether, or simply hunkering down and bearing the stress. Under stress, some people engage in behaviors that are unhealthy, known as **negative coping**. This can include blaming themselves for the events, blaming others, and self-indulgent behaviors like overeating and excessive computer use or **Internet addiction**. Negative coping can just make matters worse.

Others shut down under stress and do not attempt to respond or cope. **Learned helplessness** occurs when an animal fails to take action to escape a noxious stimulus. The same appears to be true for people. When in a situation in which you feel you have no control, you may tolerate it rather than fight (Peterson, Maier, & Seligman, 1993).

There are also several constructive ways to cope with stress, which rely on the way you think and what you do in the environment. Coping can be directed inward to alter your perception of stress, or outward, targeted at the problem causing the stress. Researchers have divided the way you cope into two different classes: changing the actual stressor and changing your emotional reaction to the event.

Emotion-focused coping directs coping at the response to the event. This can be cognitive (varying the way you think about the event) or behavioral (things that you do, like distract yourself). At best, cognitive and behavioral approaches can lead to reappraisal of the stressful situation and help you to see the situation in a new light. At worst, emotion-focused coping can result in drug and alcohol abuse.

You are more likely to employ emotion-focused responses when you think there is not much that you can do to change the actual stressor (Lazarus & Folkman, 1984). A **problem-focused coping** strategy, on the other hand, directs the coping toward the situation itself. You tend to use problem-focused coping if you think you can influence the situation.

Employing **constructive coping**, healthy efforts to reduce the impact of stress, is the best thing you can do to combat stress and make a preemptive strike to keep the effects of stress at bay. Exercise, including **aerobic exercise**, physical activity that increases the capacity of the heart and lungs, has been shown to reduce stress, as do getting adequate sleep, eating healthy foods, and meditation. Interestingly, these are the very things that people stop doing when they begin to feel stress.

Interventions

Because of the important link between stress, health, and psychology, many professionals will employ the use of these techniques to help promote health and prevent and treat illnesses. **Health psychology** is a branch of psychology that is concerned with how psychological factors impact wellness, illness, and medical treatment. **Behavioral medicine**, for example is an interdisciplinary field concerned with health and illness that combines knowledge of the social and medical sciences to improve health and combat illness. Practitioners who utilize behavioral medicine will often intervene with psychological techniques like biofeedback to reduce their stress. In **biofeedback**, a person becomes aware of physiological functions, such as heartbeat or galvanic skin response, and attempts to influence those functions. If you are aware of your heart rate, for example, you can use relaxation or meditation techniques to reduce your heart rate and activate your parasympathetic nervous system.

Immunosuppression Weakening the immune response.

Coping Efforts to reduce the impact of stressors.

Negative coping Engaging in behaviors that are unhealthy and can make matters worse.

Internet addiction Excessive use of computer systems that causes impairment in social, occupational, or school functioning.

Learned helplessness When an animal fails to take action to escape a noxious stimulus.

Emotion-focused coping A reaction to stress that involves managing the feelings that arise from the situation.

Problem-focused coping A reaction to stress that involves the management of the event causing the stress.

Constructive coping Healthy efforts to reduce the impact of stressors.

Aerobic exercise Physical activity that increases the capability of the heart and lungs.

Health psychology A branch of psychology that is concerned with how psychological factors impact wellness, illness, and medical treatments.

Behavioral medicine An interdisciplinary field concerned with health and illness that combines knowledge of social and medical sciences.

Biofeedback A procedure through which a person becomes aware of physiological functions in order to influence the physiological functions.

CONCEPT LEARNING CHECK 11.5   *Sources and Effects of Stress*

Match each numbered example below with the proper category.

A. Type A

B. Major life event

C. Daily hassle

D. Constructive coping

E. Negative coping

1. _____ Aerobic activity

2. _____ Blaming others

3. _____ Divorce

4. _____ Getting enough sleep

5. _____ Hostility

6. _____ Internet addiction

7. _____ Lost keys

8. _____ Moving

9. _____ Time urgency

10. _____ Traffic

Explain

11. The most important factors in the Type A behavior pattern are _____ and _____.

12. Describe a way that the Type A behavior pattern could influence illness.

11.6 Positive Psychology

Positive psychology emphasizes the constructive features of human strength and healthful living rather than pathology.

- Illustrate how positive psychology emphasizes the constructive features of human strength and healthful living rather than pathology.

Since well before Freud, psychology has been criticized for focusing too much on what's wrong with people—the negative inside of them. Some suggest that psychology was born of misery. After all, most of the theories of personality were derived from meticulous studies of patient populations, and psychologists' views of people come from those who sought relief from suffering. But this clearly must provide a distorted view of humanity. It would be like drawing a medical atlas only from people who visited the emergency room. When I was a graduate student in clinical psychology, some students joked that "normal" people were "undiagnosed clients." Positive psychology turns that idea on its head. **Positive psychology** is a branch of psychology that studies human strengths. Positive psychology focuses on what's good about individuals and the qualities that bring out the best in humanity. Because of this imbalance between illness and health, some suggest that maybe now we know enough about illness and disease and we should try to focus on strengths like happiness, hardiness, and optimism rather than deficits.

Positive psychology
A branch of psychology that studies human strengths.

Subjective well-being
A feeling of satisfaction with life and happiness.

Feel-good, do-good phenomenon The theory that people are more likely to be helpful if they are happy.

Happiness

Happiness consists of positive emotions and **subjective well-being**, or feeling good about your life. Researchers have discovered that happy people are more likely to be solution-focused and are also more likely to be helpful, called the **feel-good, do-good phenomenon**—happy people are helpful people.

Happiness can be a moving target. How happy you feel now depends, in part, on how you've felt in the past. If you get a raise at work or more vacation time, you will feel happier, but you can easily adjust to the new norm. The **adaption-level phenomenon** is the ability to adapt to a new situation so that the new situation becomes the norm and you may end up wanting more. It's easy to get used to the new normal.

Our happiness also depends on how we feel in comparison to others (Lyubomirsky, Tucker, & Kasri, 2001). If you feel worse off than your comparison group, it can affect how happy you feel. **Relative deprivation** is your opinion that you are worse off than your comparison group. If you earned a B on a paper, you might feel worse if your friends all earned As than you would if they earned Cs. Relative deprivation may be more important than absolute deprivation since we normally focus our attention to those around us such as our comparison groups.

Seeking money doesn't make you happier. In fact, those who seek and value love and friendship report being happier than those who seek money (Sheldon & Kasser, 2001). Positive emotions not only make you happier but are related to a longer life, too. Researchers read the autobiographies of 180 nuns (Danner, Snowdon, & Friesen, 2001) and counted the number of positive emotional states like gratitude, love, happiness, and hope. The nuns who wrote more about positive emotions lived longer (up to 9 more years) than the nuns whose stories contained fewer positive feelings, despite having lived together for most of their lives and experiencing similar events. There are lots of reasons positive emotions could be protective. Positive emotions can counteract stresses to the immune response created by ongoing stress. What's more, they could lead to greater problem solving and less helplessness.

Age, gender, amount of schooling, attractiveness, or having kids doesn't predict how happy you are. What does? Having good friends, work you like, and health behaviors predict happiness more than anything else **TABLE 11-5**.

Hardiness

You may recall Seligman's studies of dogs' responses to a series of shocks. What often isn't reported is that there were some dogs who never learned to be helpless—hardy doggies that never gave up. Also found in people, hardiness acts as a buffer against stress. **Hardiness** is a personality style characterized by commitment, challenge, and control.

1. Challenge: seeing problems as challenges to be vanquished
2. Commitment: to self, friends, family, and values
3. Control: a perception of control over life and work

Hardiness is associated with lower stress levels and fewer illnesses (Eschleman, Bowling, & Alarcon, 2010) and greater job satisfaction (Maddi, 2006). It's the polar opposite of learned helplessness, a behavioral reaction to negative events over which a

There are multiple effects on happiness.

Adaptation-level phenomenon The ability to adapt to new situations so that the new situation becomes the norm.

Relative deprivation The opinion that a person is worse off than a comparison group.

Hardiness A personality style characterized by commitment, challenge, and control.

TABLE 11-5 Summary of Research on Happiness

Weak Predictors of Happiness	Moderate Predictors of Happiness	Strong Predictors of Happiness
Money	Health	Love
Age	Social activity	Supportive relationships
Intelligence	Religious affiliation	Fulfilling work
Attractiveness		

Source: Adapted from Doherty, A. M., & Kelly, B. D. (2010). Social and psychological correlates of happiness in 17 European countries. Irish Journal of Psychological Medicine, 27(3), *130–134.*

An optimistic explanatory style has little to do with seeing a glass half full or half empty and more to do with how you explain negative events that happen to you.

person has or perceives him- or herself to have no control. While those who feel helpless tend to freeze in the face of adversity, hardy individuals employ problem-focused coping and easily accept **social support** or help from others when they are stressed (Eschleman, Bowling, & Alarcon, 2010)

Optimism

In their experiments on learned helplessness, Peterson and Seligman discovered three cognitive components of helplessness and reformulated the helplessness approach by examining explanatory style.

Your **explanatory style** reflects what you think caused or explains an event. By nature, you tend to be more consistent about the ways you explain negative events than positive events (Peterson et al., 1982). A negative event, on the other hand, requires an explanation so that you can prevent it from happening in the future.

Peterson and his colleagues (1982; **TABLE 11-6**) suggested that our responses to negative events tend to revolve around three questions about the event itself:

1. Is the event *internal* or *external*? In other words, who or what caused the event? Was it your fault or did someone else cause the event to occur? In an **internal locus of control**, you believe that any good or bad things that happen to you are the result of your own actions. **External locus of control**, on the other hand, is the idea that reinforcers and punishments are outside of your control.

2. Is the event *stable* or *unstable*? In other words, is the cause of the negative event here to stay or does it come and go?

3. Is the event *global* or *specific*? That is, does the event affect other things in your life, or does it have a relatively localized impact?

The way you answer these questions or explain such events to yourself determines your explanatory style, or your characteristic way of interpreting the cause of events. Those whose explanatory style reflects *internal*, *stable*, and *global* explanations will have a **pessimistic explanatory style** and be more prone to helplessness. When negative events occur, they tend to fold. If you've lost your keys and have a pessimistic explanatory style, you are likely to have thoughts that reflect *internal* blame, or **locus of control**; ("It's my fault that I lost my keys"), *stable* ("I'm an idiot, I'm always doing things like this"), and *global* ("this is exactly why I shouldn't get an expensive cell phone, I'd lose that, too").

However, a person with an **optimistic explanatory style** will often attribute the negative event to an outside, or *external*, factor ("I was distracted"), that the event is a temporary, or *unstable*, occurrence ("because my phone was ringing"), whose impact has a limited, or *specific*, effect ("it will likely never happen again"; Table 11-6).

People with an optimistic explanatory style tend to be happier and healthier. Optimists tend to have longer life spans (Zuckerman, 2001), recover more quickly from illnesses (Affleck, Tennen, & Apter, 2001), and have overall better health (Seligman, 2006). While some people tend to have that style automatically, it's also something that can be learned.

Social support The help provided by others.

Explanatory style Reflects what you think caused an event. Explanatory style can be either optimistic or pessimistic.

Internal locus of control The idea that your reinforcers and punishments are under your own control.

External locus of control The idea that reinforcers and punishments are outside of your control.

Pessimistic explanatory style A way of explaining negative events by using internal, stable, and global attributions.

Locus of control Your idea of the source of reinforcement and punishment.

Optimistic explanatory style A way of explaining negative events by using external, unstable, and specific attributions.

TABLE 11-6 Explanatory Styles for Negative Events

Explanatory Style	Internality	Stability	Globality
Optimism	External	Unstable	Specific
Pessimism	Internal	Stable	Global

Source: Adapted from Peterson, C., Semmel, A., Baeyer, C., Abramson, L. Y., Metalsky, G. I., & Seligman, M. E. P. (1982). The attributional style questionnaire. Cognitive Therapy and Research, 6(3), 287–299. doi:10.1007/BF01173577

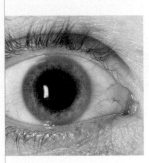

11.1 The Role of Physiology and Evolution in Emotion

- Bodily processes are involved in emotion.
- The fight-or-flight response is a reaction to danger that prepares you to fight, freeze, or flee.
- The sympathetic nervous system releases stress hormones like corticosteroids and catecholamines.
- According to the Yerkes Dodson law, optimal levels of arousal are helpful, while

too little arous
be problematic

- A polygraph w
order to detect
- Polygraphs hav
- Charles Darwi
an evolutionar
response.

11.2 The Role of Behavior and Cognition in Emotion

- Thoughts can have an impact on emotion.
- Emotional responses can occur in the absence of cognition.
- Sensory input from your eyes and ears can often take a neural shortcut to the amygdala and trigger an emotional response.
- Behavior and emotion are interconnected.

- Paul Ekman re
feeling states t
common way
- The original li
includes anger
sadness, and s
- The facial feed
that how we fe
the signal you
your face is arr

11.3 Theories of Emotion

- Psychologists have various theories of emotion.
- The James-Lange theory of emotion suggests the emotional experience is an interpretation of the specific physiological recipe for that emotion.
- The Cannon-Bard theory of emotion suggests that perception of a stimulus causes bodily arousal and emotion at the same time.

- The Schacter-S
of emotion sug
combination o
think about th
- The cognitive-
emotion sugge
influenced by
thoughts.

Summary of Multiple Influences on Emotion, Stress, and Health

After the break-in, the rest of the day went smoothly. What caused my emotions that morning? My reaction was the result a combination of biological, social, and cognitive factors.

My heart racing, my high blood pressure, and other sympathetic nervous system actions were fully present that morning. Darwin and other evolutionary theorists would suggest that my ability to create an angry face and the intruder's ability to recognize it could be an adaptive response. Cognition was involved as well. Theories that emphasize cognitive factors would suggest that my initial reaction of thinking the noise came from my cat was driven by previous experiences. The emotion that flowed from that thought was one of annoyance. After I thought it might be something dangerous, my body reacted with alarm.

The result of the incident was certainly stressful. Instead of emotion-focused coping, I called the police, a problem-focused solution. Later, as I told my students the story of what happened, some asked me if I planned to move to another neighborhood or get a guard dog. My first thought was, Oh, I'm sure it was a fluke, it will never happen again—revealing my optimistic explanatory style. There are multiple influences on emotion, stress, and health.

Calling the police in response to a break-in, is an example of a problem-focused solution.

CONCEPT LEARNING CHECK 11.6   *Positive Psychology*

For each type of explanatory style, select the correct components.

A. Optimistic explanatory style

B. Pessimistic explanatory style

1. _____ External locus of control for negative events
2. _____ Internal locus of control for negative events
3. _____ Negative events have a global impact
4. _____ Negative events have a local impact
5. _____ See negative events as a temporary occurrence
6. _____ See negative events as having a lasting impact

Explain

7. One aspect of positive psychology is the research on hardiness. Hardiness is a personality style characterized by _____, _____, and _____.

8. Identify some of the benefits of hardiness.

CRITICAL THINKING APPLICATION

College students are subjected to a growing amount of stress. Lots of reading, assignments, financial stress, and worries about future jobs and college loans can create significant stress. Stress is even worse around midterms and final exams!

Evaluate

1. Given what you know about stress, health, and positive psychology, design an intervention for college students that would reduce the dangerous impact of stress.

2. When people begin to feel stress, they often stop doing exactly the things that will decrease their stress. People turn to alcohol, stop sleeping, stop hanging out with their friends, and stop exercising. Why do you think this is and what can be done to increase the healthy activities?

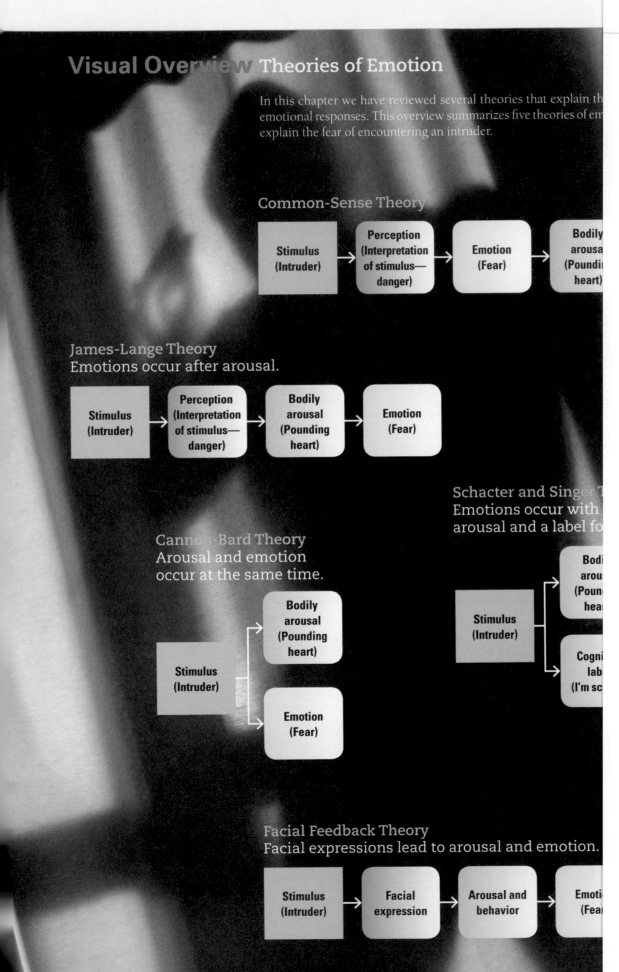

Visual Overview Theories of Emotion

In this chapter we have reviewed several theories that explain th[...]
emotional responses. This overview summarizes five theories of em[...]
explain the fear of encountering an intruder.

Common-Sense Theory

Stimulus (Intruder) → Perception (Interpretation of stimulus— danger) → Emotion (Fear) → Bodily arousal (Pounding heart)

James-Lange Theory
Emotions occur after arousal.

Stimulus (Intruder) → Perception (Interpretation of stimulus— danger) → Bodily arousal (Pounding heart) → Emotion (Fear)

Cannon-Bard Theory
Arousal and emotion occur at the same time.

Stimulus (Intruder) → Bodily arousal (Pounding heart) / Emotion (Fear)

Schacter and Singer T[...]
Emotions occur with [...] arousal and a label fo[...]

Stimulus (Intruder) → Bodi[...] arou[...] (Poun[...] hea[...] / Cogni[...] lab[...] (I'm sc[...]

Facial Feedback Theory
Facial expressions lead to arousal and emotion.

Stimulus (Intruder) → Facial expression → Arousal and behavior → Emoti[...] (Fea[...]

11.4 Expressing Emotion

- Special factors and situations have the potential to influence how and when emotions are expressed.
- Display rules are guidelines about how you should express emotions.
- The amygdala processes stimuli related to fear.
- The frustration-aggression hypothesis suggests that when a goal is blocked, it can lead to anger and aggression.

- Research does not support the catharsis theory of anger.
- Sternberg created a triangular theory of love, suggesting that all interpersonal relationships contain some combination of intimacy, passion, and commitment.

11.5 Stress

- Various factors lead to stress, and stress can have multiple effects on your life.
- Stress is a response that occurs from events seen as a challenge.
- Stress can be ongoing, or acute.
- Coping refers to the reduction of the impact of a stressor.
- Stress can come from major life events or from daily hassles.
- The way you think about things can increase or decrease stress
- Choices in your life can cause conflict and stress.
- Culture can cause stress.
- There is a link between stress and illness.
- Type A personalities tend to be competitive, hostile, and impatient and

- have a higher risk for coronary heart disease.
- Stress can lead to immunosuppression and increased illness.
- Under stress, some people engage in negative coping strategies that can make matters worse.
- Emotion-focused coping directs coping at the way you feel about the event, while problem-focused coping directs coping towards the event itself.
- Practitioners use information about the interaction between psychology and health and illness through biofeedback, behavioral medicine, and health psychology.

11.6 Positive Psychology

- Positive psychology emphasizes the constructive features of human strength and healthful living rather than pathology.
- Happiness is related to feeling good about your life. Happiness is related to many positive outcomes.

- Hardiness is a personality style characterized by commitment, openness to challenge, and a sense of control.
- Those with an optimistic explanatory style tend to be happier and healthier.

11.1 The Role of Physiology and Evolution in Emotion

1. "Optimal levels of arousal produce the best reaction" is the basis of the:
   A. parasympathetic nervous system
   B. flight-or-fight response
   C. galvanic skin response
   D. Yerkes Dodson law

2. Polygraphs use a number of measurements to detect sympathetic nervous system arousal, including _____, a measurement of skin conductivity.
   A. corticosteroids
   B. catecholamines
   C. GSR

11.2 The Role of Behavior and Cognition in Emotion

3. According to Robert Zajonc, sometimes you can have an emotional response without a conscious thought. Physiological evidence to support this comes from the idea that:
   A. sometimes sights and smells take a neural shortcut to the amygdala.
   B. the brain is not activated during emotions.
   C. sometimes sights and smells take longer to process into emotions.

4. Susan is being recorded while she watches a funny movie. According to the research, you should expect that Susan's face is:
   A. more expressive because she watched the movie alone.
   B. just as expressive as when watching alone or with other people.
   C. less expressive because she watched the movie alone.

5. According to Ekman, a basic emotion is an emotion that is:
   A. necessary in order to get along in a group.
   B. conveyed in the same way across cultures.
   C. used to create other emotions.
   D. important to express every day.

6. If someone says, "Smile, you'll feel better," there might be some truth in it, due to what we know about:
   A. the facial feedback hypothesis
   B. basic emotions
   C. catastrophic thinking

11.3 Theories of Emotion

7. The _____ theory states that emotions are the result of purely physiological events.
   A. James-Lange
   B. common-sense
   C. Schacter-Singer
   D. cognitive mediational

8. The central idea behind the Cannon-Bard theory of emotion rests on the idea that
   A. emotions are cognitive responses to events.
   B. what distinguishes feelings is the label we place on that emotion.
   C. an emotional experience is an interpretation of the specific physiological recipe for that type of arousal.
   D. the perception of a stimulus causes bodily arousal and emotion at the same time.

9. According to the Schacter-Singer two-factor theory of emotion:
   A. emotions are cognitive responses to events.
   B. what distinguishes feelings is the label we place on that type of arousal
   C. an emotional experience is an interpretation of the specific physiological recipe for that emotion.
   D. the perception of a stimulus causes bodily arousal and emotion at the same time.

11.4 Expressing Emotion

10. When people cover their mouths when they laugh, this is governed by:
    A. display rules
    B. anthropomorphism
    C. the amygdala
    D. the facial feedback hypothesis

11. When a person is afraid, the _____ is activated.
    A. MRI
    B. amygdala
    C. GSR
    D. parasympathetic nervous system

11.5 Stress

12. Long-lasting events, such as adjusting to a new job in a different country, are thought of as:
- **A.** acute stressors
- **B.** coping mechanisms
- **C.** chronic stressors
- **D.** conflicts

13. If you just won the lottery and had to choose between a $10,000 lump-sum payment or $1,000 a month for 10 months, you might experience what kind of conflict?
- **A.** approach-approach conflict
- **B.** avoidance-avoidance conflict
- **C.** approach-avoidance conflict
- **D.** nonapproach conflict

11.6 Positive Psychology

14. Which of the following is the strongest predictor of happiness, according to recent research?
- **A.** age
- **B.** intelligence
- **C.** attractiveness
- **D.** fulfilling work

15. Those who tend to explain negative events as being external, temporary, and with limited impact have:
- **A.** an optimistic explanatory style
- **B.** a pessimistic explanatory style
- **C.** learned helplessness
- **D.** Type A behavior pattern

CHAPTER DISCUSSION QUESTIONS

1. Compare the strengths of the various theories of emotion.

2. What are the strengths and limitations of using a polygraph?

3. What are the strengths and weaknesses of using daily hassles as an assessment of stress?

4. Identify the dangers of venting anger. What factors do you think influence how people express their anger?

5. Discuss the general adaptation syndrome in relationship to stressful life events. What are some ways in which you can identify healthy coping mechanisms in those who experience stress before they reach the exhaustion phase?

CHAPTER PROJECTS

1. Use the two-factor theory of emotion to design an intervention to help someone with test anxiety.

2. The critical factor in the Type A personality is hostility. Use your knowledge of emotion, stress, and health to design a frustration-aggression reduction program to help those with Type A personality.

CHAPTER KEY TERMS

Acculturative stress
Acute stressors
Adaptation-level phenomenon
Aerobic exercise
Aggression
Amygdala
Anthropomorphism
Approach-approach conflict
Approach-avoidance conflict
Avoidance-avoidance conflict
Basic emotions
Behavioral medicine
Biofeedback
Biopsychosocial model
Cannon-Bard theory
Catastrophic thinking
Catecholamines
Catharsis
Chronic stressors

Cognitive-mediational theory of emotion
Conflict
Constructive coping
Cope
Coping
Coronary heart disease
Corticosteroids
Daily hassles (microstressors)
Display rules
Emotional intelligence
Emotion-focused coping
Emotion
Explanatory style
External locus of control
Facial feedback hypothesis
Feel-good, do-good phenomenon
Fight-or-flight response
Frustration

Frustration-aggression hypothesis
Galvanic skin response (GSR)
General adaptation syndrome (GAS)
Hardiness
Health psychology
Immune system
Immunosuppression
Internal locus of control
Internet addiction
James-Lange theory
Learned helplessness
Locus of control
Lymphocytes
Multiple-approach-avoidance conflict
Negative coping
Optimistic explanatory style
Pessimistic explanatory style

Polygraph
Positive psychology
Problem-focused coping
Psychosomatic diseases
Relative deprivation

Schacter-Singer two-factor theory
Social support
Stress
Stressors
Subjective well-being

Triangular theory of love
Type A personality
Type B personality
Yerkes Dodson law

ANSWERS TO CONCEPT LEARNING CHECKS

11.1 Bodily Processes and Emotion

1. D. The Yerkes Dodson law suggests that moderate amounts of arousal are best.

2. C. Anthropomorphism is assigning human emotions to nonhumans.

3. A. The fight-or-flight response is a reaction to danger in which the sympathetic nervous system prepares the organs for vigorous activity.

4. B. The galvanic skin response is a measure of skin conductivity that is associated with stress.

5. A. The fight-or-flight response is a reaction to danger in which the sympathetic nervous system prepares the organs for vigorous activity. It sometimes leads to freezing.

6. The Yerkes Dodson law suggests that moderate amounts of arousal are best. For easy tasks, more arousal can be tolerated than for tedious tasks.

11.2 Behavior and Cognition and Emotion

1. You can have an emotion without a thought. [T]

2. The amygdala is a cluster of neurons linked to sadness. [F]

3. Sensory signals can take a neural shortcut from the eyes to the brain in order to create emotions. [T]

4. Thinking about things differently can impact emotions. [T]

5. Children born without the ability to see will often smile when they are happy. Some researchers say that this is evidence that happiness is a **basic** emotion.

6. The **facial feedback hypothesis** suggests that smiling more can make you feel happier.

7. According to the facial feedback hypothesis, how you feel an emotion is regulated, in part, by the feedback your brain gets from the way your face is arranged. If you can't arrange your face in certain ways, it might blunt your emotional experience.

11.3 Theories of Emotion

1. James-Lange: Each emotion has a **specific physiological recipe is derived from this theory of emotion**.

2. Cannon-Bard: This theory suggests that a stimulus that leads to emotions triggers both **physiological** and **emotional experiences** at the same time.

3. Schacter and Singer: This theory suggests that emotion is caused by **arousal** plus a **cognitive label**.

11.4 Expressing Emotion

1. Companionate [intimacy + commitment]

2. Consummate [intimacy + passion + commitment]

3. Empty [commitment]

4. Fatuous [passion + commitment]

5. Friendship [intimacy]

6. Infatuation [passion]

7. Nonlove [none]

8. Romantic [intimacy + passion]

9. People who think that venting their anger is useful because it provides **catharsis** or releases pent-up emotions and prevents the anger from exploding are more likely to express their anger.

10. Some alternative solutions to venting anger include waiting, exercising, listening to calming music, and solution-focused coping.

11.5 Sources and Effects of Stress

1. Aerobic activity [D]

2. Blaming others [E]

3. Divorce [B]

4. Getting enough sleep [D]

5. Hostility [A]

6. Internet addiction [E]

7. Lost keys [C]

8. Moving [B]

9. Time urgency [A]

10. Traffic [C]

11. The most important factors in the Type A behavior pattern are **anger** and **hostility**.

12. The anger and hostility can lead to increased stress. Hormones such as endorphins and corticosteroids flow into your body during stress and can weaken the immune response, which can lead to increased illness.

11.6 Positive Psychology

1. External locus of control for negative events [B]

2. Internal locus of control for negative events [A]

3. Negative events have a global impact [B]

4. Negative events have a local impact [A]

5. See negative events as a temporary occurrence [A]

6. See negative events as having a lasting impact [B]

7. Hardiness is a personality style characterized by **commitment**, **challenge**, and **control**.

8. Hardiness is associated with greater job satisfaction, lower stress levels, fewer illnesses, and increased optimism.

ANSWERS TO CHAPTER REVIEW TEST

11.1 The Role of Physiology and Evolution in Emotion

1. D. Rationale: The Yerkes Dodson law suggests that optional arousal is best, while too much or too little can hinder performance.

2. C. Rationale: GSR or galvanic skin response is a measurement of the conductivity of skin.

11.2 The Role of Behavior and Cognition in Emotion

3. A. Rationale: Sights and smells take a neural shortcut to the amygdala, which can process the stimulation as fear.

4. C. Rationale: People don't usually express their emotions in facial expressions as much unless others are around.

5. B. Rationale: A basic emotion is a feeling state thought to be expressed in a common way across cultures.

6. A. Rationale: According to facial feedback, emotion is regulated, in part, by the way your face is arranged.

11.3 Theories of Emotion

7. A. Rationale: According to the James-Lange theory of emotion, our emotional experiences are an interpretation of the specific physiological recipe for that emotion.

8. D. Rationale: The Cannon-Bard theory of emotion suggests that perception of a stimulus causes bodily arousal and emotion at the same time.

9. B. Rationale: According to the Schacter-Singer two-factor theory of emotion, what distinguishes feelings is the label we place on a type of arousal.

11.4 Expressing Emotion

10. A. Rationale: Display rules are guidelines about how you should express emotions.

11. B. Rationale: The amygdala is the part of the brain that's involved with fear.

11.5 Stress

12. C. Rationale: Chronic stressors are long-lasting events that require you to adapt.

13. A. Rationale: In an approach-approach conflict, a decision must be made between two incompatible choices that both have positive features.

11.6 Positive Psychology

14. D. Rationale: According to the research, age, intelligence, and attractiveness are weak predictors of happiness, while having fulfilling work is a strong predictor.

15. A. Rationale: A person with an optimistic explanatory style will often attribute the negative event to an outside factor that is a temporary occurrence whose impact has a limited effect.

REFERENCES

Affleck, G., Tennen, H., & Apter, A. (2001). Optimism, pessimism, and daily life with chronic illness. In E. C. Chang (Ed.), *Optimism & pessimism: Implications for theory, research, and practice* (pp. 147–168). Washington, DC: American Psychological Association.

Barraza, J. A., & Zak, P. J. (2009). Empathy toward strangers triggers oxytocin release and subsequent generosity. In O. Vilarroya, S. Altran, A. Navarro, K. Ochsner, & A. Tobeña (Eds.), *Values, empathy, and fairness across social barriers* (Annals of the New York Academy of Sciences Vol. 1167, pp. 182–189). New York: New York Academy of Sciences.

Buck, R., Losow, J. I., Murphy, M. M., & Costanzo, P. (1992). Social facilitation and inhibition of emotional expression and communication. *Journal of Personality and Social Psychology, 63,* 962–968. doi:10.1037/0022-3514.63.6.962

Cacioppo, J. T., Berntson, G. G., Klein, D. J., & Poehlmann, K. M. (1997). Psychophysiology of emotion across the life span. *Annual review of Gerontology and Geriatrics, 17,* 27–74.

Cannon, W. B. (1939). *The wisdom of the body.* W.W. Norton & Company, Inc.

Danner, D. D., Snowdon, D. A., & Friesen, W. V. (2001). Positive emotions in early life and longevity: Findings from the nun study. *Journal of Personality and Social Psychology, 80,* 804–813. doi:10.1037/0022-3514.80.5.804

Darwin, C. (2009). *The expression of the emotions in man and animals, anniversary edition* (4th ed.). New York: Oxford University Press.

DeLongis, A., Coyne, J. C., Dakof, G., Folkman, S., & Lazarus, R. S. (1982). Relationship of daily hassles, uplifts, and major life events to health status. *Health Psychology, 1,* 119–136. doi:10.1037/0278-6133.1.2.119

Ekman, P. (1999). Basic emotions. In T. Dalgleish & M. J. Power (Eds.), *Handbook of cognition and emotion* (pp. 45–60). New York: John Wiley & Sons.

Ekman, P., Friesen, W. V., O'Sullivan, M., & Chan, A., et al. (1987). Universals and cultural differences in the judgments of facial expressions of emotion. *Journal of Personality and Social Psychology, 53*(4), 712–717. doi:10.1037/0022-3514.53.4.712

Emmons, R. A., & King, L. A. (1988). Conflict among personal strivings: Immediate and long-term implications for psychological and physical well-being. *Journal of Personality and Social Psychology, 54*(6), 1040–1048. doi:10.1037/0022-3514.54.6.1040

Eschleman, K. J., Bowling, N. A., & Alarcon, G. M. (2010). A meta-analytic examination of hardiness. *International Journal of Stress Management, 17*(4), 277–307. doi:10.1037/a0020476

Feinstein, J. S., Adolphs, R., Damasio, A., & Tranel, D. (2011). The human amygdala and the induction and experience of fear. *Current Biology, 21*(1), 34–38. doi:10.1016/j.cub.2010.11.042

Flores, E., Tschann, J. M., Dimas, J. M., Bachen, E. A., Pasch, L. A., & de Groat, C. L. (2008). Perceived discrimination, perceived stress, and mental and physical health among Mexican-origin adults. *Hispanic Journal of Behavioral Sciences, 30*(4), 401–424. doi:10.1177/0739986308323056

Friedman, M., & Rosenman, R. (1974). *Type A behaviour and your heart.* New York: Knopf.

Galati, D., Miceli, R., & Sini, B. (2001). Judging and coding facial expression of emotions in congenitally blind children. *International Journal of Behavioral Development, 25*(3), 268–278. doi:10.1080/01650250042000393

Glaser, R., Rice, J., Sheridan, J., & Fertel, R. (1987). Stress-related immune suppression: Health implications. *Brain, Behavior, and Immunity, 1*(1), 7–20. doi:10.1016/0889-1591(87)90002-X

Grossman, M., & Wood, W. (1993). Sex differences in intensity of emotional experience: A social role interpretation. *Journal of Personality and Social Psychology, 65*(5), 1010–1022. doi:10.1037/0022-3514.65.5.1010

Grubin, D. (2010). The polygraph and forensic psychiatry. *Journal of the American Academy of Psychiatry and the Law, 38*(4), 446–451.

Holmes, T. H., & Rahe, R. H. (1967). The Social Readjustment Rating Scale. *Journal of Psychosomatic Research, 11*(2), 213–218. doi:10.1016/0022-3999(67)90010-4

Jackson, J., Williams, D., Torres, M. (1997). *Perception of discrimination: The stress process and physical and psychological health.* Washington, DC: National Institute for Mental Health.

James, W. (1948). What is emotion? 1884. In W. Dennis (Ed.), *Readings in the history of psychology* (pp. 290–303). East Norwalk, CT: Appleton-Century-Crofts. doi:10.1037/11304-033

Klein, S., Smolka, M. N., Wrase, J., Grusser, S. M., Mann, K., Braus, D. F., & Heinz, A. (2004). The influence of gender and emotional valence of visual cues on fMRI activation in humans: Erratum. *Pharmacopsychiatry, 37*(3). doi:10.1055/s-2004-827166

Klonoff, E. A., Landrine, H., & Ullman, J. B. (1999). Racial discrimination and psychiatric symptoms among Blacks. *Cultural Diversity and Ethnic Minority Psychology, 5*(4), 329–339. doi:10.1037/1099-9809.5.4.329

Kraut, R. E. (1982). Social presence, facial feedback, and emotion. *Journal of Personality and Social Psychology, 42*(5), 853–863. doi:10.1037/0022-3514.42.5.853

LaFrance, M., & Banaji, M. (1992). Toward a reconsideration of the gender–emotion relationship. In M. S. Clark (Ed.), *Emotion and social behavior* (Review of personality and social psychology, Vol. 14, pp. 178–201). Thousand Oaks, CA: Sage.

Lazarus, R. S. (1991a). *Emotion and adaptation.* New York: Oxford University Press.

Lazarus, R. S. (1991b). Progress on a cognitive-motivational-relational theory of emotion. *American Psychologist, 46*(8), 819–834. doi:10.1037/0003-066X.46.8.819

Lazarus, R. S., & Folkman, S. (1984). *Stress, appraisal, and coping.* New York: Springer Publishing Company.

LeDoux, J. (1998). *The emotional brain: The mysterious underpinnings of emotional life.* New York: Simon & Schuster.

Lewin, K. (1935). *A dynamic theory of personality.* New York: McGraw-Hill.

Lohr, J. M., Olatunji, B. O., Baumeister, R. F., & Bushman, B. J. (2007). The psychology of anger venting and empirically supported alternatives that do no harm. *The Scientific Review of Mental Health Practice: Objective Investigations of Controversial and Unorthodox Claims in Clinical Psychology, Psychiatry, and Social Work, 5*(1), 53–64.

Lyubomirsky, S., Tucker, K. L., & Kasri, F. (2001). Responses to hedonically conflicting social comparisons: Comparing happy and unhappy people. *European Journal of Social Psychology, 31*(5), 511–535. doi:10.1002/ejsp.82

Maddi, S. R. (2006). Hardiness: The courage to be resilient. In J. C. Thomas, D. L. Segal, & M. Hersen (Eds.), *Comprehensive handbook of personality and psychopathology, Vol. 1: Personality and everyday functioning* (pp. 306–321). Hoboken, NJ: John Wiley & Sons.

Martin, P. R., Lae, L., & Reece, J. (2007). Stress as a trigger for headaches: Relationship between exposure and sensitivity. *Anxiety, Stress & Coping: An International Journal, 20*(4), 393–407. doi:10.1080/10615800701628843

Matsumoto, D., Yoo, S. H., & Fontaine, J. (2008). Mapping expressive differences around the world: The relationship between emotional display rules and individualism versus collectivism. *Journal of Cross-Cultural Psychology, 39*(1), 55–74. doi:10.1177/0022022107311854

McIntosh, D., Peter, R. B. Z., Stephen, S. V., & Emerick, W. (1997). Facial movement, breathing, temperature, and affect: Implications of the vascular theory of emotional efference. *Cognition & Emotion, 11*(2), 171–196. doi:10.1080/026999397379980

Mesquita, B., & Frijda, N. H. (1992). Cultural variations in emotions: A review. *Psychological Bulletin, 112*(2), 179–204. doi:10.1037/0033-2909.112.2.179

Mullen, K. D. (1981). *Health awareness through self-discovery: A workbook.* New York: Burgess Publishing.

National Research Council. (2003). *The polygraph and lie detection.* Committee to Review the Scientific Evidence on the Polygraph. Division of Behavioral and Social Sciences and Education. Washington, DC: National Academies Press.

Peterson, C., & Park, N. (2007). Explanatory style and emotion regulation. In J. J. Gross (Ed.), *Handbook of emotion regulation* (pp. 159–179). New York: Guilford Press.

Peterson, C., Maier, S. F., & Seligman, M. E. P. (1993). *Learned helplessness: A theory for the age of personal control.* New York: Oxford University Press.

Peterson, C., Semmel, A., Baeyer, C., Abramson, L. Y., Metalsky, G. I., & Seligman, M. E. P. (1982). The attributional style questionnaire. *Cognitive Therapy and Research, 6*(3), 287–299. doi:10.1007/BF01173577

Plant, E. A., Hyde, J. S., Keltner, D., & Devine, P. G. (2000). The gender stereotyping of emotions. *Psychology of Women Quarterly, 24*(1), 81–92. doi:10.1111/j.1471-6402.2000.tb01024.x

Schacter, S., & Singer, J. (1962). Cognitive, social, and physiological determinants of emotional state. *Psychological Review, 69*(5), 379–399. doi:10.1037/h0046234

Seligman, M. E. P. (2006). *Learned optimism: How to change your mind and your life.* New York: Vintage.

Selye, H. (1936). A syndrome produced by diverse nocuous agents. *Nature, 138.* doi:10.1038/138032a0

Sharma, S., Ghosh, S. N., & Sharma, M. (2004). Life events stress, emotional vital signs and peptic ulcer. *Psychological Studies, 49*(2–3), 167–176.

Sheldon, K. M., & Kasser, T. (2001). Goals, congruence, and positive well-being: New empirical support for humanistic theories. *Journal of Humanistic Psychology, 41*(1), 30–50. doi:10.1177/0022167801411004

Smith, T. W., & Ruiz, J. M. (2002). Psychosocial influences on the development and course of coronary heart disease: Current status and implications for research and practice. *Journal of Consulting and Clinical Psychology, Behavioral Medicine and Clinical Health Psychology, 70*(3), 548–568. doi:10.1037/0022-006X.70.3.548

Sternberg, R. J. (1986). A triangular theory of love. *Psychological Review, 93*(2), 119–135. doi:10.1037/0033-295X.93.2.119

Stotzer, R. L. (2010). Seeking solace in West Hollywood: Sexual orientation based hate crimes in Los Angeles County. *Journal of Homosexuality, 57*(8), 987–1003. doi:10.1080/00918369.2010.503506

Strack, F., Martin, L. L., & Stepper, S. (1988). Inhibiting and facilitating conditions of the human smile: A nonobtrusive test of the facial feedback hypothesis. *Journal of Personality and Social Psychology, 54*(5), 768–777. doi:10.1037/0022-3514.54.5.768

Teigen, K. H. (1994). Yerkes-Dodson: A law for all seasons. *Theory & Psychology, 4*(4), 525–547. doi:10.1177/0959354394044004

Zajonc, R. B. (1980). Feeling and thinking: Preferences need no inferences. *American Psychologist, 35*(2), 151–175. doi:10.1037/0003-066X.35.2.151

Zuckerman, M. (2001). Optimism and pessimism: Biological foundations. In E. C. Chang (Ed.), Optimism & pessimism: Implications for theory, research, and practice (pp. 169–188). Washington, DC: American Psychological Association

Chapter Overview ▼

12.1 The Beginnings of Development
What Is Development?
Prenatal Development
The Newborn

CONCEPT LEARNING CHECK **12.1** *Before and After Birth*

12.2 Infancy and Childhood
Physical Development
Cognitive Development
　Piaget's Stage Theory
　Sensorimotor Stage

Preoperational Stage
Concrete Operational Stage
Formal Operational Stage
Challenges to Piaget's Stage Theory
Social Development
　The Power of Touch
　Attachment Theory
　Disruption of Attachment
　Family Relationships
　Peers

CONCEPT LEARNING CHECK **12.2** *Stages of Cognitive Development*

12 Development Throughout the Life Span

Learning Objectives ▼

12.1 ■ Describe the development of the field and explain the prenatal and newborn stages of human development.

12.2 ■ Discuss physical development in infants and newborns.
■ Examine Piaget's stage theory in relation to early cognitive development.
■ Illustrate the importance of attachment in psychosocial development.

12.3 ■ Discuss the impact of sexual development in adolescence and changes in moral reasoning in adolescents and young adults.
■ Examine the life stages within Erikson's theory of psychosocial development.

12.4 ■ Illustrate the physical, cognitive, and social aspects of aging.

12.5 ■ Describe the multiple influences of nature and nurture in human development.

12.3 Adolescence and Young Adulthood
Physical Development
Cognitive Development
Social Development
CONCEPT LEARNING CHECK **12.3** *Defining Adolescence*
CRITICAL THINKING APPLICATION

12.4 Adulthood and Aging
Physical Development
Reproductive Life
Life Expectancy
Death and Dying

Cognitive Development
Social Development
Continuity or Change
Relationships
Ages and Stages of Adulthood
CONCEPT LEARNING CHECK **12.4** *Is There a "Right Time" for Everything?*

12.5 Nature and Nurture
Summary of Multiple Influences on Development
CONCEPT LEARNING CHECK **12.5** *Nature or Nurture?*

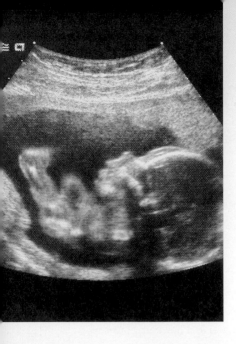

What is the first question ever asked about *you*? It was not your name, nor where you are from, nor which of your parents you most resemble. I guarantee that is was, "What is it?" As soon as we know there *is* a baby, we ask whether it is a boy or a girl. Why should the answer matter? How does knowing gender make us feel more connected to this new person? With modern ultrasound techniques, you can have a color photograph of your baby nestled in the womb as early as 4 weeks from conception. My own pregnancy was a miraculous surprise, and at my advanced age of 40, considered "high risk." I anxiously awaited the ultrasound pictures, wanting reassurance that my baby was healthy and developing normally. When I left, I was given my first picture of my baby-to-be. And there, labeled clearly in capital letters, was the answer: "BOY," along with an arrow pointing to the evidence. Before I knew he would survive, or how much I would love him, I knew he was a boy, and that changed everything: his name, his baby blankets, the wall color in his room, the toys that filled our house, the friends he made, his experience in school, and the activities (mostly involving superheroes) we spend our days pursuing. Why does gender matter so much?

12.1 The Beginnings of Development

Developmental psychology studies the changes we experience throughout life beginning at conception.

■ Describe the development of the field and explain the prenatal and newborn stages of human development.

The field of developmental psychology studies the changes we experience from the beginning to the end of our lives. When you think about yourself now and in your earliest memories, how are you the same and different? Many factors play a role in development; of course, there is biological growth, but there are also influences from your surrounding environment. Where you were born, who your parents are, what culture surrounded you, and your gender all play important roles in creating the person you are now. In this chapter, we will examine development in three areas (physical, cognitive, and social) from before birth, in infancy and childhood, through adolescence, adulthood, and advanced age.

What Is Development?

The notion of "childhood" is a relatively recent invention. It is only in modern societies (with good medical care) that parents have the luxury of assuming their babies will live to adulthood. For example, in the 1700s in rural areas of Europe, about one-third of children died before age 15. As one mother in 1772 wrote, after losing her eighth child after only 10 hours: ". . . one cannot grieve after her too much and I have just now other things to think of . . ." (Hyde, 1976). With many demands, affection was limited for children who may not live long. In addition, historically, children were often put to work as soon as possible to help support the family. From the 1700s to mid-1800s, coal mines and trades employed boys and girls from age 5. This practice still takes place today, as an estimated 150 million children aged 5 to 14 are engaged in child labor, or one in six children in the world (Basu & Tzannatos, 2003). Conditions like these led to a growing cry for reform by 1890, and child labor laws established free and compulsory education in western Europe and the United States (Nardinelli, 1990). The industrial revolution provided an economic base to "indulge" children because it became economically feasible to have children who did not work. The legacy of child labor is seen today in the practice of summer vacations from U.S. schools, required initially because children worked in the fields during the growing seasons. The changing socioeconomic conditions led to a growing attention to the processes of childhood development.

Development is one of the most challenging areas within psychology because its focus is on how the individual *changes over time*. How have you changed from your first year of high school to this year? If we repeatedly measured aspects of your life over time, we would be conducting a longitudinal study. This type of study compares the same person to him- or herself at different points in time. Alternatively, we can try to understand change by comparing people entering college to others entering high school. This approach, called a cross-sectional study, compares different groups of people at different ages. The problem is that there may be cohort effects; that is, life may be different for those entering high school now than it was for you way back then TABLE 12-1 (McBride & Nief, 2011).

Psychologists try to identify the "universal" features of development over time. These are features that hold true for everyone, no matter what culture they are raised in, what gender they are, or any other differences among individuals. However, culture plays a critical role in human development. Newborn humans are helpless compared to many other animals (e.g., horses or turtles). We are not able to protect ourselves from predators or to feed ourselves for many years. The human cortex does the bulk of the work to support our decisions, and that requires about 8 years to develop. In the meantime, survival depends on our relationships with others. Humans may take more than 20 years to fully "leave the nest," while the average robin accomplishes this over one summer. In modern society, some milestones, like the age of first marriage, are now increasingly delayed to over 28 for men and 26 for women in the United States (U.S. Census Bureau, 2009). One consequence of our long maturation phase is that there is plenty of time for culture to play a major role in our development.

Prenatal Development

Maturation refers to biological growth that occurs continuously over time. From the moment of conception, when a sperm cell meets an egg cell and they combine, growth begins.

> **Maturation** Biological growth occurring in a continuous fashion over time.

TABLE 12-1   *The Mindset List* for the Classes of 2010 and 2015

Here are some ideas in the mindset of students entering college as the class of '10, and a comparison to the class of '15 when they entered college

2010	2015
1. A stained blue dress is famous to their generation.	1. They have always had to wear bike helmets.
2. They have known only two presidents.	2. They have always wanted to be like Shaq or Kobe.
3. They had headphones in the back seat of the minivan.	3. Women have never been too old to have children.
4. Faux fur has always been a necessary element of style.	4. No state has ever failed to observe Martin Luther King Day.
5. They grew up pushing their own miniature shopping carts in the supermarket.	5. Women have always been kissing women on television.
6. "Boogers" candy has always been a favorite for grossing out parents.	6. Unlike older siblings, they spent bedtime on their backs as infants.
7. "So" as in "Sooooo New York," has always been a drawn-out adjective modifying a proper noun.	7. Music has always been available via free downloads.
8. "Outing" has always been a threat.	8. They pressured their parents to take them to Taco Bell or Burger King to get free pogs.
9. They have always "dissed" what they don't like.	9. They've broken up with their significant others via texting, Facebook, or MySpace.
10. They grew up with virtual pets to feed, water, and play games with, lest they die.	10. When they were 3, their parents battled other parents in toy stores to buy them a "Tickle Me Elmo" while they lasted.

Source: Created using data from the Beloit College Mindset Lists, administered by Tom McBride and Ron Nief. http://www.beloit.edu/mindset

Each cell contains 23 pairs of chromosomes, one of each pair from your father and one from your mother. Each chromosome is made up of more than 2,000 genes for a total of 50,000 genes within each cell. These genes make all the proteins in the body, which promote development and growth and carry out all body functions. So, is development dictated by genotype, your unique genetic pattern of DNA? Genotypes provide a "blueprint" for your body's development; however, genes are expressed flexibly, so that they may be turned on and off and may require specific environmental cues in order to act (Panning & Taatjes, 2008). As a result, your phenotype (your observed characteristics) may or may not reflect the underlying genetic code. For example, you may be born with the genotype to make you 6 feet tall; however, if nutrition is inadequate, your actual height (the expressed phenotype) may be much shorter. Another example is a trait like extraversion, or how sociable and outgoing you tend to be. Your genotype may plan a very extraverted personality; but, based on environment (being an only child, home day care, limited interactions with other children), you may develop a less outgoing nature as a toddler. So genetics provide a *predisposition* or potential for a characteristic, but expressing it may require contributions from the environment (Parens, 2004). Genetic factors may also affect development much later in life, becoming active at puberty, during periods of stress, or in old age.

Because people vary in so many ways, it is tempting to think that all of these variations are driven by genetic differences. However, keep in mind that our genetic code overlaps 96% with that of chimpanzees (Britten, 2002). Even so, heredity does influence the observed behaviors of individuals. For example, identical twins have more similar personalities than fraternal twins, whether or not they are raised together (Bouchard et al., 1990). So two people with the same DNA who are raised in very different families, neighborhoods, and classrooms still show similar personalities as adults. This suggests that our characteristic ways of thinking, feeling, and behaving are related to the specific combination of DNA determined at conception. Genes matter!

Genetics influence **prenatal** (before birth) development by directing the growth of the fertilized egg. The initial stage, called the **zygote**, lasts only between 1 and 2 weeks. If genes or chromosomes are missing or extra copies are present, or if mutations occur, then needed proteins may be absent or made in excess. As a result, abnormal development and growth of the zygote may result. Sometimes abnormalities are inherited, and sometimes they occur spontaneously, without reason. As a result, fewer than half of zygotes conceived will survive (James, 2000). Once implanted in the uterus, the zygote enters the **embryo** stage for between 2 and 8 weeks. In the embryo, the heart begins beating. By 2 months, sexual differentiation occurs: Males, who have an XY chromosome pattern, begin producing testis differentiating factor, causing the development of male sex organs. If this factor is not present at this time, the same tissue develops into female genitalia by default. About 126 male embryos are formed for every 100 female embryos, but male embryos have lower chances of survival, with 105 males born for every 100 females (Davis et al., 1998).

Sometimes, errors occur in genetic replication of the sex chromosomes or in the processing of sex hormones (androgen and testosterone) and enzymes. As a result, some babies are born with physical characteristics of both genders, such as a chromosomally male (XY) baby with female external genitalia. Sometimes called "intersex" or "hermaphrodite," the condition is now called a *disorder of sex development*. Imagine discovering as an adult that your genetics indicate you are a different gender! Women in sports are sometimes required to undergo gender screening because higher-than-normal levels of the male hormone testosterone may be an advantage. For example, Caster Semenya won the women's 800-meter final at the 2009 World Championships in Berlin FIGURE 12-1. Her appearance (and her amazing performance) raised questions about her gender. Following genetic and gynecological screening, Semenya was allowed to keep her medal (O'Reilly, 2010). Perhaps this is why the ultrasound technician was quick to label my son: Sometimes, that first question of life, "What is it?" may have a less certain answer.

From around 9 weeks until birth, the now identifiably human **fetus** continues to develop FIGURE 12-2. But exposure to toxic agents from the environment, called **teratogens**,

Prenatal stage Development taking place in the mother's womb before birth.

Zygote An initial stage in development as the fertilized egg grows through cell division and attaches to the uterine wall.

Embryo Prenatal stage following zygote lasting 2 to 8 weeks; in this stage, the heart begins beating.

Fetus The unborn child from around 9 weeks until birth.

Teratogens Toxic agents from the environment, such as disease, poisons, or drugs, that can harm the fetus.

FIGURE 12-1 Caster Semenya, winner of the 800-meter gold medal in Berlin, 2009.

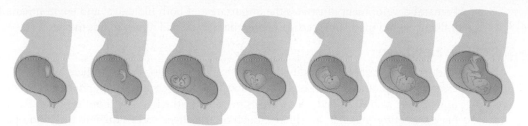

FIGURE 12-2 Stages in fetal development before birth.

is a dangerous problem for fetal development. Mothers who take in toxic substances like cigarettes, some prescribed medications, or street drugs place their babies at greater risk. Infections or disease (like measles), along with x-ray radiation, can negatively impact the fetus. Heavy alcohol use causes more than 40,000 children in the United States to be born with **fetal alcohol syndrome**, resulting in irreversible brain abnormalities (Burd, 2004). *Any* alcohol consumed by a pregnant woman can adversely affect the developing child. Lack of vitamins and minerals (such as folic acid) in the mother's diet can cause problems in the physical development of the fetus (Milunsky et al., 1989). In addition, diseases like HIV/AIDS can be passed from mother to fetus. If a pregnant woman is infected with HIV, she has a 20 to 50% chance of transmitting the virus to her baby during pregnancy, labor and delivery, or breastfeeding (De Cock et al., 2000). The best thing a pregnant woman can do to increase the likelihood of a healthy baby is to take care of her body during pregnancy: Do not smoke, avoid secondhand smoke, avoid alcohol and all illicit drugs, eat a healthy diet and take prenatal vitamins, exercise and get plenty of rest, and get early and regular prenatal care. Clearly, the biological vulnerability of the fetus makes planning for a pregnancy vital to its health; if unplanned, the mother may be unaware of the pregnancy during the earliest weeks of development.

Experiences in the womb also contribute to the developing person. The fetus learns the sound of its mother's voice and prefers it to the sounds of other voices (DeCasper, 1994). In addition, mothers' mental states during pregnancy appear to change the infant's reactivity to stress (Rice et al., 2010). Mothers diagnosed prenatally with anxiety and depression were more likely to have children with behavior problems at 1.5 years (Barker et al., 2011). In one study, exposure to hormones in the womb was found to correlate with development of cognitive abilities (Brosnan, 2008). In this study, ring fingers that were longer than index fingers, a sign of high prenatal testosterone exposure, were correlated with higher scores on standardized math tests. Girls with lower prenatal testosterone exposure (revealed by a shorter ring finger) had higher literacy SAT scores. (Check your own fingers: If you have a longer ring finger, your right brain may be more developed!)

The fetus is not just *growing* before birth but also increasing in **differentiation**; that is, its structures and functions are becoming more specific to perform given tasks. By around 6 months, the fetus has developed enough that it may survive on its own if born prematurely, called the **age of viability** FIGURE 12-3. A full-term birth is typically 37 weeks of prenatal development. Birth itself carries risks: The death rate of mothers from childbirth in the United States has gone from 1 in 100 before 1800 to 1 in 10,000 today. And child survival still depends on the survival of mothers. In a recent study in West Africa, children were more than four times more likely to die by age 5 if their mothers died (Strassman, 2011).

Fetal alcohol syndrome Irreversible brain abnormalities caused by the mother's consumption of alcohol during pregnancy.

Differentiation Growth in complexity over time, with structures and functions becoming more specific for given tasks.

Age of viability By around 6 months, the fetus has developed enough that it may survive if born prematurely.

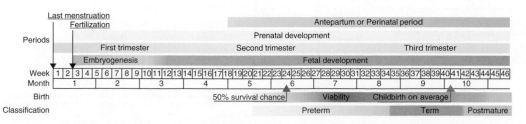

FIGURE 12-3 Stages in fetal development before birth.

Prenatal development illustrates the importance of both biological and environmental influences, and in the final section of this chapter, we will return to this theme.

The Newborn

Most animals enter the world with many "built-in" abilities to help them survive. For example, ducks and geese instinctively follow their mothers through *imprinting*. Newborn humans are also equipped with reflexes present for the first few months of life. Babies have a "rooting" instinct, in which a touch on the cheek causes them to turn and open their mouths. If you touch their lips, they try to suck. And when they feel a touch on the back of their mouths, they swallow. These instincts are obviously helpful in ensuring that newborns are able to breastfeed immediately after birth. The grasp reflex involves grabbing onto anything placed in the baby's palm, and the Moro reflex is a "startle" response to loud noises or the sudden loss of support: The baby throws its arms and legs outward, and then pulls them back together. With these physical actions, a baby may rescue itself by clinging onto a parent. These reflexes are tested at birth as signs of healthy neurological development (Majnemer et al., 1992).

Infants show considerable variability in their natural reactions to stimulation from the environment. A child may be fearful and cry with moderately stimulating play; another enjoys vigorous play and seeks out exciting events. Individual differences in **temperament**, or emotional, motor, and attentional reactions to stimulation, are evident in the first few weeks of life (Carey & McDevitt, 1978; Rothbart, 1981, 1986). Temperament appears to be biologically based (Rothbart et al., 2007). Some babies are called *difficult* because they are irritable, intense, and unpredictable, while *easy* babies are cheerful, relaxed, and more predictable. A third group is considered *slow to warm up* because they resist or withdraw from novel stimulation or new people. These observed differences in behavior may be due to underlying differences in the tuning of physiological systems, so that some infants are more aroused by stimulation than others (Kagan & Snidman, 2004).

The visual system is not well developed at birth, and infants see best at a distance of around 8 inches (Salapatek et al., 1976). This happens to be about how far they are from their mother's face while breastfeeding. But newborns have inborn visual preferences that are particularly helpful. What pattern do you suppose babies like to look at the most? In one study, 2- to 5-day-old infants were shown pairs of disks, including some with bright colors and complex patterns FIGURE 12-4 (Fantz, 1961). Their *preferential looking*—which of the two images they looked at more—was measured. The pattern babies preferred was the depiction of a human face! But perhaps they simply liked the more complex pattern in faces. To find out, another study compared a disk with a face to one with the same graphics scrambled out of order (Johnson et al., 1991). While the complex figure was interesting to them, infants spent more time following the image of the face.

In fact, babies are so attentive to faces that they can make surprising distinctions between them. In one study, faces (without hair or makeup) were shown to 9-month-old babies (Leinbach & Fagot, 1993). When they saw a series of female faces, they grew bored and stopped looking as long at each picture (they "habituated" to them). But when a male face appeared, they suddenly became interested and spent more time looking. The same behavioral pattern occurred when a series of male faces was interrupted by a female face. How do babies recognize gender? Looking at the facial profiles in FIGURE 12-5, can you

Temperament Individual differences in infants' emotional, motor, and attentional reactivity to stimulation.

FIGURE 12-4 Babies were shown disks with different patterns. Based on eye and head movements, babies were most interested in the face design. *Source: Data from Fantz, R. L. (1961). The origin of form perception. Scientific American, 204(5), 1961, 66–72.*

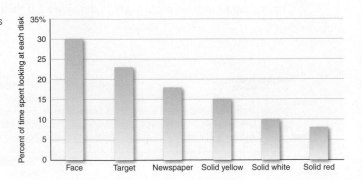

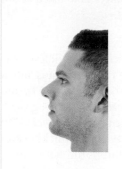

FIGURE 12-5 Male and female profiles tend to differ in fullness of the lower face area.

spot any difference between male and female faces? It turns out that the lower facial area tends to be more full in females, sometimes called a "muzzle" effect (Bruce, 1990). Male faces (on average) have more protuberant noses and brows. A fuller lower face is associated with children and young animals, and this "baby face" feature seems to protect them from aggression from others (Berry & McArthur, 1985).

Babies are not only more interested in faces; they also come prepared to mimic them. Within 72 hours of birth, newborns imitate gestures, such as pursing their lips or sticking out their tongues (Meltzoff & Moore, 1983, 1989). Imitation may serve a purpose by connecting the newborn infant to the caregiver, helping to form social bonds. By around 2 months old, they develop the social skill of smiling with intention (Anisfeld, 1982). Imitation of behavior has been shown to promote affiliation toward humans by other primates as well (Paukner et al., 2009). Like vision, newborns' hearing is also underdeveloped at birth, but infants have been found to like listening to higher-pitched voices (Trainor & Zacharias, 1998). As a result, a "baby talk" voice (called **motherese**—high in pitch, rhythmic, and simple) is better at attracting responses from babies. These inborn patterns of attention are very helpful in focusing attention on social interactions, a very adaptive behavior in evolutionary terms. Clearly, the natural tendencies for infants to be "in tune" with parents provide an advantage, making them more likely to be cared for and, therefore, to survive.

Motherese "Baby talk" that is high in pitch, rhythmic, and simple and may better attract responses from babies.

CONCEPT LEARNING CHECK 12.1   *Before and After Birth*

1. During the longest stage of prenatal development, the soon-to-be baby is called a _____.

2. A research study method that, for example, follows moms and babies from the prenatal period through the first year of life is called _____.

3. Dangerous external agents that affect babies during the prenatal period are called _____.

4. Newborns arrive with built-in reflexes that help them immediately _____.

5. A newborn's favorite visual pattern is _____.

12.2 Infancy and Childhood

Experiences in infancy set a foundation for social relationships, while children's thinking is qualitatively different from that of adults.

- Discuss physical development in infants and newborns.
- Examine Piaget's stage theory in relation to early cognitive development.
- Illustrate the importance of attachment in psychosocial development.

From the moment of birth through sexual maturity, we develop from 7-pound weaklings into strapping youths able to fend for ourselves if need be. A look back at childhood photos will show you how strikingly you changed from year to year compared to changes over a year as an adult. But in addition to physical changes, many changes take place in our cognitive and social development through infancy and childhood.

Physical Development

Physical growth occurs at a faster rate in the young, with another spurt in adolescence. After the first year, the head becomes proportionally smaller FIGURE 12-6. In humans, infant cranial capacity is only 23% of adult capacity; at age 2.5, cranial capacity is 75%; and at age 5, the brain has reached 90% of adult size. But the biological processes of growth are also affected by experience in the world. When rats were raised (for 4–10 weeks) in enriched playgrounds with stimulating toys, they developed heavier and thicker cerebral cortexes (Rosenzweig et al., 1972). While the number of neurons did not change, their size grew, and their synapses (the points at which two cells meet) were 50% larger. Stimulating environments produce larger, more interconnected brains.

Young children also appear to have greater **plasticity** in their neural functions. Plasticity is the capacity of the brain to adapt to the "dings, dents, and major insults" that alter it (Stein et al., 1995). After damage, other areas of the brain can change to compensate for the loss. This is because synaptic connections are created more quickly in younger brains. In one 6-year-old child, epilepsy required surgical removal of the cortex over her entire right hemisphere. Five years later, the only sign of its absence was the limited use of her left arm, and she loves math, music, and art, skills usually involving the right side of the brain (Nash, 2001). Younger people are also less likely to have linguistic deficits than people whose brains are injured when older (Chapman & McKinnon, 2000). The maturing brain also increases its speed of processing. Between the ages of 8 and 12, the children get much faster at performing a mental task, such as adding two numbers together or searching for information in memory (Kail, 1991).

In addition to continuous maturation or growth, development can take place as an orderly progression of *stages*, or discrete, qualitative "jumps" over time. Developmental psychologists have been struck by the regularity in the occurrence of stages of development. Consider the task of learning to walk FIGURE 12-7. Typically, 2-day-old babies spend

Plasticity The capacity of the brain and neurons to adapt to damage that alters them.

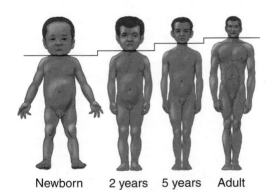

FIGURE 12-6 The head alone comprises about one-quarter of body size at birth, and a large proportion through 5 years of age.

Newborn   2 years   5 years   Adult

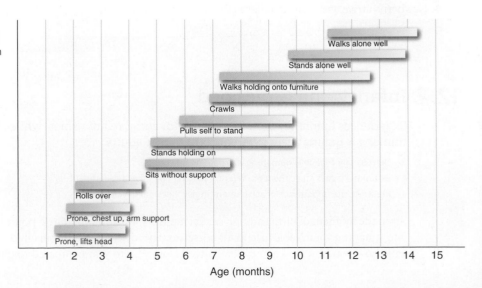

FIGURE 12-7 Children move through an orderly sequence of stages in motor development in the first year.

Walks alone well
Stands alone well
Walks holding onto furniture
Crawls
Pulls self to stand
Stands holding on
Sits without support
Rolls over
Prone, chest up, arm support
Prone, lifts head

1 2 3 4 5 6 7 8 9 10 11 12 13 14 15
Age (months)

most of their time curled in a fetal position. Three months later, they learn to roll over. At about 6 months, they are sitting up by themselves, and by 9 months, they are crawling. At 12 months, they can stand alone and will begin to walk by themselves. Do you think there are babies that can walk but cannot sit up? In fact, babies seem to go through the exact same progression of different stages in a fixed sequence as they learn to walk.

Developmental **norms** are milestones that identify *when* certain behaviors usually occur in normal development **TABLE 12-2**. Normative stages include motor skills (run, keep balance, use hands to eat and draw), language skills (gestures and communication), cognitive skills (learning, remembering, reasoning), and social skills (cooperating, responding to others). Doctors use norms to identify children that may have disruptions (such as hearing loss) or delays in their development. For example, autism spectrum disorders can be detected from videotapes of first birthday parties based on observed behaviors (Osterling & Dawson, 1994). The striking differences involve the number of sensorimotor actions performed by the children; normal children are much more active with objects in their environment. Early intervention in children with autism and other disorders can be highly beneficial to their development (Dawson et al., 2010). Keep in mind, however, that though each milestone is associated with age, the actual age when a given child reaches that milestone can vary quite a bit. Every child is unique!

Norm Behavioral milestone that identifies when certain behaviors usually occur in normal development.

TABLE 12-2 Developmental Norms by Age

	Motor Skills	Sensory and Thinking Skills	Language and Social Skills
By 3 months of age does your child:	• Lift head when held at your shoulder • Lift head and chest when lying on his stomach • Turn head from side to side when lying on his stomach • Follow a moving object or person with his eyes • Often hold hands open or loosely fisted • Grasp rattle when given to her • Wiggle and kick with arms and legs	• Turn head toward bright colors and lights • Turn toward the sound of a human voice • Recognize bottle or breast • Respond to your shaking a rattle or bell	• Make cooing, gurgling sounds • Smile when smiled at • Communicate hunger, fear, discomfort (through crying or facial expression) • Usually quiet down at the sound of a soothing voice or when held • Anticipate being lifted • React to "peek-a-boo" games
By 6 months of age does your child:	• Hold head steady when sitting with your help • Reach for and grasp objects • Play with his toes • Help hold the bottle during feeding • Explore by mouthing and banging objects • Move toys from one hand to another • Shake a rattle • Pull up to a sitting position on her own if you grasp her hands • Sit with only a little support • Sit in a high chair • Roll over • Bounce when held in a standing position	• Open his mouth for the spoon • Imitate familiar actions you perform	• Babble, making almost sing-song sounds • Know familiar faces • Laugh and squeal with delight • Scream if annoyed • Smile at herself in a mirror
By 12 months of age does your child:	• Drink from a cup with help • Feed herself finger food like raisins or bread crumbs • Grasp small objects by using her thumb and index or forefinger • Use his first finger to poke or point • Put small blocks in and take them out of a container • Knock two blocks together • Sit well without support • Crawl on hands and knees	• Copy sounds and actions you make • Respond to music with body motion • Try to accomplish simple goals (seeing and then crawling to a toy) • Look for an object she watched fall out of sight (such as a spoon that falls under the table)	• Babble, but it sometimes "sounds like" talking • Say his first word • Recognize family members' names • Try to "talk" with you • Respond to another's distress by showing distress or crying • Show affection to familiar adults • Show mild to severe anxiety at separation from parent • Show apprehension about strangers • Raise her arms when she wants to be picked up

(continues)

TABLE 12-2 Developmental Norms by Age *(continued)*

	Motor Skills	Sensory and Thinking Skills	Language and Social Skills
	• Pull himself to stand or take steps holding onto furniture • Stand alone momentarily • Walk with one hand held • Cooperate with dressing by offering a foot or an arm		• Understand simple commands
By 18 months of age does your child:	• Like to pull, push, and dump things • Pull off hat, socks, and mittens • Turn pages in a book • Stack two blocks • Carry a stuffed animal or doll • Scribble with crayons • Walk without help • Run stiffly, with eyes on the ground	• Identify an object in a picture book • Laugh at silly actions (as in wearing a bowl as a hat) • Look for objects that are out of sight • Put a round lid on a round pot • Follow simple one-step directions • Solve problems by trial and error	• Say 8–10 words you can understand • Look at a person who is talking to him • Ask specifically for her mother or father • Use "hi," "bye," and "please," with reminders • Protest when frustrated • Ask for something by pointing or by using one word • Direct another's attention to an object or action • Become anxious when separated from parent(s) • Seek attention • Bring toys to share with parent • Act out a familiar activity in play (as in pretending to take a bath) • Play alone on the floor with toys • Compete with other children for toys • Recognize herself in the mirror or in pictures • Seem selfish at times
By 2 years of age does your child:	• Drink from a straw • Feed himself with a spoon • Help in washing hands • Put arms in sleeves with help • Build a tower of three or four blocks • Toss or roll a large ball • Open cabinets, drawers, boxes • Operate a mechanical toy • Bend over to pick up a toy and not fall • Walk up steps with help • Take steps backward	• Like to take things apart • Explore surroundings • Point to five or six parts of a doll when asked	• Have a vocabulary of several hundred words • Use two- or three-word sentences • Say names of toys • Ask for information about an object (asks, "Shoe?" while pointing to shoe box) • Hum or try to sing • Listen to short rhymes • Like to imitate parents • Sometimes get angry and have temper tantrums • Act shy around strangers • Comfort a distressed friend or parent • Take turns in play with other children • Treat a doll or stuffed animal as though it were alive • Apply pretend action to others (as in pretending to feed a doll) • Show awareness of parental approval or disapproval for her actions • Refer to self by name and use "me" and "mine" • Verbalize his desires and feelings ("I want cookie") • Laugh at silly labeling of objects and events (as in calling a nose an ear) • Enjoy looking at one book over and over • Point to eyes, ears, or nose when you ask

Source: Reprinted with permission from the National Network for Child Care (NNCC). Powell, J., & Smith, C. A. (1994). The 1st year. In Developmental milestones: A guide for parents. Manhattan, KS: Kansas State University Cooperative Extension Service.

Stage theory predicts that babies must crawl before they walk. Crawling appears to be required before progressing to other neuromuscular stages. However, crawling may also depend upon the culture in which a baby is raised. In Papua New Guinea, Au mothers and siblings carry infants about 85% of the time during the first year of life (Johnson, 2004). When they are put down, babies are propped up in a seated position. These babies go through a "scooting" stage in which they learn to pull themselves forward while sitting. As a result, they "skip" the crawling stage and learn to walk without ever learning to crawl. These children do not experience any problems from this different stage sequence, and babies in a number of other traditional societies are raised in this way. Anthropologist David Tracer contends the crawling stage is a recent invention that emerged only within the past century or two, after humans began living in houses with flooring that avoids exposure to dirt and germs (Wong, 2009). This example points out the importance of examining differences in development across cultures rather than assuming a universal truth for all.

In some cultures, babies and toddlers are carried by adults or siblings most of the time, resulting in different stages of motor development.

Cognitive Development

What is a baby thinking? This question is difficult to answer because young children cannot tell us what they are thinking and cannot control much of their movements. Early work on cognitive development focused on what could be observed about infants' natural behaviors. Jean Piaget (1896–1980) was a child prodigy who published his first scientific article (on albino sparrows) at age 10! Always good at meticulous scientific observation, he later applied his skills to watching the development of his own three children and trying out informal experiments with them (Gardner, 1981). From his observations, he created a theory of development that captured the field of developmental psychology (Piaget, 1928, 1932, 1951, 1952).

Piaget's Stage Theory

Piaget's theory of cognitive development focused on the formation of concepts, or mental frameworks for organizing and categorizing information. These concepts change through two processes: (1) **assimilation**, or using current concepts to understand new information, and (2) **accommodation**, or changing concepts to fit new information.

Imagine a child with a concept of a "fish." Now she sees a picture of a dolphin. It looks a lot like a fish, so the child assimilates dolphins into her category of "fish." But then her parent says, "No, dolphins are not fish, they are a different kind of water animal." Now her existing concepts cannot incorporate this new knowledge, so she accommodates by creating a new category, "water animals." Piaget sees thinking as the constant interplay of these two processes to form more and more complex concepts. Piaget then identified four different stages of thinking during development, each marked by specific qualities of thinking **TABLE 12-3**. Piaget proposed all humans go through an orderly sequence of stages in cognitive development, and he identified *when* the stages take place.

Assimilation Using current concepts in memory to understand new information.

Accommodation Changing concepts in memory to fit new information.

TABLE 12-3 Piaget's Stages of Development

Stage	Age	Group	Description
Sensorimotor	0–2 years	Babies and toddlers	Explores the world through sensory and motor contact
Preoperational	2–6 years	Preschool and kindergarteners	Uses symbols (words and images) but not yet logic
Concrete operational	7–12 years	Grade school years	Thinks logically about concrete objects
Formal operational	12 and on	Teens and adults	Reasons abstractly and thinks hypothetically

Source: Data from Piaget, J. (1928). The child's conception of the world. London: Routledge and Kegan Paul.

For a baby under 8 months, objects not in view seem to leave their attention, showing a lack of "object permanence."

Sensorimotor Stage

In this first stage, think of babies and toddlers as they approach the world: For them, it is all about learning to grasp and manipulate objects (a bottle, a rattle, a toy) and move through the world (to crawl, walk, and run). As a result, they are focused on developing their sensory and motor processes to coordinate their movements and their eyes with their hands. Piaget called this the **sensorimotor stage** and identified a specific behavior that changes during this stage, called **object permanence**. With babies younger than 8 months, "out of sight is out of mind." They seem to forget about objects they can no longer see and do not seem to search for them if removed. By around 9 months, babies will look for a hidden object, suggesting they are now thinking about it even when it is no longer in view. Now they love playing peek-a-boo, because they now know that objects that appear hidden are really still there. Object permanence is a key sign that a child is moving out of the sensorimotor period and into the preoperational stage.

Preoperational Stage

When you think about Piaget's **preoperational stage**, think of "*preschoolers.*" They have solved the problems of moving around their environment and can recall and think about objects that are not present. They are also rapidly learning language, using verbal symbols to represent concepts. However, preschoolers are still focused on what they perceive. Piaget identified **conservation** as a mental ability that points out the limitations of preoperational thinking. Conservation is the principle that an object maintains the same mass, volume, or number, even if it is displaced across space: A stack of pennies is the same even if spread out across the table **TABLE 12-4**. Children in the preoperational stage are overwhelmed by what things look like. This explains a preschooler's concern with sharing a cupcake: It has to *look* like two identical halves, and if one ends up spread across the plate, it looks "bigger" to them! Until around age 7, the child lacks the concept of conservation and may be misled by superficial changes in appearance.

Preschool children also believe that others know, think, and feel the same way they do, called **egocentrism**. For example, a 3-year-old child calls to his mother downstairs, "Mommy, what is this?" Preoperational preschoolers have not developed the ability to perceive things from another person's viewpoint. For example, imagine a story in which the momma bear leaves home, and a monkey comes in the window and eats a cake. When the momma bear returns, who will she blame for the missing cake? Preoperational children

Sensorimotor stage Piaget's stage for babies and toddlers who are focused on developing their sensory and motor processes.

Object permanence Babies remembering objects they can no longer see in front of them.

Preoperational stage Piaget's stage for preschoolers, marked by an intense focus on what they perceive.

Conservation The knowledge that physical properties of an object stay the same even though there may be superficial changes in appearance.

Egocentrism In preschool children, the belief that others know, think, and feel the same way they do.

TABLE 12-4 Conservation Tasks

Principle	Scenario 1	Scenario 2	Interpretation
Conservation of Liquid	Two identical glasses filled with colored fluid	One glass unchanged and the other changed to a tall, thin glass, so the fluid level appears much higher	The child sees two identical glasses with the same amount of liquid. One glass is then emptied into a tall, thin glass. The child is asked, "Which glass holds more liquid?" Preoperational children will say the taller glass holds more.
Conservation of Mass	Two identical balls of colored clay	One ball unchanged and the other spread out into a longer, thinner shape	The child sees two balls of clay the same size. One ball is then flattened out so it is longer. The child is asked, "Which piece has more clay?" Preoperational children will say the longer piece has more clay.
Conservation of Number	Two rows of eight flowers each	One row unchanged and the other spread apart between flowers to make a longer row	The child see two rows of flowers with the same number in each row. One row is spread out so that it is spread across the table. The child is asked, "Which row has more flowers?" Preoperational children will say the spread out row has more flowers.

cannot yet distinguish between what *they* know and what *others* know, so they answer, "The monkey!" (Wimmer & Perner, 1983). Egocentrism and lack of conservation demonstrate that the preoperational child is able to think from only one perspective at a time.

Concrete Operational Stage

Around 7 years of age, children advance into the **concrete operational stage**. They have achieved conservation and are no longer fooled by appearances. At the same time, they usually enter grade school and receive some training in learning to think logically. But while they are able to learn concrete concepts like arithmetic, they are still limited in their reasoning. What does it mean that "the Earth is round?" FIGURE 12-8. One study examined how children's conceptions of the Earth's shape changed from preschool to fifth grade (Vosniadou & Brewer, 1992). This concept is difficult because you must combine the notion of the round planet with the powerful perceptual sense that the Earth you are standing upon is flat. One research project created a flight simulator that took children on a ride around the Earth, showing the flat Earth on takeoff and landing. Even after the trip, children reported that they believed the Earth is flat (Johnson et al., 1999). The ability to combine two dimensions at once, such as a local view and a distant view of Earth, is finally accomplished toward the end of the concrete operational stage. But even more advanced reasoning is identified with the final stage of Piaget's theory, the formal operational stage.

Formal Operational Stage

Piaget's **formal operational stage** begins at about age 12 and is characterized by reasoning on a logical or hypothetical level. Before this stage, children use trial and error to solve problems; with formal operations, they can use logical methods like experimentation. For example, can you design an experiment that would identify whether cell phones cause brain tumors? Or explain the consequences if people were able to fly? Thinking in an orderly fashion and conceiving novel causes and consequences represents the highest level of cognitive development. Of course, most adults do not always function at this formal level. As discussed earlier, people often use heuristic "rules" to take shortcuts in reasoning. But children around the time of puberty are finally cognitively *capable* of learning the formal methods of thinking, and formal schooling helps to develop these skills.

Challenges to Piaget's Stage Theory

After Piaget, researchers finally came up with new ways of asking babies about what they are thinking. The key was developing ways to measure it. For example, one study placed a mobile (a toy with objects hanging from it) suspended over a crib and connected it with a string to the right foot of a baby. Just 3 months old, the babies quickly learned to jiggle just their right foot to make the mobile move (Rouvee-Collier et al., 1980). Further, though the babies forgot about the kicking after about 8 days, they were able to recall it up to 4 weeks later if given a brief refresher training. This far exceeds the cognitive development Piaget described for the sensorimotor period.

Another innovative technique to assess infant thinking is based on habituation, or loss of response to a stimulus over time (Bornstein, 1989). Babies shown a picture of a red turtle will initially look at it closely; but if a similar picture is presented again, the infant shows a lack of interest by looking away, a lowered heartbeat, or decreasing their sucking on a pacifier. Now, if a picture of a blue bird is presented, the baby will

Concrete operational stage Piaget's stage when grade schoolers have achieved conservation and are no longer fooled by appearances.

Formal operational stage Piaget's final stage (around age 12) characterized by reasoning on a logical or hypothetical level.

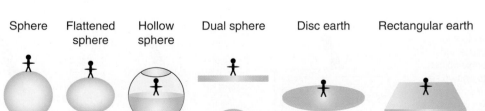

FIGURE 12-8 The notion that the flat surface you stand on is actually a giant globe is difficult to grasp, and children go through stages in its understanding.
Source: Reproduced from Vosniadou, S., & Brewer, W. F. (1992). Mental models of the earth: A study of conceptual change in childhood. Cognitive Psychology, 24, 535–585.

FIGURE 12-9 Based on behaviors that indicate surprise, researchers can determine babies' cognitive expectations.

look at it much longer, showing it is perceived as novel. So the habituation procedure involves first making the baby "bored" by showing similar things and then seeing if he notices a new item as different. A longer looking time or *preferential looking* (judged by observers who cannot see what the baby is looking at) reveals the baby is surprised by the new stimulus (Fantz, 1961).

Piaget claimed that, after about 9 months, babies will search for hidden objects, suggesting the infant achieved *object permanence*. But new studies using looking times showed that infants as young as 5 months thought the hidden object was still there. How do we know? They showed surprise! For example, if a bunny is shown to an infant, then a screen comes down to hide it, and then the screen rises to show *no* bunny, the infants look longer than when the bunny is still there FIGURE 12-9. Based upon observations of the surprise reactions, babies expected object permanence at a much younger age—they just could not show it by reaching out for the object themselves (Baillargeon et al., 1985; Wynn, 1992). By depending only on the baby's motor behaviors, Piaget underestimated the cognitive abilities of babies.

Now that we know how to ask them, what do babies really think? In one study, 4-month-old babies watched a stick moving across a stage with an obstruction across its middle (Kellman & Spelke, 1983) FIGURE 12-10. The two ends they could see always moved together. When the obstruction was removed, some saw a complete stick left behind, and these babies showed habituation—it was what they expected. But for other babies, when the obstruction was removed, two *separate* sticks were revealed. Then, the babies looked 30 seconds longer at the two stick pieces. So, 10-week-old babies expect that objects are unitary (parts that move together are parts of the same object). Other studies showed babies were surprised when a block stayed suspended in midair or a car seemed to pass through a solid object (Baillargeon, 2008; Talbot, 2006). Nine-month-old babies also show a sense of number, distinguishing between two and three objects, or two versus three repetitions of actions (McCrink & Wynn, 2004). Babies know a lot more about the world than we thought!

Theory of mind The child's conception of what he or she and others know, and that these can differ.

Piaget's notion of egocentrism has also been expanded to reflect the **theory of mind**, or the child's conception of what he or she and others know (Wellman, 1990). Three-year-olds have some understanding of their own and others' minds, knowing that they can have a dream while someone else did not, or hide objects so someone else cannot see them (Flavell, Shipstead, & Croft, 1978). Two-year-olds can predict actions and emotions; for example, if Pat looks for her friend in one location and cannot find him, they understand that she will be sad and will look for him somewhere else. But not until age 3 can children predict where Pat might look based on what *Pat* believes. The child's theory of mind—including differences between what he or she knows and what other people know—develops throughout the preschool years (Wellman, 1990). The idea of

FIGURE 12-10 With a block in front, the stick moving behind it is assumed to be a single object. When it is revealed to be two separate sticks, babies are surprised!
Source: Reproduced from Kellman, P. J., & Spelke, E. S. (1983). Perception of partly occluded objects in infancy. Cognitive Psychology, 15(4), 483–524.

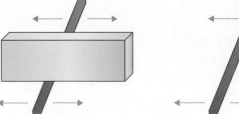

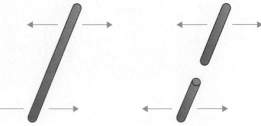

false beliefs does not arise until age 4 or 5. For example, 3-year-olds are presented with a candy box and see pencils inside. They say that other kids will also think pencils are in the box. They will also say they had *always* thought there were pencils in the box (Gopnik & Astington, 1988). Four-year-olds "get" the trick the experimenter is playing, and they predict that *other* children will also be tricked.

Other theorists, such as Lev Vygotksy (1896–1934), proposed that cognition also requires social processes during learning (Wertsch, 1985). A mental skill like retracing your steps to find a lost item may be learned by internalizing information in a social interaction. For example, you lose your jacket, and your mom asks you, "Were you wearing it when you came home?" By seeing another's strategies, we internalize new ways of thinking. Vygotsky also proposed a **zone of proximal development** that predicts *what* children will learn next. This zone is the range between what the child can already do and what he or she is ready to accomplish. For example, once a child can count, he or she is ready to learn about zero. This notion of just-right-sized steps in learning is very important in the design of modern school curricula.

Given this new evidence about development, was Piaget wrong? Yes, in that babies know more than he suspected, and that cognition develops more gradually and continuously than he proposed. For example, a child may grasp conservation of number before displaying conservation of mass. And a child may be able to recognize someone else's emotions before becoming able to understand another's beliefs. However, Piaget was accurate in that children do seem to progress through his four stages of thinking in the same order and at about the ages he predicted they would. So Piaget was pretty close!

Zone of proximal development Children's readiness to learn the next step from what they already know.

Attachment A deep, emotional bond that an infant develops with its caregiver.

Social Development

Human infants, like the young of most mammals, are dependent on their parents to help them survive and thrive in the world. One of the primary bonds across species is the mother–infant bond. In evolutionary terms, it is in a mother's best interest to foster the well-being of her child and for the child to attract and hold the interest of its mother. **Attachment** refers to this deep, emotional bond that an infant develops with its caregiver. But what motivates the infant to bond?

The Power of Touch

In a paper called "The Nature of Love," Harry Harlow (1906–1981) set out to determine why infants bond. Using rhesus monkeys, his studies tested a theory called the primary drives theory (Harlow, 1958). Attachment may happen just because you associate the satisfaction of primary drives (hunger, thirst) with the person who satisfies them. In other words, you, like my dog, may become emotionally attached to whoever feeds you. To test this theory, Harlow constructed surrogate "mothers" from wood, rubber, terry cloth, and wire. The "mothers" had a working nursing device to provide milk and a light bulb within the body to provide warmth. But one "mother" was covered by a wire form, and the other by softer sponge rubber covered by terry cloth FIGURE 12-11. Infant monkeys were placed

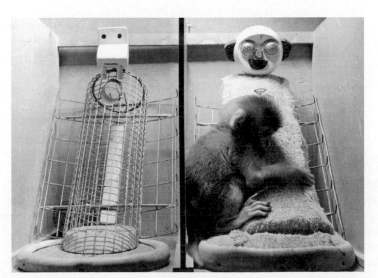

FIGURE 12-11 Two surrogate monkey "moms," one made of wire and one of terry cloth.

in cages containing both of these mothers. In half the cages, the cloth mother provided the milk, and in the other half, the wire mother did. Infant monkeys lived alone in one of these cages for the first 5 months of their lives, and the amount of time they spent in direct contact with each surrogate "mother" was recorded.

Not surprisingly, the monkeys preferred the softer, terry cloth mom. But Harlow's study showed that the source of milk had very little impact on the amount of time spent with each surrogate. *All* of the monkeys spent nearly *all* of their time clinging to the soft mother, regardless of whether the wire mother or the cloth mother provided milk FIGURE 12-12. Even the monkeys feeding from the wire surrogate left the cloth surrogate as briefly as possible to nurse and quickly returned to the terry cloth "mom" FIGURE 12-13. Harlow called this need **contact comfort**, or the need for touch as a primary drive in monkeys. Further studies showed that when the monkeys were faced with threatening objects, like a noisy robot, they raced to their cloth "mother" for comfort and protection. When left in the cage without the soft surrogate, they would

Contact comfort The need for touch as a primary drive in monkeys and humans.

FIGURE 12-12 Baby monkey clings to its terry cloth "mom."

FIGURE 12-13 Monkeys held onto their soft "mom" even when driven to nurse from the wire "mom."

FIGURE 12-14 Motherless monkeys showed signs of emotional devastation, raising ethical questions about the studies.

freeze in fear or cry, crouch, and suck their thumbs FIGURE 12-14. With their soft "mom" present, they were more likely to investigate the robot from this secure base. Harlow's findings identified the attachment bond as psychological (contact) rather than biological (food). From his studies, Harlow concluded that contact comfort was the primary need in infants and that the ability to nurse was not as important.

At the time (in 1958), this idea went against the prevailing culture in the United States. Harlow was stating that the source of the bond between baby and mother was not milk but the frequent and intimate body contact between them. He suggested that fathers and other caregivers could serve this contact need just as well as mothers. Later studies supported the idea that increased contact with fathers had benefits for the father and child (Keller et al., 1985; Lamb, 1977). In fact, fathers who were allowed to hold their babies at birth were more likely to touch them when observed while playing at 3 months (Rödholm, 1981). Cultures vary in the practice of contact between fathers and infants and in the rates of breast versus bottle feeding. However, the benefits of child–caregiver touch are readily observed across cultures and childrearing practices (Johnson, 2004; Jung & Fouts, 2011). For example, mothers given free infant carriers rather than infant seats were found to be more responsive to their babies' vocalizations at 3.5 months (Anisfeld et al., 1990). In short, babies need as much contact comfort as possible! Note that this fits with an evolutionary perspective: An infant that is clinging to its mother is much less likely to be hurt or left behind in an emergency. Contact comfort also serves to keep infants safe by keeping them close to their protectors.

Harlow's research was also controversial because of the use of monkeys as subjects and their experiences in the studies. The surrogate mothers were not real parents, and monkeys reared in these conditions had difficulty in social settings once they rejoined social groups. Some monkeys were left alone without even surrogate "mothers," and their emotional suffering was readily apparent. However, Harlow's studies also had important benefits for the lives of many children. The "power of touch" was soon implemented in institutional care settings in which orphans had in the past received little attention beyond feeding. Now, infants are intentionally held and touched as much as possible by staff and volunteers. For example, premature infants' medical care often limits their interaction with others FIGURE 12-15; by introducing "kangaroo care," even premature babies benefit from skin-to-skin contact FIGURE 12-16 (Feldman & Eidelman, 1998; Feldman et al., 2003).

What motivates the caregiver to bond with a child? Biology plays an important role in creating the bond between mother and child. Oxytocin, the hormone linked to close relationships and sexual intercourse, also plays a role in parenting. Mothers with higher levels of oxytocin in their blood before and after giving birth are more strongly attached to their babies (Levine et al., 2007). Attachment is observed in mothers who focused their gaze mostly on the child, exhibited positive energy, maintained constant affectionate touch, and used a "motherese" speech pattern. For fathers, close contact with their children has been shown to lead to decreases in levels of testosterone, the male hormone related to sex and aggression (Gettler et al., 2011). In a longitudinal study, fathers reporting 3 hours or more of daily childcare had lower testosterone levels at follow-up compared with fathers not involved in care. Biological responses to infants help parents to focus attention on their newborns and to build bonds with their children that are of great importance to their relationships in infancy and throughout life. Clearly, these bonds have value in promoting the survival of the babies.

Attachment Theory

John Bowlby (1969, 1973, 1980) developed a theory about the formation of attachment bonds and suggested there is a *sensitive period* for them. This means attachment relationships develop more readily when the child is between 6 months to 24 months of age. After the sensitive period, a first attachment relationship can develop, but with greater difficulty. This sensitive period coincides with a period during which the baby shows an increasing tendency to approach familiar caregivers and to avoid unfamiliar adults FIGURE 12-17. This **stranger anxiety** refers to the fear reaction infants develop around 12 months of age. A related fear, called separation anxiety, is expressed when babies are separated from mother or father, and is observed across cultures FIGURE 12-18 (Kagan, 1976; Werner, 1988). It may reflect improving memory and conceptual development in the baby (Kagan, 1976), and it coincides with the timing of Piaget's (1932) object permanence. All children go through this normal stage of separation anxiety during development.

However, developmental psychologists also noticed that children *differ* in their level of attachment to their caregiver. As a result of their experiences, some children are more attached than are other children. Mary Ainsworth (1913–1999) created a test of Bowlby's theory of attachment in a laboratory (Ainsworth & Bell, 1970; Ainsworth et al., 1978; Bell & Ainsworth, 1972). First, a child and its mother are left alone together in a playroom. In the **strange situation procedure**, the mother then leaves the child alone, and a friendly

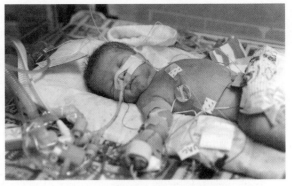

FIGURE 12-15 Premature birth often requires medical interventions that limit the ability to hold and nurse the infant.

FIGURE 12-16 Parents are now encouraged to have regular skin-to-skin contact with their babies.

FIGURE 12-17 Babies demonstrate a "stranger anxiety" with fearful crying that peaks around 12 months.

FIGURE 12-18
Anxiety when separated from mother is observed across cultures.
Source: Adapted from Kagan, J. (1976). Emergent themes in human development. American Scientist, *64, 186–196.*

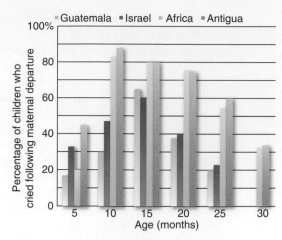

Stranger anxiety A fear reaction of infants to new people usually peaking around 12 months.

Strange situation procedure A test in which the mother leaves her child alone in the playroom, and a friendly stranger tries to interact with the child. Finally, the mother rejoins them.

stranger enters and tries to interact with the child. Finally, the mother returns to rejoin them. How do the babies react?

Sixty percent of infants tested at 1 year of age showed a *secure attachment* to their mother **TABLE 12-5** (Ainsworth, 1979). "Secure" describes an attachment in which the child seems happy with the parent present, distressed when the parent leaves, and delighted by the parent's return. Just like the monkeys with the Harlow "soft moms," securely attached babies are comfortable when their mothers are near, and they use her as a *secure base* for venturing out and exploring the world. When she is gone, the child is upset, and when she returns, the child greets her with excitement. With secure attachment, the infant feels her caregiver will meet her needs. Secure attachment is more likely to occur when the mother is available and appropriately responsive to her child (Ainsworth, 1979).

When children have a secure attachment at 1 year, they grow up to feel happier and have more successful peer relationships (Pastor, 1981; Waters et al., 1979). Securely attached children have been shown to be more positive about others when they become adolescents and have better adult relationships (Allen et al., 2003). They seem to face the world with an ongoing confidence that the world is a safe place, a result of the *basic trust* they felt toward their caregiver (Erikson, 1959, 1968). Our early attachment experiences

TABLE 12-5 Attachment Styles

Attachment Pattern	Child	Caregiver
Secure	• Caregiver is a "secure base" during exploration • Protests caregiver's departure • Seeks caregiver and is comforted on return • May be comforted by stranger, but prefers caregiver	• Responds appropriately to needs • Behaves contingently with the child's requests
Avoidant	• Little or no distress on departure • Little or no visible response to caregiver's return • Ignoring, or turning away if picked up • Treats the stranger the same as the caregiver	• Little or no response to distressed child • Discourages crying and encourages independence
Ambivalent/anxious	• Clinging before separation occurs • Distressed on separation • Ambivalent, angry on return • Seeks contact but resists when it is achieved	• Inconsistent responses • Responds to increased attachment behavior from the infant
Disorganized	• Freezing or rocking • Lack of coherent attachment strategy	• Frightened or frightening behavior, abuse toward the child

Source: Data from Ainsworth, M. D. S., Blehar, M., Waters, E., & Wall, S. (1978). Patterns of attachment: Psychological studies of the strange situation. *Hillsdale, NJ: Erlbaum.*

appear to form a basis of our other close relationships, even as adults (Waters & Cummings, 2000; Waters et al., 2000). As adults, our styles in relationships tend to mirror the same pattern of attachment we experienced in our primary relationship (Hazan & Shaver, 1987; Shaver & Mikulincer, 2007). About 30% of people report changing attachment styles in adulthood, most notably those who had insecure attachments to parents early in life (Davila & Cobb, 2003). Of course, many other factors influence our intimate relationships.

Children thrive under attentive care giving. But that does not always mean their mother, their father, a relative, or even one single person must be involved. In the Efe of Zaire, multiple caregivers are involved with each child (Field, 1996). In this culture, women work together to care for all young children, taking turns holding and nursing newborns. As a result, the child forms strong attachments to multiple adults in the community. It appears that there are many ways of providing for an infant to produce the outcome of a healthy, secure child (Werner, 1988). Similarly, children raised on Israeli kibbutzim, a communal arrangement in which children live separately from their parents, appear to form satisfactory bonds for secure attachment (Sagi et al., 1994). However, secure attachments were more frequent when the children also slept at home with their parents. The important factor is not *who* gives the care, but that someone does.

Disruption of Attachment

What happens when secure attachment is disrupted? Some babies learn they cannot rely upon the caregiver and act this out in the strange situation task mentioned earlier by showing *insecure attachment* (see **TABLE 12-5**). Some of these children seem to alternately seek out and then avoid their mothers, called *ambivalent/anxious attachment*. For example, the baby clings to the parent when she or he tries to leave, cries during separation, but reacts with anger to their reunion. For these children, there is no secure base, and they respond with anxiety. Others show *avoidant attachment*, with none of the typical signs of interest in or consolation from their mothers. They treated the stranger in the same way as their caregivers. What causes these differences in attachment style?

Ainsworth's studies of families in their homes demonstrated that a secure attachment relationship depends on the quality of caregiving the infant receives. Consistent and *responsive* caregiving—noticing and responding to the child—leads to a more secure attachment (Ainsworth et al., 1978; Ainsworth, 1979). Disrupted attachment results when parents are inattentive or respond only some of the time. Problems with attachment also affect other outcomes; for example, those with secure attachment are less likely to have behavioral problems in preschool (Erickson et al., 1985). Intervention programs have been successful at teaching mothers to be more sensitive to their babies' signals (Velderman, 2006).

Is there evidence for a sensitive period in forming attachments? We know from studies of other animals that bonding is sometimes limited to a specific time window, called a **critical period**. For example, the imprinting of baby ducks (in which they focus on following their mother) has a critical period of 13 to 16 hours shortly after hatching; if missed, imprinting will not occur. Because it would be highly unethical to intentionally disrupt human attachment, the only available information comes from cases of neglected infants. This sometimes occurs because of institutional care before adoption or from extreme neglect in the home. One such child, Genie (a pseudonym), was discovered when she was 13 years old. Since infancy, her parents had locked her alone in a small room. When she was discovered, she was unable to stand, was not toilet trained, and could understand only her name. During the first 7 months after her rescue, Genie learned to walk (PBS, 1997). Over time, her cognitive abilities improved, reaching normal levels on some perceptual tasks. While Genie did improve her skills, she did not fully develop language. She did form attachments to her caregivers and to a psychologist studying her language use (Curtiss, 1977). Though her father was convicted of child abuse, Genie was eventually returned to live with her mother. As this case shows, the consequences of missing the attachment bond in infancy can be extreme.

> **Critical period** A period during development where specific abilities must occur.

Family Relationships

Studies of parenting have identified differences in terms of how parents establish control over their children. The authoritarian parenting style focuses on obedience without question: "Because I said so!" This parenting pattern tends to produce children with low

Authoritative parenting style A balance between obedience from the child and willingness to explain and make exceptions.

self-esteem. Permissive parents go to an opposite extreme, allowing the children to impose their own control on their behavior: "What do you want to do?" As a result of a lack of boundaries, their children are often impulsive and more immature than other children. Finally, the **authoritative parenting style** falls in the middle of these extremes: They have rules to be followed, but these parents are willing to explain the reasons behind them and to allow occasional exceptions to them. Children reporting high levels of self-confidence tend to have authoritative parents (Baumrind, 1996). This pattern has been observed across cultures throughout the world (Sorkhabi, 2005).

Within families, each parent is experienced differently by each child (Ricciuti & Scarr, 1990). Children may perceive unequal treatment from their parents, termed *differential parenting*. If children receive equal affection from their parents (in comparison to siblings), they have higher self-esteem, more secure attachment styles, and less romantic relationship distress (Rauer & Volling, 2007). However, if parents "played favorites," their children felt more negative about themselves, whether or not they were the favored child. The early within-family experiences of childhood appear critical to building healthy self-esteem, and these first relationships continue to influence us throughout life (Bronfenbrenner, 1986).

Sibling relationships also contribute to development (Brody, 2004). Interactions with older siblings can improve language and cognitive development and the understanding of other people's emotions and perspectives. However, aggressive older siblings can lead to younger children performing poorly in school and having fewer positive peer experiences (Bank, Patterson, & Reid, 1996). These risks are greater for children living in disadvantaged neighborhoods (with high unemployment rates and pervasive poverty; Brody et al., 2003). However, older siblings can also provide a buffer to younger siblings from the negative effects of family disruption (Jenkins, 1992). And parents' experiences with older children also tend to improve their parenting of younger children (Whiteman & Buchanan, 2002).

A major concern for many parents is the effect of daycare on their child's development. Many families in which parents work outside the home worry that their children will be harmed by having other caregivers for long periods. No research has shown a relationship between working mothers and outcomes of development (Goldberg et al., 2008). Studies *have* found that high-quality daycare, with warm, supportive interactions with adults in a safe and stimulating environment, produces better outcomes (Scarr, 1997; Phillips et al., 2000). Lower socioeconomic status is associated with problems in daycare, along with less stimulation and fewer educational opportunities (Burchinal et al., 1989). But, daycare can even be a protective factor in families of lower socioeconomic status, enhancing academic achievement in elementary school (Burchinal et al., 2009). For at-risk children, more hours of daycare have a compensatory effect, but children from middle-income households did less well with more hours of outside care.

A longitudinal study found that children who had spent more time in daycare showed increased aggressive behavior, but only through grade 3 (NICHD, 2005). A consistent finding is that more hours of childcare are correlated with problem behaviors, even into mid-adolescence (Vandell et al., 2010). However, across 40 years of childcare research, studies show the quality and type of care are related to gains in cognitive, academic, and language functioning in young children and that benefits extend for more than 10 years after leaving daycare (Vandell et al., 2010). These long-lasting (albeit small) benefits occurred for middle-class and affluent children as well as for those who are economically disadvantaged (Ziegler & Styfco, 2004). More research on the impact of daycare and how the features of care affect different children is needed. At this point, the evidence suggests daycare can benefit all children if it is of moderately high quality and if the hours of care are not excessive.

A rite of passage for many children is the divorce of their parents. When divorce occurs, it is often accompanied by a history of family strife and other changes, such as an absent father, working mother, and change in homes (Johnston et al., 1989). As a result, it can be difficult to discern the causal factors in adjustment (Kelly, 2000). Surrounding the time of divorce, family conflicts increase, including custody and financial issues, and continue postdivorce. Parental discipline can become less consistent (Hetherington et al., 1985). In the midst of change, children can respond with anger, grief, guilt, and depression. Some feel better off, some adjust quickly, and some show long-term negative effects, such as poorer grades (Amato, 2000; Amato & Keith, 1991a;

Kelly & Emery, 2003). Children with divorced parents score significantly lower on measures of academic achievement, conduct, psychological adjustment, self-concept, and social relations (Amato, 2001). A review of studies of the economic impact of divorce suggests that families are better off if they stay together (Hetherington, 1999). A meta-analysis of studies showed consequences for the children such as fewer years of education, early parenting, and an increased likelihood of becoming divorced themselves (Amato & Keith, 1991b; Kiernan & Hobcraft, 1997).

Peers

One of the first self-identifications children make is their gender: They learn to think of themselves as male or female by age 4 (Martin & Ruble, 2004). They then use this knowledge to self-segregate by gender to form peer groups. One study found a 10-to-1 ratio in same-sex versus opposite-sex play partners in kindergarteners (Laosa & Brophy, 1972). Throughout childhood, differences in the activities of boys and girls have been observed across human and primate societies. For example, from age 3, girls spend more time working, whereas boys spend more time in play; boys engage in more rough-and-tumble play, while girls engage in more infant contact and grooming (real and play; Edwards, 1993). **Gender roles**—our expectations about how males and females should act—are learned through culture. Gender differences in "play-mothering" (i.e., carrying sticks like mother chimpanzees carrying infants) have been observed in chimpanzees and appear to be supported by cultural practices within a group FIGURE 12-19 (Kahlenberg & Wrangham, 2010). Gender differences in observed behavior occur early in development, well before the biological influences from reproductive maturation in puberty (McIntyre & Pope Edwards, 2009).

Peer relationships in childhood can be important bonds even for very young children like preschoolers. Children who had been together for 3 to 4 years but then transferred to new schools showed increases in desire for physical contact, negative statements and affect, fussiness, and illness, as well as changes in eating and sleeping patterns (Field, 1984). In addition, the children's drawings of themselves showed agitation and disorganization, with distorted facial and body parts and sad faces FIGURE 12-20. While we think of peer relationships as critical in adolescence, children are learning from their peers from a very young age and developing bonds, even though the friendships are much shorter in duration.

Gender roles Our expectations about how males and females should act are learned through culture.

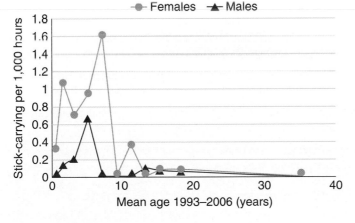

FIGURE 12-19 Age and sex differences in the rate of stick carrying as "dolls" in chimpanzees.
Source: Reproduced from Kahlenberg, S. M., & Wrangham, R. W., (2010). Sex differences in chimpanzees' use of sticks as play objects resemble those of children. Current Biology, 20(24), R1067–R1068.

FIGURE 12-20 A 4-year-old boy created this self-portrait just before moving to a new preschool (Field, 1984).
Courtesy of Tiffany Field.

Peer relationships can sometimes be marked by bullying, either as an aggressor or as a victim. Bullying may be physical or verbal—hitting or kicking, teasing or taunting—or may involve indirect actions such as manipulating others or purposefully excluding other children from activities (Rivers & Smith, 1994). Both children and adults underestimate the prevalence of and harm from bullying (Whitney & Smith, 1993). A study of fourth to sixth graders in the rural South indicated that 1 in 4 students had been bullied with some regularity within the past 3 months and that 1 in 10 had been bullied at least once a week (Limber et al., 1997). Children who are chronic victims of bullying experience more physical and psychological problems than their peers, and they tend not to grow out of the role of victim (Olweus, 1993). These negative interactions can have devastating long-term effects on self-esteem (Seals & Young, 2003). One 11-year-old boy, Jaheem Herrera, told his mother he was being bullied. He used to say "Mom they keep telling me this . . . this gay word, this gay, gay, gay. I'm tired of hearing it; they're telling me the same thing over and over" (Simon, 2009). Jaheem took his own life to escape the constant harassment. Increasingly, children are able to exert bullying behavior using the Internet, and **cyberbullying**, or online harassment, which has been documented in primary schools as well as secondary schools (DeHue et al., 2008). Schools are making efforts to intervene, and schoolwide programs about bullying have been shown to reduce reported incidents (Olweus, 1996).

Cyberbullying Aggressive and hostile acts toward others through Internet media.

A child's development of social relationships is influenced by multiple factors, from the initial family environment, extended family, caregivers, and peers to biological influences such as the evolutionary tendencies that promote taking care of infants. Other biological factors like temperament may alter how social bonds are formed, and environmental factors like daycare and school may influence the child's sense of social ties. Environmental and biological influences combine to create a unique experience in each child's social development.

CONCEPT LEARNING CHECK 12.2   *Stages of Cognitive Development*

Match the concept to the examples.

A. Sensorimotor stage

B. Preoperational stage

C. Concrete operational stage

D. Formal operational stage

1. _____ Helen is looking at a large picture book while her Dad is seated at a desk in the next room. "What is this at the top of the page, Dad?" she asks.

2. _____ Harold grabs his cup, moves it away from the table, and drops it. His mom puts it back on the table. Harold grabs his cup, moves it away from the table, and drops it.

3. _____ Jordana gets upset when her twin sister dumps her bag of Halloween candy. Jordana's neatly piled stack looks much smaller than her sister's spread-out pile.

4. _____ Jorges is not sure which of the three syrups he likes best on his pancakes. So he tries out each one separately first, then he tries every pair of syrups together, and then combines all three at a time. He finally settles on his favorite flavor and color.

12.3 Adolescence and Young Adulthood

Adolescence is an important period in which puberty, brain development, and social interactions produce rapid changes in the individual.

- Discuss the impact of sexual development in adolescence and changes in moral reasoning in adolescents and young adults.
- Examine the life stages within Erikson's theory of psychosocial development.

For 12-year-olds, childhood is behind them. Ahead lies adolescence, the dawn of a new era in development, stretching from the teen years through age 20. Many cultures mark this turning point in development. For example, Jewish families hold bar mitzvah and bat mitzvah for 13-years-olds, Hispanic and South American families celebrate the quinceañera for girls at 15, and many African cultures have a ceremonial rite of passage between childhood and full inclusion into a tribe or social group. This next stage of development toward adulthood is characterized by great changes in physical, cognitive, and social development. In the United States, the early 20s mark a time of many transitions, as students complete college, enter long-term relationships, select a career direction, and leave the family home. In *emerging adulthood* (Arnett, 2006), many questions of how you will choose to live your life are addressed for the first time.

Physical Development

The causal factor leading to these big changes in development is *puberty*, or the sexual maturation that occurs as a result of rising hormone levels; specifically, testosterone in boys and estrogen and progesterone in girls. The hormones cause biological changes that signal reproductive maturity. **Primary sexual characteristics**, the reproductive organs and external genitalia, undergo development. **Secondary sexual characteristics** (pubic hair, breast development in girls and facial hair and lowered voice in boys) announce puberty, along with a spurt in height and changes to the body's overall shape. For girls, the first menstrual period, called **menarche** (me-NAR-kee) occurs (on average) at age 12, indicating the capacity to become pregnant. For boys, the first ejaculation occurs around age 14, followed a year later by the development of mature sperm cells, called **spermarche** (sperm-AR-kee; Hirsch et al., 1985). These are notable changes, but the physical changes continue on into adulthood as the body matures under hormonal influences. These changes can be difficult to adjust to, especially if puberty occurs earlier or later than average. The average age is also lower for both boys and girls than in the past (12.5 for girls in the United States; Anderson et al., 2003) due to improvements in nutrition (Gilger et al., 1991).

What are the psychological effects of these physical changes caused by hormones? For girls, their appearance can become a dominant concern, while boys experience puberty as a more positive change (Petersen et al., 1991). Sexuality is imposed on all adolescents in terms of interest, curiosity, and readiness for sexual reponse. U.S. surveys show 48% of teenage boys and 43% of teenage girls are sexually active (Brener et al., 2002). Though teen pregnancy rates are now in decline, approximately 80% of pregnancies under age 18 are unplanned. Regardless of the outcome—abortion, early marriage, single parenthood—early pregnancies change lives dramatically. Yet in one study, the majority of college students surveyed stated they had not used contraception in their first sexual experience (Darling et al., 1992). This suggests the rapid pace of physical development in adolescence far outpaces development in cognitive and social areas.

As it happens, the physical maturation of the brain goes through its own growth spurt during adolescence FIGURE 12-21 (Lenroot & Giedd, 2006). Because the brain reaches 90% of adult size by age 6, it was thought that the brain was also fully matured. In fact, our brains

Primary sexual characteristics The reproductive organs and external genitalia.

Secondary sexual characteristics Physical changes, including pubic hair, breast development in girls, facial hair and lowered voice in boys, along with a spurt in height and changes to the body's overall shape, that occur during puberty.

Menarche The occurrence of a first menstrual period, indicating the capacity to become pregnant.

Spermarche For boys, the first ejaculation occurs around age 14, followed a year later by the development of mature sperm cells.

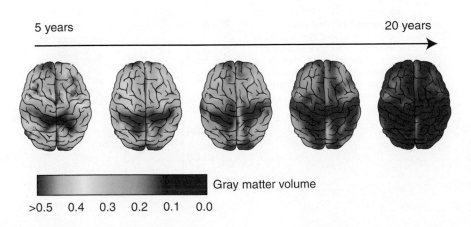

5 years   20 years

Gray matter volume

>0.5   0.4   0.3   0.2   0.1   0.0

FIGURE 12-21 Gray matter volume in the cortex (shown in purple) increases with maturation from 5 to 20 years of age. *Source: Reproduced from Lenroot, R. K., & Giedd, J. N. (2006). Brain development in children and adolescents: insights from anatomical magnetic resonance imaging.* Neuroscience & Biobehavioral Review, 30(6), 718–729.

Neural pruning
Winnowing down the number of neural connections in the brain, associated with adolescence.

undergo a massive reorganization between our 12th and 25th years (Casey et al., 2008) FIGURE 12-22. The infant brain has relatively few connections between neurons. Early brain development involves tremendous growth in the number of connections made between neurons. Over time, the neural connections become more and more dense. Then, in adolescence, a new type of physical development takes place in the brain: winnowing down the number of neural connections, called **neural pruning** (Blakemore, 2008). The brain differentiates useful connections from useless connections: The most heavily used synapses grow richer and stronger, and the connections that do not get used are lost and literally disappear. So the neural connections in the brain become increasingly complex and differentiated in their purpose in the adolescent years. As a result, the cortex becomes thinner but more efficient. In addition, the speed of processing in the brain grows to be a hundred times faster due to increased myelination (or covering) of neural axons, allowing speedier transfer of information along neural pathways (Silveri et al., 2006).

The teenage brain is driven by emotion, and cognitive control takes longer to develop. Physical changes in the brain during adolescence start in the rear brain areas and the limbic system and move slowly toward the frontal lobes. This means that more basic functions, such as emotion, vision, and movement, improve in processing speed first. The amygdala areas respond to negative or fearful stimuli more intensely during adolescence (Guyer et al., 2008), and brain areas involved in rewards are activated more in teens (Somerville et al., 2011). Later, stronger links are added between the hippocampus and the frontal lobe areas that control behavior (Asato et al., 2010). This means emotional reactivity increases *before* the development of control provided by the frontal areas FIGURE 12-23. As a result, adolescents' capacity for cognitive control has not fully matured (Somerville

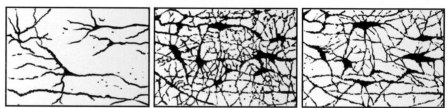

FIGURE 12-22 In the first panel, the interconnections between neurons at birth are sparse; by age 12, the interconnections are quite dense; in the teen years, the connections are "pruned" to maintain only those often used.

FIGURE 12-23 Adolescents show a larger magnitude of activation in response to happy faces relative to both children and adults. *Source: Reproduced from Somerville, L. H., Hare, T., & Casey, B. J. (2011). Frontostriatal maturation predicts cognitive control failure to appetitive cues in adolescents. Journal of Cognitive Neuroscience, 23(9), 2123–2134.*

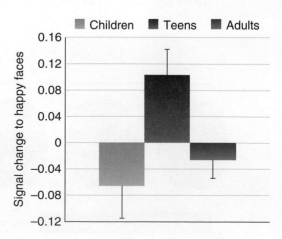

et al., 2011). By the end of adolescence, there is gradual improvement in the ability to control or inhibit behavior, to weigh decisions, and to consider more information at one time (Spear, 2007; 2000).

The consequence of neural development is that thinking is *qualitatively* different during adolescence. That is, teenagers think in a different way than adults. Immaturity in behavior, such as taking risks like speeding or stealing and overdoing drinking or using drugs, may be a consequence of lagging brain development (Ernst & Mueller, 2008). One study tested people in a video task in which their eye movements and brain activity were measured (Hwang et al., 2010). The game involved watching a video screen and looking away from the direction of a light that appeared without warning. This is difficult because the light attracts your attention, and the ability to avoid looking at it requires control from frontal areas of the brain. Young children (age 10) can do it about half of the time, and teens score around 75%. But brain scans show teens make less use of the brain regions responsible for catching errors and staying focused. By age 20, those areas were accessed automatically, and performance improved to that of adults. While it is tempting to think of uncontrolled impulses as the "problem of adolescence," some argue that neural changes during this period are actually helpful. Because teens are less controlled and focused, they may be more flexible in noticing and responding to new situations, just at the time when they are moving from the family into a larger world (Casey et al., 2008).

Cognitive Development

Now able to think and reason logically in the last of Piaget's stages, formal operations, adolescents can let loose their minds on problems of interest. Piaget (1932) pointed out that the ability to reason about abstractions provides an opportunity for the growth of moral reasoning. Building on this notion, Lawrence Kohlberg (1981, 1984) argued that adolescence is a prime time for developing a sense of morality. To investigate this topic, he presented simple scenarios to people and asked their response. Consider this classic example (Kohlberg, 1969): A woman suffering from cancer was near death, and the one drug that might save her was only available from its inventor. The drug was expensive to make, but the inventor was charging 10 times what it cost him. The woman's husband tried unsuccessfully to borrow the money. He then went to the inventor and asked for a discount and offered to pay more over time. But he was told, "No." Finally, the desperate husband broke into the inventor's warehouse to steal the drug for his sick wife. Should the husband have broken into the store to steal the drug for his wife? Why or why not?

In Kohlberg's view, it is not important what someone thinks the husband should *do*. Kohlberg (1969) believed that the *justification* someone offers is what is significant. He collected responses from people of all ages and devised a theory with three levels of moral thinking, each divided into two stages as shown in **TABLE 12-6**. A *preconventional* level of moral reasoning judges the morality of an action based on its consequences, particularly to oneself. An action is morally wrong if you will be punished. A *conventional* level of moral reasoning determines right and wrong based on social roles and society's laws. Good intentions are taken into account, but the law is the law. Finally, the *postconventional level* of moral reasoning considers that social contracts, laws, and rules can bend to uphold individual and universal rights.

Studies have shown that people do pass through the first two stages of moral reasoning in order, just as Kohlberg specified (Colby et al., 1983; Thoma & Rest, 1999). Before adolescence, most children are preconventional, and during adolescence, they begin to reason in conventional terms. Surprisingly, as far as studies can tell, few adolescents and adults reason using postconventional arguments. Only educated adults from middle-class, urban areas were found to display postconventional reasoning (Snarey et al., 1985). This may indicate that postconventional reasoning is a cultural value, and cultures with different values would not develop this same type of moral justification. For example, Americans focus on how events will affect them personally, while South Asians speak in terms of interpersonal concerns (Miller, 1994). In addition, Kohlberg developed his theory using only male subjects. Women may address moral issues with more compassion for individuals and less emphasis on abstractions (Gilligan, 1982).

TABLE 12-6 Examples of Kohlberg's Stages of Moral Reasoning

Stage one (*obedience*):	"Heinz should not steal the medicine because he will consequently be put in prison which will mean he is a bad person."
Stage two (*self-interest*):	"Heinz should not steal the medicine because prison is an awful place, and he would more likely languish in a jail cell than over his wife's death."
Stage three (*conformity*):	"Heinz should not steal the drug because stealing is bad and he is not a criminal."
Stage four (*law-and-order*):	"Heinz should steal the drug for his wife but also take the prescribed punishment for the crime as well as paying the druggist what he is owed. Criminals cannot just run around without regard for the law; actions have consequences."
Stage five (*human rights*):	"Heinz should steal the medicine because everyone has a right to choose life, regardless of the law."
Stage six (*universal human ethics*):	"Heinz should steal the medicine, because saving a human life is a more fundamental value than the property rights of another person."

Source: Data from Kohlberg, L. (1984). The psychology of moral development: The nature and validity of moral stages. San Francisco: Harper & Row.

Another theory focuses on moral *feelings* rather than thoughts. Like our thinking, our moral reasoning may involve a faster, emotional response and a slower, more deliberate justification for our behavior. For example, a 7-year-old boy dove from a dock to rescue a toddler that had fallen into deep water. He said he "didn't think at all," but panicked at the sight of the girl in danger. Afterward, he talked about how it was the right thing to do; but in the moment, he simply felt an emotion and acted upon it. The *social intuitionist* account of morality (Haidt, 2001, 2008) explains our decisions based on the feelings evoked rather than justifications for actions. Consider this dilemma: A runaway trolley is headed down a track. Five people will be killed unless you flip a switch to divert the trolley onto a backup track. But if you do so, a man standing on that track will certainly die. Will you do it? Most people say, "yes," because more people will be saved. But if the scenario is changed so that you have to physically push the stranger onto the track to stop the trolley, most people say, "no!" The reason seems to be that the second scenario evokes an emotional response (Greene & Haidt, 2002), which is evident in the brain during imaging (Greene et al., 2001). It is difficult emotionally to be the one to directly cause death. Another view of morality is that how we justify our actions or even how we feel about them is less important; instead, morality may depend on what we choose to *do*.

Social Development

Theory of psychosocial development Erikson's stage theory of important issues to resolve across the life span.

Identity formation The process of developing a distinct, individualized personality.

Erik Erikson's (1902–1994) **theory of psychosocial development** identifies a series of stages in life as we develop from childhood through old age **TABLE 12-7** (Erikson, 1959, 1968). For adolescents, Erikson defined the central task to be the forming of an **identity**, or a distinct, individualized sense of self. Erikson called this process the "*identity crisis*," in which teenagers explore alternative ways of living and describing themselves to the world. In the adolescent years, you break free from your relationship with your parents, going from spending most of your free time with family to spending most of it without them. In one study, the amount of time adolescents were with their family went down from 35 to 14% of waking hours (Larson et al., 1996). In addition, teenagers reported feeling more negatively when around their family, but this improved in the 9th and 10th grade for boys and the 11th and 12th grades for girls. Parents and teenagers tend to disagree, and their arguments place a strain on the entire family (Silverberg & Steinberg, 1990).

An evolutionary perspective suggests the reasons for these family strains lie in the problem of having sexually mature offspring living within the family group. In many primate species, such as gibbons and chimpanzees, individuals depart from their group at

TABLE 12-7 Erikson's Stages of Psychosocial Development

Virtue	Crisis	Age	Description
Hope	Trust vs. Mistrust	Infants, birth to 12–18 months	Infants achieve a sense of safety when their basic needs are met
Will	Autonomy vs. Self-doubt	Toddlers, 18 months to 3 years	Children learn to exercise their will to make things happen
Purpose	Initiative vs. Guilt	Preschool, 3 to 6 years	Children learn to initiate activities, gaining self-confidence
Competence	Industry vs. Inferiority	Childhood, 6 to 12 years	Children learn to systematically explore and develop their abilities
Fidelity	Identity vs. Role confusion	Adolescence, 12 to 18 years	Adolescents create their own values and goals
Love	Intimacy vs. Isolation	Young adults, 18 to 25 years	Young adults learn to merge their identity with another
Care	Generativity vs. Stagnation	Middle adulthood, 25 to 50 years	Middle adults focus concern on the world and their contributions
Wisdom	Ego Integrity vs. Despair	Later adults, 50 years onwards	Later adults must come to terms with their previous choices

Source: Adapted from Erikson, E. H. (1959). Identity and the life cycle. *New York: International Universities Press.*

puberty (Steinberg, 1989), presumably to form new families. In modern humans, the age of marriage is much later, and children may remain living in the home for longer periods and return after college. Living as an adult with your parents poses problems for a sense of autonomy. In more traditional cultures, with less emphasis on independence, there is less tension between adolescents and parents (Arnett, 1999; Schlegel & Barry, 1991). Cultural values may direct an individual toward independence or toward interdependence with others (Greenfield et al., 2003).

Another important aspect of social development is *gender identity*. From the moment of birth, gender is an important social label that influences the way adults interact with you, the peers you choose, and the activities you do. Are men and women as different as society treats them, or are they more alike? Throughout human history, and in varied cultures, gender differences are assumed to operate due to differences in reproduction. Evolutionary theory stresses the roles taken within the family in a hunter-gatherer society, in which childcare is the responsibility of women. Across cultures, the type of work performed outside the home and educational opportunities provided differ greatly for women and men. However, research into the *psychological* differences between males and females has found they are actually quite similar (Maccoby & Jacklin, 1974). Cross-cultural studies (including nonindustrial societies) suggest that both biological differences and social roles contribute to observed differences by gender (Wood & Eagly, 2002). There are some differences that appear regularly across cultures: Males appear to be more aggressive and have better mathematical and spatial abilities, while females have better verbal skills (Maccoby & Jacklin, 1974). Societal expectations for careers and child rearing reinforce stereotypes that even parents and teachers are unable to ignore (Fagot et al., 1985; Stern & Karraker, 1989). Each individual is left to work out his or her place within the sometimes-conflicting views of gender within a culture.

An important marker of adolescent social development is increasing emphasis on peer relationships. Moving away from gender segregation, adolescents seek out friendships with the opposite sex, distinguishing between friends and romantic partners (Furman & Shaffer, 1999). Peer groups provide a reference to compare and evaluate a developing identity. A study of pairs of friends in grades 7 to 11 showed an influence of closest friends on the likelihood of binge drinking or engaging in sexual activity (Jaccard et al., 2005).

Peer relationships are marked by conformity of behavior, or *peer pressure*, peaking in the ninth grade (Gavin & Furman, 1989; Ge et al., 2007). Peers can influence both negatively (increasing likelihood of drug use) and positively (improving grades; Lansford et al., 2003). For those excluded from peer groups, loneliness, low self-esteem, and depression may occur (Steinberg & Morris, 2001). Teens with warmer (and more demanding) parents are somewhat less likely to follow the influence of peers (Mounts & Steinberg, 1995).

What makes some adolescents able to thrive despite conditions of neglect, abuse, and trauma? This phenomenon is called **resilience**, or good developmental outcomes despite high risks, competence under stress, or recovery from trauma (Masten, 2001; Masten & Obradovic, 2006; Werner, 1995). Studies in younger children suggest resilience may be partly heritable (Kim-Cohen et al., 2004; Moffitt et al., 2006). When children overcome the odds to do well in adolescence and later life, they often have personal qualities like an engaging personality, good communication and problem-solving skills, and a belief that their own actions can make a difference in their lives. In fact, the surprising finding is that resilience is so "ordinary;" that is, so many adolescents go through events that might derail their development, yet they somehow recover and thrive (Masten, 2001). Schools can foster resilience by taking a whole-school approach, building on strengths and connections between families, teachers, and social services (Smith et al., 2004).

> **Resilience** Good developmental outcomes despite high risks, competence under stress, or recovery from trauma.

CONCEPT LEARNING CHECK **12.3**   *Defining Adolescence*

Define these important concepts from adolescent development.

1. Menarche and spermarche

2. Neural pruning

3. Conventional morality

4. Social intuitionist

5. Identity crisis

CRITICAL THINKING APPLICATION

"When I was 16, four friends jumped into my car one night, and we headed to a local 'lovers' lane.' I drove up next to a parked car with steamy windows, and we all began to sing "Love to Love You Baby" by Donna Summer. After a few minutes, the dome light in the other car went on, and a handgun was clearly visible. I peeled out and drove like mad, with the other car in pursuit. After running a yellow light and barely missing a passing police car, I finally stopped for help. Our pursuer drove off, and the officer agreed not to give us a ticket if we went down to the station to report what had happened. There we were, under age, in the middle of the night, trying to explain why the evening's events had seemed like a good idea at the time. What was I thinking?"

Teenagers are known for their risky choices. But studies of risk perception and appraisal cannot explain why teenagers engage in more risky behaviors than adults given that they appear to recognize risks (Steinberg, 2006). Several factors may be involved:

1. Changes in reward sensitivity occurring at puberty. Adolescents seek more novelty and require higher levels of stimulation to achieve the same subjective feelings of excitement. It is not that adolescents cannot perceive the higher risk of activities like smoking, drugs, and drinking, but they have a higher need for the stimulation risk taking provides. They weigh the benefits of the risky behavior (such as unprotected sex) more heavily (Steinberg, 2007).

2. An "illusion of unique invulnerability." People often fail to use effective contraception methods because they engage in a systematic distortion of their likelihood of being involved in an unwanted pregnancy relative to others (Burger & Burns, 1988).

(Continues)

CRITICAL THINKING APPLICATION *(Continued)*

3. Delayed development of the brain's prefrontal cortical areas. The prefrontal cortex is the seat of inhibition of behavior yet has a relatively slow development compared to other parts of the brain. The higher-level, self-regulatory capabilities involved in impulse control and planning continue to mature into adulthood (Keating, 2004; Silveri et al., 2006). In fact, maturation in the brain goes on through age 25 (Crews et al., 2007).

These factors are biologically driven, normative, and unlikely to be remediable by education (Steinberg, 2006). So what should we conclude about the appropriate age for rights and responsibilities to be assigned to adolescents? Some researchers argue that the evidence of neural changes in adolescence should be considered in establishing public policies (Steinberg, 2009). What do you think? Examine each of the factors below, consider the legal age for the rights by law, and decide on what age you feel is most appropriate for each.

Right/Responsibility	Legal Age	Appropriate Age
A. Driver's license	16(MI)	
B. Purchasing cigarettes	18(MN)	
C. Voting	18(Federal)	
D. Gun ownership	18(Federal)	
E. Purchasing alcohol	21(NY)	
F. Enlistment in military service	18(Federal)	
G. Eligibility for the death penalty	18(Federal)	

12.4 Adulthood and Aging

Adulthood is marked by important developmental stages, including determining one's purpose and a partner in life and, later, coming to terms with the choices made.

- Illustrate the physical, cognitive, and social aspects of aging.

The many choices in life, combined with the realities of financial and social needs, can be overwhelming. But there is no one right way to develop, no single right path to finding the future of your dreams. One metaphor imagines starting at the top of a mountain, with crossing pathways circling down (Bee, 1987). You make your way down, altering your path at every intersection, finding harder and easier routes and better or less-preferred spots. Every individual takes a unique route down the mountain, but we all pass through the same elevations as we travel through development. While we all begin in the same spot, our experiences of development can be quite different and yet equally satisfying.

Physical Development

By our mid-20s, humans are finally physically mature, and all of our systems are fully developed. Unfortunately, it is all downhill from here! The passage of time results in changes to physical abilities we may take for granted when younger. During the 1960s, Vietnam war protester Jerry Rubin gave a rallying cry, "Don't trust anyone over 30!" All too soon, we join the ranks of adults in their 30s and 40s and begin noticing physical changes, including wrinkles, stooped posture, thinning white or graying hair, and "shrinkage," with men losing an inch in height and women two. After age 20, a 1% loss in muscle mass occurs each year.

Aging gracefully becomes increasingly difficult for some people in cultures where a youthful appearance is highly valued. Jocelyn Wildenstein reportedly underwent dozens of plastic surgeries in a misguided attempt to win back her husband (CBS News, 2011). She is reported to have undergone a brow lift, facelift, lip-plumping injections,

Jocelyn Wildenstein reportedly sought plastic surgery to halt the aging process, attempting to minimize features such as wrinkles, thinning lips, and sagging skin.

Menopause The cessation of menstrual periods in women, usually occurring around age 50.

Grandmother hypothesis Evolutionary theory that older females aid in the reproductive success of their families by helping to raise grandchildren.

chin augmentation, fat grafting and/or cheek implants, upper and lower eyelid surgery, and canthopexy, a procedure that elevates the eyes to give them a catlike appearance. There have been reports of social parties in which the guests are given injections of Botox to "freeze" facial muscles and hide wrinkles (Cooper, 2002). After spending the adolescent years attempting to look older, adults struggle with looking younger. Appearance counts heavily in old age as well, with elderly persons who appear more youthful enjoying more optimism, social ties, and work opportunities. People who look older than their actual age are not as healthy and are even likely to die earlier (Kligman & Graham, 1986).

Reproductive Life

Delaying parenthood until after age 22 is associated with positive health benefits, and, for women, maximum health benefits are predicted for a first birth at age 30 (Mirowsky, 2002). But reproductive ability also diminishes with age, particularly for females. Even with assistive technology, women over 40 can have a difficult time becoming pregnant. Around age 50, women experience **menopause**, or the cessation of menstrual periods. In men, sperm continue to be produced throughout the life span, but the number and motility of sperm decrease. While modern medicine has extended pregnancy to later ages, physical limits to reproductive life eventually weigh in. What happens after the possibility of reproduction ends? In evolutionary terms, this period of life appears to be a relatively recent invention in human history. Once people started living longer lives and had completed their own reproduction, they became available to help others in the family. It has been argued that the presence of grandparents aids in raising the young, called the **grandmother hypothesis** (e.g., Shanley et al., 2007). Grandmaternal investment, in the form of help from extended family, may have allowed women to successfully raise more babies closer together in age. This pattern of grandparental care is not apparent among other primates (Hawkes et al., 1998).

However, new evidence suggests that nonreproducing members of a group may be a drain on resources. A meta-analysis of published studies over several centuries in 17 patrilineal societies showed that paternal grandparents who lived with their grandchildren did not have a beneficial effect on the grandchildren's survival (Strassmann & Garrard, 2011), though maternal grandparents did. An ongoing, 25-year study of the Dogon people of Mali, West Africa, a traditional, agricultural society, showed resources are scarce and mortality is high. Like many human groups in the past, Dogon society is patrilineal, with a tight-knit web of kinship established through fathers. Dogon women give birth to nine children, on average, over their lifetimes. Their children were 52% less likely to die if their paternal grandparents were dead. This is because the paternal grandparents are likely to live with the child and compete for scarce resources (Strassman, 2011). In some circumstances, having a village to raise a child is too expensive.

Life Expectancy

In 2008, there were 506 million people in the world over 65; in 2040, there will be 1.4 billion (Kinsella & He, 2009). For the first time in modern history, older adults will outnumber children younger than age 14. As we age, strength, speed, and endurance grow weaker. Slowly, our sensory detectors start to fail, making us less sensitive to light, sound, and smell. Around age 50, the ability to focus light on the retina fails, and reading glasses are needed. The loss of sensory acuity is viewed as responsible for increasing physical deterioration in other areas, called the common cause hypothesis (Baltes & Lindenberger, 1997). However, health and physical abilities are affected more by behavior than by the mere passing of time: Physical exercise aids brain cells by increasing oxygen and nutrient circulation (Pereira et al., 2007). Exercise also aids the creation of new neurons in the hippocampus, important to building new memories.

Life expectancy in countries with modern medical care now exceeds 80, far past the time frame designed by evolution. Women have longer lives than men, and in the highest age group, women outnumber men 5 to 1. Later age of parental death is associated with better functional performance and cognitive ability in their children, suggesting that living longer may be heritable (Vaillant & Mukamal, 2001). While advanced age shows continued deterioration of physical skills, other qualities of life in this age group remain vital. In particular, those with a positive view toward their own aging live more than 7 years longer than others and have higher rates of engagement in healthy behaviors (Levy et al., 2002). In a longitudinal Dutch study of older men, greater optimism was related to lower rates of death (Giltay et al., 2004). Having a sense of usefulness to others (Gruenewald et al., 2007) also leads to a longer life.

Death and Dying

Successful aging receives far less attention than physical health (Depp et al., 2010). Rowe and Kahn (1987) define successful aging as: (a) freedom from disability and disease; (b) high cognitive and physical functioning; and (c) social engagement (in terms of involvement in both social and productive activities). Recent clinical trials found positive effects for a variety of interventions, such as physical exercise, dietary restriction, cognitive stimulation, social interventions, and stress reduction (Depp et al., 2010). All of these may enhance cognitive and emotional health in older people.

While people may fear senility, or the widespread loss of cognitive function, it occurs in less than 5% of people. These individuals experience the loss of brain cells leading to **dementia**, or progressive loss of cognitive function due to aging or disease. Strokes, tumors, and other diseases can cause the deterioration of the brain in old age. Alzheimer's disease is caused by the disruption of the neurotransmitter acetylcholine and is diagnosed in about 3% of elderly patients. Alzheimer's has a genetic component, shown by an identical twin's 60% likelihood of also getting the disease, with 30% for a fraternal twin (Plomin & Crabbe, 2000).

Current medical thinking defines death as an active physical process occurring over time. In psychological terms, the process of dying also involves reactions that unfold over time (Kübler-Ross, 1969) **TABLE 12 8**. Through interviews with terminally ill patients, five stages of dying were identified: denial, anger, bargaining, depression, and acceptance. Kübler-Ross's theory was the first to qualitatively describe systematic observations; however, this stage theory has not been supported by other research (Schulz & Aderman, 1974). A dying person may experience many changes in attitude over time and events. Surprisingly, it is those in middle adulthood who fear death most (Bengston et al., 1977), while those who feel they have achieved their goals in life fear death less (Neimeyer & Chapman, 1980/1981). This fits well with Erikson's (1959) life-span theory suggesting the need to resolve the final conflict—ego integrity vs. despair—in development over the lifespan.

> **Dementia** Progressive loss of cognitive function due to aging or disease.

Cognitive Development

As physical systems decline with age, cognitive processes show similar impairment. With age, we have more trouble assimilating new information, cannot recall information from memory as accurately, and are slower to learn associations through classical conditioning. In addition, mental processing speed begins to slow down, so it takes longer to recall information, react to signals, and perform mental computations (Salthouse, 2011).

TABLE 12-8 Stages of Coping with Death and Dying

1. Denial	The first reaction is to refuse to believe death will occur: "There must be some mistake here."
2. Anger	The second stage is resentment against those who are healthy, caregivers, or the cause of death: "Why did this have to happen to me?"
3. Bargaining	In the third stage, people try to make a deal to stay alive: "If I get better, I will exercise every day!"
4. Depression	A time of mourning for oneself and all of the losses death will bring: "I'll never see my grandchildren."
5. Acceptance	The final stage involves understanding death as inevitable, and accepting it with equanimity.

Source: Adapted from Kubler-Ross, E. (1969). On death and dying. New York: Scribner. Reprinted 1997.

Age-related declines in many cognitive variables have been reported with correlations ranging from −0.30 to −0.50 FIGURE 12-24 (Salthouse, 2011). All adults, not just those at advanced ages, show a decline in performance on tasks requiring *fluid intelligence*, or reasoning about new information. However, *crystalized intelligence*, or reasoning using knowledge already existing in memory, shows *no* decline with advancing age (Cattell, 1963). Old people do know better!

Lehman (1962, 1966a, 1966b) showed a pattern of decreasing performance on achievement tests with age (c.f. Simonton, 1988) FIGURE 12-25. The inverted-U-shaped curve—a steep increase, a relatively early peak, and a gradual decline with age—shows up across disciplines and historical periods, and across measures of achievement, including counts of products (number of published articles, paintings, inventions, or musical recordings) and quality of products (highly cited articles or Nobel Prizes) (Salthouse, 2011). Similar results have been obtained in within-individual comparisons (Simonton, 1988); specifically, fields such as lyric poetry, pure mathematics, and theoretical physics, which may focus on novel problem solving, tend to have earlier peaks and more rapid declines than do fields with more reliance on accumulated knowledge (e.g., novel writing, history, philosophy). To illustrate, Simonton (1997) noted that the peak age for greatest career success is 26.5 for mathematicians, but 38.5 for historians.

Individual minds may also be differently resilient when damage occurs. *Cognitive reserve* refers to the brain's ability to adapt to damage by recruiting alternate brain regions to perform tasks (Stern, 2009). Higher education levels, participating in mentally demanding occupations and cognitively stimulating activities, along with lifestyle factors, contribute to cognitive reserve (Fratiglioni & Wang 2004). In fMRI studies, older adults appear to make more use of *both* hemispheres during tasks compared to younger people (Eyler et al., 2011; Hedden & Gabrieli, 2004). Cognitive aging can be impacted by adopting strategies for

FIGURE 12-24 Knowledge gained from experience (accumulated) shows less change over time than scores on tests of solving novel problems.
Source: Reproduced from Salthouse, T. (2011). Consequences of age-related cognitive declines. Annual Review of Psychology, 63, *5.1–5.26.*

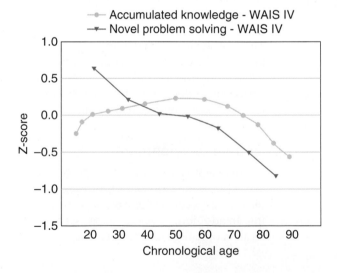

FIGURE 12-25 Scores on achievement tests show an inverted U shape, with increases in the early adult years followed by steady declines with age.
Source: Data from Lehman, H. C. (1962). More about age and achievement. Gerontologist, 2, *141–148.*

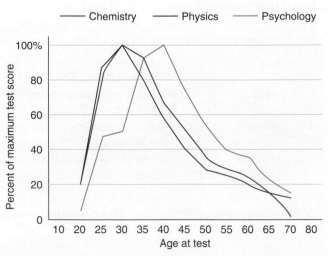

performing tasks. Commercial "brain-training" games appear (based on longitudinal data) to show a relationship between cognitive stimulation and reduced risk of dementia (Wilson et al., 2002). However, Salthouse (2006) questioned the "use-it-or-lose-it" hypothesis because there is little evidence that the rate of cognitive aging is affected by such interventions.

Surprisingly, these slowdowns in cognitive systems and achievements with age do not show up as changes in perceived performance in real-world settings (Salthouse, 2011). This is because in most work settings, you seldom need to perform at peak ability, you use more accumulated knowledge than novel reasoning FIGURE 12-26, and you can be successful in ways not limited to cognition. So the elderly corporate board member is called upon to bring to bear his experience, not to reason quickly about new problems. In addition, older adults may use methods to accommodate for cognitive declines, such as organizers, notes, and calendars. For example, prospective memory tasks—remembering to perform an action at a later time, such as take a pill or let the dog in—are harder with advanced age (Henry et al., 2004). However, planning reminders may help to implement intentions (Patalano & Seifert, 1997). For example, patients who planned when they would take a walk helped cut their recovery time in half (Orbell & Sheeran, 2000). With age, we appear to be increasingly likely to use strategies that help us perform tasks. While the expectation is that cognitive declines will make for poorer performance with age, the wisdom of experience can compensate quite well (Baltes & Baltes, 1990).

Social Development

Erikson's (1959) theory of development noted many important stages in adulthood, focusing on love, caring, and wisdom (see **TABLE 12-7**). Successfully resolving earlier conflicts in life is thought to lead to better later-life outcomes. Whether the final stages end in "ego integrity" and satisfaction with your choices or "despair" and regret depends upon how you resolve developmental crises throughout your life (Erikson, 1959).

Continuity or Change

Now that you are an adult, we can ask the question, "How much are you like the infant, child, and adolescent you once were?" Do people change a great deal as they develop, or is a shy child likely to become a shy adult? Let us consider the evidence from studies of personality traits such as openness, conscientiousness, extraversion, agreeableness, and neuroticism. Across time and age, personality traits are largely consistent (Fraley & Roberts, 2005; Roberts & Mroczek, 2008) FIGURE 12-27. A cross-sectional study comparing personality traits like extroversion over age groups found consistent patterns across nationalities, including Turkey, Germany, Spain, Britain, and Czechoslovakia (McCrae et al., 1997; Schmitt et al., 2007) FIGURE 12-28. Individual differences in personality traits show some continuity from early childhood on and are essentially fixed by age 30 (McCrae & Costa, 1994). However, there is also evidence that people can change over time: With increased age, people show increased self-confidence, warmth, self-control, and emotional stability (Roberts et al., 2006).

But is maturation the cause, or is it simply "getting older"? Life experiences in young adulthood may be the most likely reason for changes in personality with age. In young

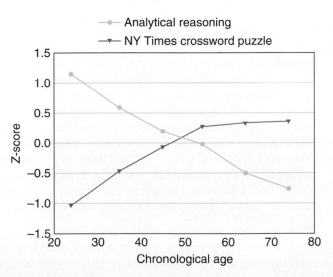

FIGURE 12-26 Reasoning test scores decline with advanced age, but practical skills like crossword solutions remain high. *Source: Reproduced from Salthouse, T. (2011). Consequences of age-related cognitive declines. Annual Review of Psychology, 63, 5.1–5.26.*

FIGURE 12-27 Change in personality traits over time for six trait domains (assuming cumulative change over time). Extraversion is broken into social vitality and social dominance. *Source: Data from Roberts, B. W., & Mroczek, D. (2008). Personality trait change in adulthood. Current Directions in Psychological Science, 17(1), 31–35.*

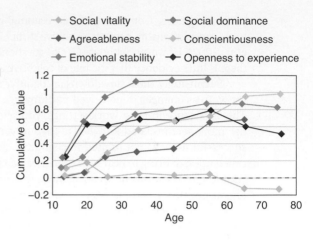

FIGURE 12-28 Mean levels of extraversion in five cultures by age group. Total scores (T) are based on the mean and standard deviation of all respondents over age 21 within each culture. *Source: Reproduced from McCrae, R. R., Costa, P. T., Jr., Ostendorf, F., Angleitner, A., Hřebíčková, M., Avia, M. D., Sanz, J., Sánchez-Bernardos, M. L., Kusdil, M. E., Woodfield, R., Saunders, P. R., & Smith, P. B. (2000). Nature over nurture: Temperament, personality, and life span development. Journal of Personality and Social Psychology, 78(1), 173–186.*

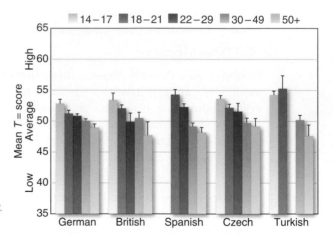

adulthood, there are many life tasks most people experience for the first time, such as finding a romantic partner, starting a family, and establishing a career. Perhaps as a result of growing responsibilities, we develop increased conscientiousness and emotional stability. This pattern is supported across cultures and ethnic groups (Helson et al., 2002). Changes in social roles also occur with age; for example, you move from child to parent to grandparent. A first job may bring expectations about showing up on time, working hard and extra hours, and being agreeable with coworkers. Other people may encourage you to change by punishing or rewarding your behavior, such as providing raises or social rejection. Personality may be further shaped by the social expectations experienced in these adult roles (Roberts & Mroczek, 2008).

In addition, personality traits continue to change in middle adulthood and old age (Roberts et al., 2006). As they age, people decrease on social vitality (a facet of extraversion), openness, agreeableness, and neuroticism. Older people tend to be a little less sociable but also less worried about life. Your chronological age may be less important than the life experiences you encounter at different stages of life. Erikson's theory proposes stages tied to age, but each involves specific types of first experiences that challenge the individual (Erikson, 1959). The task of finding a life partner often occurs in young adulthood, a period of accomplishment follows in middle adulthood, and later, concern about the impact of your efforts is more likely to arise (the generativity vs. stagnation crisis). In older adulthood, resolving the questions of "what it all means" and whether you are satisfied with your life choices fits with having lived the majority of your life span. Because these stages are not as tied to chronological age as they are to experience, the notion of "psychological age" may be a better metric for stages of development (Roberts et al., 2006).

Relationships

One of the most profound developmental tasks is selecting a life partner, an individual who remains with you through time and circumstance. More than 90% of heterosexuals marry at some point in their lives. Satisfaction in marriage is high at first (O'Leary & Smith, 1991) and hits a low point when adolescent children are in the home, rising again once they leave the "empty nest" (White & Edwards, 1990). Many factors influence the quality of marriages, such as loyalty, emotional security, sexual intimacy, respect, and communication (Levenson et al., 1993). Men are happier in marriage than women, and research has pointed out a specific trouble point: Following the birth of children, couples report greater marital stress. Once children enter the family, women feel overextended with work outside the home and unequal responsibilities for childcare (Erel & Burman, 1995). Devoting attention to sharing the workload has the potential to head off problems within marriages.

One clinical psychologist working with couples began bringing them into the laboratory to record them as they argued just as they would at home (Gottman, 1994, 1998). After observing more than 2,000 couples, he reported a very clear finding: Couples that stayed together maintained a ratio of five positive comments for every one negative comment. Imagine smiles, hugs, compliments, and laughs sprinkled with occasional sarcasm and criticism. By managing the tone of the conversations, couples that lasted kept the relationship on a positive track. The best predictor of which couples ended up divorcing was any expression of "contempt:" When one member of the couple reached the point at which he or she had no respect for the other, the damage was more likely to be irreparable.

Divorce is one of the most difficult transitions encountered in life. In the middle 1800s, only 4% of marriages ended in divorce; today, about half of all first marriages in the United States end in divorce (Raley & Bumpass, 2003). Following divorce, there is greater risk of health problems, drinking and drug use, and depression. However, most people make a recovery within 2 years after divorce (Hetherington et al., 1985). The majority of those who divorce go on to remarry, and on average, their experience with marriage is as satisfying (Huyck, 1982). When a spouse dies, both physical and psychological difficulties can follow (Strobe & Strobe, 1983). Because women tend to marry older men and are more likely to live longer, many women experience the loss of a husband in later life. There are perhaps 10 times as many women as men who have lost their spouses. Friends who have also experienced loss are particularly helpful in recovery (Utz et al., 2002).

Ages and Stages of Adulthood

When asked about critical points in their lives, people mention graduation, first jobs, getting married, having children, moving to a new home, health changes, and world events like wars (Ryff, 1989). For certain milestones, people are sensitive to a **social clock**, or norms for ages at which these events occur. People who are out of sync with these expectations experience more stress than those who are "on time" (Neugarten, 1979). Work and career goals also include expectations for age of achievements and limitations on beginning training in some professions. For example, federal air traffic controllers must begin training by age 30 and retire by 59. Because opportunities often depend on chance encounters (Bandura, 1998), the pressure to make choices and move ahead can grow throughout adulthood.

An additional task in this phase of life is identifying a "purpose" in life, or something personally meaningful to pursue (Damon, 2004). For many people, motivation in their career or work fills the majority of their hours, and jobs with better matches to personal goals are viewed as more fulfilling. During middle adulthood, climbing the professional ladder or accomplishing financial goals becomes a central focus in order to to support a family, desired lifestyle, or future retirement. An additional demand arises in middle age: Elderly parents often need care from their children, both in social support and financial contributions (Brody, 1985). Cultures differ in the expectations for caring for elderly parents, with black families expressing higher expectations for support (Lee et al., 1998) and Chinese-American families mandating that children care for elderly parents (Dai & Dimond, 1998).

In later adulthood, people find increasing satisfaction by "giving back," termed **generativity** by Erikson (1959). Contributing to the development of the next generation, making a mark upon the world, and "making a difference" are all motivations cited by adults who feel their own life goals are largely satisfied. In fact, life satisfaction ratings are similar across age ranges, suggesting that around 75 to 80% of people feel satisfied with their lives (Inglehart, 1990) FIGURE 12-29. This is a surprising finding because it provides no evidence for a turbulent "midlife crisis" taking place in the 40s; in fact, rates of divorce, job change, and suicide do not increase in midlife (Wethington, 2000). Another surprise

Social clock Cultural norms for appropriate ages to seek out life events like marriage.

Generativity Erikson's stage of life focusing on contributing to the development of the next generation and "making a difference."

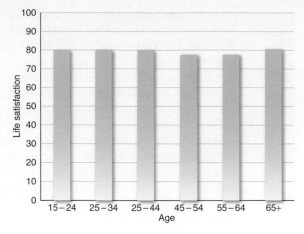

FIGURE 12-29 Levels of life satisfaction show little difference based on age.
Source: Data from Inglehart, R. (1990). Culture shift in advanced industrial society. Princeton, NJ: Princeton University Press.

is that satisfaction does not decrease in later life. Life satisfaction may relate more to the state of your relationships and your experiences at work than to your chronological age.

The psychological effects of aging also include a changing sense of time itself and the value of the present compared to the future (Charles & Carstensen, 2009). Young people are forging new connections to others and looking for new opportunities, while older adults become more selective about how and with whom they spend their time (Lang & Carstensen, 2002). Perhaps with less time remaining, using the present is more important. When not in distress over health or other events, older adults in everyday life enjoy social and emotional functioning that is equal to or better than that of younger adults (Scheibe & Carstensen, 2010). So in many ways, in the later years of life, we take advantage of the expertise we accumulate through living our lives.

CONCEPT LEARNING CHECK 12.4   *Is There a "Right Time" for Everything?*

Answer each question in a few sentences.

1. Explain an evolutionary view of why the end of human life occured at around age 40 in early human history.

2. Describe the kinds of cognitive tasks in which older people have an advantage in performance and those that are more challenging for them.

3. Identify the "social clock" and explain where you personally are on the typical timeline of life events.

12.5 Nature and Nurture

The question of whether nature (biological influences) or nurture (environmental influences) is more important in development has changed to reflect that multiple influences create psychological outcomes.

■ Describe the multiple influences of nature and nurture in patterns of development.

One of the ongoing questions about development is the relative importance of nature (biological influences including genetics, hormones, and evolutionary tendencies) to that of nurture (environmental influences such as family life, schooling, culture, and experiences). What creates the person you grow up to be? Which influences play a greater role in determining the outcomes of development?

Learning theorist John B. Watson claimed that nurture could change the future of any child: "Give me a dozen healthy infants, well-formed, and my own specified world to bring them up in and I will guarantee to take any one at random and train him to become any type of specialist I might select—doctor, lawyer, artist, merchant-chief and, yes, even beggar-man and thief, regardless of his talents, penchants, tendencies, abilities, vocations, and race of his ancestors" (Watson, 1930, p. 82). Watson believed that learning from the environment was the primary determinant in development. And much of the evidence about development points to environmental factors (caregivers, peers, rich environments) as important influences in development.

At the same time, some environmental variables that would seem to be very important in development have been found to have little effect. For example, why are children from the same family so different (Pinker, 2002; Hoffman, 1991)? The shared environment of family life has clear influences on development, yet it appears to have little impact on personality. Studies of adoptive families show that people growing up together, whether related or not, do not resemble each other much in their personalities (Plomin et al., 1998). Does it really not matter whether you are raised by your specific family or by wolves in developing your characteristic ways of thinking, acting, and feeling? Why does sharing our earliest relationships within a family have so little impact on our individual ways of approaching the world? Is every environment "nonshared," so that even growing up in the same family is a very different experience for each sibling?

Nature weighs in on development early: The temperaments of newborns—how emotionally excitable they are, whether they seek or avoid extra stimulation—is heritable (McCrae et al., 2000; Rothbart, 2006). No matter what learning takes place later, that basic response to stimulation remains in place throughout life. The emotional reactivity of newborns relates to their temperament as young adults (Larsen & Diener, 1987). Studies of twins show many similarities influenced by genetics, including intelligence, extraversion, neuroticism, abilities, interests, and even fears (Bouchard et al., 1990). Genetic predispositions affect our likelihood of developing diseases, pursuing behaviors like drinking, and reactions to stress. Increasingly, evidence from behavioral genetics suggests that virtually all individual differences, when reliably measured, are moderately to substantially heritable (Bouchard & McGue, 2003). For much of the history of developmental psychology, the importance of nature was underweighted, and it remains so today.

An example comes from a tragic case study of twin boys born in Canada in 1966 (Colapinto, 2001). After the accidental destruction of one twin's penis, medical experts advised his parents to raise him instead as a girl. This idea was consistent with theories at the time that gender is a socially constructed identity (Cerulo, 1997): "If you treat her as a girl, she will become a girl." Did it work? The psychiatrist following the case reported that the mother said her daughter, by 4 1/2 years of age, was much neater than her brother, and in contrast with him, disliked to be dirty: "She likes for me to wipe her face. She doesn't like to be dirty, and yet my son is quite different. I can't wash his face for anything. . . . She seems to be daintier. Maybe it's because I encourage it" (Money, 1975). The development of different gender identities in the identical twins was reported as a great success (Money, 1975).

However, other researchers later uncovered the truth about the case: "Brenda" never accepted himself as a girl (Diamond & Sigmundson, 1997). When his mother told him the truth at age 14, he immediately changed his name to "David," and assumed his male identity. As an adult, David Reimer commented, "There's . . . there's no way of knowing whether you're a boy or girl 'cause nobody tells you. You don't wake up one morning and say, 'Oh I'm . . . I'm . . . I'm a boy today.' You know! You know! It's . . . it's . . . it's in you. Nobody has to tell you *who* you are" (NOVA, 2001). The traumatic effects of this experiment in gender assignment were followed by a drug overdose by his brother, and David's own suicide. His experience strongly suggests that gender is not simply socially defined but is determined by multiple influences on development.

So what influences determine gender identity? In David Reimer's case, he was likely affected by the presence of normal male hormones during prenatal development. Recall that sexual differentiation of the genitals takes places in the first 2 months of pregnancy. Later, during the second half of pregnancy, sexual differentiation also takes place in brain functions. Both of these periods require the presence of specific hormones in order for male and female development to occur. Since David was a boy at birth, his prenatal experience was inconsistent with being raised as a girl. In fact, genital and brain development occur *independently* of each other during the prenatal period, potentially giving rise to mismatches. Some children, adolescents, and adults experience *transsexuality*, or the perception of their true gender identity as different from their biologically determined

David Reimer was born a normal boy, but after a surgical accident, was raised as a girl from age 2. Though socially identified as a girl, he never accepted it, and assumed his male gender identity when he was told the truth at age 14.

sexual identity (Swaab, 2007). We are born with a biological predisposition that is fixed by genetics and hormones, so that certain sexual and gender behaviors are likely to be expressed (Diamond, 1995). But *which* patterns are expressed also depends upon the societal and cultural gender roles that are imposed upon us and the degrees of tolerance our culture allows (Diamond, 1979). A child also asks herself, "Who am I like, and who am I not like?" An identification with gender in society comes from general observation of roles and expectations and from comparing yourself with your parents and your peers (Diamond, 2000). So nature and nurture can work together, or sometimes at cross-purposes, to influence the development of a child's gender identity.

In addition, nature and nurture can *interact* to create patterns of development, such as individual differences in intellectual ability. These differences appear to be greatly influenced by environment, particularly for lower-socioeconomic-status (SES) families. Children from families without economic and social resources (like access to good schools) tend to score lower on tests of intelligence. Further studies show that biology *does* play a role in intelligence test scores for some children, but only for those raised in high-SES homes. For the low-SES children, genetics does not predict their intelligence test scores, while their disadvantaged homes provide a good predictor of their cognitive ability (Tucker-Drob et al., 2011). How can this be? In the study, 750 pairs of twins were measured on cognitive tests at 10 months and at 2 years old. At age 10 months, genes did not account for any variation in mental ability for any of the children. However, genetic influences emerged over the course of development: At age 2, genes accounted for nearly 50% of the variation in intelligence scores of children raised in high-SES homes. But genes *still* did not explain any differences in mental ability for children raised in low-SES homes; rather, their poor environments predicted their intelligence test outcomes. A gene-by-environment *interaction* occurs: Genes do matter for intelligence, but only for those children whose basic needs are already being supported by their environment.

Poor-socioeconomic homes limit children's opportunities to engage with environments that support cognitive growth. As a result, possible genetic influences are limited in their expression. In particular, SES disadvantages are likely to make it harder to elicit responsive care and stimulation from caregivers. Later in childhood, disadvantage limits opportunities to seek out educational and social experiences that fit with their own (potentially genetically influenced) interests (such as music, educational toys, or preschool programs; Scarr & McCartney, 1983). From this data, it appears that the role of genetics depends on *reciprocal* interactions between the child and his or her environment (Bronfenbrenner & Ceci, 1994; Dickens & Flynn, 2001). Some environments provide fertile ground for biological factors to play out. Like seeds planted in rich soil versus dry sand, the right environment is required to allow biological processes to unfold.

Further, people are not just passively affected by the biological and environmental contributions to their development. For example, children create their own development based on the reactions they elicit from others, and these reactions in turn affect the child's development (Lerner, 1982). For example, a toddler who is impulsive may be socially rejected by his peers, leading to longer-term patterns of aggression toward others (Olson, 1992). Some children are more affected—both for better and for worse—by their experiences growing up (Belsky et al., 2007). And finally, even as children, we choose and, to some extent, create the environments that influence us (Scarr & McCartney, 1983). Biological factors such as sensitivity to stimulation can affect our choice of environments, including the activities and peers we choose (Scarr, 1996). Based on temperamental differences, an "easy" baby may readily learn from social interactions, while a "difficult" baby may shut his eyes to avoid too much stimulation and miss learning social cues. Individuals may actively seek out environments that foster the expression of their genetic tendencies. Alternatively, one may choose environments that inhibit genetic tendencies; for example, while higher testosterone levels in males can produce aggression (Olweus et al., 1980), some men choose to avoid its expression (Lore & Schultz, 1993). Both nature and nurture affect our development, but our choices in life can inhibit, alter, or enhance their effects.

Summary of Multiple Influences on Development

Throughout this chapter, we have seen multiple influences affecting the development of individuals throughout the life span. Biology determines our natures at birth, and we come into the world with temperamental differences that bias our reactions to it. Biology is also a major determinant of behavior during adolescence as hormonal changes in puberty alter our physical, cognitive, and emotional growth. At the same time, the environment causes key differences among us during development: how we bond with our caregivers, who we associate with as peers, and the opportunities and events of later life that help shape us as individuals. And these influences interact, so that certain environments are required for some genetic traits to be displayed, and biological tendencies can be altered through context.

Consider the question of gender differences, with which we began this chapter. Evolutionary theory would argue that we would see the largest gender differences surrounding the behaviors that have to do with reproduction, since the mating strategies for males and females differ. Yet there are few real "gender differences" observed in human sexual behaviors and attitudes. In a meta-analysis, Petersen and Hyde (2010) reviewed 834 studies with more than one million subjects. Most of the gender differences they found were small in size, with the exception of a few, such as masturbation, pornography use, and attitudes toward casual sex. Importantly, in studies of more gender-equal societies, even these differences were small. So differences in behavior tied to biological influences like gender are affected by the context of the social environment. Gender differences in sexuality are not immutable, and are altered by environmental influences. Biology creates gender, but our social environment influences what it means to be a "girl" or a "boy." This can be readily seen by comparing the lives of men and women across cultures; for example, in some countries, whether you are allowed to drive a car, hold a job, or go to school may depend on your gender, but not for biological reasons.

The complexity of development ensures that both nature and nurture contribute to our developing self. We also actively select environments that suit our biological tendencies; we attend or skip parties, we seek or avoid relationships, we study hard or drop out of school. While we are subject to the biological and environmental influences surrounding us, we also drive the changes that take place as we develop. Though we share many experiences with others, each person's development occurs in a context that is unique, following a biological and environmental path that is different from all others.

CONCEPT LEARNING CHECK 12.5 | *Nature or Nurture?*

Explain how nature and nurture each may affect development in this example case.

Adam grew up in Evanston, Illinois, where his father is a professor and his mother is a product researcher. He learned how to program and opened his own profitable web page on college sports. He was accepted to enter Harvard University this fall.

1. Genetics

2. Socioeconomic status

3. Activity preferences and experiences (e.g., enjoying reading)

Visual Overview Stages of Development Across the Lifespan

Each stage of development has characteristic changes in our physical, cognitive, and social well-being.

	Physical	**Cognitive**	**Social**
Adulthood and Aging	**Reproductive Maturity** **End of Reproduction** **Diminished Abilities**	**Declines in Speed and New Learning** **Growth in Knowledge**	**Choosing a Life Partner** **Assessing Contributions**
Adolescence	**Puberty:** **Sexual Maturation** **Growth Spurt** **Neural Growth and Pruning**	**Emotion over Cognition** **Moral Reasoning**	**Identity Formation** **Separation from Parents** **Peer Relationships**
Infancy and Childhood	**Neural Plasticity** **Rapid Growth**	**Piaget's Stage Theory:** **Sensorimotor** **Preoperational** **Concrete Operational** **Formal Operational**	**Touch as Primary** **Attachment Bond** **Secure** **Insecure** **Avoidant**

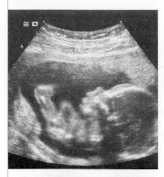

12.1 The Beginnings of Development

- Culture plays an important role in our development across the life span.
- Genetics provides a predisposition for a characteristic, but expressing it may require contributions from the environment.
- Exposure to toxic agents from the environment, called teratogens, is a dangerous problem.

- Newborns are *not* "blank slates;" instead, they are prepared with inborn abilities.
- Biologically based individual differences in temperament are already evident in the newborn, along with reflexes and visual preferences.

12.2 Infancy and Childhood

- Physical growth occurs at a faster rate in the young, with another spurt in adolescence.
- Young children appear to have greater *plasticity* in their neural functions.
- The formation of concepts proceeds through assimilation and accommodation of new information.
- Babies and toddlers learn to grasp and manipulate objects, and to move through the world in the sensorimotor stage.
- Preschool children are focused on what they perceive and are egocentric in believing that others know, think, and feel the same way they do in the preoperational stage.
- Conservation tasks show children in grade school (the concrete operational stage) are no longer overwhelmed by what things look like.
- Piaget's final stage, formal operations, is characterized by reasoning on a logical or hypothetical level.

- New methods of testing such as habituation uncovered surprising abilities in young babies.
- Harlow's studies identified contact comfort, or the need for touch, as a primary drive.
- *Attachment* refers to the deep, emotional bond that an infant develops with its caregiver. Ainsworth's strange situation task showed that most infants showed a *secure attachment* to their mothers.
- Some babies seem to feel they cannot rely upon the caregiver and act this out in the strange situation task by showing insecure or avoidant attachment.
- Differences in parenting style have been identified in how parents establish control over their children.
- Peer relationships can sometimes be marked by bullying, either as an aggressor or as a victim.

12.3 Adolescence and Young Adulthood

- Big changes in development result from *puberty*, or the sexual maturation that occurs as a result of rising hormone levels in preteen years.
- The physical maturation of the brain goes through a similar growth spurt in adolescence and then goes through neural pruning.
- The teenage brain is driven by emotion, and cognitive control takes longer to develop.

- Kohlberg's theory of moral reasoning identifies a progression in justifications for actions from concern about consequences to following laws to individual and universal rights.
- Erik Erikson's theory of psychosocial development identifies a series of stages in life, including establishing your own identity as an adolescent.

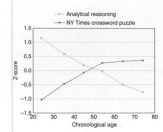

12.4 Adulthood and Aging

- By their mid-20s, humans are finally physically mature, and deterioration begins.
- Reproductive ability also diminishes with age, particularly for females.
- Human life spans now exceed the time frame designed by evolution.
- A small percentage of people experience the loss of brain cells leading to dementia.
- Cognitive declines occur with advanced age, with more trouble assimilating new information, recalling information, and learning new associations.
- Erikson's (1959) final stage involves reconciling with your life choices.

- Across time and age, personality traits are largely consistent from early childhood on and are essentially fixed by age 30, but change still occurs in middle adulthood and old age.
- One of the most profound developmental tasks is selecting a life partner, an individual who remains with you through time and circumstance.
- In later adulthood, people find increasing satisfaction by "giving back," termed *generativity* by Erikson.

12.5 Nature and Nurture

- We are born with a biological predisposition that is fixed by genetics and hormone levels, but societal and cultural roles also influence us.
- Individuals may actively select and create environments that foster or inhibit the expression of their genetic tendencies.

- The complexity of development ensures that both nature and nurture contribute to our sense of self.

492

12.1 The Beginnings of Development

1. A study that follows a person through different ages as he or she develops is called a(n) _____ study.
   A. cross-sectional
   B. longitudinal
   C. cohort
   D. experimental

2. The longest stage of prenatal development is the _____ stage.
   A. zygote
   B. fetus
   C. embryo
   D. newborn

3. In a study of visual preferences, researchers presented newborns with head-shaped forms that depicted a properly featured face, a scrambled face, or a blank, featureless face. The infants' visual tracking behavior indicated:
   A. a preference for the scrambled face.
   B. a preference for the properly featured face.
   C. no preferences among the three stimuli.
   D. a preference for the blank, featureless face.

12.2 Infancy and Childhood

4. After a child's pet kitten runs away, his parents buy him a puppy. The child finds out that puppies are different from kittens and then acts differently with the puppy. This best illustrates Piaget's concept of:
   A. assimilation.
   B. accommodation.
   C. egocentrism.
   D. conservation.

5. A child who is reading a book upstairs calls to his mother who is downstairs, "Mommy, what is this a picture of?" This illustrates that the child is:
   A. egocentric.
   B. concrete operational.
   C. experiencing separation anxiety.
   D. babbling.

6. A child returns from Halloween trick-or-treating and promptly dumps a bag of candy in a pile on the kitchen table. She then spreads it out at and it looks like more, but she knows it is the same amount of candy. You can conclude she:
   A. is in the preoperational stage of development.
   B. is no longer egocentric in her thinking.
   C. has a good understanding of conservation of mass.
   D. is at least 7 years old.

7. In a classic series of experiments on attachment by Harlow, newborn monkeys were placed in cages that contained "surrogate mothers." How did the monkeys react to these "moms"?
   A. They developed as normally as if they were with their real mothers.
   B. They became attached to the one that provided milk.
   C. They became attached to the one that was soft and cuddly.
   D. They became attached to both kinds of "mothers."

8. In the context of parent–child relationships, *attachment* refers to:
   A. a deep emotional bond between infant and primary caretaker.
   B. the fondness that a child sometimes has for inanimate objects like "blankies."
   C. clinging behavior that is characteristic of insecure relationships.
   D. an instinctive tendency for babies to follow their mothers.

9. How do children with secure attachment behave in the strange situation procedure when their mother returns after leaving them earlier?
   A. They are indifferent.
   B. They actively ignore her.
   C. They react with anger.
   D. They appear delighted.

12.3 Adolescence and Young Adulthood

10. According to Kohlberg, postconventional moral thought:
    A. violates a person's conscience.
    B. reflects norms set by sources of authority.
    C. is based on satisfying self-interests.
    D. is based on abstract principles like justice.

11. According to Erikson, the central task in adolescence is resolving the _____ crisis.
    A. intimacy
    B. identity
    C. autonomy
    D. trust

12. Making "riskier" decisions during adolescence may be correlated with:
    A. lack of peer contact.
    B. differential parenting.
    C. slower frontal lobe development.
    D. delays in reaching puberty.

12.4 Adulthood and Aging

13. The most likely cause of changes in personality with increased age is:
   A. life experiences.
   B. further maturation.
   C. dementia.
   D. changes in physical abilities.

14. Older adults tend to have declines in cognitive processes but show little decline in:
   A. crystalized intelligence.
   B. memory recall.
   C. fluid intelligence.
   D. speed of processing.

12.5 Nature and Nurture

16. The case study of identical twin boys, one of whom suffered the loss of his penis and was raised as a girl, suggests that in this case, the medical specialist underweighted the importance of _____ to gender identity.
   A. biology
   B. socialization
   C. both nature and nurture
   D. attachment

15. People's ratings of satisfaction with their lives are:
   A. higher in adolescence.
   B. higher in older adults.
   C. lower in adolescence.
   D. about the same across the life span.

CHAPTER DISCUSSION QUESTIONS

1. Consider what you have learned about brain development across the life span. What do the stages in brain development suggest about the ability of the person to recuperate from damage (physical injury, surgery, or tumors) to the brain?

2. Consider the parenting style you experienced from your parents or caregivers. Would you identify it as authoritative, authoritarian, or permissive? What style would you choose to use should you become a parent?

3. Section 12.2 reviews the major areas of development in infancy and childhood (physical, cognitive, and social). Evaluate each of these areas of development in terms of

their long-term impact on an adult's life. Is there one area that you consider to be most important? Least? Explain.

4. Adolescence is widely considered to be a difficult period of human development. Consider the areas of development and judge the contribution of each to the difficulty of adolescent development. Explain your reasoning for each (physical, cognitive, and social).

5. After reviewing the areas of development (physical, cognitive, and social) as they relate to adulthood and aging, analyze each area for choices a person can make that will create more enjoyable adult lives. Explain your reasoning.

CHAPTER PROJECTS

1. What does a "life well lived" mean to you? Think about a possible life path for yourself. What type of career might you pursue that will give you a sense of mastery and purpose, as well as meeting your financial needs? What types of relationships will be a priority to you, and who will you live with? How will you impact the world around you and contribute to the development of others?

2. Demonstrate the interdependence of the areas of development (physical, cognitive, and social) by imagining a person's behavior with one area missing. Create three scenarios, each with a different area of development lacking. You may focus on a specific age or imagine how a later age would be affected by the lack of an area during an earlier age (e.g., how a lack of cognitive development during infancy would affect the behavior of an adolescent).

CHAPTER KEY TERMS

Accommodation	**Conservation**	**Egocentrism**
Age of viability	**Contact comfort**	**Embryo**
Assimilation	**Critical period**	**Fetal alcohol syndrome**
Attachment	**Cyberbullying**	**Fetus**
Authoritative parenting style	**Dementia**	**Formal operational stage**
Concrete operational stage	**Differentiation**	**Gender roles**

Generativity
Grandmother hypothesis
Identity formation
Maturation
Menarche
Menopause
Motherese
Neural pruning
Norm
Object permanence

Plasticity
Prenatal stage
Preoperational stage
Primary sexual characteristics
Resilience
Secondary sexual characteristics
Sensorimotor stage
Social clock
Spermarche
Stranger anxiety

Strange situation procedure
Temperament
Teratogens
Theory of mind
Theory of psychosocial development
Zone of proximal development
Zygote

ANSWERS TO CONCEPT LEARNING CHECK

12.1 Before and After Birth

1. Fetus

2. Longitudinal

3. Teratogens

4. Feed

5. Faces

12.2 Stages of Cognitive Development

1. B. Helen is showing egocentric behavior by assuming her father can see the page in the same direction as she can. That identifies the preoperational stage.

2. A. The sensorimotor stage involves learning to control movements, and repeating is great practice.

3. B. Jordana shows she does not yet have conservation of mass; therefore, she is in the preoperational stage.

4. D. Jorges shows systematic reasoning in his careful approach to the problem, suggesting formal operations

12.3 Defining Adolescence

1. *Menarche* is a girl's first menstrual period, and *spermarche* is a boy's first production of mature sperm cells.

2. *Neural pruning* refers to the stage of brain development in adolescence when the number of connections between neurons is cut down to preserve only those most frequently used.

3. *Conventional morality* refers to justifications of moral decisions based on social roles or laws.

4. The *social intuitionist* refers to making moral judgments using emotion rather than reasoning.

5. *Identity crisis* refers to the stage of developing your own sense of personal identity.

12.4 Is There a "Right Time" for Everything?

1. Once humans reach the end of their reproductive life span (at age 40 for females), they may help with raising grandchildren but would also compete for limited resources within the family group.

2. Any task involving a knowledge base of expertise would show those of advanced age as highly competent, while tasks involving speedy responses or recall from memory would show poorer performance.

3. The social clock provides a timeline of typical ages when life events like marriage are expected to take place. Your place on this timeline is individual, and you may alter it as you wish, with biological constraints like reproduction in mind.

12.5 Nature or Nurture?

1. Genetics may play a role in Adam's intelligence. Both of his parents have professions requiring intelligence, which is partly heritable.

2. Adam grew up in an affluent town where his parents were both employed in high-paying professions. They likely provided opportunities for learning in the home which helped with his school performance.

3. Adam pursued his interests in programming to create a successful business, contributing to his preparation for college.

12.1 The Beginnings of Development

1. B. Rationale: Following the same person over time allows comparison at different life stages.

2. B. Rationale: This stage lasts from 9 weeks until birth at 37 weeks.

3. B. Rationale: Even newborns prefer looking at faces.

12.2 Infancy and Childhood

4. B. Rationale: The boy had to change his concepts in memory to fit in the new "dog" information.

5. A. Rationale: The child thinks his mother can see the same things he is seeing.

6. C. Rationale: She recognizes that appearances may change, but the amount does not.

7. C. Rationale: Harlow named this *contact comfort*.

8. A. Rationale: Attachment is defined as the first bond in life.

9. D. Rationale: Securely bonded children are thrilled to have Mom back again.

12.3 Adolescence and Young Adulthood

10. D. Rationale: This stage goes beyond rules or law.

11. B. Rationale: Adolescents are forming their personalities in this crisis.

12. C. Rationale: The emotional areas of the brain develop faster than the control areas in the frontal lobe.

12.4 Adulthood and Aging

13. A. Rationale: People change at different points and in different ways, likely due to experience.

14. A. Rationale: Using past knowledge allows older adults to continue to function well.

15. D. Rationale: People rate themselves equally satisfied in all age groups.

12.5 Nature and Nurture

16. A. Rationale: Prenatal hormones were normal in this case, and the resulting gender identity was male.

REFERENCES

Ainsworth, M. D. S., & Bell, S. M. (1970). Attachment, exploration, and separation: Illustrated by the behavior of one-year-olds in a strange situation. *Child Development, 41*(1), 49–67.

Ainsworth, M. D. S., Blehar, M., Waters, E., & Wall, S. (1978). *Patterns of attachment: Psychological studies of the strange situation.* Hillsdale, NJ: Erlbaum.

Ainsworth, M. S. (1979). Infant–mother attachment. *American Psychologist, 34*(10), 932–937.

Allen, J. P., McElhaney, K. B., Land, D. J., Kuperminc, G. P., Moore, C. W., O'Beirne-Kelly, H., & Liebman Kilmer, S. (2003). A secure base in adolescence: Markers of attachment security in the mother–adolescent relationship. *Child Development, 74*(1), 292–307.

Amato, P. R. (2000). The consequences of divorce for adults and children. *Journal of Marriage and Family, 62*(4), 1269–1287.

Amato, P. R. (2001). Children of divorce in the 1990s: An update of the Amato and Keith (1991) meta-analysis. *Journal of Family Psychology, 15*(3), 355–370.

Amato, P. R, & Keith, B. (1991a). Parental divorce and well-being. *Journal of Marriage and the Family, 53*, 43–58.

Amato, P. R, & Keith, B. (1991b). Parental divorce and the well-being of children: A meta-analysis. *Psychological Bulletin, 110*(1), 26–46.

Anderson, S. E., Dallal, G. E., Must, A. (2003). Relative weight and race influence average age at menarche: Results from two nationally representative surveys of US girls studied 25 years apart. *Pediatrics, 111*(4 Pt 1), 844–850.

Anisfeld, E. (1982). The onset of social smiling in preterm and full-term infants from two ethnic backgrounds. *Infant Behavior and Development, 5*(2–4), 387–395.

Anisfeld, E., Casper, V., Nozyce, M., & Cunningham N. (1990). Does infant carrying promote attachment? An experimental study of the effects of increased physical contact on the development of attachment. *Child Development, 61*(5), 1617–1627.

Arnett, J. J. (1999). Adolescent storm and stress, reconsidered. *American Psychologist, 54*(5), 317–326.

Arnett, J. J. (2006). Emerging adulthood: Understanding the new way of coming of age. In J. J. Arnett & J. L. Tanner (Eds.), *Emerging adults in America: Coming of age in the 21st century* (pp. 3–19). Washington, DC: American Psychological Association.

Asato, M. R., Terwilliger, R., Woo, J., & Luna, B. (2010). White matter development in adolescence: A DTI study. *Cerebral Cortex, 20*(9), 2122–2131.

Baillargeon, R. (1994). How do infants learn about the physical world? *Current Directions in Psychological Science, 5*, 133–140

Baillargeon, R. (2008). Innate ideas revisited: For a principle of persistence in infants' physical reasoning. *Perspectives on Psychological Science, 3*(1), 2–13.

Baillargeon, R., Spelke, E. S., & Wasserman, S. (1985). Object permanence in five-month-old infants. *Cognition, 20*(3), 191–208.

Baltes, P. B., & Baltes, M. M. (1990). Selective optimization with compensation. In P. B. Baltes & M. M. Baltes (Eds.), *Successful aging: Perspectives from the behavioral sciences* (pp. 1–34). New York: Cambridge University Press.

Baltes, P. B., & Lindenberger, U. (1997). Emergence of a powerful connection between sensory and cognitive functions across the adult life span: A new window to the study of cognitive aging? *Psychology and Aging, 12*(1), 12–21.

Bandura, A. (1998). Exploration of fortuitous determinant of life paths. *Psychological Inquiry, 9*(2), 95–115.

Bank, L., Patterson, G. R., & Reid, J. B. (1996). Negative sibling interaction patterns as predictors of later adjustment problems in adolescent and young adult males. In G. H. Brody (Ed.), *Sibling relationships: Their causes and consequences* (pp. 197–229). Norwood, NJ: Ablex.

Barker, E. D., Jaffee, S. R., Uher, R., & Maughan, B. (2011). The contribution of prenatal and postnatal maternal anxiety and depression to child maladjustment. *Depression and Anxiety, 28*(8), 696–702.

Basu, K., & Tzannatos, Z. (2003). The global child labor problem: What do we know and what can we do? *World Bank Economic Review, 17*(2). 147–173.

Baumrind, D. (1996). The discipline controversy revisited. *Family Relations, 45*(4), 405–414.

Bee, H. L. (1987). *The journey of adulthood.* New York: Macmillan.

Bell, S. M., & Ainsworth, M. D. S. (1972). Infant crying and maternal responsiveness. *Child Development, 43*(4), 1171–1190.

Belsky, J., Bakermans-Kranenburg, M. J., & van Ijzendoorn, M. H. (2007). For better and for worse: Differential susceptibility to environmental influences. *Current Directions in Psychological Science, 16*, 300–304.

Bengston, V. L., Cuellar, J. B., & Ragan, P. K. (1977). Stratum contrasts and similarities in attitudes toward death. *Journal of Gerontology, 32*(1), 76–88.

Berry, D. S., & McArthur, L. Z. (1985). Some components and consequences of a babyface. *Journal of Personality and Social Psychology, 48*(2), 312–323.

Blakemore, S.-J. (2008). The social brain in adolescence. *Nature Reviews Neuroscience, 9*, 267–277.

Bornstein, M. H. (1989). Information processing (habituation) in infancy and stability in cognitive development. *Human Development, 32*, 129–136.

Bouchard, T. J., Lykken, D. T., McGue, M., Segal, N. L., & Tellegen, A. (1990). Sources of human psychological differences: The Minnesota Study of Twins Reared Apart. *Science, 250*(4978), 223–228.

Bouchard, T. J. Jr., & McGue, M. (2003). Genetic and environmental influences on human psychological differences. *Journal of Neurobiology, Special Issue: Special Issue on Genes and Behavior,* 4–45.

Bowlby, J. (1969). *Attachment and loss: Vol. I. Attachment.* New York: Basic Books.

Bowlby, J. (1973). *Attachment and loss: Vol. 2. Separation: Anxiety and anger.* New York: Basic Books.

Bowlby, J. (1980). *Attachment and loss: Vol. 3. Loss.* New York: Basic Books.

Brener N. D., Kann, L., McManus, T., Kinchen, S. A., Sundberg, E. C., & Ross, J. G. (2002). Reliability of the 1999 Youth Risk Behavior Survey Questionnaire. *Journal of Adolescent Health, 31*(4), 336–342.

Britten, R. J. (2002). Divergence between samples of chimpanzee and human DNA sequences is 5%, counting intels. *Proceedings of the National Academy of Sciences, 99*, 13633–13635.

Brody, E. M. (1985). Parent care as a normative family stress. *The Gerontologist, 25*(1), 19–29.

Brody, G. H. (2004). Siblings' direct and indirect contributions to child development. *Current Directions in Psychological Science, 13*(3), 124–126.

Brody, G. H., Ge, X., Kim, S. Y., Murry, V. M., Simons, R. L., Gibbons, F. X., Gerrard, M., & Conger, R. (2003). Neighborhood disadvantage moderates associations of parenting and older sibling problem attitudes and behavior with conduct disorders in African American children. *Journal of Consulting and Clinical Psychology, 71*, 211–222.

Bronfenbrenner, U. (1986). Ecology of the family as a context for human development: Research perspectives. *Developmental Psychology, 22*(6), 723–742.

Bronfenbrenner, U., & Ceci, S. J. (1994). Nature-nurture reconceptualized in developmental perspective: A bioecological model. *Psychological Review, 101*(4), 568–586.

Brosnan, M. J. (2008). Digit ratio as an indicator of numeracy relative to literacy in 7-year-old British schoolchildren. *British Journal of Psychology, 99*(1), 75–85.

Bruce V. (1990). Perceiving and recognizing faces. *Mind & Language, 5*(4), 342–364.

Burchinal, M., Lee, M., & Ramey, C. (1989). Type of day-care and preschool intellectual development in disadvantaged children. *Child Development, 60*(1), 128–137.

Burchinal, M., Vandergrift, N., Pianta, R., & Mashburn, A., (2009). Threshold analysis of association between child care quality and child outcomes for low-income children in pre-kindergarten programs. *Early Childhood Research Quarterly, 25*, 166–176.

Burd, L. (2004). Fetal alcohol syndrome. *American Journal of Medical Genetics, 127*, 1–2.

Burger, J. M., & Burns, L. (1988). The illusion of unique invulnerability and the use of effective contraception. *Personality and Social Psychology Bulletin, 14*(2), 264–270.

Carey, W. B., & McDevitt, S. C. (1978). Revision of the Infant Temperament Questionnaire. *Pediatrics, 61*, 735–739.

Casey, B. J., Jones, R. M., & Hare, T. A. (2008). *The adolescent brain. Annals of the New York Academy of Sciences, 1124 The Year in Cognitive Neuroscience,* 111–126.

Cattell, R. B. (1963). Theory of crystalized and fluid intelligence: A critical experiment. *Journal of Educational Psychology, 54,* 1–22.

CBS News. (2011). Celebrity plastic surgery disasters? http://www.cbsnews.com/2300-204_162-10006001-7.html

Cerulo, K. A. (1997). Identity construction: New issues, new directions. *Annual Review of Sociology, 23,* 385–409.

Chapman, S. B., & McKinnon, L. (2000). Discussion of developmental plasticity: Factors affecting cognitive outcome after pediatric traumatic brain injury. *Journal of Communication Disorders, 33*(4), 333–344.

Charles, S. T., & Carstensen, L. L. (2009). Social and emotional aging. *Annual Review of Psychology, 6,* 383–409.

Colapinto, J. (2001). *As nature made him: The boy who was raised as a girl.* New York: Harper Perennial. Revised in 2006.

Colby, A., Kohlberg, L., Gibbs, J., Lieberman, M., Fischer K., & Saltzstein, H. D. (1983). A longitudinal study of moral judgment. *Monographs of the Society for Research in Child Development, 48*(1/2), 1–124.

Cooper, R. R. (2002). Botox parties. *New York Times,* December 15. Retrieved from http://www.nytimes.com/2002/12/15/magazine/the-year-in-ideas-botox-parties.html?scp=1&sq=2002+botox+parties&st=nyt&pagewanted=print

Crews, F., He, J., & Hodge, C. (2007). Adolescent cortical development: A critical period of vulnerability for addiction. *Pharmacology, Biochemistry, and Behavior, 86*(2), 189–199.

Curtiss, S. (1977). *Genie: A linguistic study of a modern-day "wild child."* New York: Academic Press.

Dai, Y. T., & Dimond, M. F. (1998). Filial piety. A cross-cultural comparison and its implications for the well-being of older parents. *Journal of Gerontological Nursing, 24*(3),13–18.

Damon, W. (2004). What is positive youth development? *Annals of the American Academy of Political and Social Science, 591*(1), 13–24.

Darling, C. A., Davidson, J. K., & Passarello, L. C. (1992). The mystique of first intercourse among college youth: The role of partners, contraceptive practices, and psychological reactions. *Journal of Youth and Adolescence, 21*(1), 97–117.

Davila, J., & Cobb, R. W. (2003). Predicting change in self-reported and interviewer-assessed adult attachment: Tests of the individual difference and life stress models of attachment change. *Personality and Social Psychology Bulletin, 29*(7), 859–870.

Davis, D. L., Gottlieb, M. B., & Stampnitzky, J. R. (1998). Reduced ratio of male to female births in several industrial countries: A sentinel health indicator? *Journal of the American Medical Association, 279*(13), 1018–1023.

Dawson, G., Rogers, S., Munson, J., Smith, M., Winter, J., Greenson, J., Donaldson, A., Varley, J. (2010). Randomized, controlled trial of an intervention for toddlers with autism: The Early Start Denver model. *Pediatrics, 125*(1), e17–e23.

DeCasper, A. J., Lecanuet, J.-P., Busnel, M.-C., Granier-Deferre, C., & Maugeais, R. (1994). Fetal reactions to recurrent maternal speech. *Infant Behavior and Development, 17*(2), 159–164.

De Cock, K. M., Fowler, M. G., Mercier, E., de Vincenzi, I., Saba, J., Hoff, E., Alnwick, D. J., Rogers, M., & Shaffer, N. (2000). Prevention of mother-to-child HIV transmission in resource-poor countries: Translating research into policy and practice. *Journal of the American Medical Association, 283*(9), 1175–1182.

Dehue, F., Bolman, C., & Völlink, T. (2008). Cyberbullying: Youngsters' experiences and parental perception. *CyberPsychology & Behavior, 11*(2), 217–223.

Depp, C., Vahia, I. V., & Jeste, D. (2010). Successful aging: Focus on cognitive and emotional health. *Annual Review of Clinical Psychology, 6,* 527–550.

Diamond, M. (1979). Sexual identity and sex roles. In V. Bullough (Ed.), *The frontiers of sex research* (pp. 33–56). Buffalo, NY: Prometheus.

Diamond, M. (1995). Biological aspects of sexual orientation and identity. In L. Diamant & R. McAnulty (Eds.), *The psychology of sexual orientation, behavior and identity: A handbook* (pp. 45–80). Westport, CT: Greenwood Press.

Diamond, M. (2000). Sex and gender: Same or different? *Feminism Psychology, 10*(1), 46–54.

Diamond, M., & Sigmundson, K. (1997). Sex reassignment at birth: Long-term review and clinical implications. *Archives of Pediatrics & Adolescent Medicine, 151*(3), 298–304.

Dickens, W. T., & Flynn, J. R. (2001). Heritability estimates versus large environmental effects: The IQ paradox resolved. *Psychological Review, 108*(2), 346–369.

Edwards, C. P. (1993). Behavioral sex differences in children of diverse cultures: The case of nurturance to infants. In M. E. Pereira & L. A. Fairbanks (Eds.), *Juvenile primates: Life history, development, and behavior* (pp. 327–338). New York/Oxford: Oxford University Press.

Erel, O., & Burman, B. (1995). Interrelatedness of marital relations and parent–child relations: A meta-analytic review. *Psychological Bulletin, 118*(1), 108–132.

Erickson, M. E, Sroufe, L. A., & Egeland, B. (1985). The relationship between quality of attachment and behavior problems in preschool in a high-risk sample. *Monographs of the Society for Research in Child Development, 50*(1 & 2), 147–166.

Erikson, E. H. (1959). *Identity and the life cycle.* New York: International Universities Press.

Erikson, E. H. (1968). *Identity, youth and crisis.* New York: Norton.

Ernst, M., & Mueller, S. C. (2008). The adolescent brain: Insights from functional neuroimaging research. *Developmental Neurobiology, 68*(6), 729–743.

Eyler, L. T., Serzai, A., Kaup, A. R., & Jeste, D. V. (2011). A review of functional brain imaging correlates of successful cognitive aging. *Biological Psychiatry, 70*(2), 115–122.

Fagot, B. I., Hagan, R., Leinbach M. D., & Kronsberg, S. (1985). Differential reactions to assertive and communicative acts of toddler boys and girls. *Child Development, 56*(6), 1499–1505.

Fantz, R. L. (1961). The origin of form perception. *Scientific American, 204*(5), 66–72.

Feldman, R., & Eidelman, A. (1998). Intervention programs for premature infants: How and do they affect development? *Clinics in Perinatology, 25*(3), 613–629.

Feldman, R., Weller, A., Sirota, L., & Eidelman, A. (2003). Testing a family intervention hypothesis: The contribution of mother–infant skin-to-skin contact (kangaroo care) to family interaction, proximity, and touch. *Journal of Family Psychology, 17*(1), 94–107.

Field, T. (1984). Peer separation of children attending new schools. *Developmental Psychology, 20,* 786–792.

Field, T. (1996). Attachment and separation in young children. *Annual Review of Psychology, 47,* 541–561.

Flavell, J. H., Shipstead, S. G., & Croft, K. (1978). Young children's knowledge about visual perception: Hiding objects from others. *Child Development, 49*(4), 1208–1211.

Fraley, C., & Roberts, B. W. (2005). Patterns of continuity: A dynamic model for conceptualizing the stability of individual differences in psychological constructs across the life course. *Psychological Review, 112,* 60–74.

Fratiglioni, L., Wang, H.-X., et al. (2004). Brain reserve hypothesis in dementia. *Journal of Alzheimer's Disease, 12*(1), 11–22.

Furman, W., & Shaffer, L. A. (1999). A story of adolescence: The emergence of other-sex relationships. *Journal of Youth and Adolescence, 28*(4), 513–522.

Gardner, H. (1981). *The quest for mind.* Chicago: University of Chicago Press.

Gavin, L. A., & Furman, W. (1989). Age differences in adolescents' perceptions of their peer groups. *Developmental Psychology, 25*(5), 827–834.

Ge, X., Natsuaki, M. N., Neiderhiser, J. M., & Reiss, D. (2007). Genetic and environmental influences on pubertal timing: Results from two national sibling studies. *Journal of Research on Adolescence, 17*(4), 767–788.

Gettler, L. T., McDade, T. W., Feranil, A. B., & Kuzawa, C. W. (2011). Longitudinal evidence that fatherhood decreases testosterone in human males. *Proceedings of the National Academy of Sciences,* published ahead of print September 12, 2011, doi:10.1073/pnas.1105403108

Gilger, J. W., Geary, D. C., & Eisele, L. M. (1991). Reliability and validity of retrospective self-reports of the age of pubertal onset using twin, sibling, and college student data. *Adolescence, 26,* 41–53.

Gilligan, C. (1982). *In a different voice: Psychological theory and women's development.* Cambridge, MA: Harvard University Press.

Giltay, E. J., Geleijnse, J. M., Zitman, F. G., Hoekstra, T., & Schouten, E. G. (2004). Dispositional optimism and all-cause and cardiovascular mortality in a prospective cohort of elderly Dutch men and women. *Archives of General Psychiatry, 61,* 1126–1135.

Goldberg, W. A., Prause, J., Lucas-Thompson, R., & Himsel, A. (2008). Maternal employment and children's achievement in context: A meta-analysis of four decades of research. *Psychological Bulletin, 134*(1), 77–108.

Gopnik, A., & Astington, J. W. (1988). Children's understanding of representational change and its relation to the understanding of false belief and the appearance–reality distinction. *Child Development, 59*(1), 26–37.

Gottman, J. M. (1994). *What predicts divorce? The relationship between marital processes and martial outcomes.* Hillsdale, NJ: Lawrence Erlbaum.

Gottman, J. M. (1998). Psychology and the study of marital processes. *Annual Review of Psychology, 49,* 169–197.

Greene, J. D., Sommerville, R. B., Nystrom, L. E., Darley, J. M., & Cohen, J. D. (2001). An fMRI investigation of emotional engagement in moral judgment. *Science, 293*(5537), 2105–2108.

Greene, J. & Haidt, J. (2002). How (and where) does moral judgment work? *Trends in Cognitive Sciences, 6*(12), 517–523.

Greenfield, P. M., Keller, H., Fuligni, A., & Maynard, A. (2003). Cultural pathways through universal development. *Annual Review of Psychology, 54,* 461–490.

Gruenewald, T. L., Karlamanglia, A. S., Greendale, G. A., Singer, B. H., & Seeman, T. E. (2007). Feelings of usefulness to others, disability, and mortality in older adults: The MacArthur Study of Successful Aging. *Journal of Gerontology B, 62*(1), P28–P37.

Guyer, A. E., Monk, C. S., McClure-Tone, E. B., Nelson, E. E., Roberson-Nay, R., Adler, A. D., Fromm, S. J., Leibenluft, E., Pine, D. S., & Ernst, M. (2008). A developmental examination of amygdala response to facial expressions. *Journal of Cognitive Neuroscience, 20*(9), 1565–1582.

Haidt, J. (2001). The emotional dog and its rational tail: A social intuitionist approach to moral judgment. *Psychological Review, 108*(4), 814–834.

Haidt, J. (2008). Morality. *Perspectives on Psychological Science, 3*(1), 65–72.

Harlow, H. F. (1958). The nature of love. *American Psychologist, 13,* 673–685.

Hawkes, K., O'Connell, J. F., Blurton Jones, N. G., Alvarez, H., & Charnov, E. L. (1998). Grandmothering, menopause and the evolution of human life histories. *Proceedings of the National Academy of Sciences USA, 95,* 1336–1339.

Hazan, C., & Shaver, P. (1987). Romantic love conceptualized as an attachment process. *Journal of Personality and Social Psychology, 52*(3), 511–524.

Hedden, T., & Gabrieli, J. D. E. (2004). Insights into the ageing mind: A view from cognitive neuroscience. *Nature Reviews Neuroscience, 5,* 87–96.

Helson, R., Jones, C., & Kwan, V. S. (2002). Personality change over 40 years of adulthood: Hierarchical linear modeling analyses of two longitudinal samples. *Journal of Personality and Social Psychology, 83*(3), 752–766.

Henry, J. D., MacLeod, M. S., Phillips, L. H., & Crawford, J. R. (2004). A meta-analytic review of prospective memory and aging. *Psychology and Aging, 19*(1), 27–39.

Hetherington, E. M. (1999). Should we stay together for the sake of the children? In E. M. Hetherington (Ed.), *Coping with divorce, single parenting, and remarriage: A risk and resiliency perspective* (pp. 93–116). Mahwah, NJ: Erlbaum.

Hetherington, E. M., Cox, M., & Cox, R. (1985). Long-term effects of divorce and remarriage on the adjustment of children. *Journal of the American Academy of Child Psychiatry, 24,* 518–530.

Hirsch, M., Lunenfeld, B., Modan, M., Ovadia, J., & Shemesh, J. (1985). Spermarche: The age of onset of sperm emission. *Journal of Adolescent Health Care, 6*(1), 35–39.

Hoffman, L. W. (1991). The influence of the family environment on personality: Accounting for sibling differences. *Psychological Bulletin, 110*(2), 187–203.

Huyck, M. H. (1982). From gregariousness to intimacy: Marriage and friendship over the adult years. In T. M. Field, A. Huston, H. C. Quay, L. Troll, & G. E. Finlay (Eds.), *Review of human development* (pp. 471–484). New York: Wiley.

Hwang, K., Velanova, K., & Luna, B. (2010). Strengthening of top-down frontal cognitive control networks underlying the development of inhibitory control: A functional magnetic resonance imaging effective connectivity study. *Journal of Neuroscience, 30*(46), 15535–15545.

Hyde, M. (1976). *The Thrales of Streatham Park.* Cambridge, MA: Harvard University Press.

Inglehart, R. (1990). *Culture shift in advanced industrial society.* Princeton, NJ: Princeton University Press.

Jaccard, J., Blanton, H., & Dodge, T. (2005). Peer influences on risk behavior: An analysis of the effects of a close friend. *Developmental Psychology, 41*(1), 135–147.

James, W. H. (2000). Reproductive physiology: Why are boys more likely to be preterm than girls? Plus other related conundrums in human reproduction: Opinion. *Human Reproduction, 15*(10), 2108–2122.

Jenkins, J. (1992). Sibling relationships in disharmonious homes: Potential difficulties and protective effects. In F. Boer & J. Dunn (Eds.), *Children's sibling relationships: Developmental and clinical issues* (pp. 125–138). Hillsdale, NJ: Erlbaum.

Johnson, A., Moher, T., Ohlsson, S., & Gillingham, M. (1999). The round earth project—collaborative VR for conceptual learning. *IEEE Computer Graphics, 19*(6), 60–69.

Johnson, D. (2004). Will baby crawl? National Science Foundation Discoveries, July 21. http://www.nsf.gov/discoveries/disc_summ.jsp?cntn_id=103153&org=NSF

Johnson, M. H., Dziurawiec, S., Ellis, H. D., & Morton, J. (1991). Newborns' preferential tracking of faces and its subsequent decline. *Cognition, 40,* 1–19.

Johnston, J. R., Kline, M., & Tschann, J. M. (1989). Ongoing postdivorce conflict: Effects on children of joint custody and frequent access. *American Journal of Orthopsychiatry, 39,* 576–592.

Jung, M.-J., & Fouts, H. N. (2011). Multiple caregivers' touch interactions with young children among the Bofi foragers in Central Africa. *International Journal of Psychology, 46*(1), 24–32.

Kagan, J. (1976). Emergent themes in human development. *American Scientist, 64,* 186–196.

Kagan, J., & Snidman, N. C. (2004). *The long shadow of temperament.* Cambridge, MA: Belknap Press.

Kahlenberg, S. M., & Wrangham, R. W. (2010). Sex differences in chimpanzees' use of sticks as play objects resemble those of children. *Current Biology, 20*(24), R1067–R1068.

Kail, R. (1991). Developmental changes in speed of processing during childhood and adolescence. *Psychological Bulletin, 109,* 490–501.

Keating, D. (2004). Cognitive and brain development. In R. Lerner & I. Steinberg (Eds.), *Handbook of adolescent psychology* (2nd ed., pp. 45–84). New York: Wiley.

Keller, W. D., Hildebrandt, K. A., & Richards, M. E. (1985). Effects of extended father–infant contact during the newborn period. *Infant Behavior & Development, 8*(3), 337–350.

Kelly, J. B. (2000). Children's adjustment in conflicted marriage and divorce: A decade review of research. *Journal of the American Academy of Child & Adolescent Psychiatry, 39*(8), 963–973.

Kelly, J. B., & Emery, R. E. (2003). Children's adjustment following divorce: Risk and resilience perspectives. *Family Relations, 52*(4), 352–362.

Keller, W. D., Hildebrandt, K. A., & Richards, M. E. (1985). Effects of extended father–infant contact during the newborn period. *Infant Behavior & Development, 8*(3), 337–350.

Kellman, P. J., & Spelke, E. S. (1983). Perception of partly occluded objects in infancy. *Cognitive Psychology, 15*(4), 483–524.

Kiernan, K. E., & Hobcraft, J. (1997). Parental divorce during childhood: Age at first intercourse, partnership and parenthood. *Population Studies, 51*(1), 41–55.

Kim-Cohen, J., Moffitt, T. E., Caspi, A., & Taylor, A. (2004). Genetic and environmental processes in young children's resilience and vulnerability to socioeconomic deprivation. *Child Development, 75*(3), 651–668.

Kinsella, K., & He, W. (2009). An aging world: 2008 (International Population Reports). Washington, DC, National Institute on Aging, Census Bureau. Retrieved from http://www.census.gov/prod/2009pubs/p95-09-1.pdf, 06.07.2010.

Kligman, A. M., & Graham, J. A. (1986). The psychology of appearance in the elderly. *Dermatologic Clinics, 4*(3), 501–507.

Kohlberg, L. (1969). Stage and sequence: The cognitive developmental approach to socialization. In D. A. Goslin (Ed.), *Handbook of socialization theory and research*. Chicago: Rand McNally.

Kohlberg, L. (1981). *Essays on moral development*. San Francisco: Harper & Row.

Kohlberg, L. (1984). *The psychology of moral development: The nature and validity of moral stages*. San Francisco: Harper & Row.

Kübler-Ross, E. (1969). *On death and dying*. New York: Scribner. Reprinted 1997.

Lamb, M. E., (1977). Father–infant and mother–infant interaction in the first year of life. *Child Development, 48*(1), 167–181.

Lang, F. R., & Carstensen, L. L. (2002). Time counts: Future time perspective, goals, and social relationships. *Psychology and Aging, 17*(1), 125–139.

Lansford, J. E., Michael, M., Criss, M. M., Pettit, G. S., Dodge, K. A., & Bates, J. E. (2003). Friendship quality, peer group affiliation, and peer antisocial behavior as moderators of the link between negative parenting and adolescent externalizing behavior. *Journal of Research on Adolescence, 13*(2), 161–184.

Laosa, L. M., & Brophy, J. E. (1972). Effects of sex and birth order on sex role development and intelligence among kindergarten children. *Developmental Psychology, 6*, 409–415.

Larsen, R. J., & Diener, E. (1987). Affect intensity as an individual difference characteristic: A review. *Journal of Research in Personality, 21*(1), 1–39.

Larson, R. W., Richards, M. H., Moneta, G., Holmbeck, G., & Duckett, E. (1996). Changes in adolescents' daily interactions with their families from ages 10 to 18: Disengagement and transformation. *Developmental Psychology, 32*(4), 744–754.

Lee, G. R., Peek. C. W., & Coward, R. T. (1998). Race differences in filial responsibility expectations among older parents. *Journal of Marriage and Family, 60*(2), 404–412.

Lehman, H. C. (1962). More about age and achievement. *Gerontologist, 2*, 141–148.

Lehman, H. C. (1966a). The most creative years of engineers and other technologists. *Journal of Genetic Psychology, 108*, 263–270.

Lehman, H. C. (1966b). The psychologist's most creative years. *American Psychologist, 21*, 363–369.

Leinbach, M. D., & Fagot, B. I. (1993). Categorical habituation to male and female faces: Gender schematic processing in infancy. *Infant Behavior and Development, 16*(3), 317–332.

Lenroot, R. K., & Giedd, J. N. (2006). Brain development in children and adolescents: Insights from anatomical magnetic resonance imaging. *Neuroscience Biobehavior Review, 30*(6), 718–729.

Lerner, R. M. (1982). Children and adolescents as producers of their own development. *Developmental Review, 2*, 342–370.

Levenson, R. W., Carstensen, L. L., & Gottman, J. M. (1993). Long-term marriage: Age, gender, and satisfaction. *Psychology and Aging, 8*(2), 301–313.

Levine, A., Zagoory-Sharon, O., Feldman, R., & Weller, A. (2007). Oxytocin during pregnancy and early postpartum: Individual patterns and maternal–fetal attachment. *Peptides, 28*(6), 1162–1169.

Levy, B. R., Slade, M. D., Kunkel, S. R., & Kasl, S. V. (2002). Longevity increased by positive self-perceptions of aging. *Journal of Personality and Social Psychology, 83*(2), 261–270.

Limber, S. P., Cunningham, P., Florx, V., Ivey, J., Nation, M., Chai, S., & Melton, G. (1997). *Bullying among school children: Preliminary findings from a school-based intervention program*. Fifth International Family Violence Research Conference, Durham, NH, June/July.

Lore, R. K., & Schultz, L. A. (1993). Control of human aggression: A comparative perspective. *American Psychologist, 48*(1), 16–25.

Maccoby, E. E., & Jacklin, C. N. (1974). *The psychology of sex differences*. Stanford, CA: Stanford University Press.

Majnemer, A., Brownstein, A., Kadanoff, R., & Shevell M. I. (1992). A comparison of neurobehavioral performance of healthy term and low-risk preterm infants at term. *Developmental Medicine & Child Neurology, 34*(5), 417–424.

Martin, C. L., & Ruble, D. (2004). Children's search for gender cues—cognitive perspectives on gender development. *Current Directions in Psychological Science, 13*, 67–70.

Masten, A. S. (2001). Ordinary magic: Resilience processes in development. *American Psychologist, 56*(3), 227–238.

Masten, A. S., & Obradovic, J. (2006). Competence and resilience in development. *Annals of the New York Academy of Sciences, 1094*, 13–27.

McBride, T., & Nief, R., (2011). *The Mindset Lists of American history: From typewriters to text messages, what ten generations of Americans think is normal*. New York: John Wiley & Sons.

McCrae, R. R., & Costa, P. T. (1994). The stability of personality: Observations and evaluations. *Current Directions in Psychological Science, 3*(6), 173–175.

McCrae, R. R., & Costa, P. T., Jr. (1997). Personality trait structure as a human universal. *American Psychologist, 52*(5), 509–516.

McCrae, R. R., Costa, P. T., Jr., Ostendorf, F., Angleitner, A., Hrebíčková, M., Avia, M. D., Sanz, J., Sánchez-Bernardos, M. L., Kusdil, M. E., Woodfield, R., Saunders, P. R., & Smith, P. B. (2000). Nature over nurture: Temperament, personality, and life span development. *Journal of Personality and Social Psychology, 78*(1), 173–186.

McCrink, K., & Wynn, K. (2004). Large-number addition and subtraction by 9-month-old infants. *Psychological Science, 15*(11), 776–781.

McIntyre, M. H., & Pope Edwards, C. (2009). The early development of gender differences. *Annual Review of Anthropology, 38*, 83–97.

Meltzoff, A. N., & Moore, M. K. (1983). Imitation of facial and manual gestures by human neonates. *Child Development, 54*, 702–709.

Meltzoff, A. N., & Moore, M. K. (1989). Imitation in newborn infants: Exploring the range of gestures imitated and the underlying mechanisms. *Developmental Psychology, 25*, 954–962.

Miller, J. G. (1994). Cultural diversity in the morality of caring: Individually oriented versus duty-based interpersonal moral codes. *Cross-Cultural Research: The Journal of Comparative Social Science, 28*, 3–39.

Milunsky, A., Jick, H., Jick, S. S., Bruel, C. L., MacLaughlin, D. S., Rothman, K. J., & Willett, W. (1989). Multivitamin/folic acid supplementation in early pregnancy reduces the prevalence of neural tube defects. *Journal of the American Medical Association, 262*(20), 2847–2852.

Mirowsky, J. (2002). Parenthood and health: The pivotal and optimal age at first birth. *Social Forces, 81*(1), 315–349.

Moffitt, T. E., Caspi, A., & Rutter, M. (2006). Measured gene-environment interactions in psychopathology: Concepts, research strategies, and implications for research, intervention, and public understanding of genetics. *Perspectives on Psychological Science, 1*(1), 5–27.

Money, J. (1975). Ablatio penis: Normal male infant sex-reassignment as a girl. *Archives of Sexual Behavior, 4*, 65–71.

Mounts, N. S., & Steinberg, L. (1995). An ecological analysis of peer influence on adolescent grade point average and drug use. *Developmental Psychology, 31*(6), 915–922.

Nardinelli, C. (1990). *Child labor and the industrial revolution*. Bloomington: Indiana University Press.

Nash, J. M. (2001). Fertile minds. *Time*, June 24.

Neimeyer, R. A., & Chapman, K. M. (1980/1981). Self-ideal discrepancy and fear of death: The test of an existential hypothesis. *Omega, 11*, 233–239.

Neugarten, B. L. (1979). Time, age, and the life cycle. *American Journal of Psychiatry, 136*, 887–894.

NICHD Early Child Care Network. (2005). *Child care and child development: Results from the NICHD Study of Early Child Care and Youth Development*. New York: Guilford.

NOVA. (2001). (TV series). Sex: Unknown (transcript). 2001-10-30.

O'Leary, K. D., & Smith, D. A. (1991). Marital interactions. *Annual Review of Psychology, 42*, 191–212.

Olson, S. L. (1992). Development of conduct problems and peer rejection in preschool children: A social systems analysis. *Journal of Abnormal Child Psychology, 20*(3), 327–350.

Olweus, D. (1993). Victimization by peers: Antecedents and long-term outcomes. In K. H. Rubin & J. B. Asendorf (Eds.), *Social withdrawal, inhibitions, and shyness* (pp. 315–341). Hillsdale, NJ: Erlbaum.

Olweus, D. (1996). Bullying at school: Knowledge base and an effective intervention program. *Annals of the New York Academy of Sciences, 794, Understanding Aggressive Behavior in Children,* 265–276.

Olweus, D., Mattson, A., Schalling, D., & Low, H. (1980). Testosterone, aggression, physical, and personality dimensions in normal adolescent males. *Psychosomatic Medicine, 42,* 253–269.

Orbell, S., & Sheeran, P. (2000). Motivational and volitional processes in action initiation: A field study of the role of implementation intentions. *Journal of Applied Social Psychology, 30,* 780–797.

O'Reilly, I. (2010, February 15). Tension over sex testing in sport. BBC NEWS, http://news.bbc.co.uk/go/pr/fr/-/2/hi/in_depth/8511176.stm

Osterling, J., & Dawson, G. (1994). Early recognition of children with autism: A study of first birthday home videotapes. *Journal of Autism and Developmental Disorders, 24*(3), 247–257.

Panning, B., & Taatjes, D. J. (2008). Transcriptional regulation: It takes a village. *Molecular Cell, 31*(5), 622–629.

Parens, E. (2004), Genetic differences and human identities: On why talking about behavioral genetics is important and difficult. *Hastings Center Report Supplement 34,* S1–S36.

Pastor, D. (1981). The quality of mother–infant attachment and its relationship to toddlers' initial sociability with peers. *Developmental Psychology, 17*(3), 326–335.

Patalano, A. L., & Seifert, C. M. (1997). Opportunistic planning: Being reminded of pending goals. *Cognitive Psychology, 34,* 1–36.

Paukner, A., Suomi, S. J., Visalberghi, E., & Ferrari, P. F. (2009). Capuchin monkeys display affiliation toward humans who imitate them. *Science, 325*(5942), 880–883.

PBS. (1997, March 4). Secret of the wild child. *NOVA.*

Pereira, A. C., Huddleston, D. E., Brickman, A. M., Sosunov, A. A., Hen, R., McKhann, G. M., Sloan, R., Gage, F. H., Brown, T. R., & Small, S. A. (2007). An *in vivo* correlate of exercise-induced neurogenesis in the adult dentate gyrus. *Proceedings of the National Academy of Sciences, 104*(13), 5638–5643.

Petersen, A. C., Sarigiani, P. A., & Kennedy, R. E. (1991). Adolescent depression. Why more girls? *Journal of Youth and Adolescence, 20*(2), 247–271.

Petersen, J. L., & Hyde, J. S. (2010). A meta-analytic review of research on gender differences in sexuality, 1993–2007. *Psychological Bulletin, 136*(1), 21–38.

Phillips, D., Mekos, D., Scarr, S., McCartney, K., & Abbott-Shim, M. (2000). Within and beyond the classroom door: Assessing quality in child care centers. *Early Childhood Research Quarterly, 15*(4), 475–496.

Piaget, J. (1928). *The child's conception of the world.* London: Routledge and Kegan Paul.

Piaget, J. (1932). *The moral judgment of the child.* London: Kegan Paul, Trench, Trubner.

Piaget, J. (1951). *The psychology of intelligence.* London: Routledge and Kegan Paul.

Piaget, J. (1952). *The origins of intelligence in children.* New York: International University Press. (Original work published 1936.)

Pinker, S. (2002). *The blank slate: The modern denial of human nature.* New York: Penguin.

Plomin, R., & Crabbe, J. (2000). DNA. *Psychological Bulletin, 126*(6), 806–828.

Plomin, R., Corley, R., Caspi, A., Fulker, D. W., & De Fries, J. C. (1998). Adoption results for self-reported personality: Not much nature or nurture? *Journal of Personality and Social Psychology, 75,* 211–218.

Raley, R. K., & Bumpass, L. (2003). The topography of the divorce plateau: Levels and trends in union stability in the United States after 1980. *Demographic Research, 8*(8), 245–260.

Rauer, A. J., & Volling, B. L. (2007). Differential parenting and sibling jealousy: Developmental correlates of young adults' romantic relationships. *Personal Relationships, 14*(4), 495–511.

Ricciuti, A. E., & Scarr, S. (1990). Interaction of early biological and family risk factors in predicting cognitive development. *Journal of Applied Developmental Psychology, 11*(1), 1–12.

Rice, F., Harold, G. T., Boivin, J., van den Bree, M., Hay, D. F., & Thapar, A. (2010). The links between prenatal stress and offspring development and psychopathology: Disentangling environmental and inherited influences. *Psychological Medicine, 40,* 335–345.

Rivers, I., & Smith, P. K. (1994). Types of bullying behavior and their correlates. *Aggressive Behavior, 20,* 259–368.

Roberts, B. W., & Mroczek, D. (2008). Personality trait change in adulthood. *Current Directions in Psychological Science, 17*(1), 31–35.

Roberts, B. W., Walton, K. E., & Viechtbauer, W. (2006). Patterns of mean-level change in personality traits across the life course: A meta-analysis of longitudinal studies. *Psychological Bulletin, 132*(1), 1–25.

Rödholm, M. (1981). Effects of father–infant postpartum contact on their interaction 3 months after birth. *Early Human Development, 5*(1), 79–85.

Rosenzweig, M. R., Bennett, E. L., & Diamond, M. C. (1972). Brain changes in response to experience. *Scientific American, 226*(2), 22–29.

Rothbart, M. K. (1981). Measurement of temperament infancy. *Child Development, 52*(2), 569–578.

Rothbart, M. K. (1986). Longitudinal observation of infant temperament. *Developmental Psychology, 22*(3), 356–365.

Rothbart, M. K., & Bates, J. E. (2006). Temperament. In N. Eisenberg, W. Damon, & R. M. Lerner (Eds.), *Handbook of child psychology: Vol. 3, Social, emotional, and personality development* (6th ed., pp. 99–166). New York: Wiley.

Rothbart, M. K., Sheese, B. E., & Posner, M. I. (2007). Executive attention and effortful control: Linking temperament, brain networks, and genes. *Child Development Perspectives, 1*(1), 2–7.

Rovee-Collier, C. K., Sullivan, M. W., Enright, M., Lucas, D., & Fagen, J. W. (1980). Reactivation of infant memory. *Science, 208*(4448), 1159–1161.

Rowe, J. W., & Kahn, R. L. (1997). Successful aging. *Gerontologist, 37*(4), 433–440.

Ryff, C. D. (1989). Happiness is everything, or is it? Explorations on the meaning of psychological well-being. *Journal of Personality and Social Psychology, 57*(6), 1069–1081.

Sagi, A., van Ijzendoorn, M. H., Aviezer, O., Donnell, F., & Mayseless, O. (1994). Sleeping out of home in a kibbutz communal arrangement: It makes a difference for infant–mother attachment. *Child Development, 65*(1), 992–1001.

Salapatek, P., Bechtold, G., & Bushnell, E. W. (1976). Infant visual acuity as a function of viewing distance. *Child Development, 47*(3), 860–863.

Salthouse, T. A. (2006). Mental exercise and mental aging: Evaluating the validity of the "Use It or Lose It" hypothesis. *Perspectives on Psychological Science, 1*(1), 68–87.

Salthouse, T. (2011). Consequences of age-related cognitive declines. *Annual Review of Psychology, 63,* 5.1–5.26.

Scarr, S. (1992). Developmental theories for the 1990s: Development and individual differences. *Child Development, 63*(1), 1–19.

Scarr, S. (1996). How people make their own environments: Implications for parents and policy makers. *Psychology, Public Policy, and Law, 2*(2), 204–228.

Scarr, S. (1997). Why child care has little impact on most children's development. *Current Directions in Psychological Science, 6*(5), 143–148

Scarr, S., & McCartney, K. (1983). How people make their own environments: A theory of genotype x environment effects. *Child Development, 54,* 424–435.

Scheibe, S., & Carstensen, L. L. (2010). Emotional aging: Recent findings and future trends. *Journal of Gerontology, 65B*(2), 135–144.

Schlegel, A., & Barry, H., III. (1991). *Adolescence: An anthropological inquiry.* New York: Free Press.

Schmitt, D. P., Allik, J., McCrae, R. R., & Benet-Martínez, V. (2007). The geographic distribution of Big Five personality traits: Patterns and profiles of human self-description across 56 nations. *Journal of Cross-Cultural Psychology, 38*(2), 173–212.

Seals, D., & Young, J. (2003). Bullying and victimization: Prevalence and relationship to gender, grade level, ethnicity, self-esteem, and depression. *Adolescence, 38,* 735–747.

Shanley, D. P., Sear, R., Mace, R., & Kirkwood, T. B. I. (2007). Testing evolutionary theories of menopause. *Proceedings of the Royal Society of London B: Biological Sciences, 274,* 2943–2949.

Shaver, P. R., & Mikulincer, M. (2007). Adult attachment strategies and the regulation of emotion. In J. J. Gross (Ed.), *Handbook of emotion regulation* (pp. 446–465). New York: Guilford.

Silveri, M., Rohan, M. L., Pimentel, P. J., Gruber, S. A., Rosso, I. M., & Yurgelun-Todd, D. A. (2006). Sex differences in the relationship between white matter microstructure and impulsivity in adolescents. *Magnetic Resonance Imaging, 24*(7), 833–841.

Silverberg, S. B., & Steinberg, L. (1997). Psychological well-being of parents with early adolescent children. *Developmental Psychology, 26*(4), 658–666.

Simon, M. (2009, April 23). My bullied son's last day on earth. CNN U.S. http://articles.cnn.com/2009-04-23/us/bullying.suicide_1_bullies-gay-tired?_s=PM:US

Simonton, D. K. (1988). Age and outstanding achievement: What do we know after a century of research? *Psychological Bulletin, 104*(2), 251–267.

Simonton, D. K. (1997). Creative productivity: A predictive and explanatory model of career trajectories and landmarks. *Psychological Review, 104*(1), 66–89.

Smith, E. P., Boutte, G. S., Zigler, E., & Finn-Stevenson, M. (2004). Opportunities for schools to promote resilience in children and youth. In L. I. Maton, C. J. Schellenbach, B. J. Leadbeater, A. L. Solarz, (Eds.), *Investing in children, youth, families, and communities: Strengths-based research and policy* (pp. 213–231). Washington, DC: American Psychological Association.

Snarey, J. R., Reimer, J., & Kohlberg, L. (1985). Development of social-moral reasoning among Kibbutz adolescents: A longitudinal cross-cultural study. *Developmental Psychology, 21*(1), 3–17.

Somerville, L. H., Hare, T., & Casey, B. J. (2011). Frontostriatal maturation predicts cognitive control failure to appetitive cues in adolescents. *Journal of Cognitive Neuroscience, 23*(9), 2123–2134.

Sorkhabi, N. (2005). Applicability of Baumrind's parent typology to collective cultures: Analysis of cultural explanations of parent socialization effects. *International Journal of Behavioral Development, 29*(6), 552–563.

Spear, L. P. (2000). The adolescent brain and age-related behavioral manifestations. *Neuroscience Biobehavioral Review, 24,* 417–463.

Spear, L. P. (2007). The developing brain and adolescent-typical behavior patterns: An evolutionary approach. In D. Romer and E. Walker (Eds.), *Adolescent psychopathology and the developing brain.* New York: Oxford University Press.

Stein, D. G., Brailowsky, S., & Will, B. (1995). *Brain repair.* New York: Oxford University Press.

Steinberg, L. (1989). Pubertal maturation and parent–adolescent distance: An evolutionary perspective. In L. Steinberg, G. R. Adams, R. Montemayor, & T. P. Gullotta (Eds.), *Biology of adolescent behavior and development, advances in adolescent development: An annual book series, Vol. 1* (pp. 71–97). Thousand Oaks, CA: Sage.

Steinberg, L. (2006). Risk taking in adolescence: What changes, and why? *Annals of the New York Academy of Sciences, 1021*(1), 51–58.

Steinberg, L. (2007). Risk taking in adolescence: New perspectives from brain and behavioral science. *Current Directions in Psychological Science, 16*(2), 55–59.

Steinberg, L. (2009). Should the science of adolescent brain development inform public policy? *American Psychologist, 64*(8), 739–750.

Steinberg, L., & Morris, A. S. (2001). Adolescent development. *Annual Review of Psychology, 52,* 83–110.

Stern, M., & Karraker, K. H. (1989). Sex stereotyping of infants: A review of gender labeling studies. *Sex Roles, 20*(9–10), 501–522.

Stern, Y. (2009). Cognitive reserve. *Neuropsychologia, 47*(10), 2015–2028.

Strassmann, B. I. (2011). Cooperation and competition in a cliff-dwelling people. *Proceedings of the National Academy of Sciences, 108*(2), 10894–10901.

Strassmann, B. I., & Garrard, W. M. (2011). Alternatives to the grandmother hypothesis: A meta-analysis of the association between grandparental and grandchild survival in patrilineal populations. *Human Nature, 22,* 201–222.

Strobe, M. S., & Strobe, W. (1983). Who suffers more? Sex differences in health risks of the widowed. *Psychological Bulletin, 93,* 279–301.

Swaab, D. F. (2007). Sexual differentiation of the brain and behavior. *Best Practice & Research Clinical Endocrinology & Metabolism, 21*(3), 431–444.

Talbot, M. (2006, September 4). The baby lab. *New Yorker, 82*(27), 91–101.

Thoma, S. J., & Rest, J. R. (1999). The relationship between moral decision making and patterns of consolidation and transition in moral judgment development. *Developmental Psychology, 35*(2), 323–334.

Trainor, L. J., & Zacharias, C. A. (1998). Infants prefer higher-pitched singing. *Infant Behavior and Development, 21*(4), 799–805.

Tucker-Drob, E. M., Rhemtulla, M., Harden, K. P., Turkheimer, E., & Fask, D. (2011). Emergence of a gene x socioeconomic status interaction on infant mental ability between 10 months and 2 years. *Psychological Science, 22*(1), 125–133.

U.S. Census Bureau. (2009). Median age at first marriage for women and men. Retrieved from http://factfinder.census.gov/servlet/GRTSelectServlet?ds_name=ACS_2009_1YR_G00_, 5/21/2011.

Utz, R. L., Carr, D., Nesse, R., & Wortman, C. B. (2002). The effect of widowhood on older adults' social participation: An evaluation of activity, disengagement, and continuity theories. *The Gerontologist, 42*(4), 522–533.

Vaillant, G. E., & Mukamal, K. (2001). Successful aging. *American Journal of Psychiatry, 158,* 839–847.

Vandell, D. L., Belsky, J., Burchinal, M., Steinberg, L., Vandergrift, N., & NICHD Early Child Care Research Network. (2010). Do effects of early child care extend to age 15 years? Results from the NICHD study of early child care and youth development. *Child Development, 81*(3), 737–756.

Velderman, M. K., Bakermans-Kranenburg, M. J., Juffer, F., & van Ijzendoorn, M. H. (2006). Effects of attachment-based interventions on maternal sensitivity and infant attachment: Differential susceptibility of highly reactive infants. *Journal of Family Psychology, 20*(2), 266–274.

Vosniadou, S., & Brewer, W. F. (1992). Mental models of the earth: A study of conceptual change in childhood. *Cognitive Psychology, 24,* 535–585.

Waters, E., & Cummings, M. (2000). A secure base from which to explore close relationships. *Child Development, 71*(1), 164–172.

Waters, E., Merrick, S., Treboux, D., Crowell, J., & Albersheim, L. (2000). Attachment security in infancy and early adulthood: A twenty-year longitudinal study. *Child Development, 71*(3), 684–689.

Waters, E., Wippman, J., & Sroufe, L. A. (1979). Attachment, positive affect, and competence in the peer group: Two studies in construct validation. *Child Development, 50,* 821–829.

Watson, J. B. (1930). *Behaviorism* (revised edition). Chicago: University of Chicago Press.

Wellman, H. M. (1990). *The child's theory of mind.* Cambridge: MIT Press.

Werner, E. E. (1988). A cross-cultural perspective on infancy research and social issues. *Journal of Cross-Cultural Psychology, 19*(1), 96–113.

Werner, E. E. (1995). Resilience in development. *Current Directions in Psychological Science, 4*(3), 81–85.

Wertsch, J. V. (1985). *Vygotsky and the social formation of mind.* Cambridge, MA: Harvard University Press.

Wethington, E. (2000). Expecting stress: Americans and the "midlife crisis." *Motivation and Emotion, 24*(2), 85–103.

White, L. & Edwards, J. N. (1990). Emptying the nest and parental well-being: An analysis of National Panel Data. *American Sociological Review, 55*(2), 235–242.

Whiteman, S. D., & Buchanan, C. M. (2002). Mothers' and children's expectations for adolescence: The impact of perceptions of an older sibling's experience. *Journal of Family Psychology, 16,* 157–171.

Whitney, I., & Smith, P. K. (1993). A survey of the nature and extent of bullying in junior/middle and secondary schools. *Educational Research, 35,* 3–25.

Wilson, R. S., Mendes de Leon, C. F., Barnes, L. L., Schneider, J. A., Bienias, J. L., Evans, D. A., & Bennett, D. A. (2002). Participation in cognitively stimulating activities and risk of incident Alzheimer disease. *Journal of the American Medical Association, 287*(6), 742–748.

Wimmer, H., & Perner, J. (1983). Beliefs about beliefs: Representation and constraining function of wrong beliefs in young children's understanding of deception. *Cognition, 13*(1), 103–128.

Wong, K. (2009). Hitching a ride. *Scientific American,* July, 20–23.

Wood, W., & Eagly, A. H. (2002). A cross-cultural analysis of the behavior of women and men: Implications for the origins of sex differences. *Psychological Bulletin, 128*(5), 699–727.

Wynn, K. (1992). Children's acquisition of the number words and the counting system. *Cognitive Psychology, 24*(2), 220–251.

Ziegler, E., & Styfco, S. (2004). *The Head Start debates.* Baltimore, MD: Brookes.

Chapter Overview ▼

13.1 Defining Personality
CONCEPT LEARNING CHECK **13.1** *Describing Personality Theories*

13.2 The Psychoanalytic Perspective
The Nature of the Psychoanalytic Perspective
Freud's Psychoanalytic Theory
  Structure of Personality
  Personality Development
  Defense Mechanisms
Jung's Analytical Psychology
Adler's Individual Psychology
Evaluating the Psychoanalytic Perspective—Is Freud in Error?
CONCEPT LEARNING CHECK **13.2** *Comparing the Psychoanalytic Perspectives*

13.3 The Humanistic Perspective
Rogers's Person-Centered Perspective
Maslow's Theory of Self-actualization
Evaluating the Humanistic Perspectives
CONCEPT LEARNING CHECK **13.3** *Illustrating the Humanistic Perspective*

13.4 Trait Perspectives
Factor Analysis
The Big Five Factors
Assessing Traits
Evaluating the Trait Perspective
CONCEPT LEARNING CHECK **13.4** *Identifying the Big Five Traits*

13 Personality

Learning Objectives ▼

13.1 ■ Describe the characteristics of a well-crafted personality theory.

13.2 ■ Compare and contrast the psychoanalytic theories of Freud, Jung, and Adler.

13.3 ■ Illustrate the humanistic perspective of personality using Rogers's Person-Centered Perspective and Maslow's Theory of Self-actualization.

13.4 ■ Discuss the factors involved in the trait perspective.

13.5 ■ Analyze the social cognitive theories of Bandura as compared to those of Mischel.

13.6 ■ Explain the different biological perspectives and theories of how physiological processes determine personality.

13.7 ■ Identify the different tools to understand personality and how they are used.

13.8 ■ Describe how culture and belief systems can shape and be shaped by personality.

13.5 The Social Cognitive Perspective
Bandura's Social Cognitive Theory
Mischel's Social Cognitive Theory
Evaluating the Social Cognitive Perspective

CONCEPT LEARNING CHECK **13.5** *Comparing the Social Cognitive Perspectives*

13.6 The Biological Perspective
Eysenck's Theory
Genetics and Personality

Evolutionary Theories of Personality
Evaluating the Biological Perspective

CONCEPT LEARNING CHECK **13.6**
Understanding the Biological Perspective

13.7 Personality Assessment

CONCEPT LEARNING CHECK **13.7** *Identifying Personality Assessments*

13.8 Culture and Personality
Summary of Multiple Influences on Personality

CONCEPT LEARNING CHECK **13.8** *Examining Culture and Personality*

CRITICAL THINKING APPLICATION

*I*t turned out to be a really good morning to play hooky from work. That morning, my neighbor Stephanie, who had graciously agreed to help me renovate the bathroom of my 1920s bungalow, dragged me to a home improvement store. That bathroom had not been refreshed since the previous owner swathed the entire room with gloomy grays and dingy tans. We had just returned from looking at sinks when I got a call. It was Sharon, another psychologist at Oxford College. "*Do not come into work,*" she commanded.

"Oh . . . okay?" I responded inquisitively.

Sharon then explained how a group of students had managed to wrangle an animal to the third floor of my 19th-century Victorian brick office building as a prank.

"Apparently," I later explained to Stephanie, "the building is not fit to enter. The students . . . well, the students stole a zebra as a prank." I blurted out like it was all one word, hoping she would not ask for details.

"A *zebra*?" she enunciated. "Are they *sure* it was a *zebra*?" She contorted her face to be sure that I understood that either she did not hear me correctly or I must have been mistaken.

I paused for a moment. "What else looks like a zebra?"

"Goodness, what *kind* of person would steal a *zebra* and walk it up three flights of stairs as a prank?"

I slipped into professor mode and answered her question with a question (Socratic style). "What kind of person?" I began. "I suppose that depends on who you ask."

Stephanie was right. It probably takes a special kind of person to coax an animal up three flights of stairs . . . but what kind of person? What, in general, motivates us to do what we do?

13.1 Defining Personality

Psychologists define personality in many ways.

■ Describe the characteristics of a well-crafted personality theory.

Personality An individual's pattern of thinking, feeling, and behaving.

Disposition The way a person behaves across different situations as well as over time.

Personality theory A system used to describe and explain the genesis and development of an individual's pattern of thinking, feeling, and behaving.

Personality is your pattern of thinking, feeling, and behaving. It is the enduring nature of who you are. It describes not only what you like but also why you like what you like. Personality theorists try to explain a person's **disposition**, which is the way a person behaves across different situations as well as over time. Personality psychologists are interested not just in describing personality but also in understanding where personality comes from and how it develops over time. **Personality theory** is a system used to describe and explain the genesis and development of an individual's pattern of thinking, feeling, and behaving.

According to Magnavita (2002), a well-crafted personality theory will possess several characteristics:

1. **Clinical utility.** Is the theory helpful to mental health practitioners to understand and treat psychological conditions?

2. **Practical utility.** Can the theory be applied to everyday situations?

3. **Predictive value.** Can the theory predict future behavior?

4. Insight into human nature. Does the theory provide useful information on what it means to be human?

5. Ability to provide self-understanding. Does the theory offer an individual some degree of insight into his or her own personality?

6. Ability to understand complex human behavior. Does the theory help explain nuances in our behavior?

As convenient as it might be, people do not come with instruction manuals, so different theories have emerged about the nature and components of personality. In this chapter, we will examine the major grand or all-encompassing theories of personalities, including the psychoanalytic perspective, the humanistic perspective, the trait perspective, the social cognitive perspective, and the biological perspective. And maybe, just maybe, we will figure out what kind of person would kidnap a zebra and hold it hostage as a prank.

CONCEPT LEARNING CHECK 13.1 | *Describing Personality Theories*

Please match the goals of a useful personality theory to the examples below.

A. Clinical utility

B. Practical utility of the theory

C. Predictive value

D. Insight into human nature

E. Self-understanding

F. Describes complex human behavior

1. _____ A theory of personality suggests that people are basically good.

2. _____ Understanding a theory well can help a therapist design a treatment for a client.

3. _____ Understanding a person's personality can help you to know why you do what you do.

4. _____ A theory helps you to understand what it means to be human.

5. _____ A theory helps you to know how a friend will react to being asked to be part of a flash mob.

13.2 The Psychoanalytic Perspective

According to the psychoanalytic perspective, unconscious processes determine your personality.

- Compare and contrast the psychoanalytic theories of Freud, Jung, and Adler.

The Nature of the Psychoanalytic Perspective

The **psychoanalytic theories** (sometimes referred to as psychodynamic, dynamic, or Freudian) are a family of personality theories originated by Sigmund Freud FIGURE 13-1 that focus on unconscious motivation. The notion is that the psyche, or personality, moves energy around to where the energy is needed. The movement of energy is why the theory is called dynamic.

Like many personality theories, the psychoanalytic tradition was developed alongside a psychotherapy technique. The psychoanalytic theorists have assumptions about the formation and development of personality as well as treatment techniques known as psychoanalysis.

FIGURE 13-1 Dr. Sigmund Freud.

Psychoanalytic theories A family of theories originated by Freud that focuses on unconscious motivation.

Psychoanalysis A type of therapy in which unconscious conflicts and motivation are uncovered, explored, and redirected.

Catharsis A release of emotions.

Unconscious According to Freud, thoughts, memories, feelings, and wishes that reside outside of awareness.

Conscious mind According to Freud, a part of the mind that is aware of current thoughts and experiences.

Preconscious According to Freud, the part of your mind that contains material just outside of awareness that is easy to pull into awareness.

Id According to Freud, the part of the personality that operates on the pleasure principle, always looking to reduce tension that comes from basic physiological drives.

Pleasure principle According to Freud, the drive to reduce tension.

The tension reduction of a rollercoaster is fun for your id.

Your id tries to reduce tension by creating images of the things that it wants.

Psychoanalysis is a type of therapy, based on the psychoanalytic technique, in which unconscious conflicts or motivations are uncovered, explored, and redirected.

Not all psychoanalytic perspectives are Freudian. They all, however, do share some assumptions about the nature of human personality, including the presence of the unconscious. In this section, we will discuss three: those of Sigmund Freud, Carl Jung, and Alfred Adler.

Freud's Psychoanalytic Theory

Sigmund Freud, the founder of psychoanalysis, is often considered to be the founder of the first well-organized grand theory of personality. Trained in neurology, his early work focused on using hypnosis to bring about a release of emotions, or **catharsis**. Freud's research in this area led to one of his first publications, *Studies on Hysteria* (Breuer & Freud, 1895). Later, he abandoned the use of hypnosis and shifted to examining the **unconscious**, or the thoughts, memories, feelings, and wishes that reside outside of awareness.

Structure of Personality

Freud describes the landscape of the mind as having several realms, some in awareness and some outside of it. The components of awareness include the **conscious mind**, which encompasses your current thoughts and experiences. As you are reading this text, for example, the words are in your conscious mind. Sometimes, however, you have memories that you can pull into your consciousness fairly easily. Until I mentioned it, you might not have had in your consciousness what you had for lunch yesterday. It was in your preconscious, but it now resides in your consciousness. The **preconscious**, according to Freud, is the part of your mind that contains material just outside of awareness that is easy to pull into awareness. The majority of our mind, however, is in the vast unconscious. The unconscious contains thoughts, memories, feelings, and wishes that reside outside of awareness, including instincts, drives, and memories that may have been repressed or forgotten. As you can see in FIGURE 13-2, most of personality resides outside of your awareness in your unconscious mind. Many people compare the massiveness of the unconscious to an iceberg: You might only see the tip, but there is much lurking beneath.

Freud suggested that there are three main structures within our psyche: the id, ego, and superego. The **id**, according to Freud, is the part of the personality that operates on the **pleasure principle**, meaning the id is always looking to reduce the tension that comes from basic physiological drives. The id is not especially smart, but it knows what it likes, and what it likes is reduction of tension. What kind of tension? All kinds. As a human, you have all sorts of physiological needs and drives. When these needs are unmet, tension builds up. Being thirsty creates tension; sipping a tart lemonade will reduce that tension. Being hungry creates tension; munching on a juicy chicken sandwich will reduce that tension. When the tension is reduced, the id feels satisfied, sometimes referred to as gratification. When the id feels tension, the first thing it does is to create an image of the thing that it wants. This can satisfy the id in the short run, but thinking of a moist four-layer chocolate cake will not make you less hungry. The need becomes stronger, and you

FIGURE 13-2 According to the psychoanalytic perspective, your personality is like an iceberg—there is a lot more to it than what you can perceive.

might not be able to think of anything else. Think of a time when you drank so much water that you really needed to use the restroom but you were not in a place where you could do so. After awhile, all you can think about is going to the restroom. Freud says that this is due to your id.

The main driving force of the id is that pleasure principle—the drive to reduce tension at all costs. The physical and physiological needs that motivate the id keep us alive, causing us to eat, drink, and perpetuate the species by having sex. Freud grouped these drives into a cluster of instincts called eros, or the life instinct. **Eros** is the id instinct that reduces tension associated with basic biological drives. A type of eros is **libido**, or the energy linked with sexuality.

Life instincts are not all that motivate the id; there is another way the id seeks the pleasure principle. Remember the id is not very smart, but it knows what it likes. Freud also suggested that the id has a death instinct, an unconscious desire to be dead—the ultimate state of tension reduction called **thanatos**. According to Freud, thanatos is a way in which we reduce tensions that are aggressive and destructive.

What stops you from satisfying your id instincts in inappropriate ways? Let us say I am thirsty in class and a student is gulping a refreshing root beer. What prevents me from stopping mid-sentence, snatching the beverage from my student's hand, and downing the entire can? According to Freud, my good behavior is due, in part, to the ego and the reality principle. The **ego** is the part of the personality responsible for interacting with conscious reality. Rather than the pleasure principle, the ego is governed by the reality principle. The **reality principle** suggests that the ego will defer pleasure until a reasonable way to satisfy id instincts is available.

But the ego has another master, the superego. While not fully developed until age 2 or 3, the **superego** is the internalization of your parental and societal values. The superego is governed by the **perfection principle**. Also known as the ego ideal, the perfection principle is the image of the perfect person, or ego, that inspires the superego. The superego makes us feel proud when we do well, but it can also cause us to feel shame and guilt when we do not measure up to expectations. While the id's demands are generated from biological needs, the superego's demands come from societal pressures. As you can imagine, sometimes these demands can clash, forcing the ego to compromise.

Personality Development

Freud noticed that the tension reduction pleasure principle did not always manifest itself in the same way throughout life. In fact, as people grow and develop, the area of the body involved in tension reduction shifts. He named these developmental phases **psychosexual stages**, developmental periods in which tension reduction focuses on different areas of the body (oral, anal, phallic, latency, genital) TABLE 13-1. For example, think about the job description of a newborn child. It does not do much. Nevertheless, biological needs still build tension in its body. It gets hungry, gassy, and thirsty. The main area of the body where tension reduction is centered is the mouth. Biting, sucking, chewing, and crying are ways tension is reduced. Freud decided to name the stages of development after the part of the body where tension reduction is centered.

But the tension reduction does not stay in the mouth forever. Imagine a child having the urge to defecate. As an infant, the child would just go—like exhaling. Defecation is not really something children think about much. Then somewhere around 18 months,

Some people smoke even though they know it's not good for them. Freud might suggest that this motivation is generated from thanatos, the death instinct.

Eros An id instinct that reduces tension associated with basic biological drives.

Libido According to Freud, the energy linked with sexuality.

Thanatos According to Freud, ways in which we reduce tensions that are aggressive and destructive; also known as the death instinct.

Ego According to Freud, the part of the personality responsible for interacting with conscious reality.

Guilt is a feeling that comes from the internalization of parental and societal values. The superego creates these feelings to encourage us to behave in an ideal way, according to Freud.

TABLE 13-1 Freud's Stages of Development

Age	Stage
0–18 months	Oral
18–38 months	Anal
3–6 years	Phallic
6 years–puberty	Latency
Puberty–Adulthood	Genital

In the oral stage, tension reduction is centered in the mouth.

The Oedipus complex is the psychoanalytic explanation of why boys end up identifying with Dad rather than Mom.

Reality principle According to Freud, the main focus of the ego that suggests that the ego will defer pleasure until a reasonable way to satisfy id instincts is available.

Superego According to Freud, the part of the personality governed by the perfection principle.

Perfection principle The image of the perfect person, or ego, that inspires the superego; also know as the ego ideal.

Psychosexual stages According to Freud, childhood developmental stages in which tension reduction is focused on different areas of the body (oral, anal, phallic, latency, genital).

Oedipal complex According to Freud, a boy's unconscious desire for his mother that results in identification with his father.

it is as if someone taps them on the shoulder and says, "Hey, you know that thing you used to do that you never thought about? Today is a new day. You have to go at a certain time and in a certain place." What happens if you do not? Well, for the first time in your very short life, you are something that you have never been before—bad. Being a good boy or good girl involves delay of gratification (reduction of tension) and an internalization of your parental and societal values concerning how to relieve yourself appropriately. After all, getting along with others really requires that you avoid defecation around other people.

The anal stage starts at around 18 months and goes until about age 3, where the tension reduction is focused on the genitals during the phallic stage. Masturbation is common in this stage. In the latent stage from age 5 to around age 12, sexual impulses are suppressed. The genital stage starts around puberty when sexual impulses return.

Something else occurs during the phallic stage for boys, the Oedipal complex. According to Freud, the **Oedipal complex** is a boy's unconscious desire for his mother that results in copying the behavior of or identification with his father. The Oedipal complex gets its name from the Greek story of Oedipus, who inadvertently murdered his dad and married his own mother. I know you might be thinking that this sounds very odd, but stick with me. The Oedipal crisis was a way to solve a dilemma that Freud noticed and needed to explain. Why is it that as boys grow up, they come to identify with their fathers right after puberty but cling so closely to their moms before that?

Back in the 1800s, women had the responsibility of raising children, and children were drawn to their mothers. After all, mothers are the id's ticket to most tension reduction, and children crave attention, affection, and love from her. Some boys even say they want to grow up and marry their mom. There is at least one wrinkle in this plan—Dad. Freud suggested that the id becomes jealous of Dad because he, too, receives attention from Mom. The child sees Dad as competition and a threat. The ego uses a defense mechanism to protect the ego from this danger and satisfy the id instinct of wanting Mom. The ego identifies with the aggressor. By identifying with Dad, the ego is no longer in danger from the aggressor and is safe. Plus there is a bonus. Since Dad is married to Mom, by identifying with Dad, the child will be connected to Mom as well. The Oedipal crisis happens unconsciously. Freud believed that the Oedipal crisis resulted in boys' identification with Dad.

There are some after effects of the psychosexual stages. Freud suggested that too much or too little tension reduction at a certain stage can lead to fixation at that stage. **Fixation** is a habit of obtaining tension reduction from a certain stage of psychosexual development. For example, a child who always gets a bottle during the oral stage may become fixated at that stage later. That means that during adulthood, he or she may seek oral tension reduction when under stress. If you talk a lot, eat, or chew your pencil when you are stressed, you may have an oral fixation. Fixation is not bad; it just describes where you go to seek a reduction of tension—it is a way of explaining one aspect of your personality. Fixation can occur at any stage. For example, too much tension reduction during the anal stage can lead to an anal-retentive personality. Those who are perfectionistic or exceptionally clean are attempting to control their world in the same way they receive pleasure from the tension reduction of controlling their bowels.

Defense Mechanisms

Remember, the ego has two masters: the id and the superego. It has to meet the demands of the id and the prohibitions of the superego. Often, to satisfy the id, the superego, and the realities of life, the ego has to compromise. One way the ego does this is through **defense mechanisms**, which are unconscious arrangements that the ego uses to satisfy id instincts indirectly **TABLE 13-2**.

These compromises often take the form of defense mechanisms that have been described by Sigmund Freud and his daughter, Anna Freud (Freud, 1967) FIGURE 13-3. All defense mechanisms occur unconsciously, not on purpose.

Not all defense mechanisms are problematic. In sublimation, a person unconsciously redirects an id instinct in a socially acceptable fashion, basically performing an id instinct in a superego way. A person who has an id instinct to beat up another person may unconsciously transform that into a desire to be a boxer, or a person with a hostile

TABLE 13-2 Freudian Defense Mechanisms

Defense Mechanism	Description
Denial	A psychoanalytic defense mechanism in which a person fails to accept a reality
Displacement	A psychoanalytic defense mechanism in which an impulse is unconsciously directed to a substitute object or person
Identification	According to Freud, the unconscious process of copying the behavior of a person
Projection	A defense mechanism in which a person unconsciously attributes their threatening impulses to another person
Rationalization	A defense mechanism in which an irrational behavior is unconsciously explained as acceptable in order to reduce anxiety
Reaction formation	A defense mechanism where a person will unconsciously replace a feeling
Regression	A defense mechanism in which a person reverts to an earlier age of functioning
Repression	A defense mechanism in which a person unconsciously forces a threatening experience from their awareness
Sublimation	A defense mechanism in which a person unconsciously redirects an id instinct in a socially acceptable way

Tongue piercings are an example of an oral fixation, according to some psychoanalytic theorists.

Fixation According to Freud, a habit of obtaining tension reduction from an earlier stage of psychosexual development.

Defense mechanism According to the psychoanalytic perspective, a compromise that the ego uses to satisfy an id instinct indirectly.

Neo-Freudian Psychoanalytic theories inspired by Sigmund Freud.

Personal unconscious According to Jung, the part of one's personality that stores material currently outside of awareness.

Collective unconscious According to Jung, the part of the personality that stores shared experiences and ideas from previous generations.

unconscious impulse to cut other people may long to be a surgeon. All positive activities, according to Freud, are sublimations of negative id impulses.

Jung's Analytical Psychology

Freud's work inspired other psychologists to develop other theories of personality. Carl Jung, FIGURE 13-4 for example, was an early **neo-Freudian**, meaning a theorist inspired by Sigmund Freud. Jung called his version of psychoanalytic theory "analytical psychology." It divided the psyche into three realms: the ego was the conscious mind, what you are aware of at any given moment; the **personal unconscious**, which contains information that can be made conscious; and the **collective unconscious**, which includes all personal unconsciousness from everyone who has ever lived. One way to think about the contents of the psyche as Jung described it is with a computer metaphor: The conscious is what is on your screen at that moment, the personal unconscious is what might be on your hard drive, and the collective unconscious is the Internet.

FIGURE 13-3 Sigmund Freud and his daughter, Anna.

The collective unconscious contains a collection of thoughts known as **archetypes**. Examples of archetypes include the great mother, the shadow, the persona, the hero, the wise old man, and the trickster. These figures are universal symbols: a great mother is not necessarily a woman or a man or even a mother. The **great mother** archetype symbolizes a person or thing that loves to nurture without wanting anything in return. You probably know someone to whom you go when you have had a bad day and they will make you soup and listen to your story. A great mother is a bottomless supply of support and love.

Another archetype is the shadow, your dark side, which is part of your daily life and awareness. Why are you reading your textbook? Maybe, for some of you, before you opened the book you considered other things that you would rather do, like play a game, talk to friends, surf the Internet. But you are reading. Why? What would happen if you did not read for class . . . ever? Some people imagine that they would not do well on the next exam or the one after that. If you did not read for class . . . why attend? That might lead to you failing one or several classes, maybe losing your job, or who knows what else?

Sublimation suggests that even the most noble actions may be rooted in id instincts.

Archetypes According to Jung, a universal thought form that exists in the collective unconscious.

Great mother An archetype described by Jung that symbolizes a person or thing that provides nurture without wanting anything in return.

Shadow An archetype described by Jung that represents the worst possible version of a person.

Persona An archetype that represents the public self.

Hero An archetype that represents someone who saves the day.

Wise old man An archetype that represents wisdom.

Trickster An archetype that represents someone who pretends to be something that he or she is not.

Freud (front row, left) inspired many theorists including Carl Jung (front row, right).

The shadow is the archetype that describes what you might become if you give in to your negative impulses.

FIGURE 13-4 Dr. Carl Gustav Jung.

What might happen next would be the first step in a spiral downward to the worst possible version of you. Like Freud, Jung believed you have a dark side, one that you are well aware of: the shadow. The **shadow** is the archetype that describes your view of what you think you would become if you gave in to your negative impulses. Sometimes those impulses drive you to be a better person. The only problem is that the more successful you become, the darker and more destructive your shadow becomes. Jung also suggested that sometimes you might have negative, unexplained reactions to people because they remind you of your shadow. While this may lead to empathy, you might avoid telling them, "I'm sorry I've been so mean to you; you seem to remind me of the worst possible version of myself." You will not make a friend that way. Monsters, snakes, witches, warlocks, and villains in fiction are all symbols of the shadow archetype.

The **persona** is the archetype that represents your public face. It is like a mask that you wear to the outside world. You may have different personas at work, school, home, or around your friends and family. These various personas can also cause problems if they clash. When I was a college student, I worked as a server at a gourmet pizza restaurant in the mall. I had my peppy pizza server persona, which was very different than my cool peacemaking resident advisor persona. When students who lived in my residence hall came to visit, the personas clashed, which led to very bad tips.

The **hero** is the archetype of someone who saves the day. The hero often fights other archetypes such as the shadow or the trickster in stories with help from the great mother or wise old man. Stories like "Little Red Riding Hood" or "Hansel and Gretel" often feature the hero battling against the shadow or other archetypes. The **wise old man** is a source of unending wisdom. Like the great mother archetype, the wise old man does not need to be a man, or old, just wise. Yoda and Dumbledore are examples of the wise old man archetype. The **trickster** is an archetype that represents someone who pretends to be something that he or she is not.

Jung suggested that personality operated by three fundamental principles: the principle of opposites, the principle of equivalence, and the principle of entropy. The **principle of opposites** states that every wish unconsciously proposes its opposite. As you carefully take a cake out of the oven and work as carefully as you can to place it on the table gingerly, unconsciously you would love to smash it. The second principle is the **principle of equivalence**. The principle of equivalence extends from the principle of opposites. It suggests that the energy devoted to do one thing will equally be devoted to the opposite activity. Denying negative feelings can be a problem since it feeds your shadow archetype. The last principle is a principle of entropy. The **principle of entropy** suggests that opposites tend to come together over time. The principle of entropy explains why people tend to mellow as they get older. As you can see, Jung suggested that we are a dichotomy, always wanting to do two things. The principle of entropy suggests that over time, we can resolve this dichotomy. The process of trying to resolve and rise above the dichotomy of who we are is called **transcendence**.

Perhaps the most widely known of Jung's theories is his theory of preferences for the internal or external world. **Introverts** prefer their internal world to the external world. Introverts may be reserved when interacting socially. **Extroverts**, on the other hand, prefer the external world to the internal world. While some extroverts tend to be outgoing and sociable, the active ingredient for introversion and extroversion is actually energy. Determining if you are an introvert or an extrovert has more to do with where you seek your energy—how you recharge yourself. After a bad day, extroverts tend to recharge themselves by being around others. An extrovert who has had a bad day might want to go hang out with friends and feel better, while an introvert might rather be alone.

Adler's Individual Psychology

The psychologist Alfred Adler FIGURE 13-5 believed the major drive of personality to be striving for superiority (Ansbacher & Ansbacher, 1964). **Striving for superiority**, or compensation, according to Adler, is an attempt to overcome feelings of inferiority by being a better person. Adler called his theory of personality "individual psychology." Adler suggested that when we are young, we have a sense that we are less than or inferior to others for the simple reason that we are. When you are a child, there are always people who can do things you cannot. Maybe they can reach things or stay up late or dodge that big red ball on the playground. As kids, we are constantly bombarded by inabilities. Adler called this idea **inferiority** or organ inferiority: At a basic level, we all feel inferior. Adler believed we spend the rest

FIGURE 13-5 Dr. Alfred Adler.

of our lives striving for superiority in order to make up for those feelings of inferiority. The way in which you strive for superiority in order to overcome feelings of inferiority is called your style of life, or **lifestyle**. Adler thought that those who strive for superiority by beating down others had an **unhealthy lifestyle** or mistaken lifestyle. If you try to be the best version of yourself by working together with others toward common goals, you are exhibiting a **healthy lifestyle**.

Social interests separate healthy from unhealthy styles of life. I had a friend who gained some weight after having a baby. She was having trouble losing the weight when she told me about a "brilliant idea" that she had. She started baking cakes and cookies for her friends. The idea was that she would cause her friends to gain weight so that, in comparison, she would look slimmer. I was not sure how to respond to her. According to Adler, however, her way of striving for superiority would be mistaken.

Evaluating the Psychoanalytic Perspective—Is Freud in Error?

Ask people what they think of Freud and the neo-Freudian theorists and you are likely to see a person make a face and say something like, "That fraud!" People tend to have negative views of both Freud as a person and his theories. Strangely, however, when you listen to the way that people tend to describe personality characteristics, you hear Freudian language and theory everywhere. It is hard to go even a week without stumbling over one of Freud's terms: *repressive, denial, unconscious*. Freud has become part of our culture.

Freud is often criticized for his views of women as well. It is important to remember that Freud's views reflect the ideas of society at the time that he lived; every personality theory does to some degree. *Studies on Hysteria*, for example, was published in 1895—only 2 years before the first European country allowed women to vote, and some 25 years before women were allowed to vote in the United States.

Another criticism is leveled at Freud because many of his theories were derived from case studies of his patients. This makes the evidence difficult to generalize to everyone and hardly objective. Many of his theories are not scientifically sound because they defy the **principle of falsifiability**. In order to be scientific, a theory must be testable and able to be disproved. It is difficult to disprove the existence of the ego and superego since, by definition, they are outside of your awareness.

Despite this, modern psychodynamic researchers (e.g., Betan, Heim, Zittel, Conklin, & Westen, 2005) have tested Freud's theories, and many have withstood the rigor of modern techniques. For example, his core theories that suggest that early experience impacts later behavior and the theory of unconscious motivation have amassed supportive evidence.

While psychoanalytic theory has its critics, no one person or one theory has had as much influence on psychology as has Sigmund Freud.

Principle of opposites According to Jung, the theory that every wish also represents the opposite of the same wish.

Principle of equivalence According to Jung, the energy devoted to do one thing will be equally devoted to the opposite activity.

Principle of entropy Jung's theory that opposites tend to come together over time.

Transcendence According to Jung, the process of resolving the dichotomy of who we are as people.

As children, we are constantly bombarded by inabilities; these form the basis of our inferiority, according to Adler.

Introvert A personality type that prefers the internal world to the external world; also known as introversion.

Extrovert A personality type that prefers the external world to the internal world; also known as extroversion.

Striving for superiority According to Adler, an attempt to overcome feelings of inferiority by being a better person; also known as compensation.

Inferiority According to Adler, feelings of inadequacy; also known as organ inferiority.

Lifestyle According to Adler, the way in which you strive for superiority in order to make up for feelings of inferiority.

CONCEPT LEARNING CHECK 13.2 | *Comparing the Psychoanalytic Perspectives*

There are five psychosexual stages. For each stage listed below, circle the number that corresponds to that stage's order in personality development.

1. Anal   1 2 3 4 5

2. Genital   1 2 3 4 5

3. Latency   1 2 3 4 5

4. Oral   1 2 3 4 5

5. Phallic   1 2 3 4 5

Explain

6. All psychoanalytic theories have unconscious processes as a primary motivation of behavior. How are the primary unconscious motivations different in Freud, Jung, and Adler's theories?

13.3 The Humanistic Perspective

According to the humanistic perspective, your personality is influenced by an innate capacity for personal growth.

■ Illustrate the humanistic perspective of personality using Rogers's Person-Centered Perspective and Maslow's Theory of Self-actualization.

All living things, according to humanists, have an actualizing tendency.

While Freud saw people as basically selfish and needing to be tamed by society's influence on the superego, humanists saw people as inherently good. Humanists believe that all humans, indeed all living things, have an **actualizing tendency** or a need for **self-actualization**, that is, a desire to be the best version of themselves possible. Like a plant turns toward the sunlight and grows, you have an innate drive to be the best you that you can be given your environment. It is just your nature. **Humanism** or the phenomenological approach is a family of personality theories that emphasizes growth, potential, and self-actualization.

Because of this actualizing tendency, you know, internally and maybe even unconsciously, what is best for you. You also have an understanding of your **self**, or an awareness of your own personal characteristics and maybe even your level of functioning. According to the **humanistic psychology**, if you are in touch with yourself, you will make the best choices for yourself. It is like you have an internal global positioning system, or GPS, that points you in the correct direction for your best growth. Because a person's way of being the best version of him- or herself is unique, humanists believe that it is important to examine humans on an individual level. Like the saying "In order to understand people, you need to walk a mile in their shoes," humanists believe that in order to understand a person, you need to understand the world from his or her perspective.

Rogers's Person-Centered Perspective

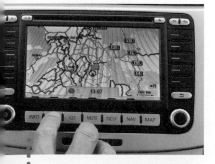

A GPS gives you guidance. Our actualizing tendency, according to humanists, guides you to the best version of you.

Carl Rogers **FIGURE 13-6** (Rogers, 1989) suggested that besides food, water, and shelter, humans have a need for **positive regard**, a sense of being loved and respected. At some point, we also develop **positive self-regard**, which is a kind of grow-your-own version of positive regard. You develop positive self-regard through the positive regard you get from others.

The ideal way to obtain positive regard that grows into positive self-regard is through **unconditional positive regard**—that is, a sense of respect and love that is not linked to specific behaviors. Unconditional positive regard would allow you to love and respect yourself and get in touch with the internal sense of what is best for you. All of this works out just fine unless positive regard is given with strings attached. If you feel like you must act a certain way in order to be loved and respected, you are receiving **conditional positive regard**, or love and respect only when you act in ways that others want. This leads to the performance of particular behaviors in order to be loved and respected. It is important to note that parents, teachers, and friends often deliver conditional regard unintentionally and not usually out of some desire to control you. Most people deliver conditional regard because it is a pretty good way of getting you to do what they want and what they think is best for you. It becomes problematic, however, because conditional regard can cause you to shift from doing things because of your own internal GPS reasons to an external reason (in order to get that respect and love), and as a result you are no longer listening to your own internal GPS to guide you. You dampen that voice inside of you.

FIGURE 13-6 Dr. Carl Rogers.

Rogers suggested that the internal GPS that guides you by means of the actualizing tendency is your **real self**. However, the way you see yourself is your **self-image**. Through conditional regard, you develop an idea of what you "should become" to get maximum worthy feelings from others. You develop an internal idea of an **ideal self**, which would possibly meet all the conditions of worth we discern from others. The difference between your real self and the artificial ideal self is **incongruency**. The more incongruency you have, the more miserable you are.

Rogers believed that a **fully functioning person** is one who is open to experience, is accurate in his or her perceptions of the world, and accurately perceives his or her own feelings and motives. The person lives in the here and now, trusts him- or herself to do what is right, feels free to make independent choices, and contributes to the actualization of others. Rogers believed that in order to help people regain connection with their internal GPS, therapists should be genuine and honest and have empathy and genuine respect for clients.

Maslow's Theory of Self-actualization

At its essence, Abraham Maslow's (Maslow, 1987) theory is a simple one—some needs take precedence over others. If you are both very thirsty and chilly and have a choice to address one need over the other, people will tend to choose to drink water before putting on a parka. According to Maslow, there is a **hierarchy of needs**, meaning an order of importance of motivations from basic physiological needs to self-fulfillment needs. Maslow's hierarchy of needs consists of five levels, which you can see in FIGURE 13-7. Biological needs and safety needs are at the bottom, forming the base of the pyramid, and esteem and self-actualization needs are at the top. The higher-level needs are less important because we can survive without them. From bottom to top, the levels of the pyramid are:

1. Physiological needs: biological drives and survival
2. Safety and security needs: stability and well-being
3. Love and belonging needs: relationships and sense of purpose
4. Esteem needs: being valued by others
5. Actualization needs: being the best version of yourself possible

Maslow described most of the needs as deficit needs or **D needs**, meaning that you really feel that need when you are running low on it. If your need is being met, you are not aware that the need exists. Lacking D needs will stunt your personal growth. Actualization, on the other hand, is a being need or **B need** because we grow toward it. Unlike hunger that goes away once you have enough food, self-actualization continues to grow the more energy you put toward it.

Unhealthy (mistaken) lifestyle Adler's description of those who strive for superiority by competing with others.

Healthy lifestyle According to Adler, attempts to compensate for feelings of inferiority in a socially useful way.

Principle of falsifiability The notion that a theory must be able to be disproved in order to be testable and scientific.

Actualizing tendency According to the humanists, the instinctual desire to be the best version of yourself possible.

Self-actualization The motivation to be the best version of yourself possible.

Humanism A theoretical orientation that emphasizes growth, potential, and self-actualization; also known as the phenomenological approach.

Self A person's awareness of his or her own characteristics.

Humanistic psychology A family of personality theories that emphasize human growth, potential, and self-actualization.

Positive regard A communication of love and respect.

Positive self-regard Respect for your own decisions.

Unconditional positive regard According to Rogers, a sense of respect and love that is not linked to specific behaviors.

Conditional positive regard According to Rogers, the idea that respect comes only when certain circumstances are met.

Real self According to Rogers, your internal idea of who you should be.

Self-image How you see yourself.

Ideal self According to Rogers, a version of yourself that could please other people.

Incongruency According to Rogers, the difference between your ideal self and your actual self.

Fully functioning person According to Jung, a person who has a developed real self.

Hierarchy of needs According to Maslow, the order of importance of motivations, from basic physiological needs to self-fulfillment needs.

D (deficit) needs According to Maslow, needs other than self-actualization needs.

B (being) needs According to Maslow, self-actualization needs.

Peak experience According to Maslow, "transient moments of self-actualization" that are associated with feelings of harmony, interconnectedness, and joy.

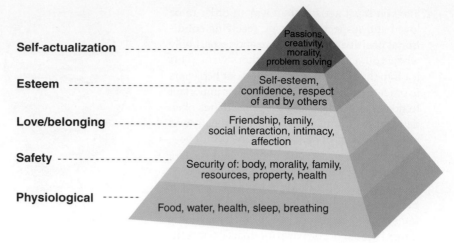

FIGURE 13-7 Maslow's need hierarchy.

Maslow suggested that maybe only a small percentage of the population will make it to this level. Many self-actualized people have some things in common. They see the journey as being more important that the result, enjoy being alone, and accept others for who they are. Self-actualized people are known to have an efficient perception of reality and the presence of **peak experiences**, which Maslow defined as "transient moments of self-actualization" that are associated with feelings of harmony, interconnectedness, and joy (Maslow, 1987).

Evaluating the Humanistic Perspectives

Despite the positive view that the humanistic theory holds of humans, not all humans hold humanistic theory in such high regard. As with Freudian theory, it is difficult to muster scientific evidence for humanist theory. Much of the evidence for the theory comes from case studies of the healthiest of people. And many believe the humanistic approach to be so overly confident regarding the nature of personality as to be impractical.

Still, humanistic ideas have found their way into our everyday language: living authentically and awareness are part of our understanding of ourselves and others. In addition, humanist influences have formed our understanding of therapy and have influenced other research trends such as positive psychology.

CONCEPT LEARNING CHECK 13.3 | *Illustrating the Humanistic Perspective*

For each stage listed below, circle the number that corresponds to that need's level in the hierarchy.

1. Actualization needs: being the best version of yourself possible   1 2 3 4 5

2. Physiological needs: biological drives and survival   1 2 3 4 5

3. Love and belonging needs: relationships and sense of purpose   1 2 3 4 5

4. Esteem needs: being valued by others   1 2 3 4 5

5. Safety and security needs: stability and well-being   1 2 3 4 5

Explain

6. Give an example to illustrate the following:

   A. Unconditional positive regard

   B. Conditional regard

13.4 Trait Perspectives

According to the trait perspective, your personality has stable characteristics of behavior.

■ Discuss the factors involved in the trait perspective.

"Have you met Marsha? What she like?" I overheard one student ask another.

"Well, she's a bit shy, but she's funny once you get to know her . . . oh . . . and she's got great taste in clothes, too."

We use traits to describe personality all the time. One way to think of a **trait** is as a stable quality that differentiates one individual from another individual. And the **trait theory** of personality focuses on identifying the traits that summarize and predict a person's behavior. Raymond Cattell (Cattell, 1964) and other trait theorists make a distinction between traits you can observe, or **surface traits**, and **source traits**, which are universal, enduring behavioral characteristics, the underpinnings that produce the traits that we see.

Factor Analysis

One of the things that trait theorists focus on is the number of traits that you can use to describe a person's personality. Sure, you could just use every word possible in the English language to describe a person, but at nearly 14,000 traits, it be would tedious to describe a person's personality in about as many words as are in this chapter. Psychologists needed a simpler, more elegant solution. With the hundreds and hundreds of traits that are in our language, how do psychologists determine which are the most important? One tool they have to whittle down the choices is factor analysis. **Factor analysis** is a statistical technique that is used to find clusters of related items. Factor analysis reveals the core quality, or factor, that lies under many variables. A person may be outgoing, talkative, sociable, and enjoy parties, but the underlying trait that links these qualities may be extroversion. Since one of the main goals of science is parsimony—meaning simpler is better—explaining personality using the fewest traits possible is best.

The Big Five Factors

Factor analysis of trait terms of the English language yielded the five-factor model of personality, also known as the **Big Five** (McCrae & Costa, 1987). The five-factor model of personality is a trait theory concept suggesting that the five most essential personality traits are openness to experience, conscientiousness, extroversion, agreeableness, and neuroticism. A great way to remember the five factors is the acronym OCEAN **TABLE 13-3**.

Trait A stable characteristic of behavior.

Trait theory A theory of personality that focuses on identifying and measuring characteristics of behavior.

Surface trait An enduring behavior that is easily observed.

Source trait A universal, enduring behavioral characteristic.

Factor analysis A statistical technique used to find clusters of related items.

Big Five A trait theory concept suggesting that the five most essential personality traits are openness to experience, conscientiousness, extroversion, agreeableness, and neuroticism; also known as the five-factor model of personality.

TABLE 13-3 The Big Five

Trait	Low Scorers	High Scorers
Openness	Conforming Favors predictability Real-world	Autonomous Favors change Creative
Conscientiousness	Chaotic Cavalier Hasty	Prepared Meticulous Methodical
Extroversion	Timid Restrained Distant	Outgoing Boisterous Demonstrative
Agreeableness	Unfeeling Skeptical Unhelpful	Soft-hearted Unquestioning Accommodating
Neuroticism	Still Confident Smug	Nervous Unconfident Self-absorbed

Source: Adapted from McCrae & Costa (1986).

Openness to experience
A personality trait that is part of the Big Five that describes how much affection a person has for newness.

Conscientiousness A Big Five trait that describes how trustworthy a person might be.

Extroversion A trait that describes that an individual is energized by the external world rather than by the internal world.

Agreeableness A personality trait that is part of the Big Five that describes how trusting a person is.

Neuroticism A personality trait that describes how emotional the person might be.

Theoretical approach to traits Deriving traits from another theory of personality.

Lexical approach to traits An approach that uses language to determining the most important traits of personality.

Openness to experience is affection for the new. People who score high on openness are curious and imaginative. People who score low on openness might be seen as conventional. If, whenever you go to a restaurant, you always order exactly the same thing, you might score low on openness to experience. **Conscientiousness** describes how trustworthy a person might be. People who score high on conscientiousness are seen as organized, reliable, and punctual. Those low on conscientiousness are seen as unreliable. **Extroversion** describes where you get your energy. This is similar to Jung's concept of extroversion and introversion. People who score high on extroversion are seen as social, active, and talkative. People who score low on extroversion, otherwise known as introverts, are reserved and quiet. **Agreeableness** describes how trusting the person might be. People who score extremely high on agreeableness are serious, trusting, helpful, and forgiving. They may also be seen as gullible, perhaps agreeing to cash checks for stranded royalty who send emails. Those low on agreeableness and are seen as cynical and suspicious and are always looking for ways they may get tricked: "Don't eat the bread at a buffet, that's how they trick you into eating less!" **Neuroticism** describes how emotional the person might be. People who score high on neuroticism are seen as worrying and nervous and excitable. He or she may call you and yell, "Oh my gosh, the *worst* thing happened to me today," when it may be a minor event. Those with extremely low scores on neuroticism can be seen as cold and stoic.

The Revised NEO Personality Inventory consists of 240 items that measure the factors in the Big Five (Piedmont, 1998).

Assessing Traits

Some personality researchers derived traits using a theoretical approach. A **theoretical approach to traits** means that the traits come from another theory of personality. An example might be how Jung's theory gave rise to the trait of extroversion in the Big Five—a trait perspective approach. Using a theoretical approach has some problems. Any deficits in the original theory will be duplicated in the trait version of the theory.

Some personality psychologists use a **lexical**, or language, approach to determining the most important traits. Important personality characteristics are embedded within the language, according to this theory. The more a word is used to describe people, the more central the concept. The more frequently the word appears, the more likely that that trait is important. Frequency reflects not just the number of times a word is used but also the number of synonyms a word might have. In addition to frequency, cross-cultural universality is another important lexical quality. The more often different languages invoke a certain trait, the more likely it is that these words are reflecting a similar understanding of the same underlying trait.

Evaluating the Trait Perspective

While we no doubt can describe people in terms of traits (be it three or five or sixteen or more), researchers do have criticisms of this approach to personality. Some psychologists wonder if the trait approach to personality is even really a theory of personality. While it does a good job of describing and perhaps predicting behavior, the trait approach falls flat at explaining where the traits originated or what happens

---

CONCEPT LEARNING CHECK 13.4 | *Identifying the Big Five Traits*

Match each personality description to one of the Big Five personality trait categories below. Remember that people can score from high to low in each of the five trait categories.

BIG FIVE TRAIT	PERSONALITY DESCRIPTION
A. Openness	1. _____ Becomes anxious easily
B. Consciousness	2. _____ Prefers time alone to recharge
C. Extroversion	3. _____ Is nearly always on time
D. Agreeableness	4. _____ Loves trying new foods
E. Neuroticism	5. _____ Suspicious and cautious

if the situation changes. Also, unlike the humanistic and psychodynamic approaches, the trait approach does not describe any underlying motivation behind behavior or any developmental patterns over time—how personality is formed or how or why or if personality changes over time.

13.5 The Social Cognitive Perspective

According to the social cognitive perspective, an interaction among traits, thoughts, and the environment determines your personality.

■ Analyze the social cognitive theories of Bandura as compared to those of Mischel.

Earlier, we discussed learning theory and **behaviorism**, the study of learning based on directly observable actions. Behaviorists believe that your personality is the result of reinforcement and punishment. One of the problems of the behavioral perspective is that people think. While it is true that we learn from our environment, we also have subjective thoughts about what we learn, as well as the consequences. According to the **social cognitive perspective**, your personality is not just your history of reinforcements and punishments; it is based on the interplay among traits, thoughts, and the environment.

If I invited you to listen to a dull 3-hour lecture and offered to pay you $1,000 to attend the lecture, you might jump at the chance. Classic behaviorism has no problem explaining that! But what if you had just won $100,000 in a game show? You might not be as excited about the opportunity. The subjective nature of your interpretation of your environment, what you think you can do, and what you expect from your environment and yourself are subjective, and these expectations can have a big impact when folded into the ideas of behaviorism. The social cognitive theories of personality take the subjective nature of cognition into consideration.

Bandura's Social Cognitive Theory

Earlier, we discussed Albert Bandura's FIGURE 13-8 theory of observational learning. **Observational learning** acknowledges that behavior can change simply from watching others, or **models**. A model is a person who performs specific behaviors that others observe. If you have ever driven on the highway and suddenly slowed down to the speed limit because someone else has been pulled over by a police officer for speeding, you have participated in observational learning. Slowing down is strange because the likelihood of being pulled over for speeding has just decreased, but your behavior has changed. Why? Bandura would explain your behavior as witnessing someone (a model) being punished for the exact behavior you are exhibiting (speeding). This vicarious punishment acts to change your behavior.

Bandura had another important theory about personality: You change your environment; the environment changes you. This is the central notion in Bandura's idea of reciprocal determinism. **Reciprocal determinism** is a concept that suggests that behavior, environment, and cognitions are interrelated, as you can see in FIGURE 13-9. A key cognitive factor in reciprocal determinism is self-efficacy, or your perception of your ability to perform a certain task. Feeling like you can do something well increases the likelihood that you will do that behavior. It is also likely that you will seek out environments in which you can show yourself or other people your ability to do things well. If you think you are good dancer, you will seek out environments in which you can show your moves. On the other hand, if you think your singing skills are best left in the shower, you will likely avoid the karaoke bars.

FIGURE 13-8 Dr. Albert Bandura.

Behaviorism The study of learning based on directly observable actions in the absence of mental processes.

Social cognitive perspective A personality theory that focuses on the interplay among traits, thoughts, and environmental contexts.

Observational learning Acquiring new behaviors by watching a model.

Model One who performs specific behaviors that others observe.

Reciprocal determinism Bandura's concept that suggests that behavior, environment, and thoughts are interrelated.

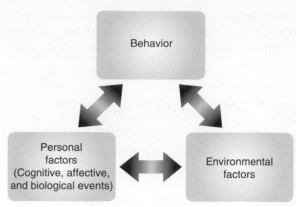

FIGURE 13-9 Reciprocal determinism.

Self-efficacy is subjective and specific. You might, for example have rather high self-efficacy for puzzles and dismal self-efficacy for learning a new dance. The higher your self-efficacy, the more likely you are going to try to excel and exhibit your prowess.

In addition to self-efficacy, Bandura also emphasized a key behavioral factor in reciprocal determinism: **self-regulation**, or the ability to control or adjust our own behavior. Personality, to a large extent, involves understanding what we can do and being able to put those beliefs in motion.

Mischel's Social Cognitive Theory

One of the important assumptions of personality theory is that personality is an enduring characteristic. But what if it is not? What if personality is not consistent across different situations and across time? That is exactly what Walter Mischel discovered. A person's behavior, when carefully scrutinized, depends on situational cues rather than being consistent across situations (Mischel, 1996).

This introduces what some call the **consistency paradox**. Most people believe their personality is the same all the time, but it is not, according to Michel. Although most believe that people behave consistently, there is actually low cross-situational consistency (Mischel & Peake, 1982). Mischel's approach does not predict that behavior will be consistent across situations. It argues that your behavior in a given situation depends on situational cues and expectations to be rewarded or punished. Consistency, Mischel suggests, occurs only when the same behavior is reinforced in a variety of situations or the person is unable to determine what situation she or he is in. **Cognitive person variables** are individual traits that shape the way you act in different situations.

Cognitive person variables affect your way of seeing the world and the way you navigate through life. Examples of cognitive person variables include your values, expectations, and competencies. Many of the factors included in cognitive person variables make up the collection of your beliefs about yourself—your **self-concept**.

Locus of control is a cognitive person variable that summarizes your idea of the source of reinforcement and punishment (Rotter, 1966). Locus of control can either be internal or external. In an **internal locus of control**, you believe that any good or bad things that happen to you are the result of your own actions. **External locus of control**, on the other hand, is the idea that reinforcers and punishments are outside of your control. For example, if you believe that how well you do on the exam is based mostly on how difficult the exam is, that will change how much and how hard you will study in school. What you try to achieve in the world, according to the cognitive theory of personality, depends on what you believe you can do, or your **self-efficacy**. If you believe that you cannot do well on an exam because the professor does not like you, then the reinforcement for studying is out of your control, and you believe that you cannot do well. How you behave in that situation depends more on those factors than your individual personality. Mischel believes that if you are looking for consistency in personality or traits, you are looking in the wrong place. Consistency depends on the situations we seek out.

Self-regulation The ability to control or adjust our own behavior.

Consistency paradox The idea that people believe that personality is stable, although research says that it is not.

Cognitive person variables Individual traits that affect the way you see the world.

Self-concept The collection of all your beliefs about yourself.

Locus of control A cognitive person variable that summarizes your idea of the source of reinforcement and punishment.

Internal locus of control The idea that reinforcers and punishments are under your own control.

External locus of control The idea that reinforcers and punishments are outside of your control.

Self-efficacy Your perception about your ability to do a certain task.

Evaluating the Social Cognitive Perspective

The behavioral and social cognitive approaches are rooted in a scientific view of personality. The social cognitive approach is powered by learning theory but goes beyond learning theory and behavioral approaches by incorporating situational and person factors into understanding personality. Nevertheless, some suggest that cognitive variables such as a tendency to expect bad things to happen can be vague and difficult to study scientifically. Pure behaviorists wonder if the introduction of vague cognitive variables raises more questions than it answers.

While the social cognitive perspective extends the behavioral perspective, it may retain some of the main weaknesses of the behavioral approach, such as reducing human personality to simply what we do. Although they take into account subjective thoughts, social cognitive theories are harder to test scientifically than pure behavioral ones.

CONCEPT LEARNING CHECK 13.5 | *Comparing Social Cognitive Perspectives*

Fill in the blank with the correct term or word.

1. Sarah thinks no matter how hard she studies, she will get bad grades. Sarah has a(n) _____ locus of control.

2. _____ is a theorist that suggested that we learn by modeling the behaviors of others.

3. Mischel believed that behavior is _____ across time.

Explain

1. Leah is an expert cheerleader and loves to be the center of attention. Sketch out how Bandura would explain why she is a cheerleader based on his idea of reciprocal determinism.

13.6 The Biological Perspective

According to the biological perspective, physiological processes determine your personality.

- Explain the different biological perspectives and theories of how physiological processes determine personality.

Biological underpinnings of personality are certainly not new. Some of the earliest theories of personality were biologically based. For example, the ancient Greeks had a theory of personality that was biologically rooted. They felt that those who had certain temperaments must have an abundance of certain humors. The four humors—blood, black bile, yellow bile, and phlegm—were thought to be fluids in the body that at various levels could create differences in personality (Strathern, 2005) FIGURE 13-10. Too much blood, for example, was associated with an aggressive personality. Too much phlegm, on the other hand, was associated with a dopey or phlegmatic personality. Intervention into disordered personality was created by balancing out these different fluids through diet, exercise, and more gruesome types of manipulations like bloodletting. It is no wonder they thought that too much phlegm was associated with a sluggish personality: Think about what happens when you are sick, with so much phlegm that it is coming out of your nose. They thought that maybe you blew out the extra phlegm, and when the phlegm levels returned to normal, your energy level increased.

Even Freud's personality theory may have been, in part, a biological model. Some suggest that Freud was trying to explain the different levels of energy and how it transferred and flowed throughout the body (Peterson, 2010). Some believe that Freud was actually describing a physiological theory of personality.

More modern biological theories focus on brain structures and physiological mechanisms that may result in changes in personality. The biological perspective on personality suggests that individual differences are based in biological differences. Brain anatomy and biochemistry are involved in personality, and differences in observed traits such

FIGURE 13-10 The four humors—blood, black bile, yellow bile, and phlegm.

as introversion or extroversion or impulsivity and sensation seeking are all based upon biological factors, according to the biological perspective.

There is a good deal of evidence that suggests that parts of the brain, for example, are associated with personality. You may recall Phineas Gage, whose damaged frontal lobe caused dramatic differences in his personality. We also know from psychosurgery such as lobotomy that changes in personality can occur after surgery on the brain. You can also see differences in personalities from comparing PET scans and MRIs of individuals who score as high or low on traits such as sensation seeking (Freeman & Beer, 2010).

Eysenck's Theory

Temperament According to the biological perspective, inborn biological traits.

Hans Eysenck FIGURE 13-11 suggested that differences in **temperament**, or inborn biological traits, determine individual differences in personality. According to Eysenck's three-factor model of personality, the three most important dimensions of personality are neuroticism (N), extroversion (E), and psychoticism (P) (Zuckerman, Kuhlman, Joireman, Teta, & Kraft, 1993).

Eysenck believed that extroversion was influenced by variations in arousal in the cortex (Eysenck & Eysenck, 1985). This arousal theory maintained that the introvert's arousal "engine" idled higher, suggesting introverts need less external stimulation to feel comfortable. Extroverts, on the other hand, have lower baseline levels of cortical arousal and thus seek out stimulation. According to this theory, pursuing or shunning arousing situations

FIGURE 13-11 Dr. Hans Eysenck.

(such as social situations or noise) is a tactic for maintaining optimal levels of arousal. For example, researchers had subjects choose the level of background noise they preferred while working on a matching task. Introverts chose noise levels that were much lower than those of extroverts, and each group performed best under its preferred noise level (Geen, 1984).

While the biological perspective suggested that the introversion-extroversion dimension is driven by cortical arousal, Eysenck suggested that neuroticism, or emotional stability, is based on how easily the sympathetic nervous system is activated. Those who trip the sympathetic nervous system easily have low activation thresholds and have a harder time inhibiting their feelings. This means that minor events can make them stressed. Those with low levels of neuroticism, on the other hand, have higher activation thresholds and take longer to experience negative feelings and are harder to unnerve.

Psychoticism is a trait that combines the attributes of the Big Five traits of openness and agreeableness. Those who score high on psychoticism can be inflexible, creative, sometimes inconsiderate, quick to anger, and reckless. The physiological basis suggested by Eysenck for psychoticism is testosterone, with higher levels of psychoticism associated with higher levels of testosterone (Eysenck & Eysenck, 1985).

Genetics and Personality

If personality is largely biological, as Eysenck and others suggest, it would stand to reason that the biologically derived traits should share characteristics of other biological processes, such as genetic links. There is research that supports this contention FIGURE 13-12. **Behavioral genetics** is an interdisciplinary field that examines the influences of heredity and environment on behavior. Genetic factors, according to researchers, make up about half of individual differences on many traits (Jang, Livesley, & Vernon, 1996).

Psychoticism A personality trait that describes how inflexible, creative, or reckless a person is.

Behavioral genetics An interdisciplinary field that examines the influences of heredity and environment on behavior.

Sociobiology A theory that your behaviors and personality can be explained through the ideas of evolution.

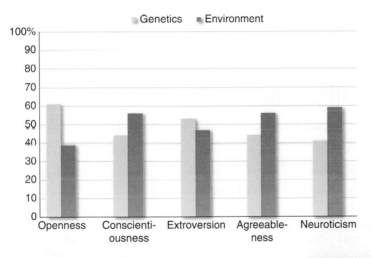

FIGURE 13-12 Heritability estimates for personality traits. *Source: Data from Jang, K. L., Livesley, W. J., & Vernon, P. A. (1996). Heritability of the big five personality dimensions and their facets: a twin study.* Journal of Personality, *64(3), 577–591.*

Evolutionary Theories of Personality

Evolutionary theories of personality are extensions of biological theories. If biology is the root of all our traits, then the patterns of behavior could also be passed down from generation to generation. Temperament would be under the influence of heritability and evolutionary forces, and certain behaviors may increase the likelihood of passing along your genes to future offspring.

The evolutionary theory of **sociobiology**, developed by E. O. Wilson FIGURE 13-13, suggests that our social behavior is under evolutionary pressure and that personality and social behavior are products of natural selection (Wilson, 2004). Wilson developed this theory by examining mating strategies of nonhuman animals, and these were extended to explain mating strategies of humans.

FIGURE 13-13 E. O. Wilson.

Evaluating the Biological Perspective

Biological theories of personality are compelling and can be combined with other theories of personality, such as the trait perspective. Given what we know about the brain, it is hard to ignore that biological processes are at the root of who we are. Another strength of the biological approach is an emphasis on a scientific explanation of personality.

Despite the strengths of the biological approach, there are still some criticisms of this approach. Biological approaches tend to ignore hard-to-evaluate concepts like thoughts or motivations. Doing so ignores the multiple influences that culture and society have on our personalities. Can what it means to be human be reduced to brain functioning alone? It is easy to oversimplify personality as brain and hormonal functioning alone. Some suggest that because of this, biological theories are not complete theories of personality. In addition, biological theories, much like the trait approach, do not provide any background for the development of personality.

CONCEPT LEARNING CHECK 13.6 | *Understanding the Biological Perspective*

Fill in the blanks with the correct response.

1. According to Eysenck, the three most important dimensions of personality are _____, _____, and _____.

2. According to the biological perspective, the arousal "engine" of extroverts idles _____.

3. _____ is the theory that personality traits are influenced by evolution.

Explain

4. Explain Eysenck's theory of the differences between introverts and extroverts.

13.7 Personality Assessment

Psychologists use a number of different tools to understand and describe an individual's personality.

■ Identify the different tools to understand personality and how they are used.

Psychological test A measure used to assess or describe mental functioning.

Personality inventory A test used to measure an individual's pattern of thinking, feeling, and behaving.

Graphology A technique in which handwriting is analyzed in order to describe personality.

Intrapsychic conflict Differences between the desires of the id, ego, and superego.

Projective test A personality instrument in the psychoanalytic perspective that uses interpretation of ambiguous stimuli to uncover unconscious conflicts.

Projective hypothesis A theory that suggests that reactions to ambiguous material reveal intrapsychic conflicts.

How can you gauge or describe a person's personality? One way is through a psychological test. A **psychological test** is a measure used to assess or describe mental functioning. A **personality inventory** is a special type of psychological test that is used to measure an individual's pattern of thinking, feeling, and behaving. The way that psychologists measure or assess personality depends on their approach to personality. For example, if you believed that the way a person formed the letters as they wrote said something about his or her personality, you would employ **graphology**, a technique in which handwriting is analyzed in order to assess personality. Graphology, unfortunately, is not a good predictor of personality (Dazzi & Pedrabissi, 2009). For a personality test to be useful, it must be valid and reliable.

In the psychoanalytic realm, psychologists are interested in revealing **intrapsychic conflicts**, meaning the differences between the desires of the id, ego, and superego. Psychologists do this by using **projective tests**, a kind of personality instrument that uses the interpretation of ambiguous stimuli to uncover unconscious conflicts. Projective tests operate by means of the **projective hypothesis**, which suggests that when you see ambiguous material, you describe it in a way that reveals the interplay of your id, ego, and superego desires. Projective tests get their name from the defense mechanism of projection. You will recall that projection is a defense mechanism in which a person unconsciously attributes his or her own threatening impulses to another person. In projective tests, a person will unconsciously attribute his or her intrapsychic conflicts onto the test material. Examples of projective tests include free association tasks, the Rorschach inkblot test, and the thematic apperception test (TAT).

Let's say Geoff is on his way to take a **free association** test, which is a test in which you say the first thing that comes to your mind in response to a target word. On the drive, Geoff accidently hits a white rat on the way to the psychologist's office. His id is thrilled by the tension reduction of the act, but his superego is horrified at his carelessness. While at the psychologist's office, the therapist introduces a free association task. "I'm going to say a word and I want you to say the first word that pops into your head." The therapist may also time how long it takes Geoff to react. "Let's get started. White." Well, Geoff's id wants to shout, "White fluffy rat that I killed!" The super ego interjects unconsciously, "What ever you do, don't mention the rat; you don't want the psychologist to know how careless you are!" Geoff is in the middle of an intrapsychic battle. The stronger the fight between id and superego, the longer it takes to resolve the conflict. Eventually Geoff responds, "I can't think of anything."

Another projective test, which may be familiar from the movies, is the **Rorschach inkblot test** FIGURE 13-14. In this test, unconscious conflicts are revealed by the client's interpretation of and reactions to ambiguous patterns of ink. The Rorschach inkblot test, developed by Herman Rorschach in 1921, consists of 10 inkblots. The cards are presented one at a time, and the person tested reports what he or she sees and where it is on the card. Scoring of the Rorschach is complex and uses various criteria dependent on the scoring method used such as

FIGURE 13-14 A woman takes the Rorschach inkblot test. She will respond with what images she sees in the card.

Exner's (Exner, 1993). Most scoring systems include the kinds and placement of objects reported in the cards.

The **thematic apperception test (TAT)** FIGURE 13-15, is a projective personality instrument in which unconscious conflicts are revealed by the interpretation of stories told in reaction to a series of ambiguous images. Most of the images in the TAT show people interacting with each other. As with other projective instruments, the kinds of stories told will reveal intrapsychic and unconscious conflicts. If all the stories are about people fighting and never talking again, for example, this may reflect the way the subject handles fights in his or her life.

All projective tests involve subjective scoring by the examiner. While they can reveal a great deal of complex information about a person and can be useful in a therapeutic setting, they can be time consuming to administer and require extensive training. Some scientists question the validity and reliability of projective tests (Lilienfield, 2005) since the scoring is subjective and the same

FIGURE 13-15 The thematic apperception test.

test can produce inconsistent results even from the same person.

If it is traits you are after, then self-report inventories are useful. **Self-report inventories** are tests in which a person will directly answer questions about her or his behaviors, thoughts, or feelings. Unlike projective tests, self-report inventories are often **empirically derived**, meaning they are created by using a large number of test questions and are whittled down to a smaller number that best reflect the characteristic being tested. Examples of self-report inventories include the Minnesota Multiphasic Personality Inventory, the California Personality Inventory, and the Sixteen Personality Factor Questionnaire.

The **Minnesota Multiphasic Personality Inventory (MMPI)** is an empirically derived personality test that assesses a range of characteristics. The MMPI is an objective personality instrument. Unlike projective tests like the TAT or Rorschach, the

Graphology claims to understand personality through analyzing handwriting.

Free association A psychoanalytic technique in which people will report the first things that occur to them. Used to uncover unconscious conflicts.

Rorschach inkblot test A projective test in which someone's unconscious conflicts are revealed by his or her interpretation of and reactions to ambiguous patterns of ink.

Thematic apperception test (TAT) A projective personality instrument in which unconscious conflicts are revealed by the interpretation of stories told in reaction to a series of ambiguous images.

Self-report inventory A type of test in which a person will directly answer questions about his or her behaviors, thoughts, or feelings.

Empirically derived test A type of instrument that starts with a large number of test questions in order to select the ones that best reflect the characteristics being tested.

Minnesota Multiphasic Personality Inventory (MMPI) An empirically derived personality test that assesses a range of characteristics.

Objective A scoring system where the results are the same no matter who scores it.

California Personality Inventory (CPI) A type of personality test designed to measure characteristics important to daily life.

Sixteen Personality Factor Questionnaire (16PF) A personality inventory with results that are closely related to the Big Five.

results of an MMPI are **objective**, meaning the results are the same no matter who scores it; in fact, most MMPIs are computer scored, although hand-sorting options are available. The newest incarnation of the MMPI is the MMPI II-RF (for restructured form); it consists of 567 true–false items that determine 4 validity scores and 10 clinical scales (Butcher, 2011).

Not all personality tests are used in clinical work. The **California Personality Inventory (CPI)** is a type of personality test designed to measure characteristics important to daily life. Unlike the MMPI, which has more of a focus on psychopathology, the CPI describes personality in terms of individual strengths and challenges (Furnham & Henderson, 1982). The **Sixteen Personality Factor Questionnaire (16PF)** is a multiple-choice personality inventory that contains 185 multiple-choice items. Results of the 16PF reveal 16 primary factors or traits and 5 global factors that are closely related to the Big Five (Gregory, 2011).

CONCEPT LEARNING CHECK 13.7   *Identifying Personality Assessments*

Indicate whether the personality test is an empirical or projective test.

A. Empirical test

B. Projective test

1. _____ MMPI

2. _____ Rorschach inkblot test

3. _____ Sixteen personality factor questionnaire

4. _____ Thematic apperception test

5. _____ Word association

13.8 Culture and Personality

Culture and belief systems can shape and be shaped by personality.

■ Describe how culture and belief systems can shape and be shaped by personality.

Terror management theory A theory that suggests that because of our awareness of death, we battle anxiety by boosting our self-esteem and cultural connections.

Self-esteem Your self-worth.

Collectivist culture A culture that places an emphasis on interreliance rather than self-reliance.

Individualist culture A culture that places an emphasis on each person's rights rather than on the society.

Allocentrism A personality trait with an interreliant focus in which people tend to see themselves as part of a community.

Ideocentrism A personality trait with an interreliant focus.

Some researchers are starting to investigate how aspects of personality may be responsible for strengthening cultural beliefs. **Terror management theory**, for example, suggests that because we are self-aware, we know about the possibility of death. Whenever we are confronted with things that could cause death, we feel anxiety, fear, and unconscious terror (Greenberg & Kosloff, 2008). In order to combat this anxiety, we attempt to boost our **self-esteem**, or self-worth, by connecting with things that we feel are immortal and long lasting, like a cultural worldview. The theorists suggest that this explains surges in school sprit after a tragedy in a high school. The more you are confronted with your own mortality, the more you may emphasize your culture.

Culture can also shape personality. **Collectivist cultures** tend to emphasize interreliance (Sivadas, Bruvold, & Nelson, 2008). Members of collectivist cultures often have an interdependent understanding of the self and view themselves as part of a whole. In contrast, **individualist cultures** place an emphasis on each person's rights and place society in the background. Independent understanding of self is emphasized, and members of individualist cultures view themselves as independent units. As a result, collectivist cultures tend to generate members who have the trait of **allocentrism**, a personality trait with an interreliant focus, in which people tend to see themselves as part of a community. Individualistic cultures tend to create **ideocentrism**, a personality trait with an individual focus in which people tend to see themselves as self-reliant entities. A focus on self-esteem, for example, promotes your belief in yourself and is probably more prevalent in individualist cultures.

Summary of Multiple Influences on Personality

I never did find out who kidnapped the zebra and deposited him in Seney Hall. What caused the students to do it? No doubt there were multiple influences that affected their decision and multiple influences for their personality. Freud and the other psychoanalytic theorists might argue that intrapsychic conflict, the Shadow, or a need for superiority possessed the zebra-nappers that day. In contrast, the humanists might have suggested that a pull into incongruency drove the decision. Trait theories would point to extroversion and openness to experience. Biologically oriented theorists might point to sensation seeking or other temperament explanations. Some personality theorists may even take an eclectic approach. An **eclectic approach** blends several theories to explain or influence behavior. All personality approaches recognize the multiple influences of individual biology and individual characteristics, be they an individual preference for certain defense mechanisms, learned traits, or a tendency to be mischievous.

> **Eclectic approach** Blending several theories together to explain or influence behavior.

CONCEPT LEARNING CHECK 13.8   *Examining Culture and Personality*

Indicate whether each statement is true or false.

1. _____ People with the trait of allocentrism tend to see themselves as self-reliant.

2. _____ Those from collectivist cultures tend to emphasize interreliance.

3. _____ Terror management theory suggests that fear of culture is the main source of anxiety for people.

4. _____ Collectivist cultures encourage the trait of ideocentrism.

5. _____ Individualist cultures encourage the trait of allocentrism.

Explain

6. Describe how culture has influenced your personality.

CRITICAL THINKING APPLICATION

As far as I am concerned, everyone should get to watch *one* television show without being judged, no matter how ridiculous the show. Be it people losing weight, swapping spouses, strangers living together, or trying to survive on an island, reality TV has been an entertainment fixture for quite some time. People watch reality TV, in part, to get a glimpse into, as one show puts it, "what happens . . . when people stop being polite . . . and start getting real." But how much of an actual glimpse into human personality is reality TV? Certainly the situations that are created are extraordinary, but do extraordinary situations breed extraordinary personality?

Evaluate

1. How would different families of personality theories explain the behavior on reality TV?

2. Compare and contrast the role of personality and environmental influences that could lead someone to say, "I'm not here to make friends," a common reality TV phrase, but something people rarely say in real life.

3. As reality TV continues to be popular, what kinds of behaviors from reality TV have started to be modeled in the real world? What are the possible effects of this?

Visual Overview The major theories of personality, theorists, and concepts.

What kind of person would kidnap a zebra? Different theories of personality might offer different explanations. This overview summarizes the major theories of personality.

According to the psychoanalytic theory, unconscious processes determine your personality.

Freud

Jung

- Catharsis
- Thanatos
- Sublimation
- Defense mechanisms
- Denial

- Displacement
- Ego
- Fixation
- Id
- Oedipal complex
- Projection
- Psychosexual stages

- Sublimation
- Rationalization
- Reaction formation
- Reality principle
- Regression
- Repression
- Superego

- Great mother
- Principle of entropy
- Collective unconscious
- Hero
- Persona
- Principle of equivalence
- Transcendence
- Wise old man

Adler

- Inferiority
- Striving for superiority
- Compensation

According to the humanistic perspective, an innate capacity for personal growth influences your personality.

Rogers
- Unconditional positive regard
- Fully functioning person
- Conditional positive regard
- Ideal self
- Incongruence

Maslow
- Hierarchy of needs
  - D-needs
  - B-needs

Bandura
- Self-efficacy
- Observational learning
- Reciprocal determinism

Mischel
- Consistency paradox

According to the social cognitive perspective, your personality is determined by an integration of traits, thoughts, and the environment.

Eysenck
- Three-factor model of personality

Wilson
- Sociobiology

McCrae & Costa
- Big Five

According to the biological perspective, physiological processes determine your personality.

According to the trait perspective, your personality consists of stable characteristics of behavior.

13.1 Defining Personality

- Psychologists define personality in many ways.
- Personality is your pattern of thinking, feeling, and behaving.

- A good personality theory has clinical utility, practical utility, and predictive value, gives insight into human nature, can provide self-understanding, and helps describe complex behavior.

13.2 The Psychoanalytic Perspective

- According to the psychoanalytic perspective, unconscious processes determine your personality.
- According to Freud, your personality has conscious, preconscious, and unconscious components.
- The structures of your personality include the id, ego, and superego, according to Freud.
- As people grow and develop, the way they processes tension shifts, resulting in different stages of psychosexual development.
- The Oedipal complex describes a boy's unconscious desire for his mother, which results in identification with his father.

- Defense mechanisms describe unconscious compromises among the id, ego, and superego.
- Jung's theory of personality includes the conscious mind, the personal unconscious, and the collective unconscious as the basic structures of personality.
- Your collective unconscious contains a collection of archetypes, or universal thought forms, including the great mother, the shadow, the persona, wise old man, trickster, and the hero.
- Adler's theory of personality suggested that the major drive of personality is striving for superiority.
- Although there are many criticisms of psychodynamic theory, it remains a major force in psychology.

13.3 The Humanistic Perspective

- According to the humanistic perspective, your personality is influenced by an innate capacity for personal growth.
- Rogers suggested that providing unconditional positive regard would lead to growth, while conditional regard would lead to the development of an artificial ideal self and incongruency.
- Maslow suggested that a need hierarchy exists, meaning an order of importance

for motivations from basic physiological needs to self-fulfillment needs.
- Self-actualized people, according to Maslow, have the basic needs fulfilled.
- Humanistic theories are difficult to test; however, they have influenced psychotherapy and the positive psychology movement.

13.4 Trait Perspectives

- According to the trait perspective, your personality has stable characteristics of behavior.
- Factor analysis is a statistical technique used to find clusters of related items and is a major tool of the trait perspective.
- Factor analysis has yielded the five-factor model of personality, which suggests

that the five most essential personality traits are openness to experience, conscientiousness, extroversion, agreeableness, and neuroticism.
- While the trait approach is based on research, some psychologists do not think it is as comprehensive a theory as the psychodynamic or humanistic approaches.

13.5 The Social Cognitive Perspective

- According to the social cognitive perspective, an interaction among traits, thoughts, and the environment determines your personality.
- Bandura suggests that behavior can change simply from watching others.
- Reciprocal determinism is a concept that suggests that behavior, environment, and cognitions are interrelated.

- Mischel hypothesized that personality may not be as consistent as once thought.
- The social cognitive perspective of personality has the strength of a well-researched theory but may not add additional value to a traditional behavioral view of personality.

13.6 The Biological Perspective

- According to the biological perspective, physiological processes determine your personality.
- Brain structures and hormones may affect temperament and determine individual differences in personality.
- Behavioral genetics is a field that examines the influences of heredity and environment on behavior.

- Genetic factors make up about half of the individual differences on many traits.
- Temperament may be under the influence of heritability and evolutionary forces.
- Biological theories are compelling but can oversimplify complex behavior, and there are many alternative explanations for the same behavior.

13.7 Personality Assessment

- Psychologists use a number of different tools to understand personality.
- Projective tests measure intrapsychic conflicts.

- Empirically derived tests are derived through research methods.

13.8 Culture and Personality

- Culture and belief systems can shape and be shaped by personality.
- Terror management theory suggests that because of our awareness of death, we

battle anxiety by boosting our self-esteem and cultural connections.
- Collectivist and individualist cultures can influence the expression of personality.

13.1 Defining Personality

1. Your pattern of thinking, feeling, and behaving is called your:
   A. persona.
   B. personality.
   C. conscious mind.
   D. ego ideal.

13.2 The Psychoanalytic Perspective

2. If a person starts to talk in baby talk when under stress, Freud might suggest he or she is using the defense mechanism known as:
   A. regression.
   B. sublimation.
   C. denial.
   D. reaction formation.

3. Which structure of the personality, according to Freud, represents moral values?
   A. Id
   B. Ego
   C. Superego
   D. Collective unconscious

4. The id, according to Freud, was driven by aggressive and sexual instincts. This corresponds to Jung's archetype called:
   A. wise old man.
   B. great mother.
   C. shadow.
   D. persona.

5. People on reality TV shows who win by tearing down the other contestants may have a _____ style of life.
   A. healthy
   B. mistaken
   C. compensation
   D. thanatos

13.3 The Humanistic Perspective

6. If parents say to their kids, "We love you when you obey us," they may communicate:
   A. conditional positive regard.
   B. unconditional positive regard.
   C. incongruency.
   D. deficit needs.

7. What is the result from lacking in a D need, according to the humanists?
   A. Stunting of personal growth
   B. Encouragement of growth
   C. Self-actualization
   D. Denial of the need

13.4 Trait Perspectives

8. Veena orders scrambled eggs for breakfast no matter what. According to the Big Five, Veena would score _____ on the trait of _____.
   A. high; conscientiousness
   B. high; openness to experience
   C. low; openness to experience
   D. low; conscientiousness

13.5 The Social Cognitive Perspective

9. Mischel's work on cross-situational consistency suggested that personality is:
   A. inconsistent.
   B. based on modeling.
   C. based on observing others.
   D. biologically based.

13.6 The Biological Perspective

10. Those who link personality to biology point to research that suggests that extroverts seek stimulation because their typical arousal level is relatively:
    A. low.
    B. high.
    C. unstable.
    D. unaffected by external factors.

11. Inborn traits, according to biological theorists, are called:
    A. sociobiology.
    B. factor analysis.
    C. genes.
    D. temperament.

13.7 Personality Assessment

12. Psychologists use projective tests in order to assess:
  A. self-actualization.
  B. conscious motivation.
  C. unconscious motivation.
  D. happiness.

13. If Aubree is taking the thematic apperception test, which of the following will she do?
  A. Tell stories about a series of cards presented to her.
  B. Explain what she sees in a series of inkblots.
  C. Draw a picture of her family doing something.
  D. Take a paper-and-pencil test with true/false answers.

13.8 Culture and Personality

14. Which of the following traits is more helpful in individualistic cultures than in collectivist cultures?
  A. The trait of allocentrism
  B. The trait of ideocentrism
  C. Source traits
  D. Surface traits

15. According to terror management theory, being confronted with death creates anxiety. To confront this anxiety, you attempt to boost:
  A. self-esteem.
  B. allocentrism.
  C. ideocentrism.
  D. introversion.

CHAPTER DISCUSSION QUESTIONS

1. Tempers erupt during the holiday season when the passengers of an airline have been told that it has been overbooked. Craig's response illustrates displacement, while Scott's response illustrates regression. Describe the scene at the airport by giving an example of Craig's and Scott's reactions. Which response do you think will be more effective in getting them what they each want? Why?

2. A good theory of personality can help explain psychopathology. How does psychopathology arise according to Freud? Rogers?

3. How does a person's personality, according to the Big Five, shape the kind of music or clothes a person buys?

4. What are some challenges and practical solutions for parenting using unconditional positive regard?

5. Walter Mischel determined that personality is not always consistent. Are his findings in line with your experience of other people? How consistent or inconsistent do you feel your personality is? Why?

6. Considering the many theories of personality, how changeable or unchangeable do you think someone's personality is?

CHAPTER PROJECTS

1. Use Jung and the Big Five to describe the personality of a popular TV character.

2. Create a grid of well-known characters from TV, movies, and books that show extremes of each of the Big Five dimensions. You should have 10 characters total.

CHAPTER KEY TERMS

Actualizing tendency
Agreeableness
Allocentrism
Archetypes
B (being) needs
Behavioral genetics
Behaviorism
Big Five
California Personality Inventory (CPI)
Catharsis
Cognitive person variable
Collective unconscious
Collectivist culture
Conditional positive regard
Conscientiousness
Conscious mind
Consistency paradox
D (deficit) needs
Defense mechanism
Denial

Displacement
Disposition
Eclectic approach
Ego
Empirically derived test
Eros
External locus of control
Extroversion
Extrovert
Factor analysis
Fixation
Free association
Fully functioning person
Graphology
Great mother
Healthy lifestyle
Hero
Hierarchy of needs
Humanism
Humanistic psychology
Id

Ideal self
Identification
Ideocentrism
Incongruency
Individualist culture
Inferiority
Internal locus of control
Intrapsychic conflict
Introvert
Lexical approach to traits
Libido
Lifestyle
Locus of control
Minnesota Multiphasic Personality Inventory (MMPI)
Model
Neo-Freudian
Neuroticism
Objective
Observational learning
Oedipal complex

Openness to experience	Psychosexual stages	Sociobiology
Peak experience	Psychoticism	Source trait
Perfection principle	Rationalization	Striving for superiority
Persona	Reaction formation	Sublimation
Personality	Reality principle	Superego
Personality inventory	Real self	Surface trait
Personality theory	Reciprocal determinism	Temperament
Personal unconscious	Regression	Terror management theory
Pleasure principle	Repression	Thanatos
Positive regard	Rorschach inkblot test	Thematic apperception
Positive self-regard	Self	test (TAT)
Preconscious	Self-actualization	Theoretical approach to traits
Principle of entropy	Self-concept	Trait theory
Principle of equivalence	Self-efficacy	Trait
Principle of falsifiability	Self-esteem	Transcendence
Principle of opposites	Self-image	Trickster
Projection	Self-regulation	Unconditional positive regard
Projective hypothesis	Self-report inventory	Unconscious
Projective test	Shadow	Unhealthy (mistaken) lifestyle
Psychoanalysis	Sixteen Personality Factor	Wise old man
Psychoanalytic theories	Questionnaire (16PF)	
Psychological test	Social cognitive perspective	

ANSWERS TO CONCEPT LEARNING CHECKS

13.1 Describing Personality Theories

1. D. Insight into human nature
2. A. Clinical utility
3. E. Self-understanding
4. D. Insight into human nature
5. C. Predictive value

13.2 Comparing the Psychoanalytic Perspectives

1. Anal [2]
2. Genital [5]
3. Latency [4]
4. Oral [1]
5. Phallic [3]
6. Sample answer: Freud: intrapsychic conflict among the id, ego, and superego. Jung: unconscious operations of the principle of opposites, the principle of equivalence, and the principle of entropy. Adler: unconscious striving for perfection

13.3 Illustrating the Humanistic Perspective

1. Actualization needs: being the best version of yourself possible [5]
2. Physiological needs: biological drives and survival [1]
3. Love and belonging needs: relationships and sense of purpose [3]
4. Esteem needs: being valued by others [4]
5. Safety and security needs: stability and well-being [2]
6. A: Answers should indicate respect despite the person's behavior, such as "I don't agree with your decision to spend your allowance all in one place, but I still love and respect you."

   B: Answers should indicate respect but with strings, such as, "No daughter of mine will act that way!"

13.4 Identifying the Big Five Traits

1. Neuroticism [E]
2. Extroversion [C]
3. Consciousness [B]
4. Openness [A]
5. Agreeableness [D]

13.5 Comparing Social Cognitive Perspectives

1. Sarah thinks no matter how hard she studies, she will get bad grades. Sarah has an **external** locus of control.
2. **Bandura** is a theorist that suggested that we learn by modeling the behaviors of others.
3. Michel believed that behavior is **inconsistent** across time.
4. Behavior: Cheers

   Environment: Seeks out situations where she can get attention

   Personal factors: Ability to be a good cheerleader

13.6 Understanding the Biological Perspective

1. According to Eysenck, the three most important dimensions of personality are **neuroticism, extroversion,** and **psychoticism**.
2. According to the biological perspective, the arousal "engine" of extroverts idles **lower**.
3. **Sociobiology** is the theory that personality traits are influenced by evolution.
4. The introversion-extroversion dimension is driven by cortical arousal. Those who trip the sympathetic nervous system easily have low activation thresholds and have a harder time inhibiting their feelings. This means that minor events can make them stressed.

13.7 Identifying Personality Assessments

1. MMPI [Empirical]
2. Rorschach inkblot test [Projective]
3. Sixteen personality factor questionnaire [Empirical]
4. Thematic apperception test [Projective]
5. Word association [Projective]

13.8 Examining Culture and Personality

1. People with the trait of allocentrism tend to see themselves as self-reliant. [F]
2. Those from collectivist cultures tend to emphasize interreliance. [T]
3. Terror management theory suggests that fear of culture is the main source of anxiety for people. [F]
4. Collectivist cultures encourages the trait of ideocentrism. [F]
5. Individualist cultures encourage the trait of allocentrism. [T]

ANSWERS TO CHAPTER REVIEW TEST

13.1 Defining Personality

1. B. Rationale: Your personality is your pattern of thinking, feeling, and behaving.

13.2 The Psychoanalytic Perspective

2. A. Rationale: Regression is the defense mechanism in which a person reverts to an earlier age of functioning.
3. C. Rationale: According to Freud, the superego is the personality governed by the perfection principle.
4. C. Rationale: The shadow is the archetype that describes your view of what you would become if you gave in to your negative impulses.
5. B. Rationale: Those who strive for superiority by beating down others have a unhealthy, or mistaken style of life, according to Adler.

13.3 The Humanistic Perspective

6. A. Rationale: Communicating love and respect only when you act in ways that others want.
7. A. Rationale: Lacking a D need or deficit need.

13.4 Trait Perspectives

8. C. Rationale: Openness to experiences is an affection for the new. People who score low are conventional and love routines.

13.5 The Social Cognitive Perspective

9. A. Rationale: Mischel's theory revealed low cross-situational consistency.

13.6 The Biological Perspective

10. B. Rationale: Eysenck's arousal theory suggested that the introvert's arousal engine idled higher, suggesting introverts need less external stimulation to feel comfortable.
11. D. Rationale: Temperament is your inborn personality.

13.7 Personality Assessment

12. C. Rationale: Projective tests are a kind of personality instrument that uses the interpretation of ambiguous stimuli to uncover unconscious conflicts.
13. A. Rationale: The thematic apperception test is a projective personality instrument in which unconscious conflicts are revealed by the interpretation of stories told in reaction to a series of ambiguous images.

13.8 Culture and Personality

14. B. Rationale: Ideocentrism is a personality trait with an individual focus in which people see themselves as self-reliant entities.
15. A. Rationale: According to terror management theory, boosting self-esteem by connecting with things we feel are immortal can reduce anxiety.

REFERENCES

Ansbacher, H., & Ansbacher, R. R. (1964). *Individual psychology of Alfred Adler.* New York: Harper Perennial.

Betan, E., Heim, A. K., Zittel Conklin, C., & Westen, D. (2005). Countertransference phenomena and personality pathology in clinical practice: An empirical investigation. *American Journal of Psychiatry, 162*(5), 890.

Breuer, J., & Freud, S. (1895). *Studies on hysteria.* New York: Basic Books.

Butcher, J. N. (2011). Departures from MMPI–2 empirical traditions: The fake bad scale, restructured clinical scales, and the MMPI–2–RF. *A beginner's guide to the MMPI-2* (3rd ed., pp. 175–194). Washington, DC: American Psychological Association.

Cattell, R. B. (1964). *Personality & social psychology: Collected papers of Raymond B. Catell.* San Diego, CA: Robert R. Knapp.

Dazzi, C., & Pedrabissi, L. (2009). Graphology and personality: An empirical study on validity of handwriting analysis. *Psychological Reports, 105*(3, Pt2), 1255–1268.

Freud, A. (1967). *The ego and the mechanisms of defense.* New York: International Universities Press.

Eysenck, H. J. & Eysenck, J. H. (1975). *Manual of the Eysenck Personality Questionnaire.* London: Hodder and Stoughton.

Freeman, H. D., & Beer, J. S. (2010). Frontal lobe activation mediates the relation between sensation seeking and cortisol increases. *Journal of Personality, 78*(5), 1497–1528. doi:10.1111/j.1467-6494.2010.00659.x

Furnham, A., & Henderson, M. (1982). A content analysis of four personality inventories. *Journal of Clinical Psychology, 38*(4), 818–825. doi:10.1002/1097-1679(198210)38:4<818::AID JCLP2270380422>3.0.CO;2-Y

Geen, R. G. (1984). Preferred stimulation levels in introverts and extroverts: Effects on arousal and performance. *Journal of Personality and Social Psychology, 46*(6), 1303–1312. doi:10.1037/0022-3514.46.6.1303

Greenberg, J., & Kosloff, S. (2008). Terror management theory: Implications for understanding prejudice, stereotyping, intergroup conflict, and political attitudes. *Social and Personality Psychology Compass, 2*(5), 1881–1894. doi:10.1111/j.1751-9004.2008.00144.x

Gregory, R. J. (2011). *Psychological testing: History, principles, and applications* (6th ed.). Boston: Allyn & Bacon.

Jang, K. L., Livesley, W. J., & Vernon, P. A. (1996). Heritability of the big five personality dimensions and their facets. A twin study. *Journal of Personality, 64*(3), 577–591.

Lilienfeld, S., Wood, J., & Garb, H. (2001). What's wrong with this picture? *Scientific American 284*(5), 80–87

Magnavita, J. J. (2002). *Theories of personality: Contemporary approaches to the science of personality.* New York: John Wiley and Sons.

Maslow, A. H. (1987). *Motivation and personality* (3rd ed.). New York: HarperCollins.

McCrae, R. R., & Costa, P. T. (1987). Validation of the five-factor model of personality across instruments and observers. *Journal of Personality and Social Psychology, 52*(1), 81–90. doi:10.1037/0022-3514.52.1.81

Mischel, W. (1996). *Personality and assessment.* London: Psychology Press.

Mischel, W., & Peake, P. K. (1982). Analyzing the construction of consistency in personality. *Nebraska Symposium on Motivation,* 233–262.

Peterson, C. (2010). Psychological approaches to mental illness. In T. L. Scheid & T. N. Brown (Eds.), *A handbook for the study of mental health: Social contexts, theories, and systems* (2nd ed., pp. 89–105). New York: Cambridge University Press.

Piedmont, R. L. (1998). *The revised NEO Personality Inventory: Clinical and research applications* (The Plenum series in social/clinical psychology, 1st ed.). New York: Springer.

Rogers, C. (1989). *The Carl Rogers reader* (1st ed.). Boston: Mariner Books.

Rotter, J. B. (1966). Generalized expectancies of internal versus external control of reinforcements. *Psychological Monographs, 80*(609), 1–28.

Sivadas, E., Bruvold, N. T., & Nelson, M. R. (2008). A reduced version of the horizontal and vertical individualism and collectivism scale: A four-country assessment. *Journal of Business Research, 61*(3), 201–210. doi:10.1016/j.jbusres.2007.06.016

Strathern, P. (2005). *A brief history of medicine: From Hippocrates' four humours to Crick and Watson's double helix.* Philadelphia: Running Press.

Wilson, E. O. (2004). *On human nature: Revised edition.* Boston: Harvard University Press.

Zuckerman, M., Kuhlman, D. M., Joireman, J., Teta, P., & Kraft, M. (1993). A comparison of three structural models for personality: The big three, the big five, and the alternative five. *Journal of Personality and Social Psychology, 65*(4), 757–768. doi:10.1037/0022-3514.65.4.757

Chapter Overview ▼

14.1 Overview: Understanding Psychological Disorders
Defining Psychological Disorders
The *DSM*, or Medical Model
The Biopsychosocial Approach
Criteria of Abnormal Behavior
Classifying and Labeling Psychological Disorders
Advantages and Disadvantages of Classification Systems
Etiology of Psychological Disorders

CONCEPT LEARNING CHECK **14.1** *Identifying Psychological Disorders*

14.2 Anxiety Disorders
Generalized Anxiety Disorder
Panic Disorder
Phobic Disorders
Obsessive-Compulsive Disorder

Posttraumatic Stress Disorder
Etiology of Anxiety Disorders
Biological Perspective
Learning Perspective
Cognitive Factors

CONCEPT LEARNING CHECK **14.2** *Identifying Anxiety Disorders*

14.3 Somatoform Disorders
Somatization Disorder
Conversion Disorder
Hypochondriasis
Etiology of Somatoform Disorders
Personality and Cognitive Perspectives

CONCEPT LEARNING CHECK **14.3** *Identifying Somatoform Disorders*

14 Psychological Disorders

Learning Objectives ▼

14.1 ■ Define psychological disorders as determined by the American Psychiatric Association (APA) and explain the criteria for abnormal behavior using the *Diagnostic and Statistical Manual of Mental Disorders.*

14.2 ■ Distinguish between different types of anxiety disorders; identify signs and symptoms of anxiety disorders.
   ■ Categorize the types of anxiety disorders according to diagnostic criteria.
   ■ Explain biological, behavioral, and cognitive perspectives of anxiety disorders.

14.3 ■ Understand personality, behavioral, cognitive, and unconscious factors involved in the development of somatoform disorders.

14.4 ■ Identify the signs and symptoms of dissociative disorders.

14.5 ■ Examine types of mood disorders based upon APA guidelines using D-SIGECAPS
   ■ Be able to differentiate between a unipolar and bipolar mood disorder.

14.6 ■ Recognize signs and symptoms of psychotic disorders.

14.7 ■ List and describe the personality disorders as described in the *DSM-IV-TR.*

14.4 Dissociative Disorders
Dissociative Amnesia and Fugue
Dissociative Identity Disorder
Etiology of Dissociative Disorders

CONCEPT LEARNING CHECK 14.4 *Identifying Dissociative Disorders*

14.5 Mood Disorders
Major Depressive Disorder
Depression and Bipolar Disorder
Etiology of Mood Disorders
   The Biological Perspective
   The Social-Cognitive Perspective

CONCEPT LEARNING CHECK 14.5 *Identifying Mood Disorders*

14.6 Psychotic Disorders
Symptoms of All Schizophrenic Disorders
   Disorganized Thinking
   Delusions and Hallucinations
CRITICAL THINKING APPLICATION
   Catatonia
   Deficits of Behavior
Schizophrenic Subtypes
   Paranoid, Catatonic, Disorganized, Undifferentiated
Etiology of Psychotic Disorders
   Genetic Vulnerability
   Brain Abnormalities
   Neurodevelopment in the Uterus
   Psychological Factors

CONCEPT LEARNING CHECK 14.6 *Classifying Signs and Symptoms of Schizophrenia*

14.7 Personality Disorders
Antisocial Personality Disorder
   Etiology of Antisocial Personality Disorder
Paranoid Personality Disorder
   Etiology of Paranoid Personality Disorder
Borderline Personality Disorder
   Etiology of Borderline Personality Disorder
Summary of Multiple Influences on Psychological Disorders

CONCEPT LEARNING CHECK 14.7 *Categorizing Personality Disorders*

Balloons. Not two or three, but dozens of them. I wasn't sure what to think. There she was, in my waiting room, with what must have been three dozen balloons of all different colors tied with brightly colored ribbons.

As a clinical psychologist, I've learned to watch for certain behaviors in my therapy waiting room. Most clients are anxious: They might sip nervously from a cup of water, or thumb through a magazine. Some bring props, photo albums, diaries, or lists. None had brought balloons.

I led her back to my office. Anyone else might have jumped right in and asked, "So, what's with the balloons?" But as a psychologist, you learn to let these things unfold in their own time. She was disheveled, her face worn with age, and she had sadness in her eyes. She waited, as many clients do on their first visit, for my cue. "So what brings you here today?" I began.

She explained to me that a year ago, on this very day, her 8-year-old son had died. She described his long, protracted illness. She told me how much he loved balloons. She and a few dozen others, who had also lost loved ones, were on their way to the park. There they would write notes to the people they had lost, tie the notes to the balloons, and set them free, one by one. It was sad, and beautiful, and yes, a little strange.

14.1 Overview: Understanding Psychological Disorders

Psychologists use a number of different tools to diagnose and understand psychological disorders.

- Define psychological disorders as determined by the American Psychiatric Association (APA) and explain the criteria for abnormal behavior using the *Diagnostic and Statistical Manual of Mental Disorders*.

What causes people to behave in unusual or disturbing ways? To what extent do outside influences (nurture) combine with biological forces (nature) to affect behavior? Does the person described above have a psychological disorder or a very healthy way of dealing with her grief? Psychologists understand a **psychological disorder** to be any behavior or mental process that causes a person to suffer or worry or produce harm to his or her social or work life. The science of understanding and diagnosing these psychological disorders is called **psychopathology**. In their quest to understand the nature of psychological disorders, psychologists use several tools to identify, study, and discover the origins of disordered behavior. These tools include diagnostic manuals, statistics, and biopsychosocial models.

By the end of this chapter, you will have examined some of these tools and how psychologists combine their use to understand psychological disorders. You will also use these tools to define and identify psychological disorders.

If a person lines up her fries before she eats them, it might be unusual, but it's not likely to be a disorder.

Defining Psychological Disorders

Not all abnormal or unusual behavior qualifies as a psychological disorder. Lining up French fries in rows before eating them may be unusual behavior. However, it probably does not indicate a psychological disorder. There are two widely used approaches to understanding and defining psychological disorders: the medical model and the biopsychosocial approach.

The *DSM,* or Medical Model

Over several years, mental health professionals developed a system for categorizing and describing disordered behavior. This system is presented in the *Diagnostic and Statistical Manual of Mental Disorders,* or *DSM,* published by the American

Psychiatric Association. The *DSM* is researched, written, and reviewed by scientists, doctors, psychiatrists, and psychologists. Because so many members of the medical community help develop the *DSM*, it reflects the **medical model**, or approach, to the study of psychological disorders. The *DSM* is used by most mental health professionals in the United States to research and form clinical diagnoses.

As its name suggests, the *DSM* has two functions. First, it acts as a diagnostic manual, listing the symptoms that must be present in order to identify or diagnose a condition or disorder. Second, the *DSM* serves as a statistical manual, supplying important **epidemiological**, or statistical, information about the disorders. Epidemiological information can include the usual first age when a person might expect to have symptoms or the percentage of the population with a certain disorder, also known as prevalence FIGURE 14-1.

The current edition of the *DSM* is known as the *DSM-IV-TR*. The "tr" stands for "text revision." In 2013 the American Psychiatric Association will issue a major revision of the *DSM*, the *DSM-5*, which will reflect recent advances in our understanding and treatment of psychological disorders.

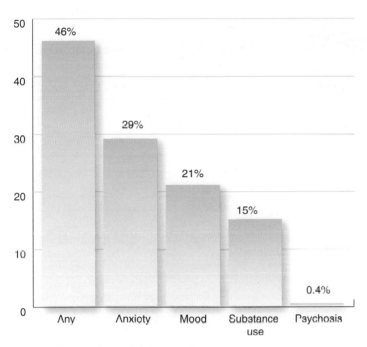

FIGURE 14-1 Prevalence of psychological disorders among U.S. adult population.
Source: Data from Kessler, R. C., Berglund, P., Demler, O., Jin, R., Merikangas, K. R., & Walters, E. E. (2005). Lifetime prevalence and age-of-onset distributions of DSM-IV disorders in the national comorbidity survey replication. Archives of General Psychiatry, 62(6), 593–602. oi:10.1001/archpsyc.62.6.593

The Biopsychosocial Approach

More recently, psychologists have developed a more holistic approach to understanding the influences that affect mental and emotional development and functioning. The **biopsychosocial approach** to psychopathology recognizes three equally important aspects of human mental processes and behavior: biological, psychological, and social. The biological aspect explores the essential influence of brain chemistry on disordered behavior. The psychological aspect explores the role played by thoughts, emotions, and behaviors in psychological disorders. The social aspect explores societal influences and whether a disorder causes problems when viewed within a social context FIGURE 14-2.

Criteria of Abnormal Behavior

Distinguishing between disordered behavior and abnormal behavior isn't easy. A psychologist might spend a great deal of time observing and listening to a patient before forming a diagnosis. In forming a diagnosis, psychologists must rely on professional, generally agreed-upon standards about the nature and symptoms of psychological disorders. As mentioned earlier, most psychologists consult the *DSM* for diagnostic and statistical information on disordered behavior.

According to the *DSM*, any one of three criteria must be satisfied in order to diagnose abnormal or unusual behavior as a psychological disorder:

1. **The behavior must be deviant.** Deviant means departing from existing and accepted standards. The behavior may be a departure from commonly accepted cultural

Psychological disorder A psychological condition that varies from the norm, is usually maladaptive, and may cause personal distress.

Psychopathology The science of diagnosing and understanding psychological disorders.

Medical model A theory that suggests that psychological disorders are illnesses that require treatment.

Epidemiology A science that examines the frequency of medical conditions.

Biopsychosocial approach A theory that recognizes three equally important aspects of human mental processes and behavior: biological (including brain chemistry), psychological (thoughts, emotions, and behaviors), and social (cultural and societal influences).

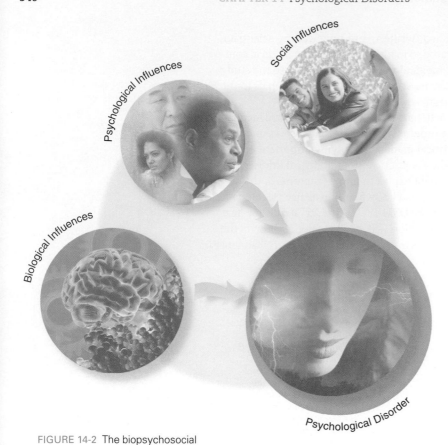

FIGURE 14-2 The biopsychosocial approach stresses the importance of examining all three factors that might contribute to a psychological disorder.

Someone whose behavior varies from the norm does not necessarily have a disorder.

standards of behavior. The behavior may represent a deviation from the statistical standards outlined in the *DSM*. Betty didn't violate any cultural standards by bringing balloons to a psychologist's office. She did, however, violate some statistical ones. By itself, though, statistical infrequency is not a compelling standard. This would mean that only conformity is normal and nonconformity is at best, abnormal, and at worst, disordered.

2. **The behavior must be maladaptive.** Much of our behavior is adaptive. We eat, we drink, we sleep. All of these things are adaptive because they help us to survive. If something is maladaptive it means that it decreases, or impairs, our ability to function. The *DSM* considers how much impairment a person has in his or her work, school, and social life.

3. **The behavior must cause personal distress.** At times people behave in ways that cause them stress or make them miserable. These people may not want to behave this way, but they seem unable to stop themselves FIGURE 14-3.

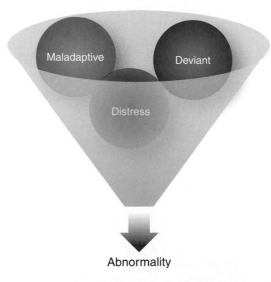

FIGURE 14-3 A person who is suffering from a psychological disorder exhibits behavior that is maladaptive, deviant, or causes him or her significant distress.

Classifying and Labeling Psychological Disorders

Often when people think of a disorder, such as depression, they think of it as a single category of unique symptoms. Disorders, however, aren't that simple. They may share certain symptoms, or present themselves differently, depending on the individual. Therefore psychologists use the *DSM*'s system of classification to help them form a diagnosis.

The *DSM*'s classification system is known as the multiaxial, or multidimensional, approach to diagnosis. The multiaxial system consists of five separate categories of information that psychologists consider before forming a diagnosis TABLE 14-1.

Using this system, a psychologist can examine a patient's symptoms and situation from several critical and interrelated points of view. Using this multiaxial approach, psychologists can form diagnoses at a level of detail that is more complete and more appropriate for individual cases TABLE 14-2 and TABLE 14-3.

TABLE 14-1 Multiaxial Assessment: Axis Categories and Descriptions

Axis	Condition	Description
Axis I	Clinical disorders	These are the conditions most people think about when they think of psychological disorders. They include disorders like schizophrenia and phobias.
Axis II	Personality disorders	Personality disorders are chronic and pervasive ways in which a person behaves. Unlike clinical disorders that may come and go, personality disorders are long lasting by nature. They are more often lifetime conditions, such as antisocial personality disorder, and tend to have a broad impact on the person's life.
Axis III	General medical conditions	The *DSM* is like a chapter in an encyclopedia of everything that could go wrong with a human. That larger encyclopedia is called the International Classification of Diseases (ICD). The ICD-9 has sections on many different conditions. There is a section on infectious diseases, a section on diseases of the blood, and even a section on injury and poisoning. The section on mental disorders is the *DSM*. Any other medical conditions that a person might have would be cross-listed here.
Axis IV	Psychosocial stress-ors	The *DSM* also considers the context of the condition by listing the person's stressors. Sometimes these stresses are directly related to the condition, sometimes not. The categories for this include housing problems, primary support group problems, and educational problems.
Axis V	Global assessment of functioning (GAF)	The GAF is a scale (1–100) that indicates how well a person is doing, with higher numbers indicating higher functioning. 100 indicates optimal function. 1 indicates poor functioning.

TABLE 14-2 Sample *DSM-IV-TR* Multiaxial Axis Diagnosis

Axis I	Major depressive disorder, Alcohol abuse
Axis II	Dependent personality disorder
Axis III	None
Axis IV	Recent job loss
Axis V	GAF – 35

Advantages and Disadvantages of Classification Systems

Diagnostic and labeling systems present both strengths and weaknesses. A system such as the *DSM* serves as useful shorthand for mental health professionals as they communicate with each other. In addition, since the *DSM* is based on statistical data, it has predictive value. A psychologist who knows that a person is depressed, for example, can expect certain symptoms to cluster together. A person who is depressed is likely to experience not just sadness, but also problems sleeping, feeling inappropriately guilty, and thoughts about death.

Labels, however, are seldom perfect. For example, depression presents itself somewhat differently in each individual who experiences it. When mental health professionals label disorders—and the people who suffer from them—they risk making an error that can have important consequences. In a classic study, psychologist David Rosenhan had "pseudopatients" present themselves at psychiatric hospitals with complaints of hallucinations. All were diagnosed and admitted. Beyond their complaints of hallucination, the pseudopatients behaved normally. Nevertheless, their normal everyday behavior was diagnosed as abnormal (Rosenhan, 1973) FIGURE 14-4. Critics of the medical model (Szasz 2010) use the study as evidence of the subjective nature of diagnostic judgements and the negative effects of labeling psychological conditions as diseases. Supporters of the medical model point out that there are no biological tests for most psychological conditions and that, because of that, it is important to rely on self-report from clients. It would be unusual for someone to report having hallucinations when they don't have them.

TABLE 14-3 *DSM-IV-TR*: Key Diagnostic Categories

Category	Examples
Disorders usually first diagnosed in infancy, childhood, or adolescence	Asperger's disorder Attention deficit hyperactivity disorder
Delirium, dementia, and amnesic and other cognitive disorders	Dementia of the Alzheimer's type
Substance-related disorders	Alcohol dependence Caffeine intoxication
Schizophrenia and other psychotic disorders	Schizophrenia Delusional disorder Brief psychotic disorder
Mood disorders	Major depressive disorder Bipolar I Dysthymic disorder Cyclothymic disorder
Anxiety disorders	Specific phobia Social phobia Agoraphobia without a history of panic disorder OCD PTSD
Factitious disorders	Factitious disorder Factitious disorder by proxy (aka Munchausen syndrome)
Dissociative disorders	Dissociative fugue Dissociative identity disorder Dissociative amnesia
Sexual and gender identity disorders	Paraphilias Gender identity disorder Sexual aversion disorder Male erectile disorder
Eating disorders	Anorexia nervosa Bulimia nervosa Binge eating disorder
Sleep disorders	Primary insomnia Narcolepsy
Impulse control disorders not elsewhere classified	Kleptomania Trichotillomania
Adjustment disorders	Adjustment disorder with anxiety Adjustment disorder with disturbance of conduct
Other conditions that may be the focus of clinical attention	Parent-child relational problem

Etiology of Psychological Disorders

Clara is a 42-year-old mother of two. She is in the waiting room of her local university counseling center. She clutches her stuffed animal tightly. She's terrified of who is about to enter the room—Giggles, a clown who has been hired to help her with her fear of clowns. When Giggles enters, she hyperventilates and is filled with panic. "No . . . please . . . no. I can't do this," she says over and over. It is obvious that Clara has a specific phobia of clowns. But where did this fear come from and how is it treated?

The *DSM* does not identify the **etiology**, or cause, of a disorder. Nor does the *DSM* recommend treatment. Clinicians use their theoretical orientations to determine the etiology. The etiology of a disorder also helps to determine the treatment for a disorder. This is true for a variety of conditions. For example, we used to think that ulcers were caused by stress and spicy food. The treatment would be to check your temper and stay away from meatball subs. Current evidence suggests a possible bacterial etiology for ulcers (*Helicobacter pylori*), which is why some people are prescribed amoxicillin, an antibiotic, as a treatment for ulcers.

Etiology Cause of a disorder.

FIGURE 14-4 St. Elizabeth's Psychiatric Hospital, in Washington, D.C., was one of the sites of the Rosenhan pseudopatient study.

Why do some clinicians treat a disorder one way, while others choose a different treatment? Most psychological disorders can be successfully treated in various ways because the disorders have complex etiological roots. The answer to the question "Are psychological disorders caused by biology (nature) or the environment (nurture)?" is "yes"—they are caused by both.

Two important theories explain the interaction of nature and nurture: the diathesis-stress hypothesis and the reciprocal gene environment model. The **diathesis-stress hypothesis** suggests that a condition may have a biological root or cause (diathesis) that is brought out by an environmental stressor. For example, up to 30% of the population will have a photic sneeze reflex, meaning that they sneeze when looking at bright lights (Whitman & Packer, 1993). The diathesis is the sneezing response and the stressor or environmental condition is the bright lights. This means that under similar situations, some people will never sneeze while other people always will. There is evidence that supports the same diathesis-stress connection for many psychological conditions (Praag, Kloet, and Os, 2001) FIGURE 14-5.

Another theory picks up where the diathesis-stress hypothesis ends. The **reciprocal-gene environment model** suggests that while there may be biological propensities for certain conditions, these biological propensities can themselves cause stress that will feed back and make things worse (Rutter, Moffitt, & Caspi, 2006). For example, let's say that you have a tendency to become forgetful during stress. During exams and other high stress periods, you begin to be forgetful and misplace your books. Being unable to find your books causes even more stress and more forgetting, leading to a vicious cycle FIGURE 14-6.

Diathesis-stress hypothesis A hypothesis that suggests a condition can have a biological root or cause that is triggered by an environmental stressor.

Reciprocal-gene environment model A model that suggests that established biological tendencies toward a condition can themselves cause stress, which in turn aggravates the condition, and then begins the cycle again.

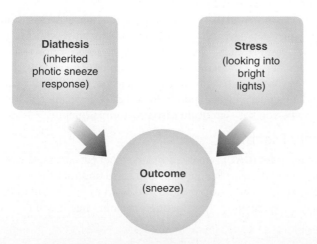

FIGURE 14-5 Example of the diathesis-stress hypothesis.

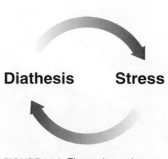

FIGURE 14-6 The reciprocal gene-environment model suggests a feedback loop between stress and diathesis.

Because of the multiple biological and environmental causes of disorders, clinicians may intervene at various points. Different kinds of medications can intervene at different points on the nervous system. Similarly, different psychological interventions can attack the environmental elements of the condition. A clinician may use one therapy or several. When they use several, the treatment is called "eclectic."

CONCEPT LEARNING CHECK **14.1** | *Identifying Psychological Disorders*

Consider each behavior according to the three criteria of psychological disorders. Then decide whether the behavior is disordered or not.

	Betty brought balloons to her first appointment with her therapist.	*Ben throws a tantrum almost every day whenever he doesn't get his way. Ben is 22.*	*Sam throws a tantrum almost every day whenever he doesn't get his way. Sam is 2.*	*Clara is afraid of clowns. She wants to take her children to the circus, but she's afraid she'll see a clown. She avoids toy aisles in department stores for the same reason.*	*Maria is very afraid of snakes. She enjoys hiking, but won't go in the reptile house at the zoo.*
Is it deviant?					
Does it cause the person distress?					
Is it maladaptive?					
Is it a disorder?					

14.2 Anxiety Disorders

Generalized anxiety disorder is marked by worry.

Anxiety disorders are marked by feelings of nervousness, distress, apprehension, and often disruptive attempts to diminish anxiety.

- Distinguish between different types of anxiety disorders; identify signs and symptoms of anxiety disorders.
- Categorize the types of anxiety disorders according to diagnostic criteria.
- Explain biological, behavioral, and cognitive perspectives of anxiety disorders.

Everyone feels anxious every now and then: the feeling you might have before an important exam or interview, the worry you have if you are running late for an appointment. Anxiety is part of our everyday lives. For most of us, anxiety can even be adaptive. It can help motivate us to do our best or to be prepared. People with **anxiety disorders**, on the other hand, have feelings of nervousness, distress, and apprehension, and often have disruptive ways of diminishing their anxiety. Like all psychological disorders, anxiety disorders are diagnosed only when a person has significant distress or impairment FIGURE 14-7.

Generalized Anxiety Disorder

Generalized anxiety disorder (GAD) is marked by unexplained, excessive worry that is not linked to anything in particular. People with GAD also find that their worry is difficult to control (APA, 2000). Their worry and dread seem to have a life of their own. Sometimes the anxiety is described as "free floating," meaning that it will float and stick

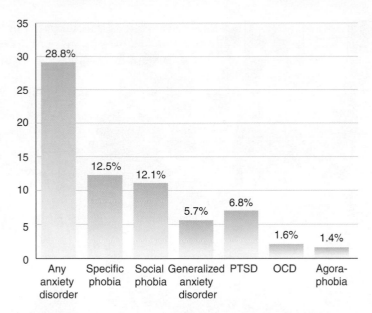

FIGURE 14-7 Prevalence of anxiety disorders among U.S. adult population. *Source: Data from Kessler, R. C., Berglund, P., Demler, O., Jin, R., Merikangas, K. R., & Walters, E. E. (2005). Lifetime prevalence and age-of-onset distributions of DSM IV disorders in the national comorbidity survey replication. Archives of General Psychiatry, 62(6), 593–602. oi:10.1001/archpsyc.62.6.593*

Anxiety disorder A psychological condition marked by nervousness, distress, apprehension, and disruptive attempts to reduce anxiety.

Generalized anxiety disorder (GAD) A psychological condition characterized by unexplained, excessive worry that has an unspecific cause.

Panic attack A period of intense fear or discomfort that is linked with specific physical and psychological symptoms.

Panic disorder The presence of frequent, recurrent panic attacks, along with the fear of panic attacks.

Agoraphobia The fear of having a panic attack, which causes a person to avoid places and situations where having a panic attack would be particularly embarrassing or dangerous.

to any thought the person might have and infect it with worry. In addition to worry, GAD is associated with restlessness, fatigue, concentration difficulties, irritability, muscle tension, and sleep disturbances. For a diagnosis, symptoms must have been experienced on more days than not, for a period of six months or longer. Evidence from several countries suggests a lifetime prevalence of around 3% (Andrews, Sanderson, Slade, & Issakidis, 2000; Kessler et al., 2005).

Panic Disorder

A **panic attack** is a period of intense fear or discomfort in which four or more of the following symptoms are present: pounding heart, sweating, shaking, feelings of choking, chest pain or discomfort, abdominal distress, feeling faint, feelings of unreality, fear of losing control, fear of dying, numbness, and chills or hot flashes. A panic attack can begin quickly, often out of nowhere, and it peaks in intensity within 10 minutes. A panic attack itself is not a disorder, but if panic attacks happen frequently and there is constant fear of having another panic attack, it is considered **panic disorder**. About 4% of adults in the United States suffer from panic disorder, and it is twice as common among women as among men (Halbreich, 2003).

Imagine you were told that at some point today you would experience a panic attack. What would you do? Would you go about your normal day? Would you stay close to home?

People who fear having a panic attack will sometimes stick close to home or travel away from home only with a friend who could help them if they did have a panic attack. They avoid places and situations where having a panic attack would be particularly embarrassing or where it might be very difficult to get help, like riding on a bus or train. Psychologists refer to this as **agoraphobia**. Some people think that agoraphobia means fear of crowds or open places (after all, it translates to "fear of the marketplace"). However, what people with agoraphobia fear is the potential embarrassment or helplessness they might experience while having a panic attack, not the crowds or open places themselves.

Some with agoraphobic avoidance have never had a panic attack (diagnosed as agoraphobia without a history of panic disorder). Others have had frequent panic attacks that have led to impairment (panic disorder with agoraphobia). Still other individuals with frequent panic attacks are resilient and do not suffer from any agoraphobic avoidance (panic disorder without agoraphobia) FIGURE 14-8.

A panic attack is a period of intense fear and discomfort.

FIGURE 14-8 Because crowded shopping centers wouldn't be a good place to have a panic attack, people with agoraphobia avoid them.

Snakes are a common specific phobia.

Phobic Disorders

Everyone is frightened of something. Maybe it's heights, or snakes, or even killer bees. **Phobias** are diagnosed when the fear is unreasonably great or it interferes with your life in some way. Psychologists distinguish between two broad categories of phobias: specific phobias and social phobias.

Specific phobias are fears of certain objects or certain situations. Seeing or anticipating the object or situation almost invariably produces a phobic response. Specific phobias come in different flavors, including phobias of animals, heights, blood and injured tissue, and storms FIGURE 14-9.

While specific phobias are fears of objects or situations, **social phobia** involves a different kind of fear—that of embarrassment or humiliation. The fears in a social phobia are usually of things that are public—speaking in public, eating in public, or maybe even

Phobia A psychological symptom in which fear is unreasonably great or it interferes with a person's life.

Social phobia An anxiety disorder characterized by fear of public embarrassment or humiliation.

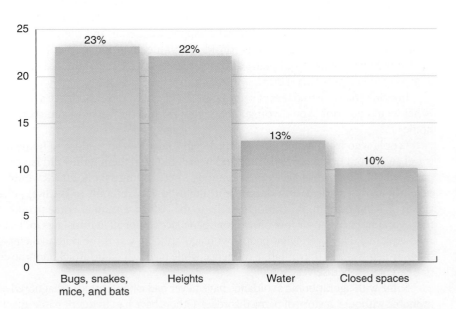

FIGURE 14-9 Prevalence of the most common specific phobias among U.S. adult population.
Source: Data from Eaton, W. W., Dryman, A., & Weissman, M. M. Panic and Phobia. In Psychiatric Disorders in America: The Epidemiologic Catchment Area Study, ed. L. N. Robins and D. A. Regier, 155–179. Simon and Schuster, 1991.

writing in public. The fear of humiliation produces the anxiety response, and the anxiety increases the fear of humiliation, making things even worse.

Many people have a mild fear of public speaking. It isn't the act of speaking that people fear; it's the possibility of making a public mistake—stammering, saying the wrong thing, becoming paralyzed or "freezing up." Thinking about these possibilities—that is, thinking about the fear itself—generates anxiety. Greater anxiety, in turn, increases one's chances of making a public mistake. Often social phobias create such vicious cycles FIGURE 14-10. Some people fear performing, or suffer performance anxiety, in nearly all types of social situations. This type of generalized social phobia has a nickname—**social anxiety disorder**. It's like being clinically shy. Like all disorders, it's appropriate to diagnose a person with a specific or social phobia only if it causes significant distress or impairment **TABLE 14-4**, FIGURE 14-11.

> **Social anxiety disorder**
> An anxiety disorder characterized by performance anxiety in nearly all types of social situations.

Obsessive-Compulsive Disorder

Let's say you have arrived at the post office. You get out of your car and close the door. You hit the button on your car key, and "chirp-chirp," the doors are locked. Now you head into the store. A moment later you think to yourself, "Did I lock the car?" It is easy to do it so automatically; perhaps you just thought you locked it. "Better safe than sorry," you think to yourself. You might push the button again, or maybe even unlock and

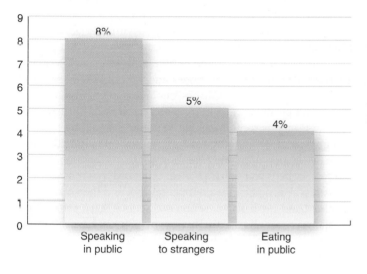

FIGURE 14-10 Prevalence of social phobias among U.S. adult population.
Source: Data from Eaton, W. W., Dryman, A., & Weissman, M. M. Panic and Phobia. In Psychiatric Disorders in America: The Epidemiologic Catchment Area Study, ed. L. N. Robins and D. A. Regier, 155–179. Simon and Schuster, 1991.

Public speaking is a common social phobia.

TABLE 14-4 Thirteen Unusual Phobias

Arachibutyrophobia	Fear of peanut butter sticking to the roof of your mouth
Limnophobia	Fear of lakes
Catoptrophobia	Fear of mirrors
Peladophobia	Fear of bald people
Anthrophobia	Fear of flowers
Automatonophobia	Fear of ventriloquist's dummies
Belonephobia	Fear of pins and needles
Chiraptophobia	Fear of being touched
Xanthophobia	Fear of the color yellow
Homichlophobia	Fear of fog
Logophobia	Fear of words
Trichopathophobia	Fear of hair
Triskaidekaphobia	Fear of the number 13

Did you lock your car today?

Obsessive-compulsive disorder A psychological disorder associated with obsessions, or obsessions linked to compulsions.

Obsession A thought that is unwanted, intrusive, and distressing.

Compulsions A condition in which a person feels compelled to perform behaviors or mental actions in response to an obsession.

The fear of fire caused by an unattended flame is an example of a fear associated with obsession.

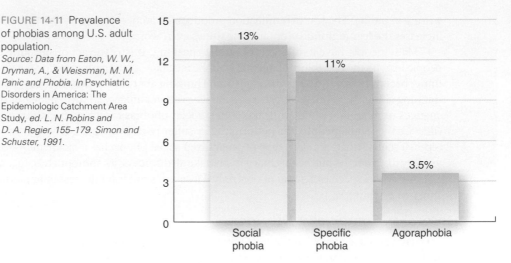

FIGURE 14-11 Prevalence of phobias among U.S. adult population. *Source: Data from Eaton, W. W., Dryman, A., & Weissman, M. M. Panic and Phobia. In* Psychiatric Disorders in America: The Epidemiologic Catchment Area Study, *ed. L. N. Robins and D. A. Regier, 155–179. Simon and Schuster, 1991.*

lock it again. Now you are reassured, and your anxiety goes down. For the person with obsessive-compulsive disorder, or OCD, that would just be the beginning. For that person, the obsession is a disquieting thought or impulse: He or she has left the car unlocked and something terrible will come from that.

In order to be diagnosed with **obsessive-compulsive disorder**, a person must have an obsession or have an obsession linked to a compulsion. About 80% of people with OCD have both. As you will learn, a person can have an obsession without a compulsion, but not a compulsion without an obsession.

Each of us likes certain things. For a close friend of mine, it is tennis. He watches every tennis game he can locate. He even records games and watches them over and over again. Some would say he's obsessed with tennis. Psychologists might disagree. For psychologists, an **obsession** is an unwanted thought that the person finds intrusive and distressing FIGURE 14-12. An obsession is something that you find disquieting to think about, such as hurting your own child, or thinking you've forgotten something that will cause harm to others. These distressing thoughts enter our minds all the time. Maybe you've left a candle unattended. Perhaps you've left your car unlocked. For most people, these thoughts are easy to dismiss. For others, the doubt takes root and then takes over.

Compulsions, on the other hand, are behaviors or mental actions that a person feels compelled to perform in response to an obsession. This is why you can have an obsession by itself, but a compulsion must be linked with an obsession. Some compulsions are directly linked to a companion obsession, like hand washing after being exposed to dirt. Other compulsions are meant to neutralize or undo the obsessions through a thought or mental act such as counting or praying FIGURE 14-13.

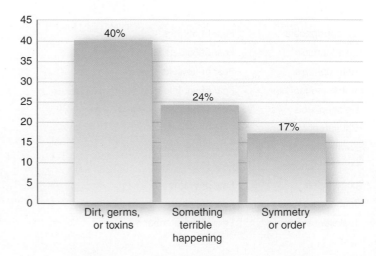

FIGURE 14-12 Percentage of common obsessions among U.S. adult population who have obsessive-compulsive disorder. *Source: Data from Rapoport. J. L. (1989, March). The biology of obsessions and compulsions.* Scientific American, *pp. 83–98.*

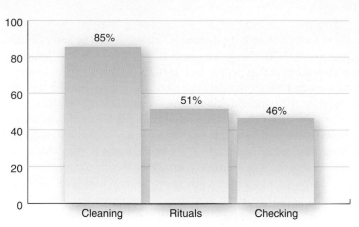

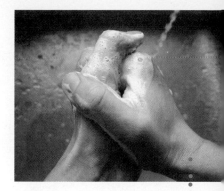

FIGURE 14-13 Percentage of common compulsions among U.S. adult population who have obsessive-compulsive disorder.
Source: Data from Rapoport. J. L. (1989, March). The biology of obsessions and compulsions. Scientific American, pp. 83–98.

Hand washing is a common compulsion.

Posttraumatic Stress Disorder

Posttraumatic stress disorder, or PTSD, is an anxiety disorder triggered by a traumatic event that involves reexperiencing the trauma, increased arousal, and symptoms of numbing and avoidance. In order to be diagnosed with PTSD, a person needs to have experienced a trauma; after all, it is called **posttraumatic stress disorder**. The *DSM* is very particular about what constitutes a trauma. Saying something embarrassing in front of your entire class—not a trauma. Showing up at a party with exactly the same outfit as someone else—not a trauma. In order to meet the criteria for a trauma, an event has to cause actual or threatened injury. In addition, the person must respond with fear, helplessness, or horror.

However, not all individuals who experience a trauma go on to develop PTSD. In fact, most don't. The criteria fall into three broad clusters:

1. **Reexperiencing.** People with PTSD will reexperience the traumatic event. They may have flashbacks, dreams, and distress at reminders of the trauma, or even a sense that they are reliving the event.

2. **Avoidance and numbing.** Often people with PTSD will avoid activities, thoughts, or conversations about the traumatic event. In addition, they may forget important details of the trauma, and sometimes exhibit depressive-type symptoms such as flat moods, detachment from others, or an inability to experience pleasure. Some even have a sense of foreshortened future.

3. **Increased arousal.** They may have difficulty sleeping or problems with concentration. They also sometimes may be irritable or startle easily.

Posttraumatic stress disorder Associated with a traumatic event, this disorder involves re-experiencing the trauma, increased arousal, and symptoms of numbing and avoidance.

Etiology of Anxiety Disorders

Biological Perspective

Quite a few biological factors have been implicated in the development of anxiety disorders. Some suggest that we are biologically "programmed" to have certain fears. Others point to abnormalities in brain structures or neurotransmitters. There are several cues that a biological predisposition to anxiety disorders might be present. There is some evidence that OCD is genetic; it tends to run in families (Grabe et al., 2006).

Natural Selection

Psychological disorders can be considered part of a continuum. On one side is everyday behavior, in the middle are atypical or "subclinical" behaviors, and at the other extreme are true psychological disorders. We can think about anxiety disorders as maladaptive or disruptive versions of adaptive behaviors. Remember that natural selection makes some behaviors—even fear—useful for survival: Some snakes are venomous, some heights are dangerous, and some dogs bite.

The idea of preparedness suggests that our evolutionary history makes us more prone to some fears than others, producing rapid fear responses that are hard to reduce (Seligman, 1971). This may explain why many people have phobias of things they rarely encounter, such as scorpions, as opposed to electrical outlets or cars that are, statistically speaking, far more common and dangerous (Mineka & Öhman, 2002).

Traumas include witnessing harm or injury.

The Brain

Many brain structures are involved in anxiety disorders FIGURE 14-14. The anterior cingulate cortex, especially active in OCD, checks for errors (Ursu, Stenger, Shear, Jones, & Carter, 2003). Evidence also indicates that people with panic disorders are more likely to have limbic system structures that are more easily activated and trigger fear (Shin et al., 2005). This would predispose certain individuals to respond with fear to stressful events and perhaps to develop "anxiety disorders." Another theory suggests that abnormalities in the limbic system, frontal lobes, and basal ganglia may interfere with the signal your brain sends to let you know you've finished a task. This would cause people with OCD to feel that they need to complete the task again (Szechtman & Woody, 2004).

Brain chemicals also play a part in anxiety disorders. Several biological theories focus on GABA (gamma-aminobutyric acid), an inhibitory neurotransmitter that reduces synaptic activity. Think of GABA as the "brakes" of the nervous system. Some theorists think that low GABA can result in a more active nervous system. Medications, such as benzodiazepines, that increase the activity of GABA in the synapse seem to improve anxiety disorder systems (Stahl, 2009). This suggests that GABA plays a key role in anxiety disorders. In addition to GABA, the neurotransmitter serotonin has also been implicated in OCD, PTSD, and generalized anxiety disorder (Stahl, 2009) FIGURE 14-15.

Learning Perspective

Biology by itself explains much, but not all, of the story. Even if someone has a biological disposition to a disorder, that disposition may not explain why he or she acquires a social phobia at age 35. The learning perspective suggests that disorders are learned behaviors. Anxiety disorders may be acquired and maintained through learning.

FIGURE 14-14 Limbic system structures such as the hypothalamus and thalamus may be involved with OCD.

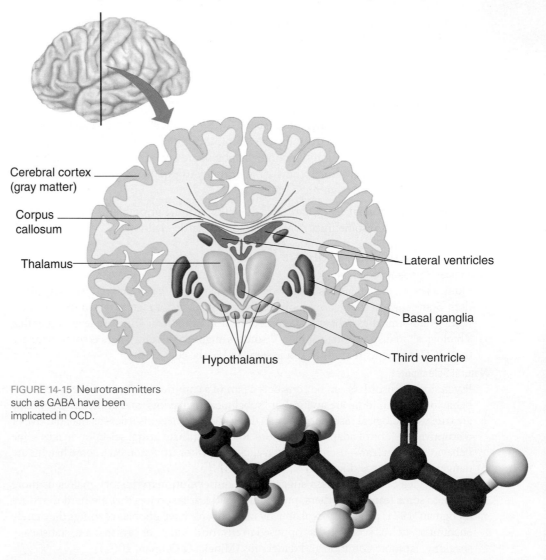

Cerebral cortex (gray matter)

Corpus callosum

Thalamus

Hypothalamus

Lateral ventricles

Basal ganglia

Third ventricle

FIGURE 14-15 Neurotransmitters such as GABA have been implicated in OCD.

Conditioning

Up to 40% of people with phobias can remember a particular event that led to their disorder (Mineka & Zinbarg, 2006). Using what we know about classical conditioning, theorists of the **learning perspective** suggest that these precipitating events became associated with what became the phobia. The learning model suggests that someone may acquire a phobic response to a previously neutral stimulus when that stimulus is paired with a frightening experience. This is known as phobia acquisition. The phobia is then maintained by avoidance of the newly acquired conditioned stimulus. This is known as phobia maintenance. In other words, anxiety disorders are acquired through classical conditioning and maintained through operant conditioning. This is referred to as the two-process conditioning model.

1. **Phobia acquisition.** Clara has a childhood experience in which she was severely frightened by a clown.

2. **Phobia maintenance.** Imagining she might see a clown increases her fear. Avoiding clowns reduces her fear. Even avoidance, one aspect of her fear response, reinforces and maintains her fear of clowns.

Learning perspective
A theory that suggests that anxiety disorders are learned behaviors.

Observational Learning

We can also develop anxiety from watching others. A father who has a phobia of storms and who forces his children to turn out all the lights in their home and unplug all the appliances probably sends his children the message that storms are dangerous and should be feared. Evidence suggests that wild monkeys can transmit their fear of snakes to their young (Mineka, Keir, & Price, 1980). When we react to something fearfully, we can effectively communicate its potential danger to others.

Cognitive Factors

Cognition means thinking. Cognitive theorists emphasize the idea that maladaptive thoughts can be linked to anxiety.

The theory of anxiety sensitivity (Schmidt, Lerew, & Jackson, 1997) suggests that anxious people are highly sensitive to internal sensations associated with anxiety and tend to misinterpret harm, focus on threat, and are more likely to recall information that is threatening. In addition, when presented with ambiguous situations, anxious people viewed them as threatening (Eysenck, Mogg, May, Richards, & Mathews, 1991) FIGURE 14-16.

FIGURE 14-16 Anxious people attributed harmful meanings to the middle statement. Non-anxious people attributed benign meanings to the same statement *Source: Adapted from Eysenck, M. W., Mogg, K., May, J., Richards, A., & Mathews, A. (1991). Bias in interpretation of ambiguous sentences related to threat in anxiety. Journal of Abnormal Psychology, 100(2), 144–150. doi:10.1037/0021-843X.100.2.144*

CONCEPT LEARNING CHECK 14.2 | *Identifying Anxiety Disorders*

1. As a child, Clara had a terrible experience in which a clown frightened her. Now, as an adult, if she even imagines seeing a clown, she grows extremely nervous, frightened, and distressed. What kind of anxiety order does Clara seem to have?

2. Manuel has been worrying "all the time" and says that it's not about anything in particular. He finds it difficult to control his worry and feels restless, tired, and irritable. He's also having problems sleeping. Manuel most likely has which disorder?

3. Marty, 27, reports a long-standing fear of speaking in public. When asked to speak in front of a large group of people he becomes extremely anxious and thinks he'll be embarrassed. Because of this fear, he has passed on promotions and other opportunities to advance in his career. On one occasion when he was forced to speak, he became so anxious that he started shaking and panicking. Marty most likely has which disorder?

Somatoform disorders
Psychological disorders characterized by having symptoms of physical illness that cannot be explained by a general medical condition.

Malingering A condition involving an external motivation for illness, such as avoiding a test.

Factitious disorder A psychological disorder in which a person plays the sick role for the emotional gain, sometimes called Münchausen syndrome.

Psychophysiological disorder A disorder in which a real medical syndrome is exacerbated by psychological factors.

Somatization disorder A type of somatoform disorder characterized by a long history of many vague physical complaints over several years.

14.3 Somatoform Disorders

The essential features of somatoform disorders are symptoms of a physical illness that are unexplained by a general medical condition.

■ Understand personality, behavioral, cognitive, and unconscious factors involved in the development of somatoform disorders.

Imagine you are a physician at a clinic and a patient—let's call him Jack—comes in with a stomachache. You've run about a dozen tests and you still can't, for the life of you, figure out why his stomach hurts. In fact, biologically, as much as you can figure, Jack's stomach is fine. It really *shouldn't* hurt. What might you have on your hands?

One of the possibilities is a somatoform disorder. All somatoform disorders share the essential feature of symptoms of a physical illness that are unexplained by a general medical condition.

When considering whether someone has a **somatoform disorder**, a few other conditions need to be eliminated. First, symptoms cannot be caused by a physical illness. You might remember that physical illnesses, also known as general medical conditions, are listed on Axis III of a *DSM-IV-TR* diagnosis. Also, somatoform disorders can't involve any sort of external motivation for being sick, such as getting out of a test or hoping to cash in on a lawsuit, which is called **malingering**. Also absent is an emotional gain such as the motivation to play the sick role as you might expect in **factitious disorders**, which are sometimes called Münchausen syndrome, hospital addiction syndrome, or hospital hopper syndrome. Lastly, it is important to know that somatoform disorders are different from **psychophysiological disorders**, in which a real medical condition can be exacerbated by psychological factors. Anyone who has had headaches, asthma, or ulcers knows that stress can make these conditions worse.

People with somatoform disorders feel sick even when they are completely healthy. A person with a somatoform disorder may convince his doctor to run diagnostic tests to discover what's wrong, but the doctors never can find any physical cause for the complaints. Often, there is some psychological connection to the beginning or worsening of the illness of a person with a somatoform disorder.

TABLE 14-5 describes the somatoform disorders listed in the *DSM-IV-TR*, but we will focus on just three: somatization disorder, conversion disorder, and hypochondriasis.

Somatization Disorder

In **somatization disorder**, a person has a long history of many vague physical complaints over several years. In somatization disorder, the focus is on the actual physical symptoms the person experiences rather than the disease she thinks she has. Individuals with somatization disorder have dozens of unexplained symptoms, often requiring investigation, and in every case there is no medical condition that explains the symptoms. To meet the criteria for this disorder, by age 30 a person must have had at least eight unexplained medical symptoms. These include several pain symptoms, gastrointestinal symptoms,

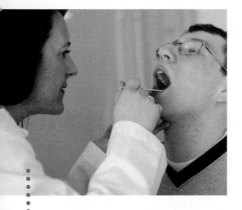

In a somatization disorder, the focus is on the physical symptoms rather than a disease.

TABLE 14-5 Somatoform Disorders

Disorder	Description
Somatization disorder	Pain, gastrointestinal and sexual concerns, and what seems to be neurological damage that cannot be explained by any medical condition
Pain disorder	Pain in several parts of the body that cannot be explained by any medical condition
Conversion disorder	Symptoms that suggest neurological damage, such as numbness with no reason for the symptoms
Hypochondriasis	Fear of having an illness based on the misreading of normal body functions
Body dysmorphic disorder	The preoccupation with an imagined or exaggerated defect in physical appearance

Source: Adapted from American Psychiatric Association. Diagnostic and Statistical Manual of Mental Disorders: *DSM-IV-TR. American Psychiatric Publishing, 2000.*

sexual symptoms, and even neurological symptoms—all with no apparent biological cause. Somatization disorder can be debilitating, since to the person with somatization disorder, the symptoms are real. Fortunately, it is quite rare. Only 1.5% of people who seek medical treatment have a diagnosis of somatization disorder (Fink, 2004).

Conversion Disorder

In **conversion disorder**, a psychological worry or concern is transformed (converted) into a physical symptom. For most conversion disorders, the symptoms suggest a neurological disorder such as partial paralysis, numbness, muscle weakness, or even blindness.

Often a clue that the symptoms are a conversion disorder will lie in the way the symptoms are presented. People with numbness caused by conversion disorder, for example, will often complain of numbness only in their hands (called glove anesthesia), which is impossible given the physiology of the arm. People with numbness resulting from neurological damage, on the other hand, lose all sensation in their entire arms and hands. This makes sense because the nerves in the arm provide sensory input along the entire limb.

Another clue to conversion disorders is the blitheness patients have about their symptoms. You might expect that if you suddenly went blind or had numbness in your arms you might be extremely bothered. However, people with conversion disorder seem strangely blasé about their condition (sometimes called "la belle indifference").

Like many somatoform disorders, the onset or exacerbation of the symptoms is linked to some sort of event in the person's life. When matters get worse, the symptoms do too. Only 1.5% of people who seek medical treatment meet the criteria for conversion disorder (Fink, 2004).

Hypochondriasis

We all know someone who we think is a hypochondriac. She always has the latest sickness. This week it's Lyme disease, next week it might be the H1N1 influenza. This is very different from the *DSM-IV-TR* disorder of **hypochondriasis**. Usually the person with hypochondriasis is convinced she has a specific disease process unfolding despite being fine. She interprets normal body symptoms as evidence of disease. She may even have invasive medical procedures to find out what she might have. These tests, as you can imagine, all come back normal. Often, these investigative medical procedures themselves produce lingering symptoms that the person will interpret as part of the very illness the tests disproved. For a diagnosis of hypochondriasis the symptoms need to persist despite medical evidence to the contrary and go on for at least 6 months. Hypochondriasis may sound similar to somatization disorder; however, in somatization disorder, the focus is on the symptoms, while in hypochondriasis the focus is on having a certain disease.

Like all disorders, hypochondriasis has to cause distress or impairment in functioning. Research suggests that 4.7% of adults who seek medical treatment meet *DSM-IV-TR* criteria for hypochondriasis (Fink, 2004).

Etiology of Somatoform Disorders

As you might expect, somatoform disorders can have multiple causes. Some speculate that vulnerabilities such as hypersensitivity to physical sensations and a history of illnesses may combine with stressors such as emotional conflicts to produce somatoform disorders. Your patient Jack, for example, may have always been sensitive to physical sensations. You find out from chatting with him that he recently lost his job, girlfriend, and dog. Now he has persistent nausea. He's been tested over and over and there's no biological reason for it. Jack quite possibly is suffering from a somatoform disorder.

Personality and Cognitive Perspectives

There may be personality and cognitive patterns involved with somatoform disorders. Some research has suggested that those with somatoform disorders are more highly susceptible to hypnosis compared to people without somatoform disorders (Roelofs et al., 2002). This leads researchers to believe that people with somatoform disorders are highly susceptible to even the idea that they may have an illness.

Physical symptoms can sometimes be somatoform disorders.

Conversion disorder A disorder in which a worry or concern is transformed into a physical symptom.

Hypochondriasis A disorder characterized by a specific disease process that progresses in a person in which there is no physiological cause.

Numbness in just the hand can be a sign of a conversion disorder.

In addition to such personality factors, there are some cognitive and learning factors that might be involved in somatoform disorders. Even though, by definition, people with somatoform disorders are not producing the illness to play the sick role, people around them may unintentionally reinforce them for being sick. In this way they may have inadvertently learned that being sick brings them greater attention. Also, people with somatoform disorders more often associate normal physical sensations with catastrophic events and exaggerate and distort the meaning of the sensations, like thinking the pain of a normal stomachache is something terrible like stomach cancer.

There are some researchers who believe that somatoform disorders are actually more like anxiety disorders about health concerns. What adds to this theory is that people with hypochondriasis often have a family history of anxiety disorders (Deacon & Abramowitz, 2008).

CONCEPT LEARNING CHECK 14.3   *Identifying Somatoform Disorders*

1. James, a 22-year-old man, was referred to your clinic for evaluation of his complaints. He's convinced that he has stomach cancer despite being told that it is very unlikely. He has cramps when he overeats and reports that his tongue "just doesn't look right." Despite medical evidence to the contrary, James has continued to believe that he has stomach cancer. What is the most likely diagnosis?

2. Martha was robbed at gunpoint about 3 months ago. Luckily she wasn't hurt and the police were able to recover her purse and capture the assailant. About a week before Martha had to identify the man who robbed her, Martha suddenly lost her sight. She didn't seem that concerned about it. What's the most likely diagnosis?

14.4 Dissociative Disorders

Dissociative disorders involve a sudden loss of the integration of consciousness, memory, for events and experiences in a person's life.

- Identify the signs and symptoms of dissociative disorders.

Dissociation A split of consciousness or attention into two or more separate streams.

Dissociative disorders A disorder characterized by the sudden loss of the integration of consciousness or memory, or a change in personal identity.

Dissociative amnesia A condition characterized by extreme memory lapses or forgetting important personal information; usually associated with a traumatic emotional experience.

Dissociation means a split of your consciousness or attention into separate streams. We all dissociate now and then. Maybe you are doing a presentation and thinking about lunch at the same time. Perhaps you are reading psychology and wondering how much longer the text will be. These are all forms of normal dissociation that can occur frequently (Kihlstrom, Glisky, & Angiulo, 1994). Some people call it "multitasking" since many people can engage in one activity automatically and still be aware of the things they need to do to conduct the other behavior.

Dissociation only becomes problematic when the streams become too separate, disjointed, and fragmented, and there is a loss of the integration of the personality. This is what is seen in the **dissociative disorders**. Dissociative disorders involve a sudden loss of the integration of consciousness or memory, or a change in a person's identity. The streams become so distinct that there is a disruption in the personality and a disconnection or even amnesia during the experience. Sometimes the streams may even take on a life of their own.

Dissociative disorders can occur when a stressful event becomes tremendously overwhelming and the individuals escape by diverting awareness from the painful memories, thoughts, and emotions. Sometimes in dissociated states, individuals escape from conflicts by giving up consistency and rejecting a part of themselves.

All of the dissociative disorders described in *DSM-IV-TR* are listed in **TABLE 14-6**. We will focus on three forms of dissociative disorders—dissociative amnesia, dissociative fugue, and dissociative identity disorder.

Dissociative Amnesia and Fugue

Imagine waking up one day and having no idea where you are. You are dazed, confused, and unsure of anything. A moment later, you also realize you aren't even sure who you are. Frightening. In **dissociative amnesia**, individuals forget important personal information—much more than you would expect with normal forgetfulness. They may not remember their own identity, including their birthday, address, or their name, even though they have not had any sort of head trauma.

TABLE 14-6 Dissociative Disorders

Dissociative Disorder	Description
Depersonalization disorder	Periods of detachment from self or surroundings, which may be experienced as "unreal" (lacking in control of or "outside of" self), while retaining awareness that this is only a feeling and not a reality.
Dissociative amnesia	Noticeable memory impairment resulting from emotional trauma.
Dissociative fugue	Physical desertion of familiar surroundings and experience of impaired recall of the past. This may lead to confusion about actual identity and the assumption of a new identity.
Dissociative identity disorder	The alternation of two or more distinct identities with impaired recall among the alters.

Source: Adapted from American Psychiatric Association. Diagnostic and Statistical Manual of Mental Disorders: *DSM-IV-TR. American Psychiatric Publishing, 2000.*

Some researchers suggest that this can be triggered by a severe emotional event such as physical abuse, war, or even relationship difficulties (Mclewin & Muller, 2006). A few years ago, after a man was distraught after discovering his wife of 13 years had been cheating on him, he woke up to find that he couldn't recall the last 13 years of his life.

Some with dissociative amnesia forget all the details of their lives. Often they are found wandering the street confused and bewildered. Luckily, it is fairly self-limiting, and episodes usually last less than a week. Their entire memory soon returns, often in fits and spurts, to full function

Others with symptoms of dissociative amnesia lose their memory, but not all parts of their identity. This is called **dissociative fugue**. In addition to experiencing amnesia, they may travel away from home and live in a new location. It's like dissociative amnesia—with travel ("fugue" means flight). People with dissociative fugue forget who they are and often will travel great distances and assume new identities that are similar to their old identity. Unlike in dissociative amnesia, people in such fugue states will often recover their memory all at once and have amnesia about the fugue period. As rare as the disorder is   (the prevalence of dissociative fugue has been estimated at 0.2% (APA, 2000)—it is even more rare for it to occur twice in the same individual. Details of the fugue state are difficult to come by since those in the fugue state don't realize they are in one.

Dissociative Identity Disorder

Recall that dissociation is a splitting of your consciousness and attention. Sometimes this split becomes so extreme that an identity can take on a life of its own. This is the case in **dissociative identity disorder (DID)**. You may know DID under its older name, multiple personality disorder. DID is a much better name since it highlights the importance of dissociation in the disorder. In DID, two or more distinct identities (sometimes called alters) exist inside of one person, each with his or her own unique characteristics. Dramatic differences have been reported in the personalities of the alters. Alters with different genders, food preferences, and eyeglass prescriptions have been reported (Miller, Blackburn, Scholes, White, & Mamalis, 1991).

The primary, or host, personality will be in control of the person most of the time. Often memories of the behaviors of the alters are shrouded by amnesia. Shifts between alters can often be initiated by stressful circumstances (Sar, Akyüz, & Dogan, 2007).

DID is very rare, but it used to be even more so. Until around 1980 only 300 cases had been reported; since then thousands more have been identified (Spanos, 1999). For some, this shift in the numbers indicates that we are much better at diagnosing the people who have DID and that those who need treatment are able to get the help they need. For others, this dramatic increase raises even more suspicion about the existence of the condition.

Dissociative fugue A disorder in which a person forgets who he or she is, often traveling great distances and assuming new identities that resemble his or her original identity.

Dissociative identity disorder (DID) A dissociative disorder in which two or more distinct identities, each with unique characteristics, exist within one person.

Forgetfulness in dissociative amnesia is greater than normal forgetfulness.

Etiology of Dissociative Disorders

One theory of the cause of dissociative disorders is that the dissociative experience helps to separate and disconnect a person from the awareness of a disturbing experience (Dorahy, 2001). In this way, the dissociation acts as a mechanism to help the person to cope.

Others believe that the behavior seen in dissociative disorders is reinforced attention-seeking behavior (Lilienfeld et al., 1999). These theories do not suggest that the conditions are faked, but rather that the behaviors help them to make sense of the many incompatible and contradictory emotions that can be experienced during and after a trauma. The new identities become real to the patient and they behave accordingly.

CONCEPT LEARNING CHECK 14.4 | *Identifying Dissociative Disorders*

1. A 24-year-old man is brought to the hospital emergency room because he was found wandering the street. He reports feeling "confused" and says that he isn't sure where he is. The last thing he remembers is coming home to a fire in his house. After examination you discover no head trauma or any kind of injury that would account for his loss of memory. What is the most likely diagnosis?

14.5 Mood Disorders

Mood disorders are marked by fluctuations in emotional states and can include problematic social functioning, thinking, behaviors, and physical symptoms.

- Examine types of mood disorders based upon APA guidelines using D-SIGECAPS.
- Be able to differentiate between a unipolar and bipolar mood disorder.

We've all had our ups and downs. When something great happens, it's uplifting and our mood soars. When something terrible occurs we might feel down in the dumps. The peaks, valleys, potency, and length of our moods are predictable in relation to the things that happen to us. For people with mood disorders, however, extremes in their emotional state can create distress and impairment in their social and work life.

Moods are long-lasting, nonspecific emotional states. Mood disorders are marked by tumultuous emotional states and can include problematic social functioning, thinking, behaviors, and physical symptoms.

Mood disorders are pretty common. Researchers indicate up to 20.8% of adults have suffered from mood disorders (Kessler et al., 2005). **TABLE 14-7** summarizes the mood disorders described in *DSM-IV-TR*. We will focus on two of these: major depressive disorder and bipolar disorder.

Moods Long-lasting, nonspecific emotional states.

Major Depressive Disorder

I'm sure you've had a time in your life when things just weren't going right. Maybe after a breakup or when you'd moved to a new city. You might have felt normal sadness. How can you tell normal sadness from major depressive disorder? Partly due to the severity and length of the symptoms you experience.

TABLE 14-7 Mood Disorders

Disorder	Description
Major depressive disorder	Two weeks of a low mood or anhedonia and a at least four other behavioral, cognitive, or emotional symptoms
Dysthymic disorder	A chronic low mood that doesn't meet criteria for a major depressive disorder; a person must experience these symptoms for at least 2 years
Bipolar I disorder	Cycling between mania and either hypomania or depression
Bipolar II disorder	Cycling between hypomania and depression
Cyclothymic disorder	A chronic mood syndrome where a person cycles between symptoms of hypomania and symptoms of dysthymia. A person must experience these symptoms for at least 2 years

Source: Adapted from American Psychiatric Association. Diagnostic and Statistical Manual of Mental Disorders: *DSM-IV-TR. American Psychiatric Publishing, 2000.*

Depression is more than just a sad mood. It's a syndrome that carries a number of behavioral, cognitive, and emotional features. It's most commonly associated with a sad or low mood, but it also may carry with it a reduced capacity to feel pleasure (sometimes called **anhedonia**), hopelessness, loss of energy, disrupted sleep patterns, weight and appetite changes, difficulty in concentration, and thoughts of death (APA, 2000).

Because it's so common, depression is often called the common cold of mental illness. Depression is the most common mental health problem seen in a physician's office. In addition, nearly a third of college students will encounter mild depression at some point in their undergraduate career (Seligman, 2006).

It's not just common; it has quite an impact as well. Depression has been ranked as the fourth leading cause of disability worldwide and it is expected to rise to second by 2020 (Murray & Lopez, 1997).

There are nine symptoms in addition to sad mood that could signal depression. You need to have five or more symptoms most of the day, nearly every day, for at least 2 weeks, for these symptoms to be considered chronic and severe enough to be major depressive disorder. One way psychologists remember the symptoms is the acronym D-SIGECAPS, as you can see in **TABLE 14-8**.

Depression is thought to be self-limiting, lasting between 6 and 18 months even without treatment. This isn't to suggest that it's a good idea to just wait it out. With no help or treatment of any sort, about 80% of people will relapse into another depressive episode (Mueller et al., 1999). Luckily, the relapse rate for treated depression is much lower, so it makes sense to treat depression and treat it early. However, despite the myriad of effective treatments, only one-third of people seek any sort of treatment for their depression, and some of those who seek treatment delay as long as 8 years before they get any sort of help (Wang et al., 2005).

> **Anhedonia** A reduced capacity to feel pleasure.
>
> **Mania** A condition associated with an elevated, expansive, or sometimes irritable mood.

Although sadness is a symptom of major depressive disorder, one can meet the criteria for depression without being sad.

Depression and Bipolar Disorder

As you have learned, the central feature of major depressive disorder is a major depressive episode (five of those nine D-SIGECAPS). However, a major depressive episode isn't the only kind of mood episode that psychologists describe. Some individuals have symptoms that are the polar opposite. Instead of feeling down and blue, their mood is abnormally elevated, and their mood is so good they do things that get them into trouble.

Think about the best mood you've ever had . . . then double it. Some people even describe their mood as "better than good." This is called a manic episode. In addition to this elevated, expansive, or sometimes irritable mood, the person has three of the following symptoms most days, for at least a week.

Symptoms of **mania** include:

- inflated self-esteem
- decreased need for sleep

TABLE 14-8 Major Symptoms of Depression

Letter	Symptom	Description
D	Depressed mood	Sadness
S	Sleep	Change in sleep, maybe insomnia, or hypersomnia (lots of sleep without feeling rested)
I	Lack of Interest	Lack of interest in normally pleasurable activities
G	Guilt	Inappropriate guilt or feelings of worthlessness
E	Energy	Lack of energy
C	Concentration	Problems in concentration or indecisiveness
A	Appetite	Change in appetite
P	Psychomotor agitation/retardation	Moving more slowly than is normal (psychomotor retardation) or more fidgety than normal (psychomotor agitation)
S	Suicidality	Thoughts of death or suicide

Excessive involvement in risky behaviors, such as excessive shopping, can be a sign of mania.

- feeling a pressure to keep talking
- a flight of ideas, or the feeling that your thoughts are racing
- increase in goal-directed behavior
- excessive involvement in pleasurable activities that have a high possibility for painful consequences (like unrestrained shopping sprees)

I'm sure that in that list you could find three symptoms that you might like to have (I'll sign up for a decreased need for sleep). You'll recall that in order for something to be a disorder it has to cause distress and/or impairment. Some people can have symptoms of mania and do not get themselves into trouble. In this case you would experience **hypomania** ("hypo" meaning under—like a hypodermic needle that goes under the dermis). In hypomania, a person shows symptoms of an elevated mood and other signs of mania, but these symptoms don't interfere with daily life. In fact, the symptoms can be helpful. Hypomania alone is not a disorder, but hypomania can occur in combination with other mood episodes, like depression and mania as part of bipolar disorder.

A diagnosis of **bipolar disorder** requires at least one manic episode. Often in the months and years following the manic episode, people with bipolar disorder will have depressive episodes, hypomanic episodes, or even additional manic episodes. In these cases, the mood episodes that follow the manic episodes are all considered to be part of the bipolar disorder.

Bipolar disorders are far less common than their unipolar (depressive only) counterparts, with only about 2 in 100 people in the United States having had the diagnosis (Kessler et al., 2005).

Etiology of Mood Disorders

Remember that the diathesis-stress hypothesis suggests that most disorders include a biological vulnerability as well as environmental factors that can put these vulnerabilities in motion. This is believed to be true of mood disorders as well.

The Biological Perspective

There is a good deal of evidence that the biological perspective can explain many parts of the mood disorders. There is evidence, for example, of genetic, neurochemical, and neuroanatomical factors for depression.

Genetic Vulnerability

Mood disorders seem to have a genetic link. Depression, for example, certainly runs in families (Sullivan, Neale, & Kendler, 2000), and while the genetic commonality is stronger for depressive disorders, bipolar disorder runs in families too. For example, if you have a parent or sibling with bipolar disorder, your chance of having it too is up to 20 times higher than if your relatives didn't have bipolar disorder (MacKinnon, Jamison, & DePaulo, 1997) FIGURE 14-17.

Hypomania A condition in which a person has symptoms of mania but avoids getting into trouble.

Bipolar disorder A mood disorder in which a person may alternate between a sad, depressive mood and elevated, irritable, or manic episodes.

FIGURE 14-17 The risk of bipolar disorder increases with genetic relatedness.
Source: Adapted from Gottesman, I. I. (1990). Schizophrenia Genesis: The Origins of Madness (1st ed.). New York: W. H. Freeman.

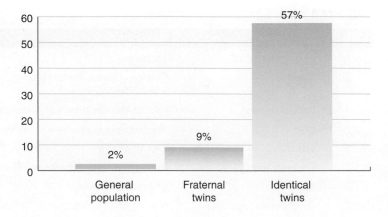

Suicide

One of the most upsetting and troubling symptoms of depression are the thoughts of death, or suicidality, that often accompany the disorder. These thoughts and emotions are part of the constellation of symptoms that come with depression. When the symptoms of depression fade with treatment, the symptoms of suicidality and hopelessness fade too.

Despite this, suicide remains a significant problem. More than half a million people in the United States each year will make a suicide attempt that is so severe that it results in hospitalization, and more than 1 million people each year will actually kill themselves. The completed suicide rates only tell part of the story, since suicide attempts outnumber completed suicides by a ratio of 20 to 1 (Sudock, 2005).

Suicide is the second leading cause of death among college students (Rawe & Kingsburry, 2006). The National Suicide Prevention Lifeline (http://www.suicidepreventionlifeline.org/) offers assistance to those in crisis and stories of attempt survivors.

Neurochemical and Neuroanatomical Factors

You'll remember that neurotransmitters help the nervous system to communicate. The **monoamine hypothesis of depression** suggests that depressive symptoms are brought on by a malfunction of certain types of neurotransmitters, specifically norepinephrine (NE), serotonin (5HT), and dopamine (DA) neurons (also known as monoamines). These neurotransmitters connect to important areas in the brain's limbic system. Lower activity in the limbic system has been implicated in the symptoms of depression. What's more, medications that boost the effectiveness of these neurotransmitters help those with depression get better (Stahl, 2008a).

Monoamine hypothesis of depression A hypothesis that suggests that depressive symptoms are brought on by a malfunction of certain types of neurotransmitters.

The Social-Cognitive Perspective

The learned helplessness model suggests that when people feel they don't have any control over the good things that happen to them, they are more likely to become depressed. This theory comes from research done in animals: When the animals were exposed to uncontrollable negative stimuli, like a mild shock, and were unable to escape it, they learned to be helpless. When they were in a position to escape the bad event—they didn't (Peterson, Maier, & Seligman, 1995).

An expansion of this idea is seen with cognitive distortions. The idea is that some people have thoughts about themselves, the world, or other people that are not accurate; they are distortions of reality. However inaccurate, these thoughts can shape their actions and emotions. They may, for example, filter out the positive things in their life and remember more disappointing moments instead. What results is a belief that they are worthless and defective.

CONCEPT LEARNING CHECK 14.5   *Identifying Mood Disorders*

1. After a recent move Sean "has lost a considerable amount of weight and has periods when he cries." He misses his old friends. He feels exhausted most of the day has trouble sleeping. What's the most likely diagnosis?

2. A few months later Sean returns to his therapist with some new symptoms. He says he's feeling much better, in fact he reports feeling "better than good." He says he has been focusing on his work for about 15 hours a day. He sleeps only for about 2 hours, but says that he still feels rested. Despite all his work he hasn't been that productive. His supervisor says that Sean's presentations are sloppy, and it seems as if Sean feels a pressure to keep talking. Sean says his thoughts are racing around in his head. Because of his lack of productivity, Sean has been put on probation at work. Given the new symptoms, what is the most likely diagnosis?

3. A 36-year-old-woman says that for the past 2 months she has been feeling irritable and has lost interest in most of her usual activities. She says that she also has trouble concentrating at work, doesn't sleep well at night, and has lost about 10 pounds. What's the most likely diagnosis?

14.6 Psychotic Disorders

Psychotic disorders involve a loss of contact with reality.

- Recognize signs and symptoms of psychotic disorders.

Schizophrenia A psychological disorder characterized by disordered thinking, delusions, hallucinations, and disordered behavior and emotions.

Delusions Beliefs that most people would think are incredible or impossible.

Bizarre delusions False and impossible beliefs.

Non-bizarre delusions False beliefs that are possible but highly unlikely.

The devastating impact of **schizophrenia** is clear. The experience can be terrifying and disruptive and is characterized by disordered thinking, delusions, hallucinations, irrational thoughts, and disturbed emotions and actions. In the United States, nearly 2.5 million people have schizophrenia and nearly a third of those require inpatient assistance (Kessler & Wang, 2008).

Schizophrenia has more than just a devastating emotional impact; it also has a very significant financial impact. If you add up all the financial costs of treating schizophrenia, it makes up around 3% of the entire U.S. healthcare budget and nearly 75% of all U.S. mental health care expenses (Knapp, Mangalore, & Simon, 2004).

Schizophrenia is chronic. Up to 80% of those hospitalized with their first episode of schizophrenia will return to the hospital with another episode eventually (Eaton et al., 1992). Luckily, up to 30% of those diagnosed will get much better with treatment (Wiersma, Nienhuis, Slooff, & Giel, 1998).

Psychotic symptoms appear in a number of psychological disorders like anxiety or mood disorders. When psychotic symptoms appear as the central feature of the disorder, it might suggest a psychotic disorder such as schizophrenia. **TABLE 14-9** summarizes the psychotic disorders described by the *DSM-IV-TR*. Our discussion will focus on just one: schizophrenia.

Symptoms of All Schizophrenic Disorders

Symptoms of psychosis include disordered thinking, delusions, and hallucinations, as well as disordered behavior and emotions.

Disorganized Thinking

The way we speak is often a sign of the way we think. Therefore, the disorganized speaking often found in people with psychosis is a clue to the disordered thoughts these individuals have. Disorganized speaking patterns can range from rapidly switching from one unrelated topic to the next (as in "loose associations") to totally incomprehensible word patterns ("incoherence" or "word salad").

Delusions and Hallucinations

Delusions are false beliefs. These are beliefs that most anyone would believe are false. They come in two types: bizarre and non-bizarre. **Bizarre delusions** are beliefs that are totally impossible. **Non-bizarre delusions** are very, very unlikely, but possible. For example, if I told you that I thought that the nightly local newscast is a way to communicate my daily whereabouts to a government agency, although this is unlikely, it is possible (involving microphones, codes, and such). On the other hand, saying that I believed my organs were turning into straw would be a bizarre delusion, since that is impossible.

TABLE 14-9 Psychotic Disorders

Psychotic Disorder	Description
Schizophrenia	A disorder that lasts for at least 6 months and includes at least 1 month of active-phase symptoms (i.e., two [or more] of the following: delusions, hallucinations, disorganized speech, grossly disorganized or catatonic behavior, negative symptoms)
Schizophrenia	Six months of symptoms of psychosis and accompanying impairment
Delusional disorder	Only non-bizarre delusions for at least 30 days
Brief psychotic disorder	Symptoms of psychosis lasting at least 1 day and no more than 30 days
Shared psychotic disorder	A disorder where two people have the same delusion

Source: Adapted from American Psychiatric Association. Diagnostic and Statistical Manual of Mental Disorders: *DSM-IV-TR. American Psychiatric Publishing, 2000.*

CRITICAL THINKING APPLICATION

Afew years ago in a small Connecticut city, a man named Scott left his office and began his drive home. He was 25 years old, single, and in good health. In fact, he had never suffered from more than a cold or a bad case of food poisoning. With no history of seizure disorder, Scott had a seizure while driving. Unable to control his muscles or his car, he lost control of the vehicle, killing one person and injuring several others.

When people who hear this story are asked if they think Scott should be punished, most say no, because they believe the accident wasn't his fault. Some may suggest that his driving privileges should be suspended until he is seizure-free. Almost everyone agrees, however, that putting him in jail wouldn't prevent or deter another similar accident.

Strangely, when this story is told so that Scott's "seizures" are instead called "hallucinations," people take a harsher view of Scott's role. They suggest that Scott should be committed to a mental institution or arrested and tried for the death and destruction he caused.

If we think about it, most of us would agree that seizures and hallucinations share some biological and physiological characteristics. Nevertheless, we tend to feel very differently about behavior that results from one condition versus another. Why?

Evaluate

1. Do attitudes about mental health affect how we treat, punish, or choose not to treat mental illnesses as opposed to other illnesses? Explain.

2. How might stigmas and biases about mental illness be reflected in our language and in our laws?

Hallucinations, on the other hand, are sensory perceptions with no sensory input. People who experience hallucinations may see things that aren't there or hear things that no one else hears. Hallucinations can come from all five senses. Most, however, are auditory or visual.

Catatonia

Another example of a symptom of psychosis is catatonia. Catatonia is a problem with movement. It comes in two types. One is **agitated catatonia**, in which the person has uncontrollable movements. They may flap their arms or spin in circles. It can also be exhibited as **stuporous catatonia**, where the person is immobile and nonreactive. They may even exhibit waxy flexibility (you can move their arms and they stay in that position).

Deficits of Behavior

The symptoms that were already mentioned are called **positive symptoms**. They are referred to as positive, not because they are good, but because they are in addition to typical behavior. For example, most people do not have hallucinations, so this would be an addition to expected behavior. Positive symptoms are distinct from **negative symptoms**, which are deficits in behavior—things that are expected but are sometimes absent in psychosis. They all begin with the letter A. Negative symptoms include avolition (lack of will), alogia (lack of elaborative speech), and affective flattening (flat moods).

Schizophrenic Subtypes

Diagnosing schizophrenia is more complicated than just identifying psychosis. For a firm diagnosis, the symptoms must be present for a minimum amount of time and cause distress and impairment. In addition, it is important to know that people with schizophrenia don't always exhibit these symptoms of psychosis and often have long stretches with no symptoms whatsoever.

This waxing and waning of symptoms can occur with other conditions. Think back to the last time you had a cold. You probably had a time when you were sneezing and coughing and felt horrible. Then maybe you started to feel better, but still had some leftover

Hallucinations Sensory perceptions with no sensory input. The perceptions may affect any or all of the five senses.

Agitated catatonia A symptom of schizophrenia that is characterized by excessive motor activity and periods of inexhaustibility.

Stuporous catatonia A symptom of schizophrenia that is characterized by restricted motor activity such as periods of immobility and muscle rigidity.

Positive symptoms of psychosis Symptoms, such as hallucinations or delusions, that are present in addition to expected behavior.

Negative symptoms of psychosis Symptoms of psychosis that involve behavior deficits, or expected behaviors that are absent.

ickyness. You could consider the time you were feeling bad and the symptoms were really the worst to be the active phase of your illness. The other is a residual (leftover) phase.

A diagnosis of schizophrenia is much the same. Continuous signs of the disorder must last for at least 6 months. At least 1 month must be an active phase. At this point the person will show two or more of the symptoms of psychosis most of the day, nearly every day. This is often followed by several months of a residual phase. The residual period sometimes consists of two or more positive symptoms with less severe impact, or maybe just negative symptoms. Some can have it worse and have several months of an active phase.

Paranoid, Catatonic, Disorganized, Undifferentiated

Schizophrenia is grouped into four main subtypes. The subtypes of schizophrenia reflect the prominence of certain symptoms.

For example, in the **paranoid type**, the delusions are typically non-bizarre and there are highly structured visual or auditory hallucinations that are coherent and fit the story of the delusions. There is usually a theme of persecution. You wouldn't expect to find any catatonia in this type. As you can imagine, people with this type are suspicious of others and often believe that others are attempting to trick them. This type of schizophrenia is the most common one, affecting nearly 40% of those diagnosed with schizophrenia.

As the name suggests, the **catatonic type** is dominated by catatonia—either stuporous, agitated, or both. They may exhibit other symptoms such as repeating the movements or words of others, or standing in strange and uncomfortable postures for long times. This type of schizophrenia is fairly rare and affects only 5% of those diagnosed with schizophrenia.

People with the **disorganized type of schizophrenia** exhibit disorganized speech and behavior and may also have a flat mood or emotions that don't fit the situation (such as laughing at serious moments). During severe active phases of their disorder, they may have bizarre delusions of bodily functions (such as the feeling that their brain is melting), incoherent speech, and frequent disorganized hallucinations. The impairment in their social and self-care functioning is severe and they may neglect their personal hygiene. This type of schizophrenia is uncommon and is seen in only 5% of those diagnosed with schizophrenia.

The **undifferentiated type** is reserved for individuals who meet the core criteria for schizophrenia but their varied symptoms don't meet the criteria for paranoid, disorganized, or catatonic type. It afflicts 40% of those diagnosed with schizophrenia.

Etiology of Psychotic Disorders

Schizophrenia most likely is the result of many things. Like most every psychological disorder, there is evidence of both a biological underpinning and non-biological influences.

Genetic Vulnerability

Genes play a significant role in schizophrenia. The more closely a person is related to someone with schizophrenia, the greater his or her likelihood for having the disorder. You may remember that there is a 1 in 100 chance of a person being diagnosed with schizophrenia. This changes to 1 in 10 with a parent or sibling with the disorder and 1 in 2 if the sibling is identical. This holds true no matter if the individuals grow up in the same household or apart (Plomin, DeFries, McClearn, & McGuffin, 2000; Gottesman, 1990).

Brain Abnormalities

There are several differences in the brains of individuals diagnosed with schizophrenia. Brain scans reveal that people with schizophrenia have larger ventricles—fluid-filled cavities—in their brain than do people without this disorder (Galderisi, 2000) FIGURE 14-18. Other researchers found that the hippocampus and areas within the cerebral cortex were a bit smaller than would be expected (Lui et al., 2009). Although these structural differences are convincing, they are not enough to explain the vast behavioral and emotional differences in those with schizophrenia.

The **dopamine hypothesis of schizophrenia** suggests that the neurotransmitter dopamine plays a key role in the disorder. Current theories suggest that a complex imbalance might lead to the symptoms of schizophrenia as well as the side effects of medications

Paranoid type of schizophrenia A disorder characterized by highly structured non-bizarre delusions, coherent visual or auditory hallucinations, and feelings of persecution.

Catatonic type of schizophrenia A disorder characterized by one or both forms of catatonia, as well as other behavioral symptoms.

Disorganized type of schizophrenia A schizophrenic disorder characterized by disorganized speech and behavior, a flat mood, and inappropriate emotions. Severe, active phases are characterized by bizarre delusions of bodily functions, frequent disorganized hallucinations, and incoherent speech.

Undifferentiated type of schizophrenia The presence of symptoms that meet the core criteria for schizophrenia but do not meet the criteria for paranoid, disorganized, or catatonic type.

Dopamine hypothesis of schizophrenia A hypothesis that suggests that the neurotransmitter dopamine plays a key role in schizophrenia.

used to balance out dopamine in the brain (Conklin & Iacono, 2002). For example, there may be too much dopamine in the mesolimbic system, which is involved in emotion and thinking. Too much dopamine in this area could explain the delusions, hallucinations, and distorted thinking often found in people suffering from psychosis. On the other hand, low dopamine levels in the prefrontal area have been implicated in the organization of behavior, attention, and motivation (Stahl, 2008b).

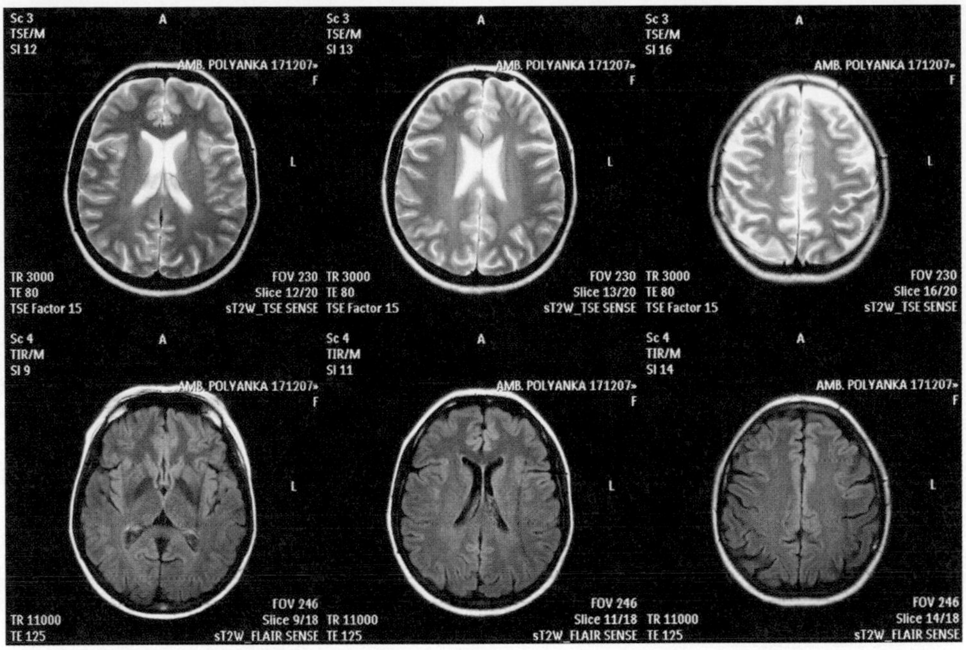

Neurodevelopment in the Uterus
Neurodevelopment refers to the growth and maturation of the nervous system. The neurodevelopmental hypothesis of

FIGURE 14-18 Enlarged brain ventricles are often present in people with schizophrenia.

schizophrenia proposes that the nervous system differences found in schizophrenia are due, in part, to factors that occur during the growth of the nervous system before birth (McGrath, Féron, Burne, Mackay-Sim, & Eyles, 2003). These factors can be genetic (like having a family member with schizophrenia), environmental (like maternal malnutrition, infection, or incompatible blood types), or both (Fatemi & Folsom, 2009).

Psychological Factors
Biology doesn't tell the whole story. It never does. There is strong evidence that psychosocial influences may interact with genetic vulnerability in producing schizophrenia. Extremely poor parenting and the failure of developing adequate psychosocial and coping skills can increase the stress that could set schizophrenia into motion (Walker & Diforio, 1997). Other sources of stress can include being raised in an abusive family, experiencing disturbed patterns of communication in the family, and early trauma.

CONCEPT LEARNING CHECK 14.6 *Classifying Signs and Symptoms of Schizophrenia*

Decide whether each of the following symptoms is a positive or a negative symptom of schizophrenia. Place a check mark in the appropriate column.

Positive and Negative Symptoms of Schizophrenia

Symptom	Positive	Negative
Avolition		
Visual hallucinations		
Delusions		
Anhedonia		
Stuporous catatonia		
Flattened affect		
Inability to experience pleasure		
Auditory hallucinations		
Alogia		

14.7 Personality Disorders

Personality disorders involve extreme, inflexible global personality traits that are both chronic and pervasive.

■ List and describe the personality disorders as described in the *DSM-IV-TR*.

Personality disorder
A psychological condition, coded on Axis II of the *DSM*, that involves extreme, inflexible global personality traits that are chronic and pervasive.

Ego syntonic A psychological symptom that does not cause a person distress.

Ego dystonic A psychological symptom that causes a person distress.

So far, all of the disorders previously discussed have been Axis I conditions. You might wonder how they differ from the Axis II **personality disorders**. Diagnoses on Axis II are often concerned with a person's global traits or way of life. For something to be a personality disorder, it has to be a disruptive pattern that is both chronic and pervasive. Chronic means it doesn't come and go; it ends up being the main way they interact with people all the time. The personality disorders also begin early and are often identifiable by the time a person reaches early adulthood.

In addition to being long lasting, the disorder is pervasive, meaning that it creeps into every nook and cranny of a person's life. Personality disorders are self-defeating and rigid and often very resistant to change.

You might think that a behavior pattern so disruptive and so impairing would be something the person doesn't like. Most of the time this is true, but often people with personality disorders don't find their own behavior disagreeable. Some types of personality disorders are **ego syntonic**, meaning that they do not bother the person. Think of a friend of yours who has a shirt with a hole in it. You might find it unthinkable to leave the house with an obvious problem with your clothing, but to that person, it is not a big deal. He might not think twice about it. It's the same with behaviors sometimes. When behaviors are ego **syn**tonic, they are similar to how they see themselves (like the word synonym, meaning words that are similar). Most of the disorders, however, are **ego dystonic**, meaning they are dissimilar to how they see themselves. Ego dystonic disorders are easier to treat since clients are usually more motivated to change things they don't like about themselves. If the behavior is ego syntonic, treatment can be rough-going or even futile.

Personality disorders affect about 1% of the population (Kessler & Wang, 2008) **TABLE 14-10** lists the ten personality disorders described in the *DSM-IV-TR*. We will focus on three: antisocial personality disorder, paranoid personality disorder, and borderline personality disorder.

TABLE 14-10 Personality Disorders

Disorder	Key Themes
Paranoid personality disorder	Distrust and suspiciousness
Schizoid personality	Apathy and detachment from others, including family members
Antisocial personality disorder	Breaking rules and harming others without remorse
Borderline personality disorder	Instability in relationships, mood, and ever-changing view of self
Histrionic personality disorder	Always needs attention from others
Narcissistic personality disorder	Inflated sense of self-importance and extreme preoccupation with themselves
Avoidant personality disorder	Extreme reaction to the criticism of others
Dependent personality disorder	Insatiable need for care from others
Obsessive-compulsive personality disorder	Fixation with rules and lists that interferes with them getting things done

Source: Adapted from American Psychiatric Association. Diagnostic and Statistical Manual of Mental Disorders: DSM-IV-TR. American Psychiatric Publishing, 2000.

Antisocial Personality Disorder

I'm sure you've been tempted to do something you know you shouldn't do. I know I have. Taking something that doesn't belong to you or sneaking gummy worms into a movie theater that has a sign that reads "No outside food allowed" are things that might cross our minds at times, but most of us stop ourselves before we act on these impulses. We might feel guilty for even entertaining the thought. We follow the rules and hope others will too. But let's say you didn't care to follow the rules and you gave into every impulse you had and didn't care about the consequences or who you hurt or cheated even if it was your best friend or your parents.

That's similar to what you might expect in **antisocial personality disorder**, a personality disorder where a person breaks the rules of society often with no remorse or anxiety. For a diagnosis of antisocial personality disorder, in addition to conduct difficulties, before age 15 you would expect three or more symptoms including law-breaking, frequent lying, impulsivity, aggressiveness, disregard for the safety of others, irresponsibility, and lack of remorse or even rationalizing having hurt others.

Antisocial personality disorder is more often found in men (with a prevalence of 3%) than in women (1%) (APA, 2000).

> **Antisocial personality disorder** A personality disorder in which a person breaks societal rules, often without remorse or anxiety.

Etiology of Antisocial Personality Disorder

Scientists have been trying to determine the cause or causes of antisocial personality disorder. Some have wondered about the role of biology. Is there a criminal mind? Are there really natural born killers? Certainly, biology does play a role. In fact, the prefrontal cortex—the part of the cerebral cortex that controls impulses and aids in ethical behavior and moral decision making—has been found to be different in people who have been diagnosed with antisocial personality disorder (Kiehl, 2006).

There is even some evidence that those individuals with antisocial personality disorder crave higher levels of sensation to maintain the normal feelings we all have. They are chaos junkies, so to speak. They are easily susceptible to boredom and pick activities that will give them a quick fix (Gabbard, 2005).

Dr. James Fallon, a neuroscientist at the University of California, Irvine, discovered a specific area of the brain, the orbital cortex, that he feels is involved in the impulse control lacking in people with antisocial personality disorder (Fallon, 2006). His research has even been able to identify low activity in this area using brain scans, after studying brain scans in many people with antisocial personality disorder. This was exciting stuff—a link to a test for antisocial personality disorder FIGURE 14-19.

There is a twist. After being encouraged to check into his family background, Fallon discovered that one of his ancestors allegedly murdered his own mother. It didn't stop there. There were seven alleged murders in that line of his family, including the notorious Lizzy Borden, who in August of 1892 allegedly killed her father and stepmother with an axe (she was acquitted of the murder).

Fallon was shocked. He studied the brain scans of all the members of his immediate family to see if they too had the low activity in the orbital frontal cortex. He discovered that none of them had the underactivity you might expect for antisocial personality disorder. None except for one—Fallon himself. He had exactly the orbital frontal profile shared by all of the people with antisocial personality disorder who were also murderers he had been studying, as well as all the known high-risk violence-related genes.

As you are no doubt well aware by now, biology doesn't determine everything—the environment plays a critical role, and in Fallon's case his entire upbringing was filled with love and support from his entire extended family. Many factors during childhood, such as lack of warmth, neglect, and harsh punishment, are also important for the development of antisocial personality disorder (Johnson, Cohen, Chen, Kasen, & Brook, 2006).

FIGURE 14-19 Dr. Fallon studies brain images in people with antisocial personality disorder.

Paranoid Personality Disorder

Individuals with paranoid personality disorder have a long history of seeing malicious intent in the actions of others. This suspiciousness and mistrust does not subside no matter how long they know you.

A diagnosis of this disorder includes four symptoms that should pervade every part of their lives. They expect to be exploited or harmed by others and are preoccupied with the trustworthiness of their friends. In addition, they think that information they give about themselves will be used against them, and they read hidden meaning into harmless remarks. What's more, they are unforgiving of insults, are quick to counterattack, and often doubt the fidelity of their romantic partners.

As you can imagine, they are always on guard and it causes significant impairment in their work lives and social lives.

Etiology of Paranoid Personality Disorder

The cause of **paranoid personality disorder** remains a mystery. Paranoid personality disorder tends to run in families (Kendler et al., 2006). Other researchers suggest that paranoid personality disorder could be acquired through learning. In this way paranoid behaviors once could have been adaptive responses to stressful situations (Bradley, Conklin, & Westen, 2007).

Borderline Personality Disorder

Individuals with **borderline personality disorder** have a long history of instability in their lives. This instability extends to their relationships, self-image, and moods. Borderline personality disorder is a troubling and difficult disorder in which the individual often has difficulty in controlling his or her impulses.

Instability can cause disruptions in relationships and changes in goals, work, and friends. The instability can leave one feeling worried and with little sense of who he or she is as a person. This can lead to frequent fights and hot tempers, and fears of abandonment. TABLE 14-11 outlines the symptoms of borderline personality disorder.

Although borderline personality disorder is not very common (about 2% of the general population), the severity of symptoms makes it overrepresented in treatment populations. About one in every ten people in outpatient mental health settings are diagnosed with borderline personality disorder, and about two of every ten people among psychiatric inpatients (Kessler & Wang, 2008).

Etiology of Borderline Personality Disorder

As with other disorders, researchers have found several possible causes for this one. Some suggest that serotonin might be related to reduced impulse control. Studies of twins with borderline personality disorder provide strong evidence that there might be a genetic component to the disorder (Siever & Koenigsberg, 2000). Other studies have suggested that the amygdala, responsible for regulating emotions, could be involved. In people with borderline personality disorder, this area is overactive and the brain areas responsible for controlling emotional responses are underactive (Meyer-Lindenberg, 2008).

Biology is only part of the story. Many people with borderline personality disorder have reported significant abuse, neglect, instability, and psychopathology in their backgrounds. Often these abuses are reflected in their earliest memories (Bradley et al., 2007). One study reported that up to 70% of people with borderline personality disorder had been sexually abused (Zanarini, 2000).

Paranoid personality disorder A disorder characterized by a long and unwavering history of attributing malicious intent to others.

Borderline personality disorder A personality disorder marked by a history of instability in a person's self-image, ability to control impulses, relationships, and moods.

TABLE 14-11 Borderline Personality Disorder

People with borderline personality disorder have an unstable view of themselves, their friends, and they experience rapidly shifting moods. These three core symptoms characterize their world. Additional symptoms include—

1. Trying to prevent important others from abandoning them
2. Stormy relationships with others in which the other person is alternately idealized and condemned
3. Shallow understanding of themselves
4. Recklessness that can get them into trouble
5. Physical self-harm that may include cutting or suicide attempts
6. Feelings of emptiness
7. Intense anger

Source: Adapted from American Psychiatric Association. Diagnostic and Statistical Manual of Mental Disorders: *DSM-IV-TR. American Psychiatric Publishing, 2000.*

Summary of Multiple Influences on Psychological Disorders

I never heard from Betty again. Odds are that the behaviors she exhibited, despite being unusual, were not indicative of a psychological condition. What creates a psychological disorder? The etiology of psychological disorders is certainly not singular. The diathesis-stress and reciprocal gene environment model, for example, suggest that biological forces such as natural selection, brain anatomy, and biochemical activity may be involved. Also, environmental factors like learning and exposure to stressful events also have an impact. In addition, sociocultural forces like family background, and how a person interprets what happens in his or her life may also increase the likelihood of developing a psychological condition. Multiple influences are at play in how disorders start and are maintained.

CONCEPT LEARNING CHECK **14.7** | *Categorizing Personality Disorders*

1. Alex, age 40, has long-standing difficulty maintaining relationships because of her frequent shifts in moods. She also has the following symptoms: a history of unstable friendships, frequent mood shifts, indecisiveness, and a fear of being left alone. Alex seems to suffer from which disorder?

Visual Overview Distinguishing Psychological Disorders

Well-trained psychologists can identify specific disorders and apply appropriate treatments. As you study psychological disorders, you might find it challenging to keep them straight. Two of these disorders—dissociative identity disorder and schizophrenia—are easily confused. When you compare their symptoms, however, you'll see that there is little resemblance.

Anxiety disorders are marked by feelings of nervousness, distress, and apprehension. They are often disruptive attempts to diminish anxiety (*Section 14.2*).

Somatoform disorders are symptoms of a physical illness that are unexplained by a medical condition (*Section 14.3*).

Mood disorders are marked by turbulent emotional states and can include problematic social functioning, thinking, behaviors, and physical symptoms. Mood disorders include major depressive disorder and bipolar disorder (*Section 14.5*).

Dissociative identity disorders involve a loss of the integration of consciousness, loss of memory, or a change in the identity of a person. In dissociative identity disorder (formerly called multiple personality disorder), at least two personalities take control of an individual's behavior (*Section 14.4*).
Core symptoms:
 - Two or more identities or personalities within one person
 - Amnesia between different identities

Are people with multiple personalities schizophrenic? Students sometimes confuse dissociative identity disorder with schizophrenia.

Personality disorders involve extreme, inflexible, global personality traits that are chronic and pervasive. People suffering from these disorders may break societal rules, often with no remorse or anxiety (*Section 14.7*).

Psychotic disorders encompass a number of psychological conditions that include symptoms of psychosis (*Section 14.6*).
Core symptoms:
 - Hallucinations
 - Disorganized speech
 - Catatonic behavior
 - Negative symptoms (affective flattening, alogia, or avolition)

14.1 Overview: Understanding Psychological Disorders

- Psychopathology is the science of diagnosing and understanding psychological disorders.
- Psychologists use a number of different tools to diagnose and understand psychological disorders.
- The *Diagnostic and Statistical Manual of Mental Disorders* (*DSM-IV-TR*) is the manual that mental health professionals use to describe mental disorders.

- For most disorders in the *DSM-IV-TR*, the behavior must be deviant, maladapative, or cause personal distress.
- The biopsychosocial approach to psychopathology recognizes three important aspects of human behavior: biological, psychological, and social.
- Classifying and labeling psychological disorders has both advantages and disadvantages.

14.2 Anxiety Disorders

- Anxiety disorders are marked by feelings of nervousness, distress, and apprehension, and disruptive attempts to diminish anxiety.
- Anxiety disorders include generalized anxiety disorder, agoraphobia without a history of panic disorder, panic disorder with agoraphobia, panic disorder without agoraphobia, specific phobia, social phobia, obsessive-compulsive disorder, and posttraumatic stress disorder.

- Both biology and environment are important in explaining the cause of anxiety disorders.

14.3 Somatoform Disorders

- The essential features of somatoform disorders are symptoms of a physical illness that are unexplained by a general medical condition.
- Somatoform disorders include somatization disorder, conversion disorder, and hypochondriasis.
- In somatization disorder, a person has a long history of many vague physical complaints over several years.

- In conversion disorder, a psychological worry or concern is transformed (converted) into a physical symptom.
- In hyopchondriasis, a person is convinced that they have a specific disease process unfolding despite being physically fine.
- Biological vulnerabilities and stressors such as emotional conflicts likely bring on somatoform disorders.

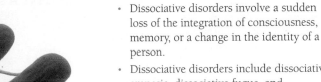

14.4 Dissociative Disorders

- Dissociative disorders involve a sudden loss of the integration of consciousness, memory, or a change in the identity of a person.
- Dissociative disorders include dissociative amnesia, dissociative fugue, and dissociative identity disorder.
- The core symptom of dissociative amnesia is loss of personal memory.
- In dissociative fugue amnesia is exacerbated by travel away from home and the creation of a new identity.

- Dissociative identity disorder is diagnosed when two or more distinct identities exist within one individual.
- Theories of the etiology of dissociative disorders include the symptoms helping to separate and disconnect a person from a disturbing experience. Other researchers believe the symptoms to be reinforced attention-seeking behavior.

14.5 Mood Disorders

- Mood disorders are marked by tumultuous emotional states and can include problematic social functioning, thinking, behaviors, and physical symptoms.

- Mood disorders include major depressive disorder and bipolar disorder.

- Symptoms of depression include a sad mood, anhedonia, hopelessness, loss of energy, disrupted sleep patterns, weight and appetite changes, difficulty in concentration, and thoughts of death.

- Symptoms of mania include inflated self-esteem, decreased need for sleep, a pressure to keep talking, a flight of ideas, increase in goal-directed behavior, and excessive involvement in pleasurable activities that have a high possibility for painful consequences.

- When a major depressive episode occurs alone, it is diagnosed as a major depressive disorder.

- When a major depressive episode alternates with a manic episode, it is diagnosed as a bipolar disorder.

- Mood disorders are caused by both biological and environmental factors.

- The monoamine hypothesis of depression suggests that depressive symptoms are brought on by a malfunction of norepinephrine, serotonin, and dopamine.

- The learned helplessness model of depression suggests that when people feel they don't have any control over the good things that happen to them, they are more likely to be depressed.

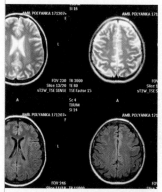

14.6 Psychotic Disorders

- Schizophrenic disorders encompass a number of psychological conditions that include symptoms of psychosis.

- Schizophrenic disorders include several types including paranoid type, catatonic type, disorganized type, and the undifferentiated type.

- The dopamine hypothesis of schizophrenia suggests that the neurotransmitter dopamine plays a key role in the disorder.

- The neurodevelopmental hypothesis proposes that the nervous system differences found in schizophrenia are due, in part, to factors that occur during the growth of the nervous system before birth.

- There is strong evidence that psychosocial influences may interact with genetic vulnerability in producing schizophrenia.

14.7 Personality Disorders

- Personality disorders involve extreme, inflexible global personality traits that are both chronic and pervasive.

- Personality disorders include antisocial personality disorder, paranoid personality disorder, and borderline personality disorder.

- Antisocial personality disorder is a personality disorder in which a person breaks the rules of society often with no remorse or anxiety.

- Individuals with paranoid personality disorder have a long history of seeing malicious intent in the actions of others.

- Individuals with borderline personality disorder have a long history of instability in their lives. This instability extends to their relationships, self-image, and moods.

14.1 Overview: Understanding Psychological Disorders

1. Using the multiaxial system of *DSM-IV-TR*, conditions such as schizophrenia and anxiety disorders are coded on:
   A. Axis I.
   B. Axis II.
   C. Axis III.
   D. Axis IV.

2. The *DSM-IV-TR* contains:
   A. the etiology of mental disorders.
   B. treatments of mental disorders.
   C. criteria for diagnosing mental disorders.
   D. theoretical approaches to psychopathology.

3. Using the multiaxial system of *DSM-IV-TR*, conditions such as paranoid personality disorder and borderline personality disorder are coded on:
   A. Axis I.
   B. Axis II.
   C. Axis III.
   D. Axis IV.

14.2 Anxiety Disorders

4. In the diathesis-stress model, "diathesis" refers to:
   A. biological predisposition.
   B. environmental stressor.
   C. ways to treat the disorders.
   D. the main cause of a disorder.

5. Which of the following best describes an obsession?
   A. A behavior or mental act that a person feels compelled to perform
   B. An unwanted thought that a person finds intrusive and distressing
   C. Something a person enjoys doing and talking about constantly
   D. Continually reliving a traumatic event

14.3 Somatoform Disorders

6. Pam has completely lost her sense of taste during the past year, but doctors cannot explain her loss of sensory function. This is most likely an example of what kind of disorder?
   A. Somatoform
   B. Mood
   C. Psychotic
   D. Personality

7. When might symptoms of conversion disorder typically emerge?
   A. Soon after a stressful event
   B. Several months after a physical injury
   C. Several years after a traumatic incident
   D. Soon after an episode of unconsciousness

14.4 Dissociative Disorders

8. Which of the following disorders usually involves travel and the creation of a new identity?
   A. Dissociative identity disorder
   B. Borderline personality disorder
   C. Schizophrenia
   D. Dissociative fugue

9. What is the diagnosis when two or more distinct identities exist within one individual?
   A. Schizophrenia
   B. Bipolar disorder
   C. Dissociative identity disorder
   D. Conversion disorder

14.5 Mood Disorders

10. One of the symptoms of a mood disorder is anhedonia, which means:
    A. a depressed mood.
    B. lack of feeling pleasure.
    C. feelings of worthlessness.
    D. change in appetite.

11. What is the main difference between mania and hypomania?
    A. Hypomanic symptoms are more serious than manic symptoms.
    B. Hypomanic symptoms are less serious than manic symptoms.
    C. Hypomanic symptoms include symptoms of anxiety.
    D. Hypomanic symptoms include symptoms of hyperactivity.

14.6 Psychotic Disorders

12. A psychologist sees from a patient's chart that he is experiencing alogia. Based on this information the psychologist can expect that the patient will answer her questions with:

A. short answers.

B. long, rambling answers.

C. tangential or unrelated answers.

D. a different answer depending on which personality is answering.

13. The neurodevelopmental hypothesis of schizophrenia suggests that this disorder is due in part to:

A. a brain injury.

B. malnutrition in early adulthood.

C. factors that occur before birth.

D. suffering or witnessing trauma.

14.7 Personality Disorders

14. Impulsive suicidal behavior is sometimes a symptom of:

A. borderline personality disorder.

B. generalized anxiety disorder.

C. social phobia.

D. paranoid personality disorder.

15. The core symptom of antisocial personality disorder is:

A. shyness.

B. failure to comply with social norms.

C. dislike for other people.

D. anxiety around strangers.

CHAPTER DISCUSSION QUESTIONS

1. What are some of the benefits of a diagnostic system like the *DSM-IV-TR*?

2. What are the various contributions of nature and nurture in the development of different psychological disorders?

3. What are the main criticisms of the *DSM*?

4. Why do you suppose the rates of psychological conditions are higher for women than for men?

5. What are some of the ways we can mediate the factors that cause psychological disorders and boost the factors that are protective?

6. Given the risks of labeling people, do you think the *DSM* does more harm than good? What are some alternatives to diagnostic labels for mental health professionals?

CHAPTER PROJECTS

1. While watching TV, YouTube, or movies, notice the differences between the way the media describe psychopathology and the way mental health professionals do.

2. Read an autobiography by a person with a psychological disorder and see if you can describe the constellation of symptoms as they would be listed in the *DSM*.

CHAPTER KEY TERMS

Agitated catatonia
Agoraphobia
Anhedonia
Antisocial personality disorder
Anxiety disorder
Biopsychosocial approach
Bipolar disorder
Bizarre delusions
Borderline personality disorder
Catatonic type of schizophrenia
Compulsions
Conversion disorder
Delusions
Diathesis-stress hypothesis
Disorganized type of schizophrenia
Dissociation
Dissociative amnesia
Dissociative disorders
Dissociative fugue
Dissociative identity disorder (DID)
Dopamine hypothesis of
  schizophrenia

Ego dystonic
Ego syntonic
Epidemiology
Etiology
Factitious disorder
Generalized anxiety disorder
  (GAD)
Hallucinations
Hypochondriasis
Hypomania
Learning perspective
Malingering
Mania
Medical model
Monoamine hypothesis of
  depression
Moods
Negative symptoms of psychosis
Non-bizarre delusions
Obsession
Obsessive-compulsive disorder
Panic attack

Panic disorder
Paranoid personality disorder
Paranoid type of schizophrenia
Personality disorder
Phobia
Positive symptoms of psychosis
Posttraumatic stress disorder
Psychological disorder
Psychopathology
Psychophysiological disorder
Reciprocal-gene environment
  model
Schizophrenia
Social anxiety disorder
Social phobia
Somatization disorder
Somatoform disorders
Stuporous catatonia
Undifferentiated type of
  schizophrenia

ANSWERS TO CONCEPT LEARNING CHECKS

14.1 Identifying Psychological Disorders

Consider each described behavior according to the three criteria of psychological disorders. Then decide whether the behavior is disordered or not.

Behavior Description	Is it deviant?	Does it cause the person distress?	Is it maladaptive?	Is it a disorder?
Betty brought balloons to her first appointment with her therapist.	Yes			No
Ben throws a tantrum almost every day whenever he doesn't get his way. Ben is 22.	Yes	Yes	Yes	Possibly
Sam throws a tantrum almost every day whenever he doesn't get his way. Sam is 2.		Yes		No
Clara is afraid of clowns. She wants to take her children to the circus, but she's afraid she'll see a clown. She avoids toy aisles in department stores for the same reason.	Yes	Yes	Yes	Yes
Maria is very afraid of snakes. She enjoys hiking, but won't go in the reptile house at the zoo.		Yes		No

14.2 Identifying Anxiety Disorders

1. As a child, Clara had a terrible experience in which a clown frightened her. Now, as an adult, if she even imagines seeing a clown, she grows extremely nervous, frightened, and distressed. What kind of anxiety order does Clara seem to have? [Specific phobia]

2. Manuel has been worrying "all the time" and says that it's not about anything in particular. He finds it difficult to control his worry and feels restless, tired, and irritable. He's also having problems sleeping. Manuel most likely has which disorder? [Generalized anxiety disorder]

3. Marty, 27, reports a long-standing fear of speaking in public. When asked to speak in front of a large group of people he becomes extremely anxious and thinks he'll be embarrassed. Because of this fear, he has passed on promotions and other opportunities to advance in his career. On one occasion where he was forced to speak, he became so anxious that he started shaking and panicking. Marty most likely has which disorder? [Social phobia]

14.3 Identifying Somatoform Disorders

1. James, a 22-year-old-man, was referred to your clinic for evaluation of his complaints. He's convinced that he has stomach cancer despite being told it is very unlikely. He has cramps when he overeats and reports that his tongue "just doesn't look right." Despite medical evidence to the contrary, James has continued to believe that he has stomach cancer. What is the most likely diagnosis? [Hypochondriasis]

2. Martha was robbed at gunpoint about 3 months ago. Luckily she wasn't hurt and the police were able to recover her purse and capture the assailant. About a week before Martha had to identify the man who robbed her, Martha suddenly lost her sight. She didn't seem that concerned about it. What's the most likely diagnosis? [Conversion disorder]

14.4 Identifying Dissociative Disorders

1. A 24-year-old-man is brought to the hospital emergency room because he was found wandering the street. He reports feeling "confused" and says he isn't sure where he is. The last thing he remembers is coming home to a fire in his house. After examination you discover no head trauma or any kind of injury that would account for his loss of memory. What is the most likely diagnosis? [Dissociative amnesia]

14.5 Identifying Mood Disorders

1. After a recent move Sean "has lost a considerable amount of weight and has periods where he cries." He misses his old friends. He feels exhausted most of the day, and has trouble sleeping. What's the most likely diagnosis? [Major depressive disorder]

2. A few months later Sean returns to his therapist with some new symptoms. He says he's feeling much better, in fact he reports feeling "better than good." He says he has been focusing on his work for about 15 hours a day. He sleeps only for about 2 hours, but says that he still feels rested. Despite all his work he hasn't been that productive. His supervisor says that Sean's presentations are sloppy, and it seems as if Sean feels a pressure to keep talking. Sean says his thoughts are racing around in his head. Because of his lack of productivity, Sean has been put on probation at work. Given the new symptoms, what is the most likely diagnosis? [Bipolar disorder]

3. A 36-year-old-woman says that for the past 2 months she has been feeling irritable and has lost interest in most of her usual activities. She says that she also has trouble concentrating at work, doesn't sleep well at night and has lost about 10 pounds. What's the most likely diagnosis? [Major depressive disorder]

14.6 Classifying Signs and Symptoms of Schizophrenia

Positive and Negative Symptoms of Schizophrenia

Avolition: Negative

Visual hallucinations: Positive

Delusions: Positive

Anhedonia: Negative

Stuperous catatonia: Positive

Flattened affect: Negative

Inability to experience pleasure: Negative

Auditory hallucinations: Positive

Alogia: Negative

14.7 Categorizing Personality Disorders

1. Alex, age 40, has long-standing difficulty maintaining relationships because of her frequent shifts in moods. She also has the following symptoms: a history of unstable friendships, frequent mood shifts, indecisiveness, and a fear of being left alone. Alex seems to suffer from which disorder? [Borderline personality disorder]

14.1 Overview: Understanding Psychological Disorders

1. **A.** Rationale: Axis I conditions are clinical disorders such as schizophrenia and anxiety disorders. Axis II conditions are personality disorders. Axis III conditions are general medical conditions, and Axis IV would list the current psychosocial stressors.

2. **C.** Rationale: The *DSM* is the classification system used by most mental health professionals in the United States. It contains the criteria for diagnosing mental disorders. It does not, however, contain any suggestions for treatment or any causes of the disorder.

3. **B.** Rationale: Psychological conditions that are coded on Axis II of the *DSM* involve extreme, inflexible global personality traits that are both chronic and pervasive.

4. **A.** Rationale: A diathesis is a biological root or cause of a disorder.

14.2 Anxiety Disorders

5. **B.** Rationale: An obsession is an unwanted thought that the person finds intrusive and distressing.

14.3 Somatoform Disorders

6. **A.** Rationale: Somatoform disorders are psychological disorders where individuals have symptoms of a physical illness that are unexplained by a general medical condition.

7. **A.** Rationale: A conversion disorder is a condition in which a worry or concern is transformed into a physical symptom. They usually appear soon after a stressful event.

14.4 Dissociative Disorders

8. **D.** Rationale: In dissociative fugue a person forgets who they are and often will travel great distances and assume a new identity that resembles their original identity.

9. **C.** Rationale: In dissociative identity disorder a person has two or more distinct identities within one individual. A split of consciousness is typical in dissociative disorders but would not be expected in psychotic disorders such as schizophrenia, mood disorders like bipolar, or the conversion disorders.

14.5 Mood Disorders

10. **B.** Rationale: A symptom of depression and sometimes of psychosis, anhedonia is a reduced capacity to feel pleasure.

11. **B.** Rationale: Hypomania is a condition in which a person has symptoms of mania but avoids getting into trouble. Therefore hypomania would be less serious than mania.

12. **A.** Rationale: Alogia is the lack of elaborative speech. Someone with alogia is likely to have brief and simple answers to any questions asked.

14.6 Psychotic Disorders

13. **C.** Rationale: The neurodevelopmental hypothesis of schizophrenia suggests that the disorder might be related to factors that occur during the growth and development of the nervous system.

14.7 Personality Disorders

14. **A.** Rationale: Individuals with borderline personality disorder have a long history of instability in their lives. This instability can even extend to impulsive suicidal behavior, which is one of the symptoms of borderline personality disorder.

15. **B.** Rationale: In antisocial personality disorder a person breaks societal rules, often without remorse or anxiety. It isn't so much that they don't like people, but that they break rules without considering others.

REFERENCES

Andrews, G., Sanderson, K., Slade, T., & Issakidis, C. (2000). Why does the burden of disease persist? Relating the burden of anxiety and depression to effectiveness of treatment. *Bulletin of the World Health Organization, 78,* 446–454.

APA. (2000). *Diagnostic and statistical manual of mental disorders: DSM-IV-TR.* (4th ed.). Washington, DC: American Psychiatric Association.

Beck, A. T., & Clark, D. A. (1997). An information processing model of anxiety: Automatic and strategic processes. *Behaviour Research and Therapy, 35*(1), 49–58.

Bijl, R. V., de Graaf, R., Hiripi, E., Kessler, R. C., Kohn, R., Offord, D. R., Ustun, T. B., et al. (2003). The prevalence of treated and untreated mental disorders in five countries. *Health Affairs, 22*(3), 122–133. doi:10.1377/hlthaff.22.3.122

Bradley, R., Conklin, C. Z., & Westen, D. (2007). Borderline personality disorder. *Personality disorders: Toward the DSM-V, 167*–201.

Burns, D. D. (1999). *The Feeling Good Handbook* (Rev Sub.). Plume. CDC-injury-national suicide statistics at a glance: Suicide rates by race/ethnicity and sex 10+. (n.d.). Retrieved from http://www.cdc.gov/violenceprevention/suicide/statistics/rates02.html

Conklin, H. M., & Iacono, W. G. (2002). Schizophrenia: A neurodevelopmental perspective. *Current Directions in Psychological Science (Wiley-Blackwell), 11*(1), 33.

Deacon, B., & Abramowitz, J. S. (2008). Is hypochondriasis related to obsessive-compulsive disorder, panic disorder, or both? An empirical evaluation. *Journal of Cognitive Psychotherapy, 22*(2), 115–127. doi:10.1891/0889-8391.22.2.115

Dorahy, M. J. (2001). Dissociative identity disorder and memory dysfunction: The current state of experimental research and its future directions. *Clinical Psychology Review, 21*(5), 771–795.

Eaton, W. W., Mortensen, P. B., Herrman, H., Freeman, H., Bilker, W., Burgess, P., & Wooff, K. (1992). Long-term course of hospitalization for schizophrenia: Part I. Risk for rehospitalization. *Schizophrenia Bulletin, 18*(2), 217–228.

Eysenck, M. W., Mogg, K., May, J., Richards, A., & Mathews, A. (1991). Bias in interpretation of ambiguous sentences related to threat in anxiety. *Journal of Abnormal Psychology, 100*(2), 144–150. doi:10.1037/0021-843X.100.2.144

Fallon, J. H. (2006). Neuroanatomical background to understanding the brain of the young psychopath. *Ohio State Journal of Criminal Law, 3*(34), 341–367.

Fatemi, S. H., & Folsom, T. D. (2009). The neurodevelopmental hypothesis of schizophrenia, revisited. *Schizophr Bull, 35*(3), 528–548. doi:10.1093/schbul/sbn187

Fink, P. (2004). The prevalence of somatoform disorders among internal medical inpatients. *Journal of Psychosomatic Research, 56*(4), 413–418. doi:10.1016/S0022-3999(03)00624-X

Gabbard, G. O. (2005). Mind, brain, and personality disorders. *Am J Psychiatry, 162*(4), 648–655. doi:10.1176/appi.ajp.162.4.648

Galderisi, S. (2000). Qualitative MRI findings in patients with schizophrenia: A controlled study. *Psychiatry Research: Neuroimaging, 98*(2), 117–126. doi:10.1016/S0925-4927(00)00047-0

Gottesman, I. I. (1990). *Schizophrenia genesis: The origins of madness* (1st ed.). New York: W. H. Freeman.

Grabe, H. J., Ruhrmann, S., Ettelt, S., Buhtz, F., Hochrein, A., Schulze-Rauschenbach, S., Meyer, K., et al. (2006). Familiality of obsessive-compulsive disorder in nonclinical and clinical subjects. *The American Journal of Psychiatry, 163*(11), 1986–1992.

Johnson, J. G., Cohen, P., Chen, H., Kasen, S., & Brook, J. S. (2006). Parenting behaviors associated with risk for offspring personality disorder during adulthood. *Arch Gen Psychiatry, 63*(5), 579–587. doi:10.1001/archpsyc.63.5.579

Kendler, K. S., Czajkowski, N., Tambs, K., Torgersen, S., Aggen, S., C. Neale, M., & Reichborn-Kjennnerun, T. (2006). Dimensional representations of DSM-IV cluster A personality disorders in a population-based sample of Norwegian twins: A Multivariate Study. *Psychological Medicine, 36*(11), 1583–1591. doi:10.1017/S0033291706008609

Kessler, R. C., Berglund, P., Demler, O., Jin, R., Merikangas, K. R., & Walters, E. E. (2005). Lifetime prevalence and age-of-onset distributions of *DSM-IV* disorders in the national comorbidity survey replication. *Archives of General Psychiatry, 62*(6), 593–602. doi:10.1001/archpsyc.62.6.593

Kessler, R. C., & Wang, P. S. (2008). The descriptive epidemiology of commonly occurring mental disorders in the United States. *Annual Review of Public Health, 29*(1), 115–129. doi:10.1146/annurev.publhealth.29.020907.090847

Kiehl, K. A. (2006). A cognitive neuroscience perspective on psychopathy: Evidence for paralimbic system dysfunction. *Psychiatry research, 142*(2–3), 107–128. doi:10.1016/j.psychres.2005.09.013

Kihlstrom, J. F., Glisky, M. L., & Angiulo, M. J. (1994). Dissociative tendencies and dissociative disorders. *Journal of Abnormal Psychology, 103*(1), 117–124.

Knapp, M., Mangalore, R., & Simon, J. (2004). The global costs of schizophrenia. *Schizophrenia Bulletin, 30,* 279–293.

Lilienfeld, S. O., Lynn, S. J., Kirsch, I., Chaves, J. F., Sarbin, T. R., Ganaway, G. K., Powell, R. A., et al. (1999). Dissociative identity disorder and the sociocognitive model: Recalling the lessons of the past. *Psychological Bulletin, 125,* 507–523.

Lui, S., Deng, W., Huang, X., Jiang, L., Ma, X., Chen, H., Zhang, T., et al. (2009). Association of cerebral deficits with clinical symptoms in antipsychotic-naive first-episode schizophrenia: An optimized voxel-based morphometry and resting state functional connectivity study. *Am J Psychiatry, 166*(2), 196–205. doi:10.1176/appi.ajp.2008.08020183

MacKinnon, D. F., Jamison, K. R., & DePaulo, J. R. (1997). Genetics of manic depressive illness. *Annual review of neuroscience, 20*(1), 355–373.

McGrath, J. J., Féron, F. P., Burne, T. H. J., Mackay-Sim, A., & Eyles, D. W. (2003). The neurodevelopmental hypothesis of schizophrenia: A review of recent developments. *Annals of Medicine, 35*(2), 86–93.

Mclewin, L., & Muller, R. (2006). Childhood trauma, imaginary companions, and the development of pathological dissociation. *Aggression and Violent Behavior, 11*(5), 531–545. doi:10.1016/j.avb.2006.02.001

Meyer-Lindenberg, A. (2008). Psychology: Trust me on this. *Science, 321*(5890), 778–780. doi:10.1126/science.1162908

Miller, S. D., Blackburn, T., Scholes, G., White, G. L., & Mamalis, N. (1991). Optical differences in multiple personality disorder. A second look. *The Journal of Nervous and Mental Disease, 179*(3), 132–135.

Mineka, S., Keir, R., & Price, V. (1980). Fear of snakes in wild- and laboratory-reared rhesus monkeys (*Macaca mulatta*). *Animal Learning & Behavior, 8*(4), 653–663.

Mineka, S., & Öhman, A. (2002). Phobias and preparedness: The selective, automatic, and encapsulated nature of fear. *Biological Psychiatry, 52*(10), 927–937. doi:10.1016/S0006-3223(02)01669-4

Mineka, S., & Zinbarg, R. (2006). A contemporary learning theory perspective on the etiology of anxiety disorders: It's not what you thought it was. *The American Psychologist, 61*(1), 10–26. doi:10.1037/0003-066X.61.1.10

Mueller, T. I., Leon, A. C., Keller, M. B., Solomon, D. A., Endicott, J., Coryell, W., Warshaw, M., et al. (1999). Recurrence after recovery from major depressive disorder during 15 years of observational follow-up. *Am J Psychiatry, 156*(7), 1000–1006.

Murray, C. J., & Lopez, A. D. (1997). Alternative projections of mortality and disability by cause 1990–2020: Global burden of disease study. *Lancet, 349*(9064), 1498–1504. doi:10.1016/S0140-6736(96)07492-2

Patterson, J. M., & Turnbull, A. P. (1993). *Cognitive coping, families, and disability.* Baltimore, MD: Paul H. Brookes Publishing Co.

Peterson, C., Maier, S. F., & Seligman, M. E. P. (1995). *Learned helplessness: A theory for the age of personal control.* New York: Oxford University Press.

Plomin, R., DeFries, J. C., McClearn, G. E., & McGuffin, P. (2000). *Behavioral genetics* (4th ed.). New York: Worth Publishers.

Praag, H., Kloet, E., & Os, J. (2004). *Stress, the brain and depression* (1st ed.). Cambridge, UK: Cambridge University Press.

Rapoport. J. L. (1989, March). The biology of obsessions and compulsions. *Scientific American*, 83–98.

Roelofs, K., Hoogduin, K. A., Keijsers, G. P., Näring, G. W., Moene, F. C., & Sandijck, P. (2002). Hypnotic susceptibility in patients with conversion disorder. *Journal of Abnormal Psychology, 111*(2), 390–395.

Rosenhan, D. L. (1973). On being sane in insane places. *Science, 179*(70), 250–258.

Sar, V., Akyüz, G., & Dogan, O. (2007). Prevalence of dissociative disorders among women in the general population. *Psychiatry Research, 149*(1–3), 169–176. doi:10.1016/j.psychres.2006.01.005

Schmidt, N. B., Lerew, D. R., & Jackson, R. J. (1997). The role of anxiety sensitivity in the pathogenesis of panic: Prospective evaluation of spontaneous panic attacks during acute stress. *Journal of Abnormal Psychology, 106*(3), 355–364.

Seligman, M. E. (1971). Phobias and preparedness. *Behavior Therapy, 2*(3), 307–320. doi:10.1016/S0005-7894(71)80064-3

Seligman, M. E. P. (2006). *Learned optimism: How to change your mind and your life*. New York: Vintage Books.

Shin, L. M., Wright, C. I., Cannistraro, P. A., Wedig, M. M., McMullin, K., Martis, B., Macklin, M. L., et al. (2005). A functional magnetic resonance imaging study of amygdala and medial prefrontal cortex responses to overtly presented fearful faces in posttraumatic stress disorder. *Archives of General Psychiatry, 62*(3), 273–281.

Siever, L. J., & Koenigsberg, H. W. (2000). The frustrating no-mans-land of borderline personality disorder. In *Cerebrum, the dana forum on brain science* (Vol. 2).

Spanos, N. P. (1999). Multiple identities and false memories: A socio-cognitive perspective. *Journal of Psychology and Christianity*, (Spring). Retrieved from http://search.ebscohost.com.proxy.library.emory.edu /login.aspx?direct=true&db=33h&AN=33h-3EB969FB-74DE95B3&site= ehost-live

Stahl, S. (2009). *The prescriber's guide* (3rd ed.). Cambridge, UK: Cambridge University Press.

Stahl, S. M. (2008a) *Stahl's essential psychopharmacology: Neuroscientific basis and practical applications* (3rd ed.). Cambridge, UK: Cambridge University Press.

Stahl, S. M. (2008b). *Antipsychotics and mood stabilizers: Stahl's essential psychopharmacology*, (3rd ed.). Cambridge, UK: Cambridge University Press.

Sullivan, P. F., Neale, M. C., & Kendler, K. S. (2000). Genetic epidemiology of major depression: Review and meta-analysis. *Am J Psychiatry, 157*(10), 1552–1562. doi:10.1176/appi.ajp.157.10.1552

Szechtman, H., & Woody, E. (2004). Obsessive-compulsive disorder as a disturbance of security motivation. *Psychological Review, 111*(1), 111–127. doi:10.1037/0033-295X.111.1.111

Ursu, S., Stenger, V. A., Shear, M. K., Jones, M. R., & Carter, C. S. (2003). Overactive action monitoring in obsessive-compulsive disorder: Evidence from functional magnetic resonance imaging. *Psychological Science: A Journal Of The American Psychological Society / APS, 14*(4), 347–353.

Villalta-Gil, V., Vilaplana, M., Ochoa, S., Dolz, M., Usall, J., Haro, J. M., et al. (2006). Four symptom dimensions in outpatients with schizophrenia. *Comprehensive Psychiatry, 47*, 384–388.

Walker, E. F., & Diforio, D. (1997). Schizophrenia: A neural diathesis-stress model. *Psychological Review, 104*(4), 667–685.

Wang, P. S., Berglund, P., Olfson, M., Pincus, H. A., Wells, K. B., & Kessler, R. C. (2005). Failure and delay in initial treatment contact after first onset of mental disorders in the National Comorbidity Survey Replication. *Archives of General Psychiatry, 62*(6), 603–613. doi:10.1001/archpsyc.62.6.603

Whitman, B. W., & Packer, R. J. (1993). The photic sneeze reflex: Literature review and discussion. *Neurology, 43*(5), 868–871.

Wiersma, D., Nienhuis, F. J., Slooff, C. J., & Giel, R. (1998). Natural course of schizophrenic disorders: A 15 year follow up of a Dutch incidence cohort. *Schizophr Bull, 24*(1), 75–85.

Zanarini, M. C. (2000). Childhood experiences associated with the development of borderline personality disorder. *Psychiatric Clinics of North America, 23*(1), 89–101. doi:10.1016/S0193-953X(05)70145-3

World Health Organization. (2009). World health organization mental health surveys. Cambridge, UK: Cambridge University Press.

Chapter Overview ▼

15.1 Mental Health Practitioners and Settings
Psychiatrists
Counseling and Clinical Psychologists
Counseling Psychologists
Clinical Psychologists
Master's-Level Therapists
Settings for Mental Health Practitioners
The Role of Psychotherapy

CONCEPT LEARNING CHECK **15.1** *Comparing the Roles and Settings of Mental Health Practitioners*

15.2 Psychodynamic Therapy
Techniques of Psychodynamic Therapy
Types of Psychodynamic Therapy
Psychoanalysis

Short-Term Psychodynamic Therapy

CONCEPT LEARNING CHECK **15.2**
Understanding Psychodynamic Therapies

15.3 Humanistic Therapy
Carl Rogers and Client-Centered Therapy

CONCEPT LEARNING CHECK **15.3** *Describing the Elements of Humanistic Therapy*

15.4 Behavior Therapy
Classic Conditioning Techniques
Operant Conditioning Techniques

CONCEPT LEARNING CHECK **15.4** *Designing a Behavioral Treatment Plan*

15.5 Cognitive Therapies
Aaron Beck and Cognitive Therapy
Albert Ellis and Rational Emotive Therapy

15 Therapies for Psychological Disorders

Learning Objectives ▼

15.1
- Compare and contrast the roles of psychiatrists, counseling psychologists, and clinical psychologists.
- Discuss the settings used by mental health practitioners.

15.2
- Define psychodynamic therapy.
- Illustrate the techniques used in psychodynamic therapy.
- Compare and contrast traditional psychoanalytic therapy and short-term psychodynamic therapy.

15.3
- Describe the role of genuineness, acceptance, and empathy in client-centered approaches.

15.4
- Explain the ways in which behavioral therapies attempt to change maladaptive associations, discourage maladaptive behaviors, or encourage more adaptive ones.
- Compare and contrast classical conditioning and operant conditioning.

15.5
- Discuss Beck's cognitive therapy and Ellis's rational emotive therapy as they relate to cognitive therapy.

15.6
- Illustrate how family systems therapy focuses on how individuals function in their relationships through communication patterns.

15.7
- Explain the focus on changing physiological problems that lead to psychological conditions in biomedical therapies.
- Compare and contrast the major classes of antidepressant drugs, the major drug treatments for anxiety, and antipsychotic medications.
- Discuss other nondrug medical treatments for psychological conditions.

15.8
- Describe how clinical trials test treatments for psychological conditions.
- Discuss types of research that have provided evidence of the efficacy of treatments for psychological disorders.

CONCEPT LEARNING CHECK **15.5** *Comparing Cognitive Therapies*

15.6 Family Systems and Group Therapy
Systems Approaches
Group Therapy

CONCEPT LEARNING CHECK **15.6** *Describing an Eclectic Systems Approach*

15.7 Biomedical Therapies
Drug Treatments
Antidepressant Drugs
Antianxiety Drugs

Mood-Stabilizing Drugs
Antipsychotic Drugs
Medical Procedures
Electroconvulsive Therapy
Other Medical Procedures

CONCEPT LEARNING CHECK **15.7** *Explaining the Use of Medications for Psychological Conditions*

15.8 Evaluating Therapies for Psychological Disorders
Effectiveness of Therapies for Psychological Disorders
Effectiveness of Different Therapies

Common Factors That Increase Effectiveness
Culture, Cultural Values, and Psychotherapy
CRITICAL THINKING APPLICATION
Summary of Multiple Influences on Therapies for Psychological Disorders

CONCEPT LEARNING CHECK **15.8** *Summarizing the Factors of Effective Psychotherapy*

I must have looked terrified. There I was, staring out the window at the wing of the airplane, doing my best to interpret the signals and noises around me. I always chose the window seat over the wing. It is the safest part of the airliner, or so I was told, and it had the added benefit of being a front-row seat to all the commotion on the ever-wobbling wings. Every sound, every noise, every bump was a prelude to disaster—or so I imagined. This time was going to be different. In the palm of my hand was the miracle pill that would rescue me from my anxiety. I had recently received a prescription for a medication to help me with my phobia of flying.

Even as a psychology student, I always thought "fear of flying" was an odd term. It really was not the flying that scared me—it was the potential to suddenly *not* be flying that was the problem. On the plane, my brain would go into overtime analyzing hints of possible problems. I would scrutinize the flight attendants' faces for any sign of nervousness, analyze the whirr and flailing of little flaps on the wing as they went up and down, and usually could convince myself, briefly, that it was some sort of visual warning to the other planes to stay way. My anxiety usually got the best of me.

I took the pill wondering how in the world something so small could help with such great anxiety. I expected it to make me feel dopey or sleepy like Xanax or Valium might. But it did not. In fact, it did not do anything at all. The next moment, as the engine started, I noticed that I was searching my body for anxiety. None was there. It was as if my brain had signaled, "cue stomach for anxiety," and my stomach simply refused to obey. Something was different. But would it last?

Etiology Cause of a disorder.

The **etiology**, or cause, of a disorder informs the disorder's treatment. Tension headaches, for example, are caused by inflammation. Reducing the inflammation with aspirin can be a good treatment. Because there are multiple influences on the creation of psychological conditions, there are many ways to intervene. Treatments can be behavioral, biological, sociocultural, or a mix of all of these. In this chapter, we will describe the professionals who use these techniques as well as many treatments that mental health practitioners employ to help those with psychological conditions. By the end of the chapter, you will have learned how each of these treatments is used, and you may realize that it took more than that one tiny pill to get me through the flight.

15.1 Mental Health Practitioners and Settings

There are various kinds of mental health practitioners who help clients in a variety of settings.

- Compare and contrast the roles of psychiatrists, counseling psychologists, and clinical psychologists.
- Discuss the settings used by mental health practitioners.

Generally, when people experience a lot of stress, a significant event, depression, or other symptoms, they employ their own ways of coping. Often things get better. Sometimes they do not. When regular coping mechanisms offer little relief, or a new, objective approach is desired, people often seek professional help. How do people decide to get help? To what settings and what kind of person do they turn?

Naturally, some people are uneasy about seeking treatment the first time. People new to therapy sometimes think that the professional will think they are weak. Others seeking treatment wonder if they will be in therapy forever. These are common and understandable concerns. Unfortunately, such concerns can delay help. The median delay for seeking treatment is about 6 years for bipolar disorder, 8 years for depression, and up to 10 years for panic disorders (Wang et al., 2005). Fortunately, many do seek treatment, and in the United States, about 15% of the population seek mental health treatment, mostly for depression and anxiety (Narrow, Regier, Rae, Manderscheid, & Locke, 1993).

Often people will say that they are going to a therapist, counselor, or a psychotherapist, which could refer to any number of mental health practitioners with various approaches to mental health concerns. There are many kinds of mental health professionals. In this section, we will discuss three: psychiatrists, counseling psychologists, and clinical psychologists.

Psychiatrists

Psychiatry is a branch of medicine that treats mental and behavioral conditions. The first 2 years of medical training focus on the biomedical clinical sciences, followed by training in clinical specialties. Students earn professional doctoral degrees such as doctor of medicine (MD) or doctor of osteopathic medicine (DO). After medical school, those interested in psychiatry practice as psychiatric residents for another 4 years of in-depth training. Psychiatrists spend the majority of their time treating severe psychological conditions and may prescribe psychotropic mediation or order and interpret laboratory tests.

Counseling and Clinical Psychologists

It can be confusing that some psychologists call themselves counseling psychologists while others are known as clinical psychologists. After all, counseling and clinical psychologists often do similar tasks and may even work together. A peek into the history of these two fields reveals their similarities and differences.

Counseling Psychologists

A **counseling psychologist** is a mental health professional who helps people experiencing difficulty adjusting to life stressors to achieve greater well-being. *Counsel* comes from the Latin *consulere*, which means to consult or seek advice. Historically, counseling psychologists delivered occupational advice to help people choose careers best suited to their abilities and interests. Since then, counseling psychologists have expanded their role by providing psychotherapy. Many counseling psychologists focus on everyday people by helping them adjust to changes in their lives.

Clinical Psychologists

Clinical psychologists are mental health practitioners who research, evaluate, and treat psychological conditions. *Clinical* gets its name from Greek *kline*, which means bed, as in recline, since most medical clinical work was done at the bedside. Historically, clinical psychologists have focused on psychopathology. Clinical psychologists began by providing testing services and added psychotherapy, previously practiced only by psychiatrists, to their portfolio.

Clinical psychology training programs vary in their emphasis on the different roles of clinical psychologists. Clinical training programs can be based on a scientist-practitioner model, a practitioner-scholar model, or a clinical researcher model. The **scientist-practitioner model**, also called the Boulder model, is a balanced program in which students learn clinical skills as well as research skills. However, not everyone who is interested in clinical psychology wants to generate new research. Some are interested only in treatment. An alternative model for clinical psychologists is a program that focuses more on treatment than on generating research. This model emphasizes work with clients

Psychiatry A branch of medicine that treats mental and behavioral conditions.

Counseling psychologist A mental health professional who helps people experiencing difficulty adjusting to life stressors to achieve greater well-being.

Clinical psychologist A mental health practitioner who researches, evaluates, and treats psychological conditions.

Scientist-practitioner model Also called the Boulder model, a balanced program in which psychologists learn about clinical skills as well as research skills.

Practitioner-scholar model
Also called the Vail model, a program in which psychologists emphasize clinical training over generating new research in order to understand, synthesize, and apply existing research.

Clinical researcher model A type of psychology program that emphasizes clinical psychology research over direct work with clients.

Psychopharmacology Treatment of psychological conditions using medication.

Mental hospital A medical center that treats psychological conditions.

Outpatient Treatment settings that are outside of a hospital.

and shifts the focus from generating new research to understanding, synthesizing, and applying existing research. The **practitioner-scholar model**, otherwise known as the Vail model, along with a professional doctorate in psychology (doctor of psychology, or PsyD) is well suited for individuals who want to focus on treatment. Still others who are interested in psychology focus on generating new research and less on working directly with clients. Research is the basis of the **clinical researcher model**, a training program that emphasizes clinical psychology research over direct work with clients FIGURE 15-1.

In addition to coursework, doctoral students in psychology undertake 2 to 3 years of supervised training and complete scholarly work such as a dissertation in PhD programs or an extensive literature review in PsyD programs.

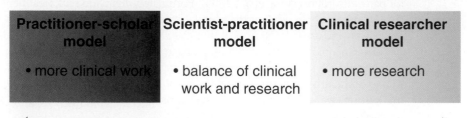

Practitioner-scholar model	Scientist-practitioner model	Clinical researcher model
• more clinical work	• balance of clinical work and research	• more research

Clinical ←——————————————————→ Research

FIGURE 15-1 Types of psychological training programs.

Recently, some psychologists with advanced training in **psychopharmacology**, treatment of psychological conditions using medication, have been licensed to prescribe medicine. New Mexico granted properly trained psychologists prescriptive authority in 2002, and Louisiana followed by granting medical psychologists prescriptive authority.

Master's-Level Therapists

So far we have discussed mental health practitioners at the doctoral level. However, there are also many mental health practitioners who are trained at the master's level. These include social workers, pastoral counselors, licensed professional counselors, and marriage and family therapists.

Settings for Mental Health Practitioners

Mental health practitioners work in many settings. Some work in modern **mental hospitals**, medical centers that treat psychological conditions. Many more work in **outpatient** settings, which are outside of hospitals.

Mental hospitals have come a long way since their beginning. The first mental hospitals, called asylums, opened in Europe around 850. The Bethlem Royal Hospital in London FIGURE 15-2, for example, was an early mental hospital for those suffering from mental conditions. It also housed the poor and people being punished for crimes. Those hospitalized were sometimes subjected to torture and deprivation. It would not be until the late 1700s when more humane mental hospitals would be built (Porter, 2003).

A psychiatrist's work with clients may include writing prescriptions to treat psychological conditions.

FIGURE 15-2 The first Bethlem Royal Hospital was built in the 14th century. Known as "Bedlam," this was the first hospital specializing in the treatment of psychiatric conditions.

By the mid-19th century, there were many state-funded mental hospitals in the United States. Led in part by Dorothea Dix FIGURE 15-3 and others, the new facilities were established to provide more humane treatment to those suffering from psychological conditions (Gollaher, 1995). By the mid-1950s, however, large state facilities fell into disrepair from lack of funding, which resulted in too many patients and too few well-trained staff members. Mental hospitals again became notorious for poor treatment. In reaction to the poorly funded large hospitals, many patients were discharged from the hospitals and a community-based system was established for those suffering from psychological conditions. Community mental health services include housing with oversight by either full- or part-time mental health professions in assisted-living facilities or half-way houses. **Deinstitutionalization** is the process of replacing inpatient psychiatric care with community outpatient services. While offering more freedom for clients and costing less than care in large hospitals, deinstitutionalization released many people with severe conditions, few work skills, and limited access to the level of care required for their condition. Many former patients became homeless or ended up in prison FIGURE 15-4. The inpatient population plummeted from 555,000 in the mid-1950s to around 70,000 by 2000 FIGURE 15-5 as the imprisoned and homeless populations grew.

Even in the mid-1940s in the United States, patients in mental hospitals were subjected to inadequate conditions.

The Role of Psychotherapy

Psychotherapy, or talk therapy, has probably been around as long as language itself and is often misunderstood. In therapy, many believe, the cure comes from complaining. It is understandable that people who have never been in therapy may be unaware of the therapeutic process or of the variety of procedures used in the different styles of psychotherapy. Theories of personality explain the nature of humans, and, in many cases, offer ways to treat psychological conditions. An understanding of the sources and motivation of behavior leads to therapeutic **insight**, which is central to therapies such as psychodynamic, humanistic, and systems approaches, while it is less important to behavioral and cognitive approaches. Psychotherapies that use insight as part of treatment are referred to as **insight therapies**. In the next sections, we will discuss therapy treatments from five established therapies: psychodynamic, humanistic, behavioral, cognitive, and systems approaches.

Before we begin, a note about terminology: You will recall that there are several different kinds of mental health care practitioners—psychiatrists, clinical psychologists, and counseling psychologists, to name a few. There are also many terms for those who receive services. Some mental health practitioners call the people with whom they work *clients*, some call them *patients*, and others use the term *consumer*. In this chapter, we will use the terms *therapist* and *client* or *patient* as general terms for those who provide and those who receive therapeutic services.

FIGURE 15-3 Dorothea Dix (1802–1887) was a leader in promoting ethical treatment for those in psychiatric hospitals. She was responsible for the founding of dozens of mental institutions in the United States.

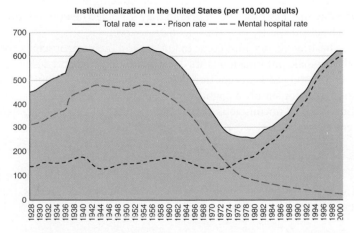

Institutionalization in the United States (per 100,000 adults)
— Total rate - - - - Prison rate — — Mental hospital rate

FIGURE 15-4 As the population in mental hospitals declined through deinstitutionalization, the prison population increased dramatically.
Source: Data from Harcourt, B. E. An institutionalization effect: The impact of mental hospitalization and imprisonment on homicide in the United States, 1934–2001 (March 1, 2007). Journal of Legal Studies, Vol. 40, 2011; University of Chicago Law & Economics, Olin Working Paper No. 335; University of Chicago, Public Law Working Paper No. 155. Available at SSRN: http://ssrn.com/abstract=970341

Deinstitutionalization The process of replacing inpatient psychiatric care with community outpatient services.

Insight An understanding of the motivation of behavior.

Insight therapies A family of psychotherapies that focus on the unconscious motivations of behavior.

FIGURE 15-5 In 1955 the first antipsychotic medications were in wide use. By 1955, the number of patients in mental hospitals had been reduced remarkably.
Source: Data from Deinstitutionalization—Special Reports\The New Asylums\FRONTLINE\PBS, Out of the shadows: Confronting America's mental illness crisis by E. F. Torrey, M.D. (New York: John Wiley & Sons, 1997).

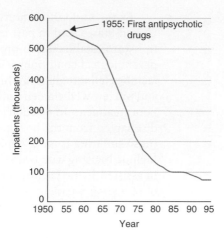

CONCEPT LEARNING CHECK 15.1   *Comparing the Roles and Settings of Mental Health Practitioners*

1. Compare some of the results, both positive and negative, of deinstitutionalization.

2. Compare and contrast the roles of psychiatrists, counseling psychologists, and clinical psychologists.

> **Psychodynamic therapies**
> A family of psychotherapies that have at their core the exploration of intrapsychic conflict and the role of insight to bring about therapeutic change.

15.2 Psychodynamic Therapy

Psychodynamic treatments are based on settling unconscious conflicts that are created in childhood.

- Define psychodynamic therapy.
- Illustrate the techniques used in psychodynamic therapy.
- Compare and contrast traditional psychoanalytic therapy and short-term psychodynamic therapy.

Modern psychotherapy emerged from the personality theories and treatments of Sigmund Freud (1856–1939) FIGURE 15-6. Earlier physicians had relied on other devices and techniques, including hypnosis and even machines designed to rock patients into passivity FIGURE 15-7 to treat psychological conditions. **Psychodynamic therapies** are a family of treatments that have at their core the exploration of unconscious internal conflict. They use insight to bring about therapeutic change.

According to Freud, unresolved unconscious conflicts from childhood cause difficulties in adulthood. These difficulties include unhealthy defense mechanisms, anxiety, and problematic ways of guarding against the wishes of the id. Unhealthy defense mechanisms need to be dismantled because they are not successful at reducing anxiety and they cause problems in everyday life. For example, a person may sabotage healthy relationships because he or she feels unlovable, all at the unconscious level.

In order to be healthy, clients must come to understand their unconscious conflicts and gain the ability to make informed, mature decisions about fears and desires created in the formative childhood years. Insight into these internal workings requires an emotional appreciation and not simply a cognitive understanding. After all, someone can intellectually understand an unconscious conflict but not really appreciate its potentially overwhelming emotional force.

Techniques of Psychodynamic Therapy

Psychodynamic techniques use several tools to help clients bring unconscious conflicts into awareness and gain insight, including interpretation, analysis of dreams, transference, and resistance, as well as free association.

FIGURE 15-6 Dr. Sigmund Freud in 1885.

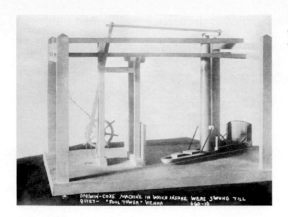

FIGURE 15-7 The Darwin-Coxe machine was used to swing patients until they were quiet.

In order to explore the unconscious and discover what is causing the symptoms in consciousness, the therapist must find a way to bring unconscious processes into consciousness. Free association is one way to explore the unconscious. **Free association** is a psychodynamic therapy technique that reveals unconscious conflicts by interpreting spontaneous responses to given words. Free association provides evidence about unconscious conflicts that can be interpreted by the therapist.

Evidence of unconscious conflicts can also be revealed through **dream analysis**—the interpretation of dreams. According to the psychodynamic theory of dreams, dreams contain both a surface or **manifest content**, as well as a deeper unconscious or **latent content**. Through therapy, the latent content can be revealed.

A goal of psychodynamic therapy is to bring into awareness problematic intrapsychic conflicts. Awareness allows the client to work through unresolved conflicts in a more adaptive way. Since the conflicts are unconscious, the therapist must take care to reveal them in a way that is useful or helpful to the client. Because the therapist is trained in psychodynamic techniques and is not entangled in the intrapsychic conflicts of the client, the therapist can see patterns in the evidence, or material revealed by the client. Using the material gathered, the therapist may develop an understanding of the landscape of the client's unconscious world. Making carefully timed **interpretations**, or explanations of the client's unconscious motivations, in order to improve psychological functioning is an important part of therapy. Interpretations can help clients to understand their own unconscious worlds.

But the therapist's work is more complex than simply revealing the interpretation. If it is revealed too quickly or in the wrong way, the client may reject it. A client may reject an interpretation no matter how it is revealed. Interpretations, especially controversial ones, can be met with unconscious or conscious **resistance**. Resistance is a client's employment of a defense mechanism during therapy. **Defense mechanisms** are unconscious arrangements that the ego uses to satisfy id instincts indirectly. In fact, the closer to the conflict, the greater the resistance can be. Resistance can show up in subtle ways. Coming late to a session or revealing important information so late in a session that there is little time to actually address it are all examples of resistance because they block the therapeutic process.

Sometimes, unconsciously, clients will act out the kinds of relationships they have in their lives and shift the fears or wishes of past important relationships into the therapeutic relationship. This shift is called **transference**. Analysis of transference provides the therapist with additional material for interpretation. Interpreting transference gives the client insight into his or her relationships. One way the therapist can encourage transference is to be as neutral as possible so that he or she can use the therapeutic relationship itself as a tool to help the client. For example, a few years ago, I needed to rebook a client for a later appointment in the same week. About 2 weeks before the event, I let my client know about the change. He responded angrily, "You are just like my dad. You are never there when I need you." I knew that he was not really upset with me but with his father. The unconscious feelings about being disappointed by

Free association A psychoanalytic therapy technique that reveals intrapsychic conflicts by interpreting spontaneous responses to given words.

Dream analysis A psychoanalytic technique that reveals intrapsychic conflicts through interpretations of dreams.

Manifest content In the psychoanalytic theory, the dream as the dreamer reports it.

Interpretation A psychoanalytic technique in which a therapist will reveal explanations of the client's unconscious motivations in order to improve psychological functioning.

Latent content In the psychoanalytic theory, the true, underlying, undisguised meaning of a dream.

Resistance In psychoanalysis, a client's employment of a defense mechanism during therapy.

Defense mechanism Unconscious arrangements that the ego uses to satisfy id instincts indirectly.

Transference In psychoanalysis, a type of displacement in which the client will unconsciously act out relationships with the therapist.

important people in his life bubbled to the surface, and we had a chance to discuss that in the session.

Types of Psychodynamic Therapy

There are several categories of psychodynamic therapies. We will discuss two: classical psychoanalysis and short-term psychodynamic therapy.

Psychoanalysis

Although not broadly practiced, classical psychoanalysis is performed in much the same way as Freud developed it. Psychoanalytic therapy, or **psychoanalysis**, is based on Freud's traditional approach to psychotherapy. The client lies on a comfortable couch while the therapist sits out of view and encourages free association FIGURE 15-8. This creates a comfortable environment in which free association can take place without the client having to look at the therapist directly. Much like it is easier to tell someone something while looking down, relaxing on a sofa in an inviting environment with only your thoughts is a better environment for psychotherapy, according to the psychoanalytic approach. Psychoanalysis is intense, with hour-long sessions taking place three to five times a week for years. Psychoanalysis is prohibitively expensive and time consuming for most people. However, it does have a track record of helping those with complex psychological conditions (Leichsenring & Rabung, 2008).

Short-Term Psychodynamic Therapy

Short-term psychodynamic therapy is a type of solution-focused psychoanalytic treatment rooted in Freud's classical psychoanalysis. The client–therapist relationship is much more casual in short-term psychodynamic therapy. While still exploring intrapsychic dynamics, the therapist and client sit face to face in chairs FIGURE 15-9. Psychodynamic therapy is much more goal oriented, lasting from 12 to 50 weekly sessions. Short-term psychodynamic therapy is more active and directive than psychoanalysis, with the goal of figuring out a client's current problems rather than restructuring his or her personality. Because of its duration, short-term psychodynamic therapy is much more affordable but not necessarily appropriate for in-depth personality change as might be required, for personality disorders, for example (Knekt et al., 2008).

The couch of Sigmund Freud.

Psychoanalysis A type of therapy based on Freud's theory of personality.

Short-term psychodynamic therapy A type of solution-focused psychoanalytic treatment.

FIGURE 15-8 In classic psychoanalysis, the therapist is out of view of the client.

FIGURE 15-9 In short-term psychodynamic therapy, client and therapist sit face to face in a more casual and goal-oriented approach.

CONCEPT LEARNING CHECK 15.2   *Understanding Psychodynamic Therapies*

1. Psychoanalytic therapy is considered an insight-oriented therapy. What kind of insight does this therapy provide?

2. Compare and contrast traditional psychoanalytic therapy and short-term psychodynamic therapy.

15.3 Humanistic Therapy

Humanistic therapy focuses on the therapeutic environment to release an individual's ability to improve his or her own life.

■ Describe the role of genuineness, acceptance, and empathy in client-centered approaches.

As a personality theory, **humanism** is based on the idea that all humans have an **actualizing tendency**, that is, an instinctual desire to be the best possible version of themselves. As such, therapies based on the humanistic perspective attempt to activate this natural actualizing tendency by fostering self-acceptance and self-awareness. Humanistic therapies do this by encouraging clients to understand and be accountable for their own behavior and use the therapeutic relationship to lead the client toward therapeutic change. For example, **client-centered therapy**, a humanistic psychotherapy based on a nondirective, genuine, and accepting environment, features humanistic therapeutic techniques.

Carl Rogers and Client-Centered Therapy

Carl Rogers FIGURE 15-10 established client-centered therapy based on humanistic personality theory. In nondirective client-centered therapy, the therapist's major role is to clarify and to provide the proper therapeutic environment, working as an equal with the client. Client-centered therapists create the environment for therapeutic change by providing feedback to the client, with minimal advice giving, instruction, or interpretation. An important part of client-centered therapy is **active listening**, a communication method in which the listener responds in ways that demonstrate understanding of what another person says. Using these techniques, the therapist helps clients deeply explore their emotions and approaches to life. The therapeutic relationship leads the client toward personality change. Client-centered approaches are powered by the active ingredients of genuineness, acceptance, and empathy (Rogers, 1989).

Genuineness refers to authenticity in the relationship. In client-centered therapy, the therapist is encouraged to behave in exactly the way she or he feels, revealing his or her inner experiences to the client. In that way, client-centered therapy encourages therapists to be transparent in their relationships with their clients. In order to be genuine, the therapist is encouraged to focus more on the "here and now" rather than past experience (the "there and then"). As clients sense genuineness in the therapist, they will offer more genuineness themselves. Genuineness encourages clients to become more aware of their experiences and to become better able to know and express what is going on in the moment. Instead of recalling and discussing past feelings, humanistic therapies explore emotions in real time as they occur.

Acceptance, or communication of respect, is also important for client-centered therapy. Rogers suggests that the client is more likely to be able to change if the therapist grants the client the respect that all humans should receive. This respect should be communicated as **unconditional positive regard**, or a sense of respect and love that is not linked to specific behaviors and does not have to be earned. Respect from the therapist will increase self-respect and self-acceptance in the client and, according to Rogers, lead to greater self-understanding.

Empathy refers to the therapist's attempt to understand the client's inner world. The client-centered approach is rooted in the idea of phenomenology, which emphasizes each individual's unique perspective. **Phenomenology** is the idea that in order to understand someone, it is important to understand what it feels like to be that person and to see the world from his or her perspective.

By exposing clients to an atmosphere of genuineness, acceptance, and empathy, the therapeutic environment helps clients to understand hidden aspects of themselves, relate more directly to others, better tolerate the nuances of situations, and emphasize conscious over unconscious processes. The relationship encourages clients to focus on growth and to appreciate and be accountable for their own behavior.

Humanism A theoretical orientation that emphasizes growth, potential, and self-actualization.

Actualizing tendency According to the humanists, the instinctual desire to be the best version of yourself possible.

Client-centered therapy A humanistic psychotherapy based on a nondirective, genuine, and accepting environment.

Active listening A communication method in which the listener responds in ways that demonstrate understanding of what another person says.

Genuineness According to the client-centered approach, authenticity in a relationship.

Acceptance Communication of respect.

Unconditional positive regard According to Rogers, a sense of respect and love that is not linked to specific behaviors.

Empathy An attempt to understand the client's inner world.

Phenomenology The idea that, in order to understand a person, it is important to understand the world from that person's perspective; also known as phenomenological approach.

FIGURE 15-10 Dr. Carl Rogers.

Many therapies have been influenced by client-centered approaches, including positive psychotherapy, which helps clients recognize strengths and relish positive experiences (Joseph & Linley, 2006). Positive psychotherapy is an applied version of **positive psychology**, a branch of psychology that studies human strengths.

CONCEPT LEARNING CHECK 15.3 | *Describing the Elements of Humanistic Therapy*

1. Humanistic therapists seem to focus more on the therapeutic environment than the actual psychotherapy. Why do you suppose the client-centered approach focuses so much on the environment?

Positive psychology
A branch of psychology that studies human strengths.

Behavior therapy A family of therapies that use learning theory to change behavior.

Symptom substitution
The emergence of a replacement symptom of a psychological condition if the root cause is not resolved.

Social skills training
A type of behavior therapy intended to improve interaction with others.

Classical conditioning
Learning in which a neutral stimulus becomes associated with an unlearned stimulus and the response it automatically elicits.

Counterconditioning
A behavioral technique in which a response to a stimulus is replaced by a new response.

Bell-and-pad treatment
A classical conditioning treatment used to treat nighttime bedwetting.

15.4 Behavior Therapy

Behavioral therapies attempt to modify clients' maladaptive actions.

- Explain the ways in which behavioral therapies attempt to change maladaptive associations, discourage maladaptive behaviors, or encourage more adaptive ones.
- Compare and contrast classical conditioning and operant conditioning.

Behavior therapies use learning theory to change behavior. Behavior therapies for psychological conditions assume that psychological disorders are the result of maladaptive behavior patterns: Change the behaviors and you can change the emotions, too. Behavioral therapists question the role of insight in producing change. Symptoms, behavioral therapists believe, are not a sign of the problem—they are the only problem. On the other hand, insight-oriented therapists believe that if you just get rid of a symptom, it will return in another way, in what is called **symptom substitution**. Symptom substitution is like a game of whack-a-mole, with new symptoms emerging if the root cause of the condition is not found. Behaviorists disagree, arguing that knowing why you do something does not necessarily stop the behavior. Knowing that you should not eat three cupcakes a day might not stop you from doing it. So behavior therapies focus on current symptoms by discouraging maladaptive behaviors and encouraging constructive ones.

Sometimes behavior therapy will treat a specific sign related to the complaint. Lack of social skills, for example, can lead to nervousness and, in extreme cases, social isolation. Since social skills are attained through learning, according to behaviorists, behavior therapy uses social skills training to increase social ease. **Social skills training** is a type of behavior therapy intended to improve interaction with others, and it has been used to treat many issues, including social anxiety (Spence, Donovan, & Brechman-Toussaint, 2000) and autism (Leaf, Dotson, Oppenheim-Leaf, Sherman, & Sheldon, 2011).

More often, behavioral therapies are used as a way to change associations, discourage maladaptive behaviors, or encourage more adaptive ones. Behavioral therapists use classical conditioning and operant conditioning techniques to achieve therapeutic change.

Classical Conditioning Techniques

Classical conditioning focuses on the basic physiological responses to various experiences, also known as stimuli. Classical conditioning is a type of associative learning in which two things are paired together. Sometimes people make maladaptive or accidental associations that lead to problematic behaviors or reactions. Behavioral therapists attempt to decouple these associations by using **counterconditioning**, a behavioral technique in which a response to a stimulus is replaced by a new response. Classical conditioning techniques attempt to extinguish behaviors in various ways. The **bell-and-pad treatment** FIGURE 15-11 is a classical conditioning treatment used to treat nighttime bedwetting. A moisture sensor in the bed (pad) is activated by bedwetting. When the moisture sensor is activated, an alarm (bell) awakens the person. An association of relaxation of the bladder with waking up prevents bedwetting. Having a full bladder (a conditioned stimulus) triggers waking up (a conditioned response) since the sensation has been linked to the bell that would awaken you FIGURE 15-12. Bell-and-pad treatments have been shown to be very effective, with few people needing additional treatments (Gim, Lillystone, & Caldwell, 2009).

The bell-and-pad treatment can be an effective behavioral treatment for bedwetting.

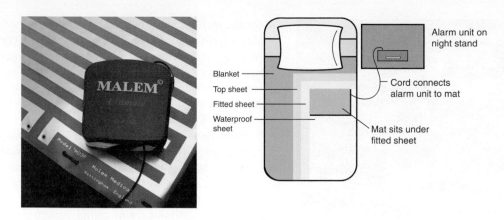

FIGURE 15-11 A bell-and-pad device uses classical conditioning techniques as a treatment for bedwetting.

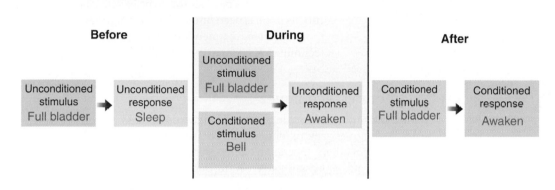

FIGURE 15-12 Classical conditioning helps to associate a full bladder with waking up.

Anxiety can be countered by using relaxation as a substitute. Since anxiety is produced by the sympathetic nervous system, which prepares the body to fight, flee, or freeze, and relaxation by the parasympathetic nervous system that conserves the bodily functions and energy, these two states cannot exist at the same time. Mary Cover Jones (1924) developed **exposure therapy**. This behavior therapy technique involves repeatedly presenting the client with a distressing object in order to reduce anxiety. Repetitive exposure leads to less anxiety and reduces the fear response over time (Deacon & Abramowitz, 2001). A common type of exposure therapy is **systematic desensitization**, in which a client practices relaxation while facing progressively more fear-inducing stimuli.

Systematic desensitization has three components:

1. Constructing a hierarchy of fears such as the one in **TABLE 15-1**
2. Training the client in progressive relaxation
3. Alternately exposing the client through the fear hierarchy and relaxing until the fear response is extinguished so that it no longer occurs.

Exposure therapies, including systematic desensitization, can be done **en vivo**, meaning actual exposure to the thing that causes anxiety; using imagination, in which the person will create a mental image of the feared object; or by using computers, as

Exposure therapy A behavior therapy technique that involves repeatedly presenting the client with a distressing object in order to reduce anxiety.

Systematic desensitization Treatment for phobia in which a client practices relaxation during progressively more fear-inducing stimuli.

En vivo A type of exposure therapy in which the actual feared object is used.

TABLE 15-1 Hierarchy of Fears for Flying

Anticipated Distress Level	Description
100	Strapping yourself into the airplane seat
90	Finding your seat on the airplane
80	Boarding the airplane
70	Waiting at the gate for your flight
60	Finding your gate
50	Arriving at the airport

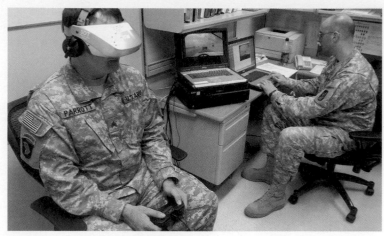

FIGURE 15-13 Virtual reality exposure therapy is a form of behavior therapy in which the soldier is subjected to simulations of the event that caused the PTSD symptoms.

in virtual reality exposure therapy FIGURE 15-13. **Virtual reality exposure therapy** is a behavior therapy technique involving the repetitive presentation of a simulated distressing object or situation in order to reduce anxiety. Virtual reality therapy has been used for posttraumatic stress disorder and for flight anxiety (Krijn, Emmelkamp, Olafsson, & Biemond, 2004).

Aversive conditioning involves pairing an unpleasant stimulus with an undesired behavior in order to reduce the target behavior. Painting an unpleasant-tasting liquid on the fingernails of people who bite their nails to reduce the nail biting, for example (Vargas & Adesso, 1976), is using aversive conditioning. Although aversive conditioning has been shown to be beneficial in the short run, its use has been limited because of the availability of more effective treatments such as operant conditioning techniques (Nakatani et al., 2009).

Painting a bad-tasting liquid on the fingernails can be an example of aversive conditioning.

Operant Conditioning Techniques

Operant conditioning involves training emitted behaviors to make them more likely to occur again. Techniques seek to increase the occurrence of certain behaviors and reduce the occurrence of others. Operant techniques include positive reinforcement, or a consequence that creates a pleasant state, making behavior more likely to occur again, of adaptive behaviors and nonreinforcement and sometimes punishment of behaviors that are maladaptive, or undesired. Often, desired or adaptive behaviors are encouraged through **shaping**, in which a part of a behavior is reinforced initially, and then increasing the goal to more complex behaviors later on. Sometimes what is called a token economy is used for reinforcement. In this type of behavior therapy, involving positive reinforcement of specific behaviors, tokens or points can be swapped for privileges or other reinforcements.

CONCEPT LEARNING CHECK 15.4 | *Designing a Behavioral Treatment Plan*

1. Create a systematic desensitization behavioral treatment plan for a person who has a fear of flying.

Cognitive and rational emotive therapists may ask clients to fill out forms in order to analyze their thoughts.

15.5 Cognitive Therapies

Cognitive therapies attempt to modify clients' maladaptive thoughts.

- Discuss Beck's cognitive therapy and Ellis's rational emotive therapy as they relate to cognitive therapy.

Cognitive therapy is a type of treatment emphasizing the link between thoughts and emotions. Cognitive therapies suggest that thoughts are the etiology, or cause, of psychological conditions. The goal of cognitive therapy is to understand these maladaptive thinking patterns and develop healthier ways of thinking: change the way you think and you can change the way you feel. While this may sound like using the power of positive thinking, it is not the same thing. Therapists use specific techniques to recognize patterns of maladaptive thoughts and apply intervention strategies to reshape ways of thinking. The two most common types of cognitive therapy are Beck's cognitive therapy and Ellis's rational emotive therapy.

Aaron Beck and Cognitive Therapy

Aaron Beck, who was trained as a psychoanalyst, noticed that his clients' language changed over the course of therapy (Beck, Rush, Shaw, & Emery, 1987). Reflecting on this observation, he wondered if a therapist could change clients' thoughts more directly using language. As in all forms of cognitive therapy, the basis of Beck's model is that psychological conditions, like depression, result from thoughts. People who are depressed tend to have a pessimistic explanatory style, and when bad things occur, they tend to blame themselves. They are also more likely to discount positive events (Beck et al., 1987). In therapy, the goal is to identify any negative self-talk and examine it fully. Rather than just thinking positively, the therapist encourages clients to notice and test their maladaptive or distorted beliefs through questioning techniques and homework. Cognitive behavior therapy is a type of treatment that emphasizes the link between thoughts, emotions, and behavior. In therapy, a cognitive therapist will give clients tools that can help them address distortions in their thinking. TABLE 15-2 gives examples of common cognitive distortions.

TABLE 15-2 Examples of Maladaptive Beliefs in Cognitive Therapy

All or nothing thinking	Seeing things in inflexible extremes such as good or bad
Overgeneralization	Seeing one negative event as an ongoing pattern
Disqualifying the positive	Filtering out the positive aspects of a situation
Jumping to conclusions	Assuming something negative without enough evidence
Magnification or minimization	Amplifying the significance of something negative or lessening the significance of something positive
Emotional reasoning	An assumption that negative emotions mean that negative things are really happening
Labeling	Instead of describing a mistake you negatively brand yourself as "loser" or an "idiot"

Albert Ellis and Rational Emotive Therapy

Like Beck, Albert Ellis was also trained as a psychoanalyst, but Ellis's approach to cognitive therapy is different from Beck's. Ellis's **rational emotive therapy** is a type of active and directive therapy that emphasizes the link between thoughts and emotions.

Ellis rejected the notion that the past is important to a person's current condition. In fact, he believed that you affect your future more than the past affects you. Your current problems are based on the idea that you teach yourself false notions of yourself, the world, or other people over and over again (Ellis, 2001). How do we do this? Ellis says that we use self-talk to focus on irrational or unrealistic expectations, leading to unwanted feelings. Statements like "I am worthless" are illogical overgeneralizations associated with anxiety and depression. Ellis also emphasizes the importance of action. Like cognitive therapy, rational emotive therapy involves homework in which clients practice their new ways of thinking.

Virtual reality exposure therapy A behavioral therapy technique that involves the repetitive presentation of a simulated distressing object or situation in order to reduce anxiety.

Aversive conditioning A behavioral technique that pairs an unpleasant stimulus with an undesired behavior in order to reduce the target behavior.

Shaping Reinforcing part of a behavior initially and then increasing the goal to more complex behaviors.

Cognitive therapy A type of treatment that emphasizes the link between thoughts and emotions; also known as cognitive behavior therapy.

Rational emotive therapy A type of active and directive therapy that emphasizes the link between thoughts and emotions.

CONCEPT LEARNING CHECK 15.5 *Comparing Cognitive Therapies*

1. Compare and contrast the cognitive therapy approaches of Aaron Beck and Albert Ellis.

15.6 Family Systems and Group Therapy

Family systems and group therapy focus on how individuals function in their relationships to evaluate and improve communication and interpersonal connections.

■ Illustrate how family systems therapy focuses on how individuals function in their relationships through communication patterns.

Family and couples therapy attempt to change the way that individuals in a group relate to one another.

Both therapy and support groups treat clients in a collective setting.

Some psychotherapies focus on the individual in treatment. Other therapies take into account the relationships that people have in their lives. For example, family systems and group therapy approaches both recognize the influence of other people in an individual's life.

Systems Approaches

Family therapy is a type of psychotherapy that treats the immediate social system, the family, to improve individuals' psychological functioning. Family therapy, also known as family system therapy or couples therapy, is an approach to psychotherapy that attempts to change the way individuals in a group (such as a family or couple) relate to each other (Becvar, 1998). Systems approaches emphasize the importance of relationships.

No psychological condition is an individual issue, according to this approach. Systems approaches suggest that even when an individual has a psychological condition, something in his or her system is involved in establishing, maintaining, or exacerbating the current psychological state. Systems therapists recognize this and use the system as an important intervention point in treatment. Families, couples, and friends may participate in the therapy session. Systems approaches also note that people will often play roles in certain social structures, such as being first born in a family.

The systems approach is **eclectic**, meaning it integrates a broad range of intervention strategies and therapies, including psychodynamic, humanistic, behavioral, and cognitive ones. Systems approaches also utilize communication skills training and relationship education in an effort to open up the lines of communication. Rather than examining intrapsychic conflicts or assigning blame in the system, the intervention focuses on patterns of communication, exploring the ways of communication within the system. Sometimes the intervention involves examining intergenerational patterns, using **genograms** or family trees to understand common roles that people play in the system.

Primary Theoretical Orientations for Psychologists

Eclectic (36%)	Psychodynamic (29%)	Cognitive behavioral (19%)	Other (10%)	Humanistic (6%)	Family systems (3%)

Primary theoretical orientations for psychologists.
Source: Adapted from Norcross, J. C., Hedges, M., & Castle, P. H. (2002). Psychologists conducting psychotherapy in 2001: A study of the Division 29 membership. Psychotherapy: Theory, Research, Practice, Training, 39(1), 97–102. doi:10.1037/0033-3204.39.1.97

Group Therapy

Group therapy can use some of the same intervention techniques as family systems approaches, except the clients in the group have similar concerns. **Group therapy** is a technique that treats multiple clients in a collective setting, often under the direction of one or several therapists (Yalom & Leszcz, 2005). One type of group therapy is the **support group**, in which members meet without a therapist to provide social support for each other.

Group therapy has both strengths and weaknesses. It is much less expensive than individual therapy since the members share the cost of the therapist. In addition, the group experience can reveal patterns of problematic relationships that may not show themselves in individual settings. However, while members of the group do save money because they share therapist, they compete for the therapist's time. Confidentiality is harder to control in group settings as well. Groups are helpful for some concerns but not appropriate for all conditions.

CONCEPT LEARNING CHECK 15.6 | *Describing an Eclectic Systems Approach*

1. The systems approach is eclectic, meaning it integrates a broad range of intervention strategies, including psychodynamic, humanistic, behavioral and cognitive ones. Illustrate how a group therapy approach can be combined with a humanistic approach.

15.7 Biomedical Therapies

Biomedical therapies focus on changing physiological problems that lead to psychological conditions using drug treatments as well as surgical interventions.

- Explain the focus on changing physiological problems that lead to psychological conditions in biomedical therapies.
- Compare and contrast the major classes of antidepressant drugs, the major drug treatments for anxiety, and antipsychotic medications.
- Discuss other nondrug medical treatments for psychological conditions.

Psychotherapy is not the only technique used to help with psychological conditions. **Biomedical therapies** are a family of therapies that use surgery, medication, or other physiological interventions for the treatment of psychological conditions. In this section, we will focus on drug treatments, including medications for depression, bipolar and anxiety disorders, and psychosis; as well as more invasive medical procedures such as electroconvulsive therapy, transcranial magnetic stimulation, and deep brain stimulation.

Drug Treatments

Psychotropic medications are drugs used to treat psychological conditions. Most biomedical therapies are pharmaceutical or drug treatments. **Psychopharmacologists** are researchers and practitioners who study and often prescribe psychiatric medications. Psychopharmacologists include physicians, nurse practitioners, doctors of nursing practice, pharmacists, medical psychologists, and prescribing psychologists with extensive knowledge of medicines that treat psychological conditions. Psychopharmacologists assume that psychological conditions are, in part, the result of physiological problems, including neurotransmitter abnormalities. Neurotransmitters are chemical messengers that transmit information from one neuron to another. Drug treatments have reduced patients' hospitalizations and relieved their suffering from the symptoms of psychological disorders.

All prescription medications undergo extensive review in the United States by the Food and Drug Administration (FDA). In order for a medication to be approved for use, its developers have to provide evidence that the medication is both safe and effective. "Safe" does not mean that the medication is without risk. In general, a medication is considered "safe" if the benefits of the medicine outweigh the risks. For example, some medications have significant or dangerous adverse effects such as nausea or seizures. Similarly, "effective" does not mean that the medication cures or removes all symptoms of the condition. A medication is considered "effective" if the medication's treatment effects outperform a **placebo**, a substance without an active ingredient. In fact, many placebos can have treatment effects as well as side effects. When a placebo helps a condition, it is considered to be a **placebo effect**, a treatment result in response to a physiologically ineffective treatment. People have reported side effects such as nausea, sweating, rash, and fever, while using placebos (Hróbjartsson & Norup, 2003).

After a medication has been approved by the FDA to be used as a treatment for a condition, the developer of the medication is granted a patent for the medication. Medicines normally have both a generic name (often related to the molecule or how it works) as well as a brand name that is used in marketing the medication. Brand names are usually written with the first letter capitalized, while the generic name is lowercase. For example, if you have been to the supermarket in search of something to help your headache, you may have chosen Tylenol® (a brand name) or a supermarket version of acetaminophen (generic). Once the patent for the medication runs out, other companies can produce

Family therapy A type of psychotherapy that treats the immediate social system, i.e., the family, to improve individuals' psychological functioning.

Eclectic approach A therapy technique that integrates ideas from several theories.

Genogram Family tree.

Group therapy A psychotherapeutic technique that treats multiple clients in a collective setting.

Support group A type of group therapy in which members meet without a therapist to provide social support.

Biomedical therapies A family of therapies that focuses on surgery, medication, or other physiological interventions for the treatment of psychological conditions.

Psychotropic medication A drug used to treat psychological conditions.

Psychopharmacologists Researchers and practitioners who study and often prescribe psychiatric medications.

Placebo A substance without an active ingredient.

Placebo effect Treatment result in response to a physiologically ineffective treatment.

generic versions of the medication. While these generic medications are usually much less expensive because their manufacturers do not have to recoup any development costs for the medication, they contain the same active ingredients as the brand-name medication. Some brand-name medications also contain inactive ingredients that might help them work better, but in general, generic medications are quite similar to brand-name medications (Howland, 2009).

Antidepressant Drugs

An **antidepressant medication** is a type of drug used to reduce the symptoms of depressive mood disorders. There are dozens of different antidepressants on the market today. They are all designed to affect neurotransmitters, the chemical messengers in the brain. The monoamine hypothesis of depression is the theory that depression is related to problems in a family of neurotransmitters called monoamines (Preston, O'Neal, & Talaga, 2010). The monoamines include serotonin (abbreviated 5-HT), norepinephrine (NE), and dopamine (DA). Some theories suggest that excessive reuptake of monoamines is a problem related to the symptoms of depression. This means that the transport proteins reabsorb the monoamines too aggressively and take too many of the monoamines out of the synaptic gap, leaving too few of the monoamines to bind to the receptor site and deliver the message that the next neuron should fire. Other biomedical theories of depression suggest that neurons are not releasing enough monoamines, so the "fire" message is not delivered as quickly as it should be. Another theory suggests that the enzyme responsible for cleaning up the synaptic gap, monoamine oxidase (MAO), is overactive. Overactive MAO metabolizes, or breaks down, the monoamines too quickly. This leaves too few monoamines available to bind with neurons to deliver the "fire" message. A different theory suggests that the receptor site that receives the neurotransmitter is abnormal in some way and needs extra stimulation in order to send the message to the receiving neuron. In all of these theories, monoamine malfunction results in symptoms of depression.

Whatever the case, increasing the availability or efficiency of monoamines does reduce the symptoms of depression. Two out of three people who are depressed will benefit from antidepressant medications (Gitlin, 2002). While many medications are indicated for treatment of depression, these medications can also be used to treat other conditions. Prozac, for example, is useful in alleviating the symptoms of both depression and anxiety (Stahl, 2008). Because medications can treat more than one condition, medications are categorized into functional classes according to what they do rather than the specific conditions that they treat. Functional classes that have an antidepressant effect include monoamine oxidase inhibitors (MAOIs), selective serotonin reuptake inhibitors (SSRIs), and serotonin-norepinephrine reuptake inhibitors (SNRIs).

Monoamine Oxidase Inhibitors

Some of the oldest medications for use in depression are monoamine oxidase inhibitors, or MAOIs. As the name suggests, MAOIs **TABLE 15-3** work by preventing the enzyme monoamine oxidase from doing its job of metabolizing, or destroying, the family of neurotransmitters known as monoamines: serotonin, norepinephrine, and dopamine (Preston et al., 2010). MAOIs typically take about 4 to 6 weeks to start working and have side effects including dizziness, diarrhea, insomnia, and weight gain (Stahl, 2009). One notable side effect of MAOIs is what some call the "cheese effect," or hypertensive crisis. Because MAO helps to regulate blood pressure, destroying MAO makes it difficult to control blood pressure under certain situations. One of these situations occurs when you ingest tyrine, a naturally occurring substance in many foods **TABLE 15-4** and

Antidepressant medication A type of drug used to reduce the symptoms of depressive mood disorders.

A pepperoni pizza can be a problematic choice for those on MAOIs.

TABLE 15-3 Commonly Prescribed Monoamine Oxidase Inhibitors (MAOIs)

phenelzine (Nardil)
tranylcypromine (Parnate)
selegiline (Emsam)

TABLE 15-4 Foods to Avoid with Monoamine Oxidase Inhibitors (MAOIs)

All tap beers	
Matured or aged cheese	
Casseroles made with aged cheeses	
Fermented or dry sausage like pepperoni, salami, or summer sausage	
Improperly stored meat, fish, or poultry	
Fava or broad bean pods	
Soy sauce or other soybean condiments	

Source: Adapted from Gardner, Shulman, Walker, & Tailor (1996).

medicines. Ingesting too much tyrine from, for example, eating pepperoni pizza and taking cough medicine if you are not feeling well can lead to a sudden spike of your blood pressure, giving you a terrible headache or even a stroke. Because many people need to stay on MAOIs for several years, adherence to a tyrine-free diet can be challenging. For this reason, MAOIs are not usually the first medicine that prescribers choose, even though they decrease symptoms in up to 75% of patients with depression (Stein, Kupfer, & Schatzberg, 2005).

Selective Serotonin Reuptake Inhibitors

Another way to keep monoamines in the synaptic gap is to prevent them from being reabsorbed. That is what SSRIs do. **Selective serotonin reuptake inhibitors (SSRIs)** **TABLE 15-5** are a class of medications that increase the efficiency of serotonin binding in the nervous system. Like their name suggests, SSRIs work by blocking the reabsorption of the neurotransmitter serotonin to the presynaptic neurons **FIGURE 15-14**. Doing this causes

Selective serotonin reuptake inhibitor (SSRI) A class of medications that increase the efficiency of serotonin binding in the nervous system.

TABLE 15-5 Commonly Prescribed Selective Serotonin Reuptake Inhibitors (SSRIs)

citalopram (Celexa)
escitalopram (Lexapro)
paroxetine (Paxil)
sertraline (Zoloft)

serotonin to build up in the synaptic gap and increases the likelihood that serotonin will bind with the receptor sites on the postsynaptic neuron. Serotonin is normally removed from the synapse by reuptake sites on the presynaptic neuron. SSRIs block the serotonin reuptake sites, allowing serotonin to remain active in the synapse longer.

FIGURE 15-14 SSRIs are a class of antidepressants used in the treatment of depression and anxiety disorders. They block the reabsorption of serotonin to the presynaptic cell and therefore increase the availability of serotonin in the synapse. Here serotonin is represented as green beads that have been blocked from reentering the presynaptic cell by the SSRI (red), at left.

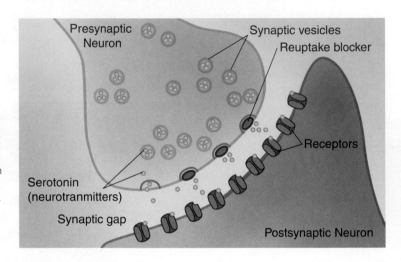

SSRIs are well tolerated, meaning that people do not have as many side effects on SSRIs as they might on other medications. Fewer side effects increases the likelihood that clients who are depressed will take them. In addition, SSRIs are not toxic in overdose and are available as generics, which makes them less expensive than some of the newer drugs. Side effects of SSRIs include high rates of sexual dysfunction, decreased appetite, nausea, diarrhea, insomnia, and headaches.

Vilazodone (Viibryd) is a new SSRI that works on both the presynaptic and postsynaptic neurons. You will recall that the monoamine hypothesis of depression suggests that problems of depression can happen both upstream (on the sending neuron) as well as downstream (on the receiving neuron). Vilazodone targets serotonin by blocking reabsorption (like an SSRI) and by antagonizing, or stimulating, the receiving neuron by pretending to be a type of serotonin. Vilazodone has a lower rate of sexual dysfunction than SSRIs (de Paulis, 2007).

Serotonin-Norepinephrine Reuptake Inhibitors

Some antidepressants work in more than one way. Serotonin-norepinephrine reuptake inhibitors (SNRIs) are medicines used to treat depression that keep both serotonin and norepinephrine in the synapse longer **TABLE 15-6**. This gives them the benefits of SSRIs while also treating depression in an additional way by targeting norepinephrine. Unfortunately, SNRIs also have additional side effects, including nervousness, insomnia, and increase in blood pressure (Stahl, 2009).

TABLE 15-6 Commonly Prescribed Serotonin-Norepinephrine Reuptake Inhibitors (SNRIs)

venlafaxine (Effexor)
desvenlafaxine (Pristiq)
duloxetine (Cymbalta)

Some SNRIs offer different kinds of action on serotonin and norepinephrine. Venlafaxine, for example, inhibits the reuptake only of serotonin in low doses, meaning it works just like an SSRI. At moderate doses, venlafaxine inhibits more serotonin and starts to block norepinephrine as well. At high doses, venlafaxine blocks reuptake of serotonin, norepinephrine, and dopamine (Stahl, 2008).

Taking an Antidepressant

When taking an antidepressant, it is important to follow the prescriber's directions very carefully. It is also important not to stop taking the medication, even if you start to feel better. Antidepressants are not taken like you might take an aspirin for a headache. Normally, prescribers will suggest that a person remain on a medication for a few months to a few years (Preston et al., 2010). Many times, when people stop taking the medicine too quickly, they will have headaches and feel dizzy, tired, and irritable. This is because they are experiencing a discontinuation syndrome. It is not that they are hooked on the medicine—antidepressants are not associated with dependency. Taking an antidepressant to treat depression decreases the severity of the depression and reduces the likelihood of a **relapse**, meaning a recurrence of the condition. If a person has had several episodes of depression, the guidelines suggest that it is better to stay on the medication than go on and off the medication. If one antidepressant does not work, your prescriber may recommend trying a different one. Among patients whose depression is not helped by one antidepressant, about 25% improve when their prescriber changes their medication (Rush, 2007).

Antianxiety Drugs

An **antianxiety medication** is a type of drug used to reduce the symptoms of agitation and nervousness. Nervousness and tension are present in a number of different anxiety disorders, including flight anxiety. The most common antianxiety medications are benzodiazepines, SSRIs, and SNRIs.

Benzodiazepines **TABLE 15-7** are the most commonly used antianxiety medications. Sometimes known as tranquilizers, benzodiazepines are fast-acting and effective (Stahl, 2009). While some caution against their use because of the risk that patients will develop **tolerance**, a reduction in a person's sensitivity to a drug over time, others suggest they are not as risky as once believed (Ballenger, 2000).

Benzodiazepines work on the neurotransmitter GABA. **Gamma-aminobutyric acid (GABA)** is an all-purpose inhibitory neurotransmitter. By affecting GABA, benzodiazepines reduce central nervous system arousal, dampening the anxiety response.

In addition to benzodiazepines, SSRIs and SNRIs are also effective antianxiety medications. Just as when they are used for depression, SSRIs and SNRIs take a few weeks to start working and may need to be taken in larger doses than when used as an antidepressant.

You are already familiar with the advantages and disadvantages of using SSRIs and SNRIs, but benzodiazepines present some different challenges. Long-term use of benzodiazepines is associated with both tolerance and **dependence**. In addition, many people report having memory problems and feeling tired and dizzy when they take benzodiazepines.

Mood-Stabilizing Drugs

Mood stabilizers **TABLE 15-8** are a family of medications used to treat the symptoms of bipolar mood disorders. True mood-stabilizing drugs will treat both the manic/hypomanic phase as well as the depressive phase of a bipolar condition (Stahl, 2008a). The gold standard medication to treat bipolar mood disorders is **lithium** (Stahl, 2008a). Unfortunately, lithium is associated with some serious potential side effects. Although it is more like an antimanic medication than a true mood stabilizer, Depakote (divalproex) is more widely prescribed than lithium (Thase & Denko, 2008).

Relapse A recurrence of a condition or disorder.

Antianxiety medication A type of drug used to reduce the symptoms of agitation and nervousness.

Tolerance A reduction in a person's sensitivity to a drug over time.

Gamma-aminobutyric acid (GABA) The nervous system's primary inhibitory neurotransmitter.

Dependence When a person's drug use has led to distress or impairment and unsuccessful efforts to reduce drug use.

Mood stabilizers A family of medications used to treat bipolar mood disorders.

Lithium A medication used to treat bipolar mood disorders.

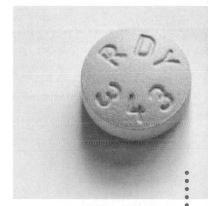

Citalopram (Celexa) is an antidepressant and antianxiety medication which acts as a selective serotonin reuptake inhibitor (SSRI), increasing the amount of the neurotransmitter in the synaptic gap.

TABLE 15-7 Commonly Prescribed Benzodiazepines

alprazolam (Xanax)
diazepam (Valium)

TABLE 15-8 Commonly Prescribed Mood Stabilizers

Lithium
divalproex (Depakote)

Australian medical scientist Dr. John Cade first used lithium as a treatment for psychological conditions in the 1940s. He discovered the treatment almost by mistake after delivering the medicine to a group of mice. He thought that the lithium calmed them, although it actually made them sick. Luckily, the lithium treatment did help his patients, and lithium is an effective treatment (Gim et al., 2009). It does, however, have some limitations. Lithium has a narrow therapeutic window. If lithium levels are too low, the medication will not be helpful, but if they are too high, thyroid and kidney damage can result. Lithium's mechanism of action is on the neurotransmitter glutamate (Grandjean & Aubry, 2009). Glutamate is an all-purpose excitatory neurotransmitter, the "gas" or "accelerator" of the nervous system. By stabilizing glutamate, lithium treats the manic and depressive phases of bipolar disorder. Valproate is helpful for those who do not respond well to lithium (Davis, Bartolucci, & Petty, 2005).

While medicines like lithium combat the symptoms of both mania and depression, other medicines, such as the anticonvulsant lamotrigine (Lamictal), target only manic symptoms. They often need to be combined with an antidepressant for the depressive phase of the condition. Lamotragine helps with rapid cycling (Calabrese et al., 2000). Lamotragine does not have the same side-effect profile as lithium. It has a broader therapeutic window but has its own unwanted side effects, including, in rare cases, a terrible rash (Stahl, 2009).

Antipsychotic Drugs

Antipsychotic medications TABLE 15-9 are a type of drug used to reduce the symptoms of psychosis as seen in schizophrenia. Symptoms of psychosis can include positive symptoms such as **hallucinations**, sensory experiences with no sensory input, and **delusions**—beliefs that most people would think are incredible or impossible. Psychosis can also include deficits of behavior, or **negative symptoms**, such as **anhedonia**, or lack of pleasurable experiences, **avolition**, or lack of will, and **alogia**, or lack of elaborative speech. Antipsychotic medications diminish psychosis in about 70% of patients (Sadock & Sadock, 2010) in just a few weeks (Emsley, Rabinowitz, & Medori, 2006).

The dopamine hypothesis of psychosis suggests that symptoms of psychosis are associated with low amounts of dopamine. Some of the early medications used to treat psychosis targeted this neurotransmitter. By blocking dopamine, they reduced dopamine activity in brain areas in which it was thought to be overactive. Since they were used so regularly, medications such as haloperidol (Haldol) were known as typical antipsychotics. Typical antipsychotics were beneficial at targeting the positive symptoms of psychosis, like hallucinations and delusions. The impact of these drugs on the lives of people experiencing these symptoms is powerful. Many have seen dramatic improvement in just a few weeks of treatment.

Adverse effects of typical antipsychotics include debilitating symptoms such as **tardive dyskinesia**, a neurological condition involving involuntary, repetitive movements caused by typical antipsychotics' effects on dopamine. Tardive dyskinesia is estimated to occur in one in five people who take the typical antipsychotics (Miyamoto, Lieberman,

Antipsychotic medication A type of drug used to reduce the symptoms of thought disorders.

Hallucination Sensory experience with no sensory input.

Delusion A belief that most people would think is incredible or implausible.

Negative symptoms of psychosis Symptoms of psychosis that involve behavior deficits, or expected behaviors that are absent.

Anhedonia A reduced capacity to experience pleasure.

Avolition Lack of will.

Alogia Lack of elaborative speech.

Tardive dyskinesia A neurological condition involving involuntary, repetitive movements.

TABLE 15-9 Commonly Prescribed Antipsychotic Medications

Typical Antipsychotics	Atypical Antipsychotics
haloperidol (Haldol)	risperidone (Risperdal)
	aripiprazole (Abilify)

Fleishhacker, Aoba, & Marder, 2006). While reducing dopamine in places in which its concentration may be too high, typical antipsychotics may also reduce dopamine levels in places in which it is in the normal range, resulting in adverse effects such as tardive dyskinesia. The name of this condition literally means "late to arrive" (like tardy) and "abnormal" (like dysfunction) "movements" (like kinetics), because tardive dyskinesia is associated with abnormal movements like lip smacking, blinking, puckering, and grimacing. Although it can be controlled with medication, the condition is considered permanent.

Another disadvantage of typical antipsychotics is that the treatment effects seem to focus only on the positive symptoms of psychosis. Although those are important symptoms, the negative symptoms of psychosis, including flat affect, avolition, and alogia, also have a great impact on the lives of people who experience them.

More recently, newer medications have been discovered that reduce both the positive and negative symptoms of psychosis. Since these new medications were not the ones normally given, they were called atypical antipsychotics. Atypical antipsychotics (or second-generation antipsychotics) target dopamine as well as other neurotransmitters. Atypical antipsychotic medications, also listed in Table 15-9, are drugs that reduce both the positive and negative symptoms of psychosis. Atypical antipsychotics have an additional benefit of producing lower rates of tardive dyskinesia than typical antipsychotics (Stahl, 2009). Atypical antipsychotics do cause weight gain and higher rates of diabetes than the earlier medications (Stahl, 2009).

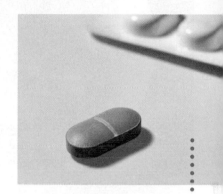

Risperdal is a second-generation antipsychotic.

Medical Procedures

Medicines are not the only medical treatment for psychological conditions. Medical treatments also include electroconvulsive therapy and medical devices such as transcranial magnetic stimulation and deep brain stimulation.

Electroconvulsive Therapy

Electroconvulsive therapy (ECT), sometimes referred to as shock therapy, is a biological treatment in which seizures are induced in anesthetized patients FIGURE 15-15. Back in the 1930, Ladislas von Meduna noticed that very few people who had epilepsy also had schizophrenia (Dukakis & Tye, 2007). Von Meduna hypothesized that epilepsy and schizophrenia were not able to exist in the same body. Perhaps, he surmised, seizures were curative of schizophrenia. If schizophrenia and epilepsy are incompatible, maybe seizures could treat psychological conditions. Although von Meduna's hypothesis proved false, the connection he saw between seizures and the absence of schizophrenia led to an effective treatment for the condition.

> **Electroconvulsive therapy (ECT)** A biological treatment in which seizures are induced in anesthetized patients.

When most people think about ECT, they think of a barbaric procedure. ECT procedures in the movies are very different than modern electroconvulsive therapy. Improvements in techniques make it a different kind of intervention than you might think. Around 100,000 people receive ECT annually in the United States. While most often used to treat depression, ECT has been effective for treating mania and catatonia as well (Glass, 2001).

The ECT procedure begins with a patient receiving a muscle relaxant and a general anesthetic so that the patient will be unconscious during the procedure. Then a short burst of electrical current is sent through electrodes placed on one or both sides of the patient's temple. The electrical current creates a seizure that lasts between 30 and 60 seconds. Often 6 to 10 sessions are used to treat depression.

Unlike antidepressant medications that can often take months to work, ECT relieves symptoms after only a few days. In fact, about 80% of depressed patients who receive ECT improve (Glass, 2001). Unfortunately, ECT has a high relapse rate. About half of people treated with ECT will have a recurrence of their depression within just 6 months (Glass, 2001). Additional ECT

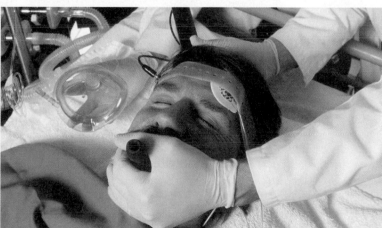

FIGURE 15-15 Patient undergoing ECT in which seizures are electrically induced in anesthetized patients for therapeutic effect.

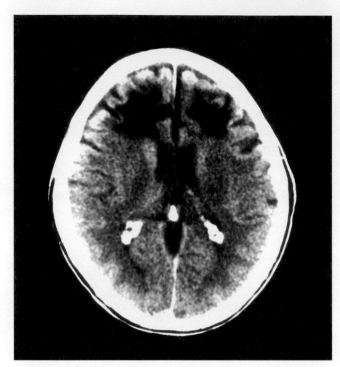

FIGURE 15-16 Frontal lobotomies used to be performed to intentionally damage the regions involved in emotion in an attempt to cure or improve individuals with severe aggression. This was performed by drilling holes into the skull. After the holes were drilled, needles were placed into the frontal lobe and rocked back and forth to sever neuronal connections. In this image you can see inactive (dark) regions in the frontal lobe near the top of the image.

treatments or the addition of antidepressants can stave off these new depressive episodes. Side effects include memory loss about the treatment. Research suggests that ECT does not produce any brain damage (Eschweiler et al., 2007).

Despite the benefits of ECT, it is still a rare procedure, prescribed by only 8% of all psychiatrists. Although the side effects are relatively minor, such as memory loss around the time of the procedure, some researchers think the low usage rates of the procedure are due to the misunderstandings and fears that people have about ECT.

How ECT works is still a mystery. Some theories suggest that ECT lowers activity in brain areas that might be involved in depression (Nobler et al., 2001), while others suggest that ECT stimulates **neurogenesis**, or new nerve growth, that may be the source of the symptom relief.

Other Medical Procedures

There are other medical procedures that can help with psychological conditions. **Psychosurgery**, or treatment of mental and behavioral conditions using an invasive biological procedure, has come a long way since early treatments. Previously, medical procedures were limited to drilling holes in the head to release spirits or less specific surgical procedures such as **lobotomy**, a surgery that involves destruction of nerves in the prefrontal cortex in order to improve symptoms of psychological conditions FIGURE 15-16.

One example of newer medical procedures is **transcranial magnetic stimulation (TMS)** FIGURE 15-17. This procedure uses magnetic fields generated by electromagnetic coils to activate or deactivate nerve cells in specific areas of the brain. Depressed moods seem to improve when TMS is applied. TMS has a benefit over ECT in that TMS causes no memory loss or seizures. About 50% of those who have received TMS procedures show an improvement in their symptoms (Schutter, 2009). Another procedure is **deep brain stimulation (DBS)**, in which a small electrode connected to a pulse generator stimulates the overexcited junction between the limbic system and the frontal lobe FIGURE 15-18. In addition, some patients with chronic depression have found relief through a chest implant that stimulates the vagus nerve, which sends signals to the brain's mood related limbic system (Conway et al., 2011).

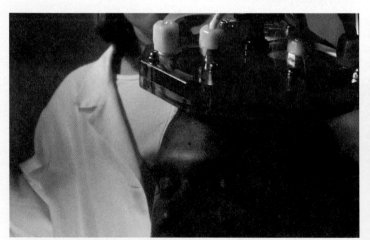

FIGURE 15-17 Using a high-power magnet, transcranial magnetic stimulation (TMS) excites neurons in the brain, triggering activity.

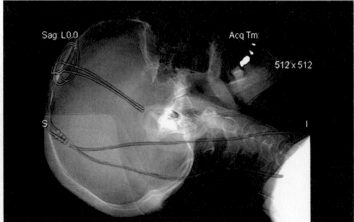

FIGURE 15-18 Electrodes for deep brain stimulation treatment.

CONCEPT LEARNING CHECK 15.7   *Explaining the Use of Medicines for Psychological Conditions*

1. A friend of yours has just returned from a psychiatrist and is confused. Even though your friend went with a presenting problem of anxiety, the doctor prescribed him Prozac, an antidepressant. Explain why this is not an unusual choice.

15.8 Evaluating Therapies for Psychological Disorders

Researchers use clinical trials to test treatments for psychological conditions and have found psychotherapy to be an effective treatment.

- Describe how clinical trials test treatments for psychological conditions.
- Discuss types of research that have provided evidence of the efficacy of treatments for psychological disorders.

Before we discuss the effectiveness of therapies for psychological conditions, it is important to understand the natural progression of a disorder. Many psychological conditions are self-limiting, meaning they go away all by themselves. This is true for some nonpsychological conditions, too. The average length of the common cold, for example, is about 10 days. In contrast, the average of an episode of major depressive disorder is between 6 months and 2 years (Katon & Schulberg, 1992). After that point, many people experience a **spontaneous remission**, or a reduction of symptoms of a condition even in the absence of treatment. People who are depressed, for example, do not stay depressed in exactly the same way for the rest of their lives. Although some people with psychological conditions do remain impaired for significant amounts of time, there is also a propensity for symptoms to change over time. This change is called **regression toward the mean** and refers to a tendency for those with severe symptoms to move to more moderate symptoms. What is more, many people with psychological conditions experience a placebo effect with treatment. "Placebo effect" refers to a client's response to nontreatment disguised as treatment, such as receiving a sugar pill while being told it is a therapeutic drug. Clients will sometimes improve by being on a waiting list for psychotherapy or even receiving a sugar pill (Kirsch, Moore, Scoboria, & Nicholls, 2002).

Effectiveness of Therapies for Psychological Disorders

How can psychologists and other mental health care practitioners tell if therapy is working? The scientific method is a powerful tool in evaluating the effectiveness of both psychotherapy and biomedical therapies. People who measure the effectiveness of therapies often use a **clinical trial**, which employs the scientific method to test a treatment for a disorder or condition. In a clinical trial meant to test a treatment for depression, for example, researchers ideally would like to study everyone who is depressed. But since that would be impossible, researchers instead use a convenience sample made up of people who volunteer to be part of their study. Then, the researchers randomly assign these participants into two groups—the "treatment" group gets the intervention (a type of psychotherapy or perhaps a drug that is being tested), and the "no treatment" group gets no treatment (they may be assigned to a waiting list for psychotherapy or receive a placebo instead of the drug being tested). Other than receiving or not receiving the intervention being tested, the two groups are treated in exactly the same way. Before the intervention takes place, researchers measure the severity of the participants' conditions. For our depression example, they might use a standard depression survey such as the Beck Depression Inventory (Beck & Aaron, 1988). Then, at regular intervals, they retake the measurements. If the participants' final depression scores were different, the researchers would conclude that the change was due to the administration of the **dependent variable**, which would be receiving the particular therapy. This technique distributes any nontreatment artifacts, such as regression to the mean, spontaneous remission, or the placebo effect, into both groups randomly since all of the participants have an equal chance of getting the intervention.

Often researchers replicate studies like the one described and compare the interventions to other drugs or other therapies. After a while, researchers know a lot about a particular intervention. At that point, researchers can statistically combine the individual studies to get a broad view of the intervention using a meta-analysis. A **meta-analysis** is a statistical technique that pools the results of several research studies so that practitioners can make the best decisions for their clients. **Evidence-based practice** involves selecting therapy treatments using information gained through research. For example, a meta-analysis (Davidson & Parker, 2001) of a sometimes-controversial therapeutic technique, **eye movement desensitization reprocessing (EMDR)**, a therapy technique involving bilateral stimulation in order to process distressing memories, revealed that EMDR is an

Neurogenesis New nerve growth.

Psychosurgery Treatment of mental and behavioral conditions using an invasive biological procedure.

Lobotomy A surgery that involves destruction of nerves in the prefrontal cortex in order to improve symptoms of psychological conditions.

Transcranial magnetic stimulation (TMS) A procedure that uses electromagnetic coils to activate nerve cells in the brain.

Deep brain stimulation (DBS) A surgical treatment in which a medical device is used to send electrical impulses to parts of the nervous system.

Spontaneous remission Reduction of symptoms of a condition in the absence of treatment.

Regression toward the mean The inclination for extreme scores to move toward the average over time.

Clinical trial The use of the scientific method to test a treatment for a disorder or condition.

Dependent variable The measurement collected to determine if there was any effect of the independent variable in an experiment.

Meta-analysis A statistical technique that pools the results of several research studies.

Evidence-based practice Selecting therapy treatments using information gained through research.

Eye movement desensitization reprocessing (EMDR) A therapy technique involving bilateral stimulation in order to process distressing memories.

effective treatment for PTSD, but perhaps not in the way originally thought. Through meta-analysis and subsequent research, it was determined that it was the exposure and not the bilateral stimulation that appeared to be the most important part of the intervention.

Effectiveness of Different Therapies

So what have we discovered through research techniques like clinical trials and meta-analyses? Psychotherapy is effective. Half of all people who enter therapy show improvement by the second month, and by 9 months, three out of four show significant improvement (McNeilly & Howard, 1991). In fact, according to a classic meta-analysis, those in the treatment group show a greater improvement than 80% of those untreated (Smith & Glass, 1977). Treatment effects are good for medication, too, and patients fare even better when the two are combined. What researchers have not found is one therapy that is best for everyone when comparing psychodynamic, humanistic, behavioral, cognitive, or drug treatments (Nathan, Stuart, & Dolan, 2000). Smith and Glass's (1977) meta-analysis of 400 clinical trials showed that no one therapy was best overall. However, there were some winners for particular kinds of conditions: Behavioral and cognitive behavioral therapies were the best treatment for panic disorder and obsessive compulsive disorder, and cognitive behavioral therapy was best for depression TABLE 15-10.

TABLE 15-10 Empirically Supported Therapies for Psychological Conditions

Problem	Strong Research Support*	Modest Research Support**
Bipolar disorder		• Cognitive therapy
Depression	• Cognitive therapy • Behavioral therapy	• Short-term psychodynamic therapy
Generalized anxiety disorder	• Behavioral therapy • Cognitive therapy	
Insomnia	• Cognitive behavioral therapy • Relaxation training	• Biofeedback
Obsessive-compulsive disorder	• Behavioral therapy • Cognitive therapy	
Panic disorder	• Cognitive behavioral therapy	• Relaxation • Psychoanalytic treatment
PTSD	• Exposure therapy • Eye movement desensitization reprocessing	
Schizophrenia	• Social skills training • Cognitive behavioral therapy	
Social phobia	• Cognitive therapy • Behavioral therapy	
Specific phobias	• Exposure therapies	

*Research support for a given treatment is labeled "strong" if criteria are met for what Chambless et al. (1998) termed "well-established" treatments. To meet this standard, well-designed studies conducted by independent investigators must converge to support a treatment's efficacy.

**Research support is labeled "modest" if criteria are met for what Chambless et al. (1998) termed "probably efficacious treatments". To meet this standard, one well-designed study or two or more adequately designed studies must support a treatment's efficacy.

Source: Data from the American Psychological Association, Division 12, Society of Clinical Psychology.

Common Factors That Increase Effectiveness

There appear to be some crosscutting factors related to the effectiveness of psychotherapy treatments. Across all therapy techniques, the better the quality of the therapeutic relationship, the better the outcomes. Similar to what the humanistic psychologists Carl Rogers suggested, genuineness and warmth are important therapeutic characteristics, and they appear to have a treatment effect of their own (Lambert & Barley, 2001). In addition to therapist factors, client factors are important, too. For example, clients' outcomes are better when they have greater access to support in their environments and when they are motivated (Lambert & Barley, 2001).

Culture, Cultural Values, and Psychotherapy

Cultures can vary on the amount of stigma associated with seeking treatments for psychological conditions. The more stigma associated with seeking help, the fewer choices for help, and the less likely those who suffer will look for assistance. Although psychotherapy is relatively accepted in the United States, this is not the case all over the world. China, for example, has relatively few therapists that are as extensively trained as those in the United States (Gao et al., 2010).

Psychotherapy treatments also reflect the values of a particular culture. Cultures that place an emphasis on interreliance rather than self-reliance, or **collectivist cultures**, for example, often discourage public emotional displays and focusing on the self too much (Lee, 2006). Other cultures place an emphasis on the family, and sharing problems outside of the family is discouraged (La Roche & Maxie, 2003). A focus away from the self can run counter to many insight-oriented therapies, such as self-exploration, emotional expression, and self-disclosure.

Collectivist culture A culture that places an emphasis on interreliance rather than self-reliance.

Understanding cultural nuances can be important in psychotherapy. Professional associations such as the American Psychological Association, the Association for Psychological Science, the American Psychiatric Association, and many state psychological licensing boards require training in cultural differences that could potentially influence the therapeutic relationship and emphasize awareness of the influences and challenges that are faced. Despite additional training, some clients prefer therapists who are culturally similar to them (Sanchez & Atkinson, 1983).

CRITICAL THINKING APPLICATION

Treatments for psychological conditions can be effective in relieving stress and helping those with psychological disorders. Professional organizations, client advocate groups, and government agencies all give advice about how to choose a therapist. This information is subject to bias toward the particular group, so sorting through the information can be confusing to those unfamiliar with psychology. Finding the right therapist and therapy is important, and those seeking help should be encouraged to ask questions and to find the best person and treatment for them.

Using the Internet, search the websites of agencies such as the American Psychiatric Association, PsychCentral, and the American Psychological Association, construct a guide for a person seeking therapy. In your guide, be sure to fold in information about the cross-cutting themes of effective therapies that are mentioned in this chapter. Your guide should encourage those seeking therapy to ask direct questions about how long the therapists have been seeing clients, their areas of expertise, the types of treatments they use, and what licenses they hold. In addition, it is important to talk about finances, fees, and if health insurance is accepted.

It will also be important to note in your guide that there are licensing boards to report a therapist if you feel the therapist is engaging in unethical behavior. A person can stop treatment with a psychotherapist at any time.

Summary of Multiple Influences on Therapies for Psychological Disorders

Ideally, psychological conditions are treated on multiple levels as seen in FIGURE 15-19. For example, many research studies have shown that depression responds better when treated with both medication and psychotherapy (Zuckerbrot, 2007). Two are better than one alone. It results in a faster recovery and a lower chance of relapse than when the depression is treated with only one intervention.

For example, cognitive therapy with a systems approach might examine family dynamics that have contributed to the problem. Learned behaviors may intersect with

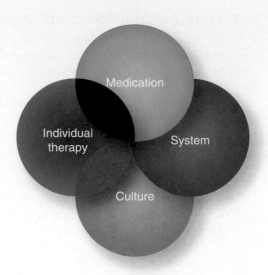

FIGURE 15-19 Interventions for psychological conditions can occur on multiple levels.

the larger social environment. Some psychologists are examining large-scale interventions that target the social issues that may set the stage for psychological conditions or may prevent those suffering from seeking treatment. In fact, many college residence halls focus on prevention in this way. Targeting society may well be the best way to attack psychological conditions, since it will allow a psychological condition to be targeted on many levels.

The medicine I took for my flight quelled my anxiety for the first few hours. Ultimately, my nearly 6,000-mile flight from Chicago to Istanbul, Turkey, meant that a behavioral exposure technique for my anxiety would also be at work due to the length of the flight. I landed exhausted but relaxed, jetlagged, and with a huge reduction of my fear of flying. To this day, I am still not convinced that it was the medication that got rid of my flight anxiety. There were probably multiple influences on my treatment. Sure, the medicine helped biologically by reducing my central nervous system activity, but I also realized that I may have had an unconscious worry about not being in control (psychodynamic). I had to trust what I felt would be best for me to take care of myself in that situation (humanistic) and even question my irrational thoughts and fears (cognitive) while I listened to relaxing music, although I was feeling frightened (behavioral). Ultimately, there were multiple influences on my treatment of my flight anxiety. I fly all the time now with only the slightest hint of anxiety, but I still prefer the window seat.

CONCEPT LEARNING CHECK **15.8**   *Summarizing the Factors of Effective Psychotherapy*

1. Summarize some of the crosscutting factors thought to increase likelihood of effective psychotherapy.

Visual Overview — Common Medications Used to Treat Psychological Disorders

Those who prescribe medication to treat psychological conditions choose from a number of medicines. This overview summarizes the common classes of psychotropic medications, the conditions they treat, as well as examples of each class of medicine.

MAOI (Monoamine Oxidase Inhibitors)
Uses include treatments for major depressive disorder

Examples include:
phenelzine (Nardil)
tranylcypromine (Parnate)
emsam (Selegiline)

Lithium
Uses include treatments for both mania and depression in bipolar disorder

Benzodiazepines
Uses include treatments for anxiety disorders

Examples include:
diazepam (Valium)
alprazolam (Xanax)

SNRI (Serotonin Norepinephrine Reuptake Inhibitors)
Uses include treatments for mood disorders like depression, anxiety disorders like generalized anxiety disorder

Examples include:
venlafaxine (Effexor)
duloxetine (Cymbalta)
desvenlafaxine (Pristiq)

Anticonvulsants
Uses include treatments for the manic phase of bipolar disorder.

Examples include:
lamotrigine (Lamictal)

Antipsychotics
Uses include treatments for psychotic disorders like schizophrenia. Some antipsychotics are used to boost the effectiveness of an SSRI in the treatment of depression.

Examples include:
Typical antipsychotic:
haloperidol (Haldol)

Atypical antipsychotics:
risperdal (Risperidone)
aripiprazole (Abilify)

SSRI (Selective Serotonin Reuptake Inhibitors)
Uses include treatments for mood disorders like major depressive disorder, anxiety disorders like PTSD

Examples include:
citalopram (Celexa)
escitalopram (Lexapro)
paroxetine (Paxil)
sertraline (Zoloft)
vilazodone (Viibryd)

15.1 Mental Health Practitioners and Settings

- Despite effective treatment, many people wait years to get help for psychological conditions.
- There are a number of mental health practitioners with various approaches to mental health concerns.
- Psychiatrists are medical doctors with a clinical specialty in treating psychological conditions.
- Clinical and counseling psychologists both study and treat individuals with psychological concerns.
- Although much improved, historically, mental hospitals have had a stormy history in providing adequate care for those in need of psychological treatment.

15.2 Psychodynamic Therapy

- Modern psychodynamic therapy emerged out of the personality theories and treatments of Sigmund Freud.
- Psychodynamic treatments are based on settling unconscious conflicts that are created in childhood.
- Psychodynamic therapists use many tools, including free association, dream analysis, carefully timed interpretations and analysis of transference, and resistance for treatments.
- There are several types of psychodynamic therapies, including classical psychoanalysis and short-term psychodynamic therapy.

15.3 Humanistic Therapy

- Humanistic therapy is based on the idea that all humans have an actualizing tendency.
- Carl Rogers pioneered client-centered therapy based on humanistic personality theory.
- Client-centered therapists create the proper conditions so that therapeutic change will occur in their clients.
- Client-centered approaches are powered by genuineness, acceptance, and empathy.

15.4 Behavior Therapy

- Behavior therapies for psychological conditions are based on the assumption that psychological disorders are the result of maladaptive behavior patterns.
- Behavioral therapies attempt to change maladaptive associations, discourage maladaptive behaviors, or encourage more adaptive ones.
- Behavioral therapies use classical conditioning techniques to decouple problematic associations using counterconditioning techniques to attempt to extinguish the behaviors.
- Classical conditioning techniques include exposure therapies, aversive conditioning, and systematic desensitization.
- Operant conditioning techniques attempt to increase the occurrence of behaviors and reduce the occurrence of others using positive reinforcement.

15.5 Cognitive Therapies

- Cognitive therapies suggest that the causes of psychological conditions are the results of maladaptive thoughts.
- Cognitive therapists use various techniques to recognize patterns of maladaptive thinking and construct intervention strategies to reshape ways of thinking.
- The two most common types of cognitive therapy are Beck's cognitive therapy and Ellis's rational emotive therapy.

15.6 Family Systems and Group Therapy

- Family systems therapy focuses on how individuals function in their relationships.

- The focus of interventions for systems approaches is on communication patterns.

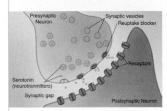

15.7 Biomedical Therapies

- Biomedical therapies focus on changing physiological problems that lead to psychological conditions using drug treatments as well as surgical interventions.

- Most antidepressants are constructed by the monoamine hypothesis of depression, suggesting that depression is related to problems in a family of neurotransmitters that includes serotonin, norepinephrine, and dopamine.

- Monoamine oxidase inhibitors (MAOIs) work by preventing the enzyme monoamine oxidase from metabolizing the neurotransmitters serotonin, norepinephrine, and dopamine in the synaptic gap.

- Selective serotonin reuptake inhibitors (SSRIs) increase the efficiency of serotonin by blocking the reabsorption of the neurotransmitter serotonin into the presynaptic neurons.

- Serotonin norepinephrine reuptake inhibitors (SNRIs) are medicines that keep both serotonin and norepinephrine in the synapse longer.

- Antianxiety medications reduce the symptoms of agitation and nervousness.

- Benzodiazepines work by affecting gamma-aminobutyric acid (GABA) in the nervous system.

- Mood stabilizers are a family of medications used to treat bipolar mood disorders.

- Lithium is a medication that will stabilize the manic and depressive phases of bipolar disorder.

- Anticonvulsants such as lamotrigine and valproate are helpful antimanic medications for those who do not respond well to lithium.

- Antipsychotic medications reduce the symptoms of thought disorders like schizophrenia.

- Older medications such as the typical antipsychotics improve the positive symptoms of psychosis (including hallucinations and delusions) but have limited impact on the negative symptoms of psychosis (i.e., affective flattening and avolition).

- Typical antipsychotics can have disruptive side effects including tardive dyskinesia.

- Newer atypical antipsychotics have a lower rate of tardive dyskinesia and offer relief for both positive and negative symptoms of psychosis but are associated with higher rates of weight gain and diabetes.

- In addition to medications, other medical treatments for psychological conditions include electroconvulsive therapy, transcranial magnetic stimulation, and deep brain stimulation.

15.8 Evaluating Therapies for Psychological Disorders

- Clinical researchers utilize clinical trials to test treatments for psychological conditions.

- Research has provided evidence of the efficacy of treatments for psychological disorders.

- Researchers did not find one kind of therapy that was better than others, except for specific treatments for specific disorders.

- Research has found some crosscutting factors for effective psychotherapy treatments, including therapist factors such as genuineness and warmth and client factors such as access to supportive environments and client motivation.

- Combining psychotherapy and drug therapy can be more effective than one alone.

15.1 Mental Health Practitioners and Settings

1. Your friend just returned from a visit with a mental health practitioner. He said the person had a DO degree after her name and gave your friend a prescription for a medication for anxiety. Your friend cannot remember the kind of practitioner. Based on this information, the practitioner was most likely a:
   A. psychiatrist.
   B. counseling psychologist.
   C. clinical psychologist.
   D. psychiatric nurse.

15.2 Psychodynamic Therapy

2. If a client comes in 20 minutes late to every session soon after the therapist has uncovered an important issue, this could be a sign of:
   A. insight.
   B. free association.
   C. resistance.
   D. transference.

3. Which type of therapy is most like the one that Freud would have practiced?
   A. Transference therapy
   B. Short-term psychodynamic therapy
   C. Psychodynamic therapy
   D. Psychoanalysis

15.3 Humanistic Therapy

4. Client-centered approaches are rooted in:
   A. creating an environment of genuineness, acceptance, and empathy.
   B. examining intrapsychic conflicts.
   C. increasing the occurrence of adaptive behaviors.
   D. challenging maladaptive cognitions.

5. What emotions do humanists explore most often?
   A. The emotions that arise naturally in therapy
   B. The emotions generated from projective tests, such as the Rorschach inkblot test
   C. Emotions that occur from early memories
   D. Emotions that the client recalls from dreams

15.4 Behavior Therapy

6. In the bell-and-pad treatment, the bell serves as a(n):
   A. unconditioned stimulus.
   B. unconditioned response.
   C. conditioned stimulus.
   D. conditioned response.

7. In systematic desensitization, each step of the hierarchy of fears is associated with:
   A. an aversive stimulus.
   B. relaxation.
   C. the feared outcome.
   D. a substitute symptom.

15.5 Cognitive Therapies

8. In cognitive therapy, clients are taught to identify negative thoughts and then:
   A. relax.
   B. question them.
   C. stop thinking the thought.
   D. think more positive thoughts.

9. Beck's cognitive therapy (CT) differs from Ellis's rational emotive therapy [RET] in that:
   A. RET has homework and CT does not.
   B. RET is more directive and CT is more guiding.
   C. RET suggests that psychological conditions are caused by maladaptive thoughts and CT suggests that psychological conditions are caused by maladaptive behaviors.
   D. Ellis was trained as a psychoanalyst while Beck was trained as a behaviorist.

15.6 Family Systems and Group Therapy

10. Systems approaches will sometimes use genograms in order to:
    A. uncover the source of blame in the family.
    B. examine patterns of intrapsychic conflicts in the family.
    C. explain and examine the common roles that people play in the family.
    D. interpret dreams.

15.7 Biomedical Therapies

11. SSRIs work by:
    A. blocking the reabsorption of serotonin.
    B. binding to receptor sites.
    C. encouraging the release of more serotonin.
    D. inhibiting the removal of serotonin by the enzyme MAO.

12. If a client takes the antipsychotic Haldol, which of the following symptoms is it most likely to help?
    A. A flat affect
    B. Auditory hallucination
    C. Lack of elaborative speech
    D. Lack of pleasurable experiences

13. Which of the following is considered an advantage of a benzodiazepine like Xanax?
    A. Benzodiazepines have a low risk for abuse.
    B. Benzodiazepines are an effective treatment for depression.
    C. Benzodiazepines work quickly.
    D. Benzodiazepines have an action on the neurotransmitter serotonin.

15.8 Evaluating Therapies for Psychological Disorders

14. If a client comes in with lots of anxiety it is likely that, on its own, the anxiety will decrease because of the phenomenon of:
    A. resistance.
    B. regression toward the mean.
    C. counterconditioning.
    D. transference.

15. Your friend Emily said that she is looking for a therapist to help with some personal struggles. Without knowing her specific condition, which type of psychotherapist would be best for her, according to the research?
    A. Psychodynamic
    B. Humanistic
    C. Behavioral
    D. Cognitive
    E. They are all equally effective.

CHAPTER DISCUSSION QUESTIONS

1. Section 15.1 describes three main types of mental health practitioners: psychiatrists, counseling psychologists, and clinical psychologists. Compare and contrast the assistance you would receive from each type of mental health practitioner. Are there some situations where one type of practitioner might be more appropriate than another?

2. Imagine that you are suffering from test anxiety and that you are researching a different therapy approaches that might help you overcome your anxiety. Review psychodynamic, humanistic, behavioral, cognitive, and family and group therapy techniques. Then, rank each theory in terms of how effective you think it would be in helping you with your test anxiety. Explain the order of your rankings.

3. Review all the approaches to therapy from Section 15.2–7 and evaluate how comfortable you would be accepting each form of therapy for yourself. Once you've gone through all the therapies, look at your ratings for biological versus nonbiological therapies. Do you see a preference for biological or nonbiological? What are the reasons for your preference?

4. Section 15.8 explains how to evaluate the effectiveness of different forms of therapy, but also highlights some other factors that may improve a person's mental state such as a placebo effect. Differentiate those factors other than therapy that may influence a person's psychological status.

1. Imagine that you have a friend who has come to you for advice about choosing a type of therapy for depression. Formulate a guide for your friend to help him or her understand the pros and cons of each type of therapy.

2. Identify a common problem among college students that might require psychological therapy. Then, act out a therapy session to work through the problem using at least four different approaches to therapy. Develop a script for each therapy session. Use a video camera to record the sessions. To complete the project, write a summary of the results of each session and your conclusions about what worked and what might have been done differently.

CHAPTER KEY TERMS

Acceptance
Active listening
Actualizing tendency
Alogia
Anhedonia
Antianxiety medication
Antidepressant medication
Antipsychotic medication
Aversive conditioning
Avolition
Behavior therapy
Bell-and-pad treatment
Biomedical therapies
Classical conditioning
Client-centered therapy
Clinical psychologist
Clinical researcher model
Clinical trial
Cognitive therapy
Collectivist culture
Counseling psychologist
Counterconditioning
Deep brain stimulation (DBS)
Defense mechanism
Deinstitutionalization
Delusions
Dependence
Dependent variable
Dream analysis
Eclectic approach
Electroconvulsive therapy (ECT)

Empathy
En vivo
Etiology
Evidence-based practice
Exposure therapy
Eye movement desensitization reprocessing (EMDR)
Family therapy
Free association
Gamma-aminobutyric acid (GABA)
Genogram
Genuineness
Group therapy
Hallucination
Humanism
Insight
Insight therapies
Interpretation
Latent content
Lithium
Lobotomy
Manifest content
Mental hospital
Meta-analysis
Mood stabilizers
Negative symptoms of psychosis
Neurogenesis
Outpatient
Phenomenology
Placebo
Placebo effect

Positive psychology
Practitioner-scholar model
Psychiatry
Psychoanalysis
Psychodynamic therapies
Psychopharmacologist
Psychopharmacology
Psychosurgery
Psychotropic medication
Rational emotive therapy
Regression toward the mean
Relapse
Resistance
Scientist-practitioner model
Selective serotonin reuptake inhibitor (SSRI)
Shaping
Short-term psychodynamic therapy
Social skills training
Spontaneous remission
Support group
Symptom substitution
Systematic desensitization
Tardive dyskinesia
Tolerance
Transcranial magnetic stimulation (TMS)
Transference
Unconditional positive regard
Virtual reality exposure therapy

ANSWERS TO CONCEPT LEARNING CHECKS

15.1 Comparing the Roles and Settings of Mental Health Care Practitioners

1. Deinstitutionalization created more freedom and choices for treatment, but it also created more homelessness and a population that did not receive the treatment it needed.

2. Psychiatrists typically use medicine to treat psychological disorders and counseling and clinical psychologists employ psychotherapy. Clinical and counseling psychologists are more similar than different in the way they research and treat psychological conditions.

15.2 Understanding Psychodynamic Therapies

1. Psychoanalytic therapies provide insight into problematic intrapsychic conflicts.

2. Traditional psychoanalytic therapy is long term and more formal, whereas short-term psychodynamic therapy is time limited and more casual in focus.

15.3 Describing the Elements of Humanistic Therapy

Humanistic therapies attempt to active the actualizing tendency or the instinctual desire to be the best possible version of oneself. By providing the correct environment, the therapist releases this the potential in the client.

15.4 Designing a Behavioral Treatment Plan

The behavioral treatment plan should include relaxation training, a hierarchy of fears, and paired exposure with relaxation.

15.5 Comparing Cognitive Therapies

Both Beck and Ellis emphasize the importance of action and maladaptive thoughts. Ellis's approach is more directive and active, while Beck's approach is to encourage clients to test out their beliefs.

15.6 Describing an Eclectic Systems Approach

1. The components of the client-centered approaches are genuineness, acceptance, and empathy. The therapist would help the members of the group to practice those components in the group.

15.7 Explaining the Use of Medications for Psychological Conditions

Although called an antidepressant, Prozac is an SSRI that can also be used for chronic anxiety.

15.8 Summarizing the Factors of Effective Psychotherapy

The better the quality of the therapeutic relationship, the better the outcomes such as genuineness and warmth. Client factors are important, too, such as supportive environments and client motivation.

ANSWERS TO CHAPTER REVIEW TEST

15.1 Mental Health Practitioners and Settings

1. A. Rationale: Psychiatrists are practitioners with professional medical doctorates (like MD or DO). Psychiatrists will sometimes treat psychological conditions using medication.

15.2 Psychodynamic Therapy

2. C. Rationale: Resistance is a client's employment of a defense mechanism during therapy.

3. D. Rationale: Psychoanalysis is a type of therapy based on Freud's theory of personality.

15.3 Humanistic Therapy

4. A. Rationale: Client-centered approaches are powered by the creation of an environment of genuineness, acceptance, and empathy.

5. A. Rationale: Instead of recalling and discussing emotions, humanists discuss the ones that occur during real time in therapy.

15.4 Behavior Therapy

6. A. Rationale: The bell would naturally wake you up, and this is an unconditioned stimulus that generates an unconditioned response of waking.

7. B. Rationale: Systematic desensitization is a treatment for phobia in which a client practices relaxation during progressively more fear-inducing stimuli.

15.5 Cognitive Therapies

8. B. Rationale: Rather than just thinking positively, the therapist encourages the client to notice and test out maladaptive beliefs through questioning techniques and homework.

9. B. Rationale: RET and CT are similar, except RET takes a more active and directive approach as compared to CT.

15.6 Family Systems and Group Therapy

10. C. Rationale: Systems approaches also note that people will often play roles in certain systems. These patterns can sometimes be revealed in genograms, or family trees.

15.7 Biomedical Therapies

11. A. Rationale: Selective serotonin reuptake inhibitors are a class of medications that increase the efficiency of serotonin by binding to the reuptake sites.

12. B. Rationale: Hallucinations are positive symptoms of psychosis.

13. C. Rationale: Benzodiazepine are fast-acting medicines for the treatment of anxiety. They have an action on the neurotransmitter GABA and have a high risk for abuse.

15.8 Evaluating Therapies for Psychological Disorders

14. B. Rationale: Regression toward the mean is the inclination for extreme scores to move toward the average over time.

15. E. Rationale: Without knowing the specific condition, the research suggests that all the interventions are about equally effective.

REFERENCES

Ballenger, J. C. (2000). Anxiety and depression: Optimizing treatments. *Primary Care Companion to the Journal of Clinical Psychiatry, 2*(3), 71.

Beck, R. A., & Aaron, T. (1988). Psychometric properties of the Beck Depression Inventory: Twenty-five years of evaluation. *Clinical Psychology Review, 8*(1), 77–100.

Beck, A. T., Rush, A. J., Shaw, B. F., & Emery, G. (1987). *Cognitive therapy of depression* (1st ed.). New York: Guilford.

Becvar, R. J. (1998). *Systems theory and family therapy: A primer* (2nd ed.). Lanham, MD: University Press of America.

Calabrese, J. R., Suppes, T., Bowden, C. L., Sachs, G. S., Swann, A. C., McElroy, S. L., et al. (2000). A double-blind, placebo-controlled, prophylaxis study of lamotrigine in rapid-cycling bipolar disorder. Lamictal 614 Study Group. *Journal of Clinical Psychiatry, 61*(11), 841–850.

Conway, C. R., Sheline, Y. I., Chibnall, J. T., Bucholz, R. D., Price, J. L., Gangwani, S., & Mintun, M. A. (2011). VNS-induced cerebral blood flow in depression. Brain blood-flow change with acute vagus nerve stimulation in treatment-refractory major depressive disorder. *Brain Stimulation.* doi:10.1016/j.brs.2011.03.001

Davidson, P. R., & Parker, K. C. (2001). Eye movement desensitization and reprocessing (EMDR): A meta-analysis. *Journal of Consulting and Clinical Psychology, 69*(2), 305–316.

Davis, L. L., Bartolucci, A., & Petty, F. (2005). Divalproex in the treatment of bipolar depression: A placebo-controlled study. *Journal of Affective Disorders, 85*(3), 259–266.

Deacon, B. J., & Abramowitz, J. S. (2004). Cognitive and behavioral treatments for anxiety disorders: A review of meta-analytic findings. *Journal of Clinical Psychology, 60*(4), 429–441.

Dukakis, K., & Tye, L. (2007). *Shock: The healing power of electroconvulsive therapy.* New York: Penguin.

Ellis, A. (2001). *Overcoming destructive beliefs, feelings, and behaviors: New directions for rational emotive behavior therapy.* Amherst, NY: Prometheus Books.

Emsley, R., Rabinowitz, J., & Medori, R. (2006). Time course for antipsychotic treatment response in first-episode schizophrenia. *American Journal of Psychiatry, 163*(4), 743–745. doi:10.1176/appi.ajp.163.4.743

Eschweiler, G. W., Vonthein, R., Bode, R., Huell, M., Conca, A., Peters, O., et al. (2007). Clinical efficacy and cognitive side effects of bifrontal versus right unilateral electroconvulsive therapy (ECT): A short-term randomised controlled trial in pharmaco-resistant major depression. *Journal of Affective Disorders, 101*(1–3), 149–157.

Gao, X., Jackson, T., Chen, H., Liu, Y., Wang, R., Qian, M., & Huang, X. (2010). There is a long way to go: A nationwide survey of professional training for mental health practitioners in China. *Health Policy, 95*(1), 74–81.

Gim, C. S. Y., Lillystone, D., & Caldwell, P. H. Y. (2009). Efficacy of the bell and pad alarm therapy for nocturnal enuresis. *Journal of Paediatrics and Child Health, 45,* 405–408.

Gitlin, M. J. (2002). Pharmacological treatment of depression. Handbook of depression. In I. Gotlib, & C. Hammen, (Eds.), *Handbook of depression,* (pp. 360–382). New York, NY: Guilford Press.

Glass, R. M. (2001). Electroconvulsive therapy. *JAMA: The Journal of the American Medical Association, 285*(10), 1346–1348. doi:10.1001/jama.285.10.1346

Gollaher, D. L. (1995). *Voice for the mad: The life of Dorothea Dix* (1st ed.). New York: Free Press.

Grandjean, E. M., & Aubry, J.-M. (2009). Lithium: Updated human knowledge using an evidence-based approach: Part I: Clinical efficacy in bipolar disorder. *CNS Drugs, 23,* 225–240.

Howland, R. H. (2009). What makes a generic medication generic? *Journal of Psychosocial Nursing and Mental Health Services, 47*(12), 17–20. doi:10.3928/02793695-20091103-99

Hróbjartsson, A., & Norup, M. (2003). The use of placebo interventions in medical practice—A national questionnaire survey of Danish clinicians. *Evaluation & the Health Professions, 26*(2), 153–165. doi:10.1177/0163278703026002002

Jones, M. (1924). A laboratory study of fear: The case of Peter. *Pedagogical Seminary, 31,* 308–315.

Joseph, S., & Linley, P. A. (2006). *Positive therapy: A meta-theory for positive psychological practice* (1st ed.). London: Routledge.

Katon, W., & Schulberg, H. (1992). Epidemiology of depression in primary care. *General Hospital Psychiatry, 14*(4), 237–247. doi:10.1016/0163-8343(92)90094-Q

Kirsch, I., Moore, T. J., Scoboria, A., & Nicholls, S. S. (2002). The emperor's new drugs: An analysis of antidepressant medication data submitted to the US Food and Drug Administration. *Prevention & Treatment, 5*(1), 23a.

Knekt, P., Lindfors, O., Harkanen, T., Valikoski, M., Virtala, E., Laaksonen, M. A., Marttunen, M., et al. (2008). Randomized trial on the effectiveness of long- and short-term psychodynamic psychotherapy and solution-focused therapy on psychiatric symptoms during a 3-year follow-up. *Psychological Medicine, 38*(05), 689–703. doi:10.1017/S003329170700164X

Krijn, M., Emmelkamp, P. M. G., Olafsson, R. P., & Biemond, R. (2004). Virtual reality exposure therapy of anxiety disorders: A review. *Clinical Psychology Review, 24*(3), 259–281. doi:10.1016/j.cpr.2004.04.001

Lambert, M. J., & Barley, D. E. (2001). Research summary on the therapeutic relationship and psychotherapy outcome. *Psychotherapy: Theory, Research, Practice, Training, 38*(4), 357–361. doi:10.1037/0033-3204.38.4.357

La Roche, M. J., & Maxie, A. (2003). Ten considerations in addressing cultural differences in psychotherapy. *Professional Psychology: Research and Practice, 34*(2), 180–186. doi:10.1037/0735-7028.34.2.180

Leaf, J. B., Dotson, W. H., Oppenheim-Leaf, M. L., Sherman, J. A., & Sheldon, J. B. (2011). A programmatic description of a social skills group for young children with autism. *Topics in Early Childhood Special Education.* doi:10.1177/0271121411405855

Lee, C. C. (2006). *Multicultural issues in counseling: New approaches to diversity* (3rd ed.). Alexandria, VA: American Counseling Association.

Leichsenring, F., & Rabung, S. (2008). Effectiveness of long-term psychodynamic psychotherapy: A meta-analysis. *JAMA: The Journal of the American Medical Association, 300*(13), 1551–1565. doi:10.1001/jama.300.13.1551

McNeilly, C. L., & Howard, K. L. (1991). The effects of psychotherapy: A re-evaluation based on dosage. *Psychotherapy Research, 1,* 74–78.

Miyamoto, S., Lieberman, J., Fleishhacker, W., Aoba, A., & Marder, S. (2003). Antipsychotic drugs. In J. Tasman, J. Kay, & J. Lieberman (Eds.), *Psychiatry* (2nd ed.). New York: Wiley.

Nakatani, Y., Matsumoto, Y., Mori, Y., Hirashima, D., Nishino, H., Arikawa, K., & Mizunami, M. (2009). Why the carrot is more effective than the stick: Different dynamics of punishment memory and reward memory and its possible biological basis. *Neurobiology of Learning and Memory, 92*(3), 370–380. doi:10.1016/j.nlm.2009.05.003

Narrow, W. E., Regier, D. A., Rae, D. S., Manderscheid, R. W., et al. (1993). Use of services by persons with mental and addictive disorders: Findings from the National Institute of Mental Health Epidemiologic Catchment Area Program. *Archives of General Psychiatry, 50*(2), 95–107.

Nathan, P. E., Stuart, S. P., & Dolan, S. L. (2000). Research on psychotherapy efficacy and effectiveness: Between Scylla and Charybdis? *Psychological Bulletin, 126*(6), 964.

Nobler, M. S., Oquendo, M. A., Kegeles, L. S., Malone, K. M., Campbell, C., Sackeim, H. A., & Mann, J. J. (2001). Decreased regional brain metabolism after ECT. *American Journal of Psychiatry, 158*(2), 305.

Norcross, J. C., Hedges, M., & Castle, P. H. (2002). Psychologists conducting psychotherapy in 2001: A study of the Division 29 membership. *Psychotherapy: Theory, Research, Practice, Training, 39*(1), 97–102. doi:10.1037/0033-3204.39.1.97

de Paulis, T. (2007). Drug evaluation: Vilazodone—a combined SSRI and 5-HT1A partial agonist for the treatment of depression. *IDrugs: The Investigational Drugs Journal, 10*(3), 193–201.

Porter, R. (2003). *Madness: A brief history* (1st ed.). Oxford, UK: Oxford University Press.

Preston, J. D., O'Neal, J. H., & Talaga, M. C. (2010). *Handbook of clinical psycho-pharmacology for therapists* (6th ed.). Oakland, CA: New Harbinger.

Rogers, C. (1989). *The Carl Rogers reader* (1st ed.). New York: Mariner Books.

Rush, A. J. (2007). STAR*D: What have we learned? *American Journal of Psychiatry, 164*(2), 201–204.

Sadock, B. J., & Sadock, V. A. (2010). *Kaplan and Sadock's pocket handbook of clinical psychiatry* (5th ed.). Philadelphia: Lippincott Williams & Wilkins.

Sanchez, A. R., & Atkinson, D. R. (1983). Mexican-American cultural commitment, preference for counselor ethnicity, and willingness to use counseling. *Journal of Counseling Psychology, 30*(2), 215–220. doi:10.1037/0022-0167.30.2.215

Schutter, D. J. L. G. (2009). Antidepressant efficacy of high-frequency transcranial magnetic stimulation over the left dorsolateral prefrontal cortex in double-blind sham-controlled designs: A meta-analysis. *Psychological Medicine, 39*(01), 65–75. doi:10.1017/S0033291708003462

Smith, M. L., & Glass, G. V. (1977). Meta-analysis of psychotherapy outcome studies. *American Psychologist, 32*(9), 752.

Spence, S. H., Donovan, C., & Brechman-Toussaint, M. (2000). The treatment of childhood social phobia: The effectiveness of a social skills training-based, cognitive-behavioural intervention, with and without parental involvement. *Journal of Child Psychology and Psychiatry and Allied Disciplines, 41*(06), 713–726.

Stahl, S. M. (2008). *Stahl's essential psychopharmacology: Neuroscientific basis and practical applications* (3rd ed.). New York: Cambridge University Press.

Stahl, S. (2009). *The prescriber's guide* (3rd ed.). New York: Cambridge University Press.

Stein, D. J., Kupfer, D. J., & Schatzberg, A. F. (2005). *The American Psychiatric Publishing textbook of mood disorders* (1st ed.). Arlington, VA: American Psychiatric Publishing.

Thase, M. E., & Denko, T. (2008). Pharmacotherapy of mood disorders. *Annual Review of Clinical Psychology, 4,* 53–91. doi:10.1146/annurev.clinpsy.2.022305.095301

Vargas, J. M., & Adesso, V. J. (1976). A comparison of aversion therapies for nailbiting behavior. *Behavior Therapy, 7*(3), 322–329. doi:10.1016/S0005-7894(76)80058-5

Wang, P. S., Berglund, P., Olfson, M., Pincus, H. A., Wells, K. B., & Kessler, R. C. (2005). Failure and delay in initial treatment contact after first onset of mental disorders in the National Comorbidity Survey Replication. *Archives of General Psychiatry, 62*(6), 603–613. doi:10.1001/archpsyc.62.6.603

Yalom, I. D., & Leszcz, M. (2005). *Theory and practice of group psychotherapy* (5th ed.). New York: Basic Books.

Zuckerbrot, R. A. (2007). Combined fluoxetine plus cognitive behavioural therapy is more effective than monotherapy or placebo for adolescents with depression. *Evidence-Based Mental Health, 10*(3), 1393–1403. doi:10.1136/ebmh.10.3.84

Chapter Overview ▼

16.1 Social Thought and Behavior
Groups
Core Social Motives

CONCEPT LEARNING CHECK **16.1** *Describing Social Roles*

16.2 Person Perception
Social Categorization
Physical Appearance
Stereotypes
Subjectivity
Culture and Person Perception

CONCEPT LEARNING CHECK **16.2** *Person Perception and Musical Tastes*

16.3 Attribution: The Person or the Situation?
Fundamental Attribution Error
Actor-Observer Bias
Defensive Attribution
Self-Serving Bias

CONCEPT LEARNING CHECK **16.3** *Explaining Attributional Biases*

16.4 Attitudes and Social Judgments
Components of Attitudes
Relieving Cognitive Dissonance
Influencing Attitudes: Persuasion
The Foot-in-the-Door Technique
Role Playing Affects Attitudes
Culture and Attitudes

CONCEPT LEARNING CHECK **16.4** *Explaining Persuasion*

16 Social Psychology

Learning Objectives ▼

16.1
- Define social psychology.
- Compare and contrast social cognition, social influence, and social norms.
- Describe the core social motives.

16.2
- Illustrate social categorization.
- Discuss how stereotypes and subjectivity impact personal perception.

16.3
- Explain the various types of attribution.

16.4
- Describe the components of attitudes.
- Illustrate the different ways to influence attitudes.

16.5
- Differentiate between conformity, obedience, and compliance.

16.6
- Describe the biological, psychological, and sociocultural aspects of prejudice, aggression, and attraction.

16.7
- Discuss the pros and cons of group influence on an individual.

16.5 Conformity and Obedience
Conformity
The Power of the Situation: The Stanford Prison Experiment
Obedience
  Milgram's Experiment
CRITICAL THINKING APPLICATION

CONCEPT LEARNING CHECK 16.5
Distinguishing Conformity, Obedience, and Compliance

16.6 Social Interactions
Prejudice
Aggression
  Biology of Aggression
  Psychological and Sociocultural Aspects of Aggression

Media Impact: The Impact of TV, Movies, Music, and Videogames
Factors in Attraction
  Competence
  Proximity
  Physical Attractiveness
  Similarity
  Reciprocity

CONCEPT LEARNING CHECK 16.6 *Designing for Friendships*

16.7 Group Influence on the Individual
Altruism
  Bystander Intervention
Effects of Group Interaction
Decision Making

Group Polarization
Groupthink
  Individual Influence
Social Loafing
Social Facilitation
Deindividuation
Summary of Multiple Influences on Social Psychology

CONCEPT LEARNING CHECK 16.7 *Preventing Groupthink*

Throughout my life, I have encountered my share of wounding acts of discrimination, along with the lesser nicks of mostly harmless and even humorous assumptions that others have made. The range of these experiences has been vast. Once, upon reading my name, "Dr. Carter," on my credit card, a man asked me if that was my "rap name." Another time, when I was wearing a tuxedo at my friend's wedding, a man handed me his coat because he thought that I was a member of the hotel staff. On a different occasion, when I arrived to pick up a rented academic robe before a college graduation ceremony, a kind woman told me, "When you see Dr. Carter, please tell him to hang the regalia up to ease out the wrinkles." My youthful appearance, my race, or a mixture of both had motivated the assumptions these people made about who I was. But none of these experiences prepared me for the assumptions of a 5-year-old girl at a cupcake shop.

You see, most days when I have exercised, and many days when I have not, I treat myself to a cupcake at a local bakery within walking distance of my house. It is a quirky place with mismatched tables and chairs, walls lined with built-in bookshelves, and stacks and stacks of used books for sale. Some wall space is reserved for posters of local bands and other announcements. In the front of the establishment are the gems: dozens of puffy, fluffy cupcakes in a kaleidoscope of colors, encrusted with crunchy candy bits. They occupy a once-revolving 5-foot-tall glass case. It is one of those local places full of Southern charm, where they come to expect you. The owners delight in coming up with surprises for regulars.

"Hey, what will it be today?" one of the bakers said with a slight smile, because I nearly always order exactly the same item.

"Oh . . . hmm . . . I . . . think I'll have . . . one cupcake to go, please," I said, doing my best to make it sound like I gave it some thought.

"I thought so," she replied. "I actually saved something special for you in the back. Wait right here, Hun." She popped to the back of the shop and was quickly replaced by a little girl who must have been 5 years old and who was dressed like a fairy princess.

"Hi," she said, "My mom is gone to get you a special cupcake. Are you a president?"

"Hello," I responded, and then I did not know how to answer. Thinking I must have misunderstood, I said, "I'm sorry, I don't understand. Am I a what?"

"Are you a president?"

"Oh . . . no." I laughed. "Are *you* a president?"

"No, silly; black people can be a president, like him." She pointed to a poster of Barack Obama. Then it suddenly hit me: She must have thought that all black people were presidents.

For the rest of the day, I wondered what led to the little girl's assumptions about me and people who she thought were similar to me. What kinds of experiences influenced her assumptions?

16.1 Social Thought and Behavior

The way people think about others influences the way they relate to them.

- Define social psychology.
- Compare and contrast social cognition, social influence, and social norms.
- Describe the core social motives.

Think about the many roles you play. In any given day, your **role** might be a student, a customer, a son or daughter, a parent, and an employee, each with its own set of customary behaviors based on your position. Your assumptions and thoughts about how these **social roles** function is called a **schema**. Schemas are sets of thoughts and presumptions and they help define the roles you play.

The roles you play involve multiple tasks, and for the most part, you slide easily from one role to another. Take ordering a cupcake in a bakery, for example. This activity involves taking on the role of a customer, holding certain expectations, and performing tasks associated with that role: You locate the bakery; you expect to be greeted by a polite, knowledgeable employee; you make your selection, and the employee wraps it and presents it to you as you pay for it. Ordering a cupcake follows an expected pattern, like a script for a play. The ability to perform various roles helps make life easier, because knowing these roles and their scripts can reduce the uncertainty of otherwise complex social situations. When everyone has a role to play, everyone generally knows what is expected.

Schemas, then, are like cognitive shorthand, internalized scripts, based on assumptions about the behaviors that occur in social situations. Schemas are efficient. They enable you to walk into new situations and figure out pretty quickly what to do. You can, for example, walk into an unfamiliar restaurant and determine the roles and expectations with minimal effort. Schemas and roles can also lead you to make mistakes in unfamiliar or uncommon social situations. For example, assumptions about one's expected behavior at a wedding, a funeral, or a large family gathering can vary drastically according to social and cultural norms or expectations. Finally, both schemas and roles can reveal the complex backstory of how humans sort out social situations. In this chapter, we will examine how you think, feel, and behave in relation to the social roles and social influences you encounter.

Psychology studies mental processes and behavior. As we have discussed in other chapters, many things can influence your thoughts and behavior. Some of the most prevalent influences are those that involve other people. Other people—even imagined others—can have a huge impact on your behavior. The presence of other people can cause you to work harder or even pull back on your effort. Your thoughts about other people can influence how you treat them. **Social psychology** is the branch of psychology that focuses on how people's thoughts, feelings, and behavior influence and are influenced by others. It also examines the ways we explain the behavior of others, make social connections, and form or justify our own attitudes and opinions. As a social science, social psychology applies the scientific method of formulating and testing theories—in this case, theories about how people think and behave in relation to others. As we will see, several of the more famous of these social scientific experiments offer unique insights into what it means to be human in a social context.

Groups

Groups are collections of people who have something in common. They can be as small as two people or as large as several million. The concept of the group is fundamental to social psychology, which examines the person as part of a group as well as the group's

Role A set of customary behaviors based on your position.

Social roles Assumptions about the way people should behave given their status.

Schema A structured set of thoughts and presumptions.

Social psychology The branch of psychology that focuses on how the way people think, feel, and behave influences and is influenced by others.

Group Collection of people who have something in common.

Social cognition Thoughts people use to understand their social world.

Social influence The way behavior is shaped.

Social norm An expectation about customary behaviors based on a person's position.

influence on the person. We will examine various aspects of groups later in the chapter; however, two important areas related to the study of groups are social cognition and social influence. **Social cognition** refers to the way our thoughts and assumptions about other people help shape our attitudes and behaviors toward them. **Social influence** refers to the way other people and events directly influence and change our attitudes and behavior. These two areas of study offer two different ways of thinking about, observing, and sometimes predicting attitudes and social behavior.

People in groups rely on their expectations of each other. **Social norms** are the expectations we have for the behaviors of others and ourselves, helping to define what we expect people to do and how we might expect them to behave. Social norms associated with specific circumstances, like that of a teacher in a classroom, are called social roles. Sometimes roles and norms are clearly spelled out and expectations are well defined, both for the people in a particular social role and for those who may find themselves part of the environment, even temporarily. For example, if all employees of a department store wear red shirts and tan pants, then you might expect that everyone dressed that way works there. The role of the salespeople is defined, so it is considered okay for customers to approach them and ask about the location of items in the store. If you are a customer unfortunate enough to have chosen to wear a red shirt and tan pants that day, then strangers are likely to approach you to ask for assistance. Those strangers might be confused to discover that you do not work there.

Roles can also carry with them power differences and social status. Managers in a department store may direct the sales associates, for example. Often, the higher the status someone has, the more power, money, and decision-making power he or she possesses within the group.

Groups can be as small as two and as large as millions.

Core Social Motives

Several things direct and influence behavior. For example, more often than not, people are motivated to belong and to be correct. These principles can direct how we operate in the social world.

Susan Fiske (Fiske, 2003) classified five core social motives—belonging, understanding, controlling, enhancing self, and trusting, or BUC(k)ET.

1. Belonging. People are motivated to join together and to create relationships.
2. Understanding. People are motivated to make sense of the world. This helps people to predict their own behavior and the behavior of others.
3. Controlling. People are motivated to exert power over the things that happen.
4. Enhancing self. People are motivated to feel and be perceived as worthy.
5. Trusting. People are motivated to see the world in a positive light.

For example, in an effort to enhance self, people like to see their own behavior as typical. That is, most people tend to believe that they are correct and figure that others would respond to situations or information in the same ways that they would. The habit of seeing our own behavior as typical is called the **false consensus effect**. A similar shortcut in our thinking is the **availability heuristic**: The more quickly we can think of an example of something, the more likely we suppose it must be true. We can easily identify examples of our own behavior and opinions, so according to the availability heuristic, we see our own opinions and thoughts as common opinions and thoughts. These core social motives influence our social interactions.

Social norms are the expectations we have for the behaviors of others.

CONCEPT LEARNING CHECK 16.1   *Describing Social Roles*

1. Describe some typical roles involved in ordering a meal at a fine restaurant. List the social roles and briefly describe the behavioral expectations associated with each role.

16.2 Person Perception

Person perception includes the way people categorize and react to others.

- Illustrate social categorization.
- Discuss how stereotypes and subjectivity impact personal perception.

How do we form opinions about others? Psychologists call this issue **person perception**. Person perception includes **social categorization**, or the way we sort or tag people into various types, often depending on physical appearance, stereotype, and our personal and cultural beliefs about people. Person perception also includes biases that affect our opinions about others, the information we use to form them, and their accuracy.

We often pay particularly close attention to negative behaviors, called a negativity bias. When we catch a glimpse of something negative about a person, we are more likely to assume that the negative behavior is a snapshot into the person's personality (Baumeister et al., 2001; Taylor, Peplau, & Sears, 2005). This happens, in part, because negative stimuli grab our attention more than positive stimuli do (Smith et al., 2003). On a recent trip, I saw a man shuffle luggage in the overhead bin to make room for his bags. Frustrated and in a rush, he took out another passenger's bag and left it in the aisle. The owner of the bags reminded him to return it, barking, "You can't leave my bag there! Put it back!"

I then overheard the owner of the bag say to the passenger sitting next to him, "I can't imagine what his wife must go through every day." He was assuming that the other passenger's behavior was typical of his behavior at all times. Negative information affects our first impressions much more strongly than the good things we notice about others (Carney, Colvin, & Hall, 2007).

Social Categorization

Social categorization involves the mental sorting of people into groups. We form opinions of others almost instantly, sometimes with only the smallest slices of information to go on. Without even being fully aware of it, we automatically tag the people we see as members of one or several groups (Seger, Smith, & Mackie, 2009). We mentally tag people into lots of categories, including race, gender, age, or in terms of their role. At the grocery store, when we look around, we see categories of people: customers waiting in line, clerks, and baggers. Categorization reflects the core social motive to understand our world. We tend to minimize behaviors that make individuals unique and focus attention on the behaviors that are linked to their category or role.

First impressions can determine how we tag or assess others. We do not pay attention to everything about other people. Instead, we use environmental cues to determine what aspects of other people to focus on. Unusual features especially grab our attention, and small, unimportant details can too: "Why is that person holding her hand *that* way?" We try our best to ascribe meaning to the behavior of others.

Sometimes we interpret the same behavior differently depending on the context. If we see a person painting her nails at a bus stop, we might see her as tidy, careful, and concerned about her appearance. If a representative at a ticket counter is painting her nails, we might see her as inattentive and careless. We may assume that this single example of her behavior represents the kind of person she is.

Physical Appearance

Person perception initially involves using physical appearance to assess others. We first notice nonverbal cues about people: how they walk, gesture, dress, facial expressions. These behaviors deliver a lot of information (Ambady & Rosenthal, 1993). People even judge personality traits based upon how a person looks. We glean information about their level of comfort or even mood (Ambady, Hallahan, & Conner, 1999). Instead of simply looking at someone, we examine, analyze, and do our best to explain why they look the way they look. The results of our analysis can go a long way in determining how we might interact with and respond to the person.

False consensus effect The habit of seeing our own behavior as typical.

Availability heuristic A thinking shortcut in which the more quickly a person can think of an example of something, the more likely he or she supposes it must be true.

Person perception Involves the way we form opinions about others.

Social categorization Mental sorting of people into groups.

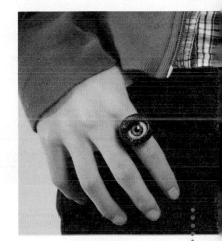

People focus on unusual features in order to predict behavior or personality.

How you interpret behavior depends on the context. You might see this woman as being tidy and careful.

If you are waiting in line for assistance, you might see this woman as being inattentive and careless.

Person perception suggests that people categorize others based, in part, on physical appearance. Would you choose a seat next to this person if you were looking for someone quiet to sit next to on the bus?

It can take less than 1/10 of a second to determine whether or not you trust this man. Person perception suggests you can make a decision like this outside of your awareness.

For example, on a train, you might notice a person's posture, dress, gender, or age to determine what kind of music you think he might like. You may use physical cues to determine whom you would like to sit next to.

We do this incredibly quickly. One study suggested that it takes only about 1/10 of a second to determine how much we trust a person just based on the way he or she looks (Willis & Todorov, 2006).

Stereotypes

In order to make decisions about unfamiliar people, we sometimes employ sweeping generalizations. **Stereotypes** are overgeneralized beliefs—positive or negative—about a group and its members. Stereotypes highlight physical characteristics such as age, gender, or ethnicity, and suggest that people who look alike are alike. You might get ideas about the type of person you think someone is likely to be based on the way someone dresses, how her hair looks, or even the way her name sounds. Stereotypes help sort people into categories that are familiar to us. Although it is easier to think about people in categories than as completely unique individuals, relying on stereotypes can skew the way we see new people, how we perceive their behavior, and our expectations of them.

How do we learn stereotypes? Some researchers believe it is through behavior. People are rewarded for believing certain things. Stereotypes may also be molded through culture as people learn to believe accepted "truths" about groups of people. As we will discus later in the chapter, stereotypes can make up so much of our daily experiences that they affect our behavior without our awareness. Stereotypes develop as early as 6 years of age (Baron & Banaji, 2006).

Although stereotypes can be useful as shortcuts, they may create problems, too. A stereotype can emphasize differences between categorized groups and can create an "us versus them" mentality. Stereotypes can easily become entrenched: If you group together all the people in a given category, it is easy to search for evidence that supports the stereotype and to ignore all the evidence that might not. This minimizes differences within the stereotyped group, making group "members" seem more similar than they really are. What is more, stereotypes can affect initial impressions, which can be long lasting. Acting on initial impressions may cause you to prejudge a person's intentions and actions and can lead to **prejudice** toward the individual. Sometimes people are so convinced that a stereotype is true that when they encounter a person who does not fit the stereotype, they assign that person to a special category rather than changing the stereotype or their belief in it.

Despite these problems, the biological and evolutionary perspective would suggest that stereotypes are essential shortcuts to person perception. If we took the time needed to process individual characteristics to form an impression and decide on the appropriate behavior, this would significantly compromise our chances of survival. For example, automatically categorizing an individual as an "out-group" member may trigger the fight-or-flight response needed for survival.

Subjectivity

How we view other people can be subjective, meaning that our thoughts about them change depending on the situation and our personal feelings. We do not gather and interpret the same information about others in every situation. For example, if you expect to interact with a person only once, like whom you choose to sit next to on a bus, you may focus on very different aspects of their behavior than if you expect to see them every day, like what information you notice about a professor on the first day of a 15-week course. The situation and even our moods affect what information we gather and how we view it.

Culture and Person Perception

Just as situations and subjectivity can impact person perception, culture can also influence the categories and explanations for behaviors we assign to others. Research has demonstrated that those in **individualist cultures**, cultures that place an emphasis on each person rather than on the society, tend to explain a person's behavior as being the result of a person's personality. People in **collectivist cultures**, which are cultures that tend to emphasize the society, are more likely to explain behavior on situational factors (Knowles, Morris, Chiu, & Hong, 2001).

Look at the photos below and see if you can match the image with the kinds of music you think they might like.

A

B

C

D

1. _____ Rock

2. _____ Country

3. _____ Punk

4. _____ Classical

Explain

5. Using the theory of person perception, physical appearance, and social categorization, explain what led you to these assumptions.

16.3 Attribution: The Person or the Situation?

Attributions are the way we explain behavior and can be influenced by assumptions.

■ Explain the various types of attribution.

If it is not clear why a person looks or behaves a certain way, we tend to fill in the blanks with our own ideas of his or her motivation. Sometimes we might focus on an environmental trigger, such as being in a hurry, and other times we rely on a personality explanation, such as that the person is a bully. An **attribution** is a mental explanation of events or behavior. **Attribution theory** is the theory that behavior is explained by situational or personal factors. **Internal attributions** explain behavior based on personality characteristics, while **external attributions** focus on environmental explanations.

Determining an attribution helps us make sense of behavior and predict future behaviors. The problem with attributions is they are often biased. Some common ways that our attributions can be biased include the actor-observer bias, the self-serving bias, and cultural influences on attribution tendencies.

Fundamental Attribution Error

In general, people tend to overestimate the influence of personality characteristics over environmental or situational characteristics when describing the causes of behavior. This tendency is called the **fundamental attribution error**. When we try to explain why someone does something, we tend to think that the behavior is linked to the "kind" of person they are.

Actor-Observer Bias

The fundamental attribution error does not always seem to show up. The way we tend to explain the behavior of other people is very different from the way we tend to explain our own behavior. We are likely to emphasize situational factors when we explain our

Stereotype Overgeneralized beliefs about a group and its members.

Prejudice Negative stereotypes or attitudes about members of a particular group.

Individualist cultures Cultures that place an emphasis on each person's right rather than on the society.

Collectivist cultures A type of culture that prioritizes the group over the individual.

Attribution Our mental explanations of events or behaviors.

Attribution theory The theory that behavior is explained by situational or personal factors.

Internal attribution An explanation of behavior based on personality characteristics.

External attribution An explanation of behavior that focuses on environmental explanations.

Fundamental attribution error An inclination to overestimate the impact of internal characteristics in explaining the behavior of others and underestimate the same characteristics in explaining your own behavior.

Actor A person who exhibits a behavior.

Actor-observer bias The likelihood of assigning an external and situational explanation to your own behavior while assigning internal, personal factors to the behavior of others.

own behavior, but when we explain the behavior of others, we emphasize personality. In a given situation, the **actor** is the person who exhibits a behavior, while the observer is the person who witnesses the behavior. The actor-observer bias is rooted in the idea that we rarely have much information about why someone else behaves in a certain way. Situational factors that motivate a behavior are especially elusive to outside observers, so we tend to attribute others' behavior to personality factors.

When we think about our own behavior, it is just the opposite. We see our own behavior from our own perspective, not as it appears to someone else. We are focused on interacting with our environment as we act, so we attribute our behavior to the situational factors of our environment. Also, we tend to assume that we would choose the best option, while we do not necessarily assume that about others. For example, we think that other people speed because they are aggressive and reckless drivers. But when we speed, it is because someone else caused us to be late. The **actor-observer bias** is our tendency to assign an external and situational explanation to our own behavior while assigning internal, personal factors to the behavior of others (Malle, 2006).

Defensive Attribution

It is common for us to blame others for their own misfortunes. That way, in our minds, it seems less likely that such misfortunes could happen to us. **Defensive attributions** involve blaming people for the bad things that happen to them in order to protect our own feelings and sense of fairness. An example of a defensive attribution is **blaming the victim**, which means attributing the cause of an unfortunate circumstance to the person experiencing it. Defensive attributions help people to feel that the world is fair. The **just-world hypothesis** suggests that we believe that people get what they deserve and deserve what they get. The just-world hypothesis may be linked to the core social motive of controlling, that is, our wish to control our outcomes and manage our world. People feel that they should be rewarded for doing good things and punished for doing bad things. This gives us a feeling of control over the good things that could happen. After all, no one wants to live in a world in which good people do not get what they deserve. It is much more comforting and reassuring to think that if bad things happen to someone, that person must be doing something wrong.

Is this person impatient or is the situation hard to tolerate? According to the actor-observer bias you tend to assign external and situational explanations to your own behavior and personality explanations to the behavior of others.

Self-Serving Bias

There is one exception to the actor-observer bias—when things go well. People tend to take credit when things go well and tend not to when they do not. This is called a **self-serving bias**, which is the tendency to see yourself in a positive light. The actor-observer and self-serving biases primarily protect people's self-esteem and the core social motive of enhancing the self (Trafimow, Armendariz, & Madson, 2004).

CONCEPT LEARNING CHECK 16.3   *Explaining Attributional Biases*

The way we explain our own behavior and the behavior of others is not always an accurate reflection of reality. Fill in each of the following assumptions and behaviors with an appropriate key term. Note what each theory says about why people distort their own and others' behavior.

1. Despite the fact she did not study much for the second exam, Nicole was convinced that the second physics exam was tricky. After all, she studied so hard for the first exam and got a great grade.

2. Wayne suggested the reason his friend's car was broken into was because his friend was careless about where he parked his car. This is strange, because when the same thing happened to Wayne, he said it was because of an increase in neighborhood crime.

3. Anita figured that her roommate's parents must have been doing something wrong if the Internal Revenue Service was auditing them.

16.4 Attitudes and Social Judgments

Attitudes contain affective, behavioral, and cognitive components and can be shaped to relieve the discomfort people feel when the components are not in harmony.

- Describe the components of attitudes.
- Illustrate the different ways to influence attitudes.

An **attitude** is a tendency to judge people, objects, or issues in a certain way. Some of our attitudes are front and center in our minds. Others fly under the radar, implicit; we may be unaware of their influences on our actions. Attitudes can be shaped by culture, experience, situations, and even pressure from others or the need to be consistent. We have attitudes about all sorts of things. Psychologists are concerned with how attitudes are created and changed. Attitudes can impact our interactions with people as well as ourselves: When we find that we have attitudes or behaviors that are inconsistent, we work hard to make them consistent.

Components of Attitudes

You might think that people would generally behave in ways consistent with their attitudes. Psychologists have found that the relationship between attitudes and behavior is sometimes complex. Attitude involves **a**ffects (emotions), **b**ehaviors (actions), and **c**ognitions (thoughts—ABC) FIGURE 16-1. When affects, behaviors, and cognitions are in harmony, it is easy to understand a person's motivation. For example, Edwin hates bananas (affective component); he thinks bananas give him indigestion (cognitive); so he will not eat them (behavioral).

However, sometimes social norms are not consistent with your attitudinal affects, behaviors, or cognitions. This disrupts the usual correspondence among these elements and creates internal tension or **conflict** (Ajzen, 2005). If Edwin's roommate is nice enough to surprise him with banana pancakes for breakfast, he might eat them even though he hates bananas.

Examining our behavior can help us learn about our attitudes. According to **self-perception theory** (Bem, 1967), we are not fully aware of our attitudes. In many cases, we infer our attitudes and preferences based on our behavior. This is interesting because we assume that our attitudes determine our behavior, not the other way around. For the most part, however, the theory applies to attitudes that could be considered trivial, such as a preference for a certain color or a type of food. Attitudes can also be shaped by a change in behavior (Webb & Sheeran, 2006). Nevertheless, cognitions are likely to predict behaviors, especially when the person holds an especially strong attitude, is very aware of the attitude, or discusses the attitude often (Ajzen, 2005).

People are less likely to help if they believe the victim is the cause of the misfortune. If this person dropped his papers because he was texting while walking up the stairs we might be less likely to offer assistance.

Defensive attribution Blaming people for bad things that happen to them in order to protect your own feelings.

Blaming the victim The tendency to attribute the cause of an unfortunate circumstance to the person experiencing it.

Just-world hypothesis A belief that people get what they deserve and deserve what they get.

Self-serving bias The tendency to see yourself in a positive light.

Attitude A tendency to judge people, objects, or issues in a certain way.

Conflict A situation that involves incompatible objectives.

Self-perception theory The theory that suggests that people discover their attitudes while observing their own behavior.

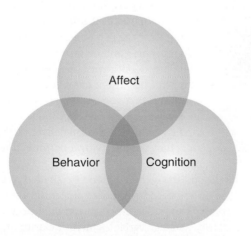

FIGURE 16-1 Attitudes consist of affects, behaviors, and cognitions.

Cognitive dissonance theory
The theory that we try to decrease our discomfort when holding two competing ideas at the same time by changing either our ideas or our behaviors.

Cognitive dissonance
Discomfort that you experience from holding two competing ideas at the same time.

Persuasion Convincing another person.

Central route to persuasion
A constructive response to an argument that focuses solely on the argument's merits.

Peripheral route to persuasion Influence based on small, noncore factors.

Relieving Cognitive Dissonance

You will recall that understanding is a core social motive. It is important for people to see behavior and attitudes as consistent, which makes understanding easier. According to **cognitive dissonance theory** (Festinger, 1957), when we hold two or more conflicting ideas, we try to decrease the discomfort this causes by changing our ideas and/or our behaviors. **Cognitive dissonance** is the discomfort that you experience from holding two or more ideas that oppose one another. Dissonance theory focuses on the differences in the components of a person's attitudes and/or behavior. At times, we sense a conflict—or dissonance—between two or more ideas or between our ideas and our behavior. When this happens, according to the theory, we will change our ideas or behavior enough to resolve the conflict. Often we do this in imperceptible ways, such as modifying our opinion about something or someone. But if we lock ourselves into a decision with no obvious escape, we may need to perform mental acrobatics to relieve the dissonance we experience. This has been the case with doomsday groups who have predicted the end of the world more than a few times. Social psychologist Leon Festinger FIGURE 16-2 (Festinger, Riecken, & Schachter, 2011) embedded himself in a doomsday group to try to understand their attitudes and actions. As the doomsday date approached, members gave away their possessions in preparation for what they fervently believed would be the end of the world. When the world did not end, there was a great amount of cognitive dissonance to be relieved. They were faced with two starkly conflicting thoughts or cognitions. Cognition one: They believed fervently (causing them to behave somewhat recklessly) that the world would end on a particular date. Cognition two: The world did not end on that date. How could the group's members resolve their cognitive dissonance? One way might have been to dismiss the group's leader as a fool or a charlatan. But this would have meant admitting they had been foolish and taken advantage of. Instead, many of the group's members latched on to a third cognition that resolved the dissonance of the first two: They decided that their fervent belief had actually *delayed* the end of the world. Armed with this explanation, they became even more entrenched in their belief that the end was near.

Influencing Attitudes: Persuasion

It seems as though there is always someone trying to change our attitudes. After all, we are inundated with as many as 3,000 advertisements per day (Huston et al., 1992). **Persuasion** is convincing another person to do or believe something. Attempts to sway opinions are not solely the realm of fast food restaurants and soda producers. Family, friends, and teachers do this all the time. Luckily, we are not changed by every attempt. Psychologists are interested in what kinds of messages do change our attitudes.

Persuasion can be more or less effective depending on how people examine the evidence that a would-be persuader offers. Using the **central route to persuasion** means that we examine the logical links of the persuader's argument. For example, you might choose a toothbrush based on how well the toothbrush cleans. People focus solely on the argument's merits and then we decide on a constructive response.

FIGURE 16-2 American social psychologist Leon Festinger (1919–1989).

But we do not always do that. Often, people use a **peripheral route to persuasion** in which their attitudes are influenced not by the merits of the persuader's argument but by insignificant, noncore factors—for example, if you buy a toothbrush not because it cleans better but because it has a comic book character on it that you really like. When people are swayed by surface aspects, such as how much they like the person delivering the message, they are following a peripheral route to persuasion.

If you are convinced by how a salesperson looks, you are employing the peripheral route to persuasion.

Several things can increase the likelihood that others will be persuaded to change their attitudes. Persuasion can be more or less successful based upon the source, the message, or the audience. Source factors that can increase persuasion include authority, likability, expertise, credibility, and similarity. Message variables include clarity, organization, and directness (direct attempts to persuade are less likely to change behavior than indirect messages). Audience factors include mood. Being in a good mood makes us easier to persuade—which is why buttering someone up with compliments is often a strategy of persuasion. In addition to these general techniques, there are other strategies for persuasion, including the foot-in-the-door technique and behavioral techniques.

The Foot-in-the-Door Technique

It is easier to persuade someone to comply with a small request than with a larger one. But once someone agrees to a small request, it is more likely that he or she will go along with a larger and more unreasonable request. This is called the **foot-in-the-door technique**, and it is commonly used as a way to secure agreement. The larger request may have been declined were it not preceded by the smaller request.

Self-perception theory can explain the mechanism behind this technique. When we comply with the small request, our attitude shifts. In order to maintain consistency with our previous attitude, we agree to the larger request. If you were willing to do a small thing, then it is likely you are willing to do the larger things (Meineri & Guéguen, 2008). Complying with a small request makes people believe they must be committed to the issue.

By contrast, the **door-in-the-face technique** starts off with an unreasonable request that will most likely be turned down, followed by a second, more reasonable request that is more likely to be accepted. The door-in-the-face technique secures agreement because the person who turned down the extreme request does not want to appear unreasonable in the face of a compromise over a smaller request.

> **Foot-in-the-door technique**
> A practice by which agreement to a small request makes agreement to a more unreasonable request more likely.
>
> **Door-in-the-face technique**
> A practice by which rejecting an unreasonable request will lead to a more reasonable request that is more likely to be accepted.

Role Playing Affects Attitudes

Even playing a role will increase your chances of preferring something. Self-perception theory suggests that the more work you put into something, even if playing a role, and pretending to like it, the more likely you are to have a shift or prefer that thing. In some ways, you convince yourself that you must possess that attitude if you went through that effort.

Attitudes can also be strengthened when a person goes through discomfort on behalf of an attitude. This discomfort means either that the cause is important or that you like to be uncomfortable. If you have gone through so much, it must be worth it.

Culture and Attitudes

Since attitudes are learned, culture can have a tremendous influence on the norms governing our attitudes. Some of the things that you might have strong attitudes about—being an organ donor, for example—are culturally influenced and may be drastically different in different parts of the world. Individualist cultures tend to emphasize the importance of being a unique individual, while collectivist cultures may emphasize their allegiance to certain groups (Hoshimo-Browne et al., 2005).

The fact that we experience dissonance and self-doubt when we act in a way that is not in harmony with our attitudes is also influenced by culture. In individualistic cultures, dissonance is more likely to be caused by acting in a way that is different from a belief, such as when a person spanks a child for fighting at school. In collectivist cultures, however, dissonance is more likely to happen in a situation that creates doubt in a person's standing and character in the community rather than how a person might define him- or herself (Kitayama, Snibbe, Markus, & Suzuki, 2004).

CONCEPT LEARNING CHECK 16.4 | *Explaining Persuasion*

Think back to the last time you purchased something because you were persuaded by an advertisement. Use some of the following terms to explain what influenced your behaviors.

- Affect
- Behavior
- Cognition
- Self-perception theory

(Continues)

- Cognitive dissonance
- Persuasion
- Central route to persuasion
- Peripheral route to persuasion
- Foot-in-the-door technique

Conformity Changing your thoughts or behavior to align with those of another.

Obedience Behavior that is in response to the orders of another.

Compliance Shifting behavior because of a request.

16.5 Conformity and Obedience

Affects, behaviors, and cognitions can be shaped by conformity and obedience.

■ Differentiate between conformity, obedience, and compliance.

There are many good reasons to change your behavior. You might do so because of a request from another person, in order to go along with a group, or because of a direct order from another person. There are many good reasons to follow rules, orders, and instructions. Following rules, even unwritten ones, makes getting along more easily, and sometimes not doing so means suffering painful consequences. Not cutting in line at a store, for example, is usually driven by the social pressure of the other people waiting. **Conformity** involves changing your thoughts or behavior to align with someone else's, while **obedience** involves a change in your behavior in response to the orders of another. **Compliance** involves shifting your behavior because of requests. What factors make these shifts in behavior likely to happen and what kinds of orders people obey are the kinds of questions that interest social psychologists.

Conformity

Obedience involves a change in behavior in response to the orders of another.

Conformity involves aligning your thoughts or behavior with those of another. When we conform, we alter what we do or believe in order to align with a person or a group. The need to conform can be, in part, due to social pressures and norms (**normative social influence**). Normative social influence is linked to the core social motive of belonging. Internally, those who conform may feel more accepted. They may determine the best thing to do based on the actions of other people. You will recall that a basic core principle of social psychology is to be correct. Often, people will conform in order to be correct, which, in turn, can increase self-esteem. Conformity in order to be correct is called **informational social influence**. Informational social influence helps us to enhance the self. Two classic experiments studied the power of roles and conformity: the Asch line experiment (Asch, 1956) and the Stanford Prison experiment (Zimbardo, 2008).

Social psychologist Solomon Asch conducted an experiment to determine if people would conform when they knew for sure that their conforming behavior was wrong. After all, social psychology would predict that people, all other things being equal, like being right. Which would win over—the pressure to be correct or the pressure to conform?

Social pressure to conform is known as normative social influence.

Subjects in the experiment were asked to perform the simple task of identifying which of three lines was the same length as a target line (such as the lines in FIGURE 16-3). One line was exactly the same length as the target line and the other two were entirely different. Five people were shown the line. After the lines were displayed, each subject stated his answer. One by one, everyone agreed. This was repeated twice more with exactly the same results. The third time, something was different. Even though it was obvious that A was the correct answer, the first person responded with a confident "C." The second: "C." How could this be? Well, the experiment was rigged. The only true participant, or test subject, was the last person to answer. The others were all "confederates," or accomplices who worked for the researcher. Would the desire to be correct win over the desire to conform? Subjects gave the obviously incorrect answer some 35% of the time, with 75% conforming at least once.

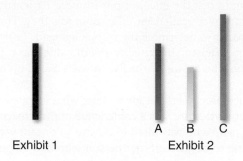

FIGURE 16-3 Lines like these were used in the Asch experiment. The reference line is on the left and the lines on the right were the three comparison lines.

Exhibit 1

A   B   C
Exhibit 2

The Power of the Situation: The Stanford Prison Experiment

To examine the power of roles and conformity, psychologist Philip Zimbardo FIGURE 16-4 recruited 24 male participants from Stanford University to be part of a study. They were randomly assigned to play the roles of either prisoners or guards in a simulated prison in the basement of a building on campus for 2 weeks. The guards wore uniforms and were outfitted with clubs. The prisoners were referred to by serial numbers. Before long, people fell into their roles, perhaps too well. The guards became offensive and insulting to the prisoners, who soon became passive and helpless. The entire situation got so out of hand that they abandoned the experiment before the end of the first week.

Obedience

Obedience is behavior that is in response to the orders of another who is perceived to have some form of power or authority. Perhaps the simplest way to get someone to do something is to just ask. Why do people comply with requests? There are several reasons: to obtain a reward, such as points or expertise; to gain information; coercion (when a person forces or intimidates someone else); and personal relationships (such as a friend who needs to be taken to the airport). Legitimate authorities, such as a boss at work, have the right to ask us to do things. Helplessness, too, can be a factor, such as when a small child asks for help in tying her shoes or someone asks you to reach something in a grocery store. But would people comply with a request out of "blind obedience"? That is what Stanley Milgram wanted to know.

Milgram's Experiment

It was a simple enough question. Would people blindly obey the directions of an authority? This question was on the minds of psychologists all over the world. At the time, World War II had just ended and the atrocities committed in Adolph Hitler's concentration camps were becoming widely known. Many people suggested that even though horrible things were done by officials and guards "just following orders," surely decent people would not and could not follow orders that would harm another person just because they were told to.

Psychology professor Stanley Milgram FIGURE 16-5 (Milgram, 1963) had a plan to test this assumption. He recruited everyday people from mailings and flyers to be part of a study FIGURE 16-6. Milgram's team recruited 40 men who were told that the

Normative social influence The need to conform due to social pressures.

Informational social influence Sway that comes from believing another person.

FIGURE 16-4 Philip Zimbardo's famous prison study examined the power of the situation in creating roles and social norms.

FIGURE 16-5 Milgram and his shock generator.

FIGURE 16-6 Public recruiting announcement used for the Milgram experiment.

study would test the effect of punishment on learning. Two participants were called into the room together. They chose slips of paper to determine the roles. One read "Learner" and the other "Teacher." In actuality, the drawing was rigged and the person who answered the flyer always ended up being the teacher.

In fact, much of the study was not what it appeared to be. The other participant was a confederate of the experimenter's, an adult male who was hired to behave in certain ways while pretending to be just another person who had responded to the flyer. Together, the experimenter and teacher walked the learner into an adjoining room, where he was strapped into a chair with wires and belts to hold him in place. This chair would deliver the shocks that were part of the learning experiment. The teacher also received a 75-volt test shock so he could feel what he would soon dole out. The experimenter and teacher walked back to the main room. A huge, scary-looking machine with switches and knobs with various voltages and labels sat on the table. The experimenter and teacher were together in the same room, and the learner was in an adjacent room FIGURE 16-7. The learner was to remember word pairs; the teacher was to deliver a shock if the learner responded incorrectly. The teacher could stop delivering the shocks whenever he wanted and could leave the experiment at any point.

When the outline of the experiment was described to 20 psychiatrists, they all said that surely the teacher would stop delivering the shocks as soon as the learner requested that he stop. No one would deliver the highest shock. It turned out that the experts severely underestimated the power of the situation on obedience.

When the shock was "delivered," the machine really did nothing. The learner responded based on a predetermined script. Early shocks produced responses like "ouch." Soon, the learner's responses escalated to pleading for the teacher to stop, around 300 volts; then begging to withdraw from the experiment, and falling eerily silent at where the dial read "450 volts." The experimenter provided only mild encouragement such as: "The experiment requires that you continue," and "Please continue." And continue they did. Of the 40 people tested, 2 out of 3 people provided shocks to the very end of the scale, and 100% delivered shocks well beyond what the experts predicted. In the years that followed, Milgram and others replicated the study in various forms with more than 1,000 participants: males, females, varying age and situations. But they came to the same conclusions. The Milgram experiment was repeated at various times and in various countries, and the proportion of "teachers" who continued to shock the "learners" all the way to the top of the scale was always the same—between 61 and 66% (Blass, 1999; Milgram, 2009). The situation is a powerful factor in determining blind obedience.

Milgram did try different variations of the study that decreased the amount of obedience. Situations that decreased obedience included teaming with others who also refused to obey; the learner being in the same room as the teacher; the teacher being alone in the room; or if two experimenters gave different commands. From Milgram's study and others, we have an idea of the kinds of things than can increase and decrease blind obedience to authority, as you can see in **TABLE 16-1**.

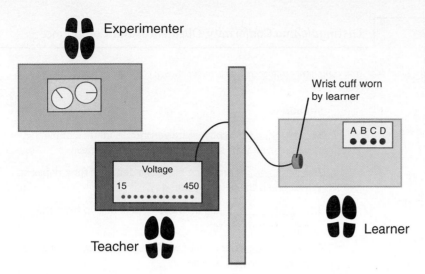

FIGURE 16-7 The Milgram experiment consisted of an experimenter and learner who were both part of the study, and a teacher.

While the participants in the experiment seemed to have no long-term effects from participating in the study, it begs the question about whether the study went too far. The experimenters subjected the teachers to a good deal of anxiety. Many of the teachers felt guilty about having "shocked" strangers and regretted their actions even after discovering no one was hurt. Certainly given the current guidelines for ethical behavior in research, the experiment could not be replicated in its original form.

TABLE 16-1 Factors that Increase and Decrease Conformity

Increase	Decrease
A unanimous group	Seeing others behaving independently
Giving your responses in the open	Low prestige of the person giving orders
Having a difficult task	Disinterest in the approval of others in the group
Having an ambiguous task	High self-confidence
Doubt of your ability	Knowledge of ethics
Attraction to the group	
Possessing low self-esteem	
Having a low amount of leadership potential	
Being in a large group	

Source: Data from Asch, S. E. (1956). Studies of independence and conformity: I. A minority of one against a unanimous majority. Psychological monographs; Deutsch, M., & Gerard, H. B. (1955). A study of normative and informational social influences upon individual judgment. The Journal of Abnormal and Social Psychology, *51 (3), 629; Hofling, C. K., Brotzman, E., Dalrymple, S., Graves, N. & Bierce, C. (1966). An experimental study of nurse-physician relationships.* Journal of Nervous and Mental Disease, 143, *171–180.*

CRITICAL THINKING APPLICATION

Consider the Milgram experiment. Remember, the participants believed they are actually hurting the subjects.

Evaluate

1. Use the core motives of social psychology to explain the behavior of the participants.

2. Using what you know about social psychology, relate the concepts of social psychology to bullying and hazing.

3. Many people who hear about the Milgram experiment suggest they would have behaved differently. How can you explain this response using social psychology?

CONCEPT LEARNING CHECK 16.5   *Distinguishing Conformity, Obedience, and Compliance*

First, match the terms to the definitions of conformity, obedience, and compliance and then distinguish between conformity, obedience, and compliance in the following situations.

A. Compliance

B. Conformity

C. Obedience

Definitions

1. _____ A change in behavior in response to the orders of another.

2. _____ Changing thoughts or behavior to align with another.

3. _____ Shifting your behavior because of a request.

Situations

1. _____ You buy white earphones instead of black because all your friends own white earphones.

2. _____ A professor assigns a deadline for a paper, so you finish the paper by that day.

3. _____ A friend asks you to pick her up from the airport.

4. _____ Your boss at work requests that you change the paper in the photocopier.

5. _____ You consider having a milkshake at dinner, but since all your friends are just having water, you order water, too.

16.6 Social Interactions

The way we relate to each other can reveal our assumptions and influences prejudice, aggression, and attraction.

- Describe the biological, psychological, and sociocultural aspects of prejudice, aggression, and attraction.

Studying social interactions can help us understand how we prejudge people as well as the impact of aggression and attraction on social interactions. Studying and understanding prejudice can help us attempt to diminish the impact of prejudice.

Prejudice

Like all attitudes, prejudice contains three components: an affective, or emotional component (like or dislike toward the group), a behavioral component (acts toward or against a group), and a cognitive component (set of beliefs about the group). Prejudicial affects, beliefs, and behaviors can be strongly resistant to change.

Prejudice is universal. You may have prejudicial attitudes toward or against certain kinds of computers, food, music, areas of the country, body types, or racial groups. Prejudice can be overt or subtle. It can be so ingrained in the culture, it can be difficult to see—especially when it is your own. Prejudice is easier to spot in other people than in yourself.

Prejudice is the way people apply characteristics of and judgments about a group to an individual. Often these characteristics and judgments are negative. Discrimination goes a step further than prejudice. **Discrimination** involves the tendency to act differently toward a member of a particular group.

How prevalent is prejudice? It depends on whom you ask. A recent poll by CNN (2006) revealed that 18% of whites saw racial bias as a serious problem in the United States. The same poll showed that 49% of blacks saw racial bias as a problem FIGURE 16-8.

What reduces prejudice? Exposure alone does not necessarily help (Brewer & Brown, 1998). Rather, working together in a setting in which people are equal, in an environment that fosters friendships, and in which an authority encourages this setting does tend to improve relationships of people with different backgrounds (Pettigrew & Tropp, 2006).

Aggression

Aggression consists of words or physical acts a person does in order to cause harm. There are several types of aggression. **Instrumental aggression**, for example, is aggression that

Discrimination The tendency to act differently toward members of a particular group.

Aggression Words or physical acts that a person does in order to cause harm.

Instrumental aggression Words or physical acts a person does to cause harm in an ultimate goal to obtain something.

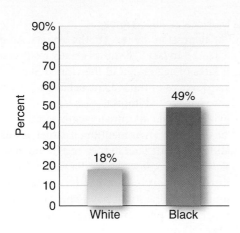

FIGURE 16-8 Prevalence of perceived racial bias based on race of respondant. *Source: Data from CNN poll, December 12, 2006.*

is used to obtain something, like a child who hits another child to obtain a toy truck. **Hostile aggression** is a desire to inflict harm, as seen in bullying.

Biology of Aggression

Biological theories of aggression highlight areas of the brain and brain chemicals associated with aggression. Twin studies have suggested that about 34% of the factors associated with aggression, such as levels of certain hormones and neurotransmitters, could be biological (Brendgen, Vitaro, Boivin, Dionne, & Pérusse, 2006). For example, since a large percentage of people arrested for aggressive crime are men, and since men have higher levels of the sex hormone **testosterone**, research has pointed to the role of testosterone as a chemical associated with aggressive behavior. Newer research has also implicated low levels of **serotonin**, a neurotransmitter involved in sleep, mood, and appetite, as playing a role in aggression. Diminished serotonin is linked to problems in controlling behavior (Seo, Patrick, & Kennealy, 2008).

Certain brain areas are also important in aggression. The **amygdala**, a cluster of neurons in the temporal lobe linked to emotions such as anger and fear, and other areas of the limbic system have been associated with aggressive behavior. For example, damage to limbic system structures can produce aggression even when the person is not threatened (Siever, 2008).

Psychological and Sociocultural Aspects of Aggression

Psychological and social factors are also involved in aggression. Some psychologists point toward observational learning as a way we learn aggression. The Bobo experiments (Bandura, Ross, & Ross, 1961) were designed to find out whether watching aggression could make people more or less aggressive. After all, psychoanalytic theory might suggest that observing aggression could be **cathartic**, involving a release of pent-up emotions, and lead to less aggression in a person. Bandura's experiment involved a room full of toys, including an inflatable Bobo doll. A group of children watched as an adult played in the room with the plastic doll, hitting it, flinging it in the air, and kicking it. Another group of kids did not watch the adult play. Then, one by one, kids were set free to play in the room. Would watching aggression mean the kids would play more or less aggressively? Bandura and his team of researchers watched the kids play and counted only the aggressive acts that were not modeled by the adult. The kicks, punches and flings that the kids saw the adult modeling would not be counted. The children could choose to play however they liked. The result? The kids who watched the aggressive model exhibited more aggressive acts, including attraction to playing with toy guns, than the kids who did not watch the model.

Sociocultural theories of aggression suggest that societal and cultural factors can be important aspects of aggression. After all, crime is much higher in countries that have considerable gaps between poor and rich (Kennedy, Kawachi, Prothrow-Stith, Lochner, & Gupta, 1998). In addition, in cultures of honor, in which reputation is a core part of personality, insults more often result in aggression (Cohen, 2001; Cohen, Nisbett, Bowdle, & Schwarz, 1996).

Hostile aggression Aggression simply to inflict harm.

Testosterone A sex hormone that stimulates production of sperm and development of sex organs in males, and sex drive in males and females.

Serotonin A neurotransmitter involved in sleep, mood, and appetite.

Amygdala A cluster of neurons in the temporal lobe linked to emotions such as anger and fear.

Cathartic An experience that involves the release of pent-up emotions.

Media Impact: The Impact of TV, Movies, Music, and Videogames

It is no surprise that TV shows are full of aggression. By age 18, the average American has seen 40,000 murders (Huston et al., 1992). In fact, TV shows greatly exaggerate the amount of violence compared to actual rates of aggression in the United States. What are missing from the shows are the consequences of the violent behavior, which may unintentionally communicate that violence has limited impact.

Unfortunately, there is a wealth of evidence that exposure to aggressive TV, movies, and music increases aggression (Anderson et al., 2003). As mentioned earlier, it was once thought that viewing aggressive acts would be cathartic and reduce aggression in people, but it appears to do the opposite. People who are exposed to media violence are more aggressive than those who are not exposed to the aggression (Anderson & Bushman, 2001; Villani, 2001). Videogames fare similarly. In one study, boys who were allowed to play aggressive videogames displayed much more physical and verbal aggression than those who were not (Irwin & Gross, 1995).

Factors in Attraction

You will recall that one of the core principles of social psychology is that people like being correct and consistent and like to boost their self-esteem. The same formula attracts us to our friends and romantic interests. We like people who like us and who are competent, physically attractive, and similar to us. Furthermore we seek out these rewards while expending as little effort and cost as possible.

Competence

Surrounding yourself with competent people makes you feel good about who wants to be around you—as long as they are not overly competent. Too much competence can create discomfort. Having flaws, if you are very confident, helps to temper the high levels of confidence (Helmreich, Aronson, & LeFan, 1970).

Proximity

Proximity plays a central role in forming supportive contacts. Festinger (Festinger, 1951) examined friendship patterns among military veterans and their wives living in two student housing projects at the Massachusetts Institute of Technology. People who lived closer to each other were much more likely to become friends than were those whose apartments were farther apart. The exact location of people's apartments also had an effect on what kind of friendships were formed. For example, within the buildings, friendships were highly dependent on whether residents' apartments were centrally located or toward the end of the floor. An explanation for the importance of proximity may be familiarity. All other things being equal, people seem to like objects and people to which they have been exposed to before—this is called the **mere exposure effect** (Moreland & Zajonc, 1982). We tend to prefer things the more we are around them. Through repeated exposure to a person, you may grow to like him or her, and there is a greater chance that the person will become a supportive contact in your interpersonal world.

Mere exposure effect
Repeated exposure to a stimulus leads to preferring that stimulus.

Physical Attractiveness

Another important factor in the early stages of forming supportive contacts is appearance or physical attractiveness (Eagly, Ashmore, Makhijani, & Longo, 1991). Numerous studies have found a strong association between people's perception of others' attractiveness and their positive evaluation of those others as people whom they would like to meet (Dijkstra, Cillessen, Lindenberg, & Veenstra, 2010). In a study of roommates (Carli, Ganley, & Pierce-Otay, 1991), those who perceived their roommates to be attractive were more satisfied with roommate relations. People seem to respond generally favorably to more attractive individuals. Physically attractive people are believed to be nicer people (Lorenzo, Biesanz, & Human, 2010), more skillful verbal communicators (Rosenblat, 2008), and more exciting, sociable, interesting, sensitive, outgoing, nurturing, kind, and modest. People who participated in these studies predicted that physically attractive people would enjoy more satisfying lives, have more social and professional success, and benefit from happier marriages and prestige than less attractive people (Dion, Berscheid, & Walster, 1972). These perceptions may indicate to others that attractive individuals are better able to provide the benefits derived from friendships.

Even though we tend to think that highly attractive people are healthier, happier, and more successful than less attractive people, looks can be deceiving. High levels of attractiveness are not really related to levels of happiness or self-esteem (Major, 1984).

What is attractive? Ignoring the fads that come and go, women who are more youthful looking, and men who are healthy and dominant looking (Cunningham, 1986; Cunningham, Barbee, & Pike, 1990) are considered attractive, and the more average and symmetrical the faces appear, the better (Alley & Cunningham, 1991).

Similarity

Another major determinant of creating contacts is similarity. People tend to gravitate to those who are like themselves. Research suggests that individuals prefer people who are similar to themselves in intelligence, ability, ethnicity, socioeconomic status, and even size. Johnson (Johnson, 1989) discovered that having similar values, interests, and background were strong predictors of friendship in his sample of 50 pairs of friends. Attitudinal similarity may be one of the more powerful factors. When students were told the attitudes of hypothetical strangers, there was a strong and direct relationship between attitude similarity and the students' reports of liking the strangers (Byrne, 1971). Research showed that attitude similarity was a very strong predictor of how much students reported liking each other, even determining seating choice in a classroom (Mackinnon, Jordan, & Wilson, 2011). Some of this similarity is real; however, some may be only perceived similarity, since attitudes and beliefs may bend toward each other over time. There is evidence that similar people are drawn together across cultures and types of relationships (Berscheid & Reis, 1998).

Similarity is an important factor for attraction.

According to the **matching hypothesis**, people are paired to equally attractive partners. People who have similar attitudes may be drawn to each other. Perhaps this is due to our chronic desire to feel validated. Some believe that we overexaggerate similarity to people we like. Despite this, couples are likely to possess similar attitudes, values, and similar levels of attractiveness (Bleske-Rechek, Remiker, & Baker, 2009).

Reciprocity

Reciprocity is an important aspect of human relationships. If someone does something for you, you are more likely to do something for him or her. This principle even extends to liking. Knowing a person thinks you are attractive can also make that person more attractive to you. In addition, people tend to react positively to those who react positively to them (Greitemeyer, 2010). This principle is **reciprocity of liking**. When people like us, they treat us in ways that we appreciate, they smile at us, their eyes brighten when we enter the room, and they cheerfully say hello when we call. It is rewarding when people like us.

> **Matching hypothesis** The belief that people are paired to equally attractive partners.
>
> **Reciprocity of liking** Reacting positively to those who react positively to you.

CONCEPT LEARNING CHECK 16.6 | *Designing for Friendships*

1. A local university that is designing a residential education program has asked you to act as a consultant. You are in charge of helping to design the resident experience. What kinds of features would you include in the living spaces and educational programs to increase friendships and reduce prejudice in the community?

16.7 Group Influence on the Individual

Groups can have a powerful influence on how much an individual will help and on the decision-making and efforts of individuals.

■ Discuss the pros and cons of group influence on an individual.

Think about how you might describe yourself to someone you do not know. You probably would describe yourself as being part of several groups. The groups you belong to are really important. They are linked to your identity, provide a boost of self-esteem, and can be the source of important friendships. Be it your college alma matter, your favorite sports team, or a club, feeling good about the groups you belong to makes you feel good about yourself as well.

Any group we consider ourselves to be included in—"us"—is the in-group. The in-group consists of people who share similar attitudes and identity. We think of people who are not in our group as "them," or the out-group, a social group to which we do not belong. The in-group is special. Once we find ourselves in a group, we immediately treat the members in the group differently. We start to prefer those in our group. **In-group bias** is accepting the attitudes of your own team. We also tend to see the out-group members as being more alike than those in the in-group: "They are all alike." **Out-group homogeneity**, or the idea that members of the out-group are similar to each other, may be the basis of stereotypes and may also lead to discrimination.

According to social identity theory, in-groups raise our self-esteem because we see the members of the group as special. We can sometimes regard those who are not part of the group as inferior. When this is applied toward ethnic groups, it can result in **ethnocentrism**, which involves believing that your own group is superior to others and that it should be the standard by which other cultures are judged. Ethnocentrism can be the basis of prejudice or negative stereotypes and attitudes about members of a particular group.

There are a lot of benefits to being part of a group, and people are highly motivated to be accepted as members of groups. Once you become a member of a group, the group has a great deal of influence over your behavior, perhaps more than you realize. The social power of groups can affect many things, including how much we help or do not help, those in need, as well as the decisions we make while in a group.

Altruism

It is amazing how much we help each other in a given day. Sometimes we help for external reasons, such as to gain favor from another person; sometimes we do so because of internal motivation. We may help because of our attitudes toward helping those in need; we may see ourselves in or identify with those who need help; or we may feel responsible to help, if we can, because of our ethical standards. There are times when we even help for no reason at all.

How do psychologists think about helpful behavior, otherwise known as prosocial behavior? Why is our behavior sometimes governed by **altruism**, which involves being unselfish and helpful to other people? In part, it is because of the **social-responsibility norm**, the assumption that assistance should be given to those in need. We also help those who have helped us. According to the **reciprocity norm**, we are more likely to offer assistance to people who have helped us in the past. Psychologists are interested in why people risk their own safety for the safety of others, as well as why they sometimes refuse to help when someone is in obvious need.

According to Latane and Darley (1970), the decision to offer assistance happens in five distinct stages. Deciding not to help can happen at any point. First, you have to notice the situation and decide if help is needed. If you determine that help is needed, you then must take personal responsibility to assist. Then, you decide what kind of assistance is needed. Finally, you offer your assistance. For example, let us say you notice that someone has dropped a jar full of change in the parking lot. You first assess whether you should help (are they with someone else?). Then you decide what kind of help that person needs (just some help picking up the change) and you offer assistance if you think you can help.

Another theory of helping suggests that we feel distress when we see someone who needs help. Helping reduces that distress. However, offering help can come at a price. We offer to help when the cost of offering is less than enduring the distress of seeing the person in need (Dovidio, Piliavin, Gaertner, Schroeder, & Clark, 1991).

In addition to these models, there are also social forces that have an impact on helping.

Bystander Intervention

Imagine you are on the street, walking home, and you find yourself in a situation in which you need help. Would you prefer that you have just one stranger around who might provide assistance, or would you prefer three dozen? Before you answer, consider the story of a woman in a similar situation that launched dozens of research investigations into bystander intervention.

Kitty Genovese was attacked and stabbed one night as she returned home from work (Rosenthal, 2008). The attack happened in her neighborhood, over a grueling

Sometimes people offer assistance for personal gain and not as an act of altruism.

There are many reasons for prosocial behavior including the social responsibility norm, the assumption that assistance should be offered to those in need.

In-group bias Accepting the attitudes of your own team.

Out-group homogeneity The tendency for members of an out-group to seem similar to each other.

30-minute timespan. Her neighbors heard her screams, most likely. Some said that up to 38 people reported hearing the screams and cries for help, yet no one even picked up the phone to call the police during the attack. Reports said that about 20 minutes after she died, the police were finally called, and that they arrived about 2 minutes after the phone call. After the call was made, it was, of course, too late. It turns out that the situation was stacked against Kitty due to the psychology of bystander intervention.

Psychologists interested in helping behavior are especially interested in whether a bystander will offer assistance. One factor determining whether bystanders decide to help is **diffusion of responsibility**, which occurs when the responsibility to help is spread across a crowd. If you are the only person around, then you have to assume responsibility to help. If you and another person are present, then each of you might think that the other person will help. If there are 38 people present, then you have 37 other people who could assume the responsibility, 37 others you could blame if help was not called, and 37 people to share in the guilt if nothing is done. The more people who are around, the less likely it is that a bystander will offer assistance (Fischer et al., 2011). How can this be? It would seem that if more people were around, it would be more likely that someone would help. Do groups make us heartless and uncaring? No. Groups lead us to assume that someone else has already offered their help. The **bystander effect** is a phenomenon in which people in groups are less likely to offer assistance than they would be by themselves.

To test the bystander effect and diffusion of responsibility, psychologists had participants fill out a questionnaire in a room. Some were tested alone; others were tested with one other person and some with two others. As they were diligently filling out the questionnaires, the room filled with ominous smoke. When the participants were by themselves, three out of four reported the smoke. However, as the number of bystanders increased to three, it dropped to one out of three reporting the smoke. In general, when alone, 75% of people will offer to help. It drops to just over half (53%) when in a group (Latane & Nida, 1981).

Besides diffusion of responsibility, there are other factors that increase and decrease bystander helping TABLE 16-2. Some argue that seeing others not helping makes it easier to assume that the situation is not urgent, and that this assumption reduces the likelihood of helping. Seeing others not react can lead us to believe that everything is okay. "See something, say something" campaigns are meant to create a sense of responsibility and to call people to action in order to reduce diffusion of responsibility.

Effects of Group Interaction

People tend to clump together and form groups. People live in cities and form sports teams, work groups, and even Internet chat groups. Humans seem to have a fondness for bonding. These groups, whether virtual or physical, are influenced by the people in them, and being a member of the group influences the individuals, too. Almost instantly, people begin to imitate the behaviors of the individuals in the group, look for a group leader, and tend to prefer their group's members over nonmembers.

You probably belong to dozens of groups—sports groups, classroom groups, maybe a sorority, fraternity, or even a secret society. Some groups last a lifetime. I will always feel like a member of the Spring Valley High School Class of 1985 (Go Vikings!). Other groups are quick to form and vanish nearly as instantly, like the one made up of the three people I stood next to for 4 minutes waiting for the campus shuttle.

Catherine (Kitty) Genovese.

Ethnocentrism Believing that your own group is superior to others and should be the standard by which other cultures are judged.

Altruism Being unselfish and helpful toward other people.

Social-responsibility norm The assumption that assistance should be given to those in need.

Reciprocity norm An assumption that you should behave positively toward those who have helped you.

Diffusion of responsibility The tendency for the responsibility to help is spread across a crowd.

TABLE 16-2 Factors that Increase and Decrease Bystander Assistance

Increase	Decrease
We know the victim	Rushed
In-group member requires assistance	Situation is ambiguous
Good mood	Might be injured
The person is dependent on others (like a child)	Out-group member needs help
	We perceive that the victim is responsible for needing help

People are less likely to offer help if they believe that help has already been offered.

Bystander effect A phenomenon in which people are less likely to offer assistance to someone in need while in groups than they are by themselves.

Group polarization The likelihood that the attitudes of members of a team will become more similar over time.

Groupthink When a group's ideals become so important that alternative ideas are dismissed.

We can form in-group and out-group preferences almost instantly and prefer members of our in-group without even meeting them. In a study by Tajfel, Billig, Bundy, and Flament (1971), a group of about 50 students were shown slides of paintings by two different artists. They were asked to view the slides and indicate their preferences. The participants thought they were being placed into groups according to their preferences, but actually they were randomly assigned into one of the two groups. Then the subjects, newly aware of their group status, were asked to allocate money to the other participants. The researchers discovered that the subjects tended to favor their own group—quite a bit, as you can see in FIGURE 16-9. The study revealed a strong in-group bias, in which they were more accepting of the members of their own group.

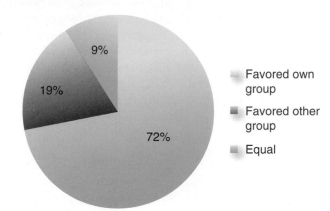

FIGURE 16-9 Even when placed into random groups people were more likely to assign money to their own group members (blue) than to members of other groups (red).
Source: Tajfel, H., Billig, M. G., Bundy, R. P., & Flament, C. (1971). Social categorization and intergroup behavior. European Journal of Social Psychology, 1(2), 149–178.

- 9% Favored own group
- 19% Favored other group
- 72% Equal

Decision Making

Making decisions is not always easy. Making decisions in a group can be even more difficult. A lot of important decisions happen in groups. From serious ones like jury decisions to more light-hearted ones like where to have a family reunion or a birthday party, group decision making is much more complicated than making a decision by yourself. Since groups can influence the individual and individuals can influence the group, group decision making happens in complex ways, especially when groupthink and group polarization occur.

Group Polarization

Groups sometimes make riskier decisions than individuals might. The nature of the group may help determine how group decisions differ from individual ones. When individuals themselves are risk averse, they tend to be even more conservative when they are in a group. When individuals are prone toward risk taking, they take even more risks when together in a group. Basically, the group amplifies the individual members' inclinations. This tendency is called **group polarization**, which is the likelihood that the attitudes of members of a team will become more similar over time. How does this happen? Some believe that since people gather ideas from others, and they tend to listen to information that supports their thoughts, their groups can help them feel even more secure in their initial attitude.

People also compare their ideas as they share them. In order to be seen in the best light, they may change their views to match those in the group and increase a sense of belonging. While discussing ideas, they may form a membership with the group (in-group) and conform to their idea of the will of the group. Groups do not always cause polarization or risky (or conservative) shifts. Polarization tends to occur more often when the group consists of people who share particular feelings. The less the group's members share particular attitudes, the less likely group polarization will occur.

Groupthink

Sometimes groups begin to overestimate their moral position, become more closed off to new people and ideas, and pressure their members to conform. These are signs of **groupthink**, when a group's ideas become so important to the group that alternative ideas are dismissed. With groupthink, the members are so focused on being good members of the group that they are not focusing on making the best decisions.

In groupthink the members are so focused on being a good group member they aren't focused on making the best decisions.

When a team feels very optimistic and almost infallible, it can often form groupthink. When that happens, opposing views are shot down and decisions are made without concern for minority opinions. Everyone is on the same page on the surface, though in actuality, some members may find the decisions troubling. Groupthink is more likely in tight-knit groups with dynamic leaders. In order to prevent groupthink, the group's leader should show an ability to listen to criticism, and criticism should be actively encouraged. Since the leader may be highly influential, the leader should hide his or her thoughts until the individual members have expressed ideas and criticism. Smaller groups should be formed that can generate ideas and criticism. Bringing in members of other teams can bring fresh ideas. A devil's advocate should be appointed to give voice to alternative opinions (Packer, 2009).

Individual Influence

Individuals do have some power. Individuals in a minority who are stalwart in their positions have greater success in changing the views of the majority than do individuals who are wishy-washy (Moscovici, 1985). Their position may lead those in the majority to reconsider their views. Conformity to the minority position occurs through informational pressure rather than normative pressure. A consistent and confident message may get the minority view heard.

Social Loafing

Having more people involved in an activity can be useful. It might appear that the more people there are to help, the less each person has to do. However, when there is no way to assess how much each person has contributed, people tend to put forth less effort than they normally might. **Social loafing** is the tendency to put forth less effort in a group than one would on one's own. Social loafing seems to be affected by an individual's understanding of how essential his or her individual effort is to the overall task. It also depends on how much the individual wants the group to succeed. If people feel that their contributions are not really essential and that no one will know whether they helped, they tend to pull back on their efforts. The larger the group, the more this can be a problem.

What helps alleviate social loafing? Anything that can both strengthen the importance of group success and increase the uniqueness of an individual's contribution. Social loafing, as you may imagine, is greater when people work with people they do not know rather than with people they do know. Also, the more difficult and rewarding the group task, the less social loafing there likely will be.

Social loafing can be decreased by forming close relations in the group and by providing consequences for or criticism of loafers (Aggarwal & O'Brien, 2008). There is a cultural aspect to social loafing, too: It is more likely in individualistic cultures and less likely among collectivist cultures. In fact, in collectivist cultures, working in a group more often generates greater effort (Earley, 1993).

Social Facilitation

While groups can decrease individuals' efforts, being around people can at times increase performance. Maybe you have had the experience of working harder or improving your performance when you are with others. **Social facilitation** is the tendency to work harder when others are around (Bond & Titus, 1983). Having others around can be encouraging (Zajonc, 1965), as in a boot camp–type exercise setting, as well as motivating, especially for tasks that are not overly complex, like folding pizza boxes. Norman Triplett (1898) demonstrated that the pressure of others changed individual behavior. He found that in a bike race, the racers were speedier when other racers were nearby than when they were racing against the clock. Added social pressure helped the racers.

Deindividuation

Crowds can affect your individualism. Being in a crowd can even strip away your individuality. **Deindividuation** is a merging of the self with a group in order to feel anonymous. At times, people may behave differently when they are in a large crowd than when they are alone. During Mardi Gras, people dress up in costumes. Both locals and visitors behave quite differently than they do in their everyday lives. Normally, what we do is influenced by social roles and our attitudes, but when we are in an anonymous group, the

Is everyone here pulling as hard as they can? Probably not. When individual effort can't be measured it can lead to social loafing, a tendency to put forth less effort in a group.

Social loafing The tendency to work less in a group than by yourself.

Social facilitation The tendency to work harder when others are around.

Deindividuation A merging of the self with a group in order to feel anonymous.

According to social facilitation, having others around can be motivating.

group can diminish our sense of control and responsibility. Social psychologists call this deindividuation. As the crowd gets larger, we feel more anonymous and tend to behave in the way the group does rather than being influenced by our own attitudes. It is not just crowds that make us feel anonymous. Disguises and darkness can also create this feeling.

What causes this? Some believe that deindividuation causes people to become less connected to their own attitudes. Others suggest that identification with the crowd and conformity to the new norms become powerful forces, and those who are part of the group are conforming to the new norm (Li, 2010).

Summary of Multiple Influences on Social Psychology

The baker returned with a cupcake in the shape of a puppy face. It had molded chocolate toffee ears and a nose made from a licorice jellybean. It was a wonderful gift, and the baker said it gave her joy to do something nice for me. "It's on the house, Hun, enjoy it."

We are most human, for better or for worse, around others. Studying social psychology reveals a lot about what it means to be human—maybe more so than any other branch of psychology. So too are there multiple influences on the way our social interactions change us and on the ways we change those around us. Biology can set the scene and, for example, can impact our perception and aggression. Social settings bring out discrimination, selfless acts, and blind obedience in all of us. As society changes, we do too, which helps explain why a little girl assumed I was a president.

Being in a crowd can cause deindividuation and diminish self-control and individual responsibility.

CONCEPT LEARNING CHECK 16.7   *Preventing Groupthink*

1. You have been selected to be the leader of a community group to look over a local park. You have to make a decision about the installation of a controversial outdoor sculpture that has been donated to the city. The citizens in your group are long-standing residents of the houses that surround the park. What steps can you take to ensure that group's decision does not fall prey to groupthink?

Visual Overview The Core Social Motives

As you have seen in this chapter, people both influence and are influenced by, their social environments. Susan Fiske (2003) summarized the influences into five core social motives: BUC(k)ET. Remembering these core social influences is a good way to understand how we operate in our social world.

BELONGING

People are motivated to join together and create relationships.

UNDERSTANDING

People are motivated to make sense of the world. This helps people to predict their own behavior and the behavior of others.

CONTROLLING

People are motivated to exert power over the things that happen to them.

ENHANCING SELF

People are motivated to feel and be perceived as worthy.

TRUSTING

People are motivated to see the world in a positive light.

16.1 Social Thought and Behavior

- Social psychology is a branch of psychology that examines how the ways that people think, feel, and behave influence and are influenced by others.

- Social roles and social norms are expectations about customary behaviors based on a person's position.
- People strive to belong, control, enhance themselves, and understand.

16.2 Person Perception

- Person perception is concerned with the way people form opinions about others. One aspect of person perception is social categorization.

- People use physical appearance and stereotypes in order to categorize others.

16.3 Attribution: The Person or the Situation?

- An attribution is a mental explanation for events or behavior.
- Internal attributions explain behavior based on personality.
- External attribution focuses on environmental and situational explanations of behavior.

- The actor-observer discrepancy is the likelihood of assigning an external and situational explanation to one's own behavior while assigning an internal and personal factor to the behavior of others.
- The self-serving bias is the tendency to see oneself in a positive light.

16.4 Attitudes and Social Judgments

- An attitude is a tendency to judge people, objects, or issues in a certain way.
- Attitudes consist of affects, behaviors, and cognitions.
- When the components of an attitude are in harmony, it is easy to predict the other components.
- Cognitive dissonance is the discomfort that people experience from holding two competing ideas at the same time.

- Attitudes can be influenced by persuasion.
- When people use logic to change their attitudes, they are employing the central route to persuasion.
- The peripheral route to persuasion occurs when attitudes are influenced by noncore factors.
- Attitudes can be altered by role playing.

16.5 Conformity and Obedience

- Conformity involves a change in thoughts or behavior to align with another person or group.
- Obedience involves a change in behavior in response to the orders of another.
- Compliance involves shifting behavior because of a request.

- People conform in response to social pressure or norms (normative social influence) as well as to the need to be correct (informational social influence).
- The Asch, Zimbardo, and Milgram studies demonstrated the power of the situation in conformity and obedience.

16.6 Social Interactions

- Prejudice involves stereotyped attitudes about a member of a group.
- Discrimination is the tendency to act differently toward a member of a group.
- Aggression consists of words or physical acts a person does to cause harm to another and can be due to a desire to obtain something (as in instrumental aggression) or simply to inflict harm (hostile aggression).

- Aggression has multiple influences, including biological, psychological, and sociocultural.
- There are multiple influences to attraction, including competence, proximity, physical attractiveness, similarity, and reciprocity.

16.7 Group Influence on the Individual

- Groups can influence an individual.
- When in a group, we treat those in the group differently than those outside of a group.
- Prosocial behavior involves helping another and can be influenced by the presence of others.
- Diffusion of responsibility can cause a bystander effect in which people are less likely to offer assistance to someone in need while in a group than when they are by themselves.
- Groups can also affect decision making and can cause the individuals in the group to shift attitudes so they are more similar over time.

- When a group is involved in groupthink, its members overestimate the moral position of the group, become more closed off to ideas, and are pressured to conform.
- When there is no way to assess how much each person has contributed to a group, people tend to work less, according to the theory of social loafing.
- Social facilitation occurs when having others around increases a person's performance.
- Deindividuation is a merging of the self with a group and can diminish a person's sense of control and responsibility.

16.1 Social Thought and Behavior

1. Ryan was surprised to discover that his roommate did not like apple pie with cheddar cheese on it. Ryan loved it that way and figured everyone else did as well. Which of the following explains why he thought most people preferred apple pie with cheese?
   A. False consensus effect
   B. Social cognition
   C. Social influence
   D. Social norms

16.2 Person Perception

2. An overgeneralized belief about a person is known as:
   A. social categorization.
   B. stereotype.
   C. groupthink.
   D. person perception.

16.3 Attribution: The Person or the Situation?

3. Marina suggested that the reason her friend's car stereo was stolen was because he must have carelessly left the car unlocked. Marina is using a(n) _____ for the event.
   A. internal attribution
   B. external attribution
   C. self-serving bias
   D. social influence

4. According to the _____, people tend to believe that bad things happen to bad people and good things happen to good people.
   A. actor-observer discrepancy
   B. defensive attribution
   C. just-world hypothesis
   D. self-serving bias

16.4 Attitudes and Social Judgments

5. Which of the following theories suggests that people discover their attitudes while observing their own behavior?
   A. Self-serving bias
   B. Cognitive dissonance theory
   C. Actor-observer discrepancy
   D. Self-perception theory

6. If you buy a product because you find the person selling it attractive, your decision is being driven by:
   A. social norms.
   B. the central route to persuasion.
   C. a peripheral route to persuasion.
   D. the foot-in-the-door technique.

16.5 Conformity and Obedience

7. The senior partner in the law firm tells Taylor, a junior partner, to revise the brief before she leaves that evening, and she does. The act of doing so represents:
   A. conformity.
   B. obedience.
   C. central route to persuasion.
   D. normative social influence.

8. Carla changed her vote from guilty to not guilty simply because the rest of the jury voted that way. Which concept explains why?
   A. Normative social influence
   B. Informational social influence
   C. Compliance
   D. Obedience

16.6 Social Interactions

9. Five-year-old Drake hit his sister Cassie in order to take the ball she was playing with. The act of hitting Cassie to get the ball is an example of:
   A. discrimination.
   B. obedience.
   C. instrumental aggression.
   D. hostile aggression.

10. Nick is surprised that a couple he knows is getting married. "I think she can do better, she's so much more attractive than he is," he thinks. Nick is using which principle to determine the couple's compatibility?
    A. Mere exposure effect
    B. Matching hypothesis
    C. False conscious effect
    D. Self-perception theory

16.7 Group Influence on the Individual

11. Thinking that everyone in the South listens to country music is an example of:
    A. out-group homogeneity.
    B. out-group bias.
    C. ethnocentrism.
    D. in-group bias.

12. Darla helped her neighbor clean her gutters because earlier in the summer, the same neighbor helped her clean out the garage. This helping behavior demonstrates:
    A. social facilitation.
    B. altruism.
    C. social responsibility norm.
    D. reciprocity norm.

13. Individuals with a minority decision within a group will need to sway the larger group to the minority opinion using:
    A. informational social influence.
    B. normative social influence.
    C. social facilitation.
    D. groupthink.

14. Barbara likes exercising in boot camp with other people because she feels she works much harder than when she works out alone. Her extra effort is due to:
    A. diffusion of responsibility.
    B. bystander effect.
    C. deindividuation.
    D. social facilitation.

15. Although they were helping Trey get his truck unstuck from the mud, not everyone was pushing as hard as he could. The factor that explains this is:
    A. group polarization.
    B. groupthink.
    C. social loafing.
    D. deindividuation.

CHAPTER DISCUSSION QUESTIONS

1. Recognizing that they are all important, select the one social motive that you consider most important to you. Then, select the one that you consider least important to you. Explain your answers.

2. Section 16.2 outlines some of the reasons people develop stereotypes. Examine these reasons for stereotype development, and then consider if they could also be used to reverse a person's stereotypes. In other words, how might you use your knowledge of stereotypes to undo a stereotype?

3. Cognitive dissonance theory states that if we hold two conflicting beliefs, we will change our beliefs to decrease the discomfort of the conflict. Relate this theory to an experience from your own life. Is there a time when you have changed your opinion because you realized that your beliefs were in conflict? What were the original conflicting beliefs? What change in belief(s) reduced the discomfort of the conflict? Did you keep the new beliefs or find yourself wanting to return to the old beliefs?

4. Consider the difference between conformity (you shifting your thoughts to align with someone else's) versus obedience (changing because someone tells you to). Now consider a situation in which you might change your thoughts or behavior. Is there a difference in how you would evaluate your change if you did it to align with someone (conformity) versus if someone told you to change (obedience)? What positive or negative self-evaluations might go along with realizing you were conforming versus obedient?

5. Imagine that you are the manager of a group working on a team project. Review the different elements of group influences on the individual in Section 16.7 and identify the top three that would help you do a good job. Explain why you chose each group influence and how understanding it would make you a better manager.

CHAPTER PROJECTS

1. Imagine that you have a sibling who is about to start high school and is very nervous about making friends and getting along with his/her teachers. Use your knowledge of social psychology to prepare a guidebook of advice for your sibling. You may organize your book however you would like, but make sure it includes specific examples from the chapter along with specific scenarios in which social psychology would be helpful.

2. Think of a historical event about which you know something about the behavior and decisions of individuals from the event. Then, use the concepts from this chapter to interpret the behaviors and decisions of these individuals. Of course, you may not have all of the details of each person's behavior, so go with what you know and feel free to speculate a bit if necessary. How might your knowledge of social psychology change the interpretation of a person's behavior?

Actor
Actor-observer bias
Aggression
Altruism
Amygdala
Attitude
Attribution
Attribution theory
Availability heuristic
Blaming the victim
Bystander effect
Cathartic
Central route to persuasion
Cognitive dissonance
Cognitive dissonance theory
Collectivist cultures
Compliance
Conflict
Conformity
Defensive attribution
Deindividuation
Diffusion of responsibility

Discrimination
Door-in-the-face technique
Ethnocentrism
External attribution
False consensus effect
Foot-in-the-door technique
Fundamental attribution error
Group
Group polarization
Groupthink
Hostile aggression
In-group bias
Individualist cultures
Informational social influence
Instrumental aggression
Internal attribution
Just-world hypothesis
Matching hypothesis
Mere exposure effect
Normative social influence
Obedience
Out-group homogeneity

Peripheral route to persuasion
Person perception
Persuasion
Prejudice
Reciprocity norm
Reciprocity of liking
Role
Schema
Self-perception theory
Self-serving bias
Serotonin
Social categorization
Social cognition
Social facilitation
Social influence
Social loafing
Social norm
Social psychology
Social-responsibility norm
Social roles
Stereotype
Testosterone

ANSWERS TO CONCEPT LEARNING CHECKS

16.1 Describing Social Roles

Host: Seats customers, hands them a menu
Server: Greets customers, requests drink order, brings food, brings check
Customer: Gives food order, pays check, leaves tip

16.2 Person Perception and Musical Tastes

Typical answers would be:

1. D. Rock
2. A. Country
3. C. Punk
4. B. Classical

Would you be surprised if you were wrong? What influenced your answers?

16.3 Explaining Attributional Biases

1. Actor-observer bias. [The actor-observer bias suggests that people tend to assign an external and situational explanation to their own behavior while assigning internal, personal factors to the behavior of others.]

2. Self-serving bias. [The self-serving bias reflects the belief that good things happen because of ability and bad things occur because of external factors.]

3. Just-world hypothesis. [The just-world hypothesis suggests that we believe that people get what they deserve and deserve what they get. If Belinda's roommate's parents were going through an audit, they must have deserved the circumstance.]

16.4 Explaining Persuasion

Include as many key terms as you can.

16.5 Distinguishing Conformity, Obedience, and Compliance

1. C. Obedience—changing behavior in response to the orders of another
2. B. Conformity—changing thoughts or behavior to align with another
3. A. Compliance—shifting your behavior because of a request

1. You buy white earphones instead of black because all your friends own white earphones [conformity].
2. A professor assigns a deadline for a paper, so you finish the paper by that day [obedience].
3. A friend asks you to pick her up from the airport [compliance].
4. Your boss at work requests that you change the paper in the photocopier [obedience].
5. You consider having an expensive drink at dinner, but since all your friends are just having water, you order water, too [conformity].

16.6 Designing for Friendships

Example: Friendships could be increased by making sure that residents are near each other (proximity) and that they are aware of ways in which they are alike (similarity). Prejudice could be decreased by having residents of differing backgrounds work together on difficult tasks in which friendships are encouraged.

16.7 Preventing Groupthink

1. The leader should listen to and actively encourage criticism.

2. The leader should hide his or her thoughts until everyone has expressed ideas and criticism.

3. Small groups should be formed to generate new ideas.

4. A devil's advocate should be appointed to give voice to alternative opinions.

ANSWERS TO CHAPTER REVIEW TEST

16.1 Social Thought and Behavior

1. A. Rationale: The false consensus effect is the habit of seeing your own behavior as typical.

16.2 Person Perception

2. B. Rationale: A stereotype is an overgeneralized belief about a group and its members.

16.3 Attribution: The Person or the Situation?

3. A. Rationale: An internal attribution emphasizes the role of personality characteristics regarding an event.

4. C. Rationale: According to the just-world hypothesis, people get what they deserve and deserve what they get.

16.4 Attitudes and Social Judgments

5. D. Rationale: According to self-perception theory, people infer their attitudes from their behavior.

6. C. Rationale: The peripheral route to persuasion occurs when a person uses insignificant, noncore factors to make a decision—in this case, source attractiveness.

16.5 Conformity and Obedience

7. B. Rationale: Obedience involves a change in your behavior in response to the orders of another.

8. A. Rationale: Normative social influence involves social pressure to conform to a group's norms—in this case, the belief that the defendant in a trial was not guilty.

16.6 Social Interactions

9. C. Rationale: Instrumental aggression is aggression used to obtain something. Hostile aggression is aggression simply to inflict harm.

10. B. Rationale: According to the matching hypothesis, people are paired to equally attractive partners.

16.7 Group Influence on the Individual

11. A. Rationale: Out-group homogeneity suggests that members of an out-group are similar.

12. D. Rationale: The reciprocity norm suggests that when someone helps us, we are more likely to help that person in return.

13. A. Rationale: Informational social influence involves conformity due to evidence.

14. D. Rationale: Social facilitation is the tendency to work harder when others are around.

15. C. Rationale: Social loafing is the tendency to work less in a group than by yourself.

REFERENCES

Aggarwal, P., & O'Brien, C. L. (2008). Social loafing on group projects. *Journal of Marketing Education, 30*(3), 255.

Ajzen, I. (2005). *Attitudes, personality and behavior.* New York: McGraw-Hill International.

Alley, T. R., & Cunningham, M. R. (1991). Averaged faces are attractive, but very attractive faces are not average. *Psychological Science, 2*(2), 123–125.

Ambady, N., Hallahan, M., & Conner, B. (1999). Accuracy of judgments of sexual orientation from thin slices of behavior. *Journal of Personality and Social Psychology, 77*(3), 538–547. doi:10.1037/0022-3514.77.3.538

Ambady, N., & Rosenthal, R. (1993). Half a minute: Predicting teacher evaluations from thin slices of nonverbal behavior and physical attractiveness. *Journal of Personality and Social Psychology, 64*(3), 431–441. doi:10.1037/0022-3514.64.3.431

Anderson, C. A., Berkowitz, L., Donnerstein, E., Huesmann, L. R., Johnson, J. D., Linz, D., Malamuth, N. M., et al. (2003). The influence of media violence on youth. *Psychological Science in the Public Interest, 4*(3), 81.

Anderson, C. A., & Bushman, B. J. (2001). Effects of violent video games on aggressive behavior, aggressive cognition, aggressive affect, physiological arousal, and prosocial behavior: A meta-analytic review of the scientific literature. *Psychological Science, 12*(5), 353–359.

Asch, S. E. (1956). Studies of independence and conformity: I. A minority of one against a unanimous majority. *Psychological monographs, 70*(9), 1–70. doi: 10.1037/h0093718

Bandura, A., Ross, D., & Ross, S. A. (1961). Transmission of aggression through imitation of aggressive models. *Journal of Abnormal and Social Psychology, 63*(3), 575–582. doi:10.1037/h0045925

Baron, A. S., & Banaji, M. R. (2006). The development of implicit attitudes. Evidence of race evaluations from ages 6 and 10 and adulthood. *Psychological Science, 17*(1), 53–58. doi:10.1111/j.1467-9280.2005.01664.x

Baumeister, R. F., Bratslavsky, E., Finkenauer, C., & Vohs, K. D. (2001). Bad is stronger than good. *Review of General Psychology, 5,* 323–370.

Bem, D. J. (1967). Self-perception: An alternative interpretation of cognitive dissonance phenomena. *Psychological Review, 74*(3), 183.

Berscheid, E., & Reis, H. T. (1998). Attraction and close relationships. *Handbook of Social Psychology, 2,* 193–281.

Blass, T. (1999). The Milgram paradigm after 35 years: Some things we now know about obedience to authority. *Journal of Applied Social Psychology, 29*(5), 955–978.

Bleske-Rechek, A., Remiker, M. W., & Baker, J. P. (2009). Similar from the start: Assortment in young adult dating couples and its link to relationship stability over time. *Individual Differences Research, 7*(3), 142–158.

Bond, C. F., & Titus, L. J. (1983). Social facilitation: A meta-analysis of 241 studies. *Psychological Bulletin, 94*(2), 265–292. doi:10.1037/0033-2909.94.2.265

Brendgen, M., Vitaro, F., Boivin, M., Dionne, G., & Pérusse, D. (2006). Examining genetic and environmental effects on reactive versus proactive aggression. *Developmental Psychology, 42*(6), 1299–1312. doi:10.1037/0012-1649.42.6.1299

Brewer, M. B., & Brown, R. J. (1998). *Intergroup relations.* New York: McGraw-Hill.

Byrne, D. (1971). *The attraction paradigm (Personality and Psychopathology, Vol. 11,* 1st ed.). Academic Press.

Carli, L. L., Ganley, R., & Pierce-Otay, A. (1991). Similarity and satisfaction in roommate relationships. *Personality and Social Psychology Bulletin, 17*(4), 419.

Carney, D. R., Colvin, C. R., & Hall, J. A. (2007). A thin slice perspective on the accuracy of first impressions. *Journal of Research in Personality, 41*(5), 1054–1072. doi:16/j.jrp.2007.01.004

CNN (2006, December 12). Poll: Most Americans see lingering racism—in others. CNN.COM. Retrieved from http://edition.cnn.com/2006/US/12/12/racism.poll/index.html

Cohen, D. (2001). Cultural variation: Considerations and implications. *Psychological Bulletin, 127*(4), 451.

Cohen, D., Nisbett, R. E., Bowdle, B. F., & Schwarz, N. (1996). Insult, aggression, and the Southern culture of honor: An "experimental ethnography." *Journal of Personality and Social Psychology, 70*(5), 945.

Cunningham, M. R. (1986). Measuring the physical in physical attractiveness: Quasi-experiments on the sociobiology of female facial beauty. *Journal of Personality and Social Psychology, 50*(5), 925.

Cunningham, M. R., Barbee, A. P., & Pike, C. L. (1990). What do women want? Facialmetric assessment of multiple motives in the perception of male facial physical attractiveness. *Journal of Personality and Social Psychology, 59*(1), 61–72. doi:10.1037/0022-3514.59.1.61

Dijkstra, J. K., Cillessen, A. H. N., Lindenberg, S., & Veenstra, R. (2010). Same-gender and cross-gender likeability: Associations with popularity and status enhancement: The TRAILS study. *Journal of Early Adolescence, 30*(6), 773–802. doi:10.1177/0272431609350926

Dion, K., Berscheid, E., & Walster, E. (1972). What is beautiful is good. *Journal of Personality and Social Psychology, 24*(3), 285.

Dovidio, J. F., Piliavin, J. A., Gaertner, S. L., Schroeder, D. A., & Clark III, R. D. (1991). The arousal: Cost-reward model and the process of intervention: A review of the evidence. In M. Clark (Ed.), *Prosocial behavior. Review of personality and social psychology* (Vol. 12, pp. 86–118). Newbury Park, CA: Sage.

Eagly, A. H., Ashmore, R. D., Makhijani, M. G., & Longo, L. C. (1991). What is beautiful is good, but . . .: A meta-analytic review of research on the physical attractiveness stereotype. *Psychological Bulletin, 110*(1), 109.

Earley, P. C. (1993). East meets West meets Mideast: Further explorations of collectivistic and individualistic work groups. *Academy of Management Journal, 36*(2), 319–348. doi:10.2307/256525

Festinger, L. (1951). Architecture and group membership. *Journal of Social Issues, 7*(1–2), 152–163. doi:10.1111/j.1540-4560.1951.tb02229.x

Festinger, L. (1957). *A theory of cognitive dissonance.* Palo Alto, CA: Stanford University Press.

Festinger, L., Riecken, H., & Schachter, S. (2011). *When prophecy fails.* Eastford, CT: Martino Fine Books.

Fischer, P., Krueger, J. I., Greitemeyer, T., Vogrincic, C., Kastenmüller, A., Frey, D., Heene, M., et al. (2011). The bystander effect: A meta-analytic review on bystander intervention in dangerous and non-dangerous emergencies. *Psychological Bulletin, 137*(4), 517–537. doi:10.1037/a0023304

Fiske, S. T. (2003). Five core social motives, plus or minus five. *Motivated Social Perception, 9,* 233–246.

Greitemeyer, T. (2010). Effects of reciprocity on attraction: The role of a partner's physical attractiveness. *Personal Relationships, 17*(2), 317–330.

Helmreich, R., Aronson, E., & LeFan, J. (1970). To err is humanizing sometimes: Effects of self-esteem, competence, and a pratfall on interpersonal attraction. *Journal of Personality and Social Psychology, 16*(2), 259–264. doi:10.1037/h0029848.

Hoshino-Browne, E., Zamana, A., Spencer, S., Zanna, M., Kitayama S. & Lackenbauer, S. (2005). On the cultural guises of cognitive dissonance: The case of easteners and westerners. *Journal of Personal and Social Psychology, 89*(3), 294–310.

Huston, A. C., Zuckerman, D., Wilcox, B. L., Donnerstein, E., Fairchild, H., Feshbach, N. D., Katz, P. A., et al. (1992). *Big world, small screen: The role of television in American society.* Lincoln, NE: University of Nebraska Press.

Irwin, A. R., & Gross, A. M. (1995). Cognitive tempo, violent video games, and aggressive behavior in young boys. *Journal of Family Violence, 10*(3), 337–350.

Johnson, M. A. (1989). Variables associated with friendship in an adult population. *Journal of Social Psychology, 129*(3), 379–390.

Kennedy, B. P., Kawachi, I., Prothrow-Stith, D., Lochner, K., & Gupta, V. (1998). Social capital, income inequality, and firearm violent crime. *Social Science & Medicine, 47*(1), 7–17. doi:16/S0277-9536(98)00097-5

Kitayama, S., Snibbe, A. C., Markus, H. R., & Suzuki, T. (2004). Is there any "free" choice? Self and dissonance in two cultures. *Psychological Science, 15*(8), 527–533.

Knowles, E. D., Morris, M. W., Chiu, C. Y., & Hong, Y. Y. (2001). Culture and the process of person perception: Evidence for automaticity among East Asians in correcting for situational influences on behavior. *Personality and Social Psychology Bulletin, 27*(10), 1344–1356. doi:10.1177/01461672012710010

Latane, B., & Darley, J. M. (1970). *The unresponsive bystander: Why doesn't he help?* New York: Appleton-Century Crofts.

Latane, B., & Nida, S. (1981). Ten years of research on group size and helping. *Psychological Bulletin, 89*(2), 308–324. doi:10.1037/0033-2909.89.2.308

Lorenzo, G. L., Biesanz, J. C., & Human, L. J. (2010). What is beautiful is good and more accurately understood. *Psychological Science, 21*(12), 1777–1782. doi:10.1177/0956797610388048

Mackinnon, S. P., Jordan, C. H., & Wilson, A. E. (2011). Birds of a feather sit together: Physical similarity predicts seating choice. *Personality and Social Psychology Bulletin, 37*(7), 879–892. doi:10.1177/0146167211402094

Major, B., Carrington, P. I., & Carnevale, P. J. D. (1984). Physical attractiveness and self-esteem. *Personality and Social Psychology Bulletin, 10*(1), 43–50. doi:10.1177/0146167284101004

Malle, B. F. (2006). The actor-observer asymmetry in attribution: A (surprising) meta-analysis. *Psychological Bulletin, 132*(6), 895–919. doi:10.1037/0033-2909.132.6.895

Meineri, S., & Guéguen, N. (2008). An application of the foot-in-the-door strategy in the environmental field. *European Journal of Social Sciences, 7*(1), 71–74.

Milgram, S. (1963). Behavioral study of obedience. *Journal of Abnormal and Social Psychology, 67*(4), 371–378. doi:10.1037/h0040525

Milgram, S. (2009). *Obedience to authority: An experimental view* (Reprint.). New York: Harper Perennial Modern Classics.

Moreland, R. L., & Zajonc, R. B. (1982). Exposure effects in person perception: Familiarity, similarity, and attraction. *Journal of Experimental Social Psychology, 18*(5), 395–415.

Moscovici, S. (1985). Innovation and minority influence. In S. Moscovici, G. Mugny, & E. Van Avermaet (Eds.), *Perspectives on minority influence* (pp. 9–52). Cambridge, UK: Cambridge University Press..

Packer, D. J. (2009). Avoiding groupthink. *Psychological Science, 20*(5), 546–548. doi:10.1111/j.1467-9280.2009.02333.x

Pettigrew, T. F., & Tropp, L. R. (2006). A meta-analytic test of intergroup contact theory. *Journal of Personality and Social Psychology, 90*(5), 751.

Rosenblat, T. S. (2008). The beauty premium: Physical attractiveness and gender in dictator games. *Negotiation Journal, 24*(4), 465–481. doi:10.1111/j.1571-9979.2008.00198.x

Rosenthal, A. M. (2008). *Thirty-eight witnesses: The Kitty Genovese case.* Brooklyn, NY: Melville House.

Seger, C. R., Smith, E. R., & Mackie, D. M. (2009). Subtle activation of a social categorization triggers group-level emotions. *Journal of Experimental Social Psychology, 45*(3), 460–467. doi:16/j.jesp.2008.12.004

Seo, D., Patrick, C. J., & Kennealy, P. J. (2008). Role of serotonin and dopamine system interactions in the neurobiology of impulsive aggression and its comorbidity with other clinical disorders. *Aggression and Violent Behavior, 13*(5), 383–395.

Siever, L. J. (2008). Neurobiology of aggression and violence. *American Journal of Psychiatry, 165*(4), 429–442. doi:10.1176/appi.ajp.2008.07111774

Smith, N. K., Cacioppo, J. T., Larsen, J. T., & Chartrand, T. L. (2003). May I have your attention, please: Electrocortical responses to positive and negative stimuli. *Neuropsychologia, 41,* 171–183.

Taylor, S. E., Peplau, L. A., & Sears, D. O. (2005). *Social psychology* (12th ed.). Upper Saddle River, NJ: Prentice Hall.

Tajfel, H., Billig, M. G., Bundy, R. P., & Flament, C. (1971). Social categorization and intergroup behavior. *European Journal of Social Psychology, 1*(2), 149–178.

Trafimow, D., Armendariz, M. L., & Madson, L. (2004). A test of whether attributions provide for self-enhancement or self-defense. *Journal of Social Psychology, 144*(5), 453–464.

Triplett, N. (1898). The dynamogenic factors in pacemaking and competition. *American Journal of Psychology, 9*(4), 507–533.

Villani, S. (2001). Impact of media on children and adolescents: A 10-year review of the research. *Journal of the American Academy of Child & Adolescent Psychiatry, 40*(4), 392–401.

Webb, T. L., & Sheeran, P. (2006). Does changing behavioral intentions engender behavior change? A meta-analysis of the experimental evidence. *Psychological Bulletin, 132*(2), 249–268. doi:10.1037/0033-2909.132.2.249

Willis, J., & Todorov, A. (2006). First impressions: Making up your mind after a 100-ms exposure to a face. *Psychological Science, 17*(7), 592–598. doi:10.1111/j.1467-9280.2006.01750.x

Zajonc, R. B. (1965). Social facilitation. *Science, 149*(3681), 269–274.

Zimbardo, P. (2008). *The Lucifer effect: Understanding how good people turn evil.* New York: Random House.

Glossary

360-degree feedback Evaluation method that solicits input from everyone who interacts with an employee.

Absolute refractory period The point after an action potential when the neuron cannot produce another action potential no matter the intensity of the stimulation.

Absolute threshold The lowest amount of physical energy that can be detected reliably 50 percent of the time using a given sense organ.

Acceptance Communication of respect.

Accommodation Movement in an eye's muscles as we focus our vision on near or far objects provides a monocular depth cue; Changing concepts in memory to fit new information.

Acculturative stress The anxiety felt in response to challenges from new cultural expectations.

Acetylcholine Neurotransmitter that is involved in memory and muscle functions.

Achievement gap The difference in U.S. school test scores and grades for white compared to African American children.

Achievement motivation A desire to accomplish difficult jobs in an area with a standard of excellence.

Achievement test A measure of what is already known or learned, as the outcome of education.

Acquisition Gaining new knowledge or behavior to use in the future.

Action potential The electrical message or neural impulse that flows along a neuron's axon.

Activation-synthesis model of dreaming A theory of dreams that suggests that dreams are interpreted brain activity.

Active listening A communication method in which the listener responds in ways that demonstrate understanding of what another person says.

Actor A person who exhibits a behavior.

Actor-observer bias The likelihood of assigning an external and situational explanation to your own behavior while assigning internal, personal factors to the behavior of others.

Actualizing tendency According to the humanists, the instinctual desire to be the best version of yourself possible.

Acute insomnia Short-term inability to fall or stay asleep.

Acute stressor Brief event that requires a period of coping.

Adaptation A process by which a characteristic increases in a population because it makes reproduction or survival more likely.

Adaptation-level phenomenon The ability to adapt to new situations so that the new situation becomes the norm.

Adaptive behavior Cognitive, social, and practical skills used to assess intellectual disability in low-scoring individuals.

Adaptive theory of sleep A theory of sleep that suggests that our sleep-wake patterns are shaped by an evolved biological process.

Adipose tissue Fat cells stored beneath the skin and throughout the abdomen.

Adoption study A method that allows researchers to test hypotheses concerning the contributions of genetic and environmental factors by examining characteristics between children and their biological and non-biological parents.

Adrenal cortex The outer layer of the adrenal gland that secretes hormones during stress.

Adrenal glands Important glands of the endocrine system consisting of the adrenal cortex and the adrenal medulla.

Adrenal medulla The interior layer of the adrenal gland that secretes epinephrine and norepinephrine.

Aerobic exercise Physical activity that increases the capability of the heart and lungs.

Afferent nerve fibers Neurons that move information toward the brain and spinal cord.

Afterimage The appearance of an illusion of color (e.g., red) on a white surface after viewing its complementary color (e.g., green) for a prolonged period.

Age of viability By around 6 months, the fetus has developed enough that it may survive if born prematurely.

Aggression Words or physical acts a person does in order to cause harm.

Agitated catatonia A symptom of schizophrenia that is characterized by excessive motor activity and periods of inexhaustibility.

Agonist A substance that mimics or increases the effect of a neurotransmitter.

Agoraphobia The fear of having a panic attack, which causes a person to avoid places and situations where having a panic attack would be particularly embarrassing or dangerous.

Agreeableness A personality trait that is part of the Big Five that describes how trusting a person is.

Alcohol A type of depressant drug that is associated with reduced inhibition, slurred speech, and impairments in balance.

Algorithm A well-defined process that is guaranteed to produce a solution.

All-or-nothing law The concept that either a neuron fires or it doesn't. There is no partial firing.

Allocentrism A personality trait with an interreliant focus in which people tend to see themselves as part of a community.

Alogia Lack of elaborative speech.

Alpha waves A type of brain wave linked to relaxed wakefulness.

Altruism Being unselfish and helpful toward other people.

Alzheimer's disease A progressive memory disorder in which people lose access to explicit memory.

Ames room An illusion created by adding physical distortions to make a room appear to have a normal rectangular shape so that its contents appear to violate size constancy.

Amnesia The loss of memory in clinical patients.

Amphetamines A class of stimulant drugs that activates the central nervous system.

Amygdala A cluster of neurons in the temporal lobe linked to emotions such as anger and fear.

Analogy A problem-solving process that makes use of a previous solution.

Analytic intelligence Sternberg's theory posited the ability to break problems down into component parts for analysis.

Anecdotal evidence A type of information that relies on unscientific observation.

Anhedonia A reduced capacity to experience pleasure.

Anorexia nervosa An eating disorder in which an individual feels he or she is overweight despite objective evidence.

Antagonist A substance that blocks the action of a neurotransmitter.

Anthropomorphism Assigning human emotions or behaviors to nonhumans.

Antianxiety medication A type of drug used to reduce the symptoms of agitation and nervousness.

Antidepressant medication A type of drug used to reduce the symptoms of depressive mood disorders.

Antipsychotic medication A type of drug used to reduce the symptoms of thought disorders.

Antisocial personality disorder A personality disorder in which a person breaks societal rules, often without remorse or anxiety.

Anxiety disorders A psychological condition marked by nervousness, distress, apprehension, and disruptive attempts to reduce anxiety.

Aphasia An inability to understand or produce language based on damage to the language areas of the brain.

Applied research A type of research concerned with solving everyday problems.

Approach-approach conflict A situation in which a decision must be made between two incompatible choices that both have positive features.

Approach-avoidance conflict A situation in which a decision must be made about a goal that has both positive and negative features.

Aptitude test A measure of the ability to benefit from further training.

Archetypes According to Jung, a universal thought form that exists in the collective unconscious.

Arousal theory The theory that we are motivated to seek out a particular level of arousal.

Assimilation Using current concepts in memory to understand new information.

Association areas Areas of the cerebral cortex involved in integration of information.

Ataxia Loss of coordination of muscle movements.

Attachment A deep, emotional bond that an infant develops with its caregiver.

Attention Awareness of the sensations and perceptions that are a focus of thinking at any given time.

Attentional blink Difficulty in detecting new information after a information is presented.

Attitude A tendency to judge people, objects, or issues in a certain way.

Attribution Our mental explanations of events or behaviors.

Attribution theory The theory that behavior is explained by situational or personal factors.

Authoritative parenting style A balance between obedience from the child and willingness to explain and make exceptions.

Automatic processing Information made available without conscious effort.

Autonomic nervous system Part of the peripheral nervous system that interfaces with the heart, intestines, and other organs.

Availability heuristic A thinking shortcut in which the more quickly a person can think of an example of something, the more likely he or she supposes it must be true.

Aversive conditioning A behavioral technique that pairs an unpleasant stimulus with an undesired behavior in order to reduce the target behavior.

Avoidance-avoidance conflict A situation in which a decision must be made between two undesirable choices.

Avoidance learning Learning to stay away from stimuli that predict negative events.

Avolition Lack of will.

Axon The part of the neuron that carries the nerve impulse away from the soma.

Axon terminal The part of the neuron that discharges and recycles neurotransmitters; also called the terminal button.

B (being) needs According to Maslow, self-actualization needs.

Babbling The initial vocalizing performed by babies learning to speak.

Barbiturates A type of depressant drug that reduces stress and induces sleep.

Basal metabolic rate The body's ability to use nutrients efficiently to maintain itself when at rest.

Basic emotions Feeling states that are thought to be expressed in a universal way.

Basic research A type of research concerned with expanding knowledge, even if the knowledge has no practical application.

Basilar membrane A neural pathway within the cochlea that registers the movement of fluid through tiny hair cells on its surface.

Behavior modification An operant conditioning program designed to achieve a goal.

Behavior therapy A family of therapies that use learning theory to change behavior.

Behavioral contract The learner signs a written specification of an operant conditioning program.

Behavioral genetics An interdisciplinary field that examines the influences of heredity and environment on behavior.

Behavioral medicine An interdisciplinary field concerned with health and illness that combines knowledge of social and medical sciences.

Behaviorism The study of learning based on directly observable actions in the absence of mental processes.

Behaviorist theory The view that language is learned just like other things.

Belief perseverance Holding onto a belief in the face of evidence against it.

Bell-and-pad treatment A classical conditioning treatment used to treat nighttime bedwetting.

Between-subjects design A research plan in which different individuals take part in differing aspects of the study and the different groups are compared.

Bias A preexisting perspective applied to a problem or decision.

Big Five A trait theory concept suggesting that the five most essential personality traits are openness to experience, conscientiousness, extroversion, agreeableness, and neuroticism; also known as the five-factor model of personality.

Bimodal distribution A pattern of scores with two distinct clusters with different modes (frequently occurring scores).

Binge eating disorder An eating disorder marked by repeated overeating without the compensatory strategies found in bulimia.

Binocular cues Ways to determine depth of field that require having two eyes.

Biofeedback A procedure through which a person becomes aware of physiological functions in order to influence the physiological functions.

Biological preparedness Built-in tendencies to learn some associations more easily.

Biological psychology The branch of psychology that studies the connection of bodily systems and behavior.

Biomedical therapies A family of therapies that focuses on surgery, medication, or other physiological interventions for the treatment of psychological conditions.

Biopsychosocial model A theory that recognizes three equally important aspects of human mental processes and behaviors: biological (including brain chemistry), psychological (thoughts, emotions, and behaviors), and social (cultural and societal influences).

Bipolar cells Cells that process incoming information from the rods and cones in the retina.

Bipolar disorder A mood disorder in which a person may alternate between a sad, depressive mood and elevated, irritable, or manic episodes.

Bisexual A person with more than incidental involvement with both male and female partners.

Bizarre delusions False and impossible beliefs.

Blaming the victim The tendency to attribute the cause of an unfortunate circumstance to the person experiencing it.

Blind spot The small area of the retina where the optic nerve leaves the eyeball.

Body dysmorphia A disturbance of body image including an overly self-critical attitude.

Body mass index (BMI) A ratio of height and weight that includes comparison to others.

Borderline personality disorder A personality disorder marked by a history of instability in a person's self-image, ability to control impulses, relationships, and moods.

Bottom-up processing The stimulus-driven process of sensation that registers external physical energy and translates it into neural encoding.

Brainstem The part of the brain between the cerebral cortex and the spinal cord responsible for survival functions.

Broca's area Part of the left frontal lobe that produces speech sounds.

Bulimia nervosa A disorder involving binge eating large amounts of food but maintaining relatively normal weight by purging.

Bystander effect A phenomenon in which people are less likely to offer assistance to someone in need while in groups than they are by themselves.

Caffeine A type of stimulant drug that is associated with increased central nervous system activity.

California Personality Inventory (CPI) A type of personality test designed to measure characteristics important to daily life.

Calling Choice of occupation you feel drawn to pursue for intrinsic meaning and identity.

Cannon-Bard theory A theory of emotion that suggests that events cause emotions by triggering biological and psychological experience of emotions at the same time.

Case study The extensive examination of the experience of a single individual or group.

Cataplexy An abrupt and temporary weakness often following a strong emotional experience.

Catastrophic thinking A cognitive distortion of the scale and impact of a stressful event.

Catatonic type of schizophrenia A disorder characterized by one or both forms of catatonia, as well as other behavioral symptoms.

Catecholamines Stress hormones released by the adrenal glands.

Category A cluster of similar concepts.

Catharsis A release of pent-up emotions.

Cathartic An experience that involves the release of pent-up emotions.

Cell body The part of a nerve cell that keeps the entire cell alive; also called the soma.

Central nervous system A division of the nervous system that is comprised of the brain and spinal cord.

Central route to persuasion A constructive response to an argument that focuses solely on the argument's merits.

Central tendency The "typical value" of a group of scores, described by the mean, mode, or median.

Cerebellum A part of the hindbrain involved in the development and coordination of movement.

Cerebral cortex The part of the brain involved in complex cognitive functioning.

Cerebral hemispheres One of the two regions of the cerebral cortex.

Cerebrospinal fluid (CSF) Clear liquid created in the ventricular system that supports and protects the central nervous system.

Cerebrum The cerebrum is the largest part of the forebrain and consists of left and right hemispheres, each made up of four lobes.

Change blindness A change occurs between two viewings of a scene, but it is not noticed.

Chemical senses The two external senses that involve the detection of chemical molecules either dissolved in water (taste) or floating in the air (smell).

Choice overload The presence of too many options, causing problems in decisions.

Chromosome Cellular organelle that contains genes.

Chronic stressors Long-lasting events that require adaption.

Chunking Grouping separate elements into a related unit in memory.

Circadian rhythm A biological process that occurs on a daily cycle.

Classical conditioning Learning in which a neutral stimulus becomes associated with an unlearned stimulus and the response it automatically elicits.

Client-centered therapy A humanistic psychotherapy based on a nondirective, genuine, and accepting environment.

Clinical psychologist A mental health practitioner who researches, evaluates, and treats psychological conditions.

Clinical researcher model A type of psychology program that emphasizes clinical psychology research over direct work with clients.

Clinical trial The use of the scientific method to test a treatment for a disorder or condition.

Cocaine A stimulant drug made from the coca plant.

Cochlea The semicircular canal of fluid-filled tubes that captures movements of the oval window to transduce vibrations into neural firing.

Cocktail party phenomenon Hearing your name mentioned despite not attending to its source.

Cognition All types of thinking, including knowing, remembering, reasoning, deciding, and communicating.

Cognitive The explanations of behavior based on changes in knowledge within the mind.

Cognitive dissonance Discomfort that you experience from holding two competing ideas at the same time.

Cognitive dissonance theory The theory that we try to decrease our discomfort when holding two competing ideas at the same time by changing either our ideas or our behaviors.

Cognitive map A mental representation of a physical path to a goal location.

Cognitive-mediational theory of emotion A theory that feelings are caused by what we think caused our thoughts.

Cognitive neuroscience The methodological study of brain action linked to thought, perception, and language.

Cognitive neuroscientist A scientist who studies brain action as it is linked to thought, perception, and language.

Cognitive person variables Individual traits that affect the way you see the world.

Cognitive therapy A type of treatment that emphasizes the link between thoughts and emotions; also known as cognitive behavior therapy.

Cohort effect A difference observed between age groups that may be due to differences in their experiences in addition to age.

Collective unconscious According to Jung, the part of the personality that stores shared experiences and ideas from previous generations.

Collectivist culture A type of culture that prioritizes the group over the individual.

Colorblindness A condition marked by difficulty in distinguishing among some shades of red, green, or, more rarely, blue.

Coming out Sharing one's same-sex orientation with others or the public.

Comparative study A research project that compares similarities and differences between human and animal behavior.

Compliance Shifting behavior because of a request.

Compulsions A condition in which a person feels compelled to perform behaviors or mental actions in response to an obsession.

Computed tomography scans (CT scans) A neuroscience imaging technique that uses computer-enhanced X-rays that are helpful at examining brain structures. Also called CT scans.

Concept A "building block" or basic unit of knowledge.

Conceptual hierarchy Organization of related concepts into levels of categories.

Concrete operational stage Piaget's stage when grade schoolers have achieved conservation and are no longer fooled by appearances.

Conditional positive regard According to Rogers, the idea that respect comes only when certain circumstances are met.

Conditioned response A physiological behavior that is associated with a learned stimulus.

Conditioned stimulus A learned signal that predicts another stimulus is about to occur.

Conditioning Training, or learning as displayed by an animal's or human's behavior.

Cone cells Cone-shaped cells on the retina that recognize colors.

Confirmation bias Seeking out information consistent with what is believed to be true.

Conflict A situation that involves incompatible objectives.

Conformity Changing your thoughts or behavior to align with those of another.

Confounding variable An alternative factor that might account for observed differences in the dependent measure.

Connectionist models Memory theories that capture the distributed interconnections between concepts.

Conscientiousness A Big Five trait that describes how trustworthy a person might be.

Conscious mind According to Freud, a part of the mind that is aware of current thoughts and experiences.

Consciousness A state of awareness of the internal and the external world.

Conservation The knowledge that physical properties of an object stay the same even though there may be superficial changes in appearance.

Consistency paradox The idea that people believe that personality is stable, although research says that it is not.

Consolidation The stabilization of information in long-term memory through structural changes in the brain.

Constancy The assumption that objects in the physical world do not change spontaneously, but maintain their size, shape, color, and brightness over time.

Constructive coping Healthy efforts to reduce the impact of stressors.

Contact comfort The need for touch as a primary drive in monkeys and humans.

Content The surface meaning of the words in a problem.

Content validity Refers to the surface appearance of the items on the test and whether they reflect the concept of interest (also called face validity).

Continuous positive airway pressure (CPAP) A treatment for insomnia utilizing a small machine and mask to keep the airway open.

Continuous reinforcement Following every behavior with a consequence.

Continuum of sexual orientation Most people report falling somewhere in the range from exclusively heterosexual to exclusively homosexual.

Control group In an experiment, the group that receives no extra treatment or experience.

Convenience sample A group of participants who are readily available for a study.

Convergence A cue to depth based on the muscle movement of your eyes as they work to coordinate focus on objects in front of you.

Conversion disorder A disorder in which a worry or concern is transformed into a physical symptom.

Cope To reduce the impact of an event.

Coping Efforts to reduce the impact of stressors.

Coronary heart disease A medical condition that results in narrowing of the vessels that supply blood to the heart.

Corpus callosum A dense network of fibers that connects the left and right cerebral hemispheres.

Correlation A measure of the degree to which different factors are associated with one another.

Correlation coefficient An index, called r, of the degree of relationship between two variables, ranging from –1.00 to +1.00.

Cortical localization The observation that certain areas of the brain are responsible for specific processes.

Corticosteroids Hormones produced in the adrenal cortex in reaction to stress.

Counseling psychologist A mental health professional who helps people experiencing difficulty adjusting to life stressors to achieve greater well-being.

Counterconditioning A behavioral technique in which a response to a stimulus is replaced by a new response.

Creative intelligence Sternberg's theory suggests an underlying component of applying mental abilities to your experience in novel and helpful ways.

Creativity Novel thinking in which we redefine problems, see gaps in knowledge, generate ideas, and take reasonable risks in implementing them.

Critical period A sensitive time in development during which learning must occur.

Critical thinking Identification and evaluation of evidence to guide thoughts and decision making.

Cross-cultural psychology A branch of psychology concerned with the impact that shared attitudes, customs, and behaviors have on individual behavior and mental processes.

Cross-sectional study Comparing people at different ages with different people in the age groups.

Crystalized intelligence The ability to draw upon previously learned knowledge and skills.

Cued recall Retrieving information from related pieces of information.

Cyberbullying Aggressive and hostile acts toward others through Internet media.

D (deficit) needs According to Maslow, needs other than self-actualization needs.

Daily hassles (microstressors) Minor irritations that produce stress.

Dark adaptation The increased sensitivity experienced when your eyes adjust to lower levels of available light.

Debriefing The process by which any deception used by researchers is fully disclosed to participants at the end of a study.

Decay theory The notion that information fades from memory on its own.

Deception To actively provide information to the participant that is untrue.

Decision Thinking that requires a choice among alternatives.

Decision tree A decision-support tool that uses a tree-like graph of options, including chance event, resources, cost, and value.

Deductive reasoning A logical task in which new assertions are derived from what is known.

Deep brain stimulation (DBS) A surgical treatment in which a medical device is used to send electrical impulses to parts of the nervous system.

Deep structure The meaning composed by a phrase or sentence.

Defense mechanism According to the psychoanalytic perspective, a compromise that the ego uses to satisfy an id instinct indirectly.

Defensive attribution Blaming people for bad things that happen to them in order to protect your own feelings.

Deindividuation A merging of the self with a group in order to feel anonymous.

Deinstitutionalization The process of replacing inpatient psychiatric care with community outpatient services.

Delay of gratification The ability to postpone rewards until a later time.

Deliberation Slow, careful thinking aimed at considering all alternatives.

Deliberative practice Working on skills just beyond your current level of comfort.

Delta waves A type of brain wave pattern linked to Stage 4 sleep.

Delusion A belief that most people would think is incredible or implausible.

Dementia Progressive loss of cognitive function due to aging or disease.

Dendrite Nerve cell structure that receives information from other cells.

Denial A psychoanalytic defense mechanism in which a person fails to accept a reality.

Dependence When a person's drug use has led to distress or impairment and unsuccessful efforts to reduce drug use.

Dependent variable The measurement collected to determine if there was any effect of the independent variable in an experiment.

Depolarize The process by which an axon becomes more positive.

Depressants A class of drugs that reduces the activity in the nervous system.

Depth perception The detection of the distance of a stimulus from the body.

Diabetes A disease in which sugar in the blood is ineffectively used due to resistance to or an absence of insulin.

Diathesis-stress hypothesis A hypothesis that suggests a condition can have a biological root or cause that is triggered by an environmental stressor.

Difference threshold The smallest difference in sensation that is reliably detectable.

Differentiation Growth in complexity over time, with structures and functions becoming more specific for given tasks.

Diffusion of responsibility The tendency for the responsibility to help is spread across a crowd.

Discrimination Learning to see the difference between two similar stimuli; The tendency to act differently toward members of a particular group.

Disorganized type of schizophrenia A schizophrenic disorder characterized by disorganized speech and behavior, a flat mood, and inappropriate emotions. Severe, active phases are characterized by bizarre delusions of bodily functions, frequent disorganized hallucinations, and incoherent speech.

Displacement The ability to refer to things not visible in our immediate surroundings.

Display rules Guidelines about how one should express emotions.

Disposition The way a person behaves across different situations as well as over time.

Dissociation A split of consciousness or attention into two or more separate streams.

Dissociation theory of hypnosis A theory of hypnosis that suggests that the hypnotic state produces a split in consciousness and separates the executive control system from the rest of the brain.

Dissociative amnesia A condition characterized by extreme memory lapses or forgetting important personal information; usually associated with a traumatic emotional experience.

Dissociative disorder A disorder characterized by the sudden loss of the integration of consciousness or memory, or a change in personal identity.

Dissociative fugue A disorder in which a person forgets who he or she is, often traveling great distances and assuming new identities that resemble his or her original identity.

Dissociative identity disorder (DID) A dissociative disorder in which two or more distinct identities, each with unique characteristics, exist within one person.

Distinctive features The essential physical properties that uniquely identify an object.

Divided attention The process of attending to two or more tasks to perform them at the same time.

Dizygotic (DZ) twins Twins who are formed from two fertilized eggs; also known as fraternal twins.

Dominant gene A unit of heredity whose influence is exerted over other genes.

Door-in-the-face technique A practice by which rejecting an unreasonable request will lead to a more reasonable request that is more likely to be accepted.

Dopamine Neurotransmitter that is involved in movement and reward systems.

Dopamine hypothesis of schizophrenia A hypothesis that suggests that the neurotransmitter dopamine plays a key role in schizophrenia.

Double-blind procedure A method in which both the experimenter and participant are not informed about the subject's assignment to a treatment within a study.

Down syndrome An extra chromosome causes physical characteristics like poor muscle tone and slanting eyes, and moderate to severe intellectual disability.

Dream An array of sensory events experienced during sleep.

Dream analysis A psychoanalytic technique that reveals intrapsychic conflicts through interpretations of dreams.

Drive A tension arising from within physiological systems that motivates action.

Drive theory A theory that states of tension motivate us to take action to reduce them.

Drug abuse A condition in which a person uses psychoactive substances that results in distress or impairment in their social, work, or school functioning.

Drug addiction A situation in which taking a psychoactive substance leads to habitual use and craving even though the use causes distress or impairment.

Drug dependence A situation in which a person's drug use has led to distress or impairment including drug tolerance, significant withdrawal symptoms, and unsuccessful efforts to reduce drug use.

Drug rebound effect A situation in which stopping the use of a drug can have the reverse effect of the action of the drug.

Dual processes The two modes of thinking, one fast and easy, one slow and careful.

Dual processing The ability to attend to and manage several stimuli at once, some automatically (out of consciousness) and some intentionally in your awareness.

Dyssomnia A condition that affects the quantity, quality, or timing of sleep.

Echoic memory Sensory memory for the sound reaching your ears.

Eclarative memory Memory for knowledge of which we are consciously aware; also called explicit memory.

Eclectic approach Blending several theories together to explain or influence behavior.

Eclectic model An approach that pulls together multiple ways of examining a particular problem or question

Ecstasy (MDMA) A stimulant-hallucinogenic drug that can induce euphoria and diminish anxiety.

Efferent nerve fibers A type of neuron that carries impulses away from the central nervous system.

Ego According to Freud, the part of the personality responsible for interacting with conscious reality.

Ego dystonic A psychological symptom that causes a person distress.

Ego syntonic A psychological symptom that does not cause a person distress.

Egocentrism In preschool children, the belief that others know, think, and feel the same way they do.

Elaboration Tying new information to that already stored in memory.

Electrical stimulation of the brain A technique used to stimulate neural networks in the nervous system. Also known as deep brain stimulation.

Electroconvulsive therapy (ECT) A biological treatment in which seizures are induced in anesthetized patients.

Electroencephalogram (EEG) A device that measures and illustrates the electrical activity in the brain.

Embryo Prenatal stage following zygote lasting 2 to 8 weeks; in this stage, the heart begins beating.

Emotion A class of subjective feelings elicited by stimuli that have high significance to an individual.

Emotion-focused coping A reaction to stress that involves managing the feelings that arise from the situation.

Emotional intelligence The ability to perceive, understand, integrate, and regulate emotions to be self-motivated and socially skilled.

Empathy An attempt to understand the client's inner world.

Empirical Research studies that gain information by carefully collecting observations, or data.

Empirical evidence A type of information that is capable of being confirmed or invalidated by systematic observation.

Empirically derived test A type of instrument that starts with a large number of test questions in order to select the ones that best reflect the characteristics being tested.

Empiricism The theory of knowledge that assumes that knowledge should be based on observation.

En vivo A type of exposure therapy in which the actual feared object is used.

Encoding The process of taking new information and storing it in short- and long-term memory.

Encoding specificity The principle that cues present at encoding will be the best cues for retrieval.

Endocrine system The network of glands throughout the body that manufacture and secrete hormones.

Endorphins Chemicals linked to pain perception and reward.

Engagement Feelings of involvement and interest in work.

Environmental influence A factor in the social, cultural, physical, or family setting that may influence an individual.

Epidemiology A science that examines the frequency of medical conditions.

Episodic memory Recall of your own personal, autobiographical experiences.

Equity theory The notion that people want their effort and pay to be fair compared to that of others.

Eros An id instinct that reduces tension associated with basic biological drives.

Escape learning An acquired behavior performed to avoid a noxious stimulus.

Esteem motivation Desire to feel appreciation from others.

Estrogen A sex hormone produced primarily by the ovaries that is central to female sexual development and fertility.

Ethnocentrism Believing that your own group is superior to others and should be the standard by which other cultures are judged.

Etiology Cause of a disorder.

Evidence-based practice Selecting therapy treatments using information gained through research.

Evolutionary psychologist Researcher who applies the theory of evolution to explain the psychology behind behaviors.

Evolutionary psychology A branch of psychology that examines the impact of natural selection on behavioral and mental processes.

Evolved behaviors Behaviors selected over generations to best fit the environment.

Excitatory postsynaptic potential (EPSP) A voltage change caused by the binding of neurotransmitters that causes a positive voltage shift in the resting potential of the postsynaptic neuron triggering the neuron to fire.

Excitement phase Sexual arousal begins with blood circulation into all the erectile structures in the body.

Executive control system An assortment of brain processes that plan and initiate actions.

Experiment A method by which one or more independent factors is manipulated by an experimenter, and the result is measured through one or more dependent variables.

Experimental group In an experiment, the group that receives some treatment or experience.

Experimenter bias The introduction of inaccuracy of measurements due to the researcher's expectations.

Explanatory style Reflects what you think caused an event. Explanatory style can be either optimistic or pessimistic.

Exposure therapy A behavior therapy technique that involves repeatedly presenting the client with a distressing object in order to reduce anxiety.

"Exotic becomes erotic" Bem's theory that typical gender preferences lead to less exposure to the opposite sex and, thus, later attraction.

External attribution An explanation of behavior that focuses on environmental explanations.

External locus of control The idea that reinforcers and punishments are outside of your control.

Extinction The tendency to stop responding to the conditioned stimulus when repeatedly presented without the unconditioned stimulus.

Extinguish To stop the display of a given behavior.

Extralinguistic factors Information outside of language that aids in comprehension.

Extrasensory perception (ESP or psi) Detecting information without knowing its sensory source.

Extrinsic incentives Rewards (such as pay) given to motivate people to perform certain behaviors.

Extrinsic motivation Behavior is repeated only when external reinforcement is provided.

Extroversion A trait that describes that an individual is energized by the external world rather than by the internal world.

Extrovert A personality type that prefers the external world to the internal world; also known as extroversion.

Eye movement desensitization reprocessing (EMDR) A therapy technique involving bilateral stimulation in order to process distressing memories.

Facial feedback hypothesis A theory that suggests that the position of the facial muscles influences emotional expression.

Factitious disorder A psychological disorder in which a person plays the sick role for the emotional gain, sometimes called Münchausen syndrome.

Factor analysis A statistical technique used to find clusters of related items.

Family study A method that allows researchers to test hypotheses concerning the contribution of genetic and environmental factors by examining biological relatives.

Family therapy A type of psychotherapy that treats the immediate social system, i.e., the family, to improve individuals' psychological functioning.

False consensus effect The habit of seeing our own behavior as typical.

False memory Inaccurate information incorporated into memory.

Feature detectors Individual cells in the visual cortex that respond only to certain types of visual patterns, such as lines, circles, or angles.

Feel-good, do-good phenomenon The theory that people are more likely to be helpful if they are happy.

Fertile A female able to conceive and bear children.

Fetal alcohol syndrome Irreversible brain abnormalities caused by the mother's consumption of alcohol during pregnancy.

Fetus The unborn child from around 9 weeks until birth.

Fight-or-flight response A reaction to danger in which the sympathetic nervous system prepares the organs for vigorous activity.

Fitness The contribution an individual makes to the gene pool of the next generation.

Fixation According to Freud, a habit of obtaining tension reduction from an earlier stage of psychosexual development; Getting stuck on an approach to a problem and failing to see alternative approaches.

Fixed-interval schedule Providing reinforcement for the first behavior after a set amount of time passes.

Fixed mindset The belief that your traits are predetermined and nothing can change them.

Fixed-ratio schedule Providing reinforcement after a set number of repeated behaviors.

Flashbulb memory An emotional or vivid event that appears to be well remembered.

Flooding A therapy to treat phobias based on intense exposure to the feared stimulus.

Flow A state of mind arising during activities when the challenge of the task is met by expertise.

Flynn effect The increase in intelligence test scores have (about three points per decade, across the globe) over generations taking the tests.

Foot-in-the-door technique A practice by which agreement to a small request makes agreement to a more unreasonable request more likely.

Forebrain The largest part of the brain, consisting of a number of structures including the cerebrum, the thalamus, and the limbic system.

Forgetting curve Graph showing that much information is immediately lost from memory after study.

Formal operational stage Piaget's final stage (around age 12) characterized by reasoning on a logical or hypothetical level.

Fovea The focal point of the retina where image processing is sharpest due to more cone cells.

Framing effect A bias in decisions based on the description of the problem.

Free association A psychoanalytic technique in which people will report the first things that occur to them. Used to uncover unconscious conflicts.

Frequency The wavelength of sound or light waves (the time distance between peaks).

Frequency theory The notion that the firing rate of neurons is determined directly by the frequency (length of time between sound waves) of the sound.

Frontal lobe The front part of the cerebral cortex involved in planning, organization, and personality.

Frustration Anxiety felt when attempts to reach a goal are hindered.

Frustration aggression hypothesis Early theory of anger suggesting that anger is a reaction to a goal blocked or unattained.

Fully functioning person According to Jung, a person who has a developed real self.

Functional fixedness Seeing objects for use only in their intended roles.

Functional magnetic resonance imaging (fMRI) Neuroscience imaging technique used to measure changes in blood flow.

Functional plasticity The capacity to change areas of the brain that are responsible for activities.

Functionalism A school of psychology concerned with the purposes of behavior and mental processes.

Fundamental attribution error An inclination to overestimate the impact of internal characteristics in explaining the behavior of others and underestimate the same characteristics in explaining your own behavior.

Galvanic skin response (GSR) A measurement of the conductivity of your skin.

Gamma-aminobutric acid (GABA) The nervous system's primary inhibitory neurotransmitter.

Ganglion cells More complex cells that process patterns of receptor activation within the retina.

Gate-control theory The notion that interneurons in the spinal cord act as a gate to block some sensory signals from going to the brain.

Geon A simple three-dimensional form that, in combination, can create any shape.

Gender roles Our expectations about how males and females should act are learned through culture.

Gene A segment of DNA.

General adaptation syndrome (GAS) Selye's term for the body's stress response that occurs in three stages: alarm, resistance, and exhaustion.

General intelligence (g) Spearman's theory that all mental abilities reflect a single underlying capacity.

Generalizability How well a study's findings can be applied to other people and circumstances.

Generalization Learning to respond to stimuli similar to the one experienced.

Generalized anxiety disorder (GAD) A psychological condition characterized by unexplained, excessive worry that has an unspecific cause.

Generate and test Guess at the answer and see if it works on a trial-and-error basis.

Generation effect Memory is better for information that we create ourselves.

Generativity The capacity to use a finite set to create endless variety of unique combinations; Erikson's stage of life focusing on contributing to the development of the next generation and "making a difference."

Genius A noted, exceptional individual whose accomplishments outlive them.

Genogram Family tree.

Genome The sum of an organism's hereditary information.

Genotype An individual's genetic makeup.

Genuineness According to the client-centered approach, authenticity in a relationship.

Gestalt The "whole," reflecting the belief that the whole emerges in perception and is more than simply "the sum of its parts."

Ghrelin A hormone secreted by the empty stomach to stimulate hunger.

Gifted A determination made by some schools and educational programs based on an intelligence test score of more than 130.

Gist The semantic meaning of a sentence.

Glia cells Cells in the nervous system that provide support and protection for neurons.

Glucose The form of sugar that carries nutrients in the bloodstream.

Glutamate An excitatory neurotransmitter.

Goal A situation you would like to achieve.

Gonads An organ that secretes sex hormones.

Grammar Rules within a language that determine whether a sentence is properly formed and complete.

Grandmother hypothesis Evolutionary theory that older females aid in the reproductive success of their families by helping to raise grandchildren.

Graphology A technique in which handwriting is analyzed in order to describe personality.

Great mother An archetype described by Jung that symbolizes a person or thing that provides nurture without wanting anything in return.

Group Collection of people who have something in common.

Group aptitude test A test meant to assess your ability to benefit from further training or education, but are also affected by past achievements in school. (e.g., ACT)

Group polarization The likelihood that the attitudes of members of a team will become more similar over time.

Group therapy A psychotherapeutic technique that treats multiple clients in a collective setting.

Groupthink When a group's ideals become so important that alternative ideas are dismissed.

Growth mindset Belief that your qualities and capacities develop through effort.

Gustatory The sense of taste.

Hair cell receptors Sound receptors in the cochlea that transduce fluid movement into neural impulses.

Hallucination Sensory perception with no sensory input. The perception may affect any or all of the five senses.

Hallucinogens A type of drug that distort conscious experiences.

Hardiness A personality style characterized by commitment, challenge, and control.

Hawthorne effect Improvement in a test group (compared to a control group) caused by the increased interest shown toward them.

Health psychology A branch of psychology that is concerned with how psychological factors impact wellness, illness, and medical treatments.

Healthy lifestyle According to Adler, attempts to compensate for feelings of inferiority in a socially useful way.

Heritability How much of a characteristic can be linked to genetics as opposed to the environment.

Hero An archetype that represents someone who saves the day.

Heterosexual A person who desires emotional and sexual intimacy with members of the opposite sex.

Heterozygous condition A circumstance where genes are different for a given trait.

Heuristic A mental shortcut, or rule of thumb, that may or may not lead to a correct solution.

Hidden observer In the dissociation theory of hypnosis, the executive control system that witnesses without being involved.

Hierarchy of needs According to Maslow, the order of importance of motivations, from basic physiological needs to self-fulfillment needs.

Higher-order conditioning Learning to associate a neutral stimulus with an already-learned conditioned stimulus and conditioned response.

Hindbrain A region of the brain that includes the cerebellum, the pons, and the medulla. It supports vital bodily processes.

Hippocampus Part of the limbic system that is involved in processing new memories.

Holophrastic The use of a single word to represent more complex ideas in early language learning.

Homosexual A person who desires emotional and sexual intimacy with members of the same sex.

Homozygous condition A circumstance where both genes are the same for a given trait.

Hormone A chemical messenger that is produced by endocrine glands and influences body growth, mood, and sexual characteristics.

Hostile aggression Aggression simply to inflict harm.

Human sexual response cycle Phases of excitement, plateau, orgasm, and resolution that complete a sexual act.

Humanism A theoretical orientation that emphasizes growth, potential, and self-actualization; also known as the phenomenological approach.

Humanistic perspective A branch of psychology that emphasizes growth, potential, and self-actualization.

Humanistic psychology Theories of motivation emphasizing the goal to develop to the highest potential for each individual.

Hypermnesia Elevated memory recall by means of hypnosis.

Hyperthymesia Recalling past autobiographical events to an excessive degree and accuracy.

Hypnagogic hallucinations Sensory experiences that occur between being awake and asleep.

Hypnosis A trancelike state in which the subject readily accepts the hypnotist's suggestion of changes in consciousness or sensations.

Hypochondriasis A disorder characterized by a specific disease process that progresses in a person in which there is no physiological cause.

Hypocretin A hormone that is linked to wakefulness.

Hypomania A condition in which a person has symptoms of mania but avoids getting into trouble.

Hypothalamus The functional center of motivation in the brain.

Hypothesis A clear statement or prediction that can be shown to be true or false in an experiment.

Iconic memory Sensory memory for visual information taken in.

Id According to Freud, the part of the personality that operates on the pleasure principle, always looking to reduce tension that comes from basic physiological drives.

Ideal self According to Rogers, a version of yourself that could please other people.

Identification According to Freud, the unconscious process of copying the behavior of a person.

Identity formation The process of developing a distinct, individualized personality.

Ideocentrism A personality trait with an interreliant focus.

Illusion A visual image that creates a misperception of the world.

Immune system Processes the body uses to protect against disease.

Immunosuppression Weakening the immune response.

Impossible figure An image that can't be resolved into a single consistent interpretation.

In-group bias Accepting the attitudes of your own team.

Inattentional blindness Failing to process an object clearly present in a scene.

Incentive The rewards and punishments associated with different actions.

Incentive theories Motivation that focuses on the reward or payoff for behaviors.

Incidental memory Explicit knowledge you did not intentionally encode.

Inclusive fitness (kinship selection) Also known as kin selection, the contributions to the next generation's gene pool of both an individual and his or her relatives.

Incongruency According to Rogers, the difference between your ideal self and your actual self.

Incubation A period of time in which a problem is set aside prior to further attempts to solve it.

Independent variable The factor that an experimenter manipulates to create different experiences for participants.

Individualist culture A culture that places an emphasis on each person's rights rather than on the society.

Inductive reasoning Generalizing from specific information to form a rule.

Industrial and organizational psychology Field of study addressing the psychology of work.

Inferential statistic A numerical test to determine what conclusions can be drawn from observed data.

Inferiority According to Adler, feelings of inadequacy; also known as organ inferiority.

Informational social influence Sway that comes from believing another person.

Informed consent The process through which an experimenter describes the nature of study participation to the potential volunteer, including his or her right to stop at any time.

Inhalants Drugs whose vapors are breathed in to produce their intoxicating effect.

Inhibitory postsynaptic potential (IPSP) A voltage change caused by the binding of neurotransmitters that causes a negative voltage shift in the resting potential of the postsynaptic neuron preventing the neuron from firing.

Insight An understanding of the motivation of behavior.

Insight therapies A family of psychotherapies that focus on the unconscious motivations of behavior.

Insomnia A condition in which a person is unable to fall or stay asleep.

Instinct theories Motivation from biologically programmed behaviors occurring in response to environmental cues.

Instinctual drift The tendency for new behaviors to revert to ones familiar to that species.

Instrumental aggression Words or physical acts a person does to cause harm in an ultimate goal to obtain something.

Insulin A hormone secreted by the pancreas and used to convert glucose into energy for muscle use.

Intellectual disability A limitation in intellectual functioning indicated by an intelligence test score of less than 70 along with problems in adaptive behavior.

Intelligence The capacity to learn from experience, acquire knowledge, adapt to the environment, and solve problems.

Intelligence quotient (IQ) The ratio of a child's "mental age" score on the Stanford-Binet test divided by his or her chronological age.

Intelligence test A measure intended to identify the relative mental ability of individuals.

Interaction between variables When the effect of one independent variable on the dependent variable depends upon the level of another independent variable.

Interactionist theory The view that language combines inborn abilities with special environmental triggers.

Interference theory New knowledge can disrupt recently learned memories.

Intermittent reinforcement Following behavior with a consequence sometimes, but not every time.

Internal attribution An explanation of behavior based on personality characteristics.

Internal locus of control The idea that reinforcers and punishments are under your own control.

Internet addiction Excessive use of computer systems that causes impairment in social, occupational, or school functioning.

Internet-mediated research Using the World Wide Web to collect data from remote participants.

Interneuron A neuron that communicates only with other neurons.

Interpretation A psychoanalytic technique in which a therapist will reveal explanations of the client's unconscious motivations in order to improve psychological functioning.

Interval schedule Reinforcement is provided after time passes, and then a behavior is repeated.

Interviewer illusion Belief in one's own intuitive abilities to find good candidates in the absence of evidence.

Intrapsychic conflict Differences between the desires of the id, ego, and superego.

Intrinsic incentives Feelings of reward created within the individual.

Intrinsic motivation The desire to perform behaviors for an internal reward.

Introspection Examination of one's own mental and emotional processes.

Introvert A personality type that prefers the internal world to the external world; also known as introversion.

Intuition The "gut feeling" that leads to a fast and easy conclusion.

Irrelevant information Knowledge referred to in a problem that is not needed in its solution.

Isomorphic A representation taking on the same shape or form as the object itself.

James-Lange theory A concept of emotion that suggests that emotions are composed of our awareness of biological reactions to stimuli.

Job analysis Determination of the tasks, knowledge, skills, and abilities needed in a job.

Job burnout A prolonged response to chronic emotional and interpersonal stress on the job.

Journal A publication containing articles written by scientists that are reviewed before publication by a group of peers.

Judgment Making an informed guess about something unknown or uncertain.

Just noticeable difference (jnd) The smallest amount of change between two stimuli that a person can detect at least half of the time.

Just-world hypothesis A belief that people get what they deserve and deserve what they get.

K-complex An EEG waveform that is characteristic of Stage 2 sleep.

Kinetic depth effect The movement of a three-dimensional object reveals its shape.

Lack of transfer The failure to use a past analogy that offers a solution.

Language A form of thinking used to communicate with others and ourselves.

Latent content In psychoanalytic theory, the true, underlying, undisguised meaning of a dream.

Latent learning Knowledge that is not displayed in behavior until reinforcement is provided.

Lateral hypothalamus The "start eating" functional center in the brain.

Lateralization of function The concept that each hemisphere of the cerebral cortex is primarily responsible for certain activities.

Law of Effect Behaviors that lead to positive outcomes are likely to be repeated.

Laws of perceptual grouping Simple organizational principles that help to interpret image elements, including similarity, proximity, continuity, and closure.

Learned helplessness When an animal fails to take action to escape a noxious stimulus.

Learning A lasting change in knowledge or behavior based on experience.

Learning perspective A theory that suggests that anxiety disorders are learned behaviors.

Leptin A protein secreted by fat cells to signal adequate stores.

Lesion A natural or intentional destruction of brain tissue.

Levels of analysis Various ways of examining the same psychological phenomenon.

Levels of processing The depth of thinking with new information affects the likelihood of remembering it.

Lexical approach to traits An approach that uses language to determining the most important traits of personality.

Libido According to Freud, the energy linked with sexuality.

Lifestyle According to Adler, the way in which you strive for superiority in order to make up for feelings of inferiority.

Limbic system A group of structures surrounding the brainstem that governs emotions such as anger, happiness, and fear, and stores and retrieves new memories.

Linguistic relativity The notion that language shapes our ideas and not the other way around.

Link method Forming links between concepts to make them more memorable.

Lithium A medication used to treat bipolar mood disorders.

Lobotomy A surgery that involves destruction of nerves in the prefrontal cortex in order to improve symptoms of psychological conditions.

Locus of contro A cognitive person variable that summarizes your idea of the source of reinforcement and punishment.

Long-term memory (LTM) The enduring stage of memory that is unlimited in capacity and duration.

Long-term potentiation The process of changes in neuronal receptivity that encodes information into memory.

Longitudinal study Following a person through development by studying him or her at different points in time.

Loss aversion Preferring options that will avoid losing rather than maximize gains.

Lymphocytes A type of cell involved in the immune system that works to attack foreign substances.

Lysergic acid diethylamide (LSD) A synthetic psychedelic hallucinogenic drug that produces altered states of consciousness.

Magnetic resonance imaging (MRI) A non-invasive neuroscience imaging technique that uses magnets and radio equipment to produce detailed images.

Maintenance rehearsal Reactivating information in short-term memory to keep it in mind.

Malingering A condition involving an external motivation for illness, such as avoiding a test.

Mania A condition associated with an elevated, expansive, or sometimes irritable mood.

Manifest content In psychoanalytic theory, the dream as the dreamer reports it.

Marijuana A drug that has both painkilling as well as stimulating effects on the nervous system.

Matching hypothesis The belief that people are paired to equally attractive partners.

Mating Male-to-female intercourse for the purpose of reproduction.

Maturation Biological growth occurring in a continuous fashion over time.

Mean The arithmetic average, or the sum of all scores in a sample divided by the number of scores.

Means-end analysis A problem-solving strategy that reduces differences between the current and the goal states.

Mechanism of action MOA A description of the way a drug functions.

Median The score at the middle of a distribution of scores from a sample.

Medical model A theory that suggests that psychological disorders are illnesses that require treatment.

Meditation A mental practice that regulates attention and awareness.

Medulla Part of the hindbrain that is involved in breathing, heartbeat, and other essential functions.

Melatonin A hormone manufactured by the pineal gland that promotes sleepiness.

Memory The enduring consequence in the mind of our experiences with the world.

Menarche The occurrence of a first menstrual period, indicating the capacity to become pregnant.

Menopause The cessation of menstrual periods in women, usually occurring around age 50.

Mental age The average level of intellectual development for a child of a particular age.

Mental hospital A medical center that treats psychological conditions.

Mental model A visual, spatial, or content-based representation of a problem or situation.

Mental set An existing state of mind, habit, or attitude that affects new problem solving.

Mere exposure effect Repeated exposure to a stimulus leads to preferring that stimulus.

Meta-analysis A study that examines the results of many earlier studies on a topic and compares their findings to draw conclusions.

Metabolism The physiological processes used to convert energy from nutrients.

Metacognition Reflective thoughts about your own thinking processes.

Methamphetamine A stimulant drug that is associated with increased nervous system activity and elevated libido and self-esteem.

Method of loci Mnemonic for remembering items by placing them on a familiar path.

Midbrain Part of the brainstem involved in control of sensory processes.

Mind Mental processes and our subjective experiences.

Mindset A belief about yourself and your abilities, such as intelligence, talents, and personality.

Minnesota Multiphasic Personality Inventory (MMPI) An empirically derived personality test that assesses a range of characteristics.

Mirror neuron A type of neuron that fires when an individual watches an action and when performing the action.

Misinformation effect Adding new, incorrect information to a memory after the event.

Mnemonic Encoding "trick" that ties to-be-remembered information to something familiar.

Mode The most frequently observed score in a data sample.

Model One who performs specific behaviors that others observe.

Modeling Performing specific behaviors that others observe.

Mood Long-lasting, nonspecific emotional state.

Mood congruence Matching emotional mood as a cue at encoding and retrieval to improve memory.

Mood stabilizers A family of medications used to treat bipolar mood disorders.

Monoamine hypothesis of depression A hypothesis that suggests that depressive symptoms are brought on by a malfunction of certain types of neurotransmitters.

Monocular cues Ways of determining the distance of an object that require a single eye.

Monozygotic (MZ) twins Twins from a single fertilized egg; also known as identical twins.

Morpheme The smallest unit of sounds that carries meaning.

Motherese "Baby talk" that is high in pitch, rhythmic, and simple and may better attract responses from babies.

Motion parallax The interpretation that objects close to you are moving past you faster than objects farther away.

Motivation An inner state that energizes people toward the fulfillment of a goal.

Motive The pursuit of pleasure and the avoidance of pain or displeasure.

Motor cortex A region of the cerebral cortex involved in planning, controlling, and executing motor functions.

Motor neuron A type of neuron that interfaces with muscles and glands.

Müller-Lyer illusion Two lines of the same length appear to be different if one has inward "arrowhead" extensions compared to outward extensions.

Multiple-approach-avoidance conflict A situation in which a decision must be made between many choices, each with positive and negative consequences.

Multiple intelligences Gardner's theory proposed seven separate types of cognitive abilities operating independently.

Myelin sheath A fatty substance that insulates the axon and enables efficient transmission.

Narcolepsy A condition characterized by daytime sleepiness and sudden lapses into sleep during the day.

Nativist theory The view that language is a special skill we are born with.

Natural selection Varying success in reproduction resulting from the interaction of an organism with the environment.

Naturalistic observation Observing human behavior as it occurs in a real-world setting.

Need for achievement Desire to succeed at challenging tasks.

Need to belong Motivation to feel a part of relationships or groups of people.

Negative coping Engaging in behaviors that are unhealthy and can make matters worse.

Negative correlation An association between two variables where higher scores on one go with lower scores on the other.

Negative reinforcement A consequence that takes away an unpleasant state, making behavior more likely to occur.

Negative symptoms of psychosis Symptoms of psychosis that involve behavior deficits, or expected behaviors that are absent.

Neo-Freudian Psychoanalytic theories inspired by Sigmund Freud.

Neodissociation theory of hypnosis A theory of hypnosis that suggests that hypnosis causes subjects to divide their consciousness voluntarily.

Nerves Bundles of neurons.

Nervous system A collection of organs including neurons and supportive systems.

Neural pruning The destruction of certain neurons to increase the processing speed of the nervous system.

Neurogenesis The process of the development of new neurons.

Neuron A nerve cell.

Neuroscience The study of the brain and nervous system; also called biological psychology.

Neuroticism A personality trait that describes how emotional the person might be.

Neurotransmitter Chemical messenger that transmits information from one neuron to another.

Neutral stimulus An event or signal that causes no reflexive, automatic response.

Nicotine A type of drug that targets the nicotinic receptors. Found in tobacco.

Nightmare A type of dream that is frightening and often will wake up the dreamer.

Non-bizarre delusions False beliefs that are possible but highly unlikely.

Norepinephrine A neurotransmitter responsible for learning and memory.

Norm Behavioral milestone that identifies when certain behaviors usually occur in normal development; Comparison of many individuals on the same test so that relative performance can be determined.

Normal distribution The inverted bell-shaped frequency distribution that often occurs for psychological tests and variables such as height.

Normative social influence The need to conform due to social pressures.

nREM sleep Stages of sleep in which dreams are unlikely to occur and that are not associated with rapid eye movement.

Obedience Behavior that is in response to the orders of another.

Obesity An excess level of fat in the body, at least 15% above ideal weight for a given height.

Object permanence Babies remembering objects they can no longer see in front of them.

Objective A scoring system where the results are the same no matter who scores it.

Observational learning Acquiring new behaviors from watching a model.

Obsession A thought that is unwanted, intrusive, and distressing.

Obsessive-compulsive disorder A psychological disorder associated with obsessions, or obsessions linked to compulsions.

Occipital lobe An area in the back of the cerebral cortex. Its visual cortex processes image information.

Oedipal complex According to Freud, a boy's unconscious desire for his mother that results in identification with his father.

Olfaction The sense of smell.

Olfactory bulb The processing center for smell located at the base of the brain.

Openness to experience A personality trait that is part of the Big Five that describes how much affection a person has for newness.

Operant A behavior freely initiated or displayed, which can be conditioned.

Operant conditioning Training emitted behaviors to make them more likely to occur again.

Operational definition The concrete implementation of a psychological concept within a study.

Opiates A psychoactive substance made from opium that relieves pain and reduces the activity of the nervous system.

Opponent process theory The theory that opposing, or complementary, colors (yellow/blue, white/black, and red/green) are produced by differences in firing rates by complex cells within the retina.

Optic chiasm The place in the front of the brain where the neural tracts following from the optic nerve of each eye cross over so that some tracts lead to both the right and left hemispheres.

Optic nerve The bundle of neural fibers collecting sensation in the retina that passes out of the eyeball in a pathway to the brain.

Optimal arousal A level of activation that is sufficient but not overwhelming.

Optimistic explanatory style A way of explaining negative events by using external, unstable, and specific attributions.

Organizational psychology Field examining how the structure of jobs and the workplace affects the success of group efforts.

Orgasmic phase The climax of arousal during which orgasm and ejaculation occur.

Out-group homogeneity The tendency for members of an out-group to seem similar to each other.

Outpatient Treatment settings that are outside of a hospital.

Oval window Membrane in the ear that collects sound waves and translates them into fluid movement in the cochlea.

Overconfidence Being more certain about your beliefs than you should be.

Overjustification effect When a task provides an extrinsic reward, no intrinsic motive is needed.

Overlearning Continuing learning even when recall appears successful.

Overregularize Applying a rule of grammar beyond its limits.

Oxytocin "Feel-good" hormone released after orgasm.

Pacinian corpuscles Tiny pressure receptors located in the fatty layer beneath the skin.

Panic attack A period of intense fear or discomfort that is linked with specific physical and psychological symptoms.

Panic disorder The presence of frequent, recurrent panic attacks, along with the fear of panic attacks.

Papillae Visible bumps on the tongue.

Parallel processing Analyzing information in groups or "columns" of cells in the cortex at the same time in order to understand an overall pattern.

Paranoid personality disorder A disorder characterized by a long and unwavering history of attributing malicious intent to others.

Paranoid type of schizophrenia A disorder characterized by highly structured non-bizarre delusions, coherent visual or auditory hallucinations, and feelings of persecution.

Paraphrase A description of the same meaning using different elements.

Parapsychology The study of paranormal or extrasensory phenomena.

Parasomnia Abnormal behaviors associated with sleep.

Parasympathetic nervous system A component of the autonomic nervous system that conserves bodily functions and energy.

Parental investment theory The required investment in offspring differs between genders, resulting in differing strategies.

Parietal lobe An area of the cerebral cortex located behind the frontal lobe. Its somatosensory cortex processes body sensation information.

Participant A volunteer who agrees to take part in research studies, also called a subject.

Paternal uncertainty Historically, men could not be sure whether a child was their genetic offspring.

Peak experience According to Maslow, "transient moment of self-actualization" that is associated with feelings of harmony, interconnectedness, and joy.

Perception The process of organizing sensory information to form a meaningful interpretation.

Perceptual asymmetry Because of imbalances between the left and right cerebral hemispheres, visual or auditory processing happens at different speeds depending on whether sensory input is coming from the left or right side of the body.

Perceptual set The influence of recent processing as a framework for continuing perception.

Perfection principle The image of the perfect person, or ego, that inspires the superego; also know as the ego ideal.

Peripheral nervous system A division of the nervous system excluding the brain and spinal cord.

Peripheral route to persuasion Influence based on small, noncore factors.

Persistence The ability to repeatedly respond to failure by exerting more effort.

Person perception Involves the way we form opinions about others.

Persona An archetype that represents the public self.

Personal unconscious According to Jung, the part of one's personality that stores material currently outside of awareness.

Personality An individual's pattern of thinking, feeling, and behaving.

Personality disorder A psychological condition, coded on Axis II of the DSM, that involves extreme, inflexible global personality traits that are chronic and pervasive.

Personality inventory A test used to measure an individual's pattern of thinking, feeling, and behaving.

Personality theory A system used to describe and explain the genesis and development of an individual's pattern of thinking, feeling, and behaving.

Personnel psychology Field focusing on the selection, training, and evaluation of employees.

Persuasion Convincing another person

Pessimistic explanatory style A way of explaining negative events by using internal, stable, and global attributions.

Phenomenology The idea that, in order to understand a person, it is important to understand the world from that person's perspective; also known as phenomenological approach.

Phenotype Expression of genetic influences.

Pheromone A characteristic biochemical odor emitted by an individual.

Phi phenomenon A series of static images viewed in sequence are interpreted as a moving image.

Philosophy The study of knowledge and existence.

Phobia A psychological symptom in which fear is unreasonably great or it interferes with a person's life.

Phonemes The basic sounds of human languages.

Photoreceptors The rod and cone cells in the retina that register the presence of light waves.

Phrase Two or more words combined to convey meaning.

Phrenology A procedure that uses bumps on an individual's head to determine and predict personality characteristics.

Physical dependence A condition in which a drug must be taken continually to avoid symptoms of withdrawal.

Physiology A branch of biology that studies internal biological processes.

Pituitary gland The endocrine system's master gland.

Place theory The notion that the pitch of a sound is determined by the location of the stimulation on the basilar membrane inside the ear.

Placebo A substance without an active ingredient.

Placebo effect Feeling benefit or improvement from a treatment known to have no effect.

Plasticity The ability of the nervous system to adapt by creating new neural pathways.

Plateau phase The second stage of the sexual response cycle, during which there is a leveling off of excitement.

Pleasure principle According to Freud, the drive to reduce tension.

Polygenic Characteristics that multiple genes shape.

Polygraph A machine that uses physiological measurements to detect lies.

Pons Part of the hindbrain that is involved in relaying information from the cortex, as well as in sleep and arousal.

Ponzo illusion The misjudgment based on linear perspective that identical objects placed within converging lines appears to be of different sizes.

Population The larger group about whom a study would like to draw conclusions.

Positive correlation An association between two variables where higher scores on one go with higher scores on the other.

Positive psychology A branch of psychology that emphasizes the constructive features of human strength and healthy living rather than pathology.

Positive regard A communication of love and respect.

Positive reinforcement A consequence that creates a pleasant state, making behavior more likely to occur.

Positive self-regard Respect for your own decisions.

Positive symptoms of psychosis Symptoms that are present in addition to typical psychotic behavior.

Positron emission tomography (PET) A neuroscience imaging technique that uses radioactive glucose to indicate areas of activity.

Posthypnotic suggestion A behavior or thinking pattern that comes out after hypnosis.

Postsynaptic neuron A neuron that receives a signal from another neuron.

Postsynaptic potential (PSP) Changes in the dendrite of the receiving neuron as the result of its binding with neurotransmitters.

Posttraumatic stress disorder Associated with a traumatic event, this disorder involves re-experiencing the trauma, increased arousal, and symptoms of numbing and avoidance.

Practical intelligence Sternberg's theory proposed the ability to assess a situation and do what is necessary to be successful.

Practitioner-scholar model Also called the Vail model, a program in which psychologists emphasize clinical training over generating new research in order to understand, synthesize, and apply existing research.

Pragmatics The social context of language that adds to its meaning.

Preconscious According to Freud, the part of your mind that contains material just outside of awareness that is easy to pull into awareness.

Predictive validity The ability of a test to identify those who will have high scores on other measures.

Prejudice Negative stereotypes or attitudes about members of a particular group.

Prenatal stage Development taking place in the mother's womb before birth.

Preoperational stage Piaget's stage for preschoolers, marked by an intense focus on what they perceive.

Presynaptic neuron A neuron that sends a signal to another neuron.

Primary insomnia Difficulty falling asleep, staying asleep, or waking up too early that is not associated with another medical or psychological condition.

Primary mental abilities Thurstone's theory of a set of seven different factors related to intelligence.

Primary reinforcer A reward that provides basic needs.

Primary sexual characteristics The reproductive organs and external genitalia.

Priming The activation of information in memory from a related cue.

Principle of entropy Jung's theory that opposites tend to come together over time.

Principle of equivalence According to Jung, the energy devoted to do one thing will be equally devoted to the opposite activity.

Principle of falsifiability The notion that a theory must be able to be disproved in order to be testable and scientific.

Principle of opposites According to Jung, the theory that every wish also represents the opposite of the same wish.

Probability theory A statistical algorithm that takes into account all contingencies and their likelihoods to determine the best estimate of an uncertain event.

Problem A situation with a starting point, a goal state, and a nonobvious way to get to it.

Problem-focused coping A reaction to stress that involves the management of the event causing the stress.

Procedural memory Implicit, nonstated memory for how to do things; also called implicit memory.

Process loss Time a group spends coordinating discussion rather than working on the task itself.

Prodigy A child with a special skill or talent far exceeding the norm for his or her age.

Progressive relaxation A method for reducing stress by contracting and then releasing groups of muscles.

Projection A defense mechanism in which a person unconsciously attributes their threatening impulses to another person.

Projective hypothesis A theory that suggests that reactions to ambiguous material reveal intrapsychic conflicts.

Projective test A personality instrument in the psychoanalytic perspective that uses interpretation of ambiguous stimuli to uncover unconscious conflicts.

Prosocial behavior Actions that help others at a cost to oneself.

Pseudoscience Information that appears scientific but is based on unsound scientific principles.

Psychiatry A branch of medicine that treats mental and behavioral conditions.

Psychoactive drug A chemical that alters consciousness.

Psychoanalysis A type of therapy in which unconscious conflicts and motivation are uncovered, explored, and redirected.

Psychoanalytic theory A family of theories originated by Freud that focuses on unconscious motivation.

Psychoanalytic theory of dreams A theory of dreams that suggest that dreams are unconscious wishes and/or conflicts.

Psychodynamic therapies A family of psychotherapies that have at their core the exploration of intrapsychic conflict and the role of insight to bring about therapeutic change.

Psychological dependence A situation in which a person's use of a substance leads to cravings, with distress and impairment in the absence of physiological dependence.

Psychological disorder A psychological condition that varies from the norm, is usually maladaptive, and may cause personal distress.

Psychological science Research conducted on topics in the field of psychology.

Psychological test A measure used to assess or describe mental functioning.

Psychology The scientific study of behavior and mental processes.

Psychometrician A scientist who studies the principles of psychological measurement.

Psychopathology The science of diagnosing and understanding psychological disorders.

Psychopharmacologist Researcher and practitioner who studies and often prescribes psychiatric medications.

Psychopharmacology Treatment of psychological conditions using medication.

Psychophysiological disorder A disorder in which a real medical syndrome is exacerbated by psychological factors.

Psychosexual stages According to Freud, childhood developmental stages in which tension reduction is focused on different areas of the body (oral, anal, phallic, latency, genital).

Psychosomatic diseases Disorders in which a real medical syndrome is exacerbated by psychological factors. Also known as psychophysiological illness.

Psychosurgery Treatment of mental and behavioral conditions using an invasive biological procedure.

Psychoticism A personality trait that describes how inflexible, creative, or reckless a person is.

Psychotropic medication A drug used to treat psychological conditions.

Punishment by application Attempting to extinguish a behavior by applying a negative consequence.

Punishment by removal Attempting to extinguish a behavior by removing a positive state.

Racial gap Differences on average test scores between groups associated by racial or ethnic definitions.

Random assignment Assigning participants to receive a given treatment or control condition by chance so that each has an equal likelihood of appearing in a given group.

Random sampling Selecting which members of a population will participate in a study through a systematic method that gives every person an equal chance of selection.

Range A measure of variation in a data sample determined by subtracting the lowest score from the highest score.

Rapid eye movement (REM) sleep A period of sleep that is characterized by rapid eye movements and dreams.

Ratio schedules Reinforcement is provided after behaviors are repeated a number of times.

Rational emotive therapy A type of active and directive therapy that emphasizes the link between thoughts and emotions.

Rational thinking Thinking marked by the use of deliberate reasoning.

Rationalization A defense mechanism in which an irrational behavior is unconsciously explained as acceptable in order to reduce anxiety.

Reaction formation A defense mechanism where a person will unconsciously replace a feeling.

Reactivity Unintentionally altering people's natural behavior by attempting to measure it.

Real self According to Rogers, your internal idea of who you should be.

Realistic job preview A potential employee samples the work experience to determine his or her interest in a job.

Reality principle According to Freud, the main focus of the ego that suggests that the ego will defer pleasure until a reasonable way to satisfy id instincts is available.

Reasoning Thinking through our knowledge and beliefs to reach a conclusion.

Receptor site An area on the dendrite that receives neurotransmitters.

Recessive gene A unit of heredity whose influence is exerted only when paired with an identical gene.

Reciprocal determinism Bandura's concept that suggests that behavior, environment, and thoughts are interrelated.

Reciprocity norm An assumption that you should behave positively toward those who have helped you.

Reciprocity of liking Reacting positively to those who react positively to you.

Reconstruction Creating a memory of what likely occurred based on information you can recall.

Reflex An involuntary motor response.

Refractory period Period of time following orgasm during which males cannot achieve another.

Regression A defense mechanism in which a person reverts to an earlier age of functioning.

Regression toward the mean The inclination for extreme scores to move toward the average over time.

Reinforce To strengthen behavior, making it more likely to occur again.

Reinforcer A consequence (either positive or negative) following a behavior that makes it more likely to occur again.

Relapse A recurrence of a condition or disorder.

Relative deprivation The opinion that a person is worse off than a comparison group.

Relearning A measure of forgetting and learning that is based on how easy it is to learn information again at a later time.

Reliability The consistency of the results when similar studies are performed.

REM rebound After periods of loss of sleep, the tendency to increase the length of REM.

REM sleep behavior disorder A type of REM parasomnia in which a person will act out a dream.

Replicable Results from a research study that appear the same when the study is repeated.

Repolarize The process by which a neuron's axon will return to the resting potential.

Representation An internal, mental description of a problem or information.

Representativeness heuristic Making a guess based on how much the situation "looks like" something known.

Repression A defense mechanism in which a person unconsciously forces a threatening experience from their awareness.

Reproductive strategies The preferences males and females show in their mating behavior.

Resilience Good developmental outcomes despite high risks, competence under stress, or recovery from trauma.

Resistance In psychoanalysis, a client's employment of a defense mechanism during therapy.

Resolution phase Final stage of the sexual response cycle, during which excitement levels return to base rate.

Resting potential An inactive neuron's negative charge.

Restorative theory of sleep The view that sleep is needed in order to maintain mental and physical operations.

Restructuring Changing the representation of a problem to remove unnecessary constraints.

Reticular formation A network of nerve fibers involved in sleep and wakefulness. Also called the reticular activating system (RAS).

Retina The layer of sensory receptor cells lining the back wall of the eye.

Retinal disparity Two slightly different images falling on each retina because of their distance from one another on the face.

Reuptake The reabsorption of neurotransmitters back into a presynaptic neuron.

Reversible figure An image that can be understood with two different interpretations.

Rod cells Rod-shaped cells in the retina that register degrees of lightness and darkness.

Role A set of customary behaviors based on your position.

Rorschach inkblot test A projective test in which someone's unconscious conflicts are revealed by his or her interpretation of and reactions to ambiguous patterns of ink.

Sample The subgroup of individuals included in a study to represent a larger population.

Sampling bias The selection of a sample of individuals from within a population that fails to capture an accurate representation of the larger group.

Satisfice Finding a satisfactory choice rather than the best one.

Savant syndrome Individuals who are average (or even deficient) in most areas of cognitive functioning but display an extraordinary talent in one area.

Scale A test designed to measure a particular skill from low to high.

Scatterplot Graph showing the points observed from scores on two variables.

Schacter-Singer two-factor theory A theory of emotion that suggests that feelings are a combination of body arousal and how we think about that arousal.

Schedule of reinforcement A plan for applying consequences following a behavior.

Schema A structured set of thoughts and presumptions.

Schizophrenia A psychological disorder characterized by disordered thinking, delusions, hallucinations, and disordered behavior and emotions.

Science The operation of general laws, especially as obtained and tested through the scientific method.

Scientific method A systematic approach to organizing the collection of data and drawing conclusions from a research study.

Scientist-practitioner model Also called the Boulder model, a balanced program in which psychologists learn about clinical skills as well as research skills.

Secondary insomnia Lack of sleep associated with another medical or psychological condition.

Secondary reinforcer (conditioned reinforcer) A reward that can be exchanged for ones meeting basic needs.

Secondary sexual characteristics Physical changes, including pubic hair, breast development in girls, facial hair and lowered voice in boys, along with a spurt in height and changes to the body's overall shape, that occur during puberty.

Selective attention The ability to focus thought or perception while filtering extraneous stimulation.

Selective serotonin reuptake inhibitors (SSRI) A class of medications that increases the efficiency of serotonin binding in the nervous system.

Self A person's awareness of his or her own characteristics.

Self-actualization Maslow's concept that the highest need is to fulfill individual potential.

Self-concept The collection of all your beliefs about yourself.

Self-determination theory Motivation involves integrating new behaviors into your internal values.

Self-efficacy Your perception about your ability to do a certain task.

Self-esteem Your self-worth.

Self-image How you see yourself.

Self-perception theory The theory that suggests that people discover their attitudes while observing their own behavior.

Self-reference effect Associating information with oneself to aid in retrieval.

Self-regulation The ability to control behavior through intentional strategies.

Self-report inventory A type of test in which a person will directly answer questions about his or her behaviors, thoughts, or feelings.

Self-serving bias The tendency to see yourself in a positive light.

Semantic memory Memory for the meaning of material.

Semantic network model Organization of information that captures meaningful relationships between concepts.

Semanticity Containing meaning or reference to things in the world.

Sensation The process of registering the stimulation of sensory receptors by an external physical stimulus.

Sensorimotor stage Piaget's stage for babies and toddlers who are focused on developing their sensory and motor processes.

Sensory adaptation A change in responsiveness to the same stimulation in a sensory organ over time.

Sensory memory The brief flash of input information through the senses.

Sensory neuron A neuron that is responsible for carrying external stimuli to the central nervous system for processing.

Sensory receptor Specialized cells in each sense organ that react to only particular kinds of external physical stimulation.

Sentence Organized sequence of words that conveys facts, hypotheses, questions, requests, intentions, and thoughts.

Serotonin A neurotransmitter involved in sleep, mood, and appetite.

Set point The tendency to maintain a particular range of body weight.

Settling point Tendency to maintain an approximate but changeable weight range.

Sex norms Typical behaviors observed across people.

Sexual disorder Problems occurring in the sexual response cycle.

Sexual harassment Unwelcome sexual comments or advances imposed in the workplace.

Sexual orientation The gender preferred for emotional sexual intimacy—same sex, opposite sex, or bisexual.

Sexual peak The highest point of interest and engagement in sex.

Shadow An archetype described by Jung that represents the worst possible version of a person.

Shaping Reinforcing part of a behavior initially and then increasing the goal to more complex behaviors.

Short-term memory (STM) The memory stage consisting of whatever information is in consciousness.

Short-term psychodynamic therapy A type of solution-focused psychoanalytic treatment.

Signal detection theory A sensory testing method that takes into account both the actual stimulus intensity and your readiness to respond.

Sixteen Personality Factor Questionnaire (16PF) A personality inventory with results that are closely related to the Big Five.

Skinner box (operant chamber) A testing apparatus with a response mechanism that also delivers reinforcement.

Sleep A natural loss of consciousness that is associated with reduced motor and sensory activity.

Sleep apnea A sleep disorder characterized by abrupt gaps in breathing during sleep, causing momentary wakefulness; also called obstructive sleep apnea.

Sleep debt The difference between how much you should sleep and your actual amount of sleep.

Sleep disorder A condition in which the amount or quality of sleep is disturbed, resulting in distress or impairment.

Sleep eating A type of nREM parasomnia associated with preparing and consuming food while still asleep.

Sleep hygiene Sleep habits.

Sleep paralysis A sleep condition characterized by a temporary inability to move upon wakening.

Sleep spindle A type of brain wave pattern associated with Stage 2 sleep and the consolidation of new memories.

Sleep terror A type of nREM parasomnia characterized by observed panic and terror while asleep, often associated with amnesia about the situation. Also called night terror.

Sleepsex A type of nREM parasomnia associated with engaging in sexual activity while asleep. Also called sexsomnia.

Sleepthink Generic thought about the day during sleep.

Sleepwalking A type of nREM parasomnia in which a person will leave his or her bed and perform activities while still asleep.

Social anxiety disorder An anxiety disorder characterized by performance anxiety in nearly all types of social situations.

Social categorization Mental sorting of people into groups.

Social clock Cultural norms for appropriate ages to seek out life events like marriage.

Social cognition Thoughts people use to understand their social world.

Social cognitive perspective A personality theory that focuses on the interplay among traits, thoughts, and environmental contexts.

Social desirability bias Participants may alter their responses if they perceive them as depicting them negatively.

Social facilitation The tendency to work harder when others are around.

Social influence The way behavior is shaped.

Social loafing The tendency to work less in a group than by yourself.

Social norm An expectation about customary behaviors based on a person's position.

Social phobia An anxiety disorder characterized by fear of public embarrassment or humiliation.

Social psychology The branch of psychology that focuses on how the way people think, feel, and behave influences and is influenced by others.

Social rejection Exclusion from contact by others causes emotional pain.

Social-responsibility norm The assumption that assistance should be given to those in need.

Social roles Assumptions about the way people should behave given their status.

Social skills training A type of behavior therapy intended to improve interaction with others.

Social support The help provided by others.

Sociobiology A theory that your behaviors and personality can be explained through the ideas of evolution.

Sociocultural perspective A school of psychology that emphasizes the way that social and cultural elements in the world (or environment) influence behavior and mental processes.

Soma The part of the neuron that keeps the cell alive and contains the genetic material for the cell.

Somatic marker A visceral, physiological response that reveals underlying emotion about an event or decision.

Somatic nervous system The division of the peripheral nervous system that connects to voluntary muscle movement and communicates sensory information.

Somatization disorder A type of somatoform disorder characterized by a long history of many vague physical complaints over several years.

Somatoform disorder Psychological disorder characterized by having symptoms of physical illness that cannot be explained by a general medical condition.

Somatosensory cortex An area of the parietal lobe that processes body sensation information.

Source monitoring Memory for the circumstances of acquiring information.

Source trait A universal, enduring behavioral characteristic.

Spacing effect Learning is improved if study effort is distributed over time.

Specific intelligences (s) Spearman's theory of performance factors only involved in each particular task.

Spermarche For boys, the first ejaculation occurs around age 14, followed a year later by the development of mature sperm cells.

Spinal cord A collection of neurons that run from the base of the brain down the back.

Spinal reflex An involuntary motor response coordinated by the spinal cord.

Split brain The result of severing the corpus callosum, so that the hemispheres of the cerebral cortex cannot communicate through the nerves that would usually connect them.

Split-brain surgery An operation that involves severing the corpus callosum. Also called a corpus callostomy.

Split-half reliability Performance on one-half of the test is compared against performance on the other half.

Spontaneous recovery The reappearance of an extinguished conditioned response.

Spontaneous remission Reduction of symptoms of a condition in the absence of treatment.

Spreading activation The links between concepts in memory help to access one given another.

Stage 1 A phase of sleep between relaxed wakefulness and being asleep.

Stage model of memory Atkinson and Shiffrins's three stages of memory—sensory, short-term, and long-term memory.

Standard deviation A statistical measure tracking how each score in a sample differs from the mean.

Standardization Conversion of scores from the number of correct answers to a relative performance score compared to others on the same test.

Standardized procedure Protocol for testing that follows the same steps for all test takers.

Stanford-Binet Scale A version of the intelligence test devised by Louis Terman and tested on many American schoolchildren.

Statistic A numerical summary of the results of data collection.

Statistically significant When the probability (p) of an observed difference occurring is determined to be less than 5% (p <0.05).

Status High economic and social status within the group is a desirable quality in male mates.

Stereotype Overgeneralized beliefs about a group and its members.

Stereotype threat Performance decrements caused by knowledge of cultural stereotypes.

Stimulant-induced psychosis Symptoms of hallucinations and delusions that are caused by medication that activates the nervous system.

Stimulants A class of psychoactive substances that increases activity in the nervous system.

Stimulus Physical energy in the world registered by a sensory organ, including light, sound, and smell.

Stimulus control therapy A treatment for insomnia that includes associating bedtime with sleep to reestablish a consistent sleep-wake schedule.

Stimulus threshold The point at which the neuron responds by changing its voltage.

Strange situation procedure A test in which the mother leaves her child alone in the playroom, and a friendly stranger tries to interact with the child. Finally, the mother rejoins them.

Stranger anxiety A fear reaction of infants to new people usually peaking around 12 months.

Stress A response that occurs from events seen as a challenge.

Stressors Anything perceived as a challenge.

Striving for superiority According to Adler, an attempt to overcome feelings of inferiority by being a better person; also known as compensation.

Structural plasticity The brain's ability to change in response to the environment.

Structuralism The school of psychology that studies human experience by breaking it down into smaller pieces.

Stuporous catatonia A symptom of schizophrenia that is characterized by restricted motor activity such as periods of immobility and muscle rigidity.

Subjective well-being A feeling of satisfaction with life and happiness.

Sublimation A defense mechanism in which a person unconsciously redirects an id instinct in a socially acceptable way.

Subliminal perception Sensation registered "below threshold," without conscious awareness of its occurrence.

Substantia nigra A midbrain structure that is responsible for initiation of movement.

Superego According to Freud, the part of the personality governed by the perfection principle.

Support group A type of group therapy in which members meet without a therapist to provide social support.

Suprachiasmatic nucleus A part of the hypothalamus that controls daily rhythms for sleep and wakefulness.

Surface structure The ordering of a sequence of words in time.

Surface trait An enduring behavior that is easily observed.

Survey A study method in which individuals are asked to respond to a set of questions designed by an experimenter.

Syllogism A simple deduction task with three statements or premises.

Sympathetic nervous system A branch of the autonomic nervous system that prepares the organs for vigorous activity.

Symptom substitution The emergence of a replacement symptom of a psychological condition if the root cause is not resolved.

Synapse An area that includes three structures: the terminal button of the sending neuron, the synaptic gap, and the dendrite of the receiving neuron.

Synaptic cleft The small space between the axon terminal of a sending neuron and the dendrite of the receiving neuron.

Synaptic pruning The destruction of less active synapses to organize and improve efficiency of the neural connections.

Synaptic transmission The process by which one neuron communicates with another by using neurotransmitters.

Synaptic vesicle A sac that contains neurotransmitters in the axon terminal.

Systematic desensitization Treatment for phobia in which a client practices relaxation during progressively more fear-inducing stimuli.

Tardive dyskinesia A neurological condition involving involuntary, repetitive movements.

Taste aversion Learning to dislike foods that were followed by nausea.

Telegraphic speech Two- and three-word combinations with meaning.

Temperament According to the biological perspective, inborn biological traits.

Temporal lobes An area of the cerebral cortex near the temples. Includes primary auditory cortex, and language centers.

Teratogens Toxic agents from the environment, such as disease, poisons, or drugs, that can harm the fetus.

Terror management theory A theory that suggests that because of our awareness of death, we battle anxiety by boosting our self-esteem and cultural connections.

Test-retest reliability The likelihood of receiving a similar score when a test is repeated.

Testosterone A sex hormone produced by the testes, adrenal cortex, and ovaries that is important in the male sex characteristics of the male body.

Tetrahydrocannabinol (THC) A psychoactive substance that is the active ingredient in marijuana.

Thalamus A forebrain structure that is a major relay station for sensory information.

Thanatos According to Freud, ways in which we reduce tensions that are aggressive and destructive, also known as the death instinct.

Thematic apperception test (TAT) A projective personality instrument in which unconscious conflicts are revealed by the interpretation of stories told in reaction to a series of ambiguous images.

Theoretical approach to traits Deriving traits from another theory of personality.

Theory An overarching conceptualization about how variables may cause behavior.

Theory of mind The child's conception of what he or she and others know, and that these can differ.

Theory of psychosocial development Erikson's stage theory of important issues to resolve across the life span.

Theta An EEG pattern that is associated with relaxed wakefulness.

Thinking The internal mental processes that make sense of our experiences.

Threshold The point at which a neuron will respond to an action potential.

Tip-of-the-tongue phenomenon The feeling of knowing a word but being unable to recall it from long-term memory.

Token economies Situations in which easy-to-use secondary reinforcers are traded in for a meaningful reward.

Tolerance A reduction in a person's sensitivity to a drug over time.

Top-down processing Perception through the use of information in memory to organize incoming sensations.

Trait A stable characteristic of behavior.

Trait theory A theory of personality that focuses on identifying and measuring characteristics of behavior.

Tranquilizers A type of drug used for sedation and reducing anxiety.

Transcendence According to Jung, the process of resolving the dichotomy of who we are as people.

Transcranial magnetic stimulation (TMS) A procedure that uses electromagnetic coils to activate nerve cells in the brain.

Transduction The process in which physical energy in the world is translated into an electrochemical signal—neurons firing—that represents sensation in the brain.

Transference In psychoanalysis, a type of displacement in which the client will unconsciously act out relationships with the therapist.

Trial and error Creating a solution, testing to see if it works, and then starting over if unsuccessful.

Triangular theory of love Sternberg's theory that relationships are composed of three components: intimacy, passion, commitment.

Triarchic theory of intelligence Sternberg's theory positing three underlying aspects of cognition: analytic, creative, and practical.

Trichromatic theory The notion that color vision relies on sensory receptors in the retina that process only red, blue, and green.

Trickster An archetype that represents someone who pretends to be something that he or she is not.

Twin study Examining the heritability of traits by comparing identical twins (who share all of their genes) to fraternal twins (who share 50% of their genes).

Type A personality A style characterized by difficulty relaxing, impatience, and anger when delayed.

Type B personality A style characterized by being relaxed about time, slow to anger, and relative ease at relaxing.

Uncertainty The state of not being determined, either because the event has not occurred or cannot be known logically.

Unconditional positive regard According to Rogers, a sense of respect and love that is not linked to specific behaviors.

Unconditioned response A physiological behavior that is involuntarily elicited by a stimulus.

Unconditioned stimulus An unlearned signal that leads to an automatic, reflexive response.

Unconscious According to Freud, thoughts, memories, feelings, and wishes that reside outside of awareness.

Undifferentiated type of schizophrenia The presence of symptoms that meet the core criteria for schizophrenia but do not meet the criteria for paranoid, disorganized, or catatonic type.

Unhealthy (mistaken) lifestyle Adler's description of those who strive for superiority by competing with others.

Unit bias Tendency to eat the amount provided as a serving.

Universals Behaviors that all people perform regardless of their cultures.

Unnecessary constraint An apparent requirement for a solution that is not really needed.

Validity The degree to which a research experiment captures what it claims to study.

Variable A factor that is manipulated or measured, or controlled, during an experiment.

Variable-interval schedule Providing reinforcement for the first behavior after a set average amount of time has passed.

Variable-ratio schedule Providing reinforcement after an average number of repeated behaviors.

Variance The variability between scores observed on a given dependent variable.

Vasocongestion Blood circulates into all the erectile structures in the body (e.g., penis, clitoris, nipples).

Ventromedial hypothalamus The functional "stop eating" center in the brain.

Virtual reality exposure therapy A behavioral therapy technique that involves the repetitive presentation of a simulated distressing object or situation in order to reduce anxiety.

Waist-to-hip ratio (WHR) A woman's waist size divided by hip size gives an index of figure shape.

Wason selection task A card game that requires checking for rule violations.

Wavelength The distance between peaks of incoming light waves that determines their color.

Weber's Law As the stimulus becomes stronger or larger, so does the just noticeable difference between it and other similar stimuli.

Wechsler Adult Intelligence Scale (WAIS) An intelligence test written for adults and widely used in group assessment.

Wernicke's area Part of the left temporal lobe that comprehends spoken words.

Wise old man An archetype that represents wisdom.

Withdrawal symptoms Distress and cravings associated with the rapid discontinuation of certain psychoactive substances.

Within-subjects design A research plan in which each subject takes part in every aspect of the study.

Word A meaningful pattern of sound defined within a language.

Working memory Synonym for short-term memory that reflects its role in thinking.

Working memory capacity The amount of information you can retain for a short period and report back correctly.

Working memory span The amount of different pieces of information (such as digits) that can be held in conscious memory for a short time and reported back correctly.

Yerkes-Dodson law of arousal The theory that performance is best at medium levels of arousal.

Zone of proximal development Children's readiness to learn the next step from what they already know.

Zygote An initial stage in development as the fertilized egg grows through cell division and attaches to the uterine wall.

Index

A

Abnormal behavior criteria, 539–540, 540f
Absolute refractory period, 82
Acceptance, 587
Accommodation, 461
Acculturative stress, 435–436
Acetylcholine, 83
Achievement gap, 392
Achievement in school, 327–328, 327t
Achievement motivation, 392–393, 392f
Achievement tests, 330
Acquisition
    defined, 186
    Pavlov's experiments, 189–190, 189–190f
    performance vs., 211
    shaping and, 200
    theories, 297–298
Action potentials, 80–82, 81f
Activation-synthesis model of dreaming, 164, 164f
Active listening, 587
Actor, 622
Actor-observer bias, 621–622
Actualizing tendency, 514, 587
Acute insomnia, 159
Acute stressors, 432
Adaptation
    defined, 97
    sensory, 117, 117f
Adaption-level phenomenon, 439
Adaptive behavior, 336
Adaptive theory of sleep, 157
Addiction, 168–169
Adipose tissue, 372
Adler, Alfred, 513, 513f
Adolescence, 472–479
    cognitive development, 475–476, 476t
    overview, 472–473
    physical development, 473–475, 473–474f
    social development, 476–479, 477t
Adoption studies, 99
Adrenal cortex, 95
Adrenal glands, 95
Adrenaline, 95
Adrenal medulla, 95
Adulthood and aging, 479–486
    ages and stages of adulthood, 485–486
    cognitive development, 481–483, 482–483f
    continuity or change, 483–484, 484f
    death and dying, 481, 481t
    life expectancy, 480–481
    overview, 479
    physical development, 479–480
    relationships, 484–485
    reproductive life, 480
    social development, 477t, 483–486, 484f
Aerobic exercise, 437
Afferent nerve fibers, 78
Age of viability, 455, 455f
Aggression, 429–430
    anger and, 429–430
    biology of aggression, 631
    media and, 212–213, 632
    overview, 630–631
    physical punishment and, 204
    psychological and sociocultural aspects of aggression, 631
Aging. See Adulthood and aging
Agitated catatonia, 561
Agonist, 83
Agoraphobia, 545
Agreeableness, 518
Ainsworth, Mary, 467–468
Alcohol

as depressant, 171
as sleep aid, 163
Alcoholism, 89
Algorithms
    decision making, 287, 287f
    defined, 282
    reasoning, 290–292, 291–292f
Allocentrism, 526
All or nothing law, 81
Alogia, 598
Alpha waves, 156
Altered state of consciousness (ASC) theory of hypnosis, 166
Altruism, 634–635, 635t
Alzheimer's disease, 78, 262, 481
Ambivalent/anxious attachment, 468t, 469
American Association on Intellectual and Developmental Disabilities, 336
American Psychiatric Association, 374, 538–539, 603
American Psychological Association (APA), 17, 17t, 19, 20t, 603
American Sign Language (ASL), 297, 297f
Amnesia
    childhood amnesia, 250
    defined, 240
    dissociative amnesia, 554–555
    generally, 261–262, 261–262f
    procedural memory and, 247
Amphetamines, 172
Amygdala, 89, 422, 422f, 429, 631
Analogy, 283
Analytical psychology, 511–512, 512f
Analytic intelligence, 321
Anatomy of memory, 239–240, 239f
Anecdotal evidence, 11
Anger and aggression, 429–430
Anhedonia, 557, 598
Animals
    language in, 298–299
    studies and ethics, 59–60, 60f
Anorexia nervosa, 374–375
Antagonists, 83
Anthropomorphism, 421
Antianxiety drugs, 597, 597t
Antidepressant drugs, 594–597
    defined, 594
    monoamine oxidase inhibitors, 594–595, 594–595t
    overview, 594
    selective serotonin reuptake inhibitors, 595–596, 596f, 596t
    serotonin-norepinephrine reuptake inhibitors, 596–597, 596t
    taking antidepressants, 597
Antipsychotic drugs, 598–599, 598t
Antisocial personality disorder, 565, 565f
Anxiety disorders, 544–551
    biological perspective, 549–550, 550f
    brain and, 550, 550f
    cognitive factors, 551, 551f
    conditioning, 551
    generalized anxiety disorder, 544–545
    learning perspective, 550–551
    natural selection, 549
    observational learning, 551
    obsessive-compulsive disorder, 547–548, 548–549f
    overview, 544, 545f
    panic disorder, 545, 546f
    phobic disorders, 546–547, 546–548f, 547t
    posttraumatic stress disorder, 549–551
APA (American Psychological Association), 17, 17t, 19, 20t, 603
Aphasia, 93

Applied research, 17
Approach-approach conflict, 435
Approach-avoidance conflict, 435
APS (Association for Psychological Science), 17, 603
Aptitude, 330
Aptitude tests, 330
Archetypes, 511–512
Aristotle, 9, 9f
Arousal theories, 364–365, 364f
ASC (altered state of consciousness) theory of hypnosis, 166
Asch, Solomon, 626, 627f
ASL (American Sign Language), 297, 297f
Assimilation, 461
Association areas, 90
Association for Psychological Science (APS), 17, 603
Ataxia, 89
Attachment, 465
Attachment theory, 467–469, 467–468f, 468t
Attention, 140–142
Attitudes and social judgments
    attitude, defined, 623
    components of attitudes, 623, 623f
    culture and attitudes, 625
    foot-in-the-door technique, 625
    overview, 623
    persuasion, 624–625
    relieving cognitive dissonance, 624, 624f
    role playing, 625
Attraction, 632–633
Attribution, 621–622
Attribution theory, 621
Atypical antipsychotics, 598t, 599
Authoritative parenting style, 470
Automatic processing, 227–229, 227–228f
Autonomic nervous system, 84
Availability heuristic, 286, 610
Aversive conditioning, 590
Avoidance-avoidance conflict, 435
Avoidance learning, 13f, 194
Avoidant attachment, 468t, 469
Avolition, 598
Awareness. See Consciousness
Axon, 79
Axon terminal, 79

B

B needs (Maslow's hierarchy), 515
Babbling, 296
Baby talk, 457, 467
Bandura, Albert, 210–213
    acquisition vs. performance, 211
    basic processes of observational learning, 211
    biological basis of observational learning, 212, 212f
    Bobo experiments, 210–211, 211f, 631
    perspective of social cognitive theory, 210–213, 519–520, 519–520f
    principles of observational learning, 212–213, 212f
Barbiturates, 172
Basal metabolic rate, 370–371
Basic emotions, 423, 424t
Basic research, 17
Beck, Aaron, 591, 591t
Beck Depression Inventory, 601
Behavior. See also Neuroscience
    abnormal, 539–540, 540f
    adaptive, 336
    behavior measures in psychology studies, 50t
    classical conditioning techniques, 588–590, 589–590f, 589t
    emotion and, 422–425, 422–424f, 424t

learning and, 213
operant conditioning techniques, 590
psychotic disorders and, 561
REM sleep behavior disorder, 161
social thought and, 617–618
stress and, 437
therapy, 588–590, 589–590f, 589t
Behavioral genetics, 523
Behavioral medicine, 437
Behavior analysis, 207
Behavior contracts, 208
Behaviorism
    contemporary psychology and, 16
    defined, 187, 519
    Watson and, 196–197
Behaviorist theories, 297. *See also* Skinner, B.F.
Behavior modification, 207
Being needs, 515
Belief perseverance, 293
Bell-and-pad treatment, 588, 589f
Bell curve, 332–333, 332f
Belmont Report, 57
Belonging and social motivation, 390–391, 391f
Benzodiazepines, 597
Bethlem Royal Hospital, 582, 582f
Between-subjects, 35
Bias. *See also* Stereotypes
    actor-observer bias, 621–622
    defined, 284
    experimenter bias, 49
    in-group bias, 634
    intelligence testing bias, 331, 343–346, 344–345f
    job hiring, 396
    learning disabled, 337
    negativity bias, 619
    in problem solving, 284–285, 284–285f
    reasoning, 292–294, 292f
    sampling bias, 40
    self-serving bias, 622
    unit bias, 374
Big Five factors, 517–518, 517t
Bimodal distribution, 53, 54f
Binet, Alfred, 327–329, 327t, 339, 343
Binge eating disorder, 375, 380
Biodeterminism, 101
Biofeedback, 193, 437
Biological preparedness, 195
Biological psychology, 76. *See also* Neuroscience
Biology. *See also* Evolution; Hormones; Physiology
    of aggression, 631
    anxiety disorders and, 549–550, 550f
    Bandura's theory and, 212, 212f
    of behavior. *See* Neuroscience
    classical conditioning and, 194–196, 195f
    mood disorders and, 558–559, 558f
    operant conditioning and, 206–207, 206f
    personality and, 521–524
    sexual orientation and, 388–389, 389f
    of sleep, 156–157, 156f
Biomedical therapies, 593–600
    drug treatments, 593–599. *See also* Drug treatment
    electroconvulsive therapy, 599–600, 599f
    medical procedures, 599–600, 599–600f
    overview, 593
Biopsychosocial model, 13, 425, 539, 540f
Bipolar disorder, 557–558
Bisexuals, 388
Bizarre delusions, 560
Blaming the victim, 368
BMI (body mass index), 376–377, 376f
Bobo experiment, 210–211, 211f, 631
Body dysmorphia, 375
Body mass index (BMI), 376–377, 376f
Borderline personality disorder, 566, 566t
Botulism, 83
Boulder model, 581
Bowlby, John, 467

Brain, 86–94. *See also* Consciousness
    abnormalities, 562–563
    achievement and, 393
    anxiety disorders and, 550, 550f
    brainstem, 87–89, 88f
    culture and language, 300–302, 300–301f, 302t
    forebrain, 89–93. *See also* Forebrain
    and hunger physiology, 368–369, 369f
    hunger physiology and, 89
    intelligence and, 324–326, 325–326f
    midbrain, 89
    organization, 86
    overview, 86
    physical development and, 473–474f, 473–475
    plasticity, 93
    research on, 86–87, 86–88f
    storing memories in brain, 239–240, 239f
    tumors, 78
Brainstem, 87–89, 88f
Broca's area, 300, 300f
Bulimia nervosa, 375
Bullying, 472
Bystander effect, 634–635, 635t

C
Cade, John, 598
Caffeine, 172
California Personality Inventory (CPI), 526
Calkins, Mary, 17
Calling, 400–401
Callostomy, 91
Cannon-Bard theory of emotion, 426, 427f
Cannon, Walter, 426, 436
Cardiovascular disease, 84
Career directions, 400–403, 401–402t
Case studies, 38–39, 38f
Cataplexy, 160
Catastophic thinking, 422
Catatonia, 561, 599
Catatonic type of schizophrenia, 562
Catecholamines, 419
Category, 242, 242f
Catharsis, 429, 508, 631
Cattell, Raymond, 320
Cattell Culture-Fair Intelligence Test, 344
Cell body, 79
Centers for Disease Control and Prevention, 383
Central nervous system, 84, 85, 85f
Central route to persuasion, 624
Central tendency, 52
Cerebellum, 88–89
Cerebral cortex
    cerebrum and, 90–93, 91f
    defined, 88
Cerebral hemispheres, 91, 91f
Cerebrospinal fluid (CSF), 85
Cerebrum and cerebral cortex, 90–93, 91f
Change blindness, 155
Child development. *See* Infancy and childhood
Childhood amnesia, 250
Choice as stress, 435
Choice overload, 288, 289f
Chomsky, Noam, 298
Chromosomes, 96, 97f
Chronic stressors, 432
Chunking, 236, 236f
Circadian rhythm, 156
Classical conditioning, 188–197
    anxiety disorders and, 551
    applying principles of, 196–197
    biological and evolutionary predispositions, 194–196, 195f
    conditioning and emotional responses, 192–194, 193–194f
    contemporary view of, 194–196, 195f
    defined, 187

learning to predict, 194
Little Albert experiment, 196–197
overview, 188–189
Pavlov experiments, 189–192
punishment and, 204
review of, 192
techniques, 588–590, 589–590f, 589t
Watson and behaviorism, 196–197
Client-centered therapy, 587–588, 587f
Clinical psychologists, 581–582, 582f
Clinical researcher model, 582
Clinical trials, 601
Cocaine, 172
Cognition. *See also* Social cognitive perspective
    adolescence and young adulthood development, 475–476, 476t
    adulthood and aging development, 481–483, 482–483f
    anxiety disorders and, 551, 551f
    behavior and emotion, 422–425, 422–424f, 424t
    defined, 16, 112
    infancy and childhood development, 461–465
    stress and, 433, 435, 437
Cognitive approach, defined, 187
Cognitive dissonance, 624
Cognitive dissonance theory, 624, 624f
Cognitive maps, 210
Cognitive meditational theory of emotion, 428
Cognitive neuroscience, 155
Cognitive neuroscientists, 16
Cognitive person variables, 520
Cognitive reserve, 482
Cognitive therapy, 590–591, 591t
Cohort effects, 49, 453, 453t
Collective unconscious, 511
Collectivist cultures, 526, 603, 620
Coming out, 388
Common rule, 57, 58
Common-sense theory, 425, 426f
Communication. *See* Neural communication
Comparative study, 37
Compensation, 513
Competence, 632
Compliance, 626
Compulsions, 548, 549f
Computerized tomography (CT) scans, 87
Concept, 242, 242f
Conceptual hierarchies, 242–243, 243f
Concrete operational stage, 463, 463f
Conditional positive regard, 515
Conditioned reinforcers, 200
Conditioned response, 189
Conditioned stimulus, 189
Conditioning. *See also specific types*
    anxiety disorders and, 551
    defined, 187
    emotional responses and, 192–194, 193f, 194f
Confirmation bias, 292
Conflict, 435, 623
Conformity, 626–627, 627f
Confounding variables, 35, 49
Connectionist models, 243
Conscientiousness, 518
Conscious mind, 508, 511
Consciousness, 152–183
    defined, 154
    dreams and, 162–165
    drug use and, 168–174. *See also* Drug use
    hypnosis, 165–167
    meditation, 167–168
    overview, 154–155
    sleep and, 155–162. *See also* Sleep
    summary of multiple influences on consciousness, 175
Conservation, 462, 462t
Consistency paradox, 520
Consolidation, 164, 239

Constructing memory, 227–233
  actively constructing memory, 263
  automatic processing, 227–229, 227–228f
  effortful processing, 229–232, 229–230f
  mnemonics, 232
  overview, 227
Constructive coping, 437
Contact comfort, 466
Contemporary psychology, 13–19
  behavioral perspective, 16
  biological perspective, 14–15f
  cognitive perspective, 16
  evolutionary perspective, 14–15, 15f
  humanistic perspective, 16
  overview, 13–14, 13–14t
  professional specialization and research areas,
    17–19, 18t, 19f
  psychodynamic perspective, 15–16
  sociocultural perspective, 16–17
Content, 291
Content validity, 334
Continued influence effect, 255
Continuous positive airway pressure (CPAP), 159,
  160f
Continuous reinforcement, 201
Continuum of sexual orientation, 388
Control group, 48
Convenience sample, 41
Conventional level of moral reasoning, 475
Conversion disorder, 553
Coping, 432, 437
Core social motives, 618
Coronary heart disease, 436
Corpus callosum, 90, 91
Correlation, 42, 43f
Correlational studies, 41–46, 41–42t, 42–45f
Correlation coefficient (r), 42, 319
Cortical localization, 93
Corticosteroids, 419, 437
Counseling psychologists, 581
Counterconditioning, 588
CPAP (continuous positive airway pressure), 159,
  160f
CPI (California Personality Inventory), 526
Creative intelligence, 321
Creativity, 323–324
Criterion, 328
Critical period
  for attachment and bonding, 469
  brain function and, 93
  for language learning, 297
Critical thinking, 19–20, 20t, 165–166
Cross-cultural psychology, 17
Cross-sectional study, 49, 453
Crystalized intelligence, 320
CSF (cerebrospinal fluid), 85
CT (computerized tomography) scans, 87
Cued recall, 249
Cue retrieval, 248–250, 249f, 264
Cultural psychology, 17
Culture. *See also* Environment; Stereotypes
  attitudes and, 625
  body image and, 375–376
  brain and language, 300–302, 300–301f, 302t,
    303f
  Cattell Culture-Fair Intelligence Test, 344
  collectivist cultures, 526, 603, 620
  cultural, defined, 16
  emotion and, 428–429, 428f
  experience and perception, 138–140, 138–139f
  facial expressions and, 423, 424f
  individualist cultures, 526, 620
  intelligence testing bias and, 331, 343–344
  learning and, 213
  mate preferences and, 387
  pay differences and, 398
  personality and, 526–527

  person perception and, 620
  psychotherapy evaluation and, 603
  sociocultural and psychological aspects of aggres-
    sion, 631
  sociocultural perspective, 16–17
  stress and, 435–436
Cyberbullying, 472

D

D needs (Maslow's hierarchy), 515
Daily hassles, 433, 434–435t
Darwin, Charles, 11, 12f, 14, 421
Daycare, 470
DBS (deep brain stimulation), 86–87, 600, 600f
Death and dying, 481, 481t
Debriefing, 58
Decay theory, 259
Deception, 58
Decision making, 286–290
  algorithms, 287, 287f
  group influence on individual, 636
  heuristics, 287–289, 287f, 289f
  overview, 286–287
Decision tree, 287, 287f
Declarative memory, 241–246
  defined, 241
  episodic memory, 245, 245f
  flashbulb memory, 245–246, 246f
  overview, 242
  semantic memory, 242–245, 242–244f
Deductive reasoning, 290
Deep brain stimulation (DBS), 86–87, 600, 600f
Deep structure, 295
Defense mechanisms, 510–511, 511f, 511t, 585
Defensive attribution, 368
Deficit needs, 515
Deindividuation, 637–638
Deinstitutionalization, 583–584f
Delay of gratification, 379
Deliberation, 278
Deliberative practice, 286
Delta waves, 156
Delusions, 560, 598
Dementia, 262, 481
Dendrites, 79
Denial, 511t, 512
Deoxyribonucleic acid (DNA), 96, 97
Dependence, 597
Dependent variable, 46–47, 601
Depolarization of neurons, 81
Depressants, 171–172
Depression. *See also* Antidepressant drugs
  bipolar disorder and, 557–558
  learned helplessness, 205
  major depressive disorder, 556–557, 557t
  monoamine hypothesis of depression, 559, 594
Deprivation of sleep, 158, 158f
Depth perception, 133–134, 134f, 135t
Descriptive research
  case studies, 38–39, 38f
  correlational studies, 41–46, 41–42t, 42–45f
  naturalistic observation, 37–38
  overview, 37
  surveys, 39–41, 39–40f, 40t
Desensitization, 213
Detection thresholds, 115–117, 115–116t, 116f
Development, 450–503
  adolescence and young adulthood, 472–479. *See
    also* Adolescence
  adulthood and aging, 479–486. *See also* Adulthood
    and aging
  beginnings of development, 452–453
  defined, 452–453, 453t
  experience and perception, 137, 137f
  infancy and childhood, 457–472. *See also* Infancy
    and childhood

  nature and nurture, 486–488
  newborn, 456–457, 456–457f
  prenatal development, 453–456, 455f
  summary of multiple influences on development,
    488–489
Deviant, 539–540
Deviation IQ scores, 333
Diabetes, 372
*Diagnostic and Statistical Manual of Mental Disorder
  (DSM-IV-TR)*, 538–542, 539f, 541–542t
Diathesis-stress hypothesis, 543, 543f
DID (dissociative identity disorder), 555
Differential parenting, 470
Differentiation, 455
Diffusion of responsibility, 635
Digit span test, 237, 238f
Disability, intellectual, 336–338, 337t
Discontinuation syndrome, 597
Discrimination. *See also* Bias
  classical conditioning and, 191–192
  defined, 630
  job hiring and, 396
  stress and, 436
Disease. *See* Health
Disguised dream, 164
Disorders. *See specific types*
Disorganized thinking, 560
Disorganized type of schizophrenia, 562
Displacement, 294, 511t, 512
Display rules, 428–429, 428f
Disposition, 506
Dissociation, 554
Dissociation theory of hypnosis, 167
Dissociative amnesia, 554–555
Dissociative disorders, 554–556, 555t
Dissociative fugue, 555
Dissociative identity disorder (DID), 555
Divided attention, 141–142
Divided consciousness, 167
Divorce, 470–471
Dix, Dorothea, 583, 583f
Dizygotic (DZ) twins, 99, 99f
DNA (deoxyribonucleic acid), 96, 97
Dominant genes, 97
Door-in-the-face technique, 625
Dopamine
  psychoactive drugs and, 172, 174
  schizophrenia and, 562–563, 598–599
  sexual response and, 382
Double-blind procedure, 49
Down syndrome, 337
Dream analysis, 585
Dreams, 162–165
  content of, 164, 165f
  defined, 162
  as interpreted brain activity, 164, 164f
  overview, 162
  as reflection of unconscious wishes, 162–164
  theories of, 162–164
Drive, 363
Drive theories, 363–364
Drug abuse and addiction, 168–169
Drug dependence, 169
Drug rebound effects, 169
Drug treatment, 593–599
  antianxiety drugs, 597, 597t
  antidepressant drugs, 594–597
  antipsychotic drugs, 598–599, 598t
  mood-stabilizing drugs, 597–598, 598t
  overview, 593–599
  for parasomnias, 161, 162
Drug use, 168–174
  caffeine, 172
  cocaine, 172
  depressants, 171–172
  ecstasy, 174
  hallucinogens, 173–174

LSD, 173
marijuana, 173–174
methamphetamine, 172–173
MOA of psychoactive drugs, 171
narcotics and opiates, 172
nicotine, 172
overview, 168–170, 169–171t
stimulants, 172–173
DSM (Diagnostic and Statistical Manual of Mental Disorder), 538–542, 539f, 541–542t
Dual processing, 155, 279
Dying, 481, 481t
Dyssomnias, 159
DZ (dizygotic) twins, 99, 99f

E

Eating, 374–378
eating disorders, 374–376, 375f
obesity, 376–378, 376–377f
overview, 374
Ebbinghaus, Herman, 257
Echoic memory, 234
Eclectic model, 13, 527, 544, 592
Ecstasy (MDMA), 174
ECT (electroconvulsive therapy), 599–600, 599f
Education. *See* School
EEG (electroencephalogram), 87, 87f
Efferent nerve fibers, 78
Effortful processing, 229–232, 229–230f
Ego, 163, 509
Egocentrism, 462
Ego dystonic, 564
Ego ideal, 509
Ego syntonic, 564
Eighth Amendment, 338
Ekman, Paul, 423, 424f
Elaboration, 231, 249
Electrical stimulation of brain, 86–87, 600, 600f
Electroconvulsive therapy (ECT), 599–600, 599f
Electroencephalogram (EEG), 14, 15f, 87, 87f, 155
Elicited behaviors, 187
Elimination by Aspects approach, 289–290
Ellis, Albert, 591
Embryo, 454
EMDR (eye movement desensitization reprocessing), 601–602
Emit, 187
Emotion, 418–431. *See also* Stress
anger and aggression, 429–430. *See also* Aggression
behavior and cognition, 422–425, 422–424f, 424t
Cannon-Bard simultaneous trigger theory, 426, 427f
cognitive meditational theory, 428
common-sense theory, 425, 426f
conditioning and emotional responses, 192–194, 193–194f
culture and, 428–429, 428f
evolution and, 421, 421f
expression, 428–431, 428f, 430f
facial feedback and, 423–425, 424f
fear, 429
gender and emotion, 429
happiness, 438–439, 439t
James-Lange peripheral feedback theory, 425–426, 426f
love, 430–431, 430f
physiology and, 418–421, 419–420f
positive psychology, 438–441
Schacter-Singer two-factor theory, 426–428, 427f
summary of multiple influences, 441
theories, 425–428, 426–427f
Emotional intelligence, 322–323t, 429
Emotional stability, 523
Emotion-focused coping, 437
Empathy, 587
Empirically derived test, 525
Empirical studies and evidence, 5, 33

Encoding, 227
Encoding specificity, 249
Endocrine system, 94–96, 94f, 369–370
Endogenous opioid peptides, 95, 437
Endorphins, 95, 437
Engagement, 397
Entropy principle, 512
Environment. *See also* Culture
environmental differences, 349
environmental influences, defined, 343
Flynn effect, 348
hunger and, 373–374
intelligence and, 347–349, 348f
sexual orientation and, 389–390
twin studies and, 109–110, 347–348, 348f
En vivo exposure therapy, 589
Epidemiology, 539
Epilepsy, 90
Epinephrine, 95
Episodic memory, 245–246, 245–246f
EPSPs (excitatory postsynaptic potentials), 82, 83
Equity theory, 399
Equivalence principle, 512
Erikson, Erik, 476, 477t, 483
Eros, 509
Escape learning, 205
Esteem motivation, 392
Estrogen, 95, 389
Ethics, 56–63
animal studies, 59–60, 60f
human participants, 57–59
overview, 56
Ethnic groups. *See also* Culture
dream content and, 164
intelligence and, 342–343, 342f
Ethnocentrism, 17, 634
Etiologies
antisocial personality disorder, 565
borderline personality disorder, 566
defined, 542, 580
dissociative disorders, 556
mood disorders, 558–559, 558f
paranoid personality disorder, 566
psychological disorders, 542–544, 543f
psychotic disorders, 562–563
somatoform disorders, 553–554
Evidence-based practice, 601
Evolution
emotion and, 421, 421f
mating theories, 384–387, 385–387f
motivation theories, 363, 373
personality theories, 523, 523f
Evolutionary psychology and psychologists, 14–15, 15f, 363
Evolved behaviors, 363
Excitatory messages, 80
Excitatory postsynaptic potentials (EPSPs), 82, 83
Excitement phase, 381
Executive control system, 167
Exercise
endorphins and, 95
in mice, 93
"Exotic becomes erotic" theory, 389
Expectancies, 345–346
Experience and perception, 137–140
culture, 138–140, 138–139f
development, 137, 137f
learning, 137–138, 138f
Experimental group, 48
Experimental research, 46–51, 47–49f, 50t
Experimenter bias, 49
Expertise, 286, 286f
Explanatory style, 440, 440f
Explicit memory. *See* Declarative memory
Exposure therapy, 589
External attributions, 621
External locus of control, 440, 520

Extinction, 190–191, 191f, 201
Extinguished behavior, 201, 589
Extralinguistic factors, 296
Extrinsic motivation, 206, 365–366
Extroversion, 518, 522–523
Extroverts, 512
Eye movement desensitization reprocessing (EMDR), 601–602
Eyewitness testimony, 256, 256f, 256t
Eysenck, Hans, 522–523, 522f

F

Facial expressions, 422–424, 424f, 424t
Facial feedback hypothesis, 423–425, 424f
Factitious disorders, 552
Factor analysis, 517
Fallon, James, 565
False consensus effect, 618
False memories, 254–256
Falsifiability principle, 513
Family relationships, 469–471
Family studies, 98–99
Family systems, 592
Family therapy, 592
Fat tissue, 372
FDA (Food and Drug Administration), 593
Fear, 429
Feel-good, do-good phenomenon, 439
Fertility, 385
Fertilized egg, 96, 454
Festinger, Leon, 624, 624f
Fetal alcohol syndrome, 455
Fetus, 454, 455f
Fight-or-flight response, 89, 419, 419f, 436
Figure and ground organization, 131–132
Fiske, Susan, 618
Fitness, 97
Five-factor model of personality, 517–518, 517t
Fixation, 285, 510
Fixed-interval schedules, 203, 203f
Fixed mindset, 393
Fixed-ratio schedule, 201–202, 202f
Flashbulb memory, 245–246, 246f
Flooding, 197
Flow, 397
Fluid intelligence, 320, 482
Flynn, James, 348
Flynn Effect, 348
fMRI (functional magnetic resonance imaging), 14, 14f, 87
Food and Drug Administration (FDA), 593
Foot-in-the-door technique, 625
Forebrain, 89–93
amygdala, 89, 422, 422f, 429, 631
cerebrum and cerebral cortex, 90
hemispheres, 91–93
hippocampus, 90, 239, 239f
hypothalamus, 89, 95, 156, 368, 388
illustration of, 89, 89f
limbic system, 89–90, 90f
lobes of cerebrum, 90, 91f
thalamus, 89
Forgetting, 257–262
amnesia, 240, 247, 250, 261–262, 261–262f, 554–555
measures of forgetting, 257–259, 257–258f
motivated forgetting, 260–261
overview, 257
sleep and, 259, 263
theories of forgetting, 259–260, 260f
Forgetting curve, 257, 257f
Formal operational stage, 463
Form and pattern perception, 130–131, 131f
Framing effect, 288
Fraternal twins, 99, 99f
Free association, 585

Free association test, 525
Freud, Anna, 510, 511f
Freud, Sigmund
    biological model and, 521
    defense mechanisms and, 510–511, 511f, 511t, 585
    drive theory and, 364
    motivated forgetting and, 260–261
    overview, 508
    personality development and, 509–510, 509t
    psychoanalytic theory and, 15, 508–511
    psychodynamic therapy and, 584, 584f
    sexual motivation and, 383
    structure of personality and, 508–509, 508f
    theory of dreams and, 162–164
Frontal lobes, 90
Frustration, 429
Frustration-aggression hypothesis, 429
Fully functioning person, 515
Functional fixedness, 285
Functionalism, 11–12, 11–12f
Functional magnetic resonance imaging (fMRI), 14, 14f, 87
Functional plasticity, 93
Fundamental attribution error, 60–61, 621

G

GABA (gamma-aminobutric acid), 83, 162, 171, 550, 550f, 597
Galton, Francis, 327
Galvanic skin response (GSR), 420
Gamma-aminobutric acid (GABA), 83, 162, 171, 550, 550f, 597
Gardner, Howard, 321–322
GAS (general adaptation syndrome), 436
Gender. See also Women
    emotion and, 429
    gaps, 341
    group differences in intelligence, 310–312, 341–342f, 344–345
    sexual motivation norms, 383–384, 382–384f
    stereotypes, 398–399
Gender identity, 477, 487–488
Gender roles, 471, 471f
General adaptation syndrome (GAS), 436
General intelligence (g), 319
Generalizability, defined, 36, 191, 191f
Generalization and discrimination, Skinner experiments, 200–201
Generalized anxiety disorder, 544–545
Generate and test method, 282
Generation effect, 231
Generativity, 294, 485
Genes, 96, 97f
Genetics
    basic concepts of, 96–97, 97f
    hunger physiology, 372–373, 373f
    intelligence and, 347–348f
    mood disorders and, 558, 558f, 562
    personality and, 523, 523f
    psychotic disorders and, 562–563, 563f
    research methods of, 98–100, 98–99f
Geniuses, 339
Genograms, 592
Genome, 96
Genotype, 97, 454
Genovese, Catherine, 634, 635f
Genuineness, 587
Gestalt organizing principles, 131–133, 132–133f
Ghrelin, 370
Gifted intelligence, 339
Gist, 296
GKT (guilty knowledge test), 419
Glia cells, 78
Glucose, 371, 372f
Glucose monitoring, 371–372, 372f

Glutamate, 171, 598
Goals, 281
Gonads, 95
Goodall, Jane, 37
Grammar, 295, 295f
Grandmother hypothesis, 480
Graphology, 524
Great mother archetype, 511
Group aptitude tests, 330
Group polarization, 636
Groups
    altruism, 634–635, 635t
    bystander intervention, 634–635, 635t
    decision making, 636
    deindividuation, 637–638
    effects of group interaction, 635–636, 636f
    individual influence of, 633–638, 635t, 636f
    intelligence testing, 330
    overview, 633–634
    social facilitation, 637
    social loafing, 637
    social psychology, 617–618
    team performance, 399–400
Group therapy, 592
Groupthink, 636–637
Growth mindset, 393
GSR (galvanic skin response), 420
Guilty knowledge test (GKT), 419
Gut reaction, 113

H

Habituation, 213, 373–374, 463–464
Hallucinations, 561, 598
Hallucinogens, 173–174
Happiness, 438–439, 439t
Hardiness, 439–440
Harlow, Harry, 465
Hawthorne effect, 395
Head Start, 337
Health
    classical conditioning and, 193
    diabetes, 372
    intellectually disabled and, 338
    stress and, 436–437, 437f
    summary of multiple influences on health, 441
Health psychology, 437
Healthy lifestyle, 313
Hearing, 123–124, 124f
Hemispheres, 90, 91–93, 91f
Heredity and IQ, 347
Heritability, 14, 98, 98f, 347
Hero archetype, 512
Heterosexuals, 387
Heterozygous twins, 97
Heuristics
    decision making, 287–289, 287f, 289f
    defined, 282
    problem solving and, 282–283, 283t
Hidden observer, 167
Hierarchical theories, 366–367, 367f
Hierarchy of needs, 366, 367f, 515, 516f
Higher-order conditioning, 190
High intellectual ability, 338–339, 338f
Hindbrain, 87–89, 88f
Hippocampus, 90, 239, 239f
Hippocrates, 9, 9f
Holmes, Thomas, 432–433
Holophrastic, 296
Homeostasis, 364
Homosexuals, 388
Homozygous twins, 97
Hormones
    defined, 77, 95
    endorphins, 95, 437
    hunger motivation and, 369–370, 370t
    oxytocin, 382, 467

physical development and, 473
    prenatal exposure, 389
    sex hormones, 95, 382, 389, 523, 631
Hospital addiction syndrome, 552
Hospital hopper syndrome, 552
Hospitals, mental, 582–583, 582–584f
Hostile aggression, 631–632
Humanistic psychology, 514–516
    evaluating humanistic perspectives, 16, 516
    humanism, defined, 16, 514, 587
    Maslow's theory of self-actualization, 366–367, 390, 393, 515–516, 516f
    overview, 514
    Rogers's person-centered perspective, 514–515, 515f
    therapy, 587–588, 587f
Human research participants and ethics, 57–59
Human sexual response cycle, 381, 381t, 382f
Hunger
    brain and, 89, 368–369, 369f
    eating and weight, 374–378. See also Eating
    environmental influences, 373–374
    genetics, 372–373, 373f
    glucose monitoring, 371–372, 372f
    hormones, 369–370, 370t
    metabolism, 370–371, 371f
    overview, 368
    physiology and regulation of hunger, 368–373, 368–369f, 370t, 371–373f
    stomach and, 368, 368f
Hypermnesia, 166
Hyperthymesia, 257
Hypnagogic hallucinations, 160
Hypnosis
    altered state of consciousness and, 166
    critical thinking about, 165–166
    defined, 165
    divided consciousness and, 167
    overview, 165
    role playing and, 166
    theories of, 166–167
Hypochondriasis, 553
Hypocretin, 160
Hypomania, 558
Hypothalamus, 89, 95, 156, 368, 388
Hypothesis, 33

I

Iconic memory, 234
Id, 163–164, 508–509
Ideal self, 515
Identification, 510, 511t, 512
Identity disorder, 555
Identity formation, 476
Ideocentrism, 526
Illness. See Health
Imagination inflation, 255
Immune system
    classical conditioning and, 193
    stress and, 436–437, 437f
Immunosuppression, 437
Implicit memory, 241, 247, 247f, 255
Inattentional blindness, 155
Inborn motivation, 362–363
Incentives, defined, 365
Incentive theories, 365–366, 365–366f
Incidental memory, 227, 227f
Incivility in the workplace, 398
Inclusive fitness, 97
Incongruency, 515
Incubation, 285
Independent variables, 46–47
Individualist cultures, 526, 620
Individual psychology, 513, 513f
Inductive reasoning, 290

Industrial psychology, 394–395. *See also* Organizational psychology
Infancy and childhood
    cognitive development, 461–465
    concrete operational stage, 463, 463*f*
    formal operational stage, 463
    overview, 457–458
    physical development, 458–461, 458*f*, 459–460*t*
    Piaget's stage theory, 461, 461*t*, 463–465, 464*f*
    preoperational stage, 462–463, 462*t*
    sensorimotor stage, 462
    social development, 465–472. *See also* Social development
Inferential statistics, 55–56, 56*f*
Inferiority, 513
Informational social influence, 626
Information organization, 240–248
    declarative memory, 241–246
    overview, 240–241, 241*f*
    procedural memory, 241, 247, 247*f*, 255
Informed consent, 57
In-group bias, 634
Inhalants, 173
Inhibitory messages, 80
Inhibitory postsynaptic potentials (IPSPs), 82, 83
Insecure attachment, 468*t*, 469
Insight, 283, 583
Insight therapies, 583
Insomnia, 159, 163
Inspection speed, 326
Instinct theories, 362–363
Instinctual drift, 206, 206*f*
Institutional review boards (IRBs), 57
Instrumental aggression, 631–632
Insulin, 371–372
Intelligence, 316–339
    Binet and school achievement prediction, 327–328, 327*t*
    brain and, 324–326, 325–326*f*
    defined, 318–319, 319*f*
    differences in, 336–340, 337*t*, 338*f*
    differences within and between groups, 340–343, 341–342*f*
    disability in, 336–338, 337*t*
    environment and, 347–349, 348*f*
    ethnic group differences, 342–343, 342*f*
    expanding concept of intelligence, 321–322, 321–323*t*
    gender group differences, 340–342, 341–342*f*
    as general ability, 319–320
    genetics and, 347–348*f*
    group differences in, 340–346, 341–342*f*
    heritability of, 98, 98*f*
    high intellectual ability, 338–339, 338*f*
    individual differences in, 336–340
    measuring, 327–336. *See also* Intelligence tests
    as multiple abilities, 320–321, 321*f*
    overview, 317
    socioeconomics and, 343, 349, 488
    stereotype threat, 344–345, 344–345*f*
    summary of multiple influences, 350
    theories, 319–323, 320–323*t*, 321*f*
Intelligence quotient (IQ), 328, 347
Intelligence tests, 327–336
    bias in testing, 343–346, 344–345*f*
    construction principles, 330–336
    cultural bias in testing, 331, 343–344
    defined, 320
    development of testing, 327–330, 327*t*
    group intelligence testing, 330
    principles of testing, 330–336, 331*f*, 335*f*
    question selection for tests, 331–332, 331*f*
    reliability of tests, 333–334
    school and, 349
    standardization of tests, 332–333, 332*f*
    Stanford-Binet intelligence test, 328–329, 339, 343
    validity of tests, 334–335, 335*f*
    Wechsler intelligence scales, 329–330, 329*f*, 331

Interaction between variables, 48
Interactionist theories, 298
Interference, 259
Intermittent reinforcement, 201
Internal attributions, 621
Internal description, 232
Internal locus of control, 440, 520
Internet addiction, 437
Internet-mediated research, 39
Interneurons, 78
Interpretations, 585
Interval schedules, 202–203
Intervention techniques for stress, 437
Interviewer illusion, 396
Intrapsychic conflicts, 524
Intrinsic incentives, 365
Intrinsic motivation, 206, 365, 394
Introspection, 11
Introversion, 512, 518, 522–523
Intuition, 279
IPSPs (inhibitory postsynaptic potentials), 82, 83
IRBs (institutional review boards), 57
Irrelevant information, 284

J
James, William, 11–12, 11*f*, 425
James-Lange peripheral feedback theory, 425–426, 426*f*
Job analysis, 396
Job burnout, 397
Job Diagnostic Survey, 396
Johnson, Virginia E., 381
Jones, Mary Cover, 589
Journal publications, 34
Judgment, 286
Jung, Carl, 511–512, 512*f*
Just-world hypothesis, 368

K
K-complexes, 156, 156*f*
Kinsey, Alfred, 387–388, 388*f*
Kinship selection, 97
Kohlberg, Lawrence, 475, 476*t*
Korsakoff's syndrome, 261, 261*f*

L
Lack of transfer, 283
Lange, Carl, 425
Language, 294–304
    acquisition theories, 297–298
    in animals, 298–299
    brain and culture, 300–302, 300–301*f*, 302*t*
    defined, 294
    development, 296–297, 298*f*
    overview, 294
    plasticity and, 93
    properties of, 294
    structure, 294–296, 295*f*
    summary of multiple influences on language, 302–304
    trait determination and, 518
Latent content, 164, 585
Latent learning, 209–210, 210*f*
Lateral hypothalamus, 368–369, 369*f*
Lateralization of function, 92, 92*f*
Law of Effect, 198, 198*f*
Leadership, 400
Learned helplessness, 205–206, 437
Learned response, 189
Learning, 184–222
    anxiety disorders and, 550–551
    classical conditioning, 188–197. *See also* Classical conditioning
    defined, 186
    experience and perception, 137–140. *See also* Experience and perception

how we learn, 186–188, 187*f*, 188*t*
    observational learning, 208–214. *See also* Observational learning
    operant conditioning, 198–208. *See also* Operant conditioning
    summary of multiple influences on learning, 213
    testing to learn, 263–264
Learning perspective, 551
Leptin, 370, 371
Lesions, 86, 86*f*
Levels of analysis, 13
Levels of processing, 230
Lexical approach, 518
Libido, 509
Life expectancy, 480–481
Lifestyle, 513
Limbic system, 89–90, 90*f*
Linguistic relativity, 300–301
Link method, 232
Lithium, 597–598
Little Albert experiment, 196–197
Lobes of the cerebrum, 90, 91*f*
Lobotomy, 600, 600*f*
Locke, John, 9, 10*f*
Locus of control, 440, 520
Longitudinal studies, 49, 453
Long-term memory (LTM), 238–247
    declarative memory, 241–246, 241–246*f*
    defined, 238, 238*t*
    procedural memory, 247, 247*f*
    storing memories in brain, 239–240, 239*f*
Long-term potentiation, 239
Loss aversion, 288
Love, 430–431, 430*f*
LSD (lysergic acid diethylamide), 173
LTM. *See* Long-term memory
Lymphocytes, 436, 437*f*
Lysergic acid diethylamide (LSD), 173

M
Magnetic resonance imaging (MRI), 87, 88*f*
Maintenance rehearsal, 235
Major depressive disorder, 556–557, 557*t*
Malingering, 552
Mania, 557–558, 599
Manifest content, 164, 585
MAO (monoamine oxidase), 82, 594
MAOIs (monoamine oxidase inhibitors), 594–595, 594–595*t*
Marijuana, 95, 173–174
Maslow, Abraham, 16, 366–367, 390, 393, 515–516, 516*f*
Massed practice, 259
Master gland, 95
Masters, William H., 381
Master's-level therapists, 582
Mastery orientation, 392
Matching hypothesis, 633
Math ability, 101
Mating, 380
Maturation, 453
MDMA (methylenedioxymethamphetamine), 174
Mean, 52
Means-end analysis, 282
Mechanism of action (MOA), 171
Media impact, 632
Median, 52
Medical model, 539
Medical procedures, 599–600, 599–600*f*
Medications. *See* Drug treatment; *specific types*
Meditation, 167–168
Medulla, 88
Melatonin, 157
Memory, 224–275
    anatomy of memory, 239–240, 239*f*
    constructing memory, 227–233. *See also* Constructing memory

context for retrieval, 250–251
cue retrieval, 248–250, 249f, 264
declarative memory, 241–246
defined, 226
false memories, 254–256
forgetting, 257–262. *See also* Forgetting
improving memory, 263–264, 264–265t
long-term memory, 238–247. *See also* Long-term
memory (LTM)
loss, 262
misinformation effect, 252–254, 253–254f
organization of information, 240–248, 241f
overview, 226–227
procedural memory, 241, 247, 247f, 255
reconstruction, 252–256
retrieval, 248–251, 248–249f, 264
scheduling study sessions, 263
sensory memory, 234–235f
short-term memory, 234–238, 235–238f
source monitoring, 252
stages of memory, 233–240, 233f
storing memories in brain, 239–240, 239f
studying principles, 263–264
summary of multiple influences on memory, 264,
264–265t
synaptic changes, 239
testing to learn, 263–264
Menarche, 473
Menopause, 480
Mental age, 328
Mental health practitioners, 580–584
clinical psychologists, 581–582, 582f
counseling psychologists, 581
master's level therapists, 582
overview, 580–581
psychiatrists, 581
psychotherapy role of, 583
settings for mental health practitioners, 582–583,
583–584f
Mental hospitals, 582–583, 582–584f
Mental model, 291
Mental rotation, 311, 311f
Mental set, 285
Mere exposure effect, 632
Meta-analysis, 36, 601
Metabolism, 370–371, 371f
Metacognition, 280
Methamphetamine, 172–173
Method of loci, 232
Methylenedioxymethamphetamine (MDMA), 174
Microstressors, 433, 434–435t
Midbrain, 89
Milgram, Stanley, 627–629, 628–629f, 629t
Mind, 5
Mindsets, 393
Minnesota Multiphasic Personality Inventory (MMPI),
525–526
Mirror neurons, 79, 212
Mischel, Walter, 520
Misinformation effect, 252–254, 253–254f
Mistaken lifestyle, 513
MMPI (Minnesota Multiphasic Personality Inventory),
525–526
Mnemonics, 232
MOA (mechanism of action), 171
Mode, 52
Modeling, 208, 519
Monoamine hypothesis of depression, 559, 594
Monoamine oxidase (MAO), 82, 594
Monoamine oxidase inhibitors (MAOIs), 594–595,
594–595t
Monozygotic (MZ) twins, 99, 99f
Mood congruence, 250
Mood disorders, 556–559
biological perspective, 558–559, 558f
depression and bipolar disorder, 557–558
etiology of mood disorders, 558–559, 558f

genetic vulnerability, 558, 558f
major depressive disorder, 556–557, 557t
neurochemical and neuroanatomical factors, 559
overview, 556, 556t
social-cognitive perspective, 559
suicide and, 559
Moods, 556
Mood-stabilizers, 597–598, 598t
Morpheme, 294
Motherese, 457, 467
Motion perception, 134–135, 135–136f
Motivated forgetting, 260–261
Motivation, 360–415
arousal theories, 364–365, 364f
defined, 362
drive theories, 363–364
evolutionary theories, 363
hierarchical theories, 366–367, 367f
of hunger, 368–380. *See also* Hunger
incentive theories, 365–366, 365–366f
instinct theories, 362–363
sexual, 380–390. *See also* Sexual motivation
social, 390–394. *See also* Social motivation
summary of multiple influences on motivation,
403
theories, 362–367, 364–367f
work and, 394–403. *See also* Work
Motives, 362
Motor cortex, 90
Motor neurons, 78
MRI (magnetic resonance imaging), 87, 88f
Multiaxial system, 540–541, 541t
Multiple-approach-avoidance conflict, 435
Multiple intelligences, 321–322, 321–322t
Multiple sclerosis, 78
Münchausen syndrome, 552
Myelin sheath, 79
MZ (monozygotic) twins, 99, 99f

N

Narcolepsy, 160
Narcotics and opiates, 172
National Center for Health Statistics, 383
National Commission for the Protection of Human
Subjects of Biomedical and Behavioral Research,
57
National Highway Traffic Safety Administration, 287
National Research Act, 57
National Weight Control Registry, 371
Nativist theories, 298
Naturalistic observation, 37–38
Natural selection
anxiety disorders and, 549
defined, 14, 97
Nature and nurture, 486–488
Need for achievement, 392
Needs, hierarchy of, 366, 367f, 515, 516f
Need to belong, 390
Negative coping, 437
Negative correlation, 43
Negative reinforcement, 199
Negative symptoms of psychosis, 561, 598
Negativity bias, 619
Neodissociation theory of hypnosis, 167
Neo-Freudian theories, 511
Nerves, 79, 84
Nervous system
defined, 77
organization, 84–86, 85f
Neural communication, 77–84
glia cells, 78
multitasking neurotransmitters, 83, 83t
neural networks, 82–83, 83f
neurons, 78–82, 78f. *See also* Neurons
overview, 77
Neural networks, 82–83, 83f

Neural pruning, 78, 474
Neurochemicals. *See* Neurotransmitters
Neurodevelopment in uterus, 563
Neurogenesis, 93, 600
Neuromodulators, 95, 437
Neurons, 78–82
action potentials, 80–82
communication, 80
defined, 77
illustration of, 78, 78f
mirror, 79, 212
motor, 78
neurotransmitters, 79
overview, 78–79
sensory, 78
structure of neuron, 79
synapses, 79
Neuropsychology, 76. *See also* Neuroscience
Neuroscience, 74–108
adrenal glands, 95
brain, 86–94. *See also* Brain
central nervous system, 85
cognitive neuroscience, 155
contemporary psychology and, 14–15f
endocrine system, 94–96
endorphins, 95, 437
genetics, 96–100. *See also* Genetics
gonads, 95
nervous system organization, 84–86
neural communication, 77–84. *See also* Neural
communication
overview, 76–77
peripheral nervous system, 84–85, 85f
spinal cord, 85
summary, 100, 100t
Neuroticism, 518, 523
Neurotransmitters
defined, 79, 593
functions of, 83, 83t
GABA, 83, 162, 171, 550, 550f, 597
monoamine hypothesis of depression and, 559
multitasking, 83
Neutral stimulus, 189
Newborn development, 456–457, 456–457f
Nicotine, 172
Nightmares, 161, 164
Night terrors, 161
Non-bizarre delusions, 560
Norepinephrine, 83, 95. *See also* Serotonin-norepi-
nephrine reuptake inhibitors (SNRIs)
Normal curve, 332–333, 332f
Normal distribution, 53, 54f, 332–333, 332f
Normative social influence, 626
Norms, 328, 459–460t, 618
nREM sleep, 157

O

Obedience, 626, 627–629, 628–629f, 629t
Obesity, 374, 376–378, 376–377f
Objectivity of personality tests, 526
Object permanence, 462
Observational learning, 208–214
anxiety disorders, 551
Bandura's social-cognitive learning theory,
210–213, 519–520, 519–520f, 631
defined, 188
overview, 208–209
Tolman's latent learning theory, 209–210, 210f
Obsession, 548, 548f
Obsessive-compulsive disorder, 547–548, 548–549f
Obstructive sleep apnea, 159
Occipital lobes, 90
Oedipal complex, 510
One-egg twins, 99, 99f
Openness to experience, 518
Operant Chamber, 199, 199f

Operant conditioning, 198–208
  anxiety disorders and, 551
  applying principles of, 207–208, 207f
  biological influences on, 206–207, 206f
  contemporary views of, 205–207, 206f
  defined, 187
  intrinsic motivation, 206
  learned helplessness, 205–206
  operant, defined, 198
  overview, 198
  punishment, 203–204, 203f
  review of, 204–205
  Skinner's experiments, 198–203. See also Skinner,
    B.F.
  techniques, 590
  Thorndike's Law of Effect, 198, 198f
Operational definitions, 49
Opiates, 172
Opposites principle, 512
Optimal arousal, 364
Optimism, 440, 440t
Optimistic explanatory style, 440
Organ inferiority, 513
Organizational psychology, 397–400, 398–399f
Orgasmic phase, 381
Out-group homogeneity, 634
Outpatient, 582
Overconfidence, 293
Overjustification effect, 365–366, 365f
Overlearning, 251, 263
Overregularization of language, 297
Oxytocin, 382, 467

P

Panic attack, 545
Panic disorder, 545, 546f
Parallel distributed processing (PDP) models, 243
Paranoid personality disorder, 565–566
Paranoid type of schizophrenia, 562
Paraphrasing development, 296
Parasomnias, 159, 160–162
Parasympathetic nervous system, 84–85, 85f, 589
Parental investment theory, 385
Parietal lobe, 90
Partial reinforcement, 201
Participants, 34
Paternal uncertainty, 384
Pavlov, Ivan, 189–192
  acquisition, 189–190, 189f, 190f
  discrimination, 191–192
  extinction and spontaneous recovery, 190–191,
    191f
  generalization, 191, 191f
Pavlovian conditioning, 189
PDP (parallel distributed processing) models, 243
Peak experiences, 516
Pearson, Karl, 42
Peers, 471–472, 471f, 478
Percentile scores, 333
Perception, 130–136. See also Sensation and percep-
    tion
  constancy and, 135–136, 137f
  depth perception, 133–134, 134f, 135t
  figure and ground, 131–132
  form and pattern perception, 130–131
  Gestalt organizing principles, 131–133, 132–133f
  grouping and, 132–133, 132–133f
  motion perception, 134–135, 135–136f
  organization and, 130–136
  person perception, 619–621
Perceptual asymmetries, 93
Perfection principle, 509
Performance vs. acquisition, 211
Performance orientation, 392
Peripheral nervous system, 84–85, 85f
Peripheral route to persuasion, 624
Persistence, 393

Persona, 512
Personality, 504–535
  assessment, 524–526, 525f
  biological perspective, 521–524, 522f
  culture and, 526–527
  defined, 506–507
  evolutionary theories of, 523, 523f
  Eysenck's theory, 522–523, 522f
  genetics and, 523, 523f
  heritability and, 98, 98f
  humanistic perspective, 514–516
  psychoanalytic perspective, 507–514. See also
    Psychoanalytic theories
  social cognitive perspective, 519–521
  somatoform disorders, 553–554
  summary of multiple influences, 527
  theory, 506
  trait perspectives, 517–519
Personality disorders, 564–567, 564t, 565f, 566t
Personality inventory, 524
Personality traits, 483–484, 484f
Personal unconscious, 511
Person-centered perspective, 514–515, 515f
Personnel psychology, 395–397, 395t, 397f
Person perception, 619
Persuasion, 624–625
Pessimistic explanatory style, 440
PET (positron emission tomography) scans, 14, 87,
    87f
Phenomenological approach, 514, 587
Phenotype, 97, 454
Philosophy, 9, 9f
Phobias, 196–197, 546–547, 546–548f, 547t
Phonemes, 294
Photographic memory, 234, 235f
Phrases, 295
Phrenology, 86
Physical appearance, 619–620
Physical attractiveness, 632–633
Physical dependence, 169
Physical development
  adolescence and young adulthood, 473–475,
    473–474f
  adulthood and aging, 479–480
  infancy and childhood, 458–461, 458f, 459–460t
Physical punishment, 204
Physiology
  defined, 9, 9f
  emotion and, 418–421, 419–420f
  hunger regulation and, 89, 368–373, 368–369f,
    370t, 371–373f
  of sexual response, 381–382, 381f, 381t
Piaget, Jean, 461–465, 461t, 464f
Pituitary gland, 95
Placebo effect, 49, 593, 601
Placebos, 593
Plasticity, 93, 458
Plateau phase, 381
Pleasure principle, 508–509
Polygenic traits, 96
Polygraphs, 420–421, 420f
Pons, 88
Population in research design, 40
Positive correlation, 42
Positive psychology, 16, 438–440, 439–440t, 588
Positive regard, 514
Positive reinforcement, 199, 590
Positive self-regard, 514
Positive symptoms of psychosis, 561
Positron emission tomography (PET) scans, 14, 87,
    87f
Postconventional level of moral reasoning, 475
Posthypnotic suggestion, 166
Postsynaptic neuron, 79
Postsynaptic potential (PSP), 82
Posttraumatic stress disorder (PTSD), 549–551, 602
Practical intelligence, 321

Practitioner-scholar model, 582
Pragmatics, 296
Preconscious mind, 508
Preconventional level of moral reasoning, 475
Prediction, 194
Predictive validity, 334
Prejudice, 620, 630
Prenatal development, 453–456, 455f
Prenatal stage, 454
Preoperational stage, 462–463, 462t
Presynaptic neuron, 79
Prevalence, 539, 539f
Primary insomnia, 159
Primary mental abilities, 320
Primary reinforcers, 199–200, 200f
Primary sexual characteristics, 473
Priming, 228
Probability theory, 287
Problem-focused coping, 437
Problem solving, 281–286
  biases, 284–285, 284–285f
  expertise, 286, 286f
  methods, 281–284, 281f, 283t, 284f
  overview, 281
  problem, defined, 281
Procedural memory, 241, 247, 247f, 255
Process loss, 399
Prodigy, 339
Progressive relaxation, 168
Projection, 511t, 512, 524
Projective hypothesis, 524
Projective tests, 524
Prosocial behavior, 634
Prosopagnosia, 39
Proximity, 632
Pseudoscience, 7
PSP (postsynaptic potential), 82
Psychiatrists, 581
Psychoactive drugs, 168, 169–171t. See also specific
    types
Psychoanalysis, 420, 586, 586f
Psychoanalytic theories, 507–514
  Adler's individual psychology, 513, 513f
  contemporary psychology and, 15–16
  defined, 507
  evaluating psychoanalytic perspective, 513
  Freud's psychoanalytic theory, 15, 508–511
  Jung's analytical psychology, 511–512, 512f
  nature of, 507–508, 507f
  psychoanalytic theory of dreams, 162–164
Psychodynamic therapy, 584–586
  overview, 584–585f
  psychoanalysis, 586, 586f
  short-term psychodynamic therapy, 586, 586f
  techniques, 584–586
  types, 586, 586f
Psychological aspects of aggression, 631
Psychological dependence, 169
Psychological disorders, 536–612
  abnormal behavior criteria, 539–540, 540f
  anxiety disorders, 544–551. See also Anxiety
    disorders
  behavior therapy, 588–590
  biomedical therapies, 593–600. See also Biomedi-
    cal therapies
  biopsychosocial approach, 539
  classification system advantages and disadvantages,
    541, 543f
  classifying and labeling psychological disorders,
    540–542, 541–542t, 543f
  client-centered therapy, 587–588, 587f
  cognitive therapies, 590–591, 591t
  defined, 538–539
  dissociative disorders, 554–556, 555t
  DSM, 538–539, 539f
  etiology of psychological disorders, 542–544, 543f
  evaluating therapies for psychological disorders,
    601–603, 602t

family systems, 592
group therapy, 592
humanistic therapy, 587–588, 587f
mental health practitioners and settings, 580–584.
    See also Mental health practitioners
mood disorders, 556–559. See also Mood disorders
overview, 538–544
personality disorders, 564–567, 564t, 565f, 566t
psychodynamic therapy, 584–586
psychotic disorders, 560–563. See also Psychotic
    disorders
rational emotive therapy, 591
somatoform disorders, 552–554
summary of multiple influences, 603–604
therapies, 578–612
Psychological science, 33
Psychological test, 524
Psychology and psychologists, 2–29. See also Social
    psychology
Adler's individual psychology, 513, 513f
biological psychology, 76
clinical, 581–582, 582f
contemporary, 13–19. See also Contemporary
    psychology
counseling, 581, 582f
critical thinking, 19–20, 20t
defined, 5
factors in psychotic disorders, 563
group social psychology, 617–618
health, 437
Jung's analytical psychology, 511–512, 512f
motivation theories, 363
multiple influences on, 20–23, 22f
neuropsychology, 76
organizational, 397–400, 398–399f
origins and history of, 8–12, 8–12f
personnel, 395–397, 395t, 397f
positive, 438–440
science of, 5–7
Psychometricians, 343
Psychopathology, 539
Psychopharmacology, 582, 593
Psychophysiological disorders, 552
Psychosexual stages, 509–510, 509t
Psychosomatic disease, 436
Psychosurgery, 600
Psychotherapy, 583. See also specific therapies
Psychotherapy evaluation, 601–603
Psychotic disorders, 560–563
    brain abnormalities, 562–563
    catatonia, 561, 599
    catatonic type, 562
    deficits of behavior, 561
    delusions, 560
    disorganized thinking, 560
    disorganized type of schizophrenia, 562
    etiology of psychotic disorders, 562–563
    genetic vulnerability, 562
    hallucinations, 561
    neurodevelopment in uterus, 563
    overview, 560, 560t
    paranoid type, 562
    psychological factors, 563
    schizophrenic subtypes, 561–562
    symptoms of all schizophrenic disorders, 560–561
    undifferentiated type, 562
Psychoticism, 523
Psychotropic drugs, 593
PTSD (posttraumatic stress disorder), 549–551, 602
Puberty, 473
Punishment, 203–204, 203f
Punishment by application, 203
Punishment by removal, 203

Q

Question selection for intelligence tests, 331–332,
    331f

R

Race. See Ethnic groups
Racial gap, 343
Rahe, Richard, 432–433
Random assignment, 47, 47f
Random sampling, 41
Range, 52–53
Rapid eye movement (REM) sleep, 156–157, 158,
    161, 164
RAS (reticular activating system), 88
Rational emotive therapy, 591
Rationalization, 511t, 513
Rational thinking, 278
Ratio schedules, 202, 202f
Raven's Progressive Matrices, 320, 331
Reaction formation, 511t, 513
Reactivity, 35
Realistic job preview, 396
Reality principle, 509
Real self, 515
Reasoning
    algorithms, 290–292, 291–292f
    biases, 292–294, 292f
    defined, 290
    overview, 290
Receptor sites, 82
Recessive genes, 97
Reciprocal determinism, 519, 520f
Reciprocal-gene environment, 513, 543f
Reciprocity, 633
Reciprocity norm, 634
Reciprocity of liking, 633
Reconstruction of memory, 252–256
Recovered memories, 260
Reflexes, 85
Refractory period, 381
Regression, 511t, 513
Regression toward the mean, 601
Reinforced, 187
Reinforcement, behavioral, 199–200, 199–200f, 200t
Reinforcer, 198
Relapse, 597
Relationships, 484–485
Relative deprivation, 439
Relearning, 258
Reliability, 35, 333–334
REM rebound, 157
REM (rapid eye movement) sleep, 156–157, 158,
    161, 164
REM sleep behavior disorder, 161
Replication, 35, 55
Repolarization of neurons, 81
Representation, 284
Representativeness heuristic, 287
Repression, 260, 511t, 513
Reproductive life, 480
Reproductive strategies, 384–387
Research
    areas and specialization in psychology, 17–19, 18t
    on brain, 86–87, 86–88f
    comparison of research methods, 51t
Resilience, 478
Resistance, 585
Resistance to extinction, 191
Resolution phase, 381
Resting potential, 81, 81f
Restorative theory of sleep, 157
Restricted range, 335
Restructuring, 283
Reticular activating system (RAS), 88
Reticular formation, 88
Retrieval of memory, 248–251, 248–249f, 264

Reuptake, 82
Revised NEO Personality Inventory, 518
Rogers, Carl, 16, 514–515, 515f, 587–588, 587f
Role, defined, 617
Role playing, 166, 625
Rorschach, Herman, 525
Rorschach inkblot test, 525, 525f
Rosenhan, David, 541, 543f

S

SAMHSA (Substance Abuse and Mental Health Ser-
    vices Administration), 168
Sample, 40, 40f
Sampling bias, 40
Sapir-Whorf hypothesis, 301
Satisfice reasoning, 290
Savant syndrome, 338–339
Scale, 328
Scatterplots, 42, 42f
Schacter-Singer two-factor theory of emotion,
    426–428, 427f
Schedules of reinforcement, 201–203, 202–203f, 202t
Schema, 243–245, 244f, 617
Schizophrenia, 560–563
    antipsychotic drugs, 598–599, 598t
    defined, 560
    etiology of, 562–563, 563f
    subtypes, 561–562
    symptoms, 560–561
    twin studies and, 99
School
    achievement, 327–328, 327t
    intelligence test scores and, 349
Science, 5
Science of psychology, 30–73
    descriptive research, 37–46. See also Descriptive
        research
    ethics in psychological research, 56–63. See also
        Ethics
    experimental research, 46–51, 47–49f, 50t
    overview, 5–7
    statistical analysis, 51–56. See also Statistical
        analysis
    summary of multiple influences on research
        methods, 60–61
Scientific method, 32–36, 34f
Scientific publication, 34
Scientist-practitioner model, 581
Secondary insomnia, 159
Secondary reinforcers, 200, 200f
Secondary sexual characteristics, 473
Second-generation antipsychotics, 598t, 599
Secure attachment, 468, 468t
Seizures, 90
Selective attention, 140–141, 140–141f, 155
Selective serotonin reuptake inhibitors (SSRIs),
    595–596, 596f, 596t, 597
Self, 514
Self-actualization, 366–367, 390, 393–394, 514,
    515–516, 516f
Self-concept, 520
Self-determination theory, 393
Self-efficacy, 519–520
Self-esteem, 526
Self-fulfilling prophecy, 346
Self-image, 515
Self-perception theory, 623
Self-reference effect, 231
Self-regulation, 379–380, 520
Self-report inventories, 525
Self-serving bias, 622
Selye, Hans, 436
Semanticity, 294
Semantic memory, 242–245, 242–244f
Semantic network. See Conceptual hierarchies
Semenya, Caster, 454, 454f

Sensation and perception, 110–151
    attention and, 140–142
    experience and perception, 137–140
    interaction of, 112–114, 112–114f
    perceptual organization, 130–136
    senses, 118–130. *See also* Senses
    sensory principles, 114–118. *See also* Sensory principles
    summary of multiple influences, 142
Senses, 118–130
    hearing, 123–124, 124f
    overview, 118–119, 118t
    smell, 124–125, 125f
    taste, 125–127, 126f
    touch, 127–129, 127–128f
    vision, 119–123, 119–120f, 122–123f
Sensitivity and detection thresholds, 115–116t, 115–117, 116f
Sensorimotor stage, 461t, 462
Sensory adaptation, 117, 117f
Sensory memory, 234, 234–235f
Sensory neurons, 78
Sensory principles, 114–118
    detection thresholds reflection of sensitivity, 115–117, 115–116t, 116f
    sensory adaptation, 117, 117f
    transduction of physical energy into neural stimulation, 115
Sentences, 295
Separation anxiety, 467, 468f
Serotonin, 173, 174, 550, 631
Serotonin-norepinephrine reuptake inhibitors (SNRIs), 596–597, 596t
Set point, 371
Settling point, 371
Sex norms, 382–384
Sexsomnia, 161
Sexual disorders, 382
Sexual harassment, 398
Sexual motivation, 380–390
    evolutionary theories of mating, 384–387, 385–387f
    gender norms in sexual motivation, 382–384, 382–384f
    overview, 380
    physiology of sexual response, 381–382, 381f, 381t
    sexual orientation, 387–390. *See also* Sexual orientation
Sexual orientation, 387–390
    biological factors, 388–389, 389f
    environmental factors, 389–390
    overview, 387–388, 388f
Sexual peak, 383
Shadow persona, 512
Shaping, 200, 204, 590
Shock therapy, 599–600, 599f
Short-term memory (STM), 234–238, 235–238f
Short-term psychodynamic therapy, 586, 586f
Sibling relationships, 470
Similarity as attraction source, 633
Simultaneous trigger theory, 426, 427f
Single-Feature Model, 289
Sixteen Personality Factor Questionnaire (16PF), 526
Skin conductivity, 420
Skinner, B.F., 198–203
    acquisition and shaping, 200
    extinction, 201
    generalization and discrimination, 200–201
    overview, 198–199, 198–199f, 205
    reinforcement, 199–200, 199–200f, 200t
    schedules of reinforcement, 201–203, 202–203f, 202t
Skinner box, 199, 199f
Sleep, 155–162
    alcohol as sleep aid, 163
    biological rhythms and stages of, 156–157, 156f

defined, 155
    deprivation of, 158, 158f
    disorders, 158–162. *See also* Sleep disorders
    forgetting and, 259, 263
    overview, 155
    theories of, 157
Sleep apnea, 159, 160f
Sleep attacks, 160
Sleep debt, 158
Sleep disorders, 158–162
    apnea, 159, 160f
    defined, 158
    insomnia, 159
    narcolepsy, 160
    overview, 158–159
    paralysis, 160
    parasomnias, 160–162
    REM sleep behavior disorder, 161
    sexsomnia, 161
    sleepwalking and sleep eating, 161–162
    terrors, 161
Sleep eating, 161–162
Sleep hygiene, 163
Sleep paralysis, 160
Sleepsex, 161
Sleep spindles, 156
Sleep terrors, 161
Sleepthink, 164
Sleepwalking, 161–162
Smell, 124–125, 125f
SNRIs (serotonin-norepinephrine reuptake inhibitors), 596–597, 596t
Social anxiety disorder, 547
Social categorization, 619
Social clock, 485
Social cognition, 618
Social cognitive perspective
    Bandura's social cognitive theory, 210–213, 519–520, 519–520f
    evaluating social cognitive perspective, 521
    Mischel's social cognitive theory, 520
    mood disorders, 559
    overview, 519
    personality, 519–521
Social desirability bias, 49
Social development
    adolescence and young adulthood, 476–479, 477t
    adulthood and aging, 477t, 483–486, 484f
    attachment theory, 467–469, 467–468f, 468t
    disruption of attachment, 469
    family relationships, 469–471
    infancy and childhood, 465–472
    peers, 471–472, 471f
    power of touch, 465–467, 465–467f
Social facilitation, 637
Social influence, 618
Social interactions, 630–633
    aggression, 630–632
    competence, 632
    factors in attraction, 632–633
    overview, 630
    physical attractiveness, 632–633
    prejudice, 630
    proximity, 632
    reciprocity, 633
    similarity, 633
Social intuitionist, 476
Social loafing, 637
Social motivation, 390–394
    achievement, 392–393, 392f
    belonging, 390–391, 391f
    overview, 390
    self-actualization, 366–367, 390, 393–394, 514, 515–516, 516f
Social norms, 618
Social phobias, 546, 547f
Social psychology, 614–647

attitudes and social judgments, 623–626
    attributions, 621–622
    conformity, 626–627, 627f
    core social motives, 618
    defined, 17
    group influence on individual, 633–638
    groups, 617–618
    Milgram's experiment, 627–629, 628–629f, 629t
    obedience, 627–629, 628–629f, 629t
    person perception, 619–621
    social interactions, 630–633
    social thought and behavior, 617–618
    Stanford prison experiment, 591f, 627
    summary of multiple influences, 638
Social Readjustment Rating Scale, 432–433, 432–433t
Social rejection, 391
Social-responsibility norm, 634
Social roles, 617
Social skills training, 588
Social support, 440
Sociobiolgy, 523
Sociocognitive theory of hypnosis, 166
Sociocultural aspects of aggression, 631
Sociocultural perspective, 16–17
Socioeconomics and intelligence, 343, 349, 488
Soma, 79
Somatic marker, 279
Somatic nervous system, 84
Somatoform disorders, 552–554
    conversion disorder, 553
    etiology of somatoform disorders, 553–554
    hypochondriasis, 553
    overview, 552, 552t
    personality and cognitive perspectives, 553–554
    somatization disorders, 552–553
Somatosensory cortex, 90
Source monitoring, 252
Source traits, 517
Spacing effect, 259, 260f, 263
Spearman, Charles, 319–320
Specialization and research areas in psychology, 17–19, 18t
Specific intelligences (s), 320
Spermarche, 473
Spinal cord, 85
Spinal reflexes, 85
Split-brain surgery, 91, 92, 92f
Split-half reliability, 334
Spontaneous recovery, 191, 191f
Spontaneous remission, 601
Spreading activation, 243
SSRIs (selective serotonin reuptake inhibitors), 595–596, 596f, 596t, 597
Stage model of memory, 240
Stage 1 sleep, 156
Stage theory of development, 461–465, 461t, 464f
Stage theory of memory, 233–240
    anatomy of memory, 239–240, 239f
    long-term memory, 238–240, 238t, 239f
    overview, 233–234, 233f
    sensory memory, 234, 234f
    short-term memory, 234–238, 235–238f
    storing memories, 239–240, 239f
    synaptic changes, 239
Standard, 328
Standard deviation, 53, 53t
Standardization, 332–333, 332f
Standardized procedures, 328
Stanford-Binet intelligence test, 328–329, 339, 343
Stanford prison experiment, 591f, 627
Statistical analysis, 51–56
    making inferences with statistics, 55–56, 56f
    measures of central tendency and variance, 52–54, 52–54f, 53t
    overview, 51–52
Statistical significance, 55
Statistics, 52

Status, 385–386
Steele, Claude, 17
Stereotypes, 398–399, 620. *See also* Bias
Stereotype threat, 344–345, 344–345f
Sternberg, Robert, 430
Stimulant-induced psychosis, 172
Stimulants, 160, 172–173
Stimulus control therapy, 163
Stimulus discrimination, 192
Stimulus generalization, 191, 191f
Stimulus threshold, 82
STM (short-term memory), 234–238, 235–238f
Stomach, 368, 368f
Stranger anxiety, 467, 467f
Strange situation procedure, 467–468
Stress, 431–438
    choice as stress, 435
    cognition and stress, 21, 433
    coping with and managing stress, 437
    culture and stress, 435–436
    defined, 431, 432
    discrimination and, 436
    effects of stress, 436
    health and stress, 436–437, 437f
    immune system and stress, 436–437, 437f
    interventions, 437
    overview, 431–432
    sources of stress, 20–21t, 432–433, 432–433t
    summary of multiple influences on stress, 441
Stressors, 432
Striving for superiority (Adler), 513
Strong Interest Inventory, 395
Structuralism, 10–11, 10f
Structural plasticity, 93
Study principles, 263–264
Stuporous catatonia, 561
Subjective well-being, 438
Subjectivity, 620
Subjects, 34
Sublimation, 383, 510–511, 511t, 513
Substance Abuse and Mental Health Services Admin-
    istration (SAMHSA), 160
Substantia nigra, 89
Suicide, 559
Sumner, Francis Cecil, 17
Superego, 163–164, 509
Superstition reinforcement, 201
Support groups, 592
Suprachiasmatic nucleus, 157
Surface structure, 295
Surface traits, 517
Surveys, 39–41, 39–40f, 40t
Syllogisms, 290–291
Sympathetic nervous system, 84–85, 85f, 589
Symptom substitution, 588
Synapses, 79, 80f
Synaptic changes, 239
Synaptic pruning, 82–83, 83f
Synaptic vesicles, 82
Synaptic cleft, 79
Synaptic gap, 79
Synaptic transmission, 80, 80f
Systematic desensitization, 197, 589

T

Talk therapy, 583
Tardive dyskinesia, 598–599
Taste, 125–127, 126f
Taste aversions, 194, 196
Telegraphic speech, 297
Temperament, 456, 522
Temporal lobes, 90
Teratogens, 455
Terman, Lewis, 328–329, 339
Terminal bend bulb, 79
Terminal button, 79

Terror management theory, 526
Testing effect, 251
Testing to learn, 263–264
Testosterone, 95, 382, 523, 631
Test-retest reliability, 333
Tetrahydrocannabinol (THC), 95, 173
Thalamus, 89
Thanatos, 509
THC (tetrahydrocannabinol), 95, 173
Thematic Apperception Test (TAT), 392, 392f, 525,
    525f
Theoretical approach to traits, 518
Theory, defined, 33
Theory of mind, 464
Theory of psychosocial development, 476, 477t
Therapies
    behavior, 588–590, 589–590f, 589t
    biomedical therapies, 593–600. *See also* Biomedi-
        cal therapies
    client-centered, 587–588, 587f
    cognitive, 590–591, 591t
    drug treatments, 593–599. *See also* Drug treatment
    electroconvulsive therapy (ECT), 599–600, 599f
    evaluation of, 601–603, 602t
    exposure therapy, 589
    family therapy, 592
    group therapy, 592
    humanistic, 587–588, 587f
    insight therapies, 583
    medical procedures, 599–600, 599–600f
    overview, 593
    psychodynamic, 584–586, 584–586f
    psychodynamic therapy, 584–586
    rational emotive therapy, 591
    shock therapy, 599–600, 599f
    stimulus control therapy, 163
    talk therapy, 583
    therapies, 578–612
    virtual reality exposure therapy, 590, 590f
Therapy, 601–603
Theta, 156
Thinking, 276–304
    decision making, 286–290. *See also* Decision
        making
    defined, 278
    overview, 278–281, 279–280f
    problem solving, 281–286. *See also* Problem
        solving
    reasoning, 290–294. *See also* Reasoning
    summary of multiple influences on thinking,
        302–304
Thirst, 378, 378f
Thorndike, Edward, 198, 198f
360-degree feedback, 397, 397f
Threshold, 80
Thurstone, Louis, 320
Tip-of-the-tongue phenomenon, 248, 249f
Titchener, Edward B., 10
TMS (transcranial magnetic stimulation), 87, 600,
    600f
Token economics, 208, 590
Tolerance, 169, 597
Tolman, Edward C., 209–210, 210f
Touch, 127–129, 127–128f, 465–467, 465–467f
Tracer, David, 461
Traits, 517
Trait theory
    assessing traits, 518
    Big Five factors, 517–518, 517t
    defined, 517
    evaluating trait perspective, 518–519
    factor analysis, 517
    overview, 517
Tranquilizers, 171
Transcendence, 512
Transcranial magnetic stimulation (TMS), 87, 600,
    600f

Transduction of physical energy into neural stimula-
    tion, 115
Transference, 585
Transsexuality, 487–488
Trial and error, 282
Triangular theory of love, 430–431, 430f
Triarchic theory of intelligence, 321
Trickster archetype, 512
Twin studies
    environment and, 109–110, 347–348, 348f
    genetics and, 99–100, 99f
    hunger physiology and, 372–373, 373f
    intelligence and, 347–348, 348f
    sexual orientation and, 389, 389f
Two-egg twins, 99, 99f
Type A personalities, 436
Type B personalities, 436

U

Uncertainty, 286
Unconditional positive regard, 514, 587
Unconditioned response, 189
Unconditioned stimulus, 189
Unconscious, 15, 420
Undifferentiated type of schizophrenia, 562
Undisguised dream, 164
Unhealthy lifestyle, 513
Unit bias, 374
Universals, 363
Unlearned response, 189
Unnecessary constraints, 284

V

Vail model, 582
Validity, 35, 334–335, 335f
Valium, 83
Variable-interval schedules, 203, 203f
Variable-ratio schedule, 202, 202f
Variables, 37. *See also* specific types
Variance, 52
Variation, 52
Vasocongestion, 381
Ventromedial hypothalamus, 369, 369f
Videogames, 212–213
Violence, 212–213
Virtual reality exposure therapy, 590, 590f
Vision, 119–123, 119–120f, 122–123f
Von Meduna, Ladislas, 599
Vygotksy, Lev, 465

W

WAIS (Wechsler Adult Intelligence Scale), 329–330,
    329f, 331
Waist-to-hip ratio (WHR), 387
Wason selection task, 291–292, 291f, 292f
Watson, John Broadus, 16, 196–197, 486
Wechsler Adult Intelligence Scale (WAIS), 329–330,
    329f, 331
Wechsler, David, 329–330
Weight, 374–378
Wernicke's area, 300, 300f
WHR (waist-to-hip ratio), 387
Willpower, 379–380
Wilson, E.O., 523, 523f
Wise old man archetype, 512
Withdrawal symptoms, 169
Within-subjects design, 35
Women
    emotion and, 429
    gender gaps, 341
    gender identity, 477, 487–488
    gender roles, 471, 471f
    intelligence differences, 340–342, 341–342f,
        344–345
    sexual motivation norms, 382–384, 382–384f

stereotypes, 398–399
Words, 294
Work, 394–403
    career directions, 400–403, 401–402*t*
    organizational psychology, 397–400, 398–399*f*
    overview, 394–395
    personnel psychology, 395–397, 395*t*, 397*f*
Working memory, 234–238, 235–238*f*
Working memory capacity, 332

Working memory span, 236–237, 237–238*f*
Wundt, Wilhelm, 10–11, 10*f*

Y

Yerkes, Robert, 330
Yerkes-Dodson law of arousal, 364, 364*f*, 419–420, 420*f*
Young adulthood. *See* Adolescence

Z

Zimbardo, Phillip, 627, 627*f*
Zone of proximal development, 465
Zygote, 96, 454

Credits

675

Chapter 12
Opener © Dmitriy Shironosov/Shutter-Stock, Inc.; **page 451** © Dmitriy Shiro-nosov/ShutterStock, Inc.; **second opener** © Darren Brode/ShutterStock, Inc.; **12-1** © Michael Sohn/AP Photos; **12-2** © lelik759/ShutterStock, Inc.; **12-5A** © Rui Vale de Sousa/ShutterStock, Inc.; **12-5B** © Olinchuk/ShutterStock, Inc.; **12-5C** © Stepanov/ShutterStock, Inc.; **12-5D** © Valua Vitaly/ShutterStock, Inc.; **page 461** © Charlie Edward/ShutterStock, Inc.; **12-11** © Photo Researchers, Inc.; **12-13** © Photo Researchers, Inc.; **12-12** © Photo Researchers, Inc.; **12-14** © Photo Researchers, Inc.; **12-16** © Iakov Filimonov/ShutterStock, Inc.; **12-17** © Ruslan Kudrin/ShutterStock, Inc.; **12-15** © Steve Lovegrove/ShutterStock, Inc.; **page 462 (top)** © Doug Goodman/Photo Researchers, Inc.; **page 462 (bottom)** © Doug Goodman/Photo Researchers, Inc.; **page 480** © Jason LaVeris/FilmMagic/Getty Images; **page 487** © Reuters/Landov.

Chapter 12 Visual Overview
Page 490 (top) © Angelo Giampiccolo/ShutterStock, Inc.; **page 490 (middle)** © Samuel Borges/ShutterStock, Inc.; page 490 (bottom) © Monkey Business Images/ShutterStock, Inc.

Chapter 13
Opener © vipflash/ShutterStock, Inc.; **page 505** © vipflash/ShutterStock, Inc.; **second opener** © Pascal Janssen/Shut-terStock, Inc.; **13-1** Library of Congress, Prints & Photographs Division, [reproduction number LC-USZ62-1234]; **page 508 (middle)** © Edwin Verin/ShutterStock, Inc.; **page 508 (bottom)** © ElenaGaak/ShutterStock, Inc.; **13-2** © Jurgen Ziewe/ShutterStock, Inc.; **page 509 (top)** © Tatiana Morozova/ShutterStock, Inc.; **page 509 (bottom)** © siamionau pavel/ShutterStock, Inc.; **page 510 (top)** © Melissa King/ShutterStock, Inc.; **page 510 (middle)** © iofoto/ShutterStock, Inc.; **13-3** © Mary Evans/Photo Researchers, Inc.; **page 511 (middle)** © Serg Shalimoff/ShutterStock, Inc.; **page 511 (bottom)** © Ingrid W./ShutterStock, Inc.; **13-4** © National Library of Medicine; **page 512 (top)** © Science Source/Photo Researchers, Inc.; **page 512 (bottom)** © Adam Michal Ziaja/ShutterStock, Inc.; **page 513** © Chris Knapton/Photo Researchers, Inc.; **13-5** © SPL/Photo Researchers, Inc.; **page 514 (top)** © Allison Achauer/ShutterStock, Inc.; **page 514 (bottom)** © kaczor58/ShutterStock, Inc.; **13-8** Courtesy of Dr. Albert Bandura; **13-10** © Mary Evans Picture Library/Alamy Images; **13-11** Courtesy of The HJ Eysenck Memorial Fund; **13-13** © SPL/Photo Researchers, Inc.; **13-14** © Will & Deni McIntyre/Photo Researchers, Inc.; **13-15** © Lewis J. Merrim/Photo Researchers, Inc.; **page 525** © viviamo/ShutterStock, Inc.

Chapter 13 Visual Overview
Page 528 (top left) Library of Congress, Prints & Photographs Division, [reproduction number LC-USZ62-1234]; **page 528 (top right)** © National Library of Medicine; **page 528 (middle)** © Pascal Janssen/Shut-terStock, Inc.; **page 528 (middle right)** © SPL/Photo Researchers, Inc.; **page 528 (bottom right)** © SPL/Photo Researchers, Inc.

Chapter 14
Opener © Emilia Dotcheva/ShutterStock, Inc.; **page 537** © Emilia Dotcheva/Shut-terStock, Inc.; second opener © Able-Stock; **page 538** © Ingram Publishing/age fotostock; **page 540** © Oleg Seleznev/Dreamstime.com; **14-2A** © LiquidLibrary; **14-2B** © Rubberball Productions; **14-2C** © Monkey Business Images/ShutterStock, Inc.; **14-2D** © Matthew Gough/Shutter-Stock, Inc.; **14-2E** © LiquidLibrary; **14-2F** © Selahattin Bayram/ShutterStock, Inc.; **14-2G** © Mads Abildgaard/ShutterStock, Inc.; **14-4** Courtesy of Library of Congress, Prints & Photographs Division, [LC-USZ62-104691]; **page 544** © Jason Stitt/ShutterStock, Inc.; **page 544 (middle right)** © Diedie/ShutterStock, Inc.; **page 544 (middle)** © Vatikaki/ShutterStock, Inc.; **page 544 (right)** © Sim Kay Seng/ShutterStock, Inc.; **page 545** © Geotrac/Dreamstime.com; **page 546** © Mircea BEZERGHEANU/ShutterStock, Inc.; **14-8** © Sculpies/Dreamstime.com; **page 547** © Jonathan Souza/Dreamstime.com; **page 548 (top)** © sommthink/ShutterStock, Inc., **page 548 (bottom)** © Valeev/Shut-terStock, Inc.; **page 549 (top)** © Muriel Lasure/ShutterStock, Inc.; **page 549 (bottom)** © Kileman/Dreamstime.com; **page 552** © Pixtal/age fotostock; **page 553 (top)** © Robert Kneschke/Shutter-Stock, Inc.; **page 553 (bottom)** © Jose Gil/Dreamstime.com; **page 555** © Lyn Baxter/Dreamstime.com; **page 557** © DNF-Style Photography/ShutterStock, Inc.; **page 558** © Andrey Kiselev/Dreamstime.com; **14-18** © Mikhail Basov/Dreamstime.com; **14-19** © Daniel Anderson and courtesy of Dr. James Fallon.

Chapter 14 Visual Overview
Page 568 (top right) © AbleStock; **page 568 (top right background)** © AbleStock; **Anxiety disorders** © Geotrac/Dream-stime.com; **Somatoform disorders** © Pixtal/age fotostock; **Dissociative identity disorder** © Bryoni Castelijn/Shutter-Stock, Inc.; **Mood disorders** © AbleStock; **Psychotic disorders** © dundanim/Shut-terStock, Inc.; **Personality disorders** © Martin Novak/ShutterStock, Inc.

Chapter 15
Opener © iStockphoto/Thinkstock; **page 579** © iStockphoto/Thinkstock; **second opener** © Anteromite/ShutterStock, Inc.; **page 582** © Arena Creative/ShutterStock, Inc.; **15-2** © Middle Temple Library/Photo Researchers, Inc.; **page 583** © Jerry Cooke/Photo Researchers, Inc.; **15-3** © National Library of Medicine; **15-6** Courtesy of Library of Congress, Prints & Photographs Division, [reproduction number LC-USZ62-1234]; **15-7** © Library of Congress/Photo Researchers, Inc.; **15-8** © Creatas/Thinkstock; **page 586** © Geraint Lewis/Alamy Images; **15-9** © Rob Marmion/ShutterStock, Inc.; **page 588** © Jupiterimages/Brand X Pictures/Thinkstock; **15-11A** Courtesy of Malem Medical, http://www.malem.co.uk; **page 590 (middle)** © Piotr Marcincki/ShutterStock, Inc.; **page 590 (bottom)** © mast3r/ShutterStock, Inc.; **15-13** © US Army/Photo Researchers, Inc.; **page 592 (top)** © Garo/Phanie/Photo Researchers, Inc.; **page 592 (middle)** © Will & Deni McIntyre/Photo Researchers, Inc.; **page 594** © Mike Flippo/Shut-terStock, Inc.; **Table 15-4A** © .shock/ShutterStock, Inc.; **Table 15-4B** © Knud Nielsen/ShutterStock, Inc.; **Table 15-4C** © Lilyana Vynogradova/ShutterStock, Inc.; **Table 15-4D** © SunnyS/ShutterStock, Inc.; **Table 15-4E** © Maxim Tupikov/ShutterStock, Inc.; **Table 15-4F** © nito/ShutterStock, Inc.; **Table 15-4G** © Gregory Gerber/ShutterStock, Inc.; **page 597** © Chris Gallagher/Photo Researchers, Inc.; **page 599** © Robert Brook/Photo Research-ers, Inc.; **15-15** © Will & Deni McIntyre/Photo Researchers, Inc.; **15-16** © Living Art Enterprises, LLC/Photo Researchers, Inc.; **15-17** © Richard T. Nowitz/Photo Researchers, Inc.; **15-18** © Medical Body Scans/Photo Researchers, Inc.

Chapter 15 Visual Overview
© iStockphoto/Thinkstock

Chapter 16
Opener © William Perugini/ShutterStock, Inc.; **page 615** © William Perugini/Shut-terStock, Inc.; **second opener** © Creatas/Thinkstock; **page 618 (top)** © Design Pics/Colleen Cahill/Valueline/Thinkstock; **page 618 (bottom)** © DigitalVision/Thinkstock; **page 619 (top)** © Jupiterimages/Polka Dot/Thinkstock; **page 619 (bottom)** © AISPIX by Image Source/ShutterStock, Inc.; **page 620 (bottom)** © iStockphoto/Thinkstock; **page 620 (middle)** © Comstock/Think-stock; **page 620 (top)** © Stockbyte/Think-stock; **page 621 (A)** © Pinkcandy/Shut-terStock, Inc.; **page 621 (B)** © Stephen Coburn/ShutterStock, Inc.; **page 621 (C)** © Gina Smith/ShutterStock, Inc.; **page 621 (D)** © Nejron Photo/ShutterStock, Inc.; **page 622** © iStockphoto/Thinkstock; **page 623** © Creatas/Thinkstock; **16-02** © Estate of Francis Bello/Photo Research-ers, Inc.; **page 624 (left)** © iStockphoto/Thinkstock; **page 624 (right)** © Jupiterim-ages/Comstock/Thinkstock; **page 626 (middle)** © Hemera/Thinkstock ; **page 626 (bottom)** © DigitalVision/Thinkstock; **16-4** © Philip G. Zimbardo, Inc.; **page 633** © Jack Hollingsworth/DigitalVision/Think-stock; **page 634 (middle)** © Comstock/Thinkstock; **page 634 (bottom)** © Jupi-terimages/Pixland/Thinkstock; **page 635 (top)** © AP Photos; **page 635 (bottom)** © Michael Blann/DigitalVision/Thinkstock; **page 636** © Jupiterimages/BananaStock/Thinkstock; **page 637 (top)** © iStockphoto/Thinkstock; **page 637 (bottom)** © Ryan McVay/DigitalVision/Thinkstock; **page 638** © Ryan McVay/Photodisc/Thinkstock.

Chapter 16 Visual Overview
© ZargonDesign/iStockphoto.

Critical Thinking Applications

Visual Summary

End Sheets

Multiple Perspectives

Transduction from Physical Energy to Neural Signals

Motivation: Sources of Hunger

The major theories of personality, theorists, and concepts.

Visual Overview Motivation: Sources of Hunger

The motivation to eat has characteristic influences in our physical bodies (shown in blue) and in our environment (shown in green).

Are You Hungry?

Hypothalamus: start and stop

Body image

Hypothalamus: drives endocrine system

Advertisements, serving size, others eating

Stomach stretching and contractions

Metabolic rate and set point

Taste preferences

Insulin production

Food available

Cultural practices